OXFORD REFERENCE

BBC
PRONOUNCING DICTIONARY
OF BRITISH NAMES

D1230682

BBC
Pronouncing Dictionary
of British Names

SECOND EDITION

Edited and Transcribed by
G. E. POINTON

Oxford   New York
OXFORD UNIVERSITY PRESS
1990

Oxford University Press, Walton Street, Oxford OX2 6DP

Oxford New York Toronto
Delhi Bombay Calcutta Madras Karachi
Petaling Jaya Singapore Hong Kong Tokyo
Nairobi Dar es Salaam Cape Town
Melbourne Auckland

and associated companies in
Berlin Ibadan

Oxford is a trade mark of Oxford University Press

First published 1971
Second edition 1983
First issued as an Oxford University Press paperback 1990

British Library Cataloguing in Publication Data

BBC pronouncing dictionary of British names.—2nd ed,
edited and transcribed by C. E. Pointon — (Oxford Reference)
1. Great Britain. Personal names. Pronunciation
2. Great Britian. Place names. Pronunciation
I. Title
929.4'0941
ISBN 0–19–282745–6

Printed in Great Britain by
Richard Clay Ltd.
Bungay, Suffolk

PREFACE

ELEVEN years have passed since the publication of the first edition of this dictionary, edited by Miss G. M. Miller, and the BBC's Pronunciation Unit has been continuing its work throughout that time. A lot of new information has come to light, concerning personal and place names which had not previously been recorded by us and also names which were already part of our collection. This new information has been incorporated where appropriate in the second edition.

Some minor changes have been introduced in the layout: most importantly, each place name is now identified by its county, or in Scotland its region. This is in order to show at a glance which place is intended. There are many names which occur in more than one county, and the BBC has established the pronunciation only of those whose county is stated. Other places whose names are identically spelt may be differently pronounced.

Secondly, there is no longer any typographical distinction between personal and place names. The addition of county and region names has rendered the previous practice superfluous.

The bracketing of both IPA and Modified Spelling has been discontinued without, we hope, giving rise to any ambiguity.

I have included on another page the names of members of the Pronunciation Unit, past and present. If there are any omissions, they are not intentional, as all my fellow-workers in the Unit are responsible for some part of the material in this book.

Those who have helped in the revision of the work are too numerous to mention by name, and include many people in public libraries, post offices, police stations, and elsewhere, who remained anonymous. I am grateful to them all for the time they gave me as well as for the information. BBC staff around the country, in local radio stations and regional headquarters, were also very helpful and deserve my thanks. Special mention must be made of two people, however: Miss Nia Rhosier, who gave a lot of time and effort to helping me with the Welsh entries, and Mr Gregory James, lecturer in the Language Centre at the University of Exeter, who checked many of the entries for Devon and Cornwall. My thanks go also to Miss Alexandra Bejda who prepared much of the typescript for this edition, and to Betty Palmer and Ena Sheen of the Oxford University Press for their help in seeing the work through to publication.

The responsibility for any errors which may remain lies entirely with me.

G. E. POINTON

Broadcasting House
London W1A 1AA
August 1982

PREFACE TO THE
FIRST EDITION

IN this book the BBC has gathered together the fruits of more than forty years of research into the pronunciation of proper names in the United Kingdom. The book was compiled primarily for the use of members of staff, but the BBC hopes that it will prove useful to many other readers. Here they will find the pronunciation which as nearly as possible represents the usage of the inhabitants of the place or of the family bearing the name listed. Although the BBC does not, and never did, impose pronunciations of its own on English words, the myth of 'BBC English' dies hard. It owed its birth no doubt to the era before the Second World War, when all announcers and perhaps a majority of other broadcasters spoke the variety of Southern English known as Received Pronunciation, which is the type of English spoken by those educated at public schools; but there was nothing esoteric about this way of speaking, nothing exclusive to the BBC, and in its pre-war setting it came to be accepted as the natural mode of communication over the air. Even today, when a much wider variety of voices is heard, the old style is still regarded as having an important place in broadcasting. The good announcer remains, as far as the BBC is concerned, the pleasant, unobtrusive speaker who does not distract attention from his subject matter by causing embarrassment, unwitting amusement, or resentment among intelligent listeners. He is the mouthpiece for the BBC's official pronouncements, the man who links programmes, announces concerts, narrates opera scripts, reads bulletins prepared in the newsroom, and generally undertakes the exacting task of interpreting other people's work, only occasionally displaying his own versatility by taking part in particular programmes.

In the early 1960s, the BBC felt that it would be more realistic to throw the stage open to the men behind the scenes, so that news men participated personally in news broadcasts, meteorologists gave us our weather forecasts, policemen enlisted our aid direct from Scotland Yard, and the BBC Motoring Unit kept us hourly aware of traffic problems. This created a greater sense of immediacy between the listener and those at the heart of the event. Naturally, there was no longer insistence on purely southern usage, as these experts are likely to be drawn from all parts of the country. Their prime advantage is that they are informed and articulate on their own subject, and consequently easy to follow. They hold the interest and sympathy of the listener because of their expertise. At the same time, a more colloquial element has been introduced, which has disposed even further of a sense of formality. Individual departments are of course responsible for avoiding the pitfall of employing the man who is patently neither adequate speaker nor expert. In both radio and television, News Division has experimented widely. London television presentation announcers, on the other hand, continue to be drawn from the ranks of RP speakers, while domestic radio presentation has extended its range to take in several Commonwealth announcers. In the BBC's European and World Service English language broadcasts, understandably, Southern English RP remains the accepted norm for all announcers, both in news bulletins and in programmes. As well as the need to overcome the occasional vagaries of short-wave reception, there is the consideration that to a very large number of listeners English is a foreign tongue, and a stable style of pronunciation greatly helps intelligibility. It is also appreciated by the world-wide followers of BBC English by Radio programmes.

There is one sphere, however, in which the BBC expects conformity from all its official broadcasters, and that is in the treatment of British proper names. It is felt that, as a matter of courtesy, the bearer of a name or title should be referred to by the pronunciation which he himself prefers; and that place names should be pronounced as they are locally, with perhaps rare exceptions where there is a recognized 'national' pronunciation. A name is usually a matter of vital moment to those closely and often emotively concerned with it, and unfavourable reaction to a mispronunciation, with all the lack of interest and care that the latter implies, is immediate. On the BBC's part, the size of the Pronunciation Unit's telephone bills must be considered one small testimony to its endeavour to keep in close touch with personal and local usage. It is this Unit, which emerged as the direct heir to the BBC's Advisory Committee on Spoken English in 1939, that continues to carry out the Committee's far-sighted recommendations in regard to both English and foreign language problems. It is worth pausing for a moment to study the calibre of the Committee itself, which was set up in 1926 by the Director-General, Mr. J. C. W. Reith, later Lord Reith. Foremost among its members were four linguistic specialists—Arthur Lloyd James, Professor of Phonetics at the School of Oriental and African Studies in the University of London, who acted as honorary secretary to the Committee and linguistic adviser to the announcers; Daniel Jones, Professor of Phonetics at University College London, a phonetician of world repute, whose close association with the BBC continued until his death in 1967; H. C. Wyld, Merton Professor of English Language and Literature in the University of Oxford; and Harold Orton, later to become Professor of English Language and Medieval Literature in the University of Leeds. Among the members of the main Committee over the years were the Poet Laureate Robert Bridges, Sir Johnston Forbes-Robertson, George Bernard Shaw, Sir Julian Huxley, Lord David Cecil, Sir Kenneth Clark, Lady Cynthia Asquith, Rose Macaulay, and many others of distinction. After some early lively battles on matters of principle, the members settled down to collecting information for inclusion in a successive range of booklets covering the pronunciation of English, Scottish, Welsh, and Northern Irish place names, and of British family names and titles. All their findings, published before 1939, have been incorporated in this present book, together with much evidence acquired since that time.

I wish to acknowledge my indebtedness to Professor A. Lloyd James and Professor Daniel Jones, who were responsible for the inception of this collection and for the principles on which it is based, and with whom I had the constant pleasure of working during their years as the Corporation's Linguistic Advisers; to my colleague, Elspeth D. Anderson, who has not only collaborated closely throughout the preparation of the dictionary, but who did much of the research over a long period of years; to R. L. W. Collison, formerly BBC Librarian and now Professor of Library Service in the University of California, Los Angeles, who advised on the more intricate aspects of indexing; to Dr. Aled Rhys Wiliam, formerly of the BBC in Wales and now Director of Audio-Visual Media at the University of Salford, whose scholarly yet practical knowledge of his country and its language, enhanced by his broadcasting experience, has left him singularly well equipped to advise on Welsh names; to Arthur G. Kent of Jersey and Frank Falla of Guernsey, who undertook the difficult task of indicating by pen rather than by word of mouth the pronunciation of Channel Islands names, and whose wishes I hope I have interpreted successfully; to A. C. Gimson, Professor of Phonetics in the University of London, who has been unfailingly swift and generous with advice on general and specific points whenever this was sought; to J. Windsor Lewis, Lecturer in the Department of Phonetics in the University of Leeds, for accepting the arduous assignment of proof-reading, in the course of which he has offered much constructive criticism and valuable guidance on phonetic problems, particularly in relation to Welsh names; and to numerous BBC colleagues in London and the Regions.

G. M. MILLER

Broadcasting House,
London, W.1.
December 1970

INTRODUCTION

A CURIOUS witness to the remarkable diversity of provenance of the inhabitants of the British Isles is the fact that the first entry in this dictionary should be *Aagaard* and the last *Zabiela*—names more immediately suggesting an affinity with Scandinavia and the Iberian Peninsula. Here, however, the recording of pronunciations rather than research into historical origins has been the aim. The book includes titles, family names (i.e., surnames), certain Christian names (or personal first names), place names, those of institutions and societies, and adjectival forms of proper names, drawn from England, Wales, Scotland, Northern Ireland, the Isle of Man, and the Channel Islands—the last appearing in a separate appendix. Some names, like that of *Yehudi Menuhin*, appear because their owners, although not technically of British nationality, have made their homes here and are very much a part of the British scene. It is not an exhaustive collection, and not every pronunciation of every name is represented; only those for which satisfactory evidence was available have been included. Local clergy, town clerks and their staff, postal and police officials, and many private citizens have contributed—sometimes very extensively—to the information on place names. Advice on personal names has been most carefully sought from the individuals concerned, or from members of their families or other sources close to them. Although it is naturally outside the scope of the book to record the many popular versions of pronunciations used by those professing no local or personal knowledge of the names, there are cases, like those of *Carlisle* and *Newcastle*, in which an accepted 'national' pronunciation has been recorded, even though it is not necessarily the most general one among the educated local population. Many historians, artists, musicians, scientists, and others have been consulted about present-day spoken forms of historic names. Descendants of historical personages, too, have sometimes provided interesting information about past and present usage. For entries like *Wriothesley*, where evidence was elusive, various written sources were also consulted.

Spellings

For place-name spellings, the authorities accepted have been the Handbook entitled *Post Offices in the United Kingdom* published by the Post Office in November 1974, the *Census 1971, England and Wales, Index of Place-names*, the *Ordnance Survey Gazetteer of Great Britain*, the *Gazetteer of Welsh Place-Names*, and Bartholomew's *Survey Gazetteer of the British Isles* and *Gazetteer of Britain*. Spellings of titles were verified in Debrett.

Titles

The pronunciation of a title has been linked, according to its origin, sometimes with a family name and sometimes with a place name. In the case of an historic hereditary title where the line of succession has come to an end, or the title is in abeyance, and the last holder's pronunciation is known to us, this has been recorded, as appropriate, as a *dukedom, earldom, viscountcy*, or *barony*. Likewise, the term *barony* appears in association with certain family names to record the specific pronunciation of one who has been a life peer. However, no mention is made of the large majority of life peers whose title is identical with their family name and whose pronunciation is in no doubt. A place name has sometimes been retained in a title, not because it is an integral part of the title, but because of its pronunciation interest. This situation arises when the place name, in this particular form, appears only in the title and is not to be found elsewhere, e.g., *Viscount Greenwood of Holbourne, Baron Tedder of Glenguin*. The opportunity to record the pronunciation might otherwise be lost. There are titles, on the other hand, where the territorial designation is included as a matter of course because it is an essential distinguishing feature of the title, e.g., *Baron Balfour of Burleigh, Baron Balfour of Inchrye*.

County names

The names of counties, or in Scotland regions, have been included for each place name recorded. Many place names occur in more than one county or region. In such cases only those counties have been included for which satisfactory evidence of the pronunciation has been obtained by the Pronunciation Unit. For instance, Bartholomew's *Survey Gazetteer of the British Isles* records 48 places called *Broughton*, but for those in counties not named in the dictionary, we have not had occasion to verify the pronunciation. When a river flows through more than one county, those counties have been identified.

Indexing

Names of the same spelling appear in the sequence of Christian name (i.e., personal first name), family name (i.e., surname), and place name. A title, if isolated, precedes all of these, but titles generally are associated with particular family or place names. Otherwise names are in strict letter-by-letter alphabetical order. Where the same sequence of letters appears twice, as a single word and as a group of two or more words, the single word is given precedence, e.g., *Vandyck*, *Van Dyck*.

All names beginning *Mac-*, *Mc-* or *M'-* have been treated as beginning with *Mac-*, and placed accordingly. Optional ways of writing this initial syllable, according to family preference, are exemplified in the name *MacGregor*, *Macgregor*, *McGregor*, *M'Gregor*.

St., the standard abbreviation of *Saint* in family and place names, is treated for alphabetical purposes as if it were written in full. In general, the names of saints associated with these islands occur, as do other Christian names, in their due alphabetical places throughout the book. Certain of them, however, having come to the notice of the BBC in the form of names of individual churches or hospitals, have found their place alphabetically under *St.*, intermingled with place names and family names.

Unless otherwise stated, it may be assumed that the ordering of variant pronunciations within an entry is as follows for place names: the first entry is that preferred by the local educated population, and is recommended to BBC announcers. Local dialectal pronunciations are given last if at all. Between these two extremes are given, in descending order of frequency heard (in so far as we can judge) any other variant pronunciations we have been made aware of.

All entries under a place name refer to one specific place. Family names with variants must be understood differently: some bearers of the name prefer one pronunciation, others prefer another. Thus *Kenneth Alwyn* (conductor) is ˈɔlwɪn, áwlwin, while *William Alwyn* (composer) is ˈælwɪn, álwin, and to refer to them otherwise would be, at the least, discourteous, if not completely wrong. Even so, in a very general way, the first pronunciation given is normally that for which we have the most evidence, and subsequent ones are in an approximate order of decreasing frequency.

Welsh names

Those who are already aware of the complex linguistic situation arising from the differing pronunciations of North and South Wales on the one hand, and from the existence of a demotic and a classical language on the other, will appreciate that the BBC's need to adapt individual pronunciations still further to the speech of English announcers must inevitably produce different solutions from those which might appear in a work of exclusively Welsh interest. It can be taken for granted, however, that a BBC announcer is expected at least to distinguish between *l* and *ll* in those Welsh names in which these consonants would be differentiated by local educated speakers of English. Professor A. Lloyd James, whose comprehensive collection of Welsh names and their pronunciations was published by the BBC in 1934 in *Broadcast English IV*, found it necessary to recommend considerably anglicized versions for the use of announcers in London and the rest of the country. In the present work extensive advice on the adaptation of these names and many others has been given by Dr Aled Rhys Wiliam, Mr Jack Windsor Lewis, and Miss Nia Rhosier; if there has been any failure to adopt their recommendations, the fault is certainly not theirs. Orthography was checked largely against *A Gazetteer of Welsh Place-Names* prepared by the Language and Literature Committee of the Board of Celtic Studies of the University of Wales, but in cases where this was at variance with *Post Offices in the United Kingdom* the final decision was allowed to rest with the latter, as it is the forms used there which are most likely to appear in national newspapers and in BBC news bulletins. Nevertheless, the Committee's admirable principle of making stress patterns clear by the use of hyphens has been followed wherever possible. In Welsh names stressed at the regular penultimate syllable no hyphens are necessary. The appearance of a hyphen before the final syllable, however, reveals that stress falls on that syllable, e.g., *Troedrhiw-fuwch*. The practical benefit of the system is perhaps most evident in two-syllable names which, in North Wales, tend usually to be stressed on the first (or penultimate) syllable, whereas in the South their counterparts are often stressed on the second (or final) syllable, thus, *Penrhos* in Gwynedd, but *Pen-rhos* in Gwent and Powys. Hyphens are in general also used before and after the definite article in three-syllable names where the stress falls on the last syllable, as in *Pen-y-bank*, *Pen-y-fan*, *Pont-y-clun*.

KEY TO PRONUNCIATION

Two systems have been employed to indicate pronunciation, one for the benefit of those acquainted with the International Phonetic Association's method of symbolizing sounds and the other for the general user. In the IPA system, a 'multiliteral' transcription has been used, with the addition of italicized [ə], [h], [r], [p], [d], to indicate variant pronunciations. For the second method an English modified spelling system has been used which, after its explanations have been studied, should be immediately obvious to most English speakers. The systems have been adapted to Received Pronunciation, which is familiar alike to BBC announcers and to listeners and viewers in this country and overseas, whether it happens to be their own type of speech or not. The only exception to this is that orthographic *r* is acknowledged in both pronunciation systems. In those cases, however, in which it is in general omitted by Southern English speakers, it it written as italicized [r] in the IPA version.

Vowels

IPA symbol	English modified spelling	Words containing sound
i	ee	see
ɪ	i	pity
e	e	get
æ	a	hat
ɑ	aa	father
ɒ	o	not
ɔ	aw	law
ʊ	o͞o	book
u	oo	food
ʌ	u	but
ə	ă, ĕ, ŏ, ŭ	*about*, butt*er*
ɜ	er, ur, ir	fern, fur, fir
	ö	*is used to indicate this same centralized vowel sound in cases where there is no 'r' in the original spelling*, e.g.

Beinn Laoigh ben 'lɜɪ, ben lö̆-i

De Veulle də 'vɜl, dĕ vö̆l

Des Voex deɪ 'vɜ, day vö̆

Exotic vowels

		More or less as in French
æ̃	a*ng*	vin
ã	aa*ng*	banc
õ	ō*ng*	bon
ɛ:	e	fèvre
y	ü	du

Diphthongs

eɪ	ay	day
aɪ	ī	high
ɔɪ	oy	boy
oʊ	ō	no
aʊ	ow	now
ɪə	eer	here
ɛə	air	there
ʊə	ōor	poor

Consonants

p, b, t, d, k, m, n, l, r, f, v, s, z, h, w are used in both transcriptions with their customary English values.

Otherwise the symbols are:

g	g	get
x	<u>ch</u>	Scottish *loch*
tʃ	ch, tch	church
dʒ	j	jet
n̩	n	see note on syllabic n
ŋ	ng	sing
l̩	l	see note on syllabic l
ɬ	<u>hl</u>	Welsh *llan*
θ	th	thin
ð	<u>th</u>	there
ʃ	sh	shut
ʒ	<u>zh</u>	*s* in *measure*
r̥	r	is used in French-type pronunciations to denote devoiced, non-syllabic r following p, t; e.g., **Earl of Ypres** ipr̥, eepr̥
*h*w	wh	where
j	y	yes

Stress symbols

In the IPA transcription main stress is indicated by the symbol ['] preceding the stressed syllable, and secondary stress by the symbol [,]. In modified spelling, secondary stress is not shown, but main stress is indicated by an acute accent '′' above the syllable. Thus:

     Aberdeen *Grampian*, ˌæbər'din, abbĕrdéen

Use of hyphens

The use of hyphens in the IPA script has been kept to a minimum, but hyphens have been introduced to avoid the ambiguity which might arise when [ɪə] and [ɔɪ] are employed not as diphthongs but in each case as two distinct vowels. *Flawith* makes the point particularly well, as its pronunciation allows two such variants: 'flɔ-ɪθ, fláw-ith; flɔɪθ, floyth. In modified spelling hyphens are used more frequently, and generally for obvious reasons. A less obvious treatment becomes necessary in a name like the Welsh *Dewi*, where the use of open [e] 'e' before [w] 'w' constitutes a sound sequence unfamiliar to most users of the Received Pronunciation of English, and where the pronunciation ['dewɪ] has been written 'dé-wi'. Similarly, the Irish name *Mulcahy*, pronounced [mʌl'kæhɪ] with *a* as in 'cat', has been written 'mulká-hi'.

The two systems

In the text, the IPA transcription precedes the modified spelling, the two being separated by a comma. Where more than one pronunciation is shown, a semi-colon keeps them apart. The two methods are systematically related, although the precision of the IPA system cannot be quite matched by the other, and certain concessions have had to be made in the modified spelling system in order to avoid misinterpretation. For example, the sound corresponding to [ju] appears as 'yoo' at the beginning of a pronunciation, as in **Udall** 'judɔl, yoodawl, but in all other cases as 'ew'; that corresponding to [ɔr] is generally written 'or', but before another vowel, or following 'w', it becomes 'awr', so that **Dorey** 'dɔrɪ, dáwri may not be mistaken for 'dɒrɪ, dórri, and that the initial syllables *Ward-*, *Wark-*, and *Warm-*, pronounced [wɔrd-], 'wawrd-', [wɔrk-], 'wawrk-', [wɔrm-], 'wawrm-', should not be confused with the English words *word*, *work*, and *worm*. A convention of the modified spelling is that it is in general related to the original spelling of the name, so that *Burghersh* is written 'búrgersh', although the two vowel sounds are the same. Wherever they occur, the modified spellings 'ăr', 'ĕr', 'ŭr' are merely different representations of the same sound. A double consonant, or in appropriate cases 'ck', is used to make the open nature of the preceding vowel more obvious, as in **Debenham** 'debənəm, débběnăm, **Brecon** 'brekən, bréckŏn.

Unstressed syllables

In many names, unstressed syllables have alternative forms whose vowels may be transcribed in the IPA system in the one case as [ə] and in the other as [ɪ]. To include both of these in all entries would have increased greatly the bulk of the dictionary. Consequently a simplified solution has been found: both pronunciations have been shown where the traditional orthography spells the unstressed vowel *a*, *i*, or *y*, while for such names with *e* in the traditional orthography the IPA transcription uses [ɪ], but the Modified Spelling has 'ĕ', which may be interpreted by the reader as either [ə] or [ɪ].

Exotic vowels

As the key to pronunciation shows, the nasalization of a vowel in IPA script is indicated by the use of a tilde [~] over it; in modified spelling, it is shown by writing an italicized '*ng*' after the vowel. Of the nasal vowels the first, [æ̃] 'a*ng*', is related to the [æ] 'a' of English *hat*; the second, [ɑ̃] 'aa*ng*', to the [ɑ] 'aa' sound of English *father*; and the third, [õ] 'ō*ng*' to the close *o* used by many Scots, Irish, and Welsh speakers in the word *no*. The vowel [ɛ:]—the only instance in which the IPA length mark [:] has been used, incidentally—is a lengthened version of the first vowel in English *ever*. In Southern English usage [eɪ] 'ay' is generally substituted for this sound, but there are names in which a closer approximation to the foreign sound is usual.

Syllabic l

In the numerous cases in which final syllables spelt -*al*, -*all*, -*el*, -*ell*, -*il*, -*ill*, -*ull* are pronounced as a syllabic *l*, no indeterminate vowel has been introduced into either system of pronunciation and they are written simply as *l*, e.g., **Dougall** 'dugl, doʹogl; **Mitchell** 'mɪtʃl, mítchl; **Sempill** 'sempl, sémpl; **Minshull** 'mɪnʃl, mínshl. When a syllabic *l* occurs in the middle of a word, however, it becomes necessary to introduce a syllabic mark, [l̩], in the IPA script, and to use a hyphen in an appropriate place in the modified spelling. Thus, **Chittlehamholt** 'tʃɪtl̩əmhoʊlt, chíttl-ăm-hōlt, to suggest that, in the more careful pronunciation at least, the *l* would constitute a syllable in itself.

Syllabic n

There is a good deal of variety in the treatment of final unstressed syllables in which the following consonants are preceded by a vowel, and followed by another vowel plus *n*: [t] 't', [d] 'd', [s] 's', [z] 'z', [ʃ] 'sh', [ʒ] 'zh'. Although the majority usually in relaxed speech make the *n* syllabic, some endeavour, even in informal speech, always to retain the indeterminate vowel, and this has been indicated by writing (ən) with an italicized, alternative [ə] in IPA script, and 'ăn', 'ĕn', 'ŏn', 'ŭn', not merely 'n', in modified spelling, e.g., **Beaton** 'bitən, béetŏn; **Rowden** 'raʊdən, rówdĕn. Occasionally, on the other hand, it becomes necessary to accommodate a syllabic *n* in the middle of a name, and this is done by writing [n̩], with a syllabic mark, in IPA script and using a hyphen to show the suitable break in modified spelling, e.g., **Aldenham,** Baron 'ɔldn̩əm, áwldn-ăm.

Italicized [ə] in IPA transcription

Although the use of italicized [ə] in the IPA transcription has been restricted largely to endings where syllabic *n* may occur, it could feasibly be extended to cover such further possible variants as [-bərə], [-bərɪ], [-dʒəm],

[-ʃəm], [-rəm], [-rən], [-wəl]. This would not in most cases affect the present modified spelling renderings.

Italicized [r] in IPA transcription

The decision to acknowledge orthographic r in all positions in both pronunciation systems leads to its italicization in the IPA transcription in the following positions:

(1) before consonants, e.g., **Parnell** pɑr'nel, paarnéll

(2) in final positions, e.g., **Grosvenor** 'groʊvnər, grŏv-nŏr, except when this is a linking r, as mentioned below.

It is not italicized

(1) in initial positions, e.g., **Renwick** 'renɪk, rénnick

(2) after consonants, e.g., **Franklin** 'fræŋklɪn, fránklin

(3) as linking r between two words, where the second word begins with a vowel, e.g., **Over Alderley** 'oʊvər 'ɔldərlɪ, ŏvĕr áwldĕrli.

The devoiced [r̥] 'r', used in the *Earl of Ypres* and similar names, occurs only after the unvoiced plosives *p*, *t*. It is employed to guard against the possible interpretation of the single-syllable [ipr̥], 'eepr' as two syllables, ['ipər], 'éepĕr'.

Initial orthographic rh

Rh occurs particularly at the beginning of Welsh names and is generally an indication that the *r* is a strong voiceless sound in the Welsh language; but, as this is a pronunciation not usually employed by non-Welsh speakers, it has not been shown in the modified spelling pronunciation. Its presence in Welsh, however, is acknowledged by writing [hr] in IPA script, so that *Rhos*, for example, appears as [hroʊs], 'rōss'.

Orthographic rhiw

This root may occur initially, medially, or finally in Welsh place names. To pronounce it as one syllable, [hrju], 'rew', is normal in Welsh, but not in RP usage, and it has in general been treated as [hrɪ'u], 'ri-óo', with [ˌhriu], 'ree-oo' occasionally when it is initial.

Initial orthographic wh

While most southern speakers, at least, habitually make
no distinction in pronunciation between such pairs of
words as *Wales* and *whales*, others regularly do. It is a
matter of usage in particular regions or speech groups.
Allowance has been made for both schools here by
writing [*h*w] in IPA script, and by showing 'wh' in
modified spelling, e.g., **Whitefield** 'hwaɪtfɪld, whítfeeld.
In those cases in which there has been no evidence of
the existence of a pronunciation with [hw], no [h] has
been shown. A further possible treatment of the spelling
occurs in the name **Whewell**, pronounced 'hjuəl,
héw-ĕl.

Final orthographic -ian, -ien, -ion, -ear, -ier, -iour, -iel, -iol

In all cases where the pronunciation of these syllables
has been indicated in IPA script as [-ɪən], [-ɪər], [-ɪəl], it
can be taken for granted that the alternatives [-jən],
[-jər], [-jəl] are acceptable variations, e.g., **Fabian**
'feɪbɪən, fáybi-ăn; **Collier** 'kɒlɪər, kólli-ĕr; **Baliol**
'beɪlɪəl, báyli-ŏl can also be 'feɪbjən, fáyb-yăn; 'kɒljər,
kól-yĕr; 'beɪljəl, báyl-yŏl.

Attributive stress

An aspect of stress to be remembered is that, although
a two- or three-syllable name may be stressed on the
final syllable when used in isolation, more often than
not the stress moves to the first syllable when it is used
attributively. For example, *Thorness* is pronounced
θɔr'nes, thornéss; but *Thorness Bay*, in the natural
rhythm of the English language, becomes 'θɔrnes 'beɪ,
thórness báy. This point has not been elaborated in
individual cases, but taken for granted, and the stress
shown is that which would apply if the name were used
in isolation.

Initial Dun- and Strath- in Celtic names

The unstressed initial syllables *Dun-* and *Strath-* in
Scottish and Northern Irish names have been shown in
this book only as [dʌn-], 'dun-' and [stræθ-], 'strath-',

which is the way in which they are pronounced in careful speech; but in colloquial use they are just as often pronounced [dən-], 'dŭn-' and [strəθ-], 'străth-', and a footnote to this effect appears on the relevant pages.

ABBREVIATIONS

County and region names

Beds.	Bedfordshire
Berks.	Berkshire
Bucks.	Buckinghamshire
Cambs.	Cambridgeshire
Ches.	Cheshire
D. & G.	Dumfries and Galloway
Derby.	Derbyshire
Glos.	Gloucestershire
Gtr. M'chester	Greater Manchester
H. & W.	Hereford and Worcester
Hants	Hampshire
Herts.	Hertfordshire
H'land	Highland
Lancs.	Lancashire
Leics.	Leicestershire
Lincs.	Lincolnshire
Northants.	Northamptonshire
Northd.	Northumberland
Notts.	Nottinghamshire
Oxon.	Oxfordshire
Salop	Shropshire
S'clyde	Strathclyde
Staffs.	Staffordshire
Wilts.	Wiltshire
Yorks.	Yorkshire

Other abbreviations

admin. dist.	administrative district
anc.	ancient
A.-S.	Anglo-Saxon
Assoc.	Association
c.	century
cf.	compare
C.n.	Christian name
Co.	County
Coll.	College

div.	division
f.n.	family name
HRH	His *or* Her Royal Highness
I.	Isle, -s
mt.	mountain
nr.	near
q.v.	which see
Rt. Revd	Right Reverend
St.	Saint *or* Street
Univ.	University

WORKS OF REFERENCE
CONSULTED

Bardsley, C. W. (1901): *A Dictionary of English and Welsh Surnames*. Henry Frowde, London.

Bartholomew, J. (1951): *Survey Gazetteer of the British Isles*, 9th edition. Bartholomew, Edinburgh.

Davies, E. (ed.) (1958): *A Gazetteer of Welsh Place-Names*, 2nd edition. University of Wales Press, Cardiff.

Gimson, A. C. (ed.) (1977): *Everyman's English Pronouncing Dictionary*, 14th edition. Dent, London.

Hudson, E. (ed.) (1958): *Commercial Gazetteer of Great Britain*. Geographia, London.

Lloyd-James, A. (1936): *Broadcast English II: Recommendations to announcers regarding the pronunciation of some English place-names*, 2nd edition. BBC, London.

—— (1932): *Broadcast English III: Recommendations to announcers regarding the pronunciation of some Scottish place-names*. BBC, London.

—— (1934): *Broadcast English IV: Recommendations to announcers regarding the pronunciation of some Welsh place-names*. BBC, London.

—— (1935): *Broadcast English V: Recommendations to announcers regarding the pronunciation of some Northern-Irish place-names*. BBC, London.

—— (1939): *Broadcast English VII: Recommendations to announcers regarding the pronunciation of some British family names and titles*. BBC, London.

Mason, O. (1977): *Gazetteer of Britain*, 1st edition. Bartholomew, Edinburgh.

Montague-Smith, P. (ed.) (1979): *Peerage, Baronetage, Knightage, and Companionage*. Debrett's Peerage, London. Earlier editions also consulted.

Reaney, P. H. (1961): *A Dictionary of British Surnames*. Routledge and Kegan Paul, London.

Thorne, J. O. (ed.) (1963): *Chambers's Biographical Dictionary*, new edition 1961, revised 1963. Chambers, Edinburgh.

Townend, P. (ed.) (1971): *Peerage, Baronetage and Knightage*. Burke's Publishing, London. Earlier editions also consulted.

Withycombe, E. G. (1950): *The Oxford Dictionary of English Christian Names*, 2nd edition. Oxford University Press, Oxford.

Census 1971, England and Wales, Index of Place-Names (1977). HMSO, London.

Concise Dictionary of National Biography Part I (1953). Oxford University Press, Oxford.

Crockford's Clerical Directory (1979). Oxford University Press, London. Earlier editions also consulted.

Ordnance Survey Gazetteer of Great Britain (1969). HMSO, London.

Post Offices in the United Kingdom (1974). HMSO, London.

Webster's Pronouncing Biographical Dictionary, 2nd edition (1961). Bell, London.

Who's Who 1981. Black, London. Earlier editions also consulted.

MEMBERS OF THE
BBC PRONUNCIATION UNIT
SINCE ITS INCEPTION

Miss G. M. Miller, MBE, *Pronunciation Assistant 1939–71*
Mrs C. H. M. Langlands, *Pronunciation Assistant 1971*
Mrs H. C. Wright, *Pronunciation Assistant-in-Charge 1971–78*
Mrs S. E. Fairman, *Acting Pronunciation Assistant-in-Charge 1978*
G. E. Pointon, *Pronunciation Adviser 1979–*

Miss E. D. Anderson
Miss P. O. Blyth
Miss J. Brennan
Miss L. A. Broome
Mrs A. C. Chappell
Miss K. C. Coombe
Miss M. G. Cooper
Miss M. T. Edmond
Miss H. D. Fairbank
Miss P. M. Hurst
Miss M. Lane
Miss F. Liddle
Miss H. Likeman
Mrs L. L. S. Montague
Miss A. C. Mylod
Miss M. Slowey
Mrs M. Spearman
Mrs E. A. Terry
Miss J. M. Wilson

A

Aagaard, *f.n.,* 'eɪɡɑrd, áygaard
Aan, River, *also spelt* **Aven,**
   Grampian, ɑn, aan
Aaronovitch, *f.n.,* ə'rɒnəvɪtʃ,
   ărónnŏvitch
Aarvold, *f.n.,* 'ɑrvoʊld, áarvōld
Abady, Temple, *composer,* 'templ
   'æbədɪ, témpl ábbădi
Abaty Cwmhir *Powys,* ə'bætɪ kʊm-
   'hɪər, ăbátti kŏŏm-heér. *Welsh
   form of* **Abbeycwmhir,** *q.v.*
Abberley *Wilts.,* 'æbərlɪ, ábbĕrli
Abbeycwmhir *Powys,* 'æbɪ kʊm-
   'hɪər, ábbi kŏŏm-heér. *English
   form of* **Abaty Cwmhir,** *q.v.*
Abbey St. Bathans *Borders,* 'æbɪ
   snt 'bæθənz, ábbi sĭnt báthănz
Abbiss, *f.n.,* 'æbɪs, ábbiss
Abbots Bromley *Staffs.,* 'æbəts
   'brɒmlɪ, ábbŏts brŏmli
Abbotsham *Devon,* 'æbətsəm,
   ábbŏtsăm
Abbotsinch *S'clyde,* 'æbətsɪnʃ,
   ábbŏtsinsh
Abbotskerswell *Devon,* 'æbəts-
   'kɜrzwəl, ábbŏtskérzwĕl
Abbs, *f.n.,* æbz, abz
Abdela, *f.n.,* æb'delə, abdéllă
Abel, *f.n.,* 'eɪbl, áybl
Abelard, *f.n.,* 'æbəlɑrd, ábbĕlaard.
   *Appropriate also for the ~
   Music Ensemble.*
Abelard-Schuman, *publishers and
   printers,* 'æbəlɑrd 'ʃumən,
   ábbĕlaard shoʻomǎn
Abelé, *f.n.,* 'eɪbəlɪ, áybĕli
Aberaeron, *also spelt* **Aberayron,**
   Dyfed, ,æbər'aɪrən, abbĕrírŏn
Aberafan *W. Glam.,* ,æbər'ævən,
   abbĕrávvăn. *Welsh form of*
   Aberavon.
Aberaman *Mid Glam.,* ,æbər-
   'æmən, abbĕrámmăn
Aberangell *Gwynedd,* ,æbər'æŋeɬ,
   abbĕráng-e̱hl
Aberarth *Dyfed,* ,æbər'ɑrθ,
   abbĕráarth
Aberavon *W. Glam.,* ,æbər'ævən,
   abbĕrávvŏn
Aberayron *see* **Aberaeron**
Aberbargod *see* **Aberbargoed**
Aberbargoed, *also spelt* **Aberbar-
   god,** *Mid Glam.,* ,æbər'bɑrɡɔɪd,
   abbĕrbaʻargoyd; ,æbər'bɑrɡɒd,
   abbĕrbaʻargod; ,æbər'bɑrɡɔd,
   abbĕrbaʻargawd
Aberbeeg *Gwent,* ,æbər'big,
   abbĕrbeeg

Aberbig *Gwent,* ,æbər'big,
   abbĕrbeeg. *Welsh form of* **Aberbeeg.**
Aberbran *Powys,* ,æbər'brɑn,
   abbĕrbraʻan
Abercairney *Tayside,* ,æbər'keərnɪ,
   abbĕrkáirni
Abercanaid *Mid Glam.,* ,æbər-
   'kænaɪd, abbĕrkánnïd
Abercarn *Gwent,* ,æbər'karn,
   abbĕrkaʻarn
Aberchalder *H'land,* ,æbər-
   'xɔldər, abbĕr<u>ch</u>áwldĕr
Aberchirder *Grampian,* ,æbər-
   'xɜrdər, abbĕr<u>ch</u>írdĕr
Aberconway, Baron, ,æbər'kɒn-
   weɪ, abbĕrkónway
Aberconwy, *Gwynedd,* ,æbər-
   'kɒnwɪ, abbĕrkónwi
Abercorn, Duke of, 'æbərkɔrn,
   ábbĕrkorn
Abercraf *Powys,* ,æbər'krɑv,
   abbĕrkraʻav. *Welsh form of*
   Abercrave, *q.v.*
Abercrave *Powys,* ,æbər'kreɪv,
   abbĕrkráyv. *English form of*
   Abercraf, *q.v.*
Abercregan *W. Glam.,* ,æbər-
   'kregən, abbĕrkréggăn
Abercrombie, *f.n.,* 'æbərkrʌmbɪ,
   ábbĕrkrumbi; 'æbərkrɒmbɪ,
   ábbĕrkrombi. *The first is
   appropriate for Sir Patrick ~,
   architect, and Lascelles ~, poet.*
Abercwmboi *Mid Glam.,* ,æbər-
   kʊm'bɔɪ, abbĕrkŏŏm-bóy
Abercynon *Mid Glam.,* ,æbər-
   'kʌnən, abbĕrkúnnŏn
Aberdare *Mid Glam.,* ,æbər'deər,
   abbĕrdáir. *Appropriate also for
   Baron ~.*
Aberdaron *Gwynedd,* ,æbər'dærən,
   abbĕrdárrŏn
Aberdeen *Grampian,* ,æbər'din,
   abbĕrdeén
Aberdeen and Temair, Marquess
   of, ,æbər'din ənd tɪ'meər,
   abbĕrdeén ănd tĕmáir
Aberdonian, *native of Aberdeen,*
   ,æbər'doʊnɪən, abbĕrdṓniăn
Aberdour *Fife, Grampian,* ,æbər-
   'dauər, abbĕrdówr
Aberdovey *Gwynedd,* ,æbər'dʌvɪ,
   abbĕrdúvvi
Aberdulais *W. Glam.,* ,æbər-
   'dɪlaɪs, abbĕrdílliss
Aberedw *Powys,* ,æbər'eɪdu,
   abbĕráydoo

Abererch Gwynedd, ˌæbər'ɛərx, abbĕráirch

Aberfan Mid Glam., ˌæbər'væn, abbĕrván

Aberfeldy Tayside, ˌæbər'feldɪ, abbĕrféldi

Aberffraw Gwynedd, ə'bɛərfrau, äbáirfrow

Aberffrwd Dyfed, ˌæbər'frud, abbĕrfroʻod

Abergavenny, Marquess of, ˌæbər'genɪ, abbĕrgénni

Abergavenny Gwent, ˌæbərgə-'venɪ, abbĕrgăvénni

Abergele Clwyd, ˌæbər'geleɪ, abbĕrgéllay

Aberglaslyn Pass Gwynedd, ˌæbər-'glæslɪn, abbĕrglásslin

Abergorlech Dyfed, ˌæbər'gɔrləx, abbĕrgórlĕch

Abergwessin Powys, ˌæbər-'gwesɪn, abbĕrgwéssin

Abergwili Dyfed, ˌæbər'gwɪlɪ, abbĕrgwílli

Abergwynfi W. Glam., ˌæbər-'gwɪnvɪ, abbĕrgwínvi

Abergynolwyn Gwynedd, ˌæbər-gʌn'ɒlwɪn, abbĕrgunólwin

Aberhafesp Powys, ˌæbər'hævesp, abbĕr-hávvesp

Aberkenfig Mid Glam., ˌæbər-'kenfɪg, abbĕrkénfig

Aberlady Lothian, ˌæbər'leɪdɪ, abbĕrláydi

Aberllefenni Gwynedd, ˌæbərɬə-'venɪ, abbĕrhlĕvénni

Aberlour Grampian, ˌæbər'lauər, abbĕrlówr

Abermorddu Clwyd, ˌæbər'mɔrðɪ, abbĕrmórthi

Abermule Powys, ˌæbər'mjul, abbĕrméwl

Abernant Dyfed, ˌæbər'nænt, abbĕrnánt

Abernethy H'land, Tayside, ˌæbər'neθɪ, abbĕrnéthi. Appropriate also for Lord ~.

Aberpedwar Powys, ˌæbər'pedwər, abbĕrpédwăr

Aberporth Dyfed, ˌæbər'pɔrθ, abbĕrpórth

Abersoch Gwynedd, ˌæbər'soux, abbĕr-sóch

Abersychan Gwent, ˌæbər'sʌxən, abbĕr-súchăn

Abertay, Barony of, ˌæbər'teɪ, abbĕrtáy

Aberthaw S. Glam., ˌæbər'θɔ, abbĕr-tháw

Abertillery Gwent, ˌæbərtɪ'lɛərɪ, abbĕrtiláiri

Abertridwr Mid Glam., Powys, ˌæbər'trɪduər, abbĕrtríddo͞or

Abertysswg Mid Glam., ˌæbər-'tʌsug, abbĕrtússo͞og

Aberuchill Tayside, ˌæbər'uxɪl, abbĕro͝ochil

Aberuthven Tayside, ˌæbə'rɪvən, abbĕrívvĕn

Aberystwyth Dyfed, ˌæbər'ɪstwɪθ, abbĕrístwith; ˌæbər'ʌstwɪθ, abbĕrústwith

Abineri, f.n., æbɪ'nɛərɪ, abbináiri

Abinger Surrey, 'æbɪndʒər, ábbinjĕr. Appropriate also for Baron ~.

Abinger Hammer Surrey, 'æbɪndʒər 'hæmər, ábbinjĕr hámmĕr

Abington Northants., S'clyde, 'æbɪŋtən, ábbingtŏn

Abington Pigotts Cambs., 'æbɪŋtən 'pɪgəts, ábbingtŏn píggŏts

Abley, f.n., 'æblɪ, ábbli

Aboyne Grampian, ə'bɔɪn, ăbóyn. Appropriate also for the Earl of ~.

Abra, f.n., 'eɪbrə, áybră

Abrahams, f.n., 'eɪbrəhəmz, áybră-hämz

Abram Gtr. M'chester, 'æbrəm, ábrăm

Abridge Essex, 'eɪbrɪdʒ, áybrij

Abse, f.n., 'æbzɪ, ábzi

Aby Lincs., 'eɪbɪ, áybi

Acaster Malbis N. Yorks., ə'kæstər 'mælbɪs, ăkástĕr málbiss

Achanalt H'land, ˌæxə'nælt, achănált

Achany Glen H'land, 'æxənɪ, áchăni

Acharacle H'land, ə'xærəkl̩, ăchárrăkl

Acharn Tayside, ə'xɑrn, ăchaʻarn

Achdalieu H'land, ˌæxdə'lu, achdálo͞o

Acheson, f.n., 'ætʃɪsən, átchĕssŏn

Achillini, f.n., ˌækɪ'linɪ, ackilléeni

Achmore, also spelt **Auchmore**, Central, 'æx'mɔr, ách-mór

Achmore H'land, 'æx'mɔr, ách-mór

Achmore W. Isles, 'æxmɔr, ách-mor

Achnacarry H'land, ˌæxnə'kærɪ, achnăkárri

Achnasheen H'land, ˌæxnə'ʃin, achnăshéen

Achonry, f.n., 'ækənrɪ, áckŏnri; ə'kɒnrɪ, ăkónri

Achray, Loch and Forest, Central, ə'xreɪ, ăchráy

Achurch Northants., 'eɪtʃərtʃ, áytchurtch

Ackrill, f.n., 'ækrɪl, áckril

Ackroyd, f.n., 'ækrɔɪd, áckroyd

Acland, *f.n.*, 'æklənd, áckländ
Acle *Norfolk*, 'eɪkl, áykl
Acol *Kent*, 'eɪkɒl, áykol
Acomb, *f.n.*, 'eɪkəm, áykŏm
Acomb *Northd., N. Yorks.*,
'eɪkəm, áykŏm
Acontius, Jacobus, *Elizabethan
philosopher and engineer,* dʒə-
'koʊbəs ə'kɒntɪəs, jäkŏbúss
äkóntiŭss; ə'kɒnʃɪəs, äkónshi-
-ŭss. *He hailed from the Tirol
and was originally Jacopo
Aconzio,* 'jækəpoʊ ə'kɒntsɪoʊ,
yáckŏpō äkóntsiō.
Acott, *f.n.*, 'eɪkɒt, áykot
A'court, *f.n.*, 'eɪkɔrt, áykort
Acraman, *f.n.*, 'ækrəmən,
áckrämän
Acrefair *Clwyd*, ‚ækrɪ'vaɪər,
ackrĕvír
Acrise *Kent*, 'eɪkris, áykreess;
'eɪkrɪs, áykriss
Acton Burnell *Salop*, 'æktən bər-
'nel, ácktŏn burnéll
Acutt, *f.n.*, 'eɪkʌt, áykut
Adair, *f.n.*, ə'dɛər, ädáir
Adam, *f.n.*, 'ædəm, áddăm
Adare, *f.n.*, ə'dɛər, ädáir. *Appro-
priate also for Viscount* ~.
Adbaston *Staffs.*, 'ædbəstən,
ádbăstŏn
Adburgham, *f.n.*, æd'bərgəm,
adbúrgăm
Adcock, *f.n.*, 'ædkɒk, ádkock
Addlebrough *N. Yorks.*, 'ædlbərə,
áddlbŭră
Addlestone *Surrey*, 'ædlstoʊn,
áddlstōn
Adeane, *f.n.*, ə'din, ädeén
Adel *W. Yorks.*, 'ædl, áddl
Adeney, *f.n.*, 'eɪdn̩ɪ, áydn-i;
'eɪdnɪ, áyd-ni
Ades, *f.n.*, 'ædɪs, áddiss
Adey, *f.n.*, 'eɪdɪ, áydi
Adeyfield *Herts.*, 'eɪdɪfɪld, áydi-
-feeld
Adgie, *f.n.*, 'ædʒɪ, ájji
Adie, *f.n.*, 'eɪdɪ, áydi
Adisham *Kent*, 'ædɪʃəm,
áddi-shăm
Adlam, *f.n.*, 'ædləm, ádlăm
Adlard, *f.n.*, 'ædlɑrd, ádlaard
Adlestrop *Glos.*, 'ædlstrɒp, áddl-
-strop
Adley, *f.n.*, 'ædlɪ, ádli
Adorian, *f.n.*, ə'dɔrɪən, ädáwriăn
Adrianssens, *f.n.*, 'eɪdrɪənsənz,
áydriănssĕnz
Adshead, *f.n.*, 'ædzhed, ádz-
-hed
Adur, River, *W. Sussex*, 'eɪdər,
áydŭr. *Appropriate also for the
administrative district, which
takes its name from the river.*

Adversane *W. Sussex*, 'ædvər-
seɪn, ádvĕrssayn
Advie *H'land*, 'ædvɪ, ádvi
Adwalton *W. Yorks.*, æd'wɒltən,
adwáwltŏn. *A local pronuncia-
tion,* 'æðərtən, áthĕrtŏn, *derives
from Heather Town, an old
name for the area.*
Adwick-le-Street *S. Yorks.*,
'ædwɪk lɪ 'strit, ádwick li stréet
Adwick upon Dearne *S. Yorks.*,
'ædwɪk əpɒn 'dərn, ádwick
ŭpon dérn
Ady, *f.n.*, 'eɪdɪ, áydi
Adye, *f.n.*, 'eɪdɪ, áydi
Ae *D. & G.*, eɪ, ay
Aehron, *f.n.*, 'ɛərən, áirŏn
Aelred, *C.n.*, 'eɪlred, áylred
Aeolian Hall *London*, i'oʊlɪən,
ee-ṓli-än; eɪ'oʊlɪən, ay-ṓli-än
Aeronwy, *C.n.*, aɪə'rɒnwɪ, īrón-
-wi
Affleck, *f.n.*, 'æflek, áffleck
Afford, *f.n.*, 'æfɔrd, áffŏrd
Affric, Loch *and* River, *H'land*,
'æfrɪk, áffrick
Aflalo, *f.n.*, ə'flɑloʊ, äflaálō
Afon, River, *Mid Glam.–W. Glam.
boundary,* 'ævən, ávvŏn
Afon Wen *Gwynedd*, 'ævən 'wen,
ávvŏn wén
Afton, *f.n.*, 'æftən, áftŏn
Agar, *f.n.*, 'eɪgər, áygăr; 'eɪgɑr,
áygaar
Agate, *f.n.*, 'eɪgət, áygăt; 'ægət,
ággăt
Agen Allwedd *Powys*, 'ægen
'ælwəð, ággen áhl-wĕth. *Said to
be the longest cave in Britain,
part of the* **Dan yr Ogof** *cave
system (q.v.).*
Ager, *f.n.*, 'eɪgər, áygĕr; 'ædʒər,
ájjĕr; 'eɪdʒər, áyjĕr
Aggett, *f.n.*, 'ægɪt, ággĕt
Aghacully *Co. Antrim*, ‚æxə'kʌlɪ,
achăkúlli
Aghaderg *Co. Down*, ‚æxə'dərg,
achădérg. *Another form is*
Aghaderrick, *q.v.*
Aghaderrick *Co. Down*, ‚æxə-
'derɪk, achădérrick. *See also*
Aghaderg.
Aghadowey *Co. Derry*, ‚æxə'duɪ,
achădoó-i
Aghagallon *Co. Antrim*, ‚æxə-
'gælən, achăgálŏn
Aghalane *Co. Fermanagh*, ‚æxə-
'leɪn, achăláyn
Aghalee *Co. Antrim*, ‚æxə'li,
achălée
Aghanloo *Co. Derry*, ɑn'lu,
aanloó; ‚æxən'lu, achănloó
Agharan *Co. Tyrone*, ‚æxə'ræn,
achărán

Aghavea *Co. Fermanagh*, ˌæxə-'veɪ, aᴄhăváy

Aghyaran *Co. Tyrone*, ˌæxɪ'ɑrn, aᴄhi-aárn

Agius, *f.n.*, 'eɪdʒəs, áyjŭss

Agivey *Co. Derry*, ə'gɪvɪ, ăgívvi

Aglionby, *f.n.*, 'æglɪənbɪ, ággli--ŏnbi

Agnellus, *C.n.*, æg'neləs, ag--néllŭss

Agnew, *f.n.*, 'ægnju, ág-new

Ago, *f.n.*, 'agoʊ, aágō

Agoult, *f.n.*, 'ægult, ággoolt

Agrell, *f.n.*, ə'grel, ăgréll

Aguilar, *f.n.*, ə'gwɪlər, ăgwíllăr

Agutter, *f.n.*, 'ægətər, ággŭttĕr; ə'gʌtər, ăgúttĕr

Aherne, *f.n.*, ə'hɜrn, ăhérn

Ahoghill *Co. Antrim*, ə'hɒxɪl, ăhóᴄhil

Aichroth, *f.n.*, 'eɪtʃrɒθ, áytch-roth; 'eɪkrɒθ, áykroth

Aikman, *f.n.*, 'eɪkmən, áykmän

Aileen, *C.n.*, 'eɪlin, áyleen; 'aɪlin, íleen

Ailesbury, Marquess of, 'eɪlzbərɪ, áylzbŭri

Ailort, Loch *and* River, *H'land*, 'aɪlərt, ílŏrt

Ailsa, Marquess of, 'eɪlsə, áylssă

Ailsa Craig, *S'clyde*, 'eɪlzə 'kreɪg, áylză kráyg

Ailwyn, Baron, 'eɪlwɪn, áylwin

Aimers, *f.n.*, 'eɪmərz, áymĕrz

Ainge, *f.n.*, eɪndʒ, aynj

Ainley, *f.n.*, 'eɪnlɪ, áynli

Ainscough, *f.n.*, 'eɪnzkoʊ, áynzkō

Ainscow, *f.n.*, 'eɪnzkoʊ, áynzkō

Ainsley, *f.n.*, 'eɪnzlɪ, áynzli

Ainslie, *f.n.*, 'eɪnzlɪ, áynzli

Aintree *Merseyside*, 'eɪntrɪ, áyntri

Aird, *f.n.*, ɛərd, aird

Airdrie *S'clyde*, 'ɛərdrɪ, áirdri

Airds, The, *S'clyde*, ɛərdz, airdz

Aire, River, *N. Yorks.*, ɛər, air

Airedale, Baron, 'ɛərdeɪl, áirdayl

Airey of Abingdon, Baroness, 'ɛərɪ əv 'æbɪŋdən, áiri ŏv ábbingdŏn

Airlie, Earl of, 'ɛərlɪ, áirli

Airor *H'land*, 'ɛərər, áirŏr

Airthrey Castle, *also spelt* **Airthrie**, *Central*, 'ɛərθrɪ, áirthri

Aish *Devon*, eɪʃ, aysh; æʃ, ash. *Appropriate for both places of the name in Devon.*

Aisher, *f.n.*, 'eɪʃər, áyshĕr

Aiskew *N. Yorks.*, 'eɪskju, áysskew

Aislaby *N. Yorks.*, 'eɪzlbɪ, áyzlbi. *Appropriate for both places of the name in North Yorks.*

Aisthorpe *Lincs.*, 'eɪsθɔrp, áyss--thorp

Aistrop, *f.n.*, 'eɪstrɒp, áysstrop

Aitchison, *f.n.*, 'eɪtʃɪsən, áytchissŏn

Aithrie, Viscount, 'eɪθrɪ, áythri

Aithsting *Shetland*, 'eɪθstɪŋ, áyth--sting

Aitken, *f.n.*, 'eɪtkɪn, áytkĕn; 'eɪkɪn, áykĕn

Aitkenhead, *f.n.*, 'eɪkənhed, áykĕn-hed

Aitkin, *f.n.*, 'eɪtkɪn, áytkin; 'eɪkɪn, áykin

Aked, *f.n.*, 'eɪkɪd, áykĕd

Akeld *Northd.*, 'eɪkəld, áykĕld

Akeman St. *Tring (Herts.)*, 'eɪkmən, áykmän

Akerman, *f.n.*, 'eɪkərmæn, áykĕrman; 'ækərmən, áckĕrmän

Akers, *f.n.*, 'eɪkərz, áykĕrz

Akery, *f.n.*, 'eɪkərɪ, áykĕri

Akhurst, *f.n.*, 'ækhərst, áck-hurst

Akister, *f.n.*, 'eɪkɪstər, áykistĕr

Akroyd, *f.n.*, 'ækrɔɪd, áckroyd

Akst, *f.n.*, ækst, ackst

Alan, *C.n. and f.n.*, 'ælən, álăn

Alanbrooke, Viscount, 'ælənbrʊk, álănbrŏŏk

Alarcon, *f.n.*, æ'lɑrkən, alaárkŏn

Alasdair, *C.n.*, *also spelt* **Alastair**, **Alistair**, 'ælɪstər, álistĕr

Alastair, *C.n. see* **Alasdair**

Albany, *f.n.*, 'ɔlbənɪ, áwlbăni

Albemarle, Earl of, 'ælbəmɑrl, álbĕmaarl

Alberbury *Salop*, 'ɔlbərbərɪ, áwlbĕrbŭri

Alberry-Speyer, *f.n.*, 'ælbərɪ 'speɪər, álbĕri spáy-ĕr

Albery, *f.n.*, 'ælbərɪ, álbĕri. *Appropriate also for the ~ Theatre, London.*

Albiston, *f.n.*, 'ɔlbɪstən, áwlbisstŏn

Albon, *f.n.*, 'ælbən, álbŏn

Albourne *W. Sussex*, 'ɔlbɔrn, áwlborn; 'ælbɔrn, álborn

Albrecht, *f.n.*, 'ɔlbrekt, áwlbrekt

Albrighton *Salop*, ɔl'braɪtən, awlbrítŏn. *Appropriate for both places of the name in Shropshire.*

Albu, *f.n.*, 'ælbju, álbew

Albury *Herts., Oxon., Surrey*, 'ɔlbərɪ, áwlbŭri

Alby *Norfolk*, 'ɔlbɪ, áwlbi

Alby Hill *Norfolk*, 'ɔlbɪ 'hɪl, áwlbi híll

Alce, *f.n.*, æls, alss

Alcester, *f.n.*, 'ɔlstər, áwlsstĕr

Alcester *Warwicks.*, 'ɔlstər, áwlsstĕr

Alciston *E. Sussex*, 'ɔlsɪstən, áwlssisstŏn

Alcock, *f.n.*, 'ælkɒk, álkock; 'ɔlkɒk, áwlkock. *The first was*

the pronunciation of Sir John ~, airman, and of Sir Walter ~, organist and composer.
Alconbury *Cambs.*, 'ɔlkənbərɪ, áwlkŏnbŭri; 'ɔkənbərɪ, áwkŏn-bŭri
Alcorn, *f.n.*, 'ɔlkɔrn, áwlkorn
Aldborough *Norfolk, N. Yorks.*, 'ɔldbərə, áwldbŭrə
Aldbourne *Wilts.*, 'ɔlbɔrn, áwlborn
Aldbrough *Humberside*, 'ɔlbərə, áwlbŭrə
Aldbury *Herts.*, 'ɔldbərɪ, áwld-bŭri
Alde, River, *Suffolk*, ɔld, awld
Aldeburgh *Suffolk*, 'ɔlbərə, áwl-bŭrə; 'ɔldbərə, áwldbŭrə. *Home of the ~ Festival.*
Aldeby *Norfolk*, 'ɔldəbɪ, áwldĕbi
Aldeguer, *f.n.*, 'ɔldɪgər, áwldĕgĕr
Aldenham, Baron, 'ɔldṇəm, áwldn-ăm
Aldenham *Herts.*, 'ɔldənəm, áwldĕnăm
Alder, *f.n.*, 'ɔldər, áwldĕr
Alderbury *Wilts.*, 'ɔldərbərɪ, áwldĕrbŭri
Aldergrove *Co. Antrim*, 'ɔldər-groʊv, áwldĕrgrōv
Alderley, Nether *and* Over, *Ches.*, 'ɔldərlɪ, áwldĕrli
Aldermaston *Berks.*, 'ɔldərmɑs-tən, áwldĕrmaastŏn
Alderney, Viscount, 'ɔldərnɪ, áwldĕrni
Aldersey *Ches.*, 'ɔldərsɪ, áwldĕrssi
Aldershot *Hants*, 'ɔldərʃɒt, áwldĕr-shot
Alderson, *f.n.*, 'ɔldərsən, áwldĕrs-sŏn
Alderton, *f.n.*, 'ɔldərtən, áwldĕr-tŏn
Alderwasley *Derby.*, 'ɔldər-wɒzlɪ, áwldĕrwozli
Aldham, *f.n.*, 'ɔldəm, áwldăm
Aldhelm, *C.n.*, 'ɔldhelm, áwld--helm
Aldington, Baron, 'ɔldɪŋtən, áwldingtŏn
Aldous, *f.n.*, 'ɔldəs, áwldŭss
Aldred, *f.n.*, 'ɔldrəd, áwldrĕd; 'ɒldrəd, ól-drĕd
Aldreth *Cambs.*, 'ɔldrəθ, áwld-rĕth
Aldridge, *f.n.*, 'ɔldrɪdʒ, áwldrij
Aldringham *Suffolk*, 'ɔldrɪŋəm, áwldring-ăm
Aldwark *Derby., N. Yorks.*, 'ɔldwɔrk, áwldwawrk
Aldwick *W. Sussex*, 'ɔldwɪk, áwldwick
Aldwinckle, *f.n.*, 'ɔldwɪŋkl, áwldwinkl

Aldwych *London*, 'ɔldwɪtʃ, áwldwitch
Aled, *Welsh C.n.*, 'æled, áled
Aleksic, *f.n.*, ə'leksɪk, ălécksick
Alençon Link, *Basingstoke*, 'ælɑ̃sõ, álaangssõng
Alethea, *C.n.*, ˌælɪ'θɪə, alĕthée-ă; ə'liθɪə, ăléethiă
Alethorpe *Norfolk*, 'eɪlθɔrp, áyl--thorp
Alexa, *C.n.*, ə'leksə, ălécksă
Alexander, *C.n. and f.n.*, ˌælɪg-'zɑndər, alĕgzaándĕr; 'elʃɪndər, él-shindĕr. *The second is a Scottish pronunciation.*
Alexander of Tunis and Errigal, Viscount, ˌælɪg'zɑndər əv 'tjunɪs ənd 'erɪgɔl, alĕgzaándĕr ŏv téwniss ănd érrigawl
Alexandre, *f.n.*, ælɪk'sɑndər, alĕksaándĕr
Alfold *Surrey*, 'ɔlfoʊld, áwlfōld; 'ælfoʊld, álfōld; 'ɑfoʊld, aáfōld
Alford, *f.n.*, 'ɔlfərd, áwlfŏrd
Alford *Grampian*, 'æfərd, áffŏrd
Alford *Lincs.*, 'ɔlfərd, áwlfŏrd
Alford *Somerset*, 'ɒlfərd, ólfŏrd; 'ælfərd, álfŏrd
Alfoxton Park *Somerset*, æl'fɒks-tən, alfóckstŏn
Alfreda, *C.n.*, æl'fridə, alfréedă
Alfreton *Derby.*, 'ɔlfrɪtən, áwl-frĕtŏn; 'ɒlfrɪtən, ólfrĕtŏn; 'ælfrɪtən, álfrĕtŏn
Alfriston *E. Sussex*, ɔl'frɪstən, awlfrístŏn
Algar, *f.n.*, 'ælgər, álgăr
Algarkirk *Lincs.*, 'ɔlgərkɜrk, áwlgărkirk; 'ɔldʒərkɜrk, áwl-järkirk; 'ɔldʒkɜrk, áwlj-kirk; 'ældʒərkɜrk, áljärkirk
Algeo, *f.n.*, 'ældʒɪoʊ, áljiõ
Aline, Loch *and* River, *H'land*, 'ælɪn, álin
Alington, *f.n.*, 'ælɪŋtən, álingtŏn. *Also appropriate for the Barony of ~.*
Alistair, *C.n. see* **Alasdair**
Alkborough *Humberside*, 'ɔlkbərə, áwlkbŭrə
Alker, *f.n.*, 'ɔlkər, áwlkĕr
Alkham *Kent*, 'ɔlkəm, áwlkăm; 'ɔkəm, áwkăm
Alkin, *f.n.*, 'ælkɪn, álkin
Alkington *Glos.*, 'ɔlkɪŋtən, áwlkingtŏn
Alkington *Salop*, 'ɔkɪŋtən, áwk-ingtŏn; 'ɔlkɪŋtən, áwlkingtŏn
Alkrington *Gtr. M'chester*, 'ɔlkrɪŋtən, áwlkringtŏn
Allaker, *f.n.*, 'æləkər, álákĕr
Allam, *f.n.*, 'æləm, áläm
Allard, *f.n.*, 'ælɑrd, álaard

Allason, *f.n.*, 'æləsən, álǎssŏn
Allaun, *f.n.*, ə'lɒn, ǎláwn
Allbeury, *f.n.*, ɔl'bjʊərɪ, awl-
byǒŏri
Allchin, *f.n.*, 'ɔltʃɪn, áwlchin
Allen, *f.n.*, 'ælɪn, álĕn
Allenby, Viscount, 'ælənbɪ,
álĕnbi
Aller *Devon*, 'ælər, álĕr
Aller *Somerset*, 'ɒlər, óllĕr; 'ɔlər,
áwlĕr
Allerton, Baron, 'ælərtən, álĕrtŏn
Allerton *Merseyside, Somerset*,
'ælərtən, álĕrtŏn
Allerton *W. Yorks.*, 'ɒlərtən,
óllĕrtŏn
Allerton, Chapel, *Leeds, Somer-*
set, 'tʃæpl 'ælərtən, cháppl
álĕrtŏn
Allerton Bywater *W. Yorks.*,
'ælərtən 'baɪwɔtər, álĕrtŏn
bí-wawtĕr
Allerton Mauleverer *N. Yorks.*,
'ɒlərtən mɔ'levərər, óllĕrtŏn
mawlévvĕrĕr
Alles, *f.n.*, 'ælɪz, álĕz
Allesley *W. Midlands*, 'ɔlzlɪ,
áwlzli
Allestree *Derby.*, 'ælɪstrɪ, álĕss-
tree
Allet *Cornwall*, 'ælɪt, álĕt
Alleyne, *f.n.*, æ'leɪn, aláyn; æ'lɪn,
aleén; 'ælən, álĕn
Alleynian, *one educated at Dul-*
wich College, ə'leɪnɪən,
ǎláyniǎn
Alleyn Park *Dulwich*, 'ælɪn, áleen
Alleyn's School *Dulwich*, 'ælɪnz,
álĕnz
Alleyne's Grammar School
Stevenage, 'æleɪnz, álaynz
Allfrey, *f.n.*, 'ɔlfrɪ, áwlfri
Allhallows *Kent*, ɔl'hælɒʊz, awl-
-hálŏz
Allhusen, *f.n.*, ɔl'hjuzən, awl-
-héwzĕn; æl'hjuzən, al-héwzĕn
Allibone, *f.n.*, 'ælɪbɒʊn, álibŏn
Allighan, *f.n.*, 'ælɪgən, áligǎn
Allingham, *f.n.*, 'ælɪŋəm, áling-ǎm
Allington *Dorset, Kent, Wilts.*,
'ælɪŋtən, álingtŏn
Alliss, *f.n.*, 'ælɪs, áliss
Allitt, *f.n.*, 'ælɪt, álit
Allner, *f.n.*, 'ɔlnər, áwlnĕr
Alloa *Central*, 'ælɒʊə, álŏ-ǎ
Allott, *f.n.*, 'ælət, álŏt
Allsebrook, *f.n.*, 'ɔlsbrʊk, áwlss-
brŏŏk
Allsop, *f.n.*, 'ɔlsɒp, áwlssop
Allsopp, *f.n.*, 'ɔlsɒp, áwlssop
Allt, *f.n.*, ɔlt, awlt
Allt-Rhyd-y-Groes *Dyfed*, 'æɨt rid
ə 'grɔɪs, áhlt-reed-ǎ-gróyss
Almack, *f.n.*, 'ɔlmæk, áwlmack

Alma-Tadema, *f.n.*, 'ælmə
'tædɪmə, álmǎ táddĕmǎ. *This is*
also the pronunciation generally
associated with the Anglo-Dutch
painter.
Almedingen, *f.n.*, ˌælmə'dɪŋgən,
almĕding-gĕn
Almeley *H. & W.*, 'æmlɪ, ámli
Almer *Dorset*, 'ælmər, álmĕr
Almey, *f.n.*, 'ælmɪ, álmi
Almodington *W. Sussex*, æl'mɒd-
ɪŋtən, almóddingtŏn
Almond, *f.n.*, 'amənd, aámŏnd
Almondbank *Tayside*, 'amənd-
'bæŋk, aámŏndbánk
Almondbury *W. Yorks.*, 'eɪmbərɪ,
áymbŭri; 'ɔmbərɪ, áwmbŭri;
'ælməndbərɪ, ál-mŏndbŭri
Almondsbury *Avon*, 'aməndzbərɪ,
aámŏndzbŭri; 'eɪmzbərɪ,
áymzbŭri
Almshoe, Little, *Herts.*, 'amʃu,
aám-shoo
Aln, River, *Northd.*, æln, aln
Alne *N. Yorks.*, ɒn, awn
Alne, Great *and* **Little,** *Warwicks.*,
ɒn, awn; ɔln, awln; æln, aln
Alness, Barony of, 'ɔlnes, áwl-
ness
Alness *H'land*, 'ɔlnɪs, áwlnĕss;
'ælnɪs, álnĕss
Alnham *Northd.*, 'ælnəm, álnǎm
Alnmouth *Northd.*, 'ælnmaʊθ,
áln-mowth; 'eɪlmaʊθ, áyl-
mowth
Alnwick, *f.n.*, 'ænɪk, ánnick
Alnwick *Northd.*, 'ænɪk, ánnick.
Appropriate also for the Barony
of ∼.
Aloysius, *C.n.*, ˌælɒʊ'ɪʃəs, alō-
-íshüss
Alpass, *f.n.*, 'ɔlpəs, áwlpǎss
Alperton *London*, 'ælpərtən,
álpĕrtŏn
Alphege, saint, 'ælfɪdʒ, álfĕj
Alpheton *Suffolk*, æl'fitən,
alféetŏn
Alpington *Norfolk*, 'ælpɪŋtən,
álpingtŏn
Alport, *f.n.*, 'ɔlpɔrt, áwlport.
Appropriate also for Baron ∼.
Alresford, *f.n.*, 'ɔlzfərd, áwlzfŏrd
Alresford *Essex*, 'ɑlsfərd, aálss-
fŏrd; 'eɪlsfərd, áylssfŏrd
Alresford *Hants*, 'ɔlzfərd, áwlz-
fŏrd; 'ɑlzfərd, aálzfŏrd
Alrewas *Staffs.*, 'ɔlrəs, áwlrǎss;
'ɔlrəwəs, áwlrĕwǎss
Alsager *Ches.*, æl'seɪdʒər, awls-
sáyjĕr; 'ɔlsədʒər, áwlssǎjĕr
Alsatia, *old name for Whitefriars*,
London, æl'seɪʃə, alssáyshǎ
Alscott *Devon*, 'ɔlskət, áwlskŏt.
But see pronunciation of

Alverdiscott, *which is the more usual form.*

Alsh, Loch, *H'land*, ælʃ, alsh

Alsop, *f.n.*, 'ɔlsɒp, áwlssop

Alston, *f.n.*, 'ɔlstən, áwlsstŏn

Alston *Cumbria, Devon*, 'ɔlstən, áwlsstŏn

Alstone *Glos., Somerset, Staffs.*, 'ɔlstən, áwlsstŏn. *Appropriate for both places of the name in Gloucestershire.*

Alswyck Hall *Buntingford (Herts.)*, 'æsɪk, ássick

Alt, River, *Lancs.–Merseyside*, ɔlt, awlt

Altarnun *Cornwall*, ˌɔltər'nʌn, awltärnún

Altcar, Great, *Lancs.*, 'ɔltkɑr, áwltkaar

Altedesert *Co. Tyrone*, 'ɔltədezərt, áwltĕdezzĕrt

Altham, *f.n.*, 'ɔlθəm, áwl-thăm

Altham *Lancs.*, 'ɔlθəm, áwl-thăm; 'æltəm, áltăm; 'ɔltəm, áwltăm

Althaus, *f.n.*, 'ɔlthaʊs, áwlt--howss

Althorne *Essex*, 'ɔlθɔrn, áwl-thorn

Althorp, *f.n.*, 'ɔlθɔrp, áwl-thorp; 'ælθɔrp, ál-thorp

Althorp *Northants.*, 'ɔltrəp, áwltrŏp; 'ɔlθɔrp, áwl-thorp; 'ɔlθrəp, áwl-thrŏp. *The first pronunciation is that used by the family of the Earl Spencer, and is appropriate also for Viscount ~. The second is that used generally in the neighbourhood of the estate, and the third is now old-fashioned.*

Althorpe *Humberside*, 'ɔlθɔrp, áwl-thorp

Altimeg Hill, *S'clyde*, 'ɔltɪmeg, áwltimeg

Altnabreac *H'land*, ˌæltnə'brek, altnăbréck

Altnagelvin *Co. Derry*, ˌæltnə-'gelvɪn, altnăgélvin

Altnamachin *Co. Armagh*, ˌæltnə-'mækɪn, altnămáckin

Altnaveigh *Co. Armagh*, ˌæltnə-'veɪ, altnăváy

Altofts *W. Yorks.*, 'ɔltɒfts, áwltŏfts; 'ɒltəs, óltŭss

Alton, *f.n.*, 'ɔltən, áwltŏn

Alton *Derby., Hants, Staffs.*, 'ɔltən, áwltŏn

Altries *Grampian*, 'æltrɪz, áltriz

Altrincham *Gtr. M'chester*, 'ɔltrɪŋəm, áwltring-ăm. *Appropriate also for the Barony of ~.*

Altsigh *H'land*, 'ælt'ʃi, ált-shée

Alty, *f.n.*, 'ɔltɪ, áwlti

Alun, *Welsh C.n.*, 'ælɪn, álin

Alva *Central*, 'ælvə, álvă

Alvar, *C.n.*, 'ælvɑr, álvaar; 'ælvər, álvăr

Alvarez, *f.n.*, æl'vɑrez, alváarez

Alvaston *Derby.*, 'ɔlvəstən, áwlvăstŏn; 'ɒlvəstən, ólvăstŏn

Alvechurch *H. & W.*, 'ɔlvtʃɑrtʃ, áwlv-church

Alvediston *Wilts.*, ˌælvɪ'dɪstən, alvĕdístŏn

Alveley *Salop*, 'ævlɪ, ávvli

Alverdiscott *Devon*, ˌælvər'dɪskət, alvĕr-dísskŏt. *A less usual form of this name is* **Alscott**, *q.v.*

Alverstoke *Hants*, 'ælvərstoʊk, álvĕrstŏk

Alverthorpe *W. Yorks.*, 'ɔlvər-θɔrp, áwlvĕr-thorp

Alves *Grampian*, 'ɑvɪs, áavĕss

Alvescot *Oxon.*, 'ɔlskət, áwlsskŏt; 'ælskət, álsskŏt; 'ælvɪskɒt, álvĕsskot

Alveston *Avon, Warwicks.*, 'ælvɪstən, álvĕstŏn

Alvie *H'land*, 'ælvɪ, álvi

Alvin, *C.n.*, 'ælvɪn, álvin

Alvingham *Lincs.*, 'ɔlvɪŋəm, áwlving-ăm; 'ælvɪŋəm, álving-ăm. *The first is appropriate also for Baron ~.*

Alvington *Glos.*, 'ælvɪŋtən, álvingtŏn

Alvington, West, *Devon*, 'ɔlvɪŋtən, áwlvingtŏn

Alwalton *Cambs.*, 'ɔlwɔltən, áwl--wawltŏn; 'ɔlwɒltən, áwl--woltŏn

Alway, *f.n.*, 'ɔlweɪ, áwl-way

Alwin Gallery *London*, 'ɔlwɪn, áwl-win

Alwinton *Northd.*, 'ælwɪntən, álwintŏn

Alwoodley *W. Yorks.*, 'ɔlwʊdlɪ, áwl-woŏdli; ɒl'wʊdlɪ, awl--woŏdli

Alwyn, Kenneth, *conductor*, 'ɔlwɪn, áwl-win

Alwyn, William, *composer*, 'ælwɪn, álwin

Alwyn House Rehabilitation Centre *Fife*, 'ɔlwɪn, áwl-win

Alyth *Tayside*, 'eɪlɪθ, áylith

Amadeus String Quartet, ˌæmə'deɪəs, ammădáy-ŭss

Amaury, *f.n.*, 'eɪmərɪ, áymări

Ambersham, South, *W. Sussex*, 'æmbərʃəm, ámbĕr-shăm

Ambion Hill, *Leics.*, 'æmbɪən, ámbi-ŏn

Am Bodach *H'land*, æm 'bɒtəx, am bóttăc<u>h</u>

Ambrosden *Oxon.*, 'æmbroʊzdən, ámbrōzdĕn

Amen Corner *City of London*, 'eɪmen, áymen

Amen House *City of London,*
'eɪmen, áymen
Amer, *f.n.,* 'eɪmər, áyměr
Amersham *Bucks.,* 'æmərʃəm,
ámměr-shăm
Amery, *f.n.,* 'eɪmərɪ, áyměri
Ames, *f.n.,* eɪmz, aymz
Amey, *f.n.,* 'eɪmɪ, áymi
Amherst, *f.n.,* 'æmərst, ámměrst;
'æmhərst, ám-herst. *The first is
the pronunciation of Earl ∼ and
of Baron ∼ of Hackney.*
Amici String Quartet, ə'miːtʃɪ,
ămeetchi
Amies, *f.n.,* 'eɪmɪz, áymiz
Amis, *f.n.,* 'eɪmɪs, áymiss
Amiss, *f.n.,* 'eɪmɪs, áymiss
Amlwch *Gwynedd,* 'æmlʊx,
ámlōo̱ch
Amman, River, *Dyfed,* 'æmən,
ámmăn
Ammanford *Dyfed,* 'æmənfərd,
ámmănfŏrd
Ammon, Barony of, 'æmən,
ámmŏn
Ammonds, *f.n.,* 'æməndz,
ámmŏndz
Amner, *f.n.,* 'æmnər, ámněr
Amoore, *f.n.,* 'eɪmʊər, áymōōr;
'eɪmər, áymor
Amor, *f.n.,* 'eɪmər, áymor
Amore, *f.n.,* 'eɪmər, áymor
Amory, *f.n.,* 'eɪmərɪ, áymŏri.
*Appropriate also for the Vis-
countcy of ∼.*
Amos, *f.n.,* 'eɪmɒs, áymoss
Amothe, *C.n.,* 'æməθi, ámmŏthee
Amphlett, *f.n.,* 'æmflɪt, ámflĕt
Ampleforth *N. Yorks.,* 'æmplfɔrθ,
ámpl-forth
Ampney Crucis *Glos.,* 'æmpnɪ
'kruːsɪs, ámpni kroÓossiss
Ampney St. Peter *Glos.,* 'æmpnɪ
snt 'piːtər, ámpni sĭnt péetěr
Ampthill *Beds.,* 'æmpθɪl, ámpt-
-hill. *Appropriate also for Baron
∼.*
Amroth *Dyfed,* 'æmrɒθ, ámroth
Amulree *Tayside,* ˌæml'riː,
amml-rée. *Appropriate also for
Baron ∼.*
Amwell, Baron, 'æmwəl, ámwěl
Amyes, *f.n.,* 'eɪmɪz, áymeez
an Athain, Loch *I. of Skye,*
ən 'ɑn, ăn aán
Ancaster, Earl of, 'æŋkəstər,
ánkăstěr
Ancoats *Gtr. M'chester,* 'æŋkoʊts,
ánkŏts
An Comunn Gaidhealach *High-
land Assoc.,* ən 'kɒmən 'gaɪləx,
ăn kómmŭn gílă̱ch
Ancram, Earl of, 'æŋkrəm, ánkrăm

Ancram, *f.n.,* 'æŋkrəm, ánkrăm
Anderson, *f.n.,* 'ændərsən,
ándĕrssŏn
Andover *Hants,* 'ændoʊvər,
ándōvĕr. *Appropriate also for
Viscount ∼.*
Andoversford *Glos.,* 'ændoʊvərz-
fərd, ándōvĕrzford
Andrade, *f.n.,* 'ændreɪd, ándrayd
Andreas *I. of Man,* 'ændrəs,
ándráss
André Deutsch *publishers,*
'ændreɪ 'dɔɪtʃ, ándray dóytch
Andreetti, *f.n.,* ˌændrɪ'etɪ, andri-
-étti
Andreoli, *f.n.,* ˌændrɪ'oʊlɪ, andri-
-óli
Aneurin, *Welsh C.n.,* ə'naɪrɪn,
ănîrin
Angarrick *Cornwall,* æŋ'gærɪk,
ang-gárrick
Angas, *f.n.,* 'æŋgəs, áng-găss
Angelis, *f.n.,* 'ændʒəlɪs, ánjĕliss
Angell, *f.n.,* 'eɪndʒl, áynjl
Angers, *f.n.,* 'æŋgərz, áng-gĕrz
Angersleigh *Somerset,* 'eɪndʒərzlɪ,
áynjĕrzlee
Angerstein, *f.n.,* 'æŋgərstin, áng-
-gĕrsteen; 'æŋgərstaɪn, áng-
-gĕrstîn. *The second is appropriate
for John Julius ∼, 18–19th-c.
merchant and art collector.*
Angharad, *Welsh C.n.,* æŋ'hærəd,
ang-hárrăd
Angier, *f.n.,* 'ændʒɪər, ánjeer
Angle *Dyfed,* 'æŋgl, áng-gl
Anglesey *Gwynedd,* 'æŋglsɪ,
áng-gl-si. *Appropriate also for
the Marquess of ∼.*
Angmering *W. Sussex,* 'æŋmərɪŋ,
áng-měring
Angove, *f.n.,* 'æŋgoʊv, áng-gōv
Angus, *C.n. and f.n.,* 'æŋgəs,
áng-gŭss
Angus *Tayside,* 'æŋgəs, áng-gŭss.
*Appropriate also for the Earl of
∼.*
Anick *Northd.,* 'eɪnɪk, áynick
Anido, *f.n.,* 'ænɪdoʊ, ánnidō
Anketell, *f.n.,* 'æŋkətl, ánkĕtl
Anlaby *Humberside,* 'ænləbɪ,
ánlăbi
Annacloy *Co. Down,* ˌænə'klɔɪ,
annăklóy
Annaghmore *Co. Armagh,* ˌænəx-
'mɔr, annăchmór
Annahilt *Co. Down,* ˌænə'hɪlt,
annă-hílt
Annakin, *f.n.,* 'ænəkɪn, ánnăkin
Annalong *Co. Down,* ˌænə'lɒŋ,
annălóng
Annaly, *f.n.,* 'ænəlɪ, ánnăli.
Appropriate also for Baron ∼.
Annan, *f.n.,* 'ænən, ánnăn

Annear, *f.n.,* ə'nɪər, ănéer
Annells, *f.n.,* 'ænlz, ánnlz
Annely Juda Fine Art *London,*
  'ænəlɪ 'dʒudə, ánněli jo'odă
Annereau, *f.n.,* 'ænərou, ánněrō
Annesley, *f.n.,* 'ænzlɪ, ánzli.
  Appropriate also for Earl ∼.
Annesley *Notts.,* 'ænɪzlɪ, ánnězli;
  'ænzlɪ, ánzli
Anness, *f.n.,* 'ænɪs, ánněss
Annet *I. of Scilly,* 'ænɪt, ánnět
Annett, *f.n.,* 'ænɪt, ánnět
Annis, *f.n.,* 'ænɪs, ánniss
Ansbacher, *f.n.,* 'ænzbækər,
  ánzbacker
Anscombe, *f.n.,* 'ænskəm,
  ánsskŏm
Ansell, *f.n.,* 'ænsl, ánssl
Ansley *Warwicks.,* 'ænzlɪ, ánzli
Anson, *f.n.,* 'ænsən, ánssŏn
Ansorge, *f.n.,* 'ænsɔrdʒ, ánssorj;
  'ænsɔrʒ, ánssorzh
Anstey *Devon, Dorset, Herts.,*
  Leics., 'ænstɪ, ánssti
Anstice, *f.n.,* 'ænstɪs, ánstiss
Anstruther, *f.n.,* 'ænstrʌðər,
  ánstruthěr
Anstruther *Fife,* 'ænstrʌðər,
  ánstruthěr; 'eɪnstər, áynsstěr
Ansty *Dorset, Warwicks., Wilts.,*
  'ænstɪ, ánssti
Ansty *W. Sussex,* æn'staɪ, ansstí
Anstye Cross *W. Sussex,* 'ænstaɪ
  'krɒs, ánsstī króss
An Teallach *H'land,* æn 'tʃæləx,
  an chálǎch
Anthea, *C.n.,* 'ænθɪə, ánthiǎ
Anthony, *C.n. and f.n.,* 'æntənɪ,
  ántŏni; 'ænθənɪ, ánthŏni
Antiquis, *f.n.,* æn'tɪkwɪs, antíck-
  wiss
Antony *Cornwall,* 'æntənɪ, ántŏni
Antrim *Co. name,* 'æntrɪm,
  ántrim. *Appropriate also for the
  Earl of* ∼.
Antrobus, *f.n.,* 'æntrəbəs,
  ántrŏbŭss
Anwick, *f.n.,* 'ænɪk, ánnick
Anwoth *D. & G.,* 'ænwɒθ, án-
  woth
Anwyl, *f.n.,* 'ænwɪl, ánwill
Apethorpe *Northants.,* 'æpθɔrp,
  áp-thorp; 'eɪpθɔrp, áyp-thorp
Aplvor, Denis, *composer,* 'denɪs
  æp'aɪvər, dénniss ap-ívŏr
Appel, *f.n.,* ə'pel, ăpéll
Appelbe, *f.n.,* ə'pelbɪ, ăpélbi
Appleby, *f.n.,* 'æplbɪ, ápplbi
Appledram *see* **Apuldram**
Applegate, *f.n.,* 'æplgeɪt, áppl-
  -gayt; 'æplgɪt, áppl-git
Appletreewick *N. Yorks.,*
  'æpltri'wɪk, áppltree-wíck
Aprahamian, Felix, *music critic,*

'fɪlɪks ,æprə'heɪmɪən, feéliks
  apprə-háymiăn
Apted, *f.n.,* 'æptɪd, áptěd
Apuldram, *also spelt* **Appledram,**
  W. Sussex, 'æpldrəm, áppl-
  drăm
Arabin, *f.n.,* ə'ræbɪn, ărábbin
Arbikie *Tayside,* ɑr'bɪkɪ, aarbícki
Arbirlot *Tayside,* ɑr'bɜrlət,
  aarbírlŏt
Arblaster, *f.n.,* 'ɑrblastər,
  aárblaastěr
Arboe *Co. Tyrone,* ɑr'bou, aarbő
Arborfield *Berks.,* 'ɑrbərfild,
  aárbŏrfeeld
Arbory *I. of Man,* 'ɑrbərɪ,
  aárbŏri
Arbroath *Tayside,* ɑr'brouθ,
  aarbrőth
Arbuthnot, *f.n.,* ɑr'bʌθnət, aar-
  búthnŏt
Arbuthnott, Viscount of,
  ɑr'bʌθnət, aarbúthnŏt
Arcedeckne, *f.n.,* ɑrtʃ'dikən,
  aartch-deékěn
Ardachie Lodge, *also spelt*
  Ardachy, *H'land,* 'ardəki,
  aárdăkee
Ardagh, *f.n.,* 'ardə, aárdă
Ardcharnich *H'land,* ɑrd'tʃɑrnɪx,
  aard-chaárnich
Ardchattan *S'clyde,* ɑrd'kætən,
  aardkáttăn
Ardd-lin *Powys,* 'arðlɪn, aárth-lin
Ardee, Baron of, ɑr'di, aardeé
Ardeer *S'clyde,* ɑr'dɪər, aardeér
Ardeonaig *Central,* ɑr'dʒouneɪg,
  aarjőnayg; ɑr'dʒounɪg,
  aarjőnig
Ardersier *H'land,* ,ɑrdər'sɪər,
  aarděrsseér
Ardgay *H'land,* ɑrd'gaɪ, aard-gí
Ardglass *Co. Down,* ɑrd'glæs,
  aardgláss
Ardgour *H'land,* ɑrd'gauər,
  aardgówr
Ardilaun, Barony of, ,ɑrdɪ'lɔn,
  aardiláwn
Ardingly *W. Sussex,* ,ɑrdɪŋ'laɪ,
  aarding-lí
Ardivachar Point *W. Isles,* ,ɑrdɪ-
  'væxər, aardiváchǎr
Ardizzone, Edward, *painter and
  illustrator,* ,ɑrdɪ'zouni,
  aardizőni
Ardkeen *Co. Down,* ɑrd'kin,
  aardkeén
Ardkenneth Chapel *W. Isles,*
  ɑrd'kenɪθ, aardkénněth
Ardlamont Point *S'clyde,* ɑrd-
  'læmənt, aardlámmŏnt
Ardleigh *Essex,* 'ɑrdlɪ, áardli
Ardmore *Grampian, H'land,
  S'clyde,* ɑrd'mɔr, aardmór.

This pronunciation is appropriate for the names of headlands on Islay (S'clyde), and Skye (H'land), a harbour on the Dornoch Firth (H'land), and a distillery at Kennethmont (Grampian).

Ardnadam S'clyde, ɑrd'nædəm, aardnáddăm

Ardnamurchan H'land, ,ɑrdnə-'mɜrxən, aardnămúrchăn

Ardoch Tayside, 'ɑrdɒx, aárdoch

Ardovie Tayside, ɑr'dʌvɪ, aardúvvi

Ardoyne Co. Antrim, ɑr'dɔɪn, aardóyn

Ardrishaig S'clyde, ɑr'drɪʃɪg, aardríshig; ɑr'drɪʃeɪg, aardrísh-ayg

Ardrossan S'clyde, ɑr'drɒsən, aardróssăn. *Appropriate also for Baron ~.*

Ards Peninsula Co. Down, ɑrdz, aardz

Ardtalnaig Tayside, ɑrd'tælneɪg, aardtálnayg

Ardvasar I. of Skye, ɑrd'vɑzər, aardvaázăr

Ardwick Gtr. M'chester, 'ɑrdwɪk, aárdwick

Arenig Gwynedd, ə'renɪg, ărénnig

Arfon Gwynedd, 'ɑrvɒn, aárvon

Argall, f.n., 'ɑrgɔl, aárgawl

Argent, f.n., 'ɑrdʒənt, aárjĕnt

Argoed Gwent, 'ɑrgɔɪd, aárgoyd

Argoed Salop, ɑr'gouɪd, aargó-ĕd

Argyll, Duke of, ɑr'gaɪl, aargíl

Argyll and Bute S'clyde, ɑr'gaɪl ənd 'bjut, aargíl ănd béwt

Arieli, Celia, pianist, 'sɪliə ,ærɪ'elɪ, séeliă arri-élli

Arinagour Coll (S'clyde), 'ærɪnəguər, árrinăgōor

Aris, f.n., 'ɛərɪs, áiriss; 'ɑrɪs, aáriss

Arisaig H'land, 'ærɪseɪg, árrissayg

Ariss, f.n., 'ɛərɪs, áiriss

Arkaig, Loch, H'land, 'ɑrkeɪg, aárkayg

Arkell, f.n., 'ɑrkl, aárkl; ɑr'kel, aarkéll

Arkesden Essex, 'ɑrksdən, aárksdĕn

Arkholme Lancs., 'ɑrkhoum, aárk-hōm

Arlecdon Cumbria, 'ɑrləkdən, aárlĕkdŏn

Arlen, f.n., 'ɑrlən, aárlĕn

Arlesey Beds., 'ɑrlzɪ, aárlzi

Arleston Salop, 'ɑrlstən, aárlsstŏn

Arlingham Glos., 'ɑrlɪŋəm, aárling-ăm

Armadale H'land, Lothian, 'ɑrmədeɪl, aármădayl.

Appropriate for both places of the name in Highland.

Armagh, f.n., ɑr'mɑ, aarmaá

Armagh Co. name and town, ɑr'mɑ, aarmaá

Armathwaite Cumbria, 'ɑrməθweɪt, aármăthwayt

Armley W. Yorks., 'ɑrmlɪ, aármli

Armoy Co. Antrim, ɑr'mɔɪ, aarmóy

Arncroach Fife, ɑrn'kroux, aarn-króch

Arndts, f.n., ɑrnts, aarnts

Arne, f.n., ɑrn, aarn

Arnell, f.n., ɑr'nel, aarnéll

Arnesby Leics., 'ɑrnzbɪ, aárnzbi

Arnett, f.n., 'ɑrnɪt, aárnĕt

Arnolfini Gallery Bristol, ɑrnəl-'fɪnɪ, aarnŏlféeni

Arnott, f.n., 'ɑrnət, aárnŏt

Aronowitz, f.n., ə'rɒnəwɪts, ărónnŏ-wits. *Appropriate for Cecil ~, viola player, and for John ~, pianist.*

Aros S'clyde, 'ɑrɒs, aáross

Arpinge Kent, 'ɑrpɪndʒ, aárpinj

Arram, f.n., 'ærəm, árrăm

Arran S'clyde, 'ærən, árrăn. *Appropriate also for the Earl of ~.*

Arrantash, f.n., 'ærəntæʃ, árrănt-ash

Arreton I. of Wight, 'ærətən, árrĕtŏn

Arrochar S'clyde, 'ærəxər, árrŏchăr

Artemiou, f.n., ɑr'tɪmju, aartée-mew

Arthington, f.n., 'ɑrθɪŋtən, aárthingtŏn

Arthog Gwynedd, 'ɑrθɒg, aárthog

Arthurlie S'clyde, 'ɑrθərlɪ, aárthŭrli

Arthy, f.n., 'ɑrθɪ, aárthi

Articlave Co. Derry, ɑrtɪ'kleɪv, aartikláyv

Arun, River, W. Sussex, 'ærən, árrŭn. *Appropriate also for the administrative district, which takes its name from the river.*

Arundel W. Sussex, 'ærəndl, árrŭndl. *Appropriate also for the Earl of ~.*

Arundell of Wardour, Barony of, 'ærəndl əv 'wɔrdər, árrŭndl ŏv wáwrdŭr

Arwel, Welsh C.n., 'ɑrwel, aárwel

Arwyn, Baron, 'ɑrwɪn, aárwin

Asa, C.n., 'eɪsə, áyssă

Ascham, Roger, 16th-c. scholar, 'æskəm, ásskăm

Ascog S'clyde, 'æskɒg, ásskog

Ascoli, f.n., 'æskəlɪ, ásskŏli

Ascot Berks., 'æskət, ásskŏt

Asfordby *Leics.*, 'æsfərdbɪ, ássfŏrdbi
Asgarby *Lincs.*, 'æzgərbɪ, ázgărbi. *Appropriate for both places of the name in Lincolnshire.*
Ashampstead *Berks.*, 'æʃəmsted, áshămsted
Ashbee, *f.n.*, 'æʃbɪ, áshbi
Ashbourne *Derby.*, 'æʃbɔːn, áshborn
Ashburnham *E. Sussex*, æʃ-'bɜːnəm, ashbúrnăm
Ashburton, Baron, 'æʃbɜːtən, áshbŭrtŏn
Ashburton *Devon*, æʃ'bɜːtən, ashbúrtŏn
Ashby *Humberside, Norfolk*, 'æʃbɪ, áshbi
Ashby-de-la-Launde *Lincs.*, 'æʃbɪ də lə 'lɔnd, áshbi dĕ lă láwnd
Ashby-de-la-Zouch *Leics.*, 'æʃbɪ də lə 'zuʃ, áshbi dĕ lă zoósh
Ashby St. Ledgers *Northants.*, 'æʃbɪ snt 'ledʒərz, áshbi sĭnt léjjĕrz
Ashby Woulds *Leics.*, 'æʃbɪ 'wouldz, áshbi wŏldz
Ashcombe, Baron, 'æʃkəm, áshkŏm
Asher, *f.n.*, 'æʃər, áshĕr
Asheridge *Bucks.*, 'æʃrɪdʒ, áshrij
Ashill *Devon, Norfolk, Somerset*, 'æʃhɪl, ásh-hil
Ashkenazi, *f.n.*, ˌæʃkɪ'nɑzɪ, ashkĕnáazi
Ashleworth *Glos.*, 'æʃlwɜːθ, áshlwurth
Ashmolean Museum *Oxford*, æʃ'moulɪən, ashmóliăn
Ashop Clough *Derby.*, 'æʃəp 'klʌf, áshŏp klúff
Ashorne *Warwicks.*, 'æʃhɔːn, ásh-horn
Ashort, *f.n.*, 'æʃərt, áshŏrt
Ashow *Warwicks.*, 'æʃou, áshō
Ashplant, *f.n.*, 'æʃplɑnt, ásh--plaant
Ashreigney *Devon*, æʃ'reɪnɪ, ashráyni
Ashton, *f.n.*, 'æʃtən, áshtŏn
Ashton-in-Makerfield *Gtr. M'chester*, 'æʃtən ɪn 'meɪkərfild, áshtŏn in máykĕrfeeld
Ashton Keynes *Wilts.*, 'æʃtən 'keɪnz, áshtŏn káynz
Ashurst *Kent, W. Sussex*, 'æʃhɜːst, ásh-hurst
Ashwellthorpe *Norfolk*, 'æʃwəl-θɔːp, áshwĕl-thorp
Aske, *f.n.*, æsk, assk
Askern *S. Yorks.*, 'æskərn, ásskĕrn

Askerswell *Dorset*, 'æskərzwel, ásskĕrzwel
Askew, *f.n.*, 'æskju, ásskew
Askham *Cumbria, Notts.*, 'æskəm, ásskăm
Askwith, Barony of, 'æskwɪθ, ásskwith
Aslackby *Lincs.*, 'eɪzlbɪ, áyzlbi
Aslacton *Norfolk*, æz'læktən, azlácktŏn
Aslockton *Notts.*, 'æzlɒktən, ázlocktŏn
Aspatria *Cumbria*, əs'peɪtrɪə, ässpáytriă
Aspel, *f.n.*, 'æspl, ásspl
Aspinall, *f.n.*, 'æspɪnəl, ásspinăl
Aspinwall, *f.n.*, 'æspɪnwɔl, ásspinwawl
Aspland, *f.n.*, 'æsplænd, ásspland
Aspley Guise *Beds.*, 'æsplɪ 'gaɪz, ásspli gíz
Asprey, *f.n.*, 'æsprɪ, ásspri
Asquith, *f.n.*, 'æskwɪθ, ásskwith. *Family name of the Earl of Oxford and ∼.*
Assersohn, *f.n.*, 'æsərsən, ássĕrssŏn
Assheton, *f.n.*, 'æʃtən, áshtŏn
Assinder, *f.n.*, 'æsɪndər, ássindĕr
Assynt *H'land*, 'æsɪnt, ássint
Astell, *f.n.*, æs'tel, asstéll
Asterby *Lincs.*, 'eɪstərbɪ, áysstĕrbi
Asthall Leigh *Oxon.*, 'æstɔl 'li, ásstawl leé; 'æstɔl 'leɪ, ásstawl láy
Astins, *f.n.*, 'æstɪnz, ásstinz
Astle, *f.n.*, 'æstl, ásstl
Astles, *f.n.*, 'æstlz, ásstlz
Astman, *f.n.*, 'æstmən, ásstmăn
Aston Ingham *Glos.*, 'æstən 'ɪŋəm, ásstŏn íng-ăm
Aston Rowant *Oxon.*, 'æstən 'rouənt, ásstŏn rŏ-ănt
Astor, Viscount, 'æstər, ásstŏr
Astor of Hever, Baron, 'æstər əv 'hivər, ásstŏr ŏv heévĕr
Atack, *f.n.*, 'eɪtæk, áytack
Atchison, *f.n.*, 'ætʃɪsən, átchissŏn
Atha, *f.n.*, 'æθə, áthă
Athawes, *f.n.*, 'æθɔz, áth-awz; 'æthɔz, át-hawz
Athelney *Somerset*, 'æθəlnɪ, áthĕlni
Athelstaneford *Lothian*, 'æθəl-steɪnfɔrd, áthĕlstaynford; 'elʃənfərd, élshănford
Athenaeum Club *London*, ˌæθɪ'niəm, athĕnee-ŭm
Atherstone *Warwicks.*, 'æθər-stoun, áthĕrsstŏn
Atherton, *f.n.*, 'æðərtən, áthĕrtŏn; 'æðərtən, áthĕrtŏn
Atherton *Gtr. M'chester*, 'æðərtən, áthĕrtŏn

Athey, *f.n.*, 'æθɪ, áthi
Athill, *f.n.*, 'æðɪl, a͟th͟il; 'æthɪl,
    át-híl; 'æθɪl, áthil
Athlone, Earldom of, æθ'loʊn,
    athlón
Athlumney, Barony of, əθ'lʌmnɪ,
    äthlúmni
Atholl, Duke of, 'æθl, áthl
Atienza, *f.n.*, ˌætɪ'enzə, atti-
    -énzä
Attenborough, *f.n.*, 'ætənbərə,
    áttĕnbŏrŏ
Atter, *f.n.*, 'ætər, áttĕr
Attercliffe *S. Yorks.*, 'ætərklɪf,
    áttĕrkliff
Attewell, *f.n.*, 'ætwel, átwel
Attleborough *Norfolk*, 'ætlbərə,
    áttlbŭrä
Attlee, *f.n.*, 'ætlɪ, áttli. *Appro-
    priate also for Earl* ~.
Atwick *Humberside*, 'ætɪk, áttick
Aubertin, *f.n.*, 'oʊbərtɪn, ŏbĕrtin
Aubery, *f.n.*, 'ɔbərɪ, áwbĕri
Auchaber *Grampian*, ɒ'xɑbər,
    ocha͟'aber
Auchendennan *S'clyde*, ˌɒxən-
    'denən, oc͟hĕndénnän
Auchengeich Colliery *Chryston
    (S'clyde)*, ˌɒxən'gix, oc͟hĕn-
    -géech
Auchenlarie *D. & G.*, ˌɒxən'lɛərɪ,
    oc͟hĕnláiri
Auchenlochan *S'clyde*, ˌɒxən-
    'lɒxən, oc͟hĕnlóc͟hän
Auchernach Lodge *Grampian*,
    ɒ'xɛərnəx, oc͟hairnäc͟h
Auchinachie, *f.n.*, ɒ'xinəxɪ,
    oc͟hinnäc͟hi
Auchincruive *S'clyde*, ˌɒxɪn'kruv,
    oc͟hin-kroʻov
Auchindachie, *also spelt
    Auchindachy, Grampian*,
    ɒ'xinəxɪ, oc͟hinnäc͟hi
Auchindoir *Grampian*, ˌɒxɪn'dɔɪər,
    oc͟hindóyr
Auchindrain *S'clyde*, 'ɒxɪndreɪn,
    óc͟hindrayn
Auchinleck, Field Marshal Sir
    Claude, ˌɒxɪn'lek, oc͟hinléck
Auchinleck *S'clyde*, ˌɒxɪn'lek,
    oc͟hinléck
Auchinleck, Boswell of, 'bɒzwəl
    əv 'æflek, bózwĕl ŏv áffleck
Auchmore *Central see* Achmore
Auchmuty, *f.n.*, ɒk'mjutɪ,
    ockméwti
Auchnagatt *Grampian*, ˌɒxnə'gæt,
    oc͟hnägát
Auchterarder *Tayside*, ˌɒxtər-
    'ɑrdər, oc͟htĕraardĕr
Auchterderran *Fife*, ˌɒxtər'derən,
    oc͟htĕrdérrän
Auchterhouse *Tayside*, 'ɒxtər-
    haʊs, óc͟htĕr-howss

Auchterless *Grampian*, ˌɒxtər'les,
    oc͟htĕrléss
Auchterlonie, *f.n.*, ˌɒxtər'loʊnɪ,
    oc͟htĕrlóni
Auchtermuchty *Fife*, ˌɒxtər'mʌxtɪ,
    oc͟htĕrmúc͟hti
Auchtertool *Fife*, ˌɒxtər'tul,
    oc͟htĕr-toʻol
Auckengill, *also spelt* Auckingill,
    H'land, 'ɒkɪŋgɪl, óckin-gil;
    'aʊkɪŋgɪl, ówkin-gil
Auden, *f.n.*, 'ɔdən, áwdĕn
Audenshaw *Gtr. M'chester*,
    'ɔdənʃɔ, áwdĕn-shaw
Audigier, *f.n.*, 'ɔdɪʒeɪ, áwdiz͟hay
Audlem *Ches.*, 'ɔdləm, áwdlĕm
Audley, Baroness, 'ɔdlɪ, áwdli
Audley End *Essex*, 'ɔdlɪ 'end,
    áwdli énd
Audus, *f.n.*, 'ɔdəs, áwdŭss
Auerbach, *f.n.*, 'ɔrbæk, órback
Augener, *f.n.*, 'ɔgənər, áwgĕnĕr
Auger, *f.n.*, 'ɔgər, áwgĕr
Augher *Co. Tyrone*, 'ɒxər, óc͟hĕr
Aughertree *Cumbria* 'ɒfərtrɪ,
    óffĕrtree; 'æfərtrɪ, áffĕrtree
Aughnacloy *Co. Tyrone*, ˌɒxnə-
    'klɔɪ, oc͟hnäklóy
Aughrim *Co. Down*, 'ɒxrɪm,
    óc͟hrim
Aughton *Humberside, S. Yorks.*,
    'ɔtən, áwtŏn
Aughton *nr. Lancaster (Lancs.)*,
    'æftən, áfftŏn
Aughton *nr. Ormskirk (Lancs.)*,
    'ɔtən, áwtŏn
Augill Castle *Cumbria*, 'ɔgɪl, áwgil
Augustine, *f.n.*, ɔ'gʌstɪn, awgústin
Aukin, *f.n.*, 'ɔkɪn, áwkin
Auld, *f.n.*, ɔld, awld
Auldearn *H'land*, ɔld'ɜrn,
    awldérn
Auldgirth *D. & G.*, 'ɔldgɜrθ, áwld-
    -girth
Auliff, *f.n.*, 'ɔlɪf, áwlif
Aultguish, Stream, *H'land*, ɔlt-
    'gʊʃ, awltgoʻo-ish
Aultbea *H'land*, ɔlt'beɪ, awltbáy
Ault Hucknall *Derby.*, 'ɔlt
    'hʌknəl, áwlt húcknäl
Aumonier, Stacy, *author*, 'steɪsɪ
    oʊ'moʊnɪeɪ, stáyssi ōmóni-ay
Aunger, *f.n.*, 'ɔndʒər, áwnjĕr
Aust *Avon*, ɔst, awsst
Austen, *f.n.*, 'ɒstɪn, ósstĕn; 'ɔstɪn,
    áwsstĕn
Austick, *f.n.*, 'ɔstɪk, áwstick
Austin, *f.n.*, 'ɒstɪn, ósstin; 'ɔstɪn,
    áwsstin
Austwick, *f.n.*, 'ɒstwɪk, ósstwick
Austwick *N. Yorks.*, 'ɔstwɪk,
    áwsstwick; 'ɒstɪk, ósstick
Authers, *f.n.*, 'ɒðərz, áwthĕrz
Auton, *f.n.*, 'ɔtən, áwtŏn

Auty, *f.n.*, 'ɔtɪ, áwti

Ava, Earl of, 'avə, aávă

Ava, *C.n.*, 'avə, aávă

Avann, *f.n.*, ə'væn, ăván

Avaulds *Grampian*, 'jævlz, yávvlz

Avebury *Wilts.*, 'eɪvbərɪ, áyvbŭri; 'eɪbərɪ, áybŭri. *The first is appropriate also for Baron* ~.

Aveley *Essex*, 'eɪvlɪ, áyvli

Aveling, *f.n.*, 'eɪvəlɪŋ, áyvěling; 'eɪvlɪŋ, áyvling

Ave Maria Lane *City of London*, 'avɪ mə'riə, aávi mărée-ă

Aven, River, *see* **Aan**

Aven and Innerdale, Lord, 'eɪvən ənd 'ɪnərdeɪl, áyvĕn ănd ínnĕrdayl

Avendaño, *f.n.*, ,ævɪn'danjoʊ, avvĕndaányō

Avenell, *f.n.*, 'eɪvənəl, áyvĕnĕl

Avening *Glos.*, 'eɪvnɪŋ, áyv-ning

Averham *Notts.*, 'ɛərəm, áirăm

Averill, *f.n.*, 'ævərɪl, ávvĕril

Avern, *f.n.*, 'ævərn, ávvĕrn; ə'vɜrn, ăvérn

Aves, *f.n.*, eɪvz, ayvz

Aveton Gifford *Devon*, 'ɔtən 'dʒɪfərd, áwtŏn jíffŏrd; 'ævɪtən 'gɪfərd, ávvĕtŏn gíffŏrd

Aviemore *H'land*, ,ævɪ'mɔr, avvimór

Avill, River, *Somerset*, 'ævɪl, ávvil

Avington *Berks.*, *Hants*, 'ævɪŋtən, ávvingtŏn

Avishays, *also spelt* **Avishayes,** *Somerset*, 'ævɪsheɪz, ávvis-hayz; 'ævɪʃeɪz, ávvi-shayz. *The spelling* **Avishays** *and the first pronunciation apply to the historic house and the agricultural and sporting estate.* **Avishayes,** *pronounced either way, is appropriate for the modern housing site.*

Avison, *f.n.*, 'eɪvɪsən, áyvissŏn. *Appropriate for Charles* ~, *18th-c. composer.*

Aviss, *f.n.*, 'eɪvɪs, áyviss

Avoch, *f.n.*, 'ævəx, ávvŏch

Avoch *H'land*, ɔx, awch

Avon, Earl of, 'eɪvən, áyvŏn

Avon, River, *Avon*, 'eɪvən, áyvŏn. *Appropriate also for the county name, which is taken from that for the river.*

Avon, River, *Central*, 'eɪvən, áyvŏn

Avon, River, *Devon*, 'ævən, ávvŏn

Avon, Loch *and* River, *Grampian*, an, aan

Avon, River, *tributary of the Severn*, 'eɪvən, áyvŏn. *This is*

the river which flows through Stratford-upon-Avon and empties into the Severn at Tewkesbury, Glos.

Avon Carrow *Warwicks.*, 'eɪvən 'kæroʊ, áyvŏn kárrō

Avonmouth *Avon*, 'eɪvənmaʊθ, áyvŏnmowth

Avon Tyrell *Hants*, 'eɪvən 'tɪrəl, áyvŏn tírrĕl

Avonwick *Devon*, 'ævənwɪk, ávvŏn-wick

Avory, *f.n.*, 'eɪvərɪ, áyvŏri

Avoth, *f.n.*, 'eɪvɒθ, áyvoth

Awbery, *f.n.*, 'ɔbərɪ, áwbĕri

Awbridge *Hants*, 'eɪbrɪdʒ, áybrij

Awe, Loch, *S'clyde*, ɔ, aw

Awliscombe *Devon*, 'ɔlɪskəm, áwlisskŏm

Awre *Glos.*, ɔr, or

Awsworth *Notts.*, 'ɒzwərθ, ózwŭrth

Axholme *Humberside*, 'ækshoʊm, ácks-hōm

Axmouth *Devon*, 'æksmaʊθ, ácksmowth

Axon, *f.n.*, 'æksən, ácksŏn

Ayckbourn, *f.n.*, 'eɪkbɔrn, áykborn

Aycliffe *Durham*, 'eɪklɪf, áyklif

Ayer, *f.n.*, ɛər, air

Ayers, *f.n.*, ɛərz, airz; 'eɪərz, áy-ĕrz

Ayerst, *f.n.*, 'eɪərst, áy-ĕrst; 'aɪərst, í-ĕrst

Aykroyd, *f.n.*, 'eɪkrɔɪd, áykroyd

Aylburton *Glos.*, 'eɪlbərtən, áylburtŏn

Aylen, *f.n.*, 'eɪlən, áylĕn

Ayles, *f.n.*, eɪlz, aylz

Aylesbeare *Devon*, 'eɪlzbɪər, áylzbeer

Aylesbury *Bucks.*, 'eɪlzbərɪ, áylzbŭri

Aylesford, Earl of, 'eɪlzfərd, áylzfŏrd

Aylesham *Kent*, 'eɪlʃəm, áyl-shăm

Aylestone *Leics.*, 'eɪlstən, áylsstŏn. *Appropriate also for Baron* ~.

Aylett, *f.n.*, 'eɪlɪt, áylĕt

Ayliffe, *f.n.*, 'eɪlɪf, áyliff

Ayling, *f.n.*, 'eɪlɪŋ, áyling

Aylmer, *f.n.*, 'eɪlmər, áylmĕr

Aylmerton *Norfolk*, 'eɪlmərtən, áylmĕrtŏn

Aylsham *Norfolk*, 'eɪlʃəm, áyl-shăm; 'eɪlsəm, áylssăm; 'alʃəm, aál-shăm

Aylward, *f.n.*, 'eɪlwərd, áylwărd; 'eɪlwɔrd, áylwawrd

Aylwen, *f.n.*, 'eɪlwɪn, áylwĕn

Aymestrey *H. & W.*, 'eɪmstrɪ, áymsstri

Aynho *Northants.*, 'eɪnhoʊ, áyn-hō

Ayot St. Lawrence *Herts.*, 'eɪət snt 'lɒrəns, áy-ŏt sĭnt lórrĕnss

Ayr *S'clyde*, ɛər, air

Ayris, *f.n.*, 'ɛərɪs, áiriss

Ayrst, *f.n.*, ɛərst, airst

Ayrton, *f.n.*, 'ɛərtən, áirtŏn

Ayscough, *f.n.*, 'eɪzkoʊ, áyzkō; 'eɪskoʊ, áysskō; 'æskoʊ, ásskō

Aysgarth *N. Yorks.*, 'eɪzgɑrθ, áyzgaarth

Ayshea, *C.n.*, 'eɪʃə, áyshă

Ayton, Great, *N. Yorks.*, 'eɪtən, áytŏn

Aytoun, William **Edmonstoune**, *Scottish poet*, 'edmənstən 'eɪtən, édmŏnstŏn áytŏn

Aza, *f.n.*, 'eɪzə, áyză

B

Babcock, *f.n.*, 'bæbkɒk, bábkock

Babell, William, *composer*, 'beɪbl, báybl

Babell *Clwyd*, 'bæbeɫ, bábbe<u>hl</u>

Babergh *Suffolk*, 'beɪbər, báybĕr

Bablockhythe *Oxon.*, 'bæbləkhaɪð, báblŏck-hï<u>th</u>

Babraham *Cambs.*, 'beɪbrəm, báybräm

Bach, *f.n.*, bɑk, baak

Bacharach, *f.n.*, 'bækəræk, báckărack

Bache, *f.n.*, beɪtʃ, baytch; beɪʃ, baysh

Bachell, *f.n.*, 'beɪtʃl, báytchl

Bachymbyd Bach *Clwyd*, bə'xʌmbɪd 'bɑx, bă<u>ch</u>úmbid baá<u>ch</u>

Backhouse, *f.n.*, 'bækəs, báckŭss; 'bækhaʊs, báck-howss

Bacon, *f.n.*, 'beɪkən, báykŏn

Baconian, *pertaining to Francis Bacon*, beɪ'koʊnɪən, baykŏn-iăn

Bacup *Lancs.*, 'beɪkəp, báykŭp

Bacuzzi, *f.n.*, bə'kʌzɪ, băkúzzi

Badcock, *f.n.*, 'bædkoʊ, bádkō

Baddeley, *f.n.*, 'bædəlɪ, báddĕli; 'bædlɪ, bádli

Baddesley, North, *Hants*, 'bædzlɪ, bádzli

Baddesley, South, *Hants*, 'bædɪzlɪ, báddĕzli; 'bædzlɪ, bádzli

Baddesley Clinton *Warwicks.*, 'bædɪzlɪ 'klɪntən, báddĕzli klíntŏn; 'bædzlɪ 'klɪntən, bádzli klíntŏn

Baddesley Ensor *Warwicks.*, 'bædɪzlɪ 'enzər, báddĕzli énzor; 'bædzlɪ 'enzər, bádzli énzor

Badel, *f.n.*, bə'del, bădéll. *Appropriate for Alan ∼, actor, and Sarah ∼, actress.*

Badeley, *f.n.*, 'bædlɪ, bádli. *Appropriate also for the Barony of ∼.*

Badenoch, *f.n.*, 'beɪdnɒk, báyd-nock

Badenoch *H'land*, 'bædənɒx, báddĕno<u>ch</u>

Baden-Powell, Baron, 'beɪdən 'poʊəl, báydŏn pó-ĕl

Bader, *f.n.*, 'bɑdər, ba´adĕr. *Appropriate for Group Captain Sir Douglas ∼.*

Badgworthy Water, *also spelt* Bagworthy, *Devon*, 'bædʒərɪ 'wɔtər, bájjĕri wáwtĕr

Badham, *f.n.*, 'bædəm, báddăm

Badoney *Co. Tyrone*, bə'dʌnɪ, bădúnni

Baelz, *f.n.*, belts, belts

Baerlein, *f.n.*, 'bɛərlaɪn, báirlïn

Bage, *f.n.*, beɪdʒ, bayj

Bagehot, *f.n.*, 'bædʒət, bájjŏt; 'bægət, bággŏt. *The first was the pronunciation of Walter ∼, economist and journalist.*

Bagenal, *f.n.*, 'bægnəl, bágnăl; 'bægənəl, bággĕnăl

Bager, *f.n.*, 'beɪdʒər, báyjĕr

Baggallay, *f.n.*, 'bægəlɪ, bággäli

Bagier, *f.n.*, 'beɪdʒər, báyjĕr

Bagillt *Clwyd*, 'bægɪɫt, bággi<u>hl</u>t

Baginton *Warwicks.*, 'bægɪntən, bággintŏn

Baglan *W. Glam.*, 'bæglən, báglăn

Bagley, *f.n.*, 'bæglɪ, bágli

Baglin, *f.n.*, 'bæglɪn, báglin

Bagnall *Staffs.*, 'bægnəl, bágnăl

Bagnari, *f.n.*, bæg'nɑrɪ, bag-naári

Bagnell, *f.n.*, 'bægnəl, bágnĕl

Bagnold, *f.n.*, 'bægnoʊld, bág-nōld

Bagot, Baron, 'bægət, bággŏt

Bagrie, *f.n.*, 'bægrɪ, bágri

Bagrit, *f.n.*, 'bægrɪt, bágrit

Baguley, *f.n.*, 'bægəlɪ, bággŭli; 'bæglɪ, bágli; 'bægjʊlɪ, bágg-yŏoli

Baguley *Gtr. M'chester*, 'bæglɪ, bágli

Bagworthy Water *see* Badgworthy Water

Baharie, *f.n.*, bə'hɑrɪ, bă-haári

Baigent, *f.n.*, 'beɪdʒənt, báyjĕnt

Baildon *W. Yorks.*, 'beɪldən, báyldŏn

Bailey, *f.n.*, 'beɪlɪ, báyli

Bailhache, *f.n.*, 'beɪlhætʃ, báyl-
-hatch
Bailliere-Tindall, *publishers*,
'beɪlɪər 'tɪndl, báyli-ĕr tíndl
Baillieston *S'clyde*, 'beɪlɪstən,
báylistŏn
Baillieu, *f.n.*, 'beɪlju, báylew.
Appropriate also for Baron ~.
Baillon, *f.n.*, 'beɪlən, báylŏn
Bain, River, *N. Yorks.*, beɪn, bayn
Baird, *f.n.*, beərd, baird
Bairstow, *f.n.*, 'beərstoʊ, báirsstō
Baiton, *f.n.*, 'beɪtən, báytŏn
Bakewell *Derby.*, 'beɪkwel,
báykwel
Bakowski, *f.n.*, bə'kɒfskɪ, băkóf-
ski
Bala *Gwynedd*, 'bælə, bálă
Balado *Tayside*, bə'lædoʊ,
băláddō
Balblair Forest, *H'land*, 'bælbleər,
bálblair
Balby *S. Yorks.*, 'bɔlbɪ, báwlbi
Balch, *f.n.*, bɔlʃ, bawlsh
Balchen, *f.n.*, 'bæltʃɪn, báltchĕn.
*This is the pronunciation
associated with the 18th-c.
Admiral of the name.*
Balchin, Nigel, *author*, 'bɔltʃɪn,
báwltchin
Balcomb, *f.n.*, 'bɒlkəm, báwlkŏm
Balcombe *W. Sussex*, 'bɒlkəm,
báwlkŏm
Balcon, *f.n.*, 'bɒlkən, báwlkŏn.
Appropriate for Sir Michael ~,
film producer, and Jill ~,
actress.
Balden, *f.n.*, 'bɒldən, báwldĕn
Baldernock *S'clyde*, bɒl'dɜrnək,
bawldérnŏk
Balderston, *f.n.*, 'bɒldərstən,
báwldĕrstŏn
Baldhu *Cornwall*, bæl'dju, baldéw;
bɔl'dju, bawldéw; bɔl'du,
bawldoó
Baldick, *f.n.*, 'bɒldɪk, báwldick
Baldock, *f.n.*, 'bɒldɒk, báwldock
Baldock *Herts.*, 'bɒldɒk, báwl-
dock
Baldovan *Tayside*, bæl'dɒvən,
bal-dóvvăn
Baldovie *Tayside*, bæl'dʌvɪ,
bal-dúvvi
Baldragon *Tayside*, bæl'drægən,
bal-drággŏn
Baldry, *f.n.*, 'bɔldrɪ, báwldri
Baldslow *E. Sussex*, 'bɔldzloʊ,
báwldz-lō
Baldwin, *f.n.*, 'bɔldwɪn, báwldwin.
Appropriate also for Earl ~ *of
Bewdley.*
Balerno *Lothian*, bə'lɜrnoʊ,
bălérnō. *Appropriate also for
Baron* ~.

Balfe, *f.n.*, bælf, balf
Balfour, *f.n.*, 'bælfər, bálfŭr;
'bælfɔr, bálfor. *The second is
appropriate for the Earl of* ~
and for Baron ~ *of Inchrye.*
Balfour of Burleigh, Baron,
'bælfər əv 'bɜrlɪ, bálfŭr ŏv
búrli
Balfron *Central*, bæl'frɒn, balfrón
Balgavies Loch *Tayside*, bæl-
'gævɪz, balgávviz
Balgay *Tayside*, bæl'geɪ, balgáy
Balgedie *Tayside*, bæl'gedɪ,
balgéddi
Balgonie, *f.n.*, bæl'goʊnɪ, bal-
gŏni
Balguy, *f.n.*, 'bɒlgɪ, báwlgi
Balham *London*, 'bæləm, bálăm
Balhatchet, *f.n.*, bæl'hætʃɪt, bal-
-hátchĕt
Balhousie Castle *Tayside*, bæl-
'haʊzɪ, bal-hówzi
Baliol, *f.n.*, 'beɪlɪəl, báyli-ŏl
Balivanich *Benbecula* (*W. Isles*),
ˌbælɪ'vænɪx, balivánnich
Ball, *f.n.*, bɔl, bawl
Ballabrooie *I. of Man*, ˌbælə'bruɪ,
balăbroó-i
Ballachulish *H'land*, ˌbælə'hulɪʃ,
balăhoólish
Ballacraine *I. of Man*, ˌbælə'kreɪn,
balăkráyn
Ballagh *Co. Fermanagh, Co.
Tyrone*, 'bælə, bálă
Ballagher, *f.n.*, 'bæləgər, bálágĕr
Ballam, Higher *and* Lower, *Lancs.*
'bæləm, bálăm
Ballantine, *f.n.*, 'bæləntaɪn,
bálăntīn
Ballantrae *S'clyde*, ˌbælən'treɪ,
balăn-tráy
Ballantyne, *f.n.*, 'bæləntaɪn,
bálăntīn
Ballard, *f.n.*, 'bælɑrd, bálaard;
'bælərd, bálărd
Ballardie, *f.n.*, bə'lɑrdɪ, bălaárdi
Ballasalla *I. of Man*, ˌbælə'sælə,
balăssálă
Ballater *Grampian*, 'bælətər,
bálătĕr
Ballaugh *I. of Man*, bə'lɑf,
bălaáf
Ballechin *Tayside*, bə'lexɪn,
băléchin
Balleine, *f.n.*, bæ'len, balén
Ballengeich *Central*, ˌbælən'gix,
balĕn-geéch
Ballham, *f.n.*, 'bɒləm, báwlăm
Ballinahatty *Co. Tyrone*, ˌbælɪnə-
'hætɪ, balinähátti
Ballinamallard *Co. Fermanagh*,
ˌbælɪnə'mælərd, balinămálărd
Ballinaskeagh *Co. Down*,
ˌbælɪnə'skeɪ, balinăskáy

Ballindalloch *Grampian*, ˌbælɪn-
'dæləx, balindálŏ<u>ch</u>
Ballinderry *Co. Antrim*, ˌbælɪn-
'derɪ, balindérri
Ballinger *Bucks.*, 'bælɪndʒər,
bálinjĕr
Ballingry *Fife*, bə'lɪŋgrɪ, bălíng-gri
Ballinluig *Tayside*, ˌbælɪn'luɪg,
balinloo-ig
Ballintogher *Co. Down*, ˌbælɪn-
'tɒxər, balintó<u>ch</u>ĕr
Ballintoy *Co. Antrim*, ˌbælɪn'tɔɪ,
balintóy
Balliol College, *Oxford Univ.*,
'beɪlɪəl, báyli-ŏl
Balloch *H'land*, bæ'lɒx, baló<u>ch</u>
Balloch *S'clyde*, 'bæləx, bálŏ<u>ch</u>
Balloch Buie *Grampian*, 'bæləx
'buɪ, bálŏ<u>ch</u> bo̅o̅-i
Ballochmyle *S'clyde*, ˌbæləx'maɪl,
balŏ<u>ch</u>míl
Balloo *Co. Down*, bə'lu, băló̅o̅
Ballyards *Co. Armagh*, ˌbælɪ'ɑrdz,
bali-aʹardz
Ballyaughlis *Co. Down*, ˌbælɪ-
'ɒxlɪs, bali-ó<u>ch</u>liss
Ballybannon *Co. Down*, ˌbælɪ-
'bænən, balibánnŏn
Ballycairn *Co. Antrim*, ˌbælɪ-
'kɛərn, balikáirn
Ballycarry *Co. Antrim*, ˌbælɪ'kærɪ,
balikárri
Ballycastle *Co. Antrim*, ˌbælɪ'kɑsl,
balikaʹassl
Ballyclare *Co. Antrim*, ˌbælɪ'klɛər,
baliklaʹir
Ballycoan *Co. Down*, ˌbælɪ'koʊən,
balikŏ̅-än
Ballycopeland *Co. Down*, ˌbælɪ-
'koʊplənd, balikŏ̅pländ
Ballycultra *Co. Down*, ˌbælɪkəl'trɔ,
balikúltráw
Ballydavey *Co. Down*, ˌbælɪ-
'deɪvɪ, balidáyvi
Ballydivity *Co. Antrim*, ˌbælɪ-
'dɪvɪtɪ, balidívviti
Ballydougan *Co. Down*, ˌbælɪ-
'dugən, balidóogän
Ballydrain *Co. Down*, ˌbælɪ'dreɪn,
balidráyn
Ballyeglish *Co. Derry*, ˌbælɪ'eɪglɪʃ,
bali-áyglish
Ballyfinaghy *Co. Antrim*, ˌbælɪ-
'fɪnəxɪ, balifínná<u>ch</u>i
Ballygally *Co. Antrim*, ˌbælɪ'gælɪ,
baligáli
Ballygawley *Co. Tyrone*, ˌbælɪ-
'gɔlɪ, baligáwli
Ballygilbert *Co. Down*, ˌbælɪ-
'gɪlbərt, baligílbĕrt
Ballygomartin *Co. Antrim*,
ˌbælɪgoʊ'mɑrtɪn, baligōmaʹartin
Ballygowan *Co. Down*, ˌbælɪ-
'gaʊən, baligówän

Ballygrainey *Co. Down*, ˌbælɪ-
'greɪnɪ, baligráyni
Ballyhackamore *Co. Down*,
ˌbælɪ'hækəmɔr, balihácká̈mor
Ballyhalbert *Co. Down*, ˌbælɪ-
'hælbərt, balihálbĕrt
Ballyhanwood *Co. Down*, ˌbælɪ-
'hænwʊd, balihánwo̅o̅d
Ballyholme *Co. Down*, ˌbælɪ-
'hoʊm, balihŏ̅m
Ballyhornan *Co. Down*, ˌbælɪ-
'hɔrnən, balihórnän
Ballykelly *Co. Derry*, ˌbælɪ'kelɪ,
balikélli
Ballykilbeg *Co. Down*, ˌbælɪkɪl-
'beg, balikilbég
Ballykinlar *Co. Down*, ˌbælɪ'kɪnlər,
balikínlär
Ballylesson *Co. Down*, ˌbælɪ'lesən,
baliléssŏn
Ballylumford *Co. Antrim*, ˌbælɪ-
'lʌmfərd, balilúmfŏrd
Ballymacarrett *Co. Down*,
ˌbælɪmə'kærɪt, balimäkárrĕt
Ballymachan *Belfast*, ˌbælɪ-
'mæxən, balimá<u>ch</u>än
Ballymaconaghy *Co. Down*,
ˌbælɪmə'kɒnəxɪ, balimäkón-
ná<u>ch</u>i
Ballymaconnell *Co. Down*,
ˌbælɪmə'kɒnl, balimäkónnl
Ballymacormick *Co. Down*,
ˌbælɪmə'kɔrmɪk, balimäkór-
mick
Ballymagorry *Co. Tyrone*,
ˌbælɪmə'gɒrɪ, balimägórri
Ballymaguigan *Co. Derry*,
ˌbælɪmə'gwɪgən, balimägwíggän
Ballymena *Co. Antrim*, ˌbælɪ-
'minə, baliméenä
Ballymenoch *Co. Down*, ˌbælɪ-
'minəx, baliméenŏ<u>ch</u>
Ballymoney *Co. Antrim*, ˌbælɪ-
'mʌnɪ, balimúnni
Ballynafeigh *Co. Down*, ˌbælɪnə-
'faɪ, balinäfí
Ballynahinch *Co. Down*,
ˌbælɪnə'hɪnʃ, balinähínsh
Ballynure *Co. Antrim*, ˌbælɪ-
'njʊər, balinyŏ̅or
Ballyquintin *Co. Down*, ˌbælɪ-
'kwɪntɪn, balikwíntin
Ballyrashane *Co. Derry*, ˌbælɪrə-
'ʃeɪn, balirăsháyn
Ballyrobert *Co. Down*, ˌbælɪ-
'rɒbərt, baliróbbĕrt
Ballyronan *Co. Derry*, ˌbælɪ-
'roʊnən, balirŏ̅nän
Ballyroney *Co. Down*, ˌbælɪ-
'roʊnɪ, balirŏ̅ni
Ballysallagh *Co. Down*, ˌbælɪ-
'sælə, balissálá
Ballysillan *Co. Antrim*, ˌbælɪ'sɪlən,
balissíllän

Ballystockart *Co. Down*, ‚bælɪ-
'stɒkərt, balistóckärt
Ballywalter *Co. Down*, ‚bælɪ-
'wɔltər, bali-wáwltĕr
Ballywillan *Co. Down*, ‚bælɪ'wɪlən,
bali-wíllän
Balmacara *H'land*, ‚bælmə'kɑrə,
balmăka'ärä
Balmaghie *D. & G.*, ‚bælmə'gi,
balmăgéé
Balmaha *Central*, ‚bælmə'hɑ,
balmăha'a
Balmedie *Grampian*, bæl'medɪ,
balméddi
Balmer,*f.n.*, 'bɑmər, ba'amĕr
Balmerino,*f.n.*, bæl'mɛərnɪ,
balmáirni
Balmerino *Fife*, ‚bælmə'rinoʊ,
balmĕréenŏ
Balmoral *Grampian*, *Co. Antrim*,
bæl'mɒrəl, balmórräl
Balnacra *H'land*, ‚bælnə'krɑ,
balnăkra'a
Balnaguard *Tayside*, ‚bælnə'gɑrd,
balnăga'ard
Balnain *H'land*, bæl'neɪn,
balnáyn
Balnave,*f.n.*, bæl'neɪv, balnáyv
Balne *S. Yorks.*, bɔn, bawn
Balniel, Lord, bæl'nil, balnéel
Balogh, Baron, 'bælɒg, bálog
Balornock *S'clyde*, bə'lɔrnək,
bălórnŏk
Balquharn *Grampian*, bæl'hwɑrn,
bal-wha'arn
Balquhidder *Central*, bæl'hwɪdər,
bal-whíddĕr; bæl'kwɪdər,
bal-kwíddĕr
Balranald *N. Uist* (*W. Isles*),
bæl'rænəld, balránnäld
Balsall Heath *W. Midlands*,
'bɔlsl 'hiθ, báwlssl héeth
Balshagray *S'clyde*, bæl'ʃægreɪ,
bal-shágray
Balsham *Cambs.*, 'bɔlʃəm, báwl-
-shäm
Balston,*f.n.*, 'bɔlstən, báwlsstŏn
Baltasound *Shetland*, 'bæltəsund,
báltăssoond
Baltonsborough *Somerset*,
'bɔltənzbərə, báwltŏnzbŭră;
'bɔlzbərɪ, báwlzbŭri
Balvenie *Grampian*, bæl'venɪ,
balvénni
Bambaras Music hall, *Newcastle-
upon-Tyne*, 'bæmbrəz, bámbräz
Bambridge,*f.n.*, 'beɪmbrɪdʒ,
báymbrij
Bambrough,*f.n.*, 'bæmbrə, bám-
brä
Bamburgh *Northd.*, 'bæmbərə,
bámbŭră
Bamford,*f.n.*, 'bæmfərd, bámfŏrd
Bamfyld,*f.n.*, 'bæmfild, bámfeeld

Bamont,*f.n.*, 'beɪmənt, báymŏnt
Bampfylde,*f.n.*, 'bæmpfild,
bámpfeeld. *Family name of
Lord Poltimore.*
Bamrah,*f.n.*, 'bæmrɑ, bámraa
Banbridge *Co. Down*, bæn'brɪdʒ,
banbríj; 'bænbrɪdʒ, bánbrij
Banagher *Co. Derry*, 'bænəxər,
bánnă̱c̱ẖĕr
Banavie *H'land*, 'bænəvɪ, bánnăvi
Banbury *Oxon.*, 'bænbərɪ, bán-
bŭri; 'bæmbərɪ, bámbŭri
Banbury of Southam, Baron,
'bænbərɪ əv 'saʊðəm, bánbŭri
ŏv sów̱ṯẖäm
Bance,*f.n.*, bæns, banss
Banchory *Grampian*, 'bæŋkərɪ,
bánkŏri; 'bæŋxərɪ, bánc̱ẖŏri
Banchory-Devenick *Grampian*,
'bæŋkərɪ 'devənɪk, bánkŏri
dévvĕnick; 'bæŋxərɪ 'devənɪk,
bánc̱ẖŏri dévvĕnick
Banchory-Ternan *Grampian*,
'bæŋkərɪ 'tɛərnən, bánkŏri
táirnän; 'bæŋxərɪ 'tɛərnən,
bánc̱ẖŏri táirnän
Banc-y-ffordd *Dyfed*,‚bæŋkə'fɔrð,
bankăfóṟṯẖ
Bandey,*f.n.*, 'bændɪ, bándi
Banff *Grampian*, bæmf, bamf;
bænf, banf
Bangor *Clwyd, Gwynedd, Co.
Down*, 'bæŋgər, báng-gŏr.
Appropriate also for Viscount ∼.
Bangour *Lothian*, bæŋ'gaʊər,
bang-gówr
Banham,*f.n.*, 'bænəm, bánnăm
Bank-Ffos-Felen *Dyfed*, ‚bæŋk
foʊs 'velɪn, bank fŏss véllĕn
Bankyfelin *Dyfed*, ‚bæŋkə'velɪn,
bankăvéllin
Bannard,*f.n.*, 'bænɑrd, bánnaard
Bannatyne,*f.n.*, 'bænətaɪn,
bánnătīn
Bannatyne, Port, *S'clyde*, pɔrt
'bænətaɪn, port bánnătīn
Bannell,*f.n.*, 'bænl, bánnl
Banner Hey *Merseyside*, 'bænər
'heɪ, bánnĕr háy
Bannerman of Kildonan, Barony
of, 'bænərmən əv kɪl'dɒnən,
bánnĕrmän ŏv kildónnän
Bannockburn *Central*, 'bænək-
bərn, bánnŏkburn
Bannon,*f.n.*, 'bænən, bánnŏn
Bantham *Devon*, 'bæntəm,
bántäm
Banwell *Avon*, 'bænwəl, bán-wĕl
Banyard,*f.n.*, 'bænjɑrd, bán-
-yaard
Bapchild *Kent*, 'bæptʃaɪld, báp-
-chīld
Barachnie *S'clyde*, bə'ræxnɪ,
bără̱c̱ẖni

Barassie *S'clyde*, bə'ræsɪ, bărássi

Barbirolli, Sir John, *conductor*, ‚bɑrbɪ'rɒlɪ, baarbirólli

Barbour, *f.n.*, 'bɑrbər, baʹarbŭr

Barcaldine *S'clyde*, bɑr'kældɪn, baarkáldin

Barclay, *f.n.*, 'bɑrklɪ, baʹarkli

Barcloy *D. & G.*, bər'klɔɪ, bărklóy

Barcombe *E. Sussex*, 'bɑrkəm, baʹarkŏm

Barcroft, *f.n.*, 'bɑrkrɒft, baʹarkroft

Bardgett, Herbert, *conductor*, 'bɑrdʒet, baʹarjet

Bardill, *f.n.*, 'bɑrdl, baʹardl; 'bɑrdɪl, baʹardil

Bardsey Island *Gwynedd*, 'bɑrdsɪ, baʹardssi

Bareau, Paul, *economist*, 'pɔl 'bæroʊ, páwl bárrō

Barfreston *Kent*, 'bɑrfrɪstən, baʹarfrĕstŏn

Bargany *S'clyde*, bɑr'genɪ, baar-génni

Bargeddie *S'clyde*, bɑr'gedɪ, baargéddi

Barger, *f.n.*, 'bɑrdʒər, baʹarjĕr

Bargery, *f.n.*, 'bɑrdʒərɪ, baʹarjĕri

Bargh, *f.n.*, 'bɑrdʒ, baarj; bɑrf, baarf; bɑrg, baarg

Bargoed *Mid Glam.*, 'bɑrgɔɪd, baʹargoyd

Barham, *f.n.*, 'bærəm, bárrăm; 'bɑrəm, baʹarăm. *The second is appropriate for Baron ~.*

Barham *Cambs.*, 'bɑrəm, baʹarăm; 'bærəm, bárrăm

Barham *Kent*, 'bærəm, bárrăm

Barharrow *D. & G.*, bɑr'hæroʊ, baar-hárrō

Barholm *Lincs.*, 'bærəm, bárrŏm

Baring, *f.n.*, 'bɛərɪŋ, báiring; 'bærɪŋ, bárring

Baring-Gould, The Revd. **Sabine,** *author and hymn-writer*, 'seɪbɪn 'bɛərɪŋ 'guld, sáybin báiring goʹold

Barkisland *W. Yorks.*, 'bɑrkɪslənd, baʹarkissländ; 'bɑslənd, baʹassländ

Barklye *E. Sussex*, bɑrk'laɪ, baarklí

Barlanark *S'clyde*, bɑr'lænərk, baar-lánnărk

Barlas, *f.n.*, 'bɑrləs, baʹarlăss

Barlass, *f.n.*, 'bɑrləs, baʹarlăss

Barlaston *Staffs.*, 'bɑrləstən, baʹarlăstŏn

Barlavington *W. Sussex*, bɑr-'lævɪŋtən, baarlávvingtŏn

Barlborough *Derby.*, 'bɑrlbərə, baʹarlbŭră; 'bɑrbərə, baʹarbŭră

Barlestone *Leics.*, 'bɑrlstoʊn, baʹarlsstŏn

Barlinnie Prison *Glasgow*, bɑr'lɪnɪ, baarlínni

Barmouth *Gwynedd*, 'bɑrməθ, baʹarmŭth

Barnabe, *f.n.*, 'bɑrnəbɪ, baʹarnăbi

Barnadier, *f.n.*, ‚bɑrnə'dɪər, baarnădéer

Barnard, *f.n.*, 'bɑrnərd, baʹar-naard; 'bɑrnərd, baʹarnărd

Barnard Castle *Durham*, 'bɑrnərd 'kɑsl, baʹarnărd kaʹassl

Barnard Gate *Oxon.*, 'bɑrnərd 'geɪt, baʹarnărd gáyt

Barnardiston, *f.n.*, ‚bɑrnər'dɪstən, baarnărdístŏn

Barnbow *W. Yorks.*, bɑrn'boʊ, baarnbó; 'bɑrnboʊ, baʹarnbō

Barneby, *f.n.*, 'bɑrnəbɪ, baʹarnĕbi

Barnehurst *London*, 'bɑrnhərst, baʹarn-hurst

Barnell, *f.n.*, bɑr'nel, baarnéll

Barnet, *f.n.*, 'bɑrnɪt, baʹarnĕt

Barnett, *f.n.*, 'bɑrnɪt, baʹarnĕt; bɑr'net, baarnétt

Barnoldswick *Lancs.*, bɑr'noʊldz-wɪk, baarnóldzwick; 'bɑrlɪk, baʹarlick

Barnstaple *Devon* 'bɑrnstəpl, baʹarnstăpl

Barou, *f.n.*, bə'ru, băroʹo

Barraclough, *f.n.*, 'bærəklʌf, bárräkluff

Barrass, *f.n.*, 'bærəs, bárräss

Barraud, *f.n.*, 'bærɒd, bárrawd

Barrell, *f.n.*, 'bærəl, bárrĕl

Barrington, *f.n.*, 'bærɪŋtən, bárringtŏn

Barripper *Cornwall*, bə'rɪpər, băríppĕr

Barritt, *f.n.*, 'bærət, bárrĕt

Barrogil Castle *H'land*, 'bæroʊgɪl, bárrōgil. *Former name of the Castle of* **Mey**, *q.v.*

Barrow-in-Furness *Cumbria*, 'bæroʊ ɪn 'fərnɪs, bárrō in fúrnĕss

Barry *S. Glam.*, 'bærɪ, bárri

Barsham, *f.n.*, 'bɑrʃəm, baʹar-shăm

Barsham *Suffolk*, 'bɑrʃəm, baʹar--shăm. *Appropriate also for East, West, and North ~ in Norfolk, and the historic East ~ Manor.*

Barsotti, *f.n.*, bɑr'zɒtɪ, baarzótti

Barstow, *f.n.*, 'bɑrstoʊ, baʹarsstō

Bartell, *f.n.*, bɑr'tel, baartéll

Bartelski, *f.n.*, bɑr'telskɪ, baar-télski

Bartestree *H. & W.*, 'bɑrtɪstrɪ, baʹartĕstree

Bartholomew, *f.n.*, bɑr'θɒləmju, baarthóllŏmew

Barthomley *Ches.*, 'bɑrθəmlɪ, baʹarthŏmli

Bartleet, *f.n.*, 'bɑrtlit, baʹartleet

Bartlett, f.n., 'bɑrtlɪt, baártlĕt
Barton-in-Fabis, Notts., 'bɑrtən ɪn 'feɪbɪs, baártŏn in fáybiss
Barton Seagrave Northants., 'bɑrtən 'sigreɪv, baártŏn seé-grayv
Barttelot, f.n., 'bɑrtəlɒt, baártĕlot
Baruck, f.n., bə'rʊk, bărŏŏk
Barugh, f.n., bɑrf, baarf
Barugh Cumbria, bɑrf, baarf
Barugh, Great and Little, N. Yorks., bɑrf, baarf
Barugh S. Yorks., bɑrk, baark
Barwick, f.n., 'bɑrɪk, bárrick; 'bɑrwɪk, baárwick
Barwick Norfolk, Somerset, 'bærɪk, bárrick
Barwick-in-Elmet W. Yorks., 'bærɪk ɪn 'elmɪt, bárrick in élmĕt
Baschurch Salop, 'bæstʃɜrtʃ, báss-churtch
Basèbé, f.n., bə'seɪbɪ, băssáybi
Baseden, f.n., 'beɪzdən, báyzdĕn
Baseley, f.n., 'beɪzlɪ, báyzli
Basevi, George, 19th-c. architect, bə'seɪvɪ, băssáyvi
Basford Ches., Staffs., 'bæsfərd, bássfŏrd
Basford, Notts., 'beɪsfərd, báyssfŏrd
Basildon Berks., Essex, 'bæzldən, bázzldŏn
Basing, Baron, 'beɪzɪŋ, báyzing
Basingstoke Hants, 'beɪzɪŋstoʊk, báyzingstōk
Baskind, f.n., 'bæskɪnd, básskind
Baslow Derby., 'bæzloʊ, bázlō
Basnett, f.n., 'bæznet, báznett
Bason, f.n., 'bæsən, bássŏn
Bassaleg Gwent, 'beɪzlɪg, báyzlig; bæ'sæleg, bassáleg
Bassenthwaite Cumbria, 'bæsən-θweɪt, bássĕnthwayt
Bassetlaw Notts., 'bæsɪt'lɔ, bássĕtláw
Bassham, f.n., 'bæsəm, bássăm
Bassingbourn Cambs., 'bæsɪŋbɔrn, bássingborn
Bassingfield Notts., 'bæsɪŋfɪld, bássingfeeld
Bassingthwaite, f.n., 'bæsɪŋθweɪt, bássingthwayt
Bastedo, f.n., bə'tidoʊ, băsteédō
Baster, f.n., 'bæstər, básstĕr
Basterfield, f.n., 'bæstərfild, básstĕrfeeld
Bastie, f.n., 'bæstɪ, bássti
Bastin, f.n., 'bæstɪn, básstin
Baston Lincs., 'bæstən, básstŏn
Bastonford H. & W., 'bæstənfɔrd, básstŏnford
Baswich Staffs., 'bæsɪdʒ, bássij; 'bæsɪtʃ, bássitch

Batchelor, f.n., 'bætʃɪlər, bátchĕlŏr
Bate, f.n., beɪt, bayt
Baterip, f.n., 'bætərɪp, báttĕrip
Bates, f.n., beɪts, bayts
Bateson, f.n., 'beɪtsən, báytsŏn
Batham, f.n., 'beɪθəm, báythăm
Bathavon Avon, 'baθeɪvən, baáth-ayvŏn
Bathealton Somerset, 'bætltən, báttltŏn
Batheaston Avon, bɑ'θistən, baatheéstŏn; 'bætɪstən, báttistŏn
Bather, f.n., 'bæðər, báthĕr; 'bæθər, báthĕr
Bathford Avon, bɑθ'fɔrd, baath-ford
Batho, f.n., 'bæθoʊ, báthō; 'beɪθoʊ, báythō
Bathurst, f.n., 'bæθɜrst, báthurst; 'bæθhɜrst, báth-hurst. The first is appropriate for Earl ~ and for Viscount Bledisloe's family name.
Batley W. Yorks., 'bætlɪ, bátli
Batsford, f.n., 'bætsfərd, bátsfŏrd
Battagel, f.n., 'bætədʒl, báttăjl
Battersea London, 'bætərsɪ, báttĕrssi
Battershill, f.n., 'bætərʃɪl, báttĕr-shil
Battes, f.n., 'bætɪs, báttĕss
Battine, f.n., 'bætin, bátteen
Battisford Suffolk, 'bætɪsfərd, báttissfŏrd
Battishill, f.n., 'bætɪʃɪl, bátti-shil; 'bætɪʃl, báttishl
Battleby Tayside, 'bætlbɪ, báttlbi
Battlefield Glasgow, 'bætlfɪld, báttl-feeld
Battlesbridge Essex, 'bætlzbrɪdʒ, báttlz-brij
Battye, f.n., 'bætɪ, bátti
Baty, f.n., 'beɪtɪ, báyti
Baublys, f.n., 'bɒblɪs, báwbliss
Baudains, f.n., 'boʊdeɪnz, bódaynz
Baufield, f.n., 'baʊfild, bówfeeld
Baugh, f.n., bɔ, baw
Baughan, f.n., bɒn, bawn; 'bɔən, báw-ăn; 'bɒfən, bóffăn
Baughen, f.n., bɒn, bawn; 'bɔən, báw-ĕn; 'bɒfən, bóffĕn
Baughurst Hants, 'bɒghɜrst, báwg-hurst
Baulard, f.n., 'boʊlɑrd, bólaard
Baulch, f.n., bɔltʃ, bawltch
Baumber, f.n., 'bɒmbər, báwmbĕr
Baumber Lincs., 'bɒmbər, báwmbĕr
Baunton Glos., 'bɒntən, báwntŏn
Baur, f.n., 'baʊər, bowr
Baverstock, f.n., 'bævərstɒk, bávvĕrsstock

Bavin, *f.n.,* 'bævɪn, bávvin;
'beɪvɪn, báyvin
Bawburgh *Norfolk,* 'beɪbər,
báybĕr; 'bɔbərə, báwbŭrä
Bawden, *f.n.,* 'bɔdən, báwdĕn
Bawdeswell *Norfolk,* 'bɔdzwəl,
báwdzwĕl
Bawdsey *Suffolk,* 'bɔdzɪ, báwdzi
Bawor, *f.n.,* 'bauər, bówĕr
Bawtree, *f.n.,* 'bɔtrɪ, báwtri
Baxandall, *f.n.,* 'bæksəndɔl,
bácksändawl
Baxendale, *f.n.,* 'bæksəndeɪl,
bácksĕndayl
Baxendine, *f.n.,* 'bæksəndaɪn,
bácksĕndïn
Baxter, *f.n.,* 'bækstər, báckstĕr
Bayard, *f.n.,* 'beɪard, báy-aard
Baylham *Suffolk,* 'beɪləm, báylăm
Baynard's Castle *see* **Castle
Baynard**
Baynard's Green *Oxon.,*
'beɪnardz 'grin, báynaardz
gréen
Bazalgette, *f.n.,* 'bæzldʒet, bázzl-
-jet
Bazeley, *f.n.,* 'beɪzlɪ, báyzli
Bazell, *f.n.,* bə'zel, băzéll
Bazett, *f.n.,* 'bæzɪt, bázzĕt
Bazin, *f.n.,* 'beɪzɪn, báyzin
Beacham, *f.n.,* 'bitʃəm, beétchăm
Beachy Head *E. Sussex,* 'bitʃɪ
'hed, beétchi héd
Beacon Lough *Tyne & Wear,*
'bikən 'lɒf, beékŏn lóff
Beaconsfield *Bucks.,* 'bekənzfild,
béckŏnzfeeld; 'bikənzfild,
beékŏnzfeeld. *The second is
appropriate also for the Earldom
of* ~.
Beaford *Devon,* 'bifərd, beéfŏrd
Beagh's Forest *Co. Antrim,* 'beɪəx,
báy-ăch
Beaglehole, *f.n.,* 'biglhoul,
beégl-hōl
Beahan, *f.n.,* 'biən, beé-ăn
Beament, *f.n.,* 'bimənt, beémĕnt
Beaminster *Dorset,* 'bemɪnstər,
bémminstĕr
Beamish, *f.n.,* 'bimɪʃ, beémish
Beamont, *f.n.,* 'bimənt, beémŏnt
Bean, *f.n.,* bin, been
Beanacharan, Loch, *H'land,*
bjænə'xærən, byannăchárrăn
Beanes, *f.n.,* beɪnz, baynz
Beaney, *f.n.,* 'binɪ, beéni
Beardsall, *f.n.,* 'bɪərdsl, beérdssl
Beardsell, *f.n.,* 'bɪərdsl, beérdssl
Beardsley, *f.n.,* 'bɪərdzlɪ, beérdzli.
Appropriate for Aubrey ~,
19th-c. artist.
Beare *Devon,* bɪər, beer
Beare Green *Surrey,* 'bɛər 'grin,
báir gréen

Bearley *Warwicks.,* 'bɪərlɪ, beérli
Bearpark *Durham,* 'bɪər'park,
beér-paárk
Bearsden *S'clyde,* bɛərz'den,
bairzdén
Bearsted *Kent,* 'barsted, bérssted;
'bɛərsted, báirssted. *The first is
appropriate for Viscount* ~.
Bearstone *Salop,* 'bɪərstən,
beérstŏn
Bearwardcote *Derby.,* 'bærəkət,
bárräkŏt
Beastall, *f.n.,* 'bistl, beéstl
Beaton, *f.n.,* 'bitən, beétŏn
Beattie, *f.n.,* 'bitɪ, beéti
Beattock *D. & G.,* 'bitək, beé-
tŏk
Beatty, Earl, 'bitɪ, beéti
Beauchamp *Gwent,* 'bitʃəm,
beétchăm. *Appropriate also for
the Earldom of* ~.
Beauchamp of Powyke, Baron,
'bitʃəm əv 'pouɪk, beétchăm ŏv
pṓ-ik
Beauchief *S. Yorks.,* 'bitʃɪf,
beétchif
Beauclerk, *f.n.,* 'bouklɛər, bṓ-
klair; bou'klɛər, bōkláir. *The
first is appropriate for the Duke
of St. Albans' family name.*
Beaudesert *Warwicks.,* bou-
'dezərt, bōdézzĕrt; ˌboudɪ'zɛər,
bōdĕzáir; 'belzər, bélzĕr
Beaufort, Duke of, 'boufərt,
bṓfŏrt
Beaufoy, *f.n.,* 'boufɔɪ, bṓfoy
Beaulieu *Hants,* 'bjulɪ, béwli
Beauly *H'land,* 'bjulɪ, béwli
Beaumanor *Leics.,* bou'mænər,
bōmánnŏr
Beaumaris *Gwynedd,* bou'mærɪs,
bōmárriss
Beaumont, *f.n.,* 'boumənt,
bṓmŏnt; 'boumɒnt, bṓmont.
*The first is appropriate also for
Baron* ~ *of Whitley.*
Beaumont *Cumbria,* 'bimənt,
beémŏnt
Beausale *Warwicks.,* 'bjusl,
béwssl
Beausire, *f.n.,* bou'sɪər, bōsseér
Beauvoir, *f.n.,* 'bouvwar,
bṓvwaar
Beavan, *f.n.,* 'bevən, bévvăn
Beavis, *f.n.,* 'bivɪs, beéviss
Beavon, *f.n.,* 'bevən, bévvŏn
Beaworthy *Devon,* 'biwɜrðɪ,
beé-wurthi; 'bauərɪ, bówĕri
Beba, *f.n.,* 'bibə, beébä
Bebe, *f.n.,* 'bibɪ, beébi
Bechely, *f.n.,* 'bitʃlɪ, beétchli
Becher's Brook *Aintree race-
course, Liverpool,* 'bitʃərz 'bruk,
beétchĕrz brṓok

Bechervaise, *f.n.,* 'betʃərveɪz, bétchĕrvayz; 'beʃərveɪz, béshĕrvayz
Bechhofer, *f.n.,* 'bekhoʊfər, béck--hōfĕr
Becke, *f.n.,* bek, beck
Beckermet *Cumbria,* be'kɜrmɪt, beckérmĕt
Beckinsale, *f.n.,* 'bekɪnseɪl, béckinssayl
Beckles, *f.n.,* 'beklz, bécklz
Bective, Earl of, 'bektɪv, bécktiv
Bedale *N. Yorks.,* 'bidl, beédl. The local ~ *Hunt, however, is pronounced* 'bideɪl, beédayl.
Bedales School *Hants,* 'bideɪlz, beédaylz
Beddall, *f.n.,* 'bedɔl, béddawl
Beddau *Mid Glam.,* 'beðaɪ, béthī
Beddgelert *Gwynedd,* beɪð-'gelərt, bayth-géllĕrt
Beddingham *E. Sussex,* ˌbedɪŋ-'hæm, bedding-hám
Beddoes, Thomas **Lovell,** *19th-c. poet and dramatist,* 'lʌvl 'bedoʊz, lúvvl béddōz
Bedel, *f.n.,* 'bidl, beédl
Bedells, *f.n.,* bə'delz, bĕdéllz
Bedenham *Hants,* 'bedənəm, béddĕnăm
Bedford *Beds.,* 'bedfərd, bédfŏrd. *Appropriate also for the Duke of* ~.
Bedham *W. Sussex,* bed'hæm, bed-hám
Bedlinog *Mid Glam.,* bed'lɪnɒg, bedleénog
Bedruthan *Cornwall,* bɪ'drʌðən, bĕdrúthăn
Bedstone *Salop,* 'bedstən, béd--stŏn
Bedwas *Mid Glam.,* 'bedwæs, bédwass
Bedwell, *f.n.,* 'bedwel, bédwel
Bedwellty *Gwent,* bed'wełtɪ, bed-wéhlti
Beebee, *f.n.,* 'bibi, beébee
Beech, *f.n.,* bitʃ, beetch
Beecham, *f.n.,* 'bitʃəm, beétchăm
Beeleigh *Essex,* 'bili, beélee; 'bilɪ, beéli
Beer, *f.n.,* bɪər, beer
Beerbohm, *f.n.,* 'bɪərboʊm, beér-bōm. *Appropriate for Sir Max* ~, *author and caricaturist, and Sir Herbert* ~-*Tree, actor.*
Beesands *Devon,* 'bisændz, beé-sandz
Beese, *f.n.,* biz, beez
Beeswing *D. & G.,* 'bizwɪŋ, beézwing
Beetham, *f.n.,* 'biθəm, beéthăm
Beetham *Cumbria,* 'biðəm, beéthăm

Beeton, *f.n.,* 'bitən, beétŏn
Begbroke *Oxon.,* 'begbrʊk, bégbrŏŏk
Begelly *Dyfed,* bɪ'gelɪ, bĕgélli
Begent, *f.n.,* 'bidʒənt, beéjĕnt
Beggearn Huish *Somerset,* 'begɜrn 'hjuɪʃ, béggern héw-ish
Beguildy *Powys,* bɪ'gaɪldɪ, bĕgíldi
Behague, *f.n.,* bɪ'heɪg, bĕ-háyg
Beharrell, *f.n.,* bɪ'hærəl, bĕ-hárrĕl
Behnes, William, *19th-c. sculptor,* 'beɪnɪz, báynĕz; beɪnz, báynz. *These pronunciations are based merely on usage, not on historical evidence. The sculptor was of German origin.*
Behrens, *f.n.,* 'beərənz, báirĕnz
Beighton, *f.n.,* 'beɪtən, báytŏn
Beighton *Norfolk,* 'baɪtən, bítŏn; 'beɪtən, báytŏn
Beighton *S. Yorks.,* 'beɪtən, báytŏn; 'baɪtən, bítŏn
Beilby, *f.n.,* 'bilbɪ, beélbi
Beinn a'Chaolais *S'clyde,* ˌben ə 'xɜɪlɪʃ, ben ă chŏ́-ilish
Beinn-an-Oir *S'clyde,* ˌben ən 'ɔr, ben ăn ór
Beinn Eighe *see* **Ben Eay**
Beinn Laoigh *S'clyde–Central border,* ben 'lɜɪ, ben lŏ́-i
Beinn Siantaidh *S'clyde,* ben 'ʃɪəntɪ, ben sheé-ănti
Beint, *f.n.,* baɪnt, bīnt
Beit, *f.n.,* baɪt, bīt. *Appropriate for Alfred and Sir Otto* ~, *the financiers and philanthropists associated with the Rhodes foundation.*
Beith, *f.n.,* biθ, beeth
Beith *S'clyde,* bið, beeth
Bejda, *f.n.,* 'beɪdə, báydă
Bekesbourne *Kent,* 'biksbɔrn, beéksborn
Bekonscot *model village in Beaconsfield,* 'bekənzkɒt, béckŏnzkot
Belah, River, *Cumbria,* 'bilə, beélă
Belaugh *Norfolk,* 'bilɑ, beélaa; 'bilɔ, beélaw; 'biloʊ, beélō; 'bilu, beéloo
Belbroughton *H. & W.,* bel'brɔtən, belbráwtŏn
Belchamp Otten *Essex,* 'belʃəm 'ɒtən, bél-shăm óttĕn. *Appropriate also for Belchamp St. Paul, and Belchamp Walter.*
Belchem, *f.n.,* 'beltʃəm, béltchĕm
Belcher, *f.n.,* 'beltʃər, béltchĕr
Belchier, *f.n.,* 'belʃɪeɪ, bélshi-ay
Belcoo *Co. Fermanagh,* bel'ku, belkoó

Belfast Co. Antrim–Co. Down, bel'fɑst, belfaʹast; 'belfɑst, belʹfaast

Belhaven and Stenton, Baron, bel'heɪvən, bel-háyvĕn

Belhelvie Grampian, bel'helvɪ, bel-hélvi

Belhus Essex, 'beləs, béllŭss

Belim, f.n., 'belɪm, béllim

Belisha, f.n., bə'liʃə, bĕléeshă

Bellaghy Co. Derry, be'læxɪ, belláchi

Bellairs, f.n., be'lɛərz, belláirz

Bellak, f.n., 'belæk, béllack

Bellamy, f.n., 'beləmɪ, béllămi

Bellars, f.n., 'belɑrz, béllaarz

Bellasis, f.n., 'beləsɪs, béllăssiss; be'leɪsɪs, belláyssiss

Bellasis Cleveland, 'beləsɪs, béllăssiss

Bellasis Northd., bɪ'læsɪs, belássiss

Bell-Burnell, f.n., ,bel bər'nel, bell burnéll

Bellchambers, f.n., 'beltʃeɪmbərz, béllchaymbĕrz

Belleau Lincs., 'belou, béllō; 'belu, bélloo

Belleek Co. Fermanagh, bɪ'lik, bĕléek

Bellenger, f.n., 'belɪndʒər, béllĕnjĕr

Belle Tout site of old Beachy Head lighthouse, 'bel 'tut, béll toʹot

Bellew, f.n., 'belju, béllew. Appropriate also for Baron ~.

Bellinger, f.n., 'belɪndʒər, béllinjĕr

Bellingham, f.n., 'belɪŋhəm, bélling-hăm; 'belɪŋəm, bélling-ăm; 'belɪndʒəm, béllinjăm

Bellingham London, 'belɪŋəm, bélling-ăm

Bellingham Northd., 'belɪndʒəm, béllinjăm

Belliver Devon, 'belɪvər, béllivĕr

Bellm, f.n., 'beləm, béllĕm

Belloc, Hilaire, author and poet, 'hɪlɛər 'belɒk, híllair béllock

Bellshill Lothian, S'clyde, 'belz-'hɪl, béllz-híll

Bellue, f.n., 'belju, béllew

Bellyse, f.n., 'belɪs, bélliss

Belmore, Earl, 'belmɔr, bélmor

Belmore, f.n., 'belmɔr, bélmor

Beloe, f.n., 'belou, béelō

Beloff, f.n., 'belɒf, bélloff

Belsay Northd., 'belsɪ, bélssi

Belthorn Lancs., 'belθɔrn, bél-thorn

Beltinge Kent, 'beltɪndʒ, béltinj

Beltingham Northd., 'beltɪndʒəm, béltinjăm

Belvedere Kent, ,belvɪ'dɪər, belvĕdéer

Belvoir, f.n., 'bivər, béevĕr

Belvoir Leics., 'bivər, béevĕr

Belvoir Park, Belfast, 'bivər, béevĕr

Bembaron, f.n., bem'bærən, bembárrŏn

Bemersyde Borders, 'bimərsaɪd, béemĕrssīd

Benacre Suffolk, 'beneɪkər, bénaykĕr

Benad, f.n., bɪ'næd, bĕnádd

Ben Alder Inverness, ben 'ældər, ben áldĕr

Ben Attow H'land, ben 'ætou, ben áttō

Benbecula W. Isles, ben'bekjʊlə, benbéck-yōōlă

Ben Cruachan S'clyde, ben 'kruəxən, ben kroo-áchăn

Bendelow, f.n., 'bendɪlou, bén-dĕlō

Benderloch S'clyde, 'bendərlɒx, béndĕrloch

Ben Eay H'land, ben 'eɪ, ben áy

Benefield, Upper and Lower, Northants., 'benɪfɪld, bénnifeeld

Benenden Kent, 'benəndən, bénnĕndĕn; ,benən'den, bennĕn-dén. The latter is rarely heard now.

Benenson, f.n., 'benənsən, bén-nĕnssŏn

Benest, f.n., 'benest, bénnest; bɪ'nest, bĕnést

Benet, f.n., 'benɪt, bénnĕt. From the history of the name it seems probable that this was the pronunciation of the 16th-c. madrigal composer, J. Benet.

Beneveian, Loch, also spelt **Benevean,** H'land, ,benɪ'viən, bennĕvée-ăn

Beney, f.n., 'binɪ, béeni

Benfleet Essex, 'benflɪt, bénfleet

Bengeo Herts., 'bendʒou, bénjō

Bengeyfield, f.n., 'bendʒɪfɪld, bénjifeeld

Bengough, f.n., 'bengɒf, bén-goff

Benhall Suffolk, 'benl, bénnl

Benhar S'clyde, ben'hɑr, ben-haʹar

Benholm Grampian, 'benhoum, bén-hōm

Benians, f.n., 'benɪənz, bénni-ănz

Ben Ime S'clyde, ben 'imə, ben éemĕ

Beningfield, f.n., 'benɪŋfɪld, bénningfeeld

Benke, f.n., 'beŋkɪ, bénki

Ben Ledi Central, ben 'ledɪ, ben léddi

Ben Macdhui Grampian, ,ben mək'duɪ, ben măkdoʹo-i

Bennachie Grampian, ,benə'xi, bennăchée

Bennane Head *S'clyde*, 'benən
'hed, bénnăn héd
Bennell,*f.n.*, 'benl, bénnl
Bennellick,*f.n.*, bɪ'nelɪk, běnéllick
Bennett,*f.n.*, 'benɪt, běnnět
Ben Nevis *H'land*, ben 'nevɪs,
ben névviss
Benoliel,*f.n.*, ˌbenoʊ'liəl,
bennōleé-ël
Ben Rhydding *W. Yorks.*, ben
'rɪdɪŋ, ben rídding
Ben Rinnes *Grampian*, ben 'rɪnɪs,
ben rínnèss
Bensham *Tyne & Wear*, 'benʃəm,
bén-shăm
Benson,*f.n.*, 'bensən, bénssŏn
Benson *Oxon.*, 'bensən, bénssŏn
Benstead,*f.n.*, 'bensted, bénsted
Bentall,*f.n.*, 'bentɔl, béntawl
Benthall,*f.n.*, 'bentɔl, béntawl;
'benθɔl, bén-thawl
Bentham,*f.n.*, 'benθəm, bén-
-thăm; 'bentəm, béntăm. *The
first is appropriate for Jeremy
~, 18–19th-c. author and
founder of University College
London.*
Bentham *Glos.*, 'benθəm, bén-
-thăm
Bentham, High *and* Lower, *N.
Yorks.*, 'benθəm, bén-thăm
Bentilee *Staffs.*, ˌbentɪ'li, bentileé
Bentinck,*f.n.*, 'bentɪŋk, béntink.
*A member of the family asserts
that* 'bentɪk, béntick *is simply a
popular misconception.*
Bentine,*f.n.*, ben'tin, bentéen
Bentwich,*f.n.*, 'bentwɪtʃ, bént-
witch
Ben Venue *Central*, ˌben və'nju,
ben věnéw
Benwick *Cambs.*, 'benɪk, bénnick
Benyon,*f.n.*, 'benjən, bén-yŏn
Benzie,*f.n.*, 'benzɪ, bénzi
Beoley *H. & W.*, 'bilɪ, beéli
Beowulf, *A.-S. epic hero*,
'beɪoʊwʊlf, báy-ō-wŏŏlf;
'beɪəwʊlf, báy-ŏ-wŏŏlf
Beragh *Co. Tyrone*, 'beərə, báiră
Berain *Clwyd*, 'beraɪn, bérrīn
Bere Alston *Devon*, 'bɪər 'ɔlstən,
beér áwlsstŏn
Beregi,*f.n.*, 'berəgɪ, bérrĕgi
Berenson,*f.n.*, 'berənsən, bérrĕns-
sŏn
Bere Regis *Dorset*, 'bɪər 'rɪdʒɪs,
beér reéjiss
Beresford,*f.n.*, 'berɪsfərd,
bérrĕsfŏrd
Berger,*f.n.*, 'bɜrdʒər, bérjěr
Bergh Apton *Norfolk*, 'bɜr 'æptən,
bér áptŏn
Bergmann,*f.n.*, 'bɜrgmən,
bérgmăn

Bergonzi,*f.n.*, bər'gɒnzɪ, běrgónzi
Beringer,*f.n.*, 'berɪndʒər, bérrin-
jěr
Beriosova, Svetlana, *ballerina*,
svet'lanə beər'jɒsəvə, svetlaánă
bair-yóssŏvă
Berkeley,*f.n.*, 'barklɪ, baárkli.
Appropriate also for Baroness ~.
Berkeley *Glos.*, 'barklɪ, baárkli
Berkhamsted *Herts.*, 'bɜrkəmsted,
bérkămsted
Berkley *Somerset*, 'barklɪ, baárkli
Berkoff,*f.n.*, 'bɜrkɒf, bérkoff
Berkshire *Co. name* 'barkʃər,
baárk-shĕr
Berkswell *W. Midlands*,
'barkswel, baárkswel; 'bɜrkswel,
bérkswel
Berkswich *Staffs.*, 'barkswɪtʃ,
baárkswitch
Berkyngechirche, *A.-S. name for
Barking-by-the-Tower, London*,
'barkɪŋtʃərtʃ, baárkingtchurtch
Bermange,*f.n.*, bər'mãʒ, běr-
maángzh
Bermel,*f.n.*, bər'mel, běrméll
Bernal,*f.n.*, bər'næl, běrnál;
'bɜrnəl, bérnăl
Bernard, *C.n.*, 'bɜrnərd, bérnărd
Bernard, Anthony, *composer and
conductor*, 'æntənɪ bər'nard,
ántŏni běrnaárd
Bernardin,*f.n.*, 'bɜrnərdɪn,
bérnărdin
Bernays,*f.n.*, bər'neɪz, běrnáyz
Bernelle,*f.n.*, bər'nel, běrnéll
Bernera *S'clyde*, 'bɜrnərə, bér-
něră. *Appropriate also for the
name of two islands, Great ~
and Little ~, in the W. Isles.*
Berners, Baroness, 'bɜrnərz,
bérněrz. *Appropriate also for
Lord ~, the composer.*
Bernhard, *C.n.*, 'bɜrnərd, bérnărd
Bernhard,*f.n.*, 'bɜrnhard, bérn-
-haard; bɜrn'hard, bern-haárd
Bernhardt,*f.n.*, 'bɜrnhart, bérn-
-haart
Bernice, *C.n.*, 'bɜrnɪs, bérniss;
bər'nis, běrneéss
Bernicia *part of anc. Northumbria*,
bər'nɪʃə, běrníshă
Bernstein,*f.n.*, 'bɜrnstaɪn, bérn-
stīn; 'bɜrnstin, bérnsteen. *The
first is appropriate for Baron ~.*
Berrick Salome *Oxon.*, 'berɪk
'sæləm, bérrick sállŏm
Berriew *Powys*, 'berɪu, bérri-oo
Berrynarbor *Devon*, ˌberɪ'narbər,
berrinaárbŏr
Bertalot,*f.n.*, 'bɜrtəloʊ, bértălō
Bertera,*f.n.*, beər'tɛərə, bairtáiră
Berthengam *Clwyd*, bər'θeŋgəm,
běrthéng-găm

Berthon, *f.n.,* 'bɜrθən, bérthŏn
Berthoud, *f.n.,* 'bɜrtu, bértoo; beər'tu, bairtóo
Bertie, *f.n.,* 'bɑrtɪ, baárti. *Family name of the Earl of Lindsey and Abingdon.*
Bertie of Thame, Viscountcy of, 'bɑrtɪ əv 'teɪm, baárti ŏv táym
Bertin, *f.n.,* 'bɜrtɪn, bértin
Berwick *E. Sussex,* 'berɪk, bérrick. *Appropriate also for the Barony of ~.*
Berwick St. John *Wilts.,* 'berɪk snt 'dʒɒn, bérrick sĭnt jón
Berwick-upon-Tweed *Northd.,* 'berɪk əpɒn 'twid, bérrick ŭpon tweéd
Berwyn Mountains *Clwyd* (*mainly*), 'beərwɪn, báirwin. *Although principally situated in Clwyd, the ~ Mountains are also partly in Powys and Gwynedd.*
Besant, *f.n.,* bɪ'zænt, bĕzánt; 'besənt, béssänt; 'bezənt, bézzänt. *The second was the pronunciation of Annie ~, social reformer.*
Bescoby, *f.n.,* 'beskoʊbɪ, béskōbi
Besier, *f.n.,* 'besjeɪ, béss-yay; 'bezjeɪ, béz-yay
Besley, *f.n.,* 'bezlɪ, bézli
Bessacarr, *S. Yorks.,* 'besəkər, béssäkär
Bessant, *f.n.,* 'besənt, béssänt
Bessborough, Earl of, 'bezbərə, bézbŭrä
Bessbrook *Co. Armagh,* 'besbrʊk, béssbrŏŏk
Bessell, *f.n.,* 'besl, béssl; bɪ'sel, bĕséll
Besselsleigh *Oxon.,* 'beslz'li, bésslz-leé
Bessone, *f.n.,* be'soʊn, bessón
Bestharris, *f.n.,* 'best'hærɪs, bést-hárriss
Besthorpe *Norfolk, Notts.,* 'besθɔrp, béss-thorp
Beswick, *f.n.,* 'bezɪk, bézzick. *Appropriate also for Baron ~.*
Beswick *Gtr. M'chester,* 'besɪk, béssick
Beswick *Humberside,* 'bezɪk, bézzick
Betham *Somerset,* 'betəm, béttäm
Bethell, *f.n.,* 'beθl, béthl. *Appropriate also for Baron ~.*
Bethersden *Kent,* 'beθərzdən, béthĕrzdĕn
Bethesda *Dyfed, Gwynedd,* be'θezdə, bethézdä
Bethune, *f.n.,* 'bitn, beétn; bɪ'θjun, bĕthéwn

Betjeman, Sir John, *Poet Laureate,* 'betʃɪmən, bétchĕmän
Betsham *Kent,* 'betsəm, bétsäm
Bettaney, *f.n.,* 'betənɪ, béttäni
Betteshanger *Kent* 'betshæŋər, béts-hang-ĕr
Bettice, *f.n.,* 'betɪs, béttiss
Bettws Bledrws *Dyfed,* 'betʊs 'bledrʊs, béttŏŏss blédrŏŏss
Bettws-y-Coed *Gwynedd,* 'betʊs ə 'kɔɪd, béttŏŏss ă kóyd
Bettws-yn-Rhos *Clwyd,* 'betʊs ən 'hroʊs, béttŏŏss ăn róss
Beuden, *f.n.,* 'bjudən, béwdĕn
Beult, River, *Kent,* belt, belt
Beuno, *Welsh saint,* 'baɪnɔ, bínaw
Beuttler, *f.n.,* 'bɔɪtlər, bóytlĕr
Bevan, Aneurin, *politician,* ə'naɪrɪn 'bevən, ănírin bévvän
Bevercotes *Notts.,* 'bevərkoʊts, bévvĕrkōts
Bevere *H. & W.,* 'bevərɪ, bévvĕri
Beveridge of Tuggal, Barony of, 'bevərɪdʒ əv 'tʌgl, bévvĕrij ŏv túggl
Beverley, Earl of, 'bevərlɪ, bévvĕrli
Beves, *f.n.,* 'bivɪs, beévĕss
Bevin, *f.n.,* 'bevɪn, bévvin
Bevins, *f.n.,* 'bevɪnz, bévvinz
Bevir, *f.n.,* 'bivər, beévĕr
Bevis, *f.n.,* 'bivɪs, beéviss; 'bevɪs, bévviss
Bevis Marks *St. in London,* 'bevɪs 'mɑrks, bévviss maárks
Bewaldeth *Cumbria,* bju'ældəθ, bew-áldĕth
Bewdley *H. & W.,* 'bjudlɪ, béwdli
Bewes, *f.n.,* bjuz, bewz
Bewhay, *f.n.,* 'bjuheɪ, béw-hay
Bewick, *f.n.,* 'bjuɪk, béw-ick. *Appropriate for Thomas ~, 18–19th-c. wood engraver, and therefore also for ~'s swan.*
Bews, *f.n.,* bjuz, bewz
Bewsher, *f.n.,* 'bjuʃər, béwshĕr
Beyer, *f.n.,* beər, bair; 'baɪər, bí-ĕr
Beyfus, *f.n.,* 'beɪfəs, báyfüss; 'baɪfəs, bífüss
Beynon, *f.n.,* 'baɪnən, bínŏn; 'beɪnən, báynŏn
Beyton *Suffolk,* 'beɪtən, báytŏn
Beyts, *f.n.,* beɪts, bayts
Bezant, *f.n.,* bɪ'zænt, bĕzánt; 'bezənt, bézzänt
Bezer, *f.n.,* 'bizər, beézĕr
Beznosiuk, *f.n.,* ˌbeznoʊ'sjʊk, bezznōssyŏŏk
Bezzant, *f.n.,* bɪ'zænt, bĕzánt
Bias, *f.n.,* 'baɪəs, bí-äss
Bibby, *f.n.,* 'bɪbɪ, bíbbi
Bibury *Glos.,* 'baɪbərɪ, bíbŭri
Bicât, *f.n.,* 'bikɑ, beékaa

Bicester *Oxon.*, 'bɪstər, bísstĕr. *Appropriate also for Baron* ~.
Bichard, *f.n.*, 'biʃɑrd, beé-shaard
Bickerdike, *f.n.*, 'bɪkərdaɪk, bíckĕrdīk
Bickleigh *Devon*, 'bɪklɪ, bíck-lee
Bicort, *f.n.* 'baɪkɔrt, bí-kort
Biddell, *f.n.*, 'bɪdl, bíddl; bɪ'del, bidéll
Biddenden *Kent*, 'bɪdəndən, bíddĕndĕn
Biddestone *Wilts.*, 'bɪdɪstən, bíddĕstŏn
Biddie, *f.n.*, 'bɪdɪ, bíddi
Biddle, *f.n.*, 'bɪdl, bíddl
Biddlesden *Bucks.*, 'bɪlzdən, bílzdĕn
Biddulph, *f.n.*, 'bɪdʌlf, bíddulf. *Appropriate also for Baron* ~.
Biddulph *Staffs.*, 'bɪdʌlf, bíddulf
Bideford *Devon*, 'bɪdɪfərd, bíddĕfŏrd
Biden, *f.n.*, 'baɪdən, bídĕn
Bidwell, *f.n.*, 'bɪdwel, bídwel
Bieber, *f.n.*, 'bibər, beébĕr
Biek, *f.n.*, bik, beek
Bielby, *f.n.*, 'bɪlbɪ, beélbi
Bierer, *f.n.*, 'bɪərər, beérĕr
Bierley *W. Yorks.*, 'baɪərlɪ, bírli
Bierton *Bucks.*, 'bɪərtən, beértŏn
Biffen, *f.n.*, 'bɪfɪn, bíffĕn
Bigelow, *f.n.*, 'bɪgɪlou, bíggĕlō
Biggar *Cumbria, S'clyde*, 'bɪgər, bíggăr
Bigge, *f.n.*, bɪg, big
Bigham, *f.n.*, 'bɪgəm, bíggăm
Bignian *Co. Down*, 'bɪnjən, bín--yăn
Bilainkin, George, *author*, bɪ'leɪŋkɪn, biláynkin
Bilbster *H'land*, 'bɪlpstər, bílpstĕr
Bildeston *Suffolk*, 'bɪldɪstən, bíldĕstŏn
Bilgora, *f.n.*, bɪl'gɒrə, bilgórră
Billenness, *f.n.*, 'bɪlɪnɪs, bíllĕnĕss
Billericay *Essex*, ˌbɪlə'rɪkɪ, billĕrícki
Billesdon *Leics.*, 'bɪlzdən, bílzdŏn
Billett, *f.n.*, 'bɪlɪt, bíllĕt
Billinge *Merseyside*, 'bɪlɪndʒ, bíllinj
Billingham *Cleveland*, 'bɪlɪŋhəm, bílling-hăm
Billmeir, *f.n.*, 'bɪlmaɪər, bílmīr
Bilsington *Kent*, 'bɪlzɪŋtən, bílzingtŏn
Bilyard, *f.n.*, 'bɪljɑrd, bíl-yaard
Binder, *f.n.*, 'baɪndər, bíndĕr. *Appropriate for Pearl* ~, *painter*.
Binderton *W. Sussex*, 'bɪndərtən, bíndĕrtŏn

Binge, Ronald, *composer*, bɪndʒ, binj
Bingham, *f.n.*, 'bɪŋəm, bíng-ăm. *Appropriate also for Baron* ~.
Bingley *W. Yorks.*, 'bɪŋlɪ, bíng-li
Binks, *f.n.*, bɪŋks, binks
Binsey *Cumbria*, 'bɪnzɪ, bínzi
Binski, *f.n.*, 'bɪnskɪ, bínski
Binyon, Laurence, *poet and art critic*, 'lɒrəns 'bɪnjən, lórrĕnss bín-yŏn
Bion, *f.n.*, 'bɪən, beé-ŏn
Birchall, *f.n.*, 'bɜrtʃl, bírtchl
Birchenough, *f.n.*, 'bɜrtʃɪnʌf, bírchĕnuff
Birches Head *Staffs.*, ˌbɜrtʃɪz 'hed, birtchĕz hédd
Birchington *Kent*, 'bɜrtʃɪŋtən, bírtchingtŏn
Birchmore, *f.n.*, 'bɜrtʃmɔr, bírtchmor
Birdsall, *f.n.*, 'bɜrdsɔl, bírdssawl; 'bɜrdsl, bírdssl
Birkbeck, *f.n.*, 'bɜrbek, bírbeck; 'bɜrkbek, bírkbeck
Birkbeck College, *Univ. of London*, 'bɜrkbek, bírkbeck
Birkenhead *Merseyside*, ˌbɜrkən-'hed, birkĕn-héd; 'bɜrkənhed, bírkĕn-hed. *The second is appropriate for the Earl of* ~.
Birkett, Baron, 'bɜrkɪt, bírkĕt
Birmingham *W. Midlands*, 'bɜrmɪŋəm, bírming-ăm
Birnam *Tayside*, 'bɜrnəm, bírnăm
Birnbryer, *f.n.*, 'bɜrnbraɪər, bírnbrī-ĕr
Birnie, *f.n.*, 'bɜrnɪ, bírni
Birnstingl, *f.n.*, 'bɜrnstɪŋgl, bírn-sting-gl
Birrane, *f.n.*, bɪ'reɪn, birráyn
Birrell, *f.n.*, 'bɪrəl, bírrĕl
Birsay *Orkney*, 'bɜrzeɪ, bírzay. *Appropriate also for Lord* ~.
Birss, *f.n.*, bɜrs, birss
Birstall *W. Yorks.*, 'bɜrstəl, bírstawl
Birtles, *f.n.*, 'bɜrtlz, bírtlz
Biscombe, *f.n.*, 'bɪskəm, bísskŏm
Biscovey *Cornwall*, 'bɪskəveɪ, bískŏvay
Bisham *Berks.*, 'bɪsəm, bíssăm
Bishop Auckland *Durham*, 'bɪʃəp 'ɔklənd, bíshŏp áwkländ
Bishop's Frome *H. & W.*, 'bɪʃəps 'frum, bíshŏps froóm
Bishop's Lydeard *Somerset*, 'bɪʃəps 'lɪdɪərd, bíshŏps líddi-ärd
Bishop's Nympton *Devon*, 'bɪʃəps 'nɪmptən, bíshŏps nímtŏn
Bishop's Stortford *Herts.*, 'bɪʃəps 'stɔrtfərd, bíshŏps stórtfŏrd;

'bıʃəps 'stɔrfərd, bíshŏps stór-
fŏrd
Bishop's Tachbrook *Warwicks.*,
'bıʃəps 'tætʃbrʊk, bíshŏps
tátchbröök
Bishopsteignton *Devon*,
'bıʃəps'teıntən, bíshŏpstáyntŏn
Bishopston *Avon, W. Glam.*,
'bıʃəpstən, bíshŏpstŏn
Bishop's Waltham *Hants*, 'bıʃəps
'wɔlθəm, bíshŏps wáwl-thăm;
'bıʃəps 'wɔltəm, bíshŏps
wáwltăm
Bishopwearmouth *Tyne & Wear*,
'bıʃəp'wıərmaʊθ, bíshŏp-
-weérmowth
Bispham, *f.n.*, 'bıspəm, bíspăm;
'bısfəm, bísfăm
Bispham *Lancs.*, 'bıspəm, bíspăm
Bissell, *f.n.*, 'bısl, bíssl
Bisset, *f.n.*, 'bızıt, bízzĕt; 'bısıt,
bíssĕt
Bissoe *Cornwall*, 'bısoʊ, bíssō
Bistre *Clwyd*, 'bıstər, bísstĕr
Bitham Hall *Warwicks.*, 'bıθəm,
bíthăm
Bithell, *f.n.*, 'bıθl, bíthl
Bitterley *Salop*, 'bıtərlı, bíttĕrli
Bittesby *Leics.*, 'bıtsbı, bítsbi
Bitteswell *Leics.*, 'bıtızwel,
bíttĕzwel
Bizeray, *f.n.*, 'bızəreı, bízzĕray
Bizony, *f.n.*, bı'zoʊnı, bizŏ́ni
Blabhein *see* **Blaven**
Blaby *Leics.*, 'bleıbı, bláybi
Blackadder, River, *Borders*,
'blækədər, bláckădĕr
Blackawton *Devon*, blæk'ɔtən,
blackáwtŏn
Blackbird Leys *Oxford*,
'blækbərd 'lız, bláckbird leéz
Black Bourton *Oxon.*, 'blæk
'bɔrtən, bláck bórtŏn
Blackfenn *London*, blæk'fen,
black-fénn
Blackley *Gtr. M'chester*, 'bleıklı,
bláykli
Blackness *Central*, blæk'nes,
black-néss
Blackwater *Cornwall, Dorset,
Hants, I. of Wight*, 'blækwɔtər,
bláckwawtĕr
Blackwatertown *Co. Armagh*,
blæk'wɔtərtaʊn, black-wáwtĕr-
-town
Blackwood *Gwent*, 'blæk'wʊd,
bláck-wŏ́od
Blackwood *S'clyde*, 'blækwʊd,
bláckwŏ́od
Blacon *Ches.*, 'bleıkən, bláykŏn
Blacow, *f.n.*, 'bleıkoʊ, bláykō
Bladon *Oxon.*, 'bleıdən, bláydŏn
Blaenannerch *Dyfed*, blaın'ænərx,
blīnánner<u>ch</u>

Blaenau Ffestiniog *Gwynedd*,
'blaınaı fes'tınjɒg, blīnī
festín-yog
Blaenavon *Gwent*, blaın'ævən,
blīnávvŏn
Blaenclydach *Mid Glam.*, blaın-
'klıdəx, blīn-klíddä<u>ch</u>
Blaen-Cwm *Mid Glam.*, blaın-
'kʊm, blīn-kŏ́om
Blaengarw *Mid Glam.*, blaın-
'gæru, blīn-gárroo
Blaengwawr *Mid Glam.*, blaın-
'gwaʊər, blīn-gwówr
Blaengwrach *W. Glam.*, blaın-
'gwrɑx, blīn-gwráa<u>ch</u>; blaın-
'grɑx, blīn-gráa<u>ch</u>. *Welsh
speakers pronounce 'gwrach' as
one syllable by treating the 'w'
as a rounding of the lips to
accompany the 'r'.*
Blaenhirwaun Colliery *Dyfed*,
blaın'hərwaın, blīn-hírwīn
Blaenhonddan *W. Glam.*, blaın-
'hɒnðən, blīn-hónthăn
Blaenllecha *Mid Glam.*, blaın-
'ɬexə, blīn-<u>h</u>léchă. *Another
form*, Blaenllechau, *may be
pronounced* blaın'ɬexaı, blīn-
<u>h</u>léchī.
Blaenllechau *Mid Glam.*, blaın-
'ɬexaı, blīn-<u>h</u>léchī. *Another form*,
Blaenllecha, *may be pronounced*
blaın'ɬexə, blīn-<u>h</u>léchă.
Blaen Llynfi *W. Glam.*, blaın
'ɬʌnvı, blīn <u>h</u>lúnvi; blaın 'ɬınvı,
blīn <u>h</u>línvi.
Blaenpenal *Dyfed*, blaın'penæl,
blīn-pénnal
Blaen-Plwyf *Dyfed*, 'blaın 'plʊıv,
blīn plóo-iv
Blaenporth *Dyfed*, blaın'pɔrθ,
blīn-pórth
Blaenserchan Colliery *Gwent*,
blaın'sɛərxən, blīn-sáirchăn
Blaen-y-Cwm *Gwent, Mid Glam.*,
ˌblaın ə 'kʊm, blīn ă kŏ́om.
*Appropriate for both places of
the name in Mid Glam.*
Blagden, *f.n.*, 'blægdən, blágdĕn
Blagg, *f.n.*, blæg, blagg
Blagrave, *f.n.*, 'blægreıv, blágrayv
Blagrove, *f.n.*, 'bleıgroʊv,
bláygrōv
Blaikie, *f.n.*, 'bleıkı, bláyki
Blaina *Gwent*, 'blaınə, blī́nă
Blair Atholl *Tayside*, blɛər 'æθl,
blair áthl
Blairgowrie *Tayside*, blɛər'gaʊrı,
blairgówri
Blairquhan Castle *S'clyde*,
blɛər'hwæn, blair-whán
Blaisdon *Glos.*, 'bleızdən, bláyzdŏn
Blakenall *Staffs.*, 'bleıknəl,
bláyknăl

Blakeney, *f.n.,* 'bleɪknɪ, bláykni
Blakeney *Glos.,* *Norfolk,* 'bleɪknɪ, bláykni
Blakenhall *Staffs.,* 'bleɪkənhɔl, bláykĕn-hawl
Blakenham, Great *and* Little, *Suffolk,* 'bleɪkənəm, bláykĕnăm. *Appropriate also for Viscount* ~.
Blaker, *f.n.,* 'bleɪkər, bláykĕr
Blakesley *Northants.,* 'bleɪkslɪ, bláykssli
Blakiston, *f.n.,* 'bleɪkɪstən, bláykistŏn; 'blækɪstən, bláckistŏn
Blakstad, *f.n.,* 'blækstæd, bláckstad
Blamey, *f.n.,* 'bleɪmɪ, bláymi
Blamire, *f.n.,* blə'maɪər, blămír
Blamires, *f.n.,* blə'maɪərz, blămírz
Blanch, *f.n.,* blɑnʃ, blaansh
Blanchard, *f.n.,* 'blæntʃɑrd, blántchaard; 'blæntʃərd, blántchărd
Blanchett, *f.n.,* 'blæntʃɪt, blántchĕt
Blanchland *Northd.,* 'blænʃlənd, blánshlănd
Blandford, Marquess of, 'blændfərd, blándfŏrd
Blans, *f.n.,* blænz, blannz
Blanshard, *f.n.,* 'blænʃɑrd, blán-shaard
Blantyre *S'clyde,* 'blæntaɪər, blántīr
Blarmacfoldach *H'land,* ˌblɑrmək-'fooltjəx, blaarmăk-fólt-yăch
Blaston *Leics.,* 'bleɪstən, bláystŏn
Blatherwycke *Northants.,* 'blæðərwɪk, bláthĕrwick
Blathwayt, *f.n.,* 'blæθweɪt, bláth-wayt
Blaven, *also spelt* **Blabhein,** *I. of Skye,* 'blɑvən, blaávĕn
Blawith *Cumbria,* blɑð, blaath. *Appropriate for both places of the name in Cumbria.*
Blaxhall *Suffolk,* 'blæksl, blácksl
Blaydon Haughs *Tyne & Wear,* 'bleɪdən 'hɒfs, bláydŏn hóffs
Bleach, *f.n.,* blitʃ, bleetch
Bleackley, *f.n.,* 'blɪklɪ, bleékli
Bleacrag Hill, *Cumbria,* 'bleɪ-'kræg, bláykrágg
Bleadon *Avon,* 'blidən, bleédŏn
Bleakley, *f.n.,* 'bleɪklɪ, bláykli
Bleaklow *Derby.,* 'blɪkloʊ, bleéklō
Blea Moor *N. Yorks.,* 'bli 'moər, bleé moŏr
Blean *Kent,* blin, bleen
Blean *N. Yorks.,* bleɪn, blayn
Bleaney, *f.n.,* 'blinɪ, bleéni

Bleary *Co. Armagh,* 'blɪərɪ, bleéri
Bleasby *Lincs.,* *Notts.,* 'blizbɪ, bleézbi
Bleasdale, *f.n.,* 'blizdeɪl, bleézdayl
Blease, *f.n.,* bliz, bleez; blis, bleess
Bleazard, *f.n.,* 'blizɑrd, bleézaard; 'blezɑrd, blézzaard
Blech, *f.n.,* blek, bleck. *Appropriate also for the* ~ *String Quartet.*
Bleddfa *Powys,* 'bleðvə, bléthvă
Bledisloe, Viscount, 'bledɪsloʊ, bléddisslō
Blemundsbury House *Holborn* (*London*), 'blemzbərɪ, blémzbŭri
Blencathra *Cumbria,* blen'kæθrə, blen-káthră
Blencowe, *f.n.,* 'bleŋkoʊ, blénkō
Blenheim Palace *Oxon.,* 'blenɪm, blénnĕm
Blenkiron, *f.n.,* bleŋk'aɪərn, blenkírn
Blennerhassett, *f.n.,* 'blenər-hæsɪt, blénnĕr-hassĕt; ˌblenər-'hæsɪt, blennĕr-hássĕt
Bles, *f.n.,* bles, bless. *Appropriate also for Geoffrey* ~, *publishers.*
Blessed, *f.n.,* 'blesɪd, bléssĕd
Bletchingley *Surrey,* 'bletʃɪŋlɪ, blétching-li
Bletsoe *Beds.,* 'bletsoʊ, blétsō
Blewbury *Oxon.,* 'blubərɪ, bloóobŭri
Blezard, *f.n.,* 'blezɑrd, blézzaard
Blidworth *Notts.,* 'blɪdwɜrθ, blídwurth
Bligh, *f.n.,* blaɪ, blī
Blindell, *f.n.,* 'blɪndl, blíndl
Blindley Heath *Surrey,* 'blaɪndlɪ 'hiθ, blíndli heéth
Blin-Stoyle, *f.n.,* 'blɪn 'stɔɪl, blín stóyl
Blishen, *f.n.,* 'blɪʃən, blíshĕn
Blisland *Cornwall,* 'blɪzlənd, blízländ
Blisworth *Northants.,* 'blɪzwɜrθ, blízwurth
Blithfield *Staffs.,* 'blɪfild, bliffeeld
Blizard, *f.n.,* 'blɪzɑrd, blízzaard
Blofield *Norfolk,* 'bloʊfild, blŏfeeld
Blogue, *f.n.,* bloʊg, blōg
Blohm, *f.n.,* bloʊm, blōm
Blois, *f.n.,* blɔɪs, bloyss
Blom, *f.n.,* blɒm, blom
Blomefield, *f.n.,* 'blumfild, bloómfeeld
Blomfield, *f.n.,* 'blɒmfild, blómfeeld; 'blʌmfild, blúmfeeld; 'blumfild, bloómfeeld; 'blumfild, bloómfeeld

Blomiley, *f.n.,* 'blɒmɪlɪ, blómmili
Blo' Norton *Norfolk,* 'bloʊ
  'nɔrtən, blŏ nórtŏn
Blonstein, *f.n.,* 'blɒnstɪn, blón-
  steen
Bloomstein, *f.n.,* 'blumstaɪn,
  bloóm-stīn
Blorenge, Mt., *Gwent,* 'blɒrendʒ,
  blórrenj
Bloundelle, *f.n.,* 'blʌndl, blúndl
Blount, *f.n.,* blʌnt, blunt
Blower, *f.n.,* 'bloʊər, blŏ-ĕr;
  'blaʊər, blówĕr
Bloxham, *f.n.,* 'blɒksəm, blócksăm
Bloxwich *W. Midlands,* 'blɒks-
  wɪtʃ, blóckswitch
Blubberhouses *N. Yorks.,*
  'blʌbərhaʊzɪz, blúbbĕr-howzĕz
Blumer, *f.n.,* 'blumər, bloómĕr
Blundell, *f.n.,* 'blʌndl, blúndl
Blundellian, *one educated at
  Blundell's School,* blʌn'delɪən,
  blundélliăn
Blundeston *Suffolk,* 'blʌndɪstən,
  blúndĕstŏn
Blunsom, *f.n.,* 'blʌnsəm, blúnssŏm
Bluntisham *Cambs.,* 'blʌntɪʃəm,
  blúnti-shăm; 'blʌntɪsəm,
  blúntissăm
Blyth, *f.n.,* blaɪ, blī; blaɪð, blīth;
  blaɪθ, blīth. *The first is appro-
  priate for Baron* ~.
Blythborough, *f.n.,* 'blaɪbərə,
  blíbŭră
Blythburgh *Suffolk,* 'blaɪbrə,
  blíbră
Blytheman, William, *Tudor
  composer,* 'blaɪθmən, blíthmăn
Blythswood *S'clyde,* 'blaɪðzwʊd,
  blíthz-wŏŏd
Blyton, *f.n.,* 'blaɪtən, blítŏn
Boadicea, queen of the **Iceni**
  (*q.v.*), boʊədɪ'sɪə, bŏădissee-ă.
  Another form is **Boudicca,** *q.v.*
Boady, *f.n.,* 'boʊdɪ, bŏdi
Boaks, *f.n.,* boʊks, bŏks
Boal, *f.n.,* boʊl, bŏl
Boarhunt *Hants,* 'bɔrhʌnt, bór-
  -hunt; 'bɒrənt, bórrŭnt
Boase, *f.n.,* boʊz, bŏz
Boateng, *f.n.,* 'bwateŋ, bwaáteng
Boath, *f.n.,* boʊθ, bŏth
Boat of Garten *H'land,* 'boʊt əv
  'gartən, bŏt ŏv gaártĕn
Boatte, *f.n.,* boʊt, bŏt
Bobbingworth *Essex,* 'bɒbɪŋwərθ,
  bóbbing-wurth. *The post office
  is* **Bovinger,** *q.v.*
Bochaton, *f.n.,* 'bɒkətən, bóckătŏn
Bochmann, *f.n.,* 'bɒxmæn,
  bóchman
Boconnoc *Cornwall,* bə'kɒnək,
  bŏkónnŏk
Bocquet, *f.n.,* 'boʊkeɪ, bŏkay

Boddam-Whetham, *f.n.,* 'bɒdəm
  'wetəm, bóddăm wéttăm
Boddey, *f.n.,* 'bɒdɪ, bóddi
Boddice, *f.n.,* 'bɒdɪs, bóddiss
Boddis, *f.n.,* 'bɒdɪs, bóddiss
Bodedern *Gwynedd,* bɒd'edɛərn,
  boddéddairn
Bodelwyddan *Clwyd,* ˌbɒdl'wɪðən,
  boddl-weéthăn
Bodenham *H. & W.,* 'bɒdənəm,
  bóddĕnăm
Bodfari *Clwyd,* bɒd'færɪ, bod-
  fárri
Bodfean *Gwynedd,* bɒd'veɪən,
  bodváy-ăn. *Also spelt* **Boduan,**
  q.v.
Bodffordd *Gwynedd,* 'bɒtfɔrð,
  bótforth
Bodiam *E. Sussex,* 'boʊdɪəm,
  bŏdiăm; 'bɒdɪəm, bóddiăm
Bodinnar, *f.n.,* 'bɒdɪnar, bóddi-
  naar
Bodist Colliery *Dyfed,* 'bɒdɪst,
  bóddist
Bodleian Library, *Oxford,*
  bɒd'liən, bodlee-ăn; 'bɒdlɪən,
  bódliăn
Bodley Head, *publishing house,*
  'bɒdlɪ 'hed, bóddli héd
Bodmer, *f.n.,* 'bɒdmər, bódmĕr
Bodnant *Gwynedd,* 'bɒdnænt,
  bód-nant
Bodorgan *Anglesey,* bɒ'dɔrgən,
  boddórgăn. *Appropriate for both
  places of the name on Anglesey.*
Bodriggy *Cornwall,* bə'drɪgɪ,
  bŏdreégi
Bodrugan's Leap, *Cornwall,*
  bə'drʌgən, bŏdrúggăn
Boduan *Gwynedd,* bə'dɪən,
  bŏdee-ăn. *Also spelt* **Bodfean,**
  q.v.
Body, *f.n.,* 'bɒdɪ, bóddi
Boe, *f.n.,* boʊ, bŏ
Boehm, *f.n.,* boʊm, bŏm;
  'boʊəm, bŏ-ĕm
Boersma, *f.n.,* 'bʊərzmə,
  bŏŏrzmă
Boevey, *f.n.,* 'bʊvɪ, boóvi
Boex, *f.n.,* 'boʊeks, bŏ-ecks
Boffey, *f.n.,* 'bɒfɪ, bóffi
Bogany Point *I. of Bute,* 'bɒgənɪ,
  bóggăni
Bogdanov, *f.n.,* bɒg'danəv,
  boggdaánŏv
Boger, *f.n.,* 'boʊdʒər, bŏjĕr
Boggart Hole Clough *Gtr.
  M'chester,* 'bɒgərt 'hoʊl 'klʌf,
  bóggărt hŏl klúff
Boggis, *f.n.,* 'bɒgɪs, bóggiss
Boghall Bridge *Lothian,* 'bɒghɒl,
  bóg-hawl
Bogue, *f.n.,* boʊg, bŏg
Bohana, *f.n.,* boʊ'hanə, bŏ-haánă

Bohanna, *f.n.*, boʊ'hænə, bō-hánnă

Boharm *Grampian*, boʊ'hɑrm, bō-haárm

Bohn, *f.n.*, boʊn, bōn

Bohun, *f.n.*, bun, boon. *Appropriate for the historical family name of the Earls of Hereford, Essex and Northampton.*

Bohunt Manor *Liphook* (*Hants*), 'boʊhʌnt, bŏ-hunt

Boileau, *f.n.*, 'bɔɪloʊ, bóylō

Bois, *f.n.*, bɔɪz, boyz

Boisdale *S. Uist* (*W. Isles*), 'bɔɪzdeɪl, bóyzdayl

Boisragon, *f.n.*, 'bɒrəgən, bórrăgŏn

Boissevain, *f.n.*, 'bwɑzɪveɪn, bwaázĕvayn

Boissier, *f.n.*, 'bɔɪsjər, bóyss-yĕr

Boivie, *f.n.*, 'beɪvɪ, báyvi

Bojen, *f.n.*, 'bɔɪən, bóy-ĕn

Bolam, *f.n.*, 'boʊləm, bŏlăm

Bolam *Northd.*, 'boʊləm, bŏlăm

Boland, *f.n.*, 'boʊlənd, bŏlănd

Bolas Magna, *also called* **Great Bolas,** *Salop*, 'boʊləs 'mægnə, bŏlăss mágnă

Boldon *Tyne & Wear*, 'boʊldən, bŏldŏn

Boldre, *f.n.*, 'boʊldər, bŏldĕr

Boldre *Hants*, 'boʊldər, bŏldĕr

Boleat, *f.n.*, 'boʊlɪət, bŏli-ăt

Bolenowe *Cornwall*, bə'lenoʊ, bŏlénnō

Boleskine *H'land*, bɒ'leskɪn, boléskin

Boleyn, *f.n.*, bə'lɪn, bŏlín; 'bʊlɪn, boŏlin; bʊ'lɪn, boōléen. *The first two are most popularly associated with Anne ~.*

Bolger, *f.n.*, 'bɒldʒər, bóljĕr

Bolingbroke and St. John, Viscount, 'bʊlɪŋbrʊk ənd 'sɪndʒən, boŏlingbroŏk ănd sínjŏn

Bolingey *Cornwall* bə'lɪndʒɪ, bŏlínji

Bolitho, *f.n.*, bə'laɪθoʊ, bŏlíthō

Bolitho *Cornwall*, bə'laɪθoʊ, bŏlíthō

Bollin, River, *Ches.*, 'bɒlɪn, bóllin

Bollinger, *f.n.*, 'bɒlɪndʒər, bóllinjĕr

Bollingham *H. & W.*, 'bɒlɪndʒəm, bóllinjăm; 'bɒlɪŋəm, bólling-ăm

Bolloten, *f.n.*, 'bɒlətən, bóllŏtĕn

Bolney *W. Sussex*, 'boʊlnɪ, bŏlni; 'boʊnɪ, bŏni

Bolnhurst *Beds.*, 'boʊnhərst, bŏn-hurst

Bols, *f.n.*, boʊlz, bōlz

Bolsover, *f.n.*, 'bɒlsoʊvər, bólssōvĕr

Bolsover *Derby.*, 'boʊlzoʊvər, bŏlzōvĕr

Bolster, *f.n.*, 'boʊlstər, bŏlsstĕr

Bolton by Bowland *Lancs.*, 'boʊltən baɪ 'bɒlənd, bŏltŏn bī bólländ; 'boʊltən baɪ 'boʊlənd, bŏltŏn bī bŏländ

Boltz, *f.n.*, boʊlts, bōlts

Bolventor *Cornwall*, bɒl'ventər, bolvéntŏr

Bomberg, *f.n.*, 'bɒmbərg, bómberg

Bomere Heath *Salop*, 'boʊmɪər 'hiθ, bŏmeer héeth

Bompas, *f.n.*, 'bʌmpəs, búmpăss

Bonallack, *f.n.*, bə'nælək, bŏnálăk

Bonaly *Lothian*, bə'nælɪ, bŏnáli

Bonar, *f.n.*, 'bɒnər, bónnăr; 'boʊnər, bŏnăr. *The second is appropriate for the ~ Professorship of International Economics in the University of Glasgow.*

Bonar Bridge *H'land*, 'boʊnər 'brɪdʒ, bŏnăr brij; 'bɒnər 'brɪdʒ, bónnăr brij

Bonarjee, *f.n.*, 'bɒnərdʒɪ, bónnărji

Bonavia, *f.n.*, ˌbɒnə'viə, bonnă-vée-ă

Bonawe *S'clyde*, bɒ'nɔ, bonnáw

Boncath *Dyfed*, 'bɒŋkæθ, bónkath

Bondi, *f.n.*, 'bɒndɪ, bóndi

Bonell, *f.n.*, bə'nel, bŏnéll

Bo'ness *Central*, boʊ'nes, bōnéss

Bonett, *f.n.*, 'bɒnɪt, bónnĕt

Boney, *f.n.*, 'bʌnɪ, búnni

Bonifazi, *f.n.*, ˌbɒnɪ'fætsɪ, bonni-fátsi

Boningale *Salop*, 'bɒnɪŋgeɪl, bónning-gayl

Bonkle *S'clyde*, 'bʌŋkl, búnkl

Bonkyl *Borders*, 'bɒŋkl, bónkl

Bonnamy, *f.n.*, 'bɒnəmɪ, bónnämi

Bonnetard, *f.n.*, 'bɒnɪtɑrd, bónnĕtaard

Bonnett, *f.n.*, 'bɒnɪt, bónnĕt

Bonney, *f.n.*, 'bɒnɪ, bónni

Bonome, *f.n.*, 'bɒnəm, bónnŏm

Bonong, *f.n.*, bə'nɒŋ, bŏnóng

Bonskeid *Tayside*, bɒn'skɪd, bonsskéed

Bonsor, *f.n.*, 'bɒnsər, bónssŏr

Bontddu *Gwynedd*, bɒnt'ðɪ, bont-thée

Bontine, *f.n.*, bɒn'tɪn, bontéen; 'bɒntɪn, bóntin

Bont-newydd *Clwyd*, bɒnt'newɪð, bont-né-with

Bontnewydd *Dyfed, Gwynedd*, bɒnt'newɪð, bontné-with

Bonvilston *S. Glam.*, 'bɒnvɪlstən, bónvilstŏn; 'boʊlstən, bŏlsstŏn

Bonwick, *f.n.,* 'bɒnwɪk, bónwick
Bonwit, *f.n.,* 'bɒnwɪt, bónwit
Bonymaen *W. Glam.,* ˌboʊnə-'maɪn, bōnămín
Bonynge, *f.n.,* 'bɒnɪŋ, bónning
Bonython, *f.n.,* bɒ'naɪðən, bonníthŏn
Boobbyer, *f.n.,* bu'baɪər, boobí-ĕr
Boobyer, *f.n.,* 'bubjər, boʹob-yĕr
Boodle, *f.n.,* 'budl, boʹodl
Boodle's Club *London,* 'budlz, boʹodlz
Bookham *Surrey,* 'bʊkəm, boʹokăm
Boord, *f.n.* bɔrd, bord
Boorde, *f.n.,* bʊərd, boʹord
Booroff, *f.n.,* 'bʊərɒf, boʹoroff
Boosbeck *Cleveland,* 'buzbek, boʹozbeck
Boosey, *f.n.,* 'buzɪ, boʹozi
Boost, *f.n.,* bust, boost
Booth, *f.n.,* buð, booth
Bootham *N. Yorks.,* 'buðəm, boʹothăm
Boothby, Baron, 'buðbɪ, boʹothbi
Boothman, *f.n.,* 'buðmən, boʹothmăn
Boothroyd, *f.n.,* 'buθrɔɪd, boʹothroyd; 'buðrɔɪd, boʹothroyd
Bootle *Cumbria, Merseyside,* 'butl, bootl
Bootle-Wilbraham, *f.n.,* 'butl 'wɪlbrəm, boʹotl wílbrăm. *Family name of Baron Skelmersdale.*
Booy, *f.n.,* bɔɪ, boy
Boquhanran *S'clyde,* bou-'hwænrən, bō-whánrăn; bou'hwɒnrən, bō-whónrăn; bou'hænrən, bō-hánrăn
Boreel, *f.n.,* bɒ'reɪl, borráyl
Boreham, *f.n.,* 'bɔrəm, báwrăm
Borenius, *f.n.,* bə'rɪnɪəs, bŏrée-niŭss
Boreray *Two islands in W. Isles,* 'bɒˑərə, bórrĕră
Borestone *Central,* 'bɔr'stoʊn, bór-stŏn
Borgue *D. & G., H'land,* bɔrg, borg
Borlase, *f.n.,* 'bɔrleɪs, bórlayss
Borocourt Hospital *Berks.,* 'bʌrəkɔrt, búrrŏkort
Borodale, Viscount, 'bɒrədeɪl, bórrŏdayl
Borrego, *f.n.,* bə'rigou, bŏréegō
Borrell, *f.n.,* bə'rel, bŏréll
Borreraig *I. of Skye,* 'bɒrəreɪg, bórrĕrayg
Borrett, *f.n.,* 'bɒrɪt, bórrĕt; bə'ret, bŏrétt
Borrowash *Derby.,* 'bɒroʊwɒʃ, bórrō-wosh

Borrowes, *f.n.,* 'bʌroʊz, búrrōz
Borrows, *f.n.,* 'bɒroʊz, bórrōz
Borth *Dyfed,* bɔrθ, borth
Borthwick, *f.n.,* 'bɔrθwɪk, bórthwick
Borth-y-gest *Gwynedd,* ˌbɔrθ ə 'gest, borth ă gést
Borve *W. Isles,* bɔrv, borv
Borwick, *f.n.,* 'bɒrɪk, bórrick. *Appropriate also for Baron ~.*
Borwick *Lancs.,* 'bɒrɪk, bórrick
Bosahan *Cornwall,* bə'seɪn, bŏssáyn
Bosanquet, *f.n.,* 'boʊzəŋket, bŏzänket
Boscastle *Cornwall,* 'bɒskɑsl, bósskaassl; 'bɒskæsl, bósskassl
Boscaswell, Higher *and* Lower, *Cornwall,* bɒs'kæzwəl, bŏss-kázwĕl
Boscawen, *f.n.,* bɒs'koʊən, bɒskŏ-ĕn; bɒs'kɔən, bŏskŏ-ĕn; bɒs'kɔən, boskáw-ĕn. *The first is the pronunciation of Viscount Falmouth's family name.*
Boscobel *Salop,* 'bɒskəbel, bóskŏbel. *Appropriate also for ~ House, where Charles II hid after the Battle of Worcester.*
Bose, *f.n.,* boʊz, bōz
Bosfranken *Cornwall,* bɒs'fræŋkən, bŏsfránkĕn
Bosham *W. Sussex,* 'bɒzəm, bózzăm
Boshell, *f.n.,* 'boʊʃl, bŏshl
Bosher, *f.n.,* 'boʊʃər, bŏshĕr
Boshier, *f.n.,* 'boʊʃər, bŏshĕr
Bosisto, *f.n.,* bə'sɪstoʊ, bŏssísstō
Bosistow *Cornwall,* bə'sɪstoʊ, bŏssísstō
Boskenwin *Cornwall,* bɒs'kenwɪn, bŏsskénwin
Bosleake *Cornwall,* bɒs'lik, bŏssléek
Bosley, *f.n.,* 'bɒzlɪ, bózli; 'bɒslɪ, bóssli
Bossiney *Cornwall,* bə'sɪnɪ, bŏssínni
Bossom, *f.n.,* 'bɒsəm, bóssŏm. *Appropriate also for the Barony of ~.*
Boston *Lincs.,* 'bɒstən, bósstŏn
Bosullow *Cornwall,* bə'sʌloʊ, bŏssúllō
Boswall, *f.n.,* 'bɒzwəl, bózwăl
Boswell of Auchinleck, 'bɒzwəl əv 'æflek, bózwĕl ŏv áffleck
Bosworth *Leics.,* 'bɒzwərθ, bózwŭrth
Boteler, *f.n.,* 'boʊtlər, bŏtlĕr
Botetourt, Baron, 'bɒtɪtɔrt, bóttĕtort
Botham, *f.n.,* 'bɒθəm, bóthăm; 'boʊθəm, bŏthăm

Bothamsall *Notts.*, ˌbɒðəmsɔl, bóthămssawl

Bothel and Threapland *Cumbria*, ˈbɒθl ənd ˈθriplənd, bóthl ănd threépland

Bothenhampton *Dorset*, ˌbɒθən-ˈhæmptən, bothĕn-hámptŏn

Bothnagowan *Grampian*, ˌbɒθnə-ˈgauən, bothnăgów-ăn. *Old name of* **Pitgaveny**, *q.v.*

Bothwell *S'clyde*, ˈbɒθwəl, bóthwĕl; ˈbɒðwəl, bóthwĕl. *Both are used for the Earl of ~, third husband of Mary, Queen of Scots.*

Bothwellhaugh *S'clyde*, ˈbɒðwəl-ˈhɒx, bóthwĕlhóch

Botley *Hants*, ˈbɒtlɪ, bóttli

Botolph, saint, ˈbɒtɒlf, bóttolf

Botreaux, Barony of, bəˈtrou, bŏtrṓ

Botriphnie *Grampian*, bouˈtrɪfnɪ, bōtrífni

Botterill, *f.n.*, ˈbɒtərɪl, bóttĕril

Bottesford *Humberside, Leics.*, ˈbɒtɪsfərd, bóttĕssfŏrd

Bottisham *Cambs.*, ˈbɒtɪʃəm, bótti-shăm

Bottome, Phyllis, *author*, bəˈtoum, bŏtṓm

Bottrall, *f.n.*, ˈbɒtrəl, bótrăl

Bottwnnog, *Gwynedd, see* **Bottwnog**

Bottwnog, *also spelt* **Bottwnnog**, **Botwnnog**, *Gwynedd*, bɒˈtʊnɒg, bottŏ́onog

Botwnnog, *Gwynedd, see* **Bottwnog**

Boty, *f.n.*, ˈboutɪ, bóti

Bouch, Sir Thomas, *19th-c. civil engineer*, bautʃ, bowtch

Boucher, *f.n.*, ˈbautʃər, bówtchĕr

Bouchier, *f.n.*, ˈbautʃər, bówtchĕr; ˈbuʃɪeɪ, boóshi-ay. *The second is appropriate for Chili ~, film actress.*

Boucicault, Dion, *actor-manager*, ˈdaɪən ˈbusɪkou, dí-ŏn boóssikō

Boucock, *f.n.*, ˈboukɒk, bókock

Boud, *f.n.*, baud, bowd

Boudicca, queen of the **Iceni** (*q.v.*), ˈbudɪkə, boódickă; bouˈdɪkə, bōdíckă. *Another form is* **Boadicea**, *q.v.*

Bough, *f.n.*, bɒf, boff

Boughey, *f.n.*, ˈbouɪ, bṓ-i

Boughrood *Powys*, ˈbɒxrud, bóchrood

Boughton, *f.n.*, ˈbautən, bówtŏn; ˈbɒtən, báwtŏn. *The first is appropriate for Rutland ~, the composer.*

Boughton *Cambs., Northants.*, ˈbautən, bówtŏn

Boughton *Ches., Kent*, ˈbɒtən, báwtŏn

Boughton *Notts.*, ˈbutən, boótŏn; ˈbautən, bówtŏn

Boughton Aluph *Kent*, ˈbɒtən ˈæləf, báwtŏn álŭf

Boughton Malherbe *Kent*, ˈbɒtən ˈmælərbɪ, báwtŏn málĕrbi

Boughton Monchelsea *Kent*, ˈbɒtən ˈmʌntʃlsɪ, báwtŏn múntchlssi

Bould, *f.n.*, bould, bōld

Boulge *Suffolk*, buldʒ, boolj; bouldʒ, bōlj

Boulmer *Northd.*, ˈbumər, boómĕr

Boult, *f.n.*, boult, bōlt. *Appropriate for Sir Adrian ~, conductor.*

Boulter, *f.n.*, ˈboultər, bṓltĕr

Boultham *Lincs.*, ˈbutəm, boótăm

Boulton, *f.n.*, ˈboultən, bṓltŏn

Boulton *Derby.*, ˈboultən, bṓltŏn

Boumphrey, *f.n.*, ˈbʌmfrɪ, búmfri

Boundstone *Surrey*, ˈbaundstoun, bówndstōn

Bouquet, *f.n.*, buˈkeɪ, boōkáy

Bourchier, *f.n.*, ˈbautʃər, bówtchĕr

Bourdeaux, *f.n.*, bɔrˈdou, bordṓ

Bourdillon, *f.n.*, bɔrˈdɪlən, bordíl-lŏn; bərˈdɪljən, bordíl-yŏn; bərˈdɪljən, bûrdíl-yŏn. *The first is appropriate for Tom ~, mountaineer.*

Bourgeois, *f.n.*, ˈbuərʒwɑ, boŏrzhwaa

Bourke, *f.n.*, bɜrk, burk. *Appropriate for the family name of the Earl of Mayo.*

Bourlet, *f.n.*, ˈbuərleɪ, boŏrlay; ˈbuərlet, boŏrlet

Bourn *Cambs.*, bɔrn, born

Bourne, *f.n.*, bɔrn, born; buərn, boŏrn; bɜrn, burn

Bournville *W. Midlands*, ˈbɔrnvɪl, bórnvil

Bourtie *Grampian*, ˈbuərtɪ, boŏrti

Bourton, *f.n.*, ˈbɔrtən, bórtŏn

Bourton, *Avon, Bucks., Dorset, Oxon.*, ˈbɔrtən, bórtŏn

Bourton, Great *and* Little, *Oxon.*, ˈbɔrtən, bórtŏn

Bourton-on-the-Water *Glos.*, ˈbɔrtən ɒn ðə ˈwɔtər, bórtŏn on thĕ wáwtĕr

Bourtree Bush *Grampian*, ˈbuərtrɪ ˈbuʃ, boŏrtri boósh

Bousfield, *f.n.*, ˈbausfild, bówssfeeld

Bouskell, *f.n.*, ˈbauskl, bówsskl

Boustead, *f.n.*, ˈbaustɪd, bówsstĕd

Boutal, *f.n.*, ˈbautl, bówtl

Boutall, *f.n.*, 'baʊtl, bówtl; bu'tæl, bootál
Boutell, *f.n.*, bʊ'tel, bōōtéll
Boutflower, *f.n.*, 'boʊflaʊər, bóflowĕr; 'buflaʊər, bóoflowĕr
Boutle, *f.n.*, 'butl, boótl
Bouton, *f.n.*, 'butən, boótŏn
Bouttell, *f.n.*, bʊ'tel, bōōtéll
Boutwood, *f.n.*, 'baʊtwʊd, bówt--wōōd
Bouverie, *f.n.*, 'buvərɪ, boóvĕri
Boveney *Bucks.*, 'bʌvnɪ, búvni; 'bɒvənɪ, bóvvĕni
Bovenschen, *f.n.*, 'boʊvənʃən, bóvĕn-shĕn; boʊ'vɒnʃən, bōvón-shĕn
Boverton *S. Glam.*, 'bɒvərtən, bóvvĕrtŏn
Bovey Tracey *Devon*, 'bʌvɪ 'treɪsɪ, búvvi tráyssi
Bovingdon *Herts.*, 'bɒvɪŋdən, bóvvingdŏn
Bovinger *Essex*, 'bɒvɪndʒər, bóvvinjĕr
Bovington *Dorset*, 'bɒvɪŋtən, bóvvingtŏn
Bovis, *f.n.*, 'boʊvɪs, bóviss
Bow *Cumbria, Devon, London*, boʊ, bō. *Appropriate for both places of the name in Devon.*
Bowater, *f.n.*, 'boʊwɔtər, bó-wawtĕr
Bowbeck *Suffolk*, 'boʊbek, bóbeck
Bowd *Devon*, baʊd, bowd
Bowden, *f.n.*, 'boʊdən, bódĕn; 'baʊdən, bówdĕn. *The first is appropriate for Baron ∼, the second for the family name of Baron Aylestone.*
Bowden *Borders, Devon*, 'baʊdən, bówdĕn
Bowden, Great *and* Little, *Leics.*, 'baʊdən, bówdĕn
Bowder Stone *Cumbria*, 'baʊdər stoʊn, bówdĕr stŏn
Bowditch, *f.n.*, 'baʊdɪtʃ, bów-ditch
Bowdon, *f.n.*, 'boʊdən, bódŏn
Bowdon *Gtr. M'chester*, 'boʊdən, bódŏn
Bowe, *f.n.*, boʊ, bō
Bowen, *f.n.*, 'boʊɪn, bó-ĕn
Bower, *f.n.*, 'baʊər, bówĕr
Bowerchalke *Wilts.*, 'baʊərtʃɒk, bówĕrtchawk
Bowerman, *f.n.*, 'baʊərmən, bówĕrmăn
Bowers, *f.n.*, 'baʊərz, bówĕrz
Bowers Gifford *Essex*, 'baʊərz 'gɪfərd, bówĕrz giffórd
Bowes, *f.n.*, boʊz, bōz
Bowes *Durham*, boʊz, bōz
Bowes-Lyon, *f.n.*, 'boʊz 'laɪən,

bōz lí-ŏn. *Family name of the Earl of Strathmore.*
Bowes Park *London*, 'boʊz 'pɑrk, bōz paárk
Bowett, *f.n.*, 'baʊɪt, bówĕt
Bow Fell *Cumbria*, 'boʊ 'fel, bō féll
Bowhill, *f.n.*, 'boʊhɪl, bó-hil
Bowie, *f.n.*, 'baʊɪ, bów-i; 'boʊɪ, bó-i. *The second is appropriate for David ∼, singer.*
Bowker, *f.n.*, 'baʊkər, bówkĕr
Bowlby, *f.n.*, 'boʊlbɪ, bólbi
Bowlee *Gtr. M'chester*, boʊ'li, bōleé
Bowles, *f.n.*, boʊlz, bōlz
Bowley, *f.n.*, 'boʊlɪ, bóli
Bowling *S'clyde, W. Yorks.*, 'boʊlɪŋ, bóling
Bowlly, *f.n.*, 'boʊlɪ, bóli
Bowman, *f.n.*, 'boʊmən, bómăn
Bowmore *S'clyde*, 'boʊ'mɔr, bó-mór
Bown, *f.n.*, baʊn, bown
Bownas, *f.n.*, 'boʊnəs, bónăss
Bowness, *f.n.*, boʊ'nes, bōnéss
Bowness *Cumbria*, boʊ'nes, bōnéss. *Appropriate for all localities of this name in Cumbria.*
Bow of Fife *Fife*, 'baʊ əv 'faɪf, bów ŏv fíf
Bowood *Wilts.*, 'boʊwʊd, bó--wōōd
Bowra, Sir Maurice, *scholar and author*, 'baʊrə, bówră
Bowring, *f.n.*, 'baʊərɪŋ, bówring. *Appropriate also for the ∼ Group of Companies, and hence for the ∼ Bowl, awarded to the winners of the 'Varsity Rugby match.*
Bowser, *f.n.*, 'baʊzər, bówzĕr
Bowsher, *f.n.*, 'baʊʃər, bówshĕr
Bowskill, *f.n.*, 'boʊskɪl, bó-skill
Bow Street *Dyfed*, 'boʊ strit, bó street
Bowtell, *f.n.*, boʊ'tel, bōtéll
Bowyer, *f.n.*, 'boʊjər, bó-yĕr
Bowyer Tower, *Tower of London*, 'boʊjər, bó-yĕr
Boyagis, *f.n.*, 'bɔɪədʒɪs, bóy-ăjiss
Boyars, *f.n.*, 'bɔɪərz, bóy-ărz
Boycott, *f.n.*, 'bɔɪkɒt, bóykott
Boydell, *f.n.*, bɔɪ'del, boydéll
Boyd-Orr, Barony of, 'bɔɪd 'ɔr, bóyd ór
Boyer, *f.n.*, 'bɔɪər, bóy-ĕr
Boyndlie *Grampian*, 'bɔɪndlɪ, bóyndli
Boys, *f.n.*, bɔɪz, boyz
Boyson, *f.n.*, 'bɔɪsən, bóyssŏn
Boz, *pen-name of Charles Dickens*, bɒz, bozz. *The English*

Pronouncing Dictionary *notes that* booz, bōz, *the original pronunciation, is not often heard now.*
Bozeat *Northants.*, 'booziæt, bōzi-at; 'booʒət, bōẕhät
Braaid *I. of Man*, breɪd, brayd
Braal *H'land*, brɔl, brawl
Brabant, *f.n.*, 'bræbənt, brábbănt; brə'bænt, brăbánt
Brabazon of Tara, Baron, 'bræbəzən əv 'tɑrə, brábbăzŏn ŏv taáră
Brabin, *f.n.*, 'breɪbɪn, bráybin
Brabourne *Kent*, 'breɪbərn, bráyborn; 'breɪbərn, bráybŭrn. *The second is appropriate for Baron ~.*
Brabrooke, *f.n.*, 'breɪbrʊk, bráybrŏŏk
Brabyn, *f.n.*, 'breɪbɪn, bráybin
Brabyn's Brow Canal, *Ches.*, 'bræbɪnz 'braʊ, brábbinz brów
Bracadale *I. of Skye*, 'brækədeɪl, bráckădayl
Bracher, *f.n.*, 'breɪtʃər, bráytchĕr
Braco *Tayside*, 'breɪkoʊ, bráykō
Bracon Ash *Norfolk*, 'brækən æʃ, bráckŏn ash
Bracondale *Norfolk*, 'brækəndeɪl, bráckŏndayl
Braddell, *f.n.*, 'brædl, bráddl
Braddock, *f.n.*, 'brædək, bráddŏk
Braddock *Cornwall*, 'brædək, bráddŏk
Bradenham *Bucks.*, *Norfolk*, 'brædənəm, bráddĕnăm
Bradford, *f.n.*, 'brædfərd, brádförd
Bradford *Cornwall*, *Derby.*, *Devon*, *Gtr. M'chester*, *W. Yorks.*, 'brædfərd, brádförd
Bradish, *f.n.*, 'breɪdɪʃ, bráydish
Bradlaugh, *f.n.*, 'brædlɔ, brádlaw
Bradley *Ches.*, *Clwyd*, *Cumbria*, *Derby.*, *Hants*, *Humberside*, *H. & W.*, *W. Yorks.*, 'brædlɪ, brádli. *Appropriate also for ~ Green* (*H. & W.*), ~ *Mills* (*W. Yorks.*), *and* ~ *Mount* (*Ches.*).
Bradley *N. Yorks.*, *Staffs.*, *W. Midlands*, 'breɪdlɪ, bráydli
Bradley, Great *and* Little, *Suffolk*, 'brædlɪ, brádli
Bradley, Great *and* West, *Somerset*, 'brædlɪ, brádli
Bradley, High *and* Low, *N. Yorks.*, 'brædlɪ, brádli
Bradley, North, *Wilts.*, 'brædlɪ, brádli
Bradley Common *Ches.*, 'breɪdlɪ 'kɒmən, bráydli kómmŏn
Bradley Fold *Gtr. M'chester*, 'brædlɪ 'foʊld, brádli fōld

Bradley Green *H. & W.*, *Warwicks.*, 'brædlɪ 'grin, brádli grèen
Bradley in the Moors *Staffs.*, 'brædlɪ ɪn ðə 'mʊərz, brádli in thē mŏŏrz
Bradmore *W. Midlands*, 'brædmɔr, brádmor
Bradninch *Devon*, 'brædnɪntʃ, brádnintch
Bradsell, *f.n.*, 'brædzl, brádzl
Brady, *f.n.*, 'breɪdɪ, bráydi
Braefoot Bay *Fife*, 'breɪfʊt, bráyfŏŏt
Braemar *Grampian*, breɪ'mɑr, braymaár
Braeriach *Grampian-Highland border*, breɪ'riəx, bray-rée-ăch
Brafield *Northants.*, 'breɪfɪld, bráyfeeld
Braham, *f.n.*, 'breɪəm, bráy-ăm
Brahams, *f.n.*, 'breɪəmz, bráy- -ămz
Brahan, *f.n.*, brɔn, brawn
Brahan Castle *H'land*, brɑn, braan. *Appropriate also for the ~ Seer, Scottish soothsayer: see* **Coinneach Odhar.**
Braich-y-Pwll *Gwynedd*, ˌbraɪx ə 'pʊɬ, brĭch ă poóhl
Braid, *f.n.*, breɪd, brayd
Brainin, **Norbert**, *violinist*, 'nɔrbərt 'braɪnɪn, nórbĕrt brínin
Brainshaugh *Northd.*, 'breɪnzhɑf, bráynz-haaf
Braishfield *Hants*, 'breɪʃfɪld, bráysh-feeld
Braithwaite, *f.n.*, 'breɪθweɪt, bráythwayt
Braithwell *S. Yorks.*, 'breɪθwel, bráythwel
Bramah, Ernest, *19th–20th-c. author*, 'brɑmə, braámă
Bramah, Joseph, *18th–19th-c. inventor*, 'bræmə, brámmă; 'brɑmə, braámă
Bramall, *f.n.*, 'bræmɔl, brámawl
Brambletye *E. Sussex*, 'bræmbltaɪ, brámbltī
Bramcote *Notts.*, *Warwicks.*, 'bræmkət, brámkŏt
Bramerton *Norfolk*, 'bræmərtən, brámmĕrtŏn
Bramford *Suffolk*, 'brɑmfərd, braámförd
Bramhall *Gtr. M'chester*, 'bræmhɔl, brám-hawl
Bramham *W. Yorks.*, 'bræməm, brám-măm
Bramhope *W. Yorks.*, 'bræm- -hoʊp, brám-hōp
Bramley *Derby.*, *S. Yorks.*, *W. Yorks.*, 'bræmlɪ, brámli
Brammall, *f.n.*, 'bræml, brámml

Brampton *Cambs.*, 'bræmptən, brámptŏn
Bramshill *Hants*, 'bræmzhɪl, brámz-hil
Brancaster Staithe *Norfolk*, 'bræŋkəstər 'steɪð, bránkăstĕr stáyth
Brancepeth *Durham*, 'brɑnspəθ, braánsspĕth. *Appropriate also for Baron* ∼.
Brancker, *f.n.*, 'bræŋkər, bránkĕr
Brandane, *f.n.*, bræn'deɪn, brandáyn
Brander, *f.n.*, 'brændər, brándĕr
Brander, Pass of, *S'clyde*, 'brændər, brándĕr
Brandeston *Suffolk*, 'brændɪstən, brándĕstŏn
Brandis Corner *Devon*, 'brændɪs 'kɔrnər, brándiss kórnĕr
Brandiston *Norfolk*, 'brændɪstən, brándistŏn
Brandlesholme *Gtr. M'chester*, 'brændlzhoʊm, brándlz-hōm
Branfil, *f.n.*, 'brænfɪl, bránn-fil
Branfill, *f.n.*, 'brænfɪl, bránn-fil
Brangwyn, *f.n.*, 'bræŋgwɪn, bráng-gwin
Brant-Broughton *Lincs.*, 'brænt 'brutən, bránt broótŏn
Brantham *Suffolk*, 'brænθəm, brán-thăm
Brashaw, *f.n.*, 'breɪʃɔ, bráy-shaw
Brasher, *f.n.*, 'breɪʃər, bráyshĕr
Brass, *f.n.*, brɑs, braass
Brassey, *f.n.*, 'bræsɪ, brássi. *Appropriate also for Baron* ∼ *of* **Apethorpe,** 'æpθərp, áp-thorp
Brassington, *f.n.*, 'bræsɪŋtən, brássingtŏn
Brasted *Kent*, 'breɪsted, bráyssted
Bratoft *Lincs.*, 'breɪtɒft, bráytoft
Brat Tor *Devon*, 'bræt 'tɔr, brát tór
Braughing *Herts.*, 'bræfɪŋ, bráffing
Braun, *f.n.*, braʊn, brown
Braund, *f.n.*, brɔnd, brawnd
Braunholtz, *f.n.*, 'braʊnhoʊlts, brówn-hōlts
Braunstone *Leics.*, 'brɔnstən, bráwnstŏn
Braunton *Devon*, 'brɔntən, bráwntŏn
Bravington, *f.n.*, 'brævɪŋtən, brávvingtŏn
Brawdy *Dyfed*, 'brɔdɪ, bráwdi
Brazell, *f.n.*, brə'zel, brăzéll
Brazier, *f.n.*, 'breɪzɪər, bráyziĕr
Brazil, *f.n.*, 'bræzl, brázzl; brə'zɪl, brăzíll; 'bræzɪl, brázzil. *The first is appropriate for Angela* ∼, *writer.*
Brea *Cornwall*, breɪ, bray

Breadalbane *Central–Tayside*, brɪ'dælbɪn, brĕdálbin; brɪ'dɒlbɪn, brĕdáwlbin. *The second is appropriate for the Earl of* ∼.
Breadsell, *f.n.*, bred'sel, bredsséll
Breage *Cornwall*, brig, breeg
Breakell, *f.n.*, 'breɪkl, bráykl
Breakey, *f.n.*, 'breɪkɪ, bráyki
Breaks, *f.n.*, breɪks, brayks
Brealey, *f.n.*, 'brɪəlɪ, brée-äli
Breamore *Hants*, 'bremər, brémmŏr
Brean *Somerset*, brin, breen
Brearley, *f.n.*, 'brɪərlɪ, bréerli
Breaston *Derby.*, 'brɪstən, brées-stŏn
Breay, *f.n.*, breɪ, bray
Brech, *f.n.*, brek, breck
Brechfa *Dyfed*, 'brexvə, bréchvă
Brechin, *f.n.*, 'brɪxɪn, breéchin
Brechin *Tayside*, 'brɪxɪn, breéchin
Brecknock, *f.n.*, 'breknɒk, brécknock
Brecknock, *former alternative name for* **Brecon,** *Powys*, 'breknɒk, brécknock; 'breknək, brécknŏk
Breckon, *f.n.*, 'brekən, bréckŏn
Brecon *Powys*, 'brekən, bréckŏn. *Appropriate also for Baron* ∼.
Bredenbury *H. & W.*, 'brɪdənbərɪ, breédĕnbŭri
Bredin, *f.n.*, 'brɪdɪn, breédin
Bredon *H. & W.*, 'bridən, breédŏn
Bredons Hardwick *H. & W.*, 'brɪdənz 'hɑrdwɪk, breédŏnz haárdwick
Bredwardine *H. & W.*, ˌbredwər'daɪn, bredwărdín
Breggin, *f.n.*, 'bregɪn, bréggin
Brehony, *f.n.*, brɪ'hoʊnɪ, brĕ-hóni
Breich *Lothian*, brix, breech
Breidden *Powys*, 'braɪðən, bríthĕn
Breightmet *Gtr. M'chester*, 'breɪtmɪt, bráytmĕt; 'braɪtmɪt, brítmĕt
Breighton *Humberside*, 'breɪtən, bráytŏn
Breinton *H. & W.*, 'breɪntən, bráyntŏn
Brenack, *f.n.*, 'brenək, brénnăk
Brenard, *f.n.*, 'brenɑrd, brénnaard
Brenchley *Kent*, 'brentʃlɪ, bréntchli
Brenel, *f.n.*, brɪ'nel, brĕnéll
Brent Eleigh *Suffolk*, 'brent 'ilɪ, brént éeli
Brenzett *Kent*, 'brenzɪt, brénzĕt
Brereton, *f.n.*, 'brɪərtən, bráirtŏn; 'brɪɑrtən, breértŏn
Brereton *Staffs.*, 'brɪɑrtən, breértŏn
Bresler, *f.n.*, 'brezlər, brézlĕr

Bressay *Shetland*, 'breseɪ,
bréssay
Bretforton *H. & W.*, 'brefərtən,
bréffôrtŏn; 'bretfərtən, brét-
fôrtŏn
Brettargh Holt *Cumbria*, 'bretər
'hoʊlt, bréttär hŏlt
Brettell, *f.n.*, brɪ'tel, brĕtéll
Brettingham-Smith, *f.n.*, 'bretɪŋ-
əm 'smɪθ, brétting-ăm smíth
Brewham, North *and* South,
Somerset, 'bruəm, bróo-ăm
Brewis, *f.n.*, 'bruɪs, bróo-iss
Brewood *Staffs.*, brud, brood
Breydon Water *Norfolk*, 'breɪdən
'wɔtər, bráydŏn wáwtĕr
Brian, Havergal, *composer*,
'hævərɡəl 'braɪən, hávvĕrgăl
brí-ăn
Briault, *f.n.*, 'brioʊ, breé-ō
Bricett, Great *and* Little, *Suffolk*,
'braɪsɪt, bríssĕt
Brickell, *f.n.*, brɪ'kel, brickéll
Bricusse, *f.n.*, 'brɪkəs, bríckŭss
Bridburg, *f.n.*, 'brɪdbərg, brídburg
Bridell *Dyfed*, 'brɪdeł, bríddehl
Bridestowe *Devon*, 'brɪdɪstoʊ,
bríddĕstō; 'brɪstoʊ, brístō
Bridgend *Cornwall*, *S'clyde*,
'brɪdʒend, bríjjend
Bridgend *Cumbria*, *Dyfed*, *Mid
Glam.*, brɪdʒ'end, brijjénd
Bridge of Earn *Tayside*, 'brɪdʒ əv
'ɜrn, bríj ŏv érn
Bridge of Feugh *Grampian*, 'brɪdʒ
əv 'fjux, bríj ŏv féwch
Bridge of Gaur *Tayside*, 'brɪdʒ əv
'ɡɔr, bríj ŏv gór
Bridge of Orchy *S'clyde*, 'brɪdʒ əv
'ɔrxɪ, bríj ŏv órchi
Bridge of Weir *S'clyde*, 'brɪdʒ əv
'wɪər, bríj ŏv weér
Bridger, *f.n.*, 'brɪdʒər, bríjjĕr
Bridgette, *f.n.*, brɪ'dʒet, brijét
Bridgnorth *Salop*, 'brɪdʒnɔrθ,
bríj-north
Bridgwater *Somerset*, 'brɪdʒ-
wɔtər, bríj-wawtĕr
Bridie, James, *author*, 'braɪdɪ,
brídi. *Pen name of Dr O. H.
Mavor.*
Bridlington *Humberside*, 'brɪd-
lɪŋtən, brídlingtŏn
Bridport *Dorset*, 'brɪdpɔrt,
bríd-port
Bridson, *f.n.*, 'braɪdsən, brídssŏn
Bridstow *H. & W.*, 'brɪdstoʊ,
brídstō
Briege, *Irish C.n.*, briʒ, breezh
Brien, *f.n.*, 'braɪən, brí-ĕn
Brierley, *f.n.*, 'braɪərlɪ, brí-ĕrli;
'brɪərlɪ, breérli
Brierley *S. Yorks.*, 'braɪərlɪ,
brí-ĕrli; 'brɪərlɪ, breérli

Brierley Hill *W. Midlands*,
'braɪərlɪ 'hɪl, brí-ĕrli híll
Brierly, *f.n.*, 'braɪərlɪ, brí-ĕrli
Briers, *f.n.*, 'braɪərz, brí-ĕrz
Brigginshaw, *f.n.*, 'brɪɡɪnʃɔ,
bríggin-shaw
Brighouse *W. Yorks.*, 'brɪghaʊs,
bríg-howss
Brighstone *I. of Wight*, 'braɪstən,
brísstŏn
Brightholmlee *S. Yorks.*, 'braɪ-
təmlɪ, brítŏmli
Brightling *E. Sussex*, 'braɪtlɪŋ,
brítling
Brightlingsea *Essex*, 'braɪtlɪŋsi,
brítlingssee
Brighton *Cornwall*, *E. Sussex*,
'braɪtən, brítŏn
Briginshaw, *f.n.*, 'brɪɡɪnʃɔ,
bríggin-shaw
Brigstock *Northants.*, 'brɪgstɒk,
bríg-stock
Briley, *f.n.*, 'braɪlɪ, bríli
Brilles, *f.n.*, 'brɪlɪs, bríllĕss
Brimacombe, *f.n.*, 'brɪməkum,
brímmăkoom
Brimblecombe, *f.n.*, 'brɪmbl-
koum, brímblkōm
Brimelow, *f.n.*, 'brɪmɪloʊ, brím-
mēlō. *Appropriate also for
Baron ~.*
Brimicombe, *f.n.*, 'brɪmɪkəm,
brímmikŏm
Brimilow, *f.n.*, 'brɪmɪloʊ,
brímmilō
Brind, *f.n.*, brɪnd, brind
Bringsty *H. & W.*, 'brɪŋstɪ,
bríngsti
Brinkheugh *Northd.*, 'brɪŋkhjuf,
brínk-hewf
Brinscall *Lancs.*, 'brɪnskl, bríns-
skl
Brinsea *Avon*, 'brɪnzɪ, brínzi
Brio, *f.n.*, 'brioʊ, breé-ō
Briody, *f.n.*, 'braɪədɪ, brí-ŏdi
Brisby, *f.n.*, 'brɪzbɪ, brízbi
Brisco, *f.n.*, 'brɪskoʊ, brískō
Briscoe, *f.n.*, 'brɪskoʊ, brískō
Bristol *Avon*, 'brɪstl, brísstl
Bristolian, *native of Bristol*, brɪs-
'toʊlɪən, bristóliăn
Brithdir *Gwynedd*, *Mid Glam.*,
'brɪθdɪər, bríthdeer
Briton Ferry *W. Glam.*, 'brɪtən
'ferɪ, bríttŏn férri
Britten, *f.n.*, 'brɪtən, bríttĕn
Britwell Salome *Oxon.* 'brɪtwəl
'sæləm, brítwĕl sálŏm
Brize Norton *Oxon.*, 'braɪz
'nɔrtən, bríz nórtŏn
Broadbridge, *f.n.*, 'brɔdbrɪdʒ,
bráwdbrij
Broad Chalke *Wilts.* 'brɔd tʃɔk,
bráwd chawk

Broadclyst *Devon* 'brɔdklɪst,
bráwdklist
Broad Halfpenny Down *Hamble-
don (Hants)*, 'brɔd 'hɑfpenɪ
'daʊn, bráwd haáfpenni dówn
Broadhembury *Devon*, brɔd-
'hembərɪ, brawdhémbŭri
Broadis, *f.n.*, 'brɔdɪs, bráwdiss
Broadmoor *Berks.*, 'brɔdmʊər,
bráwd-mōōr
Broadstairs *Kent*, 'brɔdstɛərz,
bráwd-stairz
Broadwas *H. & W.*, 'brɔdwəs,
bráwd-wăss
Broadwoodwidger *Devon*,
'brɔdwʊd'wɪdʒər, bráwdwōōd-
-wijjĕr
Broady, *f.n.*, 'brʊdɪ, brŏdi
Brocas, Viscount, 'brɒkəs,
bróckăss
Brocklebank-Fowler, *f.n.*,
'brɒklbæŋk 'faʊlər, brócklbank
fówlĕr
Broderick, *f.n.*, 'brɒdərɪk,
bróddĕrik
Broderip, *f.n.*, 'brɒdrɪp, bródrip
Brodgar, Ring of, *Orkney*,
'brɒdgər, bród-găr
Brodick *S'clyde*, 'brɒdɪk, bróddik
Brodie, *f.n.*, 'brʊdɪ, brŏdi
Brodrick, *f.n.*, 'brɒdrɪk, bródrik
Broe, *f.n.*, brʊ, brō
Brogan, *f.n.*, 'brʊgən, brŏgăn
Brogyntyn *Salop* brɒ'gʌntɪn,
broggúntin
Broke, *f.n.*, brʊk, brŏōk
Bromborough *Merseyside*,
'brɒmbərə, brómbŭră
Brome, *f.n.*, brʊm, brōm
Brome *Suffolk*, brum, broom
Bromet, *f.n.*, 'brɒmɪt, brómmĕt
Bromford *W. Midlands*, 'brɒm-
fərd, brómfŏrd
Bromham *Beds.*, 'brɒməm,
brómmăm
Bromham *Wilts.*, 'brʌməm,
brúmmăm
Bromhead, *f.n.*, 'brʌmhed,
brúm-hed
Bromholm *Norfolk*, 'brumhoʊm,
brōōm-hōm
Bromley, *f.n.*, 'brʌmlɪ, brúmli;
'brɒmlɪ, brómli
Bromley *London*, 'brɒmlɪ, brómli.
The old pronunciation, 'brʌmlɪ,
brúmli, *seems to have suc-
cumbed completely to the
spelling pronunciation.*
Bromley *S. Yorks.*, *W. Midlands*,
brɒmlɪ, brómli
Bromley, Great *and* Little, *Essex*,
'brɒmlɪ, brómli
Bromley Cross *Gtr. M'chester*,
'brɒmlɪ 'krɒs, brómli króss

Brompton *Kent*, 'brɒmptən,
brómptŏn
Brompton Ralph *Somerset*,
'brɒmptən 'rælf, brómptŏn
rálf
Bromsgrove *H. & W.*, 'brɒmz-
groʊv, brómzgrōv
Bromwich *see* **West Bromwich**
Bromyard *H. & W.*, 'brɒmjɑrd,
bróm-yaard; 'brɒmjərd, bróm-
-yărd
Bronach, saint, 'broʊnəx,
brŏnăch
Bronant *Dyfed*, 'brɒnənt, brón-
nănt
Brongwendraeth *Dyfed*, brɒn-
'gwendraɪθ, bron-gwéndrīth
Brongwyn *Dyfed*, 'brɒngwɪn,
brón-gwin
Bronllys *Powys*, 'brɒnɬɪs, brón-
-hleess
Brontë, *f.n.*, 'brɒntɪ, brónti.
*Appropriate for authors
Charlotte, Anne, and Emily ~,
and their brother Branwell ~.*
Bronwen, *Welsh C.n.*, 'brɒnwen,
brónwen
Bronydd *Powys*, 'brɒnɪð, brón-
niṯẖ
Bron-y-Foel *Gwynedd*, ˌbrɒnə'vɔɪl,
bronnăvóyl
Brooke of Ystradfellte, Baroness,
'brʊk əv ˌʌstrəd'veɫteɪ, brŏōk
ŏv usstrăd-véẖltay
Brookes, *f.n.*, brʊks, brŏōks
Brookholding, *f.n.*, 'brʊkhoʊldɪŋ,
brŏōkhōlding
Broom, Loch, *H'land*, 'brum,
brŏōm
Broome, *f.n.*, brum, broom
Broomhead, *f.n.*, 'brumhed,
brŏōm-hed
Broomieknowe *Lothian*, ˌbrumɪ-
'naʊ, broominów
Brophy, *f.n.*, 'broʊfɪ, brŏfi
Brora *H'land*, 'brɔrə, bráwră
Broseley *Salop*, 'brʊzlɪ, brŏzli
Brotchie, *f.n.*, 'brɒtʃɪ, brótchi
Brotherton, *f.n.*, 'brʌðərtən,
brúṯẖĕrtŏn
Brough, *f.n.*, brʌf, bruff
Brough *Cumbria, Humberside*,
brʌf, bruff
Brough *H'land*, brɒx, broc̱ẖ
Broughall, *f.n.*, 'braʊəl, brów-ăl
Broughall *Salop*, 'brɒfl, bróffl
Brougham, *f.n.*, brum, brŏōm;
'broʊəm, brŏ-ăm; 'bruəm,
broŏ-ăm; broʊm, brōm
Brougham *Cumbria*, brum,
broom; brɔm, brawm
Brougham and Vaux, Baron,
'brum ənd 'vɔks, brŏōm ănd
váwks

Brougher Mountain *Co. Fermanagh*, 'brɔχər, bráwchĕr

Broughshane *Co. Antrim*, brə'ʃeɪn, brŏ-sháyn. *Appropriate also for Baron* ~.

Broughton, *f.n.*, 'brɔtən, bráwtŏn; 'brautən, brówtŏn. *The first is appropriate for Baron Fairhaven's family name.*

Broughton *Borders, Clwyd, Cumbria, Hants, Humberside, Lancs., Lincs., Oxon., Salop, Staffs.*, 'brɔtən, bráwtŏn

Broughton *Northants.*, 'brautən, brówtŏn

Broughton *Mid Glam.*, 'brʌftən, brúfftŏn

Broughton Bay *W. Glam.*, 'brʌftən, brúfftŏn

Broughton Gifford *Wilts.*, 'brɔtən 'gɪfərd, bráwtŏn gíffŏrd; 'brɔtən 'dʒɪfərd, bráwtŏn jíffŏrd

Broughty Ferry *Tayside*, 'brɔtɪ 'ferɪ, bráwti férri

Brough-under-Stainmore *Cumbria*, 'brʌf ʌndər 'steɪnmɔr, brúff undĕr stáynmor. *More simply* **Brough**.

Browell, *f.n.*, 'brauəl, brówĕl

Browett, *f.n.*, 'brouɪt, brŏ-ĕt

Browitt, *f.n.*, 'brouɪt, brŏ-it

Browne, Hablot K. 'hæblou 'braun, háblŏ brówn. *Better known as 'Phiz'*, fɪz, fizz, *illustrator of* Pickwick Papers.

Brownjohn, *f.n.*, 'braundʒɒn, brównjon

Broxbourne *Herts.*, 'brɒksbɔrn, brócks-born

Broxis, *f.n.*, 'brɒksɪs, brócksiss

Bruan *H'land*, 'bruən, broó-ăn

Bruar *Tayside*, 'bruər, broó-ăr

Bruce-Chwatt, *f.n.*, 'brus 'kwɒt, broóss kwótt

Bruce-Gardyne, *f.n.*, 'brus gɑr'daɪn, broóss gaardín

Bruce Lockhart, *f.n.*, 'brus 'lɒkərt, broóss lóckărt

Bruce of Melbourne, Viscountcy of, 'brus əv 'melbərn, broóss ŏv mélbŭrn

Bruche *Ches.*, bruʃ, broosh

Bruck, *f.n.*, bruk, broŏk

Bruckheimer, *f.n.*, 'brukhaɪmər, broŏk-hímĕr

Brudenell, Baron, 'brudənəl, broódĕnĕl

Bruen, *f.n.*, 'bruən, broó-ĕn

Bruera *Ches.*, bru'ɛərə, broó--áiră

Bruford, *f.n.*, 'brufərd, broófŏrd

Bruisyard *Suffolk*, 'bruʒɑrd, broózhaard

Brummagem, *local form of* **Birmingham**, 'brʌmədʒəm, brúmmájĕm

Brundall *Norfolk*, 'brʌndl, brúndl

Brundrett, *f.n.*, 'brʌndrɪt, brúndrĕt

Brunel, *f.n.*, bru'nel, broŏnéll. *Appropriate for Sir Marc Isambard* ~, *and Isambard Kingdom* ~, *18th–19th-c. civil engineers. Isambard is pronounced* 'ɪzəmbɑrd, ízzămbaard.

Bruning, *f.n.*, 'brunɪŋ, broóning

Brunner, *f.n.*, 'brʌnər, brúnnĕr

Brunt, *f.n.*, brʌnt, brunt

Bruntisfield, Baron, 'brʌntsfɪld, brúntsfeeld

Bruxner, *f.n.*, 'bruksnər, broŏksnĕr

Bryce, *f.n.*, braɪs, bríss

Brychan, *Welsh C.n.*, 'brʌχən, brúchăn

Brydon, *f.n.*, 'braɪdən, brídŏn

Brydone, *f.n.*, 'braɪdən, brídŏn

Bryher *I. of Scilly*, 'braɪər, brí-ĕr

Brymbo *Clwyd*, 'brɪmbou, brímbō; 'brʌmbou, brúmbō

Brymer, *f.n.*, 'braɪmər, brímĕr

Brynamman *Dyfed*, brɪn'æmən, brinámmăn

Bryncethin *Mid Glam.*, brɪn'keθɪn, brin-kéthin

Bryncoch *Mid Glam., W. Glam.*, brɪn'koux, brin-kŏch

Bryncroes *Gwynedd*, brɪn'krɔɪs, brin-króyss

Bryneglwys *Clwyd*, brɪn'egluɪs, brinégloŏ-iss

Bryn Euryn *Clwyd*, brɪn 'aɪrɪn, brin írin

Brynffynon *Gwynedd*, brɪn'fʌnən, brin-fúnnŏn

Brynglas *Gwent*, brɪn'glɑs, brin--glaáss

Bryngwyn *Gwent*, 'brɪŋgwɪn, bríng-gwin

Brynhyfryd *W. Glam.*, brɪn'hʌvrɪd, brin-húvvrid

Bryniau *Clwyd*, 'brʌnjaɪ, brún-yī

Bryning, *f.n.*, 'braɪnɪŋ, bríning

Brynkir *Gwynedd*, 'brɪŋkɪər, brínkeer

Brynmawr *Gwent*, brɪn'mauər, brin-mówr

Brynmenyn *Mid Glam.*, brɪn-'menɪn, brin-ménnin

Bryn Pydew *Gwynedd*, 'brɪn 'pʌdju, brín púddew

Brynrefail *Gwynedd*, brɪn'revaɪl, brin-révvīl. *Appropriate for both places of the name in Gwynedd.*

Brynsiencyn *Gwynedd*, brɪn-'ʃeŋkɪn, brin-shénkin

Bryony, *C.n.*, 'braɪənɪ, brí-ŏni

Buachaille Etive Mór *S'clyde*, 'buəxeɪl 'etɪv 'mɔr, boó-ăchayl éttiv mór

Buccleuch *Borders*, bə'klu, bükloó. *Appropriate also for the Duke of* ~.

Buchan, *f.n.*, 'bʌxən, búchăn; 'bʌkən, búckăn. *The first is appropriate for John* ~, *first Baron Tweedsmuir, author and statesman.*

Buchan *Grampian*, 'bʌxən, búchăn. *Appropriate also for the Earl of* ~.

Buchanan, *f.n.*, bə'kænən, bükánnăn; bju'kænən, bew-kánnăn. *The first is appropriate for Professor Sir Colin* ~, *author of the* ~ *Report* (Traffic in Towns). *It is also normal Scottish usage.*

Buchell, *f.n.*, bu'ʃel, boo-shéll

Bucher, *f.n.*, 'buʃər, boósher

Buchinch *Central*, 'bʌk'ɪnʃ, búckínsh

Buchlyvie *Central*, bʌk'laɪvɪ, bucklívi

Buckden *Cambs.*, 'bʌkdən, búckděn

Bucke, *f.n.*, bjuk, bewk

Buckeridge, *f.n.*, 'bʌkərɪdʒ, búckěrij

Buckfastleigh *Devon*, 'bʌkfɑst'li, búckfaast-leé

Buckie *Grampian*, 'bʌkɪ, búcki

Buckingham *Bucks.*, 'bʌkɪŋəm, búcking-ăm

Buckinghamshire, Earl of, 'bʌkɪŋəmʃər, búcking-ămshěr

Buckland Filleigh *Devon*, 'bʌk-lənd 'fɪlɪ, búcklănd filli

Buckland Tout Saints *Devon*, 'bʌklənd 'tu 'seɪnts, búcklănd toó sáynts

Bucknall, *f.n.*, 'bʌknəl, búcknăl

Bucknall *Staffs.*, 'bʌknəl, búcknăl

Bucknell, *f.n.*, 'bʌknəl, búckněl

Buckoke, *f.n.*, 'bʌkouk, búckōk

Buddig, *Welsh C.n.*, 'bɪðɪg, bíthig

Bude *Cornwall*, bjud, bewd

Budle *Northd.*, 'bjudl, béwdl

Budleigh Salterton *Devon*, 'bʌdlɪ 'sɔltərtən, búdli sáwltěrtŏn; 'bʌdlɪ 'sɒltərtən, búdli sóltěrtŏn

Budock *Cornwall*, 'bjudɒk, béwdock

Bueb, *f.n.*, 'bjueb, béw-eb

Buerk, *f.n.*, bɜrk, burk

Buerton *Ches.*, 'bjuərtən, béwěrtŏn

Buessst, *f.n.*, bjust, bewsst

Buggé, *f.n.*, 'bugeɪ, boógay

Buggs, *f.n.*, bjugz, bewgz; bʌgz, buggz

Bught Park *Inverness*, bʌxt, bucht

Bugle *Cornwall*, 'bjugl, béwgl

Bugner, *f.n.*, 'bʌgnər, búgněr; 'bugnər, boógněr

Buick, *f.n.*, 'bjuɪk, béw-ick

Buildwas *Salop*, 'bɪldwəs, bíld-wäss

Builth Wells *Powys*, 'bɪlθ 'welz, bílth wéllz

Buist, *f.n.*, 'bjuɪst, béw-ist; bjust, bewsst

Buittle *D. & G.*, 'bɪtl, bíttl; 'bjutl, béwtl

Bukatzsch, *f.n.*, 'bjukætʃ, béwkatch

Bukht, *f.n.*, bʌkt, buckt

Bulbarrow *Dorset*, 'bʊl'bærou, boólbárrō

Bulbrook, *f.n.*, 'bʊlbrʊk, boólbrŏŏk

Bulcote *Notts.*, 'bʊlkət, boólkŏt

Buley, *f.n.*, 'bjulɪ, béwli

Bulkeley, *f.n.*, 'bʌlklɪ, búlkli

Bulkeley *Ches.*, 'bʊklɪ, boókli

Bulkley, *f.n.*, 'bʌlklɪ, búlkli

Bullard, *f.n.*, 'bʊlərd, boólărd; 'bʊlɑrd, boólaard

Bulleid, *f.n.*, 'bʊlid, boóleed; bʊ'lid, boóleéd

Buller, *f.n.*, 'bʊlər, boólěr

Bullimore, *f.n.*, 'bʊlɪmɔr, boólimor

Bullough, *f.n.*, 'bʊlə, boólă; 'bʊlou, boólō

Bullus, *f.n.*, 'bʊləs, boólŭss

Bulmer, *f.n.*, 'bʊlmər, boólměr

Bulphan *Essex*, 'bʊlvən, boólvăn

Bulteel, *f.n.*, 'bʊltil, boólteel

Bultitude, *f.n.*, 'bʌltɪtjud, búltitewd

Bulverhythe *E. Sussex*, ,bʊlvər-'haɪð, boólvěr-híth

Bulwell *Notts.*, 'bʊlwəl, boólwěl

Bulwer, *f.n.*, 'bʊlwər, boólwěr

Bulwick *Northants.*, 'bʊlɪk, boólick

Bumpus, *f.n.*, 'bʌmpəs, búmpŭss

Bunchrew *H'land*, bʌŋ'kru, bunkroó; bən'kru, bŭnkroó

Bunessan *S'clyde*, bə'nesən, bŭnéssăn

Bungay *Suffolk*, 'bʌŋgɪ, búng-gi

Bunting, *f.n.*, 'bʌntɪŋ, búnting

Bunwell *Norfolk*, 'bʌnwəl, búnwěl

Buqué, *f.n.*, 'bju'keɪ, béwkáy

Burberry, *f.n.*, 'bɜrbərɪ, búrběri

Burbury, *f.n.*, 'bɜrbərɪ, búrbŭri

Burchard, *f.n.*, 'bɜrtʃard, búrtchaard

Burcher, *f.n.*, 'bɜrtʃər, búrtchěr

Burder, *f.n.*, 'bɜrdər, búrděr

Burdett, *f.n.*, 'bɜrdet, búrdet; bɜr'det, burdétt

Burdett-Coutts, Baroness, *philanthropist*, 'bɜrdet 'kuts, búrdet koóts

Bure, River, *Norfolk*, bjʊər, byōor

Bures *Essex–Suffolk border*, bjʊərz, byōorz

Burgate *Suffolk*, 'bɜrgeɪt, búrgayt

Burge, *f.n.*, bɜrdʒ, burj

Burges, *f.n.*, 'bɜrdʒɪz, búrjěz

Burgess, *f.n.*, 'bɜrdʒɪs, búrjěss

Burgh, *f.n.*, 'bʌrə, búrrǎ; bɜrg, burg; bɜr, bur. *The first is appropriate for Baron* ∼.

Burgh *Suffolk*, bɜrg, burg

Burgh-by-Sands *Cumbria*, 'brʌf baɪ 'sændz, brúff bī sándz

Burgh Castle *Norfolk*, 'bʌrə 'kɑsl, búrrǎ kaássl

Burghclere *Hants*, 'bɜrklɛər, búrklair. *Appropriate also for the Barony of* ∼.

Burghead *Grampian*, bɜrg'hed, burg-héd

Burghersh, Baron, 'bɜrgɜrʃ, búrgersh

Burghfield *Berks.*, 'bɜrfild, búrfeeld

Burgh Heath *Surrey*, 'bʌrə 'hiθ, búrrǎ heéth; 'bɜr 'hiθ, búr heéth

Burgh House *Hampstead (London)*, bɜrg, burg

Burghill *H. & W.*, bɜrg'hɪl, burg-híll

Burgh-le-Marsh *Lincs.*, 'bʌrə lə 'mɑrʃ, búrrǎ lě maársh; 'bɜrlɪ 'mɑrʃ, búrli maársh

Burghley, Baron, 'bɜrlɪ, búrli

Burgh-on-Bain *Lincs.*, 'bʌrə ɒn 'beɪn, búrrǎ on báyn; 'brʌf ɒn 'beɪn, brúff on báyn

Burgh St. Peter *Norfolk*, 'bʌrə snt 'pitər, búrrǎ sīnt peétěr

Burgin, *f.n.*, 'bɜrgɪn, búrgin; 'bɜrdʒɪn, búrjin

Burgon, *f.n.*, 'bɜrgən, búrgŏn

Burgoyne, *f.n.*, 'bɜrgɔɪn, búrgoyn

Burham *Kent*, 'bʌrəm, búrrǎm

Burhop, *f.n.*, 'bʌrəp, búrrŏp

Buriton *Hants*, 'berɪtən, bérritŏn

Burke, *f.n.*, bɜrk, burk

Burke-Collis, *f.n.*, 'bɑrklɪs, baárkliss; 'bɜrk 'kɒlɪs, búrk kólliss

Burkhard, *f.n.*, 'bɜrkərd, búrkǎrd

Burkinshaw, *f.n.*, 'bɜrkɪnʃɔ, búrkin-shaw

Burleigh Castle *Tayside*, 'bɜrlɪ, búrli

Burlingjobb *Powys*, ˌbɜrlɪŋ'dʒɒb, burling-jóbb

Burlton, *f.n.*, 'bɜrltən, búrltŏn

Burnaston *Derby.*, 'bɜrnəstən, búrnǎstŏn

Burnell, *f.n.*, bɜr'nel, burnéll

Burneside *Cumbria*, 'bɜrnəsaɪd, búrněssīd; 'bɜrnsaɪd, búrnssīd

Burness, *f.n.*, bɜr'nes, burnéss

Burnet, *f.n.*, 'bɜrnɪt, búrnět; bər'net, búrnétt

Burnett, *f.n.*, 'bɜrnɪt, búrnět; bɜr'net, burnétt; bər'net, búrnétt

Burngullow *Cornwall*, bɜrn'gʌloʊ, burn-gúllō

Burnham Overy Staithe *Norfolk*, 'bɜrnəm 'oʊvərɪ 'steɪð, búrnǎm ōvěri stáyth

Burnhope *Durham*, 'bɜrnhoʊp, búrn-hōp

Burnish, *f.n.*, 'bɜrnɪʃ, búrnish

Burntisland *Fife*, bɜrnt'aɪlənd, burnt-íländ

Burpham *Surrey, W. Sussex*, 'bɜrfəm, búrfǎm

Burras, *f.n.*, 'bʌrəs, búrrǎss

Burrator *Devon*, 'bʌrə'tɔr, búrrǎ-tór

Burravoe *Shetland*, 'bʌrəvoʊ, búrrǎvō. *Appropriate for both places of the name in Shetland.*

Burray Island *Orkney*, 'bʌreɪ, búrray

Burrell, *f.n.*, 'bʌrəl, búrrěl

Burringham *Humberside*, 'bʌrɪŋ-əm, búrring-ǎm

Burrough, *f.n.*, 'bʌroʊ, búrrō; 'bʌrə, búrrǎ

Burroughes, *f.n.*, 'bʌroʊz, búrrōz

Burroughs, *f.n.*, 'bʌroʊz, búrrōz

Burry *W. Glam.*, 'bʌrɪ, búrri

Burry Holmes *W. Glam.*, 'bʌrɪ 'hoʊmz, búrri hőmz

Burry Port *Dyfed*, 'bʌrɪ 'pɔrt, búrri pórt

Burscough *Lancs.*, 'bɜrskoʊ, búrsskō

Bursledon *Hants*, 'bɜrzldən, búrzldŏn

Burslem *Staffs.*, 'bɜrzləm, búrzlěm

Burstall, *f.n.*, 'bɜrstɔl, búrsstawl

Burt, *f.n.*, bɜrt, burt

Burtchaell, *f.n.*, 'bɜrtʃl, búrtchl

Burton, *f.n.*, 'bɜrtən, búrtŏn

Burton Lazars *Leics.*, 'bɜrtən 'læzərz, búrtŏn lázzǎrz

Burton Pedwardine *Lincs.*, 'bɜrtən 'pedwərdaɪn, búrtŏn pédwǎrdīn

Burton Pynsent *Somerset*, 'bɜrtən 'pɪnsənt, búrtŏn pínssěnt

Burton upon Stather *Humberside*, 'bɜrtən əpɒn 'stæðər, búrtŏn ŭpon státhěr

Burtonwood *Ches.*, 'bɜrtən'wʊd, búrtŏnwŏŏd

Burwardsley *Ches.*, 'bɜrwərdzlɪ, búrwărdzli

Burwarton *Salop*, 'bɜrwərtən, búrwărtŏn

Burwash *E. Sussex*, 'bɜrwɒʃ, búrwosh; 'bʌrəʃ, búrrăsh

Burwasher, native of **Burwash**, 'bʌrəʃər, búrrăshĕr

Burwell, *f.n.*, 'bɜrwel, búrwel; 'bɜrwəl, búrwĕl

Burwell *Cambs.*, *Lincs.*, 'bɜrwel, búrwel

Bury, *f.n.*, 'berɪ, bérri; 'bjʊərɪ, byŏŏri. *The first is appropriate for Viscount* ∼.

Bury *Gtr. M'chester, W. Sussex*, 'berɪ, bérri

Bury Fen *Cambs.*, 'berɪ 'fen, bérri fén

Bury St. Edmunds *Suffolk*, 'berɪ snt 'edməndz, bérri sĭnt éd-mŭndz

Busby, *f.n.*, 'bʌzbɪ, búzzbi

Bushby, *f.n.*, 'bʊʃbɪ, bŏŏshbi

Bushelle, *f.n.*, bʊ'ʃel, bŏŏ-shéll

Bushnell, *f.n.*, 'bʊʃnəl, bŏŏshnĕl

Buskell, *f.n.*, 'bʌskl, bússkl

Busler, *f.n.*, 'bʌzlər, búzzlĕr

Bussell, *f.n.*, 'bʌsl, bússl

Buston, *f.n.*, 'bʌstən, bússtŏn

Busutilli, *f.n.*, ‚bʊsʊ'tɪlɪ, bŏŏssŏŏ-tílli

Busvine, *f.n.*, 'bʌzvaɪn, búzzvīn

Buszard, *f.n.*, 'bʌzərd, búzzărd

Butchart, *f.n.*, 'bʊtʃɑrt, bŏŏ-tchaart; 'bʊtʃərt, bŏŏtchărt

Bute, *I. of*, bjut, bewt. *Appropriate also for the Marquess of* ∼.

Buthlay, *f.n.*, 'bʌθleɪ, búthlay

Butler-Bowdon, *f.n.*, 'bʌtlər 'boʊdən, bútlĕr bŏ́dŏn. *Family name relating to the Barony of Grey de Ruthyn.*

Butley *Ches.*, *Suffolk*, 'bʌtlɪ, bútli

Butlin, *f.n.*, 'bʌtlɪn, bútlin

Buttar, *f.n.*, 'bʌtɑr, búttaar

Butter, *f.n.*, 'bʌtər, búttĕr

Butters, *f.n.*, 'bʌtərz, búttĕrz

Butterwick *Lincs.*, 'bʌtərwɪk, búttĕrwick

Buxhall *Suffolk*, 'bʌksɔl, búcksawl

Buzan, *f.n.*, bju'zæn, bewzán

Buzeman, *f.n.*, 'bjuzmən, béwz-măn

Bwlch Gwyn *Clwyd*, bʊlx 'gwɪn, bŏŏlch gwín

Bwlchllan *Dyfed*, bʊlx'ɬæn, bŏŏlch-hlán

Bwlch Newydd *Dyfed*, bʊlx 'newɪð, bŏŏlch né-wĭth

Bwlch-y-Cibau *Powys*, ‚bʊlxə-'kibaɪ, bŏŏlchăkéebī

Bwlchysarnau *Powys*, ‚bʊlxə-'sɑrnaɪ, bŏŏlchăssaárnī

Bwllfa *W. Glam.*, 'bʊɬvə, bŏŏhlvă

Byam, *f.n.*, 'baɪəm, bí-ăm

Byars, *f.n.*, 'baɪərz, bí-ărz

Byatt, *f.n.*, 'baɪət, bí-ăt

Bygott, *f.n.*, 'baɪgɒt, bígott

Byham, *f.n.*, 'baɪəm, bí-ăm

Byker *Tyne & Wear*, 'baɪkər, bíkĕr

Bylaugh *Norfolk*, 'bilɑ, beélaa; 'biloʊ, beélō; 'baɪlɑ, bílaa; 'baɪloʊ, bílō; 'baɪlɔ, bílaw

Bylchau *Clwyd*, 'bʌlxaɪ, búlchī

Byles, *f.n.*, baɪlz, bīlz

Byllam, *f.n.*, 'bɪləm, bíllăm

Bynea *Dyfed*, 'bɪnjə, bín-yă

Byng, *f.n.*, bɪŋ, bing

Byrne, *f.n.*, bɜrn, burn

Byron, *f.n.*, 'baɪərən, bírŏn

Byshottles *Durham*, 'baɪʃɒtlz, bíshottlz

Bysouth, *f.n.*, 'baɪsaʊθ, bíssowth

Bysshe, *f.n.*, bɪʃ, bish. *Appropriate also for Percy* ∼ *Shelley, poet.*

Bythesea, *f.n.*, 'baɪθsi, bíth-see

Bytheway, *f.n.*, 'baɪðəweɪ, bíthĕway; 'baɪθweɪ, bíth-way

Byton *H. & W.*, 'baɪtən, bítŏn

Byward Tower *Tower of London*, 'baɪwərd, bí-wărd

C

Caban Coch *Powys*, 'kæbən 'koʊx, kábbän kóch

Cabeldu, *f.n.*, kə'beldju, kăbél-dew

Cabell, *f.n.*, 'kæbl, kábbl

Cabot, *f.n.*, 'kæbət, kábbŏt. *This is the pronunciation generally used for John and Sebastian* ∼, *explorers.*

Cabourn, also spelt **Cabourne**, *Lincs.*, 'keɪbərn, káybŏrn

Cabrach *Grampian*, 'kæbrəx, kábrăch; 'kabrəx, kaábrăch

Cabus *Lancs.*, 'keɪbəs, káybŭss

Caccia, *f.n.*, 'kætʃə, kátchă. *Appropriate also for Baron* ∼.

Cachemaille, *f.n.*, 'kæʃmaɪl, káshmīl; 'kæʃmeɪl, káshmayl

Cadbury, *f.n.*, 'kædbərɪ, kádbŭri

Cadby, *f.n.*, 'kædbɪ, kádbi

Caddonfoot *Borders*, ‚kædən'fʊt, kaddŏnfŏŏt

Caddoo, *f.n.*, kæ'du, kaddoó

Cadeby *Leics.*, *S. Yorks.*, 'keɪdbɪ, káydbi

Cadell, *f.n.*, 'kædl, káddl; kə'del, kădéll. *The first is appropriate for Jean ∼, actress, and the second for Selina ∼, actress.*

Cader Idris *Gwynedd*, 'kædər 'ɪdrɪs, káddĕr ídriss

Cadgwith *Cornwall*, 'kædʒwɪð, kájwith; 'kædʒwɪθ, kájwith

Cadishead *Gtr. M'chester*, 'kædɪzhed, káddiz-hed

Cadle, *f.n.*, 'keɪdl, káydl

Cadle *W. Glam.*, 'kædleɪ, kádlay

Cadnant Brook *Anglesey*, 'kædnænt, kádnant

Cadogan, Earl, kə'dʌgən, kădúggăn

Cadoux, *f.n.*, kə'du, kădóo

Cadoxton *S. Glam.*, 'kædəkstən, káddŏkstŏn

Cadwaladr, **Dilys**, *Welsh poet*, 'dɪlɪs kæd'wælədər, dílliss kadwáládĕr

Cadwaladyr, *f.n.*, kæd'wælədər, kadwáládĕr

Cadwallader, *f.n.*, kæd'wɒlədər, kadwóládĕr

Cadwgan, *f.n.*, kə'dʊgən, kădóogăn

Cady, *f.n.*, 'keɪdɪ, káydi

Cadzow, *f.n.*, 'kædzoʊ, kádzō

Cadzow *S'clyde*, 'kædzoʊ, kádzō

Caegarw *Mid Glam.*, kaɪ'gæru, kīgárroo; ki'gæru, keegárroo

Caenby *Lincs.*, 'keɪnbɪ, káynbi

Caerau *Mid Glam.*, *Powys*, *S. Glam.*, 'kaɪraɪ, kírī

Caerbwdi Bay, *Dyfed*, kaɪər'budɪ, kīrboόdi

Caer Caradoc *Salop*, 'kaɪər kə'rædɒk, kír kăráddock

Caerdeon *Gwynedd*, kɑr'deɪən, kaardáy-ŏn; kaɪər'deɪən, kīrdáy-ŏn

Caerdydd, *Welsh name for Cardiff*, ‚kaɪər'dɪð, kīrdéeth

Caergeiliog *Gwynedd*, kaɪər-'gaɪljɒg, kīrgíl-yog

Caergwrle *Clwyd*, kaɪər'gʊərlɪ, kīrgoόrli

Caergybi, *Welsh form of* **Holyhead**, *Anglesey*, kaɪər'gʌbɪ, kīrgúbbi

Caerhays, *also spelt* **Carhays**, *Cornwall*, kɑr'heɪz, kaar-háyz; kə'reɪz, kắráyz. *Historians prefer the spelling* Carhays.

Caerhays Castle *Cornwall*, kɑr'heɪz, kaar-háyz

Caerhun *Gwynedd*, kaɪər'hɪn, kīr-héen. *Appropriate for both places of the name in Gwynedd.*

Caerlaverock *D. & G.*, kɛər-'lævərɒk, kairlávvĕrock

Caerleon *Gwent*, kɑr'liən, kaarleé--ŏn; kər'liən, kắrleé-ŏn; kaɪər'liən, kīrleé-ŏn

Caernarvon *Gwynedd*, kər'nɑrvən, kărnaárvŏn

Caerphilly *Mid Glam.*, kər'fɪlɪ, kărfílli

Caersalem *W. Glam.*, kaɪər-'sæləm, kīr-sálém

Caersws *Powys*, kaɪər'sus, kīr--soόss

Caerwent *Gwent*, kaɪər'went, kīrwént

Caerwys *Clwyd*, 'kaɪərwɪs, kírwiss

Caffarey, *f.n.*, 'kæfərɪ, káffări

Caffery, *f.n.*, 'kæfərɪ, káffĕri

Caffyn, *f.n.*, 'kæfɪn, káffin

Cahal, *f.n.*, kə'hæl, kä-hál

Cahan, *f.n.*, kɑn, kaan

Cahill, *f.n.*, 'kɑhɪl, kaá-hil

Cahir, *Irish C.n.*, 'kæhər, ká-hŭr

Cahusac, *f.n.*, *also spelt* **Cahuzac**, kɑ'hjuzæk, kaa-héwzack

Cainey, *f.n.*, 'keɪnɪ, káyni

Caink, *f.n.*, keɪŋk, kaynk

Caie, *f.n.*, kaɪ, kī

Caird, *f.n.*, kɛərd, kaird

Cairnbulg *Grampian*, 'kɛərn'bʌlg, káirn-búlg

Caiger, *f.n.*, 'keɪdʒər, káyjĕr

Caillard, *f.n.*, 'kaɪɑr, kí-aar

Cairncross, *f.n.*, kɛərn'krɒs, kairn-króss

Cairngorms *H'land–Grampian*, 'kɛərn'gɔrmz, káirn-górmz

Cairntoul *Grampian*, kɛərn'tul, kairntoόl; kɛərn'taul, kairntówl

Caister *Norfolk*, 'keɪstər, káystĕr

Caistor *Lincs.*, 'keɪstər, káystŏr

Caithness, Earl of, 'keɪθnes, káythness

Caithness *H'land*, 'keɪθnɪs, káythnĕss

Caius, *f.n.*, kiz, keez

Caius College *see* **Gonville and Caius** College

Calbourne *I. of Wight*, 'kælbɔrn, kálborn

Calcot, *f.n.*, 'kɒlkət, káwlkŏt; 'kælkət, kálkŏt

Calcot Row *Berks.*, 'kælkət 'roʊ, kálkŏt rố

Calcott, *f.n.*, 'kɒlkət, káwlkŏt; 'kælkət, kálkŏt

Caldarvan *S'clyde*, kəl'dɑrvən, kăldaárvän

Caldbeck *Cumbria*, 'kɒldbek, káwldbeck; 'kɒdbek, káwdbeck

Caldcleugh, *f.n.*, 'kɒldklʌf, káwldkluff; 'kɑldklʌf, kaáldkluff

Caldecote, Viscount, 'kɔldɪkət, káwldĕkŏt
Caldecott Ches., Oxon., 'kɔldɪkət, káwldĕkŏt
Caldecott Leics., 'kɔldɪkɒt, káwldĕkott
Calder, f.n., 'kɔldər, káwldĕr
Calder, Rivers, 'kɔldər, káwldĕr. Appropriate for rivers of this name in Cumbria, Lancs. (two), and W. Yorks.
Calder and Boyars, publishers, 'kɔldər ənd 'bɔɪərz, káwldĕr ănd bóy-ărz
Caldercruix S'clyde, ˌkɔldər-'kruks, kawldĕrkroóks
Calderon, f.n., 'kældərən, káldĕrŏn; 'kɔldərən, káwldĕrŏn
Calderstones Merseyside, 'kɔldərstoʊnz, káwldĕrstōnz
Caldew, River, Cumbria, 'kɔldju, káwldew
Caldmore W. Midlands, 'kamər, kaámŏr
Caldons D. & G., 'kɔldənz, káwldŏnz
Caldow, f.n., 'kældoʊ, káldō
Caldwell, f.n., 'kɔldwel, káwldwel
Caldy Merseyside, 'kɔldɪ, káwldi
Caldy Island Dyfed, 'kɔldɪ 'aɪlənd, káwldi îlănd
Caledon Co. Tyrone, 'kælɪdən, kálĕdŏn. Appropriate also for the Earl of ~.
Calenick Cornwall, kə'lenɪk, kálénnick
Caley, f.n., 'keɪlɪ, káyli
Calfe, f.n., kaf, kaaf
Calgary I. of Mull, 'kælgərɪ, kálgări
Calke Derby., kɔk, kawk
Calkwell, also spelt Cawkwell, Lincs., 'kɔkwel, káwkwel
Calladine, f.n., 'kælədin, kálădeen
Callaghan, f.n., 'kæləhən, kálăhăn
Callaly Northd., 'kæləlɪ, kálăli; kə'lælɪ, káláli
Callander Central, 'kæləndər, kálăndĕr
Callanish, also spelt Callernish, I. of Lewis, 'kælənɪʃ, kálănish
Callard, f.n., 'kælard, kálaard
Callear, f.n., 'kælɪər, káli-ĕr; kə'lɪər, kálĕer
Callernish, see also Callanish, I. of Lewis, 'kælərnɪʃ, kálĕrnish
Callestick Cornwall, kə'lestɪk, kálĕstick; 'klestɪk, kléstick
Callieu, f.n., kæl'ju, kal-yoó
Callil, f.n., kə'lɪl, kălíl
Callington Cornwall, 'kælɪŋtən, kálingtŏn
Callis Mill Hebden Bridge (W. Yorks.), 'kælɪs 'mɪl, káliss míll

Callus, f.n., 'kæləs, kálŭss
Calman, f.n., 'kælmən, kálmăn
Calne Wilts., kan, kaan
Calne and Calstone, Viscount, 'kan ənd 'kælstən, kaʹan ănd kálstŏn
Calow Derby., 'keɪloʊ, káylō
Calshot Hants, 'kælʃɒt, kál-shot
Calstock Cornwall, 'kælstɒk, kálstock
Calstone Wellington Wilts., 'kælstən 'welɪŋtən, kálstŏn wéllingtŏn
Calthorpe, f.n., 'kɔlθɔrp, káwl-thorp; 'kælθɔrp, kál-thorp. The first is appropriate for Baron ~.
Calthorpe Norfolk, 'kælθɔrp, kál-thorp
Calton S'clyde, 'kaltən, kaʹaltŏn
Calton Hill Edinburgh, 'kɔltən 'hɪl, káwltŏn híll
Calveley Ches., 'kavlɪ, kaʹavli; 'kovlɪ, káwvli
Calver, f.n., 'kælvər, kálvĕr; 'kavər, kaʹavĕr
Calverhall Salop, 'kælvərhɔl, kálvĕr-hawl
Calverley W. Yorks., 'kavərlɪ, kaʹavĕrli; 'kɒvlɪ, káwvli. The first is appropriate for Baron ~.
Calverley, Charles Stuart, 19th-c. poet, 'kavərlɪ, kaʹavĕrli; 'kælvərlɪ, kálvĕrli. The first is the pronunciation used by his direct descendants, hence probably his own. The second seems to be otherwise common usage, e.g. in the English departments of universities, etc.
Calver Sough Derby., 'kavər 'sʌf, kaʹavĕr súff
Calvert, f.n., 'kælvərt, kálvĕrt; 'kɔlvərt, káwlvĕrt
Calverton Notts., 'kælvərtən, kálvĕrtŏn; 'kavərtən, kaʹavĕrtŏn
Calvine Tayside, kæl'vin, kal-veén
Calvocoressi, f.n., ˌkælvəkə'resɪ, kalvŏkŏréssi
Calwell, f.n., 'kɔlwəl, káwlwĕl
Cam, River, mainly Cambs., kæm, kam
Camascross Skye, ˌkæməs'krɒs, kammăskróss
Camasunary Skye, ˌkæmə'sjunərɪ, kammăsséwnări
Camberley Surrey, 'kæmbərlɪ, kámbĕrli
Camberwell London, 'kæmbər-wəl, kámbĕr-wĕl; 'kæmbərwel, kámbĕr-wel
Cambois Northd., 'kæməs, kámmŭs; 'kæmɪs, kámmiss

Camborne *Cornwall*, 'kæmbɔrn, kámborn

Cambrian, *pertaining to Wales*, 'kæmbrɪən, kámbriăn

Cambridge *Cambs., Glos.*, 'keɪmbrɪdʒ, káymbrij

Cambusavie *H'land*, ˌkæmbəs-'ævɪ, kambŭssávvi

Cambusbarron *Central*, ˌkæmbəs-'bærən, kambŭssbárrŏn

Cambuslang *S'clyde*, ˌkæmbəs-'læŋ, kambŭsslãng

Cambusnethan *S'clyde*, ˌkæmbəs-'neθən, kambŭssnéthăn

Camden, *f.n.*, 'kæmdən, kámdĕn

Cameley *Avon*, 'keɪmlɪ, káymli

Camelford *Cornwall*, 'kæmlfərd, kámmlfŏrd

Camelon *Central*, 'kæmələn, kámmĕlŏn

Camerer-Cuss, *f.n.*, 'kæmərər 'kʌs, kámmĕrĕr kúss

Cameron of Lochiel, *f.n.*, 'kæmərən əv lɒ'xil, kámmĕrŏn ŏv lochéel

Camerton *Avon, Cumbria*, 'kæmərtən, kámmĕrtŏn

Camidge, *f.n.*, 'kæmɪdʒ, kámmij

Camlachie *S'clyde*, kæm'læxɪ, kamláchi

Camlan *Gwynedd*, 'kæm'læn, kám-lán

Camlough *Co. Armagh*, 'kæmlɒx, kámloch

Cammaerts, *f.n.*, 'kæmərts, kámmĕrts

Camoys, Baron, 'kæmɔɪz, kámmoyz

Campagnac, *f.n.*, kæm'pænjæk, kampán-yack; kəm'pænjæk, kămpán-yack

Campbell, *f.n.*, 'kæmbl, kámbl

Campbell and Cowal, Earl of, 'kæmbl ənd 'kauəl, kámbl ănd kówăl

Campbell of Monzie, *f.n.*, 'kæmbl əv mə'ni, kámbl ŏv mŏneé

Campbell-Savours, *f.n.*, 'kæmbl 'seɪvərz, kámbl- sáyvŏrz

Campbeltown *S'clyde*, 'kæmbl-taun, kámbltown; 'kæmbltən, kámbltŏn

Campden, *f.n.*, 'kæmdən, kámdĕn. *Appropriate also for Viscount* ~.

Campey, *f.n.*, 'kæmpɪ, kámpi

Campoli, Alfredo, *violinist*, æl'freɪdoʊ 'kæmpəlɪ, alfráydō kámpŏli

Campsall *S. Yorks.*, 'kæmpsl, kámpssl

Campsie *S'clyde*, 'kæmpsɪ, kámpsi

Camrose *Dyfed*, 'kæmroʊz, kámrōz

Camsey, *f.n.*, 'kæmzɪ, kámzi

Camulodunum, *Roman name for* Colchester, 'kæmjʊloʊ'djunəm, kám-yōōlōdéwnŭm; 'kæmʊloʊ-'dunəm, kámōōlōdóonŭm

Camus, *f.n.*, 'kæməs, kámmŭss

Canavan, *f.n.*, 'kænəvən, kánnăvăn

Canaway, *f.n.*, 'kænəweɪ, kánnăway

Candian, *f.n.*, 'kændɪən, kándi-ăn

Candler, *f.n.*, 'kændlər, kándlĕr

Candlin, *f.n.*, 'kændlɪn, kándlin

Candlish, *f.n.*, 'kændlɪʃ, kándlish

Canel, *f.n.*, kə'nel, kănéll

Canelle, *f.n.*, kə'nel, kănéll

Canetti, Elias, *author*, eɪ'liæs kə'netɪ, aylee-ass kănétti

Canewdon *Essex*, kə'njudən, kănéwdŏn

Canna *H'land*, 'kænə, kánnă

Cannadine, *f.n.*, 'kænədaɪn, kánnădīn

Cannel, *f.n.*, kə'nel, kănéll

Cannell, *f.n.*, 'kænl, kánnl

Cannetty, *f.n.*, 'kænɪtɪ, kánnĕti

Cannich *H'land*, 'kænɪx, kánnich

Canonbury *London* 'kænənbərɪ, kánnŏnbŭri

Canon Frome *H. & W.*, 'kænən 'frum, kánnŏn fróom

Canon Pyon *H. & W.*, 'kænən 'paɪən, kánnŏn pí-ŏn

Cant, *f.n.*, kænt, kant

Cantab., *abbreviation of* Cantabrigian, 'kæntæb, kántab

Cantabrigian, *pertaining to* Cambridge *or its University*, ˌkæntə'brɪdʒɪən, kantăbríjiăn

Cantamir, *f.n.*, 'kæntəmɪər, kántămeer

Cantelo, *f.n.*, 'kæntɪloʊ, kántĕlō

Cantelowes Gardens, *London* park, 'kæntɪloʊz, kántĕlōz

Canter, *f.n.*, 'kæntər, kántĕr

Canterbury *Kent*, 'kæntərbərɪ, kántĕrbŭri; 'kæntərberɪ, kántĕrberri

Cantuar, *Archbishop of* Canterbury*'s signature* 'kæntjʊɑr, kánt-yōō-aar

Canvey Island *Essex*, 'kænvɪ 'aɪlənd, kánvi fländ

Canwick *Lincs.*, 'kænɪk, kánnick

Caol *H'land*, kɔl, köl

Capaldi, *f.n.*, kə'pældɪ, kăpáldi; kə'pɒldɪ, kăpáwldi

Cap Coch *Mid Glam.*, kæp 'koʊx, kap kóch

Cape Cornwall *Cornwall*, keɪp 'kɔrnwəl, kayp kórnwăl

Capel, *f.n.*, 'keɪpl, káypl

Capel *Kent, Surrey*, 'keɪpl, káypl

Capel Curig *Gwynedd*, 'kæpl 'kɪrɪg, káppl kírrig

Capel-ed

44

Carlyle

Capel-ed *Gwent*, 'kæpl 'ed, káppl édd
Capel-le-Ferne *Kent*, 'keɪpl lə 'fɜrn, káypl lĕ férn
Capell, *f.n.*, 'keɪpl, káypl
Capel Mair *Dyfed*, 'kæpl 'maɪər, káppl mír
Capel Mawr *Gwynedd*, 'kæpl 'maʊər, káppl mówr
Capener, *f.n.*, 'keɪpənər, káypĕnĕr
Capenerhurst, *f.n.*, kə'penərhərst, kăpénnĕr-hurst
Capenhurst *Ches.*, 'keɪpənhərst, káypĕnhurst
Capern, *f.n.*, 'keɪpərn, káypĕrn
Capewell, *f.n.*, 'keɪpwel, káypwel
Cape Wrath *H'land*, keɪp 'rɑθ, kayp raáth; keɪp 'rɔθ, kayp ráwth; keɪp 'ræθ, kayp ráth; keɪp 'rɒθ, kayp róth
Capheaton *Northd.*, kæp'hitən, kap-héetŏn
Caplan, *f.n.*, 'kæplən, káplăn
Capon, *f.n.*, 'keɪpən, káypŏn
Caporn, *f.n.*, 'keɪpɔrn, káyporn
Cappagh *Co. Tyrone*, 'kæpə, káppă
Cappercleuch *Borders*, 'kæpərklux, káppĕrklooch
Capron, *f.n.*, 'keɪprən, káyprŏn
Caputh *Tayside*, 'keɪpəθ, káypŭth
Caradoc, *Welsh C.n.*, *also spelt* **Caradog,** kə'rædɒk, kăráddock
Caradon *Cornwall*, 'kærədən, kárrădŏn. *Appropriate also for Baron* ~.
Caravias, *f.n.*, ˌkærə'viəs, karrăvée-äss
Carbery, Baron, 'kɑrbəri, káarbĕri
Carbery, *f.n.*, 'kɑrbəri, káarbĕri
Carbis Bay *Cornwall*, 'kɑrbɪs 'beɪ, káarbiss báy
Carbost *Skye*, 'kɑrbɒst, káarbosst. *Appropriate for both places of the name on Skye.*
Carburton *Notts.*, 'kɑrbərtən, káarbŭrtŏn
Carcanet Press, *publishers*, 'kɑrkənet, káarkănet
Cardenden *Fife*, ˌkɑrdən'den, kaardĕndén
Cardiff *S. Glam.*, 'kɑrdɪf, káardif
Cardigan *Dyfed*, 'kɑrdɪgən, káardigăn. *Appropriate also for the Earl of* ~.
Cardinall, *f.n.*, 'kɑrdɪnl, káardinnl
Cardinham *Cornwall*, kɑr'dɪnəm, kaardínnăm
Cardnell, *f.n.*, 'kɑrdnel, káard-nel
Cardowan *S'clyde*, kɑr'daʊən, kaardów-än
Cardus, Sir Neville, *writer*, 'nevl 'kɑrdəs, névvl káardŭss

Careglefn *Anglesey*, ˌkærɪg'levn, karrĕglévvn
Careston *Tayside*, 'kɑrɪstən, káarĕstŏn
Carew, *f.n.*, kə'ru, kăroó; 'kɛəri, káiri. *The first is appropriate for Baron* ~, *and for Thomas* ~, *17th-c. poet.*
Carew *Dyfed*, 'kɛəri, káiri; 'kɛəru, káiroo
Carew, Seaton, *Cleveland*, 'sitən kə'ru, séetŏn kăroó
Carewe, *f.n.*, kə'ru, kăroó
Carey, *f.n.*, 'kɛəri, káiri
Carfin *S'clyde*, 'kɑr'fɪn, káar-fín
Carfraemill *Borders*, 'kɑrfreɪ'mɪl, kaárfraymíll
Cargen *D. & G.*, 'kɑrgən, kaárgĕn
Cargill, *f.n.*, kɑr'gɪl, kaargíll; 'kɑrgɪl, kaárgil
Carham *Northd.*, 'kærəm, kárräm
Carharrack *Cornwall*, kɑr'hærək, kaar-hárräk; kər'hærək, kăr-hárräk
Carhart, *f.n.*, 'kɑrhɑrt, kaár-haart
Carhays *see* **Caerhays**
Carholme Racecourse *Lincoln*, 'kɑrhoʊm, kaár-hōm
Caridia, *f.n.*, kə'rɪdɪə, kăríddiä
Carie *Tayside*, 'kɑri, kaári
Carin, *f.n.*, 'kærɪn, kárrin
Carinish *N. Uist*, 'kɑrɪnɪʃ, kaári-nish; 'kærɪnɪʃ, kárrinish
Carkeet-James, *f.n.*, 'kɑrkit 'dʒeɪmz, kaárkeet jáymz
Carland *Cornwall*, 'kɑrlænd, kaárland
Carleton, Baron, 'kɑrltən, kaárltŏn
Carleton, *f.n.*, 'kɑrltən, kaárltŏn
Carleton Forhoe *Norfolk*, 'kɑrltən 'fɔrhoʊ, kaárltŏn fór-hō
Carleton Road, *London*, kɑr'litən, kaarléetŏn
Carlill, *f.n.*, 'kɑr'lɪl, kaár-líll
Carline, *f.n.*, 'kɑrlaɪn, kaárlīn
Carlinghow *W. Yorks.*, ˌkɑrlɪŋ'haʊ, kaarling-hów
Carlisle, *f.n.*, kɑr'laɪl, kaarlíl
Carlisle *Cumbria*, kɑr'laɪl, kaar-líl; 'kɑrlaɪl, kaárlil. *The first is recognized national usage; the second is preferred locally. The first is also appropriate for the Earl of* ~.
Carlops *Borders*, 'kɑrlɒps, kaár-lops
Carlton Colville *Suffolk*, 'kɑrltən 'kɒlvɪl, kaárltŏn kólvil
Carluke *S'clyde*, kɑr'luk, kaar-loók
Carlyle, *f.n.*, kɑr'laɪl, kaarlíl; 'kɑrlaɪl, kaárlil. *The first is appropriate for Thomas* ~, *essayist and historian.*

Carlyon   45   Carstairs

Carlyon, *f.n.,* kɑr'laɪən, kaarlí--ŏn
Carlyon Bay *Cornwall,* kɑr'laɪən 'beɪ, kaarlí-ŏn báy
Carman, *f.n.,* 'kɑrmən, ka'armăn
Carmarthen *Dyfed,* kər'mɑrðən, kărma'arthĕn
Carmedy, *f.n.,* 'kɑrmədɪ, ka'armĕdi
Carmel *Clwyd, Dyfed, Gwynedd,* 'kɑrmel, ka'armel
Carmichael, *f.n.,* kɑr'maɪkl, kaarmíkl; kɑr'mɪxl, kaarmíchl
Carmyllie *Tayside,* kɑr'maɪlɪ, kaarmíli
Carnaby Street *London,* 'kɑrnəbɪ, ka'arnăbi
Carnac, *f.n.,* 'kɑrnæk, ka'arnack
Carnalea *Co. Down,* ˌkɑrnə'li, kaarnăle'e
Carnane *I. of Man,* kɑr'neɪn, kaarnáyn
Carnarvon, Earl of, kər'nɑrvən, kărna'arvŏn
Carn Brea *Cornwall,* 'kɑrn 'breɪ, ka'arn bráy
Carnearney *Co. Antrim,* kɑr-'nɛərnɪ, kaarnáirni
Carnegie, *f.n.,* kɑr'negɪ, kaarnéggi; kɑr'neɪgɪ, kaarnáygi. *The first is that of the Earl of Northesk's family name. Both pronunciations are current in Scotland, and usage for the ~ Trust consequently varies with individual speakers.*
Carnegy, *f.n.,* kɑr'negɪ, kaarnéggi; kɑr'neɪgɪ, kaarnáygi
Carnell, *f.n.,* kɑr'nel, kaarnéll
Carnkie *Cornwall,* kɑrn'kaɪ, kaarn-kí. *Appropriate for both places of this name in Cornwall.*
Carnlough *Co. Antrim,* 'kɑrnlɒx, ka'arnloch
Carnmenellis *Cornwall,* ˌkɑrnmɪ-'nelɪs, kaarn-mĕnélliss
Carnmoney *Co. Antrim,* kɑrn-'mʌnɪ, kaarn-múnni
Carno *Powys,* 'kɑrnoʊ, ka'arnō
Carnoustie *Tayside,* kɑr'nustɪ, kaarno'osti
Carntyne *S'clyde,* kɑrn'taɪn, kaarntín
Carnwadric *S'clyde,* kɑrn'wɒdrɪk, kaarn-wóddrick
Carnwath *S'clyde,* kɑrn'wɒθ, kaarnwóth. *Appropriate also for the Earldom of ~.*
Carnyorth *Cornwall,* kɑrn'jɔrθ, kaarn-yórth
Caro, *f.n.,* 'kɑroʊ, ka'arō
Caroe, *f.n.,* 'kɛəroʊ, káirō; 'kæroʊ, kárrō
Carolan, *f.n.,* 'kærələn, kárrŏlăn

Caron, *f.n.,* 'kærɒn, kárron; kə'rɒn, kărón
Carothers, *f.n.,* kə'rʌðərz, kărúthĕrz
Carpmael, *f.n.,* 'kɑrpmeɪl, ka'arpmayl
Carpmale, *f.n.,* 'kɑrpmeɪl, ka'arpmayl
Carr, *f.n.,* kɑr, kaar
Carra Beag *Tayside,* 'kærə 'beɪk, kárră báyk
Carrad, *f.n.,* 'kærəd, kárrăd
Carrawburgh Fort *Northd.,* 'kærəbrʌf, kárrăbruff
Carrbridge *H'land,* 'kɑr'brɪdʒ, ka'ar-bríj
Carreghofa *Powys,* ˌkærɪg'hoʊvə, karrĕg-hóvă
Carrell, *f.n.,* kə'rel, kăréll
Carreras, *f.n.,* kə'rɪərəz, kăréerăz
Carrick-a-Rede, *islet, Co. Antrim,* ˌkærɪk ə 'rid, karrick ă re'ed
Carrickfergus *Co. Antrim,* ˌkærɪk-'fərgəs, karrickférgüss
Carrick-Mannan *Co. Down,* ˌkærɪk'mænən, karrick-mánnăn
Carritt, *f.n.,* 'kærɪt, kárrit
Carrivick, *f.n.,* kə'rɪvɪk, kărívvick
Carrocher, *f.n.,* 'kærəxər, kárrŏchĕr
Carrodus, *f.n.,* 'kærədəs, kárrŏdüss
Carrothers, *f.n.,* kə'rʌðərz, kărúthĕrz
Carrowdore *Co. Down,* 'kærədɔr, kárrădor
Carrowreagh *Co. Antrim,* ˌkærou-'reɪə, karrō-ráy-ă
Carrowreagh *Co. Down,* ˌkærou-'reɪ, karrō-ráy
Carruth, *f.n.,* kə'ruθ, kăro'oth
Carruthers, *f.n.,* kə'rʌðərz, kărúthĕrz
Carryduff *Co. Down,* ˌkærɪ'dʌf, karridúff
Carse, *f.n.,* kɑrs, kaarss
Carse of Gowrie *Tayside,* 'kɑrs əv 'gaurɪ, ka'arss ŏv gówri
Carsfad *D. & G.,* kɑrs'fæd, kaarss-fád
Carshalton *London,* kɑr'ʃɔltən, kaar-sháwltŏn. *Although apparently no longer heard, there was previously a pronunciation* keɪs'hɒtən, kayss-háwtŏn.
Carsluith *D. & G.,* kɑr'sluθ, kaar-slo'oth
Carsphairn *D. & G.,* kɑrs'fɛərn, kaarss-fáirn
Carstairs, *f.n.,* kɑr'stɛərz, kaar--stáirz; 'kɑrstɛərz, ka'ar-stairz
Carstairs *S'clyde,* kɑr'stɛərz, kaar-stáirz

Carteret, *f.n.*, 'kɑrtəret, ka'artĕret; 'kɑrtərɪt, ka'artĕrĕt. *The first is generally considered appropriate for John* ~, *Earl Granville, 18th-c. diplomatist and statesman.*

Carterhaugh *Borders*, 'kɑrtər'hɒx, ka'artĕr-hóch

Carthew, *f.n.*, 'kɑrθju, ka'arthew

Carthusian, *one educated at Charterhouse School*, kɑr-'θjuzɪən, kaar-théwziăn

Cartier, *firm*, 'kɑrtɪeɪ, ka'arti-ay

Cartmel *Cumbria*, 'kɑrtməl, ka'artmĕl

Cartmel Fell *Cumbria*, 'kɑrtməl 'fel, ka'artmĕl féll

Carton de Wiart, *f.n.*, 'kɑrtən də 'waɪərt, ka'artŏn dĕ wí-ärt

Cartwright, *f.n.*, 'kɑrtraɪt, ka'artrīt

Carus, *f.n.*, 'keərəs, ka'irŭss; 'kærəs, kárrŭss

Caruth, *f.n.*, kə'ruθ, kăro'oth

Caruthers, *f.n.*, kə'rʌðərz, kărúthĕrz

Carvell, *f.n.*, kɑr'vel, kaarvéll

Carwadine, *f.n.*, 'kɑrwədin, ka'arwădeen

Carwardine, *f.n.*, 'kɑrwərdin, ka'arwărdeen; kɑrwər'din, kaarwărdéen

Carway *Dyfed*, 'kɑrweɪ, ka'arway

Carwinnen *Cornwall*, kɑr'wɪnən, kaarwínnĕn

Carwithen, *f.n.*, kɑr'wɪðən, kaarwíthĕn

Cary, *f.n.*, 'keərɪ, ka'iri

Carysfort, *f.n.*, 'kærɪsfɔrt, kárrisfort

Casasola, *f.n.*, ,kæsə'soʊlə, kassässṓlă

Cascob *Powys*, 'kæskɒb, kásskob

Casdagli, *f.n.*, kæz'dægli, kazdágli

Casken, *f.n.*, 'kæskɪn, kásskĕn

Casley, *f.n.*, 'keɪzlɪ, káyzli

Caslon, *f.n.*, 'kæzlɒn, kázzlon

Casselden, *f.n.*, 'kæsldən, kássldĕn

Cassillis *S'clyde*, 'kæslz, kásslz. *Appropriate also for the Earl of* ~.

Cassini, *f.n.*, kə'sinɪ, kásseeni

Cassiobury Park *Herts.*, 'kæsɪoʊbərɪ 'pɑrk, kássiōbŭri pa'ark

Casson, *f.n.*, 'kæsən, kásson

Castagnola, *f.n.*, ,kæstə'noʊlə, kasstănṓlă

Castaldini, *f.n.*, ,kæstəl'dinɪ, kasstáldeeni

Castell, *f.n.*, kæs'tel, kasstéll

Castellain, *f.n.*, 'kæstɪleɪn, kásstĕlayn

Castellan, *f.n.*, 'kæstelən, kásstellăn

Castell Coch *S. Glam.*, 'kæstel 'koux, kásstehl kóch

Castelnau *London thoroughfare*, 'kɑslnɔ, ka'asslnaw; 'kɑslnoʊ, ka'asslnō

Castle-an-Dinas *Cornwall*, 'kɑsl ən 'daɪnəs, ka'assl ăn dínăss

Castlebay *Barra* (*W. Isles*), 'kɑslbeɪ, ka'asslbay

Castle Baynard, *Ward of the City of London*, 'kɑsl 'beɪnɑrd, ka'assl báynaard

Castle Bromwich *W. Midlands*, 'kɑsl 'brɒmɪtʃ, ka'assl brómmitch

Castle Bytham *Lincs.*, 'kɑsl 'baɪðəm, ka'assl bíthăm

Castle Cary *Somerset*, 'kɑsl 'keərɪ, ka'assl ka'iri

Castlecaulfield *Co. Tyrone*, ,kɑsl'kɔfild, kaasslkáwfeeld

Castle Combe *Wilts.*, 'kɑsl 'kum, ka'assl ko'om

Castledawson *Co. Derry*, ,kɑsl-'dɔsən, kaassldáwssŏn

Castlederg *Co. Tyrone*, ,kɑsl-'dɜrg, kaassldérg

Castle Donington *Leics.*, 'kɑsl 'dɒnɪŋtən, ka'assl dónningtŏn

Castledoor *Cornwall*, ,kɑsl'dɔr, kaassldór

Castle Douglas *D. & G.*, 'kɑsl 'dʌgləs, ka'assl dúglăss

Castleford *W. Yorks.*, 'kɑslfərd, ka'asslförd

Castle Leod *H'land*, 'kɒsl 'laʊd, ka'assl lówd

Castle Malwood *Hants*, 'kɑsl 'mɔlwʊd, ka'assl máwlwŏŏd

Castle of Mey *H'land*, 'kɑsl əv 'meɪ, ka'assl ŏv máy

Castlereagh, Viscount, 'kɑslreɪ, ka'assl-ray

Castlereagh *Co. Down*, ,kɑsl'reɪ, kaassl-ráy

Castlerock *Co. Antrim*, ,kɑsl'rɒk, kaassl-róck

Castlerosse, Viscountcy of, 'kɑslrɒs, ka'assl-ross

Castletown *H'land*, 'kɑsltaʊn, ka'assltown

Castletown *I. of Man*, 'kɑsl'taʊn, ka'assltówn

Castleward *Co. Down*, ,kɑsl'wɔrd, kaasslwáwrd

Castlewellan *Co. Down*, ,kɑsl'welən, kaasslwéllăn

Castley, *f.n.*, 'kæstlɪ, kásstli

Caston *Norfolk*, 'kɑstən, ka'astŏn; 'kæsən, kássŏn; 'kæstən, kásstŏn

Castor *Cambs.*, 'kæstər, kásstŏr

Caswall, *f.n.*, 'kæzwəl, kázwăl
Catch, *f.n.*, kætʃ, katch
Catchpole, *f.n.*, 'kætʃpoʊl, kátchpōl
Catcleugh *Northd.*, 'kætklʌf, kátkluff; 'kætklif, kátkleef
Catelinet, *f.n.*, 'kætlɪneɪ, kátlinay
Cater, *f.n.*, 'keɪtər, káytĕr
Caterham *Surrey*, 'keɪtərəm, káytĕrăm
Catesby, *f.n.*, 'keɪtsbɪ, káytsbi
Cathays *S. Glam.*, kə'teɪz, kătáyz
Cathcart, *f.n.*, 'kæθkɑrt, káthkaart. *Also appropriate for Earl* ~.
Cathcart *S'clyde*, kæθ'kɑrt, kathkaárt
Cathedine *Powys*, kə'θedɪn, kăthéddin
Catherwood, *f.n.*, 'kæθərwʊd, káthĕr-wōōd; 'kæðərwʊd, káthĕr-wōōd
Cathie, *f.n.*, 'keɪθɪ, káythi
Cathles, *f.n.*, 'kæθlz, káthlz
Cathro, *f.n.*, 'kæθroʊ, káthrō
Cation, *f.n.*, 'keɪʃən, káyshŏn
Catisfield *Hants*, 'kætɪsfild, káttissfeeld
Catmur, *f.n.*, 'kætmər, kátmŭr
Cato, *f.n.*, 'keɪtoʊ, káytō
Caton, *f.n.*, 'keɪtən, káytŏn
Caton *Lancs.*, 'keɪtən, káytŏn
Cator, *f.n.*, 'keɪtər, káytŏr
Catrine *S'clyde*, 'kætrɪn, kátrin
Catriona, *C.n.*, kə'triənə, kătrée--ŏnă
Cattanach, *f.n.*, 'kætənəx, káttă-nach
Cattell, *f.n.*, kə'tel, kătéll
Catterline *Grampian*, 'kætərlaɪn, káttĕrlīn
Cattewater *see* **Catwater**
Cattistock *Dorset*, 'kætɪstɒk, káttistock
Catto, Baron, 'kætoʊ, káttō
Catwater, The, *Devon*, 'kætwɒtər, kátwawtĕr. *The spelling* **Cattewater** *appears to be an older variation.*
Catwick *Humberside*, 'kætɪk, káttick
Caudle, *f.n.*, 'kɔdl, káwdl
Caughey, *f.n.*, 'kæxɪ, káchi
Caughley *Salop*, 'kɑflɪ, káafli. *Appropriate also for the 18-c.* ~ *porcelain ware.*
Caulcutt, *f.n.*, 'kɔlkət, káwlkŭt
Caulfeild, *f.n.*, 'kɔfild, káwfeeld
Caulfield, *f.n.*, 'kɔfild, káwfeeld; 'kɔlfild, káwlfeeld
Caunce, *f.n.*, kɒns, kawnss; kɒns, konss

Caunsall *H. & W.*, 'kɒnsl, káwnssl
Causer, *f.n.*, 'kɔzər, káwzĕr
Causley, *f.n.*, 'kɒzlɪ, káwzli; 'keɪzlɪ, káyzli
Causton, Thomas, *18th-c. composer*, 'kɒstən, káwstŏn. *Also sometimes spelt* **Caustun** *or* **Cawston.**
Caute, *f.n.*, koʊt, kōt
Cautley, *f.n.*, 'kɔtlɪ, káwtli
Cava Island *Orkney*, 'kɑvə, kaávă
Cavanagh, *f.n.*, 'kævənə, kávvănă; kə'vænə, kăvánnă
Cavander, *f.n.*, 'kævəndər, kávvăndĕr
Cavanna, *f.n.*, kə'vænə, kăvánnă
Cavell, *f.n.*, 'kævl, kávvl; kə'vel, kăvéll. *The first is appropriate for Nurse Edith* ~.
Cavenagh, *f.n.*, 'kævənə, kávvĕnă
Cavendish, *f.n.*, 'kævəndɪʃ, kávvĕndish
Cavers, *f.n.*, 'keɪvərz, káyvĕrz
Cavers *Borders*, 'keɪvərz, káyvĕrz
Caversham *Berks.*, 'kævərʃəm, kávvĕr-shăm
Cavers Hill *Borders*, 'keɪvərz 'hɪl, káyvĕrz híll
Caverswall *Staffs.*, 'kævərzwɒl, kávvĕrz-wawl
Cavey, *f.n.*, 'keɪvɪ, káyvi
Cavin, *f.n.*, 'keɪvɪn, káyvin
Cawardine, *f.n.*, kə'wɔrdɪn, kaw--wáwrdin
Cawdell, *f.n.*, kɔ'del, kawdéll
Cawdor *H'land*, 'kɔdər, káwdŏr. *Appropriate also for Earl* ~.
Cawkwell *see* **Calkwell**
Cawley, *f.n.*, 'kɒlɪ, káwli
Cawood, *f.n.*, 'keɪwʊd, káy-wōōd
Cawood *Lancs.*, *N. Yorks.*, 'keɪwʊd, káy-wōōd
Cawsand *Cornwall*, 'kɒsænd, káwssand
Cawston, *f.n.*, 'kɒstən, káwstŏn. *See also* **Thomas Causton.**
Cawston *Norfolk*, 'kɒstən, káwsstŏn
Cawthra, *f.n.*, 'kɔθrə, káwthră
Caxton Gibbet *Cambs.*, 'kækstən 'dʒɪbɪt, káckstŏn jíbbĕt
Cayzer, *f.n.*, 'keɪzər, káyzĕr
Cazabon, *f.n.*, 'kæzəbɒn, kázzăbon
Cazalet, *f.n.*, 'kæzəlɪt, kázzălĕt
Cazalet-Keir, *f.n.*, 'kæzəlɪt 'kɪər, kázzălĕt keér
Cazenove, *f.n.*, 'kæzɪnoʊv, kázzĕnōv
Cearns, *f.n.*, keərnz, kairnz
Cearr, *f.n.*, kɑr, kaar
Cecil, *f.n.*, 'sesl, séssl; 'sɪsl, síssl. *The second is appropriate for the family name of the Marquess of*

Exeter and that of the Marquess of Salisbury; *consequently also for Lord David* ∼ *and for the late Viscount* ∼ *of Chelwood.*

Cedric, *C.n.*, 'sedrɪk, sédrick; 'sɪdrɪk, seédrick

Cefn *Clwyd*, 'kevn, kévvn

Cefn Caeau *Dyfed*, ˌkevn 'kaɪaɪ, kevvn kí-ī

Cefn Coch *Powys*, 'kevn 'kɒx, kévvn kó<u>ch</u>

Cefn Coed *Mid Glam.*, ˌkevn 'kɔɪd, kevvn kóyd

Cefneithyn *Dyfed*, ˌkevn'aɪθɪn, kevvn-íthin; ˌkevn'eɪθɪn, kevvn--áythin

Cefn Golau *Mid Glam.*, ˌkevn 'gɒlaɪ, kevvn gólī

Cefn Hirgoed *Mid Glam.*, ˌkevn 'hɜrgɔɪd, kevvn hírgoyd

Cefn Mably *Mid Glam.*, ˌkevn 'mæblɪ, kevvn mábbli

Cefn Mawr *Clwyd*, ˌkevn 'mauʊr, kevvn mówr

Cefnpennar *Mid Glam.*, ˌkevn-'penər, kevvnpénnăr

Cefn-y-Bedd *Clwyd*, ˌkevn ə 'beð, kevvn ă bé<u>th</u>; ˌkevn ə 'beɪð, kevvn ă báy<u>th</u>. *This is also appropriate for the former name of* **Cilmery**, *Powys* (*q.v.*).

Ceinwen, *Welsh C.n.*, 'kaɪnwen, kínwen

Ceirchiog *Anglesey*, 'kaɪərxjɒg, kír<u>ch</u>-yog

Ceiriog, River, *Clwyd*, 'kaɪrɪɒg, kíri-og

Cellan, *f.n.*, 'kełən, ké<u>hl</u>ăn

Cellier, *f.n.*, 'seljeɪ, séll-yay

Celner, *f.n.*, 'selnər, sélnĕr

Celoria, *f.n.*, sɪ'lɔrɪə, sĕláwriă

Celt, *member of Celtic race*, kelt, kelt; selt, selt. *In Scotland and Northern Ireland the second is the more popular, and the only pronunciation ever heard for the Glasgow Celtic and Belfast Celtic football teams is* 'seltɪk, séltick.

Cemaes Bay *Anglesey*, 'kemaɪs 'beɪ, kémmiss báy

Cemm, *f.n.*, kem, kemm

Cemmaes *Powys*, 'kemaɪs, kémmīss

Cemmes Road *Powys*, 'kemɪs, kémmiss

Cenarth *Dyfed*, 'kenɑrθ, kén-naarth

Cennydd, *Welsh C.n.*, 'kenɪð, kénni<u>th</u>

Centlivre, Susannah, *17th–18th-c. playwright and actress*, sɪnt-'livər, sintleévĕr; sɪnt'lɪvər, sintlívvĕr. *There appears to be*

no positive evidence about her own pronunciation, and today she is known by both.

Ceredig, *f.n.*, kə'redɪg, kĕréddig

Ceredigion *Dyfed*, ˌkerə'dɪgɪɒn, kerrĕdíggi-on

Cerely, *f.n.*, 'sɪərlɪ, seérli

Ceres *Fife*, 'sɪərɪz, seériz

Ceresole, *f.n.*, 'serɪsoʊl, sérrĕssōl

Ceri, *Welsh C.n.*, 'kerɪ, kérri

Ceridwen, *Welsh C.n.*, kə'rɪdwen, kĕrídwen

Cerig Gwynion *Powys*, 'kerɪg 'gwɪnɪən, kérrig gwínniŏn

Cerne Abbas *Dorset*, 'sɜrn 'æbəs, sérn ábbăss

Cerney, North *and* South, *Glos.*, 'sɜrnɪ, sérni

Cernioge *Clwyd*, kɛərn'jɒgeɪ, kairn-yóggay

Cerrig-y-Drudion *Clwyd*, 'kerɪg ə 'drɪdjɒn, kérrig ă dríd-yon

Cesarewitch, *horse race*, sɪ'zærə-wɪtʃ, sĕzárrĕwitch

Ceserani, *f.n.*, ˌsizə'rɑnɪ, seezĕ-raáni

Cestrian, *native of Chester*, 'sestrɪən, séstriăn

Chabot, *f.n.*, 'ʃæboʊ, shábbō

Chaceley *Glos.*, 'tʃeɪslɪ, cháyssli

Chacewater *Cornwall*, 'tʃeɪswɔtər, cháysswawtĕr

Chacombe *Northants.*, 'tʃeɪkəm, cháykŏm. *An older spelling is* **Chalcombe.**

Chadbon, *f.n.*, 'tʃædbɒn, chádbon

Chadderton *Lancs.*, 'tʃædərtən, cháddĕrtŏn

Chaddesden *Derby.*, 'tʃædəzdən, cháddĕzdĕn

Chaddlehanger *Devon*, 'tʃædl-hæŋər, cháddl-hang-ĕr; 'tʃælɪŋər, cháling-ĕr

Chadshunt *Warwicks.*, 'tʃædz-hʌnt, chádz-hunt; 'tʃædzʌnt, chádzunt

Chafer, *f.n.*, 'tʃeɪfər, cháyfĕr; 'ʃeɪfər, sháyfĕr

Chaffe, *f.n.*, 'tʃeɪf, chayf

Chaffey, *f.n.*, 'tʃeɪfɪ, cháyfi

Chagford *Devon*, 'tʃægfərd, chággfŏrd

Chagrin, Francis, *composer*, 'frɑnsɪs 'ʃægræ̃, fraánssiss shágraŋ

Chailey *E. Sussex*, 'tʃeɪlɪ, cháyli

Chaillet, *f.n.*, 'ʃaɪjeɪ, shí-yay

Chain, *f.n.*, tʃeɪn, chayn

Chalcombe *see* **Chacombe**

Chaldon *Surrey*, 'tʃɔldən, cháwl-dŏn. *Appropriate also for* East *and* West ∼, *both in Dorset.* East ∼ *is alternatively known*

as ~ Herring, 'tʃɔldən 'herɪŋ, cháwldŏn hérring.
Chale *I. of Wight*, tʃeɪl, chayl
Chalfield, Great *and* Little, *Wilts.*, 'tʃalfɪld, chaálfeeld
Chalfont, Baron, 'tʃælfɒnt, chálfont
Chalfont St. Giles *Bucks.*, 'tʃælfənt snt 'dʒaɪlz, chálfŏnt sĭnt jílz; 'tʃafənt snt 'dʒaɪlz, chaáfŏnt sĭnt jílz
Chalfont St. Peters *Bucks.*, 'tʃælfənt snt 'pitərz, chálfŏnt sĭnt peétĕrz; 'tʃafənt snt 'pitərz, chaáfŏnt sĭnt peétĕrz
Chalford *Glos.*, 'tʃælfərd, chálfŏrd
Chalford *Wilts.*, 'tʃafərd, chaáfŏrd
Chalgrove *Oxon.*, 'tʃælgroʊv, chálgrōv
Chalk, *f.n.*, tʃɔk, chawk
Chalker, *f.n.*, 'tʃɔkər, cháwkĕr
Chalkley, *f.n.*, 'tʃɔklɪ, cháwkli
Challacombe *Devon*, 'tʃæləkəm, chálăkŏm
Challands, *f.n.*, 'tʃæləndz, chálăndz
Challes, *f.n.*, 'tʃælɪs, chálĕss
Challis, *f.n.*, 'tʃælɪs, cháliss
Challock *Kent*, 'tʃɒlək, chóllŏk
Challoner, *f.n.*, 'tʃælənər, chálŏnĕr
Challow, East *and* West, *Oxon.*, 'tʃæloʊ, chálō
Chalmers, *f.n.*, 'tʃamərz, chaámĕrz; 'tʃælmərz, chálmĕrz. *The first is appropriate for the Barony of* ~.
Chaloner, *f.n.*, 'tʃælənər, chálŏnĕr
Chalvey *Berks.*, 'tʃavɪ, chaávi; 'tʃalvɪ, chaálvi
Chalvington *E. Sussex*, 'tʃælvɪŋtən, chálvingtŏn; 'tʃalvɪŋtən, chaálvingtŏn
Chamberlain, *f.n.*, 'tʃeɪmbərlɪn, cháymbĕrlin; 'tʃeɪmbərleɪn, cháymbĕrlayn
Chamier, *f.n.*, 'ʃæmɪər, shámmi-ĕr
Champany *Lothian*, 'tʃæmpənɪ, chámpăni
Champelovier, *f.n.*, ˌtʃæmpə-'loʊvɪər, champĕlóvi-ĕr
Champernowne, *f.n.*, 'tʃæmpər-naʊn, chámpĕrnown
Champneys, *f.n.*, 'tʃæmpnɪz, chámpniz
Chanctonbury Ring *W. Sussex*, 'tʃæŋktənbərɪ 'rɪŋ, chánktŏn-bŭri ríng
Chanderhill *Derby.*, 'tʃændər'hɪl, chándĕr-hill; 'tʃandər'hɪl, chaándĕr-hill
Chandler, *f.n.*, 'tʃandlər, chaándlĕr

Chandos, *title of nobility*, 'ʃændɒs, shándoss. *Appropriate for both the present Viscount* ~, *and the Duchy of* ~.
Chandos, *f.n.*, 'ʃændɒs, shándoss; 'tʃændɒs, chándoss
Chandos-Pole, *f.n.*, 'ʃændɒs 'pul, shándoss poól
Changue *S'clyde*, tʃæŋ, chang
Channon, *f.n.*, 'tʃænən, chánnŏn; 'ʃænən, shánnŏn
Chaorunn, *Loch*, *S'clyde*, 'xɜrən, chúr-ŭn
Chapel Allerton *Leeds*, *Somerset*, 'tʃæpl 'ælərtən, cháppl álĕrtŏn
Chapel-en-le-Frith *Derby.*, 'tʃæpl en lə 'frɪθ, cháppl en lĕ fríth
Chapel of Garioch *Grampian*, 'tʃæpl əv 'gɪərɪ, cháppl ŏv geéri
Chapin, *f.n.*, 'tʃeɪpɪn, cháypin
Chaplin, *f.n.*, 'tʃæplɪn, cháplin
Chaplyn, *f.n.*, 'tʃæplɪn, cháplin
Chapman, *f.n.*, 'tʃæpmən, cháp-măn
Chappell, *f.n.*, 'tʃæpl, cháppl
Chappory, *f.n.*, 'tʃæpərɪ, cháppŏri
Chaproniere, *f.n.*, ˌʃæprə'nɪər, shaprŏneér; ˌʃæprən'jɛər, shaprŏn-yáir
Chard, *f.n.*, tʃard, chaard
Chardet, *f.n.*, 'ʃardeɪ, shaárday
Charig, *f.n.*, 'tʃærɪg, chárrig
Charing *Kent*, 'tʃærɪŋ, chárring; 'tʃɛərɪŋ, cháiring
Charlbury *Oxon.*, 'tʃarlbərɪ, chaárlbŭri
Charlecote Park *Warwicks.*, 'tʃarlkoʊt 'park, chaárlkŏt paárk
Charlemont *Co. Armagh*, 'tʃarlɪmənt, chaárlĕmŏnt. *Appropriate also for Viscount* ~.
Charleton, *f.n.*, 'tʃarltən, chaárl-tŏn
Charleton, East *and* West, *Devon*, 'tʃarltən, chaárltŏn
Charlier, *f.n.*, 'tʃarlɪeɪ, chaárli-ay
Charman, *f.n.*, 'tʃarmən, chaár-măn; 'ʃarmən, shaármăn
Charmouth *Dorset*, 'tʃarmaʊθ, chaármowth
Charoux, Siegfried, *sculptor*, 'sigfrid ʃə'ru, seégfreed shăroó
Charques, *f.n.*, 'ʃarkwɪz, chaár-kwĕz; 'ʃarkwɪz, shaárkwĕz
Charrosin, Frederick, *composer*, 'tʃæroʊsɪn, chárrōssin
Charteris, *f.n.*, 'tʃartərɪs, chaár-tĕriss; 'tʃartərz, chaártĕrz. *The first is appropriate for the family name of the Earl of Wemyss, and for Leslie* ~, *writer.*

Chartres, *f.n.*, 'tʃɑrtərz, chaártĕrz
Charwelton *Northants.*, tʃɑr-'weltən, chaar-wéltŏn
Chastleton *Oxon.*, 'tʃæsltən, chássltŏn
Chaston, *f.n.*, 'tʃæstən, chásstŏn
Chater, *f.n.*, 'tʃeɪtər, cháytĕr
Chathill, *Northd.*, 'tʃæt'hɪl, chát-híll
Chatteris *Cambs.*, 'tʃætərɪs, cháttĕriss
Chatto and Windus, *publishers*, 'tʃætou ənd 'wɪndəs, cháttŏ ănd wíndŭss
Chaudoir, *f.n.*, 'ʃoudwɑr, shŏd-waar
Chaul End *Beds.*, 'tʃɔl 'end, cháwl énd
Chaundler, *f.n.*, 'tʃɔndlər, cháwndlĕr
Chavasse, *f.n.*, ʃə'væs, shăváss
Chave, *f.n.*, tʃeɪv, chayv
Chawleigh *Devon*, 'tʃɔlɪ, cháwli
Chaworth, Baron, 'tʃɑwərθ, chaá-wŭrth
Chawton *Hants*, 'tʃɔtən, cháwtŏn
Chendle Hulme *Gtr. M'chester*, 'tʃɪdl 'hjum, cheédl héwm
Cheam *London*, tʃim, cheem
Chearsley *Bucks.*, 'tʃɪərzlɪ, cheérzli
Checker, *f.n.*, 'tʃekər, chéckĕr
Chedburgh *Suffolk*, 'tʃedbərə, chédbŭră
Chediston *Suffolk*, 'tʃedɪstən, chéddistŏn
Chedzoy *Somerset*, 'tʃedzɔɪ, chédzoy
Cheesman, *f.n.*, 'tʃizmən, cheéz-măn
Cheetham, *f.n.*, 'tʃitəm, cheétăm
Cheetham Hill *Gtr. M'chester*, 'tʃitəm 'hɪl, cheétăm híll
Chegwin, *f.n.*, 'tʃegwɪn, chégwin
Cheke, *f.n.*, tʃik, cheek
Cheldon *Devon*, 'tʃeldən, chéldŏn
Chelfham *Devon*, 'tʃelfəm, chélfăm
Chelioti, *f.n.*, ‚kelɪ'outɪ, kelli-óti
Chell, *f.n.*, tʃel, chell
Chellaston *Derby.*, 'tʃeləstən, chélləstŏn
Chelmer, River, *Essex*, 'tʃelmər, chélmĕr. *Appropriate also for Baron* ∼.
Chelmondiston *Suffolk*, 'tʃelmstən, chélmsstŏn
Chelmsford *Essex*, 'tʃelmsfərd, chélmssfŏrd; 'tʃemsfərd, chémssfŏrd
Chelsea *London*, 'tʃelsɪ, chélssi. *Appropriate also for Viscount* ∼.
Chelsham *Surrey*, 'tʃelʃəm, chél-shăm

Chelveston *Northants.*, tʃel-'vestən, chelvésstŏn; 'tʃelstən, chélsstŏn
Chenappa, *f.n.*, 'tʃenəpə, chénnăpă
Chenevix, *f.n.*, 'tʃenəvɪks, chénnĕvicks; 'ʃenəvɪks, shénnĕvicks
Chenevix-Trench, *f.n.*, 'ʃenəvɪks 'trentʃ, shénnĕvicks trénch
Cheney, *f.n.*, 'tʃeɪnɪ, cháyni; 'tʃinɪ, cheéni
Chenies, *f.n.*, 'tʃeɪnɪz, cháyniz
Chenies *Bucks.*, 'tʃeɪnɪz, cháyniz; 'tʃinɪz, cheéniz
Chenil Galleries *London*, 'tʃenɪl, chénnil
Chepstow *Gwent*, 'tʃepstou, chépstŏ
Chequerbent *Gtr. M'chester*, 'tʃekərbent, chéckĕrbent
Chequers *Bucks.*, 'tʃekərz, chéckĕrz
Chere, *f.n.*, ʃɪər, sheer
Cherhill *Wilts.*, 'tʃerɪl, chérril
Cherkley Court *Surrey*, 'tʃɑrklɪ 'kɔrt, chérkli kórt
Cherns, *f.n.*, tʃɜrnz, chernz
Cherrill, *f.n.*, 'tʃerɪl, chérril
Cherwell, Barony of, 'tʃɑrwel, chaárwell
Cherwell, River, *Northants.–Oxon.*, 'tʃɑrwəl, chaárwĕl. *Appropriate also for the admin. dist. of Oxon., which takes its name from the river.*
Chesham *Bucks.*, 'tʃeʃəm, chésh-ăm
Cheshire *Co. name*, 'tʃeʃər, chéshĕr
Cheshunt *Herts.*, 'tʃesənt, chéssŭnt
Chesil Beach *Dorset*, 'tʃezl 'bitʃ, chézzl beétch
Chesneau, *f.n.*, 'tʃesnou, chéssnō
Chesney, *f.n.*, 'tʃeznɪ, chézni
Chesterfield *Derby.*, 'tʃestərfild, chéstĕrfeeld. *Appropriate also for the Earldom of* ∼.
Chester-le-Street *Durham*, 'tʃestər lɪ ‚strit, chéstĕrli street
Chestle, *f.n.*, 'tʃesl, chéssl
Cheswardine *Salop*, 'tʃezwərdaɪn, chézwărdĭn
Chesworth, *f.n.*, 'tʃezwɜrθ, chézwurth
Chetham's Hospital & College *Manchester*, 'tʃitəmz, cheétămz. *Named after Humphrey* ∼ *(1580–1655), a Manchester merchant.*
Chetham-Strode, Warren, *author*, 'wɒrən 'tʃetəm 'stroud, wórrĕn chéttăm strŏd

Chettiscombe *Devon*, 'tʃetɪskəm, chéttiskŏm; 'tʃeskəm, chésskŏm

Chettle, *f.n.*, 'tʃetl, chéttl

Chetwode, *f.n.*, 'tʃetwʊd, chétwŏŏd. *Appropriate also for Baron* ~.

Chetwyn, *f.n.*, 'tʃetwɪn, chétwin

Chetwynd, *f.n.*, 'tʃetwɪnd, chétwind. *Appropriate also for Viscount* ~.

Chevalier, *f.n.*, ʃɪ'vælɪeɪ, shĕváli-ay. *Appropriate for Albert* ~, *music-hall artist.*

Chevallier, *f.n.*, ˌʃevə'lɪər, shevvăleér

Cheveley Park *Cambs.*, 'tʃivlɪ 'pɑrk, cheévli páark

Chevening *Kent*, 'tʃivnɪŋ, cheévning

Chevenix, *f.n.*, 'ʃevənɪks, shévvĕnicks

Chevet *W. Yorks.*, 'tʃevɪt, chévvĕt

Chevington *Suffolk, Northd.*, 'tʃevɪŋtən, chévvingtŏn. *In Northd., appropriate for* ~ *Drift, East* ~, *and* West ~.

Chevins, *f.n.*, 'tʃevɪnz, chévvinz

Cheviot Hills *Borders–Northd.*, 'tʃivɪət, cheéviŏt; 'tʃevɪət, chévvɪŏt. *A theory that the first pronunciation is used north of the Border, and the other on the English side, has been discredited by observation over a long period. The truth appears to be that the former is almost invariably used in the Border country, in both England and Scotland, and that it is speakers from further south who favour the second. A third pronunciation,* 'tʃɪvɪət, chívvɪŏt, *has been heard in Edinburgh for the cloth of the name.*

Chevreau, Cecile, *actress*, sɪ'sil 'ʃevrou, sĕsseél shévrō

Chewton, Viscount, 'tʃutən, chóotŏn

Cheylesmore *W. Midlands*, 'tʃaɪlzmɔr, chílzmor. *Appropriate also for the Barony of* ~.

Cheyne, *f.n.*, 'tʃeɪnɪ, cháyni; tʃeɪn, chayn; tʃɪn, cheen. *The first is appropriate for* ~ Walk *and* ~ Row, Chelsea (*London*).

Chichele, Henry, *15th-c. benefactor and founder of All Souls College, Oxford,* 'tʃɪtʃɪlɪ, chítchĕli

Chicksands *Beds.*, 'tʃɪksændz, chícksandz

Chiddention, *f.n.*, 'tʃɪdənʃən, chíddĕn-shŏn

Chiddingly *E. Sussex*, ˌtʃɪdɪŋ'laɪ, chidding-lí

Chidell, *f.n.*, tʃɪ'del, chidéll

Chideock *Dorset* 'tʃɪdək, chíddŏck

Chidgey, *f.n.*, 'tʃɪdʒɪ, chíjji

Chidlow *Ches.*, 'tʃɪdloʊ, chídlō

Chiedozie, *f.n.*, tʃɪ'doʊzɪ, chidŏzi

Chiene, *f.n.*, ʃin, sheen

Chieveley *Berks.*, 'tʃivlɪ, cheévli

Chigwell *Essex*, 'tʃɪgwəl, chígwĕl

Chilbolton *Hants*, tʃɪl'boʊltən, chilbŏltŏn

Childe, *f.n.*, tʃaɪld, chīld

Childerditch *Essex*, 'tʃɪldərdɪtʃ, chílděrditch

Childerhouse, *f.n.*, 'tʃɪldərhaʊs, chíldĕr-howss

Childers, Erskine, *author*, 'ɜrskɪn 'tʃɪldərz, érsskin chíldĕrz

Childerstone, *f.n.*, 'tʃɪldərstoʊn, chíldĕrstŏn

Childer Thornton *Ches.*, 'tʃɪldər 'θɔrntən, chíldĕr thórntŏn

Child Okeford *Dorset*, 'tʃaɪld 'oʊkfərd, chíld ŏkfŏrd. *A local variation is* 'tʃɪlɪ 'ɒkfərd, chílli óckfŏrd.

Child's Ercall *Salop*, 'tʃaɪldz 'ɑrkl, chíldz áarkl

Childwall *Merseyside*, 'tʃɪlwɔl, chíl-wawl

Childwickbury *Herts.*, 'tʃɪlɪkbərɪ, chíllickbŭri

Childwick Green *Herts.*, 'tʃɪlɪk 'grin, chillick greén

Chilham *Kent*, 'tʃɪləm, chíllăm

Chillesford *Suffolk*, 'tʃɪlzfərd, chílzfŏrd

Chillingham *Northd.*, 'tʃɪlɪŋəm, chílling-ăm

Chiltern Hills *Oxon.–Bucks.– Beds.–Herts.*, 'tʃɪltərn, chíltĕrn

Chilthorne Domer *Somerset*, 'tʃɪlθərn 'doʊmər, chíll-thorn dŏmĕr

Chilton Foliat *Wilts.*, 'tʃɪltən 'foʊlɪət, chíltŏn fŏliăt

Chilton Polden *Somerset*, 'tʃɪltən 'poʊldən, chíltŏn pŏldĕn

Chilver, *f.n.*, 'tʃɪlvər, chílvĕr

Chilvers Coton *Warwicks.*, 'tʃɪlvərz 'koʊtən, chílvĕrz kŏtŏn

Chineham *Hants*, 'tʃɪnəm, chínnăm

Chinnery, *f.n.*, 'tʃɪnərɪ, chínnĕri

Chipchase, *f.n.*, 'tʃɪptʃeɪs, chíptchayss

Chipping Campden *Glos.*, 'tʃɪpɪŋ 'kæmdən, chípping kámdĕn

Chipping Norton *Oxon.*, 'tʃɪpɪŋ 'nɔrtən, chípping nórtŏn

Chipping Sodbury *Avon*, 'tʃɪpɪŋ 'sɒdbərɪ, chípping sódbŭri

Chirbury *Salop*, 'tʃɜrbərɪ, chírbŭri
Chirk *Clwyd*, tʃɜrk, chirk
Chirol, *f.n.*, 'tʃɪrəl, chírrŏl
Chirton *Tyne & Wear, Wilts.*,
'tʃɜrtən, chírtŏn
Chishill, Great *and* Little, *Cambs.*,
'tʃɪzl, chízzl
Chisholm, *f.n.*, 'tʃɪzəm, chízzŏm
Chisledon *Wilts.*, 'tʃɪzldən,
chízzldŏn
Chissell, *f.n.*, tʃɪ'zel, chizéll;
'tʃɪzl, chízzl
Chiswell, *f.n.*, 'tʃɪzwel, chízwel;
'tʃɪzwəl, chízwĕl
Chiswick *London*, 'tʃɪzɪk, chíz-
zick
Chiswick Eyot *London*, 'tʃɪzɪk
'eɪt, chízzick áyt
Chittlehamholt *Devon*, 'tʃɪtləm-
hoʊlt, chíttl-ăm-hōlt
Chivas, *f.n.*, 'ʃɪvæs, shívvass
Chivenor *Devon*, 'tʃɪvnər, chívnŏr
Chivers, *f.n.*, 'tʃɪvərz, chívvĕrz
Choat, *f.n.*, tʃoʊt, chōt
Choate, *f.n.*, tʃoʊt, chōt
Chobham *Surrey*, 'tʃɒbəm,
chóbbăm
Chobham Farm *London*, 'tʃɒbəm,
chóbbăm
Cholderton *Wilts.*, 'tʃoʊldərtən,
chóldĕrtŏn
Cholmeley, *f.n.*, 'tʃʌmlɪ, chúmli
Cholmondeley, *f.n.*, 'tʃʌmlɪ,
chúmli. *Family name of Baron
Delamere.*
Cholmondeley *Ches.*, 'tʃʌmlɪ,
chúmli. *Appropriate also for the
Marquess of* ∼.
Cholmondeston *Ches.*, 'tʃɒmsən,
chómssŏn
Cholsey *Oxon.*, 'tʃoʊlzɪ, chŏlzi
Chomley, *f.n.*, 'tʃʌmlɪ, chúmli
Chorley Wood *Herts.*, 'tʃɔrlɪ 'wʊd,
chórli wŏŏd
Chorlton, *f.n.*, 'tʃɔrltən, chórltŏn
Chorlton-cum-Hardy *Gtr.
M'chester*, 'tʃɔrltən kʌm 'hɑrdɪ,
chórltŏn kum haárdi
Chote, *f.n.*, tʃoʊt, chōt
Chouffot, *f.n.*, 'ʃufoʊ, shoófō
Choveaux, *f.n.*, ʃə'voʊ, shŏvó;
'tʃoʊvoʊ, chóvō
Chovil, *f.n.*, 'tʃoʊvɪl, chóvil
Chown, *f.n.*, tʃaʊn, chown
Chowns, *f.n.*, tʃaʊnz, chownz
Chrimes, *f.n.*, kraɪmz, krīmz
Chrishall *Essex*, 'krɪshɔl, kríss-
-hawl
Christ, *f.n.*, krɪst, krisst
Christian Malford *Wilts.*, 'krɪstjən
'mɔlfərd, kríst-yăn máwlfŏrd
Christie, *f.n.*, 'krɪstɪ, kríssti
Christison, *f.n.*, 'krɪstɪsən,
krístissŏn

Christleton *Ches.*, 'krɪsltən,
kríssltŏn
Christopherson, *f.n.*, krɪs'tɒfərsən,
kristóffĕrsŏn
Christou, *f.n.*, 'krɪstu, krísstoo
Christow *Devon*, 'krɪstoʊ,
krísstō
Chroisg, Loch, *H'land*, xrɔɪsk,
chroysk
Chronnell, *f.n.*, 'krɒnl, krónnl
Chruikhorn, *f.n.*, 'krʊkhɔrn,
krŏŏkhorn
Chrysostom, saint, 'krɪsəstəm,
kríssŏsstŏm
Chryston *S'clyde*, 'kraɪstən,
krísstŏn
Chulmleigh *Devon*, 'tʃʌmlɪ,
chúmli
Churchill, *f.n.*, 'tʃɜrtʃɪl, chúrtchil
Churchman, *f.n.*, 'tʃɜrtʃmən,
chúrtchmăn
Church Stowe *Northants.*,
'tʃɜrtʃ 'stoʊ, chúrtch stŏ
Chute, *f.n.*, tʃut, choot
Chuter, *f.n.*, 'tʃutər, choótĕr
Chuter-Ede, *f.n.*, 'tʃutər 'id,
choótĕr éed. *Pronunciation of
the late Baron* ∼.
Chwilog *Gwynedd*, 'xwilɒg,
chwéelog
Chyandour *Cornwall*, 'ʃaɪəndaʊər,
shí-ăndowr; 'tʃaɪəndaʊər,
chí-ăndowr
Chynoweth, *f.n.*, ʃɪ'noʊəθ,
shinnŏ-ĕth
Chysoyster *Cornwall*, tʃaɪ'sɔstər,
chíssáwstĕr
Ciaran, *Irish C.n.*, 'kɪərən, keérän
Cieslewicz, *f.n.*, si'ezləvɪtʃ,
see-ézzlĕvitch
Cigman, *f.n.*, 'sɪgmən, sígmăn
Cilan *Gwynedd*, 'kɪlən, killän
Cilcain *Clwyd*, 'kɪlken, kílken
Cilcarw *Dyfed*, kɪl'kæru,
kilkárroo
Cilcennin *Dyfed*, kɪl'kenɪn,
kilkénnin. *Appropriate also for
the Viscountcy of* ∼.
Cilcewydd *Powys*, kɪl'kewɪð,
kilké-with
Cilfrew *W. Glam.*, ˌkɪlvrɪ'u,
kilvri-oo
Cilfynydd *Mid Glam.*, kɪl'vʌnɪð,
kilvúnnith
Cilgerran *Dyfed*, kɪl'gerən,
kilgérrän
Cilie Aeron *Dyfed*, 'kɪljə 'aɪrɒn,
kíl-yĕ íron
Ciliene *Powys*, kɪl'jenə, kil-
-yénnĕ
Cilmery, *also spelt* Cilmeri,
Powys, kɪl'merɪ, kilmérri
Cilrhedyn *Dyfed*, kɪl'hredɪn,
kilréddin

Cilshafe Uchaf *Dyfed*, kıl'ʃævə
'ıxəv, kil-shávvě íchăv
Cilybebyll *W. Glam.*, ‚kılə'bebıl,
killăbébbihl
Cil-y-Cwm *Dyfed*, ‚kılə'kom,
killăkŏŏm
Cil-y-Maenllwyd *Dyfed*, ‚kılə-
'mænloıd, killămán-hlŏŏid
Cimla *W. Glam.*, 'kımlə, kímlă
Cinque Ports *E. Sussex, Kent*,
'sıŋk pɔrts, sínk ports. *This is
the collective name for the towns
of Hastings, Romney, Hythe,
Dover and Sandwich, which
combined for defensive purposes.
Other towns later joined, so that
there are now more than the
original five of the name.*
Cippenham *Berks.*, 'sıpənəm,
síppěnăm
Cipriani, *18th-c. Florentine-
English painter*, ‚sıprı'ɑnı,
sipri-aʹani
Cirencester *Glos.*, 'saıərənsestər,
sírěnssesstěr; 'sısıtər, síssitěr.
*The latter, although no longer
commonly heard, has not entirely
disappeared from use. For some,
it is particularly associated with
one of the older spellings,
Ciceter.*
Ciro's *London club and restaurant*,
'sıərou, seérŏ
Ciste Dubh, *also spelt **Dhubh**,
H'land*, 'kıʃtə 'du, kíshtě doʹo
Citrine, *f.n.*, sı'trin, sitreʹen.
Appropriate also for Baron ~.
Clachan *Skye*, 'klæxən,
kláchăn
Clachtoll *H'land*, 'klæx'toʊl,
klách-tŏl
Clackmannan *Central*, klæk-
'mænən, klackmánnăn;
klək'mænən, klăkmánnăn
Claddagh *Co. Fermanagh*, 'klædə,
kláddă
Clady *Co. Tyrone*, 'klædı, kláddi
Clady *Circuit Belfast*, 'klædı,
kláddi
Cladymore *Co. Armagh*, ‚klædı-
'mɔr, kladdimór
Claerwen, *River, Dyfed–Powys*,
'klaıərwen, klír-wen
Clagh Ouyre *I. of Man*, 'klæk
'aʊər, kláck ówr
Clague, *f.n.*, kleıg, klayg; kleg,
kleg
Clancarty, *Earl of*, klæn'kɑrtı,
klan-kaʹarti
Clandeboye *Co. Down*, 'klændı-
bɔı, klándéboy. *Appropriate
also for Viscount ~.*
Clanmorris, *Baron*, klæn'mɒrıs,
klanmórriss

Clannaborough *Devon*, 'klænəbərə,
klánnăbŭră
Clanricarde, *f.n.*, klæn'rıkərd,
klanríckărd. *Appropriate also
for the Earl of ~.*
Clanwilliam, *Earl of*, klæn'wıljəm,
klanwill-yăm
Clapham *London, N. Yorks.*,
'klæpəm, kláppăm
Clapshoe, *f.n.*, 'klæpʃu, kláp-shoo
Clapworthy *Devon*, 'klæpərı,
kláppěri
Clarabut, *f.n.*, 'klærəbʌt, klárră-
but
Clarach *Dyfed*, 'klærəx, klárrăch
Clarbeston *Dyfed*, 'klɑrbəstən,
klaʹarběstŏn
Clare, *f.n.*, kleər, klair
Clarendon, *Earl of*, 'klærəndən,
klárrěndŏn
Clarina, *Barony of*, klə'raınə,
klărínă
Claringbull, *f.n.*, 'klærıŋbʊl,
klárringbŏŏl
Clarke, *f.n.*, klɑrk, klaark
Claro, *f.n.*, 'kleərou, kláirŏ
Claro *Barracks N. Yorks.*,
'kleərou, kláirŏ
Clatteringshaws *Loch D. & G.*,
'klætərıŋʃɔz, kláttěring-shawz
Claudy *Co. Derry*, 'klɔdı, kláwdi
Claughton, *f.n.*, 'klɒtən, kláwtŏn
Claughton *Lancs.*, 'klæftən,
kláfftŏn. *Appropriate for the
name of the village in the Lune
valley.*
Claughton *Merseyside*, 'klɒtən,
kláwtŏn. *Appropriate also for
Baron Evans of ~.*
Claughton-on-Brock *Lancs.*,
'klaıtən ɒn 'brɒk, klíftŏn on
bróck
Clausen, *f.n.*, 'klaʊsən, klówssěn;
'klɔsən, kláwssěn. *The first is
appropriate for Sir George ~
(1852–1944), landscape and
figure painter.*
Clauson, *f.n.*, 'klɔsən, kláwssŏn
Claverdon *Warwicks.*, 'klævərdən,
klávvěrdŏn; 'klɑrdən, klaʹardŏn
Claverham *Avon*, 'klævərəm,
klávvěrăm
Claverhouse, *f.n.*, 'kleıvərhaʊs,
kláyvěr-howss
Claverhouse *Tayside*, 'kleıvərhaʊs, kláyvěr-howss. *Appropriate also for John Graham of ~,
Scottish soldier.*
Clavering, *f.n.*, 'klævərıŋ,
klávvěring
Clavering *Essex*, 'kleıvərıŋ,
kláyvěring
Claverley *Salop*, 'klævərlı,
klávvěrli

Claverton *Avon*, 'klævərtən,
klávvĕrtŏn. *Appropriate also
for ~ Down.*
Clayhidon *Devon*, 'kleɪhaɪdən,
kláy-hídŏn
Cleadon *Tyne and Wear*, 'klidən,
kleédŏn
Cleal, *f.n.*, klil, kleel
Cleanthous, *f.n.*, klɪ'ænθəs, kli-
-ánthŭss
Clearwell *Glos.*, 'klɪər'wel,
kleérwéll; klɪər'wel, kleerwéll;
'klɪərwel, kleérwell
Cleary, *f.n.*, 'klɪərɪ, kleéri
Cleasby, *f.n.*, 'klizbɪ, kleézbi
Clease, *f.n.*, klis, kleess
Cleather, *f.n.*, 'kleðər, kléthĕr
Cleator *Cumbria*, 'klitər, kleétŏr
Cleckheaton *W. Yorks.*, klek-
'hitən, kleck-heétŏn
Cleddau, *River*, *Dyfed*, 'kleðaɪ,
kléthī
Cledwyn, *Welsh C.n.*, 'kledwɪn,
klédwin. *Appropriate also for
Baron ~ of Penrhos.*
Cleese, *f.n.*, kliz, kleez
Cleethorpes *Humberside*,
'kliθɔrps, kleé-thorps
Clegyr *Dyfed*, 'klegər, kléggŭr
Clehonger *H. & W.*, 'klɒŋgər,
klóng-gĕr
Cleland, *f.n.*, 'klelənd, kléllánd;
'klilənd, kleéländ
Cleland *S'clyde*, 'klelənd, kléllánd
Cleland House *London*, 'klilənd,
kleéländ
Clemak, *f.n.*, 'klimæk, kleémack
Clemenger, *f.n.*, 'klemɪndʒər,
klémmĕnjĕr
Clemitson, *f.n.*, 'klemɪtsən,
klémmitsŏn
Clemmow, *f.n.*, 'klemoʊ, klémmō
Clemo, *f.n.*, 'klemoʊ, klémmō
Clenchwarton *Norfolk*, 'klenʃ-
wɔrtən, klénshwawrtŏn
Clennell, *f.n.*, klə'nel, klĕnéll
Cleobury, *f.n.*, 'kloʊbərɪ, klóbŭri;
'klibərɪ, kleébŭri
Cleobury Mortimer *Salop*, 'klibərɪ
'mɔrtɪmər, klíbbŭri mórtimĕr
Cleobury North *Salop*, 'klibərɪ
'nɔrθ, klíbbŭri nórth
Clerici, *f.n.*, 'klerɪsɪ, klérrissi
Clerk, *f.n.*, klɑrk, klaark
Clerke, *f.n.*, klɑrk, klaark
Clervaux *N. Yorks.*, 'klɛərvɒks,
kláirvawks
Clery, *f.n.*, 'klɪərɪ, kleéri
Clettraval *N. Uist*, 'kletrəvæl,
kléttrăval
Clevedon *Avon*, 'klivdən,
kleévdŏn
Cleveleys *Lancs.*, 'klivlɪz,
kleévliz

Cleverdon, *f.n.*, 'klevərdən,
klévvĕrdŏn
Cleverley, *f.n.*, 'klevərlɪ,
klévvĕrli
Cleverly, *f.n.*, 'klevərlɪ, klévvĕrli
Clewlow, *f.n.*, 'kluloʊ, kloólō
Cley *Norfolk*, klaɪ, klī; kleɪ, klay
Clibborn, *f.n.*, 'klɪbɔrn, klíbborn
Cliburn *Cumbria*, 'klaɪbərn,
klíbŭrn
Clickhimin, *Loch*, *Shetland*,
'klɪkɪmɪn, klíckimin
Cliddesden *Hants*, 'klɪdɪzdən,
klíddĕzdĕn
Clifford, *C.n. and f.n.*, 'klɪfərd,
klíffŏrd
Cliffords Mesne *Glos.*, 'klɪfərdz
'min, klíffŏrdz meén
Clifton of Leighton Bromswold,
Baron, 'klɪftən əv 'leɪtən
'brʌmzwoʊld, klíftŏn ŏv láytŏn
brúmzwōld
Clifton Reynes *Bucks.*, 'klɪftən
'reɪnz, klíftŏn ráynz
Clilverd, *f.n.*, 'klɪvərd, klívvĕrd
Climie, *f.n.*, 'klaɪmɪ, klími
Clipsham *Leics.*, 'klɪpʃəm, klíp-
-shăm; 'klɪpshəm, klíps-hăm
Clipstone *Notts.*, 'klɪpstoʊn,
klípstŏn
Clitheroe *Lancs.*, 'klɪðəroʊ,
klíthĕrō. *Appropriate also for
Baron ~.*
Clitherow, *f.n.*, 'klɪðəroʊ,
klíthĕrō
Cliveden *Bucks.*, 'klɪvdən,
klívdĕn
Cliviger *Lancs.*, 'klɪvɪdʒər,
klívvijĕr
Cloan *Tayside*, kloʊn, klōn
Clocaenog *Clwyd*, kloʊ'kaɪnɒg,
klōkínog
Clode, *f.n.*, kloʊd, klōd
Cloete, *f.n.*, kloʊ'itɪ, klō-eéti;
'klutɪ, kloóti
Cloford *Avon*, 'kloʊfərd, klófŏrd
Clogher, *f.n.*, 'klɒxər, klóchĕr
Clogher *Co. Tyrone*, 'klɒxər,
klóchĕr
Clogwyn Du'r Arddu *Gwynedd*,
kloʊ'gʊɪn dɪər 'arðɪ, klōgoó-in
deer aarthee
Clogwyn-y-Person *Gwynedd*,
kloʊ'gʊɪn ə 'pɛərsɒn, klōgoó-in
ă páirsson
Clompus, *f.n.*, 'klɒmpəs, klómpŭss
Clonaneese *Co. Tyrone*, ˌklɒnə-
'nis, klonnăneéss
Clonard *Co. Antrim*, 'klɒnərd,
klónnărd
Clonbrock, *f.n.*, klɒn'brɒk,
klonbróck
Cloncurry, *f.n.*, klɒn'kʌrɪ, klon-
-kúrri

Clonmacate *Co. Armagh*, ˌklɒnmə'keɪt, klon-mǎkáyt
Clonmell, *f.n.*, klɒn'mel, klon-méll
Clonmore, *f.n.*, klɒn'mɔr, klon-mór
Clontivrim *Co. Fermanagh*, klɒn'tɪvrɪm, klontívvrim
Clontoe *Co. Tyrone*, klʌn'toʊ, kluntṓ. *Also spelt* **Cluntoe**
Clopet, *f.n.*, 'kloʊpeɪ, klṓpay
Clophill *Beds.*, 'klɒphɪl, klóp-hill
Close, *f.n.*, kloʊs, klōss
Clother, *f.n.*, 'kloʊðər, klṓthĕr
Clothier, *f.n.*, 'kloʊðɪər, klṓthiĕr
Clough, *f.n.*, klʌf, kluff
Clough *Co. Down*, klɒx, kloch
Clough, River, *Cumbria*, klʌf, kluff
Clougha Pike *Lancs.*, 'klɒfə 'paɪk, klóffǎ pík
Cloughenery *Co. Tyrone*, ˌklɒxə-'nɛərɪ, klochĕnáiri
Cloughey *Co. Down*, 'klɒxɪ, klóchi
Clough Fold *Lancs.*, 'klʌf 'foʊld, klúff fṓld
Cloughmills *Co. Antrim*, klɒx-'mɪlz, klochmíllz
Cloughogue *Co. Armagh*, klɒx-'oʊg, klochṓg
Cloughton *N. Yorks.*, 'klaʊtən, klówtŏn; 'kloʊtən, klṓtŏn
Clousta *Shetland*, 'klustə, kloóstǎ
Clouston, *f.n.*, 'klustən, kloósstŏn; 'klaʊstən, klówsstŏn
Clouston, J. Storer, *author*, 'stɔrər 'klustən, stáwrĕr kloósstŏn
Clovelly *Devon*, klə'velɪ, klŏvélli
Clovenfords *Borders*, ˌkloʊvən-'fɔrdz, klōvĕnfórdz
Cloverley *Salop*, 'klɒvərlɪ, klóvvĕrli
Clow, *f.n.*, kloʊ, klō
Clowes, *f.n.*, klaʊz, klowz; kluz, klooz
Clowne *Derby.*, klaʊn, klown
Cluanie, Loch, *H'land*, 'klunɪ, kloóni; 'kluənɪ, kloó-äni
Clubbe, *f.n.*, klʌb, klubb
Clucas, *f.n.*, 'klukəs, kloókǎss
Clulow, *f.n.*, 'kluloʊ, kloólō
Clumber Park *Notts.*, 'klʌmbər 'pɑrk, klúmbĕr paárk. *This gives its name to the Clumber spaniel.*
Clun *Salop*, klʌn, klun. *Appropriate also for Baron* ~, *and for the River* ~ *which flows through Shropshire and joins the River Teme.*
Clunbury *Salop*, 'klʌnbərɪ, klúnbŭri
Clunes, *H'land*, klunz, kloonz
Clungunford *Salop*, klʌn'gʌnfərd, klun-gúnfŏrd

Clunie, *f.n.*, 'klunɪ, kloóni
Clunie, *Grampian, Tayside*, 'klunɪ, kloóni
Clunies, *f.n.*, 'klunɪz, kloóniz
Cluntoe *Co. Tyrone*, klʌn'toʊ, kluntṓ. *Also spelt* **Clontoe**
Clunton *Salop*, 'klʌntən, klúntŏn
Cluse, *f.n.*, kluz, klooz
Clutsam, *f.n.*, 'klʌtsəm, klútsǎm
Clutton *Avon*, 'klʌtən, klúttŏn
Clwyd, River, *Clwyd*, 'kluɪd, kloō-id. *Appropriate also for the county name, which is taken from that of the river, and for Baron* ~.
Clwydian Range *Clwyd*, kluˈɪdɪən, kloō-íddiän
Clydach *Gwent, W. Glam.*, 'klɪdəx, klíddǎch; 'klʌdəx, klúddǎch. *Appropriate also for the River* ~ *(Dyfed),* ~ *Terrace (Gwent), and* ~ *Vale (Mid Glam.).*
Clyde, River, *S'clyde*, klaɪd, klīd
Clydesmuir, Baron, 'klaɪdzmjʊər, klídzmyoōr
Clyffe Pypard *Wilts.*, 'klɪf 'paɪpərd, klíff pípǎrd
Clynder *S'clyde*, 'klɪndər, klíndĕr
Clynderwen, *also spelt* **Clunderwen,** *Dyfed*, klɪn'dɛərwən, klindáirwĕn
Clyne *W. Glam.*, klaɪn, klīn
Clynnog *Gwynedd*, 'klʌnɒg, klúnnog
Clynnogfawr *Gwynedd*, 'klʌnɒg-'vaʊər, klúnnogvówr
Clypse Circuit *I. of Man*, klɪps, klips
Clyro *Powys*, 'klaɪroʊ, klírō
Clyst, River, *Devon*, klɪst, klisst
Clywedog Valley *Dyfed*, klɪ-'wedɒg, kliwéddog
Cnwch Coch *Dyfed*, 'knux 'koʊx, knoóch kŏch. *Initial -k is pronounced.*
Coad, *f.n.*, koʊd, kōd
Coade, *f.n.*, koʊd, kōd. *Appropriate also for the building-stone mixture known as* ~ *stone, associated in the 18th c. with Mrs Eleanor* ~.
Coady, *f.n.*, 'koʊdɪ, kṓdi
Coagh *Co. Tyrone*, koʊx, kōch
Coaker, *f.n.*, 'koʊkər, kṓkĕr
Coakley, *f.n.*, 'koʊklɪ, kṓkli
Coalbrookdale *Salop*, 'koʊlbrʊk-'deɪl, kṓlbroōk-dáyl
Coalisland *Co. Tyrone*, koʊl-'aɪlənd, kōlíländ
Coalsnaughton *Central*, koʊlz-'nɔtən, kōlznáwtŏn
Coase, *f.n.*, koʊz, kōz

Coate *Wilts.*, koʊt, kōt. *Appropriate for both places of this name in Wilts.*

Coatesgate *D. & G.*, 'koʊts'geɪt, kŏts-gáyt

Coatham *Cleveland*, 'koʊtəm, kŏtăm

Cobairdy *Grampian*, koʊ'bɛərdɪ, kōbáirdi

Cobban, *f.n.*, 'kɒbən, kóbbăn

Cobbold, *f.n.*, 'kɒboʊld, kóbbōld. *Appropriate also for Baron ～.*

Coberley *Glos.*, 'kʌbərlɪ, kúbbĕrli

Coberman, *f.n.*, 'koʊbərmən, kŏbĕrmän

Cobham, *f.n.*, 'kɒbəm, kóbbăm

Cobley, *f.n.*, 'kɒblɪ, kóbbli

Cobrin, *f.n.*, 'kɒbrɪn, kóbbrin

Cochran, *f.n.*, 'kɒxrən, kóchrăn; 'kɒkrən, kóckrăn

Cochrane, *f.n.*, 'kɒxrən, kóchrăn; 'kɒkrən, kóckrăn

Cockayne, *f.n.*, kɒ'keɪn, kockáyn

Cock Bridge *Grampian*, 'kɒk brɪdʒ, kóck brij

Cockburn, *f.n.*, 'koʊbərn, kŏbŭrn; 'koʊbərn, kóburn

Cockburnspath *Borders*, 'koʊbərnz'pɑθ, kŏbŭrnzpáath

Cockcroft, *f.n.*, 'kɒkkrɒft, kóck-kroft; 'koʊkrɒft, kŏkroft. *The first is appropriate for Sir John ～, physicist.*

Cocke, *f.n.*, koʊk, kōk

Cockell, *f.n.*, 'kɒkl, kóckl

Cockenzie *Lothian*, kə'kenzɪ, kŏkénzi

Cockerell, *f.n.*, 'kɒkərəl, kóckĕrĕl

Cockerham, *f.n.*, 'kɒkərəm, kóckĕrăm

Cockerington, *Lincs.*, 'kɒkərɪŋtən, kóckĕringtŏn

Cockerline, *f.n.*, 'kɒkərlaɪn, kóckĕrlīn

Cockermouth *Cumbria*, 'kɒkərmaʊθ, kóckĕr-mowth; 'kɒkərməθ, kóckĕr-mŭth

Cockernhoe Green *Herts.*, 'kɒkərnhoʊ, kóckĕrn-hō

Cockett *W. Glam.*, 'kɒkɪt, kóckĕt

Cockfield, *f.n.*, 'koʊfild, kŏ-feeld

Cockley Cley *Norfolk*, 'kɒklɪ 'klaɪ, kóckli klī

Cockram, *f.n.*, 'kɒkrəm, kóckrăm

Cockroft, *f.n.*, 'kɒkrɒft, kóckroft; 'koʊkrɒft, kŏkroft

Cocks, *f.n.*, kɒks, kocks

Cockshott, *f.n.*, 'koʊʃɒt, kŏ-shot

Cockshut, *f.n.*, 'kɒkʃʌt, kóck-shut; 'koʊʃu, kŏ-shoo

Cockshutt *Salop*, 'kɒkʃʌt, kóck-shut

Codham Hall *Essex*, 'kɒdəm, kóddăm

Codicote *Herts.*, 'kɒdɪkət, kóddikŏt

Codsall *Staffs.*, 'kɒdsl, kódssl

Coe, *f.n.*, koʊ, kō

Coed Dolgarrog *Gwynedd*, ˌkɔɪd dɒl'gɛrɒg, koyd dolgárrog

Coed-ffranc *W. Glam.*, kɔɪd-'fræŋk, koydfránk

Coed Gorswen *Gwynedd*, ˌkɔɪd gɔrs'wen, koyd gorss-wén

Coedpenmaen *Mid Glam.*, ˌkɔɪdpen'maɪn, koyd-pen-mín

Coed Poeth *Clwyd*, kɔɪd 'pɔɪθ, koyd póyth

Coed Rheidol Nature Reserve *Dyfed*, kɔɪd 'hraɪdɒl, koyd rídol

Coed Tremadoc Nature Reserve *Gwynedd*, ˌkɔɪd trɪ'mædɒk, koyd trĕmáddock

Coed-y-Brenin Forest *Gwynedd*, ˌkɔɪdə'brenɪn, koyd-ă-brénnin

Coegnant Colliery *Mid Glam.*, 'kɔɪgnænt, kóyg-nant

Coetmore, *f.n.*, 'kɔɪtmɔr, kóytmor

Coffill, *f.n.*, 'kɒfɪl, kóffil

Cogan Pill *S. Glam.*, 'koʊgən 'pɪl, kŏgăn píll

Cogenhoe, *f.n.*, 'kʊknoʊ, kŏŏknō

Cogenhoe *Northants.*, 'kʊknoʊ, kŏŏknō; 'koʊgənhoʊ, kŏgĕn-hō

Cogers, The, *London inn*, 'kɒdʒərz, kójjĕrz

Coggeshall, *f.n.*, 'kɒgzɒl, kógzawl

Coggeshall *Essex*, 'kɒgɪʃl, kóggĕshl; 'kɒksl, kócksl

Coggle, *f.n.*, 'kɒgl, kóggl

Coghill, *f.n.*, 'kɒghɪl, kóg-hil

Coghlan, *f.n.*, 'koʊlən, kŏlăn

Cogill, *f.n.*, 'koʊgɪl, kŏgil

Cogry *Co. Antrim*, 'kɒgrɪ, kógri

Cohen, *f.n.*, 'koʊɪn, kŏ-ĕn

Cohn, *f.n.*, koʊn, kōn

Coinneach Odhar, *the Brahan Seer*, 'kɒnjəx 'oʊər, kón-yăch ŏ-ĕr

Coity *Mid Glam.*, 'kɔɪtɪ, kóyti

Cokayne, *f.n.*, kɒ'keɪn, kockáyn

Coke, *f.n.*, kʊk, kŏŏk; koʊk, kōk. *The first is appropriate for the Earl of Leicester's family name.*

Colan *Cornwall*, 'kɒlən, kóllăn

Colaton Raleigh *Devon*, 'kɒlətən 'rɒlɪ, kóllătŏn ráwli

Colborn, *f.n.*, 'koʊbərn, kŏbŭrn

Colborne, *f.n.*, 'koʊlbərn, kŏl-bŭrn; 'kɒlbərn, kólborn

Colbren *W. Glam.*, 'kɒlbren, kólbren

Colbrook *Powys*, 'koʊlbrʊk, kŏlbrŏŏk

Colbury *Hants.*, 'koʊlbərɪ, kŏlbŭri

Colby, *f.n.*, 'kɒlbɪ, kólbi

Colchester *Essex*, 'koʊltʃəstər, kŏltchĕstĕr

Colclough, f.n., 'koʊlklʌf kṓl-kluff; 'koʊklɪ, kṓkli
Cold Hesledon Durham, 'koʊld 'hesldən, kṓld héssldŏn
Cold Hiendley W. Yorks., 'koʊld 'hindlɪ, kṓld heéndli
Coldingham Borders, 'koʊldɪŋəm, kṓlding-äm
Coldred Kent, 'koʊldrɪd, kṓldrĕd
Coldrick, f.n., 'koʊldrɪk, kṓldrick
Coldwaltham W. Sussex, 'koʊld-'wɔlθəm, kṓldwáwl-thäm
Coleclough, f.n., 'koʊlklaʊ, kṓlklow; 'koʊlklʌf, kṓlkluff
Coleford Glos., 'koʊlfərd, kṓl-fŏrd
Colehan, f.n., 'koʊləhən, kṓlĕhăn
Colehill Dorset, 'kɒlhɪl, kól-hil; 'koʊlhɪl, kṓl-hil
Coleman, f.n., 'koʊlmən, kṓlmän
Coleorton Leics., kɒl'ɔrtən, kolórtŏn
Coleraine Co. Derry, koʊl'reɪn, kōlráyn. Appropriate also for Baron ∼.
Coleridge, f.n., 'koʊlrɪdʒ, kṓlrij. Appropriate also for Baron ∼.
Coleridge-Taylor, Avril, composer, 'ævrɪl 'koʊlərɪdʒ 'teɪlər, ávreel kṓlĕrij táylŏr
Colerne Wilts., 'kɒlərn, kóllĕrn; 'kʌlərn, kúllĕrn; kə'lɜrn, kŏlérn. The third is the pronunciation used by RAF personnel for their airfield.
Coleshill, f.n., 'koʊlzhɪl, kṓlz-hill
Coleshill Oxon., 'koʊlzhɪl, kṓlz-hil
Colet, f.n., 'kɒlɪt, kóllĕt
Colfox, f.n., 'koʊlfɒks, kṓlfocks
Colgan, f.n.., 'kɒlgən, kólgän
Colgrain, Baron, 'kɒlgreɪn, kólgrayn
Colin, C.n. and f.n., 'kɒlɪn, kóllin
Colinton Edinburgh, 'kɒlɪntən, kóllintŏn
Colintraive S'clyde, ˌkɒlɪn'traɪv, kollintrív
Coll Island S'clyde, kɒl, kol
Collard, f.n., 'kɒlɑrd, kóllaard
Collaro, f.n., kə'lɑroʊ, kŏlaárō
Colleano, f.n., kə'lɪnoʊ, kŏleénō
Colleau, f.n., 'kɒloʊ, kóllō
Collender, f.n., 'kɒlɪndər, kóllĕndĕr
Colles, f.n., 'kɒlɪs, kólliss
Collessie Fife, kə'lesɪ, kŏléssi
Collet, f.n., 'kɒlɪt, kóllĕt
Colley, f.n., 'kɒlɪ, kólli
Collier, f.n., 'kɒlɪər, kólli-ĕr
Collingbourne Ducis Wilts., 'kɒlɪŋbɔrn 'djusɪs, kólling-born déwsiss
Collinge, f.n., 'kɒlɪndʒ, kóllinj

Collingham W. Yorks., 'kɒlɪŋəm, kólling-äm
Collinson, f.n., 'kɒlɪnsən, kóllinsŏn
Collison, f.n., 'kɒlɪsən, kóllissŏn
Collopy, f.n., 'kɒləpɪ, kóllŏpi
Collow, f.n., 'kɒloʊ, kóllō
Colman, f.n., 'kɒlmən, kólmăn; 'koʊlmən, kṓlmän
Colmanell, saint, ˌkɒlmə'nel, kolmănéll
Colmer, f.n., 'kɒlmər, kól-mĕr
Colmonell S'clyde, ˌkɒlmɒ'nel, kolmonnéll
Colnaghi London fine art dealers, kɒl'nagɪ, kolnaági
Colnbrook Bucks., 'koʊnbrʊk, kṓnbrōōk; 'koʊlnbrʊk, kṓln-brōōk
Colne, f.n., koʊn, kōn
Colne, Lancs., koʊn, kōn
Colne, River, W. Yorks., koʊn, kōn. Appropriate also for the ∼ Valley Parliamentary Division.
Colne Engaine Essex, ˌkoʊn ən'geɪn, kōn ĕn-gáyn
Colney Norfolk, 'koʊnɪ, kṓni
Colney Heath Herts., 'koʊnɪ 'hiθ, kṓni heéth
Coln St. Aldwyn Glos., 'koʊn snt 'ɔldwɪn, kṓn sĭnt áwldwin
Colomb, f.n., 'kɒləm, kóllŏm; 'kɒlɒm, kóllom
Colonsay Island, S'clyde, 'kɒlən-zeɪ, kóllŏnzay
Colquhoun, f.n., kə'hun, kŏ-hoón
Colsell, f.n., 'koʊlsl, kṓlssl
Colsterworth Lincs., 'koʊlstər-wərθ, kṓlsstĕrwŭrth
Colston, f.n., 'koʊlstən, kṓlsstŏn
Colston Basset, Notts., 'koʊlstən 'bæsɪt, kṓlsstŏn bássĕt
Colston Hall, Bristol, 'koʊlstən, kṓlsstŏn
Coltart, f.n., 'koʊltɑrt, kṓltaart
Coltishall Norfolk, 'koʊltɪʃəl, kṓlti-shawl; 'koʊltɪʃɔl, kṓltiss-hawl; 'koʊltɪsɔl, kṓltiss-awl; 'koʊltɪʃl, kṓltishl; 'koʊlsl, kṓlssl. The last of these is now considered old-fashioned.
Colum, f.n., 'kɒləm, kóllŭm
Columba, saint, kə'lʌmbə, kŏlúmbă
Colvend D. & G., kɒlv'end, kolvénd
Colville, f.n., 'kɒlvɪl, kólvil
Colville of Culross, Viscount, 'kɒlvɪl əv 'kurɒs, kólvil ŏv koó-ross
Colvin, f.n., 'kɒlvɪn, kólvin
Colwall H. & W., 'kɒlwəl, kólwăl
Colwich Staffs., 'kɒlwɪtʃ, kól-witch
Colwick Notts., 'kɒlɪk, kóllick

Colworth W. Sussex, 'kɒlwɜrθ, kólwurth

Colwyn, Baron, 'kɒlwɪn, kólwin

Colwyn Bay Clwyd, 'kɒlwɪn 'beɪ, kólwin báy

Colyford Devon, 'kɒlɪfərd, kólliförd

Colyton Devon, 'kɒlɪtən, kóllitŏn. Appropriate also for Baron ∼.

Coman, f.n., 'koʊmən, kŏmăn

Combe, f.n., kum, koom; koʊm, kŏm

Combe Cross Devon, 'kum 'krɒs, koʻom króss

Combe in Teignhead, also spelt **Combeinteignhead,** Devon, 'kum ɪn 'tinhed, koʻom in teen-hed

Comben, f.n., 'kɒmbən, kómbĕn

Combepyne, see **Combpyne,** Devon

Comber, f.n., 'kɒmbər, kómbĕr

Comber Co. Down, 'kʌmbər, kúmbĕr

Comberbach Ches., 'kʌmbərbætʃ, kúmbĕrbatch

Combermere, Viscount, 'kʌmbərmɪər, kúmbĕrmeer. Hence also for ∼ Barracks, Windsor (Berks.).

Comberti, f.n., kɒm'bɛərtɪ, kombáirti

Comberton Cambs., 'kɒmbərtən, kómbĕrtŏn

Comboy, f.n., 'kɒmbɔɪ, kómboy

Combpyne, also spelt **Combepyne,** Devon, 'kum'paɪn, koʻom-pín

Combrook Warwicks., 'kɒmbrʊk, kómbrŏŏk

Combwich Somerset, 'kʌmɪdʒ, kúmmij; 'kʌmɪtʃ, kúmmitch; 'kumɪdʒ, koʻomij; 'kumɪtʃ, koʻomitch

Comby, f.n., 'kɒmbɪ, kómbi

Comer, f.n., 'koʊmər, kŏmĕr

Comerford, f.n., 'kɒmərfərd, kómmĕrförd

Comeskey, f.n., kə'meskɪ, kŏméski

Comgall, saint, 'kɒmgəl, kómgăl

Comiston Lothian, 'kɒmɪstən, kómmistŏn

Compton, f.n., 'kʌmptən, kúmptŏn; 'kɒmptən, kómptŏn. The first is correct for the Marquess of Northampton's family name. It is also appropriate for Sir ∼ Mackenzie, author, and for Fay ∼, actress.

Compton Berks., 'kɒmptən, kómptŏn

Compton Hants, 'kʌmptən, kúmptŏn

Compton-Burnett, Ivy, author, 'kʌmptən 'bɜrnɪt, kúmptŏn búrnĕt

Compton Castle Devon, 'kɒmptən 'kɑsl, kómptŏn kaʻassl

Compton Chamberlayne Wilts., 'kɒmptən 'tʃeɪmbərlɪn, kómptŏn cháymbĕrlin

Compton Down Hants, 'kɒmptən 'daʊn, kómptŏn dówn

Compton Pauncefoot Somerset, 'kɒmptən 'pɔnsfʊt, kómptŏn páwnssfŏŏt

Compton Valence Dorset, 'kɒmptən 'væləns, kómptŏn válĕnss

Compton Wynyates, also spelt **Wyniates, Winyates,** Warwicks., 'kɒmptən 'wɪnjeɪts, kómptŏn wín-yayts; 'kʌmptən 'wɪnjeɪts, kúmptŏn wín-yayts. The first is the local village pronunciation. The second is used, appropriately, by the Marquess of Northampton for his family seat.

Comrie, f.n., 'kɒmrɪ, kómri

Comrie Fife, Tayside, 'kɒmrɪ, kómri

Comyn, f.n., 'kʌmɪn, kúmmin

Comyns, f.n., 'kʌmɪnz, kúmminz

Conacher, f.n., 'kɒnəxər, kónnăchĕr

Conan, C.n. and f.n., 'kɒnən, kónnăn; 'koʊnən, kŏnăn

Conan Doyle, Sir Arthur, author, 'koʊnən 'dɔɪl, kŏnăn dóyl. This is the family pronunciation, although he is also popularly known as 'kɒnən, kónnăn.

Conant, f.n., 'kɒnənt, kónnănt; 'koʊnənt, kŏnănt

Conbeer, f.n., 'kɒnbɪər, kónbeer

Concannon, f.n., kɒn'kænən, kon-kánnŏn

Condell, f.n., kɒn'del, kondéll

Condicote Glos., 'kɒndɪkət, kóndikŏt

Condorrat S'clyde, kən'dɒrət, köndórrăt

Condover Salop, 'kʌndoʊvər, kúndŏvĕr

Condra, f.n., 'kɒndrə, kóndră

Conesford, Barony of, 'kɒnɪsfərd, kónnĕsförd

Coneygarth Northd., 'koʊnɪgɑrθ, kŏni-gaarth

Coneysthorpe N. Yorks., 'kʌnɪs-θərp, kúnniss-thorp; 'koʊnɪs-θərp, kŏniss-thorp

Conger Hill Beds., 'kɒŋgər, kóng-gĕr

Congleton Ches., 'kɒŋgltən, kóng-gltŏn. Appropriate also for Baron ∼.

Congresbury *Avon*, 'kɒŋzbrı, kóŋgzbri; 'kumzbərı, koómzbūri. *The first is the local pronunciation; the other is said to originate in Bristol.*

Conibear, *f.n.*, 'koʊnıbɛər, kónibair

Coningham, *f.n.*, 'kʌnıŋəm, kúnning-ăm

Coningsby *Lincs.*, 'kɒnıŋzbı, kónningzbi; 'kʌnıŋzbı, kúnningzbi

Conington *Cambs.*, 'kɒnıŋtən, kónning-tŏn

Conisbee, *f.n.*, 'kɒnızbı, kónnizbi

Conisbrough, *also spelt* Conisborough, *S. Yorks.*, 'kɒnısbərə, kónnissbŭră

Coniscliffe, High *and* Low, *Durham*, 'kɒnısklıf, kónniss-kliff

Conisholme *Lincs.*, 'kɒnıshoʊm, kónniss-hōm; 'kɒnızhoʊm, kónniz-hōm; 'kɒnıʃoʊm, kónni-shōm

Coniston Water *Cumbria*, 'kɒnıstən 'wɔtər, kónnistŏn wáwtĕr

Conlig *Co. Down*, kən'lıg, kŏnlíg

Connah, *f.n.*, 'kɒnə, kónnă

Connah's Quay *Clwyd*, 'kɒnəz 'ki, kónnăz keé

Connaught, Dukedom of, 'kɒnɔt, kónnawt

Connaughton, *f.n.*, 'kɒnətən, kónnătŏn

Connel Ferry *S'clyde*, 'kɒnl 'fɛrı, kónnl férri

Connell, *f.n.*, 'kɒnl, kónnl; kə'nel, kŏnéll

Connelly, *f.n.*, 'kɒnəlı, kónnĕli; kə'nelı, kŏnélli

Connolly, *f.n.*, 'kɒnəlı, kónnŏli

Connor *Co. Antrim*, 'kɒnər, kónnŏr

Connor Downs *Cornwall*, 'kɒnər 'daʊnz, kónnŏr dównz

Connswater *Co. Down*, 'kɒnzwɔtər, kónz-wawtĕr

Conolly, *f.n.*, 'kɒnəlı, kónnŏli

Conon *H'land*, 'kɒnən, kónnŏn

Cononley *N. Yorks.*, 'kɒnənlı, kónnŏnli

Consett *Durham*, 'kɒnsıt, kónssĕt; 'kɒnset, kónsset

Considine, *f.n.*, 'kɒnsıdaın, kónssidin

Constable, *f.n.*, 'kʌnstəbl, kúnstăbl; 'kɒnstəbl, kónstăbl. *The first is appropriate for John ~, the painter and his family.*

Constable Burton *N. Yorks.*, 'kʌnstəbl 'bɜrtən, kúnstăbl búrtŏn

Constantine, *f.n.*, 'kɒnstəntaın, kónstăntīn

Constantine *Cornwall*, 'kɒnstəntaın, kónstăntīn

Contin *H'land*, 'kɒntın, kóntin

Conway, *former spelling of* Conwy *q.v.*, *Gwynedd*, 'kɒnweı, kónway

Conwil Cayo *Dyfed*, 'kɒnwıl 'kaıoʊ, kónwil kí-ō

Conwy *Gwynedd*, 'kɒnwı, kónwi

Conybeare, *f.n.*, 'kɒnıbıər, kónnibeer; 'kʌnıbıər, kúnnibeer

Conyer *Kent*, 'kʌnjər, kún-yĕr; 'kɒnjər, kón-yĕr

Conyers, *f.n.*, 'kɒnjərz, kón-yĕrz

Conyngham, Marquess, 'kʌnıŋəm, kúnning-ăm

Cooden *E. Sussex*, 'kudən, koódĕn; ku'den, koodén

Cookstown *Co. Tyrone*, 'kʊkstaʊn, koókstown

Coole Pilate *Ches.*, 'kul 'paılət, koól pílăt

Coolin Hills *see* Cuillin

Coombe, *f.n.*.., kum, koom

Coombs, *f.n.*, kumz, koomz

Coomes, *f.n.*, kumz, koomz

Coope, *f.n.*, kup, koop

Coopersale *Essex*, 'kupərseıl, koopĕrssayl

Copelin, *f.n.*, 'koʊplın, kóplin

Copestake, *f.n.*, 'koʊpsteık, kópstayk

Copinsay *Orkney*, 'kɒpınseı, kóppinssay

Copland, *f.n.*, 'koʊplənd, kóplănd

Copleston, *f.n.*, 'kɒplstən, kópplstŏn

Copley, *f.n.*, 'kɒplı, kópli

Coplin, *f.n.*, 'kɒplın, kóplin

Copped Hall *Essex*, 'kɒpt 'hɔl, kópt háwl

Coppela, *f.n.*, 'kɒpələ, kóppĕlă

Coppell, *f.n.*, 'kɒpl, kóppl

Copperashouse *W. Yorks.*, 'kɒpərzhaʊs, kóppĕrzhowss

Coppinger, *f.n.*, 'kɒpındʒər, kóppinjĕr

Coppins *Bucks.*, 'kɒpınz, kóppinz

Copplestone *Devon*, 'kɒplstən, kópplstŏn

Coppull *Lancs.*, 'kɒpl, kóppl

Coquet *Northd.*, 'koʊkıt, kókĕt. *Appropriate for both river and island of this name.*

Coquetdale *Northd.*, 'koʊkıtdeıl, kókitdayl

Coral, *f.n.*, 'kɒrəl, kórrăl

Corbally, *f.n.*, 'kɔrbəlı, kórbăli

Corbally *Co. Antrim*, kɔr'bælı, korbáli

Corbet, *f.n.*, 'kɔrbıt, kórbĕt

Corbett, *f.n.*, 'kɔrbıt, kórbĕt

Corbishley, *f.n.*, 'kɔrbıʃlı, kórbishli

Corbould, *f.n.,* 'kɔrboʊld, kór-
bōld
Corbridge *Northd.,* 'kɔrbrɪdʒ,
kórbrij
Corcoran, *f.n.,* 'kɔrkərən, kór-
kŏrän
Cordeaux, *f.n.,* 'kɔrdoʊ, kórdō
Cordell, *f.n.,* kɔr'del, kordéll
Cordiner, *f.n.,* 'kɔrdɪnər, kórdinĕr
Cordingley industrial prison
Surrey, 'kɔrdɪŋlɪ, kórding-li
Coren, *f.n.,* 'kɒrən, kórrĕn
Corina, *f.n.,* kə'rinə, kŏreénä
Cork and Orrery, Earl of, 'kɔrk
ənd 'ɒrərɪ, kórk änd órrĕri
Corken, *f.n.,* 'kɔrkən, kórkĕn
Corkett, *f.n.,* kɔr'ket, korkétt
Corkin, *f.n.,* 'kɔrkɪn, kórkin
Corlett, *f.n.,* 'kɔrlɪt, kórlĕt
Corley, *f.n.,* 'kɔrlɪ, kórli
Cornelius, *f.n.,* kɔr'niliəs,
kornéeli-üss
Cornhill *Grampian,* kɔrn'hɪl,
korn-híll
Cornillie, *f.n.,* kɔr'nilɪ, kornéeli
Cornwall *Co. name,* 'kɔrnwəl,
kórnwäl
Cornwallis, *f.n.,* kɔrn'wɒlɪs,
kornwólliss. *Appropriate also
for Baron* ∼.
Corpach *H'land,* 'kɔrpəx, kór-
pă<u>ch</u>
Corpusty *Norfolk,* 'kɔrpəstɪ,
kórpŭsti
Corrard *Co. Fermanagh,* kə'rɑrd,
kŏraárd
Corregan Rocks *I. of Scilly,* kə-
'regən, kŏréggän
Corrie *S'clyde,* 'kɒrɪ, kórri
Corriehalloch *H'land,* ‚kɒrɪ'hæləx,
korri-hál<u>ŏ</u>ch
Corriemulzie *H'land,* ‚kɒrɪ'mʌlzɪ,
korri-múlzi
Corrievreckan, Strait of, *S'clyde,*
‚kɒrɪ'vrekən, korrivréckän
Corrieyairack Pass *H'land,* ‚kɒrɪ-
'jærək, korri-yárräck
Corrigan, *f.n.,* 'kɒrɪgən, kórrigän
Corringham *Essex,* 'kɒrɪŋəm,
kórring-ăm
Corris *Gwynedd,* 'kɒrɪs, kórriss
Corrour Forest *Tayside–H'land
border,* kɒ'rʊər, korróŏr
Corsellis, *f.n.,* kɔr'selɪs, korsélliss
Corsham *Wilts.,* 'kɔrʃəm, kór-
-shăm
Corsley *Wilts.,* 'kɔrslɪ, kórssli
Corslwyn, *f.n.,* 'kɔrslʊɪn,
kórssloō-in
Corstorphine *Edinburgh,* kər-
'stɔrʃɪn, kŏrsstórfin
Cors Tregaron Nature Reserve
Dyfed, 'kɔrs trɪ'gærən, kórss
trĕgárrŏn

Cortachy *Tayside,* 'kɔrtəxɪ, kór-
tă<u>ch</u>i; kɔr'tæxɪ, kortá<u>ch</u>i
Corteen, *f.n.,* kɔr'tin, kortéen
Coruisk, Loch, *I. of Skye,*
kə'rʊʃk, kŏroŏoshk
Corvedale, Viscount, 'kɔrvdeɪl,
kórvdayl
Corwen *Clwyd,* 'kɔrwən, kórwĕn
Cory, *f.n.,* 'kɒrɪ, káwri
Coryat, Thomas, *16th–17th-c.
traveller,* 'kɒrɪət, kórri-ăt. *The
surname is sometimes spelt*
Coryate.
Coryton, *f.n.,* 'kɒrɪtən, kórritŏn
Coryton *Devon,* 'kɒrɪtən, kórritŏn
Coryton *Essex,* 'kɒrɪtən, káwritŏn
Coseley *W. Midlands,* 'koʊzlɪ,
kózli
Cosen, Benjamin, *17th-c. com-
poser, also spelt* **Cosin, Cosyn,**
'kʌzən, kúzzĕn
Cosens, *f.n.,* 'kʌzənz, kúzzĕnz
Cosford *Suffolk,* 'kɒsfərd, kóss-
fŏrd
Cosham *Hants,* 'kɒsəm, kóssäm
Cosin, Benjamin, *see* **Cosen**
Coslany *Norwich,* 'kɒzlənɪ,
kózläni
Cossall *Notts.,* 'kɒsl, kóssl
Cossington *Leics.,* 'kɒsɪŋtən,
kóssingtŏn; 'kʌsɪŋtən, kússing-
tŏn
Cossins, *f.n.,* 'kʌzɪnz, kúzzinz
Costain, *f.n.,* 'kɒsteɪn, kóstayn;
kɒs'teɪn, kostáyn
Coste, *f.n.,* koʊst, kōst; kɒst,
kosst
Costello, *f.n.,* kə'steloʊ, kŏstéllō;
'kɒstɪloʊ, kóstĕlō
Costelloe, *f.n.,* 'kɒstɪloʊ, kóstĕlō
Costessey *Norfolk,* 'kɒsɪ, kóssi
Costin, *f.n.,* 'kɒstɪn, kóstin
Costock *Notts.,* 'kɒstɒk, kóstock
Coston *Leics.,* 'koʊsən, kóssŏn
Cosyn, Benjamin, *see* **Cosen**
Cotehele House *Cornwall,* kə'til,
kōtéel; kət'hil, kŏt-héel
Cotehill *Cumbria,* 'koʊthɪl, kŏt-
-hil
Cotesbach *Leics.,* 'koʊtsbætʃ,
kŏtsbatch
Cotgrave *Notts.,* 'kɒtgreɪv, kót-
grayv
Cotham *Avon,* 'kɒtəm, kóttăm
Cothay, *f.n.,* 'koʊθeɪ, kŏ-thay
Cothelstone *Somerset,* 'kʌðlstən,
kú<u>th</u>lsstŏn; 'kɒtlstən, kóttls-
stŏn
Cotheridge *H. & W.,* 'kɒðərɪdʒ,
kó<u>th</u>ĕrij
Cotherstone *Durham,* 'kʌðərstən,
kú<u>th</u>ĕrstŏn
Cothi, River, *Dyfed,* 'kɒθɪ, kóthi
Cothill *Oxon.,* 'kɒt'hɪl, kót-híll

Cotmanhay *Derby.*, 'kɒtmənheɪ, kótmăn-hay
Cotmaton *Devon*, kɒt'meɪtən, kotmáytŏn
Coton, *f.n.*, 'koʊtən, kṓtŏn
Coton *Cambs.*, 'koʊtən, kṓtŏn
Cotswolds, The, *Oxon.–Avon*, 'kɒtswoʊldz, kótswōldz
Cottell, *f.n.*, kə'til, kŏtéel
Cottenham, Earl of, 'kɒtnəm, kót-năm
Cottenham *Cambs.*, 'kɒtn̩əm, kóttn-ăm
Cottesbrooke *Northants.*, 'kɒtɪsbrʊk, kóttĕssbrŏŏk
Cottesloe, Baron, 'kɒtsloʊ, kótslō
Cottesmore *Leics.*, 'kɒtsmɔr, kóttsmor
Cottle, *f.n.*, 'kɒtl, kóttl
Cottrell, *f.n.*, 'kɒtrəl, kóttrĕl; kə'trel, kŏtréll
Couch, *f.n.*, kutʃ, kootch
Coucher, *f.n.*, 'kaʊtʃər, kówtchĕr
Couchman, *f.n.*, 'kuʃmən, kóosh-măn; 'kaʊtʃmən, kówtchmăn
Coughlan, *f.n.*, 'kɒxlən, kóchlăn; 'kɒglən, kóglăn
Coughlin, *f.n.*, 'kɒxlɪn, kóchlin; 'kɒglɪn, kóglin
Coughton, *H. & W.*, 'koʊtən, kṓtŏn
Coughton *Warwicks.*, 'koʊtən, kṓtŏn; 'kaʊtən, kówtŏn. *The first is usual for the National Trust property of ~ Court.*
Coughtrey, *f.n.*, 'kaʊtrɪ, kówtri; 'kɔtrɪ, káwtri; 'kutrɪ, koótri; 'koʊtrɪ, kṓtri; 'kɒftrɪ, kófftri
Coughtrie, *f.n.*, 'kɒftrɪ, kófftri
Coul *H'land, Tayside*, kul, kool
Coulbeck, *f.n.*, 'kulbek, koólbeck
Coulcher, *f.n.*, 'kultʃər, koóltchĕr
Couldrey, *f.n.*, 'kuldrɪ, koóldri; 'kuldreɪ, koóldray; 'koʊldrɪ, kṓldri
Couldry, *f.n.*, 'kuldrɪ, koóldri
Couldwell, *f.n.*, 'koʊldwel, kṓldwel
Coull, *f.n.*, kul, kool
Coull *Fife, Grampian*, kul, kool
Coulling, *f.n.*, 'kulɪŋ, koóling
Coulman, *f.n.*, 'koʊlmən, kṓlmăn
Coulport *S'clyde*, 'kulpɔrt, koólport
Coulsdon *London*, 'koʊlzdən, kṓlzdŏn; 'kulzdən, koólzdŏn
Coulshaw, *f.n.*, 'kulʃɔ, koól-shaw
Coulson, *f.n.*, 'koʊlsən, kṓlssŏn; 'kulsən, koólssŏn
Coulston, *f.n.*, 'kulstən, koólstŏn
Coult, *f.n.*, koʊlt, kōlt; kult, koolt
Coultas, *f.n.*, 'kultæs, koóltass

Coulter, *f.n.*, 'kultər, koóltĕr; 'koʊltər, kṓltĕr
Coulthard, *f.n.*, 'kultɑrd, koóltaard; 'koʊlθɑrd, kṓl-thaard
Coulton, *f.n.*, 'koʊltən, kṓltŏn
Councell, *f.n.*, 'kaʊnsl, kównssl
Coundon *W. Midlands*, 'kaʊndən, kówndŏn
Counihan, *f.n.*, 'kunɪhən, koóni-hăn
Countess Wear *Devon*, 'kaʊntɪs 'wɪər, kówntĕss weér
Countesthorpe *Leics.*, 'kaʊntɪs-θɔrp, kówntĕss-thorp
Countisbury *Devon*, 'kaʊntɪsbərɪ, kówntiss-bŭri
Coupar Angus *Tayside*, ,kupər 'æŋgəs, koopăr áng-gŭss
Coupe, *f.n.*, kup, koop
Couper, *f.n.*, 'kupər, koópĕr
Coupland, *f.n.*, 'kuplənd, koóplănd; 'koʊplənd, kṓplănd
Coupland *Cumbria*, 'kuplənd, koópländ
Coupland *Northd.*, 'koʊplənd, kṓplănd
Coupland Beck *Cumbria*, 'koʊplənd 'bek, kṓplănd béck
Cournane, *f.n.*, kʊər'næn, koōrnánn
Courtauld, *f.n.*, 'kɔrtoʊ, kórtō; 'kɔrtoʊld, kórtōld. *Although the first is the pronunciation of the late Samuel ~'s family, the latter is now invariably used for the ~ Institutes and for the firm of ~s Ltd.*
Courtenay, *f.n.*, 'kɔrtnɪ, kórtni
Courthope, *f.n.*, 'kɔrthoʊp, kórthoup, kɔrt-hōp; 'kɔrtoʊp, kórtōp. *The first is appropriate for the Barony of ~.*
Courtier, *f.n.*, 'kɔrtjər, kórt-yĕr
Courtneidge, *f.n.*, 'kɔrtnɪdʒ, kórtnij
Courtney, *f.n.*, 'kɔrtnɪ, kórtni
Courtown, Earl of, 'kɔrtaʊn, kórtown
Cousens, *f.n.*, 'kʌzənz, kúzzĕnz
Couser, *f.n.*, 'kaʊzər, kówzĕr
Cousins, *f.n.*, 'kʌzənz, kúzzĕnz
Cousland, *f.n.*, 'kaʊzlænd, kówz-land
Cousland *Lothian*, 'kaʊzlənd, kówzländ
Coutts, *f.n.*, kuts, koots
Couzens, *f.n.*, 'kʌzənz, kúzzĕnz
Cove, *f.n.*, koʊv, kōv
Covehithe *Suffolk*, 'koʊv'haɪð, kŏv-hɪ̄th
Coveley, *f.n.*, 'koʊvəlɪ, kṓvĕli
Covell, *f.n.*, koʊ'vel, kōvéll; kə'vel, kŏvéll
Coven, *f.n.*, 'koʊvən, kṓvĕn

Coven *Staffs.*, 'koʊvən, kóvĕn
Coveney, *f.n.*, 'koʊvənɪ, kóvĕni
Coveney *Cambs.*, 'koʊvnɪ, kóv-ni
Covenham *Lincs.*, 'koʊvənəm, kóvĕnăm
Covenhope *H. & W.*, 'kɒnəp, kónnŏp; 'koʊvənhoʊp, kóvĕn-hōp
Covent Garden *London*, 'kɒvənt 'gɑrdən, kóvvĕnt gaárdĕn; 'kʌvənt 'gɑrdən, kúvvĕnt gaárdĕn
Coventry, *f.n.*, 'kɒvəntrɪ, kóvvĕn-tri; 'kʌvəntrɪ, kúvvĕntri
Coventry *W. Midlands*, 'kɒvəntrɪ, kóvvĕntri; 'kʌvəntrɪ, kúvvĕntri. *The first is appropriate for the Earl of ~.*
Coverack *Cornwall*, 'kʌvəræk, kúvvĕrack; 'kɒvəræk, kóvvĕrack
Coverdale, *f.n.*, 'kʌvərdeɪl, kúvvĕrdayl
Covesea *H'land*, koʊ'si, kōsseé
Covey-Crump, *f.n.*, 'kʌvɪ 'krʌmp, kúvvi krúmp
Covington, *f.n.*, 'kɒvɪŋtən, kóvvingtŏn
Covington *Cambs.*, 'kɒvɪŋtən, kóvvingtŏn
Cowal *S'clyde*, 'kaʊəl, kówăl; kaʊl, kowl
Coward, *f.n.*, 'kaʊərd, kówărd
Cowbit *Lincs.*, 'kʌbɪt, kúbbit
Cowbridge *S. Glam.*, 'kaʊbrɪdʒ, kówbrij
Cowcher, *f.n.*, 'kaʊtʃər, kówtchĕr
Cowdell, *f.n.*, kaʊ'del, kowdéll
Cowden *Kent*, kaʊ'den, kowdén
Cowdenbeath *Fife*, ˌkaʊdən'biθ, kowdĕn-beéth
Cowderoy, *f.n.*, 'kaʊdərɔɪ, kówdĕroy
Cowdray, *Viscount*, 'kaʊdrɪ, kówdri
Cowdrey, *f.n.*, 'kaʊdrɪ, kówdri
Cowell, *f.n.*, 'kaʊəl, kówĕl; 'koʊəl, kő-ĕl
Cowen, *f.n.*, 'kaʊən, kówĕn; 'koʊən, kő-ĕn
Cowes *I. of Wight*, kaʊz, kowz
Cowie, *f.n.*, 'kaʊɪ, kówi
Cowin, *f.n.*, 'kaʊɪn, kówin
Cowlairs *S'clyde*, 'kaʊ'lɛərz, ków-láirz
Cowles, *f.n.*, kaʊlz, kowlz; koʊlz, kōlz
Cowley, *f.n.*, 'kaʊlɪ, kówli. *Appropriate also for Earl ~.*
Cowley, *Oxon.*, 'kaʊlɪ, kówli
Cowling, *Lancs.*, 'kaʊlɪŋ, kówling; 'koʊlɪŋ, kőling
Cowlinge *Suffolk*, 'kulɪndʒ, koólinj
Cowpe *Lancs.*, kaʊp, kowp

Cowpen *Northd.*, 'kupən, koópĕn; 'kaʊpən, kówpĕn
Cowpen Bewley *Cleveland*, 'kupən 'bjulɪ, koópĕn béwli
Cowper, *f.n.*, 'kupər, koópĕr; 'kaʊpər, kówpĕr. *The first is appropriate for the 18th-c. poet, William ~.*
Cowper Powys, *John, author*, 'kupər 'poʊɪs, koópĕr pő-iss
Cowplain *Hants*, 'kaʊpleɪn, kówplayn
Cowsill, *f.n.*, 'kaʊzɪl, kówzil
Cowtan, *f.n.*, 'kaʊtən, kówtăn
Coxe, *f.n.*, kɒks, kocks
Coxhoe *Durham*, 'kɒkshoʊ, kócks-hō
Coyne, *f.n.*, kɔɪn, koyn
Coytrahen *Mid Glam.*, ˌkɔɪtrə-'heɪn, koytră-háyn
Cozens, *f.n.*, 'kʌzənz, kúzzĕnz
Cozens-Hardy, *Barony of*, 'kʌzənz 'hɑrdɪ, kúzzĕnz haárdi
Crabbe, *George, poet (1784–1832)*, kræb, krabb
Crabtree, *f.n.*, 'kræbtri, krábtree
Craddock, *f.n.*, 'krædək, kráddŏck
Cradley *H. & W.*, 'krædlɪ, krádli
Cradley *W. Midlands*, 'kreɪdlɪ, kráydli
Cradley Heath *W. Midlands*, 'kreɪdlɪ 'hiθ, kráydli heéth
Cradock, *f.n.*, 'krædək, kráddŏck; 'kreɪdɒk, kráydock
Craen, *f.n.*, kreɪn, krayn
Crafthole *Cornwall*, 'krafthoʊl, kraáft-hōl
Crag Lough *Northd.*, 'kræg 'lɒf, krág lóff
Crago, *f.n.*, 'kreɪgoʊ, kráygō
Craigantlet *Co. Down*, kreɪg-'æntlət, kraygántlĕt
Craigavad *Co. Down*, ˌkreɪgə'væd, kraygăvád
Craig Cerrig-Gleisiad *Nature Reserve Powys*, 'kraɪg 'kerɪg 'glaɪsjæd, kríg kérrig glíss-yad
Craigdhu *H'land*, 'kreɪg'du, kráyg doó
Craigellachie *Grampian*, kreɪg-'eləxɪ, kraygélláchi
Craigendoran *S'clyde*, ˌkreɪgən-'dɒrən, kraygĕndórrăn
Craigie, *f.n.*, 'kreɪgɪ, kráygi
Craigie *S'clyde, Tayside*, 'kreɪgɪ, kráygi
Craigievar *Grampian*, ˌkreɪgɪ'vɑr, kraygivaár
Craiglockhart *Lothian*, kreɪg-'lɒkərt, krayg-lóckärt
Craiglour-Achin *Grampian*, kreɪg-'laʊrəxɪn, krayglówrăchin; *also written* Craig Lowrigan, *and*

pronounced kreɪg 'laʊrɪgən, krayg lówrigăn

Craigmillar *Edinburgh*, kreɪg-'mɪlər, krayg-míllăr

Craigmyle, Baron, kreɪg'maɪl, kraygmíl

Craigneuk *S'clyde*, kreɪg'njuk, krayg-néwk

Craignure *S'clyde*, kreɪg'njʊər, krayg-nyőőr

Craig-ny-Baa, *also spelt* **Creg-ny-Baa**, *I. of Man*, 'kreɪg nɪ 'bɑ, kráyg-ni-baa

Craigowan *Grampian*, kreɪ'gaʊən, kraygów-än

Craig Willies Hill, *I. of Man*, kreɪg 'wɪlɪz, krayg williz

Craig-y-Deryn *Gwynedd*, ˌkraɪgə-'derɪn, krĭg-ă-dérrin

Craig-y-Llyn *Mid Glam.*, ˌkraɪgə-'ɬɪn, krĭg-ă-ḫlín

Craig-y-Nos *Powys*, ˌkraɪgə'noʊs, krĭgănóss

Crail *Fife*, kreɪl, krayl

Cramond *Lothian*, 'kræmənd, krámmŏnd; 'krɑmənd, kráamŏnd

Cranage *Ches.*, 'krænɪdʒ, kránnij

Cranagh *Co. Tyrone*, 'krænə, kránnă

Cranham, *f.n.*, 'krænəm, kránnăm

Crank ny Mona *I. of Man*, 'kræŋk nɪ 'moʊnə, kránk ni mőnă

Cranleigh *Surrey*, 'krænlɪ, kránli

Cranleighan, *one educated at Cranleigh School*, kræn'liən, kranlée-än

Cranwich *Norfolk*, 'krænɪtʃ, kránnitch

Crayke *N. Yorks.*, kreɪk, krayk

Crarae *S'clyde*, 'krærɪ, krárri

Crashaw, Richard, *17th-c. poet*, 'kræʃɔ, krásh-aw

Crask of Aigas *H'land*, 'kræʃk əv 'eɪgəʃ, kráshk ŏv áygăsh

Craske, *f.n.*, krɑsk, kraask; kræsk, krassk

Craster, *f.n.*, 'krɑstər, kráastĕr

Crathes *Grampian*, 'kræθɪz, kráthĕz

Crathie *Grampian*, 'kræθɪ, kráthi

Crathorn, *f.n.*, 'kreɪθɔrn, kráy--thorn

Crathorne, Baron, 'kreɪθɔrn, kráy-thorn

Crauford, *f.n.*, 'krɔfərd, kráwfŏrd

Craven, *f.n.*, 'kreɪvən, kráyvĕn

Craven Arms *Salop*, 'kreɪvən 'ɑrmz, kráyvĕn áarmz

Crawford and Balcarres, Earl of, 'krɔfərd ənd bæl'kærɪs, kráwfŏrd ănd balkárrĕss

Crawght, *f.n.*, krɔt, krawt

Crawhall, *f.n.*, krə'hɔl, kră-háwl

Crawley, *f.n.*, 'krɔlɪ, kráwli

Crawshaw, *f.n.*, 'krɔʃɔ, kráw-shaw

Crawshay, *f.n.*, 'krɔʃeɪ, kráw-shay

Crawt, *f.n.*, krɔt, krawt

Crayford *London*, 'kreɪfərd, kráyfŏrd

Creacombe *Devon*, 'krikəm, kréekŏm

Creagan *S'clyde*, 'krigən, kréegăn

Creagh, *f.n.*, kreɪ, kray

Creaghan, *f.n.*, 'krigən, kréegăn

Creag Meaghaidh Mt. *H'land*, 'kreɪg 'megɪ, kráyg méggi

Creak, *f.n.*, krik, kreek

Crean, *f.n.*, krin, kreen; 'kriən, krée-än

Creaney, *f.n.*, 'krinɪ, kréeni

Creasy, *f.n.*, 'krisɪ, kréessi

Creaton, Great *and* Little, *Northants.*, 'kritən, kréetŏn

Creber, *f.n.*, 'kribər, kréebĕr

Crebilly *Co. Antrim*, krə'bɪlɪ, krĕbílli

Credenhill *H. & W.*, 'kredənhɪl, kréddĕn-hil; 'kridənhɪl, kréedĕn-hil

Crediton *Devon*, 'kredɪtən, kréddĭtŏn

Cree, *f.n.*, kri, kree

Creegor, *f.n.*, 'krigər, kréegŏr

Crees, *f.n.*, kris, kreess; kriz, kreez

Creese, *f.n.*, kris, kreess

Creetown *D. & G.*, 'kritaʊn, kréetown

Creffield, *f.n.*, 'krefɪld, kréffeeld

Cregagh *Co. Down*, 'kreɪgə, kráygă

Cregan, *f.n.*, 'krigən, kréegăn

Cregeen, *f.n.*, krɪ'dʒin, krĕjéen

Cregneish *I. of Man*, kreg'niʃ, kreg-néesh

Creg-ny-Baa *see* **Craig-ny-Baa**

Crehan, *f.n.*, 'kriən, krée-än

Creich *Fife*, *H'land*, *S'clyde*, krix, kreech

Creighton, *f.n.*, 'kraɪtən, krítŏn; 'kreɪtən, kráytŏn

Creigiau *Mid Glam.*, 'kraɪgjaɪ, krĭg-yī

Creme, *f.n.*, krim, kreem

Cremer, *f.n.*, 'krimər, kréemĕr

Cremyll *Cornwall*, 'kremɪl, krémmil; 'kreml, krémml

Creran, Loch *and* River, *S'clyde*, 'krɪərən, kréerän

Crerand, *f.n.*, 'krɪərənd, kréerănd

Crerar, *f.n.*, 'krɪərər, kráirăr; 'krɪərər, kréerăr

Cresselly *Dyfed*, krɪs'elɪ, krĕssélli

Creswell, *f.n.*, 'krezwəl, krézwĕl

Creswell *Derby.*, 'kreswel, kréss-wel; 'kreswəl, krésswĕl

Creswick, f.n., 'krezık, krézzick
Creunant, also spelt Crynant, W.
 Glam., 'kraınǝnt, krínănt
Crevenagh Co. Tyrone, 'krevnǝ,
 krévnă
Crewe Ches., kru, kroo
Crewkerne Somerset, 'krukǝrn,
 kroókern
Crianlarich Central, ˌkriǝn'lærıx,
 kree-ănlárrich
Cribbett, f.n., 'krıbıt, kríbbĕt
Crib-Goch Gwynedd, 'krib 'goʊx,
 kreéb góch
Crib-y-Ddysgl Gwynedd, ˌkrib ǝ
 'ðıskl, kreeb ă thískl
Cribyn Dyfed, 'krıbın, kreébin;
 'krıbın, kríbbin
Criccieth Gwynedd, 'krıkıǝθ,
 krícki-ĕth
Crich Derby., kraıtʃ, krītch
Crichel Down Dorset, 'krıtʃl
 'daʊn, krítchl dówn
Crichton, f.n., 'kraıtǝn, krítŏn
Crickadarn Powys, krık'ædǝrn,
 krickáddärn
Cricket Malherbie Somerset,
 'krıkıt 'mælǝrbı, krícket málĕrbi
Crickhowell Powys, krık'haʊǝl,
 krick-hówĕl
Crieff Tayside, krif, kreef
Crier, f.n., 'kraıǝr, krí-ĕr
Criggion Powys, 'krıgjɒn, kríg-yon
Crighton, f.n., 'kraıtǝn, krítŏn
Crimond Grampian, 'krımǝnd,
 krímmŏnd
Crimplesham Norfolk, 'krımpl-
 ʃǝm, krímpl-shăm
Crinan S'clyde, 'krınǝn, krínnăn
Cringleford Norfolk, 'krıŋglfǝrd,
 kríng-glförd
Cringletie Borders, krıŋ'letı,
 kring-létti
Crisell, f.n., krı'sel, krisséll
Crisp, f.n., krısp, krisp
Critchley, f.n., 'krıtʃlı, krítchli
Critoph, f.n., 'krıtɒf, kríttoff
Crittall, f.n., 'krıtɔl, kríttawl
Croal, River, Lancs.–Gtr.
 M'chester, kroʊl, krōl
Croall, f.n., kroʊl, krōl
Croan, f.n., kroʊn, krōn
Croasdell, f.n., 'kroʊzdel, krózdel
Crockernwell Devon, 'krɒkǝrnwel,
 króckĕrn-wel
Crocketford D. & G., 'krɒkıtfǝrd,
 króckĕtförd
Crockford, f.n., 'krɒkfǝrd, króck-
 förd
Crockford's Club London,
 'krɒkfǝrdz, króckfördz
Croeserw W. Glam., krɔıs'eru,
 kroyssérroo
Croesfaen Mid Glam., krɔıs'vaın,
 kroyss-vín

Croesor Gwynedd, 'krɔısǝr,
 króyssor
Croesyceiliog Gwent, ˌkrɔısǝ-
 'kaıljɒg, kroyssă-kíl-yog
Croftamie S'clyde, krɒft'æmı,
 kroftámmi
Croghan, f.n., 'kroʊǝn, kró-än
Croham Hurst London, 'kroʊǝm
 'hɜrst, kró-ăm húrst
Croke, f.n., kroʊk, krōōk
Croker, f.n., 'kroʊkǝr, krókĕr
Crom Co. Fermanagh, krʌm,
 krumm
Cromac Co. Antrim, 'krɒmǝk,
 krómmăk
Cromartie, Earl of, 'krɒmǝrtı,
 krómmărti
Cromarty H'land, 'krɒmǝrtı,
 krómmărti
Crombie, f.n., 'krɒmbı, krómbi;
 'krʌmbı, krúmbi
Crome, f.n., kroʊm, krōm
Cromer Herts., Norfolk, 'kroʊ-
 mǝr, krómĕr. Appropriate also
 for the Earl of ∼.
Cromey, f.n., 'krʌmı, krúmmi
Cromford Derby., 'krɒmfǝrd,
 krómförd
Cromie, f.n., 'kroʊmı, krómi
Cromlech Co. Down, 'krʌmlǝx,
 krúmlĕch
Crommelin, f.n., 'krʌmlın, krúm-
 lin
Crompton, f.n., 'krɒmptǝn, krómp-
 tŏn. Appropriate for Samuel ∼,
 inventor of the weaving shuttle.
Crondall Hants, 'krʌndl, krúndl;
 'krɒndl, króndl
Croney, f.n., 'kroʊnı, króni
Cronin, f.n., 'kroʊnın, krónin
Cronk-ny-Mona I. of Man, 'krɒŋk
 nǝ 'moʊnǝ, krónk nĕ mónă
Crookating Shetland, 'krʊkǝtıŋ,
 kroókăting
Crook of Devon Tayside, 'krʊk ǝv
 'devǝn, kroók ŏv dévvŏn
Croome d'Abitot H. & W., 'krum
 'dæbıtoʊ, kroóm dábbitō
Cropredy Oxon., 'krɒprǝdı,
 króprĕdi
Crosby Cumbria, Humberside,
 Merseyside, 'krɒzbı, krózbi
Croser, f.n., 'kroʊzǝr, krózĕr
Crosier, f.n., 'kroʊʒǝr, krózhĕr;
 'kroʊzıǝr, krózi-ĕr
Crosland, f.n., 'krɒslǝnd, króssländ
Crossbychan Mid Glam., krɒs-
 'bʌxǝn, kross-búchăn
Crossflatts W. Yorks., 'krɒsflæts,
 króss-flats
Crossgar Co. Down, krɒs'gɑr,
 krossgaár
Crosshill Fife, S'clyde, 'krɒs'hıl,
 króss-híll

Crossmaglen Co. *Armagh*, ˌkrɒsmə'glen, kross-mäglén

Crossmyloof *S'clyde*, ˌkrɒsmɪ'luf, krossmilóof

Crossraguel Abbey *S'clyde*, krɒs-'reɪgl, krossráygl

Crosthwaite-Eyre, *f.n.*, 'krɒsθweɪt 'ɛər, króss-thwayt áir

Croston *Lancs.*, 'krɒstən, krósstŏn

Crostwick *Norfolk*, 'krɒstwɪk, króst-wick; 'krɒstɪk, króstick; 'krɒsɪk, króssick

Crothers, *f.n.*, 'krʌðərz, krúthĕrz

Crotty, *f.n.*, 'krɒtɪ, krótti

Crouch, *f.n.*, krautʃ, krowtch

Crouch *Kent*, krutʃ, krootch

Croucher, *f.n.*, 'krautʃər, krów-tchĕr

Croughton *Northants.*, 'krautən, krótŏn

Crow, *f.n.*, krou, krō

Crowan *Cornwall*, 'krauən, krówăn

Crowborough *E. Sussex*, 'krou-bərə, króbŭră

Crowcombe *Somerset*, 'kroukəm, krókŏm

Crowcroft, *f.n.*, 'kroukrɒft, krókroft

Crowden, *f.n.*, 'kraudən, krówdĕn

Crowden *Derby.*, 'kroudən, kródĕn

Crowder, *f.n.*, 'kraudər, krówdĕr

Crowdy, *f.n.*, 'kraudɪ, krówdi

Crowe, *f.n.*, krou, krō

Crowest, *f.n.*, 'krouɪst. kró-ĕst

Crowland, *also spelt* **Croyland**, *Lincs.*, 'kroulənd, królănd

Crowlas *Cornwall*, 'kraulǝs, krówlăss

Crowle *H. & W.*, kroul, krōl; kraul, krowl

Crowle *Humberside*, kroul, krōl

Crowley, *f.n.*, 'kroulɪ, króli

Crows-an-Wra *Cornwall*, 'krausən'reɪ, krówss ăn ráy

Crowson, Lamar, *pianist*, lə'mɑr 'krausən, lămáar krówssŏn

Crowther, *f.n.*, 'krauðər, krówthĕr. *Appropriate also for Baron* ~.

Crowthorne *Berks.*, 'krouθɔrn, kró-thorn

Croxdale *Durham*, 'krɒksdəl, króckssdäl

Croxton *Humberside, Norfolk*, 'krɒkstən, króckstŏn

Croxton, South, *Leics.*, 'krousən, króssŏn; 'kroustən, krósstŏn; 'krouzən, krózŏn

Croxton Kerrial *Leics.*, 'krousən 'kerɪəl, króssŏn kérriäl

Croyland *see* **Crowland**

Crozier, *f.n.*, 'krouzɪər, krózi-ĕr; 'krouʒər, krózhĕr

Cruachan, Falls of, *S'clyde*, 'kruəxən, króo-áchăn

Cruchley, *f.n.*, 'krʌtʃlɪ, krútchli

Cruddas, *f.n.*, 'krʌdəs, krúddäss

Cruden Bay *Grampian*, 'krudən 'beɪ, króodĕn báy

Crudwell *Wilts.*, 'krʌdwel, krúd-wel

Crug-y-Bar *Dyfed*, ˌkrig ə 'bɑr, kreeg ă baár

Crug-y-Byddar *Powys*, ˌkrig ə 'bʌðər, kreeg ă búthär

Cruickshank, *f.n.*, 'krukʃæŋk, króok-shank

Cruikshank, *f.n.*, 'krukʃæŋk, króok-shank

Crum, *f.n.*, krʌm, krum

Crumlin Co. *Antrim, Gwent*, 'krʌmlɪn, krúmlin

Crunwere *Dyfed*, 'krʌnwɛər, krúnwair

Crutchley, *f.n.*, 'krʌtʃlɪ, krútchli

Crutwell, *f.n.*, 'krʌtwəl, krútwĕl

Cruwys Morchard *Devon*, 'kruz 'mɔrtʃərd, króoz mórtchärd

Crwys *Welsh C.n.*, 'kruɪs, króo-iss

Crwys *W. Glam.*, 'kruɪs, króo-iss

Cryer, *f.n.*, 'kraɪər, krí-ĕr

Crymmych *Dyfed*, 'krʌmɪx, krúmmich

Crynant *see* **Creunant**

Crysell, *f.n.*, 'kraɪsl, kríssl

Cubbin, *f.n.*, 'kʌbɪn, kúbbin

Cubert *Cornwall*, 'kjubərt, kéwbĕrt

Cubitt, *f.n.*, 'kjubɪt, kéwbit

Cublington, *Bucks.*, 'kʌblɪŋtən, kúblingtŏn

Cuchullin Hills *see* **Cuillin**

Cuckfield *W. Sussex*, 'kukfild, kóokfeeld

Cuckmere, River, *E. Sussex*, 'kukmɪər, kóokmeer

Cuckney, *f.n.*, 'kʌknɪ, kúckni

Cuckney *Notts.*, 'kʌknɪ, kúckni

Cucksey, *f.n.*, 'kuksɪ, kóoksi

Cuckston, *f.n.*, 'kukstən, kóokstŏn

Cuddeford, *f.n.*, 'kʌdɪfɔrd, kúddĕford

Cuddesdon *Oxon.*, 'kʌdzdən, kúdzdŏn

Cuddihay, *f.n.*, 'kʌdɪheɪ, kúddi-hay

Cude, *f.n.*, kjud, kewd

Cudworth *S. Yorks.*, 'kʌdwərθ, kúdwŏrth; 'kʌdərθ, kúddŏrth

Cuffe, *f.n.*, kʌf, kuff

Cuillin Hills, *also spelt* **Coolin, Cuchullin**, *Skye*, 'kulɪn, kóolin

Culbone *Somerset*, 'kʌlboun, kúlbōn

Culcavey Co. *Down*, kəl'keɪvɪ, kŭlkáyvi

Culcheth Gtr. M'chester, 'kʌltʃəθ, kúltchĕth

Culdrose Cornwall, kʌl'drouz, kuldróz

Culduthel H'land, kʌl'dʌθl, kuldúthl

Culf, f.n., kʌlf, kulf

Culgaith Cumbria, kʌl'geıθ, kulgáyth; kʊl'geıθ, kōōlgáyth; 'kʊlgeıθ, kōōlgayth

Culham Oxon., 'kʌləm, kúlläm

Culhane, f.n., kʌl'heın, kul-háyn

Culkein H'land, 'kʊlkeın, kōōlkayn

Cullamore Co. Tyrone, ‚kʌlə'mɔr, kullämór

Cullavoe see **Cullivoe**

Cullen, f.n., 'kʌlən, kúllĕn

Cullen Grampian, 'kʌlən, kúllĕn

Cullercoats Tyne & Wear, 'kʌlər-kouts, kúllĕrkōts

Cullinan, f.n., 'kʌlınən, kúllinän

Cullivoe, also spelt **Cullavoe,** Shetland, 'kʌlıvou, kúllivō

Culloden H'land, kə'lɒdən, kŭlódděn; kə'loudən, kŭlódděn

Cullompton Devon, 'kʌləmptən, kúllŏmptŏn; kə'lʌmptən, kŭlúmptŏn

Cullybackey Co. Antrim, ‚kʌlı-'bækı, kullibácki

Cullyhanna Co. Armagh, ‚kʌlı-'hænə, kulli-hánnä

Culm, River, Somerset–Devon, kʌlm, kulm

Culme-Seymour, f.n., 'kʌlm 'simɔr, kúlm sèemor

Culmstock Devon, 'kʌlmstɒk, kúlm-stock

Culnady Co. Derry, kəl'nædı, kŭlnáddi

Culpeper, f.n., 'kʌlpepər, kúll-peppĕr

Culrain H'land, kʌl'reın, kulráyn

Culross, f.n., 'kʌlrɒs, kúlross

Culross Fife, 'kurəs, kóo-rŏss

Culsalmond Grampian, kʌl-'sæmənd, kul-sámmŏnd

Culter Grampian, S'clyde, 'kutər, kóotĕr

Cultoquhey Tayside, ‚kʌltə'hwaı, kultō-whí

Cultra Co. Down, kəl'trɒ, kŭltráw

Cults Fife, Grampian, kʌlts, kults

Culzean Castle S'clyde, kə'leın, kŭláyn

Cumberbeach, f.n., 'kʌmbərbitʃ, kúmbĕrbeetch

Cumberland former Co. name, 'kʌmbərlənd, kúmbĕr-länd

Cumberlege, f.n., 'kʌmbərlıdʒ, kúmbĕrlĕj

Cumbernauld S'clyde, ‚kʌmbər-'nɔld, kumbĕrnáwld

Cumbes, f.n., kumz, koomz

Cumbrae, Great and Little, S'clyde, 'kʌmbreı, kúmbray

Cumbrian, pertaining to Cumberland or Cumbria, 'kʌmbrıən, kúmbriän

Cumdivock Cumbria, kʌm'dıvək, kumdívvŏk

Cumine, f.n., 'kʌmın, kúmmin

Cuminestown Grampian, 'kʌmınztaun, kúmminz-town

Cuming Museum London, 'kʌmıŋ, kúmming

Cummertrees D. & G., 'kʌmər-'triz, kúmmĕr-treéz

Cumnock S'clyde, 'kʌmnək, kúmnŏk

Cumnor Oxon., 'kʌmnər, kúm-nŏr

Cumrew Cumbria, kʌm'ru, kumróo; kʌmrı'u, kumri-oo

Cumwhinton Cumbria, kʌm-'hwıntən, kum-whíntŏn; kʊm-'hwıntən, kōōm-whíntŏn

Cunard, f.n., kju'nɑrd, kewnaárd

Cundell, f.n., 'kʌndl, kúndl

Cuneo, Terence, painter, 'kjunıou, kéwniō

Cuningham, f.n., 'kʌnıŋəm, kúnning-ăm

Cuninghame, f.n., 'kʌnıŋəm, kúnning-ăm

Cunliffe, f.n., 'kʌnlıf, kúnlif

Cunningham of Hyndhope, Viscountcy of, 'kʌnıŋəm əv 'haındhoup, kúnning-ăm ŏv hínd-hōp

Cunobelin, ancient king, also spelt **Cunobeline,** kʊ'nɒbəlın, kōōnóbbĕlin

Cunynghame, f.n., 'kʌnıŋəm, kúnning-ăm

Cupar Fife, 'kupər, kóopăr

Cupit, f.n., 'kjupıt, kéwpit

Cupitt, f.n., 'kjupıt, kéwpit

Curgenven, f.n., kər'genvən, kŭrgénvĕn; kər'gınvən, kŭr-gínvĕn

Curigwen, Welsh C.n., kə'rıgwen, kŭrígwen

Curle, f.n., kɜrl, kurl

Curphey, f.n., 'kɜrfı, kúrfi

Curraghmore Co. Fermanagh, ‚kʌrə'mɔr, kurrämór

Curran, f.n., 'kʌrən, kúrrăn

Currell, f.n., 'kʌrəl, kúrrĕl

Currie Lothian, 'kʌrı, kúrri

Curry Rivel Somerset, 'kʌrı 'raıvl, kúrri rívl

Cursiter, f.n., 'kɜrsıtər, kúrssi-tĕr

Cursley, f.n., 'kɜrzlı, kúrzli

Cursue, f.n., kər'sju, kursséw

Curteis, f.n., 'kɜrtıs, kúrtiss

Curthoys, *f.n.,* 'kɜr'tɔɪz, kurtóyz; kɜr'θɔɪz, kur-thóyz; 'kɜrθɔɪz, kúr-thoyz; 'kɜrtɔɪz, kúrtoyz

Curtois, *f.n.,* 'kɜrtɔɪz, kúrtoyz; 'kɜrtɪs, kúrtiss

Cury *Cornwall,* 'kjʊərɪ, kyóŏri

Cury Cross *Cornwall,* 'kjʊərɪ 'krɒs, kyóŏri króss

Curzon, Viscount, 'kɜrzən, kúrzŏn

Cusack, *f.n.,* 'kjusæk, kéwssack

Cusgarne *Cornwall,* kəz'gɑrn, kŭzga'arn

Cush, *f.n.,* kʊʃ, kŏŏsh

Cushendall *Co. Antrim,* ˌkʊʃən-'dɔl, kŏŏshĕndáwl

Cushendun, Barony of, ˌkʌʃən'dʌn, kushĕndún

Cushendun *Co. Antrim,* ˌkʊʃən-'dʌn, kŏŏshĕndún

Cushine, *f.n.,* 'kʊʃaɪn, kŏŏshīn

Cushing, *f.n.,* 'kʊʃɪŋ, kŏŏshing

Cushuish *Somerset,* kəs'hjuɪʃ, kŭss-héwish

Cusick, *f.n.,* 'kjusɪk, kéwssick

Cutforth, *f.n.,* 'kʌtfɔrθ, kútforth

Cuthbe, *f.n.,* 'kʌθbɪ, kúthbi

Cuthbert, *C.n. and f.n.,* 'kʌθbərt, kúthbĕrt

Cuthill, *f.n.,* 'kʌθɪl, kúth-il; 'kʌthɪl, kút-hil

Cutner, *f.n.,* 'kʌtnər, kútnĕr

Cuttell, *f.n.,* kə'tel, kŭtéll

Cuttress, *f.n.,* 'kʌtrɪs, kúttrĕss

Cuxham *Oxon.,* 'kʊksəm, kŏŏksăm; 'kʌksəm, kúcksăm

Cuxton *Kent,* 'kʌkstən, kúckstŏn

Cuxwold *Lincs.,* 'kʌkswʊld, kúckswōld

Cuyler, *f.n.,* 'kaɪlər, kílĕr

Cwm *Clwyd, Gwent,* kʊm, kŏŏm. *Appropriate also for the River* ~ *(Powys).*

Cwmcarn *Gwent,* kʊm'kɑrn, kŏŏmka'arn

Cwmaman *Mid Glam.,* kʊm-'æmən, kŏŏmámmän

Cwmamman *Dyfed,* kʊm'æmən, kŏŏmámmän

Cwmann *Dyfed* kʊm'æn, kŏŏmán

Cwmannogisaf *Clwyd,* kʊm-'ænɒg'ɪsæv, kŏŏm-ánnog-íssav

Cwm Avon *Gwent, W. Glam.,* kʊm 'ævən, kŏŏm ávvŏn

Cwmbach *Dyfed, Mid Glam., Powys,* kʊm'bɑx, kŏŏmba'ach

Cwmbran *Gwent,* kʊm'bran, kŏŏmbra'an

Cwmbwrla *W. Glam.,* kʊm-'bʊərlə, kŏŏmbŏŏrlä

Cwmcarn *Gwent,* kʊm'kɑrn, kŏŏmka'arn

Cwmcelyn *Gwent,* kʊm'kelɪn, kŏŏmkéllin

Cwmclydach *W. Glam.,* kʊm-'klɪdəx, kŏŏm-klíddăch; kʊm'klʌdəx, kŏŏm-klúddăch

Cwmcothi *Dyfed,* kʊm'kɒθɪ, kŏŏmkóthi

Cwmdare *Mid Glam.,* kʊm'dɛər, kŏŏmdáir

Cwmdu *Dyfed, Powys, W. Glam.,* kʊm'di, kŏŏm-dée

Cwmfelin *Mid Glam.,* kʊm'velɪn, kŏŏmvéllin

Cwmfelinfach *Gwent,* kʊmˌvelɪn-'vax, kŏŏmvellinva'ach

Cwm Ffrwd *Dyfed,* kʊm 'frud, kŏŏm froód

Cwmffrwdoer *Gwent,* ˌkʊmfrud-'ɔɪər, kŏŏmfroodóyr

Cwmgiedd *Powys,* kʊm'giəð, kŏŏmgee-ĕth

Cwmgors *W. Glam.,* kʊm'gɔrs, kŏŏmgórss

Cwmgwrach *W. Glam.,* kʊm-'gwrax, kŏŏmgwra'ach; kʊm-'grax, kŏŏmgra'ach. *Welsh speakers pronounce 'gwrach' as one syllable by treating the 'w' as a rounding of the lips to accompany the 'r'.*

Cwm Idwal Nature Reserve *Gwynedd,* kʊm 'ɪdwəl, kŏŏm ídwăl

Cwmllinfell *see* **Cwmllynfell**

Cwmllynfell, *also spelt* **Cwmllinfell,** *W. Glam.,* kʊm'ɬʌnveɬ, kŏŏm-hlún-vehl

Cwmmawr *Dyfed,* kʊm'maʊər, kŏŏm-mówr

Cwmparc *Mid Glam.,* kʊm'pɑrk, kŏŏmpa'ark

Cwmpennar *Mid Glam.,* kʊm-'penər, kŏŏmpénnăr

Cwm Prysor *Gwynedd,* kʊm 'prʌsɔr, kŏŏm prússor

Cwmrheidol *Dyfed,* kʊm'hraɪdɒl, kŏŏmrídol

Cwm Silyn *Gwynedd,* kʊm 'sɪlɪn, kŏŏm síllin

Cwmstradllyn *Gwynedd,* kʊm-'strædɬɪn, kŏŏmstrádhlin

Cwmsyfiog *Mid Glam.,* kʊm-'sɪvjɒg, kŏŏmssív-yog

Cwmtillery *Gwent,* ˌkʊmtɪ'lɛərɪ, kŏŏmtiláiri

Cwm Tryweryn *Gwynedd,* ˌkʊm trɪ'werɪn, kŏŏm tri-wérrin; ˌkʊm trʌ'werɪn, kŏŏm tru-wérrin

Cwmtwrch *W. Glam.,* kʊm'tʊərx, kŏŏmtŏŏrch

Cwmyglo *Dyfed, Gwynedd,* ˌkʊmə'gloʊ, kŏŏmăglṓ

Cwmyoy *Gwent,* kʊm'jɔɪ, kŏŏm-yóy

Cwm-yr-Eglwys *Dyfed,* ˌkʊm ər 'egluɪs, kŏŏm-ŭr-églŏŏiss

Cwmystwyth *Dyfed*, kʊm'ʌstwɪθ, kōōmústwith

Cydweli, *Welsh form of* Kidwelly, *q.v.*, *Dyfed*, kɪd'welɪ, kidwélli

Cyfarthfa *Mid Glam.*, kə'vɑrθvə, kŭváarth-vă

Cyfeiliog *Powys*, kə'vaɪljɒg, kŭvíl-yog

Cyfoeth-y-Brenin *Dyfed*, 'kʌvɔɪθ ə 'brenɪn, kúvvoyth ă brénnin

Cyfronydd *Powys*, kə'vrɒnɪð, kŭvrónnith

Cylwik, *f.n.*, 'sɪlwɪk, síll-wick

Cymau *Clwyd*, 'kʌmaɪ, kúmmī

Cymmer *Mid Glam.*, 'kʌmər, kúmmĕr

Cymmrodorion Society, *London Welsh society*, ˌkʌmrə'dɒrɪən, kumrŏdórri-ŏn

Cymric party, *Welsh political party*, 'kʌmrɪk, kúmrick

Cynan, *Welsh C.n.*, 'kʌnən, kúnnăn

Cyncoed *S. Glam.*, kɪn'kɔɪd, kin-kóyd

Cynddylan, *Welsh C.n.*, kʌn-'ðʌlən, kunthúllăn

Cynghordy *Dyfed*, kʌŋ'hɔrdɪ, kung-hórdi

Cynheidre Colliery *Dyfed*, kʌn-'haɪdreɪ, kun-hídray

Cynlais *Powys*, 'kʌnlaɪs, kúnlīss

Cynog *Powys*, 'kʌnɒg, kúnnog

Cynon, River, *Mid Glam.*, 'kʌnən, kúnnŏn

Cynric, *Welsh C.n.*, 'kʌnrɪk, kúnrick

Cyntwell *S. Glam.*, 'sɪntwel, síntwel

Cynull Mawr *Dyfed*, 'kʌnɪɫ 'maʊər, kúnnihl mówr

Cynwyd *Clwyd*, 'kʌnʊɪd, kúnnōō-id

Cyriax, *f.n.*, 'sɪrɪæks, sírri-acks

Cyster, *f.n.*, 'sɪstər, sísstĕr

Cysyllte *Clwyd*, kə'sʌɫteɪ, kŭs-súhltay

Czerkawska, *f.n.*, tʃər'kæfskə, chĕrkáfskă

D

D'Abbes, *f.n.*, dæbz, dabz

D'Abernon, Viscountcy of, 'dæbərnən, dábbĕrnŏn

d'Abo, *f.n.*, 'dɑboʊ, dáabō

Daborn, *f.n.*, 'deɪbɔrn, dáyborn

D'Abreu, *f.n.*, 'dæbru, dábroo

Dacombe, *f.n.*, 'deɪkəm, dáykŏm

Dacorum *Herts.*, də'kɔrəm, dăkáwrŭm

Dacre, Baroness, 'deɪkər, dáykĕr

Dacre of Gillesland, Baron, 'deɪkər əv 'gɪlzlənd, dáykĕr ŏv gílzländ

Dacre of Glanton, Baron, 'deɪkər əv 'glæntən, dáykĕr ŏv glántŏn

Dacres, *f.n.*, 'deɪkərz, dáykĕrz

Dadd, *f.n.*, dæd, dadd

Daer and Shortcleuch, Baron, 'dɛər ənd 'ʃɔrtklu, daír ănd shórtkloo

Daer Water, River, *S'clyde*, 'dɑr 'wɔtər, dáar wáwtĕr

D'Aeth, *f.n.*, deθ, deth; deɪθ, dayth; diθ, deeth

Dafen *Dyfed*, 'dævən, dávvĕn

Dafydd, *Welsh C.n.*, 'dævɪð, dávvith

Dagenham *London*, 'dægənəm, dággĕnäm

Dagg, *f.n.*, dæg, dag

Daggar, *f.n.*, 'dægər, dággăr

Daglish, *f.n.*, 'dæglɪʃ, dáglish

D'Aguiar, *f.n.*, 'dægjʊɑr, dág-yōō-aar

D'Aguilar, *f.n.*, 'dægwɪlər, dág-willăr

Dagul, *f.n.*, 'deɪgl, dáygl

Daiches, *f.n.*, 'deɪʃɪs, dáyshĕss; 'daɪxɪs, díchĕss

Dailly *S'clyde*, 'deɪlɪ, dáyli

Daimpré, *f.n.*, 'dæmpreɪ, dámpray

Daine, *f.n.*, deɪn, dayn

Dakeyne, *f.n.*, də'keɪn, dăkáyn

Dakin, *f.n.*, 'deɪkɪn, dáykin

Dalbeattie *D. & G.*, dəl'bitɪ, dălbeéti

Dalberg, *f.n.*, 'dælbɑrg, dálberg

D'Albiac, *f.n.*, 'dɒlbɪæk, dáwlbi-ack

Dalbury Lees *Derby.*, 'dɒlbərɪ 'liz, dáwlbŭri leéz

Dalby, *f.n.*, 'dɒlbɪ, dáwlbi; 'dælbɪ, dálbi

Dalby *Leics.*, 'dɔlbɪ, dáwlbi; 'dɒlbɪ, dólbi

Dalby *Lincs.*, 'dɒlbɪ, dáwlbi

Daldy, *f.n.*, 'dældɪ, dáldi

Dalgetty, *f.n.*, dæl'getɪ, dalgétti; dəl'getɪ, dălgétti

Dalgety, *f.n.*, dæl'getɪ, dalgétti; dəl'getɪ, dălgétti

Dalgety Bay *Fife*, dəl'getɪ, dălgétti

Dalgleish, *f.n.*, dæl'gliʃ, dalgleésh

Dalhousie, Earl of, dæl'haʊzɪ, dalhówzi. *Appropriate also for* ~ *Castle.*

Daliburgh *W. Isles*, 'dælɪbərə, dálibŭră

Daligan, *f.n.*, 'dælɪgən, dáligăn

Dalkeith *Lothian*, dæl'kiθ, dal-keéth. *Appropriate also for the Earl of* ~.

Dall, *f.n.*, dæl, dal; dɔl, dawl

Dallas *Grampian*, 'dæləs, dálăss
Dalley, *f.n.*, 'dælɪ, dáli
Dalling, *f.n.*, 'dælɪŋ, dáling
Dallinghoo *Suffolk*, ,dælɪŋ'hu,
daling-hóo
Dallington *Northants.*, 'dælɪŋtən,
dálingtŏn
Dallington *E. Sussex*, 'dælɪŋtən,
dálingtŏn; 'dɒlɪŋtən, dólling-
tŏn
Dally, *f.n.*, 'dælɪ, dáli
Dalmahoy *Lothian*, ,dælmə'hɔɪ,
dalmähóy
Dalmeny *Lothian*, dæl'menɪ, dal-
ménni; dəl'menɪ, dălménni.
*The first is appropriate for
Baron* ∼.
Dalmore *W. Isles*, dæl'mɔr,
dalmór. *Appropriate also for* ∼
Distillery.
Dalnacardoch *Tayside*, ,dælnə-
'kɑrdəx, dalnăka̋ardŏch
Dalnaspidal *Tayside*, ,dælnə'spɪdl,
dalnă-spíddl
Dalness *S'clyde*, dæl'nes, dal-néss
Daloni, *C.n.*, 'dælənɪ, dálŏni
Dalriada *Co. Antrim*, ,dælrɪ'ædə,
dalri-áddă
Dalry *Edinburgh*, dəl'raɪ, dălrí
Dalrymple, *f.n.*, dəl'rɪmpl, dăl-
rímpl; dæl'rɪmpl, dalrímpl;
'dælrɪmpl, dálrimpl. *The first is
appropriate for the family name
of the Earl of Stair and thus also
for Viscount* ∼.
Dalrymple *S'clyde*, dəl'rɪmpl,
dălrímpl
Dalserf *S'clyde*, dəl'sɜrf, dăl-sérf
D'Alton, *f.n.*, 'dɔltən, dáwltŏn
Dalton, *f.n.*, 'dɔltən, dáwltŏn
Daltry, *f.n.*, 'dɔltrɪ, dáwltri
Dalway, *f.n.*, 'dɔlweɪ, dáwlway
Dalwhinnie *H'land*, dəl'hwɪnɪ,
dăl-whínni
Dalwood, *f.n.*, 'dælwʊd, dálwŏŏd
Dalwood *Devon*, 'dɔlwʊd, dáwl-
wŏŏd; 'dælwʊd, dálwŏŏd
Daly, *f.n.*, 'deɪlɪ, dáyli
Dalyell of the Binns, *f.n.*, di'el əv
ðə 'bɪnz, dee-éll ŏv thĕ bínz
Dalzell, *f.n.*, di'el, dee-éll; 'dælzel,
dálzel. *The first is appropriate
for Baron Hamilton of* ∼.
Dalzell-Payne, *f.n.*, di'el 'peɪn,
dee-éll páyn
Dalziel, *f.n.*, di'el, dee-éll;
'dælzil, dálzeel
Dalziel *S'clyde*, di'el, dee-éll
Dalziel of Kirkcaldy, Barony of,
di'el əv kər'kɒdɪ, dee-éll ŏv
kŭrkóddi
Dalziel of Wooler, Barony of,
'dælzil əv 'wʊlər, dálzeel ŏv
wŏŏlĕr

Daman, William, *Elizabethan
composer*, 'deɪmən, dáymăn
Damant, *f.n.*, də'mænt, dămánt
D'Ambrumenil, *f.n.*, dæm-
'brʌmənəl, dambrúmmĕnĕl;
dɒm'brumənəl, dombróŏmĕnĕl
Damer, *f.n.*, 'deɪmər, dáymĕr
Damerell, *f.n.*, 'dæmərəl,
dámmĕrĕl
Damerham *Hants*, 'dæmərəm,
dámmĕrăm
Damiano, *f.n.*, ,dæmɪ'ɑnoʊ,
dammi-a̋anō
Dammarell, *f.n.*, 'dæmərəl,
dámmărĕl
Dampier, *f.n.*, 'dæmpɪər, dámpi-ĕr
Danaher, *f.n.*, 'dænəhər, dánnă-
-hĕr
Danby Wiske *N. Yorks.*, 'dænbɪ
'wɪsk, dánbi wisk
Danckwerts, *f.n.*, 'dæŋkwərts,
dánkwĕrts
Dancy, *f.n.*, 'dænsɪ, dánssi
Dancyger, *f.n.*, 'dænsɪgər, dáns-
sigĕr
Daneman, *f.n.*, 'deɪnmən, dáyn-
-măn
Dangan, Viscount, 'dæŋgən,
dáng-găn
Daniell, *f.n.*, 'dænjəl, dán-yĕl
Dankworth, *f.n.*, 'dæŋkwɜrθ,
dánkwurth; 'dæŋkwərθ,
dánkwŭrth
Dannreuther, *f.n.*, 'dænrɔɪtər,
dánroytĕr
Danos, *f.n.*, 'deɪnɒs, dáynoss
d'Antal, *f.n.*, 'dæntl, dántl
Danvers, *f.n.*, 'dænvərz, dánvĕrz
Danyel, *f.n.*, 'dænjəl, dán-yĕl
Danygraig *Gwent*, ,dænə'graɪg,
dannăgríg
Dan yr Ogof Caves *Powys*,
,dæn ər 'ɒgɒv, dan ăr óggov
Danziger, *f.n.*, 'dæntsɪgər,
dántsiggĕr
D'Arcy de Knayth, Baroness,
'dɑrsɪ də 'neɪθ, da̋arssi dĕ náyth
Darent, River, *Kent*, 'dærənt,
dárrĕnt
Darenth *Kent*, 'dærənθ, dárrĕnth
Daresbury *Ches.*, 'dɑrzbərɪ,
da̋arzbŭri. *Appropriate also for
Baron* ∼.
Darewski, *f.n.*, də'ruskɪ, dăroóski
Dargavel, *f.n.*, 'dɑrgəvel, da̋ar-
găvel
Darite *Cornwall*, də'raɪt, dărít
Darke, *f.n.*, dɑrk, daark
Darlaston *W. Midlands*, 'dɑrlə-
stən, da̋arlăstŏn
Darlingscott *Warwicks.*, 'dɑrskət,
da̋arsskŏt
Darlington *Durham*, 'dɑrlɪŋtən,
da̋arlingtŏn

Darlow, *f.n.*, 'dɑrloʊ, daárlō
Darnac, *f.n.*, 'dɑrnæk, daárnack
Darnall *S. Yorks.*, 'dɑrnl, daárnl
Darowen *Powys*, də'roʊən, dắrŏ-ën
Darragh, *f.n.*, 'dærə, dárră;
  'dærəx, dárrǎch
Darsham *Suffolk*, 'dɑrʃəm, daár-shăm
Dartmouth *Devon*, 'dɑrtməθ, daártmŭth. *Appropriate also for the Earl of* ~.
Darvall, *f.n.*, 'dɑrvl, daárvl
Darvel *S'clyde*, 'dɑrvl, daárvl
Darvell, *f.n.*, 'dɑrvl, daárvl
Darwen *Lancs.*, 'dɑrwɪn, daárwĕn;
  'dærən, dárrĕn
Darwin, *f.n.*, 'dɑrwɪn, daárwin
Daryll, *f.n.*, 'dærɪl, dárril
Daryush, *f.n.*, 'dærɪʊʃ, dárri--ōōsh
Dasent, *f.n.*, 'deɪsənt, dáyssĕnt
Dashper, *f.n.*, 'dæʃpər, dáshpĕr
Dassells *Herts.*, 'dæslz, dásslz
Dassie, *f.n.*, 'dæsɪ, dássi
Dastor, *f.n.*, 'dæstər, dástor
Daszak, *f.n.*, 'dæʃæk, dáshack
Datson, *f.n.*, 'dætsən, dátssŏn
Datyner, *f.n.*, 'dætɪnər, dáttinĕr
Daube, *f.n.*, dɔb, dawb; 'daʊbə, dówbĕ
Daubeney, *f.n.*, 'dɔbnɪ, dáwb-ni
Dauncey, *f.n.*, 'dɔnsɪ, dáwnssi
Dauntsey, *f.n.*, 'dɔntsɪ, dáwntssi
Dauthieu, *f.n.*, 'doʊtjə, dṓt-yö
Davaar *S'clyde*, də'vɑr, dăvaár
Davan-Wetton, *f.n.*, 'deɪvən 'wetən, dáyvăn wéttŏn
Davenham *Ches.*, 'deɪvənəm, dáyvĕnăm; 'deɪnəm, dáynăm
Davenport, *f.n.*, 'dævənpɔrt, dávvĕnport
Daventry *Northants.*, 'dævəntrɪ, dávvĕntri; 'deɪntrɪ, dáyntri. *The first is appropriate for Viscount* ~.
Davern, *f.n.*, 'dævərn, dávvĕrn
Davey, *f.n.*, 'deɪvɪ, dáyvi
Davidge, *f.n.*, 'dævɪdʒ, dávvij
Davidson, *f.n.*, 'deɪvɪdsən, dáyvidssŏn
Davidstow *Cornwall*, 'deɪvɪdstoʊ, dáyvidsstō
Davie, *f.n.*, 'deɪvɪ, dáyvi. *See also* Thorpe Davie.
Davier, *f.n.*, 'dævɪeɪ, dávvi-ay
Davies, *f.n.*, 'deɪvɪs, dáyviss
d'Avigdor-Goldsmid, *f.n.*, 'dævɪgdɔr 'goʊldsmɪd, dávvigdor góldsmid
Davin, *f.n.*, 'dævɪn, dávvin
Davinson, *f.n.*, 'dævɪnsən, dávvinssŏn
Davion, *f.n.*, 'dævɪən, dávvi-ŏn

Daviot, Gordon, *author*, 'dævɪət, dávvi-ŏt. *Although Elizabeth McIntosh derived this pen-name from the Inverness-shire village of Daviot, she chose to pronounce it differently.*
Daviot, *Grampian, H'land*, 'deɪvɪət, dáyvi-ŏt
Davis, *f.n.*, 'deɪvɪs, dáyviss
Davison, *f.n.*, 'deɪvɪsən, dáyvissŏn
Davson, *f.n.*, 'dævsən, dávssŏn
Davyhulme *Gtr. M'chester*, 'deɪvɪhjum, dáyvi-hewm
Dawbarn, *f.n.*, 'dɔbərn, dáwbărn
Dawick, Viscount, 'dɔ-ɪk, dáw--ick
Dawley Magna *Salop*, 'dɔlɪ 'mægnə, dáwli mágnă
Dawlish *Devon*, 'dɔlɪʃ, dáwlish
Dawnay, *f.n.*, 'dɔnɪ, dáwni. *Appropriate also for Baron* ~.
Dawsholm *Glasgow*, 'dɔzhəlm, dáwz-hŏlm
Dawson, *f.n.*, 'dɔsən, dáwssŏn
Daymond, *f.n.*, 'deɪmənd, dáymŏnd
Ddôl *Clwyd*, ðoʊl, thōl
Dduallt *Gwynedd*, 'ðiætlt, theé-ahlt
Deacy, *f.n.*, 'disɪ, deéssi
Deakin, *f.n.*, 'dikɪn, deékin
Dealtry, *f.n.*, 'dɔltrɪ, dáwltri
Deamer, *f.n.*, 'dimər, deémĕr
Dearden, *f.n.*, 'dɪərdən, deérdĕn
Dearling, *f.n.*, 'dɪərlɪŋ, deérling
Dearmer, *f.n.*, 'dɪərmər, deérmĕr
Dearne, River, *W. & S. Yorks.*, dɜrn, dern
Dearnley, *f.n.*, 'dɜrnlɪ, dérnli
Dearsley, *f.n.*, 'dɪərzlɪ, deérzli
Dearth, *f.n.*, dɜrθ, derth
Deas, *f.n.*, diz, deez
Dease, *f.n.*, dis, deess
Deason, *f.n.*, 'disən, deéssŏn
De'ath, *f.n.*, di'æθ, dee-áth
Debach *Suffolk*, 'debɪdʒ, débbij
De Banzie, *f.n.*, də 'bænzɪ, dĕ bánzi
De Bartolome, *f.n.*, də bɑr-'tɒləmeɪ, dĕ baartóllŏmay
De Bathe, *f.n.*, də 'bɑθ, dĕ baáth
Debbane, *f.n.*, dɪ'bæn, dĕbánn
De Beer, *f.n.*, də 'bɪər, dĕ beér
de Bellaigue, *f.n.*, də bel'eɪg, dĕ belláyg
Deben, River, *Suffolk*, 'dibən, deébĕn
Debeney, *f.n.*, 'debənɪ, débbĕni
Debenham, *f.n.*, 'debənəm, débbĕnăm
Debenham *Suffolk*, 'debənəm, débbĕnăm
Debens, *f.n.*, 'debɪnz, débbĕnz
Debes, *f.n.*, dɪ'bez, dĕbézz

de Bettoyne, *f.n.,* də bə'tɔɪn, dĕ bĕtóyn

De Blank, The Rt. Revd **Joost,** 'joʊst də 'blæŋk, yŏst dĕ blánk

De Blaquiere, Barony of, də 'blækjər, dĕ bláck-yĕr

De Blieck, *f.n.,* də 'blik, dĕ bleék

De Bono, *f.n.,* də 'boʊnoʊ, dĕ bŏnō

De Bounevialle, *f.n.,* də 'bʊnvɪæl, dĕ boónvi-al

Debrett, *f.n.,* də'bret, dĕbrétt

De Broke, *f.n.,* də 'brʊk, dĕ broŏk

De Bruyne, *f.n.,* də 'brunɪ, dĕ broónay

De Buf, *f.n.,* də 'bʌf, dĕ búff

De Bunsen, *f.n.,* də 'bʌnsən, dĕ búnssĕn

De Burgh, *f.n.,* də 'bɜrg, dĕ búrg

De Buriatte, *f.n.,* də 'bjʊərɪæt, dĕ byoóri-at

Deby, *f.n.,* 'dibɪ, deébi

De Candole, *f.n.,* də 'kændoʊl, dĕ kándōl

De Carteret, *f.n.,* də 'kɑrtrət, dĕ kaártrĕt

De Casembroot, *f.n.,* də 'kæsəmbrut, dĕ kássĕmbroot

De Chair, *f.n.,* də'tʃɛər, dĕ cháir; də 'ʃɛər, dĕ sháir

Decies, Baron, 'diʃiz, deésheez

Decimus, *f.n.,* 'desɪməs, déssimŭss

De Comarmond, *f.n.,* də kə-'mɑrmənd, dĕ kŏmaármŏnd

De Coucey, *f.n.,* də 'kʊsɪ, dĕ koóssi

De Courcey, *f.n.,* də 'kɔrsɪ, dĕ kórssi

De Courcy, *f.n.,* də 'kɔrsɪ, dĕ kórssi; də 'kʊərsɪ, dĕ koŏrssi; də 'kɑrsɪ, dĕ kúrssi. *The first is appropriate for Baron Kingsdale's family name.*

De Crespigny, *f.n.,* də 'krepɪnɪ, dĕ kréppini

de Csilléry, *f.n.,* də 'tʃɪlɛərɪ, dĕ chíll-airi

De Cusance, *f.n.,* də 'kuzɑns, dĕ koózaanss

Dederich, *f.n.,* 'dedərɪtʃ, déddĕritch

Dedow, *f.n.,* 'didoʊ, deédō

De Eresby, *f.n.,* 'dɪərzbɪ, deérzbi

De Felice, *f.n.,* ˌdi fɪ'lis, dee fĕleéss

De Ferranti, *f.n.,* də fə'ræntɪ, dĕ fĕránti

Deffee, *f.n.,* də'fi, dĕfeé

Defferary, *f.n.,* ˌdefə'rɛərɪ, deffĕráiri

Defoe, Daniel, *18th-c. author,* dɪ'foʊ, dĕfŏ

De Francia, *f.n.,* də 'frɑnsɪə, dĕ fraánsiä

De Francquen, *f.n.,* də 'fræŋkwɪn, dĕ fránkwĕn

Defrates, *f.n.,* dɪ'freɪts, dĕfráyts

De Frece, *f.n.,* də 'fris, dĕ freéss

De Freitas, *f.n.,* də 'freɪtəs, dĕ fráytäss

Defries, *f.n.,* də'fris, dĕfreéss

Deganwy *Gwynedd,* dɪ'gænʊɪ, dĕgánōō-i

De Garis, *f.n.,* də 'gærɪs, dĕ gárriss

De Gaury, *f.n.,* də 'gɔrɪ, dĕ gáwri

De Gernier, *f.n.,* də 'dʒɜrnɪər, dĕ jérniĕr

De Glehn, *f.n.,* də 'glen, dĕ glén

de Grunwald, Anatole, *film producer,* 'ænətɒl də 'grunvæld, ánnätol dĕ groónvald

De Guingand, *f.n.,* də 'gægɑ̃, dĕ gáng-gaang

D'Egville, *f.n.,* 'degvɪl, dégvil

De Haes, *f.n.,* də 'heɪz, dĕ háyz

Dehaney, *f.n.,* də'heɪnɪ, dĕ-háyni

Deheubarth, *ancient Welsh kingdom,* de'haɪbɑrθ, de-híbaarth

Dehn, *f.n.,* deɪn, dayn

de Hoghton, *f.n.,* də 'hɒtən, dĕ háwtŏn

Deighton, *f.n.,* 'daɪtən, dítŏn; 'deɪtən, dáytŏn. *The second is appropriate for Len ~, author.*

Deighton *W. Yorks.,* 'ditən, deétŏn

Deildre Isaf *Gwynedd,* 'daɪldrɪ 'ɪsæv, díldri íssav

Deiniolen *Gwynedd,* daɪn'jɒlən, dīn-yóllĕn

Deirdre, *C.n.,* 'dɪərdrɪ, deérdri

De Jonge, *f.n.,* də 'jʌŋ, dĕ yúng

De Jongh, *f.n.,* də 'jɒŋ, dĕ yóng

de Keyser, *f.n.,* də 'kaɪzər, dĕ kízĕr

Dekker, *f.n.,* 'dekər, déckĕr

De Krassel, *f.n.,* də 'kræsl, dĕ krássl

de la Bedoyère, *f.n.,* də lɑ ˌbedwɑ'jɛər, dĕ laa bedwä-yáir

De la Bère, *f.n.,* ˌdelə'bɪər, dellăbeér

De Labilliere, *f.n.,* də lɑ'bɪljər, dĕ laabíl-yĕr

Delabole *Cornwall,* 'deləboʊl, déllăbōl; ˌdelə'boʊl, dellăbŏl

Delacombe, *f.n.,* 'deləkum, déllăkoom

Delacour, *f.n.,* 'deləkʊər, déllăkŏōr

Delacourt-Smith, Baron, 'deləkɔrt 'smɪθ, déllăkort smíth

de la Ferté, *f.n.,* də lɑ 'fɛərteɪ, dĕ laa fáirtay

Delafons, *f.n.,* 'deləfɒnz, déllăfonz

de la Fuente, *f.n.,* də lə fʊ'entɪ, dĕ lă fōō-énti
Delahaye, *f.n.,* 'deləheɪ, déllă-hay
De la Haye, *f.n.,* də lɑ 'heɪ, dĕ laa háy
de la Mahotiere, *f.n.,* də lɑ ˌmɑoʊ'tjɛər, dĕ laa maa-ō-tyáir
Delamain, *f.n.,* 'deləmeɪn, déllămayn
de la Mare, *f.n.,* ˌdelə'mɛər, dellămáir; 'deləmɛər, déllămair. *The first is appropriate for the poet, Walter ~.*
De la Marr, *f.n.,* də lə 'mɑr, dĕ lă maár
Delamere, Baron, ˌdelə'mɪər, dellăméer
Delamere *Ches.,* 'deləmɪər, déllămeer
De la Motte, *f.n.,* də lɑ 'mɒt, dĕ laa mótt
Delane, *f.n.,* də'leɪn, dĕláyn
Delaney, *f.n.,* dɪ'leɪnɪ, dĕláyni
De Lange, *f.n.,* də 'lɑ̃ʒ, dĕ laángzh
De-la-Noy, *f.n.,* 'delənɔɪ, déllănoy
Delap, *f.n.,* də'læp, dĕláp
De la Pasture, *f.n.,* də 'læpətʃər, dĕ láppătchĕr
de la Poer Beresford, *f.n.,* də lɑ 'pʊər 'berɪsfərd, dĕ laa pōŏr bérrĕsfŏrd. *Family name of the Marquess of Waterford and of Baron* **Decies.**
de la Pole, *f.n.,* də lɑ 'pʊl, dĕ laa pōŏl
Delapré Abbey *Northants.,* 'deləpreɪ, déllăpray
Delargy, *f.n.,* də'lɑrgɪ, dĕlaárgi
De Larrinaga, *f.n.,* də ˌlærɪ'nɑgə, dĕ larrinaágă
De La Rue, *f.n.,* ˌdelə'ru, dellăróo
De La Salle, *f.n.,* də lɑ 'sɑl, dĕ laa saál
De la Torre, *f.n.,* də lɑ 'tɔr, dĕ laa tór
De Laubenque, *f.n.,* də 'lʊbeŋk, dĕ lŏbenk
De La Warr, Earl, 'deləwɛər, déllăwair
Delbanco, *f.n.,* del'bæŋkoʊ, delbánkŏ
Delderfield, *f.n.,* 'deldərfild, délděrfeeld
Delephine, *f.n.,* 'deləpin, déllĕpeen
De Lestang, *f.n.,* də 'leɪtɑ̃, dĕ láytaang
Delevingne, *f.n.,* 'deləvin, déllĕveen
Delfont, *f.n.,* 'delfɒnt, délfont. *Appropriate also for Baron ~.*
Delgaty Castle, *also spelt* **Delgatie,** *Grampian,* 'delgətɪ, délgăti

De Lingen, *f.n.,* də 'lɪŋən, dĕ líng-ĕn
De Lisle, *f.n.,* də 'laɪl, dĕ líl
De L'Isle, Viscount, də 'laɪl, dĕ líl
Delith, *C.n.,* 'delɪθ, déllith
Delius, Frederick, *composer,* 'dilɪəs, déeliūss
Deller, *f.n.,* 'delər, déllĕr
Dellow, *f.n.,* 'deloʊ, déllŏ
Del Mar, *f.n.,* del 'mɑr, del maár
Deloitte, *f.n.,* də'lɔɪt, dĕlóyt
Delomosne, *f.n.,* 'deləmoʊn, déllŏmōn
De Lotbinière, *f.n.,* də 'loʊbɪnjɛər, dĕ lóbin-yair
Del Renzio, *f.n.,* del 'renzɪoʊ, del rénziŏ
Delrez, *f.n.,* 'delreɪ, déllray
Del Riego, Teresa, *composer,* tə'reɪzə del rɪ'eɪgoʊ, tĕráyză del ri-áygō
DelStrother, *f.n.,* del 'strʌðər, del strúthĕr
del Tufo, *f.n.,* del 'tufoʊ, del tóofō
de Lukacz-Leisner, *f.n.,* də 'lukætʃ 'leznər, dĕ lóokatch lézznĕr
Delury, *f.n.,* də'lʊərɪ, dĕlŏŏri
Delval, *f.n.,* del'væl, delvál
Delves *W. Midlands,* delvz, delvz
Demaid, *f.n.,* də'meɪd, dĕmáyd
de Manio, *f.n.,* də 'mænɪoʊ, dĕ mánniŏ
Demant, *f.n.,* dɪ'mænt, dĕmánt
Demarco, *f.n.,* də'mɑrkoʊ, dĕmaárkŏ
De Mauley, Baron, də 'mɔlɪ, dĕ máwli
Demel, *f.n.,* 'deml, démml
De Minvielle, *f.n.,* də 'menvəl, dĕ ménvĕl
De Moleyns, *f.n.,* də 'mʌlɪnz, dĕ múllĕnz; 'deməlinz, démmŏleenz. *The first is also appropriate for Baron ~. See* **Eveleigh-de-Moleyns.**
De Montalt, Baron, ˌdemənt'ælt, demmŏntált
De Montmorency, *f.n.,* də ˌmɒntmə'rensɪ, dĕ montmŏrénssi; də ˌmɒmə'rɑ̃sɪ, dĕ mŏngmŏraángssi. *The second was the pronunciation of the late Viscount of Mountmorres.*
Demoulpied, *f.n.,* də'moʊlpɪed, dĕmŏlpi-edd
Dempster, *f.n.,* 'dempstər, démpstĕr
De Muralt, *f.n.,* də 'mjʊərælt, dĕ myŏŏralt
Demuth, *f.n.,* də'mjuθ, dĕméwth; 'demət, démmŭt; də'muθ, dĕmōŏth; də'muθ, dĕmóoth

Denaby *S. Yorks.*, 'denəbɪ, dénnăbi. *Appropriate also for Denaby Main near by.*

Denbigh *Clwyd*, 'denbɪ, dénbi. *Appropriate also for the Earl of ~.*

Dench, *f.n.*, dentʃ, dentch

Deneke, *f.n.*, 'denɪkɪ, dénnĕki. *Appropriate for the Clara Sophie ~ scholarship at Oxford University.*

De Nevers, *f.n.*, də 'nevərz, dě névvĕrz

Dengie *Essex*, 'dendʒɪ, dénji

Denholm *Borders*, 'denəm, dénnŏm

Denholme *W. Yorks.*, 'denhɒlm, dén-hollm

Dening, *f.n.*, 'denɪŋ, dénning

Denne, *f.n.*, den, den

Dennehy, *f.n.*, 'denəhɪ, dénnĕ-hi

Denney, *f.n.*, 'denɪ, dénni

Dennistoun *S'clyde*, 'denɪstən, dénnistŏn

Denny, *f.n.*, 'denɪ, dénni

Denselow, *f.n.*, 'denzɪloʊ, dénzĕlō

Dent, *f.n.*, dent, dent

Dent-de-Lion *Kent*, 'dændɪlaɪən, dándili-ŏn

Denton *Cambs., Norfolk, Oxon.*, 'dentən, déntŏn

Denwick *Northd.*, 'denɪk, dénnick

Denys, *C.n.*, 'denɪs, dénniss

de Nys, *f.n.*, də 'nis, dě neéss

Denzil, *C.n.*, 'denzɪl, dénzil

Deopham *Norfolk*, 'dipəm, deépăm; 'difəm, deéfăm

Depden *Suffolk*, 'depdən, dépdĕn

de Peyer, *f.n.*, də 'paɪər, dě pí-ĕr

Deptford *London*, 'detfərd, déttfŏrd

De Piro, *f.n.*, də 'pɪəroʊ, dě peérō

Depledge, *f.n.*, dɪ'pledʒ, dĕpléjj

Deplidge, *f.n.*, 'deplɪdʒ, déplij

De Polnay, *f.n.*, də 'poʊlneɪ, dě pólnay; də 'pɒlneɪ, dě pólnay

Depport, *f.n.*, 'depɔrt, dépport

De Quesne, *f.n.*, də 'keɪn, dě káyn

Derby *Derby.*, 'dɑrbɪ, daárbi. *Appropriate also for the Earl of ~.*

Derbyshire, *f.n.*, 'dɑrbɪʃər, daárbishĕr

Dereham *Norfolk*, 'dɪərəm, deérăm

De Reyghère, *f.n.*, də 'reɪgər, dě ráygĕr

Derges, *f.n.*, 'dɜrdʒɪs, dérjĕss

Deri, *f.n.*, 'dɛərɪ, dáiri

Deri *Mid Glam.*, 'derɪ, dérri

Dering, *f.n.*, 'dɪərɪŋ, deéring

Deritend *W. Midlands*, ˌderɪt'end, derrit-énd

d'Erlanger, *f.n.*, 'dɛərlɑ̃ʒeɪ, dáirlaang-zhay

Dernawilt *Co. Fermanagh*, ˌdɜrnə-'wɪlt, dernăwílt

Derner, *f.n.*, 'dɜrnər, dérnĕr

De Roet, *f.n.*, də 'roʊɪt, dě ró-ĕt

de Rohan, *f.n.*, də 'roʊən, dě ró-ăn

de Ros, Baroness, də 'rus, dě roóss

Derriaghy, *also spelt* **Derryaghy**, *Co. Antrim*, ˌderɪ'æxɪ, derri-áchi

Derry *Co. name.* 'derɪ, dérri

Derryaghy *see* **Derriaghy**

Derrygonnelly *Co. Fermanagh*, ˌderɪ'gɒnəlɪ, derrigónnĕli

Derrylin *Co. Fermanagh*, ˌderɪ'lɪn, derrilín

Dersingham *Norfolk*, 'dɜrzɪŋəm, dérzing-ăm

Derville, *f.n.*, 'dɜrvɪl, dérvil

Dervock *Co. Antrim*, 'dɜrvɒk, dérvock

Derwen *Clwyd, Mid Glam.*, 'dɛərwɪn, dáirwĕn

Derwenlas *Powys*, ˌdɛərwɪn'lɑs, dairwĕnlaáss

Derwent, Baron, 'dɑrwənt, daárwĕnt

Derwenthaugh *Tyne & Wear*, 'dɛərwənthɑf, dáirwĕnt-haaf; 'dɜrwənthɒf, dérwĕnt-hoff

Derwentwater *Cumbria*, 'dɜrwəntwɔtər, dérwĕnt-wawtĕr. *Appropriate also for the Earldom of ~, attainted after the Jacobite rebellion of 1715.*

Deryck, *C.n.*, 'derɪk, dérrick

de St. Croix, *f.n.*, də snt 'krwɑ, dě sĭnt krwaá; də snt 'krɔɪ, dě sĭnt króy

de Ste. Croix, *f.n.*, də snt 'krwɑ, dě sĭnt krwaá; də snt 'krɔɪ, dě sĭnt króy

De Sales, *f.n.*, də 'sɑlz, dě saálz

De Salis, *f.n.*, də 'sælɪs, dě sáliss; də 'sɑlz, dě saálz; də 'seɪlɪs, dě sáyliss

De Saram, *f.n.*, də 'sɛərəm, dě sáirăm

Desart, Earldom of, 'dezərt, dézzărt

de Satgé, *f.n.*, də 'sætdʒeɪ, dě sátjay

De Saubergue, *f.n.*, də 'soʊbɜrg, dě sóberg

De Saumarez, *f.n.*, də 'sɒmərɪz, dě sómmărĕz; də 'sɒmərez, dě sómmărezz. *The first is appropriate for Baron ~.*

De Sausmarez, *f.n.*, də 'sɒmərɪz, dě sómmărĕz; də 'sɒmərez, dě sómmărezz

de Saxe, *f.n.*, də 'sæks, dĕ sácks
Desbois, *f.n.*, deı'bwɑ, daybwaá
Desborough, *f.n.*, 'dezbərə, dézbŭră. *Appropriate also for the Barony of* ∼.
Desch, *f.n.*, deʃ, desh
Deschamps, *f.n.*, 'deʃən, déshăn; 'deıʃɑ̃, dáy-shaa*ng*
Des Champs, *f.n.*, 'deʃən, déshăn; 'deı ʃɑ̃, dáy shaa*ng*
De Selincourt, *f.n.*, də 'selınkərt, dĕ séllin-kort
Desertmartin *Co. Derry*, ,dezərt-'mɑrtın, dezzĕrtmaártin
De Sevin, *f.n.*, də sı'vin, dĕ sĕveén
Desford *Leics.*, 'desfərd, déssförd
Desforges, *f.n.*, deı'fərdʒ, dayfórj
Des Graz, *f.n.*, deı 'grɑ, day graá
Deslandes, *f.n.*, deı'lɑ̃d, day-laà*ng*d
de Soissons, *f.n.*, də 'swɑsõ, dĕ swaássõng
Desoutter, *f.n.*, dı'sutər, dĕssoó-tĕr
De Souza, *f.n.*, də 'suzə, dĕ soóză
De Stein, *f.n.*, də 'staın, dĕ stín
De Stroumillo, *f.n.*, də 'strumılou, dĕ stroómilõ
Desvaux, *f.n.*, dı'vou, dĕvó; deı'vou, dayvó
Des Voeux, *f.n.*, deı 'vɜ, day vố
Dethick, *Derby.*, 'deθık, déthick
De Thuillier, *f.n.*, də 'twılıər, dĕ twílliĕr
Dettmer, *f.n.*, 'detmər, déttmĕr
Deuchar, *f.n.*, 'djuxər, déwch̲ăr
Deuchrie Dod, *Lothian*, 'djuxrı 'dɒd, déwch̲ri dód
Deugh, Water of, *D. & G.*, djux, dewch̲
De Valence, *f.n.*, də væ'lɑ̃s, dĕ valaáng ss
De Valera, *f.n.*, də və'lɛərə, dĕ vălăiră
Devall, *f.n.*, də'væl, dĕvál
Devally, *f.n.*, dı'væli, dĕváli
Devaney, *f.n.*, dı'veını, dĕváyni
Devas, *f.n.*, dı'væs, dĕváss
Develin, *f.n.*, dı'velın, dĕvéllin
Deveney, *f.n.*, 'divnı, deévni
Devenish, *f.n.*, 'devənıʃ, dév-vĕnish; 'divənıʃ, deévĕnish
Deverell, *f.n.*, 'devərəl, dévvĕrĕl
Devereux, *f.n.*, 'devəruks, dév-vĕrooks; 'devəreks, dévvĕrecks; 'devərə, dévvĕră; 'devəru, dévvĕroo; 'devərou, dévvĕrõ. *The first is that of the family name of Viscount Hereford, although the second is said to be usual in the former counties of Hereford and Montgomery. A descendant of the Elizabethan*

Robert ∼, *Earl of Essex, also favours the first.*
Deveron, River, *Grampian*, 'devərən, dévvĕrŏn
Devers, *f.n.*, 'divərz, deévĕrz; 'devərz, dévvĕrz
De Vesci, Viscount, də 'vesı, dĕ véssi
Deveson, *f.n.*, 'divısən, deévĕssŏn
de Veulle, *f.n.*, də 'vɜl, dĕ vốl
Devey, *f.n.*, dı'vi, dĕvée; 'divı, deévi
De Villiers, *f.n.*, də 'vılərz, dĕ víllĕrz; də 'vıljərz, dĕ víl-yĕrz. *The first is appropriate for Baron* ∼.
Devine, *f.n.*, dı'vin, dĕvéen; dı'vaın, dĕvín
de Vitré, *f.n.*, də 'vitrı, dĕ véetri
Devizes *Wilts.*, dı'vaızız, dĕvízĕz
Devlin, *f.n.*, 'devlın, dévlin
Devoke Water *Cumbria*, 'devək 'wɔtər, dévvŏk wáwtĕr
Devol, *f.n.*, də'voul, dĕvốl
Devon *Co. name*, 'devən, dévvŏn
Devon, River, *Notts.*, 'divən, deévŏn
Devon, River, *Tayside–Central*, 'devən, dévvŏn
Devonald, *f.n.*, 'devənəld, dévvŏnăld
Devons, *f.n.*, 'devənz, dévvŏnz
Devoran *Cornwall*, 'devərən, dévvŏrăn; 'devrən, dévrŏn
de Waal, *f.n.*, də 'vɑl, dĕ vaál
Dewar, *f.n.*, 'djuər, dyŏŏ-ăr
De Warfaz, *f.n.*, də 'wɔrfæz, dĕ wáwrfaz
De Warrenne, *f.n.*, də 'wɒrən, dĕ wórrĕn
Dewes, *f.n.*, djuz, dewz
Dewi, *Welsh C.n.*, 'dewı, dé-wi
De Wolff, *f.n.*, də 'wʊlf, dĕ wŏŏlf
Dewrance, *f.n.*, 'djuərəns, dyŏŏrănss
Dey, *f.n.*, deı, day
de Yevele, *f.n.*, də 'jivəlı, dĕ yéevĕli. *Appropriate for Henry* ∼, *14th-c. master-mason and architect.*
D'Eyncourt, *f.n.*, 'deıŋkərt, dáynk-ort; 'deıŋkərt, dáynkŭrt
De Zoete, *f.n.*, də 'zut, dĕ zoót; də 'zutə, dĕ zoótĕ
De Zouche, *f.n.*, də 'zuʃ, dĕ zoósh
de Zulueta, *f.n.*, də ,zulu'etə, dĕ zooloo-éttă
Dhenin, *f.n.*, 'denın, dénnin
Dhooge, *f.n.*, douɡ, dõg
Dhu Varren *Co. Antrim*, 'du 'værən, doó várrĕn
Diack, *f.n.*, 'daıək, dí-ăk
Diane, *C.n.*, daı'æn, dī-ánn; dı'æn, di-ánn

Diaper, *f.n.*, 'daɪəpər, dí-ăpĕr
Dibden, *f.n.*, 'dɪbdən, díbdĕn
Dibden Purlieu *Hants,* 'dɪbdən 'pərlju; díbdĕn púrlew
Dibdin, *f.n.*, 'dɪbdɪn, díbdin
Dibnah, *f.n.*, 'dɪbnə, díbnă
Dichmont, *f.n.*, 'dɪtʃmɒnt, dítchmont
Dickens, *f.n.*, 'dɪkɪnz, díckĕnz
Dickenson, *f.n.*, 'dɪkɪnsən, díckĕnssŏn
Dicker, *f.n.*, 'dɪkər, díckĕr
Dickins, *f.n.*, 'dɪkɪnz, díckinz; 'dɪkənz, díckĕnz
Dickinson, *f.n.*, 'dɪkɪnsən, díckinssŏn; 'dɪkənsən, díckĕnssŏn
Dicksee, *f.n.*, 'dɪksɪ, dícksi
Didion, *f.n.*, 'dɪdɪən, díddi-ŏn
Dielhenn, *f.n.*, 'dɪlən, déelĕn
Dienes, *f.n.*, dinz, deenz
Digbeth Institute *Birmingham,* 'dɪgbəθ, dígbĕth
Digges, *f.n.*, dɪgz, digz
Diggins, *f.n.*, 'dɪgɪnz, dígginz
Dighty Water *Tayside,* 'dɪxtɪ 'wɔtər, díchti wáwtĕr
Diglis *H. & W.,* 'dɪglɪs, dígliss
Dihewid, *also spelt* **Dihewyd,** *Dyfed,* di'hewɪd, dee-hé-wid
Dilger, *f.n.*, 'dɪldʒər, díljĕr
Dilhorne, Viscount, 'dɪlən, díllŏn
Dilhorne *Staffs.,* 'dɪlərn, díllŏrn; 'dɪlɔrn, díllorn
Dilke, *f.n.*, dɪlk, dilk
Dillwyn *see* **Dilwyn**
Dilly, *f.n.*, 'dɪlɪ, dílli
Dilworth, *f.n.*, 'dɪlwɜrθ, dílwurth
Dilwyn *Welsh C.n.,* *also spelt* **Dillwyn,** 'dɪlwɪn, dílwin
Dilwyn, *f.n.*, 'dɪlwɪn, dílwin
Dilys, *Welsh C.n.,* 'dɪlɪs, dílliss
Dimbleby, *f.n.*, 'dɪmblbɪ, dímblbi
Dimelow, *f.n.*, 'dɪmɪloʊ, dímmĕlō
Diment, *f.n.*, 'daɪmənt, dímĕnt
Dimmock, *f.n.*, 'dɪmək, dímmŏk
Dimoline, *f.n.*, 'dɪməlin, dímmŏleen
Dimont, *f.n.*, 'daɪmənt, dímŏnt
Dimuantes, *f.n.*, 'dɪmju'æntiz, dimmew-ánteez
Dinas, *Dyfed, Gwynedd, Mid Glam.,* 'dinæs, déenass. *Appropriate for both places of the name in Dyfed, and also for both in Gwynedd.*
Dinas Mawddwy *Gwynedd,* 'dinæs 'maʊðuɪ, déenass mówthoo-i
Dinas Oleu *Gwynedd,* 'dinæs 'oʊlaɪ, déenass ólī
Dinas Powis *S. Glam.,* 'dɪnæs 'paʊɪs, dínnass pów-iss
Dinchope *Salop,* 'dɪntʃəp, díntchŏp

Dinedor *H. & W.,* 'daɪn'dɔr, dín-dór
Dineen, *f.n.*, dɪ'nin, dinéen
Dinefwr Castle *Dyfed,* dɪ'nevʊər, dinévvōōr. *Welsh form of* **Dynevor,** *q.v.*
Dinenage, *f.n.*, 'daɪnɪdʒ, dínij
Dines, *f.n.*, daɪnz, dīnz
Dingestow *Gwent,* 'dɪndʒɪstoʊ, dínjĕstō
Dinglay, *f.n.*, 'dɪŋgleɪ, díng-glay
Dingley, *f.n.*, 'dɪŋlɪ, díng-li; 'dɪŋglɪ, díng-gli
Dingwall *H'land,* 'dɪŋwɔl, díng-wawl; 'dɪŋwəl, díng-wăl
Dinnie, *f.n.*, 'dɪnɪ, dínni
Dinorwic *Gwynedd,* dɪ'nɔrwɪk, dinórwick
Diosgydd Uchaf *Gwynedd,* di'ɒsgɪð 'ɪxəv, dee-óssgith íchăv
Diosy, *f.n.*, di'oʊzɪ, dee-ōzi
Diplock, *f.n.*, 'dɪplɒk, díplock
Diptford *Devon,* 'dɪpfərd, dípförd
Dirac, *f.n.*, dɪ'ræk, diráck
Dirleton *Lothian,* 'dɜrltən, dírltŏn
Discoed *Powys,* 'dɪskɔɪd, dísskoyd
Diseworth *Leics.,* 'daɪzwɜrθ, dízwurth
Dishforth *N. Yorks.,* 'dɪʃfərθ, dísh-förth
Disley, *f.n.*, 'dɪzlɪ, dízzli
Dispain, *f.n.*, 'dɪspeɪn, dísspayn
Disraeli, *f.n.*, dɪz'reɪlɪ, dizráyli
Diss *Norfolk,* dɪs, diss
Disserth *Powys,* 'dɪsərθ, díssĕrth
Ditcheat *Somerset,* 'dɪtʃɪt, dítchĕt
Dittisham *Devon,* 'dɪtɪsəm, díttissăm; 'dɪtɪʃəm, dítti-shăm; 'dɪtsəm, dítsăm
Divell, *f.n.*, 'daɪvl, dívl
Divin, *f.n.*, 'dɪvɪn, dívvin
Divine, *f.n.*, dɪ'vaɪn, divín
Divis *Co. Antrim,* 'dɪvɪs, dívviss
Dixey, *f.n.*, 'dɪksɪ, dícksi
Doagh *Co. Antrim,* doʊx, dōch
Dobell, *f.n.*, doʊ'bel, dōbéll
Dobie, *f.n.*, 'doʊbɪ, dōbi
Dobing, *f.n.*, 'doʊbɪŋ, dōbing
Dobrée, *f.n.*, 'doʊbreɪ, dōbray. *Appropriate for Bonamy,* 'bɒnəmɪ, bónnămi ~, *scholar and writer, and Georgina* ~, *clarinettist.*
Dobry, *f.n.*, 'dɒbrɪ, dóbri
Dochart, River, *Central,* 'dɒxərt, dóchărt
Docherty, *f.n.*, 'dɒxərtɪ, dóchĕrti
Dochfour, Loch, *H'land,* dɒx'fʊər, dochfōōr
Docwra, *f.n.*, 'dɒkrə, dóckră

Dodgson, *f.n.*, 'dɒdʒsən, dójssŏn;
'dɒdsən, dódssŏn. *The first is
appropriate for Stephen* ~,
composer, the second for Charles
~, *mathematician and author of
'Alice in Wonderland'.*
Dodington, *f.n.*, 'dɒdɪŋtən,
dóddingtŏn
Dodkin, *f.n.*, 'dɒdkɪn, dódkin
Dodman Point *Cornwall*, 'dɒd-
mən, dódmăn
Dodwell, *f.n.*, 'dɒdwəl, dódwĕl;
'dɒdwel, dódwel
Doel, *f.n.*, 'dəʊəl, dő-ĕl
Doepel, *f.n.*, dəʊ'pel, dōpéll
D'Offay, *f.n.*, 'dɒfeɪ, dóffay
Doggart, *f.n.*, 'dɒgərt, dóggărt
Doggett, *f.n.*, 'dɒgɪt, dóggĕt
Doghan, *f.n.*, 'dəʊgən, dőgăn
Doherty, *f.n.*, 'dɒxərtɪ, dóchĕrti;
'dɒhərtɪ, dó-hĕrti; 'dəʊhərtɪ,
dő-hĕrti; 'dəʊərtɪ, dő-ĕrti
Doig, *f.n.*, dɔɪg, doyg; 'dəʊɪg,
dő-ɪg
Dolan, *f.n.*, 'dəʊlən, dőlăn
Dolau *Mid Glam., Powys*, 'dəʊlaɪ,
dőlī
Dolaucothi *Dyfed*, ˌdɒlaɪ'kɒθɪ,
dolli-kóthi
Dolbadarn Castle *Gwynedd*,
dɒl'bædərn, dolbáddărn
Dolbenmaen *Gwynedd*, ˌdɒlben-
'maɪn, dolbenmín
Dolcoath *Cornwall*, dəl'kəʊθ,
dŏlkőth
Doldowlod *Powys*, dɒl'daʊlɒd,
doldówlod
Dolemore, *f.n.*, 'dɒlɪmɔr, dóllĕmor
Dolerw Park *Mid Glam.*, 'dɒl'ɛəru,
dól-áiroo
Doley, *f.n.*, 'dəʊlɪ, dőli
Dolforwyn *Powys*, dɒl'vɔrwɪn,
dolvórwin
Dolgarrog *Gwynedd*, dɒl'gærɒg,
dolgárrog
Dolgellau *Gwynedd*, dɒl'geɪaɪ,
dolgéhlī. Dolgellau *has super-
seded* Dolgelley (*q.v.*) *as the
official spelling.*
Dolgelley, *former spelling for*
Dolgellau, *q.v., Gwynedd*,
dɒl'geɪɪ, dolgéhli. *Since the
change in spelling in August
1958, this pronunciation is no
longer appropriate.*
Dolgoch *Gwynedd*, dɒl'gəʊx,
dolgóch
Dolhendre *Gwynedd*, dɒl'hendrɪ,
dol-héndri
D'Olier, *f.n.*, dɒ'lɪər, dolleér;
'dəʊljeɪ, dől-yay
Dolin, Anton, *British ballet
dancer*, 'æntɒn 'dɒlɪn; ánton
dóllin

Dollan, *f.n.*, 'dəʊlən, dőlăn
Dollar *Central*, 'dɒlər, dóllăr
Dollimore, *f.n.*, 'dɒlɪmɔr, dóllimor
Dolmetsch, *f.n.*, 'dɒlmetʃ, dól-
metch
Dolobran *Powys*, də'lɒbræn,
dŏlóbran
Dolton, *f.n.*, 'dɒltən, dólltŏn
Dolton *Devon*, 'dəʊltən, dőltŏn
Dolwyddelan *Gwynedd*, ˌdɒlwɪ-
'ðelən, dolwithéllăn
Dol-y-Gaer *Powys*, ˌdɒlə'gɛər,
dollăgáir
Dominey, *f.n.*, 'dɒmɪnɪ, dómmini
Dominy, *f.n.*, 'dɒmɪnɪ, dómmini
Domleo, *f.n.*, 'dɒmlɪəʊ, dómliŏ
Donagh *Co. Fermanagh*, 'dəʊnə,
dőnă
Donaghadee *Co. Down*,
ˌdɒnəxə'di, donnăchădeé
Donaghcloney *Co. Down*, ˌdɒnə-
'kləʊnɪ, donnăklőni
Donaghey, *f.n.*, 'dɒnəxɪ, dónnăchi
Donaghmore *Co. Tyrone*, ˌdɒnəx-
'mɔr, donnăchmór
Donaghy, *f.n.*, 'dɒnəxɪ, dónnăchi;
'dɒnəhɪ, dónnă-hi
Donald, *C.n. and f.n.*, 'dɒnld,
dónnld
Donaldson, *f.n.*, 'dɒnldsən,
dónnldssŏn
Donard, *saint*, 'dɒnərd, dónnărd
Donat, Robert, *actor*, 'dəʊnæt,
dőnat
Donati, *f.n.*, də'nɑtɪ, dŏnáati
Doncaster *S. Yorks.*, 'dɒŋkəstər,
dónkăstĕr. *Appropriate also for
the Earl of* ~.
Done, *f.n.*, dəʊn, dőn
Donegall, Marquess of, 'dɒnɪgɔl,
dónnĕgawl
Donelly, *f.n.*, 'dɒnəlɪ, dónnĕli
Doneraile, Viscount, 'dʌnəreɪl,
dúnnĕrayl
Donert, *f.n.*, 'dɒnərt, dónnĕrt
Dongray, *f.n.*, 'dɒŋgreɪ, dóng-gray
Doniach, *f.n.*, 'dɒnjæk, dón-yack
Donibristle *Fife*, ˌdɒnɪ'brɪsl,
donnibríssl
Donington, Barony of, 'dʌnɪŋtən,
dúnnington
Donington, *Lincs., Salop*, 'dɒnɪŋ-
tən, dónnington
Donington-on-Bain *Lincs.*,
'dɒnɪŋtən ɒn 'beɪn, dónningtŏn
on báyn; 'dʌnɪŋtən ɒn 'beɪn,
dúnnington on báyn
Donlevy, *f.n.*, dɒn'livɪ, donleévi
Donmall, *f.n.*, 'dɒnməl, dónmăl
Donnachie, *f.n.*, 'dɒnəxɪ, dón-
năchi
Donne, *f.n.*, dɒn, donn; dʌn, dun.
*Although usage varies for the
17th-c. poet and divine, John* ~,

there is some evidence that he used the second.
Donnegan, *f.n.,* 'dɒnɪgən, dónnĕgăn
Donnellan, *f.n.,* 'dɒnələn, dónnĕlăn
Donnelly, *f.n.,* 'dɒnəlɪ, dónnĕli
Donnet, *f.n.,* 'dɒnɪt, dónnĕt
Donnett, *f.n.,* 'dʌnɪt, dúnnĕt
Donohoe, *f.n.,* 'dʌnəhu, dúnnŏhoo; 'dɒnəhu, dónnŏhoo; 'dɒnəhou, dónnŏhō
Donoughmore, Earl of, 'dʌnəmɔr, dúnnŏmor
Donovan, *f.n.,* 'dʌnəvən, dúnnŏvăn; 'dɒnəvən, dónnŏvăn. *The second is appropriate for the Barony of* ~.
Donyatt *Somerset,* 'dɒnjət, dón-yăt
Doran, *f.n.,* 'dɔrən, dáwrăn
Dore, *f.n.,* dɔr, dor
Dormand, *f.n.,* 'dɔrmænd, dórmand
Dornoch *H'land,* 'dɔrnəx, dórnŏ<u>ch</u>
Dorow, *f.n.,* 'dɒrou, dórrō
Dorrell, *f.n.,* 'dɒrəl, dórrĕl
Dorset *Co. name,* 'dɔrsɪt, dórssĕt
Dorté, *f.n.,* 'dɔrtɪ, dórti
Dotrice, *f.n.,* dəˈtris, dŏtréess
Douai College, *also spelt* **Douay,** *Berks.,* 'dauɛɪ, dów-ay. *The* ~ *Bible is pronounced both* 'duɛɪ, doó-ay *and* 'dauɛi, dów-ay.
Doublebois *Cornwall,* 'dʌblbɔɪz, dúbbl-boyz
Douch, *f.n.,* dautʃ, dowtch; dutʃ, dootch
Doudney, *f.n.,* 'daudnɪ, dówdni; 'dudnɪ, doódni
Douet, *f.n.,* 'duɛɪ, doó-ay
Dougall, *f.n.,* 'dugl, doógl
Dougan, *f.n.,* 'dugən, doogăn
Dougherty, *f.n.,* 'dɒxərtɪ, dó<u>ch</u>ĕrti; 'douərtɪ, dó-ĕrti; 'dauərtɪ, dów-ĕrti
Doughton *Glos.,* 'dʌftən, dúfftŏn
Doughty, *f.n.,* 'dautɪ, dówti. *Appropriate also for* ~ *St., London.*
Douglas, *C.n. and f.n.,* 'dʌgləs, dúglăss
Douglas-Home, *f.n.,* 'dʌgləs 'hjum, dúglăss héwm. *This is the family name of the Earls of Home. The pronunciation is thus appropriate for Sir Alec* ~ *(Baron* **Home of the Hirsel,** *q.v.), politician, Henry* ~, *ornithologist, and William* ~, *playwright.*
Douglas and Clydesdale, Marquess of, 'dʌgləs ənd 'klaɪdzdeɪl, dúglăss ănd klídzdayl

Douglass, *f.n.,* 'dʌgləs, dúglăss
Douie, *f.n.,* 'djuɪ, déw-i; 'duɪ, doó-i; 'dauɪ, dów-i
Doulting *Somerset,* 'doultɪŋ, dólting; 'daultɪŋ, dówlting
Doulton, *f.n.,* 'doultən, dóltŏn
Dounby *Orkney,* 'dunbɪ, doónbi
Doune, Lord, dun, doon
Doune *Central, S'clyde,* dun, doon
Dounreay *H'land,* 'dunreɪ, doónray. *There is an older form* **Downreay,** *pronounced* 'daunreɪ, dównray
Douro, Marquess, 'duərou, doórō
Dousland *Devon,* 'dauzlənd, dówzlănd
Douthwaite, *f.n.,* 'dauθweɪt, dówthwayt
Dovaston, *f.n.,* 'dʌvəstən, dúvvăstŏn
Dove, River, *Derby.–Staffs. border,* dʌv, duvv
Dovedale, *stretch of R. Dove Valley on Derby.–Staffs. border,* 'dʌvdeɪl, dúvdayl
Dovenby *Cumbria,* 'dʌvənbɪ, dúvvĕnbi
Dovendale *Lincs.,* 'dʌvəndeɪl, dúvvĕndayl
Dover, *f.n.,* 'douvər, dóvĕr
Dover *Kent,* 'douvər, dóvĕr
Doverdale, Barony of, 'dʌvərdeɪl, dúvvĕrdayl
Doveridge *Derby.,* 'dʌvərɪdʒ, dúvvĕrij
Doveton, *f.n.,* 'dʌvtən, dúvvtŏn
Dovey, *f.n.,* 'douvɪ, dóvi; 'dʌvɪ, dúvvi
Dovey, River, *Gwynedd–Powys,* 'dʌvɪ, dúvvi. *The Welsh spelling is* **Dyfi,** *q.v.*
Dow, *f.n.,* dau, dow
Dowally *Tayside,* 'dauəlɪ, dów-ăli
Dowanhill *S'clyde,* 'dauənhɪl, dówăn-hil
Dowd, *f.n.,* daud, dowd
Dowdall, *f.n.,* 'daudl, dówdl
Dowden, *f.n.,* 'daudən, dówdĕn
Dowdeswell *Glos.,* 'daudzwəl, dówdzwĕl
Dowding, *f.n.,* 'daudɪŋ, dówding
Dowell, *f.n.,* 'dauəl, dów-ĕl
Dower, *f.n.,* 'dauər, dówĕr
Dowie, *f.n.,* 'dauɪ, dów-i
Dowlais *Mid Glam.,* 'daulaɪs, dówlīss
Dowland, John, *16th–17th-c. lutenist and composer,* 'daulənd, dówlănd
Dowland *Devon,* 'daulənd, dówlănd
Dowle, *f.n.,* daul, dowl
Dowler, *f.n.,* 'daulər, dówlĕr

Dowling, f.n., 'daʊlɪŋ, dówling
Dowlish Wake Somerset, 'daʊlɪʃ, dówlish
Down Co. name, daʊn, down
Downend Avon, I. of Wight, daʊn'end, down-énd
Downes, f.n., daʊnz, downz
Downham Kent, 'daʊnəm, dówn-ăm
Downpatrick Co. Down, daʊn-'pætrɪk, downpátrick
Downreay see Dounreay
Dowsby Lincs., 'daʊzbɪ, dówzbi
Dowse, f.n., daʊs, dowss
Dowsing, Inner and Outer, shoals, off Lincs. coast, 'daʊzɪŋ, dówzing
Dowson, f.n., 'daʊsən, dówssŏn
Doyle, f.n., dɔɪl, doyl
Dozmary Pool Cornwall, 'dɒzmrɪ 'pul, dóz-mri pool
Draffen, f.n., 'dræfən, dráffĕn
Draffin, f.n., 'dræfɪn, dráffin
Drage, f.n., dreɪdʒ, drayj
Draisey, f.n., 'dreɪzɪ, dráyzi
Drakelow Derby., 'dreɪkloʊ, dráyklō
Drake's Broughton H. & W., 'dreɪks 'brɔtən, dráyks bráwtŏn
Draughton Northants., 'drɔtən, dráwtŏn
Draughton N. Yorks., 'dræftən, dráfftŏn
Dravers, f.n., 'dreɪvərz, dráyvĕrz
Dreaper, f.n., 'dreɪpər, dráypĕr
Drefach Dyfed, dre'vɑx, drev-vaách
Drellingore Kent, 'drelɪŋgər, drélling-gor
Drever, f.n., 'drɪvər, dréevĕr
Drewe, f.n., dru, droo
Drewsteignton Devon, 'druz-'teɪntən, dróoztáyntŏn
Dreyer, f.n., 'draɪər, drí-ĕr
Drian Gallery, London art gallery, 'drɪən, dree-ăn
Dribbell, f.n., drɪ'bel, dribéll
Driberg, f.n., 'draɪbərg, dríberg
Driby Lincs., 'draɪbɪ, dríbi
Driffield Glos., Humberside, 'drɪfɪld, dríffeeld
Drighlington W. Yorks., 'drɪglɪŋtən, dríglingtŏn; 'drɪlɪŋtən, dríllingtŏn
Drimnin H'land, 'drɪmnɪn, drímnin
Droeshout, Martin, 17th-c. Anglo-Flemish engraver, also spelt Maerten, mɑrtɪn 'drushaʊt, maártin dróoss-howt
Drogheda, Earl of, 'drɔɪɪdə, dróy-ĕ-dă
Drogo Castle Devon, 'droʊgoʊ, drṓgō

Droitwich H. & W., 'drɔɪtwɪtʃ, dróyt-witch
Dromantine see Drumantine
Dromara Co. Down, drə'mærə, drŏmárră
Dromgoole, f.n., drɒm'gul, dromgoól
Dromore, Co. Down, Co. Tyrone, drə'mɔr, drŏmór
Dronfield Derby., 'drɒnfɪld, drónfeeld
Drower, f.n., 'draʊər, drówĕr
Drown, f.n., draʊn, drown
Droylsden Gtr. M'chester, 'drɔɪlzdən, dróylzdĕn
Drucker, f.n., 'drʊkər, dróökĕr
Drughorn, f.n., 'drʌghɔrn, drúg-horn
Druiff, f.n., 'druɪf, dróo-iff
Druimuachdar see Drumochter
Drumachose Co. Derry, ˌdrʌmə-'koʊz, drummäkṓz
Drumalbyn, Baron, drʌm'ælbɪn, drumálbin
Drumaness Co. Down, ˌdrʌmə-'nes, drummănéss
Drumantine, also spelt Dromantine, Co. Down, 'drʌməntaɪn, drúmmăntīn
Drumaroad Co. Down, ˌdrʌmə-'roʊd, drummărṓd
Drumbeg H'land, drəm'beg, drŭmbég
Drumbo Co. Down, drəm'boʊ, drŭmbṓ
Drumbuie H'land, drʌm'buɪ, drumbóo-i
Drumelzier Borders, drʌ'miljər, drumméel-yĕr
Drumhain Skye, 'drʊmɪn, dróömin
Drumlanrig and Sanquhar, Earl of, drʌm'lænrɪg ənd 'sæŋkər, drum-lánrig ănd sánkăr
Drumlithie Grampian, drʌm'lɪθɪ, drumlíthi
Drumloughar Co. Armagh, drʌm-'loʊər, drum-lṓ-ĕr
Drumm, f.n., drʌm, drum
Drummond, f.n., drʌmənd, drúmmŏnd
Drummore D. & G., drə'mɔr, drŭmór
Drummossie Moor H'land, drʌ'mɔsɪ, drumáwssi
Drumnadrochit H'land, ˌdrʌmnə-'drɒxɪt, drumnădróchit
Drumoak Grampian, drʌ'moʊk, drummṓk
Drumochter, Pass of, H'land–Tayside, drə'mɒxtər, drŭm-óchtĕr. The Gaelic spelling is Druimuachdar.
Drumquhassle Central, drʌm-'ʍæsl, drumwhássl

Drumry *S'clyde*, drʌm'raɪ, drum-rí

Drumsheugh *Edinburgh*, drʌm-'ʃux, drum-shoóch

Drury, *f.n.*, 'druərɪ, drŏŏri

Drws-y-Nant *Gwynedd*, ˌdrusə-'næænt, droossắnánt

Dryburgh, *f.n.*, 'draɪbərə, dríbŭră

Dryburgh Abbey *Borders*, 'draɪ-bərə, dríbŭră

Dryden, *f.n.*, 'draɪdən, drídĕn

Drygrange *Borders*, 'draɪgreɪndʒ, drígraynj

Drymen *Central*, 'drɪmən, drím-mĕn

Drysdale, *f.n.*, 'draɪzdeɪl, drízdayl

Duan, *f.n.*, 'djʊən, dyŏŏ-ăn

Duane, *f.n.*, du'eɪn, doo-áyn

Duarte, *f.n.*, 'djuɑrt, déw-aart

Dubbey, *f.n.*, 'dʌbɪ, dúbbi

Dubell, *f.n.*, dju'bel, dewbéll

Dubens, *f.n.*, 'djubənz, déwbĕnz

Dubh Artach Rocks *off S'clyde coast*, 'du 'ɑrtəx, doó a̋artăch

Du Boulay, *f.n.*, dʊ 'buleɪ, dŏŏ boólay; dju 'buleɪ, dew boólay

Du Buisson, *f.n.*, 'djubɪsən, déwbissŏn

Du Cane, *f.n.*, dju 'keɪn, dew káyn

Du Cann, *f.n.*, dju 'kæn, dew kánn

Duce, *f.n.*, djus, dewss

Ducharme, *f.n.*, du'ʃɑrm, doo--shaárm

Duchemin, *f.n.*, 'duʃəmɪn, doóshĕmin

Duchesne, *f.n.*, du'ʃeɪn, doo--sháyn; dju'ʃeɪn, dew-sháyn

Duchin, *f.n.*, 'dutʃɪn, doótchin

Ducie, Earl of, 'djusɪ, déwssi

Duckinfield *Ches.*, 'dʌkɪnfɪld, dúckinfeeld

Du Cros, *f.n.*, dju 'krʊʊ, dew krŏ́

Ducrow, *f.n.*, dju'krʊʊ, dewkrŏ́

Du Croz, *f.n.*, dju 'krʊʊ, dew krŏ́

Duddeston *W. Midlands*, 'dʌdɪs-tən, dúddĕstŏn

Duddleswell *E. Sussex*, 'dʌdlz-wel, dúddlzwel

Dudeney, *f.n.*, 'djudnɪ, déwd-ni; 'djudɲɪ, déwdn-i; 'djudɲeɪ, déwdn-ay; 'dudnɪ, doód-ni

Du Deney, *f.n.*, dju 'denɪ, dew dénni

Dudhope, Viscount, 'dʌdəp, dúddŏp

Duerden, *f.n.*, 'djʊərdən, dyŏŏr-dĕn

Duff, *f.n.*, dʌf, duff

Duffell, *f.n.*, 'dʌfl, dúffl

Dufferin and Ava, Marquess of, 'dʌfərɪn ənd 'avə, dúffĕrin ănd a̋avă

Duffes, *f.n.*, 'dʌfɪs, dúffĕss

Duffield, *f.n.*, 'dʌfɪld, dúffeeld

Dufftown *Grampian*, 'dʌftaʊn, dúfftown; 'dʌftən, dúfftŏn

Duffus, *f.n.*, 'dʌfəs, dúffŭss

Dufour, *f.n.*, du'fuər, dŏŏfoŏr

Dufton, *f.n.*, 'dʌftən, dúfftŏn

Dugan, *f.n.*, 'dugən, doógăn. *Appropriate also for the Barony of ~ of Victoria.*

Duggan, *f.n.*, 'dʌgən, dúggăn

Duggin, *f.n.*, 'dʌgɪn, dúggin

Duggleby, *f.n.*, 'dʌglbɪ, dúgglbi

Duguid, *f.n.*, 'djugɪd, déwgid

Duignan, *f.n.*, 'daɪgnən, dígnăn

Dukesfield *Northd.*, 'dʌksfɪld, dúcksfeeld

Dukinfield *Gtr. M'chester*, 'dʌkɪnfɪld, dúckinfeeld

Dulais, River, *Dyfed*, 'dɪlaɪs, dílliss; 'dɪləs, dílläss

Dulake, *f.n.*, 'djuleɪk, déwlayk

Dulas Valley *Powys*, 'djuləs, déwläss

Duley, *f.n.*, 'djulɪ, déwli

Dulieu, *f.n.*, də'lju, dĕléw

Dull *Tayside*, dʌl, dull

Dullatur *S'clyde*, 'dʌlətər, dúllă-tŭr

Dullea, *f.n.*, dju'leɪ, dewláy; dʌ'leɪ, dulláy

Dullingham *Cambs.*, 'dʌlɪŋəm, dúlling-ăm

Dulnain, River, *H'land*, 'dʌlnən, dúlnăn

Dulnain Bridge *H'land*, 'dʌlnən 'brɪdʒ, dúlnăn brij

Duloe *Cornwall*, 'djulʊʊ, déwlō

Dulson, *f.n.*, 'dʌlsən, dúlssŏn

Dulverton *Devon*, 'dʌlvərtən, dúlvĕrtŏn. *Appropriate also for Baron ~.*

Dulwich *London*, 'dʌlɪdʒ, dúllij; 'dʌlɪtʃ, dúllitch

Duly, *f.n.*, 'djulɪ, déwli

Dumaresq, *f.n.*, dʊ'merɪk, dŏŏmérrik; dju'merɪk, dew-mérrik

Dumas, *f.n.*, dju'mɑ, dewma̋a

du Maurier, *f.n.*, du 'mɒrɪeɪ, doo mórri-ay. *This is the family pronunciation of Sir Gerald ~, actor-manager, and of Daphne ~, author.*

Dumbarton *S'clyde*, dəm'bɑrtən, dŭmba̋artŏn

Dumbuck *S'clyde*, dʌm'bʌk, dumbúck

Dumfries *D. & G.*, dəm'fris, dŭmfrèess. *Appropriate also for the Earl of ~.*

Dummer *Hants*, 'dʌmər, dúmmĕr

Dumont, *f.n.*, dju'mɒnt, dewmónt; dy'mõ, dümóng

Dùn *St. Kilda (W. Isles)*, dun, doon

Dunadry Co. Antrim, dʌn'ædrı, dunádri

Dunalastair Tayside, dʌn'ælıstər, dunálistăr

Dunalley, Baron, dʌn'ælı, dunáli

Dunamanagh Co. Tyrone, ˌdʌnə'mænə, dunnămánnă

Dunant, f.n., dʊ'nænt, dōōnánt

Dunball Somerset, 'dʌnbɔl, dúnbawl

Dunbar, f.n., dʌn'bɑr, dunbáar

Dunbar Lothian, dʌn'bɑr, dun-báar

Dunbartonshire former Co. name, dʌn'bɑrtənʃaıər, dunbáartŏn-shīr. Dunbartonshire is now part of Strathclyde Region.

Dunblane Central, dʌn'bleın, dunbláyn

Duncalfe, f.n., dʌn'kɑf, dun-káaf

Duncan, C.n. and f.n., 'dʌŋkən, dúnkăn

Duncannon, Viscount, dʌn'kænən, dunkánnŏn

Duncansby Head H'land, 'dʌŋ-kənzbı, dúnkănzbi

Dunchideock Devon, 'dʌntʃıdək, dúntchiddŏk

Duncombe, f.n., 'dʌŋkəm, dúnkŏm

Dundarave Co. Antrim, ˌdʌndə-'reıv, dundăráyv

Dundas, f.n., dʌn'dæs, dundáss

Dundee Tayside, dʌn'di, dundeé. Appropriate also for the Earl of ~.

Dundela, Belfast, dʌn'dilə, dundeélă. But the football team is pronounced dʌn'delə, dun-déllă.

Dundonald S'clyde, dʌn'dɒnld, dundónnld. Appropriate also for the Earl of ~.

Dundonian native of Dundee, dʌn'doʊnıən, dundóniăn

Dundrod Co. Antrim, dʌn'drɒd, dundród

Dundrum Co. Armagh, Co. Down, dʌn'drʌm, dundrúm

Dundry Avon, 'dʌndrı, dúndri

Dunedin, Viscountcy of, dʌn'idın, duneédin

Dunfermline Fife, dʌn'fɜrmlın, dunférmlin

Dungannon Co. Tyrone, dʌn-'gænən, dun-gánnŏn

Dungarvan, Viscount, dʌn'gɑrvən, dun-gáarvăn

Dungate, f.n., 'dʌngeıt, dún-gayt

Dungavel S'clyde, dʌn'geıvl, dun-gáyvl; dʌn'gævl, dun-gávvl

Dungeness Kent, ˌdʌndʒə'nes, dunjĕnéss

Dungiven Co. Derry, dʌn'gıvən, dun-gívvĕn

Dunglass, Barony of, dʌn'glɑs, dun-gláass

Dunhill, f.n., 'dʌnhıl, dún-hil

Dunholme Lincs., 'dʌnəm, dúnnŏm

Dunino Fife, dʌn'inoʊ, duneénō

Dunipace f.n., 'dʌnıpeıs, dúnni-payss

Dunipace Central, 'dʌnıpeıs, dúnnipayss

Dunira Tayside, dʌn'ıərə, duneéră

Dunkeld Tayside, dʌn'keld, dun--kéld

Dunkerley, f.n., 'dʌŋkərlı, dúnkĕrli

Dunkeswell Devon, 'dʌŋkızwel, dúnkĕzwel

Dunkley, f.n., 'dʌŋklı, dúnkli

Dunlop, f.n., dʌn'lɒp, dunlóp; 'dʌnlɒp, dúnlop. The second is appropriate for the tyre and sports goods group of companies.

Dunlop S'clyde, dʌn'lɒp, dunlóp

Dunloy Co. Antrim, dʌn'lɔı, dun-lóy

Dunluce Co. Antrim, dʌn'lus, dunloóss. Appropriate also for Viscount ~.

Dunmail Raise Cumbria, 'dʌnmeil 'reız, dúnmayl ráyz

Dunmore Co. Down, dʌn'mɔr, dun-mór. Appropriate also for the Earl of ~.

Dunmow, Great & Little, Essex, 'dʌnmoʊ, dún-mō

Dunmurry Co. Antrim, dʌn'mʌrı, dun-múrri

Dunnet H'land, 'dʌnıt, dúnnĕt

Dunnett, f.n., 'dʌnıt, dúnnĕt

Dunnichen Tayside, dʌn'ıxən, duníchĕn

Dunnico, f.n., 'dʌnıkoʊ, dúnnikō

Dunnose I. of Wight, dʌ'noʊz, dunnóz

Dunnottar Castle Grampian, dʌn-'ɒtər, dunóttăr

Dunoon S'clyde, dʌn'un, dunoón

Dunphail Grampian, dʌn'feıl, dunfáyl

Dunphie, f.n., 'dʌnfı, dúnfi

Dunraven and Mountearl, Earl of, dʌn'reıvən ənd maʊnt'ɜrl, dunráyvĕn ănd mowntérl

Dunrich, f.n., dʌn'rıtʃ, dunrítch

Dunrobin Castle H'land, dʌn-'rɒbın, dunróbbin

Dunrossil of Vallaquie, Viscount, dʌn'rɒsıl əv 'væləkwı, dunróssil ŏv válăkwi

Duns Borders, dʌnz, dunz

Dunsany, Baron of, dʌn'seını, dunsáyni

Dunseverick *Co. Antrim*, dʌn-'sevərɪk, dunsévvĕrik

Dunsfold *Surrey*, 'dʌnzfoʊld, dúnz-fŏld

Dunsheath, *f.n.*, dʌn'ʃiθ, dun-shéeth; dʌnz'hiθ, dunz-heeth

Dunsinane Hill *Tayside*, dʌn-'sɪnən, dun-sínnăn. *The pro-nunciation called for in Shakespeare's 'Macbeth' is* ˌdʌnsɪ'neɪn, dunsináyn *or* 'dʌnsɪneɪn, dúnssinayn

Dunstaffnage Castle *S'clyde*, dʌn'stæfnɪdʒ, dunstáffnij

Dunstan, *f.n.*, 'dʌnstən, dún-stăn

Dunstanburgh *Northd.*, 'dʌnstən-bərə, dúnstănbŭră

Duntelchaig, Loch, *H'land*, ˌdʌntl'xeɪg, duntlcháyg

Duntisbourne Rouse *Glos.*, 'dʌntɪsbɔːn 'raʊs, dúntissborn rówss

Duntocher *S'clyde*, dʌn'tɒxər, duntóchĕr

Duntze, *f.n.*, dʌnts, dunts

Dunure *S'clyde*, dʌn'jʊər, dun-yŏŏr

Dunvant *W. Glam.*, 'dʌnvənt, dúnvănt

Dunvegan *Skye*, dʌn'vegən, dunvéggăn; dʌn'veɪgən, dunváygăn

Dunwear *Somerset*, dʌn'wɛər, dunwáir; dʌn'wɪər, dunweer

Dunwich *Suffolk*, 'dʌnɪtʃ, dún-nitch

Dunwood *Staffs.*, 'dʌnwʊd, dúnwŏŏd

Dunwoody, *f.n.*, dʌn'wʊdɪ, dun-wŏŏdi

Du Plat, *f.n.*, dju 'plɑ, dew plaá

Duployen, *f.n.*, duplɔɪ'en, dooploy-énn

Dupont, *f.n.*, dju'pɒnt, dewpónt; 'djupɒnt, déwpont

Dupplin, Viscount, 'dʌplɪn, dúpplin

Dupplin Castle *Tayside*, 'dʌplɪn, dúpplin

Dupré, *f.n.*, du'preɪ, doopráy

Duprée, *f.n.*, du'preɪ, doopráy; dju'pri, dewpreé

Duprez, *f.n.*, du'preɪ, doopráy; dju'preɪ, dewpráy; dju'pri, dewpreé

Duquenoy, *f.n.*, djʊ'kenwɑ, dyŏŏkénwaa

Durance, *f.n.*, dju'rɑns, dew-raánss; dju'ræns, dewránss

Durand, *f.n.*, djʊə'rænd, dyŏŏr-ánd; dju'rænd, dewránd

Durant, *f.n.*, djʊə'rænt, dyŏŏránt

Durbin, *f.n.*, 'dɜrbɪn, dúrbin

Durden, *f.n.*, 'dɜrdən, dúrdĕn

Durell, *f.n.*, djʊə'rel, dyŏŏréll

Dures, *f.n.*, djʊə'reɪ, dyŏŏráy

Duret, *f.n.*, 'djʊəreɪ, dyŏŏray

d'Urfey, Thomas, *17th-c. poet, song-writer, and dramatist,* 'dɜrfɪ, dúrfi. *Also known as Tom Durfey.*

Durgnat, *f.n.*, 'dɜrgnæt, dúrg-nat

Durham *Co. name*, 'dʌrəm, dúr-răm. *Appropriate also for the Earldom of* ~.

Durie, *f.n.*, 'djʊərɪ, dyŏŏri

Durisdeer *D. & G.*, 'dʌrɪzdɪər, dúrrizdeer

Durkar *W. Yorks.*, 'dɜrkər, dúrkăr

Durlacher, *f.n.*, 'dɜrlækər, dúr-lackĕr

Durness *H'land*, 'dɜrnɪs, dúr-nĕss

Duror, River, *S'clyde*, 'dʊərər, dŏŏrŏr

Durrad, *f.n.*, 'dʌrəd, dúrrăd

Durrant, *f.n.*, 'dʌrənt, dúrrănt

Durrell, *f.n.*, 'dʌrəl, dúrrĕl. *Appropriate for Lawrence* ~, *author and poet, and for Gerald* ~, *author and zoologist.*

Dursley *Glos.*, 'dɜrzlɪ, dúrzli

Durweston *Dorset*, 'dʌrəstən, dúrrĕstŏn

Du Sautoy, *f.n.*, du 'soʊtɔɪ, dŏŏ sŏtoy

Du Seautois, *f.n.*, 'djusətɔɪ, déwssĕtoy

Duthie, *f.n.*, 'dʌθɪ, dúthi

Duthil *H'land*, 'dʌθɪl, dúth-il

Duthoit, *f.n.*, du'θɔɪt, doo-thóyt

Dutoit, *f.n.*, dju'twɑ, dewtwaá

Du Toit, *f.n.*, dju 'twɑ, dew twaá; du 'twɑ, doo twaá

Dutot, *f.n.*, dy'toʊ, dütŏ́

Duttine, *f.n.*, dʌ'tin, duttéen

Dutton, *f.n.*, 'dʌtən, dúttŏn

Duval, *f.n.*, dju'væl, dewvál

Du Vivier, *f.n.*, du 'vɪvɪeɪ, dŏŏ vívvi-ay

Duxford *Cambs.*, 'dʌksfərd, dúcksfŏrd

Dwan, *f.n.*, dwɒn, dwon

Dwight, *f.n.*, dwaɪt, dwīt

Dwygyfylchi *Gwynedd*, ˌdʊɪgə-'vʌlxɪ, dŏŏ-i-găvúlchi

Dwynwen, *Welsh C.n.*, 'dʊɪnwen, dŏŏ-in-wen

The form dʌn, dun *used to indicate the unstressed prefix* Dun- *in Celtic names is that used in careful speech. Its occurrence as* dən, dŭn *is equally frequent and acceptable.*

Dwyran *Gwynedd*, 'dʊɪræn, dŏo͞-i-ran

Dwyryd, *f.n.*, 'dʊɪrɪd, dŏo͞-i-rid

Dwyryd, River, *Gwynedd*, 'dʊɪrɪd, dŏo͞-i-rid

Dyas, *f.n.*, 'daɪəs, dí-ăss

Dyball, *f.n.*, 'daɪbɔl, díbawl

Dyce, *Grampian*, daɪs, dīss

Dyche, *f.n.*, daɪtʃ, dītch

Dyde, *f.n.*, daɪd, dīd

Dyer, *f.n.*, 'daɪər, dí-ĕr

Dyfatty *Dyfed*, dʌ'vætɪ, duvvátti

Dyfed *Co. name*, 'dʌvɪd, dúvvĕd

Dyffryn *Gwynedd, Mid Glam., S. Glam.*, 'dʌfrɪn, dúffrin

Dyffryn Ardudwy *Gwynedd*, 'dʌfrɪn ɑr'dɪdʊɪ, dúffrin aardéedŏo͞-i

Dyffryn Maelor *Clwyd*, 'dʌfrɪn 'maɪlər, dúffrin mílor

Dyfi, River, *Gwynedd, Powys*, 'dʌvɪ, dúvvi. *The English spelling is* **Dovey**, *q.v.*

Dyfnallt, *Welsh Bardic or C.n.*, 'dʌvnæɬt, dúvnaḥlt

Dyfrig *Welsh C.n.*, 'dʌvrɪg, dúvv-rig

Dykes, *f.n.*, daɪks, dīks

Dylan, *C.n.*, 'dʌlən, dúllăn; 'dɪlən, díllăn. *See* **Dylan Thomas** *under his surname.*

Dylife *Powys*, dʌ'liːvə, dulleévĕ

Dymchurch *Kent*, 'dɪmtʃɜrtʃ, dímtchurch

Dyment, *f.n.*, 'daɪmənt, dímĕnt

Dymock, *f.n.*, 'dɪmək, dímmŏk

Dymock *Glos.*, 'dɪmək, dímmŏk

Dymoke, *f.n.*, 'dɪmək, dímmŏk

Dymond, *f.n.*, 'daɪmənd, dímŏnd

Dyneley, *f.n.*, 'daɪnlɪ, dínli

Dynevor, *f.n.*, 'dɪnɪvər, dínnĕvŏr. *Appropriate also for Baron ∼.*

Dynevor Castle *Dyfed*, 'dɪnɪvər, dínnĕvŏr. *This is the English form and pronunciation used outside and, to some extent, inside Wales. ∼ Grammar School in Swansea, however, is pronounced* dɪ'nevər, dinévvŏr. *The Welsh language spelling is* **Dinefwr**, *q.v.*

Dyrham *Avon*, 'dɪrəm, dírrăm

Dysart, Countess of, 'daɪsərt, díssărt

Dysart *Fife*, 'daɪzərt, dízărt

Dyscarr *Notts.*, 'daɪskɑr, díss-kaar

Dyserth *Clwyd*, 'dɪsərθ, dissĕrth

Dyson, *f.n.*, 'daɪsən, díssŏn

Dysyny, River, *Gwynedd*, də'sʌnɪ, dŭssúnni

Dytham, *f.n.*, 'daɪθəm, díthăm

Dzvonkus, *f.n.*, dɪ'vɒŋkəs, divónkŭss

E

Eaborn, *f.n.*, 'ibɔrn, éeborn

Eadie, *f.n.*, 'idɪ, éedi

Eadon, *f.n.*, 'idən, éedŏn

Eadweard, *C.n.*, 'edwərd, édwărd

Eady, *f.n.*, 'idɪ, éedi

Eager, *f.n.*, 'igər, éegĕr

Eagger, *f.n.*, 'igər, éegĕr

Eaglescarnie *Lothian*, ,iglz-'kɑrnɪ, eeglzkáirni

Eaglesham *S'clyde*, 'iglsəm, éeglssăm

Eakring *Notts.*, 'ikrɪŋ, éekring

Eales, *f.n.*, ilz, eelz

Ealing *London*, 'ilɪŋ, éeling

Eames, *f.n.*, imz, eemz; eɪmz, aymz

Eamonn, *C.n.*, 'eɪmən, áymŏn

Eamont, River, *Cumbria*, 'imənt, éemŏnt; 'jæmənt, yámmŏnt

Eanswythe, saint, 'iənswɪθ, ée-ănsswith

Earby *Lancs.*, 'ɪərbɪ, éerbi

Eardisland *H. & W.*, 'ɜrdzlənd, érdzländ

Eardisley *H. & W.*, 'ɜrdzlɪ, érdzli

Eardly, *f.n.*, 'ɜrdlɪ, érdli

Earengey, *f.n.*, 'ɛərɪndʒeɪ, áirĕnjay

Earith *Cambs.*, 'ɪərɪθ, éerith

Earle, *f.n.*, ɜrl, erl

Earley, *f.n.*, 'ɜrlɪ, érli

Earley *Berks.*, 'ɜrlɪ, érli

Earls, *f.n.*, ɜrlz, erlz

Earls Colne *Essex*, 'ɜrlz 'koʊn, érlz kṓn

Earl Stonham *Suffolk*, 'ɜrl 'stɒnəm, érl stónnăm

Earlstoun, Loch, *D. & G.*, 'ɜrlztən, érlztŏn

Earn, Loch *and* River, *Tayside*, ɜrn, ern

Earp, *f.n.*, ɜrp, erp

Earsdon *Tyne & Wear*, 'ɜrzdən, érzdŏn

Earsham *Norfolk*, 'ɜrʃəm, ér-shăm

Earsman, *f.n.*, 'ɪərzmən, éerzmăn

Earswick *N. Yorks.*, 'ɪərzwɪk, éerzwick

Earwaker, *f.n.*, 'ɜrəkər, ér-ăkĕr; 'erəkər, érrăkĕr; 'ɪərweɪkər, éerwaykĕr

Earwicker, *f.n.*, 'erɪkər, érrickĕr

Eashing *Surrey*, 'iʃɪŋ, éeshing

Easington *Durham, Northd.*, 'izɪŋtən, éezingtŏn

Eason, *f.n.*, 'isən, éessŏn

Eassie *Tayside*, 'isɪ, éessi

Eastaugh, *f.n.*, 'istɔ, éestaw

East Bergholt *Suffolk*, 'ist 'bɜrg-hoʊlt, éest bérg-hṓlt

East Bierley W. Yorks., 'ist
'baɪərlɪ, éest bírli
Eastbourne E. Sussex, 'istbɔrn,
éestborn
East Challow Oxon., 'ist 'tʃælou,
éest chálō
East Cowick Humberside, 'ist
'kauɪk, éest ków-ick
East Donyland Essex, 'ist 'dɒnɪ-
lənd, éest dónnilǎnd
Easterbrook, f.n., 'istərbruk,
éestěrbrŏŏk
East Freugh D. & G., 'ist 'frux,
éest fróoch
East Goscote Leics., 'ist 'gɒskout,
éest gósskōt
East Grinstead W. Sussex, 'ist
'grɪnstɪd, éest grínsstěd
East Guldeford E. Sussex, 'ist
'gɪlfərd, éest gílförd
Easthampstead Berks., 'ist-
'hæmpstɪd, éest-hámpstěd;
'istəmsted, éestämsted
East Hartlepool Cleveland, 'ist
'hɑrtlɪpul, éest haártlipool
East Heslerton N. Yorks., 'ist
'heslərtən, éest hésslěrtŏn
Eastham Merseyside, 'istəm,
éestăm
East Hoathly E. Sussex, 'ist
houθ'laɪ, éest hōth-lí
East Horsley Surrey, 'ist 'hɔrzlɪ,
éest hórzli
Eastleigh Hants, 'ist'li, éest-lée
East Lockinge Oxon., 'ist
'lɒkɪndʒ, éest lóckinj
East Malling Kent, 'ist 'mɔlɪŋ,
éest máwling
East Marden W. Sussex, 'ist
'mɑrdən, éest maárděn
East Meon Hants, 'ist 'miən, éest
mée-ŏn
East Mersea Essex, 'ist 'mɜrzɪ,
éest mérzi
East Molesey Surrey, 'ist 'moulzɪ,
éest mólzi
Eastnor H. & W., 'istnɔr, éest-nor.
Appropriate also for ~ Castle.
Easton Mauduit Northants., 'istən
'mɔdɪt, éestŏn máwdit
East Ravendale Humberside, 'ist
'reɪvəndeɪl, éest ráyvěndayl
Eastry Kent, 'istrɪ, éestri
East Somerton Norfolk, 'ist
'sʌmərtən, éest súmměrtŏn
Eastwood, f.n., 'istwud, éest-
wŏŏd
East Yelland Devon, 'ist 'jelənd,
éest yéllǎnd
Eathie see **Ethie**
Eathorne, f.n., 'iθɔrn, ée-thorn
Eaton, f.n., 'itən, eétŏn
Eaton Socon Cambs., 'itən
'soukən, eétŏn sókŏn

Eaudyke Lincs., 'judaɪk, yéwdīk;
'udaɪk, óodīk
Eayrs, f.n., ɛərz, airz
Ebbe, saint, eb, ebb
Ebbesbourne Wake Wilts.,
'ebzbɔrn 'weɪk, ébzborn wáyk
Ebbisham, Baron, 'ebɪʃəm, ébbi-
-shǎm
Ebbrell, f.n., 'ebrəl, ébbrěl
Ebbutt, f.n., 'ebət, ébbŭt
Ebbw Vale Gwent, 'ebu 'veɪl,
ébboo váyl
Eberle, f.n., 'ebərlɪ, ébběrli
Ebernoe House W. Sussex,
'ebərnou, ébběrnō
Ebers, f.n., 'ebərz, ébběrz
Ebery, f.n., 'ibərɪ, eéběri
Ebor, Archbishop of York's
signature, 'ibɔr, eébor
Eboracum, Roman name for
York, i'bɒrəkəm, eebórrăkŭm
Ebor Handicap, horse-race, 'ibɔr,
eébor
Ebrahim, f.n., 'ibrəhɪm, eébrǎ-
-him
Ebrington Glos., 'ebrɪŋtən,
ébbringtŏn; 'jʌbərtən, yúbběr-
tŏn. The first is appropriate for
Viscount ~. The other, strictly
local and used largely by older
residents, is a legacy of an
earlier form of the name.
Ebury, Baron, 'ibərɪ, eébŭri
Ecchinswell Hants, 'etʃɪnzwel,
étchinzwel
Ecclefechan D. & G., ˌekl'fexən,
eckl-féchǎn
Eccles, f.n., 'eklz, écklz. Appro-
priate also for Viscount ~.
Eccles Gtr. M'chester, 'eklz,
écklz
Ecclesall S. Yorks., 'eklzɔl,
écklzawl
Eccleshall Staffs., 'eklʃl, éckl-
-shl; 'eklʃɔl, éckl-shawl
Ecclesmachan Lothian, ˌeklz-
'mæxən, ecklzmáchǎn
Echlin, f.n., 'exlɪn, échlin; 'eklɪn,
écklin
Eckersall, f.n., 'ekərsl, éckěrssl
Eckersley, f.n., 'ekərzlɪ, éckěrzli
Eckhard, f.n., 'ekhɑrd, éck-haard
Edale Derby., 'ideɪl, eédayl
Eday Orkney, 'ideɪ, eéday
Eddrachillis Bay H'land, ˌedrə-
'kɪlɪs, edrăkilliss
Ede, f.n., id, eed
Edeirnion, Vale of, also spelt
Edeyrnion, Gwynedd–Clwyd,
ə'daɪərnjɒn, ědírn-yon
Edelman, f.n., 'edlmən, éddlmǎn;
'eɪdlmən, áydlmǎn
Edelsten, f.n., 'edlstən, éddlstěn
Eden, f.n., 'idən, eéděn

Edenbridge *Kent*, 'idənbrɪdʒ, eédĕn-brij
Edenderry *Co. Down*, 'idən'derɪ, eédĕndérri
Edenfield *Lancs.*, 'idənfild, eédĕnfeeld
Edensor *Derby.*, 'enzər, énzŏr; 'ensər, énssŏr
Edern, *also spelt* **Edeyrn**, *Gwynedd*, 'edɛərn, éddairn
Ederney *Co. Fermanagh*, 'edərnɪ, éddĕrni
Edeyrn *see* **Edern**
Edeyrnion *see* **Edeirnion**
Edgbaston *W. Midlands*, 'edʒbəs- tən, éj-băstŏn
Edgcumbe, Baron, 'edʒkəm, éjkŭm
Edgebolton *Salop*, edʒ'bɔultən, ej-bóltŏn
Edgecombe, *f.n.*, 'edʒkəm, éj- -kŏm
Edgell, *f.n.*, 'edʒəl, éjjĕl
Edgoose, *f.n.*, ed'gus, ed-goóss
Edholm, *f.n.*, 'edhɔum, éd-hōm
Edial *Staffs.*, 'edɪəl, éddiäl
Edinburgh *Lothian*, 'edɪnbərə, éddinbŭră; 'ednbərə, éddnbŭră
Edinger, *f.n.*, 'edɪndʒər, éddinjĕr
Edington *Borders*, 'idɪŋtən, eédingtŏn
Edington *Somerset*, *Wilts.*, 'edɪŋtən, éddingtŏn
Edington Burtle *Somerset*, 'edɪŋ- tən 'bɜrtl, éddingtŏn búrtl
Edisbury, *f.n.*, 'edɪsbərɪ, éddiss- bŭri
Edkins, *f.n.*, 'edkɪnz, édkinz
Edlingham *Northd.*, 'edlɪndʒəm, éddlinjăm
Edmead, *f.n.*, 'edmid, édmeed
Edmond, *f.n.*, 'edmənd, édmŏnd
Edmondbyers *see* **Edmundbyers**
Edmonds, *f.n.*, 'edməndz, édmŏndz
Edmondstone, *f.n.*, 'edmənstɔun, édmŏnstŏn
Edmundbyers, *also spelt* **Edmondbyers**, *Durham*, 'edməndbaɪərz, édmŭndbī-ĕrz
Edmunds, *f.n.*, 'edməndz, édmŭndz
Edney, *f.n.*, 'ednɪ, édni
Ednyfed, *C.n.*, ed'nʌvɪd, ednúv- vĕd
Edolls, *f.n.*, 'edəlz, éddŏlz
Edradour Distillery *Tayside*, ,edrə- 'dauər, edrădówr
Edradynate *Tayside*, ,edrə- 'daɪnɪt, edrădínit
Edrich, *f.n.*, 'edrɪtʃ, édritch
Edridge, *f.n.*, 'edrɪdʒ, édrij
Edstaston *Salop*, 'edstæstən, édstasstŏn

Edwalton *Notts.*, ed'wɔltən, edwáwltŏn
Edward, *C.n.*, 'edwərd, édwărd
Edwardes, *f.n.*, 'edwərdz, édwărdz
Edwardian, *pertaining to the era of King Edward VII*, ed- 'wɔrdɪən, edwáwrdiän; ed'wɔrdɪən, edwáardiän
Edwards, *f.n.*, 'edwərdz, édwărdz
Edyvean, *f.n.*, 'edɪvin, éddiveen
Edzell *Tayside*, 'edzl, éddzl
Eele, *f.n.*, il, eel
Efail Isaf *Mid Glam.*, 'evaɪl 'ɪsæv, évvīl íssav
Efemey, *f.n.*, 'efɪmɪ, éffĕmi
Egan, *f.n.*, 'igən, éegăn
Egerton, *f.n.*, 'edʒərtən, éjjĕrtŏn
Egerton *Gtr. M'chester*, 'edʒərtən, éjjĕrtŏn
Eggesford *Devon*, 'egzfərd, éggzförd
Eggington *Beds.*, 'egɪŋtən, égging- tŏn
Egginton, *f.n.*, 'egɪntən, éggintŏn
Egginton *Derby.*, 'egɪntən, éggintŏn
Egilsay *Orkney*, 'egɪlseɪ, éggilssay
Eglingham *Northd.*, 'eglɪndʒəm, égglinjăm
Eglinton and Winton, Earl of, 'eglɪntən ənd 'wɪntən, égglintŏn ănd wíntŏn
Eglish *Co. Armagh*, *Co. Tyrone*, 'eglɪʃ, égglish
Eglon, *f.n.*, 'eglɒn, égglon
Egloshayle *Cornwall*, ,eglǝs'heɪl, eglŏss-háyl
Egloskerry *Cornwall*, ,eglǝs'kerɪ, eglŏsskérri
Eglwyseg *Clwyd*, e'gluɪseg, egloó-isseg
Eglwysfach *Dyfed*, ,egluɪs'vɑx, egloō-issváach
Eglwyswrw *Dyfed*, ,egluɪs'ʊəru, egloō-issoóroo
Egmanton *Notts.*, 'egməntən, éggmäntŏn
Egmere *Norfolk*, 'egmɪər, égg- meer
Egmont, Earl of, 'egmɒnt, égmont
Egremont, *Cumbria*, *Merseyside*, 'egrɪmɒnt, éggrĕmŏnt
Egremont and Leconfield, Baron, 'egrɪmɒnt ənd 'lekənfild, éggrĕmont ănd léckŏnfeeld
Ehen, River, *Cumbria*, 'iən, eé-ĕn
Ehrmann, *f.n.*, 'ɛərmən, áirmăn
Eidda *Gwynedd*, 'aɪðə, íthă
Eiddwen, *Welsh C.n.*, 'aɪðwen, íth-wen
Eidinow, *f.n.*, 'aɪdɪnau, ídinow
Eifion, *Welsh C.n.*, 'aɪvɪɒn, ívi-on

Eigg *H'land*, eg, egg
Eighton Banks *Tyne & Wear*,
 'eɪtən 'bæŋks, áytŏn bánks;
 'aɪtən 'bæŋks, ítŏn bánks
Eigra *Welsh C.n.*, 'aɪgrə, ígră
Eil, Loch, *H'land*, il, eel
Eildon Hills *Borders*, 'ildən,
 éeldŏn
Eilean Donan *H'land*, 'elən
 'dɒnən, éllăn dónnăn
Eilean More, *name of several islets
 in Scotland*, 'elən 'mɔr, éllăn
 mór
Eilian *Welsh Bardic and C.n.*,
 'aɪlɪən, íliăn
Eiloart, *f.n.*, 'aɪlouɑrt, ílō-aart
Eils, *f.n.*, ilz, eelz
Eiluned *Welsh C.n.*, aɪ'linəd,
 īléenĕd
Einion *Welsh C.n.*, 'aɪnɪɒn, íni-on
Einzig, *f.n.*, 'aɪnzɪg, ínzig
Eira, *Welsh C.n.*, 'aɪrə, íră
Eirene, *C.n.*, aɪ'rini, īréeni
Eirlys, *Welsh C.n.*, 'aɪərlɪs, írliss
Eirwyn, *Welsh C.n.*, 'aɪərwɪn,
 írwin
Eisteddfa Gurig *Powys*, aɪs'teðvə
 'gɪrɪg, īstéthvă gírrig
Eisteddfod, *pl.* **Eisteddfodau**,
 Welsh Bardic festival,
 aɪ'steðvɒd, īstéthvod;
 ˌaɪsteð'vɒdaɪ, īstethvóddī
Eite, *f.n.*, aɪt, īt
Eitshal *I. of Lewis*, 'eɪtʃəl, áytch-
 ăl
Ekserdjian, *f.n.*, ɪk'sɜrdʒən,
 ĕksérjăn
Elan Valley Reservoir *Powys*,
 'ilən, éelăn
Eland House *London*, 'iland,
 éelănd
Elboz, *f.n.*, 'elbɒz, élbozz
Elburton *Devon*, 'elbərtən, élbŭr-
 tŏn
Elchies Forest *Grampian*, 'elxɪz,
 élchiz
Elcho, Lord, 'elkou, élkō
Elder, *f.n.*, 'eldər, éldĕr
Elderslie, *Kilmarnock & Loudoun
 (S'clyde)*, 'eldərzlɪ, éldĕrzli
Elderslie, *Renfrew (S'clyde)*,
 ˌeldərz'li, eldĕrzlée; 'eldərzlɪ,
 éldĕrzli
Eldred, *f.n.*, 'eldrɪd, éldrĕd;
 'eldred, éldred
Eldridge, *f.n.*, 'eldrɪdʒ, éldrij
Eleazar, *f.n.*, ˌelɪ'zɑr, ellĕzáar
Element, *f.n.*, 'elɪmənt, éllĕmĕnt
Elerch *Dyfed*, 'elɜrx, éllairch
Elers, *f.n.*, 'elɜrz, éllĕrz
Eley, *f.n.*, 'ilɪ, éeli
Elfed, *Welsh C.n.*, 'elved, élved
Elford, *f.n.*, 'elfərd, élfŏrd
Elfyn, *Welsh C.n.*, 'elvɪn, élvin

Elgar, Sir Edward, *composer*,
 'elgɑr, élgaar. *Although this is
 the pronunciation by which the
 composer is usually known, there
 is a suggestion that he may have
 called himself* 'elgər, élgăr.
Elger, *f.n.*, 'elgər, élgĕr
Elgin *Grampian*, 'elgɪn, élgin.
 *Appropriate also for the Earl of
 ∼ and Kincardine, q.v., and for
 the ∼ Marbles.*
Elgin and Kincardine, Earl of,
 'elgɪn ənd kɪn'kɑrdɪn, élgin ănd
 kin-kaárdin
Elgoll *Skye*, 'elgɒl, élgol
Elgy, *f.n.*, 'eldʒɪ, élji
Elham *Kent*, 'iləm, éelăm
Elia, *pen-name of Charles Lamb*,
 'ilɪə, éeliă
Eliades, *f.n.*, ɪ'laɪədiz, ĕlí-ădeez
Elias, *f.n.*, ɪ'laɪəs, ĕlí-ăss
Elibank, Baron, 'elɪbæŋk, éllibank
Elidyr-Fawr *Gwynedd*, e'lɪdər
 'vauər, elíddĕr vówr
Elie *Fife*, 'ilɪ, éeli
Elien, *Bishop of Ely's signature*,
 'eɪlɪən, áyliĕn
Eling *Hants*, 'ilɪŋ, éeling
Eliot, *f.n.*, 'elɪət, élliŏt
Eliott, *f.n.*, 'elɪət, élliŏt
Elizabeth, *C.n.*, ɪ'lɪzəbəθ,
 ĕlízzăbĕth
Elizabethan, *pertaining to
 Elizabeth*, ɪˌlɪzə'biθən, ĕliză-
 béethăn
Elkan, *f.n.*, 'elkən, élkăn; 'elkɑn,
 élkaan. *The second is appro-
 priate for Benno ∼, sculptor.*
Elkesley *Notts.*, 'elkslɪ, élksli
Elkind, *f.n.*, 'elkaɪnd, élkīnd
Elkins, *f.n.*, 'elkɪnz, élkinz
Ell, *f.n.*, el, ell
Ellenbogen, *f.n.*, 'elənbougən,
 éllĕnbōgĕn
Ellerdine *Salop*, 'elərdaɪn, éllĕrdīn
Ellerman, *f.n.*, 'elərmən, éllĕrmăn
Ellerton, *f.n.*, 'elərtən, éllĕrtŏn
Elles, *f.n.*, 'elɪs, éllĕss
Ellesborough *Bucks.*, 'elzbərə,
 élzbŭră
Ellesmere, Earl of, 'elzmɪər,
 élzmeer
Ellesmere Port *Ches.*, 'elzmɪər
 'pɔrt, élzmeer pórt
Ellice, *f.n.*, 'elɪs, éllis
Ellicock, *f.n.*, 'elɪkɒk, éllikock
Ellinger, *f.n.*, 'elɪndʒər, éllinjĕr
Ellingham *Hants, Norfolk*,
 'elɪŋəm, élling-ăm
Ellingham *Northd.*, 'elɪndʒəm,
 éllinjăm
Elliot, *f.n.*, 'elɪət, élliŏt
Elliott, *f.n.*, 'elɪət, élliŏt
Ellis, *f.n.*, 'elɪs, élliss

Ellough *Suffolk*, 'eloʊ, éllō
Elloughton *Humberside*, 'elətən, éllŏtŏn
Elmet Hall *W. Yorks.*, 'elmet, élmett
Elmham, North *and* South, *Norfolk*, 'elməm, élmăm
Elmsall, North *and* South, *W. Yorks.*, 'emsl, émssl
Elphick, *f.n.*, 'elfɪk, élfick
Elphinstone, *f.n.*, 'elfɪnstən, élfinstŏn; 'elfɪnstoʊn, élfinstōn. *The first is appropriate for Baron ~.*
Elrig *D. & G.*, 'elrɪg, élrig
Else, *f.n.*, els, elss
Elsecar *S. Yorks.*, 'elsɪkər, élssĕkăr
Elsham *Humberside*, 'elʃəm, él-shăm
Elsing *Norfolk*, 'elzɪŋ, élzing
Elslack *N. Yorks.*, el'slæk, elssláck
Elsom, *f.n.*, 'elsəm, élssŏm
Elsternwick *Humberside*, 'elstərnwɪk, élstĕrnwick. *This is the ecclesiastical name. The postal name is* **Elstronwick,** *q.v.*
Elston, *f.n.*, 'elstən, élstŏn
Elstow *Beds.*, 'elstoʊ, élsstō
Elstronwick *Humberside*, 'elstrənwɪk, élstrŏnwick. *This is the postal name. The ecclesiastical name is* **Elsternwick,** *q.v.*
Elswick *Tyne & Wear*, 'elzɪk, élzick
Elswood, *f.n.*, 'elzʊd, élzwŏŏd
Elsynge Hall *Enfield (London)*, 'elsɪŋ, élssing
Elt, *f.n.*, elt, elt
Eltham *London*, 'eltəm, éltăm
Eltisley *Cambs.*, 'eltɪzlɪ, éltizli
Eltringham *Northd.*, 'eltrɪndʒəm, éltrinjăm
Eluned, *Welsh C.n.*, el'ined, eleéned; el'ined, elínned
Elveden *Suffolk*, 'elvdən, élvdĕn; 'eldən, éldĕn. *The second is appropriate for Viscount ~.*
Elvetham *Hants*, 'elvɪθəm, élvĕthăm
Elwell, *f.n.*, 'elwəl, élwĕl; 'elwel, élwel
Elwes, *f.n.*, 'elwɪz, élwĕz
Elwick *Durham*, 'elwɪk, élwick
Elwick *Northd.*, 'elɪk, éllick
Elwy, River, *Clwyd*, 'eloɪ, éllōō-i
Ely, *f.n.*, 'ilɪ, eéli
Ely *Cambs.*, *S. Glam.*, 'ilɪ, eéli. *Appropriate also for the Marquess of ~.*
Ely, River, *Mid Glam.–S. Glam.*, 'ilɪ, eéli

Elyhaugh *Northd.*, 'ilɪhɑf, eéli-haaf; 'ilɪhɒf, eéli-hoff
Embery, *f.n.*, 'embərɪ, émbĕri
Embsay *N. Yorks.*, 'empseɪ, émpsay
Emburey, *f.n.*, 'embərɪ, émbŭri
Emeleus, *f.n.*, ˌemɪ'liəs, emmĕleé--ŭss
Emeney, *f.n.*, 'emənɪ, émmĕni
Emeny, *f.n.*, 'emənɪ, émmĕni
Emere, *f.n.*, e'mɪər, emmeér
Emlyn, *C.n. and f.n.*, 'emlɪn, émlin
Emmens, *f.n.*, 'emənz, émmĕnz
Emmet, *f.n.*, 'emɪt, émmĕt. *Appropriate also for the Barony of ~.*
Empringham, *f.n.*, 'emprɪŋəm, émpring-ăm
Emptage, *f.n.*, 'emptɪdʒ, émptij
Emrys, *Welsh C.n.*, 'emrɪs, émriss
Emyr, *Welsh C.n.*, 'emɪər, émmeer
Endellion *Cornwall*, ən'deliən, ĕndélliŏn
Energlyn *Mid Glam.*, 'enərglɪn, énnĕrglin. *Appropriate also for Baron ~.*
Engelbach, *f.n.*, 'eŋglbæk, éng-gl-back
Englefield, *f.n.*, 'eŋglfild, éng-gl--feeld
Enham Alamein *Hants*, 'enəm 'æləmeɪn, énnăm álămayn
Enid, *C.n.*, 'inɪd, eénid; 'enɪd, énnid. *The second is the Welsh pronunciation.*
Ennals, *f.n.*, 'enlz, énnlz
Ennisdale, Barony of, 'enɪsdeɪl, énnissdayl
Enniskillen *Co. Fermanagh*, ˌenɪs'kɪlən, ennisskíllĕn. *Appropriate also for the Earl of ~.*
Enochdhu *Tayside*, 'inəx'du, eénŏch-doō
Enraght, *f.n.*, 'enrɪt, énrit
Enright, *f.n.*, 'enraɪt, énrīt
Ensor, *f.n.*, 'ensɔr, énssor
Enterkin, Stream, *D. & G.*, 'entərkɪn, éntĕrkin
Enterkinfoot *D. & G.*, ˌentərkɪn-'fʊt, entĕrkinfŏŏt
Enthoven, *f.n.*, 'enthoʊvən, ént--hōvĕn; en'toʊvən, entóvĕn
Enticknap, *f.n.*, 'entɪknæp, énticknap; ˌentɪk'næp, entick-náp
Enticknapp, *f.n.*, 'entɪknæp, énticknap
Entract, *f.n.*, 'ɒntrækt, óntrackt
Entwistle, *f.n.*, 'entwɪsl, éntwissl
Enyd, *C.n.*, 'enɪd, énnid
Enys, *f.n.*, 'enɪz, énniz
Enzie *Grampian*, 'eŋɪ, éng-i

Eochar *S. Uist*, 'iəxər, ee-ŏchăr.
  The Gaelic spelling is **Iochdor**,
  q.v.
Eothen School *Surrey*, 'ioʊθen,
  ee-ōthen
Eport, Loch, *N. Uist*, 'ipɔrt,
  eeport
Eppstein, *f.n.*, 'epstaɪn, épstīn
Eppynt *Powys*, 'epɪnt, éppint
Epsom *Surrey*, 'epsəm, épssŏm
Epstein, Sir Jacob, *sculptor*,
  'epstaɪn, épstīn
Ercall, High *and* Child's, *Salop*,
  'ɑrkl, áarkl
Erchless Castle *H'land*, 'ɛərklɪs,
  áirklĕss
Ercolani, *f.n.*, ɜrkə'lɑnɪ, erkŏláani
Erddig, *also spelt* **Erthig**, *Clwyd*,
  'ɛərðɪg, áirthig
Ereira, *f.n.*, ɪ'reərə, ĕráiră
Eresby *Lincs.*, 'ɪərzbɪ, eerzbi
Erewash, River, *Derby.–Notts.
  boundary*, 'erɪwɒʃ, érrĕ-wosh
Eriboll, Loch, *H'land*, 'erɪbɒl,
  érribol
Ericht, Loch *and* River, *Tayside*,
  'erɪxt, érricht
Ericsson, *f.n.*, 'erɪksən, érriksŏn
Eridge Green *E. Sussex*, 'erɪdʒ
  érrij
Eridge Green *E. Sussex*, 'erɪdʒ
  'grin, érrij green
Eriska *S'clyde*, 'erɪskə, érriskă
Eriskay *W. Isles*, 'erɪskeɪ, érris-
  kay; 'erɪskɪ, érriski
Erisort, Loch, *W. Isles*, 'erɪsɔrt,
  érrissort
Eriswell *Suffolk*, 'erɪswəl,
  érrisswĕl
Erith *London*, 'ɪərɪθ, eerith
Erlanger, *f.n.*, ɛər'læŋər, airláng-
  -ĕr
Erlbeck, *f.n.*, 'ɜrlbek, érlbeck
Erlestoke *Wilts.*, 'ɜrlstoʊk, érl-
  -stōk
Erlich, *f.n.*, 'ɛərlɪx, áirlich
Erne, Earl of, ɜrn, ern
Ernesettle *Devon*, 'ɜrnɪsetl,
  érnissettl
Ernle, Barony of, 'ɜrnlɪ, érnli
Erraid *S'clyde*, 'ɛərɪdʒ, áirij
Errigal, *Co. Tyrone*, 'erɪgəl,
  érrigăl. *In the title of Viscount
  Alexander of Tunis and of* ~,
  derived from ~ *in Co. Donegal
  in the Republic of Ireland, the
  pronunciation is* 'erɪgɔl,
  érrigawl.
Errington, *f.n.*, 'erɪŋtən, érringtŏn
Eritt, *f.n.*, 'erɪt, érrit
Errochty Water, River, *Tayside*,
  'erəxtɪ 'wɔtər, érrŏchti wáwtĕr
Erroll, Earl of, 'erəl, érrŏl
Erskine, *f.n.*, 'ɜrskɪn, érsskin

Erskine of Rerrick, Baron,
  'ɜrskɪn əv 'rerɪk, érsskin ŏv
  rérrick
Erskine *S'clyde*, 'ɜrskɪn, érsskin
Erthig *see* **Erddig**
Ervine, *f.n.*, 'ɜrvɪn, érvin
Ervine, St. John, *author and
  dramatist*, 'sɪndʒən 'ɜrvɪn,
  sínjŏn érvin
Erw *Dyfed*, 'eru, érroo
Erwood *Powys*, 'erʊd, érrŏŏd
Erwyd, *C.n.*, 'erʊɪd, érrŏŏ-id
Eryri, *name sometimes given to
  Mount Snowdon*, ə'rʌrɪ, ĕrúrri.
  The name means 'eagle top'.
Escley Brook, River, *H. & W.*,
  'esklɪ 'brʊk, éskli brŏŏk
Esclusham *Clwyd*, es'kluʃəm,
  esklóo-shăm
Escoffey, *f.n.*, ɪs'kɒfɪ, ĕskóffi
Escott, *f.n.*, 'eskət, ésskŏt
Esdaile, *f.n.*, 'ezdeɪl, ézdayl
Esgairgeiliog *Powys*, ˌesgaɪər-
  'gaɪldʒɒg, essgīrgíl-yog
Esh *Durham*, eʃ, esh
Esha Ness *Shetland*, 'eʃə nes,
  éshă ness
Esher *Surrey*, 'iʃər, eeshĕr.
  Appropriate also for Viscount ~.
Esholt *W. Yorks.*, 'eʃɒlt, ésholt
Eskdaill, Lord, 'eskdeɪl, éskdayl
Eskdalemuir *D. & G.*, 'eskdeɪl-
  'mjʊər, éskdaylmyŏŏr
Eskew, *f.n.*, 'eskju, ésskew
Esk Hause *Cumbria*, 'esk 'hɔz,
  ésk háwz
Eskmeals *Cumbria*, 'eskmilz,
  éskmeelz
Esler, *f.n.*, 'eslər, ésslĕr
Esmond, *C.n. and f.n.*, 'ezmənd,
  ézmŏnd
Esmonde, *f.n.*, 'ezmənd, ézmŏnd
Espinasse, *f.n.*, 'espɪnæs, éspinass
Essame, *f.n.*, 'eseɪm, éssaym
Essendine *Leics.*, 'esəndaɪn,
  éssĕndīn
Essendon, Barony of, 'esəndən,
  éssĕndŏn
Essenhigh, *f.n.*, 'esənhaɪ, éssĕn-hī
Essinger, *f.n.*, 'esɪndʒər, éssinjĕr
Essex *Co. name*, 'esɪks, éssĕks
Esslemont, *f.n.*, 'eslmənt, éssl-
  mŏnt
Esswood, *f.n.*, 'eswʊd, ésswŏŏd
Estcourt, *f.n.*, 'eskɔrt, éskort
Esthwaite Water *Cumbria*,
  'esθweɪt 'wɔtər, éssthwayt
  wáwtĕr
Estorick, *f.n.*, 'estərɪk, ésstŏrick
Etal *Northd.*, 'itl, eetl'; 'etl, éttl
Etall, *f.n.*, 'etɒl, éttawl
Etches, *f.n.*, 'etʃɪz, étchĕz
Etchingham *E. Sussex*, ˌetʃɪŋ-
  'hæm, etching-hám

Etheldreda, saint, 'eθldridə, éthldreedă

Etheredge, *f.n.*, 'eθərıdʒ, éthĕrĕj

Etherege, *f.n.*, 'eθərıdʒ, éthĕrĕj

Etheridge, *f.n.*, 'eθərıdʒ, éthĕrij

Etherton, *f.n.*, 'eðərtən, éthĕrtŏn

Ethie, *also spelt* **Eathie**, *H'land*, 'iθı, éethi

Etive, Loch *and* River, *S'clyde*, 'etıv, éttiv

Eton College *Berks.*, 'itən, éetŏn

Etonian, *one educated at* **Eton** *College*, i'tounıən, eetóniăn

Ettershank, *f.n.*, 'etərʃæŋk, éttĕr-shank

Ettlinger, *f.n.*, 'etlıŋər, étling-ĕr

Ettrick *Borders*, 'etrık, étrick

Etty, *f.n.*, 'etı, étti

Etwall *Derby.*, 'etwɔl, étwawl

Eugene, *C.n.*, ju'ʒeın, yoozháyn; 'judʒın, yoójeen; ju'dʒın, yoojéen

Euler, *f.n.*, 'julər, yoólĕr; 'ɔılər, óylĕr

Eunson, *f.n.*, 'junsən, yoónssŏn

Eurfryn, *Welsh C.n.*, 'aıərvrın, írvrin

Eurich, *f.n.*, 'juərık, yoórick

Eurig, *Welsh C.n.*, 'aıərıg, írig

Eustelle, *C.n.*, jus'tel, yoostéll

Euston *Suffolk*, 'justən, yoós-tŏn

Euxton *Lancs.*, 'ekstən, éckstŏn

Evand, *f.n.*, 'evənd, évvănd

Evans, Beriah Gwynfe, *Welsh divine*, bə'raıə 'gwınvə 'evənz, bĕríă gwínvĕ évvănz

Evanton *H'land*, 'evəntən, évvăn-tŏn

Evedon *Lincs.*, 'ivdən, éevdŏn

Eveleigh, *f.n.*, 'ivlı, éevli

Eveleigh-de-Moleyns, *f.n.*, 'ivlı 'deməlinz, éevli démmŏleenz. *Family name of Baron Ventry.*

Eveline, *C.n.*, 'ivlın, éevlin

Eveling, *f.n.*, 'ivlıŋ, éevling

Evely, *f.n.*, 'ivlı, éevli

Evelyn, *C.n.*, 'ivlın, éevlin; 'evlın, évlin

Evelyn, John, *English diarist (1620–1706)*, 'ivlın, éevlin

Evemy, *f.n.*, 'evımı, évvĕmi

Evenjobb *Powys*, ,evən'dʒɒb, evvĕnjób

Evenley *Northants.*, 'ivənlı, éevĕnli

Evenlode *Glos.*, 'ivənloud, éevĕnlŏd

Evennett, *f.n.*, 'evınet, évvĕnet

Everest, *f.n.*, 'evərıst, évvĕrĕst

Everett, *f.n.*, 'evərıt, évvĕrĕt

Everill, *f.n.*, 'evərıl, évvĕril

Everingham, *f.n.*, 'evərıŋəm, évvĕring-ăm

Evers, *f.n.*, 'evərz, évvĕrz; 'ivərz, éevĕrz

Evershed, *f.n.*, 'evərʃed, évvĕr-shed. *Appropriate also for the Barony of* ~.

Eversholt *Beds.*, 'evərʃɒlt, évvĕr-sholt

Every, *f.n.*, 'evrı, évvri; 'evərı, évvĕri

Evesham *H. & W.*, 'ivʃəm, éev-shăm; 'ivıʃəm, eevĕ-shăm; 'isəm, éessăm. *Appropriate also for the Vale of* ~.

Evetts, *f.n.*, 'evıts, évvĕts

Evie *Orkney*, 'ivı, éevi

Evill, *f.n.*, 'evıl, évvil

Evington *Glos.*, *Leics.*, 'evıŋtən, évvingtŏn

Evington Place *Kent*, 'ivıŋtən, éevingtŏn

Ewart, *f.n.*, 'juərt, yoó-ărt

Ewart *Northd.*, 'juərt, yoo-ărt

Ewe, Loch, *H'land*, ju, yoo

Ewell *Surrey*, 'juəl, yoó-ĕl

Ewelme *Oxon.*, 'juelm, yoó-elm

Ewen, *f.n.*, 'juən, yoó-ĕn

Ewenny *Mid Glam.*, ı'wenı, ĕ-wénni

Ewing, *f.n.*, 'juıŋ, yoo-ing

Ewins, *f.n.*, 'juınz, yoo-inz; 'juınz, yoó-inz

Ewloe *Clwyd*, 'julou, yoólō

Ewood Bridge *Lancs.*, 'iwud 'brıdʒ, ée-wŏod bríj

Ewyas Harold *H. & W.*, 'juəs 'hærəld, yoó-ăss hárrŏld

Exceat *E. Sussex*, 'eksit, éckseet

Excell, *f.n.*, ek'sel, eckséll

Exe, River, *Somerset–Devon*, eks, ecks

Exelby, *f.n.*, 'ekslbı, écksslbi

Exeter *Devon*, 'eksıtər, écksĕtĕr. *Appropriate also for the Marquess of* ~.

Exford *Somerset*, 'eksfɔrd, écksford

Exmouth *Devon*, 'eksməθ, écksmŭth. *Appropriate also for Viscount* ~.

Exon, *f.n.*, 'eksən, écksŏn

Exstance, *f.n.*, 'ekstəns, éckstănss

Exwick *Devon*, 'ekswık, éckswick

Ey, River, *Grampian*, eı, ay

Eyam, *f.n.*, im, eem

Eyam *Derby.*, im, eem

Eyck, *f.n.*, aık, īk

Eyden, *f.n.*, 'eıdən, áydĕn

Eydon *Northants.*, 'idən, éedŏn

Eye *Cambs.*, *H. & W.*, *Northants.*, aı, ī

Eyemouth *Borders*, 'aımauθ, ímowth

Eyers, *f.n.*, ɛərz, airz

Eyet, *f.n.,* 'aɪət, í-ĕt
Eyke *Suffolk,* aɪk, īk
Eykyn, *f.n.,* 'ɪkɪn, éekin
Eyles, *f.n.,* aɪlz, ílz
Eynesbury *Cambs.,* 'eɪnzbərɪ, áynzbŭri
Eynhallow Island *Orkney,* aɪn-'hælou, īn-hálō
Eynon, *f.n. and Welsh C.n.,* 'aɪnən, ínŏn
Eynsford *Kent,* 'eɪnzfərd, áynzförd
Eynsham *Oxon.,* 'enʃəm, én-shăm; 'eɪnʃəm, áyn-shăm
Eype *Dorset,* ip, eep
Eyre, *f.n.,* ɛər, air
Eyre and Spottiswoode, *publishers,* 'ɛər ənd 'spɒtɪswʊd, áir ănd spóttisswōōd
Eyre Methuen, *publishers,* 'ɛər 'meθjuən, áir méth-yoo-ĕn
Eyres, *f.n.,* ɛərz, airz
Eysenck, *f.n.,* 'aɪzeŋk, ízenk
Eyston, *f.n.,* 'istən, éestŏn
Eythorne *Kent,* 'eɪθɔrn, áy-thorn
Eytle, *f.n.,* 'aɪtl, ítl
Eyton, *f.n.,* 'aɪtən, ítŏn; 'itən, éetŏn
Eyton *Clwyd,* 'itən, éetŏn. *Appropriate for both places of this name in Clwyd.*
Eyton *H. & W.,* 'eɪtən, áytŏn
Eyton-on-the-Weald Moors *Salop,* 'aɪtən ɒn ðə 'wild 'mʊərz, ítŏn on thē weeld mōōrz
Eywood *H. & W.,* 'eɪwʊd, áywōōd
Ezard, *f.n.,* 'izɑrd, éezaard
Ezra, *f.n.,* 'ezrə, ézzră

F

Faber, *f.n.,* 'feɪbər, fáybĕr. *Appropriate also for ～ and ～, publishers.*
Fabian, *f.n.,* 'feɪbɪən, fáybi-ăn
Fâche, *f.n.,* faʃ, faash
Facit *Lancs.,* 'feɪsɪt, fáyssit
Faed, *f.n.,* feɪd, fayd
Fagan, *f.n.,* 'feɪgən, fáygăn
Fage, *f.n.,* feɪdʒ, fayj
Fageant, *f.n.,* 'feɪdʒənt, fáyjănt
Fagence, *f.n.,* 'feɪdʒəns, fáyjĕnss
Fahey, *f.n.,* feɪ, fay
Fahie, *f.n.,* 'feɪɪ, fáy-i; 'fɑɪ, faá-i
Fahy, *f.n.,* 'fɑhɪ, faá-hi
Faichney, *f.n.,* 'feɪxnɪ, fáychni
Faiers, *f.n.,* 'feɪərz, fáy-ĕrz
Faifley *S'clyde,* 'feɪflɪ, fáyfli
Fairbairn, *f.n.,* 'fɛərbɛərn, fáirbairn

Fairbank, *f.n.,* 'fɛərbæŋk, fáirbank
Fairbanks, *f.n.,* 'fɛərbæŋks, fáirbanks
Fairbotham, *f.n.,* 'fɛərbɒθəm, fáirboth-ăm
Fairclough, *f.n.,* 'fɛərklʌf, fáirkluff; 'fɛərklou, fáirklō
Fairfoull, *f.n.,* 'fɛərfaʊl, fáirfowl
Fairgrieve, *f.n.,* 'fɛərgriv, fáirgreev
Fairhall, *f.n.,* 'fɛərhɔl, fáir-hawl
Fairhaven, Baron, 'fɛərheɪvən, fáir-hayvĕn
Fairley, *f.n.,* 'fɛərlɪ, fáirli
Fairman, *f.n.,* 'fɛərmən, fáirmăn
Fairmaner, *f.n.,* 'fɛərmænər, fáirmannĕr; fɛər'mænər, fairmánnĕr
Fairminer, *f.n.,* 'fɛərmɪnər, fáirminnĕr
Fairservice, *f.n.,* 'fɛərsɜrvɪs, fáir-serviss
Fairwarp *E. Sussex,* 'fɛərwɔrp, fáirwawrp
Fakenham *Norfolk,* 'feɪkənəm, fáykĕnăm
Fala *Lothian,* 'fælə, fálă
Falco, *f.n.,* 'fælkou, fálkō
Falcon, *f.n.,* 'fɔkən, fáwkŏn; 'fɒlkən, fáwlkŏn
Falconbridge, *f.n.,* 'fɔkənbrɪdʒ, fáwkŏnbrij
Falconer, *f.n.,* 'fɔlkənər, fáwlkŏnĕr; 'fɔknər, fáwknĕr; 'fɒlkənər, fólkŏnĕr
Faldingworth *Lincs.,* 'fɔldɪŋwərθ, fáwlding-wŭrth
Falfield *Avon,* 'fælfild, fálfeeld
Falk, *f.n.,* fɔlk, fawlk; fɒk, fawk
Falkender, *f.n.,* 'fɔlkəndər, fáwlkĕndĕr. *Appropriate also for Baroness ～.*
Falkiner, *f.n.,* 'fɔknər, fáwknĕr
Falkirk *Central,* 'fɔlkərk, fáwlkŭrk
Falkland, Viscount, 'fɔklənd, fáwklănd
Falkland *Fife,* 'fɔlklənd, fáwlklănd
Falkus, *f.n.,* 'fɔlkəs, fáwlkŭss
Falla, *f.n.,* 'fælə, fálă
Fallapit *Devon,* 'fæləpɪt, fálápit
Fallas, *f.n.,* 'fælæs, fálass
Falle, *f.n.,* fɒl, fawl
Faller, *f.n.,* 'fælər, fálĕr
Fallin *Central,* fə'lɪn, fălín
Falloon, *f.n.,* fə'lun, fălóon
Falmer *E. Sussex,* 'fælmər, fál-mĕr
Falmouth *Cornwall,* 'fælməθ, fálmŭth. *Appropriate also for Viscount ～.*
Falstone *Northd.,* 'fælstoun, fálstŏn

Fan Frynych *Powys*, væn 'vrʌnɪx,
van vrúnnich
Fannich, Mountains, River *and*
Loch, *H'land*, 'fænɪx, fánnich
Fanning, *f.n.*, 'fænɪŋ, fánning
Fanshawe, *f.n.*, 'fænʃɔ, fán-shaw
Fant, *f.n.*, fænt, fant
Fantham, *f.n.*, 'fænθəm, fán-thăm
Fanthorpe, *f.n.*, 'fænθɔrp, fán-
-thorp
Fanum House, *Basingstoke*
(*Hants*), 'feɪnəm, fáynŭm.
*Headquarters of the Automobile
Association. Many other offices
of the AA throughout the United
Kingdom bear the same name.*
Fara, Island, *also spelt* **Faray,
Pharay,** *Orkney*, 'færə, fárrǎ
Faragher, *f.n.*, 'færəgər, fárrǎgěr
Farago, *f.n.*, 'færəgou, fárrǎgō
Faray, Island, *also spelt* **Fara,
Pharay,** *Orkney*, 'færə, fárrǎ
Farcet *Cambs.*, 'fɑrsɪt, faárssět
Far Cotton *Northants.*, 'fɑr 'kɒtən,
faár kóttŏn
Fareham *Hants*, 'fɛərəm, fáir-ăm
Farey, *f.n.*, 'fɛərɪ, fáiri
Fargie, *f.n.*, 'fɑrgɪ, faárgi
Faringdon, *Berks.*, 'færɪŋdən,
fárringdŏn. *Appropriate also for
Baron* ∼.
Faris, *f.n.*, 'færɪs, fárriss
Farjeon, *f.n.* 'fɑrdʒən, faárjŏn
Farmbrough, *f.n.*, 'fɑrmbrə,
faármbrǎ
Farnaby, *f.n.*, 'fɑrnəbɪ, faárnăbi
Farncombe, *f.n.*, 'fɑrŋkəm,
faárnkŏm
Farne Islands, *Northd.*, fɑrn, faarn
Farnell *Tayside*, 'fɑrnl, faárnl
Farquhar, *f.n.*, 'fɑrkər, faárkăr;
'fɑrkwər, faárkwăr. *Both are
used for George* ∼, *the 17th-c.
Irish dramatist.*
Farquharson, *f.n.*, 'fɑrkərsən, faár-
kǎrssŏn; 'fɑrkwərsən, faárkwǎr-
ssŏn
Farr *H'land*, fɑr, faar
Farragon Hill *Tayside*, 'færəgən,
fárrǎgŏn
Farrar, *f.n.*, 'færər, fárrǎr
Farrington Gurney *Avon*, 'færɪŋtən
'gɜrnɪ, fárringtŏn gúrni
Farsley *W. Yorks.*, 'fɑrzlɪ, faárzli
Farvis, *f.n.*, 'fɑrvɪs, faárviss
Fashanu, *f.n.*, 'fæʃənu, fáshǎnoo
Faskally, Loch, *Tayside*, 'fɑskəlɪ,
faáskǎli; 'fɑsklɪ, faáskli
Faslane Bay *S'clyde*, fæz'leɪn,
fazláyn; fəs'leɪn, fǎssláyn
Fasnakyle *H'land*, ˌfæsnə'kaɪl,
fassnǎkíl
Faucett, *f.n.*, 'fɔsɪt, fáwssět
Faucitt, *f.n.*, 'fɔsɪt, fáwssit

Faugh *Cumbria*, fæf, faff; fɑf,
faaf
Faughan, River, *Co. Derry*,
'fɒxən, fóchǎn
Faul, *f.n.*, fɔl, fawl
Faulconbridge, *f.n.*, 'fɔlkənbrɪdʒ,
fáwlkŏnbrij
Fauldhouse *Lothian*, 'fɔldhaʊs,
fáwld-howss
Faulds, *f.n.*, fouldz, fōldz; fɔldz,
fawldz. *The first is appropriate
for Andrew* ∼, *actor and
politician.*
Faulkbourne *Essex*, 'fɔbɜrn,
fáwburn; 'fɔbɔrn, fáwborn
Faulkes, *f.n.*, 'fɔlks, fawlks
Faulkner, *f.n.*, 'fɒknər, fáwkněr
Faulks, *f.n.*, fouks, fōks
Faupel, *f.n.*, fou'pel, fōpéll
Faure, *f.n.*, fɔr, for
Fausset, *f.n.*, 'fɔsɪt, fáwssět;
'fɒsɪt, fóssět
Faust, *f.n.*, faust, fowst
Fauvel, *f.n.*, fou'vel, fōvéll
Faux, *f.n.*, fɔks, fawks; fou, fō
Favarger, *f.n.*, fə'vɑrʒər, fǎvaár-
zhěr
Favell, *f.n.*, 'feɪvl, fáyvl
Faversham *Kent*, 'fævərʃəm,
fávvěr-shăm
Faville, *f.n.*, 'fævɪl, fávvil; 'feɪvɪl,
fáyvil
Favor Royal *Co. Tyrone*, 'feɪvər
'rɔɪəl, fáyvŏr róyǎl
Fawcett, *f.n.*, 'fɔsɪt, fáwssět;
'fɒsɪt, fóssět
Fawdry, *f.n.*, 'fɔdrɪ, fáwdri
Fawks, *f.n.*, fɔks, fawks
Fawssett, *f.n.*, 'fɔsɪt, fáwssět
Fayer, *f.n.*, fɛər, fair; 'feɪər,
fáy-ěr
Fayerman, *f.n.*, 'feɪərmən, fáy-
-ěrmǎn
Fayers, *f.n.*, fɛərz, fairz; 'feɪərz,
fáy-ěrz
Fayrer, *f.n.*, 'fɛərər, fáirěr
Fazackerley, *f.n.*, fə'zækərlɪ,
fǎzáckěrli
Fazakerley, *f.n.*, fə'zækərlɪ,
fǎzáckěrli
Fazakerley *Merseyside*, fə'zækərlɪ,
fǎzáckěrli
Fazan, *f.n.*, fə'zæn, fǎzánn
Fazekas, *f.n.*, fə'zeɪkəs, fǎzáykǎss
Fazeley *Staffs.*, 'feɪzlɪ, fáyzli
Fearenside, *f.n.*, 'fɜrnsaɪd, férn-sīd
Fearn, *f.n.*, fɜrn, fern; fɛərn, fairn
Fearn *H'land*, fɜrn, fern
Fearnan *Tayside*, 'fɜrnən, férnăn
Fearne, *f.n.*, fɜrn, fern; fɛərn,
fairn
Fearon, *f.n.*, 'fɪərən, féerŏn
Featherstone, *f.n.*, 'feðərstən,
féthěrsstŏn; 'fɜrstən, férsstŏn

Featherstonehaugh, *f.n.,* *also spelt* **Featherstonhaugh, Fetherstonhaugh,** 'feðərstənhɔ, féthĕrstŏn-haw; 'fænʃɔ, fán-shaw; 'festənhɔ, féstŏn-haw; 'fisənheɪ, féessŏn-hay; 'fɪərstənhɔ, féerstŏn-haw
Feavearyear, *f.n.,* 'fevjər, fév-yĕr
Feaver, *f.n.,* 'fivər, féevĕr
Fecher, *f.n.,* 'fetʃər, fétchĕr
Fechlie, *f.n.,* 'fexlɪ, féchli
Feckenham *H. & W.,* 'fekənəm, féckĕnăm; 'feknəm, fécknăm
Feenan, *f.n.,* 'finən, féenăn
Feeny *Co. Derry,* 'finɪ, féeni
Fehily, *f.n.,* 'filɪ, féeli
Feighan, *f.n..* 'fiən, fee-ăn
Feilden, *f.n.,* 'fildən, féeldĕn
Feilding, *f.n.,* 'fildɪŋ, féelding
Feiling, *f.n.,* 'faɪlɪŋ, fíling
Feist, *f.n.,* fist, feest
Felindre *Powys,* ve'lɪndrə, velíndrĕ. *Cf.* **Velindre.** *There are many places of this name throughout Wales.*
Felin-foel *Dyfed,* ˌvelɪn'vɔɪl, vellinvóyl; ˌvelɪn'voʊl, vellin-vốl
Felin-hen *Gwynedd,* ˌvelɪn'heɪən, vellin-háy-ĕn
Fellgett, *f.n.,* 'felgɪt, féllgĕt
Fellowes, *f.n.,* 'feloʊz, féllōz
Felmersham *Beds.,* 'felmərʃəm, félmĕr-shăm
Felmingham, *f.n.,* 'felmɪŋəm, félming-ăm
Felpham *W. Sussex,* 'felphəm, félp-hăm; 'felpəm, félpăm; 'felfəm, félfăm
Felsted *Essex,* 'felstɪd, félstĕd
Feltham *London,* 'feltəm, féltăm
Feltwell *Norfolk,* 'feltwel, féltwel
Fenay Bridge *W. Yorks.,* 'fenɪ 'brɪdʒ, fénni bríj
Fen Ditton *Cambs.,* 'fen 'dɪtən, fén díttŏn
Fendrich, *f.n.,* 'fendrɪtʃ, féndritch
Fenemore, *f.n.,* 'fenɪmɔr, fénnĕmor
Feniscowles *Lancs.,* 'fenɪskoʊlz, fénnisskōlz
Fennah, *f.n.,* 'fenə, fénnă
Fennell, *f.n.,* 'fenl, fénnl
Fennelly, *f.n.,* 'fenəlɪ, fénnĕli
Fennessy, *f.n.,* 'fenɪsɪ, fénnĕssi
Fenoulhet, *f.n.,* 'fenəleɪ, fénnŏlay
Fenstanton *Cambs.,* fen'stæntən, fenstántŏn
Fentiman, *f.n.,* 'fentɪmən, fénti-măn
Fentum, *f.n.,* 'fentəm, féntŭm
Fenwick, *f.n.,* 'fenɪk, fénnick; 'fenwɪk, fén-wick
Fenwick *Northd.,* 'fenɪk, fénnick

Feock *Cornwall,* 'fiɒk, fée-ock
Feoffees Town Hall, The, *Colyton (Devon),* 'fifiz, féefeez
Feord, *f.n.,* 'fiɔrd, fée-ord
Ferbrache, *f.n.,* 'fɜrbræʃ, fér-brash
Fereday, *f.n.,* 'ferɪdeɪ, férrĕday
Ferens, *f.n.,* 'ferənz, férrĕnz
Ferensway *Hull (Humberside),* 'ferɪnzweɪ, férrĕnz-way
Fergus, *C.n.,* 'fɜrgəs, férgŭss
Ferguslie *S'clyde,* ˌfɜrgəs'li, fergüsslée
Ferguson, *f.n.,* 'fɜrgəsən, férgüs-sŏn
Fergusson, *f.n.,* 'fɜrgəsən, férgüs-sŏn
Ferintosh *H'land,* ˌferɪn'tɒʃ, ferrintósh
Ferman, *f.n.,* 'fɜrmən, férmăn
Fermanagh *Co. name and town,* fər'mænə, fĕrmánnă. *Appropriate also for Baron* ~.
Fermont, *f.n.,* 'fɜrmɒnt, férmont
Fermoy, Baron, fər'mɔɪ, fĕrmóy
Fermoy Centre *King's Lynn,* fər'mɔɪ, fĕrmóy
Fernald, *f.n.,* 'fɜrnəld, férnäld
Fernau, *f.n.,* 'fɜrnoʊ, férnō
Ferneyhough, *f.n.,* 'fɜrnɪhoʊ, férni-hō
Fernie, *f.n.,* 'fɜrnɪ, férni
Fernihough, *f.n.,* 'fɜrnɪhoʊ, férni-hō; 'fɜrnɪhʌf, férni-huff
Fernyhalgh *Lancs.,* 'fɜrnɪhʌf, férni-huff; 'fɜrnɪhælʃ, férni-halsh
Fernyhough, *f.n.,* 'fɜrnɪhoʊ, férni-hō; 'fɜrnɪhʌf, férni-huff
Ferrand, *f.n.,* 'ferənd, férrănd
Ferrar, *f.n.,* 'ferər, férrăr
Ferrier, *f.n.,* 'ferɪər, férri-ĕr
Ferriggi, *f.n.,* fə'rɪdʒɪ, fĕréeji
Ferryside *Dyfed,* ˌferɪ'saɪd, ferri-síd
Fertel, *f.n.,* 'fɜrtəl, fértĕl
Feshie, River, *H'land,* 'feʃɪ, féshi
Feshie Bridge *H'land,* 'feʃɪ 'brɪdʒ, féshi bríj
Fethaland Point *Shetland,* 'feɪdəlænd, fáydăland
Fetherstonhaugh, *f.n., see* **Featherstonehaugh**
Fetlar *Shetland,* 'fetlər, féttlăr
Fetterangus *Grampian,* ˌfetər'æŋgəs, fettĕráng-güss
Fettes, *f.n.,* 'fetɪz, féttĕz; 'fetɪs, féttĕss
Fettes College *Lothian,* 'fetɪs, féttĕss
Fettesian, *one educated at* **Fettes** *College,* fə'tizɪən, fĕtéeziăn
Feugh, Bridge of, *Grampian,* fjux, fewch

Feugh, Water of, *Grampian,* fjux, fewch

Feversham, Baron, 'fevərʃəm, févvĕr-shăm

Fewings, *f.n.,* 'fjuɪŋz, féw-ingz

Fewkes, *f.n.,* fjuks, fewks

Fewston *N. Yorks.,* 'fjustən, féwsstŏn

Fewtrell, *f.n.,* 'fjutrəl, féwtrĕl

Ffairfach *Dyfed,* ˌfaɪər'vax, fīrvaʹach

Ffaldau *W. Glam.,* 'fældaɪ, fáldī

Ffestiniog *Gwynedd,* fes'tɪnjɒg, festín-yog

Ffion, *Welsh C.n.,* 'fiɒn, fée-on

Ffolkes, *f.n.,* foʊks, fōks

Fforest-fach *W. Glam.,* ˌfɒrɪst'vax, forrĕst-vaʹach

Fforest Fawr *Powys,* ˌfɒrɪst'vaʊər, forrĕst vówr

Ffoulkes, *f.n.,* foʊks, fōks; fuks, fooks

Ffrangcon, *f.n.,* 'fræŋkən, fránk-ŏn

Ffrangcon-Davies, Gwen, *actress,* 'gwen 'fræŋkən 'deɪvɪs, gwén fránkŏn dáyviss

ffrench-Beytagh, *f.n.,* 'frenʃ 'bitə, frénsh beetá

Ffynnongroyw, *also spelt* **Ffynnon Groew,** *Clwyd,* ˌfʌnən'grɔɪu, funnŏn-gróy-oo

Fiander, *f.n.,* faɪ'ændər, fī-ándĕr

Fiddes *Grampian,* 'fɪdɪs, fíddĕss

Fidelis, *C.n.,* fɪ'deɪlɪs, fidáyliss

Fidelo, *f.n.,* fɪ'deloʊ, fidéllō

Fidler, *f.n.,* 'fɪdlər, fídlĕr; 'fidlər, féedlĕr

Fidra, Isle of, *Lothian,* 'fidrə, féedră

Field Dalling *Norfolk,* 'fild 'dɔlɪŋ, féeld dáwling

Fielding, *f.n.,* 'fildɪŋ, féelding. *Appropriate for Henry ~, 18th-c. author.*

Fienburgh, *f.n.,* 'finbərə, féenbŭră

Fiennes, *f.n.,* faɪnz, fīnz

Fife *Scotland,* faɪf, fīf

Fifield Bavant *Wilts.,* 'faɪfild 'bævənt, fífeeld bávvănt

Figgis, *f.n.,* 'fɪgɪs, fíggiss

Figgures, *f.n.,* 'fɪgərz, fíggŭrz

Figheldean *Wilts.,* 'faɪldin, fíldeen

Figueroa, *f.n.,* ˌfɪgə'roʊə, figgĕró-ă

Figures, *f.n.,* 'fɪgərz, fíggŭrz

Filby, *f.n.,* 'fɪlbɪ, fílbi

Filcher, *f.n.,* 'fɪltʃər, fíltchĕr

Fildes, *f.n.,* faɪldz, fīldz

Filey *N. Yorks.,* 'faɪlɪ, fíli

Filleigh *Devon,* 'fɪlɪ, fílli

Fillongley *Warwicks.,* 'fɪlɒŋlɪ, fillong-li

Filmer, *f.n.,* 'fɪlmər, fílmĕr

Finaghy *Co. Antrim,* 'fɪnəxɪ, fínnăchi

Finavon *Forfar,* fɪn'eɪvən, fináyvŏn

Finborough Parva *Suffolk,* 'fɪnbərə 'pɑrvə, fínbŭră paʹarvă

Fincastle *Tayside,* fɪn'kɑsl, fin-kaʹassl. *Appropriate also for Viscount ~.*

Finchale *Durham,* 'fɪŋkl, fínkl. *Appropriate also for ~ Abbey.*

Fincham, *f.n.,* 'fɪntʃəm, fíntchăm

Finchampstead *Berks.,* 'fɪnʃəm-sted, fínshämsted

Finchingfield *Essex,* 'fɪnʃɪŋfild, fínshingfeeld

Finchley *London,* 'fɪntʃlɪ, fíntchli; 'fɪnʃlɪ, fínshli

Findern *Derby.,* 'fɪndərn, fíndĕrn

Findhorn *Grampian,* 'fɪndhɔrn, fínd-horn

Findlater, *f.n.,* 'fɪnlətər, fínlătĕr; 'fɪndlətər, fíndlătĕr

Findlater *Grampian,* 'fɪndlətər, fíndlătĕr

Findlay, *f.n.,* 'fɪnlɪ, fínli; 'fɪndlɪ, fíndli

Findley, *f.n.,* 'fɪndlɪ, fíndli

Findochty *Grampian,* fɪn'dɒxtɪ, findóchti; fɪ'nextɪ, finnéchti

Finedon *Northants.,* 'faɪndən, fíndŏn

Finer, *f.n.,* 'faɪnər, fínĕr

Fingal, *Norse hero,* 'fɪŋgl, fíng-gl

Fingal's Cave *Staffa,* 'fɪŋglz 'keɪv, fíng-glz káyv

Fingalian, *pertaining to* **Fingal,** fɪŋ'geɪliən, fing-gáyliăn

Fingall, Earl of, fɪŋ'gɔl, fing-gáwl

Fingest *Bucks.,* 'fɪndʒɪst, fínjèst

Finglan *d, f.n.,* 'fɪŋlənd, fíng-lănd

Fingringhoe *Essex,* 'fɪŋrɪŋhoʊ, fing-ring-hō

Finis, *f.n.,* 'fɪnɪs, fínniss

Finkelstein, *f.n.,* 'fɪŋkəlstaɪn, fínkĕl-stīn

Finlay, *f.n.,* 'fɪnlɪ, fínli

Finlayson, *f.n.,* 'fɪnlɪsən, fínlissŏn

Finnart *S'clyde,* 'fɪnərt, fínnärt

Finnerty, *f.n.,* 'fɪnərtɪ, fínnĕrti

Finney, *f.n.,* 'fɪnɪ, fínni

Finnie, *f.n.,* 'fɪnɪ, fínni

Finnieston *S'clyde,* 'fɪnɪstən, fínnistŏn

Finnissy, *f.n.,* 'fɪnɪsɪ, fínnissi

Finnucane, *f.n.,* fɪ'nukən, finoʹo-kăn; fɪ'njukən, finéwkăn

Finsberg, *f.n.,* 'fɪnzbərg, fínzberg

Finsbury Park *London,* 'fɪnzbərɪ 'park, fínzbŭri paʹark

Finstown *Orkney,* 'fɪnstən, fínsstŏn

Fintona *Co. Tyrone,* 'fɪntənə, fíntŏnă

Finucane, *f.n.*, fɪ'nukən, finoókăn; fɪ'njukeın, finéwkayn; fɪ'njukən, finéwkăn

Finvoy *Co. Antrim*, 'fɪnvɔɪ, fínvoy

Finzean *Grampian*, 'fɪŋən, fíng-ăn

Finzi, Gerald, *composer*, 'fɪnzɪ, fínzi

Fionda, *f.n.*, fɪ'ɒndə, fi-óndă

Fior, *f.n.*, 'fiɔr, feé-or

Firle, West, *E. Sussex*, fɜrl, firl

Firmager, *f.n.*, 'fɜrmədʒər, fírmăjĕr

Firman, *f.n.*, 'fɜrmən, fírmăn

Firminger, *f.n.*, 'fɜrmɪndʒər, fírminjĕr

Firth, *f.n.*, fɜrθ, firth

Firth of Forth *separates Lothian and Fife regions*, 'fɜrθ əv 'fɔrθ, fírth ŏv fórth

Firth of Lorn *S'clyde*, 'fɜrθ əv 'lɔrn, fírth ŏv lórn

Fisch, *f.n.*, fɪʃ, fish

Fisherie *Grampian*, 'fɪʃərɪ, físhĕri

Fishguard *Dyfed*, 'fɪʃgɑrd, físh-gaard

Fishwick, *f.n.*, 'fɪʃwɪk, físh-wick

Fison, *f.n.*, 'faɪsən, físsŏn

Fitchew, *f.n.*, 'fɪtʃu, fítchoo

Fitzailwyn, *f.n.*, fɪts'eɪlwɪn, fits-áylwin

Fitzgerald, *f.n.*, fɪts'dʒerəld, fits-jérrăld

Fitzgibbon, *f.n.*, fɪts'gɪbən, fits-gíbbŏn

Fitzhardinge, *f.n.*, fɪts'hɑrdɪŋ, fits-haárding

Fitzpatrick, *f.n.*, fɪts'pætrɪk, fits-pátrick

Fitzrandolph, *f.n.*, fɪts'rændɒlf, fits-rándolf

Fitzroy, *f.n.*, 'fɪtsrɔɪ, fítsroy

Fitzsimons, *f.n.*, fɪts'saɪmənz, fits-símŏnz

Fitzwalter, Baron, fɪts'wɔltər, fits-wáwltĕr

Flach, *f.n.*, flæk, flack

Flackes, *f.n.*, flæks, flacks

Flaherty, *f.n.*, 'flɑhərtɪ, flaá-hĕrti; 'flɑərtɪ, flaá-ĕrti

Flamsteed, *f.n.*, 'flæmstɪd, flám-steed

Flannan *Isles W. Isles*, 'flænən, flánnăn

Flat Holm *Island S. Glam.*, 'flæt hoʊm, flát hōm

Flavell, *f.n.*, 'fleɪvl, fláyvl; flə'vel, flăvéll

Flavin, *f.n.*, 'fleɪvɪn, fláyvin

Flawith *N. Yorks.*, 'flɔ-ɪθ, fláw-ith; flɔɪθ, floyth

Flax Bourton *Avon*, 'flæks 'bɔrtən, flácks bórtŏn

Fleggburgh *Norfolk*, 'flegbərə, flégbŭră

Fleggon, *f.n.*, 'flegɒn, fléggon

Fleischman, *f.n.*, 'flaɪʃmən, flíshmăn

Flekier, *f.n.*, 'flekɪər, fléckeer

Fleming, *f.n.*, 'flemɪŋ, flémming

Flemons, *f.n.*, 'flemənz, flémmŏnz

Flessati, *f.n.*, flə'sɑtɪ, flĕssaáti

Fletcher, *f.n.*, 'fletʃər, flétchĕr

Flett, *f.n.*, flet, flett

Fleur de Lis *Gwent*, ,flɜr də 'li, flur dĕ leé

Fleure, *f.n.*, flɜr, flur

Flewin, *f.n.*, 'fluɪn, floó-in

Flint *Clwyd*, flɪnt, flint

Flintham *Notts.*, 'flɪntəm, flíntăm

Flitwick *Beds.*, 'flɪtɪk, flíttick

Floate, *f.n.*, floʊt, flōt

Flood, *f.n.*, flʌd, fludd

Floore *see* **Flore**

Flore, *also spelt* **Floore**, *Northants.*, flɔr, flor

Florey, *f.n.*, 'flɔrɪ, fláwri. *Appropriate also for the Barony of* ~.

Floris, *f.n.*, 'flɒrɪs, flórriss

Flotta *Island Orkney*, 'flɒtə, flóttă

Floud, *f.n.*, flʌd, fludd

Flower, *f.n.*, 'flaʊər, flówĕr

Flury, *f.n.*, 'fluərɪ, floóri

Flux, *f.n.*, flʌks, flucks

Fochabers *Grampian*, 'fɒxəbərz, fóchăbĕrz

Fochriw *Mid Glam.*, 'vɒxrɪu, vóchri-oo

Foco Novo, *theatre company*, 'foʊkoʊ 'noʊvoʊ, fōkō nŏvō

Foden, *f.n.*, 'foʊdən, fōdĕn

Foel *Powys*, vɔɪl, voyl

Fogarty, *f.n.*, 'foʊgərtɪ, fōgắrti

Fogerty, *f.n.*, 'foʊgərtɪ, fōgĕrti

Foges, *f.n.*, 'foʊgɪs, fōgĕss

Foggin, *f.n.*, 'fɒgɪn, fóggin

Fogou *Caves Cornwall*, 'fugu, foógoo

Folan, *f.n.*, 'foʊlən, fōlăn

Folger, *f.n.*, 'fɒlgər, fólgĕr

Foljambe, *f.n.*, 'fʊldʒəm, fooljăm. *Family name of the Earl of Liverpool*.

Folkard, *f.n.*, 'foʊkərd, fōkărd; 'foʊlkɑrd, fōl-kaard; 'fɒlkɑrd, fól-kaard

Folke *Dorset*, foʊk, fōk

Folkes, *f.n.*, foʊks, fōks

Folkestone *Kent*, 'foʊkstən, fōkstŏn. *Appropriate also for Viscount* ~.

Folking *W. Sussex*, 'fɒlkɪŋ, fól-king

Folkingham *Lincs.*, 'fɒkɪŋəm, fócking-ăm

Folkington *E. Sussex*, 'foʊɪŋtən, fō-ingtŏn

Folwell, *f.n.*, 'fɒlwəl, fól-wĕl

Fomison, *f.n.*, 'fɒmɪsən, fómmis-sŏn

Fontaine, *f.n.*, 'fɒnteɪn, fóntayn

Fonteyn, Dame **Margot,** *ballerina,* 'mɑrgoʊ 'fɒnteɪn, maárgō fóntayn; fɒn'teɪn, fontáyn. *Dame Margot herself finds that the stress varies according to the context.*

Fookes, *f.n.*, fuks, fooks

Foord, *f.n.*, fɔrd, ford

Foort, *f.n.*, fɔrt, fort

Foot, *f.n.*, fʊt, foŏt

Footdee *Grampian,* fʊt'di, foŏt--dee; 'fɪtɪ, fítti

Footler, *f.n.*, 'fʊtlər, foŏtlĕr

Forbes, *f.n.*, 'fɔrbɪs, fórbĕss; fɔrbz, forbz. *The first, which is appropriate for Baron ~ and for the Master of ~, is more usual in what used to be Aberdeenshire, the home county of the Clan Forbes.*

Forbes-Sempill, *f.n.*, 'fɔrbɪs 'sempl, fórbĕss sémpl. *Family name of the Barons of Sempill.*

Ford, Ford Madox, *author,* 'fɔrd 'mædəks 'fɔrd, fórd máddŏcks fórd. *Formerly* **Ford Madox Hueffer,** *q.v.*

Forde, *f.n.*, fɔrd, ford

Fordell *Fife,* fɔr'del, fordéll

Fordham *Cambs.*, 'fɔrdəm, fórdăm

Fordoun *Grampian,* fɔr'dun, fordoŏn

Fordred, *f.n.*, 'fɔrdrɪd, fórdrĕd

Fordwich *Kent,* 'fɔrdwɪtʃ, fórd-witch; 'fɔrdɪtʃ, fórditch

Fordyce, *f.n.*, fɔr'daɪs, fordíss

Fordyce *Grampian,* fɔr'daɪs, fordíss

Foren, *f.n.*, 'fɔrən, fáwrĕn

Fores, *f.n.*, fɔrz, forz

Forestier, *f.n.*, 'fɒrɪstjər, fórrĕst--yĕr

Forfar *Tayside,* 'fɔrfər, fórfăr

Forgan, *f.n.*, 'fɔrgən, fórgăn

Forgandenny *Tayside,* ‚fɔrgən-'denɪ, forgăndénni

Forkhill, *also spelt* **Forkill,** *Co. Armagh,* 'fɔrkɪl, fórkill

Formatine, Viscount, fər'mɑtɪn, fŏrmaátin

Forncett St. Mary *Norfolk,* 'fɔrnsɪt snt 'meərɪ, fórnssĕt sǐnt máiri

Forncett St. Peter *Norfolk,* 'fɔrnsɪt snt 'pitər, fórnssĕt sǐnt peétĕr

Fornsete, John of, *13th-c. composer,* 'fɔrnset, fórnsett

Forrabury *Cornwall,* 'fɒrəbərɪ, fórrăbŭri

Forran, *f.n.*, fɔ'ræn, fawránn

Forres *Grampian,* 'fɒrɪs, fórrĕss. *Appropriate also for Baron ~.*

Forster, *f.n.*, 'fɔrstər, fórstĕr; 'fɒstər, fósstĕr. *The first is appropriate for E. M. ~, author, the second for the late Baron ~ of Harraby.*

Forsyth, *f.n.*, fər'saɪθ, forssíth

Forsythe, *f.n.*, fər'saɪθ, forssíth; fər'saɪð, forssíth; 'fɔrsaɪθ, fórssíth

Fortbreda *Co. Down,* fɔrt'brɪdə, fortbreédă

Forte, *f.n.*, 'fɔrtɪ, fórti

Forter *Castle Tayside,* 'fɔrtər, fórtĕr

Fortescue, Earl, 'fɔrtɪskju, fór-tĕskew

Forteviot *Tayside,* fɔr'tɪvɪət, forteéviŏt. *Appropriate also for Baron ~.*

Forth, River, *Central,* fɔrθ, forth

Fortingall *Tayside,* 'fɔrtɪŋgl, fór-ting-gl

Fortrose *H'land,* 'fɔrtroʊz, fórtrōz

Fortuin, *f.n.*, 'fɔrtjʊɪn, fórt-yoō-in; fər'taɪn, fortín

Foryd, Stream, *Gwynedd,* 'vɒrɪd, vórrid

Fosdyke *Lincs.*, 'fɒzdaɪk, fózdīk

Foster, *f.n.*, 'fɒstər, fósstĕr

Fotheringhay *Northants.*, 'fɒðər-ɪŋheɪ, fóthĕring-hay; 'fɒðərɪŋgeɪ, fóthĕring-gay. *The first is the village pronunciation today. The other is more usual for historic ~ Castle.*

Foubert Place *London,* 'fubərt, foŏbĕrt

Foudland *Grampian,* 'faʊdlənd, fówdländ

Foula *Shetland,* 'fulə, foŏlä

Foulden *Borders,* 'fuldən, foŏl-dĕn

Foulds, *f.n.*, foʊldz, fōldz. *Appropriate for John ~, composer.*

Foulger, *f.n.*, 'fuldʒər, foŏljĕr; 'fuldʒər, foŏljĕr; 'fʊldʒər, fóljĕr; 'fɒldʒər, fóljĕr; 'fulgər, foŏlgĕr

Foulis, *f.n.*, faʊlz, fowlz

Foulis *H'land,* faʊlz, fowlz. *Appropriate also for ~ Castle.*

Foulis Ferry *H'land,* 'faʊlz 'ferɪ, fówlz férri

Foulkes, *f.n.*, foʊks, fōks; faʊks, fowks

Foulness *Essex, Humberside,* 'faʊl'nes, fówl-néss. *In Essex this is an island; in Humberside, a river.*

Foulridge *Lancs.*, 'foʊlrɪdʒ, fṓlrij

Foulsham, *f.n.*, 'fʊlʃəm, fṓol-shăm

Foulsham *Norfolk*, 'foʊlʃəm, fṓl-shăm; 'fʊlʃəm, fṓol-shăm; 'foʊlsəm, fṓlssăm

Foulshiels *Borders*, 'faʊl'ʃilz, fówl-sheelz

Fountaine, *f.n.*, 'faʊntɪn, fówntin

Fourcin, *f.n.*, 'fɔrsɪn, fórssin

Four Gotes *Cambs.*, 'fɔr goʊts, fór gōts

Foux, *f.n.*, fuks, fooks

Fovant *Wilts.*, 'fɒvənt, fóvvănt

Foweraker, *f.n.*, 'faʊəreɪkər, fówĕraykĕr

Fowey *Cornwall*, fɔɪ, foy

Fowke, *f.n.*, foʊk, fōk; faʊk, fowk

Fowkes, *f.n.*, foʊks, fōks; faʊks, fowks

Fowlds, *f.n.*, foʊldz, fōldz

Fowles, *f.n.*, faʊlz, fowlz

Fowlis Easter *Tayside*, 'faʊlz 'istər, fówlz ĕestĕr

Fowlis Wester *Tayside*, 'faʊlz 'westər, fówlz wéstĕr

Fowlmere *Cambs.*, 'faʊlmɪər, fówlmeer

Fownhope *H. & W.*, 'faʊnhoʊp, fówn-hōp

Fox, Uffa, *yacht designer*, 'ʌfə 'fɒks, úffă fócks

Foxell, *f.n.*, 'fɒksl, fócksl

Foxen, *f.n.*, 'fɒksən, fócksĕn

Foxhole *W. Glam.*, 'fɒkshoʊl, fócks-hōl

Foxt *Staffs.*, fɒkst, fockst

Foy, *f.n.*, fɔɪ, foy

Foyle, *f.n.*, fɔɪl, foyl

Fozzard, *f.n.*, 'fɒzərd, fózzaard

Fradin, *f.n.*, 'freɪdɪn, fráydin

Fraenkel, *f.n.*, 'fræŋkl, fránkl

Frahill, *f.n.*, frɑl, fraal

Framingham *Norfolk*, 'fræmɪŋəm, frámming-ăm

Franche *H. & W.*, franʃ, fraansh

Francillon, *f.n.*, fræn'sɪlən, fran-síllŏn

Francke, *f.n.*, 'fræŋkɪ, fránki

Francome, *f.n.*, 'fræŋkəm, fránkŏm

Franey, *f.n.*, 'freɪnɪ, fráyni

Frankau, *f.n.*, 'fræŋkoʊ, fránkō; 'fræŋkaʊ, fránkow. *The first is appropriate for Gilbert ~, author, and for Pamela ~, author.*

Frankel, *f.n.*, 'fræŋkl, fránkl

Frankell, *f.n.*, 'fræŋkl, fránkl

Frankenburgh, *f.n.*, 'fræŋkənbərg, fránkĕnburg

Franklin, *f.n.*, 'fræŋklɪn, fránklin

Franklyn, *f.n.*, 'fræŋklɪn, fránklin

Frant *E. Sussex*, frænt, frant

Fraser, *f.n.*, 'freɪzər, fráyzĕr

Fraser of Allander, Barony of, 'freɪzər əv 'æləndər, fráyzĕr ŏv áländĕr

Fraser of Dineiddwg, Baronetcy of, 'freɪzər əv dɪ'naɪðʊg, fráyzĕr ŏv dinĭthōog

Fraserburgh *Grampian*, 'freɪzərbərə, fráyzĕrbŭră

Frater, *f.n.*, 'freɪtər, fráytĕr

Frating *Essex*, 'freɪtɪŋ, fráyting

Frazer, *f.n.*, 'freɪzər, fráyzĕr

Freake, *f.n.*, frik, freek

Freakes, *f.n.*, friks, freeks

Frears, *f.n.*, frɛərz, frairz; frɪərz, freerz

Frecheville *S. Yorks.*, 'fretʃvɪl, frétchvil

Fredman, *f.n.*, 'fredmən, frédmăn

Freegard, *f.n.*, 'frigɑrd, freegaard

Freeson, *f.n.*, 'frisən, freessŏn

Freethy, *f.n.*, 'friθɪ, freethi

Freiston *Lincs.*, 'frɪstən, freesstŏn

Freke, *f.n.*, frik, freek

Fremantle, *f.n.*, 'frimæntl, freemantl; frɪ'mæntl, freemántl

Fremington *Devon*, 'fremɪŋtən, frémmingtŏn

French, *f.n.*, frenʃ, frensh

Frenchay *Avon*, 'frenʃeɪ, frén-shay

Frere, *f.n.*, frɪər, freer; frɛər, frair

Fressanges, *f.n.*, 'fresɑ̃ʒ, fréssaangzh

Freswick *H'land*, 'frezwɪk, frézwick; 'frezɪk, frézzick

Freuchie *Fife*, 'fruxɪ, froochi

Freud, *f.n.*, frɔɪd, froyd

Freugh, East *and* West, *D. & G.*, frux, frooch

Freyberg, *f.n.*, 'fraɪbərg, fríberg. *Appropriate also for Baron ~.*

Freyer, *f.n.*, 'frɪər, frée-ĕr; 'fraɪər, frí-ĕr

Freyhan, *f.n.*, 'fraɪhən, frí-hăn

Fricker, *f.n.*, 'frɪkər, frickĕr

Frideswide, *8th-c. abbess*, 'frɪdɪswɪdə, fríddĕssweedĕ

Fridge, *f.n.*, frɪdʒ, frij

Fried, *f.n.*, frid, freed

Friedman, *f.n.*, 'fridmən, freedmăn

Frieght, *f.n.*, freɪt, frayt; fraɪt, frīt

Friel, *f.n.*, fril, freel

Friend, *f.n.*, frend, frend

Friern Barnet *London*, 'fraɪərn 'bɑrnɪt, frí-ĕrn baárnĕt; 'frɪərn 'bɑrnɪt, freérn baárnĕt

Friesden *see* **Frithsden**

Friese-Greene, William, *motion-picture pioneer*, 'friz 'grin, fréez gréen

Frieth *Bucks.*, friθ, freeth
Frindsbury *Kent*, 'frɪndzbərɪ, fríndzbŭri
Frinton-on-Sea *Essex*, 'frɪntən ɒn 'si, fríntŏn on see
Friockheim *Tayside*, 'frɪkɪm, freekim
Frisch, *f.n.*, frɪʃ, frish
Frise, *f.n.*, friz, freez
Friskney *Lincs.*, 'frɪsknɪ, frískni
Friters, *f.n.*, 'frɪtərz, freetĕrz
Fritham *Hants*, 'frɪðəm, fríthăm
Frithelstock *Devon*, 'frɪθlstɒk, fríthl-stock; 'frɪstɒk, frístock
Frithsden, *also spelt* **Friesden**, *Herts.*, 'frɪzdən, freezděn; 'frɪzdən, frízděn
Frizelle, *f.n.*, frɪ'zel, frizéll
Frizinghall *W. Yorks.*, 'fraɪzɪŋhɔl, frízing-hawl
Frizington *Cumbria*, 'frɪzɪŋtən, frizzingtŏn
Frocester *Glos.*, 'frɒstər, frósstĕr
Frodin, *f.n.*, 'frɒvdɪn, frŏdin
Frodingham *Humberside*, 'frɒdɪŋəm, fródding-ăm
Frodsham *Ches.*, 'frɒdʃəm, fród-shăm
Froest, *f.n.*, 'frɒvɪst, frŏ-ĕst
Fromanteel, *f.n.*, 'frɒvməntɪl, frŏmănteel
Frome *Somerset*, frum, froom
Frome, Rivers, *Dorset, Somerset*, frum, froom
Frome Vauchurch *Dorset*, 'frum 'vɒvtʃərtʃ, fróom vŏchurch
Fron *Clwyd, Gwynedd, Powys*, vrɒn, vron
Fronallt *Gwynedd*, 'vrɒnəɫt, vrón-năḥlt
Froncysyllte, *also spelt* **Fronsysylltau, Vroncysyllte**, *Clwyd*, ‚vrɒnkə'sʌɫteɪ, vron-kǎssúḥltay
Frongoch *Gwynedd*, vrɒn'govx, vron-góch
Frood, *f.n.*, frud, frood
Frossard, *f.n.*, 'frɒsard, fróssaard
Frostenden *Suffolk*, 'frɒsəndən, fróssěnděn
Froswick *Cumbria*, 'frɒsɪk, fróssick
Froud, *f.n.*, fravd, frowd
Froude, *f.n.*, frud, frood. *Appropriate for James Anthony ~, 19th-c. historian.*
Frow, *f.n.*, frav, frow
Frowde, *f.n.*, fravd, frowd
Fryd, *f.n.*, frɪd, frid
Fryirs, *f.n.*, 'fraɪərz, frí-ĕrz
Fryston *N. Yorks.*, 'fraɪstən, frísstŏn
Fuchs, *f.n.*, fuks, fŏŏks; fuks, fooks. *The first is appropriate*

for Sir Vivian ~, *geologist and explorer.*
Fuest, *f.n.*, fjust, fewst
Fugaccia, *f.n.*, fv'gætʃɪə, fŏŏgátch-iǎ
Fuge, *f.n.*, fjudʒ, fewj
Fuinary *S'clyde*, 'fjunərɪ, féwnări
Fujino, *f.n.*, 'fjudʒɪnov, féwjinŏ
Fuke, *f.n.*, fjuk, fewk
Fulbourn *Cambs.*, 'fulbɔrn, fŏŏlborn
Fulham *London*, 'fuləm, fŏŏlăm
Fulke, *C.n. and f.n.*, fulk, fŏŏlk
Fulker, *f.n.*, 'fulkər, fŏŏlkĕr
Fulkes, *f.n.*, fulks, fŏŏlks
Fulking *W. Sussex*, 'fulkɪŋ, fŏŏlking
Fullom, *f.n.*, 'fuləm, fŏŏlŏm
Fulmodestone *Norfolk*, 'fulməstən, fŏŏlmĕstŏn
Fulstow *Lincs.*, 'fulstov, fŏŏlsstŏ
Fulwell *London*, 'fulwel, fŏŏl-wel
Fundenhall *Norfolk*, 'fʌndənhɔl, fúndĕn-hawl
Furlonge, *f.n.*, 'fɜrlɒŋ, fúrlong
Furnace *Dyfed, S'clyde*, 'fɜrnɪs, fúrniss
Furnas, *f.n.*, 'fɜrnɪs, fúrniss
Furneaux, Viscount, 'fɜrnov, fúrnŏ
Furnell, *f.n.*, fɜr'nel, furnéll
Furness, *f.n.*, 'fɜrnɪs, fúrnĕss; fɜr'nes, furnéss. *The first is appropriate for Viscount* ~.
Furneux Pelham *Herts.*, 'fɜrnɪks 'peləm, fúrnicks péllăm; 'fɜrnov 'peləm, fúrnŏ péllăm
Furnivall, Barony of, 'fɜrnɪvl, fúrnivl
Furth, *f.n.*, fɜrθ, furth
Fuseli, Henry, *18th–19th-c. painter and author*, 'fjuzəlɪ, féwzĕli; fju'zelɪ, fewzélli. *Perhaps the most commonly accepted of a variety of pronunciations. He was originally Johann Heinrich Füssli, a native of Zurich.*
Fushiebridge *Lothian*, 'fuʃɪbrɪdʒ, fŏŏshibrij
Fussell, *f.n.*, 'fʌsl, fússl
Fussey, *f.n.*, 'fʌsɪ, fússi
Futrille, *f.n.*, 'fjutrɪl, féwtril
Fyfield *Lancs.*, 'faɪfɪld, fífeeld
Fylde *Lancs.*, faɪld, fíld
Fyleman, *f.n.*, 'faɪlmən, fílmăn
Fylingdales *N. Yorks.*, 'faɪlɪŋdeɪlz, fíling-daylz
Fyne, Loch, *S'clyde*, faɪn, fín
Fysh, *f.n.*, faɪʃ, físh
Fyson, *f.n.*, 'faɪsən, físsŏn
Fyvel, *f.n.*, 'faɪvl, fívl
Fyvie *Grampian*, 'faɪvɪ, fívi

G

Gabain, *f.n.*, gə'beın, găbáyn
Gabalfa *S. Glam.*, gə'bælvə, găbálvă
Gabbitas, *f.n.*, 'gæbıtæs, gábbitass
Gaber, *f.n.*, 'geıbər, gáybĕr
Gabor, *f.n.*, 'gabər, gaábor
Gabriel, *C.n. and f.n.*, 'geıbrıəl, gáybri-ĕl
Gadbury, *f.n.*, 'gædbərı, gádbŭri
Gaddarn, *f.n.*, gə'darn, gădaárn
Gaddesby *Leics.*, 'gædzbı, gádzbi
Gaddesden, Great *and* Little, *Herts.*, 'gædzdən, gádzdĕn
Gadfan, *Welsh C.n.*, 'gædvən, gádvăn
Gadie Burn *Grampian*, 'gadı 'bɜrn, gaádi búrn
Gadlys *Mid Glam.*, *S. Glam.*, 'gædlıs, gádliss
Gaenor, *Welsh C.n.*, 'geınər, gáynŏr; 'gaınər, gínor
Gaenor, *f.n.*, 'geınər, gáynŏr
Gaerwen *Gwynedd*, 'gaıərwən, gírwĕn
Gaetjens, *f.n.*, 'geıtjənz, gáyt-yĕnz
Gaffin, *f.n.*, 'gæfın, gáffin
Gagan, *f.n.*, 'geıgən, gáygăn
Gage, *f.n.*, geıdʒ, gayj
Gahan, *f.n.*, 'geıən, gáy-ăn; gan, gaan
Gaick Forest *H'land*, 'gaık, gaá-ick; gaık, gík
Gaiger, *f.n.*, 'geıdʒər, gáyjĕr
Gaillard, *f.n.*, 'geılard, gáylaard; 'gaıard, gí-aard
Gainford, Baron, 'geınfərd, gáynfŏrd
Gainsborough *Lincs.*, 'geınzbərə, gáynzbŭră. *Appropriate also for the Earl of* ~.
Gair, *f.n.*, geər, gair
Gairdner, *f.n.*, 'gardnər, gaárdnĕr; 'geərdnər, gáirdnĕr
Gaire, *f.n.*, geər, gair
Gairloch *H'land*, 'geərlɒx, gáir-loch
Gaisgill *Cumbria*, 'geızgıl, gáyzgil
Gaitens, *f.n.*, 'geıtənz, gáytĕnz
Gaitskell, *f.n.*, 'geıtskəl, gáytskĕl. *Appropriate also for Baroness* ~.
Galashiels *Borders*, ˌgælə'ʃilz, gală-sheélz
Galbally *Co. Tyrone*, 'gælbəlı, gálbăli
Galbraith, *f.n.*, gæl'breıθ, gal-bráyth

Galby *Leics.*, 'gɔlbı, gáwlbi
Gale, *C.n. and f.n.*, geıl, gayl
Galena, *f.n.*, gə'linə, găleénă
Galgate *Lancs.*, 'gɔlgeıt, gáwlgayt
Galgorm *Co. Antrim*, gæl'gɔrm, galgórm
Galica, *f.n.*, gə'lıtsə, gălítsă
Galitzine, *f.n.*, gæ'lıtsın, galítseen
Gall, *f.n.*, gɔl, gawl
Gallacher, *f.n.*, 'gæləxər, gálă<u>ch</u>ĕr; 'gæləhər, gálă-hĕr
Gallagher, *f.n.*, 'gæləxər, gálă<u>ch</u>ĕr
Gallannaugh, *f.n.*, 'gælənɔ, gálănaw
Gallati, *f.n.*, gə'lætı, gălátti
Galleozzie, *f.n.*, ˌgælı'ɒtsı, gali-ótsi
Gallovidian, native of **Galloway**, ˌgælou'vıdıən, galōvíddiăn
Galloway *D. & G.*, 'gæləweı, gálŏ-way. *Appropriate also for the Earl of* ~.
Gallwey, *f.n.*, 'gɔlweı, gáwlway
Galmpton *Devon*, 'gæmptən, gámptŏn
Galpern, *f.n.*, 'gælpərn, gálpĕrn
Galpin, *f.n.*, 'gælpın, gálpin
Galston *S'clyde*, 'gɔlstən, gáwls-stŏn
Galsworthy, *f.n.*, 'gɔlzwɜrðı, gáwlzwur<u>thi</u>; 'gælzwɜrðı, gálzwur<u>thi</u>. *Although the first was the pronunciation of John* ~, *author, some members of the family prefer to use the second.*
Galwally *Co. Antrim*, gæl'wælı, galwáli
Galway, Viscount, 'gɔlweı, gáwlway
Gaman, *f.n.*, 'geımən, gáymăn
Gambier, *f.n.*, 'gæmbıər, gámbi-ĕr
Gamblin, *f.n.*, 'gæmblın, gámblin
Gambold, *f.n.*, 'gæmbould, gám-bōld
Gambon, *f.n.*, 'gæmbɒn, gámbon
Gamesley *Derby.*, 'geımzlı, gáymzli
Gamjee, *f.n.*, 'gæmdʒi, gámjee
Gamlen, *f.n.*, 'gæmlın, gámlĕn
Gamlin, *f.n.*, 'gæmlın, gámlin
Gamlingay *Cambs.*, 'gæmlıŋgeı, gámling-gay
Gammans, *f.n.*, 'gæmənz, gámmănz
Gammell, *f.n.*, 'gæml, gámml
Gammie, *f.n.*, 'gæmı, gámmi
Gamon, *f.n.*, 'geımən, gáymŏn
Gampell, *f.n.*, 'gæmpl, gámpl
Gandar, *f.n.*, 'gændər, gándăr
Gandee, *f.n.*, 'gændı, gándi
Gandy, *f.n.*, 'gændı, gándi
Gangel, *f.n.*, 'gæŋgl, gáng-gl
Gannaway *Co. Down*, 'gænəweı, gánnă-way

Gannon, *f.n.,* 'gænən, gánnŏn
Gaping Gill Hole, *also spelt*
 Ghyll, *N. Yorks.,* 'geɪpɪŋ 'gɪl,
 gáyping gill
Garard, *f.n.,* 'gærɑrd, gárraard
Garboldisham *Norfolk,* 'gɑrblʃəm,
 gaárbl-shăm
Garcia, *f.n.,* 'gɑrsɪə, gaárssiä;
 'gɑrʃɪə, gaárshiä
Garcke, *f.n.,* 'gɑrkɪ, gaárki
Gard, *f.n.,* gɑrd, gaard
Gardiner, *f.n.,* 'gɑrdnər, gaárdnĕr.
 Appropriate also for Baron ∼.
Gardy Loo Gully *Ben Nevis,*
 'gɑrdɪ 'lu, gaárdi loó
Gardyne, *f.n.,* gɑr'daɪn, gaardín
Garel-Jones, *f.n.,* 'gærəl 'dʒoʊnz,
 gárrĕl-jŏnz
Gare Loch, The, *S'clyde,* 'gɛər
 lɒx, gáir loch
Garendon *Leics.,* 'gærəndən,
 gárrĕndŏn
Garfield, Leon, *author,* 'liən
 'gɑrfild, leé-ŏn gaárfeeld
Garforth *W. Yorks.,* 'gɑrfərθ,
 gaár-fŏrth
Garigue, *f.n.,* 'gærɪgju, gárrigew
Garin, *f.n.,* 'gærɪn, gárrin
Garioch, *f.n.,* 'gærɪəx, gárriŏch
Garioch *Grampian,* 'gɪərɪ, geéri
Garlieston *D. & G.,* 'gɑrlɪstən,
 gaárlistŏn
Garlinge Green *Kent,* 'gɑrlɪndʒ
 'grin, gaárlinj greén
Garmonsway, *f.n.,* 'gɑrmənzweɪ,
 gaármŏnzway
Garmoyle, Viscount, gɑr'mɔɪl,
 gaarmóyl
Garnant *Dyfed,* 'gɑrnænt, gaár-
 nant
Garndiffaith *Gwent,* gɑrn'dɪfaɪθ,
 gaarndíffīth
Garnedd-wen *Clwyd,* ˌgɑrnəð-
 'wen, gaarnĕth-wén
Garneddwen *Gwynedd,* gɑr-
 'neðwən, gaarnéth-wĕn
Garnet, *f.n.,* 'gɑrnɪt, gaárnĕt
Garnethill *Glasgow,* ˌgɑrnɪt'hɪl,
 gaarnĕt-híll
Garnett, *f.n.,* 'gɑrnɪt, gaárnĕt
Garn-fach *Gwent,* gɑrn'vɑx,
 gaarnvaách
Garngoch Common *W. Glam.,*
 gɑrn'gɒx, gaarn-góch
Garnsworthy, *f.n.,* 'gɑrnzwɜrðɪ,
 gaárnzwurthi. *Appropriate also*
 for the Barony of ∼.
Garrard, *f.n.,* 'gærɑrd, gárraard
Garrett, *f.n.,* 'gærɪt, gárrĕt
Garron Point *Co. Antrim,* 'gærən,
 gárrŏn
Garry, River, *Tayside,* 'gærɪ, gárri
Garryduff *Co. Antrim,* ˌgærɪ'dʌf,
 garridúff

Garscadden *Glasgow,* gɑrs-
 'kædən, gaarsskáddĕn
Garside, *f.n.,* 'gɑrsaɪd, gaárssīd
Garsven *Skye,* 'gɑrʃven, gaársh-
 -ven
Gartcosh *S'clyde,* gɑrt'kɒʃ,
 gaart-kósh
Garten, Loch, *H'land,* 'gɑrtən,
 gaártĕn
Garthbeibio *Powys,* gɑrθ-
 'baɪbjoʊ, gaarthbíb-yō
Garthbrengy *Powys,* gɑrθ'breŋgɪ,
 gaarthbréng-gi
Gartheli *Dyfed,* gɑr'θelɪ, gaar-
 -théli
Garthmyl *Powys,* gɑrθ'mil,
 gaarth-meél
Gartnavel Hospital *Glasgow,*
 gɑrt'neɪvəl, gaart-náyvĕl
Gartocharn *S'clyde,* ˌgɑrtə'xɑrn,
 gaartŏchaárn
Gartsherrie *S'clyde,* gɑrt'ʃerɪ,
 gaart-shérri
Garvagh, *f.n.,* 'gɑrvə, gaárvă
Garvagh *Co. Derry,* 'gɑrvə,
 gaárvă. *Appropriate also for*
 Baron ∼.
Garvald *Lothian,* 'gɑrvəld,
 gaárvăld
Garve *H'land,* gɑrv, gaarv
Garvellach Isles, *also spelt*
 Garvelloch, *S'clyde,* gɑr'veləx,
 gaarvéllăch
Garvestone *Norfolk,* 'gɑrvɪstən,
 gaárvĕstŏn
Garvice, *f.n.,* 'gɑrvɪs, gaárviss
Garw *Mid Glam.,* 'gæru, gárroo
Garwell, *f.n.,* 'gɑrwel, gaárwel
Gary, *f.n.,* 'gɛərɪ, gáiri
Gascoigne, *f.n.,* 'gæskɔɪn, gáss-
 koyn
Gascoin, *f.n.,* 'gæskɔɪn, gásskoyn
Gascoine, *f.n.,* 'gæskɔɪn, gásskoyn
Gascoyne, *f.n.,* 'gæskɔɪn, gáss-
 koyn
Gaselee, *f.n.,* 'geɪzlɪ, gáyzli
Gash, *f.n.,* gæʃ, gash
Gaskell, *f.n.,* 'gæskl, gásskl
Gaskil, *f.n.,* 'gæskɪl, gásskil;
 'gæskl, gásskl
Gassiot, *f.n.,* 'gæsɪət, gássiŏt
Gastrell, *f.n.,* 'gæstrəl, gástrĕl
Gatacre, *f.n.,* 'gætəkər, gáttăckĕr
Gateacre *Merseyside,* 'gætəkər,
 gáttăkĕr
Gatehouse of Fleet *D. & G.,*
 'geɪthaʊs əv 'flit, gáyt-howss ŏv
 fleét
Gater, *f.n.,* 'geɪtər, gáytĕr
Gateshead *Tyne & Wear,*
 'geɪtshed, gáyts-hed
Gathercole, *f.n.,* 'gæðərkoʊl,
 gáthĕr-kōl
Gathorne, *f.n.,* 'geɪθɔrn, gáy-thorn

Gathurst *Gtr. M'chester*, 'gæθərst, gáth-ŭrst

Gatlish, *f.n.*, 'gætlıʃ, gátlish

Gatrell, *f.n.*, 'gætrəl, gátrĕl

Gatt, *f.n.*, gæt, gat

Gatward, *f.n.*, 'gætwɔrd, gát-wawrd

Gatwick Airport *W. Sussex*, 'gætwɪk, gátwick

Gau, *f.n.*, gaʊ, gow

Gaubert, *f.n.*, 'goʊbɛər, gőbair

Gauci, *f.n.*, 'gaʊtʃı, gówtchi

Gaudin, *f.n.*, 'gɔdın, gáwdin

Gaughan, *f.n.*, 'gɒhən, gó-hăn

Gauhan, *f.n.*, 'gɒhən, gó-hăn

Gauld, *f.n.*, gɔld, gawld

Gault, *f.n.*, gɔlt, gawlt; gɒlt, golt

Gauna, *f.n.*, 'gɔnə, gáwnă

Gauntlett, *f.n.*, 'gɔntlıt, gáwntlĕt

Gausden, *f.n.*, 'gɔzdən, gáwzdĕn

Gaussen, *f.n.*, 'goʊsən, gőssĕn

Gavall, *f.n.*, gə'væl, găvál

Gaved, *f.n.*, 'gævıd, gávvĕd

Gavegan, *f.n.*, 'gævıgən, gávvĕ-găn; gə'vegən, găvéggăn

Gaveston, *f.n.*, 'gævıstən, gávvĕstŏn

Gavey, *f.n.*, 'geıvı, gáyvi

Gavin, *C.n.*, 'gævın, gávvin

Gavinton *Borders*, 'gævıntən, gávvintŏn

Gawith, *f.n.*, 'gaʊıθ, gów-ith; 'geıwıθ, gáy-with

Gaymer, *f.n.*, 'geımər, gáymĕr

Gayton *Norfolk*, 'geıtən, gáytŏn

Geake, *f.n.*, gik, geek

Geanies *H'land*, 'gınıs, géeniss

Geard, *f.n.*, gıərd, geerd

Geary, *f.n.*, 'gıərı, géeri

Geaussent, *f.n.*, 'ʒoʊsɒŋ, zhőssong

Gebbie, *f.n.*, 'gebı, gébbi

Gebhard, *f.n.*, 'gebhɑrd, géb-haard

Geddes, *f.n.*, 'gedıs, géddĕss. *Appropriate also for Baron* ～.

Geddinge *Kent*, 'gedındʒ, géddinj

Geddington *Northants.*, 'gedıŋtən, géddingtŏn

Geduld, *f.n.*, 'gedəld, géddŭld

Gedye, *f.n.*, 'gedı, géddi

Gee, *f.n.*, dʒı, jee

Geen, *f.n.*, gin, geen

Geesin, *f.n.*, 'gısın, géessin

Geeson, *f.n.*, 'dʒısən, jéessŏn

Geeston *Leics.*, 'gıstən, géesstŏn

Geevor *Cornwall*, 'gıvər, géevŏr

Geffen, *f.n.*, 'gefən, géffĕn

Geffrye Museum *London*, 'dʒefrı, jéffri

Gegan, *f.n.*, 'gıgən, géegăn

Gegg, *f.n.*, geg, geg

Geiger, *f.n.*, 'gaıgər, gígĕr

Geikie, *f.n.*, 'gıkı, géeki

Geldeston *Norfolk*, 'geldstən, géldsstŏn; 'geldestən, géldes-stŏn; 'gelstən, gélsstŏn

Geliot, *f.n.*, 'dʒelıət, jélliŏt

Gell, *f.n.*, gel, gell; dʒel, jell

Gellan, *f.n.*, 'gelən, géllăn

Gellatly, *f.n.*, 'gelətlı, géllătli; gə'lætlı, gĕlátli

Gellender, *f.n.*, 'geləndər, géllĕndĕr

Geller, *f.n.*, 'gelər, géllĕr

Gelli *Mid Glam.*, 'gelı, géhli

Gelli Aur, *Carmarthen County Agricultural College*, 'gelı 'aıər, géhli ír

Gelli-gaer *Mid Glam.*, ,gelı'gaıər, gehli-gír

Gelli Uchaf *Dyfed*, ,gelı 'ıxæv, gehli íchavv; ,gelı 'ıxav, gehli eechaav

Gelliceidrim Colliery *Dyfed*, ,gelı'keıdrım, gehlikáydrim; ,gelı'kaıdrım, gehlikídrim

Gellilydan *Gwynedd*, ,gelı'lʌdən, gehli-lúddăn

Gelling, *f.n.*, 'gelıŋ, gélling

Gemmell, *f.n.*, 'geml, gémml

Gemmill, *f.n.*, 'geml, gémml

Gendros *W. Glam.*, 'gendrɒs, géndross

Genese, *f.n.*, dʒə'nis, jĕnéess

Genn, *f.n.*, gen, gen

Gent, *f.n.*, dʒent, jent

Gentry, *f.n.*, 'dʒentrı, jéntri

Geoffrey, *C.n.*, 'dʒefrı, jéffri

Geoghegan, *f.n.*, 'geıgən, gáygăn

George-Brown, *Baron*, 'dʒɔrdʒ 'braʊn, jórj brówn

Georgeham *Devon*, 'dʒɔrdʒhæm, jórj-ham

Georgiadis, *f.n.*, ,dʒɔrdʒı'ɑdıs, jorji-aádiss

Geraghty, *f.n.*, 'gerətı, gérrăti

Geraint, *Welsh C.n.*, 'geraınt, gérrïnt

Gerald, *C.n. and f.n.*, 'dʒerəld, jérräld

Gerber, *f.n.*, 'dʒɜrbər, jérbĕr

Gercken, *f.n.*, 'gɜrkın, gérkĕn

Gerdes, *f.n.*, gɜr'dız, gerdéez

Gerhard, **Roberto**, *composer*, rə'bɜrtoʊ 'dʒerɑrd, rŏbértŏ jérraard

Gerhardi, *f.n.*, dʒɜr'hɑrdı, jĕr-haárdi

Gerhardie, William, *author*, dʒɜr'hɑrdı, jĕr-haárdi

Gerhold, *f.n.*, 'gɜrhoʊld, gér-hōld

Gérin, *f.n.*, 'ʒeræ̃, zhérrang

Germain, *f.n.*, 'dʒɜrmeın, jérmayn

Germoe *Cornwall*, 'gɜrmoʊ, gérmō

Gerngross, *f.n.,* 'gɜrngrɒs, gérn-
-gross
Gerrans *Cornwall,* 'gerənz,
gérränz
Gerrish, *f.n.,* 'gerɪʃ, gérrish
Gershon, *f.n.,* 'gɜrʃən, gér-shŏn
Gershuny, *f.n.,* gər'ʃunɪ, gĕr-
-shoóni
Gerson, *f.n.,* 'gɛərsən, gáirssŏn
Gertler, *f.n.,* 'gɜrtlər, gértlĕr
Gerty, *f.n.,* 'gɜrtɪ, gérti
Gervase, *C.n.,* 'dʒɜrveɪz, jérvayz;
'dʒɜrvɪz, jérviz
Gervis, *f.n.,* 'dʒɑrvɪs, ja'arviss
Getgood, *f.n.,* 'getgʊd, gét-goōd
Gethin, *f.n.,* 'geθɪn, géth-in
Gething, *f.n.,* 'geθɪŋ, géth-ing
Gharbaoui, *f.n.,* gɑr'baʊɪ,
gaarbów-i
Ghey, *f.n.,* dʒaɪ, jī
Ghika, *f.n.,* 'gikə, geékä
Giarchi, *f.n.,* 'dʒɑrkɪ, ja'arki
Gibberd, *f.n.,* 'gɪbərd, gíbbĕrd
Gibbes, *f.n.,* gɪbz, gibz
Gibbon, *f.n.,* 'gɪbən, gíbbŏn
Gibbons, *f.n.,* 'gɪbənz, gíbbŏnz
Gibbons, Grinling, *17th–18th-c.
woodcarver and sculptor,*
'grɪnlɪŋ 'gɪbənz, grínling gíbbŏnz
Gibbs, *f.n.,* gɪbz, gibz
Gibson, *f.n.,* 'gɪbsən, gíbssŏn
Gick, *f.n.,* dʒɪk, jick
Gidal, *f.n.,* gɪ'dæl, gidál
Giddens, *f.n.,* 'gɪdənz, gíddĕnz
Gidding, Great *and* Little,
Cambs., 'gɪdɪŋ, gídding
Gidea Park *Essex,* 'gɪdɪə 'pɑrk,
gíddiä paárk
Gidman, *f.n.,* 'gɪdmən, gídmän
Gielgud, Sir John, *actor,* 'gilgʊd,
geelgoōd
Gieve, *f.n.,* giv, geev
Giffard, *f.n.,* 'dʒɪfərd, jíffǎrd;
'gɪfərd, giffaard. *The first is
appropriate for the family name
of the Earl of Halsbury.*
Giffnock *S'clyde,* 'gɪfnək, giffnŏk
Gifford, *f.n.,* 'dʒɪfərd, jíffŏrd;
'gɪfərd, giffŏrd. *The first is
appropriate for Baron ~, the
second for the ~ Lectureships at
the University of St. Andrews.*
Gifford *Lothian,* 'gɪfərd, giffŏrd.
*Appropriate also for the Earl
of ~.*
Gifford, Aveton, *Devon,* 'ɔtən
'dʒɪfərd, áwtŏn jíffŏrd; 'ævɪtən
'gɪfərd, ávvĕtŏn gíffŏrd
Gifford, Bowers, *Essex,* 'baʊərz
'gɪfərd, bówĕrz gíffŏrd
Gifford, Broughton, *Wilts.,*
'brɔtən 'gɪfərd, bráwtŏn gíffŏrd;
'brɔtən 'dʒɪfərd, bráwtŏn
jíffŏrd

Gifford, Stoke, *Avon,* 'stoʊk
'gɪfərd, stŏk gíffŏrd
Gifford Water *Lothian,* 'gɪfərd,
giffŏrd
Giggleswick *N. Yorks.,* 'gɪglzwɪk,
gígglz-wick
Gigha *S'clyde,* 'giə, gée-ă
Gight Castle *Grampian,* gɪxt,
gicht
Gil, *f.n.,* gɪl, gill
Gilberdyke, *also spelt* **Gilberdike,**
Humberside, 'gɪlbərdaɪk,
gílbĕrdīk
Gilbert, *C.n. and f.n.,* 'gɪlbərt,
gílbĕrt
Gilbey, *f.n.,* 'gɪlbɪ, gílbi
Gilbreath, *f.n.,* gɪl'breɪθ, gil-
bráyth
Gilcomston *Aberdeen,* 'gɪlkəm-
stən, gílkömsstŏn
Gilcrux *Cumbria,* 'gɪlkruz,
gílkrooz
Gildea, *f.n.,* 'gɪldeɪ, gílday;
gɪl'deɪ, gíldáy
Gilder, *f.n.,* 'gɪldər, gíldĕr
Gilderoy, *f.n.,* 'gɪldərɔɪ, gíldĕroy
Gildersome *W. Yorks.,* 'gɪldər-
səm, gíldĕrssŏm
Giles, *f.n.,* dʒaɪlz, jīlz
Gileston *S. Glam.,* 'dʒaɪlztən,
jílztŏn
Gilfach Fargoed *S. Glam.,*
'gɪlvax 'vargɔɪd, gílvaa<u>ch</u>
vaárgoyd
Gilfach Goch *Mid Glam.,* 'gɪlvax
'goʊx, gílvaax gŏ<u>ch</u>
Gilford *Co. Down,* 'gɪlfərd,
gílfŏrd
Gilham, *f.n.,* 'gɪləm, gíllăm
Gilhooley, *f.n.,* gɪl'hulɪ, gil-hoóli
Gilkes, *f.n.,* dʒɪlks, jílks
Gilks, *f.n.,* dʒɪlks, jílks
Gill, *f.n.,* gɪl, gill
Gillam, *f.n.,* 'gɪləm, gíllăm
Gillan Creek *Cornwall,* 'gɪlən
'krik, gíllăn kreék
Gillard, *f.n.,* 'gɪlɑrd, gíllaard;
gɪ'lɑrd, gilaárd; 'gɪlərd, gíllǎrd
Gilleney, *f.n.,* dʒɪ'linɪ, jileéni
Giller, *f.n.,* 'gɪlər, gíllĕr
Gilles, *f.n.,* 'gɪlɪs, gíllĕss
Gillesland *see* **Dacre of Gilles-
land,** Baron
Gillespie, *f.n.,* gɪ'lespɪ, gilésspi
Gillet, *f.n.,* 'gɪlɪt, gíllĕt; dʒɪ'let,
jilétt
Gillett, *f.n.,* 'gɪlɪt, gíllĕt; dʒɪ'let,
jilétt
Gilletts Crossing *Lancs.,*
'dʒɪlets 'krɒsɪŋ, jillets króssing
Gilley, *f.n.,* 'gɪlɪ, gilli
Gilliam, *f.n.,* 'gɪləm, gílliăm
Gilliat, *f.n.,* 'gɪlɪət, gílliăt
Gillick, *f.n.,* 'gɪlɪk, gíllick

Gillie, f.n., 'gılı, gílli
Gillies, f.n., 'gılıs, gílliss
Gilligan, f.n., 'gılıgən, gílligăn
Gilling, f.n., 'gılıŋ, gílling
Gilling N. Yorks., 'gılıŋ, gílling
Gillingham, f.n., 'gılıŋəm, gilling-
-ăm; 'dʒılıŋəm, jilling-ăm
Gillingham Dorset, Norfolk,
'gılıŋəm, gilling-ăm
Gillingham Kent, 'dʒılıŋəm,
jílling-ăm
Gillingwater, f.n., 'gılıŋwɔtər,
gílling-wawtĕr
Gillinson, f.n., 'gılınsən, gíllins-
sŏn
Gillis, f.n., 'gılıs, gílliss
Gillott, f.n., 'dʒılət, jíllŏt; 'gılət,
gíllŏt
Gilman, f.n., 'gılmən, gílmăn
Gilmorehill Glasgow, 'gılmɔr'hıl,
gílmŏr-hill
Gilmorton Leics., gıl'mɔrtən,
gilmórtŏn
Gilmour, f.n., 'gılmər, gílmŭr;
'gılmɔr, gílmor
Gilnahirk Co. Down, ,gılnə'hɜrk,
gilnă-hírk
Gilpin, f.n., 'gılpın, gílpin
Gilroy, f.n., 'gılrɔı, gílroy
Gilsland Northd., 'gılzlənd,
gílzländ
Gilwell Park Essex, 'gılwəl 'pɑrk,
gílwĕl paárk
Gilwern Gwent, 'gılwɛərn, gíl-
wairn
Gilwhite, f.n., 'gılʍwaıt, gíl-whīt
Gilzean, f.n., gı'lin, gileén;
gıl'zin, gilzeén
Gimbert, f.n., 'gımbərt, gímbĕrt
Gimingham Norfolk, 'gımıŋəm,
gímming-ăm
Gimson, f.n., 'gımsən, gímssŏn;
'dʒımsən, jímssŏn
Ginclough Ches., 'dʒınklʌf,
jín-kluff
Ginever, f.n., 'dʒınıvər, jínnĕvĕr
Gingell, f.n., 'gındʒl, gínjl;
'dʒındʒel, jínjel
Ginley, f.n., 'gınlı, gínli
Ginn, f.n., gın, gin
Ginner, f.n., 'dʒınər, jínnĕr
Ginsburg, f.n., 'gınzbɜrg, gínzburg
Ginsbury, f.n., 'gınzbɜrı, gínzbūri
Giordan, f.n., 'dʒɔrdən, jórdăn
Giovene, f.n., dʒı'ouvənı, ji-óvĕni
Gipping, River, Suffolk, 'gıpıŋ,
gipping
Gipps, f.n., gıps, gips
Gipson, f.n., 'gıpsən, gípssŏn
Girouard, f.n., 'dʒırʊɑrd, jírroŏ-
-aard
Girthon D. & G., 'gɜrθən, gírthŏn
Girvan S'clyde, 'gɜrvən, gírvăn
Girvin, f.n., 'gɜrvın, gírvin

Gisborough, Baron, 'gızbərə,
gízbŭră
Gisburn Lancs., 'gısbɜrn, gíssburn
Gisleham Suffolk, 'gızləm, gíz-
lăm; 'gısləm, gísslăm
Gislingham Suffolk, 'gızlıŋəm,
gízling-ăm
Gissane, f.n., gı'seın, gissáyn
Gissing Norfolk, 'gısıŋ, gíssing
Gitsham, f.n., 'gıt-ʃəm, git-shăm
Gittins, f.n., 'gıtınz, gíttinz
Gittisham Devon, 'gıtısəm,
gíttissăm; 'gıtıʃəm, gítti-shăm;
'gıtsəm, gítsăm
Gittoes, f.n., 'gıtouz, gíttōz
Gittus, f.n., 'gıtəs, gíttŭss
Givens, f.n., 'gıvənz, gívvĕnz
Givons Grove Surrey, 'dʒıvənz
'grouv, jívvŏnz gróv
Gladestry Powys, 'gleıdstrı,
gláyd-stri
Gladstone, f.n., 'glædstən, glád-
stŏn
Gladstone of Hawarden, Barony
of, 'glædstən əv 'hɑrdən,
gládstŏn ŏv haárdĕn
Gladwell, f.n., 'glædwəl, glád-
wĕl
Glais W. Glam., glaıs, glīss
Glaisdale N. Yorks., 'gleızdeıl,
gláyzdayl
Glaisher, f.n., 'gleıʃər, gláyshĕr
Glaister, f.n., 'gleıstər, gláysstĕr
Glamis Tayside, glɑmz, glaamz.
Appropriate also for Baron ∼.
Glamorgan, Mid, South, West,
Co. names, glə'mɔrgən,
glămórgăn
Glancy, f.n., 'glænsı, glánssi
Glanely, Barony of, glæn'ilı,
glaneéli
Glanffrwd, Welsh C.n., 'glænfrud,
glánfrood
Glangrwyney Powys, glæn'grʊını,
glan-groŏ-inni
Glangwili Dyfed, glæn'gwılı,
glan-gwílli
Glan Llugwy Gwynedd, glæn
'ɬıgʊı, glan hḻígoŏ-i
Glan-llyn Mid Glam., Gwynedd,
glæn'ɬın, glan-hḻín
Glan-rhyd Powys, glæn'hrıd,
glanreéd
Glanusk, Baron, glæn'ʌsk,
glanúsk. Appropriate also for
Glan Usk Park (Powys).
Glanville, f.n., 'glænvıl, glánvil
Glanwydden Gwynedd, glæn-
'wıðən, glanwíthĕn
Glanyllin Gwynedd, ,glænə'ɬın,
glannă-hḻín
Glanyrafon, also spelt Glan-yr-
afon, Gwynedd, ,glænər'ævən,
glannĕrávvŏn

Glapthorn *Northants.*, 'glæpθɔrn, gláp-thorn

Glaramara *Cumbria*, 'glærə'mɑrə, glárrämaʹärä

Glarryford *Co. Antrim*, 'glærɪfərd, glárriförd

Glas Island *H'land*, glɑs, glaass

Glasbury *Powys*, 'gleɪzbərɪ, gláyzbūri

Glasby, *f.n.*, 'glæzbɪ, glázbi

Glascodine, *f.n.*, 'glæskoʊdaɪn, glásskōdĭn

Glascoed, *also spelt* **Glasgoed**, *Clwyd*, *Gwent*, 'glæskɔɪd, glásskoyd. *Appropriate for both places of this name in Clwyd.*

Glascwm, *also spelt* **Glasgwm**, *Powys*, 'glæskʊm, glásskōōm. *Appropriate for both places of this name in Powys.*

Glasfryn *Clwyd*, 'glæsvrɪn, glássvrin

Glasgoed *see* **Glascoed**

Glasgow *S'clyde*, 'glɑsgoʊ, glaʹassgō; 'glɑskoʊ, glaʹasskō; 'glɑzgoʊ, glaʹazgō. *For* ~ **Celtic** (*football club*) *see* **Celt.**

Glasgwm *see* **Glascwm**

Glaslyn, River, *Gwynedd*, 'glæslɪn, glásslin

Glassalt Shiel Lodge *Grampian*, 'glæsəlt 'ʃil, glássält sheʹel

Glasscock, *f.n.*, 'glɑskɒk, glaʹasskock; 'glɑskoʊ, glaʹasskō

Glasser, *f.n.*, 'glæsər, glássĕr

Glass Houghton *W. Yorks.*, 'glɑs 'haʊtən, glaʹass hówtŏn

Glaston *Leics.*, 'gleɪstən, gláysstŏn

Glastonbury *Somerset*, 'glastənbərɪ, glaʹastönbŭri; 'glæstənbərɪ, glásstönbūri

Glaswegian, *native of* **Glasgow**, glɑs'widʒən, glaass-weʹejän; glɑz'widʒən, glaaz-weʹejän

Glatton, *Cambs.*, 'glætən, gláttŏn

Glatz, *f.n.*, glæts, glatts

Glavin, *f.n.*, 'glævɪn, glávvin

Glazebury *Ches.*, 'gleɪzbərɪ, gláyzbŭri

Glazer, *f.n.*, 'gleɪzər, gláyzĕr

Glazier, *f.n.*, 'gleɪzɪər, gláyzi-ĕr

Gleadless *S. Yorks.*, 'glidlɪs, gleʹedlĕss

Gleadow, *f.n.*, 'gledoʊ, gléddō

Gleadowe, *f.n.*, 'gledoʊ, gléddō

Gleadthorpe Grange *Notts.*, 'glidθɔrp 'greɪndʒ, gleʹed-thorp gráynj

Gleichen, *f.n.*, 'glaɪxən, glíchĕn

Glenalmond *Tayside*, glen'amənd, glenaʹamŏnd

Glenamara of Glenridding, Baron, ˌglenə'mɑrə əv glen'rɪdɪŋ, glennämaʹärä öv glenrídding

Glenanne *Co. Armagh*, glen'æn, glenán

Glenapp, Viscount, glen'æp, glenáp

Glenariff *Co. Antrim*, glen'ærɪf, glenárrif

Glenarm *Co. Antrim*, glen'ɑrm, glenaʹarm

Glenartney *Tayside*, glen'ɑrtnɪ, glenaʹartni

Glen Avon *Grampian*, glen 'ɑn, glen aʹan

Glenavy *Co. Antrim*, glen'eɪvɪ, glenáyvi. *Appropriate also for Baron* ~.

Glenbervie *Grampian*, glen'bɜrvɪ, glenbérvi

Glenboig *S'clyde*, glen'boʊɪg, glenbō-ig

Glenbruar *Tayside*, glen'bruər, glenbroʹo-är

Glenbuchat *Grampian*, glen-'bʌkət, glenbúckät

Glencaple *D. & G.*, glen'keɪpl, glen-káypl

Glencarse *Tayside*, glen'kɑrs, glen-kaʹarss

Glen Chas *I. of Man*, glen 'tʃæs, glen cháss

Glencoe *H'land*, glen'koʊ, glen-kō

Glenconner, *f.n.*, glen'kɒnər, glen-kónnĕr. *Appropriate also for Baron* ~.

Glencross, *f.n.*, glen'krɒs, glen-króss

Glendaruel *S'clyde*, ˌglendə'ruəl, glendäroʹo-ĕl

Glenday, *f.n.*, 'glendeɪ, glénday

Glendenning, *f.n.*, glen'denɪŋ, glendénning

Glendevon *Central–Tayside border*, glen'devən, glendévvŏn. *Appropriate also for Baron* ~.

Glendinning, *f.n.*, glen'dɪnɪŋ, glendínning

Glendochart *D. & G.*, glen'dɒxərt, glendóchärt

Glen Dochart *Central*, glen 'dɒxərt, glen dóchärt

Glendower, Owen, *14th–15th-c. Welsh chieftain*, 'oʊɪn glen-'daʊər, ó-ĕn glendówr. *The Welsh form is* **Owain Glyndwr**, *q.v.*

Glendronach Distillery *Grampian*, glen'drɒnəx, glendrónnäch

Glendyne, Baron, glen'daɪn, glen-dín

Gleneagles *Tayside*, glen'iglz, gleneéglz

Glenegedale Airport *S'clyde*, glen'egɪdeɪl, glenéggĕdayl

Glenelg *H'land*, glen'elg, glenélg

Glen Errochty *Tayside*, glen 'erəxtı, glen érrŏchti

Glen Etive *S'clyde*, glen 'etıv, glen éttiv

Glenfarclas Distillery *Grampian*, glen'fɑrkləs, glenfáarklăss

Glenfarg *Tayside*, glen'fɑrg, glenfáarg

Glen Fernait *Tayside*, glen 'fɜrnıt, glen férnit

Glenfernate *Tayside*, glen'fɜrnıt, glenférnit

Glenfeshie *H'land*, glen'feʃı, glenféshi

Glenfiddich Distillery *Grampian*, glen'fıdıx, glenfíddi̱ch

Glen Finglass *Central*, glen 'fıŋləs, glen fíng-läss; glen 'fıŋgləs, glen fíng-gläss

Glenfinnan *H'land*, glen'fınən, glenfínnăn

Glengarnock *S'clyde*, glen'gɑrnək, glen-gáarnŏk

Glen Girnaig *Tayside*, glen 'gɜrnıg, glen gírnig

Glengormley *Co. Antrim*, glen-'gɔrmlı, glen-górmli

Glenguin *see* **Tedder of ~**, Baron.

Glenholm *Borders*, glen'houm, glen-hŏm

Glenisla *Tayside*, glen'aılə, glenĭlă

Glenkinchie Distillery *Lothian*, glen'kınʃı, glen-kínshi

Glenkinglas of Cairndow, Baron, glen'kınləs əv kɜrn'du, glen--kínläss ŏv kairndoʻo

Glenlee *D. & G.*, glen'li, glen-leé

Glen Lee *Tayside*, glen 'li, glen leé

Glenlivet *Grampian*, glen'lıvıt, glen-lívvĕt

Glenlochar *D. & G.*, glen'lɒxər, glen-lóchăr

Glenmanus *Co. Derry*, glen-'mænəs, glen-mánnŭss

Glenmorangie Distillery *H'land*, ˌglenmə'rændʒı, glen-mŏránji

Glenochil *Central*, glen'ouxl, glenŏchl

Glen Ogle *Central*, glen 'ougl, glen ŏgl

Glenorchy *S'clyde*, glen'ɔrxı, glenórchi. *Appropriate also for Lord ~.*

Glenrinnes *Grampian*, glen'rınıs, glenrínnĕss

Glenrothes *Fife*, glen'rɒθıs, glenróthĕss

Glenrothes Distillery *Grampian*, glen'rɒθıs, glenróthĕss

Glenshane Pass *Co. Derry*, glen-'ʃeın, glen-sháyn

Glenshee *Tayside*, glen'ʃi, glen--sheé

Glenshesk, River, *Co. Antrim*, glen'ʃesk, glen-shésk

Glen Shira *S'clyde*, glen 'ʃıərə, glen sheéră

Glentanar, Barony of, glen'tænər, glen-tánnăr

Glentham *Lincs.*, 'glenθəm, glén-thăm

Glentoran, Baron, glen'tɔrən, glen-táwrăn

Glen Truim *H'land*, glen 'truım, glen troʻo-im

Glenwherry *Co. Antrim*, glen-'ʍwerı, glen-whérri

Glerawly, Viscount, glə'rɔlı, glĕráwli

Glevum, *Roman name for* **Gloucester**, 'glivəm, gleévŭm

Gliksten, *f.n.*, 'glıkstən, glíck-stĕn

Glimps Holm *Orkney*, 'glımps houm, glímps hŏm

Gloag, *f.n.*, gloug, glŏg

Gloddaeth *Gwynedd*, 'glɒðaıθ, glóthi̱th

Glogue *Dyfed*, glouɡ, glŏg

Glomach, Falls of, *H'land*, 'glouməx, glŏmá̱ch

Glooston *Leics.*, 'glustən, gloʻosstŏn

Glossop, *f.n.*, 'glɒsəp, glóssŏp

Gloucester *Glos.*, 'glɒstər, glós-stĕr. *Appropriate also for HRH the Duke of ~.*

Glover, *f.n.*, 'glʌvər, glúvvĕr

Glubb, *f.n.*, glʌb, glub

Gluckman, *f.n.*, 'glʌkmən, glúckmăn

Gluckstein, *f.n.*, 'glʌkstın, glúcks-teen

Glusburn *N. Yorks.*, 'glʌzbərn, glúzzbŭrn

Glyders, The, *Gwynedd*, 'glıdərz, glíddĕrz. *Twin peaks, known individually as* ~ **Fach**, 'glıdər 'vɑx, glíddĕr vá̱ach, *and* ~ **Fawr**, 'glıdər 'vauər, glíddĕr vówr.

Glyme, River, *Oxon.*, glaım, glīm

Glympton *Oxon.*, 'glımptən, glímptŏn

Glyn, *f.n.*, glın, glin

Glyncorrwg *W. Glam.*, glın'kɒrug, glin-kórrŏog

Glynde *E. Sussex*, glaınd, glīnd

Glyndebourne *E. Sussex*, 'glaınd-bɔrn, glíndborn. *Home of the* ~ *Opera.*

Glyndwr, Owain, *14th–15th-c. Welsh chieftain*, 'ouaın glın-'duər, ŏ-īn glindŏor; 'ouın glın'duər, ŏ-ĕn glindŏor. *The*

English form is **Owen Glendower**, *q.v.*

Glyndyfrdwy *Clwyd*, glɪn-'dʌvərdʊɪ, glindúvvĕrdoͦo-i

Glynn, *f.n.*, glɪn, glin

Glynn *Cornwall, Dyfed, Gwynedd, Co. Antrim*, glɪn, glin. *Appropriate for both places of the name in Dyfed.*

Glynne, *f.n.*, glɪn, glin

Glynogwr *Mid Glam.*, gli'nɒgʊər, glinóggoͦor

Glyntawe *Powys*, glɪn'taʊɪ, glintów-i

Glyn Traian *Clwyd*, glɪn 'traɪən, glin trí-ăn

Glyn-y-Groes *Clwyd*, ˌglɪnə'grɔɪs, glin-ă-gróyss

Gnoll, The, *Neath* (*W. Glam.*), ðə 'nɒl, thĕ nóll

Gnosall *Staffs.*, 'noʊsl, nóssl

Goacher, *f.n.*, 'goʊʃər, góshĕr

Goalen, *f.n.*, 'goʊlən, gólĕn

Goatcher, *f.n.*, 'goʊtʃər, gótchĕr

Goater, *f.n.*, 'goʊtər, gótĕr

Goathland *N. Yorks.*, 'goʊθlənd, góthländ

Goathurst *Somerset*, 'goʊθɜrst, gó-thurst

Gobernuisgach Lodge *H'land*, ˌgoʊbər'nɪsgəx, goͦbĕrníss-gäch

Gobey, *f.n.*, 'goʊbɪ, góbi

Gobion *Gwent*, 'goʊbjɒn, gób-yon

Goble, *f.n.*, 'goʊbl, góbl

Gobowen *Salop*, gɒ'boʊɪn, gobbó-ĕn

Godalming *Surrey*, 'gɒdlmɪŋ, góddl-ming

Godber, *f.n.*, 'gɒdbər, gódbĕr

Godbold, *f.n.*, 'gɒdboʊld, gódboͤld

Goddard, *f.n.*, 'gɒdərd, góddărd; 'gɒdɑrd, góddaard. *The first is appropriate for the Barony of* ∼.

Godde, *f.n.*, goʊd, gōd

Godden, *f.n.*, 'gɒdən, góddĕn

Godding, *f.n.*, 'gɒdɪŋ, gódding

Godefroy, *f.n.*, 'gɒdɪfrɔɪ, góddĕfroy

Goderich, Viscountcy of, 'gʊdrɪtʃ, goͦodritch

Godin, *f.n.*, 'goʊdɪn, gódin

Godiva, Lady, *Saxon heroine*, gə'daɪvə, gódívă

Godmanchester *Cambs.*, 'gɒdmən'tʃestər, gódmăn--chéstĕr

Godmanstone *Dorset*, 'gɒdmənstən, gódmănstŏn

Godmersham *Kent*, 'gɒdmərʃəm, gódmĕr-shäm

Godolphin *Cornwall*, gə'dɒlfɪn, gŏdólfin. *Appropriate also for the Barony of* ∼.

Godreaman *Mid Glam.*, ˌgɒdrɪ-'æmən, goddri-ámmăn

Godre'r-graig *W. Glam.*, ˌgɒdrər'graɪg, godrĕrgríg

Godrevy *Cornwall*, gə'drɪvɪ, gŏdreévi

Godshill *Hants*, 'gɒdzhɪl, gódz-hil

Goehr, *f.n.*, gɜr, gur. *Appropriate for Alexander* ∼, *composer, and Walter* ∼, *conductor.*

Gogar Bank *Lothian*, 'goʊgər 'bæŋk, gōgăr bánk

Gogay, *f.n.*, gə'geɪ, gŏgáy

Gogerddan *Dyfed*, goʊ'gɛərðən, gōgáirthăn

Gohorry, *f.n.*, gə'hɒrɪ, gŏ-hórri

Golant *Cornwall*, gə'lænt, gŏlánt; goʊ'lænt, gōlánt

Golborne *Gtr. M'chester*, 'goʊlbɔrn, gólborn

Golcar *W. Yorks.*, 'goʊkər, gókăr

Goldesgeyme, *f.n.*, 'goʊldəzgeɪm, góldĕzgaym

Golding, *f.n.*, 'goʊldɪŋ, gólding

Goldington *Beds.*, 'goʊldɪŋtən, góldingtŏn

Goldrei, *f.n.*, 'goʊldrɪ, góldri

Goldschmidt, *f.n.*, 'goʊldʃmɪt, góld-shmitt

Goldsithney *Cornwall*, 'goʊld-'sɪðnɪ, góld-sithni

Goldsmid, *f.n.*, 'goʊldsmɪd, góld--smid

Goldsmith, *f.n.*, 'goʊldsmɪθ, góld-smith

Goldstein, *f.n.*, 'gɒldstaɪn, góllд--stīn

Goldstone, *f.n.*, 'goʊldstoʊn, góld-stōn

Goldsworthy, *f.n.*, 'goʊldzwɜrðɪ, góldz-wurthi

Golfa *Powys*, 'gɒlvə, gólvă

Golightly, *f.n.*, gə'laɪtlɪ, gŏlítli

Gollancz, Sir Victor, *author and publisher*, gə'lænts, gŏlánts

Golombek, *f.n.*, gə'lɒmbek, gŏlómbeck

Golspie *H'land*, 'gɒlspɪ, gólsspi

Gomeldon *Wilts.*, 'gɒməldən, gómmĕldŏn

Gomersal, *W. Yorks.*, 'gɒmərsl, gómmĕrssl

Gomersall, *f.n.*, 'gɒmərsl, góm-mĕrssl

Gomez, *f.n.*, 'goʊmez, gómezz

Gomme, *f.n.*, gɒm, gomm

Gomperts, *f.n.*, 'gɒmpərts, gómpĕrts

Gompertz, *f.n.*, 'gɒmpərts, gómpĕrts

Gomshall *Surrey*, 'gɒmʃl, góm--shl; 'gʌmʃl, gúm-shl

Gonalston *Notts.*, 'gɒnlstən, gónnlstŏn

Gonella, *f.n.*, gə'nelə, gŏnéllă
Gonley, *f.n.*, 'gɒnlɪ, gónli
Gonne, *f.n.*, gɒn, gonn
Gonvena *Cornwall*, 'gɒnvɪnə, gónveenă
Gonville and Caius College, *Univ. of Cambridge*, 'gɒnvɪl ənd 'kiz, gónvil ănd kéez
Gooch, *f.n.*, gutʃ, gootch
Goodale, *f.n.*, 'gʊdeɪl, gŏodayl
Goodameavy *Devon*, ˌgʊdə'mivɪ, gōōdămeévi
Goodden, *f.n.*, 'gʊdən, gŏodĕn
Goode, *f.n.*, gʊd, gōōd
Goodenough, *f.n.*, 'gʊdɪnʌf, gŏodĕnuff
Gooderham, *f.n.*, 'gʊdərəm, gŏodĕrăm
Goodeve, *f.n.*, 'gʊdiv, gŏodeev
Goodfellow, *f.n.*, 'gʊdfeloʊ, gŏodfellō
Goodhand-Tait, *f.n.*, 'gʊdhænd 'teɪt, gŏod-hand táyt
Goodhart, *f.n.*, 'gʊdhɑrt, gŏod--haart
Goodhew, *f.n.*, 'gʊdhju, gŏod-hew
Gooding, *f.n.*, 'gʊdɪŋ, gŏoding
Goodlad, *f.n.*, 'gʊdlæd, gŏod-lad
Goodnestone *Kent*, 'gʊdnestən, gŏodnesstŏn; 'gʌnstən, gúnsstŏn
Goodrham, *f.n.*, 'gʊdrəm, gŏodrăm
Goodrick, *f.n.*, 'gʊdrɪk, gŏodrick
Goodwick *Dyfed*, 'gʊdɪk, gŏodick
Goodyear, *f.n.*, 'gʊdjər, gŏod-yĕr
Googe, *f.n.*, gudʒ, gooj
Goolden, *f.n.*, 'guldən, gooldĕn
Goonbell *Cornwall*, gun'bel, goonbéll
Goonhavern *Cornwall*, gun-'hævərn, goon-hávvĕrn; gə'nævərn, gŏnávvĕrn
Goonhilly Downs *Cornwall*, gun-'hɪlɪ, gōōn-hílli
Goonvrea *Cornwall*, gun'vreɪ, goonvráy
Goorney, *f.n.*, 'gʊərnɪ, gŏorni
Goosey *Berks.*, 'guzɪ, gŏozi
Goosnargh *Lancs.*, 'gusnər, gŏossnăr
Goossens, *f.n.*, 'gusənz, gŏossĕnz. *Appropriate for Sir Eugene* ~, ju'ʒeɪn, yoozháyn, *composer and conductor; Léon* ~, 'leɪɒn, láy--on, *oboist; and Sidonie* ~, sɪ'doʊnɪ, sidóni, *harpist*.
Goraghwood *Co. Armagh*, 'gɔrə-wʊd, gáwră-wōōd
Goran Haven *see* Gorran Haven
Gordeno, *f.n.*, gɔr'dinoʊ, gor-deénō
Gordon, *C.n. and f.n.*, 'gɔrdən, górdŏn

Gordonstoun School *Grampian*, 'gɔrdənztən, górdŏnztŏn
Gore, *f.n.*, gɔr, gor
Gorell, *f.n.*, 'gɒrəl, górrĕl. *Appropriate also for Baron* ~.
Goren, *f.n.*, 'gɔrən, gáwrĕn
Gorgie *Edinburgh*, 'gɔrgɪ, górgi
Gorham, *f.n.*, 'gɔrəm, gáwrăm
Gorhambury *Herts.*, 'gɒrəmbərɪ, górrămbŭri
Goring, *f.n.*, 'gɔrɪŋ, gáwring
Goring *Oxon.*, 'gɔrɪŋ, gáwring
Gorleston *Norfolk*, 'gɔrlstən, górlsstŏn
Gorman, *f.n.*, 'gɔrmən, górmăn
Gormanston, Viscount, 'gɔrmən-stən, górmănstŏn
Gornall, *f.n.*, 'gɔrnl, górnl
Goronwy, *Welsh C.n.*, gɒ'rɒnwɪ, gorrónwi
Gorran Haven *Cornwall*, 'gɒrən 'heɪvən, górrăn háyvĕn
Gorsedd *Clwyd*, 'gɔrseð, górsseth
Gorseinon *W. Glam.*, gɔr'saɪnən, gorssínŏn
Gors-las *Dyfed*, gɔrs'lɑs, gorss-laáss
Gortin *Co. Tyrone*, 'gɔrtjɪn, górt-yin
Gosberton Clough *Lincs.*, 'gɒz-bərtən 'klaʊ, gózbĕrtŏn klów; 'gɒzbərtən 'klʌf, gózbĕrtŏn klúff
Goschen, Viscount, 'goʊʃən, gó-shĕn
Goscote *W. Midlands*, 'gɒskoʊt, gósskōt
Goscote, East, *Leics.*, 'gɒskoʊt, gósskōt
Gosforth *Northd.*, 'gɒsfərθ, góss-fŏrth
Gosnell, *f.n.*, 'gɒznəl, gózznĕl
Gosney, *f.n.*, 'gɒznɪ, gózzni
Gosport *Hants*, 'gɒspɔrt, góssport
Goss, *f.n.*, gɒs, goss
Gossage, *f.n.*, 'gɒsɪdʒ, góssij
Gostelow, *f.n.*, 'gɒstɪloʊ, góss-tēlō
Goswick *Northd.*, 'gɒzɪk, gózzick
Gotell, *f.n.*, gə'tel, gŏtéll
Gotham *Notts.*, 'goʊtəm, gótăm
Gothard, *f.n.*, 'gɒθɑrd, góth-aard
Gotla, *f.n.*, 'gɒtlə, góttlă
Gotobed, *f.n.*, 'gɒtəbed, góttŏbed; 'goʊtəbed, gótŏbed
Gottwaltz, *f.n.*, 'gɒtwɒlts, gót-wawlts
Goudge, *f.n.*, gudʒ, gooj. *Appropriate for Elizabeth* ~, *author*.
Goudhurst *Kent*, 'gaʊdhɜrst, gówd-hurst
Goudie, *f.n.*, 'gaʊdɪ, gówdi
Goudy, *f.n.*, 'gaʊdɪ, gówdi

Gouge, *f.n.*, gaʊdʒ, gowj

Gough, *f.n.*, gɒf, goff. *Appropriate also for Viscount* ~.

Goulburn, *f.n.*, 'gʊlbɜːn, goólburn

Goulceby *Lincs.*, 'goʊlsbɪ, gólss-bi

Gould, *f.n.*, gʊld, goold; goʊld, gōld

Gouldbourn, *f.n.*, 'goʊldbɔːn, góldborn

Goulden, *f.n.*, 'gʊldən, goóldĕn; 'goʊldən, góldĕn

Goulding, *f.n.*, 'gʊldɪŋ, goólding

Gouldsmith, *f.n.*, 'goʊldsmɪθ, góldsmith

Goulik, *f.n.*, 'gʊlɪk, goólick

Goullart, *f.n.*, 'gʊlɑːt, goólaart

Goullet, *f.n.*, gu'let, goolétt

Gourgey, *f.n.*, 'gʊədʒɪ, goórji

Gourlay, *f.n.*, 'gʊəlɪ, goórli

Gourley, *f.n.*, 'gʊəlɪ, goórli

Gourlie, *f.n.*, 'gʊəlɪ, goórli

Gourock *S'clyde*, 'gʊərək, goórŏk

Goutthrappel *S'clyde*, gaʊt'θræpl, gowt-tháppl

Govan, *f.n.*, 'gʌvən, gúvvăn

Govan *S'clyde*, 'gʌvən, gúvvăn

Gove, *f.n.*, gɒʊv, gōv

Gover, *f.n.*, 'gɒʊvər, góvĕr

Goveton *Devon*, 'gʌvɪtən, gúvvĕ-tŏn

Govett, *f.n.*, 'gʌvɪt, gúvvĕt

Gow, *f.n.*, gaʊ, gow

Gowdridge, *f.n.*, 'gaʊdrɪdʒ, gówdrij

Gower, *f.n.*, 'gaʊər, gówĕr; gɔː, gor. *See also* Leveson-Gower.

Gowerton *W. Glam.*, 'gaʊətən, gówĕrtŏn

Gowing, *f.n.*, 'gaʊɪŋ, gówing

Gowling, *f.n.*, 'gaʊlɪŋ, gówling

Gowrie *Tayside*, 'gaʊrɪ, gówri. *Appropriate also for the Earl of* ~.

Goyt, River, *Derby.–Gtr. M'chester*, gɔɪt, goyt

Grabham, *f.n.*, 'græbəm, grábbăm

Gracie, *f.n.*, 'greɪsɪ, gráyssi

Grade, Baron, greɪd, grayd

Gradon, *f.n.*, 'greɪdən, gráydŏn

Gradwell, *f.n.*, 'grædwel, grádwel

Graebner, *f.n.*, 'greɪbnər, gráyb-nĕr

Graef, *f.n.*, greɪf, grayf

Graeme, *f.n.*, 'greɪəm, gráy-ĕm; greɪm, graym

Graffham *W. Sussex*, 'græfəm, gráffăm

Grafftey, *f.n.*, 'grɑftɪ, graáfti

Grafham *Cambs.*, 'grɑfəm, graáfăm

Grafham *Surrey*, 'græfəm, gráffăm

Graham, *C.n. and f.n.*, 'greɪəm, gráy-ăm

Graham of Claverhouse, John, *Scottish soldier*, 'greɪəm əv 'kleɪvərhaʊs, gráy-ăm ŏv kláyvĕr-howss

Grahamston *Central*, 'greɪəmstən, gráy-ămsstŏn

Graig *Clwyd, Gwynedd*, graɪg, grīg

Graig Goch *Powys*, graɪg 'gɒʊx, grīg góch

Graig Wen *Gwent, Mid Glam.*, graɪg 'wen, grīg wén

Graigwen Gold Mine *Gwynedd*, graɪg'wen, grīg-wén

Grainger, *f.n.*, 'greɪndʒər, gráynjĕr

Gralak, *f.n.*, 'grælæk, grálack

Grampians, The, *Scottish mountain system*, 'græmpɪənz, grámpiănz

Grampound *Cornwall*, 'græm-paʊnd, grámpownd

Grandison, *f.n.*, 'grændɪsən, grándissŏn

Grandtully *Tayside*, 'grantlɪ, graántli; 'græntlɪ, grántli

Grangemouth *Central*, 'greɪndʒ-maʊθ, gráynj-mowth

Gransha *Co. Down*, 'grænʃə, grán-shă

Grant, *f.n.*, grɑnt, graant; grænt, grant

Granta, River, *Cambs.*, 'græntə, grántă; 'grɑntə, graántă. *Alternative name for some stretches of the* Cam.

Grantchester *Cambs.*, 'grɑnt-ʃɪstər, graántchĕstĕr; 'grænt-ʃɪstər, grántchĕstĕr. *The first is appropriate for Baron* ~.

Grantham, *f.n.*, 'grænθəm, grán-thăm

Grantham *Lincs.*, 'grænθəm, grán-thăm

Granthier, *f.n.*, 'grænθɪər, gránthi-ĕr

Granton *Lothian*, 'græntən, grántŏn

Grantown-on-Spey *H'land*, 'græntaʊn ɒn 'speɪ, grántown on spáy; 'græntən ɒn 'speɪ, grántŏn on spáy

Grantshouse *Borders*, 'grants-haʊs, graánts-howss

Granville, *f.n.*, 'grænvɪl, gránvil. *Appropriate also for Earl* ~.

Granville of Eye, Baron, 'grænvɪl əv 'aɪ, gránvil ŏv í

Grasmere *Cumbria*, 'grasmɪər, graássmeer

Grassington *N. Yorks.*, 'grasɪŋtən, graássingtŏn

Grasso, *f.n.*, 'grasɒʊ, graássō

Grateley *Hants*, 'greɪtlɪ, gráytli

Gratiaen, *f.n.*, 'greɪʃən, gráy-shĕn

Gration, *f.n.*, 'greɪʃən, gráy-shŏn

Grattan, *f.n.*, 'grætən, gráttăn

Gratton *Staffs.*, 'grætən, gráttŏn

Graveley, *f.n.*, 'greɪvlɪ, gráyv-li

Graveley *Cambs.*, *Herts.*, 'greɪvlɪ, gráyv-li

Gravelly Hill *W. Midlands*, 'grævlɪ 'hɪl, grávvl-i híll

Gravesham *Kent*, 'greɪvʃəm, gráyvshăm

Graveson, *f.n.*, 'greɪvsən, gráyv-ssŏn

Gravett, *f.n.*, 'grævɪt, grávvĕt

Gravina, *f.n.*, grəˈvinə, grăvéenă

Gray, *f.n.*, greɪ, gray

Greager, *f.n.*, 'gregər, gréggĕr

Greasbrough, *S. Yorks.*, 'grizbrə, gréezbrŏ

Greasby *Merseyside*, 'grizbɪ, gréezbi

Greasley *Notts.*, 'grizlɪ, gréezli

Great Alne *Warwicks.*, 'greɪt 'ɔn, gráyt áwn; 'greɪt 'ɔln, gráyt áwln

Great Bolas, *also called* Bolas Magna, *Salop*, 'greɪt 'boʊləs, gráyt bŏláss

Great Bourton *Oxon.*, 'greɪt 'bɔrtən, gráyt bórtŏn

Great Bowden *Leics.*, 'greɪt 'baʊdən, gráyt bówdĕn

Great Bradley *Somerset*, *Suffolk*, 'greɪt 'brædlɪ, gráyt brádli

Great Bromley *Essex*, 'greɪt 'brɒmlɪ, gráyt brómli

Great Creaton *Northants.*, 'greɪt 'kritən, gráyt kréetŏn

Great Cumbrae *S'clyde*, 'greɪt 'kʌmbreɪ, gráyt kúmbray

Great Gaddesden *Herts.*, 'greɪt 'gædzdən, gráyt gádzdĕn

Greatham *Cleveland*, 'gritəm, gréetăm

Great Harrowden *Northants.*, 'greɪt 'hæroʊdən, gráyt hárrōdĕn

Great Hautbois *Norfolk*, 'greɪt 'hɒbɪs, gráyt hóbbiss

Greathead, *f.n.*, 'greɪthed, gráyt-hed

Great Houghton *Northants.*, 'greɪt 'hoʊtən, gráyt hŏtŏn

Great Houghton *S. Yorks.*, 'greɪt 'haʊtən, gráyt hówtŏn

Greatorex, *f.n.*, 'greɪtəreks, gráytŏrecks

Great Ponton *Lincs.*, 'greɪt 'pɒntən, gráyt póntŏn

Great Saughall *Ches.*, 'greɪt 'sɔkl, gráyt sáwkl

Great Shelford *Cambs.*, 'greɪt 'ʃelfərd, gráyt shélfŏrd

Great Staughton *Cambs.*, 'greɪt 'stɔtən, gráyt stáwtŏn

Great Stukeley *Cambs.*, 'greɪt 'stjuklɪ, gráyt stéwkli

Great Thorness *I. of Wight*, 'greɪt θɔr'nes, gráyt thornéss

Great Totham *Essex*, 'greɪt 'tɒtəm, gráyt tóttăm

Great Wakering *Essex*, 'greɪt 'weɪkərɪŋ, gráyt wáykĕring

Great Walsingham *Norfolk*, 'greɪt 'wɒlzɪŋəm, gráyt wáwlzing-ăm

Great Waltham *Essex*, 'greɪt 'wɒltəm, gráyt wáwltăm

Great Warley *Essex*, 'greɪt 'wɔrlɪ, gráyt wáwrli

Great Wilbraham *Cambs.*, 'greɪt 'wɪlbrəm, gráyt wilbrăm; 'greɪt 'wɪlbrəhæm, gráyt wílbrăham

Great Wymondley *Herts.*, 'greɪt 'waɪməndlɪ, gráyt wímŏndli

Great Wyrley *Staffs.*, 'greɪt 'wɜrlɪ, gráyt wúrli

Great Yarmouth *Norfolk*, 'greɪt 'jɑrməθ, gráyt yáarmŭth

Greaves, *f.n.*, greɪvz, grayvz; grivz, greevz. *The first is appropriate for the Countess of* Dysart's *family name.*

Grech, *f.n.*, gretʃ, gretch

Greenall, *f.n.*, 'grinɔl, gréenawl

Greenaway, *f.n.*, 'grinəweɪ, gréenă-way

Greenbaum, Kyla, *pianist*, 'kaɪlə 'grinbaʊm, kílă gréenbowm

Greene, *f.n.*, grin, green

Greengrass, *f.n.*, 'gringrɑs, gréen-graass

Greengross, *f.n.*, 'gringrɒs, gréen-gross

Greenhalgh, *f.n.*, 'grinhælʃ, gréen-halsh; 'grinhɒlʃ, gréen-holsh; 'grinhældʒ, gréen-halj; 'grinhɔl, gréen-hawl

Greenhalgh *Lancs.*, 'grinhælʃ, gréen-halsh; 'grinhɔlʃ, gréen-hawlsh

Greenhaugh, *f.n.*, 'grinɒf, gréen-off

Greenhough, *f.n.*, 'grinɒf, gréen-off; 'grinhɒf, gréen-hoff; 'grinhoʊ, gréen-hō; 'grinhaʊ, gréen-how; 'grinhʌf, gréen-huff; 'grinʌf, gréenuff

Greenhow, *f.n.*, 'grinoʊ, gréenō; 'grinhaʊ, gréen-how

Greenisland *Co. Antrim*, grin-ˈaɪlənd, greeníländ

Greenlaw *Borders*, 'grinlɔ, gréen-law

Greenock *S'clyde*, 'grinək, gréenŏk

Greenough, *f.n.*, 'grinoʊ, gréenō

Greenslade, *f.n.*, 'grinsleɪd, gréen-slayd

Greenwich *London*, 'grɪnɪdʒ, grínnij; 'grɪnɪtʃ, grínnitch; 'grenɪtʃ, grénnitch

Greenwood of Holbourne, Viscount, 'grinwʊd əv 'hɒlbʊərn, gréenwŏod ŏv hólbōorn

Gregg, *f.n.*, greg, greg

Grego, *f.n.*, 'grɪgoʊ, greégō

Gregoire, *f.n.*, 'gregwɑr, grégwaar

Gregor, *C.n.*, 'gregər, gréggŏr

Gregorowski, *f.n.*, ˌgregə'rɒskɪ, greggŏrósski

Gregory, *C.n. and f.n.*, 'gregərɪ, gréggŏri

Gregynog Hall *Powys*, grɪ'gʌnɒg, grĕgúnnog

Greig, *f.n.*, greg, greg

Greim, *f.n.*, grim, greem

Grein, *f.n.*, graɪn, grīn

Grenfell, *f.n.*, 'grenfəl, grénfĕl. *Appropriate also for Baron* ∼.

Grenofen *Devon*, 'grenəfən, grénnŏfĕn

Grenoside *S. Yorks.*, 'grenoʊsaɪd, grénnōssīd

Gresham, *f.n.*, 'greʃəm, gréshăm; 'gresəm, gréssăm

Gresham *Norfolk*, 'greʃəm, gréshăm

Gresley, *f.n.*, 'grezlɪ, grézli

Gressingham *Lancs.*, 'gresɪŋəm, gréssing-ăm

Gretabridge *Durham*, 'gritəbrɪdʒ, greétăbrij

Greta Hall *Cumbria*, 'gritə 'hɔl, greétă hául

Greville, Baron, 'grevɪl, grévvil

Grey de Ruthyn, Barony of, 'greɪ də 'ruθɪn, gráy dĕ roóthin

Greyn, *f.n.*, greɪn, grayn

Greysouthen *Cumbria*, 'greɪsun, gráyssoon

Greystoke *Cumbria*, 'greɪstoʊk, gráysstōk

Greywell *Hants*, 'greɪ'wel, gráy-wéll; 'grʊəl, groo-ĕl

Grianan *W. Isles*, 'grinən, greénăn

Gribbin Head *Cornwall*, 'grɪbɪn 'hed, gríbbin héd

Grice, *f.n.*, graɪs, grīss

Gridley, *f.n.*, 'grɪdlɪ, grídli

Grier, *f.n.*, grɪər, greer

Grierson, *f.n.*, 'grɪərsən, greérssŏn

Grieve, *f.n.*, griv, greev

Griew, *f.n.*, gru, groo

Griffith, *f.n.*, 'grɪfɪθ, gríffith

Griffiths, *f.n.*, 'grɪfɪθs, gríffiths

Grimethorpe *S. Yorks.*, 'graɪmθɔrp, grím-thorp

Grimond, *f.n.*, 'grɪmənd, grímmŏnd

Grimsargh *Lancs.*, 'grɪmzər, grímzăr

Grimscar *W. Yorks.*, 'graɪmzkɑr, grímzkaar

Grimsetter *Orkney*, 'grɪmstər, grímstĕr

Grimshaw, *f.n.*, 'grɪmʃɔ, grím-shaw

Grindale *Humberside*, 'grɪndl, gríndl

Grindrod, *f.n.*, 'grɪndrɒd, gríndrod

Grinke, *f.n.*, 'grɪŋkɪ, grínki

Grinstead, East *and* West, *W. Sussex*, 'grɪnstɪd, grínsstĕd. *Appropriate also for Baron* ∼.

Grisdale, *f.n.*, 'grɪzdeɪl, grízdayl

Grisdale *Cumbria*, 'graɪzdeɪl, grízdayl

Grisewood, *f.n.*, 'graɪzwʊd, grízwŏod

Grist, *f.n.*, grɪst, grisst

Gristhorpe *N. Yorks.*, 'grɪsθɔrp, gríss-thorp

Griswold, *f.n.*, 'grɪzwoʊld, grízwōld

Grives, *f.n.*, grivz, greevz

Grizedale *Cumbria*, 'graɪzdeɪl, grízdayl

Groby *Leics.*, 'grubɪ, groóbi

Grocott, *f.n.*, 'groʊkɒt, grŏkott

Grocyn, William, *15th–16th-c. priest and scholar*, 'groʊsɪn, grŏssin

Groeslon *Gwynedd*, 'grɔɪslɒn, gróysslon

Groeswen *Mid Glam.*, grɔɪs'wen, groyss-wén

Grogan, *f.n.*, 'groʊgən, grŏgăn

Grogarry *S. Uist*, 'grɒgərɪ, grŏg-gări

Gronow, Rees Howell, *19th-c. Welsh author*, 'ris 'haʊəl 'grɒnoʊ, reéss hówĕl grónnō

Groombridge *E. Sussex–Kent*, 'grum'brɪdʒ, groóm-bríj

Groomsport *Co. Down*, 'grumzpɔrt, groómzport

Grose, *f.n.*, groʊs, grōss

Groser, *f.n.*, 'groʊsər, grŏssĕr; 'grɒsər, gróssĕr

Grosmont *Gwent*, 'grɒsmənt, gróssmŏnt

Grosmont *N. Yorks.*, 'groʊmənt, grŏmŏnt; 'groʊsmənt, grŏssmŏnt

Gross, *f.n.*, grɒs, gross; groʊs, grōss

Grosseteste, Robert, *also spelt* **Grossetete, Grossetête**, *13th-c. Bishop of Lincoln*, 'groʊsteɪt, grŏstayt; 'groʊstest, grŏsstest. *The first pronunciation is appropriate for all three spellings.*

Grosvenor, *f.n.*, 'grouvnər, gróv-
-nŏr; 'grouvənər, gróvĕnŏr.
*The first is appropriate for the
family name of the Duke of
Westminster.*
Grote, *f.n.*, grout, grōt
Groton *Suffolk*, 'grətən, gráwtŏn;
'groutən, grótŏn
Grotton *Gtr. M'chester*, 'grɒtən,
gróttŏn
Groucott, *f.n.*, 'groukət, grókŏt
Groucutt, *f.n.*, 'groukət, grókŭt
Grouse, *f.n.*, graus, growss
Grout, *f.n.*, graut, growt
Groves, *f.n.*, grouvz, grōvz
Growbart, *f.n.*, 'graubart, grów-
baart
Gruenberg, *f.n.*, 'grunbзrg, groόn-
berg
Gruffydd, *f.n.*, 'grıfıð, grífﬁth
Grugeon, *f.n.*, 'gruзɒn, groόzhon
Gruinard, Bay, Island, River, *and*
Forest, *H'land,* 'grınjərd, grín-
-yărd
Grundisburgh *Suffolk,* 'grʌndz-
bərə, grúndzbŭră
Grunert, *f.n.*, 'grunərt, groόnĕrt
Grunhut, *f.n.*, 'grunhut, groόn-
-hoōt
Grunwell, *f.n.*, 'grʌnwel, grúnwel
Grupe, *f.n.*, grup, groop
Gryfe Water, *also spelt* **Gryffe,**
S'clyde, 'graıf 'wɔtər, grif
wáwtĕr
Grygar, *f.n.*, 'graıgar, grígaar
Guare, *f.n.*, gwɛər, gwair
Guaspari, *f.n.*, gwəs'parı, gwǎss-
paári
Guay *Tayside,* gaı, gī
Gubba, *f.n.*, 'gʌbə, gúbbă
Gubbay, *f.n.*, 'gʌbı, gúbbi
Guckian, *f.n.*, 'gukıən, goόkiăn
Gudgin, *f.n.*, 'gʌdзın, gújjin
Guedalla, *f.n.*, gwı'dælə, gwĕdálă
Gueritz, *f.n.*, 'gerıts, gérrits
Gueroult, *f.n.*, 'gerou, gérrō
Guerrier, *f.n.*, 'gerıər, gérri-ĕr
Guest, *f.n.*, gest, gest
Guggisberg, *f.n.*, 'gʌgısbзrg,
gúggissberg
Guignard, *f.n.*, 'ginjar, géen-yaar
Guihard, *f.n.*, 'gihard, gée-haard
Guilden Morden *Cambs.*, 'gıldən
'mɔrdən, gíldĕn mórdĕn
Guildford *Surrey,* 'gılfərd, gíl-
fŏrd
Guilding, *f.n.*, 'gıldıŋ, gílding
Guilford, Earl of, 'gılfərd, gílfŏrd
Guilford, *f.n.*, 'gılfərd, gílfŏrd
Guillamore, Viscountcy of, 'gılə-
mər, gíllămor
Guillaume, *f.n.*, 'gioum, gée-ōm
Guillebaud, *f.n.*, 'gilbou, gée·lbō;
'gılıbou, gíllibō. *The first is*

*appropriate for Claude ~,
economist.*
Guillemard, *f.n.*, 'gılmar, gílmaar
Guillermin, *f.n.*, 'gılərmın,
gíllĕrmin
Guillery, *f.n.*, 'gılərı, gíllĕri
Guilmant, *f.n.*, 'gılmɒnt, gílmont
Guilsborough *Northants.*, 'gılz-
bərə, gílzbŭră
Guilsfield *Powys,* 'gılzfıld, gílz-
feeld
Guinan, *f.n.*, gı'næn, ginán
Guinane, *f.n.*, gı'næn, ginán
Guinee, *f.n.*, 'gını, gínni
Guiney, *f.n.*, 'gaını, gíni
Guinnane, *f.n.*, gı'næn, ginán
Guinness, *f.n.*, 'gınıs, ginnĕss
Guion, *f.n.*, 'gaıən, gí-ŏn
Guisachan *H'land,* 'uʃəxən,
oόshǎchăn
Guisborough *Cleveland,* 'gızbərə,
gízbŭră
Guise, *f.n.*, gaız, gīz
Guiseley *W. Yorks.*, 'gaızlı, gízli
Guist *Norfolk,* gaıst, gísst
Guiting Power *Glos.*, 'gaıtıŋ
'pauər, gíting pówĕr
Guiver, *f.n.*, 'gaıvər, gívĕr
Gulbenkian Foundation, gul-
'beŋkıən, goōlbénkiăn
Gulland, *f.n.*, 'galənd, gúllănd
Gullane *Lothian,* 'gılən, gíllăn;
'gʌlən, gúllăn
Gulleford, *f.n.*, 'gʌlıfərd, gúlli-
fŏrd
Gulvain *H'land,* 'gulvın, goόlvin
Gulval *Cornwall,* 'gʌlvəl, gúlvăl
Gumbs, *f.n.*, gʌmz, gummz
Gummer, *f.n.*, 'gʌmər, gúmmĕr
Gummery, *f.n.*, 'gʌmərı, gúmmĕri
Gunderson, *f.n.*, 'gʌndərsən,
gúndĕrssŏn
Gunnell, *f.n.*, 'gʌnl, gúnnl
Gunness *Lincs.*, 'gʌnıs, gúnnĕss
Gunningham, *f.n.*, 'gʌnıŋəm,
gúnning-ăm
Gunnislake *Cornwall,* 'gʌnızleık,
gúnnizlayk
Gunson, *f.n.*, 'gʌnsən, gúnssŏn
Gunter, *f.n.*, 'gʌntər, gúntĕr
Gunwalloe *Cornwall,* gʌn'wɒlou,
gun-wóllō
Gunwalloe Towans *Cornwall,*
gʌn'wɒlou 'tauənz, gun-wóllō
tówănz
Gunyon, *f.n.*, 'gʌnjən, gún-yŏn
Gurnards Head *Cornwall,*
'gзrnərdz 'hed, gúrnărdz héd
Gurnos *Mid Glam., Powys,* 'gзr-
nɒs, gúrnoss
Gurr, *f.n.*, gзr, gur
Gurteen, *f.n.*, 'gзrtin, gúrteen
Gustard, *f.n.*, 'gʌstərd, gústărd
Gutch, *f.n.*, gʌtʃ, gutch

Guthrie, Sir Tyrone, *theatrical producer*, tɪˈroʊn 'gʌθɪ, tirrṓn gúthri

Gutteridge, *f.n.*, 'gʌtərɪdʒ, gúttĕrij

Guy, *C.n.*, gaɪ, gī

Guyan, *f.n.*, 'gaɪən, gí-ăn

Guyatt, *f.n.*, 'gaɪət, gí-ăt

Guyer, *f.n.*, 'gaɪər, gí-ĕr

Guyhirn *Cambs.*, 'gaɪhɜrn, gí-hirn

Guyler, *f.n.*, 'gaɪlər, gílĕr

Guyon, *f.n.*, 'gaɪən, gí-ŏn

Guyot, *f.n.*, 'gaɪət, gí-ŏt

Guyott, *f.n.*, 'gaɪət, gí-ŏt

Gwaelod-y-Garth *Mid Glam.*, 'gwaɪlɒd ə 'gɑrθ, gwílod ă gaárth

Gwaen-cae-Gurwen *see* **Gwaun- -cae-Gurwen**

Gwaenysgor *see* **Gwaunysgor**

Gwalchmai *Gwynedd*, 'gwælxmaɪ, gwálchmī

Gwanwyn, *C.n.*, gwæn'wɪn, gwann-wínn

Gwastaden *Powys*, gwəs'tædən, gwăstáddĕn

Gwatkin, *f.n.*, 'gwɒtkɪn, gwótkin

Gwaun-cae-Gurwen, *also spelt* **Gwaen-cae-Gurwen**, *W. Glam.*, 'gwaɪn kə 'gɜrwən, gwín kă gúrwĕn

Gwaunysgor, *also spelt* **Gwaenysgor**, *Clwyd*, gwaɪn'ʌsgɔr, gwínússgor

Gwbert *Dyfed*, 'gʊbərt, gŏobĕrt

Gweek *Cornwall*, gwik, gweek

Gwenddwr *Powys*, 'gwendʊər, gwéndōor; 'gwenðʊər, gwén- -thōor

Gwendraeth Fach, River, *Dyfed*, 'gwendraɪθ 'vɑx, gwéndrīth vaách

Gwendraeth Fawr, River, *Dyfed*, 'gwendraɪθ 'vaʊər, gwéndrīth vówr

Gwen-ffrwd, Stream, *Dyfed*, gwen'frud, gwen-froód

Gwennap *Cornwall*, 'gwenəp, gwénnăp

Gwernaffield *Clwyd*, 'gwɛərnə- 'fild, gwáirnăfeéld

Gwernymynydd *Clwyd*, ,gwɛərnə- 'mʌnɪð, gwairnĕmúnnith

Gwersyllt *Clwyd*, 'gwɛərsɪɬt, gwáirssihlt

Gwespyr *Clwyd*, 'gwespər, gwésspĕr

Gwilym, *f.n.*, 'gwɪlɪm, gwílim

Gwinear *Cornwall*, 'gwɪnɪər, gwínneer

Gwineas Rock, *also called* **Gwinges** Rock, *Cornwall*, 'gwɪnɪəs, gwínniăss

Gwinfryn, *Welsh C.n.*, 'gwɪnvrɪn, gwínvrin

Gwinges Rock, *also called* **Gwineas** Rock, *Cornwall*, 'gwɪndʒɪz, gwínjĕz

Gwion, *Welsh C.n.*, 'gwɪɒn, gweé-on

Gwithian *Cornwall*, 'gwɪðɪən, gwíthiăn

Gwnnws *Mid Glam.*, 'gʊnʊs, gŏonōoss

Gwrych Castle *Clwyd*, gwrix, gwreech; grix, greech. *In order to pronounce the first of these as one syllable, Welsh speakers treat the 'w' as a rounding of the lips to accompany the 'r'.*

Gwy, River, *Gwynedd*, 'gʊɪ, gŏo-i. *This is the Welsh name of the* **Wye**, *q.v.*

Gwyddelwern *Clwyd*, gwɪð- 'elwɜrn, gwithélwern

Gwydion, *Welsh C.n.*, 'gwɪdɪən, gwíddiŏn

Gwynant, Lake, *Gwynedd*, 'gwɪn- ænt, gwínnant

Gwyndâf, *Welsh Bardic name*, 'gwɪndæv, gwíndav

Gwynedd *Co. name*, 'gwɪnəð, gwinnĕth. *Appropriate also for Viscount* ~.

Gwynedd, Hywel ab Owain, *12th-c. Welsh prince*, 'haʊəl æb 'oʊɪn 'gwɪnəð, hówĕl ab ṓ-ĕn gwínnĕth

Gwynfe *Dyfed*, 'gwɪnvə, gwínvă

Gwynfil *Dyfed*, 'gwɪnvɪl, gwínvil

Gwynfor, *Welsh C.n.*, 'gwɪnvɔr, gwínvor

Gwynfynnydd *Powys*, gwɪn'vʌnɪð, gwin-vúnnith

Gwynn, *f.n.*, gwɪn, gwin

Gwyther, *f.n.*, 'gwaɪðər, gwíthĕr; 'gwɪðər, gwíthĕr

Gwytherin *Clwyd*, gwɪθ'erɪn, gwithérrin

Gyde, *f.n.*, gaɪd, gīd

Gye, *f.n.*, dʒaɪ, jī

Gyffylliog *Clwyd*, gə'fʌɬjɒg, gŭfúhl-yog

Gyle, *f.n.*, gaɪl, gīl

Gymer, *f.n.*, 'gaɪmər, gímĕr

Gyngell, *f.n.*, 'gɪndʒl, gínjl

Gyppeswyke Plate, *sheep-farming trophy*, 'gɪpswɪk, gíps-wick

H

Haacke, *f.n.*, 'hækɪ, hácki

Habermehl, *f.n.*, 'hɑbərmeɪl, haábĕrmayl

Habershon, *f.n.*, 'hæbərʃən, hábbĕr-shŏn

Haceby *Lincs.*, 'heɪsbɪ, háyssbi
Hackett, *f.n.*, 'hækɪt, háckĕt
Hackshaw, *f.n.*, 'hækʃɔ, háck--shaw
Hadath, Gunby, *author*, 'gʌnbɪ 'hædəθ, gúnbi háddäth
Hadaway, *f.n.*, 'hædəweɪ, háddǎway
Haddenham *Cambs.*, 'hædn̩əm, háddn-ăm
Haddiscoe *Norfolk*, 'hædɪskoʊ, háddisskō
Haddo, Methlic, Tarves and Kellie, Lord, 'hædoʊ 'meθlɪk 'tɑrvɪs ənd 'kelɪ, háddo méthlick taárvĕss ănd kélli
Haddon, *f.n.*, 'hædən, háddŏn
Haddow, *f.n.*, 'hædoʊ, háddō
Haddrill, *f.n.*, 'hædrɪl, hádril
Haden, *f.n.*, 'heɪdən, háydĕn
Haden-Guest, Baron, 'heɪdən 'gest, háydĕn gést
Hadnall *Salop*, 'hædnəl, hád-năl
Hadow, *f.n.*, 'hædoʊ, háddō
Hadrian's Wall *Cumbria–Northd.–Tyne & Wear*, 'heɪdrɪənz 'wɔl, háydriänz wáwl
Hadzor *H. & W.*, 'hædzər, hádzŏr
Haeems, *f.n.*, 'haɪəmz, hí-ămz
Hafner, *f.n.*, 'hæfnər, háfnĕr
Hafod, *Clwyd, Dyfed, Mid Glam., W. Glam.*, 'hævɒd, hávvod. *Appropriate for both places of the name in Dyfed.*
Hafodyrynys *Gwent*, 'hævɒdər-'ʌnɪs, hávvodărúnniss
Hagan, *f.n.*, 'heɪgən, háygăn
Hagen, *f.n.*, 'heɪgən, háygĕn
Haggar, *f.n.*, 'hægɑr, hággaar; 'hægər, hággăr
Hagnaby Priory *Lincs.*, 'hægnəbɪ, hágnăbi
Hague, *f.n.*, heɪg, hayg
Hahessy, *f.n.*, 'heɪəsɪ, háy-ĕssi
Hahlo, *f.n.*, 'hɑloʊ, haálō
Haig, *f.n.*, heɪg, hayg. *Appropriate also for Earl* ~.
Haigh, *f.n.*, heɪg, hayg
Haigh *Gtr. M'chester*, heɪ, hay
Haight, *f.n.*, haɪt, hīt
Haighton *Lancs.*, 'haɪtən, hítŏn
Hailes, Barony of, heɪlz, haylz
Hailes Castle *Lothian*, heɪlz, haylz
Haileyburian, *one educated at Haileybury College*, ‚heɪlɪ-'bjʊərɪən, haylibyŏŏriän
Haileybury *Herts.*, 'heɪlɪbərɪ, háylibŭri
Hailsham *E. Sussex*, 'heɪlʃəm, háyl-shăm. *Appropriate also for the Viscountcy of* ~.
Hailsham of Saint Marylebone, Baron, 'heɪlʃəm əv snt 'mærɪ-

boʊn, háyl-shăm ŏv sĭnt márribŏn
Hain, *f.n.*, heɪn, hayn
Hainault *London*, 'heɪnɔt, háynawt
Haire, *f.n.*, heər, hair. *Appropriate also for the Barony of* ~.
Hairmyres *S'clyde*, hɛər'maɪərz, hairmírz
Hakin *Dyfed*, 'heɪkɪn, háykin
Hakluyt, Richard, *16th-c. historian and geographer*, 'hæklut, háckloot; 'hæklwɪt, háckl-wit. *The former is much the more usual traditional pronunciation, but there is some evidence that the second was current in his own day.*
Halahan, *f.n.*, 'hæləhən, hálăhăn
Halam *Notts.*, 'heɪləm, háylăm
Halas, *f.n.*, 'hæləs, háläss
Halbeath *Fife*, 'hɒlbiθ, háwlbeeth
Halcrow, *f.n.*, 'hælkroʊ, hálkrō
Haldane, *f.n.*, 'hɔldən, háwldăn; 'hɒldeɪn, háwldayn
Haldon, Great *and* Little, *Devon*, 'hɒldən, háwldŏn. *Appropriate also for the Barony of* ~.
Halebarns *Gtr. M'chester*, heɪl-'bɑrnz, haylbaárnz
Haler, *f.n.*, 'heɪlər, háylĕr
Halesowen *W. Midlands*, heɪlz-'oʊɪn, haylzṓ-ĕn
Halewood *Merseyside*, 'heɪl'wʊd, háylwŏŏd
Haley, *f.n.*, 'heɪlɪ, háyli
Halford, *f.n.*, 'hælfərd, hálfŏrd; 'hɒlfərd, háwlford
Halford *Salop*, 'hɒlfərd, háwlfŏrd
Halford *Warwicks.*, 'hælfərd, hálfŏrd; 'hɒfərd, haáfŏrd
Halfpenny, *f.n.*, 'hɑfpənɪ, haáfpĕni
Halket, *f.n.*, 'hælkɪt, hálkĕt
Halkett, *f.n.*, 'hælkɪt, hálkĕt; 'hɒlkɪt, háwlkĕt; 'hækɪt, háckĕt
Halkirk *H'land*, 'hɒlkərk, háwlkirk
Halkyn *Clwyd*, 'hælkɪn, hálkin
Hallam, *f.n.*, 'hæləm, hálăm
Hallam *parliamentary division of Sheffield*, 'hæləm, hálăm
Hallamshire Hospital *Sheffield*, 'hæləmʃər, hálăm-shĕr
Halland *E. Sussex*, 'hælənd, hálănd
Hallas, *f.n.*, 'hæləs, háläss
Hallaton *Leics.*, 'hælətən, hálătŏn
Hallatrow *Avon*, 'hælətroʊ, hálătrō
Hallé, *f.n.*, 'hæleɪ, hálay. *Appropriate also for the* ~ *Orchestra.*
Hallen *Avon*, 'hælən, hálĕn
Hallesy, *f.n.*, 'hælɪsɪ, hálĕssi

Hallett, *f.n.,* 'hælɪt, hálĕt
Hallewell, *f.n.,* 'hælɪwel, háli-wel
Halley, Edmond, *astronomer and mathematician,* 'hælɪ, háli
Halliday, *f.n.,* 'hælɪdeɪ, háliday
Hallin *Skye,* 'hælɪn, hálin
Hallinan, *f.n.,* 'hælɪnən, hálinăn
Halling *Kent,* 'hɔlɪŋ, háwling
Hallingbury, Great *and* Little, *Essex,* 'hɒlɪŋbərɪ, hóllingbŭri; 'hɔlɪŋbərɪ, háwlingbŭri
Hallisey, *f.n.,* 'hælɪsɪ, hálissi
Hall i' th' Wood *Gtr. M'chester,* 'hɔlɪt 'wʊd, háwlit wōŏd
Halliwell, *f.n.,* 'hælɪwel, háli-wel
Hallmark, *f.n.,* 'hɔlmɑrk, háwl-maark
Halloughton *Notts.,* hæ'lɔtən, haláwtŏn
Halmore *Glos.,* 'hælmɔr, hálmor
Halnaker *W. Sussex,* 'hænəkər, hánnăkĕr
Halpern, *f.n.,* 'hælpərn, hálpĕrn
Halpin, *f.n.,* 'hælpɪn, hálpin
Halsall, *f.n.,* 'hælsl, hálssl; 'hɔlsl, háwlssl
Halsall *Lancs.,* 'hɔlsl, háwlssl
Halsbury, Earl of, 'hɔlzbərɪ, háwlzbŭri
Halse, *f.n.,* hæls, halss; hɔls, hawlss
Halse *Northants.,* hæls, halss; hɔs, hawss
Halse *Somerset,* hɔls, hawlss
Halsetown *Cornwall,* 'hɔlztaʊn, háwlztown
Halsey, *f.n.,* 'hælsɪ, hálssi; 'hɔlzɪ, háwlzi; 'hɔlsɪ, háwlssi
Halstan, *f.n.,* 'hɔlstən, háwlstăn
Halstead, *f.n.,* 'hælsted, hálsted; 'hælstɪd, hálstĕd
Halstock *Dorset,* 'hɔlstɒk, háwlstock
Halstow, Lower, *Kent,* 'loʊər 'hælstoʊ, ló-ĕr hálsstō
Halswell, *f.n.,* 'hælzwel, hálzwel
Haltemprice *Humberside,* 'hɔltəmpraɪs, háwltĕmpríss
Halton Holgate, *also spelt* **Halton Holegate,** *Lincs.,* 'hɔltən 'hɒlgeɪt, háwltŏn hólgayt
Halward, *f.n.,* 'hælwərd, hálwărd
Halwell *Devon,* 'hælwel, hálwel; 'hɔlwel, háwlwel
Halwill *Devon,* 'hælwɪl, hálwil; 'hɔlwɪl, háwlwil
Hambley, *f.n.,* 'hæmblɪ, hámbli
Hambloch, *f.n.,* 'hæmblɒk, hámblock
Hambourg, *f.n.,* 'hæmbɔrg, hámburg
Hambro, *f.n.,* 'hæmbroʊ, hámbrō; 'hæmbrə, hámbră

Hambrook, *f.n.,* 'hæmbrʊk, hámbrŏŏk
Hamburger, *f.n.,* 'hæmbɔrgər, hámburgĕr
Hamer, *f.n.,* 'heɪmər, háymĕr
Hameringham *Lincs.,* 'hæmər-ɪŋəm, hámmĕring-ăm
Hamerton *Cambs.,* 'hæmərtən, hámmĕrtŏn
Hamey, *f.n.,* 'heɪmɪ, háymi
Hamfallow *Glos.,* hæm'fæloʊ, hamfálō
Hamilton, *f.n.,* 'hæmltən, hámmltŏn
Hamilton *S'clyde,* 'hæmltən, hámmltŏn
Hamilton of Dalzell, Baron, 'hæmltən əv di'el, hámmltŏn ŏv dee-éll
Hamiltonsbawn *Co. Armagh,* ˌhæmltənz'bɔn, hammltŏnz-báwn
Hamish, *C.n.,* 'heɪmɪʃ, háymish
Hammant, *f.n.,* 'hæmənt, hámmănt
Hammill, *f.n.,* 'hæmɪl, hámmil
Hammond, *f.n.,* 'hæmənd, hámmŏnd
Hammonds, *f.n.,* 'hæməndz, hámmŏndz
Hamnett, *f.n.,* 'hæmnɪt, hám-nĕt
Hamoaze *R. Tamar estuary, Cornwall–Devon,* 'hæmoʊz, hámmōz
Hamond, *f.n.,* 'hæmənd, hámmŏnd
Hampden, Viscount, 'hæmdən, hámdĕn
Hampden, *f.n.,* 'hæmdən, hámdĕn
Hampden Park *S'clyde, E. Sussex,* 'hæmdən 'pɑrk, hámdĕn paʹark
Hampshire *Co. name,* 'hæmpʃər, hámp-shĕr
Hampson, *f.n.,* 'hæmsən, hámssŏn
Hampstead *London,* 'hæmpstɪd, hámpstĕd; 'hæmpsted, hámp-sted
Hamsey *E. Sussex,* 'hæmzɪ, hámzi
Hamsterley *Durham,* 'hæmstərlɪ, hámstĕrli
Hanak, *f.n.,* 'hænək, hánnăk
Hanbury, *f.n.,* 'hænbərɪ, hánbŭri
Hanchant, *f.n.,* 'hænʃənt, hán-shănt
Hancock, *f.n.,* 'hæŋkɒk, hánk-ock
Handcock, *f.n.,* 'hændkɒk, hándkock
Handel, George Frideric, *composer,* 'hændl, hándl. *The original German was* **Händel,** *pronounced* 'hendl, héndl.

Handelian, *pertaining to* **Handel,** hæn'dilıən, handeeliăn
Hankin, *f.n.,* 'hæŋkın, hánkin
Hannahstown *Co. Antrim,* 'hænəztaʊn, hánnăztown
Hanrahan, *f.n.,* 'hænrəhən, hánră--hăn
Hanratty, *f.n.,* hæn'rætı, hanrátti
Hansard, *f.n.,* 'hænsɑrd, hánssaard
Hanslope *Bucks.,* 'hænsloʊp, hánsslōp
Happisburgh *Norfolk,* 'heızbərə, háyzbŭră
Harberton *Devon,* 'hɑrbərtən, haárbĕrtŏn. *Appropriate also for Viscount* ~.
Harbertonford *Devon,* 'hɑrbərtən- fərd, haárbĕrtŏnford
Harborne *W. Midlands,* 'hɑrbɔrn, haárborn
Harcourt, *f.n.,* 'hɑrkɔrt, haárkort; 'hɑrkərt, haárkŭrt. *The second is appropriate for the Viscountcy of* ~.
Hardaker, *f.n.,* 'hɑrdeıkər, haárd- aykĕr
Harden, *f.n.,* 'hɑrdən, haárdĕn
Hardenhuish *Wilts.,* 'hɑrnıʃ, haárnish; ˌhɑrdən'hjuıʃ, haardĕn-héwish
Harding, *f.n.,* 'hɑrdıŋ, haárding
Hardinge, *f.n.,* 'hɑrdıŋ, haárding; 'hɑrdındʒ, haárdinj. *The first is appropriate for Viscount* ~.
Hardinge of Penshurst, Baron, 'hɑrdıŋ əv 'penzhərst, haárding ŏv pénz-hurst
Hardres, *f.n.,* hɑrdz, haardz
Hardres, Lower *and* Upper, *Kent,* hɑrdz, haardz
Hardress, *f.n.,* 'hɑrdres, haárd- ress
Hardwicke, Earl of, 'hɑrdwık, haárdwick
Hardwicke, Sir Cedric, *actor,* 'sidrık 'hɑrdwık, seédrick haárdwick
Hardy, *f.n.,* 'hɑrdı, haárdi
Harefield *London, Hants,* 'heər- fild, háirfeeld
Harehaugh *Northd.,* 'heərhɑf, háir-haaf
Harenc, *f.n.,* 'hærɒŋ, hárrong
Haresceugh *Cumbria,* 'heərskjuf, háirskewf
Harewood, *f.n.,* 'heərwʊd, háir- wōōd
Harewood *W. Yorks.,* 'hɑrwʊd, haárwōōd; 'heərwʊd, háirwōōd. *The first is appropriate for the Earl of* ~ *and for* ~ *House. The second is usual in the village.*

Harford, *f.n.,* 'hɑrfərd, haárfŏrd
Hargan, *f.n.,* 'hɑrgən, haárgăn
Harger, *f.n.,* 'hɑrdʒər, haárjĕr
Hargham *Norfolk,* 'hɑrfəm, haárfăm
Hargreaves, *f.n.,* 'hɑrgrivz, haár- greevz; 'hɑrgreıvz, haárgrayvz. *In its native North of England, the first is appropriate. The second was that of Mrs Alice* ~, *the original Alice in Wonderland.*
Haringey *London,* 'hærıŋgeı, hárring-gay
Harington, *f.n.,* 'hærıŋtən, hár- ringtŏn
Harkness, *f.n.,* 'hɑrknıs, haárk- nĕss
Harkouk, *f.n.,* hɑr'kuk, haarkoók
Harlaxton *Lincs.,* 'hɑrləkstən, haárlăkstŏn
Harle, *f.n.,* hɑrl, haarl
Harlech *Gwynedd,* 'hɑrləx, haár- lĕ<u>ch</u>. *Appropriate also for Baron* ~.
Harlesden *London,* 'hɑrlzdən, haárlzdĕn
Harlestone *Northants.,* 'hɑrlstən, haárlstŏn
Harlow *Essex,* 'hɑrloʊ, haárlō
Harmes, *f.n.,* hɑrmz, haarmz
Harmondsworth *London,* 'hɑr- məndzwərθ, haármŏndzwurth
Harneis, *f.n.,* 'hɑrnıs, haárniss
Haroldswick *Shetland,* 'hærəldz- wık, hárrŏldzwick
Harpenden *Herts.,* 'hɑrpəndən, haárpĕndĕn
Harpham, *f.n.,* 'hɑrpəm, haárpăm
Harpole *Northants.,* 'hɑrpoʊl, haárpōl
Harpwood, *f.n.,* 'hɑrpwʊd, haárp- wōōd
Harraby *Cumbria,* 'hærəbı, hár- răbi
Harragin, *f.n.,* 'hærəgın, hárrăgin
Harrap, *f.n.,* 'hærəp, hárrăp
Harray *Orkney,* 'hærı, hárri
Harré, *f.n.,* hə'reı, hăráy
Harrhy, *f.n.,* 'hærı, hárri
Harries, *f.n.,* 'hærıs, hárriss
Harrietsham *Kent,* 'hærıət-ʃəm, hárriĕt-shăm
Harris, *f.n.,* 'hærıs, hárriss
Harriseahead *Staffs.,* 'hærısı'hed, hárrissee-héd
Harrod, *f.n.,* 'hærəd, hárrŏd
Harrogate *N. Yorks.,* 'hærəgıt, hárrŏgit
Harrold *Beds.,* 'hærəld, hárrŏld
Harrop, *f.n.,* 'hærəp, hárrŏp
Harrovian, *one educated at* Harrow *School,* hə'roʊvıən, hărṓviăn
Harrow, *f.n.,* 'hæroʊ, hárrō

Harrow *London*, 'hæroʊ, hárrō
Harrowden, Great *and* Little,
  Northants., 'hæroʊdən, hár-
  rōděn
Harrup, *f.n.*, 'hærəp, hárrŭp
Hart, *f.n.*, hɑrt, haart
Hartcup, *f.n.*, 'hɑrtkʌp, haárt-kup
Hartford *Cambs.*, 'hɑrtfərd, haárt-
  fŏrd
Hartham *Herts.*, 'hɑrtəm, haárt-
  ăm
Harthan, *f.n.*, 'hɑrðən, haárthăn
Hartismere, Baron, 'hɑrtɪzmɪər,
  haártizmeer
Hartlebury *H. & W.*, 'hɑrtlbəri,
  haártlbŭri
Hartlepool *Cleveland*, 'hɑrtlɪpul,
  haártlipool
Hartley Wespall *Hants*, 'hɑrtlɪ
  'wespəl, haártli wéspawl
Hartley Wintney *Hants*, 'hɑrtlɪ
  'wɪntnɪ, haártli wíntni
Hartoch, *f.n.*, 'hɑrtɒk, haártock
Hartopp, *f.n.*, 'hɑrtɒp, haártop
Hartpury *Glos.*, 'hɑrtpəri, haárt-
  pŭri
Hartshorn, *f.n.*, 'hɑrtshɔrn,
  haárts-horn
Hartshorne, *f.n.*, 'hɑrtshɔrn,
  haárts-horn
Hartsilver, *f.n.*, 'hɑrtsɪlvər,
  haártsilvěr
Hartung, *f.n.*, 'hɑrtʌŋ, haártung
Harvey of Tasburgh, Baron,
  'hɑrvɪ əv 'teɪzbərə, haárvi ŏv
  táyzbŭră
Harwell *Berks.*, 'hɑrwəl, haárwěl
Harwich *Essex*, 'hærɪdʒ, hárrij;
  'hærɪtʃ, hárritch
Harwood, *f.n.*, 'hɑrwʊd, haár-
  wŏŏd
Hasbury *W. Midlands*, 'hæzbəri,
  házbŭri
Haselbech, *f.n.*, 'heɪzlbɪtʃ, háyzl-
  beetch
Haseldine, *f.n.*, 'hæzldaɪn, házzl-
  dīn
Haseler, *f.n.*, 'heɪzlər, háyzlěr
Haseley *Warwicks.*, 'heɪzlɪ,
  háyzli
Haseley, Great *and* Little, *Oxon.*,
  'heɪzlɪ, háyzli
Haselor *Warwicks.*, 'heɪzlɔr,
  háyzlor
Hashagen, *f.n.*, 'hæʃəgən,
  hásh-ăgěn
Haskeir *W. Isles*, hə'skɪər, hă-
  skeér
Hasketon *Suffolk*, 'hæskɪtən,
  hásskětŏn
Haslam, *f.n.*, 'hæzləm, házlăm
Haslemere *Surrey*, 'heɪzlmɪər,
  háyzlmeer
Hasler, *f.n.*, 'hæzlər, házlěr

Haslett, *f.n.*, 'heɪzlɪt, háyzlět;
  'hæzlɪt, házlět
Haslingden *Lancs.*, 'hæzlɪŋdən,
  házlingděn
Haslingfield *Cambs.*, 'heɪzlɪŋfɪld,
  háyzlingfeeld; 'hæzlɪŋfɪld,
  házlingfeeld
Hassall, *f.n.*, 'hæsl, hássl
Hassard, *f.n.*, 'hæsɑrd, hássaard
Haster *H'land*, 'hæstər, hásstěr
Hastie, *f.n.*, 'heɪstɪ, háyssti
Hastings, *f.n.*, 'heɪstɪŋz, háys-
  stingz
Hastings *E. Sussex*, 'heɪstɪŋz,
  háysstingz
Haston, *f.n.*, 'hæstən, hásstŏn
Haswell, *f.n.*, 'hæzwel, házwel
Hatch Beauchamp *Somerset*,
  'hætʃ 'bitʃəm, hátch beétchăm
Hatfield Peverel *Essex*, 'hætfɪld
  'pevərəl, hátfeeld pévvěrěl
Hathaway, *f.n.*, 'hæθəweɪ,
  háthă-way
Hathern *Leics.*, 'hæðərn, háthěrn
Hathersage *Derby.*, 'hæðərseɪdʒ,
  háthěr-sayj
Hatherton, Baron, 'hæðərtən,
  háthěrtŏn
Hathorn, *f.n.*, 'hɔθərn, háwthorn;
  'heɪθərn, háythorn; 'hæθərn,
  háthorn
Hathorne, *f.n.*, 'hɔθərn, háw-
  thŏrn
Hattersley, *f.n.*, 'hætərzlɪ, hát-
  těrzli
Hatton, *f.n.*, 'hætən, háttŏn
Hauger, *f.n.*, 'hɔgər, háwgěr
Haugh, Nether *and* Upper, *S.
  Yorks.*, hɔf, hawf
Haugham *Kent*, 'hʌfəm, húffăm
Haugham *Lincs.*, 'hæfəm, háffăm
Haughley *Suffolk*, 'hɔlɪ, háwli
Haughmond Hill *Salop*, 'hɒmənd
  'hɪl, háwmŏnd híll; 'heɪmənd
  'hɪl, háymŏnd híll
Haughney, *f.n.*, 'hɒxnɪ, hóchni
Haugh of Urr *D. & G.*, 'hɑx əv 'ɜr,
  haách ŏv úr
Haughton, *f.n.*, 'hɔtən, háwtŏn
Haughton *Gtr. M'chester*, *Notts.*,
  Powys, 'hɔtən, háwtŏn
Haughton-le-Skerne *Durham*,
  'hɔtən lə 'skɜrn, háwtŏn lě skérn
Haulbowline Rock *Co. Down*,
  hɔl'boʊlɪn, hawlbólin
Haulgh *Gtr. M'chester*, hɒf, hoff
Hauser, *f.n.*, 'hɒzər, háwzěr
Hautbois, Great *and* Little,
  Norfolk, 'hɒbɪs, hóbbiss
Hauxton *Cambs.*, 'hɔkstən,
  háwkstŏn
Hauxwell *N. Yorks.*, 'hɔkswel,
  háwkswel
Havant *Hants*, 'hævənt, hávvănt

Havard, f.n., 'hævərd, hávvărd
Havell, f.n., 'hævl, hávvl. Appropriate for E. B. ~, Indian-art historian.
Havely, f.n., 'hævəlı, hávvĕli
Havenhand, f.n., 'heɪvənhænd, háyvĕn-hand
Haverah Park N. Yorks., 'hævərə 'pɑrk, hávvĕră pɑ́ark
Haverfordwest Dyfed, ‚hævərfərd'west, havvĕrfŏrd-wést; ‚hɑrfərd'west, haarfŏrd-wést
Havergate Island Suffolk, 'hævərgeɪt, hávvĕrgayt
Haverhill Suffolk, 'heɪvrɪl, háyvril
Haverigg Cumbria, 'hævərɪg, hávvĕrig
Havering-atte-Bower London, 'heɪvərɪŋ ætı 'bauər, háyvĕring atti bówĕr
Haveringland Norfolk, 'heɪvərɪŋlənd, háyvĕring-lănd
Havers, f.n., 'heɪvərz, háyvĕrz
Haverton Hill Cleveland, 'hævərtən 'hɪl, hávvĕrtŏn híll
Haviland, f.n., 'hævɪlənd, hávviländ
Haward, f.n., 'heɪwərd, háywărd; 'hɔərd, háw-ărd; hɑrd, haard; hɔrd, hord
Hawarden, Viscount, 'heɪwɔrdən, háy-wawrdĕn
Hawarden, f.n., 'hɑrdən, haárdĕn
Hawarden, Clwyd, 'hɑrdən, haárdĕn. Appropriate also for the Barony of Gladstone of ~.
Haweis, f.n., 'hɔ-ɪs, háw-iss
Hawes N. Yorks., hɔz, hawz
Hawes Water, Lake, Cumbria, 'hɔzwɔtər, háwz-wawtĕr
Hawick Borders, 'hɔ-ɪk, háw-ick
Hawkes, f.n., hɔks, hawks
Hawkinge Kent, 'hɔkɪndʒ, háwkinj
Haworth, f.n., 'hauərθ, hów-ŭrth
Haworth W. Yorks., 'hauərθ, hów-ŭrth; 'hɔərθ, háw-ŭrth
Hawridge Bucks., 'hærɪdʒ, hárrij
Haws, f.n., hɔz, hawz
Hawtrey, f.n., 'hɔtrı, háwtri
Haxell, f.n., 'hæksl, hácksl
Haxey Humberside, 'hæksı, hácksi
Hayball, f.n., 'heɪbɔl, háybawl
Haycock, f.n., 'heɪkɒk, háykock
Hayden, f.n., 'heɪdən, háydĕn
Haydn, C.n., 'heɪdn, háydn
Haydock, f.n., 'heɪdɒk, háydock
Haydock Merseyside, 'heɪdɒk, háydock
Haydon, f.n., 'heɪdən, háydŏn. Appropriate for Benjamin ~, 19th-c. historical painter.

Hayes, f.n., heɪz, hayz
Hayhow, f.n., 'heɪhou, háy-hō
Hayhurst, f.n., 'heɪhərst, háy--hŭrst
Hayland, f.n., 'heɪlənd, háylănd
Hayle Cornwall, heɪl, hayl. Appropriate also for the river of this name.
Hayman, f.n., 'heɪmən, háymăn
Hays, f.n., heɪz, hayz
Haysom, f.n., 'heɪsəm, háyssŏm
Hayter, f.n., 'heɪtər, háytĕr
Haytor Devon, 'heɪ'tɔr, háy-tór
Hayward, f.n., 'heɪwərd, háywărd
Hazan, f.n., hə'zæn, hăzánn
Hazard, f.n., 'hæzərd, házzaard
Hazeldine, f.n., 'heɪzldaɪn, házzl-dīn; 'heɪzldin, házzldeen
Hazell, f.n., 'heɪzl, háyzl
Hazlerigg, f.n., 'heɪzlrɪg, háyzlrig. Appropriate also for Baron ~.
Hazlitt, f.n., 'heɪzlɪt, háyzlĕt; 'hæzlɪt, házlĕt. Although the second is now usual, the first was that of William ~, essayist and critic, and is still used by his descendants.
Hazlitt Gallery London, 'hæzlɪt, házlit
Hazzard, f.n., 'hæzərd, házzărd
Heacham Norfolk, 'hetʃəm, hétchăm; 'hɪtʃəm, héetchăm
Headfort, Marquess of, 'hedfərt, hédfŏrt
Headingley W. Yorks., 'hedɪŋlı, hédding-li
Headlam, f.n., 'hedləm, hédlăm
Heaf, f.n., hif, heef
Heage Derby., hidʒ, heej
Heaks, f.n., hiks, heeks
Heal, f.n., hil, heel
Healaugh N. Yorks., 'hilə, héelă
Heald, f.n., hild, heeld
Healy, f.n., 'hilı, héeli
Heamoor Cornwall, 'heɪmɔr, háymor
Heanen, f.n., 'hinən, héenĕn
Heaney, f.n., 'hinı, héeni
Heanor Derby., 'hinər, héenŏr; 'heɪnər, háynŏr
Heanton Punchardon Devon, 'hentən 'pʌnʃərdən, héntŏn pún-shărdŏn; 'heɪntən 'pʌnʃər-dən, háyntŏn pún-shărdŏn
Heape, f.n., hip, heep
Hearn, f.n., hərn, hern
Heaslip, f.n., 'heɪslɪp, háysslip
Heath, f.n., hiθ, heeth
Heathcoat, f.n., 'heθkət, héthkŏt
Heathcoat Amory, f.n., 'heθkət 'eɪmərı, héthkŏt áymŏri
Heathcock, f.n., 'hiθkɒk, héeth-kock
Heathcote, C.n., 'heθkət, héthkŏt

Heathcote, *f.n.,* 'heθkət, héthkŏt;
'hiθkoʊt, héethkŏt
Heathcote *Derby.,* 'heθkət,
héthkŏt
**Heathcote-Drummond-Willouhg-
by,** *f.n.,* 'heθkət 'drʌmənd
'wɪləbɪ, héthkŏt drúmmŏnd
wíllŏbi. *Family name of the
Earl of Ancaster.*
Heather *Leics.,* 'hiðər, héethĕr
Heathery Cleugh *Durham,*
'heðərɪ 'klʌf, héthĕri klúff
Heathfield *Devon, Dyfed, Cum-
bria,* 'hiθfild, héethfeeld
Heathorn, *f.n.,* 'hiθərn, hée-thorn
Heathrow *London,* 'hiθ'roʊ
héeth-rố
Heatlie, *f.n.,* 'hitlɪ, héetli
Heaver, *f.n.,* 'hivər, héevĕr
Heaviside, *f.n.,* 'hevɪsaɪd, hévvis-
sīd
Heawood, *f.n.,* 'heɪwʊd, háywŏŏd
Heaword, *f.n.,* 'heɪwərd, háywŭrd
Hebburn *Tyne & Wear,* 'hebɜrn,
hébburn
Hebditch, *f.n.,* 'hebdɪtʃ, hébditch
Hebel, *f.n.,* 'hebl, hébbl
Heber, *f.n.,* 'hibər, héebĕr
Hebers *Gtr. M'chester,* 'hibərz,
héebĕrz
Hebert, *f.n.,* 'hibərt, héebĕrt
Hebron *Dyfed, Gwynedd,* 'hebrɒn,
hébbron
Heckmondwike *W. Yorks.,*
'hekməndwaɪk, héckmŏndwīk
Hedgecock, *f.n.,* 'hedʒkɒk,
héjkock
Hedgehope *Northd.,* 'hedʒəp,
héjjŏp
Hedleyhope *Durham,* 'hedlɪ-
'hoʊp, hédli-hốp
Hednesford *Staffs.,* 'hensfərd,
hénssfŏrd; 'hedʒfərd, héjfŏrd
Hedon *Humberside,* 'hedən, héd-
dŏn
Heelas, *f.n.,* 'hiləs, héeläss
Heffernan, *f.n.,* 'hefərnən, héffĕr-
nän
Hegarty, *f.n.,* 'hegərtɪ, héggärti
Heggie, *f.n.,* 'hegɪ, héggi
Heigham *Norfolk,* 'heɪəm, háy-äm
Heighington *Durham,* 'heɪɪŋtən,
háy-ingtŏn; 'haɪɪŋtən, hī-ingtŏn;
'haɪntən, híntŏn
Heighington *Lincs.,* 'heɪɪŋtən,
háy-ingtŏn; 'hiɪŋtən, hée-ingtŏn
Heighton, *f.n.,* 'heɪtən, háytŏn
Heighway, *f.n.,* 'heɪweɪ, háy-
-way; 'haɪweɪ, hí-way
Heilbron, *f.n.,* 'haɪlbrɒn, hílbron
Heilgers, *f.n.,* 'haɪlgərz, hílgĕrz
Heilpern, *f.n.,* 'haɪlpərn, hílpĕrn
Heim Gallery *London,* haɪm, hīm
Heinekey, *f.n.,* 'haɪnɪkɪ, hínĕki

Heinemann, *f.n.,* 'haɪnəmən,
hínĕmän
Heiney, *f.n.,* 'haɪnɪ, híni
Heisker *W. Isles,* 'haɪskər, hísskĕr
Hele, *f.n.,* hil, heel; 'hilɪ, héeli
Hele *Devon,* hil, heel
Hele Stone *Stonehenge (Wilts.),*
'hil stoʊn, heel stōn
Helena, *C.n.,* 'helɪnə, héllĕnă;
hə'linə, hĕléenă
Helensburgh *S'clyde,* 'helənzbərə,
héllĕnzbŭră
Helenus, *C.n.,* 'helɪnəs, héllĕnŭss
Helhoughton *Norfolk,* hel'hoʊtən,
hel-hốtŏn; hel'haʊtən, hel-
-hówtŏn
Helier, saint, 'helɪər, hélli-ĕr
Helions Bumpstead *Essex,*
'hilɪənz 'bʌmpsted, héeli-ŏnz
búmpsted
Hellewell, *f.n.,* 'helɪwel, hélli-
-wel
Hellicar, *f.n.,* 'helɪkɑr, héllikaar
Hellingly *E. Sussex,* ˌhelɪŋ'laɪ,
helling-lí
Helliwell, *f.n.,* 'helɪwel, hélliwel
Hellowell, *f.n.,* 'heləwel, héllŏ-
-wel
Hellyar, *f.n.,* 'heljər, hél-yăr
Helme, *f.n.,* helm, helm
Helmingham *Suffolk,* 'helmɪŋəm,
hélming-äm
Helmore, *f.n.,* 'helmɔr, hélmor
Helmsley *N. Yorks.,* 'helmzlɪ,
hélmzli; 'hemzlɪ, hémzli
Helston *Cornwall,* 'helstən, héls-
stŏn
Helvellyn *Cumbria,* hel'velɪn,
helvéllin
Helwick Shoals *and* lightship,
off W. Glam., 'helɪk, héllick
Hely, *f.n.,* 'hilɪ, héeli
Helyer, *f.n.,* 'helɪər, hélli-ĕr
Heman, *f.n.,* 'himən, héemän
Hemans, *f.n.,* 'hemənz, hém-
mänz
Hemerdon *Devon,* 'hemərdən,
hémmĕrdŏn
Hemery, *f.n.,* 'hemərɪ, hémmĕri
Heming, *f.n.,* 'hemɪŋ, hémming
Hemingbrough *N. Yorks.,* 'hemɪŋ-
brʌf, hémming-bruff
Hemingford Abbots *Cambs.,*
'hemɪŋfərd 'æbəts, hémming-
fŏrd ábbŏts
Hemingford Grey *Cambs.,*
'hemɪŋfərd 'greɪ, hémmingfŏrd
gráy
Hemmerde, *f.n.,* 'hemərdɪ,
hémmĕrdi
Hempel, *f.n.,* 'hempl, hémpl
Hemswell *Lincs.,* 'hemzwel,
hémzwel
Hemy, *f.n.,* 'hemɪ, hémmi

Hemyock *Devon*, 'hemjɒk, hém-
-yock; 'hemɪɒk, hémmi-ock
Henbrow, *f.n.*, 'henbrou, hénbrō
Henderskelfe Castle, *N. Yorks.*,
'hendərskelf, héndĕr-skelf.
*Castle Howard was built on the
site of this former castle.*
Henderson, *f.n.*, 'hendərsən,
héndĕrssŏn
Hendreforgan *Mid Glam.*,
,hendrɪ'vɔrgən, hendrivórgăn
Hendri *Powys*, 'hendrɪ, héndri
Hendy, *f.n.*, 'hendɪ, héndi
Hene, *f.n.*, 'hinɪ, héeni
Heneage, *f.n.*, 'henɪdʒ, hénnij.
*Appropriate also for the Barony
of* ∼.
Henebery, *f.n.*, 'henɪbərɪ, hénnĕ-
bĕri
Heneghan, *f.n.*, 'henɪgən, hénnĕ-
găn
Heneglwys *Gwynedd*, hen'eglʊɪs,
henégloō-iss
Heneker, *f.n.*, 'henɪkər, hénnĕkĕr
Hengoed *Mid Glam.*, 'heŋgɔɪd,
héng-goyd
Heniarth *Powys*, 'henjɑrθ, hén-
-yaarth; 'henɪɑrθ, hénni-aarth
Henig, *f.n.*, 'henɪg, hénnig
Henlere, *f.n.*, 'henlɪər, hénleer
Henley-in-Arden *Warwicks.*,
'henlɪ ɪn 'ɑrdən, hénli in aárdĕn
Henley-on-Thames *Oxon.*, 'henlɪ
ɒn 'temz, hénli on témz
Henllan *Clwyd, Dyfed, Gwent*,
'henɬæn, hén-ḥlan
Henllan Amgoed *Dyfed*, 'henɬæn
'æmgɔɪd, hén-ḥlan ámgoyd
Henlow *Beds.*, 'henlou, hénlō
Hennebry, *f.n.*, 'henɪbrɪ, hénnĕ-
bri
Hennessey, *f.n.*, 'henɪsɪ, hénnĕssi
Hennessy, *f.n.*, 'henɪsɪ, hénnĕssi
Henniker, Baron, 'henɪkər, hén-
nikĕr
Henocq, *f.n.*, 'henɒk, hénnock
Henri, *f.n.*, 'henrɪ, hénri
Henriques, *f.n.*, hen'rikɪz, hen-
réekĕz
Henschel, Sir George, *composer*,
'henʃl, hénshl
Henshall, *f.n.*, 'henʃl, hénshl;
'henʃɔl, hén-shawl
Hensher, *f.n.*, 'henʃər, hén-shĕr
Henshilwood, *f.n.*, 'henʃlwʊd,
hénshl-woōd
Henstead *Suffolk*, 'henstɪd, hén-
stĕd
Henwick *H. & W.*, 'henwɪk,
hénwick
Heolgerrig *Mid Glam.*, ,heɪəl-
'gerɪg, hay-ŏl-gérrig
Heol-y-cyw *Mid Glam.*, ,heɪəl ə
'kju, hay-ŏl ă kéw

Hepburn, *f.n.*, 'hebɜrn, hébburn;
'hebərn, hébbŭrn
Hepburn *Northd.*, 'hebɜrn, héb-
burn
Hepburne, *f.n.*, 'hebərn, hébbŭrn
Heppell, *f.n.*, 'hepl, héppl
Heppenstall, *f.n.*, 'hepənstɔl,
héppĕn-stawl
Hepplewhite, *f.n.*, 'heplʰwaɪt,
hépplwhīt
Heptonstall *W. Yorks.*, 'heptən-
stɔl, héptŏn-stawl
Hepworth, *f.n.*, 'hepwɜrθ, hép-
wurth
Herapath, *f.n.*, 'herəpɑθ, hérră-
paath
Herbecq, *f.n.*, 'hɜrbek, hérbeck
Herbison, *f.n.*, 'hɜrbɪsən, hérbis-
sŏn
Herdwick, *breed of sheep*, 'hɜrd-
wɪk, hérdwick
Hereford *H. & W.*, 'herɪfərd,
hérrĕfŏrd. *Appropriate also for
Viscount* ∼.
Heren, *f.n.*, 'herən, hérrĕn
Herford, *f.n.*, 'hɜrfərd, hérfŏrd
Hergest Ridge, *hill range, H. &
W.*, 'hɑrgɪst, haárgĕst
Herincx, Raimund, *opera singer*,
'reɪmənd 'herɪŋks, ráymŭnd
hérrinks
Heriot *Borders*, 'herɪət, hérrĭŏt
Herklots, *f.n.*, 'hɜrklɒts, hérklots
Herkness, *f.n.*, 'hɑrknɪs, haárk-
nĕss
Herkomer, *f.n.*, 'hɜrkəmər, hér-
kŏmĕr
Herlihy, *f.n.*, 'hɜrlɪhɪ, hérli-hi
Hermaness *Shetland*, 'hɜrmənes,
hérmăness
Hermes, *f.n.*, 'hɜrmiz, hérmeez.
Appropriate for Gertrude ∼,
sculptor.
Hermges, *f.n.*, 'hɜrmdʒiz, hérm-
jeez
Herner, *f.n.*, 'hɜrnər, hérnĕr
Heron, *f.n.*, 'herən, hérrŏn
Herriard *Hants*, 'herɪərd, hérriărd
Herries, Baroness, 'herɪs, hérriss
Herrin, *f.n.*, 'herɪn, hérrin
Herringshaw, *f.n.*, 'herɪŋʃɔ,
hérring-shaw
Herriot, *f.n.*, 'herɪət, hérrĭŏt
Herschell, *f.n.*, 'hɜrʃl, hérshl.
Appropriate also for Baron ∼.
Herstmonceux, *also spelt* **Hurst-
monceaux, Hurstmonceux**,
E. Sussex, ,hɜrstmən'sju,
herstmŏn-séw; ,hɜrstmən'su,
herstmŏn-soō
Hertford *Herts.*, 'hɑrfərd, haár-
fŏrd; 'hɑrtfərd, haártfŏrd. *The
first is appropriate for the
Marquess of* ∼.

Hertford College *Univ. of Oxford*, 'hɑrfərd, haárförd

Hertingfordbury *Herts.*, 'hɑrtɪŋfərdberɪ, haártingfördberri

Hervey, *f.n.*, 'hɑrvɪ, haárvi

Herwald, *f.n.*, 'hɜrwɔld, hérwäld

Heseltine, *f.n.*, 'hesltaɪn, héssltīn. *Appropriate for Philip* ~, *whose pseudonym as composer is Peter Warlock.*

Heselton, *f.n.*, 'hesltən, héssltön

Heshel, *f.n.*, 'heʃl, héshl

Hesilrige, *f.n.*, 'hezɪlrɪdʒ, hézzilrij

Hesketh, *f.n.*, 'heskəθ, héskěth. *Appropriate also for Baron* ~.

Heslerton, East *and* West, *N. Yorks.*, 'heslərtən, hésslěrtön

Hesmondhalgh, *f.n.*, 'hezməndhɔ, hézmönd-haw; 'hezməndhælʃ, hézmönd-halsh; 'hezməndhɔltʃ, hézmönd-hawltch

Hespe, *f.n.*, hesp, hessp

Hessary Tor *Devon*, 'hesərɪ 'tɔr, héssäri tór

Hessé, *f.n.*, 'hesɪ, héssi

Hessenford *Cornwall*, 'hesənfərd, héssěnförd

Hessett *Suffolk*, 'hesɪt, héssět

Hession, *f.n.*, 'hesɪən, héssiön; 'heʃən, héshön

Hessle *Humberside*, 'hezl, hézzl

Heston *London*, 'hestən, hésstön

Heswall *Merseyside*, 'hezwəl, hézwäl

Hethel *Norfolk*, 'heθl, héthl

Hetley, *f.n.*, 'hetlɪ, hétli

Hetton-le-Hole *Tyne & Wear*, 'hetən lə 'hoʊl, héttön lě hốl

Heugh, *f.n.*, hju, hew

Heugh *Northd.*, hjuf, hewf

Heughan, *f.n.*, 'hjuən, héw-ăn

Heulwen, *Welsh C.n.*, 'haɪlwen, hílwen

Heulyn, *f.n.*, 'heɪlɪn, háylin

Heuston, *f.n.*, 'hjustən, héwstön

Heveningham Hall, *Suffolk*, 'henɪŋəm, hénning-ăm

Hever *Kent*, 'hivər, heévěr

Heversham *Cumbria*, 'hevərʃəm, hévvěr-shäm

Hevingham, *f.n.*, 'hevɪŋəm, hévving-ăm

Hewardine, *f.n.*, 'hjuərdin, héwärdeen

Hewart, Viscountcy of, 'hjuərt, héw-ärt

Hewaswater *Cornwall*, 'hjuəswɔtər, héw-äss-wawtěr

Hewelsfield *Glos.*, 'hjuəlzfild, héw-ělzfeeld

Hewett, *f.n.*, 'hjuɪt, héw-ět

Hewish, *f.n.*, 'hjuɪʃ, héw-ish

Hewitson, *f.n.*, 'hjuɪtsən, héw-itsön

Hewitt, *f.n.*, 'hjuɪt, héw-it

Hewlett, *f.n.*, 'hjulɪt, héwlět

Heworth *N. Yorks.*, 'hjuərθ, héw-ürth

Hext, *f.n.*, hekst, hekst

Hey, *f.n.*, heɪ, hay

Heycock, *f.n.*, 'heɪkɒk, háykock

Heyes, *f.n.*, heɪz, hayz

Heyford, Lower *and* Upper, *Northants.*, *Oxon.*, 'heɪfərd, háyförd

Heyford, Nether, *Northants.*, 'neðər 'heɪfərd, néthěr háyförd

Heyford at Bridge, *also called* **Lower Heyford,** *Oxon.*, 'heɪfərd ət 'brɪdʒ, háyförd ăt brij

Heyford Warren, *also called* **Upper Heyford,** *Oxon.*, 'heɪfərd 'wɒrən, háyförd wórrěn

Heygate, *f.n.*, 'heɪgeɪt, háygayt; 'heɪgɪt, háygit

Heygen, *f.n.*, 'heɪgən, háygěn

Heyhoe, *f.n.*, 'heɪhoʊ, háyhō

Heyner, *f.n.*, 'heɪnər, háyněr

Heyno, *f.n.*, 'heɪnoʊ, háynō

Heyop *Powys*, 'heɪəp, háy-öp

Heyrod *Gtr. M'chester*, 'herəd, hérröd

Heys, *f.n.*, heɪz, hayz

Heysham *Lancs.*, 'hiʃəm, heé-shäm

Heyshott *W. Sussex*, 'heɪʃɒt, háy-shot

Heytesbury, Baron, 'hetsbərɪ, hétsbūri

Heytesbury *Wilts.*, 'heɪtsbərɪ, háytsbūri

Heyther, *f.n.*, 'heðər, héthěr. *Appropriate for William* ~, *founder of the Chair of Music at Oxford Univ., 1622.*

Heythrop *Oxon.*, 'hiθrəp, heé-thrŏp. *Appropriate also for the* ~ *Hunt.*

Heyting, *f.n.*, 'heɪtɪŋ, háyting

Heywood *Gtr. M'chester, Wilts.*, 'heɪwʊd, háywoōd

Hibaldstow *Humberside*, 'hɪblstoʊ, híbblstō

Hibberd, *f.n.*, 'hɪbərd, híbběrd

Hibbert, *f.n.*, 'hɪbərt, híbběrt

Hibbitt, *f.n.*, 'hɪbɪt, híbbit

Hickin, *f.n.*, 'hɪkɪn, híckin

Hickinbotham, *f.n.*, 'hɪkɪnbɒθəm, híckinbothäm

Hidcote *Glos.*, 'hɪdkət, hídkŏt

Hider, *f.n.*, 'haɪdər, híděr

Hiendley, South, *W. Yorks.*, 'hindlɪ, heéndli

Higgens, *f.n.*, 'hɪgɪnz, híggěnz

Higgins, *f.n.*, 'hɪgɪnz, hígginz

Higham, *f.n.*, 'haɪəm, hí-ăm
Higham *Kent*, 'haɪəm, hí-ăm
Higham *S. Yorks.*, 'haɪəm, hí-ăm;
'hɪkəm, híckăm
Higham Ferrers *Northants.*,
'haɪəm 'ferərz, hí-ăm férrĕrz
Higham Gobion *Beds.*, 'haɪəm
'goʊbɪən, hí-ăm gṓbiŏn
Higham's Park *London*, 'haɪəmz
'pɑrk, hí-ămz pa'ark
High Bradley *N. Yorks.*, 'haɪ
'brædlɪ, hí brádli
Highbury *London*, 'haɪbərɪ,
híbŭri
Highclere *Hants*, 'haɪklɪər,
híkleer
High Coniscliffe *Durham*, 'haɪ
'kɒnɪsklɪf, hí kónniss-kliff
High Ercall *Salop*, 'haɪ 'ɑrkl, hí
a'arkl
Highgate, *f.n.*, 'haɪgeɪt, hígayt
High Halden *Kent*, 'haɪ 'hɔldən,
hí háwldĕn
High Legh *Ches.*, 'haɪ 'li, hí le'e
Highley *Salop*, 'haɪlɪ, híli
Highnam *Glos.*, 'haɪnəm, hínăm
High Wych *Herts.*, 'haɪ 'waɪtʃ,
hí wítch
High Wycombe *Bucks.*, 'haɪ
'wɪkəm, hí wíckŏm
Hilaire, *f.n.*, hɪ'lɛər, hiláir
Hilbre Island *Merseyside*, 'hɪlbrɪ,
hílbri
Hildenborough *Kent*, 'hɪldənbʌrə,
híldĕn-burră
Hildersham *Cambs.*, 'hɪldərʃəm,
híldĕr-shăm
Hilderstone *Staffs.*, 'hɪldərstən,
híldĕrsstŏn
Hildreth, *f.n.*, 'hɪldrɪθ, híldrĕth
Hiley, *f.n.*, 'haɪlɪ, híli
Hilgay *Norfolk*, 'hɪlgeɪ, hílgay
Hillcoat, *f.n.*, 'hɪlkoʊt, hílkōt
Hilleary, *f.n.*, 'hɪlərɪ, híllĕri
Hiller, *f.n.*, 'hɪlər, híllĕr
Hillery, *f.n.*, 'hɪlərɪ, híllĕri
Hillhead *Devon*, *S'clyde*, 'hɪl'hed,
híll-héd
Hillier, *f.n.*, 'hɪlɪər, hílli-ĕr
Hillsborough *S. Yorks.*, 'hɪlzbərə,
hílzbŭră
Hillswick *Shetland*, 'hɪlzwɪk,
hílzwick
Hinchcliffe, *f.n.*, 'hɪnʃklɪf, hínsh-
-kliff
Hinchingbrooke, Viscountcy of,
'hɪnʃɪŋbrʊk, hínshing-brŏok;
'hɪntʃɪŋbrʊk, híntching-brŏok
Hind, *f.n.*, haɪnd, hīnd; hɪnd,
hinnd
Hindell, *f.n.*, 'hɪndl, híndl
Hinden, *f.n.*, 'hɪndən, híndĕn
Hinderclay *Suffolk*, 'hɪndərkleɪ,
híndĕrklay

Hinderwell *N. Yorks.*, 'hɪndərwel,
híndĕrwel
Hindle, *f.n.*, 'hɪndl, híndl
Hindley, *f.n.*, 'hɪndlɪ, híndli;
'haɪndlɪ, híndli
Hindley *Gtr. M'chester*, 'hɪndlɪ,
híndli
Hindlip *H. & W.*, 'hɪndlɪp, hínd-
lip. *Appropriate also for Baron*
~.
Hindmarsh, *f.n.*, 'haɪndmɑrʃ,
híndmaarsh
Hindolveston, *also spelt* **Hindol-
vestone,** *Norfolk*, 'hɪndl'vestən,
híndlvéstŏn; 'hɪlvɪstən, hílvĕs-
tŏn
Hindsford *Gtr. M'chester*,
'haɪndzfərd, híndzfŏrd
Hindshaw, *f.n.*, 'haɪndʃɔ, hínd-
-shaw
Hindsley, *f.n.*, 'haɪndzlɪ, híndzli
Hindson, *f.n.*, 'haɪndsən, híndssŏn
Hinks, *f.n.*, hɪŋks, hinks
Hints *Staffs.*, hɪnts, hints
Hinwick *Beds.*, 'hɪnɪk, hínnick
Hiorns, *f.n.*, 'haɪərnz, hí-ŏrnz
Hiort *St. Kilda (W. Isles)*, hɜrt,
hurt
Hipkin, *f.n.*, 'hɪpkɪn, hípkin
Hippisley, *f.n.*, 'hɪpslɪ, hípsli
Hirnant *Powys*, 'hɜrnænt, hírnant
Hirnant, River, *Dyfed*, 'hɜrnænt,
hírnant
Hiron, *f.n.*, 'haɪərɒn, híron
Hirons, *f.n.*, 'haɪərɒnz, híronz
Hirsh, *f.n.*, hɜrʃ, hirsh
Hirwaun, *also spelt* **Hirwain,** *Mid
Glam.*, 'hɪərwaɪn, heerwīn;
'hɜrwɪn, hírwin
Hirwaun, *also spelt* **Hirwain,**
River, *Dyfed*, 'hɪərwaɪn, heer-
wīn; 'hɜrwɪn, hírwin
Hiscock, *f.n.*, 'hɪskoʊ, hískō;
'hɪskɒk, hískock
Hiscox, *f.n.*, 'hɪskoʊ, hískō
Hiseman, *f.n.*, 'haɪzmən, hízmăn
Hitchcock, *f.n.*, 'hɪtʃkɒk, hítch-
-kock
Hitchens, *f.n.*, 'hɪtʃənz, hítchĕnz
Hoar, *f.n.*, hɔr, hor
Hoare, *f.n.*, hɔr, hor
Hoathly, East *and* West, *Sussex*,
hoʊθ'laɪ, hōth-lí.
Hoban, *f.n.*, 'hoʊbən, hṓbăn
Hobart, *f.n.*, 'hoʊbɑrt, hṓbaart;
'hæbərt, húbbărt. *The second is
thought by some to be appro-
priate for the name of the 17th-c.
Sir Henry* ~, *judge, and founder
of Blickling Hall in Norfolk.*
Hobart-Hampden, *f.n.*, 'hæbərt
'hæmdən, húbbărt hámdĕn.
*Family name of the Earl of
Buckinghamshire.*

Hobbins, *f.n.,* 'hɒbɪnz, hóbbinz
Hobday, *f.n.,* 'hɒbdeɪ, hóbday
Hobley, *f.n.,* 'hoʊblɪ, hóbli
Hobourn, *f.n.,* 'hoʊbɜrn, hóburn
Hobsbaum, *f.n.,* 'hɒbzbaʊm, hóbzbowm
Hobsbawm, *f.n.,* 'hɒbzbɔm, hóbzbawm
Hoby, *f.n.,* 'hoʊbɪ, hóbi
Hockney, *f.n.,* 'hɒknɪ, hóckni
Hockwold *Norfolk,* 'hɒkwoʊld, hóckwōld
Hodder & Stoughton, *publishers,* 'hɒdər ənd 'stoʊtən, hóddĕr ănd stótŏn
Hoddesdon *Herts.,* 'hɒdzdən, hódzdŏn
Hoddinott, *f.n.,* 'hɒdɪnɒt, hóddinot
Hoddle, *f.n.,* 'hɒdl, hóddl
Hodgart, *f.n.,* 'hɒdʒɜrt, hójjärt
Hodgens, *f.n.,* 'hɒdʒənz, hójjĕnz
Hodghton, *f.n.,* 'hɒdʒtən, hójtŏn
Hodgson, *f.n.,* 'hɒdʒsən, hójssŏn
Hodsoll, *f.n.,* 'hɒdsl, hódssl
Hoenes, *f.n.,* 'hoʊnes, hóness
Hoey, *f.n.,* 'hoʊɪ, hó-i; hɔɪ, hoy
Hoffe, *f.n.,* hɒf, hoff
Hogan, *f.n.,* 'hoʊgən, hógăn
Hogarth, *f.n.,* 'hoʊgɑrθ, hógaarth; 'hɒgərt, hóggärt. *The first is traditional for William* ~, *painter and engraver. The second is usual in Cumbria.*
Hoggan, *f.n.,* 'hɒgən, hóggăn
Hoggard, *f.n.,* 'hɒgɑrd, hóggaard
Hoggart, *f.n.,* 'hɒgərt, hóggärt
Hoggarth, *f.n.,* 'hɒgərt, hóggärt
Hoggeston *Bucks.,* 'hɒgstən, hógstŏn
Hogh, *f.n.,* hoʊ, hō
Hoghton, *f.n.,* 'hɒtən, háwtŏn
Hoghton *Lancs.,* 'hɒtən, háwtŏn
Hoghton Towers *Lancs.,* 'hɒtən 'taʊərz, háwtŏn tówĕrz; 'hoʊtən 'taʊərz, hŏtŏn tówĕrz
Hogsflesh, *f.n.,* 'hoʊfleɪ, hóflay; 'hɒgzfleʃ, hógzflesh
Hogwood, *f.n.,* 'hɒgwʊd, hóg-wōōd
Holbeach *Lincs.,* 'hɒlbɪtʃ, hólbeetch
Holbech, *f.n.,* 'hɒlbɪtʃ, hólbeetch
Holbeche *House Staffs.,* 'hɒlbɪtʃ, hólbeetch
Holbeck *Notts., W. Yorks.,* 'hɒlbek, hólbeck
Holbeton *Devon,* 'hoʊlbɪtən, hólbĕtŏn
Holborn, *f.n.,* 'hɒlbɜrn, hólbŭrn
Holborn *London,* 'hoʊbɜrn, hóbŭrn; 'hoʊlbɜrn, hólbŭrn

Holborn *H'land,* hoʊl'bɜrn, hōlbórn
Holborne, *f.n.,* 'hoʊbɜrn, hóbŭrn
Holbourne *see* **Greenwood of** ~, Viscount
Holbrook *Suffolk,* 'hoʊlbrʊk, hólbrŏŏk
Holbrooke, Joseph (*also spelt* Josef), *composer,* 'hoʊlbrʊk, hólbrŏŏk
Holburn *district of Aberdeen,* 'hoʊbɜrn, hóburn
Holburne of Menstrie Museum *Bath,* 'hoʊbɜrn əv 'menstrɪ, hóbŭrn ŏv ménstri
Holcombe, *f.n.,* 'hoʊlkəm, hólkŏm
Holcombe *Gtr. M'chester,* 'hɒlkəm, hóllkŏm
Holcombe Burnell *Devon,* 'hoʊkəm 'bɜrnəl, hóküm búrnĕl
Holcombe Rogus *Devon,* 'hoʊkəm 'roʊgəs, hókŏm rŏgŭss
Holden, *f.n.,* 'hoʊldən, hóldĕn
Holdenby *Northants.,* 'hoʊldənbɪ, hóldĕnbi. *Formerly* **Holmby,** *q.v.*
Holderness, *f.n.,* 'hoʊldərnɪs, hóldĕrnĕss
Holderness *Humberside,* 'hoʊldərnɪs, hóldĕrnĕss
Holdsworth, *f.n.,* 'hoʊldzwərθ, hóldzwûrth
Holdtum, *f.n.,* 'hoʊltəm, hóltŭm
Hole of Murroes *Tayside,* 'hoʊl əv 'mʌroʊz, hól ŏv múrrōz; 'hoʊl əv 'mɒrɪs, hól ŏv mórriss. *Also called* **Kellas,** *q.v.*
Holford, *f.n.,* 'hɒlfərd, hóllfŏrd
Holford *Somerset,* 'hoʊlfərd, hólfŏrd
Holgate, *f.n.,* 'hoʊlgeɪt, hólgayt
Holinshed, Raphael, *16th-c. chronicler,* 'hɒlɪnʃed, hóllin-shed. *Traditional pronunciation.*
Holker *Cumbria,* 'hʊkər, hŏŏkĕr; 'hɒlkər, hóllkĕr
Holkham *Norfolk,* 'hɒlkəm, hóllkăm; 'hoʊlkəm, hólkăm. *The second is used by the family of the Earl of Leicester and is therefore appropriate for* ~ *Hall. The first is usual in the village.*
Hollabon, *f.n.,* 'hɒləbən, hóllăbŏn
Hollabone, *f.n.,* 'hɒləboʊn, hóllăbōn
Holland, *f.n.,* 'hɒlənd, hólländ
Hollenden, Baron, 'hɒləndən, hóllĕndĕn
Holles, *f.n.,* 'hɒlɪs, hóllĕss
Hollesley *Suffolk,* 'hoʊzlɪ, hŏzli
Hollies *Staffs.,* 'hɒlɪz, hólliz

Hollingshead, *f.n.*, 'hɒlɪŋzhed, hóllingz-hed
Hollingsworth, *f.n.*, 'hɒlɪŋzwɜrθ, hóllingzwurth
Hollingworth, *f.n.*, 'hɒlɪŋwɜrθ, hólling-wurth
Hollins, *f.n.*, 'hɒlɪnz, hóllinz
Hollinshead, *f.n.*, 'hɒlɪnzhed, hóllinz-hed
Hollinwell *Notts.*, 'hɒlɪnwel, hóllinwel
Holm Cultram Abbey *Cumbria*, 'hoʊm 'kʌltrəm, hóm kúltrăm
Holme *Cambs.*, hoʊm, hōm
Holmesdale *Surrey–Kent*, 'hoʊmzdeɪl, hómzdayl. *Appropriate also for Viscount* ~.
Holm Patrick, Baron, 'hoʊm 'pætrɪk, hóm pátrick
Holman, *f.n.*, 'hoʊlmən, hólmăn
Holmbury St. Mary *Surrey*, 'hoʊmbərɪ snt 'mɛərɪ, hómbŭri sĭnt máiri
Holmby *Northants.*, 'hoʊmbɪ, hómbi. *Older name of* **Holdenby,** *q.v.*
Holme, *f.n.*, hoʊm, hōm
Holme *Norfolk*, hoʊm, hōm
Holme Moss *moor on borders of Derby. and W. Yorks.*, 'hoʊm 'mɒs, hóm móss
Holme Pierrepont *Notts.*, 'hoʊm 'pɪərpɒnt, hóm péerpont
Holmer Green *Bucks.*, 'hoʊmər 'grin, hómĕr gréen
Holmes, *f.n.*, hoʊmz, hōmz
Holmes à Court, *f.n.*, 'hoʊmz ə 'kɔrt, hómz ă kórt. *Family name of Baron Heytesbury.*
Holmfirth *W. Yorks.*, 'hoʊm'fɜrθ, hóm-firth
Holmpton *Humberside*, 'hoʊmtən, hómtŏn
Holmstrom, *f.n.*, 'hoʊmstrəm, hómström
Holne *Devon*, hoʊn, hōn
Holness, *f.n.*, 'hoʊlnɪs, hólnĕss
Holnest *Dorset*, 'hɒlnest, hólnest
Holnicote *Somerset*, 'hʌnɪkət, húnnikŏt
Holroyd, *f.n.*, 'hɒlrɔɪd, hólroyd
Holst, Gustav, *composer*, 'gʊstav 'hoʊlst, gŏostaav hólst
Holsworthy *Devon*, 'hoʊlzwɜrðɪ, hólzwurthi
Holt *Clwyd, Norfolk*, hoʊlt, hōlt
Holtby, *f.n.*, 'hoʊltbɪ, hóltbi
Holter, *f.n.*, 'hoʊltər, hóltĕr
Holtham, *f.n.*, 'hoʊlθəm, hól-thăm; 'hoʊθəm, hó-thăm; 'hɒlθəm, hól-thăm
Holton-cum-Beckering *Lincs.*, 'hoʊltən kʌm 'bekərɪŋ, hóltŏn kum béckĕring

Holton Heath *Dorset*, 'hɒltən 'hiθ, hólltŏn héeth
Holtum, *f.n.*, 'hoʊltəm, hóltŭm
Holtye *E. Sussex*, hoʊl'taɪ, hōltí
Holverston *Norfolk*, 'hɒlvərstən, hólvĕrstŏn
Holwell *Dorset*, 'hɒlwəl, hólwĕl
Holwick *Durham*, 'hɒlwɪk, hólwick
Holwill, *f.n.*, 'hɒlwɪl, hólwil
Holybourne *Hants.*, 'hɒlɪbɔrn, hólliborn
Holyhead *Gwynedd*, 'hɒlɪ'hed, hólli-héd; 'hɒlɪhed, hólli-hed
Holyport *Berks.*, 'hɒlɪpɔrt, hólliport
Holyroodhouse, Palace of, *Edinburgh*, 'hɒlɪrud'haʊs, hóllirood-hówss
Holystone *Northd.*, 'hoʊlɪstoʊn, hólistōn
Holytown *S'clyde*, 'hɒlɪtaʊn, hóllitown
Holywell Row *Suffolk*, 'hɒlɪwel 'roʊ, hólliwel rṓ
Holywood *Belfast, D. & G.*, 'hɒlɪwʊd, hólliwŏod
Homa, *f.n.*, 'hoʊmə, hómă
Homan, *f.n.*, 'hoʊmən, hómăn
Homard, *f.n.*, 'hoʊmɑrd, hómaard
Home, *f.n.*, hjum, hewm; hoʊm, hōm. *The first is appropriate for the Earldom of* ~.
Home of the Hirsel, Baron, 'hjum əv ðə 'hɜrsl, héwm ŏv thĕ hírssl
Homer Green *Merseyside*, 'hoʊmər 'grin, hómĕr gréen
Homersfield *Suffolk*, 'hɒmərzfild, hómmĕrzfeeld; 'hʌmərzfild, húmmĕrzfeeld
Homerton *London*, 'hɒmərtən, hómmĕrtŏn. *Appropriate also for* ~ *College, Cambridge.*
Homfray, *f.n.*, 'hɒmfri, hómfri
Honddu, River, *Powys*, 'hɒnðɪ, hónthi
Hone, *f.n.*, hoʊn, hōn
Honer, *f.n.*, 'hoʊnər, hónĕr
Honess, *f.n.*, 'hoʊnes, hóness
Honey, *f.n.*, 'hʌnɪ, húnni
Honeycombe, *f.n.*, 'hʌnɪkoʊm, húnnikōm
Honicknowle *Devon*, 'hɒnɪknoʊl, hónnick-nōl
Honiley *Warwicks.*, 'hɒnɪlɪ, hónnili
Honing *Norfolk*, 'hoʊnɪŋ, hóning
Honingham *Norfolk*, 'hʌnɪŋəm, húnning-ăm
Honington *Lincs.*, 'hɒnɪŋtən, hónningtŏn

Honington *Suffolk*, 'hɒnɪŋtən, hónnĭngtŏn; 'hʌnɪŋtən, hún- nĭngtŏn
Honiton *Devon*, 'hʌnɪtən, húnni- tŏn; 'hɒnɪtən, hónnĭtŏn
Honley *W. Yorks.*, 'hɒnlɪ, hónli
Honney, *f.n.*, 'hʌnɪ, húnni
Honri, *f.n.*, 'hɒnrɪ, hónri
Honywood, *f.n.*, 'hʌnɪwʊd, húnni- wŏŏd
Hoo *Kent*, hu, hoo
Hoodless, *f.n.*, 'hʊdlɪs, hŏŏdlĕss
Hooe *E. Sussex*, hu, hoo
Hooke, *f.n.*, hʊk, hŏŏk
Hookway, *f.n.*, 'hʊkweɪ, hŏŏkway
Hooley, *f.n.*, 'hulɪ, hoóli
Hoo St. Werburgh *Kent*, 'hu snt 'wɜrbərg, hoó sĭnt wérburg
Hooson, *f.n.*, 'husən, hoóssŏn
Hooton Pagnell *S. Yorks.*, 'hutən 'pægnəl, hoótŏn págnĕl; 'hʌtən 'pænl, húttŏn pánl
Hope & Lyne, *theatrical agents*, 'hoʊp ənd 'laɪn, hóp ănd lín
Hopetoun House *Lothian*, 'hoʊp- tən, hŏptŏn. *Appropriate also for the Earl of ~.*
Hopkins, *f.n.*, 'hɒpkɪnz, hópkinz
Hoptrough, *f.n.*, 'hɒptroʊ, hóptrō
Hopwas *Staffs.*, 'hɒpwəs, hóp- wăss; 'hɒpəs, hóppăss
Horabin, *f.n.*, 'hɒrəbɪn, hórrăbin
Horam, *f.n.*, 'hɔrəm, háwrăm
Horan, *f.n.*, 'hɔrən, háwrăn
Horbury, *f.n.*, 'hɔrbərɪ, hórbŭri
Hore-Belisha, Barony of, 'hɔr bə'liʃə, hór bĕlé·eshă
Hore-Ruthven, *f.n.*, 'hɔr 'rɪvən, hór rívvĕn
Horham *Suffolk*, 'hɒrəm, hórrăm
Horkstow *Humberside*, 'hɔrkstoʊ, hórkstō
Horlick, *f.n.*, 'hɔrlɪk, hórlick
Horndean *Hants*, hɔrn'din, horn- deén
Horninglow *Staffs.*, 'hɔrnɪŋloʊ, hórning-lō
Horningsea *Cambs.*, 'hɔrnɪŋsi, hórning-see
Hornsea *Humberside*, 'hɔrnsi, hórnssee
Hornsey *London*, 'hɔrnzɪ, hórnzi
Hornstein, *f.n.*, 'hɔrnstin, hórn- steen
Horrell, *f.n.*, 'hɒrəl, hórrĕl
Horrigan, *f.n.*, 'hɒrɪgən, hórrigăn
Horringer *Suffolk*, 'hɒrɪndʒər, hórrinjĕr
Horrocks, *f.n.*, 'hɒrəks, hórrŏks
Horsbrugh, *f.n.*, 'hɔrsbrə, hórss- bră; 'hɔrzbrə, hórzbră
Horseheath *Cambs.*, 'hɔrshiθ, hórss-heeth
Horsell *Surrey*, 'hɔrsl, hórssl

Horsey, *f.n.*, 'hɔrsɪ, hórssi
Horsey *Norfolk*, 'hɔrsɪ, hórssi
Horsfall, *f.n.*, 'hɔrsfɔl, hórssfawl
Horsfield, *f.n.*, 'hɔrsfild, hórss- feeld
Horforth *W. Yorks.*, 'hɔrsfərθ, hórss-fŏrth
Horsham *W. Sussex*, 'hɔrʃəm, hór-shăm
Horsham-St.-Faith *Norfolk*, 'hɔrʃəm snt 'feɪθ, hór-shăm sĭnt fáyth
Horsley, East *and* West, *Surrey*, 'hɔrzlɪ, hórzli
Horsley Woodhouse *Derby.*, 'hɔrzlɪ 'wʊdhaʊs, hórzli wŏŏd- howss
Horsmonden *Kent*, ˌhɔrzmən'den, horzmŏndén
Horsted Keynes *W. Sussex*, 'hɔrstɪd 'keɪnz, hórsstĕd káynz
Horwich *Gtr. M'chester*, 'hɒrɪtʃ, hórritch
Horwood, *f.n.*, 'hɔrwʊd, hórwŏŏd
Hose, *f.n.*, hoʊz, hōz
Hose, *Leics.*, hoʊz, hōz
Hoseason, *f.n.*, hoʊ'sizən, hōsseézŏn; ˌhoʊsɪ'eɪsən, hōssi- -áyssŏn; ˌhoʊsɪ'æsən, hōssi- -ássŏn
Hosey, *f.n.*, 'hoʊzɪ, hŏzi
Hosford, *f.n.*, 'hɒsfərd, hóssfŏrd
Hosier, *f.n.*, 'hoʊzɪər, hŏzi-ĕr
Hoste, *f.n.*, hoʊst, hŏst
Hotham, *f.n.*, 'hʌðəm, húthăm. *Appropriate also for Baron ~.*
Hotham *Humberside*, 'hʌðəm, húthăm
Hothfield *Kent*, 'hɒθfild, hóth- feeld. *Appropriate also for Baron ~.*
Hotine, *f.n.*, 'hoʊtin, hŏteen
Hoton *Leics.*, 'hoʊtən, hŏtŏn
Hotwells *Avon*, 'hɒtwelz, hótwelz
Houblon, *f.n.*, 'hublŏ, hoóblŏng
Houchen, *f.n.*, 'haʊtʃɪn, hówtchĕn
Houchin, *f.n.*, 'haʊtʃɪn, hówtchin
Hough, *f.n.*, hʌf, huff; hɒf, hoff; haʊ, how
Hough *Ches.*, hʌf, huff
Houghall *Durham*, 'hɒfl, hóffl
Hougham, *f.n.*, 'hʌfəm, húffăm
Hougham *Lincs.*, 'hʌfəm, húffăm
Hough Green *Ches.*, 'hʌf 'grin, húff greén
Hough-on-the-Hill *Lincs.*, 'hʌf ɒn ðə 'hɪl, húff on thē hill; 'hɒf ɒn ðə 'hɪl, hóff on thē hill
Houghton, *f.n.*, 'hɒtən, háwtŏn; 'haʊtən, hówtŏn; 'hoʊtən, hŏtŏn. *The second is appropriate for Douglas ~, politician and broadcaster, later Baron ~ of* **Sowerby**, *q.v.*

Houghton *Cambs.*, 'hoʊtən, hóŏtŏn
Houghton *Hants*, 'hoʊtən, hóŏtŏn;
  'haʊtən, hówtŏn
Houghton *Lancs.*, 'hɔtən, háwtŏn;
  'haʊtən, hówtŏn
Houghton *Norfolk*, 'haʊtən, hów-
  tŏn; 'hoʊtən, hóŏtŏn
Houghton, Glass, *W. Yorks.*,
  'glɑs 'haʊtən, glaáss hówtŏn
Houghton, Great *and* Little,
  Northants., 'hoʊtən, hóŏtŏn
Houghton, Great *and* Little, *W.*
  Yorks., 'haʊtən, hówtŏn
Houghton Bridge *W. Sussex*,
  'hoʊtən 'brɪdʒ, hóŏtŏn bríj;
  'haʊtən 'brɪdʒ, hówtŏn bríj
Houghton Conquest *Beds.*,
  'haʊtən 'kɒŋkwest, hówtŏn
  kónkwest
Houghton-le-Side *Durham*,
  'haʊtən lə 'saɪd, hówtŏn lĕ síd;
  'haʊtənlɪ 'saɪd, hówtŏnli síd
Houghton-le-Spring *Tyne & Wear*,
  'hoʊtən lə 'sprɪŋ, hóŏtŏn lĕ
  spríng; 'hoʊtənlɪ 'sprɪŋ, hóŏtŏnli
  spríng
Houghton of Sowerby, Baron,
  'haʊtən əv 'soʊərbɪ, hówtŏn ŏv
  só-ĕrbi. *See also* **Houghton,** *f.n.*
Houghton-on-the-Hill *Leics.*,
  'hoʊtən ɒn ðə 'hɪl, hóŏtŏn on thĕ
  híll
Houghton Regis *Beds.*, 'haʊtən
  'rɪdʒɪs, hówtŏn reéjiss
Houlden, *f.n.*, 'hoʊldən, hóŏldĕn;
  'huldən, hoóldĕn
Houlder, *f.n.*, 'hoʊldər, hóŏldĕr
Houldsworth, *f.n.*, 'hoʊldzwɜrθ,
  hóŏldzwurth
Houlgate, *f.n.*, 'hoʊlgeɪt, hóŏlgayt
Hoult, *f.n.*, hoʊlt, hŏŏlt
Houlton, *f.n.*, 'hoʊltən, hóŏltŏn
Houndstone *Somerset*, 'haʊnd-
  stən, hówndstŏn
Hounsfield, *f.n.*, 'haʊnzfɪld,
  hównzfeeld
Hourd, *f.n.*, hʊərd, hoórd
Hourigan, *f.n.*, 'hʊərɪgən, hoóri-
  găn
Hourn, Loch, *H'land*, hʊərn,
  hoórn
Housden, *f.n.*, 'haʊzdən, hówzdĕn
House, *f.n.*, haʊs, howss
House of Gight *Grampian*, 'haʊs
  əv 'gɪxt, hówss ŏv gícht
Housego, *f.n.*, 'haʊsgoʊ, hówss-
  gō
Househillwood *Glasgow*, 'haʊzl-
  wʊd, hówzl-wŏŏd
Housley, *f.n.*, 'haʊzlɪ, hówzli
Housman, *f.n.*, 'haʊsmən, hówss-
  măn. *This is appropriate for*
  A. E. ~, *poet, and for his*
  brother Laurence, artist and

playwright. The latter particu-
larly confirmed that they
pronounced it with -s, not -z.
Houson, *f.n.*, 'haʊsən, hówssŏn
Houston, *f.n.*, 'hustən, hoóstŏn;
  'hjustən, héwsstŏn; 'haʊstən,
  hówsstŏn
Houston *Lothian, S'clyde*, 'hustən,
  hoóstŏn
Houstoun, *f.n.*, 'hustən, hoóstŏn
Houthuesen, *f.n.*, 'haʊtʃɪsən,
  hówtchĕssŏn; 'haʊthjuzən,
  hówt-hewzĕn. *The second is*
  appropriate for the painter
  Albert ~.
Houton *Orkney*, 'haʊtən, hówtŏn.
  Appropriate also for ~ *Bay.*
Hove *E. Sussex*, hoʊv, hōv
Hovell, *f.n.*, 'hɒvl, hóvvl; 'hoʊvl,
  hóvl
Hoveringham *Notts.*, 'hɒvərɪŋəm,
  hóvvĕring-ăm
Hovers, *f.n.*, 'hoʊvərz, hóvĕrz
Hoveton *Norfolk*, 'hɒftən, hóff-
  tŏn; 'hʌftən, húfftŏn; 'hɒvɪtən,
  hóvvĕtŏn
Hovey, *f.n.*, 'hoʊvɪ, hóvi
Hovingham *N. Yorks.*, 'hɒvɪŋəm,
  hóvving-ăm
Howard, *C.n. and f.n.*, 'haʊərd,
  hówărd
Howard de Walden, Baron,
  'haʊərd də 'wɔldən, hówărd dĕ
  wáwldĕn
Howard of Glossop, Baron,
  'haʊərd əv 'glɒsəp, hówărd ŏv
  glóssŏp
Howard of Penrith, Baron,
  'haʊərd əv 'penrɪθ, hówărd ŏv
  pénrith
Howarth, *f.n.*, 'haʊərθ, hówărth
Howatch, *f.n.*, 'haʊətʃ, hówătch
Howden, *f.n.*, 'haʊdən, hówdĕn
Howden *Humberside, Lothian*,
  'haʊdən, hówdĕn
Howden-le-Wear *Durham*,
  'haʊdən lə 'wɪər, hówdĕn lĕ
  weér
Howdon-on-Tyne *Tyne & Wear*,
  'haʊdən ɒn 'taɪn, hówdŏn on
  tín
Howe, Earl, haʊ, how
Howe, *f.n.*, haʊ, how
Howell, *f.n.*, 'haʊəl, hówĕl
Howells, *f.n.*, 'haʊəlz, hówĕlz
Howe of Corrichie *Grampian*,
  'haʊ əv 'kɒrɪxɪ, hów ŏv kór-
  richi
Howes, *f.n.*, haʊz, howz
Howgill, *f.n.*, 'haʊgɪl, hówgil
Howick *Northd.*, 'hoʊɪk, hŏ-ick
Howick of Glendale, Baron,
  'hoʊɪk əv glen'deɪl, hŏ-ick ŏv
  glendáyl

Howie, *f.n.*, 'haʊɪ, hów-i
Howitt, *f.n.*, 'haʊɪt, hów-it
Howlett, *f.n.*, 'haʊlɪt, hówlĕt
Howley *Somerset*, 'hoʊlɪ, hŏli
Howorth, *f.n.*, 'haʊərθ, hówŭrth
Howse, *f.n.*, haʊz, howz; haʊs, howss
Howson, *f.n.*, 'haʊsən, hówssŏn
Hoxne *Suffolk*, 'hɒksən, hócksĕn
Hoy Island *Orkney*, hɔɪ, hoy
Hoyer, *f.n.*, 'hɔɪər, hóyĕr
Hozier, *f.n.*, 'hoʊzɪər, hŏzi-ĕr
Huband, *f.n.*, 'hjubænd, héwband
Hubback, *f.n.*, 'hʌbək, húbbăk
Hubbard, *f.n.*, 'hʌbərd, húbbărd
Hubbart, *f.n.*, 'hʌbərt, húbbărt
Huby *N. Yorks.*, 'hjubɪ, héwbi
Huccaby *Devon*, 'hʌkəbɪ, húckăbi
Hucclecote *Glos.*, 'hʌklkoʊt, húcklkŏt
Hudard, *f.n.*, 'hʌdərd, húddărd
Hudis, *f.n.*, 'hjudɪs, héwdiss
Hudson, *f.n.*, 'hʌdsən, húdssŏn
Hudspith, *f.n.*, 'hʌdspɪθ, húdss-pith
Hueffer, Ford Madox, *author*, 'fɔrd 'mædəks 'hʷefər, fórd máddŏcks whéffĕr. *Original name of* **Ford Madox Ford,** *q.v.*
Huehns, *f.n.*, 'hjuɪnz, héw-ĕnz
Huelin, *f.n.*, 'hjulɪn, héwlin
Huff, *f.n.*, hʌf, huff
Hugessen, *f.n.*, 'hjugɪsən, héw-gĕssĕn
Huggate *Humberside*, 'hʌgɪt, húggit
Hugh, *C.n.*, hju, hew
Hughes, *f.n.*, hjuz, hewz
Hughes, Arwel, *composer*, 'ɑrwel 'hjuz, aárwel héwz
Hughes, Owain Arwel, *conductor*, 'oʊaɪn 'ɑrwel 'hjuz, ŏ-īn aárwel héwz
Hughesdon, *f.n.*, 'hjuzdən, héwz-dŏn
Hughson, *f.n.*, 'hjusən, héwssŏn
Hugill, *f.n.*, 'hjugɪl, héwgil
Hugill *Cumbria*, 'hjugɪl, héwgil
Huguenin, *f.n.*, 'hjugənɪn, héw-gĕnin
Huhne, *f.n.*, hjun, hewn
Huish, *f.n.*, 'hjuɪʃ, héw-ish; hʌʃ, hush
Huish Champflower *Somerset*, 'hjuɪʃ 'tʃæmpflaʊər, héwish chámpflowĕr
Huish Episcopi *Somerset*, 'hjuɪʃ ə'pɪskəpɪ, héwish ĕpísskŏpi
Hulbert, *f.n.*, 'hʌlbərt, húlbĕrt
Hulke, *f.n.*, hʌlk, hulk
Hullah, *f.n.*, 'hʌlə, húllă
Hullavington *Wilts.*, hə'lævɪŋtən, hŭlávvingtŏn; 'hʌlɪŋtən, húllingtŏn

Hulme, *f.n.*, hjum, hewm
Hulme, *Staffs.*, hjum, hewm
Hulse, *f.n.*, hʌls, hulss
Humber, River, *Humberside*, 'hʌmbər, húmbĕr
Hume, *f.n.*, hjum, hewm
Hummel, *f.n.*, 'hʌml, húmml
Hummerston, *f.n.*, 'hʌmərstən, húmmĕrstŏn
Humpherston, *f.n.*, 'hʌmfərstən, húmfĕrstŏn
Humphrey, *C.n. and f.n.*, 'hʌmfrɪ, húmfri
Humphreys, *f.n.*, 'hʌmfrɪz, húmfriz
Humphries, *f.n.*, 'hʌmfrɪz, húmfriz
Humpoletz, *f.n.*, 'hʌmpəlɪts, húmpŏlĕts
Humshaugh *Northd.*, 'hʌmzhɑf, húmz-haaf
Huna *H'land*, 'hunə, hoónă
Huncote *Leics.*, 'hʌŋkət, húnkŏt
Hungarton, Barony of, 'hʌŋgərtən, húng-gărtŏn
Hungarton, *also spelt* **Hungerton,** *Leics.*, 'hʌŋgərtən, húng-gărtŏn
Hungerford *Berks.*, 'hʌŋgərfɔrd, húng-gĕrford; 'hʌŋgərfərd, húng-gĕrfŏrd. *The second is also appropriate for Baron* ∼.
Hungerford Bridge *London*, 'hʌŋgərfərd, húng-gĕrfŏrd
Hungerford Newtown *Berks.*, 'hʌŋgərfərd 'njutaʊn, húng-gĕrfŏrd néwtown
Hungerton *see* **Hungarton**
Hunmanby *N. Yorks.*, 'hʌnmənbɪ, húnmănbi
Hunslet *W. Yorks.*, 'hʌnslɪt, húnsslĕt
Hunstanton *Norfolk*, hʌn'stæntən, hunsstántŏn; 'hʌnstən, húnsstŏn
Hunter, *f.n.*, 'hʌntər, húntĕr
Hunterian, *pertaining to John Hunter, 18th-c. Scottish surgeon*, hʌn'tɪərɪən, huntéeriän
Huntingdon *Cambs.*, 'hʌntɪŋdən, húntingdŏn. *Appropriate also for the Earl of* ∼.
Huntly *Grampian*, 'hʌntlɪ, húntli
Huntshaw *Devon*, 'hʌnʃɔ, hún--shaw
Huntspill *Somerset*, 'hʌntspɪl, húntspil
Hunwick *Durham*, 'hʌnwɪk, húnwick
Hurcomb, *f.n.*, 'hɜrkəm, húrkŏm
Hurdis, *f.n.*, 'hɜrdɪs, húrdiss
Hurll, *f.n.*, hɜrl, hurl
Hurndall, *f.n.*, 'hɜrndl, húrndl
Hurrell, *f.n.*, 'hʌrəl, húrrĕl; 'hʊərəl, hŏŏrĕl

Hurren, *f.n.,* 'hʌrən, húrrĕn
Hursley *Hants,* 'hɜrzlɪ, húrzli
Hurstmonceaux *or* **Hurstmon-**
ceaux *see* **Herstmonceux**
Hurstpierpoint *W. Sussex,*
'hɜrstpɪər'pɔɪnt, húrstpeer-
póynt
Hush, *f.n.,* hʌʃ, hush
Huskinson, *f.n.,* 'hʌskɪnsən,
hússkinssŏn
Huskisson, *f.n.,* 'hʌskɪsən, húss-
kissŏn
Hussein, *f.n.,* hʊ'seɪn, hŏōssáyn
Hussey, *f.n.,* 'hʌsɪ, hússi
Hutber, *f.n.,* 'hʌtbər, hútbĕr
Hutchens, *f.n.,* 'hʌtʃɪnz, hútchĕnz
Hutcheon, *f.n.,* 'hʌtʃən, hútchĕn
Hutcheson, *f.n.,* 'hʌtʃɪsən,
hútchĕssŏn
Hutchings, *f.n.,* 'hʌtʃɪŋz, hútch-
ingz
Hutchinson, *f.n.,* 'hʌtʃɪnsən,
hútchinssŏn
Huth, *f.n.,* huθ, hooth
Hutton Buscel, *also spelt* **Hutton**
Bushel *N. Yorks.,* 'hʌtən 'bʊʃl,
húttŏn bŏŏshl
Hutton-le-Hole *N. Yorks.,* 'hʌtən
lɪ 'hoʊl, húttŏn-li-hŏl
Huw, *Welsh C.n.,* hju, hew
Huxley, Aldous, *author,* 'ɔldəs
'hʌkslɪ, áwldŭss húcksli
Huyton *Merseyside,* 'haɪtən,
hītŏn
Huyton with Roby *Merseyside,*
'haɪtən wɪð 'roʊbɪ, hītŏn with
rŏbi
Huzzard, *f.n.,* 'hʌzɑrd, húzzaard
Hyacinth, saint, 'haɪəsɪnθ, hí-
-ăssinth
Hyde, *f.n.,* haɪd, hīd
Hydleman, *f.n.,* 'haɪdlmən,
hídlmăn
Hykeham, North *and* South,
Lincs., 'haɪkəm, híkăm
Hylton, *f.n.,* 'hɪltən, híltŏn
Hyman, *f.n.,* 'haɪmən, hímăn
Hymans, *f.n.,* 'haɪmənz, hímănz
Hynd, *f.n.,* haɪnd, hīnd
Hyndburn *Lancs.,* 'haɪndbɜrn,
hínd-burn
Hyndhope *Borders,* 'haɪndhoʊp,
hínd-hŏp
Hyndland *Glasgow,* 'haɪndlənd,
híndlănd
Hyndley, Viscountcy of, 'haɪndlɪ,
híndli
Hyndman, *f.n.,* 'haɪndmən,
híndmăn
Hyslop, *f.n.,* 'hɪzləp, hízlŏp
Hytch, *f.n.,* haɪtʃ, hītch
Hytner, *f.n.,* 'haɪtnər, hítnĕr
Hywel, *Welsh C.n.,* 'haʊəl,
hówĕl

I

Ia, saint, 'iə, ée-ă
Iago, *Welsh C.n.,* 'jɑgoʊ, yaʹágō
Iain, *C.n., also spelt* **Ian,** 'iən,
ée-ăn
I'Anson, *f.n.,* aɪ'ænsən, ī-ánssŏn
Ianthe, *C.n.,* aɪ'ænθɪ, ī-ánthi
Iball, *f.n.,* 'aɪbɔl, íbawl
Ibbs, *f.n.,* ɪbz, ibbz
Ibrox Park *Glasgow,* 'aɪbrɒks
'pɑrk, íbrocks paʹark
Ibstone *Bucks.,* 'ɪbstən, íbbstŏn
Iceni, *ancient British tribe,*
aɪ'sɪnaɪ, īsseénī
Iceton, *f.n.,* 'aɪstən, ísstŏn
Icke, *f.n.,* aɪk, īk ; ɪk, ick
Ickes, *f.n.,* 'ɪkɪs, ickĕss
Icklesham *E. Sussex,* 'ɪklʃəm,
íckl-shăm
Icomb *Glos.,* 'ɪkəm, íckŏm
Iddesleigh *Devon,* 'ɪdzlɪ, ídzli.
Appropriate also for the Earl of
~.
Iddon, *f.n.,* 'ɪdən, íddŏn
Ide *Devon,* id, eed
Ideford *Devon,* 'ɪdfərd, ídfŏrd
Iden, *f.n.,* 'aɪdən, ídĕn
Iden *E. Sussex,* 'aɪdən, ídĕn
Idiens, *f.n.,* 'ɪdɪənz, íddiĕnz
Idle *W.Yorks.,* 'aɪdl, ídl
Idle, River, *Notts.,* 'aɪdl, ídl
Idless *Cornwall,* 'ɪdlɪs, éedlĕss
Idloes, *Welsh C.n.,* 'ɪdlɔɪs, ídloyss
Idmiston *Wilts.,* 'ɪdmɪstən,
ídmisstŏn
Idridgehay *Derby.,* 'aɪdrɪdʒheɪ,
ídrij-hay ; 'ɪðəseɪ, ithĕssay
Idris, *C.n.,* 'ɪdrɪs, ídriss
Idwal, *Welsh C.n.,* 'ɪdwəl, ídwăl
Iestyn, *Welsh C.n.,* 'jestɪn,
yéstin
Ieuan, *Welsh C.n.,* 'jaɪjən, yī-yăn
Ievers, *f.n.,* 'aɪvərz, ívĕrz
Ife, *f.n.,* aɪf, īf
Ifield, *f.n.,* 'aɪfild, ífeeld
Ifold *W. Sussex,* 'aɪfoʊld, í-fōld
Ifor, *Welsh C.n.,* 'ivɔr, éevor ;
'aɪvər, ívŏr
Ightham, *f.n.,* 'aɪtəm, ítăm
Ightham *Kent,* 'aɪtəm, ítăm
Igoe, *f.n.,* 'aɪgoʊ, ígō
Iken *Suffolk,* 'aɪkən, íkĕn
Ikerrin, Viscount, 'aɪkerɪn,
í-kerrin
Ikin, *f.n.,* 'aɪkɪn, íkin
Ilam *Staffs.,* 'aɪləm, ílăm
Ilbert, *f.n.,* 'ɪlbərt, ílbĕrt
Ilchester *Somerset,* 'ɪltʃɪstər,
íltchĕstĕr. *Appropriate also for*
the Earl of ~.
Iles, *f.n.,* aɪlz, īlz

Ilett, *f.n.*, 'aılıt, ílĕt

Ilford *London*, 'ılfərd, ilfŏrd

Iliffe, *f.n.*, 'aılıf, íliff. *Appropriate also for Baron* ~.

Iline, *f.n.*, 'aılaın, ílīn

Ilkeston *Derby*, 'ılkıstən, ílkĕstŏn. *Appropriate also for the Barony of* ~.

Ilketshall *Suffolk*, 'ılkıʃɔl, ílkĕ-shawl. *Appropriate for the villages of* ~ *St. Andrew,* ~ *St. John,* ~ *St. Lawrence, and* ~ *St. Margaret.*

Ilkley *W. Yorks.*, 'ılklı, ílkli

Illingworth, *f.n.*, 'ılıŋwɜrθ, illing-wurth; 'ılıŋwərθ, ílling-wŭrth

Illogan *Cornwall*, ı'lʌgən, illúggăn

Illtud, *Welsh C.n.*, 'ıɬtıd, iḥltid

Illtyd, saint, 'ıɬtıd, iḥltid

Ilmer *Bucks.*, 'ılmər, ílmĕr

Ilott, *f.n.*, 'aılɒt, ílot

Ilsley, East *and* West, *Berks.*, 'ılzlı, ílzli

Ilsley Down *Berks.*, 'ılzlı, ílzli

Imbusch, *f.n.*, 'ımbʊʃ, ím-bōōsh

Imeson, *f.n.*, 'aımısən, ímĕssŏn; 'aımsən, ímssŏn

Imhof, *f.n.*, 'ımhoʊf, ím-hōf

Imi, *f.n.*, 'imı, eémi

Imison, *f.n.*, 'aımısən, ímissŏn

Imisson, *f.n.*, 'ımısən, ímmissŏn

Imlach, *f.n.*, 'ımləx, ímlăch

Immingham *Humberside*, 'ımıŋəm, ímming-ăm

Imogen, *C.n.*, 'ımədʒən, ímmŏjĕn

Imray, *f.n.*, 'ımreı, ímray

Ince, *f.n.*, ıns, inss

Inchcape, Earl of, ınʃ'keıp, insh-káyp

Inchcruin *Central*, ınʃ'kruın, insh-króo-in

Inchinnan *S'clyde*, ınʃ'ınən, insh-ínnăn

Inchiquin, Baron of, 'ıntʃıkwın, íntchikwin

Inchmahome *Central*, 'ınʃmə-'hoʊm, ínshmă-hŏm

Inchnadamph *H'land*, ‚ınʃnə-'dæmf, inshnădámf

Inchrye Abbey *Fife*, ınʃ'raı, insh-rī́

Inchture *Tayside*, ınʃ'tjʊər, insh-tyŏ̄or

Inchtuthil *Tayside*, ınʃ'tjuθıl, insh-téw-thil

Inchyra *Tayside*, ınʃ'aıərə, inshíră. *Appropriate also for Baron* ~.

Ind Coope, *brewers*, 'ınd 'kup, índ koóp

Ingatestone *Essex*, 'ıŋgətstoʊn, íng-găt-stōn

Inge, *f.n.*, ıŋ, ing

Ingelow, *f.n.*, 'ındʒıloʊ, ínjĕlō

Ingestre, Viscount, 'ıŋgıstrı, íng-gĕstri

Ingham, *f.n.*, 'ıŋəm, íng-ăm

Ingleton *N. Yorks.*, 'ıŋgltən, íng-gltŏn

Inglis, *f.n.*, 'ıŋglz, ing-glz; 'ıŋglıs, ing-gliss. *The first is Scottish, the second Northern Irish and southern English.*

Ingold, *f.n.*, 'ıŋgoʊld, íng-gōld

Ingoldisthorpe *Norfolk*, 'ıŋglz-θɔrp, íng-glz-thorp

Ingliston *Lothian*, 'ıŋglztən, íng-glz-tŏn; 'ıŋglstən, ing-glsstŏn

Ingoldmells *Lincs.*, 'ıŋgəmelz, íng-gŏmelz

Ingpen, *f.n.*, 'ıŋpen, íng-pen

Ingram, *f.n.*, 'ıŋgrəm, íng-grăm

Ingrams, *f.n.*, 'ıŋgrəmz, íng-grămz

Ingrebourne, River, *Essex*, 'ıŋgrıbɔrn, ing-grĕborn

Ingress, *f.n.*, 'ıŋgrıs, íng-grĕss

Ingrey, *f.n.*, 'ıŋgrı, íng-gri

Ings, *f.n.*, ıŋz, ingz

Ingwersen, *f.n.*, 'ıŋwərsən, íng-wĕrssĕn

Inishanier *Co. Down*, ‚ınıʃ'ænıər, innish-ánni-ĕr

Inishargie *Co. Down*, ‚ınıʃ'ɑrgı, innish-aárgi

Inisharoan *Co. Down*, ‚ınıʃə'roʊn, innish-ărŏn

Inkpen *Berks.*, 'ıŋkpen, ínkpen

Inman, *f.n.*, 'ınmən, ínmăn

Innellan *S'clyde*, ın'elən, inéllăn

Innerleithen *Borders*, ‚ınər'liðən, innĕrleéthĕn

Innes, *f.n.*, 'ınıs, ínnĕss; 'ınız, ínnĕz

Innes of Edingight, *f.n.*, 'ınıs əv 'idın'gıxt, ínnĕss ŏv eédin-gícht

Innes of Learney, Sir Thomas, *late Lord Lyon King of Arms*, 'ınıs əv 'lɜrnı, ínnĕss ŏv láirni

Innes-Ker, *f.n.*, 'ınıs 'kɑr, ínnĕss kaár; 'ınıs 'kɛər, ínnĕss káir. *The first is appropriate for the Duke of Roxburghe's family name.*

Inns, *f.n.*, ınz, innz

Insch *Grampian*, ıntʃ, intch

Instone, *f.n.*, 'ınstoʊn, ínstōn

Instow *Devon*, 'ınstoʊ, ínstō

Intake *S. Yorks.*, 'ınteık, íntayk. *Appropriate for the districts of this name in both Doncaster and Sheffield.*

Inver *H'land*, 'ınvər, ínvĕr. *Appropriate also for the Loch and River of this name.*

Inverallochy *Grampian*, ‚ınvər-'æləxı, invĕrálŏchi

Inveraray *S'clyde*, ˌɪnvər'ɛərɪ, invĕráiri; ˌɪnvər'ɛərə, invĕráiră
Inverarity *Tayside*, ˌɪnvər'ærɪtɪ, invĕrárriti
Inverbervie *Grampian*, ˌɪnvər-'bɜrvɪ, invĕrbérvi
Invereighty *Tayside*, ˌɪnvər'aɪtɪ, invĕríti
Inverewe House *H'land*, ˌɪnvər'ju, invĕr-yóo
Inverey *Grampian*, ˌɪnvər'eɪ, invĕráy
Inverinate *H'land*, ˌɪnvər'ɪnɪt, invĕréenit
Inverkeilor *Tayside*, ˌɪnvər'kilər, invĕrkéelŏr
Inverkeithing *Fife*, ˌɪnvər'kiðɪŋ, invĕrkéething
Inverlochy *H'land*, ˌɪnvər'lɒxɪ, invĕrlóchi
Invermoriston *H'land*, ˌɪnvər-'mɒrɪstən, invĕrmórristŏn
Inverness *H'land*, ˌɪnvər'nes, invĕrnéss
Invernessian, *native of* **Inverness**, ˌɪnvər'niziən, invĕrneéziăn
Inverquharity *Tayside*, ˌɪnvər-'hwɒrɪtɪ, invĕrwháwriti; ˌɪnvər-'hwɑrɪtɪ, invĕrwháariti
Inversnaid *Central*, ˌɪnvər'sneɪd, invĕr-snáyd
Inveruglas *S'clyde*, ˌɪnvər'ugləs, invĕróoglăss
Inverurie *Grampian*, ˌɪnvər'ʊərɪ, invĕróŏri
Ioan, *Welsh C.n.*, 'jouən, yó-ăn
Iochdor *S. Uist*, 'iəxkər, ee--ŏchkăr. *See also* **Eochar.**
Iolo, *Welsh C.n.*, 'joulou, yólō
Iona *S'clyde*, aɪ'ounə, ī-ṓnă
Ionides, *f.n.*, aɪ'ɒnɪdiz, ī-ónnideez
Ions, *f.n.*, 'iənz, ee-ŏnz
Iorns, *f.n.*, 'aɪərnz, í-ŭrnz
Iorwerth, *Welsh C.n.*, 'jɔrwɛərθ, yór-wairth
Iping *W. Sussex*, 'aɪpɪŋ, íping
Ipplepen *Devon*, 'ɪplpen, ípplpen
Ipswich *Suffolk*, 'ɪpswɪtʃ, ips-witch
Iredell, *f.n.*, 'aɪərdel, írdel
Iremonger, *f.n.*, 'aɪərmʌŋgər, írmung-gĕr
Ireby, Low, *Cumbria*, 'aɪərbɪ, írbi
Irens, *f.n.*, 'aɪərənz, írĕnz
Ireshopeburn *Durham*, 'aɪshəp-bɜrn, íss-hŏp-burn
Ireson, *f.n.*, 'aɪərsən, írssŏn
Irfonwy, *Welsh C.n.*, ɜr'vɒnʊɪ, irvónnŏō-i
Irlam *Gtr. M'chester*, 'ɜrləm, írlăm
Irlam o' the Height *Gtr. M'chester*, 'ɜrləm ə 'ðaɪt, írlăm ŏ thít

Irnham *Lincs*,. 'ɜrnəm, írnăm
Irongray *D. & G.*, 'aɪərəngreɪ, íron-gray
Irthlingborough *Northants.*, 'ɜrθ-lɪŋbərə, irthling-bŭră
Irvine, *f.n.*, 'ɜrvɪn, írvin
Irvine *S'clyde*, 'ɜrvɪn, írvin
Irvinestown *Co. Fermanagh*, 'ɜrvɪnztaun, írvinztown
Irving, *f.n.*, 'ɜrvɪŋ, írving
Irwell, River, *Lancs.*, 'ɜrwel, írwel
Isacke, *f.n.*, 'aɪzək, ízăk
Isador, *f.n.*, 'ɪzədɔr, ízzădor
Isard, *f.n.*, 'ɪzɑrd, ízzaard
Isbister, *f.n.*, 'aɪzbɪstər, ízbisstĕr; 'ɪzbɪstər, ízzbisstĕr
Ise Brook *Northants.*, 'aɪzə brʊk, ízĕ brŏŏk
Isel *Cumbria*, 'aɪzl, ízl
Isepp, *f.n.*, 'izep, eézepp
Isfield *E. Sussex*, 'ɪsfɪld, íssfeeld
Isham, *f.n.*, 'aɪʃəm, í-shăm
Isham *Northants.*, 'aɪʃəm, í-shăm
Isherwood, *f.n.*, 'ɪʃərwʊd, íshĕr-wŏōd
Isington *Hants*, 'ɪzɪŋtən, ízzingtŏn
Isis, River, *Oxon.*, 'aɪsɪs, íssiss
Islandmagee *Co. Antrim*, ˌaɪlənd-mə'gi, iländmăgée
Islay *S'clyde*, 'aɪlə, ílă; 'aɪleɪ, ílay
Isleham *Cambs.*, 'aɪzləm, ízl-ăm
Isle of Thanet *Kent*, 'aɪl əv 'θænɪt, íl ŏv thánnĕt
Isle of Wight 'aɪl əv 'waɪt, íl ŏv wít
Isleworth *London*, 'aɪzlwɜrθ, ízl--wurth; 'aɪzlwərθ, ízl-würth
Isley Walton *Leics.*, 'ɪzlɪ 'wɒltən, ízzli wáwltŏn
Islington *London*, 'ɪzlɪŋtən, ízzling-tŏn
Islip, *f.n.*, 'ɪzlɪp, ízlip. *Appropriate also for the ~ Chapel in Westminster Abbey.*
Islip *Northants.*, *Oxon.*, 'aɪslɪp, ísslip
Islwyn, *Welsh C.n.*, 'ɪsluɪn, ísslŏō--in
Ismay, *f.n.*, 'ɪzmeɪ, ízmay. *Appropriate also for the Barony of ~.*
Ison, *f.n.*, 'aɪsən, íssŏn
Issigonis, Sir Alec, *car designer*, ˌɪsɪ'gounɪs, issigŏniss
Istance, *f.n.*, 'aɪstəns, ístănss
Isted, *f.n.*, 'aɪsted, ístedd
Itchen *Hants*, 'ɪtʃən, ítchĕn
Itchenor *W. Sussex*, 'ɪtʃɪnər, ítchĕnor
Ithell, *f.n.*, 'aɪθl, íthl
Ithon, River, *Powys*, 'aɪθɒn, íthon
Ivay, *f.n.*, 'aɪveɪ, ívay
Iveagh, Earl of, 'aɪvə, ívă
Iveagh *Co. Down*, 'aɪveɪ, ívay
Ivelaw, *f.n.*, 'aɪvɪlɔ, ívĕlaw

Iver *Bucks.*, 'aɪvər, ívĕr
Iver Heath *Bucks.*, 'aɪvər 'hiθ,
  ívĕr heéth
Ives, *f.n.*, aɪvz, īvz
Iveson, *f.n.*, 'aɪvsən, ív-sŏn
Ivimey, *f.n.*, 'aɪvɪmɪ, ívimi
Ivin, *f.n.*, 'aɪvɪn, ívin
Ivington *H. & W.*, 'ɪvɪŋtən,
  ívvingtŏn
Iwade *Kent*, 'aɪ'weɪd, í-wáyd
Iwan, *Welsh C.n. and f.n.*, 'juən,
  yoö-ăn
Iwerne, River, *Dorset*, 'juɜrn,
  yoö-ern
Iwerne Courtney *Dorset*, 'juɜrn
  'kɔrtnɪ, yoö-ern kórtni
Ixer, *f.n.*, 'ɪksər, icksĕr
Izard, *f.n.*, 'aɪzɑrd, ízaard; 'aɪzərd,
  ízărd; 'ɪzərd, ízzărd
Izatt, *f.n.*, 'aɪzət, ízăt
Izbicki, *f.n.*, 'ɪzbɪkɪ, ízbicki
Izen, *f.n.*, 'aɪzən, ízĕn
Izod, *f.n.*, 'ɪzəd, ízzŏd
Izzard, *f.n.*, 'ɪzɑrd, ízzaard; 'ɪzərd,
  ízzărd
Izzett, *f.n.*, 'aɪzɪt, ízĕt

J

Jackett, *f.n.*, 'dʒækɪt, jáckĕt
Jackson, *f.n.*, 'dʒæksən, jácksŏn
Jacobi, *f.n.*, 'dʒækəbɪ, jáckŏbi
Jacobs, *f.n.*, 'dʒeɪkəbz, jáykŏbz
Jacobstow *Cornwall*, 'dʒeɪkəb-
  stoʊ, jáykŏb-stō
Jacoby, *f.n.*, dʒə'koʊbɪ, jăkŏbi;
  'dʒækəbɪ, jáckŏbi
Jacot, *f.n.*, 'dʒækoʊ, jáckō
Jacottet, *f.n.*, 'dʒækəteɪ, jáckŏtay
Jacques, *f.n.*, dʒeɪks, jayks;
  dʒæks, jacks. *The first is appro-
  priate for Baron ~.*
Jaeger, *f.n.*, 'jeɪgər, yáygĕr
Jaekel, *f.n.*, 'dʒeɪkl, jáykl
Jaffe, *f.n.*, 'dʒæfɪ, jáffi
Jaffé, *f.n.*, 'dʒæfeɪ, jáffay
Jaffray, *f.n.*, 'dʒæfrɪ, jáffri
Jago, *f.n.*, 'dʒeɪgoʊ, jáygō
Jagoe, *f.n.*, 'dʒeɪgoʊ, jáygō
Jaguer, *f.n.*, 'dʒægjʊər, jág-yōōr
Jakins, *f.n.*, 'dʒeɪkɪnz, jáykinz
Jakobi, *f.n.*, 'dʒækəbɪ, jáckŏbi
Jalland, *f.n.*, 'dʒælənd, jálănd
Jamblin, *f.n.*, 'dʒæmblɪn, jám-
  blin
James, *C.n. and f.n.*, dʒeɪmz,
  jaymz
Jameson, *f.n.*, 'dʒemɪsən, jémmis-
  sŏn; 'dʒɪmɪsən, jímmissŏn;
  'dʒeɪmsən, jáymssŏn; 'dʒæmɪ-

sən, jámmissŏn; 'dʒeɪmɪsən,
  jáymissŏn
Jamieson, *f.n.*, 'dʒɪmɪsən, jímmis-
  sŏn; 'dʒemɪsən, jémmissŏn;
  'dʒeɪmɪsən, jáymissŏn; 'dʒæmɪ-
  sən, jámmissŏn
Janis, *f.n.*, 'dʒænɪs, jánniss
Janisch, *f.n.*, 'jeɪnɪʃ, yáynish
Janson, *f.n.*, 'dʒænsən, jánssŏn
Japhet, *f.n.*, 'dʒæfɪt, jáffĕt
Jaque, *f.n.*, dʒeɪk, jayk
Jaques, *f.n.*, dʒeɪks, jayks;
  dʒæks, jacks
Jaquest, *f.n.*, 'dʒeɪkwɪst, jáyk-
  wĕst
Jaray, *f.n.*, 'dʒæreɪ, járray
Jarché, *f.n.*, 'dʒɑrʃeɪ, jaár-shay
Jardine, *f.n.*, 'dʒɑrdin, jaárdeen
Jarlshof *Shetland*, 'jɑrlzhɒf,
  yaárlz-hoff
Jarman, *f.n.*, 'dʒɑrmən, jaármăn
Jarred, *f.n.*, 'dʒærəd, járrĕd
Jarrett, *f.n.*, 'dʒærɪt, járrĕt
Jarvis, *f.n.*, 'dʒɑrvɪs, jaárviss
Jasper, *C.n. and f.n.*, 'dʒæspər,
  jásspĕr
Jast, *f.n.*, dʒæst, jasst
Jay, *f.n.*, dʒeɪ, jay
Jaywick *Essex*, 'dʒeɪwɪk, jáy-
  -wick
Jeacock, *f.n.*, 'dʒikɒk, jéekock
Jeacocke, *f.n.*, 'dʒeɪkoʊ, jáykō
Jeaffreson, *f.n.*, 'dʒefərsən,
  jéffĕrssŏn; 'dʒefrɪsən, jéfrĕssŏn
Jeal, *f.n.*, dʒil, jeel
Jeans, *f.n.*, dʒinz, jeenz
Jeater, *f.n.*, 'dʒitər, jéetĕr
Jeavons, *f.n.*, 'dʒevənz, jévvŏnz
Jeayes, *f.n.*, dʒeɪz, jayz
Jedburgh *Borders*, 'dʒedbərə,
  jédbŭră. *Appropriate also for
  Baron ~.*
Jedrzejczak, *f.n.*, jen'dʒeɪtʃæk,
  yen-jáytchack
Jeffares, *f.n.*, 'dʒefərz, jéffărz
Jeffcock, *f.n.*, 'dʒefkɒk, jéfkock
Jefferies, *f.n.*, 'dʒefrɪz, jéffriz
Jefferis, *f.n.*, 'dʒefərɪs, jéffĕriss
Jefferson, *f.n.*, 'dʒefərsən, jéffĕr-
  sŏn
Jeffes, *f.n.*, dʒefs, jeffs
Jeffress, *f.n.*, 'dʒefrɪs, jéffrĕss
Jeffries, *f.n.*, 'dʒefrɪz, jéffriz
Jeffroy, *f.n.*, 'dʒefrɔɪ, jéffroy
Jeger, *f.n.*, 'dʒeɪgər, jáygĕr.
  *Appropriate also for Baroness
  ~.*
Jekyll, *f.n.*, 'dʒikl, jéekl; 'dʒɪkɪl,
  jéekil; 'dʒekl, jéckl. *The first is
  appropriate for Gertrude ~,
  horticulturalist and author.
  There is some evidence that
  R. L. Stevenson intended the
  first for his character in 'Dr ~*

and Mr Hyde', but the pronunciation in popular use is the third.

Jellicoe, Earl, 'dʒelɪkoʊ, jéllikō

Jenks, *f.n.*, dʒeŋks, jenks

Jennens, *f.n.*, 'dʒenɪnz, jénněnz

Jenner, *f.n.*, 'dʒenər, jénněr

Jennings, *f.n.*, 'dʒenɪŋz, jénningz

Jenyns, *f.n.*, 'dʒenɪnz, jénninz

Jenyth, *C.n.*, 'dʒenɪθ, jénnith

Jeonney, *f.n.*, dʒɪ'oʊnɪ, ji-ṓni

Jephcott, *f.n.*, 'dʒefkɒt, jéffkot

Jeram, *f.n.*, 'dʒerəm, jérräm

Jerdein, *f.n.*, dʒər'diːn, jěrdéen

Jerningham, *f.n.*, 'dʒɜːnɪŋəm, jérning-äm

Jerrom, *f.n.*, 'dʒerəm, jérrŏm

Jersey, Earl of, 'dʒɜːzɪ, jérzi

Jervaulx, *f.n.*, 'dʒɜːvɪs, jérviss

Jervaulx *N. Yorks.*, 'dʒɜːvoʊ, jérvō. *Appropriate also for* ~ *Abbey. It appears that an old pronunciation,* 'dʒɑːvɪs, jaárviss, *is still used by some local speakers.*

Jervis, *f.n.*, 'dʒɜːvɪs, jérviss; 'dʒɑːvɪs, jaárviss. *The first is appropriate for the family name of the 18th-c. admiral, the Earl of St. Vincent.*

Jervois, *f.n.*, 'dʒɑːvɪs, jaárviss

Jervoise, *f.n.*, 'dʒɜːvɪs, jérviss

Jesse, *f.n.*, 'dʒesɪ, jéssi

Jessel, *f.n.*, 'dʒesl, jéssl

Jesson, *f.n.*, 'dʒesən, jéssŏn

Jessup, *f.n.*, 'dʒesəp, jéssŭp

Jeuda, *f.n.*, 'dʒuːdə, joódä

Jeudwine, *f.n.*, 'dʒuːdwaɪn, joódwīn; 'dʒuːdwɪn, joódwin

Jeune, *f.n.*, ʒɜn, zhön; ʒun, zhoon

Jevington *E. Sussex*, 'dʒevɪŋtən, jévvingtŏn

Jeyes, *f.n.*, dʒeɪz, jayz

Jeynes, *f.n.*, dʒeɪnz, jaynz

Joad, *f.n.*, dʒoʊd, jōd

Job, *f.n.*, dʒoʊb, jōb

Jobar, *f.nt*, 'dʒoʊbɑr, jóbaar

Jobling, *f.n.*, 'dʒɒblɪŋ, jóbbling

Jocelyn, *C.n. and f.n.*, 'dʒɒslɪn, jósslin. *Appropriate also for Viscount* ~.

Jockel, *f.n.*, 'dʒɒkl, jóckl

Jodrell, *f.n.*, 'dʒɒdrəl, jódrěl. *Appropriate also for the* ~ *Chair of Zoology and Comparative Anatomy in the University of London.*

Jodrell Bank *experimental station Ches.*, 'dʒɒdrəl 'bæŋk, jódrěl bánk

Joekes, *f.n.*, 'jukɪs, yoókěss

Joffe, *f.n.*, 'dʒɒfeɪ, jóffay

Johnes, *f.n.*, dʒoʊnz, jōnz

Johnian Society *St John's Coll., Cambridge*, 'dʒoʊnɪən, jṓniän

Johnsey, *f.n.*, 'dʒɒnzɪ, jónzi

Johnson, *f.n.*, 'dʒɒnsən, jónssŏn

Johnston, *f.n.*, 'dʒɒnstən, jónstŏn; 'dʒɒnsən, jónssŏn

Johnstone, *f.n.*, 'dʒɒnstən, jónstŏn; 'dʒɒnsən, jónssŏn; 'dʒɒnstoʊn, jónstōn

Johnstone *Devon*, 'dʒɒnstən, jónsstŏn

Johnstown *Clwyd, Dyfed*, 'dʒɒnztaʊn, jónztown

Joldwynds *Surrey*, 'dʒoʊldwɪndz, jṓldwindz

Joll, *f.n.*, dʒɒl, joll

Jolliff, *f.n.*, 'dʒɒlɪf, jóllif

Jolliffe, *f.n.*, 'dʒɒlɪf, jóllif

Jonasson, *f.n.*, 'dʒɒnəsən, jónnässön

Jones, *f.n.*, dʒoʊnz, jōnz

Jonesborough *Co. Armagh*, 'dʒoʊnzbərə, jṓnzbŭrä

Jonker, *f.n.*, 'dʒɒŋkər, jónkěr

Jonson, Ben, *16th–17th-c. dramatist*, 'ben 'dʒɒnsən, bén jónssŏn

Jope, *f.n.*, dʒoʊp, jōp

Jopling, *f.n.*, 'dʒɒplɪŋ, jóppling

Jordanhill *S'clyde*, 'dʒɔːrdən'hɪl, jórdän-híll

Jory, *f.n.*, 'dʒɔːrɪ, jáwri

Joshi, *f.n.*, 'dʒoʊʃɪ, jóshi

Josipovici, *f.n.*, ˌdʒoʊzɪpə'viːtʃɪ, jōzipŏvéetchi

Joss, *f.n.*, dʒɒs, joss

Joubert de la Ferté, *f.n.*, 'ʒubɛər də lɑ 'feərteɪ, zhoóbair dě laa fáirtay

Joughin, *f.n.*, 'dʒoʊɪn, jṓ-in; 'dʒɒkɪn, jóckin

Joule, *f.n.*, dʒuːl, jool; dʒoʊl, jōl; dʒaʊl, jowl. *Information obtained for the BBC in 1933 by the late Professor Arthur Lloyd James and evidence submitted by scientists to 'Nature' in Sept.–Nov. 1943 show that the first is correct for James Prescott* ~, *the 19th-c. scientist, after whom the unit of energy was named.*

Joules, *f.n.*, dʒulz, joolz

Jourdain, *f.n.*, ʒʊər'deɪn, zhōordáyn

Journeaux, *f.n.*, 'ʒʊərnoʊ, zhōórnō

Jousiffe, *f.n.*, 'ʒuːzɪf, zhṓzif

Jowell, *f.n.*, 'dʒaʊəl, jów-ěl; 'dʒoʊəl, jó-ěl

Jowers, *f.n.*, 'dʒaʊərz, jówěrz

Jowett, *f.n.*, 'dʒaʊɪt, jów-ět; 'dʒoʊɪt, jó-ět

Jowitt, *f.n.*, 'dʒaʊɪt, jów-it; 'dʒoʊɪt, jó-it. *The second is appropriate for the Earldom of* ~.

Jowle, *f.n.*, dʒaʊl, jowl; dʒul, jool; dʒoʊl, jōl

Joynson, *f.n.*, 'dʒɔɪnsən, jóynssŏn
Jubb, *f.n.*, dʒʌb, jubb
Juchau, *f.n.*, 'dʒuʃoʊ, joóoshō
Juckes, *f.n.*, dʒuks, jooks
Juett, *f.n.*, 'dʒuɪt, joó-ĕt
Jukes, *f.n.*, dʒuks, jooks
Juler, *f.n.*, 'dʒulər, joólĕr
Julnes, *f.n.*, dʒʊlnz, jōōlnz
Julyan, *f.n.*, 'dʒuljən, joól-yăn
June, *f.n.*, dʒun, joon
Junor, *f.n.*, 'dʒunər, joónŏr
Jura *S'clyde*, 'dʒʊərə, jŏŏră
Jurby *I. of Man*, 'dʒɜrbɪ, júrbi
Justham, *f.n.*, 'dʒʌstəm, jústăm
Justicz, *f.n.*, 'dʒʌstɪs, jústiss
Juta, *f.n.*, 'dʒutə, joótă

K

Kaberry, *f.n.*, 'keɪbərɪ, káybĕri
Kadisch, *f.n.*, 'kɑdɪʃ, kaádish
Kadleigh, *f.n.*, 'kædlɪ, kádli
Kagan, *f.n.*, 'keɪgən, káygăn. *Appropriate also for Baron* ~.
Kahan, *f.n.*, kə'hɑn, kă-haán
Kahn, *f.n.*, kɑn, kaan. *Appropriate also for Baron* ~.
Kalamuniak, *f.n.*, ˌkælə'munɪæk, kalămoóni-ack
Kaldor, Baron, 'kældɔr, káldor
Kalindjian, *f.n.*, kə'lɪndʒən, kălínjăn
Kames Bay *S'clyde*, keɪmz, kaymz
Kanareck, *f.n.*, 'kænərek, kánnăreck
Kanocz, *f.n.*, 'kɒnɒts, kónnawts
Kapica, *f.n.*, kə'pikə, kăpeékă
Kaplan, *f.n.*, 'kæplən, káplăn
Karen, *C.n.*, 'kærən, kárrĕn; 'kɑrən, kaáren
Karen, *f.n.*, 'kærən, kárrĕn
Karmel, *f.n.*, 'kɑrməl, kaármĕl
Karpeles, *f.n.*, 'kɑrpɪliz, kaárpĕleez
Kasia, *C.n.*, 'kæʃə, káshă
Kassell, *f.n.*, 'kæsl, kássl
Kassimatis, *f.n.*, ˌkæsɪ'mɑtɪs, kassimaátiss
Katin, *f.n.*, 'keɪtɪn, káytin
Katrine, Loch, *Central*, 'kætrɪn, kátrin
Katz, *f.n.*, kæts, kats
Kaufman, *f.n.*, 'kɔfmən, káwfmăn
Kavanagh, *f.n.*, 'kævənə, kávvănă; kə'vænə, kăvánnă
Kawerau, *f.n.*, 'kɑvraʊ, kaávrow
Kay, *f.n.*, keɪ, kay
Kazantzis, *f.n.*, kə'zæntsɪs, kăzántsiss

Kaznowski, *f.n.*, kæz'nɒfskɪ, kaznófski
Kea *Cornwall*, ki, kee
Keadby *Humberside*, 'kidbɪ, keédbi
Keady *Co. Armagh, Co. Derry*, 'kidɪ, keédi
Kealey, *f.n.*, 'kilɪ, keéli
Keane, *f.n.*, kin, keen; keɪn, kayn
Keaney, *f.n.*, 'kinɪ, keéni
Kear, *f.n.*, kɪər, keer
Kearey, *f.n.*, 'kɪərɪ, keéri
Kearley, *f.n.*, 'kɪərlɪ, keérli
Kearney, *f.n.*, 'kɜrnɪ, kérni; 'kɑrnɪ, kaárni
Kearney *Co. Down*, 'kɜrnɪ, kérni
Kearsey, *f.n.*, 'kɜrzɪ, kérzi
Kearsley, *f.n.*, 'kɪərzlɪ, keérzli
Kearsley *Gtr. M'chester*, 'kɜrzlɪ, kérzli
Kearsney *Kent*, 'kɜrznɪ, kérzni
Kearton, *f.n.*, 'kɪərtən, keértŏn; 'kɜrtən, kértŏn. *The first is appropriate for Baron* ~.
Keates, *f.n.*, kits, keets
Keating, *f.n.*, 'kitɪŋ, keéting
Keatinge, *f.n.*, 'kitɪŋ, keéting
Keatley, *f.n.*, 'kitlɪ, keétli
Keats, *f.n.*, kits, keets
Keay, *f.n.*, keɪ, kay
Keble, *f.n.*, 'kibl, keébl. *Appropriate for John* ~, *19th-c. divine and poet.*
Kedington, *also spelt* Ketton, *Suffolk*, 'kedɪŋtən, kéddingtŏn; 'ketən, kéttŏn. *Older residents use only the second pronunciation.*
Kedleston *Derby.*, 'kedlstən, kédlstŏn
Kedourie, *f.n.*, kə'dʊərɪ, kĕdŏŏri
Keeble, *f.n.*, 'kibl, keébl
Keeffe, *f.n.*, kif, keef
Keele *Staffs.*, kil, keel
Keeler, *f.n.*, 'kilər, keélĕr
Keeling, *f.n.*, 'kilɪŋ, keéling
Keene, *f.n.*, kin, keen
Keenlyside, *f.n.*, 'kinlɪsaɪd, keénlissíd
Kegan, *f.n.*, 'kigən, keégăn
Kegie, *f.n.*, 'kigɪ, keégi
Kehelland *Cornwall*, kɪ'helənd, kĕhélländ
Kehoe, *f.n.*, kjoʊ, kyō; 'kihoʊ, keé-hō
Keig, *f.n.*, kig, keeg
Keig *Grampian*, kig, keeg
Keighley, *f.n.*, 'kiθlɪ, keéthli; 'kilɪ, keéli
Keighley *W. Yorks.*, 'kiθlɪ, keéthli
Keighlian, *one educated at* Keighley *Grammar School*, 'kilɪən, keéliăn

Keightley, *f.n.*, 'kıtlı, kéetli
Keigwin, *f.n.*, 'kegwın, kégwin
Keill, *f.n.*, kil, keel
Keiller, *f.n.*, 'kılər, kéelěr
Keinton Mandeville *Somerset*, 'kentən 'mændıvıl, kéntŏn mándĕvil
Keir, *f.n.*, kıər, keer
Keisby *Lincs.*, 'keızbı, káyzbi; 'keısbı, káyssbi
Keiss *H'land*, kis, keess
Keith, *C.n. and f.n.*, kiθ, keeth
Keith *Grampian*, kiθ, keeth
Keith of Kinkel, Baron, 'kiθ əv kın'kel, kéeth ŏv kin-kéll
Kekewich, *f.n.*, 'kekıwıtʃ, kéckě-witch; 'kekwıtʃ, kéckwitch; 'kekwıdʒ, kéckwij
Kelburn, Viscount of, 'kelbərn, kélbŭrn
Kelcey, *f.n.*, 'kelsı, kélssi
Kelk, *f.n.*, kelk, kelk
Kell, *f.n.*, kel, kell
Kelland, *f.n.*, 'kelənd, kéllănd
Kellas *Grampian, Tayside*, 'keləs, kéllăss
Kellaway, *f.n.*, 'keləweı, kéllă--way
Kelleher, *f.n.*, 'keləhər, kéllě-hěr
Kellett, *f.n.*, 'kelıt, kéllět
Kellett-Bowman, *f.n.*, 'kelıt 'boʊmən, kéllět-bômăn
Kelleway, *f.n.*, 'keləweı, kéllěway
Kelley, *f.n.*, 'kelı, kélli
Kellingley *N. Yorks.*, 'kelıŋlı, kélling-li
Kellock, *f.n.*, 'kelɒk, kéllock
Kellogg, *f.n.*, 'kelɒg, kéllogg
Kelmscot *Oxon.*, 'kemskət, kémsskŏt
Kelsale *Suffolk*, 'kelseıl, kélsayl
Kelsall, *f.n.*, 'kelsl, kélssl
Kelsey, *f.n.*, 'kelsı, kélssi; 'kelzı, kélzi
Kelso *Borders*, 'kelsoʊ, kélssō
Kelvedon *Essex*, 'kelvıdən, kélvĕdŏn
Kelvinhaugh *S'clyde*, 'kelvınhɔ, kélvin-haw; 'kelvınhɒx, kélvin-hoch
Kelvinside *Glasgow*, ‚kelvın'saıd, kelvinssíd
Kelynack *Cornwall*, ke'laınək, kelínăk; 'klaınək, klínăk
Kemback *Fife*, 'kembæk, kémback
Kemeys-Tynte, *f.n.*, 'kemıs 'tınt, kémmiss tínt
Kempinski, *f.n.*, kem'pınskı, kempínski
Kempsey *H. & W.*, 'kemsı, kémssi; 'kemzı, kémzi
Kempshall, *f.n.*, 'kempʃəl, kémp--shăl

Kemptown *E. Sussex*, 'kemptaʊn, kémptown
Kemsley, Viscount, 'kemzlı, kémzli
Kenardington *Kent*, kə'nɑrdıŋtən, kěna͡ardingtŏn
Kendal *Cumbria*, 'kendl, kéndl
Kendall, *f.n.*, 'kendl, kéndl
Kendoon, Loch, *D. & G.*, 'ken-'dun, kén-do͡on
Kendrick, *f.n.*, 'kendrık, kéndrick
Kenfig Hill *Mid Glam.*, 'kenfıg 'hıl, kénfig híll
Kenidjack *Cornwall*, kın'ıdʒæk, kěníjjack
Kenlis, Baron, ken'lıs, kenlíss
Kenmare, Earldom of, ken'mɛər, kenmáir
Kenmore *H'land*, 'kenmɔr, kén-mor
Kennair, *f.n.*, ken'ɛər, kennáir
Kennaird, *f.n.*, ken'ɛərd, ken-náird
Kennard, *f.n.*, 'kenɑrd, kénnaard; kı'nɑrd, kěna͡ard
Kennerleigh *Devon*, 'kenərlı, kénněrli
Kennet, Baron, 'kenıt, kénnět
Kennethmont *Grampian*, ke-'neθmənt, kennéthmŏnt
Kennett, *f.n.*, 'kenıt, kénnět
Kennoway, *f.n.*, 'kenəweı, kénnŏ-way
Kennoway *Fife*, 'kenəweı, kénnŏ-way
Kenshole, *f.n.*, 'kenzhoʊl, kénz--hōl; 'kenʃoʊl, kén-shōl
Kent, *f.n.*, kent, kent
Kent *Co. name*, kent, kent. *Appropriate also for HRH the Duke of* ~.
Kentigern, saint, 'kentıgərn, kéntigĕrn
Kenward, *f.n.*, 'kenwərd, kén-wărd
Kenwick *Salop*, 'kenık, kénnick
Kenwyn *Cornwall*, 'kenwın, kén-win
Kenyon, *f.n.*, 'kenjən, kén-yŏn
Keogh, *f.n.*, 'kioʊ, kée-ō; kjoʊ, kyō
Keohane, *f.n.*, ki'oʊn, kee-ón; ki'eın, kee-áyn; ki'æn, kee-án
Keough, *f.n.*, 'kioʊ, kée-ō; kjoʊ, kyō
Keown, *f.n.*, kjoʊn, kyōn; ki'oʊn, kee-ón; 'kioʊn, kée-ōn
Keppel, *f.n.*, 'kepl, képpl
Keppochhill *Glasgow*, 'kepəx'hıl, képpŏch-híll
Ker, *f.n.*, kɜr, ker; kɛər, kair; kɑr. kaar. *The third is appropriate for Baron* ~.
Kerby, *f.n.*, 'kɜrbı, kérbi

Keren, Viscountcy of, 'kerən, kérrĕn

Keresley W. Midlands, 'kɜrzlɪ, kérzli; 'kɑrzlɪ, káarzli

Kerfoot, f.n., 'kɜrfʊt, kérfŏŏt

Kerman, f.n., 'kɜrmən, kérmän

Kermeen, f.n., kər'min, kĕrmeén

Kermode, f.n., 'kɜrmoʊd, kérmōd

Kernaghan, f.n., 'kɜrnəhən, kérnähän

Kernahan, f.n., 'kɜrnəhən, kérnähän

Kernick, f.n., 'kɜrnɪk, kérnick

Kernoghan, f.n., 'kɜrnəhən, kérnŏ-hän

Kernohan, f.n., 'kɜrnəhən, kérnŏhän

Kernot, f.n., 'kɜrnət, kérnŏt; 'kɜrnoʊ, kérnō

Kerr, f.n., kɜr, ker; kɛər, kair; kɑr, kaar

Kerrera S'clyde, 'kerərə, kérrĕrä

Kerrier Cornwall, 'kerɪər, kérri-ĕr

Kerrigan, f.n., 'kerɪgən, kérrigän

Kerruish, f.n., kə'ruʃ, kĕroʹosh

Kersal Gtr. M'chester, 'kɜrzl, kérzl

Kersey Suffolk, 'kɜrzɪ, kérzi

Kershaw, f.n., 'kɜrʃɔ, kér-shaw. Appropriate also for Baron ~.

Kershope, Burn, Scotland–England border, 'kɜrsəp, kérssŏp

Kerslake, f.n., 'kɑrzleɪk, káarzlayk

Kersner, f.n., 'kɜrznər, kérznĕr

Kesgrave Suffolk, 'kezgreɪv, kézgrayv

Kestelman, f.n., 'kestəlmən, késtĕlmän

Kesteven, Barony of, 'kestɪvən, késtĕvĕn

Kesteven Lincs., kes'tivən, kesteévĕn. Appropriate for the administrative districts of North and South ~.

Keswick, f.n., 'kezɪk, kézzick; 'kezwɪk, kéz-wick

Keswick Cumbria, 'kezɪk, kézzick

Ketelbey, Alfred, composer, kə-'telbɪ, kĕtélbi

Kettel, f.n., kɪ'tel, kĕtéll

Kettering Northants., 'ketərɪŋ, kéttĕring

Kettle, f.n., 'ketl, kéttl

Ketton, f.n., 'ketən, kéttŏn

Ketton see Kedington

Kettyle, f.n., 'ketl, kéttl

Kevill, f.n., 'kevɪl, kévvil

Keville, f.n., 'kevɪl, kévvil

Kewley, f.n., 'kjulɪ, kéwli

Key, f.n., ki, kee

Keyes, Baron, kiz, keez

Keyham Leics., 'kiəm, kee-äm

Keyingham Humberside, 'keɪŋhəm, káy-ing-häm; 'kenɪnhəm, kénnin-häm; 'kenɪŋhəm, kénning-häm

Keymer, f.n., 'kimər, keémĕr

Keymer W. Sussex, 'kimər, keémĕr; 'kaɪmər, kímĕr

Keynes, f.n., keɪnz, kaynz. Appropriate for John Maynard ~ (later Baron ~), economist, 1883–1946.

Keynes, Ashton, Wilts., 'æʃtən 'keɪnz, áshtŏn káynz

Keynes, Horsted, W. Sussex, 'hɔrstɪd 'keɪnz, hórsstĕd káynz

Keynes, Milton, Bucks., 'mɪltən 'kinz, míltŏn keénz

Keynsham Avon, 'keɪnʃəm, káyn-shäm

Keyser, f.n., 'kizər, keézĕr; 'kaɪzər, kízĕr

Keyser Ullmann, merchant bankers, 'kizər 'ʊlmən, keézĕr ŏŏlmän

Keysoe Beds., 'kisoʊ, keéssō

Keyston Cambs., 'kistən, keéstŏn

Keyte, f.n., kaɪt, kīt; kit, keet

Keyworth Notts., 'kiwɜrθ, keé-wurth

Khambatta, f.n., kæm'bɑtə, kambáatä

Kibworth Beauchamp Leics., 'kɪbwɜrθ 'bitʃəm, kíbwurth beétchäm

Kibworth Harcourt Leics., 'kɪbwɜrθ 'hɑrkɔrt, kíbwurth haʹarkort

Kidderminster H. & W., 'kɪdərmɪnstər, kíddĕrminstĕr

Kidel, f.n., kɪ'del, kidéll

Kidman, f.n., 'kɪdmən, kídmän

Kidsgrove Staffs., 'kɪdzgroʊv, kídz-grōv

Kidwelly Dyfed, kɪd'welɪ, kidwélli. See also Cydweli.

Kielder Northd., 'kɪldər, keéldĕr

Kielty, f.n., 'kɪltɪ, keélti

Kiely, f.n., 'kɪlɪ, keéli; 'kaɪlɪ, kíli

Kiessimal Castle see Kishmul Castle

Kiggell, f.n., 'kɪgl, kíggl

Kighley, f.n., 'kɪlɪ, keéli

Kightly, f.n., 'kaɪtlɪ, kítli

Kilbarchan S'clyde, kɪl'bɑrxən, kilbaʹarchän

Kilbirnie S'clyde, kɪl'bɜrnɪ, kilbírni

Kilbowie S'clyde, kɪl'baʊɪ, kilbów-i

Kilbracken, Baron, kɪl'brækən, kilbráckĕn

Kilbride S'clyde, kɪl'braɪd, kilbríd

Kilbroney Co. Down, kɪl'broʊnɪ, kilbróni

Kilbucho *Borders*, kɪl'bʊxoʊ, kil-bŏŏchō
Kilburn, *f.n.*, 'kɪlbərn, kílburn
Kilburn *London*, 'kɪlbərn, kílbŭrn; 'kɪlbərn, kílburn
Kilcalmonell *S'clyde*, kɪl'kælmə-'nel, kilkálmŏnéll
Kilchattan *S'clyde*, kɪl'xætən, kilcháttän
Kilchattan Bay *S'clyde*, kɪl'kætən 'beɪ, kilkáttän báy
Kilchoan *H'land*, kɪl'xoʊən, kilchŏ̄-än; ˌkɪlə'xoʊən, killăchŏ̄--än
Kilchrenan *S'clyde*, kɪl'krenən, kilkrénnän
Kilchrist *H'land*, 'kɪlkrɪst, kílkrist
Kilchurn, *f.n.*, kɪl'xɜrn, kilchúrn
Kilchurn Castle *S'clyde*, kɪl'tʃɜrn, kiltchúrn
Kilclief *Co. Down*, kɪl'klif, kil--kléef
Kilcoan *Co. Antrim*, kɪl'koʊn, kil-kŏ́n
Kilconquhar *Fife*, kɪl'kɒŋkər, kil-kónkär; kɪ'nʌxər, kinúchär
Kilcoursie *Viscount*, kɪl'kɔrsɪ, kilkórssi
Kilcreggan *S'clyde*, kɪl'kregən, kilkréggän
Kildalton *S'clyde*, kɪl'dæltən, kil-dáltŏn
Kildare, Marquess of, kɪl'dɛər, kildáir
Kildonan *H'land, S'clyde*, kɪl-'dɒnən, kildónnän
Kildwick *N. and W. Yorks. border*, 'kɪldwɪk, kildwick
Kilfedder, *f.n.*, kɪl'fedər, kilféddĕr
Kilgarriff, *f.n.*, kɪl'gærɪf, kilgárriff
Kilgetty *Dyfed*, kɪl'getɪ, kilgétti
Kilgour, *f.n.*, kɪl'gaʊər, kilgówr
Kilgraston *Tayside*, kɪl'græstən, kilgrásstŏn
Kilham, *f.n.*, 'kɪləm, kíllăm
Kilian, *f.n.*, 'kɪlɪən, killi-än
Kilkeel *Co. Down*, kɪl'kil, kilkéel
Kilkewydd *Powys*, kɪl'kewɪð, kilké-wi̱th. *English spelling of* Cilcewydd, *q.v.*
Kilkhampton *Cornwall*, kɪlk-'hæmptən, kilk-hámptŏn
Killadeas *Co. Fermanagh*, ˌkɪlə-'dis, killădé-ess
Killagan *Co. Antrim*, kɪ'lægən, kilággän
Killamarsh *Derby.*, 'kɪləmɑrʃ, kíllămaarsh
Killanin, *Baron*, kɪ'lænɪn, kilánnin
Killar, *f.n.*, 'kɪlɑr, kíllaar
Killay *W. Glam.*, kɪ'leɪ, kiláy
Killea *Co. Derry*, kɪ'leɪ, kiláy
Killead *Co. Antrim*, kɪ'lid, kiléed
Killearn, *Baron*, kɪ'lɜrn, kilérn

Killelagh *Co. Derry*, kɪ'leɪlɪ, kiláyli
Killermont *Glasgow*, 'kɪlərmənt, killĕrmŏnt. *The pronunciation of* ~ *Golf Course is* kɪ'lɛərmənt, kiláirmŏnt.
Killeter *Co. Tyrone*, kɪ'litər, killé-etĕr
Killichronan *S'clyde*, ˌkɪlɪ'xroʊnən, killichrŏ́nän
Killick, *f.n.*, 'kɪlɪk, kíllick
Killiechassie *Tayside*, ˌkɪlɪ'hæsɪ, killi-hássi
Killiecrankie *Tayside*, ˌkɪlɪ'kræŋkɪ, killikránki
Killin *Central*, kɪ'lɪn, kilín
Killinchy *Co. Down*, kɪ'lɪnʃɪ, kilínshi
Killingholme *Humberside*, 'kɪlɪŋhoʊm, killing-hōm
Killisport *S'clyde*, 'kɪlɪspɔrt, kíllisport
Killough *Co. Down*, kɪ'lɒx, kilóch
Killowen *Co. Derry, Co. Down*, kɪl'oʊɪn, kilŏ́-ĕn
Killwick, *f.n.*, 'kɪlwɪk, kílwick
Killylea *Co. Armagh*, ˌkɪlɪ'leɪ, killiláy
Killyleagh *Co. Down*, ˌkɪlɪ'leɪ, killiláy
Killywhan *D. & G.*, ˌkɪlɪ'hwɒn, killi-whón
Kilmacolm *S'clyde*, ˌkɪlmə'koʊm, kilmăkŏ́m
Kilmaine, *Baron*, kɪl'meɪn, kilmáyn
Kilmany *Fife*, kɪl'menɪ, kilménni. *Appropriate also for Baron* ~.
Kilmarnock *S'clyde*, kɪl'mɑrnək, kilmaárnŏk. *Appropriate also for Baron* ~.
Kilmaronock *S'clyde*, ˌkɪlmə'rɒnək, kilmărónnŏk
Kilmersdon *Somerset*, 'kɪlmərz-dən, kílmĕrzdŏn
Kilmister, *f.n.*, 'kɪlmɪstər, kíl-misstĕr
Kilmorack *H'land*, kɪl'mɔrək, kilmáwrăk
Kilmorey, *Earl of*, kɪl'mʌrɪ, kil-múrri
Kilmuir, *Earldom of*, kɪl'mjʊər, kilmyŏ́ŏr
Kilmun *S'clyde*, kɪl'mʌn, kilmún
Kilnasaggart Bridge *Co. Armagh*, ˌkɪlnə'sægərt, kilnăsággärt
Kilndown *Kent*, 'kɪlndaʊn, kíln-down
Kilninver *S'clyde*, kɪl'nɪnvər, kilnínvĕr
Kilnwick *Humberside*, 'kɪlɪk, kíl-lick
Kiloh, *f.n.*, 'kaɪloʊ, kḯlō
Kilpheder *W. Isles*, kɪl'fedər, kilféddĕr

Kilraughts *Co. Antrim*, kɪl'ræts, kilráts

Kilravock Castle *H'land*, kɪl'rɒk, kill-róck

Kilrea *Co. Derry*, kɪl'reɪ, kilráy

Kilroot *Co. Antrim*, kɪl'rut, kilroót

Kilroy-Silk, *f.n.*, 'kɪlrɔɪ 'sɪlk, kílroy-sílk

Kilry *Tayside*, 'kɪlrɪ, kílri

Kilsyth *S'clyde*, kɪl'saɪθ, kil-síth

Kiltarlity *H'land*, kɪl'tɑrlɪtɪ, kil--taárliti

Kilve *Somerset*, kɪlv, kilv

Kilwaughter *Co. Antrim*, kɪl-'wɔtər, kilwáwtĕr

Kilwinning *S'clyde*, kɪl'wɪnɪŋ, kilwínning

Kimball, *f.n.*, 'kɪmbl, kímbl

Kimberley, *f.n.*, 'kɪmbərlɪ, kímbĕrli

Kimbolton *H. & W.*, *Cambs.*, kɪm'boʊltən, kimbóltŏn

Kimche, *f.n.*, 'kɪmtʃɪ, kímtchi

Kimmance, *f.n.*, 'kɪməns, kímmănss

Kinahan, *f.n.*, 'kɪnəhən, kínnăhăn

Kinally, *f.n.*, kɪ'nælɪ, kináli

Kinawley *Co. Fermanagh*, kɪ'nɔlɪ, kináwli

Kinbane *Co. Antrim*, kɪn'bɒn, kinbáwn

Kincaid, *f.n.*, kɪn'keɪd, kin-káyd

Kincairney, *f.n.*, kɪn'kɛərnɪ, kin--káirni

Kincardine *H'land*, kɪn'kɑrdɪn, kin-kaárdin. *Appropriate also for ~ and Deeside, administrative district of Grampian region, and ~ Castles, Grampian and Tayside.*

Kincardine O'Neil *Grampian*, kɪn-'kɑrdɪn oʊ'nil, kin-kaárdin ōneél

Kincardine-on-Forth *Fife*, kɪn-'kɑrdɪn ɒn 'fɔrθ, kin-kaárdin on fórth

Kinclaven *Tayside*, kɪn'kleɪvən, kin-kláyvĕn

Kincraig *H'land*, kɪn'kreɪg, kin--kráyg

Kinder Scout *Derby.*, 'kɪndər skaʊt, kínndĕr skowt

Kindersley, Baron, 'kɪndərzlɪ, kínndĕrzli

Kindregan, *f.n.*, kɪn'drigən, kin-dreégăn

Kine, *f.n.*, kaɪn, kīn

Kinellar *Grampian*, kɪ'nelər, kinéllăr

Kineton *Warwicks.*, 'kaɪntən, kíntŏn

Kinfauns *Tayside*, kɪn'fɔnz, kin-fáwnz

Kingdon, *f.n.*, 'kɪŋdən, kíngdŏn

Kingennie *Tayside*, kɪn'genɪ, kin--génni

Kingham, *f.n.*, 'kɪŋəm, kíng-ăm

Kinglake, *f.n.*, 'kɪŋleɪk, kíng-layk

Kinglassie *Fife*, kɪŋ'læsɪ, king--lássi

Kingoldrum *Tayside*, kɪn'goʊldrəm, kin-góldrŭm

Kingsale, Baron, kɪn'seɪl, kin-sáyl

Kingsbury, *f.n.*, 'kɪŋzbərɪ, kíngzbŭri

King's Caple *H. & W.*, 'kɪŋz 'keɪpl, kíngz káypl

Kingscavil *Lothian*, kɪŋz'keɪvɪl, kingz-káyvil

Kingscote, *f.n.*, 'kɪŋzkət, kíngzkŏt

Kingscott, *f.n.*, 'kɪŋzkɒt, kíngzkot

Kingsford, *f.n.*, 'kɪŋzfərd, kíngzfŏrd

Kingskerswell *Devon*, kɪŋz-'kərzwəl, kingzkérzwĕl

Kingsley, *f.n.*, 'kɪŋzlɪ, kíngzli

Kingsnympton *Devon*, 'kɪŋz-'nɪmtən, kíngzanímtŏn

King's Somborne *Hants*, 'kɪŋz 'sɒmbɔrn, kíngz sómborn

Kings Tamerton *Devon*, 'kɪŋz 'tæmərtən, kíngz támmĕrtŏn

Kingsteignton *Devon*, 'kɪŋz-'teɪntən, kíngz-táyntŏn

Kingsterndale *Derby.*, kɪŋ'stərndeɪl, king-stérndayl

Kingston Bagpuize, *also spelt* **Bagpuze**, *Oxon.*, 'kɪŋstən 'bægpjuz, kíngstŏn bágpewz

Kingston Blount *Oxon.*, 'kɪŋstən 'blʌnt, kíngstŏn blúnt

Kingston Buci *W. Sussex*, 'kɪŋstən 'bjusɪ, kíngstŏn béwssi

Kingston Matravers *Dorset*, 'kɪŋstən mə'trævərz, kíngstŏn mătrávvĕrz

Kingston-upon-Hull *Humberside*, 'kɪŋstən əpɒn 'hʌl, kíngstŏn ŭpon húll

Kingswear *Devon*, 'kɪŋzwɪər, kíngzweer

Kingswinford *W. Midlands*, kɪŋ-'swɪnfərd, king-swínfŏrd

Kingussie *H'land*, kɪŋ'jusɪ, king--yoóssi

Kininmonth, *f.n.*, kɪ'nɪnmənθ, kinnínmŏnth; 'kɪnɪnmənθ, kínninmŏnth

Kininmonth *Grampian*, kɪ'nɪnmənθ, kinnínmŏnth

Kinloch, *f.n.*, kɪn'lɒx, kinlóc͟h

Kinlochbervie *H'land*, 'kɪnlɒx-'bərvɪ, kínloc͟h-bérvi

Kinlocheil *H'land*, 'kɪnlɒx'il, kínlochéél

Kinlochewe *H'land*, 'kɪnlɒx'ju, kínloc͟h-yoó

Kinlochleven H'land, 'kınlɒx-
'livən, kínlochléevēn
Kinlochmoidart H'land, 'kınlɒx-
'mɔɪdərt, kínlochmóydärt
Kinlochourn H'land, 'kınlɒx-
'huərn, kínloch-hŏŏrn
Kinloch Rannoch Tayside, 'kınlɒx
'rænəx, kínloch ránnŏch
Kinloss Grampian, kın'lɒs, kin-
lóss. Appropriate also for
Baroness ~.
Kinmel Park Clwyd, 'kınməl
'pɑrk, kínmēl paárk; 'kıml
'pɑrk, kímml paárk
Kinmond, f.n., 'kınmənd, kín-
mŏnd
Kinnaber Junction Tayside, kı-
'neıbər, kináybĕr
Kinnaird Tayside, kı'neərd, kin-
áird. Appropriate also for Baron
~.
Kinne, f.n., 'kını, kínni
Kinnear, f.n., kı'nıər, kineér;
kı'nɛər, kináir
Kinnegar Co. Down, ‚kınə'gɑr,
kinnĕgaár
Kinneil Central, kı'nil, kineél
Kinnesswood Tayside, kı'neswʊd,
kinéss-wŏŏd
Kinniburgh, f.n., 'kınıbərə, kínni-
bŭră
Kinninmonth, f.n., kı'nınmənt,
kinnínmŏnt; kı'nınmənθ,
kinnínmŏnth
Kinnock, f.n., 'kınək, kínnŏk
Kinnon, f.n., 'kınən, kínnŏn
Kinnoull Tayside, kı'nul, kinoól.
Appropriate also for the Earl of
~.
Kinoulton Notts., kı'nultən,
kinoóltŏn
Kinrade, f.n., 'kınreıd, kínrayd
Kinross Tayside, kın'rɒs, kinróss.
Appropriate also for Baron ~.
Kinsella, f.n., 'kınsələ, kínssēlä;
kın'selə, kinssélä
Kinsey, f.n., 'kınzı, kínzi
Kintore Grampian, kın'tɔr, kintór.
Appropriate also for the Earl of
~.
Kintyre S'clyde, kın'taıər, kintír
Kintyre and Lorne, Marquess of,
kın'taıər ənd 'lɔrn, kintír ănd
lórn
Kinvig, f.n., kın'vıg, kinvíg
Kinwarton Warwicks., 'kınərtən,
kínnärtŏn; 'kınwərtən, kínwär-
tŏn
Kipling, Rudyard, author, 'rʌdjərd
'kıplıŋ, rúd-yärd kípling
Kipling Cotes Humberside, 'kıplıŋ
koʊts, kípling kōts
Kippax W. Yorks., 'kıpæks, kíp-
packs

Kirby, f.n., 'kɜrbı, kírbi
Kirby Bedon Norfolk, 'kɜrbı
'bidən, kírbi béedŏn
Kirbye, f.n., 'kɜrbı, kírbi
Kirby Wiske N. Yorks., 'kɜrbı
'wısk, kírbi wísk
Kirch, f.n., kɜrtʃ, kirtch
Kirkaldie, Viscount, kər'kɔdı,
kŭrkáwdi
Kirkbean D. & G., kɜrk'bin, kirk-
béen
Kirkbride, f.n., kɜrk'braıd, kirk-
bríd
Kirkbride Cumbria, kɜrk'braıd,
kirkbríd
Kirkburton W. Yorks., kɜrk'bɜrtən,
kirkbúrtŏn
Kirkby, f.n., 'kɜrbı, kírbi; 'kɜrkbı,
kírkbi
Kirkby Merseyside, 'kɜrbı, kírbi
Kirkby-in-Ashfield Notts., 'kɜrkbı
ın 'æʃfild, kírkbi in áshfeeld
Kirkby-in-Malhamdale N. Yorks.,
'kɜrbı ın 'mæləmdeıl, kírbi in
málămdayl
Kirkby Lonsdale Cumbria, 'kɜrbı
'lɒnzdeıl, kírbi lónzdayl
Kirkby Malham N. Yorks., 'kɜrbı
'mæləm, kírbi málăm
Kirkby Mallory Leics., 'kɜrkbı
'mælərı, kírkbi málŏri
Kirkby Malzeard N. Yorks.,
'kɜrbı 'mælzərd, kírbi málzärd
Kirkby Moorside N. Yorks.,
'kɜrbı 'muərsaıd, kírbi mŏŏr-sīd
Kirkby Stephen Cumbria, 'kɜrbı
'stivən, kírbi stéevĕn
Kirkby Thore Cumbria, 'kɜrbı
'θɔr, kírbi thór; 'kɜrbı 'fjuər,
kírbi féw-ĕr
Kirkcaldy Fife, kər'kɒdı, kŭr-
kóddi; kər'kɔdı, kŭrkáwdi
Kirkcubbin Co. Down, kɜr'kʌbın,
kirkúbbin
Kirkcudbright D. & G., kər'kubrı,
kŭrkoóbri
Kirk Deighton N. Yorks., kɜrk
'ditən, kirk déetŏn
Kirkden Tayside, kərk'den,
kŭrkdén
Kirkgate Bradford, Leeds (both
W. Yorks.), 'kɜrgeıt, kirgayt
Kirkgate Edinburgh, 'kɜrgıt, kírgit
Kirkgunzeon D. & G., kər'gʌnjən,
kŭrgún-yŏn
Kirkhaugh Northd., 'kɜrkhɑf,
kírk-haaf; 'kɜrkhɔ, kírk-haw
Kirkheaton W. Yorks., kɜrk'hitən,
kirk-héetŏn
Kirkhill H'land, 'kɜrk'hıl, kírk-híll
Kirkhope Borders, 'kɜrkhoʊp,
kírkhōp
Kirkleatham Cleveland, kɜrk-
'liðəm, kirk-léethăm

Kirk Leavington *Cleveland*, kɜrk
'levɪŋtən, kirk lévvington.
Another spelling is **Levington**.
Kirklees *W. Yorks.*, kɜrk'liz,
kirkleéz
Kirkley Foggo, *f.n.*, 'kɜrklɪ 'foʊ-
goʊ, kírkli fógõ
Kirkliston *Lothian*, kərk'lɪstən,
kürklístõn
Kirkmichael *S'clyde*, kərk'maɪkl,
kürkmíkl
Kirkoswald *Cumbria, S'clyde*,
kɜrk'ɒzwəld, kirk-ózwäld
Kirkpatrick, *f.n.*, kɜrk'pætrɪk,
kirkpátrick
Kirkstall Abbey *W. Yorks.*, 'kɜrk-
stəl, kírkstawl
Kirkstone Pass *Cumbria*, 'kɜrk-
stən, kírkstõn
Kirkup, *f.n.*, 'kɜrkəp, kírkŭp
Kirkwall *Orkney*, 'kɜrkwɔl, kírk-
wawl. *Appropriate also for
Viscount* ~.
Kirk Yetholm *Borders*, kɜrk
'jetəm, kirk yéttŏm
Kirriemarian, *native of* **Kirriemuir,**
ˌkɪrɪ'mɛərɪən, kirrimáiriän
Kirriemuir *Tayside*, ˌkɪrɪ'mjʊər,
kirri-myõõr
Kirtomy *H'land*, kɜr'tɒmɪ, kir-
tómmi
Kirwan, *f.n.*, 'kɜrwən, kírwän
Kishmul Castle, *also spelt* **Kis-
mull, Kiessimal,** *W. Isles*,
'kɪʃməl, kíshmŭl
Kishorn *H'land*, 'kɪʃɔrn, kísh-orn
Kislingbury *Northants.*, 'kɪzlɪŋ-
bərɪ, kízling-bŭri
Kismeldon Bridge *Cornwall*, kɪz-
'meldən, kizméldŏn
Kismull Castle *see* **Kishmul**
Castle
Kissane, *f.n.*, kɪ'sæn, kissán
Kitcat, *f.n.*, 'kɪtkæt, kítkat
Kitcatt, *f.n.*, 'kɪtkæt, kítkat
Kitchell, *f.n.*, 'kɪtʃl, kítchl
Kitchen, *f.n.*, 'kɪtʃɪn, kítchĕn
Kitchener, *f.n.*, 'kɪtʃɪnər, kítch-
ĕnĕr
Kitchener of Khartoum, Earl,
'kɪtʃɪnər əv kɑr'tum, kítchĕnĕr
ŏv kaartoóm
Kitchin, *f.n.*, 'kɪtʃɪn, kítchin
Kitshowe Bridge *Cumbria*, 'kɪts-
haʊ, kíts-how
Kitson, *f.n.*, 'kɪtsən, kítsŏn
Kiver, *f.n.*, 'kaɪvər, kívĕr
Kiveton Park *S. Yorks.*, 'kɪvɪtən
kívvĕtŏn
Klasicki, *f.n.*, klæ'ʃɪtskɪ, klasheét-
ski
Kleinwort, *f.n.*, 'klaɪnwɔrt, klín-
-wawrt
Klimcke, *f.n.*, 'klɪmkɪ, klímki

Klug, *f.n.*, klʌg, klug
Klugg, *f.n.*, klʌg, klug
Klugh, *f.n.*, klu, kloo
Klugman, *f.n.*, 'klugmən, kloóg-
män
Kluth, *f.n.*, klʌθ, kluth
Kmiecik, *f.n.*, k'mjetʃɪk, k-myé-
tchick
Knaith *Lincs.*, neɪð, nayth; neɪθ,
nayth
Knapp, *f.n.*, næp, napp
Knapwell *Cambs.*, 'næpwel, náp-
wel
Knaresborough *N. Yorks.*, 'nɛərz-
bərə, náirzbŭră. *Appropriate
also for the Barony of* ~.
Knatchbull, *f.n.*, 'nætʃbʊl, nátch-
bŏŏl
Knavesmire Race Course *N.
Yorks.*, 'neɪvzmaɪər, náyvz-mīr
Kneale, *f.n.*, nil, neel
Knebworth *Herts.*, 'nebwərθ,
nébwŭrth
Kneebone, *f.n.*, 'niboʊn, neébõn
Kneen, *f.n.*, nin, neen
Kneesworth *Cambs.*, 'nizwərθ,
neézwürth
Kneeton *Notts.*, 'nitən, neétŏn
Kneller, *f.n.*, 'nelər, néllĕr.
Appropriate also for ~ *Hall,
London.*
Knevett, *f.n.*, 'nevɪt, névvĕt
Knibs, *f.n.*, nɪbz, nibz
Knight, *f.n.*, naɪt, nīt
Knighton, *f.n.*, 'naɪtən, nítŏn
Knighton *Powys, I. of Wight,*
'naɪtən, nítŏn
Knights Enham *Hants*, 'naɪts
'enəm, níts énnăm
Knightshayes Court *Devon,*
'naɪtsheɪz, nítz-hayz
Knipe, *f.n.*, naɪp, nīp
Kniveton *Derby.*, 'naɪvtən, nívtŏn;
'nɪftən, níftŏn
Knock *Cumbria*, nɒk, nock
Knockagh *Co. Antrim*, 'nɒkə,
nóckă
Knockando *Grampian*, nɒ'kændoʊ,
nockándõ
Knockbracken *Co. Down*, nɒk-
'brækən, nockbráckĕn
Knockbreda *Co. Down*, nɒk-
'breɪdə, nockbráydă
Knockcloghrim *Co. Derry*, nɒk-
'lɒkrɪm, nock-lóckrim
Knockdow, *f.n.*, nɒk'du, nockdoó
Knockholt *Kent*, 'nɒkhoʊlt, nóck-
-hõlt
Knocklayd *Co. Antrim*, nɒk'leɪd,
nockláyd
Knocknacarry *Co. Antrim*,
ˌnɒknə'kærɪ, nocknăkárri
Knodishall *Suffolk*, 'nɒdɪʃl,
nóddi-shl

Knokin see **Strange of Knokin**
Knole *Kent*, noʊl, nōl
Knollys, Viscount, noʊlz, nōlz
Knook *Wilts.*, nʊk, nōŏk
Knott, *f.n.*, nɒt, nott
Knowle *W. Midlands*, noʊl, nōl
Knowler, *f.n.*, 'noʊlər, nōʹlĕr
Knowles, *f.n.*, noʊlz, nōlz
Knowsley *Merseyside*, 'noʊzlɪ, nōʹzli
Knox-Johnston, *f.n.*, 'nɒks 'dʒɒnstən, nócks jónn-stŏn
Knox-Mawer, *f.n.*, 'nɒks 'mɔr, nócks mór
Knoydart *H'land*, 'nɔɪdərt, nóydärt; 'nɔɪdɑrt, nóydaart
Knucklas *Powys*, 'nʌkləs, núckläss
Knussen, *f.n.*, 'nʌsən, nússĕn. *Appropriate for Oliver* ∼, *composer.*
Knuston *Northants.*, 'nʌstən, nússtŏn
Knutsford *Ches.*, 'nʌtsfərd, núts-förd
Knypersley *Staffs.*, 'naɪpərzlɪ, nīʹpĕrzli
Knyvett, *f.n.*, 'nɪvɪt, nívvĕt
Knyvette, *f.n.*, nɪ'vet, nivétt
Knyvet-Wilson, *f.n.*, 'nɪvɪt 'wɪlsən nívvĕt wílssŏn
Kobziak, *f.n.*, 'kɒbziæk, kóbzi-ack
Kohler, *f.n.*, 'koʊlər, kōʹlĕr
Kolankiewicz, *f.n.*, ‚kɒlæŋ'kjevɪtʃ, kolankyévvitch
Koltai, *f.n.*, 'koʊltaɪ, kóltī
Kops, *f.n.*, kɒps, kopss
Koralek, *f.n.*, 'kɒrəlek, kórrăleck
Kornberg, *f.n.*, 'kɔrnbɜrg, kórn--berg
Kortright, *f.n.*, 'kɔrtraɪt, kórtrīt
Kossoff, *f.n.*, 'kɒsɒf, kóssoff
Kough, *f.n.*, kjoʊ, kyō
Kraay, *f.n.*, kreɪ, kray
Kraemer, *f.n.*, 'kreɪmər, kráymĕr
Krailsheimer, *f.n.*, 'kreɪlzhaɪmər, kráylz-hīmĕr
Kreeger, *f.n.*, 'krigər, kréegĕr
Kreiman, *f.n.*, 'kraɪmən, krímăn
Krein, *f.n.*, kraɪn, krīn
Kremer, *f.n.*, 'krimər, kréemĕr
Krichefski, *f.n.*, krɪ'tʃefskɪ, kritchéfski
Kris, *f.n.*, krɪs, kriss
Krishnamurti, *f.n.*, ‚krɪʃnə'mʊərtɪ, krishnămōŏrti
Krumb, *f.n.*, krʌm, krum
Kruse, *f.n.*, kruz, krooz
Kuggar *Cornwall*, 'kʌgər, kúggăr; 'kɪgər, kíggăr
Kuipers, *f.n.*, 'kaɪpərz, kípĕrz
Kumm, *f.n.*, kʊm, kōŏm
Kupfermann, *f.n.*, 'kʊpfərmæn, kōŏpfĕr-man

Kurakin, *f.n.*, kjʊ'rɑkɪn, kyōŏ-raákin
Kureishi, *f.n.*, kʊ'reɪʃɪ, kōŏráyshi
Kutscherauer, *f.n.*, 'kʊtʃəraʊər, kōŏtchĕrowĕr
Kwella, *f.n.*, 'kwelə, kwéllă
Kyffin, *f.n.*, 'kʌfɪn, kúffin; 'kɪfɪn, kíffin
Kyleakin *Skye*, kaɪl'ækɪn, kīl-áckin
Kyle of Durness *H'land*, 'kaɪl əv 'dərnɪs, kíl ŏv dúrnĕss
Kyle of Lochalsh *H'land*, 'kaɪl əv lɒx'ælʃ, kíl ŏv lochálsh
Kyle Rhea *H'land*, 'kaɪl 'reɪ, kíl ráy
Kyle Sku *H'land*, 'kaɪl 'skju, kíl skéw
Kyles Morar *H'land*, 'kaɪlz 'mɔrər, kílz máwrăr
Kyles of Bute *S'clyde*, 'kaɪlz əv 'bjut, kílz ŏv béwt
Kyllachy, *f.n.*, 'kaɪləxɪ, kílǎchi
Kyllo, *f.n.*, 'kaɪloʊ, kílŏ
Kylsant, Barony of, kɪl'sænt, kilssánt
Kynance Cove *Cornwall*, 'kaɪnæns, kínanss
Kynaston, *f.n.*, 'kɪnəstən, kínnăstŏn
Kynnersley, *f.n.*, 'kɪnərzlɪ, kín-nĕrzli
Kynoch, *f.n.*, 'kaɪnɒx, kínoch
Kynsey, *f.n.*, 'kɪnzɪ, kínzi
Kynynmound, *f.n.*, kɪ'nɪnmənd, kinnínmünd
Kysow, *f.n.*, 'kaɪsoʊ, kíssō

L

Labbett, *f.n.*, 'læbɪt, lábbĕt
La Belle Sauvage Yard *London*, lɑ 'bel soʊ'vɑʒ, laa béll sōvaázh
Labone, *f.n.*, lə'boʊn, lăbṓn
Labouchere, *f.n.*, ‚læbu'ʃɛər, lab-boosháir; 'læbuʃɛər, lábboo--shair
Labovitch, *f.n.*, 'læbəvɪtʃ, lábbŏvitch
La Brooy, *f.n.*, lɑ 'broʊɪ, laa brṓ-i
Lacaille, *f.n.*, lə'keɪ, lăkáy
Lacey, *f.n.*, 'leɪsɪ, láyssi
La Chard, *f.n.*, lə 'tʃɑrd, lă chaárd
Lache *Ches.*, leɪtʃ, laytch
Lachmann, *f.n.*, 'lɑkmən, laákmăn
Lackenby *Cleveland*, 'lækənbɪ, láckĕnbi
Lacock *Wilts.*, 'leɪkɒk, láykock. *Appropriate also for* ∼ *Abbey.*

Lacon, *f.n.,* 'leɪkən, láykŏn
Ladbroke, *f.n.,* 'lædbrʊk, lád-
 brŏŏk
Ladbrook, *f.n.,* 'lædbrʊk, lád-
 brŏŏk
Laddow Rocks *Gtr. M'chester,*
 'lædoʊ, láddō
Ladefoged, *f.n.,* 'lædɪfoʊgɪd,
 láddĕfōgĕd
Ladell, *f.n.,* læ'del, laddéll
Lader, *f.n.,* 'leɪdər, láydĕr
Ladhar Bheinn *H'land,* lɑ 'veɪn,
 laa váyn
Ladhope *Borders,* 'lædəp, láddŏp
Ladock *Cornwall,* 'lædək, láddŏck
Lafcadio, *f.n.,* læf'kɑdɪoʊ, laf-
 kaádiō
Laffan, *f.n.,* lə'fæn, läfán
Laffeaty, *f.n.,* 'læfɪtɪ, láffĕti
Lafford, *f.n.,* 'læfərd, láffŏrd
Lafontaine, *f.n.,* lə'fɒnteɪn, läfón-
 tayn
La Fontaine, *f.n.,* lə 'fɒnteɪn, lä
 fóntayn
Lagan, River, *Co. Down,* 'lægən,
 lággän
Laggan, Loch, *Central,* 'lægən,
 lággän
Lahee, *f.n.,* lə'hi, lähée
Laid *H'land,* leɪd, layd
Laidlaw, *f.n.,* 'leɪdlɔ, láyd-law
Laidler, *f.n.,* 'leɪdlər, láydlĕr
Laidlow, *f.n.,* 'leɪdloʊ, láydlō
Laighwood *Tayside,* 'leɪxwʊd,
 láychwŏŏd
Laindon *Essex,* 'leɪndən, láyndŏn
Laindon Hills, *also called* **Lang-
 don Hills** *q.v., Essex,* 'leɪndən
 'hɪlz, láyndŏn híllz
Laing, *f.n.,* leɪŋ, layng; læŋ, lang
Laing Art Gallery *Newcastle upon
 Tyne,* leɪŋ, layng
Laira *Devon,* 'leərə, láïrä
Laird, *f.n.,* leərd, laird
Lairg *H'land,* leərg, lairg
Laister Dyke *W. Yorks.,* 'leɪstər
 daɪk, láysstĕr dīk
Laithwaite, *f.n.,* 'leɪθweɪt, láyth-
 wayt
Lakenham *Norfolk,* 'leɪkənəm,
 láykĕnăm
Lakenheath *Suffolk,* 'leɪkənhiθ,
 láykĕn-heeth
Laker, *f.n.,* 'leɪkər, láykĕr
Lalage, *C.n.,* 'læləgɪ, lálägi;
 'lælədʒɪ, láläji
Laleham *Surrey,* 'leɪləm, láylăm
Laleston *Mid Glam.,* 'lælɪstən,
 lálĕstŏn
Lam, *f.n.,* læm, lam
Lamancha *Borders,* lə'mæŋkə,
 lămánkă
Lamarsh *Essex,* 'læmɑrʃ, lám-
 maarsh

Lamas, *also spelt* **Lammas,** *Nor-
 folk,* 'læməs, lámmäss
Lamb, *f.n.,* læm, lam
Lambeg *Co. Antrim,* læm'beg,
 lambég
Lambelet, *f.n.,* 'læmbəlɪt, lámbĕ-
 lĕt
Lambert, *f.n.,* 'læmbərt, lámbĕrt
Lamberton, *f.n.,* 'læmbərtən,
 lámbĕrtŏn
Lambeth *London,* 'læmbəθ,
 lámbĕth
Lambethan, *pertaining to* **Lam-
 beth,** læm'biθən, lambéethăn
Lambhill *S'clyde,* 'læm'hɪl, lám-
 -híll
Lamb Holm *Orkney,* 'læm hoʊm,
 lám hōm
Lambie, *f.n.,* 'læmbɪ, lámbi
Lambley, *f.n.,* 'læmlɪ, lámli
Lamborn, *f.n.,* 'læmbɔrn, lám-
 -born
Lamerton *Borders,* 'læmərtən,
 lámmĕrtŏn
Lamesley *Tyne & Wear,* 'leɪmzlɪ,
 láymzli
Laming, *f.n.,* 'leɪmɪŋ, láyming;
 'læmɪŋ, lámming
Lamington *S'clyde,* 'læmɪŋtən,
 lámmingtŏn. *Appropriate also
 for the Barony of* ~.
Lamlash *S'clyde,* ləm'læʃ, lăm-
 -lásh; læm'læʃ, lam-lásh
Lammas *see* **Lamas**
Lamond, *f.n.,* 'læmənd, lámmŏnd
Lamont, *f.n.,* 'læmənt, lámmŏnt;
 lə'mɒnt, lămónt. *The first is the
 usual Scottish pronunciation, the
 second the Northern Irish.*
Lamorbey *London,* 'læmərbɪ,
 lámmŏrbi
Lamorna *Cornwall,* lə'mɔrnə,
 lámórnä
Lamorran *Cornwall,* lə'mɒrən,
 lámórrän
Lamotte, *f.n.,* lə'mɒt, lămótt
Lampe, *f.n.,* læmp, lamp; 'læmpɪ,
 lámpi
Lampeter *Dyfed,* 'læmpɪtər, lám-
 pĕtĕr
Lamphey *Dyfed,* 'læmfɪ, lámfi.
 Appropriate also for ~ *Palace.*
Lamplugh, *f.n.,* 'læmplu, lám-ploo
Lamplugh *Cumbria,* 'læmplu, lám-
 -ploo; 'læmplə, lám-plä
Lampson, *f.n.,* 'læmpsən, lámpssŏn
Lanark *S'clyde,* 'lænərk, lánnärk
La Nauze, *f.n.,* lə 'nɔz, lä náwz
Lancashire *Co. name,* 'læŋkəʃər,
 lánkăshĕr
Lancaster, *f.n.,* 'læŋkəstər, lánk-
 ăstĕr
Lancaster *Lancs.,* 'læŋkəstər,
 lánkăstĕr

Lancastrian, *pertaining to* **Lancaster** *or* **Lancashire,** læŋ-'kæstrɪən, lankásstri-ăn
Lancaut *Glos.,* læŋ'koʊt, lankót
Lance, *C.n. and f.n.,* lɑns, laanss
Lancefield, *f.n.,* 'lɑnsfild, laánssfeeld
Lancelot, *C.n.,* 'lɑnsɪlɒt, laánssĕlot; 'lɑnslɒt, laánsslot
Lancelot, *f.n.,* 'lɑnsɪlɒt, laánssĕlot
Lanchbery, *f.n.,* 'lɑnʃbərɪ, laánshbĕri
Lancing *W. Sussex,* 'lɑnsɪŋ, laánssing
Landamare, *f.n.,* 'lændəmɑr, lándămaar
Landau, *f.n.,* 'lændoʊ, lándō; 'lændaʊ, lándow
Lander, *f.n.,* 'lændər, lándĕr
Landeryou, *f.n.,* 'lændərju, lándĕr-yoo
Landewednack *Cornwall,* ˌlændɪ-'wednək, landĕwédnăk
Landoger Trow, The, *historic Bristol inn,* 'lændɒgər 'traʊ, lándoggĕr trów
Landone, *f.n.,* 'lændən, lándŏn
Landore *W. Glam.,* læn'dɔr, landór
Landrake *Cornwall,* læn'dreɪk, landráyk
Landulph *Cornwall,* læn'dʌlf, landúlf
Lanercost *Cumbria,* 'lænərkɒst, lánnĕrkost
Lanesborough, Earl of, 'leɪnzbərə, láynzbŭră
Lanfear, *f.n.,* 'lænfɪər, lánfeer
Lanfine House, *S'clyde,* læn'fin, lanféen
Langar *Notts.,* 'læŋgər, láng-găr
Langdon Hills, *also called* **Laindon Hills** *q.v., Essex,* 'læŋdən 'hɪlz, lángdŏn híllz
Lange, *f.n.,* lændʒ, lanj
Langenhoe *Essex,* 'læŋgənhoʊ, láng-gĕn-hō
Langer, *f.n.,* 'læŋər, láng-ĕr
Langford, *f.n.,* 'læŋfərd, lángfŏrd
Langham, *f.n.,* 'læŋəm, láng-ăm
Langho *Lancs.,* 'læŋoʊ, láng-ō
Langholm *D. & G.,* 'læŋəm, láng-ŏm
Langley, *f.n.,* 'læŋlɪ, láng-li
Langloan *S'clyde,* 'læŋ'loʊn, láng-lṓn
Langold *Notts.,* 'læŋgoʊld, láng-gṓld
Langridge, *f.n.,* 'læŋgrɪdʒ, láng-grij
Langrishe, *f.n.,* læŋ'grɪʃ, lang-gréesh
Langstaff, *f.n.,* 'læŋstɑf, lángstaaf

Langstone, *parliamentary div. of Portsmouth,* 'læŋstən, lángstŏn
Langstrothdale *N. Yorks.,* læŋ-'strɒθdeɪl, lang-stróth-dayl
Langton Matravers *Dorset,* 'læŋtən mə'trævərz, lángtŏn mătrávvĕrz
Langwathby *Cumbria,* læŋ'wɒθbɪ, lang-wóthbi
Langwith, Nether, *Notts.,* 'læŋwɪθ, láng-with
Langwith, Upper, *Derby.,* 'læŋgwɪθ, láng-gwith
Lanherne *Cornwall,* læn'hɜrn, lan-hérn
Lanhydrock *Cornwall,* læn'haɪdrək, lan-hídrŏk
Lanier, *f.n.,* 'lænjər, lán-yĕr
Lanivet *Cornwall,* læn'ɪvɪt, lan-nívvĕt
Lanjeth *Cornwall,* læn'dʒeθ, lanjéth
Lankester, *f.n.,* 'læŋkɪstər, lánkĕstĕr
Lanlivery *Cornwall,* læn'lɪvərɪ, lan-lívvĕri
Lanreath *Cornwall,* læn'reθ, lanréth
Lansdown, *f.n.,* 'lænzdaʊn, lánzdown
Lanteglos *Cornwall,* læn'teglɒs, lantégloss; læn'teɪglɒs, lantáygloss
Lanyon Cromlech *Cornwall,* 'lænjən 'krɒmlek, lán-yŏn krómleck
Lapage, *f.n.,* lə'peɪdʒ, lăpáyj
Lapal *W. Midlands,* 'læpl, láppl
Laphroaig Distillery *S'clyde,* lə'frɔɪg, lăfróyg
Lapotaire, *f.n.,* ˌlæpɒ'teər, lappotáir
Lappage, *f.n.,* lɑ'peɪdʒ, laapáyj
Laraine, *C.n.,* lə'reɪn, lăráyn
Largo *Fife,* 'lɑrgoʊ, laárgō
Larkby, *f.n.,* 'lɑrkbɪ, laárkbi
Larkhill *Wilts.,* 'lɑrk'hɪl, laárk--híll
Larkins, *f.n.,* 'lɑrkɪnz, laárkinz
Larmor, *f.n.,* 'lɑrmər, laármŏr
Larmour, *f.n.,* 'lɑrmər, laármŭr
La Roche, *f.n.,* lɑ 'rɒʃ, laa rósh
Laryea, *f.n.,* laɪ, lī
Lascelles, *f.n.,* 'læslz, lásslz. *Appropriate also for Viscount* ~.
Lasdun, *f.n.,* 'læzdən, lázdŭn
Lash, *f.n.,* læʃ, lash
Lasham *Hants,* 'læsəm, lássăm; 'læʃəm, láshăm. *The first is the traditional village pronunciation. The second is familiar to those using the Gliding Centre.*
Lashmar, *f.n.,* 'læʃmɑr, láshmaar

Laslett, *f.n.*, 'læzlɪt, lázlĕt
Lassodie *Fife*, læ'soʊdɪ, lassódi
Lasswade *Lothian*, læs'weɪd, lasswáyd
Latchem, *f.n.*, 'lætʃəm, látchĕm
Lategan, *f.n.*, 'lætɪgən, láttĕgän
La Terriere, *f.n.*, lɑ 'terɪɛər, laa térri-air
Latey, *f.n.*, 'leɪtɪ, láyti
Latham, *f.n.*, 'leɪθəm, láythăm; 'leɪðəm, láythăm. *The first is appropriate for Baron* ~.
Latham-Koenig, *f.n.*, 'leɪθəm 'kənɪg, láythăm kŏnig
Lathan, *f.n.*, 'leɪθən, láythăn
Lathbury, *f.n.*, 'læθbərɪ, láthbŭri
Latheron *H'land*, 'læðərən, láthĕrŏn
Lathey, *f.n.*, 'leɪθɪ, láythi
Lathom, *f.n.*, 'leɪθəm, láythŏm; 'leɪðəm, láythŏm
Lathom *Lancs.*, 'leɪðəm, láythŏm
Latimer, *f.n.*, 'lætɪmər, láttimĕr
La Touche, *f.n.*, lɑ 'tuʃ, laa toósh
Latreille, *f.n.*, lə'treɪl, lătráyl; lə'tril, lătréel; lɑ'treɪ, laatráy
Latymer, Baron, 'lætɪmər, láttimĕr
Lauder, *f.n.*, 'lɔdər, láwdĕr
Lauder *Borders*, 'lɔdər, láwdĕr
Lauderdale *Borders*, 'lɔdərdeɪl, láwdĕrdayl. *Appropriate also for the Earl of* ~.
Laugharne, *f.n.*, lɑrn, laarn
Laugharne *Dyfed*, lɑrn, laarn
Laugherne House *H. & W.*, lɔrn, lorn
Laughlan, *f.n.*, 'lɒxlən, lóchlăn
Laughland, *f.n.*, 'lɒxlənd, lóchländ
Laughton, *f.n.*, 'lɔtən, láwtŏn
Laughton *E. Sussex*, 'lɔtən, láwtŏn
Launcells *Cornwall*, 'lɑnslz; la'ansslz; 'lænslz, lánsslz
Launceston *Cornwall*, 'lɑnsən, la'ansstŏn; 'lɒnsən, láwnssŏn; 'lɒnstən, láwnsstŏn
Laureen, *C.n.*, lɔ'rin, lawréen
Laurence, *C.n.*, 'lɒrəns, lórrĕnss
Laurie, *f.n.*, 'lɒrɪ, lórri
Laurier, *f.n.*, 'lɒrɪər, lórri-ĕr
Lauriston, *f.n.*, 'lɒrɪstən, lórristŏn
Lauriston Castle *Edinburgh*, 'lɒrɪstən, lórristŏn
Lauwers, *f.n.*, 'laʊərz, lów-ĕrz
Lauwerys, *f.n.*, 'laʊraɪz, lów-rīz
Lavant *W. Sussex*, 'lævənt, lávvănt
Lavarack, *f.n.*, 'lævəræk, lávvărack
Lavecock, *f.n.*, 'lævɪkɒk, lávvĕkock

Lavell, *f.n.*, 'lævl, lávvl; lə'vel, lăvéll
Lavendon *Bucks.*, 'lævəndən, lávvĕndŏn
Lavenham *Suffolk*, 'lævənəm, lávvĕnăm
Laver, *f.n.*, 'leɪvər, láyvĕr
Laver, River, *N. Yorks.*, 'lɑvər, laávĕr
Laverick, *f.n.*, 'lævərɪk, lávvĕrick
Lavernock Point *S. Glam.*, 'lævərnək, lávvĕrnŏk
Lavers, *f.n.*, 'leɪvərz, láyvĕrz
Laverstock *Wilts.*, 'lævərstɒk, lávvĕrstock
Laverstoke *Hants*, 'lævərstoʊk, lávvĕrstŏk
Laverton *Glos.*, 'lævərtən, lávvĕrtŏn
Laville, *f.n.*, lə'vil, lăvéel
Lavin, *f.n.*, 'lævɪn, lávvin
Lavington, West, *W. Sussex*, *Wilts.*, 'lævɪŋtən, lávvingtŏn
Lawday, *f.n.*, 'lɔdeɪ, láwday
Lawhitton *Cornwall*, lɒ'hwɪtən, law-whíttŏn; lɑ'hwɪtən, laa-whíttŏn
Lawler, *f.n.*, 'lɔlər, láwlĕr
Lawless, *f.n.*, 'lɔles, láwless
Lawley, *f.n.*, 'lɔlɪ, láwli
Lawrence, *C.n. and f.n.*, 'lɒrəns, lórrĕnss
Lawrie, *f.n.*, 'lɒrɪ, lórri
Lawshall *Suffolk*, 'lɔʃl, láwshl
Lawson, *f.n.*, 'lɔsən, láwssŏn
Lawther, *f.n.*, 'lɔðər, láwthĕr
Laxey, *I. of Man*, 'læksɪ, lácksi
Layard, *f.n.*, 'leɪɑrd, láy-aard; 'leɪərd, láy-ärd
Laycock, *f.n.*, 'leɪkɒk, láykock
Layer Breton *Essex*, 'leɪər 'bretən, láy-ĕr bréttŏn
Layer de la Haye *Essex*, 'leɪər də lɑ 'heɪ, láy-ĕr dĕ laa háy
Layham *Suffolk*, 'leɪəm, láy-ăm
Layton, *f.n.*, 'leɪtən, láytŏn
Lazar, *f.n.*, lə'zɑr, lăzaár
Lazard, *f.n.*, 'læzɑrd, lázzaard
Lazarenko, *f.n.*, ˌlæzə'reŋkoʊ, lazzăr-énkó
Lazell, *f.n.*, lə'zel, lăzéll
Lazenby, *f.n.*, 'leɪzənbɪ, láyzĕnbi
Lazonby, *f.n.*, 'leɪzənbɪ, láyzŏnbi
Lazonby *Cumbria*, 'leɪzənbɪ, láyzŏnbi
Lea, *f.n.*, li, lee
Leach, *f.n.*, litʃ, leetch
Leacock, *f.n.*, 'likɒk, léekock; 'leɪkɒk, láykock
Leadbeater, *f.n.*, 'ledbitər, lédbeetĕr; 'ledbɪtər, lédbitĕr; 'lidbitər, léedbeetĕr; 'lebɪtər, lébbitĕr

Leadbetter, f.n., 'ledbetər, léd-bettĕr; led'betər, ledbéttĕr
Leadbitter, f.n., 'ledbɪtər, léd-bittĕr
Leaden, River, *H. & W.*, 'ledən, léddĕn. *Also spelt* **Leddon.**
Leadenhall Street *London*, 'ledən-hɔl, léddĕnhawl
Leadenham *Lincs.*, 'ledənəm, léddĕnăm
Leadgate *Cumbria*, 'ledgɪt, léd-git
Leadlay, f.n., 'ledleɪ, léd-lay
Leah, f.n., 'liə, leé-ă
Leahy, f.n., 'lihɪ, leé-hi
Leakey, Louis Seymour Bazett, anthropologist and archaeologist (1903–72), 'luɪs 'simɔr 'bæzɪt 'likɪ, loʹo-iss seémor bázzĕt leéki
Leal, f.n., lil, leel
Leamington *Warwicks.*, 'lemɪŋtən, lémmingtŏn
Lean, f.n., lin, leen
Leaning, f.n., 'linɪŋ, leéning
Leaper, f.n., 'lipər, leépĕr
Leaphard, f.n., 'lepərd, léppărd
Learmonth, f.n., 'lɜrmənθ, lér-mŏnth; 'leərmənθ, láirmŏnth; 'liərmənθ, leérmŏnth; 'lɜrmənt, lérmŏnt
Learmouth, f.n., 'liərmaʊθ, leér-mowth
Learney *Grampian*, 'leərnɪ, láirni
Learoyd, f.n., 'liərɔɪd, leér-oyd
Learthart, f.n., 'liərθɑrt, leér--thaart
Leasingthorne *Durham*, 'lizɪŋθɔrn, leézingthorn
Leask, f.n., lisk, leesk
Leasowe *Merseyside*, 'lisoʊ, leéssō
Leatham, f.n., 'liθəm, leé-thăm; 'liðəm, leéthăm
Leathart, f.n., 'liθɑrt, leé-thaart
Leather, f.n., 'leðər, léthĕr
Leatherland, f.n., 'leðərlənd, léthĕrländ. *Appropriate also for* Baron ~.
Leathers, Viscount, 'leðərz, léthĕrz
Leathes, f.n., liðz, leethz
Leavenheath *Suffolk*, 'levənhiθ, lévvĕn-heeth
Leavening *N. Yorks.*, 'livnɪŋ, leév-ning
Leaver, f.n., 'livər, leévĕr
Leavesden Green *Herts.*, 'livz-dən, leévzdĕn
Leavey, f.n., 'livɪ, leévi
Leavins, f.n., 'levɪnz, lévvinz
Leavis, f.n., 'livɪs, leéviss
Leay, f.n., leɪ, lay
Le Bars, f.n., lə 'bɑrz, lĕ baʹarz
Lebon, f.n., 'libɒn, leébon
Lebor, f.n., lə'bɔr, lĕbór

Le Breton, f.n., lə 'bretɒn, lĕ brét-ton
Leburn, f.n., 'libɜrn, leéburn
Lebus, f.n., 'libəs, leébŭss
Le Cain, f.n., lə 'keɪn, lĕ káyn
Le Carré, f.n., lə 'kæreɪ, lĕ kárray
Leche, f.n., leʃ, lesh
Lechlade *Glos.*, 'letʃleɪd, létch--layd
Lechmere, f.n., 'letʃmɪər, létch-meer; 'leʃmɪər, léshmeer
Leconfield *Humberside*, 'lekən-fild, léckŏnfeeld. *Appropriate also for* Baron ~.
Le Court *Hants*, 'li 'kɔrt, leé kórt
Le Cren, f.n., lə 'kren, lĕ krén
Lecropt *Central*, 'lekrɒpt, léck-ropt
Lecumpher *Co. Derry*, lə'kʌmfər, lĕkúmfĕr
Ledbury *H. & W.*, 'ledbərɪ, léd-bŭri
Leddon, River, *see* **Leaden**
Ledeboer, f.n., 'ledəbʊər, léddĕ-bōōr
Le Despencer, Baron, lə dɪ'spen-sər, lĕ dĕspénssĕr
Ledgard, f.n., 'ledʒɑrd, léjjaard
Ledigo, f.n., 'ledɪgoʊ, léddigō
Ledingham, f.n., 'ledɪŋəm, lédding-ăm
Ledoux, f.n., lə'du, lĕdoʹo
Leech, f.n., litʃ, leetch
Leedell, f.n., li'del, leedéll
Leeds *Kent, W. Yorks.*, lidz, leedz
Leedstown *Cornwall*, 'lidztaʊn, leédztown
Leeming, f.n., 'limɪŋ, leéming
Leese, f.n., lis, leess; liz, leez
Lefanu, f.n., 'lefənju, léffänew; lə'fɑnu, lĕfáʹanoo
Le Fanu, f.n., 'lefənu, léffänoo; 'lefənju, léffänew
Lefeaux, f.n., lə'foʊ, lĕfó
Lefebure, f.n., 'lefəbjʊər, léffĕ-byōōr
Lefebvre, f.n., lə'fivər, lĕfeévĕr
Le Feuvre, f.n., lə 'fivər, lĕ feévĕr
Lefeuvre, f.n., lə'fɜvr, lĕfóvr
Le Fevre, f.n., lə 'feɪvr, lĕ fáyvr
Lefevre, f.n., lə'fivər, lĕfeévĕr; lə'fevr, lĕfévvr
Lefevre Galleries *London*, lə'fɛ:vr, lĕfévvr
Le Fleming, f.n., lə 'flemɪŋ, lĕ flémming
Lefroy, f.n., lə'frɔɪ, lĕfróy
Legacurry *Co. Down*, ˌlegə'kʌrɪ, leggäkúrri
Legacy *Clwyd*, 'legəsɪ, légässi
Le Gallienne, f.n., lə 'gæljen, lĕ gál-yen
Legard, f.n., 'ledʒərd, léjjärd

Legat, *f.n.*, lə'gæt, lĕgát
Legburthwaite *Cumbria*, 'leg-
 bərθweıt, légbŭrthwayt
Leger Galleries *London*, 'ledʒər,
 léjĕr
Legerton, *f.n.*, 'ledʒərtən, léjĕrtŏn
Legerwood *Borders*, 'ledʒərwʊd,
 léjĕrwōod
Legfordrum *Co. Tyrone*, ‚legfər-
 'drʌm, legfŏrdrúm
Leggate, *f.n.*, 'legeıt, léggayt;
 'legət, léggăt
Leggatt, *f.n.*, 'legət, léggăt
Legge, *f.n.*, leg, leg
Leggett, *f.n.*, 'legət, léggĕt
Legh, *f.n.*, li, lee
Le Grice, *f.n.*, lə 'graıs, lĕ gríss
Le Gros, *f.n.*, lə 'grou, lĕ gró
Lehane, *f.n.*, lə'hɑn, lĕ-haán
Leheup, *f.n.*, 'liəp, lée-ŭp
Lehmann, *f.n.*, 'leımən, láymăn
Le Huray, *f.n.*, lə 'hjuəreı, lĕ
 hyŏŏray
Leicester *Leics.*, 'lestər, lésstĕr.
 Appropriate also for the Earl of
 ∼.
Leifer, *f.n.*, 'lifər, léefĕr
Leigh, *f.n.*, li, lee. *Appropriate
 also for Baron* ∼.
Leigh Delamere *Wilts.*, 'li 'delə-
 mıər, lée déllămeer
Leigh-on-Mendip *Somerset*, 'laı
 ɒn 'mendıp, lī on méndip; 'li ɒn
 'mendıp, lée on méndip
Leigh-on-Sea *Essex*, 'li ɒn 'si, lée
 on sée
Leigh Sinton *H. & W.*, 'laı 'sıntən,
 lī síntŏn
Leighterton *Glos.*, 'leıtərtən, láy-
 tĕrtŏn
Leighton, *f.n.*, 'leıtən, láytŏn
Leighton *Powys*, 'leıtən, láytŏn
Leighton Bromswold *Cambs.*,
 'leıtən 'brɒmzwould, láytŏn
 brómzwōld
Leighton Buzzard *Beds.*, 'leıtən
 'bʌzərd, láytŏn búzzărd
Leinster, Duke of, 'lınstər,
 línsstĕr
Leinthall Earls *H. & W.*, 'lentl
 'ɜrlz, léntl érlz
Leinthall Starkes *H. & W.*, 'lentl
 'stɑrks, léntl staárks
Leintwardine *H. & W.*, 'lent-
 wərdaın, léntwărdīn; 'lentwər-
 din, léntwărdeen; 'læntərdin,
 lántĕrdeen
Leire *Leics.*, lıər, leer; lɛər, lair
Leishman, *f.n.*, 'liʃmən, léeshmăn;
 'lıʃmən, líshmän
Leisten, *f.n.*, 'listən, léesstĕn
Leister, *f.n.*, 'lestər, lésstĕr
Leiston *Suffolk*, 'leıstən, láysstŏn
Leitch, *f.n.*, litʃ, leetch

Leith, *f.n.*, liθ, leeth
Leith *Lothian*, liθ, leeth
Leith, River, *Cumbria*, liθ, leeth
Leithen *Borders*, 'liðən, léethĕn
Leither, *f.n.*, 'liðər, léethĕr
Leitholm *Borders*, 'litəm, léetŏm
Leitrim *Co. Down*, 'litrım, léetrim.
 *Appropriate also for the Earl-
 dom of* ∼.
Le Lacheyr, *f.n.*, lə 'læʃər, lĕ
 láshĕr
Leland, *f.n.*, 'lilənd, léelănd
Lelant *Cornwall*, le'lænt, lellánt;
 lı'lænt, lĕlánt
Lelean, *f.n.*, lə'lin, lĕléen
Leleu, *f.n.*, lə'lu, lĕlóo
Lely, Sir Peter, *17th-c. painter*,
 'lılı, léeli
Le Maitre, *f.n.*, lə 'meıtr, lĕ máytr
Leman, *f.n.*, 'lemən, lémmăn;
 'limən, léemăn
Leman Sands *off the coast of Nor-
 folk*, lı'mæn, lĕmán
Le Marchant, *f.n.*, lə 'mɑrtʃənt,
 lĕ maártchănt; lə 'mɑrʃənt, lĕ
 maárshănt
Lemare, *f.n.*, lə'mɛər, lĕmáir
Le Mare, *f.n.*, lə 'mɛər, lĕ máir
Le Masurier, *f.n.*, lə mə'zjuərıər,
 lĕ măzyŏŏri-ĕr
Le Mauviel, *f.n.*, lə 'mouvjəl, lĕ
 mόv-yĕl
Le Mesurier, *f.n.*, lə 'meʒərər, lĕ
 mézhĕrĕr; lə mə'zuərıeı, lĕ
 mĕzŏŏri-ay
Lemin, *f.n.*, lə'mın, lĕmínn
Lemoine, *f.n.*, lə'mɔın, lĕmóyn
Lemon, *f.n.*, 'lemən, lémmŏn
Lempfert, *f.n.*, 'lempfərt, lémp-
 fĕrt
Lempriere, *f.n.*, 'lemprıɛər,
 lémpri-air
Lenaderg *Co. Down*, ‚lenə'dɜrg,
 lennădérg
Lenadoon *Belfast*, ‚lenə'dun,
 lennădóon
Lenanton, *f.n.*, lə'næntən, lĕnán-
 tŏn
Lench, *f.n.*, lenʃ, lensh
Lenderyou, *f.n.*, 'lendərju,
 léndĕr-yoo
Lenehan, *f.n.*, 'lenəhən, lénnĕ-hăn
Le Neve, *f.n.*, lə 'niv, lĕ néev
Leney, *f.n.*, 'linı, léeni
Lennon, *f.n.*, 'lenən, lénnŏn
Lentaigne, *f.n.*, len'teın, lentáyn
Lenthall, *f.n.*, 'lentəl, léntawl;
 'lentl, léntl
Lenton, *f.n.*, 'lentən, léntŏn
Lenwade *Norfolk*, 'lenweıd, lén-
 -wayd
Leny, Pass *and* Falls of, *Central*,
 'lenı, lénni
Lenzie *S'clyde*, 'lenzı, lénzi

Leochel-Cushnie *Grampian*, 'lɒxl
  'kʌʃnɪ, lóchl kúshni
Leod *see* **Castle Leod**
Leode *Co. Down*, led, led
Leodegar, saint, leɪ'ɒdɪgɑr, lay-
  -óddĕgaar
Leofric, *C.n.*, 'lefrɪk, léffrick. *The*
  pronunciation 'leɪəfrɪk, láy-ŏ-
  -frick *is appropriate for the*
  Saxon lord of Coventry, husband
  of Lady **Godiva,**, *q.v.*
Leominster *H. & W.*, 'lemstər,
  lémsstĕr
Leon, *C.n. and f.n.*, 'liən, lée-ŏn
Leonard, *C.n. and f.n.*, 'lenərd,
  lénnărd
Leonard Stanley *Glos.*, 'lenərd
  'stænlɪ, lénnărd stánli
Leonardslee *W. Sussex*, ,lenərdz-
  'li, lennărdzleé
Leonowens,*f.n.*, 'liənouɪnz, lée-
  -ŏnŏ-ĕnz
Le Patourel, *f.n.*, lə 'pætuərel, lĕ
  páttŏŏrel
Lephard, *f.n.*, 'lepɑrd, léppaard
Lepine, *f.n.*, lə'pin, lĕpeén
Le Poer, *f.n.*, lə 'puər, lĕ pŏŏr
Le Poer Trench, *f.n.*, lə 'puər
  'trenʃ, lĕ pŏŏr trénsh
Leppard, *f.n.*, 'lepɑrd, léppaard
Le Prevost, *f.n.*, lə 'preɪvou, lĕ
  práyvŏ
Le Quesne, *f.n.*, lə 'keɪn, lĕ káyn
Le Queux, *f.n.*, lə 'kju, lĕ kéw
Le Riche, *f.n.*, lə 'riʃ, lĕ reésh
Le Rougetel, *f.n.*, lə 'ruʒtel, lĕ
  rŏŏzhtel
Leroy, *f.n.*, lə'rɔɪ, lĕróy
Lerwegian, *native of* **Lerwick,**
  lɜr'widʒən, lerweéjăn
Lerwick *Shetland*, 'lɜrwɪk, lérwick
Le Sage, *f.n.*, lə 'sɑʒ, lĕ saazh
Lescudjack *Cornwall*, lɪs'kʌdʒæk,
  lĕskújjack
Lesirge, *f.n.*, lə'sɜrʒ, lĕssírzh
Lesmahagow *S'clyde*, ,lesmə-
  'heɪɡou, lessmă-háygŏ
Lesnes *see* **Lessness**
Lesnewth *Devon*, lez'njuθ, lez-
  -néwth
Lesney *toy-manufacturing com-*
  pany, 'lesnɪ, léssni
Lessells, *f.n.*, 'lesls, lésslss
Lesser, *f.n.*, 'lesər, léssĕr
Lessness, *formerly spelt* **Lesnes,**
  London, 'lesnɪs, léssnĕss
Lessore, *f.n.*, lə'sɔr, lĕssór
Lessudden House *Borders*, lə-
  'sʌdən, lĕssúddĕn
Lestocq, *f.n.*, 'lestɒk, lésstock
Lestor, *f.n.*, 'lestər, lésstŏr
L'Estrange, *f.n.*, lɪ'streɪndʒ,
  lĕstráynj
Le Sueur, *f.n.*, lə 'swɜr, lĕ swúr

Le Surf, *f.n.*, lə 'sɜrf, lĕ súrf
Leswalt *D. & G.*, les'wɔlt, less-
  wáwlt
Letham, *f.n.*, 'leθəm, léthăm
Lethbridge, *f.n.*, 'leθbrɪdʒ, léth-
  brij
Lethem, *f.n.*, 'leθəm, léthĕm
Lethendy *Tayside*, 'leθəndɪ,
  léthĕndi
Lethnot *Tayside*, 'leθnət, léthnŏt
Leuchars, *f.n.*, 'lukəs, loókăss
Leuchars *Fife*, 'luxərz, loóchărz
Leueen, *C.n.*, lu'in, loo-eén
Leutscher, *f.n.*, 'lutʃər, lóotchĕr
Levack, *f.n.*, lə'væk, lĕváck
Levander, *f.n.*, lɪ'vændər, lĕván-
  dĕr
Levarne, *f.n.*, lə'vɑrn, lĕvaárn
Levatt, *f.n.*, lɪ'væt, lĕvát
Leven, *f.n.*, 'livən, leévĕn; 'levən,
  lévvĕn
Leven, River, *Cumbria*, 'levən,
  lévvĕn
Leven, Rivers, *Fife, H'land,*
  S'clyde, N. Yorks., 'livən,
  leévĕn
Leven and Melville, Earl of,
  'livən ənd 'melvɪl, leévĕn ănd
  mélvil
Levens, *f.n.*, 'levənz, lévvĕnz
Levens *Cumbria*, 'levənz, lévvĕnz
Levenshulme *Gtr. M'chester*,
  'levənzhjum, lévvĕnz-hewm
Leventon, *f.n.*, 'levəntən, lévvĕn-
  tŏn
Lever, *f.n.*, 'livər, leévĕr
Leverhulme, Viscount, 'livərhjum,
  leévĕr-hewm
Leverington *Cambs.*, 'levərɪŋtən,
  lévvĕringtŏn
Leverstock Green *Herts.*, 'levər-
  stɒk 'grin, lévvĕrstock greén
Leverton, *f.n.*, 'levərtən, lévvĕrtŏn
Leverton, North *and* South,
  Notts., 'levərtən, lévvĕrtŏn
Levesley, *f.n.*, 'livzlɪ, leévzli;
  'levəzlɪ, lévvĕzli
Leveson, *C.n.*, 'lusən, loóssŏn
Leveson-Gower, *f.n.*, 'lusən 'gɔr,
  loóssŏn gór. *Family name of*
  Earl Granville.
L'Evesque, *f.n.*, lə'vesk, lĕvésk
Levey, *f.n.*, 'livɪ, leévi; 'levɪ, lévvi
Levi, *f.n.*, 'levɪ, lévvi; 'livɪ, leévi
Levic, *f.n.*, 'levɪk, lévvick
Levick, *f.n.*, 'levɪk, lévvick
Levien, *f.n.*, lə'vin, lĕveén
Levin, *f.n.*, 'levɪn, lévvin
Levine, *f.n.*, lə'vin, lĕveén
Levinge, *f.n.*, 'levɪŋ, lévving
Levita, *f.n.*, lə'vitə, lĕveétă
Levy, *f.n.*, 'livɪ, leévi; 'levɪ, lévvi
Lewannick *Cornwall*, lɪ'wɒnɪk,
  lĕ-wónnick

Lewarne, *f.n.,* lə'wɔrn, lĕ-wáwrn
Lewarne *Cornwall,* lə'wɔrn, lĕ-wáwrn
Lewdown, *also spelt* **Lew Down,** *Devon,* 'lu'daʊn, loó-dówn
Lewell, *f.n.,* 'luəl, loó-ĕl
Lewenstein, *f.n.,* 'luənstin, loó-ĕnsteen
Lewes *E. Sussex,* 'luɪs, loó-ĕss
Lewey, *f.n.,* 'luɪ, loó-i
Lewin, *f.n.,* 'luɪn, loó-in
Lewinski, *f.n.,* lu'ɪnskɪ, loo-ínski
Lewis, *f.n.,* 'luɪs, loó-iss
Lewitter, *f.n.,* lə'wɪtər, lĕ-wíttĕr
Lewknor *Oxon.,* 'luknər, loóknor
Lewry, *f.n.,* 'luərɪ, loóri
Lews Castle *I. of Lewis,* luz, looz
Lewsen, *f.n.,* 'lusən, loóssĕn
Lewsey, *f.n.,* 'ljusɪ, léwssi
Lewthwaite, *f.n.,* 'luθweɪt, loóthwayt
Lewtrenchard, *also spelt* **Lew Trenchard,** *Devon,* 'lu'trenʃərd, loó-trén-shärd
Ley, *f.n.,* leɪ, lay; li, lee
Leybourne *Kent,* 'leɪbɔrn, láyborn
Leyburn *N. Yorks.,* 'leɪbɜrn, láyburn
Leycester, *f.n.,* 'lestər, lésstĕr
Leycett *Staffs.,* 'lisɪt, léessĕt
Leyhill *Bucks.,* 'leɪhɪl, láy-hil
Leyland, *f.n.,* 'leɪlənd, láylănd
Leyland *Lancs.,* 'leɪlənd, láylănd
Leys, *f.n.,* liz, leez
Leysdown *Kent,* 'leɪzdaʊn, láyzdown
Leyshon, *f.n.,* 'laɪʃən, lí-shŏn; 'leɪʃən, láy-shŏn. *The first is usual in Wales.*
Leyton *London,* 'leɪtən, láytŏn
Leytonstone *London,* 'leɪtənstoʊn, léytŏn-stōn
Lezant *Cornwall,* le'zænt, lezzánt
Leziate *Norfolk,* 'lezɪət, lézziät; 'ledʒɪt, léjjĕt
Liardet, *f.n.,* li'ɑrdet, lee-aárdet
Lias, *f.n.,* 'laɪəs, lí-äss
Libanus *Powys,* 'lɪbənəs, líbbănŭss
Liberton *Edinburgh,* 'lɪbərtən, líbbĕrtŏn
Lickess, *f.n.,* 'lɪkɪs, líckĕss
Lickis, *f.n.,* 'lɪkɪs, líckiss
Lickiss, *f.n.,* 'lɪkɪs, líckiss
Licswm *see* **Lixwm**
Liddell, *f.n.,* 'lɪdl, líddl; lɪ'del, lidéll. *The first, which is still much the more usual for this spelling, is appropriate for Henry George ~, joint editor of Liddell and Scott's Greek-English lexicon, and for his daughter Alice ~, the heroine of 'Alice in Wonderland'.*
Liddle, *f.n.,* 'lɪdl, líddl

Lidell, *f.n.,* 'lɪdl, líddl; lɪ'del, lidéll
Lidgate *Suffolk,* 'lɪdgeɪt, líd-gayt
Lidgett, *f.n.,* 'lɪdʒɪt, líjjĕt
Lidstone, *f.n.,* 'lɪdstən, lídstŏn
Liebert, *f.n.,* 'libərt, léebĕrt
Lienhardt, *f.n.,* 'liənhɑrt, lee-ĕn-haart
Liesching, *f.n.,* 'liʃɪŋ, léeshing
Lieven, *f.n.,* 'livən, léevĕn
Lightbown, *f.n.,* 'laɪtbaʊn, lít-bown
Lightburn, *f.n.,* 'laɪtbɜrn, lítburn
Lightoller, *f.n.,* 'laɪtɒlər, lítollĕr
Ligoniel *Co. Antrim,* ˌlɪgə'nil, liggŏneél
Ligonier, *f.n.,* ˌlɪgə'nɪər, liggŏneér
Lijertwood, *f.n.,* 'laɪdʒɜrtwʊd, líjĕrt-wŏŏd
Likeman, *f.n.,* 'laɪkmən, líkmăn
Lilburn, *f.n.,* 'lɪlbɜrn, lílburn
Lilleshall *Salop,* 'lɪlɪʃəl, lílli-shäl
Lilley, *f.n.,* 'lɪlɪ, lílli
Lilliput *Dorset,* 'lɪlɪpʊt, líllipŏŏt
Lillistone, *f.n.,* 'lɪlɪstən, líllistŏn
Lillywhite, *f.n.,* 'lɪlɪʰwaɪt, lílli-whít
Limavady *Co. Derry,* ˌlɪmə'vædɪ, limmăváddi
Limerick, Earl of, 'lɪmərɪk, límmĕrick
Limpenhoe *Norfolk,* 'lɪmpənhoʊ, límpĕn-hō
Limpkin, *f.n.,* 'lɪmpkɪn, límpkin
Linacre, *f.n.,* 'lɪnəkər, línnăkĕr
Lincoln, *f.n.,* 'lɪŋkən, línkŏn
Lincoln *Lincs.,* 'lɪŋkən, línkŏn
Lind, *f.n.,* lɪnd, lind
Lindesay, *f.n.,* 'lɪndzɪ, líndzi
Lindesay-Bethune, *f.n.,* 'lɪndzɪ 'bitən, líndzi béetŏn. *Family name of the Earl of Lindsay.*
Lindgren, *f.n.,* 'lɪngren, lín-grĕn
Lindisfarne *Northd.,* 'lɪndɪsfɑrn, líndiss-faarn
Lindley *Leics., W. Yorks.,* 'lɪndlɪ, líndli
Lindop, *f.n.,* 'lɪndɒp, líndop
Lindores *Fife,* lɪn'dɔrz, lindórz
Lindridge, *f.n.,* 'lɪndrɪdʒ, líndrij
Lindsay, Earl of, 'lɪndzɪ, líndzi
Lindsay, *C.n. and f.n.,* 'lɪndzɪ, líndzi
Lindsell, *f.n.,* 'lɪndzl, líndzl
Linehan, *f.n.,* 'lɪnəhən, línnĕhän
Ling, *f.n.,* lɪŋ, ling
Lingane, *f.n.,* 'lɪŋgeɪn, líng-gayn
Lingard, *f.n.,* 'lɪŋgɑrd, líng-gaard
Lingay, *f.n.,* 'lɪŋgɪ, líng-gi
Lingen, *f.n.,* 'lɪŋən, líng-ĕn
Lings, *f.n.,* lɪŋz, lingz
Lingstrom, *f.n.,* 'lɪŋstrəm, líng-strŏm
Linhope *Northd.,* 'lɪnəp, línnŏp

Linkie, *f.n.*, 'lɪŋkɪ, línki
Linkinhorne *Cornwall,* 'lɪŋkɪn-hɔrn, línkin-horn
Linklater, Eric, *author,* 'lɪŋklətər, línklătĕr. *The author has confirmed this as his family pronunciation, although others frequently call him* 'lɪŋkleɪtər, línklaytĕr.
Linlathen *Tayside,* lɪn'læθən, lin-láthĕn
Linley, Viscount, 'lɪnlɪ, línli
Linlithgow *Lothian,* lɪn'lɪθgoʊ, linlíthgō. *Appropriate also for the Marquess of* ~.
Linnell, *f.n.*, 'lɪnl, línnl
Linnhe, Loch, *H'land–S'clyde,* 'lɪnɪ, línni
Linos, *f.n.*, 'lɪnɒs, léenoss
Linsidemore *H'land,* 'lɪnsaɪd'mɔr, línssīdmór
Linslade *Beds.*, 'lɪnzleɪd, línz-layd
Linstead, *f.n.*, 'lɪnsted, línsted
Linstrum, *f.n.*, 'lɪnstrəm, línstrŭm
Linthwaite, *f.n.*, 'lɪnθweɪt, línth-wayt
Lintott, *f.n.*, 'lɪntɒt, líntot
Lintrathen *Tayside,* lɪn'treɪðən, lintráythĕn
Linwood *Lincs.*, *S'clyde,* 'lɪnwʊd, línwŏŏd
Linzell, *f.n.*, lɪn'zel, linzéll
Lipkin, *f.n.*, 'lɪpkɪn, lípkin
Lippiatt, *f.n.*, 'lɪpɪət, líppi-ăt
Lippiett, *f.n.*, 'lɪpɪət, líppi-ĕt
Lipscomb, *f.n.*, 'lɪpskəm, lípskŏm
Lipsidge, *f.n.*, 'lɪpsɪdʒ, lípssij
Liptrot, *f.n.*, 'lɪptrɒt, líptrot
Lipyeat, *f.n.*, 'lɪpɪət, líppi-ăt
Lisahally *Co. Derry,* ,lɪsə'hælɪ, lissăháli
Lisam, *f.n.*, 'laɪsəm, líssăm
Lisbane *Co. Down,* lɪs'bæn, liss-bán
Lisbellaw *Co. Fermanagh,* ,lɪsbɪ-'lɔ, lissbĕláw
Lisbuoy *Co. Tyrone,* lɪs'bɔɪ, liss-bóy
Lisburn *Cos. Antrim–Down,* 'lɪzbərn, lízburn
Lisburne, Earl of, 'lɪzbərn, líz-bŭrn
Lisdoonan *Co. Down,* lɪs'dunən, lissdoónăn
Lisemore, *f.n.*, 'lɪzmɔr, lízmor
Lisk, *f.n.*, lɪsk, lisk
Liskeard *Cornwall,* lɪs'kɑrd, liss-kaárd
Lisle, *f.n.*, laɪl, líl. *Appropriate also for Baron* ~.
Lismoyne *Co. Antrim,* lɪs'mɔɪn, lissmóyn
Lisnadill *Co. Armagh,* ,lɪsnə'dɪl, lissnădíll

Lisnagarvey *Co. Antrim,* ,lɪsnə-'gɑrvɪ, lissnăgaárvi
Lisnalinchy *Co. Antrim,* ,lɪsnə-'lɪnʃɪ, lissnălínshi
Lisnamallard *Co. Tyrone,* ,lɪsnə-'mælərd, lissnămálărd
Lisnaskea *Co. Fermanagh,* ,lɪsnə-'ski, lissnä-skeé
Lisney, *f.n.*, 'lɪznɪ, lízni
Lissan *Cos. Derry–Tyrone,* 'lɪsən, líssän
Lister, *f.n.*, 'lɪstər, lísstĕr. *Appropriate for Joseph Jackson* ~, *microscopist, and for his son Joseph, later Baron* ~, *surgeon.*
Listooder *Co. Down,* lɪs'tudər, lisstoódĕr
Listowel, Earl of, lɪs'toʊəl, lisstṓ-ĕl
Lisvane *S. Glam.*, lɪz'veɪn, liz-váyn. *The Welsh name is* **Llys-faen,** *q.v.*
Litheby, *f.n.*, 'lɪðəbɪ, líthĕbi
Litherland, *f.n.*, 'lɪðərlænd, líthĕr-land
Lithgow, *f.n.*, 'lɪθgoʊ, líthgō
Littell, *f.n.*, lɪ'tel, litéll
Litterick, *f.n.*, 'lɪtərɪk, líttĕrick
Little Almshoe *Herts.*, 'lɪtl 'ɑmʃu, líttl aám-shoo
Little Alne *Warwicks.*, 'lɪtl 'ɔn, líttl áwn; 'lɪtl 'ɔln, líttl áwln
Little Bourton *Oxon.*, 'lɪtl 'bɔrtən, líttl bórtŏn
Little Bowden *Leics.*, 'lɪtl 'baʊdən, líttl bówdĕn
Little Bradley *Suffolk,* 'lɪtl 'brædlɪ, líttl brádli
Little Bromley *Essex,* 'lɪtl 'brɒmli, líttl brómli
Littlebury Green *Essex,* 'lɪtlbərɪ 'grin, líttlbŭri greén
Little Compton *Warwicks.*, 'lɪtl 'kɒmptən, líttl kómptŏn
Little Creaton *Northants.*, 'lɪtl 'kritən, líttl kreétŏn
Little Cumbrae *S'clyde,* 'lɪtl 'kʌmbreɪ, líttl kúmbray
Little Fransham *Norfolk,* 'lɪtl 'frænʃəm, líttl fránshăm
Little Gaddesden *Herts.*, 'lɪtl 'gædzdən, líttl gádzdĕn
Little Harrowden *Northants.*, 'lɪtl 'hæroʊdən, líttl hárrōdĕn
Little Hautbois *Norfolk,* 'lɪtl 'hɒbɪs, líttl hóbbiss
Little Houghton *Northants.*, 'lɪtl 'hoʊtən, líttl hṓtŏn
Little Houghton *S. Yorks.*, 'lɪtl 'hɔtən, líttl háwtŏn
Little Ponton *Lincs.*, 'lɪtl 'pɒntən, líttl póntŏn
Littler, *f.n.*, 'lɪtlər, líttlĕr

Little Saughall *Ches.*, 'lɪtl 'sɔkl, líttl sáwkl
Little Shelford *Cambs.*, 'lɪtl 'ʃelfərd, líttl shélförd
Little Staughton *Beds.*, 'lɪtl 'stɔtən, líttl stáwtŏn
Littlestone-on-Sea *Kent*, 'lɪtlstən ɒn 'si, líttlstŏn on se͞e
Little Stonham *Suffolk*, 'lɪtl 'stɒnəm, líttl stónnăm
Little Stukeley *Cambs.*, 'lɪtl 'stjuklɪ, líttl stéwkli
Little Totham *Essex*, 'lɪtl 'tɒtəm, líttl tóttăm
Little Wakering *Essex*, 'lɪtl 'weɪkərɪŋ, líttl wáykĕring
Little Walsingham *Norfolk*, 'lɪtl 'wɔlzɪŋəm, líttl wáwlzing-ăm
Little Waltham *Essex*, 'lɪtl 'wɔltəm, líttl wáwltăm
Little Warley *Essex*, 'lɪtl 'wɔrlɪ, líttl wáwrli
Little Wilbraham *Cambs.*, 'lɪtl 'wɪlbrəm, líttl wílbräm; 'lɪtl 'wɪlbrəhæm, líttl wílbrăham
Little Wymondley *Herts.*, 'lɪtl 'waɪməndlɪ, líttl wímŏndli
Little Wyrley *Staffs.*, 'lɪtl 'wɜrlɪ, líttl wúrli
Litton Cheney *Dorset*, 'lɪtən 'tʃeɪnɪ, líttŏn cháyni
Lium, *f.n.*, 'liəm, le͞e-ŭm
Liveing, *f.n.*, 'lɪvɪŋ, lívving
Lively, *f.n.*, 'laɪvlɪ, lívli
Livens, *f.n.*, 'lɪvənz, lívvĕnz
Liver Building *Liverpool*, 'laɪvər, lívĕr
Livermore, *f.n.*, 'lɪvərmɔr, lívvĕrmor
Liverpool *Merseyside*, 'lɪvərpul, lívvĕrpool
Liverpudlian, *native of* **Liverpool**, ˌlɪvər'pʌdlɪən, livvĕrpúdliăn
Liversedge *W. Yorks.*, 'lɪvərsedʒ, lívvĕr-sej
Liversuch, *f.n.*, 'lɪvərsʌtʃ, lívver-sutch
Livesey, *f.n.*, 'lɪvsɪ, lívssi; 'lɪvzɪ, lívzi
Livingstone, *f.n.*, 'lɪvɪŋstən, lívving-stŏn; 'lɪvɪŋstoun, lívving-stŏn
Lixwm, *also spelt* **Licswm**, *Clwyd*, 'lɪksum, lícksŏŏm
Lizard *Cornwall*, 'lɪzərd, lízzărd
Lizars, *f.n.*, lɪ'zɑrz, lizzáarz
Llai, *also spelt* **Llay**, *Clwyd*, ɬaɪ, hlī
Llain-goch *Gwynedd*, ɬaɪn'goux, hlīn-gó͞och
Llanaelhaiarn *Gwynedd*, ˌɬænaɪl-'haɪərn, hlanīl-hí-ărn
Llanafan *Dyfed*, ɬæn'ævən, hlanávvän

Llanafan Fawr *Powys*, ɬæn'ævən 'vauər, hlanávvän vówr
Llanallgo *Gwynedd*, ɬæn'æɬgou, hlanáhlgō
Llanarmon *Clwyd, Gwynedd*, ɬæn-'ɑrmɒn, hlanáarmon
Llanarmon Dyffryn Ceiriog *Clwyd*, ɬæn'ɑrmɒn 'dʌfrɪn 'kaɪərjɒg, hlanáarmon dúffrin kír-yog
Llanarmon-yn-ial *Clwyd*, ɬæn-'ɑrmɒn ən 'jɑl, hlanáarmon-ăn-yaál
Llanarth *Dyfed, Gwent*, 'ɬænɑrθ, hlánaarth
Llan-arth Fawr *Dyfed*, ɬæn'ɑrθ 'vauər, hlanáarth vówr
Llanarthney *Dyfed*, ɬæn'ɑrθnɪ, hlanáarthni
Llanasa *Clwyd*, ɬæn'æsə, hlanássä
Llanbadarn Fawr *Dyfed*, ɬæn-'bædərn 'vauər, hlanbáddärn vówr
Llanbadarn-y-Creuddyn *Dyfed*, ɬæn'bædərn ə 'kraɪðɪn, hlanbáddärn ă kríthin
Llanbadoc *Gwent*, ɬæn'bædɒk, hlanbáddock
Llanbadrig *Gwynedd*, ɬæn'bædrɪg, hlanbádrig
Llanbeblig *Gwynedd*, ɬæn'beblɪg, hlan-béblig
Llanbedr *Gwynedd, Powys*, 'ɬæn-bedər, hlánbeddĕr
Llan-bedr *Gwent*, ɬæn'bedər, hlanbéddĕr
Llanbedr-goch *Gwynedd*, 'ɬæn-bedər 'goux, hlánbeddĕr-gó͞och
Llanbedrog *Gwynedd*, ɬæn'bedrɒg, hlanbédrog
Llanbedrycennin *Gwynedd*, 'ɬæn-bedərə'kenɪn, hlánbeddĕr-ă-kénnin
Llanberis *Gwynedd*, ɬæn'berɪs, hlanbérriss
Llanbister *Powys*, ɬæn'bɪstər, hlanbísstĕr
Llanblethian *S. Glam.*, ɬæn-'bleðɪən, hlanbléthi-än
Llanboidy *Dyfed*, ɬæn'bɔɪdɪ, hlanbóydi
Llan-borth *Dyfed*, ɬæn'bɔrθ, hlan-bórth
Llanbradach *Mid Glam.*, ɬæn-'brædəx, hlanbráddăch
Llanbrynmair *Powys*, ˌɬænbrɪn-'maɪər, hlanbrin-mír
Llancaiach, *also spelt* **Llancaeach**, *Mid Glam.*, ɬæn'kaɪəx, hlan-kí-ăch
Llancynfelin *Dyfed*, ˌɬænkɪn'velɪn, hlan-kin-véllin
Llandaff *S. Glam.*, 'ɬændəf, lándáf; 'ɬændæf, hlándaff. *Although the first is widespread*

*local usage, the second is pre-
ferred by the clergy of ~
Cathedral and by the BBC in
Cardiff. The Welsh language
form is Llandaf, pronounced*
ɬæn'dɑv, hlandáav.

Llandarcy *W. Glam.*, ɬæn'dɑrsɪ,
hlandáarssi

Llanddaniel *Gwynedd*, ɬæn'ðænjəl,
hlanthán-yěl

Llanddarog *Dyfed*, ɬæn'ðærɒg,
hlanthárrog

Llanddeiniol *Dyfed*, ɬæn'ðaɪnjɒl,
hlanthín-yol

Llanddeiniolen *Gwynedd*, ɬæn-
ðaɪn'jɒlən, hlanthín-yóllĕn

Llandderfel *Gwynedd*, ɬæn'ðɛərvel,
hlantháirvel

Llanddetty *Powys*, ɬæn'ðetɪ,
hlanthétti

Llanddeusant *Dyfed*, *Gwynedd*,
ɬæn'ðaɪsænt, hlanthíssant

Llanddew *Powys*, 'lændoʊ, lándō;
ɬæn'ðju, hlan-théw

Llanddewi Aberarth *Dyfed*,
ɬæn'ðewɪ ˌæbər'ɑrθ, hlanthé-wi
abběráarth; ɬæn'ðjuɪ ˌæbər'ɑrθ,
hlanthéw-i abběráarth

Llanddewi Brefi *Dyfed*, ɬæn'ðewɪ
'breɪvɪ, hlanthé-wi bráyvi; ɬæn-
'ðjuɪ 'breɪvɪ, hlanthéw-i bráyvi

Llanddewi'r Cwm *Powys*, ɬæn-
'ðewɪər 'kʊm, hlanthé-weer
kóōm; ɬæn'ðjuər 'kʊm,
hlanthéw-ĕr kóōm

Llanddewi Velfrey *Dyfed*, ɬæn-
'ðewɪ 'velfreɪ, hlanthé-wi
vélfray

Llanddoget *Gwynedd*, ɬæn'ðɒgɪt,
hlanthóggĕt

Llanddona *Gwynedd*, ɬæn'ðɒnə,
hlanthónnă

Llanddowror *Dyfed*, ɬæn'ðaʊrɔr,
hlanthówror

Llanddulas *Clwyd*, ɬæn'ðɪləs,
hlanthíllăss

Llanddyfnan *Gwynedd*, ɬæn-
'ðʌvnən, hlanthúvnăn

Llandebie *Dyfed*, ˌɬændə'bieɪ,
hlandĕbée-ay

Llandecwyn *Gwynedd*, ɬæn'dek-
wɪn, hlandéckwin

Llandefailog *Powys*, ˌɬændə-
'vaɪlɒg, hlandĕvílog

Llandefailog-fach *Powys*, ˌɬændə-
'vaɪlɒg 'vɑx, hlandĕvílog va'ach

Llandefalle *Powys*, ˌɬændə'væleɪ,
hlandĕváhlay

Llandefeilog *Dyfed*, ˌɬændə'vaɪlɒg
hlandĕvílog

Llandegai *Gwynedd*, ˌɬændə'gaɪ,
hlandĕgí

Llandegfan *Gwynedd*, ɬæn'deg-
væn, hlandégvan

Llandegla *Clwyd*, ɬæn'deglə,
hlandéglă

Llandegley *Powys*, ɬæn'degleɪ,
hlandéglay

Llandeilo, *also spelt* **Llandilo**,
Dyfed, ɬæn'daɪloʊ, hlandílō

Llandeilo Bertholau *Gwent*, ɬæn-
'daɪloʊ bɛər'θɒlaɪ, hlandílō
bair-thóllī

Llandeilo Graban *Powys*, ɬæn-
'daɪloʊ 'græbən, hlandílō
grábbăn

Llandeilo'r-fân *Dyfed*, ɬæn'daɪlɔr-
'vɑn, hlandílor-vaán

Llandeloy *Dyfed*, ˌɬændə'lɔɪ,
hlandĕlóy

Llandenny *Gwent*, ɬæn'denɪ,
hlandénni

Llandevaud *Gwent*, ˌɬændə'vɔd,
hlandĕváwd

Llandewi Ystradenny *Gwent*,
ɬæn'dewɪ ˌʌstrəd'enɪ, hlandé-wi
usstrădénni; ɬæn'djuɪ ˌʌstrəd-
'enɪ, hlandéw-i usstrădénni

Llandilo *see* **Llandeilo**

Llandinabo *H. & W.*, ˌɬændɪ'neɪ-
boʊ, landináybō

Llandinam *Powys*, ɬæn'dinæm,
hlandeénam

Llandinorwig *Gwynedd*, ˌɬændɪ-
'nɔrwɪg, hlandinórwig

Llandogo *Gwent*, ɬæn'doʊgoʊ,
hlandógō

Llandough *S. Glam.*, læn'dɒk,
landóck

Llandovery *Dyfed*, ɬæn'dʌvrɪ,
hlandúvvri

Llandow *S. Glam.*, læn'daʊ,
landów

Llandre *Dyfed*, 'ɬændreɪ, hlán-
dray

Llandrillo *Clwyd*, ɬæn'drɪɬoʊ,
hlandríhlō

Llandrindod Wells *Powys*, ɬæn-
'drɪndɒd 'welz, hlandríndod
wéllz

Llandrinio *Powys*, ɬæn'drɪnjoʊ,
hlandrín-yō

Llandudno *Gwynedd*, ɬæn'dɪdnoʊ,
hlandídnō

Llandulas *Powys*, ɬæn'dɪləs,
hlandíllăss

Llandwrog *Gwynedd*, ɬæn'duərɒg,
hlandóōrog

Llandyfodwg *Mid Glam.*, ˌɬændə-
ˌvoʊdʊg, hlandăvódōōg

Llandyfriog *Dyfed*, ˌɬændə'vrɪɒg,
hlandăvrée-og

Llandyfrydog *Gwynedd*, ˌɬændə-
'vrʌdɒg, hlandăvrúddog

Llandygwydd *Dyfed*, ɬæn'dʌgwɪð,
hlandúgwith

Llandyrnog *Clwyd*, ɬæn'dɜrnɒg,
hlandúrnog

Llandysilio *Powys*, ˌɬændə'sɪljoʊ, hlandŭssíl-yō

Llandysiliogogo *Dyfed*, ˌɬændə-'sɪljoʊ'goʊgoʊ, hlandŭssíl-yō-gŏgō

Llandysul *Dyfed, Powys*, ɬæn'dɪsɪl, hlandíssil ; ɬæn'dʌsɪl, hlandússil

Llanedeyrn *S. Glam.*, ɬæn'edɛərn, hlan-éddairn. *The Welsh form is* **Llanedern.**

Llanedwen *Gwynedd*, ɬæn'edwɪn, hlanédwĕn

Llanedy *Dyfed*, ɬæn'eɪdɪ, hlanáydi

Llanegryn *Gwynedd*, ɬæn'egrɪn, hlanégrin

Llanegwad *Dyfed*, ɬæn'egwəd, hlanégwäd

Llaneilian *Gwynedd*, ɬæn'aɪljən, hlanîl-yăn

Llanelian *Gwynedd*, ɬæn'eljən, hlanél-yăn

Llanelidan *Clwyd*, ˌɬænɪ'lidən, hlannĕléedän

Llanelieu *Powys*, ɬæn'ilju, hlanéelew; læn'ilju, lanéelew

Llanellen *Gwent*, ɬæn'elɪn, hlanéllĕn

Llanelli, *formerly spelt* **Llanelly,** *Dyfed, Powys*, ɬæn'eɬɪ, hlanéhli

Llanelltyd *Gwynedd*, ɬæn'eɬtɪd, hlanéhltid

Llanelly *see* **Llanelli**

Llanelwedd *Powys*, ɬæn'elwɪð, hlanélwĕth

Llanenddwyn *Gwynedd*, ɬæn-'enðʊɪn, hlanénthōō-in

Llanengan *Gwynedd*, ɬæn'eŋən, hlanéng-ăn

Llanerchymedd *Gwynedd*, ˌɬænəərxə'meɪð, hlanairchămáyth

Llanerfyl *Powys*, ɬæn'ɛərvɪl, hlanáirvil

Llaneugrad *Gwynedd*, ɬæn'aɪgræd, hlanígrad

Llanfabon *Mid Glam.*, ɬæn'væbən, hlanvábbŏn

Llanfachraeth, *also spelt* **Llanfachreth,** *Gwynedd*, ɬæn'væxrəθ, hlanvách̆rĕth. *Appropriate for both places of the name in Gwynedd.*

Llanfaelog *Gwynedd*, ɬæn'vaɪlɒg, hlanvílog

Llan-faes, *Powys*, ɬæn'vaɪs, hlanvíss

Llanfaethlu *Gwynedd*, ɬæn'vaɪθlɪ, hlanvíthli

Llanfair *Gwynedd*, 'ɬænvaɪər, hlánvīr

Llanfair-ar-y-bryn *Dyfed*,'ɬænvaɪər ær ə 'brɪn, hlánvīr-arrä-brín

Llanfair Caereinion *Powys*,'ɬæn-vaɪər kɑr'aɪnjɒn, hlánvīr kaarín--yon

Llanfair Clydogau *Dyfed*,'ɬæn-vaɪər klɪ'doʊgaɪ, hlánvīr klidŏgī

Llanfairfechan *Gwynedd*, ˌɬæn-vaɪər'vexən, hlanvīr-véch̆än

Llanfair-is-gaer *Gwynedd*,'ɬæn-vaɪər'isgaɪər, hlánvīr-eéss-gīr

Llanfair Kilgeddin *Gwent*, 'ɬæn-vaɪər kɪl'gedɪn, hlánvīr kilgéddin

Llanfair Mathafarn Eithaf *Gwynedd*,'ɬænvaɪər məθ'æfɑrn 'aɪθæv, hlánvīr mătháffaarn íthav

Llanfair Nant-y-gof *Dyfed*,'ɬæn-vaɪər ˌnæntə'goʊv, hlánvīr nant-ä-gŏv

Llanfair Pwllgwyngyll *Gwynedd*, 'ɬænvaɪər puɬ'gwɪngɪɬ, hlánvīr poohl-gwin-gihl. *The accepted abbreviation is Llanfair P.G. At the other end of the scale, however, it is traditionally the longest Welsh place name, and, as such, it appears at the bottom of this page.*

Llanfair Talhaiarn *Clwyd*, 'ɬæn-vaɪər tæl'haɪərn, hlánvīr tal-hí--ărn

Llanfair Waterdine, Baron Hunt of,'ɬænvaɪər 'wɔtərdaɪn, hlánvīr wáwtĕrdīn

Llanfairynghornwy *Gwynedd*, ˌɬænvaɪərəŋ'hɔrnʊɪ, hlanvīr-ŭng--hórnōō-i

Llanfallteg *Dyfed*, ɬæn'vælteg, hlanváhlteg

Llan-fawr *Gwynedd*, ɬæn'vaʊər, hlanvówr

Llanfechain *Powys*, ɬæn'vexaɪn, hlanvéch̆īn

Llanfechan *Powys*, ɬæn'vexən, hlanvéch̆än

Llanfechell *Gwynedd*, ɬæn'vexeɬ, hlanvéchehl

Llanfeigan *Powys*, ɬæn'vaɪgən, hlan-vígăn

Llanferres *Clwyd*, ɬæn'veres, hlanvérress

Llan-ffwyst, *also known as* **Llan-foist** *q.v.*, *Gwent*, ɬæn'fʊɪst, hlanfōō-ist

Llanfigael, *also spelt* **Llanfigel** *q.v.*, *Gwynedd*, ɬæn'vigaɪl, hlanveégīl

Llanfair-pwllgwyngyll-gogerychwyrndrobwll-llandysilio-gogogoch *Gwynedd*, 'ɬænvaɪərpuɬ'gwɪngɪɬgoʊ'gerə'xwɜrn'droʊbuɬɬændə'sɪlɪoʊgoʊgoʊ'goʊx, hlánvīr-poohl-gwín-gihl-gōgérrä-ch̆wírn-drŏboohl-hlandŭssílli-ō-gōgōgŏch. *See* **Llanfair Pwllgwyngyll** *above*.

Llanfigel, *also spelt* **Llanfigael**
q.v., *Gwynedd*, łæn'vɪgel,
hlanvíggel

Llanfihangel *Powys*, ˌłænvɪ'hæŋəl,
hlanvi-háng-ĕl

Llanfihangel Abercywyn *Dyfed*,
ˌłænvɪ'hæŋəl ˌæbər'kaʊɪn,
hlanvi-háng-ĕl abbĕrkówin

Llanfihangel-ar-arth *Dyfed*,
ˌłænvɪ'hæŋəl ɑr 'ɑrθ, hlanvi-
-háng-ĕl-aar-aárth

Llanfihangel Cwm Du *Powys*,
ˌłænvɪ'hæŋəl kʊm 'di, hlanvi-
-háng-ĕl kōōm deé

Llanfihangel Esceifiog *Gwynedd*,
ˌłænvɪ'hæŋəl es'kaɪvjɒg, hlanvi-
-háng-ĕl eskív-yog

Llanfihangel Fechan *Powys*,
ˌłænvɪ'hæŋəl 'vexən, hlanvi-
-háng-ĕl véchăn

Llanfihangel Glyn Myfyr *Clwyd*,
ˌłænvɪ'hæŋəl glɪn 'mʌvər,
hlanvi-háng-ĕl glin múvvĕr

Llanfihangel Nant Brân *Powys*,
ˌłænvɪ'hæŋəl nænt 'brɑn,
hlanvi-háng-ĕl nant braán

Llanfihangel Tal-y-llyn *Powys*,
ˌłænvɪ'hæŋəl ˌtælə'łɪn, hlanvi-
-háng-ĕl tal-ă-hlín

Llnafihangel-y-fedw *Gwent*,
ˌłænvɪ'hæŋəl ə 'vedu, hlanvi-
-háng-ĕl ă véddoo. *Welsh name
for* **Michaelston-y-Vedw**, *q.v.*

Llanfihangel Ystrad *Dyfed*,
ˌłænvɪ'hæŋəl 'ʌstrəd, hlanvi-
-háng-ĕl ússträd

Llanfilo *Powys*, łæn'vɪloʊ, hlan-
víllō

Llanfoist, *also known as* **Llan-
-ffwyst** *q.v.*, *Gwent*, łæn'vɔɪst,
hlanvóysst

Llanfrechfa *Gwent*, łæn'vrexvə,
hlanvréchvă

Llanfrothen *Gwynedd*, łæn'vrɒθən,
hlanvróthĕn

Llanfrynach *Powys*, łæn'vrʌnəx,
hlanvrúnnăch

Llanfwrog *Clwyd*, *Gwynedd*, łæn-
'vʊərɒg, hlanvōōrog

Llanfyllin *Powys*, łæn'vʌłɪn, hlan-
vúhlin

Llanfynydd *Clwyd*, *Dyfed*, łæn-
'vʌnɪð, hlanvúnnith

Llanfyrnach *Powys*, łæn'vɜrnəx,
hlanvúrnăch

Llangadfan *Powys*, łæn'gædvən,
hlan-gádvăn

Llangadog *Dyfed*, łæn'gædɒg,
hlan-gáddog

Llangadwaladr *Clwyd*, *Gwynedd*,
ˌłængæd'wælədər, hlan-gadwá-
lădĕr

Llangaffo *Gwynedd*, łæn'gæfoʊ,
hlan-gáffō

Llangammarch Wells *Powys*,
łæn'gæmɑrx 'welz, hlan-gám-
maarch wéllz

Llanganten *Powys*, łæn'gæntən,
hlan-gántĕn

Llangar *Clwyd*, 'łæŋgər, hláng-
-găr

Llangathen *Dyfed*, łæn'gæθən,
hlan-gáthĕn

Llangattock, Barony of, łæn-
'gætək, lang-gáttŏk

Llangattock *Powys*, łæn'gætɒk,
hlan-gáttock

Llangedwyn *Clwyd*, łæn'gedwɪn,
hlan-gédwin

Llangefni *Gwynedd*, łæn'gevnɪ,
hlan-gévni

Llangeinor *Mid Glam.*, łæn'gaɪnər,
hlan-gínor

Llangeinwen *Gwynedd*, łæn'gaɪn-
wen, hlan-gín-wen

Llangeitho *Dyfed*, łæn'gaɪθoʊ,
hlan-gíthō

Llangeler *Dyfed*, łæn'gelər, hlan-
-géllĕr

Llangelynin *Gwynedd*, ˌłæŋgɪ-
'lʌnɪn, hlan-gélúnnin. *Appropriate for both places of the
name in Gwynedd.*

Llangendeirne, *also spelt* **Llangen-
deyrn**, *Dyfed*, ˌłæŋgən'daɪərn,
hlan-gĕndírn

Llangennech *Dyfed*, łæn'genəx,
hlan-génnĕch

Llangenny *Powys*, łæn'genɪ,
hlan-génni

Llangernyw *Clwyd*, łæn'gɛərnju,
hlan-gáirnew

Llangian *Gwynedd*, łæn'giən,
hlan-gée-ăn

Llangibby *Gwent*, łæn'gɪbɪ, hlan-
-gíbbi

Llanginning, *now* **Llangynin** *q.v.*,
Dyfed, łæn'gɪnɪŋ, hlan-gínning

Llangiwg *W. Glam.*, łæn'gjuk,
hlan-géwk

Llanglydwen *Dyfed*, łæn'glɪdwen,
hlan-glíd-wen

Llangoed *Gwynedd*, 'łæŋgɔɪd,
hláng-goyd

Llangoedmor *Dyfed*, łæn'gɔɪdmər,
hlan-góydmor; łæn'gɔɪtmər,
hlan-góytmor

Llangollen *Clwyd*, łæn'gɒłən,
hlan-góhlĕn

Llangorse *Powys*, łæn'gɔrs, hlan-
-górss

Llangower, *also spelt* **Llangywer**,
Llangywair, *Gwynedd*, łæn-
'gaʊər, hlan-gówĕr

Llangranog *Dyfed*, łæn'grænɒg,
hlan-gránnog

Llangristiolus *Gwynedd*, ˌłæn-
grɪstɪ'ɒlɪs, hlan-grissti-ólliss

Llangrwyn, *also spelt* **Llangrwyney**
q.v., Powys, łæn'gruɪn, hlan-
-groʹo-in
Llangrwyney *also spelt* **Llangrwyn,**
q.v., Powys, łæn'gruɪneɪ,
hlan-groʹo-inay
Llangua *Gwent,* łæn'giə,hlan-geʹe-ă
Llangunllo *Powys,* łæn'gʌnłoʊ,
hlan-gún-hlō
Llangunnock *Dyfed,* łæn'gʌnɒk,
hlan-gúnnock
Llangunnor *Dyfed,* łæn'gʌnɔr,
hlan-gúnnor
Llangurig *Powys,* łæn'gɪrɪg, hlan-
-gírrig
Llangwm *Clwyd, Dyfed,* 'łæŋgʊm,
hláng-gŏōm
Llan-gwm *Gwent,* łæn'gʊm, hlan-
-gŏōm
Llangwnnadl *Gwynedd,* łæn-
'gʊnædl, hlan-gŏōn-addl
Llangwstenin *Gwynedd,* ˌłæŋgʊst-
'enɪn, hlan-gŏōsténnin
Llangwyfan *Clwyd,* łæn'guɪvən,
hlan-goʹo-ivän
Llangwyllog *Gwynedd,* łæn-
'gwɪłɒg, hlan-gwíhlog
Llangwyryfon *Dyfed,* ˌłæŋgwɪər-
'ʌvən, hlan-gweerúvvŏn
Llangybi *Dyfed, Gwent, Gwynedd,*
łæn'gʌbɪ, hlan-gúbbi
Llangyfelach *W. Glam.,* ˌłæŋgə-
'veləx, hlan-gŭ-véllắch
Llangynhafal *Clwyd,* ˌłæŋgʌn-
'hævəl, hlan-gun-hávvăl
Llangynidr *Powys,* łæn'gʌnɪdər,
hlan-gúnnidĕr
Llangyniew *Powys,* łæn'gʌnju,
hlan-gúnnew
Llangynin, *formerly* **Llanginning**
q.v., Dyfed, łæn'gʌnɪn, hlan-
-gúnnin
Llangynog *Dyfed, Powys,* łæn-
'gʌnɒg, hlan-gúnnog
Llangynwyd *Mid Glam.,* łæn-
'gʌnuɪd, hlan-gúnnŏō-id
Llangywair *see* **Llangower**
Llangywer *see* **Llangower**
Llanhamlach *Powys,* łæn'hæmlæx,
hlan-hám-lach
Llanharan *Mid Glam.,* łæn'hærən,
hlan-hárrän
Llanharry *Mid Glam.,* łæn'hærɪ,
hlan-hárri
Llanhilleth *Gwent,* łæn'hɪləθ,
hlan-híllĕth
Llanhowell *Dyfed,* łæn'haʊəl,
hlan-hówĕl
Llanidan *Gwynedd,* łæn'idən,
hlaneʹedän
Llanidloes *Powys,* łæn'ɪdlɔɪs,
hlanídloyss
Llaniestyn *Gwynedd,* łæn'jestɪn,
hlan-yésstin

Llanigon *Powys,* łæn'aɪgən,
hlanígŏn
Llanilar *Dyfed,* łæn'ilɑr, hlaneʹe-
laar
Llanion *Dyfed,* 'lænjən, lán-yŏn
Llanishen *Gwent, S. Glam.,*
læn'ɪʃən, laníshĕn
Llanllawddog *Dyfed,* łæn'łaʊðɒg,
hlan-hlów-thog
Llanllechid *Gwynedd,* łæn'łexɪd,
hlan-hléchid
Llanlleonfel *Powys,* ˌłænłeɪ'ɒnvel,
hlan-hlay-ónvel
Llanllowel *Gwent,* łæn'łaʊəl,
hlan-hlówĕl
Llanllugan *Powys,* łæn'łɪgən,
hlan-hlíggän
Llanlliwchaiarn *Powys,* ˌłænłux-
'haɪərn, hlan-hlooch-hí-ärn
Llanllwni *Dyfed,* łæn'łʊnɪ, hlan-
-hlŏōni
Llanllyfni *Gwynedd,* łæn'łʌvnɪ,
hlan-hlúvni
Llanmerewig *Powys,* ˌłænme-
'rewɪg, hlanmerré-wig
Llanmorlais *W. Glam.,* łæn'mɔr-
laɪs, hlan-mórlïss
Llannefydd *Clwyd,* łæn'evɪð,
hlanévvith
Llan-non *Dyfed,* łæn'ɒn, hlanón
Llannor *Gwynedd,* 'łænɔr, hlánnor
Llanon *Dyfed,* łæn'ɒn, hlanón
Llanover *Gwent,* łæn'oʊvər,
hlanŏvĕr
Llanpumsaint, *formerly spelt*
Llanpumpsaint, *Dyfed,* łæn-
'pɪmsaɪnt, hlan-pímssïnt
Llanrhaeadr ym Mochnant *Clwyd,*
łæn'hraɪədər ʌm 'mɒxnənt,
hlanrí-ădĕr um móchnänt
Llanrhaeadr yng Nghinmerch,
formerly spelt **Llanrhaiadr yn**
Cinmerch *q.v., Clwyd,* łæn-
'hraɪədər ʌŋ 'hɪnmeɪərx,
hlanrí-ădĕr ung hínmay-ĕrch
Llanrhaiadr yn Cinmerch, *former*
spelling of **Llanrhaeadr yng**
Nghinmerch *q.v., Clwyd,*
łæn'hraɪədər ʌŋ 'kʌmərx,
hlanrí-ădĕr ung kúmmĕrch
Llanrhidian *W. Glam.,* ˌłæn-
'hrɪdjən, hlan-ríd-yän
Llanrhychwyn *Gwynedd,* łæn-
'hrʌxwɪn, hlanrúchwin
Llanrhyddlad *Gwynedd,* łæn-
'hrɪðlæd, hlanríthlad
Llanrhystyd, *also spelt* **Llanrhy-**
stud, *Dyfed,* łæn'hrʌstɪd,
hlanrússtid
Llanrug *Gwynedd,* łæn'rig, hlanréeg
Llanrwst *Gwynedd,* łæn'rust,
hlanroʹost
Llansadwrn *Dyfed, Gwynedd,*
łæn'sæduərn, hlan-sáddŏōrn

Llansaint _Dyfed_,'łæn'saınt, hlán-
-sínt
Llansamlet _W. Glam._,łæn'sæmlıt,
hlan-sámlĕt
Llansantffraid _Powys_,,łænsænt-
'fraıd, hlan-santfríd
Llansantffraid-ym-Mechain
Powys,,łænsænt'fraıd ʌm
'mexaın, hlan-santfríd um
méchīn
Llansawel _Dyfed_,łæn'sauəl,
hlan-sówĕl
Llansilin _Clwyd_,łæn'sılın, hlan-
-síllin
Llanspyddid _Powys_,łæn'spʌðıd,
hlan-spúthid
Llanstadwell _Dyfed_,łæn'stædwel,
hlan-stád-wel
Llanstephan _Powys_,łæn'stefən,
hlan-stéffän
Llantarnam _Gwent_,łæn'tɑrnəm,
hlantaárnăm
Llanthony _Gwent_,łæn'touni, hlan-
tŏni
Llantilio Crossenny _Gwent_,łæn-
'tıljou krʊ'senı, hlantíl-yō
krossénni
Llantood _Dyfed_, 'læntud, lántood
Llantrisaint Fawr, _also spelt_
Llantrissent Fawr, _Gwent_,łæn-
'trısənt 'vauər, hlantríssänt vówr
Llantrisant _Gwent, Gwynedd, Mid
Glam._,łæn'trısənt, hlantríssänt
Llantrissent Fawr _see_ **Llantrisaint
Fawr**
Llantrithyd _S. Glam._,łæn'trıθıd,
hlantríthid
Llantwit Fardre _Mid Glam_,.
'łæntwıt 'vɑrdreı, hlántwit
vaárdray
Llantwit Major _S. Glam._, 'læntwıt
'meıdʒər, lántwit máyjŏr
Llantysilio _Clwyd_,,łæntə'sıljou,
hlantŭssil-yō
Llanuwchllyn _Gwynedd_,łæn'jux-
lın, hlanéwchlin
Llanvaches _Gwent_,łæn'væxıs,
hlanváchĕss
Llanvair Discoed _Gwent_, 'łæn-
vaıər 'dıskɔıd, hlánvīr dísskoyd
Llanvetherine _Gwent_,łæn've0rın,
hlanvéthrin. _The Welsh form is_
Llanwytherin, _q.v._
Llanvihangel Crucorney _Gwent_,
,łænvı'hæŋəl krʊ'kɔrnı, hlanvi-
-háng-ĕl krŏŏkórni
Llanwarne _H. & W._,łæn'wɔrn,
hlan-wáwrn
Llanwddyn _Powys_,łæn'ʊðın,
hlanŏŏthin
Llanwenarth _Gwent_,łæn'wenɑrθ,
hlanwénnaarth
Llanwenllwyfo _Gwynedd_,łænwın-
'łʊıvou, hlanwĕn-hlŏŏ-ivō

Llanwenog _Dyfed_,łæn'wenɒg,
hlan-wénnog
Llanwern _Gwent_,łæn'weərn,
hlan-waírn
Llanwinio _Dyfed_,łæn'wınjou,
hlan-wín-yō
Llanwnda _Dyfed, Gwynedd_,łæn-
'ʊndə, hlanŏŏndă
Llanwnen _Dyfed_,łæn'ʊnən,
hlanŏŏnĕn
Llanwnog _Powys_,łæn'ʊnɒg,
hlanŏŏnog
Llanwonno _Mid Glam._,łæn-
'wʌnou, hlan-wúnnō
Llanwrda _Dyfed_,łæn'ʊərdə,
hlanŏŏrdă
Llanwrin _Powys_,łæn'ʊərın,
hlanŏŏrin
Llanwrthwl _Powys_, łæn'ʊərθʊl,
hlanŏŏrthŏŏl
Llanwrtyd _Powys_,łæn'ʊərtıd,
hlanŏŏrtid
Llanwyddelan _Powys_,,łænwı-
'ðelən, hlanwithéllän
Llanwytherin _Gwent_,,łænwı-
'0erın, hlanwithérrin. _The English form is_ **Llanvetherine**, _q.v._
Llanyblodwell _Salop_,,łænə'blɒd-
wəl, hlanăblódwĕl
Llanybri _Dyfed_,,łænə'bri, hlannă-
breé
Llanybyther _Dyfed_,,łænə'bʌðər,
hlanăbúthĕr
Llan-y-cefn _Dyfed_,,łænə'kevn,
hlanăkévvn
Llanychâr _Dyfed_,,łænə'xɑr, hlană-
chaár
Llanychllwydog _Dyfed_,,łænəx-
'łʊıdɒg, hlanăch-hlŏŏ-idog
Llanycil _Gwynedd_,łæn'ʌkıl,
hlanúckil
Llan-y-crwys _Dyfed_,,łænə'krʊıs,
hlanăkrŏŏ-iss
Llanymawddwy _Gwynedd_,,łænə-
'mauðʊı, hlanămówthŏŏ-i
Llanymynech _Powys_,,łænə-
'mʌnıx, hlanămúnnĕch;,,łænə-
'mʌnex, hlanămúnnech
Llanynghenedl _Gwynedd_, ,łænəŋ-
'henıdl, hlanŭng-hénnĕdl
Llanynis _Clwyd_,łæn'ʌnıs, hlanúnniss
Llanynys Rhewl _Clwyd_,łæn'ʌnıs
hre'ul, hlanúnniss re-oól
Llanyrafon _Gwent_,,łænər'ævən,
hlanărávvŏn
Llanyre _Powys_,łæn'ıər, hlanéer;
łæn'aıər, hlanír
Llanystumdwy _Gwynedd_,,łænə-
'stımdʊı, hlanăstímdŏŏ-i
Llawhaden _Dyfed_,łau'hædən,
hlow-háddĕn
Llawryglyn _Powys_,,łauərə'glın,
hlowr-ăglín

Llay *see* **Llai**

Llechryd *Mid Glam.*,'ɬexrɪd, hléchrid

Llechylched *Gwynedd*,ɬeɪ'xʌlxɪd, hlaychúlchĕd

Lletty Brongu *Mid Glam.*,'ɬetɪ 'brɒŋgɪ, hlétti bróng-gi

Llewellin, Barony of, lə'welɪn, lĕ-wéllin

Llewellyn, *f.n.*,ɬə'welɪn, hlĕ--wéllin; lə'welɪn, lĕ-wéllin; lʊ'elɪn, lōō-éllin

Llewelyn, *f.n.*,ɬə'welɪn, hlĕ-wéllin; lə'welɪn, lĕ-wéllin; lʊ'elɪn, lōō--éllin

Llewelyn-Davies of Hastoe, Baroness, lʊ'elɪn 'deɪvɪs əv 'hæstoʊ, lōō-éllin dáyviss ŏv hásstō

Lleyn Peninsula *Gwynedd*,ɬin, hleen

Llidiart-y-Waun *Powys*,'ɬɪdjɑrtə-'waɪn, hlídyaart-ă-wín

Lligwy *see* **Llugwy**

Llinos, *Welsh C.n.*,'ɬinɒs, hléenoss

Lliswerry *Gwent*,ɬis'werɪ, hleess--wérri

Llithfaen *Gwynedd*,'ɬiθvaɪn, hlíth-vīn

Lliwedd *Gwynedd*,'ɬiweð, hlée--weth;'ɬʊɪð, hloo-ĕth

Llowes *Powys*,'ɬoʊɪs, hlō-ĕss

Lloyd, *f.n.*, loyd, loyd. *Appropriate also for Baron* ~.

Lloyd George of Dwyfor, Earl, 'lɔɪd 'dʒɔrdʒ əv 'dʊɪvər, lóyd jórj ŏv dōō-i-vor

Lluest Wen *Mid Glam.*,'ɬiest 'wen, hlée-est wén

Llugwy, *also spelt* **Lligwy,** River, *Gwynedd*,'ɬigʊɪ, hleegōō-i

Llwchwr *W. Glam.*,'ɬuxʊər, hloochōōr

Llwydcoed *Mid Glam.*,'ɬʊɪdkɒd, hlōō-idkod;'ɬʊɪdkɔɪd, hlōō--idkoyd

Llwydiarth *Powys*,'ɬʊɪdjɑrθ, hlōō-id-yaarth

Llwyncelyn *Dyfed*,,ɬʊɪn'kelɪn, hlōō-in-kéllin

Llwyngwril *Gwynedd*,,ɬʊɪn'gʊərɪl, hlōō-in-gōōril

Llwynhendy *Dyfed*,,ɬʊɪn'hendɪ, hlōō-in-héndi

Llwyn Madoc *Gwynedd*,,ɬʊɪn 'mædɒk, hlōō-in máddock

Llwyn-on Reservoir *Mid Glam.*, 'ɬʊɪn'ɒn, hlōō-in-ón

Llwynypia *Mid Glam.*,,ɬʊɪnə'piə, hlōō-in-ăpée-ă

Llyn Brianne *Dyfed–Powys*,ɬin brɪ'æneɪ, hlin bri-ánnay

Llyn Cau *Gwynedd*,ɬin 'kaɪ, hlin kí

Llyn Celyn *Gwynedd*,ɬin 'kelɪn, hlin kéllin

Llynclys *Salop*, 'lʌŋklɪs, lúnkliss; 'ɬʌŋklɪs, hlúnkliss

Llyn Cwellyn *Gwynedd*,ɬin 'kwelɪn, hlin kwéhlin

Llyn Mymbyr *Gwynedd*,ɬin 'mʌmbər, hlin múmbĕr

Llyn Ogwen *Gwynedd*,ɬin 'ɒgwen, hlin ógwen

Llyn Padarn *Gwynedd*,ɬin 'pædərn, hlin páddărn

Llyn Safaddan *Powys*,,ɬin sə-'væðən, hlin săváthăn

Llyn Tegid *Gwynedd*,ɬin 'tegɪd, hlin téggid. *This is the Welsh name for* **Bala** Lake.

Llysfaen *Clwyd*,'ɬɪsvaɪn, hlíssvīn

Llysfaen *Gwynedd*,ɬis'vaɪn, hleessvín

Llys-faen *S. Glam.*,ɬis'vaɪn, hleess-vín. *The English name is* **Lisvane**, *q.v.*

Llys-wen *Dyfed, Powys*,ɬis'wen, hleesswén

Llysworney *S. Glam.*, lɪz'wɜrnɪ, lizwúrni

Llys-y-frân *Dyfed*,,ɬisə'vrɑn, hleessăvraan

Llywelyn, *f.n.*,ɬə'welɪn, hlĕ-wéllin

Llywelyn ap Gruffydd, *13th-c.* Prince of Wales,ɬə'welɪn æp 'grɪfɪð, hlĕ-wéllin ap gríffith

Loach, *f.n.*, loʊtʃ, lōtch

Loader, *f.n.*, 'loʊdər, lódĕr

Loads, *f.n.*, loʊdz, lōdz

Loanhead *Lothian*, 'loʊn'hed, lōn-héd

Loasby, *f.n.*, 'loʊzbɪ, lózbi

Lobjoit, *f.n.*, 'lɒbdʒɔɪt, lóbjoyt

Lobscombe Corner *Wilts.*, 'lɒbzkəm 'kɔrnər, lóbzkŏm kórnĕr

Loch, Baron, lɒx, loch

Lochaber *H'land*, lɒ'xɑbər, loch-a'ábĕr

Lochailort *H'land*, lɒ'xaɪlərt, lochílŏrt

Lochaline *H'land*, lɒ'xælɪn, lochá-lin

Lochalsh *H'land*, lɒ'xælʃ, lochálsh

Loch an Athain *Skye*, 'lɒx ən 'ɑn, lóch ăn a'an

Loch an Eilean *H'land*, 'lɒx ən 'ilən, lóch ăn eélăn

Lochboisdale *W. Isles*, lɒx-'bɔɪzdeɪl, lochbóyzdayl

Lochbuie *S'clyde*, lɒx'bʊɪ, lochbóo-i

Lochearnhead *Central*, lɒx'ɜrn-'hed, lochérn-héd

Lochee *Tayside*, lɒ'xi, lochée

Locheilside *H'land*, lɒ'xil'saɪd, locheél-síd

Locheport W. Isles, lɒx'ipɔrt, lochéeport
Lochgelly Fife, lɒx'gelɪ, lochgélli
Lochgilphead S'clyde, lɒx'gɪlphed, lochgílp-hed
Lochiel, f.n., lɒ'xil, lochéel
Lochinvar D. & G., ˌlɒxɪn'vɑr, lochinvaár
Lochinver H'land, lɒ'xɪnvər, lochínvĕr
Lochlea S'clyde, 'lɒxlɪ, lóchli
Lochlee Tayside, lɒx'li, lochlée
Lochluichart H'land, lɒx'luɪxərt, lochlo'o-ichărt; lɒx'luxərt, lochlo'ochărt
Lochmaben D. & G., lɒx'meɪbən, lochmáybĕn
Lochmaddy W. Isles, lɒx'mædɪ, lochmáddi
Loch na Creitheach Skye, 'lɒx nə 'krihəx, lóch nă krée-hăch
Lochnagar Grampian, ˌlɒxnə'gɑr, lochnägaár
Loch nan Uamh H'land, 'lɒx nən 'uəv, lóch năn o'o-ăv
Loch of Lintrathen Tayside, 'lɒx əv lɪn'treɪðən, lóch ŏv lintráythĕn
Loch of the Lowes Tayside, 'lɒx əv ðə 'lauz, lóch ŏv thĕ lówz
Lochrane, f.n., 'lɒxrən, lóchrăn; 'lɒkrən, lóckrăn
Lochranza S'clyde, lɒx'rænzə, loch-ránzä
Lochrutton D. & G., lɒx'rʌtən, lochrúttŏn
Lochtreighead H'land, lɒx'trig-hed, lochtreég-hed
Lochwinnoch S'clyde, lɒx'wɪnəx, lochwínnŏch
Lochy, Loch, H'land, 'lɒxɪ, lóchi
Lockerbie D. & G., 'lɒkərbɪ, lóckĕrbi
Lockhart, f.n., 'lɒkərt, lóckărt; 'lɒkhɑrt, lóck-haart. The first is appropriate for the family name, **Bruce** ~.
Lockie, f.n., 'lɒkɪ, lócki
Lockinge, East and West, Oxon., 'lɒkɪndʒ, lóckinj
Lockspeiser, f.n., 'lɒkspaɪzər, lóckspīzĕr
Lockyer, f.n., 'lɒkjər, lóck-yĕr
Locock, f.n., 'loʊkɒk, lókock
Loddiswell Devon, 'lɒdɪzwel, lóddizwel
Loddon, River, Hants, 'lɒdən, lóddŏn
Lode Cambs., loʊd, lōd
Loder, f.n., 'loʊdər, lódĕr
Loe Bar, also spelt **Loo Bar**, Cornwall, 'lu 'bɑr, lo'o baár
Loeber, f.n., 'loʊbər, lóbĕr
Loelia, C.n., 'lilɪə, leéliä

Loewe, f.n., loʊ, lō; 'loʊɪ, ló-i
Loewen, f.n., 'loʊən, ló-ĕn
Lofthouse, f.n., 'lɒfthaʊs, lóft-howss; 'lɒftəs, lóftŭss
Loftus, f.n., 'lɒftəs, lóftŭss
Logan, f.n., 'loʊgən, lógăn
Logie, f.n., 'loʊgɪ, lógi
Logiealmond Tayside, ˌloʊgɪ-'ɑmənd, lōgi-aámŏnd
Logie Coldstone Grampian, ˌloʊgɪ 'koʊlstən, lōgi kŏlsstŏn
Logierait Tayside, ˌloʊgə'reɪt, lōgĕráyt; ˌloʊgɪ'reɪt, lōgiráyt
Logue, f.n., loʊg, lōg
Lohan, f.n., lɒn, lawn
Lois, C.n., 'loʊɪs, ló-iss
Loiseau, f.n., 'lwɑzoʊ, lwaázō
Loman, f.n., 'loʊmən, lómän
Lomas, f.n., 'loʊməs, lómäss
Lombe, f.n., loʊm, lōm
Lomond, Loch, Central–S'clyde, 'loʊmənd, lómŏnd
Londesborough, Baron, 'lɒndzbərə, lóndzbŭrä
London, 'lʌndən, lúndŏn
London Colney Herts., 'lʌndən 'koʊnɪ, lúndŏn kŏni
Londonderry Co. Derry, ˌlʌndən'derɪ, lundŏndérri; 'lʌndəndərɪ, lúndŏndĕri. The second is appropriate for the Marquess of ~.
Lonergan, f.n., 'lɒnərgən, lónnĕrgăn
Longannet Point Fife, lɒŋ'ænɪt, long-ánnĕt
Longay Skye, 'lɒŋgeɪ, lóng-gay
Long Compton Warwicks., 'lɒŋ 'kɒmptən, lóng kómptŏn
Longforgan Tayside, lɒŋ'fɔrgən, longfórgăn
Longformacus Borders, ˌlɒŋfər'meɪkəs, long-förmáykŭss
Longhorsley Northd., 'lɒŋ'hɔrslɪ, lóng-hórssli
Longhoughton Northd., 'lɒŋ'haʊtən, lóng-hówtŏn; 'lɒŋ'hoʊtən, lóng-hŏtŏn
Longleat Wilts., 'lɒŋlit, lóng-leet
Longlevens Glos., 'lɒŋ'levənz, lóng-lévvĕnz
Long Mynd Salop, 'lɒŋ mɪnd, lóng minnd
Longney Glos., 'lɒŋnɪ, lóng-ni
Longnor Staffs., 'lɒŋnər, lóng-nŏr
Longriggend S'clyde, 'lɒŋrɪg'end, lóng-rig-énd
Longsight Gtr. M'chester, 'lɒŋ'saɪt, lóng-sít
Longsleddale Cumbria, lɒŋ'slɪdl, long-slíddl
Longsowerby Cumbria, lɒŋ'sauərbɪ, long-sówĕrbi
Longtown Cumbria, H. & W., 'lɒŋtaʊn, lóngtown

Longuet, f.n., 'lɒŋgɪt, lóng-gĕt
Lonie, f.n., 'loʊnɪ, lốni
Lonmay Grampian, lɒn'meɪ, lon-máy
Lon-y-Glyder Gwynedd, 'loʊn ə 'glɪdər, lốn ǎ glíddĕr
Loo Bar see Loe Bar
Looe Cornwall, lu, loo
Loose Kent, luz, looz
Loosley Row Bucks., 'luzlɪ 'roʊ, loózli rố
Lopes, f.n., 'loʊpəz, lốpĕz
Loppert, f.n., 'lɒpərt, lóppĕrt
Lorenz, f.n., 'lɒrənz, lórrĕnz
Loretto School Lothian, lə'retoʊ, lŏréttō
Lorettonian, one educated at Loretto School, ˌlɒrɪ'toʊnɪən, lorrĕtốniän
Lorie, f.n., 'lɒrɪ, lórri
Lorimer, f.n., 'lɒrɪmər, lórrimĕr
Lorne, C.n. and f.n., lɔrn, lorn
Lorne S'clyde, lɔrn, lorn. Appropriate also for the Marquess of ~ and for the Firth of ~.
Lorrimer, f.n., 'lɒrɪmər, lórrimĕr
Loseley Park Surrey, 'loʊzlɪ 'pɑrk, lốzli paárk
Losey, f.n., 'loʊzɪ, lốzi
Loshak, f.n., 'loʊʃæk, lố-shack
Losinska, f.n., lɒ'sɪnskə, lossínskă
Lossiemouth Grampian, ˌlɒsɪ-'maʊθ, lossimówth
Lostock Hall Lancs., 'lɒstɒk 'hɔl, lósstock háwl
Lostwithiel Cornwall, lɒs'wɪθɪəl, losswíthi-ĕl; lɒst'wɪθɪəl, losst-wíthi-ĕl
Lotery, f.n., 'loʊtərɪ, lốtĕri
Lothbury City of London, 'loʊθ-bərɪ, lốthbŭri; 'lɒθbərɪ, lóthbŭri
Lothersdale N. Yorks., 'lɒðərz-deɪl, lóthĕrzdayl
Lothian Scottish region, 'loʊðɪən, lốthiän. Appropriate also for the Marquess of ~.
Lothingland Suffolk, 'loʊðɪŋlænd, lốthing-land
Lotterby, f.n., 'lɒtərbɪ, lóttĕrbi
Louarch, f.n., 'loʊərk, lố-ărk
Louch, f.n., laʊtʃ, lowtch
Loudan, f.n., 'laʊdən, lówdăn
Loudon, f.n., 'laʊdən, lówdŏn
Loudoun, f.n., 'laʊdən, lówdŏn
Loudoun Hill S'clyde, 'laʊdən, lówdŏn. Appropriate also for the Countess of ~.
Lough, f.n., lʌf, luff; loʊ, lō; lɒx, loch
Loughans, f.n., 'lʌfənz, lúffănz
Loughborough Leics., 'lʌfbərə, lúffbŭră
Lough Bradan Forest Co. Armagh, lɒx 'brædən, loch bráddăn

Loughbrickland Co. Down, lɒx-'brɪklənd, loch-bríckländ
Lough Foyle Cos. Donegal–Londonderry, lɒx 'fɔɪl, loch fóyl
Loughgall Co. Armagh, lɒx'gɔl, lochgáwl
Loughgiel Co. Antrim, lɒx'gil, lochgéel
Loughlin, f.n., 'lɒxlɪn, lóchlin; 'lɒklɪn, lócklin
Loughmuck Co. Tyrone, lɒx'mʌk, lochmúck
Lough Neagh N. Ireland, lɒx 'neɪ, loch náy
Loughor W.Glam., 'lʌxər, lúchŏr
Loughor, River, Dyfed, 'lʌxər, lúchŏr
Loughran, f.n., 'lɒxrən, lóchrăn
Loughrey, f.n., 'lɒxrɪ, lóchri
Loughrigg Cumbria, 'lʌfrɪg, lúffrig
Loukes, f.n., laʊks, lowks
Lound Hall Notts., laʊnd, lownd
Lourie, f.n., 'laʊərɪ, lówri
Lousada, f.n., lu'sɑdə, loossaádă; lu'zɑdə, loozaádă
Lousley, f.n., 'laʊzlɪ, lówzli
Louth, Baron, laʊð, lowth
Louth Lincs., laʊθ, lowth
Loutit, f.n., 'lutɪt, loótit
Louttit, f.n., 'lutɪt, loótit
Lovat, Baron, 'lʌvət, lúvvăt
Lovejoy, f.n., 'lʌvdʒɔɪ, lúvjoy
Lovelace, Earl of, 'lʌvleɪs, lúv-layss
Lovel and Holland, Baron, 'lʌvl ənd 'hɒlənd, lúvvl ănd hólländ
Lovell, f.n., 'lʌvl, lúvvl
Lover, Wilts., 'loʊvər, lốvĕr
Loveridge, f.n., 'lʌvrɪdʒ, lúvrij
Lovett, f.n., 'lʌvɪt, lúvvĕt
Loveys, f.n., 'lʌvɪz, lúvviz
Lovibond, f.n., 'lʌvɪbɒnd, lúvvi-bond
Lovill, f.n., 'lʌvɪl, lúvvil
Low, f.n., loʊ, lō
Lowater, f.n., 'loʊətər, lố-ătĕr
Low Bradley N. Yorks., 'loʊ 'brædlɪ, lố brádli
Lowbridge, f.n., 'loʊbrɪdʒ, lốbrij
Lowbury, f.n., 'loʊbərɪ, lốbŭri
Lowca Cumbria, 'laʊkə, lówkă
Low Coniscliffe Durham, 'loʊ 'kɒnɪsklɪf, lố kónniss-cliff
Lowdell, f.n., laʊ'del, lowdéll
Lowden, f.n., 'laʊdən, lówdĕn
Lowder, f.n., 'laʊdər, lówdĕr
Lowdham Notts., Suffolk, 'laʊd-əm, lówdăm
Lowe, f.n., loʊ, lō
Lowell, f.n., 'loʊəl, lố-ĕl
Lowenthal, f.n., 'loʊəntæl, lố-ĕntal
Lower, f.n., 'loʊər, lố-ĕr

Lower Benefield *Northants.*, 'lоʊər 'benɪfɪld, lṓ-ĕr bénnifeeld
Lower Halstow *Kent*, 'lоʊər 'hælstоʊ, lṓ-ĕr hálsstō
Lower Heyford, *also sometimes called* **Heyford at Bridge**, *Oxon.*, 'lоʊər 'heɪfərd, lṓ-ĕr háyförd
Lower Shuckburgh *Warwicks.*, 'lоʊər 'ʃʌkbərə, lṓ-ĕr shúckbŭrä
Lower Slaughter *Glos.*, 'lоʊər 'slɔtər, lṓ-ĕr sláwtĕr
Lower Wyche *H. & W.*, 'lоʊər 'wɪtʃ, lṓ-ĕr wítch
Lowes, *f.n.*, lоʊz, lōz
Lowesby *Leics.*, 'lоʊzbɪ, lṓzbi
Lowestoft *Suffolk*, 'lоʊstɒft, lṓsstoft; 'lоʊstəft, lṓsstŏft; 'lоʊstəf, lṓsstŏf
Loweswater *Cumbria*, 'lоʊzwɔtər, lṓzwawtĕr
Lowick *Cumbria*, 'lоʊɪk, lṓ-ick
Lowick *Northd.*, 'lоʊɪk, lṓ-ick; 'laʊɪk, lówick
Low Ireby *Cumbria*, 'lоʊ 'aɪərbɪ, lṓ írbi
Lowis, *f.n.*, 'lоʊɪs, lṓ-iss; 'laʊɪs, lówiss
Lowke, *f.n.*, lоʊk, lōk
Lowles, *f.n.*, lоʊlz, lōlz; laʊlz, lowlz
Lown, *f.n.*, laʊn, lown
Lownie, *f.n.*, 'laʊnɪ, lówni
Lowry, *f.n.*, 'laʊərɪ, lówri
Lowson, *f.n.*, 'lоʊsən, lṓssŏn
Lowther, *f.n.*, 'laʊðər, lówthĕr; 'lоʊðər, lṓthĕr
Lowther *Cumbria*, 'laʊðər, lówthĕr
Lowthers, The, *D. & G.–S'clyde*, 'laʊðərz, lówthĕrz
Lowthian, *f.n.*, 'lоʊðɪən, lṓthiän
Lowton *Gtr. M'chester*, 'lоʊtən, lṓtŏn
Loydall, *f.n.*, 'lɔɪdl, lóydl
Lozells *W. Midlands*, lоʊ'zelz, lōzéllz
Luard, *f.n.*, 'lʊɑrd, lоо-aard
Lubbock, *f.n.*, 'lʌbək, lúbbŏk
Lubenham *Leics.*, 'lʌbənəm, lúbbĕnăm
Lubnaig, Loch, *Central*, 'lubneɪg, lоób-nayg; 'lubnɪg, lоób-nig
Lucan, Earl of, 'lukən, lоó-kăn
Lucas, *f.n.*, 'lukəs, lоó-käss
Lucasian, *pertaining to* **Lucas**, lu'keɪzɪən, loo-káyziän. *Appropriate for the ~ Chair of Mathematics, Univ. of Cambridge.*
Luccombe *Somerset*, 'lʌkəm, lúckŏm
Luce, *f.n.*, lus, looss

Luce Bay *D. & G.*, lus, looss
Luchford, *f.n.*, 'lʌtʃfərd, lútchförd
Lucie, *f.n.*, 'lusɪ, lоóssi
Lucken, *f.n.*, 'lʌkən, lúckĕn
Luckes, *f.n.*, 'lʌkɪs, lúckĕss
Lucock, *f.n.*, 'lukɒk, lоó-kock
Lucraft, *f.n.*, 'lukrɑft, lоó-kraaft
Luddesdown *Kent*, 'lʌdzdaʊn, lúdzdown
Luder, *f.n.*, 'ludər, lоódĕr
Ludgershall *Bucks.*, *Wilts.*, 'lʌdgərʃl, lúd-gĕr-shl; 'lʌgərʃl, lúggĕr-shl
Ludgvan *Cornwall*, 'lʌdʒən, lújjän
Ludlow *Salop*, 'lʌdlоʊ, lúdlō
Ludovic, *C.n.*, 'ludəvɪk, lоódŏvick
Luetchford, *f.n.*, 'letʃfərd, létchförd
Luffness *Lothian*, lʌf'nes, luff-néss
Luffrum, *f.n.*, 'lʌfrəm, lúffrŭm
Lugar *S'clyde*, 'lugər, lоógăr
Lugard, Barony of, lu'gɑrd, loo-gaárd
Lugard, *f.n.*, 'lugɑrd, lоógaard
Luget, *f.n.*, lu'ʒeɪ, loozháy
Lugg, *f.n.*, lʌg, lug
Lugwardine *H. & W.*, 'lʌgwərdin, lúgwärdeen
Luing *S'clyde*, lɪŋ, ling. *Appropriate also for the ~ breed of cattle.*
Luker, *f.n.*, 'lukər, lоó-kĕr
Lulsgate *Avon*, 'lʌlzgeɪt, lúllzgayt
Lumbis, *f.n.*, lʌmz, lummz
Lumley, *f.n.*, 'lʌmlɪ, lúmli
Lummis, *f.n.*, 'lʌmɪs, lúmmiss
Lumphanan *Grampian*, ləm'fænən, lümfánnän
Lumsden, *f.n.*, 'lʌmzdən, lúmzdĕn
Lunan, *f.n.*, 'lunən, lоónăn
Lunan *Tayside*, 'lunən, lоónăn
Luncarty *Tayside*, 'lʌŋkərtɪ, lúnkärti
Lund, *f.n.*, lʌnd, lund
Lundie, *f.n.*, 'lʌndɪ, lúndi
Lundy Island *Devon*, 'lʌndɪ, lúndi
Lune, *f.n.*, lun, loon
Lune, River, *Cumbria*, lun, loon
Lunghi, *f.n.*, 'lʌŋgɪ, lúng-gi
Lungley, *f.n.*, 'lʌŋlɪ, lúng-li
Lunnes, *f.n.*, 'lʌnɪs, lúnnĕss
Lunt, *f.n.*, lʌnt, lunt
Lupino, *f.n.*, lʊ'pinоʊ, lооpéenō
Lupton, *f.n.*, 'lʌptən, lúptŏn
Lurgan *Co. Armagh*, 'lɜrgən, lúrgän. *Appropriate also for Baron ~.*

Lurgashall W. Sussex, 'lɜrgəʃl, lúrgă-shl

Lurie, f.n., 'ljʊərɪ, lyŏŏri

Lurigethan Co. Antrim, ˌlʌrɪ'giən, lurrigée-än

Luscombe, f.n., 'lʌskəm, lússkŏm

Lush, f.n., lʌʃ, lush

Lusher, f.n., 'lʌʃər, lúshěr

Luskentyre W. Isles, 'lʌskəntaɪər, lúskĕntīr

Luss S'clyde, lʌs, luss

Lussa S'clyde, 'lʌsə, lússă

Lustgarten, f.n., 'lʌstgɑrtən, lústgaartĕn

Lustleigh Devon, 'lʌstlɪ, lústlee

Lutener, f.n., 'luːtənər, lŏŏtĕnĕr

Luthrie Fife, 'lʌθrɪ, lúthri

Luton Beds., 'luːtən, lóŏtŏn

Lutterworth Leics., 'lʌtərwərθ, lúttĕrwŏrth

Luttrell, f.n., 'lʌtrəl, lúttrĕl

Lutwyche, f.n., 'lʌtwɪtʃ, lútwitch

Luty, f.n., 'luːtɪ, lóŏti

Lutyens, f.n., 'lʌtjənz, lút-yĕnz. Appropriate for Sir Edward ~, architect, and Elizabeth ~, composer.

Luxon, f.n., 'lʌksən, lúcksŏn

Luxulyan Cornwall, lʌk'sɪljən, lucksíl-yän

Luya, f.n., 'lujə, loŏ-yă

Lyall, f.n., 'laɪəl, lí-ăl; laɪl, líl

Lybster H'land, 'laɪbstər, líbstĕr

Lyburn, f.n., 'laɪbərn, líburn

Lycett, f.n., 'laɪsɪt, líssĕt

Lydart Gwent, 'laɪdərt, lídărt

Lydd Kent, lɪd, lid

Lydden Kent, 'lɪdən, líddĕn

Lydekker, f.n., lɪ'dekər, liddéckĕr; laɪ'dekər, lidéckĕr; 'laɪdekər, lídeckĕr

Lyden, f.n., 'laɪdən, lídĕn

Lydford, f.n., 'lɪdfərd, lídfŏrd

Lydgate Gtr. M'chester, 'lɪdgeɪt, lídgayt; 'lɪdgɪt, líd-git

Lydgate W. Yorks., 'lɪdgɪt, líd-git; 'lɪgɪt, líggit

Lydiard Millicent Wilts., 'lɪdɪərd 'mɪlɪsənt, líddi-ărd míllissĕnt

Lydiard Park Wilts., 'lɪdɪərd 'pɑrk, líddiărd paárk

Lydiard Tregoze, also spelt **Tregoz,** Wilts., 'lɪdɪərd trɪ'guz, líddi-ărd trĕgoóz; 'lɪdɪərd trɪ'gouz, líddi-ărd trĕgóz. But see **St. John of** ~, Baron.

Lydiate Lancs., 'lɪdɪət, líddiăt

Lydney Glos., 'lɪdnɪ, líd-ni

Lydway Wilts., 'laɪdweɪ, lídway

Lyell, f.n., 'laɪəl, lí-ĕl. Appropriate also for Baron ~.

Lyford, f.n., 'laɪfərd, lífŏrd

Lyford Oxon., 'laɪfərd, lífŏrd

Lygoe, f.n., 'laɪgou, lígŏ

Lygon, f.n., 'lɪgən, líggŏn

Lyle, f.n., laɪl, líl

Lyly, f.n., 'lɪlɪ, lílli. Usually associated also with John ~, 16th-c. dramatist and novelist.

Lymbery, f.n., 'lɪmbərɪ, límbĕri

Lyme Regis Dorset, 'laɪm 'rɪdʒɪs, lím reéjiss

Lyminge Kent, 'lɪmɪndʒ, límminj; 'laɪmɪndʒ, líminj

Lymington Hants, 'lɪmɪŋtən, límmingtŏn. Appropriate also for Viscount ~.

Lyminster W. Sussex, 'lɪmɪnstər, límminstĕr

Lymm Ches., lɪm, lim

Lympany, Moura, pianist, 'mʊərə 'lɪmpənɪ, moŏră límpăni

Lympne Kent, lɪm, lim

Lympstone Devon, 'lɪmpstən, límpstŏn

Lynas, f.n., 'laɪnəs, línăss

Lynch, f.n., lɪnʃ, linsh

Lynch-Blosse, f.n., 'lɪntʃ 'blɒs, líntch blóss

Lyndon, f.n., 'lɪndən, líndŏn

Lyne, f.n., laɪn, lín

Lyneham Wilts., 'laɪnəm, línăm

Lynemouth Northd., 'laɪnmaʊθ, lín-mowth

Lynher, River, Cornwall, 'laɪnər, línĕr

Lynmouth Devon, 'lɪnməθ, lín-mŭth

Lynott, f.n., 'laɪnət, línŏt

Lynturk Grampian, lɪn'tɜrk, lintúrk

Lyons, f.n., 'laɪənz, lí-ŏnz

Lyonshall H. & W., 'laɪənz'hɔl, lí-ŏnz-háwl

Lysaght, f.n., 'laɪsət, líssăt; 'laɪsɑt, líssaat. The first is appropriate for Baron Lisle's family name.

Lysons, f.n., 'laɪsənz, líssŏnz

Lyster, f.n., 'lɪstər, lísstĕr

Lytchett Matravers Dorset, 'lɪtʃɪt mə'trævərz, lítchĕt mătrávvĕrz

Lyte, f.n., laɪt, lít

Lyth, f.n., laɪθ, líth

Lyth H'land, laɪθ, líth

Lythall, f.n., 'laɪθl, líth-l

Lytham St. Annes Lancs., 'lɪðəm snt 'ænz, líthăm sínt ánz

Lyttelton, f.n., 'lɪtltən, líttltŏn

Lyttle, f.n., 'lɪtl, líttl

Lyttleton, f.n., 'lɪtltən, líttltŏn

Lytton, Earl of, 'lɪtən, líttŏn

Lyulph, C.n., 'laɪəlf, lí-ŭlf

Lyveden Northants., 'lɪvdən, lívdĕn. Appropriate also for Baron ~.

Lywood, f.n., 'laɪwʊd, lí-woŏd

M

Maas, *f.n.,* mɑz, maaz
Maaz, *f.n.,* mɑz,maaz
Mabane, *f.n.,* mə'beɪn, măbáyn
Mabayn, *f.n.,* mə'beɪn, măbáyn
Mabe *Cornwall,* meɪb, mayb
Mabel, *C.n.,* 'meɪbl, máybl
Maberly, *f.n.,* 'mæbərlɪ, mábbĕrli
Mabey, *f.n.,* 'meɪbɪ, máybi
Mably, *f.n.,* 'mæblɪ, mábli
Mabon, *f.n.,* 'mæbɒn, mábbon;
'meɪbən, máybŏn. *The first is
the Welsh pronunciation, the
second the Scottish.*
Maby, *f.n.,* 'meɪbɪ, máybi
McAdam, *f.n.,* mə'kædəm, mă-
káddăm
McAdden, *f.n.,* mə'kædən, mă-
káddĕn
Macadie, *f.n.,* mə'kædɪ, măkáddi
Macafee, *f.n.,* 'mækəfi, máckăfee
McAleese, *f.n.,* ˌmækə'lis, mack-
ăléess
McAlery, *f.n.,* ˌmækə'lɪərɪ, mack-
ăléeri
McAlister, *f.n.,* mə'kælɪstər,
măkálistĕr
McAllister, *f.n.,* mə'kælɪstər,
măkálistĕr
McAloon, *f.n.,* ˌmækə'lun, mack-
ăloón
Macalpine, *f.n.,* mə'kælpɪn,
măkálpin; mə'kælpaɪn, mă-
kálpīn
McAlpine, *f.n.,* mə'kælpɪn, mă-
kálpin; mə'kælpaɪn, măkálpīn
Macan, *f.n.,* mə'kæn, măkán
McAnally, *f.n.,* ˌmækə'nælɪ,
mackănáli
Macanaspie, *f.n.,* ˌmækə'næspɪ,
mackănásspi
Macara, *f.n.,* mə'kɑrə, măkaˊară;
mə'kærə, măkárră
McArdle, *f.n.,* mə'kɑrdl, măkaˊardl
MacArthur, *f.n.,* mə'kɑrθər, mă-
kaˊarthŭr
McAslin, *f.n.,* mə'kɔzlɪn, măkáwz-
lin
McAteer, *f.n.,* 'mækətɪər, máck-
ăteer
McAuliffe, *f.n.,* mə'kɔlɪf, mă-
káwliff
McAvoy, *f.n.,* 'mækəvɔɪ, máck-
ăvoy
MacBain, *f.n.,* mək'beɪn, măkbáyn
McBean, *f.n.,* mək'beɪn, măk-
báyn; mək'bin, măkbéen
MacBeath, *f.n.,* mək'beθ, măkbéth
MacBeth, *f.n.,* mək'beθ, măkbéth
McBirney, *f.n.,* mək'bɜrnɪ, măk-
bírni

McBrain, *f.n.,* mək'breɪn, măk-
bráyn
McBratney, *f.n.,* mək'brætnɪ,
măkbrátni
MacBrayne, *f.n.,* mək'breɪn, măk-
bráyn
McBrien, *f.n.,* mək'braɪən, măk-
brí-ĕn
McBrinn, *f.n.,* mək'brɪn, măkbrín
McCabe, *f.n.,* mə'keɪb, măkáyb
McCahearty, *f.n.,* ˌmækə'hɑrtɪ,
mackă-haˊarti
MacCaig, *f.n.,* mə'keɪg, măkáyg
McCaig, *f.n.,* mə'keɪg, măkáyg
McCaldin, *f.n.,* mə'kɔldɪn, mă-
káwldin
McCall, *f.n.,* mə'kɔl, măkáwl
McCallin, *f.n.,* mə'kælɪn, măkálin
MacCallum, *f.n.,* mə'kæləm,
măkálŭm
McCalmont, *f.n.,* mə'kælmənt,
măkálmŏnt
McCammon, *f.n.,* mə'kæmən,
măkámmŏn
McCance, *f.n.,* mə'kæns, măkánss
MacCandless, *f.n.,* mə'kændlɪs,
măkándlĕss
McCann, *f.n.,* mə'kæn, măkán
McCarthy, *f.n.,* mə'kɑrθɪ, mă-
kaˊarthi
McCartney, *f.n.,* mə'kɑrtnɪ, mă-
kaˊartni
McCaughan, *f.n.,* mə'kæxən,
măkáchăn; mə'kɔn, măkáwn
McCaughey, *f.n.,* mə'kæxɪ, mă-
káchi; mə'kæhɪ, măkă-hi; mə-
'kɒfɪ, măkóffi
McCheane, *f.n.,* mək'tʃin, măk-
-tchéen; mək'tʃeɪn, măk-tcháyn
MacCheyne, *f.n.,* mək'ʃeɪn, măk-
-sháyn
McChlery, *f.n.,* mə'klɪərɪ, măk-
léeri
McClatchie, *f.n.,* mə'klætʃɪ,
măklátchi
MacClean, *f.n.,* mə'kleɪn, măkláyn; mə'klin, măkléen
McClenaghan, *f.n.,* mə'klenəxən,
măklénăchăn
McClenahan, *f.n.,* mə'klenəhən,
măklénăhăn
McClenaughan, *f.n.,* mə'klenəxən,
măklénăchăn
Macclesfield *Ches.,* 'mæklzfild,
mácklzfeeld
McClintock, *f.n.,* mə'klɪntɒk,
măklíntock
McCloskey, *f.n.,* mə'klɒski,
măklóski
McCloughin, *f.n.,* mə'kluɪn,
măkloó-in
McCloughry, *f.n.,* mə'klɒrɪ,
măklórri
McCloy, *f.n.,* mə'klɔɪ, măklóy

Maccoby, *f.n.,* 'mækəbı, máckŏbi
MacColl, *f.n.,* mə'kɒl, mäkól
McComb, *f.n.,* mə'koʊm, mäkóm
McCombe, *f.n.,* mə'koʊm,
  mäkóm
McCombie, *f.n.,* mə'kɒmbı,
  mäkómbi
MacConachie, *f.n.,* mə'kɒnəxı,
  mäkónnä_chi_
McConachy, *f.n.,* mə'kɒnəxı,
  mäkónnä_chi_
McConaghy, *f.n.,* mə'kɒnəxı,
  mäkónnä_chi_
McConalogue, *f.n.,* mə'koʊnə-
  loʊg, mäkŏnälŏg
McConnach, *f.n.,* mə'kɒnəx, mä-
  kónnä_ch_
McCormack, *f.n.,* mə'kɔrmək,
  mäkórmäk
McCorquodale, *f.n.,* mə'kɔrkədeıl,
  mäkórkŏdayl
McCoubrey, *f.n.,* mə'kubrı, mä-
  koóbri
McCowen, *f.n.,* mə'kaʊən,
  mäkówĕn
McCracken, *f.n.,* mə'krækən,
  mäkráckĕn
McCrae, *f.n.,* mə'kreı, mäkráy
McCraw, *f.n.,* mə'krɔ, mäkráw
McCrea, *f.n.,* mə'kreı, mäkráy
McCreadie, *f.n.,* mə'krıdı, mä-
  kreédi ; me'kredı, mäkréddi
McCready, *f.n.,* me'krıdı, mä-
  kreédi ; mə'kredı, mäkréddi
McCreechan, *f.n.,* mə'krixən,
  mäkreé_chän_
McCrindle, *f.n.,* mə'krındl, mä-
  kríndl
McCrirrick, *f.n.,* mə'krırık, mä-
  krírrik
McCrudden, *f.n.,* mə'krʌdən,
  mäkrúddĕn
MacCue, *f.n.,* mə'kju, mäkéw
McCue, *f.n.,* mə'kju, mäkéw
McCullagh, *f.n.,* mə'kʌlə, mäkúllä
McCulloch, *f.n.,* mə'kʌlək, mäkúl-
  lŏ_ch_ ; mə'kʌlək, mäkúllŏk
McCullough, *f.n.,* mə'kʌlək,
  mäkúllŏ_ch_
MacCunn, *f.n.,* mə'kʌn, mäkúnn
McCusker, *f.n.,* mə'kʌskər, mä-
  kúskĕr
McCutcheon, *f.n.,* mə'kʌtʃən,
  mäkútchĕn
McDermid, *f.n.,* mək'dɜrmıd,
  mäkdérmid
MacDermot, *f.n.,* mək'dɜrmət,
  mäkdérmŏt
McDiarmid, *f.n.,* mək'dɜrmıd,
  mäkdérmid
McDona, *f.n.,* mək'dʌnə, mäk-
  dúnnä ; mək'dɒnə, mäkdónnä
McDonagh, *f.n.,* mək'dʌnə, mäk-
  dúnnä ; mək'dɒnə, mäkdónnä

Macdonald, *f.n.,* mək'dɒnld, mäkdónnld
Macdonald of Gwaenysgor,
  Baron, mək'dɒnld əv gwaın-
  'ʌsgɔr, mäkdónnld ŏv gwīnúss-
  gor
Macdonell, *f.n.,* mək'dɒnl, mäk-
  dónnl; ,mækdə'nel, macdŏnéll.
  *The second is appropriate for the
  author, A. G.* ~.
McDonell, *f.n.,* mək'dɒnl, mäk-
  dónnl; ,mækdə'nel, mack-
  dŏnéll
McDonnell, *f.n.,* mək'dɒnl, mäk-
  dónnl; ,mækdə'nel, mackdŏnéll
McDonogh, *f.n.,* mək'dʌnə, mäk-
  dúnnä ; mək'dɒnə, mäkdónnä
McDonough, *f.n.,* mək'dʌnə, mäk-
  dúnnä ; mək'dɒnə, mäkdónnä
McDouall, *f.n.,* mək'duəl, mäk-
  doó-äl
McDougall, *f.n.,* mək'dugl,
  mäkdoógl
McDowall, *f.n.,* mək'daʊəl, mäk-
  dówäl
McDowell, *f.n.,* mək'daʊəl, mäk-
  dówĕl ; mək'doʊəl, mäkdŏ́-ĕl
MacDuff, *f.n.,* mək'dʌf, mäkdúff
Mace, *f.n.,* meıs, mayss
McEacharn, *f.n.,* mə'kexərn,
  mäké_ch_ärn ; mə'kexrən, mä-
  ké_ch_rän; mə'kekrən, mäkéckrän
McEachern, *f.n.,* mə'kexərn, mä-
  ké_ch_ĕrn; mə'kexrən, mäké_ch_rĕn;
  mə'kekrən, mäkéckrĕn
McEachran, *f.n.,* mə'kexrən,
  mäké_ch_rän
McEchern, *f.n.,* mə'kexərn, mä-
  ké_ch_ĕrn; mə'kexrən, mäké_ch_rĕn
Macedo, *f.n.,* mə'sidoʊ, mässeédō
MacElderry, *f.n.,* 'mæklderı,
  mácklderri
McEldowney, *f.n.,* ,mækl'daʊnı,
  mackldówni; 'mækldaʊnı,
  máckldowni
McElhone, *f.n.,* 'mæklhoʊn,
  mácklhōn
McElligott, *f.n.,* mə'kelıgət, mä-
  kélligŏt
McElroy, *f.n.,* 'mæklrɔı, mácklroy
McElveny, *f.n.,* mə'kelvənı, mä-
  kéllvĕni
McEnaney, *f.n.,* ,mækə'nenı,
  mackĕnénni
McEneaney, *f.n.,* ,mækə'nını,
  mackĕneéni
McEnery, *f.n.,* mə'kenərı, mä-
  kénnĕri
McEnroe, *f.n.,* 'mækınroʊ,
  máckĕnrō
MacEntagart, *f.n.,* ,mækən'tægərt,
  mackĕntággärt
McEntee, *f.n.,* ,mækən'ti, mack-
  ĕnteé; mə'kentı, mäkénti

MacEntegart, *f.n.*, ˌmækən'tegərt, mackĕntéggärt; məˈkentəgɑrt, mäkéntĕgaart

MacEnteggart, *f.n.*, ˌmækən-'tegərt, mackĕntéggärt

McEvedy, *f.n.*, məˈkevədɪ, mäkévvĕdi

McEvoy, *f.n.*, 'mækɪvɔɪ, máckĕvoy

McEwen, *f.n.*, məˈkjuən, mäkéwĕn

M'Ewen, *f.n.*, məˈkjuən, mäkéwĕn

McFadyean, *f.n.*, mək'fædjən, mäkfád-yĕn

Macfadyen, *f.n.*, mək'fædjən, mäkfád-yĕn

McFadzean, *f.n.*, mək'fædjən, mäkfád-yĕn. *Appropriate also for Baron* ~.

MacFarlane, *f.n.*, mək'fɑrlən, mäkfaˈarlän

MacFarquhar, *f.n.*, mək'fɑrkər, mäkfaˈarkär

McFie, *f.n.*, mək'fi, mäkféé

Macfin *Co. Antrim*, mæk'fɪn, mackfín

McFinn, *f.n.*, mək'fɪn, mäkfín

McGahern, *f.n.*, məˈgæxərn, mägáchĕrn

McGahey, *f.n.*, məˈgæxɪ, mägáchi

McGaughey, *f.n.*, məˈgɔɪ, mägóy

MacGeach, *f.n.*, məˈgeɪ, mägáy

McGeagh, *f.n.*, məˈgeɪ, mägáy

MacGee, *f.n.*, məˈgi, mägéé

McGee, *f.n.*, məˈgi, mägéé

McGeechan, *f.n.*, məˈgixən, mägéechän

McGeoch, *f.n.*, məˈgiəx, mägéé-öch

McGeough, *f.n.*, məˈgou, mägó

McGeown, *f.n.*, məˈgjoun, mägyón

MacGhee, *f.n.*, məˈgi, mägéé

McGhee, *f.n.*, məˈgi, mägéé

McGhie, *f.n.*, məˈgi, mägéé

MacGill, *f.n.*, məˈgɪl, mägíll

MacGillesheatheanaich, *f.n.*, məx,gɪlə'hehənɪx, mäch-gillĕ-hé-häneech

McGillewie, *f.n.*, məˈgɪləwɪ, mägíllĕ-wi

McGillicuddy, *f.n.*, 'mæglɪkʌdɪ, máglikuddi

McGilligan, *f.n.*, məˈgɪlɪgən, mägílligän

MacGillivray, Pittendrigh, *19th-c. poet*, 'pɪtən'drɪx məˈgɪlɪvreɪ, píttĕndrích mägíllivray

McGillivray, *f.n.*, məˈgɪlɪvrɪ, mägíllivri; məˈgɪlvrɪ, mägílvri; məˈgɪlɪvreɪ, mägíllivray

McGimpsey, *f.n.*, məˈdʒɪmpsɪ, mäjímpsi

McGinn, *f.n.*, məˈgɪn, mägínn

MacGladdery, *f.n.*, məˈglædərɪ, mägláddĕri

McGladdery, *f.n.*, məˈglædərɪ, mägláddĕri

MacGladery, *f.n.*, məˈglædərɪ, mägláddĕri

McGladery, *f.n.*, məˈglædərɪ, mägláddĕri

McGlashan, *f.n.*, məˈglæʃən, mägláshän

M'Glashan, *f.n.*, məˈglæʃən, mägláshän

McGlone, *f.n.*, məˈgloun, mäglón

McGoffen, *f.n.*, məˈgɒfən, mägóf-fĕn

McGonagall, *f.n.*, məˈgɒnəgl, mägónnägl. *Appropriate for William* ~, *Scottish doggerel poet.*

McGonagle, *f.n.*, məˈgɒnəgl, mägónnägl

MacGonnigle, *f.n.*, məˈgɒnɪgl, mägónnigl

MacGoohan, *f.n.*, məˈguən, mägoˈo-än

McGoohan, *f.n.*, məˈguən, mägoˈo--än

McGougan, *f.n.*, məˈgugən, mägoogän

McGough, *f.n.*, məˈgɒf, mägóff

McGovern, *f.n.*, məˈgʌvərn, mägúvvĕrn

McGowan, *f.n.*, məˈgauən, mägówän

McGrady, *f.n.*, məˈgreɪdɪ, mägráddi

McGrath, *f.n.*, məˈgrɑ, mägraˈa; məˈgræθ, mägráth; məˈgrɑθ, mägraˈath

McGredy, *f.n.*, məˈgrɪdɪ, mägréédi

Macgregor, *f.n.*, məˈgregər, mägréggŏr

MacGregor, *f.n.*, məˈgregər, mägréggŏr

McGregor, *f.n.*, məˈgregər, mägréggŏr

M'Gregor, *f.n.*, məˈgregər, mägréggŏr

McGrigor, *f.n.*, məˈgregər, mägréggŏr; məˈgrɪgər, mägríggŏr. *The first is appropriate for the late Admiral Sir Rhoderick* ~.

McGroarty, *f.n.*, məˈgrɔrtɪ, mägrórti

McGrogan, *f.n.*, məˈgrougən, mägrógän

McGugan, *f.n.*, məˈgugən, mägoˈogän

McGuigan, *f.n.*, məˈgwigən, mägwéégän; məˈgwɪgən, mägwígän

McGuinness, *f.n.*, məˈgɪnɪs, mägínnĕss

McGuire, *f.n.*, məˈgwaɪər, mägwír

McHale, *f.n.*, mək'heɪl, mäk-háyl

Machansire and Polmont, Lord, 'mæxənʃaɪər ənd 'poʊlmɒnt, máchăn-shīr ănd pṓlmont

Machell, *f.n.*, 'meɪtʃl, máytchl

Machen, *f.n.*, 'meɪtʃɪn, máytchĕn; 'mækɪn, máckĕn, 'mæxən, má<u>ch</u>ĕn. *The third is the Welsh pronunciation.*

Machen *Mid Glam.*, 'mæxən, má<u>ch</u>ĕn

Machent, *f.n.*, 'meɪtʃənt, máytchĕnt

Machin, *f.n.*, 'meɪtʃɪn, máytchin

Machlis, *f.n.*, 'mæklɪs, máckliss

Machphelah *N. Yorks.*, mæk'pilə, mackpéelä

Machray, *f.n.*, mə'kreɪ, măkráy

Machrihanish *S'clyde*, ˌmæxrɪ-'hænɪʃ, ma<u>ch</u>ri-hánnish

Machynlleth *Powys*, mə'xʌnɬəθ, má<u>ch</u>ún-<u>hl</u>ĕth

McIldowie, *f.n.*, ˌmækɪl'duɪ, mackildoo-i; ˌmækɪl'daʊɪ, mackildów-i

MacIlhatton, *f.n.*, ˌmækɪl'hætən, mackilháttŏn

McIlroy, *f.n.*, 'mækɪlrɔɪ, máckil-roy; ˌmækɪl'rɔɪ, mackilróy

MacIlvenna, *f.n.*, ˌmækɪl'venə, mackilvénnä

McIlwee, *f.n.*, ˌmækl'wi, mackl-wée

MacIlwham, *f.n.*, 'mækɪl*h*wæm, máckil-wham

Macilwraith, *f.n.*, 'mækɪlreɪθ, máckilrayth

McIlwraith, *f.n.*, 'mækɪlreɪθ, máckilrayth

McInally, *f.n.*, ˌmækɪ'næli, mackináli

MacInerney, *f.n.*, ˌmækɪ'nɜrni, mackinérni

McInerny, *f.n.*, ˌmækɪ'nɜrni, mackinérni

MacInnes, *f.n.*, mə'kɪnɪs, măkínnĕss

McInroy, *f.n.*, 'mækɪnrɔɪ, máckinroy

McIntosh, *f.n.*, 'mækɪntɒʃ, máckintosh

Macintyre, *f.n.*, 'mækɪntaɪər, máckintīr

MacIntyre, *f.n.*, 'mækɪntaɪər, máckintīr

McIntyre, *f.n.*, 'mækɪntaɪər, máckintīr

McInulty, *f.n.*, ˌmækɪ'nʌlti, mackinúlti

McIver, *f.n.*, mə'kaɪvər, măkívĕr; mə'kɪvər, măkéevĕr

McIvor, *f.n.*, mə'kaɪvər, măkívŏr; mə'kɪvər, măkéevŏr

McKail, *f.n.*, mə'keɪl, măkáyl

Mackarness, *f.n.*, 'mækərnes, máckärness

McKarness, *f.n.*, 'mækərnes, máckärness

Mackay, *f.n.*, mə'kaɪ, măkí

McKay, *f.n.*, mə'kaɪ, măkí; mə'keɪ, măkáy

McKeag, *f.n.*, mə'kig, măkéeg; mə'keɪg, măkáyg

McKeague, *f.n.*, mə'keɪg, măkáyg

M'Keague, *f.n.*, mə'keɪg, măkáyg

McKean, *f.n.*, mə'kin, măkéen

McKeand, *f.n.*, mə'kind, mă-kéend; mə'kiənd, măkée-ănd

McKee, *f.n.*, mə'ki, măkée

McKellar, *f.n.*, mə'kelər, măkéllär

McKelvey, *f.n.*, mə'kelvɪ, măkélvi

Macken, *f.n.*, 'mækɪn, máckĕn

Mackendrick, *f.n.*, mə'kendrɪk, măkéndrick

MacKendrick, *f.n.*, mə'kendrɪk, măkéndrick

McKenna, *f.n.*, mə'kenə, măkénnä

Mackenzie, *f.n.*, mə'kenzɪ, mă-kénzi

McKenzie, *f.n.*, mə'kenzɪ, măkén-zi

Mackeown, *f.n.*, mə'kjoʊn, mă-kyŏ́n

McKeown, *f.n.*, mə'kjoʊn, mă-kyŏ́n

Mackereth, *f.n.*, mə'kerəθ, mă-kérrĕth

McKernan, *f.n.*, mə'kɜrnən, măkérnän

McKerness, *f.n.*, mə'kɜrnɪs, mă-kérnĕss

Mackeson, *f.n.*, 'mækɪsən, máck-ĕssŏn

Mackesy, *f.n.*, 'mækəsɪ, máckĕssi

Mackey, *f.n.*, 'mækɪ, mácki

McKey, *f.n.*, mə'ki, măkée

McKibbin, *f.n.*, mə'kɪbɪn, măkíb-bin

Mackichan, *f.n.*, mə'kixən, măkée<u>ch</u>ăn

Mackie, *f.n.*, 'mækɪ, mácki

Mackie of Benshie, Baron, 'mækɪ əv 'benʃɪ, mácki ŏv bénshi

MacKie, *f.n.*, mə'ki, măkée

McKie, *f.n.*, mə'ki, măkée; mə'kaɪ, măkí. *The second is appropriate for Sir William ~, organist and one time Master of the Choristers at Westminster Abbey.*

McKinlay, *f.n.*, mə'kɪnlɪ, măkínli

McKinnon, *f.n.*, mə'kɪnən, măkín-nŏn

McKnight, *f.n.*, mək'naɪt, măknít

Mackrell, *f.n.*, mə'krel, măkréll

Mackrill, *f.n.*, mə'krɪl, măkríll

Mackworth *Derby.*, 'mækwɜrθ, máckwurth

McLachlan, *f.n.*, mə'klɒxlən, măklóchlăn; mə'klɒklən, măklócklăn

McLafferty, *f.n.*, mə'klæfərtɪ, măkláffĕrti

McLagan, *f.n.*, mə'klægən, măklággăn

McLaine, *f.n.*, mə'kleɪn, măkláyn

Maclaren, *f.n.*, mə'klærən, măklárrĕn

MacLaren, *f.n.*, mə'klærən, măklárrĕn

McLarnon, *f.n.*, mə'klɑrnən, măkla̒arnŏn

McLauchlan, *f.n.*, mə'klɒxlən, măklóchlăn; mə'klɒklən, măklócklăn

McLauchlin, *f.n.*, mə'klɒxlɪn, măklóchlin; mə'klɒklɪn, măklócklin

McLaughlin, *f.n.*, mə'klɒxlɪn, măklóchlin; mə'glɒxlɪn, măglóchlin; mə'klɒklɪn, măklócklin

McLaurin, *f.n.*, mə'klɒrɪn, măklάwrin; mə'klɒrɪn, măklórrin

McLaverty, *f.n.*, mə'klævərtɪ, măklávvĕrti

Maclay, *f.n.*, mə'kleɪ, măkláy. *Appropriate also for Baron* ~.

McLay, *f.n.*, mə'kleɪ, măkláy

McLea, *f.n.*, mə'kleɪ, măkláy

Maclean, *f.n.*, mə'kleɪn, măkláyn; mə'klin, măkleén

McLean, *f.n.*, mə'kleɪn, măkláyn

McLear, *f.n.*, mə'klɪər, măkleér

McLeavy, *f.n.*, mə'klivɪ, măkleévi

McLeay, *f.n.*, mə'kleɪ, măkláy

MacLehose, *f.n.*, 'mæklɪhoʊz, mácklĕhōz; 'mæklhoʊz, máckl-hōz

McLeish, *f.n.*, mə'kliʃ, măkleésh

McLelland, *f.n.*, mə'klelənd, măkléllănd

Maclennan, *f.n.*, mə'klenən, măklénnăn

Macleod, *f.n.*, mə'klaʊd, măklówd

MacLeod, *f.n.*, mə'klaʊd, măklówd

Macleod of Borve, Baroness, mə'klaʊd əv 'bɔrv, măklówd ŏv bórv

MacLeod of Fuinary, Baron, mə'klaʊd əv 'fjunərɪ, măklówd ŏv féwnări

McLeod, *f.n.*, mə'klaʊd, măklówd

McLernon, *f.n.*, mə'klɑrnən, măkla̒arnŏn

McLevy, *f.n.*, mə'klivɪ, măkleévi

Maclise, *f.n.*, mə'klis, măkleéss

McLoughlin, *f.n.*, mə'klɒxlɪn, măklóchlin

MacLucas, *f.n.*, mə'klukəs, măklookáss

McLucas, *f.n.*, mə'klukəs, măklookáss

MacLurg, *f.n.*, mə'klɜrg, măklúrg

McMahon, *f.n.*, mək'mɑn, măkma̒an

Macmanaway, *f.n.*, mək'mænəweɪ, măkmánnăway

McManus, *f.n.*, mək'mænəs, măkmánnŭss; mək'mɑnəs, măkma̒anŭss; mək'meɪnəs, măkmáynŭss

MacMath, *f.n.*, mək'mɑθ, măkma̒ath

McMenemey, *f.n.*, mək'menəmɪ, măkménnĕmi

McMenemy, *f.n.*, mək'menəmɪ, măkménnĕmi

MacMillan, *f.n.*, mək'mɪlən, măkmíllăn

McMorrough, *f.n.*, mək'mɒroʊ, măkmórrō

McMullen, *f.n.*, mək'mʌlən, măkmúllĕn

MacMurdie, *f.n.*, mək'mɜrdɪ, măkmúrdi

McMynn, *f.n.*, mək'mɪn, măkmín

MacNab, *f.n.*, mək'næb, măk-náb

Macnaghten, Barony of, mək-'nɒtən, măk-náwtĕn

McNaghton, *f.n.*, mək'nɒtən, măk-náwtŏn

McNall, *f.n.*, mək'nɔl, măk-náwl

Macnalty, *f.n.*, mək'nɔltɪ, măk-náwlti

Macnamara, *f.n.*, ˌmæknə'mɑrə, mack-năma̒ară

McNamee, *f.n.*, ˌmæknə'mi, mack-nămeé

McNaught, *f.n.*, mək'nɔt, măk-náwt

McNaughton, *f.n.*, mək'nɔtən, măk-náwtŏn

McNearney, *f.n.*, mək'nɜrnɪ, măk-nérni

MacNeice, *f.n.*, mək'nis, măk-neéss

McNeil, *f.n.*, mək'nil, măk-neél

MacNeilage, *f.n.*, mək'nilɪdʒ, măk-neélij

McNeill, *f.n.*, mək'nil, măk-neél

McNeillie, *f.n.*, mək'nilɪ, măk-neéli

McNichol, *f.n.*, mək'nɪkl, măk-níckl

McNiff, *f.n.*, mək'nɪf, măk-niff

MacNiven, *f.n.*, mək'nɪvən, măk-nívvĕn

Maconachie, *f.n.*, mə'kɒnəxɪ, măkónnăchi; mə'kɒnəkɪ, măkónnăki

Maconchy, Elizabeth, *composer*, mə'kɒnkɪ, măkónki

Maconochie, *f.n.*, mə'kɒnəxɪ, măkónnŏchi; mə'kɒnəkɪ, măkónnŏki

Macosquin *Co. Derry*, məˈkɒskɪn, măkósskin

McOstrich, *f.n.*, məˈkɒstrɪtʃ, măkóstritch

McOuat, *f.n.*, məˈkaʊət, măkówăt

MacOwan, *f.n.*, məˈkoʊən, măkṓ-ăn

McPhail, *f.n.*, məkˈfeɪl, măkfáyl

MacPhee, *f.n.*, məkˈfi, măkféé

McPherson, *f.n.*, məkˈfɜrsən, măkférssŏn

Macpherson of Drumochter, Baron, məkˈfɜrsən əv drə-ˈmɒxtər, măkférssŏn ŏv drŭmóchtĕr

McQuade, *f.n.*, məˈkweɪd, măkwáyd

McQuarrie, *f.n.*, məˈkwɒrɪ, măkwórri

McQuisten, *f.n.*, məˈkwɪstən, măkwísstĕn

McQuoid, *f.n.*, məˈkwɔɪd, măkwóyd

McQuown, *f.n.*, məˈkjuən, măkéwĕn

Macready, *f.n.*, məˈkrɪdɪ, măkréedi. *Appropriate for William Charles* ～, *19th-c. actor-manager.*

McReady, *f.n.*, məˈkrɪdɪ, măkréedi; məˈkredɪ, măkréddi

McReay, *f.n.*, məˈkreɪ, măkráy

MacRobb, *f.n.*, məˈkrɒb, măkróbb

McRorie, *f.n.*, məˈkrɔrɪ, măkráwri

McRory, *f.n.*, məˈkrɔrɪ, măkráwri

McShane, *f.n.*, məkˈʃeɪn, măk-sháyn

McSwiney, *f.n.*, məkˈswɪnɪ, măksweéni; məkˈswɪnɪ, măkswínni

McTaggart, *f.n.*, məkˈtægərt, măktággărt

McVay, *f.n.*, məkˈveɪ, măkváy

MacVeagh, *f.n.*, məkˈveɪ, măkváy

McVean, *f.n.*, məkˈveɪn, măkváyn; məkˈvin, măkveén

McVeigh, *f.n.*, məkˈveɪ, măkváy

McVey, *f.n.*, məkˈveɪ, măkváy

McVicar, *f.n.*, məkˈvɪkər, măkvíckăr

McVie, *f.n.*, məkˈvi, măkveé

McVitie, *f.n.*, məkˈvɪtɪ, măkvítti

McVittie, *f.n.*, məkˈvɪtɪ, măkvítti

McWatters, *f.n.*, məkˈwɔtərz, măkwáwtĕrz

McWhirter, *f.n.*, məkˈhwɜrtər, măkwhírtĕr

MacWilliam, *f.n.*, məkˈwɪljəm, măkwíl-yăm

Madan, *f.n.*, ˈmædən, máddăn

Madden, *f.n.*, ˈmædən, máddĕn

Madderty *Tayside*, ˈmædərtɪ, máddĕrti

Madel, *f.n.*, məˈdel, mădéll

Madeley *Staffs.*, ˈmeɪdlɪ, máydli

Maden, *f.n.*, ˈmeɪdən, máydĕn

Madian, *f.n.*, ˈmeɪdɪən, máydi-ăn

Madin, *f.n.*, ˈmeɪdɪn, máydin

Madingley *Cambs.*, ˈmædɪŋlɪ, mádding-li

Madley *H. & W.*, ˈmædlɪ, mádli

Madoc, *f.n.*, ˈmædək, máddŏk

Madresfield *H. & W.*, ˈmædərz-fild, máddĕrzfeeld

Madron *Cornwall*, ˈmædrən, máddrŏn

Maeckelberghe, *f.n.*, məˈkelbərg, măkéllberg

Maegraith, *f.n.*, məˈgreɪθ, mă-gráyth

Maelor, Baron, ˈmaɪlər, mílor

Maenan *Gwynedd*, ˈmaɪnən, mínăn. *Appropriate also for the Barony of* ～.

Maenclochog *Dyfed*, maɪnˈklɒxɒg, mīn-klóchog

Maendy *S. Glam.*, ˈmaɪndɪ, míndi

Maentwrog *Gwynedd*, maɪn-ˈtuərɒg, mīntoórog

Maer *Cornwall, Staffs.*, mɛər, mair

Maer Rocks *Devon*, mɛər, mair

Maerdy *Clwyd*, ˈmɑrdɪ, maˊardi; ˈmeɪərˈdi, máyĕr-deé

Maerdy *Dyfed, Gwent*, ˈmɑrdɪ, maˊardi

Maerdy *Mid Glam.*, ˈmɑrdɪ, maˊardi; ˈmaɪərdɪ, mírdi

Maes-car *Powys*, maɪsˈkɑr, mīss-kaˊar

Maesgeirchen *Gwynedd*, maɪs-ˈgaɪərxən, mīssgírchĕn; maɪs-ˈgɛərxən, mīssgáirchĕn

Maes-glas *Clwyd, Gwent*, maɪs-ˈglɑs, mīssglaˊass

Maesglasau *Powys*, maɪsˈglæsaɪ, mīsseglássī

Maeshowe *Tumulus Orkney*, meɪzˈhaʊ, mayz-hów

Maes-llwch *Castle Powys*, maɪs-ˈɬux, mīss-hloˊoch

Maesmynis *Powys*, maɪsˈmʌnɪs, mīssmúnniss

Maesteg *Mid Glam.*, maɪsˈteɪg, mīsstáyg

Maes-y-coed *Clwyd, Mid Glam.*, ˌmaɪsəˈkɔɪd, miss-ă-kóyd

Maesycrugiau *Dyfed*, ˌmaɪsə-ˈkrɪgjaɪ, mīssäkríg-yī

Maesycwmmer *Gwent*, ˌmaɪsə-ˈkumər, mīssăkŏŏmĕr

Maes-y-dderwen *W. Glam.*, ˌmaɪsəˈðɛərwen, mīss-ă-tháirwen

Maes-y-dre *Clwyd*, ˌmaɪsəˈdreɪ, mīss-ă-dráy

Magarshack, *f.n.*, ˈmægərʃæk, mággărshack

Magauran, *f.n.*, məˈgɔrən, mă-gáwrăn

Magdalen *Norfolk*, 'mægdələn, mágdălĕn
Magdalen College *Univ. of Oxford*, 'mɔdlɪn, máwdlĕn
Magdalene College *Univ. of Cambridge*, 'mɔdlɪn, máwdlĕn
Magee, *f.n.*, mə'gi, măgeé
Magennis, *f.n.*, mə'genɪs, măgénniss
Mager, *f.n.*, 'meɪdʒər, máyjĕr; 'meɪgər, máygĕr
Maggs, *f.n.*, mægz, maggz
Maghaberry *Co. Antrim*, mə-'gæbərɪ, măgábbĕri
Maghera *Co. Derry, Co. Down*, ˌmæxə'rɑ, machĕraá
Magherafelt *Co. Derry*, 'mæxərə-'felt, máchĕrăfélt
Magheragall *Co. Antrim*, ˌmæxərə-'gɔl, machĕrăgáwl
Magherahamlet *Co. Down*, ˌmæxərə'hæmlɪt, machĕră--hámlĕt
Magheralin *Co. Armagh–Co. Down*, ˌmæxərə'lɪn, machĕrălín; ˌmærə'lɪn, marrălín
Magherally *Co. Down*, ˌmæxə'rælɪ, machĕráli
Magheramorne, Barony of, ˌmɑrə'mɔrn, maarămórn
Magheramorne *Co. Antrim*, ˌmæxərə'mɔrn, machĕrămórn
Magheraveely *Co. Fermanagh*, ˌmæxərə'vilɪ, machĕrăveéli
Maghery *Co. Armagh*, 'mæxərɪ, máchĕri
Maghull *Merseyside*, mə'gʌl, măgúll
Magill, *f.n.*, mə'gɪl, măgíll
Magilligan *Co. Derry*, mə'gɪlɪgən, măgílligăn. *Appropriate also for* ~ *Strand.*
Maginess, *f.n.*, mə'gɪnɪs, măgínnĕss
Maginnis, *f.n.*, mə'gɪnɪs, măgínniss
Magnac, *f.n.*, 'mænjæk, mán-yack
Magnay, *f.n.*, 'mægneɪ, mágnay; 'mægnɪ, mágni; mæg'neɪ, magnáy
Magniac, *f.n.*, 'mænjæk, mán-yack
Magnus, *C.n.*, 'mægnəs, mágnŭss
Magnusson, *f.n.*, 'mægnəsən, mágnŭssŏn
Magonet, *f.n.*, 'mægənet, mággŏnet
Magor *Gwent*, 'meɪgər, máygŏr
Magrath, *f.n.*, mə'grɑ, măgraá
Magri, *f.n.*, 'mægrɪ, mággri
Maguire, *f.n.*, mə'gwaɪər, măgwír
Maguiresbridge *Co. Fermanagh*, mə'gwaɪərz'brɪdʒ, măgwírzbríj
Magwood, *f.n.*, 'mægwʊd, mágwŏod

Mahaddie, *f.n.*, mə'hædɪ, măháddi
Mahan, *f.n.*, mɑn, maan
Mahany, *f.n.*, 'mɑnɪ, maáni
Mahee Island *Co. Down*, mə'hi, măheé
Maher, *f.n.*, mɑr, maar; 'meɪər, máy-ĕr
Mahir, *f.n.*, 'meɪhər, máy-hĕr
Mahlowe, *f.n.*, 'mɑloʊ, maálō
Mahon, *f.n.*, mɑn, maan; 'mæhən, má-hŏn
Mahoney, *f.n.*, 'mɑənɪ, maá-ŏni; mə'hoʊnɪ, măhóni
Mahony, *f.n.*, 'mɑnɪ, maáni
Mahood, *f.n.*, mə'hʊd, mă-hŏŏd
Maia, *f.n.*, 'maɪə, mí-ă
Maidenmoor (Maiden Moor) Hill *Cumbria*, 'meɪdən'mʊər, máydĕn mŏŏr
Maidstone *Kent*, 'meɪdstoʊn, máydstōn; 'meɪdstən, máydstŏn
Mailer, *f.n.*, 'meɪlər, máylĕr
Maillard, *f.n.*, 'meɪlɑrd, máylaard
Maina, *C.n.*, 'meɪnə, máynă
Maindee *Gwent*, 'meɪndɪ, máyndi
Maindy *S. Glam.*, 'meɪndɪ, máyndi; 'maɪndɪ, míndi
Maingot, *f.n.*, 'mæŋgoʊ, máng-gō
Mainland Island *Shetland*, 'meɪnlænd, máynland
Mainwaring, *f.n.*, 'mænərɪŋ, mánnăring; 'meɪnweərɪŋ, máynwairing. *The second is usual in Wales.*
Mair, *Welsh C.n.*, 'maɪər, mír
Mair, *f.n.*, meər, mair
Mairants, *f.n.*, 'meərənts, máirănts; mə'rænts, mĕránts
Maire, *f.n.*, meər, mair
Mairet, *f.n.*, 'meərɪ, máiri
Mairhi, *C.n.*, 'mɑrɪ, maári
Mais, *f.n.*, meɪz, mayz. *Appropriate also for Baron* ~.
Maisel, *f.n.*, 'maɪzl, mízl; 'meɪzl, máyzl
Maisemore *Glos.*, 'meɪzmɔr, máyzmor
Maison, *f.n.*, 'meɪsən, máyssŏn
Maison Dieu Hall *Dover*, 'meɪzɔ̃ 'dju, máyzōngdéw; 'meɪzən 'dju, máyzŏn déw
Maitland, *f.n.*, 'meɪtlənd, máytlănd
Majdalany, *f.n.*, ˌmædʒdə'leɪnɪ, majdăláyni
Majendie, *f.n.*, 'mædʒəndɪ, májjĕndi
Major, *f.n.*, 'meɪdʒər, máyjŏr
Makerstoun *Borders*, 'mækərstən, máckĕrstŏn
Makgill, *f.n.*, mə'gɪl, măgíll
Makins, *f.n.*, 'meɪkɪnz, máykinz
Makower, *f.n.*, mə'kaʊər, măkówĕr

Malahide, *f.n.,* 'mæləhaɪd, málă-
-hīd
Malan, *f.n.,* 'mælən, málăn;
mə'lɑn, mălaἀn; mə'læn,
mălán
Malbon, *f.n.,* 'mælbən, málbŏn
Malborough *Devon,* 'mɔlbərə,
máwlbŭră
Malcolm, *C.n. and f.n.,* 'mælkəm,
málkŏm; 'mɔlkəm, máwlkŏm
Malden, *f.n.,* 'mɔldən, máwldĕn
Malden *Surrey,* 'mɔldən, máwldĕn
Maldon *Essex,* 'mɔldən, máwldŏn
Maldwyn, *C.n.,* 'mældwɪn, máld-
win; 'mɔldwɪn, máwldwin. *The
first is the Welsh pronunciation.*
Malempre, *f.n.,* mə'lempreɪ,
mălémpray
Malet, *f.n.,* 'mælət, málĕt
Maley, *f.n.,* 'meɪlɪ, máyli
Malgwyn Castle *Dyfed,* 'mælgwɪn,
málgwin
Malikyan, *f.n.,* ˌmælɪk'jɑn, malik-
-yaán
Malim, *f.n.,* 'meɪlɪm, máylim
Malindine, *f.n.,* 'mælɪndaɪn,
málindīn
Malins, *f.n.,* 'mælɪnz, málinz;
'meɪlɪnz, máylinz
Malkin, *f.n.,* 'mælkɪn, málkin
Mall, The, *London,* ðə 'mæl, thĕ
mál
Mallabar, *f.n.,* 'mæləbɑr, málăbaar
Mallaby, *f.n.,* 'mæləbɪ, málăbi
Mallaig *H'land,* 'mæleɪg, málayg
Mallalieu, *f.n.,* 'mæləlju, málălew;
'mæləljɔ, málăl-yö
Mallandaine, *f.n.,* 'mæləndeɪn,
málăndayn
Mallet, *f.n.,* 'mælət, málĕt
Malletsheugh *S'clyde,* 'mælət-ʃux,
málĕt-shooch
Malling, East *and* West, *Kent,*
'mɔlɪŋ, máwling
Malloch, *f.n.,* 'mæləx, málŏch
Mallone, *f.n.,* mə'loʊnɪ, mălŏni
Mallowan, *f.n.,* 'mæloʊən, málō-ăn
Malltraeth Bay *Anglesey,* 'mæł-
draɪθ, máhldrīth
Mallusk *Co. Antrim,* mə'lʌsk,
mălúsk
Mallwyd *Gwynedd,* 'mæłʊɪd,
máhlŌŌ-id
Malmesbury *Wilts.,* 'mɑmzbərɪ,
maámzbŭri. *Appropriate also
for the Earl of* ~.
Malone, *f.n.,* mə'loʊn, mălŏn
Malpas, *f.n.,* 'mælpəs, málpăss
Malpas *Ches.,* 'mɔlpəs, máwlpăss;
'mælpəs, málpăss; 'mɔpəs,
máwpăss. *The first is appro-
priate for Viscount* ~.
Malpas *Cornwall,* 'moʊpəs,
mŏpăss

Malpas *Gwent,* 'mælpəs, málpăss
Malpass, *f.n.,* 'mælpæs, málpass
Malsbury, *f.n.,* 'mɔlzbərɪ, máwlz-
bŭri
Maltby, *f.n.,* 'mɔltbɪ, máwltbi
Malthus, Thomas, *18th–19th-c.
economist,* 'mælθəs, mál-thŭss
Malthusian, *pertaining to* **Malthus,**
mæl'θjuzɪən, mal-théwzĭăn
Malton *N. Yorks.,* 'mɔltən, máwl-
tŏn
Maltravers, Baron, mæl'trævərz,
maltrávvĕrz
Malvern *H. & W.,* 'mɔlvərn,
máwlvĕrn; 'mɔvərn, máwvĕrn.
*The first is appropriate for
Viscount* ~.
Malycha, *f.n.,* 'mælɪkɪ, máliki
Malyon, *f.n.,* 'mæljən, mál-yŏn
Mamhilad *Gwent,* mæm'haɪləd,
mam-hílăd
Mamore deer forest *H'land,*
mə'mɔr, mămór
Manaccan *Cornwall,* mə'nækən,
mănáckăn
Manadon *Devon,* 'mænədən, mán-
nădŏn
Manafon *Powys,* mæn'ævən, man-
návvŏn
Manaton *Devon,* 'mænətən, mán-
nătŏn
Manbré, *f.n.,* 'mænbreɪ, mánbray
Mance, *f.n.,* mæns, manss
Manchée, *f.n.,* mæn'ʃi, man-shée;
mɒn'ʃeɪ, mon-sháy
Manchester *Gtr. M'chester,*
'mæntʃɪstər, mántchĕstĕr;
'mæntʃestər, mántchestĕr
Manchip, *f.n.,* 'mænʃɪp, mán-ship
Mancunian, *native of* **Manchester,**
mæŋ'kjunɪən, mankéwnĭăn
Mandel, *f.n.,* mæn'del, mandéll
Mandelstam, *f.n.,* 'mændlstəm,
mándlstăm
Mander, *f.n.,* 'mændər, mándĕr;
'mɑndər, maándĕr. *The first is
usual in Staffs.*
Manders, *f.n.,* 'mændərz, mándĕrz
Manderson, *f.n.,* 'mændərsən,
mándĕrssŏn
Mandeville, Viscount, 'mændɪvɪl,
mándĕvil
Manduell, *f.n.,* 'mændjʊəl,
mándyŌŌ-ĕl
Manea *Cambs.,* 'meɪnɪ, máyni
Maney, *f.n.,* 'meɪnɪ, máyni
Mangan, *f.n.,* 'mæŋən, máng-ăn
Mangin, *f.n.,* 'mæŋgɪn, máng-gin
Mangold, *f.n.,* 'mæŋgoʊld, máng-
-gōld
Mangotsfield *Avon,* 'mæŋgətsfild,
máng-gŏtsfeeld
Manhood, *f.n.,* 'mænhʊd, mán-
-hŏŏd

Mankowitz, Wolf, *author,* 'wʊlf 'mæŋkəvɪtʃ, wo͝olf mánkŏvitch
Manktelow, *f.n.,* 'mæŋktɪloʊ, mánktĕlō
Manley, *f.n.,* 'mænlɪ, mánli
Mann, *f.n.,* mæn, man
Manners, *f.n.,* 'mænərz, mánnĕrz
Manning, *f.n.,* 'mænɪŋ, mánning
Manningham, *f.n.,* 'mænɪŋəm, mánning-ăm
Mannion, *f.n.,* 'mænjən, mán-yŏn
Manod *Gwynedd,* 'mænɒd, mánnod
Manorbier *Dyfed,* ˌmænər'bɪər, mannŏrbéer
Manordeifi *Dyfed,* ˌmænər'daɪvɪ, mannŏrdívi
Manordilo *Dyfed,* ˌmænər'daɪloʊ, mannŏrdílō
Manordougherty *Co. Armagh,* ˌmænər'dɒxərtɪ, mannŏrdóchĕrti
Mansel, *f.n.,* 'mænsl, mánssl
Mansell, *f.n.,* 'mænsl, mánssl
Mansergh, *f.n.,* 'mænzər, mánzĕr; 'mænsər, mánssĕr; 'mænsɜrdʒ, mánsserj
Mansergh *Cumbria,* 'mænzər, mánzĕr
Mansey, *f.n.,* 'mænsɪ, mánssi
Mansfield, *f.n.,* 'mænsfɪld, mánssfeeld
Mansfield *Notts.,* 'mænsfɪld, mánssfeeld. *Appropriate also for the Earl of* ∼.
Manson, *f.n.,* 'mænsən, mánssŏn
Manston *Kent,* 'mænstən, mánstŏn
Mantas, *f.n.,* 'mæntæs, mántass
Manton, *f.n.,* 'mæntən, mántŏn
Mantovani, *f.n.,* ˌmæntə'vɑnɪ, mantŏvaáni
Manuden *Essex,* 'mænjʊdən, mán-yo͝odĕn
Manuel, *f.n.,* 'mænjʊəl, mán-yo͝o-ĕl
Manus, *f.n.,* 'meɪnəs, máynŭss
Manwaring, *f.n.,* 'mænərɪŋ, mánnăring
Manx *pertaining to the I. of Man,* mæŋks, manks
Manydown *Hants,* 'mænɪdaʊn, mánnidown
Manzoni, *f.n.,* mæn'zoʊnɪ, manzóni
Maple, *f.n.,* 'meɪpl, máypl
Mapledurwell *Hants,* ˌmeɪpl-'dɜrwel, maypldúrwel
Mapleton *Derby.,* 'meɪpltən, máypltŏn; 'mæpltən, máppltŏn
Maplin Sands *off Essex coast,* 'mæplɪn 'sændz, máplin sándz
Maquarie, *f.n.,* mə'kwɒrɪ, mă-kwórri
Maralin *Co. Down,* ˌmærə'lɪn, marrälín

Marazion *Cornwall,* ˌmærə'zaɪən, marräzí-ŏn
March *Cambs.,* mɑrtʃ, maartch
Marchesi, *f.n.,* mɑr'kɪsɪ, maar-kéessi
Marchwiel *Clwyd,* mɑrx'wɪəl, maarchwée-ĕl
Marcousé, *f.n.,* mɑr'kuzeɪ, maar-koózay
Mardall, *f.n.,* 'mɑrdl, maárdl
Marden *Kent,* 'mɑrdən, maárdĕn; mɑr'den, maardén
Marden *H. & W., Wilts.,* 'mɑrdən, maárdĕn
Marden, East, West *and* North, *W. Sussex,* 'mɑrdən, maárdĕn
Maree, Loch, *H'land,* mə'ri, mărée
Mareham le Fen *Lincs.,* 'mɛərəm lə 'fen, máirăm lĕ fén
Mareham on the Hill *Lincs.,* 'mɛərəm ɒn ðə 'hɪl, máirăm on thĕ híll
Marett, *f.n.,* 'mærɪt, márrĕt
Margach, *f.n.,* 'mɑrgə, maárgă
Margadale, Baron, 'mɑrgədeɪl, maárgădayl
Margadale of Islay, Baron, 'mɑrgədeɪl əv 'aɪlə, múrgădayl ŏv ílă
Margam *W. Glam.,* 'mɑrgəm, maárgăm
Margaretting *Essex,* ˌmɑrgə'retɪŋ, maargărétting
Margary, *f.n.,* 'mɑrgərɪ, maárgări
Margate *Kent,* 'mɑrgeɪt, maárgayt
Margerison, *f.n.,* mɑr'dʒerɪsən, maarjérrissŏn; 'mɑrdʒərɪsən, maárjĕrissŏn
Margesson, *f.n.,* 'mɑrdʒɪsən, maárjĕssŏn. *Appropriate also for Viscount* ∼.
Margetson, *f.n.,* 'mɑrgɪtsən, maár-gĕtsŏn
Margetts, *f.n.,* 'mɑrgɪts, maárgĕts
Margochis, *f.n.,* mɑr'goʊʃɪ, maar-gŏshi
Margolin, *f.n.,* mɑr'goʊlɪn, maar-gŏlin
Margoliouth, *f.n.,* mɑr'goʊlɪəθ, maargóli-ŭth. *Appropriate for D. S.* ∼, *classical scholar and orientalist.*
Margolis, *f.n.,* mɑr'goʊlɪs, maar-gŏliss
Margolyes, *f.n.,* 'mɑrgəliz, maár-gŏleez
Margulies, *f.n.,* 'mɑrgulɪs, maár-gooliss; 'mɑrgʊlɪs, maárgoō-leess; mɑr'gulɪz, maargooliz
Marham *Norfolk,* 'mærəm, márrăm; 'mɑrəm, maárăm. *The first is the traditional local pronunciation. The second is used*

for the Royal Air Force station by RAF personnel.

Marhamchurch *Cornwall*, 'mærəmtʃərtʃ, márrămchurtch

Marholm *Cambs.*, 'mærəm, márröm

Marian-glas *Gwynedd*, ˌmærɪən'glas, marriăn-gláass

Marillier, *f.n.*, mə'rɪljər, măríl-yĕr

Marindin, *f.n.*, mə'rɪndɪn, măríndin

Mariner, *f.n.*, 'mærɪnər, márrinĕr

Marino *Co. Down*, mə'rinoʊ, măreénō

Marischal, *f.n.*, 'marʃl, maˊarshl

Marischal College *Univ. of Aberdeen*, 'marʃl, maˊarshl

Marjoram, *f.n.*, 'mardʒərəm, maˊarjŏrăm

Marjoribanks, *f.n.*, 'martʃbæŋks, maˊartch-banks

Market Bosworth *Leics.*, 'markɪt 'bɒzwərθ, maˊarkĕt bózwŭrth

Market Rasen *Lincs.*, 'markɪt 'reɪzən, maˊarkĕt ráyzĕn

Market Weighton *Humberside*, 'markɪt 'witən, maˊarkĕt weétŏn

Markham, *f.n.*, 'markəm, maˊarkăm

Markillie, *f.n.*, mar'kɪlɪ, maar-kílli

Markinch *Fife*, 'mark'ɪnʃ, maˊark--ínsh

Marklew, *f.n.*, 'marklu, maˊarkloo

Marklye *E. Sussex*, mark'laɪ, maarklí

Markova, Alicia, *ballerina*, ə'lisɪə mar'kouvə, ăleéssiă maarkóvă

Markshall *Essex*, 'markshɔl, maˊarks-hawl; 'marksl, maˊarkssl

Marks of Broughton, Baron, 'marks əv 'brɔtən, maˊarks ŏv bráwtŏn

Marks Tey *Essex*, 'marks 'teɪ, maˊarks táy

Markwick, *f.n.*, 'markwɪk, maˊarkwick

Markyate Street *Herts.*, 'markjeɪt strit, maˊark-yayt street

Marlais, *Welsh C.n.*, 'marlaɪs, maˊarlíss

Marlborough, Duke of, 'mɔlbrə, máwlbră

Marlborough *Wilts.*, 'mɔlbrə, máwlbră; 'mɔlbərə, máwlbŭră

Marlborough House *London*, 'mɔlbrə, máwlbră; 'mɔlbərə, máwlbŭră

Marlburian, *one educated at Marlborough College*, mɔl-'bjʊərɪən, mawlbyóoriăn

Marler, *f.n.*, 'marlər, maˊarlĕr

Marloes *Dyfed*, 'marlouz, maˊarlōz

Marlow *Bucks.*, 'marlou, maˊarlō

Marlowe, *f.n.*, 'marlou, maˊarlō

Marnham, *f.n.*, 'marnəm, maˊarnăm

Marnhull *Dorset*, 'marnəl, maˊarnŭl

Marochan, *f.n.*, 'mærəkən, márrŏkăn

Marown *I. of Man*, mə'raun, mărówn

Marquand, *f.n.*, 'markwənd, maˊarkwŏnd

Marques, *f.n.*, marks, maarks

Marquis, *f.n.*, 'markwɪs, maˊarkwiss; 'marki, maˊarkee

Marre, *f.n.*, mar, maar

Marreco, *f.n.*, mə'rekou, măréckō

Marriott, *f.n.*, 'mærɪət, márriŏt

Marris, *f.n.*, 'mærɪs, márriss

Marsden, *f.n.*, 'marzdən, maˊarzdĕn

Marshall, *f.n.*, 'marʃl, maˊarshl

Marshalsea Prison *Southwark (London)*, 'marʃlsɪ, maˊarshlsi

Marsham *Norfolk*, 'marʃəm, maˊar-shăm

Marsh Baldon *Oxon.*, 'marʃ 'bɔldən, maˊarsh báwldŏn

Marsingall, *f.n.*, 'marsɪŋgl, maˊar-ssing-gl

Marson, *f.n.*, 'marsən, maˊarssŏn

Marston Moor *N. Yorks.*, 'marstən, maˊarstŏn

Martel, *f.n.*, mar'tel, maartéll

Martell, *f.n.*, mar'tel, maartéll

Martens, *f.n.*, 'martɪnz, maˊartĕnz mar'tenz, maarténz

Martensson, *f.n.*, 'martənsən, maˊartĕnssŏn

Martham *Norfolk*, 'marθəm, maˊar-thăm

Martin, *C.n. and f.n.*, 'martɪn, maˊartin

Martineau, *f.n.*, 'martɪnou, maˊar-tinō

Martlesham *Suffolk*, 'martlʃəm, maˊartl-shăm

Martletwy *Dyfed*, ˌmartl'twaɪ, maartl-twí

Martonmere, Baron, 'martənmɪər, maˊartŏnmeer

Martyr, *f.n.*, 'martər, maˊartĕr

Martyr Worthy *Hants*, 'martər 'wɜrðɪ, maˊartĕr wúrthi

Marvell, *f.n.*, 'marvl, maˊarvl. *Appropriate for Andrew ~, 17th-c. poet and satirist.*

Marvin, *f.n.*, 'marvɪn, maˊarvin

Marwenne, saint, 'marwɪn, maˊar--win

Marwick, *f.n.*, 'marwɪk, maˊar--wick

Marwick Head *Orkney*, 'marwɪk, maˊar-wick

Maryculter *Grampian*, ˌmɛərɪ-'kutər, mairi-koótĕr
Maryhill *S'clyde*, 'mɛərɪ'hɪl, máiri-híll
Marylebone *London*, 'mærɪləbən, márrĭlĕbŏn; 'mærələbən, márrĕlĕbŏn; 'mærɪbən, márribŏn; 'mɑrlɪbən, maárlibŏn. *The first two are appropriate for the Parish Church of St.* ~.
Maryon-Davies, *f.n.*, 'mærɪən 'deɪvɪs, márri-ŏn dáyviss
Mary Tavy *Devon*, 'mɛərɪ 'teɪvɪ, máiri táyvi
Masbrough *S. Yorks.*, 'mæzbərə, mázbŭră
Mascherpa, *f.n.*, mə'ʃɜrpə, măshérpă
Maschwitz, *f.n.*, 'mæʃwɪts, máshwits
Mase, *f.n.*, meɪs, mayss
Masham, *f.n.*, 'mæsəm, mássăm; 'mæʃəm, máshăm
Masham *N. Yorks.*, 'mæsəm, mássăm. *Appropriate also for Baron* ~.
Masham, *breed of sheep*, 'mæsəm, mássăm; 'mæʃəm, máshăm. *Those acquainted with the place in N. Yorks. generally use the first pronunciation.*
Masheder, *f.n.*, 'mæʃɪdər, máshĕdĕr
Maskell, *f.n.*, 'mæskl, másskl
Maskelyne, *f.n.*, 'mæskəlɪn, másskĕlin
Maskery, *f.n.*, 'mæskərɪ, másskĕri
Maskrey, *f.n.*, 'mæskrɪ, másskri
Maslen, *f.n.*, 'mæzlən, mázlĕn
Mason, *f.n.*, 'meɪsən, máyssŏn
Massee, *f.n.*, 'mæsi, mássee
Massereene *Co. Antrim*, 'mæsərin, mássĕreen
Massereene and Ferrard, *Viscount*, 'mæsərin ənd 'ferɑrd, mássĕreen ănd férraard
Massey, *f.n.*, 'mæsɪ, mássi
Massie, *f.n.*, 'mæsɪ, mássi
Massinger, *f.n.*, 'mæsɪndʒər, mássinjĕr. *Considered appropriate also for Philip* ~, *16th–17th-c. dramatist.*
Massocchi, *f.n.*, mæ'sɒkɪ, mas-sócki
Masson, *f.n.*, 'mæsən, mássŏn
Massow, *f.n.*, 'mæsoʊ, mássō
Masters, *f.n.*, 'mɑstərz, maásstĕrz
Masterton, *f.n.*, 'mɑstərtən, maásstĕrtŏn
Mastrick *Grampian*, 'mæstrɪk, mástrick
Matalon, *f.n.*, 'mætəlɒn, máttălon
Matanle, *f.n.*, mə'tænlɪ, mătánli

Matchan, *f.n.*, 'mætʃən, mátchăn
Mateer, *f.n.*, mə'tɪər, mătéer
Mater Hospital *Belfast*, 'mɑtər, maátĕr
Mates, *f.n.*, meɪts, mayts
Mathafarn *Powys*, mæ'θævərn, mathávvărn
Mathen, *f.n.*, 'mɑθən, maáthĕn
Mather, *f.n.*, 'mæðər, máthĕr; 'meɪðər, máythĕr; 'meɪθər, máythĕr
Mathers, *f.n.*, 'meɪðərz, máythĕrz. *Appropriate also for the Barony of* ~.
Mathers, **E. Powys**, *author and scholar*, 'poʊɪs 'meɪðərz, pṓ-iss máythĕrz
Matheson, *f.n.*, 'mæθɪsən, máthĕssŏn
Mathias, *f.n.*, mə'θaɪəs, măthí-áss
Mathie, *f.n.*, 'mæθɪ, máthi
Mathon *H. & W.*, 'meɪðɒn, máython
Mathrafal, *also spelt* **Mathraval**, *Powys*, mæθ'rævəl, mathrávvăl
Mathry *Dyfed*, 'mæθrɪ, máthri
Matier, *f.n.*, mə'tɪər, mătéer
Matlaske *Norfolk*, 'mætlæsk, mátlassk
Maton, *f.n.*, 'meɪtən, máytŏn
Matravers *Dorset*, mə'trævərz, mătrávvĕrz
Mattacks, *f.n.*, 'mætəks, máttăcks
Mattam, *f.n.*, 'mætəm, máttăm
Mattersey *Notts.*, 'mætərsɪ, máttĕrssi
Matthay, *f.n.*, 'mæteɪ, máttay
Matthes, *f.n.*, 'mæθɪz, máthĕz
Matthias, *f.n.*, mə'θaɪəs, măthí-áss
Mattishall *Norfolk*, 'mætɪʃl, máttishl
Maturin, *f.n.*, 'mætjʊərɪn, mát-yŏorin
Mauchline *S'clyde*, 'mɒxlɪn, móchlin
Maude, *f.n.*, mɔd, mawd
Maudling, *f.n.*, 'mɔdlɪŋ, máwdling
Mauduit, *f.n.*, 'moʊdwi, mṓdwee
Maufe, **Sir Edward**, *architect*, mɔf, mawf
Mauger, *f.n.*, 'meɪdʒər, máyjĕr
Maugersbury *Glos.*, 'mɔzbərɪ, máwzbŭri
Maugham, *f.n.*, mɔm, mawm; 'mɒfəm, móffăm. *The first is appropriate for the Viscountcy of* ~.
Maugham, **W. Somerset**, *author*, 'sʌmərsɪt 'mɔm, súmmĕrssĕt máwm
Maughan, *f.n.*, mɔn, mawn
Maughenby *Cumbria*, 'mæfənbɪ, máffĕnbi

Maughold *I. of Man*, 'mækəld, máckŏld
Maule, *f.n.*, mɔl, mawl
Mauleverer, *f.n.*, mə'levərər, mŏlévvĕrĕr; mɔ'levərər, mawlévvĕrĕr
Maumbury Rings *Dorset*, 'mɔmbərɪ, máwmbŭri
Maund, *f.n.*, mɔnd, mawnd
Maunder, *f.n.*, 'mɔndər, máwndĕr
Maunsell, *f.n.*, 'mænsl, mánssl
Maurice, *f.n.*, 'mɒrɪs, mórriss; mə'ris, mŏréess
Mautby *Norfolk*, 'mɔbɪ, máwbi
Mavius, *f.n.*, 'meɪvɪəs, máyviüss
Mavor, *f.n.*, 'meɪvər, máyvŏr. *Appropriate for Dr O. H. ~, whose pen name was* **James Bridie**, *q.v.*
Mavrogordato, *f.n.*, ,mævrʊʊgɔr-'datʊʊ, mavrōgordaátō
Maw, *f.n.*, mɔ, maw
Mawddach, River, *Gwynedd*, 'maʊðəx, mówth<u>ă</u>ch
Mawdesley, *f.n.*, 'mɔdzlɪ, máwdzli
Mawhinney, *f.n.*, mə'hwɪnɪ, mă-whínni
Mawnan *Cornwall*, 'mɔnən, máwnăn
Maxen, *f.n.*, 'mæksən, mácksĕn
Maxey *Cambs.*, 'mæksɪ, mácksi
Maxim, *f.n.*, 'mæksɪm, mácksim
Maxse, *f.n.*, 'mæksɪ, mácksi
Maxwell, *f.n.*, 'mækswəl, máckswĕl; 'mækswel, máckswel
Maxwelltown *D. & G.*, 'mækswəltaʊn, máckswĕltown; 'mækswəltən, máckswĕltŏn
Maxwelton *S'clyde*, 'mækswəltən, máckswĕltŏn
May, *f.n.*, meɪ, may
Mayall, *f.n.*, 'meɪəl, máy-ăl; 'meɪɔl, máy-awl
Maybole *S'clyde*, meɪ'boʊl, may-bόl
Maydon, *f.n.*, 'meɪdən, máydŏn
Mayer, *f.n.*, 'meɪər, máy-ĕr; mɛər, mair
Mayger, *f.n.*, 'meɪdʒər, máyjĕr; 'meɪgər, máygĕr
Mayhew, *f.n.*, 'meɪhju, máy-hew
Maynard, *f.n.*, 'meɪnərd, máy-nărd; 'meɪnɑrd, máynaard
Mayne, *f.n.*, meɪn, mayn
Mayneard, *f.n.*, 'meɪnɪɑrd, máyni-aard
Mayo, Earl of, 'meɪʊʊ, máy-ō
Mayobridge *Co. Down*, ,meɪʊʊ-'brɪdʒ, may-ō-bríj
Mayon, *also spelt* **Mean**, *Cornwall*, meɪn, mayn
Mays, *f.n.*, meɪz, mayz
Mayson, *f.n.*, 'meɪsən, máyssŏn

Mayvor, *f.n.*, 'meɪvər, máyvŏr
Meachem, *f.n.*, 'mitʃəm, mée-tchĕm
Meacher, *f.n.*, 'mitʃər, méetchĕr
Meade, *f.n.*, mid, meed
Meaden, *f.n.*, 'midən, méedĕn
Meaford *Staffs.*, 'mefərd, méffŏrd; 'mifərd, méefŏrd
Meagher, *f.n.*, mɑr, maar
Meaker, *f.n.*, 'mikər, méekĕr
Meakin, *f.n.*, 'mikɪn, méekin
Mean *see* **Mayon**
Mearles, *f.n.*, mɜrlz, merlz
Mearne, *f.n.*, mɜrn, mern
Mearns, The, *Grampian*, ðə 'mɛərnz, th<u>ě</u> máirnz. *Ancient name of Kincardineshire* (*now part of Grampian Region*).
Mears, *f.n.*, mɪərz, meerz
Measach, Falls of, *H'land*, 'mesəx, méss<u>ă</u>ch
Measham *Leics.*, 'miʃəm, mée-shăm
Meath, Earl of, mið, mee<u>th</u>
Meathop *Cumbria*, 'miθəp, mée-thŏp
Meaux *Humberside*, mjus, mewss
Meavy *Devon*, 'mivɪ, méevi
Meazey, *f.n.*, 'meɪzɪ, máyzi
Mebyon Kernow, *Cornish political party*, 'mebɪən 'kɜrnʊʊ, méb-biŏn kérnō
Meczies, *f.n.*, 'mekzɪz, méck-zizz
Medak, *f.n.*, 'meɪdæk, máydack
Medawar, *f.n.*, 'medəwər, méddă-wăr
Medcraft, *f.n.*, 'medkrɑft, méd-kraaft
Meddings, *f.n.*, 'medɪŋz, méd-dingz
Medhurst, *f.n.*, 'medhərst, méd-hurst
Medlicott, *f.n.*, 'medlɪkɒt, médli-kot
Medmenham *Bucks.*, 'mednəm, méd-năm
Medomsley *Durham*, 'medəmzlɪ, méddŏmzli
Medstead *Hants*, 'medsted, médsted
Medus, *f.n.*, 'midəs, méedüss
Meehan, *f.n.*, 'miən, mée-ăn
Meekums, *f.n.*, 'mikəmz, mée-kŭmz
Meert, *f.n.*, mɪərt, meert
Meeth *Devon*, miθ, meeth
Meetham, *f.n.*, 'miθəm, mée-thăm
Megahey, *f.n.*, mɪ'gæhɪ, mĕgá-hi; mɪ'gæxɪ, mĕg<u>á</u><u>chi</u>
Megan, *Welsh C.n.*, 'megən, méggăn
Megarry, *f.n.*, mɪ'gærɪ, mĕgárri
Megaw, *f.n.*, mɪ'gɔ, mĕgáw

Meggison, *f.n.*, 'megɪsən, méggis-sŏn

Mehan, *f.n.*, 'miən, mée-ăn

Meharg, *f.n.*, mɪ'hɑrg, mĕháarg

Meheux, *f.n.*, 'meɪhju, máyhew

Mehew, *f.n.*, mɪ'hju, mée-hew; 'miu, mée-oo

Mehmedagi, *f.n.*, ˌmemə'dɑdʒɪ, memmĕdáaji

Meier, *f.n.*, 'maɪər, mí-ĕr

Meifod *Powys*, 'maɪvɒd, mívod

Meiggs, *f.n.*, megz, meggz

Meigh, *f.n.*, mi, mee; meɪ, may

Meigle *Tayside*, 'mɪgl, méegl

Meikle, *f.n.*, 'mɪkl, meékl

Meiklejohn, *f.n.*, 'mɪkldʒɒn, míckljon; 'mɪkldʒɒn, meékljon

Meikleour *Tayside*, mɪ'kluər, mĕklŏŏr

Meilen, *f.n.*, 'maɪlən, mílĕn

Mein, *f.n.*, min, meen

Meinardi, *f.n.*, meɪ'nɑrdɪ, may-naárdi

Meinciau *Dyfed*, 'maɪŋkjaɪ, mínk-yī

Meinertzhagen, *f.n.*, 'maɪnərts-hɑgən, mínĕrts-haagĕn

Meir *Staffs.*, mɪər, meer

Meirion, *Welsh C.n.*, 'maɪrɪɒn, míri-on

Mekie, *f.n.*, 'mɪkɪ, meéki

Melachrino, *f.n.*, ˌmelə'krinoʊ, mellăkréenŏ

Melbourn *Cambs.*, 'melbɔrn, mélborn

Melbourne *Derby.*, 'melbɔrn, mélborn

Melbury Abbas *Dorset*, 'melbərɪ 'æbəs, mélbŭri ábbăss

Melchett, Baron, 'meltʃɪt, mél-tchĕt

Melcio, *f.n.*, 'melsɪoʊ, mélssi-ō

Meldreth *Cambs.*, 'meldrəθ, méldrĕth

Meldrum *Grampian*, 'meldrəm, méldrŭm

Melgund, Viscount, 'melgʌnd, mélgund

Melhuish, *f.n.*, 'melhjuɪʃ, mél-hewish; mel'hjuɪʃ, mel-héwish; me'ljuɪʃ, melléwish; 'melɪʃ, méllish; 'meluɪʃ, méllŏŏ-ish

Melia, *f.n.*, 'milɪə, meéliă

Meliden, *Clwyd*, 'melɪdən, méllidĕn

Melincryddan *W. Glam.*, ˌmelɪn-'krɪðən, mellin-kríthăn; ˌmelɪn-'krʌðən, mellin-krúthăn

Melindwr *Dyfed*, me'lɪnduər, mellíndŏŏr

Melin Ifan Ddu *Mid Glam.*, 'melɪn 'ɪvən 'ði, méllin ívvăn thée

Melksham *Wilts.*, 'melkʃəm, mélk-shăm

Mellaart, *f.n.*, 'melɑrt, méllaart

Mellett, *f.n.*, 'melɪt, méllĕt

Mellinger, *f.n.*, 'melɪndʒər, mél-linjĕr

Mellingey *Cornwall*, me'lɪndʒɪ, mellínji

Mellis *Suffolk*, 'melɪs, mélliss

Mellor, *f.n.*, 'melər, méllŏr

Mellors, *f.n.*, 'melərz, méllŏrz

Melluish, *f.n.*, 'meljuɪʃ, méllew-ish

Melly, *f.n.*, 'melɪ, mélli

Melmerby *N. Yorks.*, 'melmərbɪ, mélmĕrbi; 'melərbɪ, méllĕrbi

Meloy, *f.n.*, mɪ'lɔɪ, mĕlóy

Melrose *Borders*, 'melroʊz, mélrōz

Meltham *W. Yorks.*, 'melθəm, mél-thăm

Melton Constable *Norfolk*, 'mel-tən 'kʌnstəbl, méltŏn kúnstăbl

Melton Mowbray *Leics.*, 'meltən 'moʊbreɪ, méltŏn mŏbray

Melvaig *H'land*, mel'veɪg, mel-váyg

Melvich *H'land*, 'melvɪx, mélvi<u>ch</u>

Melville, *f.n.*, 'melvɪl, mélvil

Memus *Tayside*, 'miməs, mée-mŭss

Menabilly *Cornwall*, ˌmenə'bɪlɪ, mennăbílli

Menage, *f.n.*, mɪ'nɑʒ, mĕná<u>azh</u>

Menai *Gwynedd*, 'menaɪ, ménnī. *Appropriate for both the ~ Bridge and the ~ Strait.*

Menary, *f.n.*, 'menərɪ, ménnări

Menaul, *f.n.*, me'nɔl, mennáwl

Mendel, *f.n.*, 'mendl, méndl

Mendelssohn, *f.n.*, 'mendlsən, méndlssŏn

Meneely, *f.n.*, mɪ'nilɪ, mĕneéli

Menell, *f.n.*, 'menl, ménnl

Menevia, *Welsh bishopric*, mɪ-'nivɪə, mĕnéeviă

Menges, *f.n.*, 'meŋgɪz, méng-giz; 'meŋɪs, méng-ĕss. *The first is appropriate for Herbert ~, conductor and composer.*

Menheniot *Cornwall*, mən'henɪət, mĕn-hénniŏt

Menmuir, *f.n.*, 'menmjuər, mén-myŏŏr

Menneer, *f.n.*, mə'nɪər, mĕneér

Mennell, *f.n.*, mɪ'nel, mĕnéll

Mennich, *f.n.*, 'menɪʃ, ménnish

Mennie, *f.n.*, 'menɪ, ménni

Menpes, *f.n.*, 'menpes, ménpess; 'menpɪz, ménpiz

Menston *W. Yorks.*, 'menstən, ménstŏn

Menstrie *Central*, 'menstrɪ, méns-stri

Menteith, Lake of, *Central*, mən-'tiθ, mĕnteéth

Menteth, *f.n.*, mən'tiθ, mĕnteéth

Menuhin, Yehudi, *violinist,* jə'hudi 'menjʊɪn, yĕ-hŏodi mén-yōo-in. *Mr Menuhin himself accepts the above popular English pronunciation. The Russian and Hebrew version is* mə'nuxɪn, mĕnóochin

Menzies, *f.n.,* 'mɪŋɪs, míng-iss; 'mɪŋɪz, míng-iz; 'menzɪz, ménziz. *The first two are indigenous Scottish pronunciations.*

Meo, *f.n.,* 'meɪoʊ, máy-ō

Meole Brace *Salop,* 'mil 'breɪs, meél bráyss

Meols *Lancs.,* milz, meelz

Meon, River, *Hants,* 'miən, meé--ŏn

Meon, East *and* West, *Hants,* 'miən, meé-ŏn

Meopham *Kent,* 'mepəm, méppăm

Mepal *Cambs.,* 'mipl, meépl

Meppershall *Beds.,* 'mepərʃl, méppĕrshl

Merbecke, John, *16th-c. musician and composer,* 'mɑrbek, maár-beck

Merchant, *f.n.,* 'mɜrtʃənt, mér-tchănt

Merchiston *Lothian,* 'mɜrkɪstən, mérkistŏn

Merchistoun Hall *Hants,* 'mɜrtʃɪs-tən, mértchistŏn

Mercy, *f.n.,* 'mɜrsɪ, mérssi

Meredith, *C.n. and f.n.,* mə'redɪθ, mĕréddith; 'merədɪθ, mérrĕdith. *The first is the Welsh pronunciation.*

Meredydd, *Welsh C.n. and f.n.,* mə'redɪð, mĕréddith; mə'redɪθ, mĕréddith

Merevale *Warwicks.,* 'merɪveɪl, mérrĕvayl

Mereweather, *f.n.,* 'merɪweðər, mérriwethĕr

Merewether, *f.n.,* 'merɪweðər, mérriwethĕr

Mereworth, Baron, 'merɪwɜrθ, mérrĕwŭrth

Mereworth *Kent,* 'merɪwɜrθ, mérrĕwurth

Merfyn, *Welsh C.n.,* 'mɜrvɪn, mér-vin

Meriden *W. Midlands,* 'merɪdən, mérridĕn

Merioneth *former Co. name,* ˌmerɪ'ɒnəθ, merri-ónnĕth. *Appropriate also for the Earl of ~.*

Merkelis, *f.n.,* mər'keɪlɪs, mĕrkáy-liss

Mermagen, *f.n.,* 'mɜrməgən, mér-măgĕn

Merrell, *f.n.,* 'merəl, mérrĕl

Merrion, *f.n.,* 'merɪən, mérriŏn

Merryweather, *f.n.,* 'merɪweðər, mérriwethĕr

Merse, The, *Borders,* mɜrs, merss

Mersea, East *and* West, *Essex,* 'mɜrzɪ, mérzi

Mersey, River, *Gtr. M'chester–Merseyside,* 'mɜrzɪ, mérzi. *Appropriate also for Viscount ~.*

Mersham *Kent,* 'mɜrzəm, mérzăm

Mersham-le-Hatch *Kent,* 'mɜrzəm lə 'hætʃ, mérzăm lĕ hátch

Merstham *Surrey,* 'mɜrstəm, mér-stăm

Merthyr *Dyfed,* 'mɜrθər, mérthĕr. *Appropriate also for Baron ~.*

Merthyr Tydfil *Mid Glam.,* 'mɜrθər 'tɪdvɪl, mérthĕr tídvil

Meryweather, *f.n.,* 'merɪweðər, mérriwethĕr

Mescall, *f.n.,* 'meskl, mésskl

Meshaw *Devon,* 'meʃɔ, mésh-aw

Messel, *f.n.,* 'mesl, méssl

Messenger, *f.n.,* 'mesɪndʒər, méssĕnjĕr

Messent, *f.n.,* 'mesənt, méssĕnt

Messer, *f.n.,* 'mesər, méssĕr

Messervy, *f.n.,* mɪ'sɜrvɪ, mĕssérvi

Messina, *f.n.,* mɪ'sinə, mĕsseénä

Mestel, *f.n.,* mes'tel, mestéll

Meszaros, *f.n.,* mɪ'zɑrɒs, mĕzaá-ross

Metcalfe, *f.n.,* 'metkɑf, métkaaf; 'metkɔf, métkăf

Meteyard, *f.n.,* 'metjɑrd, mét--yaard

Metherall, *f.n.,* 'meðərɔl, méthĕr-awl

Methil *Fife,* 'meθɪl, méth-il

Methley *W. Yorks.,* 'meθlɪ, méthli

Methold, *f.n.,* 'meθoʊld, méth-ōld

Methuen, Baron, 'meθʊɪn, méthōo-ĕn

Methuen, *f.n.,* 'meθjʊɪn, méth-yōo-ĕn. *Appropriate also for ~ & Co., publishers.*

Methven, *f.n.,* 'meθvən, méthvĕn

Methven *Tayside,* 'meθvən, méthvĕn

Metrebian, *f.n.,* ˌmetrɪ'bjɑn, metrĕbyaán

Meurant, *f.n.,* mjʊə'rænt, myōo-ránt

Meurig, *Welsh C.n.,* 'maɪrɪg, mí--rig

Meurwyn, *Welsh C.n.,* 'maɪərwɪn, mír-win

Meux, *f.n.,* mjuks, mewks; mjuz, mewz; mju, mew. *The first is appropriate for the firm of brewers.*

Mevagissey *Cornwall,* ˌmevə'gɪsɪ, mevvăgíssi; ˌmevə'gɪzɪ, mevvă-gízzi

Mewes, *f.n.,* 'mevɪs, mévvĕss.
This is appropriate for the
architectural firm of ∼ and
Davis, builders of the London
Ritz Hotel.
Mewett, *f.n.,* 'mjuɪt, méw-ĕt
Mexborough, Earl of, 'meksbərə,
mécksbŭră
Mey *H'land,* meɪ, may. Appropri-
ate also for the Castle of ∼.
Meyer, *f.n.,* 'maɪər, mí-ĕr; mɛər,
mair; 'meɪər, máy-ĕr; mɪər, meer
Meyerstein, *f.n.,* 'maɪərstaɪn, mí-
-ĕrsstīn
Meyjes, *f.n.,* meɪz, mayz
Meyllteyrn *Gwynedd,* meɬ'taɪərn,
meḥltírn
Meynell, *f.n.,* 'menl, ménnl
Meyrick, *f.n.,* 'merɪk, mérrick
Meysey, *f.n.,* 'meɪzɪ, máyzi
Mhachair, Loch, *W. Isles,* 'væxər,
váchăr
Miall, *f.n.,* 'maɪəl, mí-ăl
Micallef, *f.n.,* mɪ'kælɪf, mikálĕf
Michael, *C.n. and f.n.,* 'maɪkl,
míkl
Michaelchurch Escley *H. & W.,*
'maɪklt∫ɜrt∫ 'esklɪ, míkltchurtch
éskli
Michaelhouse College *Univ. of
Cambridge,* 'maɪklhaʊs, míkl-
-howss. In 1546 this college
merged with King's Hall to form
Trinity College.
Michaelis, *f.n.,* mɪ'keɪlɪs, mickáy-
liss; mɪ'kaɪlɪs, mickíliss
Michaelson, *f.n.,* 'maɪklsən,
míklssŏn
Michaelston-y-Vedw *Gwent,*
'maɪklstən ə 'vedu, míklsstŏn ă
véddoo
Michaelstow *Cornwall,* 'maɪkl-
stoʊ, míklsstō
Micheldever *Hants,* 'mɪt∫ldevər,
mítchldevvĕr
Michelham, Baron, 'mɪt∫ələm,
mítchĕlăm
Michell, *f.n.,* mɪ'∫el, mishéll
Michelli, *f.n.,* mɪ'kelɪ, mikélli
Michelmore, *f.n.,* 'mɪt∫lmɔr,
mítchlmor
Michelson, *f.n.,* 'mɪt∫lsən, mítchls-
sŏn
Michie, *f.n.,* 'mɪxɪ, míchi; 'mɪxɪ,
meechi; 'mɪkɪ, mícki
Mickel, *f.n.,* 'mɪkl, míckl
Micklebring *S. Yorks.,* 'mɪklbrɪŋ,
mícklbring
Mickleover *Derby.,* 'mɪkloʊvər,
míckl-ōvĕr
Midanbury *Hants,* 'mɪdənbərɪ,
míddănbŭri
Middleham *N. Yorks.,* 'mɪdləm,
míddl-ăm

Middlemiss, *f.n.,* 'mɪdlmɪs, míddl-
miss
Middlesbrough *Cleveland,*
'mɪdlzbrə, míddlzbră
Middlesceugh *Cumbria,* 'mɪdlz-
koʊ, míddlzkō
Middle Stoughton *Somerset,*
'mɪdl 'stɔtən, míddl stáwtŏn
Middleton, *f.n.,* 'mɪdltən, míddltŏn
Middleton Tyas *N. Yorks.,*
'mɪdltən 'taɪəs, míddltŏn tí-ăss
Middle Wallop *Hants,* 'mɪdl
'wɒləp, míddl wóllŏp
Middleweek, *f.n.,* 'mɪdlwik,
míddlweek
Middlewich *Ches.,* 'mɪdlwɪt∫,
míddlwitch
Mides, *f.n.,* 'maɪdiz, mídeez
Midgley, *f.n.,* 'mɪdʒlɪ, míjjli
Midleton, Earldom of, 'mɪdltən,
míddltŏn
Midlothian *Lothian,* mɪd'loʊðɪən,
midlóthiăn. Appropriate also for
the Earl of ∼.
Midsomer Norton *Avon,* 'mɪd-
sʌmər 'nɔrtən, mídsummĕr
nórtŏn
Miers, *f.n.,* 'maɪərz, mí-ĕrz
Miesch, *f.n.,* mi∫, meesh
Miéville, *f.n.,* 'mjeɪvɪl, myáyvil
Mighall, *f.n.,* 'maɪəl, mí-ăl
Mighell, *f.n.,* 'maɪəl, mí-ĕl
Mikardo, *f.n.,* mɪ'kɑrdoʊ, mikaʹar-
dō
Mikellatos, *f.n.,*, mɪkə'lɑtɒs,
mickĕlaʹatoss
Mikes, George, *author,* 'mike∫,
meekesh
Mikhial, *f.n.,* 'mikl, meʹekl
Milan, *f.n.,* mɪ'læn, milánn
Milbourne, *f.n.,* 'mɪlbɔrn, mílborn
Milburn, *f.n.,* 'mɪlbɜrn, mílburn
Milburne, *f.n.,* 'mɪlbɜrn, mílburn
Mildenhall *Suffolk,* 'mɪldənhɔl,
míldĕnhawl
Mildenhall *Wilts.,* 'mɪldənhɔl,
míldĕnhawl. Sometimes spelt
Minal and pronounced 'maɪnɔl,
mínawl
Mildmay, *f.n.,* 'maɪldmeɪ, míld-
may
Mildmay of Flete, Barony of,
'maɪldmeɪ əv 'flit, míldmay ŏv
fleʹet
Mildwater, *f.n.,* 'maɪldwɔtər, míld-
wawtĕr
Miles, *C.n. and f.n.,* maɪlz, mīlz
Milford Haven *Dyfed,* 'mɪlfərd
'heɪvən, mílfŏrd háyvĕn
Milkina, Nina, *pianist,* 'ninə
'mɪlkinə, neʹenă mílkeenă
Millais, Sir John, *painter,* 'mɪleɪ,
míllay

Millan 172 **Moelwyn**

Millan, *f.n.*, 'mɪlən, míllăn
Millar, *f.n.*, 'mɪlər, míllăr
Millard, *f.n.*, 'mɪlɑrd, míllaard
Millbay *Devon*, mɪl'beɪ, milbáy
Miller, *f.n.*, 'mɪlər, míllĕr
Milles, *f.n.*, mɪlz, millz
Milliband, *f.n.*, 'mɪlɪbænd, mílli-
band
Millichap, *f.n.*, 'mɪlɪtʃæp, mílli-
tchap
Millichope, *f.n.*, 'mɪlɪtʃoup, mílli-
tchōp
Milligan, *f.n.*, 'mɪlɪgən, mílligăn
Milliken, *f.n.*, 'mɪlɪkən, míllikĕn
Millings, *f.n.*, 'mɪlɪŋz, míllingz
Millington, *f.n.*, 'mɪlɪŋtən, mílling-
tŏn
Millisle *D. & G.*, mɪl'aɪl, millíl
Millwall *London*, 'mɪl'wɔl, míll-
-wáwl; 'mɪlwəl, mílwăl
Millward, *f.n.*, 'mɪlwɔrd, míl-
wawrd
Milmo, *f.n.*, 'mɪlmou, mílmō
Milnathort *Tayside*, ˌmɪlnə'θɔrt,
milnäthórt
Milne, *f.n.*, mɪln, miln; mɪl, mill
Milner, *f.n.*, 'mɪlnər, milnĕr
Milnes, *f.n.*, mɪlnz, milnz; mɪlz,
millz
Milngavie *S'clyde*, mʌl'gaɪ, mulgí;
mɪl'gaɪ, milgí
Milton, *f.n.*, 'mɪltən, míltŏn
Milton Keynes *Bucks.*, 'mɪltən
'kinz; míltŏn keénz
Milward, *f.n.*, 'mɪlwərd, mílwărd
Milwich *Staffs.*, 'mɪlɪtʃ, míllitch
Mimram, River, *Herts.*, 'mɪmræm,
mímram
Minack *Cornwall*, 'mɪnək, mínnăk
Minal *see* Mildenhall *Wilts.*
Minay, *f.n.*, 'maɪneɪ, mínay
Minchinton, *f.n.*, 'mɪntʃɪntən,
míntchintŏn
Minear, *f.n.*, mɪ'nɪər, mineér
Minell, *f.n.*, mɪ'nel, minéll
Minera *Clwyd*, mɪ'nerə, minérră
Mines, *f.n.*, maɪnz, mīnz
Mineter, *f.n.*, 'mɪnɪtər, mínnĕtĕr
Minety *Wilts.*, 'maɪntɪ, mínti
Minffordd *Gwynedd*, 'mɪnfɔrð,
mínforth
Mingary, Loch, *S'clyde*, 'mɪŋgərɪ,
ming-gări
Mingay Island *H'land*, 'mɪŋgeɪ,
ming-gay
Mingulay *W. Isles*, 'mɪŋgʊleɪ,
ming-gōolay
Miningsby *Lincs.*, 'mɪnɪŋzbɪ,
mínningzbi
Minns, *f.n.*, mɪnz, minnz
Minogue, *f.n.*, mɪ'noug, minóg
Minoprio, *f.n.*, mɪ'noupriou,
minōpriō
Minshull, *f.n.*, 'mɪnʃl, mínshl

Minshull Vernon *Ches.*, 'mɪnʃl
'vɜrnən, mínshl vérnŏn
Minsmere *Suffolk*, 'mɪnzmɪər,
mínzmeer
Minster Lovell *Oxon.*, 'mɪnstər
'lʌvl, mínsstĕr lúvvl
Minter, *f.n.*, 'mɪntər, míntĕr
Mintlaw *Grampian*, 'mɪnt'lɔ, mínt-
láw
Minto *Borders*, 'mɪntou, míntō.
Appropriate also for the Earl of
~.
Mirfield *W. Yorks.*, 'mɜrfild, mír-
feeld
Mirfin, *f.n.*, 'mɜrfɪn, mírfin
Mirzoeff, *f.n.*, 'mɜrtsɒf, mírtsoff
Miscampbell, *f.n.*, mɪs'kæmbl,
miskámbl
Miserden *Glos.*, 'mɪzərdən, míz-
zĕrdĕn
Mishcon, *f.n.*, 'mɪʃkɒn, míshkon
Mishnish *S'clyde*, 'mɪʃnɪʃ, mísh-
nish
Miskin, *f.n.*, 'mɪskɪn, mísskin
Miskin *Mid Glam.*, 'mɪskɪn, míss-
kin
Miskiw, *f.n.*, 'mɪskju, mískew
Misterton *Dorset*, 'mɪstərtən,
místĕrtŏn
Mita, *C.n.*, 'mitə, meétă
Mitcham *London*, 'mɪtʃəm, mí-
tchăm
Mitchamian, *native of* Mitcham,
mɪ'tʃeɪmɪən, mitcháymiän
Mitchard, *f.n.*, 'mɪtʃɑrd, mí-
tchaard
Mitchell, *f.n.*, 'mɪtʃl, mítchl
Mitchenere, *f.n.*, ˌmɪtʃɪ'nɛər, mi-
tchĕnáir
Mitford, *f.n.*, 'mɪtfərd, mítfŏrd
Mithian *Cornwall*, 'mɪðɪən, míth-
iän
Mitrany, *f.n.*, mɪ'trænɪ, mitránni
Mivart, *f.n.*, 'maɪvərt, mívärt
Mizen, *f.n.*, 'maɪzən, mízĕn
Mizler, *f.n.*, 'mɪzlər, mízzlĕr
Mizzi, *f.n.*, 'mɪtsɪ, mítsi
Moate, *f.n.*, mout, mōt
Mobberley *Ches.*, 'mɒbərlɪ, mób-
bĕrli
Moberly, *f.n.*, 'moubərlɪ, mṓbĕrli
Mobsby, *f.n.*, 'mɒbzbɪ, móbzbi
Mocatta, *f.n.*, mou'kætə, mōkáttă
Mochan, *f.n.*, 'mɒkən, móckăn
Mochdre *Clwyd, Powys*, 'mɒxdreɪ,
móchdray
Mochrum *D. & G.*, 'mɒxrəm,
móchrŭm
Modbury *Devon*, 'mɒdbərɪ, mód-
bŭri
Moelfre *Clwyd, Gwynedd*, 'mɔɪl-
vreɪ, móylvray
Moelwyn, *Welsh C.n.*, 'mɔɪlwɪn,
móylwin

Moelyci *Gwynedd*, mɔɪ'lʌkɪ, moylúcki
Moeran, *f.n.*, 'mɔrən, máwrăn
Moffat, *f.n.*, 'mɒfət, móffăt
Moffat *D. & G.*, 'mɒfət, móffăt
Moger, *f.n.*, 'moʊdʒər, mójĕr
Mogey, *f.n.*, 'moʊgɪ, mógi
Moggach, *f.n.*, 'mɒgəx, móggă<u>ch</u>
Mohan, *f.n.*, 'moʊhæn, mō-han
Moidart *H'land*, 'mɔɪdərt, móydărt
Moignard, *f.n.*, 'mɔɪnjɑrd, móyn--yaard
Moilliet, *f.n.*, 'mɔɪlɪet, móyli-et
Moin, The, *H'land*, mɔɪn, moyn
Moir, *f.n.*, 'mɔɪər, moyr
Moira *Leics.*, 'mɔɪrə, móyră
Moiseiwitsch, Benno, *pianist*, 'benoʊ mɔɪ'zeɪɪvɪtʃ, bénnō moyzáy-ivitch
Moiseiwitsch, Tanya, *stage designer*, 'tænjə mɔɪ'zeɪɪvɪtʃ, tányă moyzáy-ivitch
Moiser, *f.n.*, 'mɔɪzər, móyzĕr
Molash *Kent*, 'moʊlæʃ, mŏlash
Mold *Clwyd*, moʊld, mōld
Molenan *Co. Derry*, mə'lenən, mŏlénnăn
Molendinar, Burn, *Glasgow*, ˌmoʊlən'daɪnər, mŏlĕndínăr
Molesey, East *and* West, *Surrey*, 'moʊlzɪ, mŏlzi
Molesworth *Cambs.*, 'moʊlzwərθ, mŏlzwŏrth
Moline, *f.n.*, moʊ'lin, mōlé·en
Molineux football stadium *Wolverhampton*, 'mɒlɪnju, móllinew
Molland-Botreaux *Devon*, 'mɒlənd 'bɒtrɪks, móllănd bóttricks
Mollard, *f.n.*, 'mɒlɑrd, móllaard
Molle, *f.n.*, mɒl, moll
Mollo, *f.n.*, 'mɒloʊ, móllō
Molloy, *f.n.*, mə'lɔɪ, mŏlóy
Molony, *f.n.*, mə'loʊnɪ, mŏlŏni
Molseed, *f.n.*, 'moʊlsɪd, mŏlseed
Molson, *f.n.*, 'moʊlsən, mŏlssŏn. *Appropriate also for Baron* ~.
Molteno, *f.n.*, mɒl'tinoʊ, molténō
Molyneaux, *f.n.*, 'mɒlɪnoʊ, móllinō
Molyneux, *f.n.*, 'mɒlɪnju, móllinew; 'mʌlɪnjuks, múllinewks; 'mɒlɪnjuks, móllinewks; 'mʌlɪnju, múllinew. *The first is appropriate for the Earl of Sefton's family name and therefore for Viscount* ~.
Momerie, *f.n.*, 'mʌmərɪ, múmmĕri
Monadhliadh Mountains *H'land*, 'moʊnə'liə, mŏnăleé-ă
Monaghan, *f.n.*, 'mɒnəhən, mónnă-hăn

Monahan, *f.n.*, 'mɒnəhən, mónnă-hăn
Monair, *f.n.*, mɒ'neər, monnáir
Monar, Loch, *H'land*, 'moʊnər, mŏnăr
Moncaster, *f.n.*, 'mʌŋkəstər, múnkăstĕr
Monck, *f.n.*, mʌŋk, munk. *Appropriate also for Viscount* ~.
Monckton, *f.n.*, 'mʌŋktən, múnktŏn
Monckton of Brenchley, Viscount, 'mʌŋktən əv 'brentʃlɪ, múnktŏn ŏv bréntchli
Moncreiff, *f.n.*, mən'krif, mŏn--kreéf. *Appropriate also for Baron* ~.
Moncreiffe, *f.n.*, mən'krif, mŏn--kreéf. *Appropriate also for Sir Iain* ~ *of that Ilk*.
Moncrieff, *f.n.*, mən'krif, mŏn--kreéf; mɒn'krif, mon-kreéf
Moncrieffe, *f.n.*, mən'krif, mŏn--kreéf
Moncur, *f.n.*, mɒn'k3r, mon-kúr
Mondynes *Grampian*, mɒn'daɪnz, mondínz
Monea *Co. Fermanagh*, mʌ'neɪ, munnáy
Money, *f.n.*, 'mʌnɪ, múnni
Moneydie *Tayside*, mɒ'nidɪ, monneédi; mɒ'naɪdɪ, monnídi
Moneyglass *Co. Antrim*, ˌmʌnɪ'glɑs, munniglaáss
Moneymore *Co. Derry*, ˌmʌnɪ'mɔr, munnimór
Moneypenny, *f.n.*, 'mʌnɪpenɪ, múnnipenni; 'mɒnɪpenɪ, mónnipenni
Moneyreagh *Co. Tyrone*, ˌmʌnɪ'reɪ, munniráy
Mongeham, Great *and* Little, *Kent*, 'mʌndʒəm, múnjăm
Monger, *f.n.*, 'mʌŋgər, múng-gĕr
Mongewell *Oxon.*, 'mʌndʒwel, múnjwel
Moniaive *D. & G.*, ˌmɒnɪ'aɪv, monni-ív
Monifieth *Tayside*, ˌmʌnɪ'fiθ, munnifeéth
Monikie *Tayside*, mə'nikɪ, mŏneéki
Monkhouse, *f.n.*, 'mʌŋkhaʊs, múnk-howss
Monkman, *f.n.*, 'mʌŋkmən, múnkmăn
Monks Eleigh *Suffolk*, mʌŋks 'ilɪ, munks eéli
Monkton *Dyfed, Mid & S. Glam.*, 'mʌŋktən, múnktŏn
Monkwearmouth *Tyne & Wear*, mʌŋk'wɪərmaʊθ, munk--weermowth
Monlough *Co. Down*, 'mɒnlɒx, mónlo<u>ch</u>

Monmouth *Gwent*, 'mʌnməθ,
múnmŭth; 'mɒnməθ, mónmŭth
Monnet, *f.n.*, 'mɒneɪ, mónnay
Monnow, River, *Gwent*, 'mʌnoʊ,
múnnō; 'mɒnoʊ, mónnō
Monquhitter *Grampian*, mɒn-
'hwɪtər, monwhíttĕr
Monro, *f.n.*, mən'roʊ, mŏnró;
mʌn'roʊ, munró; mɒn'roʊ,
monró
Monsarrat, *f.n.*, 'mɒnsəræt, móns-
sărat; ˌmɒnsə'ræt, monssărát
Monsell, *f.n.*, 'mʌnsl, múnssl.
Appropriate also for Viscount ~.
Monsey, *f.n.*, 'mɒnsɪ, mónssi
Monslow, *f.n.*, 'mɒnzloʊ, mónzlō
Monson, *f.n.*, 'mʌnsən, múnssŏn;
'mɒnsən, mónssŏn. *The first is
appropriate for Baron* ~.
Montacute *Somerset*, 'mɒntəkjut,
móntăkewt
Montagnon, *f.n.*, mɒn'tænjŏ,
montán-yŏng; mõ'tænjŏ, mōng-
-tán-yŏng
Montagu of Beaulieu, Baron,
'mɒntəgju əv 'bjulɪ, móntăgew
ŏv béwli
Monté, *f.n.*, 'mɒnteɪ, móntay
Monteagle, Baron, mən'tigl,
mŏntéegl
Montefiore, *f.n.*, ˌmɒntɪ'fjɔrɪ,
montĕfyáwri
Monteith, *f.n.*, mɒn'tiθ, montéeth
Montgomerie, *f.n.*, mənt'gʌmərɪ,
mŏntgúmmĕri; mən'gʌmərɪ,
mŏn-gúmmĕri; mənt'gɒmərɪ,
mŏntgómmĕri
Montgomery, *f.n.*, mənt'gʌmərɪ,
mŏntgúmmĕri; mən'gʌmərɪ,
mŏn-gúmmĕri; mənt'gɒmərɪ,
mŏntgómmĕri
Montgomery *Powys*, mənt'gʌmrɪ,
mŏntgúmri; mənt'gɒmərɪ,
mŏntgómmĕri
Montgomery of Alamein, Viscount, mənt'gʌmərɪ əv 'æTlə-
meɪn, mŏntgúmmĕri ŏv
álămayn
Montpelier *Bristol* mɒnt'pelɪər,
montpélli-ĕr
Montresor, *f.n.*, 'mɒntrezər, món-
trezzŏr
Montrose *Tayside*, mɒn'troʊz,
montrōz; mən'troʊz, mŏntróz.
*The first is appropriate for the
Duke of* ~.
Monyash *Derby.*, 'mʌnɪæʃ,
múnni-ash
Monymusk *Grampian*, ˌmɒnɪ-
'mʌsk, monnimússk
Monzie *Tayside*, mɒ'ni, monnée;
mə'ni, mŏnée
Monzievaird *Tayside*, ˌmɒnɪ'veərd,
monniváird

Mooney, *f.n.*, 'munɪ, moóni
Moonie, *f.n.*, 'munɪ, moóni
Moonzie *Fife*, 'munzɪ, moónzi
Moorat, *f.n.*, 'mʊəræt, moórat
Moore, *f.n.*, mʊər, moōr
Moorfea *Hoy* (*Orkney*), mʊər'feɪ,
moōr-fáy
Moorfoot, *f.n.*, 'mʊərfʊt, moōr-
foōt
Moorhead, *f.n.*, 'mʊərhed, moōr-
-hed
Moortown *W. Yorks.*, 'mʊərtaʊn,
moōrtown
Moos, *f.n.*, mus, mooss
Morahan, *f.n.*, 'mɒrəhən, mórră-
-hăn
Moran, *f.n.*, 'mɒrən, máwrăn;
'mɒrən, mórrăn; mə'ræn,
mŏrán; *The first is appropriate
for Baron* ~.
Morant, *f.n.*, mə'rænt, mŏránt
Morar *H'land*, 'mɒrər, máwrăr
Moray *Grampian*, 'mʌrɪ, múrri.
Appropriate also for the Earl of
~ *and the* ~ *Firth.*
Morcom, *f.n.*, 'mɔrkəm, mórkŏm
Mordaunt, *f.n.*, 'mɔrdənt, mór-
dănt; 'mɔrdɒnt, mórdawnt
Mordecai, *f.n.*, 'mɔrdɪkaɪ, mór-
dĕkī
Mordiford *H. & W.*, 'mɔrdɪfərd,
mórdifŏrd
Mordue, *f.n.*, 'mɔrdju, mórdew
More, *f.n.*, mɔr, mor
Morebath *Devon*, 'mɔrbɑθ, mór-
baath
Morecambe, *f.n.*, 'mɔrkəm,
mórkăm
Morecambe *Lancs.*, 'mɔrkəm,
mórkăm
Morehen, *f.n.*, 'mɔrhen, mór-hen
Moreing, *f.n.*, 'mɔrɪŋ, máwring
Morel, *f.n.*, mɔ'rel, mawréll;
mə'rel, mŏréll
Moreland, *f.n.*, 'mɔrlənd, mórländ
Moreleigh *Devon*, 'mɔrlɪ, mórli
Morell, *f.n.*, mɒ'rel, morréll;
mə'rel, mŏréll
Morelle, *f.n.*, mə'rel, mŏréll
Morena, *f.n.*, mɒ'rinə, morréenă
Moresby, *f.n.*, 'mɔrzbɪ, mórzbi
Moresby *Cumbria*, 'mɒrɪsbɪ,
mórrĕssbi
Moreton, *f.n.*, 'mɔrtən, mórtŏn
Moreton Morrell *Warwicks.*,
'mɔrtən 'mɒrəl, mórtŏn mórrĕl
Morey, *f.n.*, 'mɔrɪ, máwri
Morfa Rhuddlan *Clwyd*, 'mɔrvə
'hrɪðlæn, mórvă ríthlan
Morfudd, *Welsh C.n.*, 'mɔrvɪð,
mórvith
Morgan, *f.n.*, 'mɔrgən, mórgăn
Morgenstern, *f.n.*, 'mɔrgənstɜrn,
mórgĕnsstern

Moriarty, *f.n.*, ˌmɒrɪ'ɑrtɪ, morri-
-aárti
Morice, *f.n.*, 'mɒrɪs, mórriss
Morin, *f.n.*, 'mɔrɪn, máwrin
Morison, *f.n.*, 'mɒrɪsən, mórrissŏn
Morissy, *f.n.*, 'mɒrɪsɪ, mórrissi
Morland, *f.n.*, 'mɔrlənd, mórländ
Morley, *f.n.*, 'mɔrlɪ, mórli
Moro, *f.n.*, 'mɒroʊ, mórrō
Morpeth *Northd.*, 'mɔrpəθ, mór-
pĕth
Morpurgo, *f.n.*, mɔr'pɜrgoʊ, mor-
púrgō
Morrah, *f.n.*, 'mɒrə, mórră
Morrell, *f.n.*, mə'rel, mŏréll;
mɒ'rel, morréll; 'mʌrəl, múrrĕl.
*The third is appropriate for
Lady Ottoline* ~.
Morrell, Moreton, *Warwicks.*,
'mɔrtən 'mɒrəl, mórtŏn mórrĕl
Morrick, *f.n.*, 'mɒrɪk, mórrick
Morris, *f.n.*, 'mɒrɪs, mórriss
Morrison, *f.n.*, 'mɒrɪsən, mórris-
sŏn
Morrissey, *f.n.*, 'mɒrɪsɪ, mórrissi
Morrow, *f.n.*, 'mɒroʊ, mórrō
Morse, *f.n.*, mɔrs, morss
Morshead, *f.n.*, 'mɔrzhed, mórz-
-hed
Mortehoe *Devon*, 'mɔrthoʊ, mórt-
-hō
Morteshed, *f.n.*, 'mɔrtɪʃed,
mórtĕ-shed
Mortimer, *f.n.*, 'mɔrtɪmər, mórti-
mĕr
Mortlach *Grampian*, 'mɔrtləx,
mórtlă͟ch
Mortlake *London*, 'mɔrtleɪk, mórt-
-layk
Morton, *f.n.*, 'mɔrtən, mórtŏn
Morvah *Cornwall*, 'mɔrvə, mórvă
Morwena, *Welsh C.n.*, mɔr'wenə,
morwénnă
Morwenstow *Cornwall*, 'mɔrwɪn-
stoʊ, mórwĕnsstō
Mosborough *S. Yorks.*, 'mɒzbrə,
mózbră; 'mɒzbərə, mózbŭră
Moscow *S'clyde*, 'mɒskoʊ,
mósskō
Moseley, *f.n.*, 'moʊzlɪ, mŏzli
Moser, Prof. Sir Claus, 'klaʊs
'moʊzər, klówss mŏzĕr
Mosley, *f.n.*, 'moʊzlɪ, mŏzli;
'mɒzlɪ, mózzli
Mosley Common *Gtr. M'chester*,
'mɒzlɪ 'kɒmən, mózzli kómmŏn
Mossley *Co. Antrim*, 'mɒslɪ,
móssli
Moss Side *Gtr. M'chester*, 'mɒs
'saɪd, móss síd
Mosterton *Dorset*, 'mɒstərtən,
mósstĕrtŏn
Mostyn *Clwyd*, 'mɒstɪn, mósstin.
Appropriate also for Baron ~.

Mothecombe *Devon*, 'mʌðəkəm,
mú͟thĕkŭm
Motley, *f.n.*, 'mɒtlɪ, móttli
Mottershead, *f.n.*, 'mɒtərzhed,
móttĕrz-hed
Motteux, Peter Anthony, *17th–
18th-c. translator and dramatist*,
'mɒtɜ, móttö
Mottistone, Baron, 'mɒtɪstən,
móttistŏn
Motyer, *f.n.*, mə'tɪər, mŏtéer
Mouat, *f.n.*, 'moʊət, mŏ-ăt
Moubray, *f.n.*, 'moʊbreɪ, mŏbray
Moughtin, *f.n.*, 'mɔtɪn, máwtin
Moughton, *f.n.*, 'moʊtən, mŏtŏn
Mouillot, *f.n.*, 'mujoʊ, móo-yō
Mouland, *f.n.*, 'mulənd, móoländ;
mu'lænd, mooländ
Mouldsworth *Ches.*, 'moʊldz-
wɜrθ, mŏldzwurth
Moule, *f.n.*, moʊl, mōl; mul, mool
Moulin *Tayside*, 'mulɪn, móolin
Moulinearn *Tayside*, ˌmulɪn'ɑrn,
moolinaárn
Moulsecoomb, *also spelt* **Moulse-
coombe, Moulsecombe,**
E. Sussex, 'moʊlskum, mŏls-
skoom
Moulsford *Oxon.*, 'moʊlzfərd,
mŏlzförd
Moulsham *Chelmsford (Essex)*,
'moʊlʃəm, mŏl-shăm
Moulsoe *Bucks.*, 'moʊlsoʊ,
mŏlssō
Moulson, *f.n.*, 'moʊlsən, mŏlssŏn
Moulton *Ches., Northants.*, 'moʊl-
tən, mŏltŏn
Moulton Eaugate *Lincs.*, 'moʊltən
'igeɪt, mŏltŏn éegayt; 'moʊltən
'igət, mŏltŏn éegăt
Moultrie, *f.n.*, 'mutrɪ, móotri
Mouncer, *f.n.*, 'maʊnsər, mównssĕr
Mounsey, *f.n.*, 'maʊnsɪ, mównssi
Mountain Ash *Mid Glam.*, 'maʊn-
tɪn 'æʃ, mówntin ásh
Mountbatten of Burma, Countess,
maʊnt'bætən əv 'bɜrmə, mownt-
báttĕn ŏv búrmă
Mount Edgcumbe, Earl of,
maʊnt 'edʒkəm, mownt éjkŭm
Mount Edgcumbe and Valletort,
Viscount, maʊnt 'edʒkəm ənd
'vælɪtɔrt, mownt éjkŭm ănd
válitort
Mountevans, Baron, maʊnt'evənz,
mowntévvănz
Mountfort, *f.n.*, 'maʊntfɔrt,
mówntfort; 'maʊntfərt, mównt-
fŏrt
Mountgarret, Viscount, maʊnt-
'gærɪt, mowntgárrĕt
Mountjoy, *f.n.*, maʊnt'dʒɔɪ,
mownt-jóy; 'maʊntdʒɔɪ,
mównt-joy

Mount Kedar *D. & G.*, maʊnt 'kidər, mownt keédăr
Mountpottinger *Co. Down*, maʊnt'pɒtɪndʒər, mownt- -póttinjĕr
Mount Sorrel *Wilts.*, maʊnt 'sɒrəl, mownt sórrĕl
Mourby, *f.n.*, 'mɔrbɪ, mórbi
Mourne Mountains *Co. Down*, mɔrn, morn
Mousa *Shetland*, 'muzə, moʻoză
Mousehold *Norfolk*, 'maʊshoʊld, mówss-hōld. *Appropriate also for* ~ *Heath.*
Mousehole *Cornwall*, 'maʊzl, mówzl
Mousley, *f.n.*, 'maʊslɪ, mówssli
Mouswald *D. & G.*, 'musl, moʻossl
Moutell, *f.n.*, moʊ'tel, mōtéll
Moverley, *f.n.*, 'moʊvərlɪ, móvĕrli
Movilla *Co. Down*, moʊ'vɪlə, mōvíllă
Mowat, *f.n.*, 'moʊət, mó-ăt; 'maʊət, mów-ăt
Mowbray, Segrave and Stourton, Baron, 'moʊbrɪ 'sigreɪv ənd 'stɜrtən, mốbri seégrayv ănd stúrtŏn
Mow Cop *Ches.–Staffs.*, 'maʊ 'kɒp, mów kóp
Mowden Hall *Darlington*, 'maʊdən, mówdĕn
Mower, *f.n.*, 'moʊər, mó-ĕr
Mowhan *Co. Armagh*, 'moʊən, mó-ăn
Mowlem, *f.n.*, 'moʊləm, mốlĕm
Mowling, *f.n.*, 'moʊlɪŋ, mốling
Mowll, *f.n.*, moʊl, mōl
Mowsley *Leics.*, 'maʊzlɪ, mówzli; 'moʊzlɪ, mốzli
Moya, *f.n.*, 'mɔɪə, móy-ă
Moyallon *Co. Down*, mɔɪ'ælən, moy-álŏn
Moyarget *Co. Antrim*, mɔɪ'ɑrgɪt, moy-aárgĕt
Moyers, *f.n.*, 'mɔɪərz, móyĕrz
Moyes, *f.n.*, mɔɪz, moyz
Moygashel *Co. Tyrone*, mɔɪ'gæʃl, moygáshl
Moyise, *f.n.*, 'mɔɪɪz, móy-iz
Moylena *Co. Antrim*, mɔɪ'linə, moyleénă
Moynahan, *f.n.*, 'mɔɪnəhən, móynă-hăn
Moynihan, Baron, 'mɔɪnɪən, móyni-ăn
Moyola *Co. Derry*, mɔɪ'oʊlə, moy-ốlă. *Appropriate also for* Baron ~.
Moys, *f.n.*, mɔɪz, moyz
Moyse, *f.n.*, mɔɪz, moyz
Moyses, *f.n.*, 'mɔɪzɪs, móyzĕss
Mozley, *f.n.*, 'moʊzlɪ, mốzli

Muchalls *Grampian*, 'mʌxlz, múchlz
Muchelney *Somerset*, 'mʌtʃəlnɪ, mútchĕlni
Muck *H'land*, mʌk, muck
Muckamore *Co. Antrim*, ˌmʌkə-'mɔr, muckămór
Muckle Flugga *Shetland*, 'mʌkl 'flʌgə, múckl flúggă
Muddiman, *f.n.*, 'mʌdɪmən, múddimăn
Mudeford *Dorset*, 'mʌdɪfərd, múddĕfŏrd
Mudell, *f.n.*, mə'del, mŭdéll
Mudie, *f.n.*, 'mjudɪ, méwdi
Mugdock Castle *S'clyde*, 'mʌgdɒk, múgdock
Muggerhanger *Beds.*, 'mʊər-hæŋər, moʻor-hang-ĕr
Muggeridge, *f.n.*, 'mʌgərɪdʒ, múggĕrij
Mugginton *Derby.*, 'mʌgɪntən, múggintŏn
Muggleswick *Durham*, 'mʌglzwɪk, múgglzwick
Muggoch, *f.n.*, 'mʌgəx, múggŏch
Mughan, *f.n.*, 'mjuhən, méw-hăn
Mugiemoss *Grampian*, 'mʌgɪmɒs, múggimoss
Mugliston, *f.n.*, 'mʌglɪstən, múgg-listŏn
Mugridge, *f.n.*, 'mʌgrɪdʒ, múgrij
Muick, Loch *and* River, *Grampian*, mɪk, mick
Muil, *f.n.*, mjul, mewl
Muill, *f.n.*, mjul, mewl
Muille, *f.n.*, mjul, mewl
Muinzer, *f.n.*, 'mʊnzər, moʻonzĕr
Muir, *f.n.*, mjʊər, myoʻor
Muirden, *f.n.*, mjʊər'den, myoʻor-dén
Muirhead, *f.n.*, 'mjʊərhed, myoʻor-hed
Muirhouses *Central*, 'mʌrɪz, múrriz
Muir of Ord *H'land*, 'mjʊər əv 'ɔrd, myoʻor ŏv órd
Muirshiel, Viscount, 'mjʊərʃil, myoʻor-sheel
Mukle, *f.n.*, 'mjuklɪ, méwkli
Mulbarton *Norfolk*, mʌl'bɑrtən, mulbaártŏn
Mulben *Grampian*, mʌl'ben, mul-bén
Mulcaghey, *f.n.*, mʌl'kæxɪ, mul-káchi
Mulcahy, *f.n.*, mʌl'kæhɪ, mulká-hi
Mulchrone, *f.n.*, mʌl'kroʊn, mulkrŏn
Mulcock, *f.n.*, 'mʌlkɒk, múlkock
Mulder, *f.n.*, 'mʌldər, múldĕr
Muldoon, *f.n.*, mʌl'dun, muldoʻon
Muldowney, *f.n.*, mʌl'daʊnɪ, muldówni

Mule, *f.n.*, mjul, mewl
Mulgrew, *f.n.*, mʌl'gru, mulgróo
Mulhall, *f.n.*, məl'hɔl, mŭl-háwl
Mulhare, *f.n.*, mʌl'hɛər, mul-háir
Mulhern, *f.n.*, mʌl'hɜrn, mul-hérn
Mulholland, *f.n.*, mʌl'hɒlənd, mul--hóllănd
Mull *S'clyde*, mʌl, mull. *Appropriate also for the Sound of* ∼.
Mullaghglass *Co. Armagh*, ˌmʌlə'glas, mullăgláass
Mullagh Ouyre *I. of Man*, 'mulək 'aʊər, moolǎck ówr
Mullally, *f.n.*, mʌ'lælɪ, mulláli
Mullaly, *f.n.*, mʌ'leɪlɪ, mulláyli
Mullan, *f.n.*, 'mʌlən, múllăn
Mullans, *f.n.*, 'mʌlənz, múllănz
Mullardoch, *Loch*, *H'land*, mʌ'lɑrdɒx, mullaárdoch
Mullen, *f.n.*, 'mʌlən, múllĕn
Muller, *f.n.*, 'mʌlər, múllĕr
Mulley, *f.n.*, 'mʌlɪ, múlli
Mulligan, *f.n.*, 'mʌlɪgən, múlligăn
Mullinar, *f.n.*, 'mʌlɪnər, múllinăr
Mulliner, *f.n.*, 'mʌlɪnər, múllinĕr
Mullineux, *f.n.*, 'mʌlɪnə, múllină
Mullins, *f.n.*, 'mʌlɪnz, múllinz
Mullion *Cornwall*, 'mʌlɪən, múlliŏn
Mullo, *f.n.*, 'mʌloʊ, múllō
Mull of Kintyre *S'clyde*, 'mʌl əv kɪn'taɪər, múll ŏv kintír
Mull of Oa *S'clyde*, 'mʌl əv 'oʊ, múll ŏv ố
Mullyard *Co. Antrim*, ˌmʌlɪ'ɑrd, mulli-aárd
Mulock, *f.n.*, 'mjulɒk, méwlock
Mulot, *f.n.*, 'mjuloʊ, méwlō
Mulrine, *f.n.*, mʌl'raɪn, mulrín
Mulso, *f.n.*, 'mʌlsoʊ, múlssō
Muncaster, *f.n.*, 'mʌŋkəstər, múnkăstĕr
Munda, saint, 'mʌndə, múndă
Munday, *f.n.*, 'mʌndeɪ, múnday
Mundesley *Norfolk*, 'mʌnzlɪ, múnzli
Mundford *Norfolk*, 'mʌndfərd, múndfŏrd
Mungean, *f.n.*, 'mʌndʒən, múnjăn
Mungo, *C.n.*, 'mʌŋgoʊ, múng-gō
Mungrisdale *Cumbria*, mʌŋ-'graɪzdeɪl, mung-grízdayl
Munnelly, *f.n.*, 'mʌnəlɪ, múnnĕli
Munns, *f.n.*, mʌnz, munnz
Munro, *f.n.*, mən'roʊ, mŭnrố; mʌn'roʊ, munrố
Munroe, *f.n.*, mən'roʊ, mŭnrố; mʌn'roʊ, munrố
Munrow, *f.n.*, 'mʌnroʊ, múnrō
Muntham Woods *W. Sussex*, 'mʌnθəm, múnthăm
Munthe, *f.n.*, 'mʌntɪ, múnti
Muraille, *f.n.*, mjuə'reɪl, myoōráyl
Murdin, *f.n.*, 'mɜrdɪn, múrdin

Murdoch, *f.n.*, 'mɜrdəx, múrdŏch; 'mɜrdɒk, múrdock
Mure, *f.n.*, mjuər, myoŏr
Murgett, *f.n.*, 'mɜrgɪt, múrgĕt
Murie, *f.n.*, 'mjuərɪ, myoŏri
Murless, *f.n.*, 'mɜrlɪs, múrlĕss
Murlough *Co. Down*, 'mɜrlɒx, múrloch
Murnaghan, *f.n.*, 'mɜrnəhən, múrnăhăn
Murphy, *f.n.*, 'mɜrfɪ, múrfi
Murrant, *f.n.*, 'mʌrənt, múrrănt
Murray, *f.n.*, 'mʌrɪ, múrri
Murrell, *f.n.*, 'mʌrəl, múrrĕl; mʌ'rel, murréll
Murricane, *f.n.*, 'mʌrɪkeɪn, múrrikayn
Murrill, *f.n.*, 'mʌrɪl, múrril
Murroes *Tayside*, 'mʌrouz, múrrōz; 'mɒrɪs, mórriss
Murrow *Cambs.*, 'mʌrə, múrră
Murtagh, *f.n.*, 'mɜrtə, múrtă
Murthly *Tayside*, 'mɜrθlɪ, múrthli
Murtle *Grampian*, 'mɜrtl, múrtl
Muschamp, *f.n.*, 'mʌskəm, músskăm
Musgrave, *f.n.*, 'mʌzgreɪv, múzzgrayv
Musidora Stakes, *horse-race*, ˌmjusɪ'dɔrə, mewssidáwră
Musselburgh *Lothian*, 'mʌslbərə, músslbŭră
Mussett, *f.n.*, 'mʌsɪt, mússĕt
Must, *f.n.*, mʌst, musst
Mustill, *f.n.*, 'mʌstɪl, músstil
Muthill *Tayside*, 'mjuθɪl, méw-thil
Mutley *Devon*, 'mʌtlɪ, múttli
Mutter, *f.n.*, 'mʌtər, múttĕr
Muybridge, Eadweard, *photographic pioneer*, 'edwərd 'maɪbrɪdʒ, édwărd míbrij
Myatt, *f.n.*, 'maɪət, mí-ăt
Mycock, *f.n.*, 'maɪkɒk, míkock; 'maɪkoʊ, míkō
Myddfai *Dyfed*, 'mʌðvaɪ, múthvī; 'mɪðvaɪ, míthvī
Myddleton, *f.n.*, 'mɪdltən, míddltŏn
Mydrim *Dyfed*, 'maɪdrɪm, mídrim
Myers, *f.n.*, 'maɪərz, mí-ĕrz
Myerscough, *f.n.*, 'maɪərskoʊ, mí-ĕrsskō; 'maɪərskɒf, mí-ĕrsskoff
Myerscough *Lancs.*, 'maɪərskoʊ, mí-ĕrsskō
Myfanwy, *Welsh C.n.*, mə'vænwɪ, mŭvánwi
Mylechreest, *f.n.*, 'mɪlkrist, míllkreest
Myles, *f.n.*, maɪlz, mīlz
Mylne, *f.n.*, mɪln, miln
Mylod, *f.n.*, 'maɪlɒd, mílod
Mylor *Cornwall*, 'maɪlər, mílŏr
Mylrea, *f.n.*, mɪl'reɪ, milráy

Mynachdy *Cardiff*, mə'nækdı, mŭnákdi

Mynett, *f.n.*, 'maınıt, mínĕt; maı'net, mīnétt

Mynors, *f.n.*, 'maınərz, mínŏrz

Mynott, *f.n.*, 'maınət, mínŏt

Mynyddcerrig *Dyfed*, ˌmʌnıð- 'kerıg, munnithkérrig

Mynyddislwyn *Gwent*, ˌmʌnıð- 'ısloın, munnithíssloō-in

Myrddin-Evans, Sir **Guildhaume** *international labour expert*, 'gıldoʊm 'mɜrðın 'evənz, gíldōm múrthin évvänz

Myroe *Co. Derry*, maı'roʊ, mīró

Mysliwiec, *f.n.*, mıʃ'lıvıes, mishleévi-ess

Mytchett *Surrey*, 'mıtʃıt, mítchĕt

Mytholm *W. Yorks.*, 'maıðəm, míthŏm

Mytholmroyd *W. Yorks.*, ˌmaıðəm'rɔıd, mīthŏmróyd

Mythop *Lancs.*, 'mıθɒp, míth-op

Myton *Warwicks.*, 'maıtən, mítŏn

Myton upon Swale *N. Yorks.*, 'maıtən əpɒn 'sweıl, mítŏn ŭpon swáyl

Mytton, *f.n.*, 'mıtən, míttŏn

N

Naan, *f.n.* nɑn, naan

Naar, *f.n.*, nɑr, naar

Naas, Baron, neıs, nayss

Nabarro, *f.n.*, nə'bɑroʊ, năbaárō

Naburn *N. Yorks.*, 'neıbərn, náy-bŭrn

Naden, *f.n.*, 'neıdən, náydĕn

Naesmith, *f.n.*, 'neısmıθ, náys-smith

Nagel, *f.n.*, 'neıgl, náygl; 'nɑgl, naágl

Nagele, *f.n.*, nə'gelı, năgélli

Nagington, *f.n.*, 'nægıŋtən, nág-gingtŏn

Nahum, *C.n.*, 'neıhəm, náy-hŭm

Naidoo, *f.n.*, 'naıdu, nídoo

Nairac, *f.n.*, 'nɛəræk, náirack

Nairn *H'land*, nɛərn, nairn

Nairne, Baroness, nɛərn, nairn

Naish, *f.n.*, neıʃ, naysh; næʃ, nash

Nalder, *f.n.*, 'nɔldər, náwldĕr

Nall, *f.n.*, nɔl, nawl

Nallen, *f.n.*, 'nælən, nálĕn

Nally, *f.n.*, 'nælı, náli

Nalty, *f.n.*, 'næltı, nálti

Namier, *f.n.*, 'neıˌmıər, náy-meer

Nancegollan *Cornwall*, ˌnænsı-'gɒlən, nanssĕgóllăn

Nancekivell, *f.n.*, næns'kıvl, nansskívvl; 'nænskıvl, nánss-kıvvl; ˌnænskı'vel, nansski-véll

Nancekuke *Cornwall*, næns'kjuk, nansskéwk

Nancledra *Cornwall*, næn'kledrə, nan-klédrä

Nanjizal Bay *Cornwall*, næn'dʒızl, nanjízzl

Nankeville, *f.n.*, 'næŋkıvıl, nánkĕvil

Nanmor, River, *Gwynedd*, 'næn-mɔr, nán-mor

Nannerch *Clwyd*, 'nænɛərx, nánnairch

Nantbwlch-yr-Haiarn *Gwynedd*, nænt'bʊlx ər 'haıərn, nant-boŏlch ŭr hí-ärn

Nantclwyd *Clwyd*, nænt'kluıd, nantkloō-id

Nantcwnlle *Dyfed*, nænt'kʊnɬeı, nantkoŏnlhay

Nant Eos *Dyfed*, nænt 'eıɒs, nant áy-oss

Nantffrancon *Gwynedd*, nænt-'fræŋkən, nantfránkŏn

Nantgaredig *Dyfed*, ˌnæntgə-'redıg, nantgăréddig

Nantgarw *Mid Glam.*, nænt'gæru, nantgárroo

Nantgwynant *Dyfed*, nænt-'gwınænt, nantgwínnant

Nantlle *Gwynedd*, 'næntɬeı, nánt--hlay

Nantmel *Powys*, 'næntmel, nánt-mel; 'nænt'meıl, nántmáyl

Nant Peris *Gwynedd*, nænt 'perıs, nant pérriss

Nantwich *Ches.*, 'næntwıtʃ, nánt-witch; 'næntwaıtʃ, nántwítch

Nant-y-bwch *Gwent*, ˌnæntə'bux, nantăboŏch

Nant-y-Bwch, River, *Powys*, ˌnæntə'bux, nantăboŏch

Nant-y-caws *Dyfed*, ˌnæntə'kaʊs, nantăkówss

Nantyffyllon *Mid Glam.*, ˌnæntə-'fʌɬɒn, nantăfúhlon

Nant-y-glo *Gwent*, ˌnæntə'gloʊ, nantăgló

Nant-y-groes *Gwent*, ˌnæntə'grɔıs, nantăgróyss

Nant-y-moel *Mid Glam.*, ˌnæntə-'mɔıl, nantămóyl

Nantyronen *Dyfed*, ˌnæntə-'roʊnən, nantărónĕn

Napier, *f.n.*, 'neıpjər, náyp-yĕr; nə'pıər, năpeér. *The first is appropriate for John ~, inventor of logarithms.*

Napier and Ettrick, Baron, 'neıpjər ənd 'etrık, náyp-yĕr ănd éttrick

Napier of Magdala, Baron, 'neɪpjər əv mæg'dɑlə, náyp-yĕr ŏv magdáalä
Napley, *f.n.*, 'næplɪ, nápli
Narberth *Dyfed*, 'nɑrbərθ, naár-bĕrth
Nares, *f.n.*, nɛərz, nairz
Naser, *f.n.*, 'neɪzər, náyzĕr
Nasmith, *f.n.*, 'neɪsmɪθ, náyssmith
Nason, *f.n.*, 'neɪsən, náyssŏn
Nasse, *f.n.*, 'næsɪ, nássi
Nassim, *f.n.*, nə'sim, nässeém
Nateley Scures *Hants*, 'neɪtlɪ 'skjʊərz, náytli skéw-ĕrz
Nathan, *f.n.*, 'neɪθən, náythăn. *Appropriate also for Baron ~.*
Natt, *f.n.*, næt, nat
Nattrass, *f.n.*, 'nætrəs, nátrăss
Naulls, *f.n.*, nɔlz, nawlz
Navan *Co. Armagh*, 'nævən, návvăn
Navar *Tayside*, 'neɪvər, náyvăr
Navenby *Lincs.*, 'neɪvənbɪ, náy-vĕnbi; 'nævənbɪ, návvĕnbi
Navin, *f.n.*, 'nævɪn, návvin
Navratil, *f.n.*, 'nævrətɪl, návrătil
Naworth *Cumbria*, 'naʊərθ, nów--ŭrth; 'nawərθ, naá-wŭrth
Naworth *Castle Cumbria*, 'nɑərθ, naá-ĕrth; nɑrθ, naarth
Naylor, *f.n.*, 'neɪlər, náylŏr
Nazeing *Essex*, 'neɪzɪŋ, náyzing
Neagh, Lough, *N. Ireland*, lɒx 'neɪ, loch náy
Neagle, *f.n.*, 'nigl, neégl
Neal, *C.n. and .fn.*, nil, neel
Neale, *f.n.*, nil, neel
Neaman, Yfrah, *violinist*, 'ifrə 'nimən, eéfră neémän
Nears, *f.n.*, nɪərz, neerz
Neary, *f.n.*, 'nɪərɪ, neéri
Neath *W. Glam.*, niθ, neeth
Neath, *River, Powys–W. Glam.*, niθ, neeth
Neatishead *Norfolk*, 'nitshed, neéts-hed; 'nitished,neétiss-hed; 'nitsted, neétsted. *The second is used by Service personnel for the local RAF Station. The third is the traditional local pronuncia-tion, rarely heard nowadays.*
Neave, *f.n.*, niv, neev
Neaverson, *f.n.*, 'nevərsən, névvĕrssŏn; 'nivərsən, neévĕrssŏn
Nebo *Dyfed, Gwynedd*, 'nebʊ, nébbŏ
Nechells *W. Midlands*, 'nitʃlz, neétchlz
Neden, *f.n.*, 'nidən, neédĕn
Needham, *f.n.*, 'nidəm, neédăm
Needingworth *Cambs.*, 'nidɪŋwərθ, neéding-wŏrth
Needle, *f.n.*, 'nidl, neédl

Neesham, *f.n.*, 'niʃəm, neé-shăm
Negus, *f.n.*, 'nigəs, neégŭss
Neidpath *Castle Borders*, 'nidpɑθ, neédpaath
Neild, *f.n.*, nild, neeld
Neilgrove, *f.n.*, 'nilgroʊv, neél-grōv
Neill, *f.n.*, nil, neel
Neilson, *f.n.*, 'nilsən, neélssŏn
Neivens, *f.n.*, 'nivənz, neévĕnz
Nelligan, *f.n.*, 'nelɪgən, nélligăn
Nelmes, *f.n.*, nelmz, nelmz
Nelson *Lancs., Mid Glam.*, 'nelsən, nélssŏn
Nemeer, *f.n.*, 'nemɪər, némmeer
Nendrum *Abbey Co. Down*, 'nendrʌm, néndrum
Nene, *River, Northants.–Cambs.–Norfolk–Lincs.*, nen, nen; nin, neen. *The first of these is used in the neighbourhood of Northampton; the second in the neighbour-hood of Peterborough and in Norfolk–Lincs.*
Nepean, *f.n.*, nɪ'pin, nĕpeén
Nercwys, *also spelt* **Nerquis,** *Clwyd*, 'neərkwɪs, náirkwiss; 'nɜrkwɪs, nérkwiss
Nesbitt, *f.n.*, 'nezbɪt, nézbit
Neslen, *f.n.*, 'nezlɪn, nézlĕn
Ness, *Loch and River, H'land*, nes, ness
Nessler, *f.n.*, 'neslər, néssler
Nethan, *River, S'clyde*, 'neθən, néthăn
Nether Alderley *Ches.*, 'neðər 'ɔldərlɪ, néthĕr áwldĕrli
Netheravon *Wilts.*, 'neðəreɪvən, néthĕrayvŏn
Nether Broughton *Leics.*, 'neðər 'brɔtən, néthĕr bráwtŏn
Nethercote *Warwicks.*, 'neðərkət, néthĕrkŏt
Nether Haugh *S. Yorks.*, 'neðər 'hɔf, néthĕr háwf
Nether Heage *Derby.*, 'neðər 'hidʒ, néthĕr heéj
Nether Heyford *Northants.*, 'neðər 'heɪfərd, néthĕr háyfŏrd
Nether Langwith *Notts.*, 'neðər 'læŋwɪθ, néthĕr láng-with
Nether Lypiatt *Glos.*, 'neðər 'lɪpɪət, néthĕr líppi-ăt
Netherne *Surrey*, 'neðərn, néthĕrn
Netherthorpe, Baron, 'neðərθɔrp, néthĕr-thorp
Nether Wallop *Hants*, 'neðər 'wɒləp, néthĕr wóllŏp
Nether Wasdale, *also spelt* **Netherwastdale,** *Cumbria*, 'neðər 'wɒsdl, néthĕr wóssdl. **Netherwastdale** *is the ecclesi-astical spelling.*

Nethy Bridge *H'land*, 'neθɪ
'brɪdʒ, néthi bríj
Nettel, *f.n.*, nə'tel, nĕtéll
Netteswell *Essex*, 'netswel,
nétswel
Nettheim, *f.n.*, 'nethaɪm, nét-hīm
Nettlecombe *Somerset*, 'netlkum,
néttlkoom
Nettleham *Lincs.*, 'netləm,
néttl-ăm
Nettleingham, *f.n.*, 'netlɪŋhəm,
néttling-hăm
Neubert, *f.n.*, 'njubərt, néwbĕrt
Neuss, *f.n.*, nɔɪs, noyss
Neustatter, *f.n.*, 'njustætər, néw-
stattĕr
Neve, *f.n.*, niv, neev
Neven, *f.n.*, 'nevən, névvĕn
Nevendon *Essex*, 'nevəndən,
névvĕndŏn
Nevern, *f.n.*, 'nevərn, névvĕrn
Neves, *f.n.*, nivz, neevz
Nevile, *C.n., and f.n.*, 'nevɪl,
névvil; 'nevl, névvl
Nevill, *C.n. and f.n.*, 'nevɪl,
névvil; 'nevl, névvl
Neville, *C.n. and f.n.*, 'nevɪl,
névvil; 'nevl, névvl
Nevin *Gwynedd*, 'nevɪn, névvin
Nevis, Loch, *H'land*, 'nevɪs,
névviss
Nevisburgh *H'land*, 'nevɪsbərə,
névvissbŭră
Newark *Cambs.*, 'njuərk, néwărk
Neway, *f.n.*, 'njuweɪ, néw-way
Newbegin, *f.n.*, 'njubɪgɪn, néw-
biggin
Newberry, *f.n.*, 'njubərɪ, néwbĕri
Newbert, *f.n.*, 'njubərt, néwbĕrt
Newbery, *f.n.*, 'njubərɪ, néwbĕri
Newbiggin-by-the-Sea *Northd.*,
'njubɪgɪn, néwbiggin
Newbigging, *f.n.*, 'njubɪgɪŋ, néw-
bigging; nju'bɪgɪŋ, newbígging
Newbigin, *f.n.*, 'njubɪgɪn, néw-
biggin
Newbold, *f.n.*, 'njubould, néw-
bōld
Newbolt, *f.n.*, 'njuboult, néwbōlt
Newborough *Cambs.*, *Gwynedd*,
'njubərə, néwbŭră
Newbould, *f.n.*, 'njubould, néw-
bōld
Newboult, *f.n.*, 'njuboult, néwbōlt
Newbrough *Northd.*, 'njubrʌf,
néwbruff
Newbury, *f.n.*, 'njubərɪ, néwbŭri
Newby, *f.n.*, 'njubɪ, néwbi
New Byth *Grampian*, 'nju 'baɪθ,
néw bíth
Newcastle Co. *Down*, *Gwent*, *Mid
Glam.*, 'njukɑsl, néwkaassl
Newcastle Emlyn *Dyfed*, 'njukɑsl
'emlɪn, néwkaassl émlin

Newcastleton *Borders*, nju-
'kɑsltən, newkaássltŏn
Newcastle-under-Lyme *Staffs.*,
'njukɑsl ʌndər 'laɪm, néwkaassl
undĕr līm
Newcastle upon Tyne *Tyne &
Wear*, 'njukɑsl əpɒn 'taɪn,
néwkaassl ŭpon tín; nju'kæsl
əpɒn 'taɪn, newkássl ŭpon tín.
*The second, being the local
pronunciation, should normally
take precedence over the other.
Here, however, is a case where
the first is firmly established
national usage.*
New Clipstone *Notts.*, 'nju
'klɪpstoun, néw klípstōn
Newcomen, Thomas, *inventor
(1663–1729)*, 'njukʌmən, néw-
kummĕn
Newcraighall *Lothian*, 'njukreɪg-
'hɔl, néw-krayg-háwl
New Cumnock *S'clyde*, 'nju
'kʌmnək, néw kúmnŏk
Newdigate, Sir Roger, *18th-c.
antiquary*, 'njudɪgeɪt, néwdi-
gayt; 'njudɪgɪt, néwdigit.
Hence also for the ~ *Prize for
English verse.*
Newell, *f.n.*, 'njuəl, néwĕl
Newens, *f.n.*, 'njuənz, néwĕnz
Newent *Glos.*, 'njuənt, néw-ĕnt
Newfound *Hants*, 'njufaund,
néwfownd
New Galloway *D. & G.*, nju
'gæləweɪ, new gálŏ-way
Newham *London*, 'njuəm, néw-
-ăm; 'nju'hæm, néw-hám
Newham *Northd.*, 'njuəm,
néw-ăm. *Appropriate for both
places of the name in North-
umberland.*
Newhaven *E. Sussex*, *Lothian*,
'njuheɪvən, néw-hayvĕn
New Houghton *Derby.*, 'nju
'hʌftən, néw húftŏn
Newill, *f.n.*, 'njuɪl, néw-il
Newington *Edinburgh*, 'njuɪŋtən,
néwingtŏn
New Kyo *Durham*, 'nju 'kaɪou,
néw kī-ō
Newlove, *f.n.*, 'njulʌv, néwluv
Newlyn *Cornwall*, 'njulɪn, néw-
lin
Newman, *f.n.*, 'njumən, néwmăn
Newmark, *f.n.*, 'njumɑrk, néw-
maark
Newmarket *Suffolk*, 'njumɑrkɪt,
néwmaarkĕt
Newmills *Gwent*, nju'mɪlz, new-
míllz
Newmilns *S'clyde*, nju'mɪlz,
newmíllz
Newnes, *f.n.*, njunz, newnz

New Pitsligo *Grampian*, 'nju
pɪt'slaɪgoʊ, néw pitslígō
Newport Pagnell *Bucks.*, 'njupɔrt
'pægnəl, néwport págnĕl
Newquay *Cornwall*, 'njuki,
néw-kee
New Quay *Dyfed* 'nju 'ki, néw
kée
Newrick, *f.n.*, 'njurɪk, néw-rick
New Romney *Kent*, 'nju 'rɒmnɪ,
néw rómni; 'nju 'rʌmnɪ, néw
rúmni
Newry *Co. Down*, 'njʊərɪ, nyóŏri
Newsham, *f.n.*, 'njuzəm, néwzăm
Newsome, *f.n.*, 'njusəm, néws-
sŏm
Newsome *W. Yorks.*, 'njuzəm,
néwzŏm
Newson, *f.n.*, 'njusən, néwssŏn
Newstone, *f.n.*, 'njustən, néws-
stŏn
Newth, *f.n.*, njuθ, newth
Newtimber *W. Sussex*, 'nju-
tɪmbər, néwtimbĕr
Newton, *f.n.*, 'njutən, néwtŏn
Newton Flotman *Norfolk*, 'njutən
'flɒtmən, néwtŏn flóttmăn
Newton Kyme *N. Yorks.*, 'njutən
'kaɪm, néwtŏn kím
Newton Mearns *S'clyde*, 'njutən
'mɛərnz, néwtŏn máirnz
Newtonmore *H'land*, 'njutən'mɔr,
néwtŏnmór
Newton Morrell *N. Yorks.*, *Oxon.*,
'njutən 'mɒrəl, néwtŏn mórrĕl
Newton Purcell *Oxon.*, 'njutən
'pərsl, néwtŏn púrssl
Newton Reigny *Cumbria*, 'njutən
'reɪnɪ, néwtŏn ráyni
Newton St. Cyres *Devon*, 'njutən
snt 'saɪərz, néwtŏn sĭnt sírz
Newton St. Loe *Avon*, 'njutən snt
'loʊ, néwtŏn sĭnt lṓ
Newtonstewart *D. & G.*,
'njutən'stjʊərt, néwtŏn-styóŏ-
-ărt
Newtownabbey *Co. Antrim*,
'njutən'æbɪ, néwtŏnábbi
Newtownards *Co. Down*, 'njutən-
'ɑrdz, néwtŏnaardz
Newtownbreda *Co. Down*, 'njutən-
'bridə, néwtŏnbreédă; 'njutən-
'breɪdə, néwtŏnbráydă
Newtownbutler *Co. Fermanagh*,
'njutən'bʌtlər, néwtŏnbúttlĕr
Newtown Crommelin *Co. Antrim*,
'njutən 'krʌmlɪn, néwtŏn krúmlin
Newtownhamilton *Co. Armagh*,
'njutən'hæmɪltən, néwtŏn-
-hámmiltŏn
Newtown St. Boswells *Borders*,
'njutən snt 'bɒzwəlz, néwtŏn
sĭnt bózwĕlz

Newydd *Powys*, 'newɪð, né-with
Neylan, *f.n.*, 'neɪlən, náylăn
Neyland *Dyfed*, 'neɪlənd, náy-
länd
Neyroud, *f.n.*, 'neɪrud, náy-rood
Niall, *C.n. and f.n.*, nil, neel;
'naɪəl, ní-ăl
Nian, *f.n.*, 'niən, neé-ăn
Nias, *f.n.*, 'naɪəs, ní-ăss
Niblo, *f.n.*, 'nɪbloʊ, níbblō
Nice, *f.n.*, nis, neess
Nicholls, *f.n.*, 'nɪklz, nícklz
Nicholson, *f.n.*, 'nɪklsən, níckls-
sŏn
Nickalls, *f.n.*, 'nɪklz, nícklz
Nickels, *f.n.*, 'nɪklz, nícklz
Nicklin, *f.n.*, 'nɪklɪn, níck-lin
Nickolls, *f.n.*, 'nɪklz, nícklz
Nicol, *C.n. and f.n.*, 'nɪkl, níckl
Nicoll, *f.n.*, 'nɪkl, níckl
Nicolson, *f.n.*, 'nɪklsən, níckls-
sŏn
Niddrie *Lothian*, 'nɪdrɪ, níddri
Niddry *Lothian*, 'nɪdrɪ, níddri
Nidon *Somerset*, 'naɪdən, nídŏn
Nield, *f.n.*, nild, neeld
Nieman, *f.n.*, 'naɪmən, nímăn;
'nimən, neémăn
Nieman, Alfred, *composer*,
'naɪmən, nímăn
Niemeyer, *f.n.*, 'nimaɪər, neémī-
-ĕr
Nifosi, *f.n.*, nɪ'foʊzɪ, nifózi
Nigel, *C.n. and f.n.*, 'naɪdʒl, níjl
Nighy, *f.n.*, naɪ, nī
Nihill, *f.n.*, 'naɪhɪl, níhil
Niklaus, *f.n.*, 'nɪkloʊ, nícklō
Nilsson, *f.n.*, 'nɪlsən, nílssŏn
Nimmie, *f.n.*, 'nɪmɪ, nímmi
Nimmo, *f.n.*, 'nɪmoʊ, nímmō
Nimmy, *f.n.*, 'nɪmɪ, nímmi
Nind, *f.n.*, nɪnd, ninnd; naɪnd,
nínd
Nineham, *f.n.*, 'naɪnəm, nínăm
Niner, *f.n.*, 'naɪnər, nínĕr
Nisbet, *f.n.*, 'nɪzbɪt, nízbĕt
Nisbett, *f.n.*, 'nɪzbɪt, nízbĕt
Nissel, *f.n.*, 'nɪsl, níssl
Nith, River, *S'clyde–D. & G.*,
nɪθ, nith
Nith, Thorthorwald and Ross,
Viscount, 'nɪθ tər'θɒrəld ənd
'rɒs, níth tŏr-thórrăld ănd róss
Niton *I. of Wight*, 'naɪtən, nítŏn
Nitshill *Glasgow*, 'nɪts'hɪl, níts-
-híll
Niven, *f.n.*, 'nɪvən, nívvĕn
Nivison, *f.n.*, 'nɪvɪsən, nívvissŏn
Nixon, *f.n.*, 'nɪksən, níckssŏn
Noakes, *f.n.*, noʊks, nōks
Nobel School, The, *Stevenage*
(*Herts.*), noʊ'bel, nōbéll
Nobes, *f.n.*, noʊbz, nōbz
Noblet, *f.n.*, 'nɒblɪt, nóbblĕt

Nolan, *f.n.*, 'noʊlən, nṓlăn
Nollekens, Joseph, *18th–19th-c.*
  sculptor, 'nɒlɪkənz, nóllĕkĕnz
Nolloth, *f.n.*, 'nɒləθ, nóllŏth.
  Appropriate also for the ∼
  professorship and scholarships at
  the Univ. of Oxford.
Nonely *Salop*, 'nʌnəlɪ, núnnĕli
Nonington *Kent*, 'nɒnɪŋtən,
  nónningtŏn; 'nʌnɪŋtən, nún-
  ningtŏn
Nonsuch Palace *Surrey*, 'nʌnsʌtʃ,
  nún-sutch; 'nɒnsʌtʃ, nón-sutch.
  The first is usual among scholars.
  Locally, however, at **Nonsuch**
  Park, *the site of the original*
  Tudor palace, the second is
  current today.
Nonsuch Park *Surrey*, 'nɒnsʌtʃ,
  nón-sutch
Nont Sarah's *W. Yorks.*, 'nɒnt
  'sɛərəz, nónt sáirăz
Nonweiler, *f.n.*, 'nɒnwilər, nón-
  weelĕr
Noormohammed, *f.n.*, ,nuərmə-
  'hæmɪd, nŏŏrmŏ-hámmĕd
Norbury, *f.n.*, 'nɔrbərɪ, nórbŭri
Nordelph *Norfolk*, 'nɔrdelf,
  nórdelf
Nore, The, *Thames Estuary*, nɔr,
  nor
Norfolk *Co. name*, 'nɔrfək, nórfŏk.
  Appropriate also for the Duke
  of ∼.
Norglen *Belfast*, 'nɔr'glen, nór-
  glénn
Norham *Northd.*, 'nɒrəm, nórr-
  ăm
Norie, *f.n.*, 'nɒrɪ, nórri
Norledge, *f.n.*, 'nɔrlɪdʒ, nórlĕj
Normanbrook, Barony of,
  'nɔrmənbrʊk, nórmănbrŏŏk
Normansell, *f.n.*, 'nɔrmənsl,
  nórmănssl
Normanton, *f.n.*, 'nɔrməntən,
  nórmăntŏn
Norquoy, *f.n.*, 'nɔrkɪ, nórki
Norreys, Baron, 'nɒrɪs, nórriss
Norris, *f.n.*, 'nɒrɪs, nórriss
Northall, *f.n.*, 'nɔrθɔl, nórthawl
Northam, *f.n.*, 'nɔrðəm, nórth̲ăm
Northampton *Northants.*, nɔr-
  'θæmptən, northámptŏn;
  nɔrθ'hæmptən, north-hámptŏn.
  The first is appropriate for the
  Marquess of ∼.
North Baddesley *Hants*, 'nɔrθ
  'bædzlɪ, nórth bádzli
Northbourne, Baron, 'nɔrθbərn,
  nórthbŭrn
North Bradley *Wilts.*, 'nɔrθ
  'brædlɪ, nórth brádli
Northcliffe, *f.n.*, 'nɔrθklɪf, nórth-
  kliff

Northcote, *f.n.*, 'nɔrθkət, nórth-
  kŏt; 'nɔrθkɒt, nórth-kott
North Elmham *Norfolk*, 'nɔrθ
  'elməm, nórth élmăm
Northenden *Gtr. M'chester*,
  'nɔrðəndən, nórth̲ĕndĕn
Northesk, Earl of, nɔrθ'esk,
  northésk
North Holmwood *Surrey*, 'nɔrθ
  'hoʊmwʊd, nórth hṓm-wŏŏd
North Hykeham *Lincs.*, 'nɔrθ
  'haɪkəm, nórth híkăm
Northiam *E. Sussex*, 'nɔrðɪəm,
  nór̲th̲iăm
Northill *Beds.*, 'nɔrθhɪl, nórth-hil
Northleigh *nr. Colyton (Devon)*,
  'nɔrθli, nórthlee
Northleigh *nr. Goodleigh (Devon)*,
  'nɔrθli, nórthlee; 'nɔrli, nórlee
North Leigh *Oxon.*, 'nɔrθ 'li
  nórth lee
North Leverton *Notts.*, 'nɔrθ
  'levərtən, nórth lévvĕrtŏn
North Marden *W. Sussex*, 'nɔrθ
  'mɑrdən, nórth maárdĕn
Northmaven *Shetland*, nɔrθ-
  'meɪvən, northmáyvĕn
Northolme *Lincs.*, 'nɔrθoʊm,
  nór-thōm
Northowram *W. Yorks.*, nər-
  'θaʊərəm, nŏr-thówrăm
Northrepps *Norfolk*, 'nɔrθreps,
  nórthreps
North Ronaldsay *Orkney*, 'nɔrθ
  'rɒnldseɪ, nórth rónnld-say;
  'nɔrθ 'rɒnldʃeɪ, nórth rónnld-
  -shay
Northsceugh *Cumbria*, 'nɔrθ-
  skjuf, nórth-skewf
North Shields *Tyne & Wear*,
  'nɔrθ 'ʃildz, nórth sheeldz
North Tawton *Devon*, 'nɔrθ 'tɔtən,
  nórth táwtŏn
Northumberland *Co. name*,
  nɔr'θʌmbərlənd, northúmbĕr-
  lănd
Northumbrian, *pertaining to*
  Northumberland, nɔr'θʌmbrɪən,
  northúmbriăn
North Walsham *Norfolk*, 'nɔrθ
  'wɔlʃəm, nórth wáwl-shăm
North Waltham *Hants*, 'nɔrθ
  'wɔlθəm, nórth wáwl-thăm
Northwich *Ches.*, 'nɔrθwɪtʃ,
  nórth-witch
Norton Hawkfield *Avon*, 'nɔrtən
  'hɔkfild, nórtŏn háwkfeeld
Norwell *Notts.*, 'nɒrəl, nórrĕl
Norwell Woodhouse *Notts.*,
  'nɒrəl 'wʊdhaʊs, nórrĕl wŏŏd-
  -howss
Norwich *Norfolk*, 'nɒrɪdʒ, nórrij;
  'nɒrɪtʃ, nórritch. *The first is*
  appropriate for Viscount ∼.

O

Norwick *Shetland*, 'nɔrwɪk, nórwick

Norwood, *f.n.*, 'nɔrwʊd, nórwōōd

Nostell Priory *W. Yorks.*, 'nɒstl, nóstl

Nosworthy, *f.n.*, 'nɒzwɜrðɪ, nózwur<u>th</u>i

Notariello, *f.n.*, ‚noʊtɑrɪ'eloʊ, nōtaari-éllō

Nothe Promontory, The, *Dorset*, noʊð, nō<u>th</u>

Notley, *f.n.*, 'nɒtlɪ, nóttli

Nott, *f.n.*, nɒt, nott

Nottingham *Notts.*, 'nɒtɪŋəm, nótting-äm

Noup Head *Orkney*, 'nup 'hed, noóp hédd

Novar *H'land*, noʊ'vɑr, nōvaár

Novar Toll *H'land*, noʊ'var 'toʊl, nōvaár tốl

Nove, *f.n.*, noʊv, nōv

Novello, *f.n.*, nə'veloʊ, nŏvéllō

Novis, *f.n.*, 'noʊvɪs, nŏviss

Novocastrian, *native of* **Newcastle upon Tyne,** ‚noʊvoʊ-'kæstrɪən, nōvōkásstriän

Nowell, *f.n.*, 'noʊəl, nŏ-ĕl

Nowlin, *f.n.*, 'noʊlɪn, nŏlin

Nowton *Suffolk*, 'noʊtən, nŏtŏn

Nudd, *f.n.*, nʌd, nudd

Nugee, *f.n.*, 'nudʒi, noŏjee

Nugent, *f.n.*, 'njudʒənt, néwjĕnt. *Appropriate also for Baron ~ of Guildford.*

Nunan, *f.n.*, 'njunən, néwnän

Nunburnholme, Baron, nʌn-'bɜrnəm, nunbúrnŏm

Nuneaton *Warwicks.*, nʌn'itən, nuneétŏn

Nuneham Courtenay *Oxon.*, 'njunəm 'kɔrtnɪ, néwnäm kórtni

Nunney *Avon*, 'nʌnɪ, núnni

Nunns, *f.n.*, nʌnz, nunnz

Nunwick *N. Yorks.*, 'nʌnɪk, núnnick

Nupen, *f.n.*, 'njupən, néwpĕn

Nuthall, *f.n.*, 'nʌtɔl, núttawl

Nuthall *Notts.*, 'nʌtl, núttl

Nuthampstead *Herts.*, 'nʌtəmsted, núttämsted

Nuttall, *f.n.*, 'nʌtɔl, núttawl

Nuttgens, *f.n.*, 'nʌtdʒənz, nútjĕnz; 'nʌtʃənz, nútchĕnz

Nygaard, *f.n.*, 'naɪgɑrd, nígaard

Nyholm, *f.n.*, 'naɪhoʊm, ní-hōm

Nymans *W. Sussex*, 'naɪmənz, nímänz

Nymet Rowland *Devon*, 'nɪmɪt 'roʊlənd, nímmĕt rŏländ

Nymet Tracey *Devon*, 'nɪmɪt 'treɪsɪ, nímmĕt tráyssi

Oa *S'clyde*, oʊ, ō

Oadby *Leics.*, 'oʊdbɪ, ŏdbi

Oakenclough *Lancs.*, 'oʊkənklju, ŏkĕn-klew; 'oʊkənklaʊ, ŏkĕn-klow; 'oʊkənklʌf, ŏkĕn-kluff

Oaksey, Baron, 'oʊksɪ, ŏksi

Oaten, *f.n.*, 'oʊtən, ŏtĕn

Oates, *f.n.*, oʊts, ōts

Oath *Somerset*, oʊð, ō<u>th</u>

Oaze Deep *Thames Estuary*, 'oʊz 'dip, ŏz deép

Oban *S'clyde*, 'oʊbən, ŏbän

Obbard, *f.n.*, 'oʊbɑrd, ŏbaard

O'Brien, *f.n.*, oʊ'braɪən, ōbrí-ĕn

Oby *Norfolk*, 'oʊbɪ, ŏbi

O'Callaghan, *f.n.*, oʊ'kæləhən, ōkálä-hän; oʊ'kæləgən, ōkálägän

O'Cathain, *f.n.*, ‚oʊkə'hɔɪn, ō-kä-hóyn

Ochil Hills *Central–Tayside*, 'oʊxl, ŏ<u>ch</u>l

Ochiltree *S'clyde*, 'ɒxɪltri, ó<u>ch</u>iltree; 'ɒxltri, ó<u>ch</u>ltree. *Appropriate also for ~ Castle.*

Ochs, *f.n.*, ɒks, ocks

Ochterlony, *f.n.*, ‚ɒxtər'loʊnɪ, o<u>ch</u>tĕrlŏni

Ocklynge *E. Sussex*, 'ɒklɪndʒ, ócklinj

Ockrent, *f.n.*, 'ɒkrənt, óckrĕnt

O'Clarey, *f.n.*, oʊ'klɛərɪ, ōkláiri

O'Clee, *f.n.*, oʊ'kli, ōkleé

Ocle Pychard *H. & W.*, 'oʊkl 'pɪtʃərd, ŏkl pítchärd

O'Connor, *f.n.*, oʊ'kɒnər, ōkónnŏr

Odam, *f.n.*, 'oʊdəm, ŏdäm

O'Dea, *f.n.*, oʊ'di, ōdeé; oʊ'deɪ, ōdáy

Odell *Beds.*, 'oʊdl, ŏdl

Odey, *f.n.*, 'oʊdɪ, ŏdi

Odham, *f.n.*, 'ɒdəm, óddäm

Odhams Press *publishers*, 'ɒdəmz, óddämz

Odiham *Hants*, 'oʊdɪəm, ŏdi-äm

Odlum, *f.n.*, 'ɒdləm, óddlüm

O'Doherty, *f.n.*, oʊ'dɒxərtɪ, ōdó<u>ch</u>ĕrti

Odom, *f.n.*, 'oʊdɒm, ŏdom

O'Donell, *f.n.*, oʊ'dɒnl, ōdónnl

O'Donovan, *f.n.*, oʊ'dʌnəvən, ōdúnnŏvän

O'Dowda, *f.n.*, oʊ'daʊdə, ōdówdä

Odsal *W. Yorks.*, 'ɒdzl, óddzl

Oertling, *f.n.*, 'ɜrtlɪŋ, értling

Oettle, *f.n.*, 'oʊtl, ŏtl

Oetzmann, *f.n.*, 'oʊtsmən, ŏtsmän

O'Ferrall, *f.n.*, oʊ'færəl, ōfárrĕl

Offaly, Earl of, 'ɒfəlɪ, óffäli

Offenbach, *f.n.*, 'ɒfənbak, óffén-
baak

Offord Cluny *Cambs.*, 'ɒfərd
'kluni, óffŏrd klóoni

Offord D'Arcy, *also spelt* **Offord
Darcy,** *Cambs.*, 'ɒfərd 'dɑrsi,
óffŏrd daárssi

O'Flaherty, *f.n.*, ouˈflɑhərti,
ōflaʹa-hĕrti; ouˈflɑərti, ōflaʹa-ĕrti

O'Gara, *f.n.*, ouˈgɑrə, ōgaʹarǎ

Ogg, *f.n.*, ɒg, ogg

Oghill *Co. Derry*, 'ɒxil, óchil

Ogilvie, *f.n.*, 'ouglvi, óglvi

Ogilvy, *f.n.*, 'ouglvi, óglvi

Ogley, *f.n.*, 'ɒgli, óggli

Ogley Locks *Staffs.*, 'ɒgli, óggli

Ogmore *Mid Glam.*, 'ɒgmɔr,
ógmor

Ogof Ffynnonddu *W. Glam.*,
'ougɒv ˌfʌnənˈ ði, ógov funnŏn-
-theé

O'Grady, *f.n.*, ouˈgreidi, ōgráydi

Ogwell *Devon*, 'ougwel, ógwel

Ogwen, Lake *and* River,
Gwynedd, 'ɒgwen, ógwen

O'Hagan, *f.n.*, ouˈheigən, ō-
-háygăn

O'Halloran, *f.n.*, ouˈhælərən,
ō-hálŏrăn

O'Hana, *f.n.*, ouˈhænə, ō-hánnǎ

O'Hare, *f.n.*, ouˈheər, ō-háir

O'Hear, *f.n.*, ouˈheər, ō-háir

O'Herlihi, *f.n.*, ouˈhərlihi, ō-
-hérli-hi

O'Keefe, *f.n.*, ouˈkif, ōkeéf

O'Keeffe, *f.n.*, ouˈkif, ōkeéf

Okeford Fitzpaine *Dorset*, 'ouk-
fərd fitsˈpein, ókfŏrd fitspáyn.
A local version is 'fipəni 'ɒkfərd,
fíppĕni óckfŏrd.

Okehampton *Devon*, oukˈhæmp-
tən, ōk-hámptŏn

Okell, *f.n.*, 'oukl, ókl

Okeover, *f.n.*, 'oukouvər, ókŏvĕr

Olantigh Towers *Kent*, 'ɒlənti
'tauərz, óllănti tówĕrz

Olave, *C.n.*, 'ɒliv, ólliv

Olchfa *Swansea*, ɒlxˈva, olch-vaʹa

Oldbury-on-Severn *Glos.*,
'ouldbəri ɒn 'sevərn, óldbŭri on
sévvĕrn

Olderfleet *Co. Antrim*, 'ouldər-
flit, óldĕrfleet

Oldhamstocks *Lothian*, ould-
'hæmstɒks, ōld-hámstocks

Olding, *f.n.*, 'ouldiŋ, ólding

Old Man of Storr *Skye*, 'ould
' mæn əv 'stɔr, óld mán ŏv
stór

Old Meldrum *Grampian*, 'ould
'meldrəm, óld méldrŭm

Oldpark *Salop*, 'ouldpɑrk, óld-
paark

Old Romney *Kent*, 'ould 'rɒmni,

óld rómni; 'ould 'rʌmni, óld
rúmni

Old Steine, The, *Brighton*, 'ould
'stin, óld steén

Old Swinford, *also spelt* **Old-
swinford,** *W. Midlands*, 'ould
'swinfərd, óld swinfŏrd

Oldys, William, *17th-c. antiquar-
ian & bibliographer*, ouldz, ōldz

O'Leary, *f.n.*, ouˈliəri, ōleéri

Olender, *f.n.*, əˈlendər, ólĕndĕr

Olerenshaw, *f.n.*, ˌɒləˈrenʃɔ,
ollĕrénshaw

Olivere, *f.n.*, ˌɒliˈviər, ollivéer

Olivier, *f.n.*, əˈliviei, ólívvi-ay;
ɒˈliviər, ollívvi-ĕr. *The first is
appropriate for Baron* ∼, *otherwise Sir Laurence* ∼, *actor.*

Ollerenshaw, *f.n.*, ˌɒləˈrenʃɔ,
ollĕrénshaw; 'ɒlərənʃɔ, óllĕrĕn-
-shaw

Olliffe, *f.n.*, 'ɒlif, ólliff

Ollivant, *f.n.*, 'ɒlivənt, óllivănt

Oliver Duchet watch tower
Richmond (*N. Yorks.*), 'ɒlivər
'dʌkit, óllivĕr dúckĕt

O'Loghlen, *f.n.*, ouˈlɒxlən,
ōlóchlĕn

O'Loughlin, *f.n.*, ouˈlɒxlin,
ōlóchlin

Olrig *H'land*, 'ɒlrig, ólrig

Olsen, *f.n.*, 'oulsən, ŏlssĕn

Olsson, *f.n.*, 'oulsən, ŏlssŏn

Olton *W. Midlands*, 'oultən, ŏltŏn

Olumide, *C.n.*, ɒˈlumidei,
olóomidday

Olver, *f.n.*, 'ɒlvər, ólvĕr

Olveston *Avon*, 'oulvistən,
ŏlvĕsstŏn; 'oulstən, ŏlsstŏn

Omagh *Co. Tyrone*, 'oumə, ŏmă

O'Malley, *f.n.*, ouˈmæli, ōmáli;
ou'meili, ōmáyli

Oman, *f.n.*, 'oumən, ŏmăn

Omand, *f.n.*, 'oumənd, ŏmănd

O'Mara, *f.n.*, ouˈmɑrə, ōmaʹarǎ

Ombersley *H. & W.*, 'ɒmbərzli,
ómbĕrzli

O'Meara, *f.n.*, ouˈmɑrə, ōmaʹarǎ;
ouˈmeərə, ōmáirǎ

Ommanney, *f.n.*, 'ɒməni, ómmăni

Omoa *S'clyde*, ouˈmouə, ōmŏ-ǎ

Onchan *I. of Man*, 'ɒŋkən, ónkăn

Onecote *Staffs.*, 'ɒnkət, ón-kŏt

O'Neill, *f.n.*, ouˈnil, ōneél

Ongar *Essex*, 'ɒŋgər, óng-găr

Onibury *Salop*, 'ɒnibəri, ónnibŭri

Onich *H'land*, 'ounix, óni ch

Onions, *f.n.*, ˈʌnjənz, ún-yŏnz;
ouˈnaiənz, ōnī-ŏnz; əˈnaiənz,
ŏnī-ŏnz. *The first is appropriate
for C. T.* ∼, *philologist, gram-
marian and an editor of the
Oxford English Dictionary*; *also
for Oliver* ∼, *author.*

Onllwyn *W. Glam.*, 'ɒnɫʊɪn, ónhlōō-in
Onny, River, *Salop*, 'ɒnɪ, ónni
Onslow, *f.n.*, 'ɒnzlou, ónzlō. *Appropriate also for the Earl of* ∼.
Oonagh, *C.n.*, 'unə, óonǎ
Oosterhuis, *f.n.*, 'oustərhaʊs, ṓstĕr-howss
Openshaw, *f.n.*, 'oʊpənʃɔ, ṓpĕn-shaw
Openshaw *Gtr. M'chester*, 'oʊpənʃɔ, ṓpĕn-shaw
Opie, *f.n.*, 'oʊpɪ, ṓpi
Oppenheim, *f.n.*, 'ɒpənhaɪm, óppĕn-hīm
Orage, *f.n.*, ɔ'rɑʒ, awrá͡azh
Oram, *f.n.*, 'ɔrəm, áwrăm
Oranmore and Browne, Baron, 'ɒrənmɔr ənd 'braʊn, órrănmor ănd brówn
Orbach, *f.n.*, 'ɔrbæk, órback
Orcadian, *native of the* **Orkney** *Islands*, ɔr'keɪdɪən, orkáydiăn
Orchy *see* **Bridge of Orchy**
Orczy, Baroness, *author*, 'ɔrtsɪ, órtsi
Orda, *f.n.*, 'ɔrdə, órdǎ
Orde-Powlett, *f.n.*, 'ɔrd 'pɔlɪt, órd páwlĕt. *Family name of Baron Bolton.*
Ordiquhill *Grampian*, ˌɔrdɪ'hwɪl, ordi-whill
O'Reilly, *f.n.*, oʊ'raɪlɪ, ō-ríli
Oreston *Devon*, ə'restən, ŏrésstŏn
Orfordness *Suffolk*, 'ɔrfərd'nes, órfŏrdnéss
Organe, *f.n.*, ɔr'geɪn, orgáyn
Orgel, *f.n.*, 'ɔrgl, órgl
Orgelist, *f.n.*, 'ɔrdʒəlɪst, órjĕlist
Orgreave *S. Yorks.*, 'ɔrgriv, órgreev
Oriel, *f.n.*, 'ɔrɪəl, áwri-ĕl
Oriel, Baron, 'ɔrɪəl, áwri-ĕl
Oritor *Co. Tyrone*, 'ɒrɪtər, órritŏr
Orkney Islands, 'ɔrknɪ, órkni. *Appropriate also for the Earl of* ∼.
Orlebar, *f.n.*, 'ɔrlɪbɑr, órlĕbaar
Orlestone *Kent*, 'ɔrlstən, órlsstŏn
Orleton *H. & W.*, 'ɔrltən, órltŏn
Orlock *Co. Down*, 'ɔrlɒk, órlock
Ormathwaite, Baron, 'ɔrməθweɪt, órmăthwayt
Ormeau *Belfast*, ɔr'moʊ, ormṓ
Ormelie, *f.n.*, 'ɔrməlɪ, órmĕli
Ormerod, *f.n.*, 'ɔrmrɒd, órmrod; 'ɔrmərɒd, órmĕrod
Ormiston, *f.n.*, 'ɔrmɪstən, órmis-stŏn
Ormiston *Lothian*, 'ɔrmɪstən, órmisstŏn
Ormonde, Marquess of, 'ɔrmənd, órmŏnd

Ormonde, *f.n.*, 'ɔrmənd, órmŏnd
Ormrod, *f.n.*, 'ɔrmrɒd, órmrod
Ormsby-Gore, *f.n.*, 'ɔrmzbɪ 'gɔr, órmzbi gór
Ornadel, *f.n.*, 'ɔrnədel, órnădel
Ornbo, *f.n.*, 'ɔrnboʊ, órnbō
O'Rorke, *f.n.*, oʊ'rɔrk, ō-rórk
O'Rourke, *f.n.*, oʊ'rɔrk, ō-rórk
Orpin, *f.n.*, 'ɔrpɪn, órpin
Orpington *London*, 'ɔrpɪŋtən, órpingtŏn
Orr, *f.n.*, ɔr, or
Orrick, *f.n.*, 'ɒrɪk, órrick
Orridge, *f.n.*, 'ɒrɪdʒ, órrij
Orton Longueville *Cambs.*, 'ɔrtən 'lɒŋvɪl, órtŏn lóng-vil
Ortzen, *f.n.*, 'ɔrtsən, órtsĕn
Osbaldeston *Lancs.*, ˌɒzbəl'destən, ozbăldésstŏn
Osborn, *f.n.*, 'ɒzbɔrn, ózborn; 'ɒzbərn, ózbŭrn
Osborne, *f.n.*, 'ɒzbɔrn, ózborn; 'ɒzbərn, ózbŭrn
Osbourne, *f.n.*, 'ɒzbɔrn, ózborn; 'ɒzbərn, ózbŭrn
Osea Island *Essex*, 'oʊzɪ, ṓzi; 'oʊsɪ, ṓssi
Osers, *f.n.*, 'oʊzərz, ṓzĕrz
Osgerby, *f.n.*, 'ɒzgərbɪ, ózgĕrbi
O'Shagar, *f.n.*, oʊ'ʃagər, ō-sháagăr
O'Shaughnessy, *f.n.*, oʊ'ʃɒnəsɪ, ō-sháwnĕssi
O'Shea, *f.n.*, oʊ'ʃeɪ, ō-sháy; oʊ'ʃi, ō-shée
Osland, *f.n.*, 'ɒzlənd, ózzlănd
Osler, *f.n.*, 'oʊslər, ṓsslĕr; 'ɒslər, ósslĕr; 'ɒzlər, ózlĕr
Osmaston *Derby.*, 'ɒzməstən, ózmăsstŏn
Osney *Oxon.*, 'oʊznɪ, ṓzni
Osoba, *f.n.*, oʊ'soʊbə, ōsṓbǎ
Ospringe *Kent*, 'ɒsprɪndʒ, óssprinj
Ossett *W. Yorks.*, 'ɒsɪt, óssĕt
Ostle, *f.n.*, 'ɒstl, óstl
Ostler, *f.n.*, 'oʊstlər, ṓstlĕr
Oswaldestre, Baron, 'ɒzwəldestər, ózwăldésstĕr
Oswaldtwistle *Lancs.*, 'ɒzwəldtwɪsl, ózwăld-twissl; 'ɒzltwɪsl, ózzl-twissl
Oswestry *Salop*, 'ɒzwəstrɪ, ózwĕstri
Otham *Kent*, 'ɒtəm, óttăm
Othery *Somerset*, 'oʊðərɪ, ṓthĕri
Othick, *f.n.*, 'ɒθɪk, óthick
Otley, *f.n.*, 'ɒtlɪ, óttli
Otley *W. Yorks.*, 'ɒtlɪ, óttli
Otterham *Cornwall*, 'ɒtərəm, óttĕrăm
Ottery St. Mary *Devon*, 'ɒtərɪ snt 'mɛərɪ, óttĕri sĭnt máiri
Ottinge *Kent*, 'ɒtɪndʒ, óttinj

Ottolangui, *f.n.,* ˌɒtoʊˈlæŋgwɪ, ottōláng-gwi

Ottoline, *C.n.,* ˈɒtəlɪn, óttŏleen

Ottoway, *f.n.,* ˈɒtəweɪ, óttŏ-way

Otway, *f.n.,* ˈɒtweɪ, óttway

Oudot, *f.n.,* ˈudoʊ, oʹodō

Ough, *f.n.,* oʊ, ō

Ougham, *f.n.,* ˈɔəm, áw-ăm

Oughtershaw *N. Yorks.,* ˈaʊtərʃɔ, ówtĕr-shaw

Oughterside *Cumbria,* ˈaʊtərsaɪd, ówtĕrssīd

Oughtibridge *S. Yorks.,* ˈutɪbrɪdʒ, oʹotibrij; ˈaʊtɪbrɪdʒ, ówtibrij; ˈɔtɪbrɪdʒ, áwtibrij; ˈoʊtɪbrɪdʒ, oʹotibrij; ˈɔtibrij

Oughton, *f.n.,* ˈaʊtən, ówtŏn; ˈɔtən, áwtŏn

Oughton, River, *Herts.,* ˈɔtən, áwtŏn

Oughtrington *Ches.,* ˈutrɪŋtən, oʹotringtŏn

Ouin, *f.n.,* ˈoʊɪn, ő-in

Ould, *f.n.,* oʊld, ōld; uld, oold

Ouless, *f.n.,* ˈulɪs, oʹolĕss

Oulton, *f.n.,* ˈoʊltən, őltŏn

Oulton *Staffs., Suffolk, W. Yorks.,* ˈoʊltən, őltŏn

Oulton Broad *Suffolk,* ˈoʊltən ˈbrɔd, őltŏn bráwd

Oulton Park *Ches.,* ˈoʊltən ˈpɑrk, őltŏn páark

Oundle *Northants.,* ˈaʊndl, ówndl

Oury, *f.n.,* ˈurɪ, oʹo-ri; ˈʊərɪ, oʹori

Ousby *Cumbria,* ˈuzbɪ, oʹozbi

Ousdale *H'land,* ˈaʊzdeɪl, ówzdayl

Ousden, *also spelt* **Owsden,** *Suffolk,* ˈaʊzdən, ówzdĕn

Ouseley, *f.n.,* ˈuzlɪ, oʹozli

Ousey, *f.n.,* ˈuzɪ, oʹozi

Ousley, *f.n.,* ˈuzlɪ, oʹozli

Ousman, *f.n.,* ˈuzmən, oʹozmăn

Ouston, *f.n.,* ˈaʊstən, ówsstŏn

Ouston *Durham,* ˈaʊstən, ówsstŏn

Outen, *f.n.,* ˈaʊtən, ówtĕn

Outhwaite, *f.n.,* ˈaʊθweɪt, ówthwayt; ˈoʊθweɪt, őthwayt; ˈuθweɪt, oʹothwayt

Outlane *W. Yorks.,* ˈaʊtleɪn, ówtlayn

Outram, *f.n.,* ˈutrəm, oʹotrăm; ˈaʊtrəm, ówtrăm. *The first is appropriate for George ~ & Co., newspaper publishers, the second for Benjamin ~, canal designer (1764–1805).*

Outred, *f.n.,* ˈutred, oʹotred; ˈaʊtred, ówtred

Outstack, The, *Shetland,* ˈaʊtstæk, ówt-stack

Ouvry, *f.n.,* ˈuvrɪ, oʹovri

Oved, *f.n.,* oʊˈved, ōvéd

Ovenden, *f.n.,* ˈɒvəndən, óvvĕndĕn; ˈoʊvəndən, ővĕndĕn

Ovenden *W. Yorks.,* ˈɒvəndən, óvvĕndĕn

Ovens, *f.n.,* ˈʌvənz, úvvĕnz

Over *Cambs., Ches.,* ˈoʊvər, ővĕr

Over *Glos.,* ˈuvər, oʹovĕr

Over Alderley *Ches.,* ˈoʊvər ˈɔldərlɪ, ővĕr áwldĕrli

Overcombe *Dorset,* ˈoʊvərkum, ővĕrkoom

Overend, *f.n.,* ˈoʊvərend, ővĕrend

Overstone *Northants.,* ˈoʊvərstən, ővĕrstŏn

Overton, *f.n.,* ˈoʊvərtən, ővĕrtŏn

Overton *Ches., Clwyd, Hants, W. Glam.,* ˈoʊvərtən, ővĕrtŏn

Over Wallop *Hants,* ˈoʊvər ˈwɒləp, ővĕr wóllŏp

Over Whitacre *Warwicks.,* ˈoʊvər hwɪtəkər, ővĕr whíttăkĕr

Ovett, *f.n.,* ˈoʊvet, ővett

Oving *Bucks., W. Sussex,* ˈoʊvɪŋ, őving

Ovingdean *E. Sussex,* ˈoʊvɪŋdin, őving-deen; ˈɒvɪŋdin, óvving-deen

Ovingham *Northd.,* ˈɒvɪndʒəm, óvvinjăm

Ovington *Norfolk,* ˈoʊvɪŋtən, ővingtŏn

Ovington *Northd.,* ˈɒvɪŋtən, óvvingtŏn

Owler Bar *Derby.,* ˈaʊlər ˈbɑr, ówlĕr báar

Owlerton *S. Yorks.,* ˈoʊlərtən, őlĕrtŏn

Owles, *f.n.,* oʊlz, ōlz; aʊlz, owlz; ulz, oolz

Owmby *Lincs.,* ˈoʊmbɪ, őmbi. *Appropriate for both places of the name in Lincolnshire.*

Owsden *see* **Ousden**

Owslebury *Hants,* ˈʌslbərɪ, ússlbŭri; ˈʌzlbərɪ, úzzlbŭri

Owst, *f.n.,* oʊst, ōsst

Owthorpe *Notts.,* ˈaʊθɔrp, ówthorp

Owtram, *f.n.,* ˈaʊtrəm, ówtrăm

Oxford *Oxon.,* ˈɒksfərd, ócksfŏrd

Oxford and Asquith, Earl of, 'ɒksfərd ənd 'æskwɪθ, ócksförd ănd ásskwith
Oxfuird, Viscount of, 'ɒksfuərd, ócksfōörd
Oxhey *Herts.*, 'ɒksɪ, ócksi
Oxley, *f.n.*, 'ɒkslɪ, ócksli
Oxnard, *f.n.*, 'ɒksnərd, ócksnärd
Oxonian, *member of* **Oxford** *Univ.*, ɒk'soʊnɪən, ocksóniăn
Oxtoby, *f.n.*, 'ɒkstəbɪ, óckstŏbi
Oxwich *W. Glam.*, 'ɒkswɪtʃ, óckswitch
Oyne *Grampian*, ɔɪn, oyn
Oystermouth *W. Glam.*, 'ɔɪstərmaʊθ, óystĕrmowth
Ozell, *f.n.*, oʊ'zel, ōzéll
Ozengell Grange *Kent*, 'oʊzəngel 'greɪndʒ, ózĕn-gel gráynj
Ozols, *f.n.*, 'ɒzlz, ózzlz

P

Pabo *Gwynedd*, 'pæboʊ, pábbō
Pace, *f.n.*, peɪs, payss
Pachesham *Surrey*, 'pætʃɪsəm, pátchĕssăm
Packer, *f.n.*, 'pækər, páckĕr
Packham, *f.n.*, 'pækəm, páckăm
Padarn, Lake, *Gwynedd*, 'pædərn, páddärn
Paddick, *f.n.*, 'pædɪk, páddick
Paddock, *f.n.*, 'pædək, páddŏk
Padel, *f.n.*, 'pɑdl, paádl
Padell, *f.n.*, pɑ'del, paadéll
Padgham, *f.n.*, 'pædʒəm, pájjăm
Padiham *Lancs.*, 'pædɪəm, páddi-ăm
Padmore, *f.n.*, 'pædmɔr, pádmor
Padog *Gwynedd*, 'pædɒg, páddog
Padstow *Cornwall*, 'pædstoʊ, pádsstō
Padwick, *f.n.*, 'pædwɪk, pád-wick
Paget, *f.n.*, 'pædʒɪt, pájjĕt
Paget of Beaudesert, Baron, 'pædʒɪt əv 'boʊdɪzɛər, pájjĕt ŏv bṓdĕzair
Pagham *W. Sussex*, 'pægəm, pággăm
Pagin, *f.n.*, 'peɪgɪn, páygin
Paglesham *Essex*, 'pæglʃəm, pággl-shăm
Paice, *f.n.*, peɪs, payss
Paignton *Devon*, 'peɪntən, páyntŏn
Pailin, *f.n.*, 'peɪlɪn, páylin
Pain, *f.n.*, peɪn, payn
Painscastle *Powys*, 'peɪnzkɑsl, páynz-kaassl
Painswick *Glos.*, 'peɪnzwɪk, páynzwick

Paish, *f.n.*, peɪʃ, paysh
Paisible, *f.n.*, 'peɪzɪbl, páyzibl
Paisley *S'clyde*, 'peɪzlɪ, páyzli
Pakenham, *f.n.*, 'pækənəm, páckĕnăm. *Appropriate for the Earl of Longford's family name and for Baron* ∼.
Pakenham *Suffolk*, 'peɪkənəm, páykĕnăm
Pakington, *f.n.*, 'pækɪŋtən, páckingtŏn
Palairet, *f.n.*, 'pælərət, pálăret
Paley, *f.n.*, 'peɪlɪ, páyli
Palfery, *f.n.*, 'pɒlfrɪ, páwlfri
Palfrey, *f.n.*, 'pɒlfrɪ, páwlfri
Palfry, *f.n.*, 'pɒlfrɪ, páwlfri
Palgrave, *f.n.*, 'pælgreɪv, pálgrayv; 'pɒlgreɪv, páwlgrayv. *The first is appropriate for Francis* ∼, *19th-c. Professor of Poetry at the Univ. of Oxford and compiler of 'The Golden Treasury'.*
Palgrave *Suffolk*, 'pælgreɪv, pálgrayv
Palin, *f.n.*, 'peɪlɪn, páylin
Paling, *f.n.*, 'peɪlɪŋ, páyling
Palk, *f.n.*, pɒk, pawk; pɒlk, pawlk
Pallant, *f.n.*, 'pælənt, pálănt
Palles, *f.n.*, 'pælɪs, páléss
Pallion *Tyne & Wear*, 'pælɪən, páli-ŏn
Palliser, *f.n.*, 'pælɪsər, pálissĕr
Pall Mall *London*, 'pæl 'mæl, pál mál; 'pel 'mel, péll méll
Pallot, *f.n.*, 'pæloʊ, pálō
Palm, *f.n.*, pɑm, paam
Palmer, *f.n.*, 'pɑmər, paámĕr
Palmes, *f.n.*, pɑmz, paamz
Palnackie *D. & G.*, pæl'nækɪ, palnácki
Palsgrave, *f.n.*, 'pælzgreɪv, pálzgrayv
Pampisford *Cambs.*, 'pæmpɪsfərd, pámpissförd
Panchen, *f.n.*, 'pæntʃɪn, pántchĕn
Paneth, *f.n.*, 'pænɪθ, pánnĕth
Pankhurst, *f.n.*, 'pæŋkhɜrst, pánkhurst
Panmure Castle *Tayside*, pæn'mjʊər, pan-myṓor
Pannal *N. Yorks.*, 'pænl, pánnl
Pannell, *f.n.*, 'pænl, pánnl
Panteg *Gwent*, pæn'teɪg, pantáyg
Pant-Glas *Gwynedd*, pænt'glɑs, pant-glaáss
Pantlin, *f.n.*, 'pæntlɪn, pántlin
Pantony, *f.n.*, 'pæntənɪ, pántŏni
Pantperthog *Gwynedd*, pænt-'pɛərθɒg, pantpáirth-og
Pantycelyn *Dyfed*, ˌpæntə'kelɪn, pantăkéllin
Pant-y-dŵr *Powys*, ˌpæntə'dʊər, pantădṓor

Pantyffynnon *Dyfed*, ,pæntə'fʌnən, pantăfúnnŏn

Pantygasseg *Gwent*, ,pæntə- 'gæseg, pantăgásseg

Pantygraig-wen *Mid Glam.*, ,pæntəgraɪg'wen, pantăgrīg- -wén

Pant-y-mwyn *Clwyd*, ,pæntə- 'mʊɪn, pantămóō-in

Pantyscallog *Mid Glam.*, ,pæntə- 'skæɪbg, pantăskáhlog

Pant-y-waun *Mid Glam.*, ,pæntə- 'waɪn, pantă-wín

Papa Stour *Shetland*, 'papə 'stʊər, paápə stŏŏr

Papa Westray *Orkney* 'papə 'westreɪ, paápə wéstray

Papillon, *f.n.*, pə'pɪlən, păpíllŏn

Papworth, *f.n.*, 'pæpwɜrθ, păp- wurth

Papworth Everard *Cambs.*, 'pæpwərθ 'evərard, pápwŏrth évvĕraard

Papworth St. Agnes *Cambs.*, 'pæpwərθ snt 'ægnɪs, pápwŏrth sint ágnĕss

Paradwys *Gwynedd*, pæ'rædʊɪs, parráddŏŏ-iss

Paravicini, *f.n.*, ,pærəvɪ'tʃɪnɪ, parrăvitchéeni

Parbroath, Lord, par'broʊθ, paarbrŏth

Parcell, *f.n.*, par'sel, paarsséll

Pardoe, *f.n.*, 'pardoʊ, paárdō

Pardovan *Lothian*, par'dʌvən, paardúvvăn

Pares, *f.n.*, pɛərz, pairz

Pargiter, *f.n.*, 'pardʒɪtər, paárjitĕr. *Appropriate also for Baron* ∼.

Parham, *f.n.*, 'pærəm, párrăm

Parham *Suffolk, W. Sussex*, 'pærəm, párrăm

Parham Park *W. Sussex*, 'pærəm 'park, párrăm paárk

Paris, *f.n.*, 'pærɪs, párriss

Parish, *f.n.*, 'pærɪʃ, párrish

Parker, *f.n.*, 'parkər, paárkĕr

Parkeston *Essex*, 'parkstən, paárkstŏn

Parkeston Quay *Essex*, 'parkstən 'ki, paárkstŏn kée

Parkgate *Co. Antrim*, 'parkgeɪt, paárk-gayt

Parkin, *f.n.*, 'parkɪn, paárkin

Parkinson, *f.n.*, 'parkɪnsən, paárkinssŏn

Parkmore *Co. Antrim*, park'mɔr, paarkmór

Parkstone *Dorset*, 'parkstən, paárkstŏn

Parlane, *f.n.*, 'parleɪn, paárlayn; par'leɪn, paarláyn

Parlour, *f.n.*, 'parlər, paárlŭr

Parmée, *f.n.*, 'parmeɪ, paármay

Parmenter, *f.n.*, 'parmɪntər, paár- mĕntĕr

Parminter, *f.n.*, 'parmɪntər, paár- mintĕr

Parmiter, *f.n.*, 'parmɪtər, paár- mitĕr

Parmley, *f.n.*, 'parmlɪ, paármli

Parnell, *f.n.*, par'nel, paarnéll; 'parnl, paárnl

Parnwell, *f.n.*, 'parnwəl, paárnwĕl

Parotte, *f.n.*, pə'rɒt, părótt

Parracombe *Devon*, 'pærəkum, párrăkoom

Parrett, *f.n.*, 'pærɪt, párrĕt

Parrett, River, *Dorset–Somerset*, 'pærɪt, párrĕt

Parrott, *f.n.*, 'pærət, párrŏt

Parry, *f.n.*, 'pærɪ, párri

Parsley, *f.n.*, 'parzlɪ, paárzli

Parslow, *f.n.*, 'parzloʊ, paárzlō

Partick *S'clyde*, 'partɪk, paártick

Partickhill *S'clyde*, 'partɪk'hɪl, paártick-híll

Partridge, *f.n.*, 'partrɪdʒ, paártrij

Pasco, *f.n.*, 'pæskoʊ, pásskō

Pascoe, *f.n.*, 'pæskoʊ, pásskō

Pashley, *f.n.*, 'pæʃlɪ, páshli

Pask, *f.n.*, pæsk, passk

Pasley, *f.n.*, 'peɪzlɪ, páyzli

Pasmore, *f.n.*, 'pasmɔr, paássmor

Passant, *f.n.*, 'pæsənt, pássănt

Passenham *Northants.*, 'pasənəm, paássĕnăm

Paston, *f.n.*, 'pæstən, pásstŏn

Patchett, *f.n.*, 'pætʃɪt, pátchĕt

Patel, *f.n.*, pə'tel, pătéll

Pater, *f.n.*, 'peɪtər, páytĕr

Paterson, *f.n.*, 'pætərsən, páttĕrs- sŏn

Patey, *f.n.*, 'peɪtɪ, páyti

Path of Condie *Tayside*, 'paθ əv 'kɒndɪ, paáth ŏv kóndi

Patmore, *f.n.*, 'pætmɔr, pátmor

Patney *Wilts.*, 'pætnɪ, pát-ni

Paton, *f.n.*, 'peɪtən, páytŏn

Patrick, *C.n. and f.n.*, 'pætrɪk, pátrick

Patrington *Humberside*, 'pætrɪŋ- tən, pátringtŏn

Patriss, *f.n.*, 'pætrɪs, pátriss

Patrixbourne *Kent*, 'pætrɪksbɔrn, pátricksborn

Patterson, *f.n.*, 'pætərsən, páttĕrs- sŏn

Pattie, *f.n.*, 'pætɪ, pátti

Pattishall *Northants.*, 'pætɪʃl, páttishl

Pattison, *f.n.*, 'pætɪsən, páttissŏn

Pattreiouex, *f.n.*, 'pætrɪoʊ, pátri-ō

Pauer, *f.n.*, 'paʊər, pówĕr

Paulerspury *Northants.*, 'pɔlərz- pərɪ, páwlĕrzpŭri

Paulin, *f.n.*, 'pɔlɪn, páwlin

Paulina, *one educated at St. Paul's Girls' School,* pɔ'laɪnə, pawlínǎ
Pauline, *one educated at St. Paul's School,* 'pɔlaɪn, páwlĭn
Paulton, *f.n.,* 'pɔʊltən, pɔ́ltŏn
Pauncefort, *f.n.,* 'pɔnsfərt, páwnssfŏrt
Pauncefote, *f.n.,* 'pɔnsfət, páwnssfŏt. *Appropriate also for the Barony of* ~.
Pauperhaugh *Northd.,* 'pɔpərhɑf, páwpĕr-haaf
Pavely, *f.n.,* 'peɪvlɪ, páyvli
Pavenham *Beds.,* 'peɪvənəm, páyvĕnǎm
Paver, *f.n.,* 'peɪvər, páyvĕr
Pavey, *f.n.,* 'peɪvɪ, páyvi
Pavey Arc *Cumbria,* 'peɪvɪ 'ɑrk, páyvi aárk
Paviere, *f.n.,* 'pævjɛər, páv-yair
Paviour, *f.n.,* 'peɪvjər, páyv-yŭr
Pavitt, *f.n.,* 'pævɪt, pávvit
Pavlow, *f.n.,* 'pævloʊ, pávlō
Pavy, *f.n.,* 'peɪvɪ, páyvi
Pawley, *f.n.,* 'pɔlɪ, páwli
Pawlyk, *f.n.,* 'pɔlɪk, páwlick
Pawsey, *f.n.,* 'pɔzɪ, páwzi; 'pɔsɪ, páwssi
Paxton, *f.n.,* 'pækstən, páckstŏn
Payan, *f.n.,* 'peɪən, páy-ǎn
Paylor, *f.n.,* 'peɪlər, páylŏr
Paynter, *f.n.,* 'peɪntər, páyntĕr
Paynting, *f.n.,* 'peɪntɪŋ, páynting
Peabody, *f.n.,* 'pibədɪ, péebŏdi; 'pibɒdɪ, péeboddi; 'peɪbɒdɪ, páyboddi
Peacey, *f.n.,* 'pisɪ, péessi
Peachell, *f.n.,* 'pitʃl, péetchl
Peachey, *f.n.,* 'pitʃɪ, péetchi
Peacock, *f.n.,* 'pikɒk, péekock
Peaker, *f.n.,* 'pikər, péekĕr
Peakirk *Cambs.,* 'pikɜrk, péekirk
Pear, *f.n.,* pɪər, peer
Pearce, *f.n.,* pɪərs, peerss
Pearcey, *f.n.,* 'pɪərsɪ, péerssi
Pearmain, *f.n.,* 'pɛərmeɪn, páirmayn
Pearn, *f.n.,* pɜrn, pern
Pears, *f.n.,* pɪərz, peerz; pɛərz, pairz. *The first is appropriate for Sir Peter* ~, *singer.*
Pearsall, *f.n.,* 'pɪərsl, péerssl
Pearson, *f.n.,* 'pɪərsən, péerssŏn
Peart, *f.n.,* pɪərt, peert
Pease, *f.n.,* piz, peez
Peasgood, *f.n.,* 'pizgʊd, péezgŏŏd
Peasholm *N. Yorks.,* 'pizhoʊm, péez-hōm
Peaston *Lothian,* 'peɪstən, páysstŏn
Peate, *f.n.,* pit, peet
Peay, *f.n.,* peɪ, pay
Pebardy, *f.n.,* 'pebərdɪ, pébbǎrdi
Peberdy, *f.n.,* 'pebərdɪ, pébbĕrdi

Pechell, *f.n.,* 'pitʃl, péetchl
Peckham *London,* 'pekəm, péckǎm
Pecorini, *f.n.,* ˌpekə'rinɪ, peckŏréeni
Pecry, *f.n.,* 'pekrɪ, péckri
Pedair Ffordd *Powys,* 'pedaɪər 'fɔrð, péddīr fórth
Peddelty, *f.n.,* 'pedltɪ, péddlti
Peden, *f.n.,* 'pidən, péedĕn
Peden *S'clyde,* 'pidən, péedĕn
Pedlow, *f.n.,* 'pedloʊ, pédlō
Pedraza, *f.n.,* pɪ'drɑzə, pĕdraázǎ
Pedwardine *H. & W.,* 'pedwərdaɪn, pédwărdīn
Peebles *Borders,* 'piblz, péeblz
Peggie, *f.n.,* 'pegɪ, péggi
Pegna, *f.n.,* 'penjə, pén-yǎ
Pegnall, *f.n.,* 'pegnəl, pégnǎl
Pegram, *f.n.,* 'pigrəm, péegrǎm
Peierls, *f.n.,* 'paɪərlz, pī-ĕrlz
Peile, *f.n.,* pil, peel
Peill, *f.n.,* pil, peel
Peirce, *f.n.,* pɪərs, peerss
Peirse, *f.n.,* pɪərz, peerz
Peirson, *f.n.,* 'pɪərsən, péerssŏn
Peiser, *f.n.,* 'paɪzər, pízĕr
Peisley, *f.n.,* 'pizlɪ, péezli
Pejic, *f.n.,* 'pedʒɪk, péjjik
Pelaw *Tyne & Wear,* 'pilə, péelǎ; 'pilɔ, péelaw
Pelham, *f.n.,* 'peləm, péllǎm
Pelletier, *f.n.,* 'peltɪeɪ, pélti-ay
Pellew, *f.n.,* pə'lju, pĕléw
Pelloe, *f.n.,* 'peloʊ, péllō
Pellsyeat *Cumbria,* 'pelzjit, péllz-yeet
Pelynt *Cornwall,* pə'lɪnt, pĕlínt; plɪnt, plint
Pembrey *Dyfed,* pem'breɪ, pembráy
Pembroke, *f.n.,* 'pembrʊk, pémbrŏŏk
Pembroke *Dyfed,* 'pembrʊk, pémbrŏŏk; 'pembrək, pémbrŏk
Pembroke *College Univs. of Cambridge and Oxford,* 'pembrʊk, pémbrŏŏk
Pen-allt *Gwent,* pen'ælt, pennáhlt
Penally *Dyfed,* pən'ælɪ, pĕnáli; pen'ælɪ, pennáli
Penally Point *Cornwall,* pen'ælɪ, pennáli
Penarth *S. Glam.,* pə'nɑrθ, pĕnaárth
Penberthy, *f.n.,* pen'bɜrðɪ, penbérthi; 'penbərðɪ, pénbĕrthi; pen'bɜrθɪ, penbérthi; 'penbərθɪ, pénbĕrthi
Penboyr *Dyfed,* pen'bɔɪər, penbóyr
Penbuallt *Powys,* pen'biælt, penbée-ahlt

Pencader *Dyfed*, pen'kædər, pen-
-káddĕr

Pencaitland *Lothian*, pen'keɪtlənd,
pen-káyt-länd

Pencalenick *Cornwall*, ,penkə-
'lenɪk, pen-kälénnik

Pencarnisiog *Gwynedd*, ,penkɑr-
'nɪsjɒg, pen-kaarníss-yog;
,penkɑr'nɪʃɒg, pen-kaarníshog

Pencarreg *Dyfed*, pen'kæreg, pen-
-kárreg

Pencerig *Powys*, pen'kerɪg, pen-
-kérrig

Pen-clawdd *W. Glam.*, pen'klauð,
pen-klówth

Pencoed *Mid Glam.*, pen'kɔɪd,
pen-kóyd

Pencoys *Cornwall*, pen'kɔɪz, pen-
-kóyz

Pencraig *H. & W.*, 'pen'kreɪg,
pén-kráyg

Pencraig *Powys*, 'penkraɪg, pén-
-krīg; 'peŋkraɪg, pénkrīg

Pendarves Point *Cornwall*,
pen'dɑrvɪs, penda'arvĕss

Pendeen *Cornwall*, pen'din,
pendéen

Pendell Court *Surrey*, 'pendl
'kɔrt, péndl kórt

Pendennis Point *Cornwall*, pen-
'denɪs, pendénniss

Penderyn *Mid Glam.*, pen'derɪn,
pendérrin

Pendeulwyn *Mid Glam.*, pen-
'daɪlwɪn, pendílwin. *The English
form is* **Pendoylan**, *q.v.*

Pendine *Dyfed*, pen'daɪn, pendín

Pendlebury, *f.n.*, 'pendlbəri,
péndlbŭri

Pendomer *Somerset*, pen'doumər,
pendómĕr

Pendoylan *Mid Glam.*, pen-
'dɔɪlən, pendóylän. *The Welsh
form is* **Pendeulwyn**, *q.v.*

Pendoylan *S. Glam.*, pen'dɔɪlən,
pendóylän

Pendrous, *f.n.*, 'pendrəs, péndrŭss

Pendry, *f.n.*. 'pendrɪ, péndri

Pendse, *f.n.*, 'pendzɪ, péndzi

Penegoes *Powys*, pen'egɔɪs,
pennéggoyss

Penfold, *f.n.*, 'penfould, pénföld

Penfound House *Cornwall*,
pən'faund 'haus, pĕnfównd
hówss

Pengam *Gwent, S. Glam.*, 'peŋ-
gəm, péng-găm

Pengegon *Cornwall*, pen'gegən,
pen-géggŏn

Pengelly, *f.n.*, peŋ'gelɪ, peng-gélli

Pengersick *Cornwall*, pen'gɜrsɪk,
pen-gérssick

Pengwern *Clwyd*, 'pengwɜrn, pén-
-gwern

Penhaligon, *f.n.*, pen'hælɪgən,
pen-háligŏn

Peniarth *Gwynedd*, 'penjɑrθ, pén-
-yaarth

Penicuik *Lothian*, 'penɪkuk,
pénnikōōk

Peniel *Clwyd, Dyfed*, 'penjəl, pén-
-yĕl

Penifiler *Skye*, ,penɪ'filər, penni-
féelĕr

Penisarwaen, *also spelt* **Penisa'r-
-waun**, *Gwynedd*, pen'ɪsər'waɪn,
peníssär-wín

Penistone *S. Yorks.*, 'penɪstən,
pénnistŏn

Penkhull *Staffs.*, 'peŋkl, pénkl

Pen-lan *W. Glam.*, pen'læn,
penlán

Penlee *Cornwall*, pen'li, penlée

Penlle'r-gaer *W. Glam.*, ,penɬər-
'gɑr, penhlĕr-ga'ar

Pen-llin *S. Glam.*, pen'ɬin, pen-
-hléen. *But see also* **Penllyne**.

Penlline *see* **Penllyne**

Penllwyn-gwent *Gwent*, pen'ɬuɪn
'gwent, pen-hlŏŏ-in gwént

Pen Llŷn *Gwynedd*, pen 'ɬin, pen
hléen

Penllyn *Gwynedd*, 'penɬɪn, pén-
-hlin

Penllyne, *also spelt* **Penlline**, *S.
Glam.*, pen'ɬaɪn, pen-hlín. *These
are locally accepted semi-
anglicized forms. The Welsh-
language form is* **Pen-llin**, *q.v.*

Penmachno *Gwynedd*, pen-
'mæxnou, penmáchnō

Penmaen-mawr *Gwynedd*,
,penmaɪn'mauər, penmīn-mówr

Penmon *Gwynedd*, 'penmɒn,
pénmon

Penmynydd *Gwynedd*, pen'mʌnɪð,
penmúnnith

Pennal *Gwynedd*, 'penæl, pénnal

Pennan *Grampian*, 'penən,
pénnän

Pennant *Dyfed, Powys*, 'penænt,
pénnant

Pennefather, *f.n.*, 'penɪfeðər,
pénnifethĕr; 'penɪfɑðər, pénni-
faathĕr

Pennell, *f.n.*, 'penl, pénnl

Pennells, *f.n.*, 'penlz, pénnlz

Pennethorne, *f.n.*, 'penɪθɔrn,
pénni-thorn

Pennines, The, *mountain chain,
Derby.–Cheviot Hills*, 'penaɪnz,
pénninz

Penninghame *D. & G.*, 'penɪŋhəm,
pénning-hăm

Penning-Rowsell, *f.n.*, 'penɪŋ
'rausl, pénning rówssl

Pennington, *f.n.*, 'penɪŋtən, pén-
ningtŏn

Pennycuick, *f.n.*, 'penıkʊk, pénnikōōk; 'penıkwık, pénni--kwick; 'penıkjuk, pénnikewk

Pennyfather, *f.n.*, 'penıfeðər, pénnifethĕr; 'penıfɑðər, pénni-faathĕr

Pennyman, *f.n.*, 'penımən, pénnimăn

Penparcau *Dyfed*, pen'pɑrkaı, penpa'arkī

Penpedairheol *Gwent*, pen-'pedaıər'heıɒl, penpéddīr-háy-ol

Penpedairhoel *Mid Glam.*, pen-'pedaıər'hɔıl, penpéddīr-hóyl

Penpergwm *Gwent*, pen'pɛərgʊm, penpáirgōōm

Penponds *Cornwall*, pen'pɒndz, penpóndz

Penrhiw-ceiber *Mid Glam.*, ˌpenhrıu'kaıbər, penri-oo-kíbĕr

Penrhiwlas *Gwynedd*, ˌpenhrı'uləs, penri-o'oláss

Penrhiwtyn *W. Glam.*, ˌpenhrı-'utın, penri-o'otin

Pen-rhos *Gwent, Powys*, pen-'hroʊs, penrŏss

Pen-rhos *Gwynedd*, 'pen'hroʊs, pén-rŏss

Penrhos *Gwynedd*, 'penhrɒs, pénross; 'penhroʊs, pénrŏss

Penrhos Lligwy *Anglesey*, pen-'hroʊs 'łıgʊı, penrŏss hlíggōō-i

Penrhyn, Baron, 'penrın, pénrin

Penrhyn-coch *Dyfed*, ˌpenhrın-'koʊx, penrin-kóch

Penrhyndeudraeth *Gwynedd*, ˌpenhrın'daıdraıθ, penrin--dídrīth

Penrice *Cornwall, W. Glam.*, pen'raıs, penríss

Penrith *Cumbria*, 'penrıθ, pénrith; 'pıərıθ, peérith

Penrose, *f.n.*, 'penroʊz, pénrōz; pen'roʊz, penrŏz

Penryn *Cornwall*, pen'rın, penrín

Pen-sarn *Clwyd, Gwynedd*, pen-'sɑrn, penssa'arn

Pensarn *Dyfed*, 'pensɑrn, pénssaarn

Penselwood *Somerset*, pen-'selwʊd, penssélwōōd

Penshaw *Tyne & Wear*, 'penʃə, pén-shă; 'penʃɔ, pén-shaw

Pentewan *Cornwall*, pen'tjuən, pentéw-ăn

Pentir *Gwynedd*, 'pentıər, pénteer

Pentire Head *Cornwall*, pen'taıər, pentír

Pentland Firth *sea area between Orkney and Scottish mainland*, 'pentlənd, péntländ

Pentland Hills *S'clyde–Lothian*, 'pentlənd, péntländ

Penton *Cumbria*, pen'tɒn, pentón

Pentonville *London*, 'pentənvıl, péntŏnvil

Pentraeth *Gwynedd*, 'pentraıθ, péntrīth

Pentre *Clwyd, Powys*, 'pentrə, péntră

Pentre *Mid Glam., W. Glam.*, 'pentreı, péntray

Pentreath, *f.n.*, pen'triθ, pentréeth

Pentre-bach *Powys*, ˌpentrə'bɑx, pentrăba'ach

Pentrebach *Dyfed, Mid Glam.*, ˌpentrə'bɑx, pentrăba'ach

Pentre Celyn *Clwyd*, ˌpentrə 'kelın, pentră kéllin

Pentrefelin *Dyfed, Gwynedd*, ˌpentrə'velın, pentrăvéllin

Pentrefoelas *Clwyd*, ˌpentrə-'vɔıləs, pentrăvóyláss

Pentre-llyn-cymmer *Clwyd*, ˌpentrəłın'kʌmər, pentrăhlin--kúmmĕr

Pentre-poeth *Gwent*, ˌpentrə'pɔıθ, pentrăpóyth

Pentre Poeth *W. Glam.*, ˌpentrə 'pɔıθ, pentră póyth

Pentre Uchaf *Clwyd*, ˌpentrə 'ıxæv, pentră íchav

Pentrich *Derby.*, 'pentrıtʃ, péntritch

Pentwyn *Dyfed, Gwent, Mid Glam.*, pen'tʊın, pentōō-in. *Appropriate for both places of the name in Gwent, and both in Mid Glam.*

Pen-twyn *Gwent*, pen'tʊın, pentōō-in

Pentwyn-mawr *Gwent*, pen,tʊın-'maʊər, pentōō-in-mówr

Pentyla *Mid Glam.*, pen'tʌlə, pen-túllă; pen'tılə, pentíllă

Pentyrch *Mid Glam.*, pen'tɜrx, pentírch; pen'tɜrk, pentírk

Pentyrch *Powys*, 'pentɜrx, pén-tirch

Penwarden, *f.n.*, pen'wɔrdən, penwáwrdĕn

Pen-waun *Mid Glam.*, pen'waın, penwín

Penwill, *f.n.*, 'penwıl, pénwil

Penwith *Cornwall*, pen'wıθ, pen-with

Penwortham *Lancs.*, 'penwərðəm, pénwŭrthăm

Pen-y-banc *Dyfed*, ˌpenə'bæŋk, pennăbánk

Penyberth *Gwynedd*, pe'nʌbɜrθ, pennúbberth; pe'nʌbərθ, pen-núbbĕrth

Pen-y-bont *Clwyd, Dyfed, Gwent*, ˌpenə'bɒnt, pennăbónt. *Appropriate for all three places of the name in Clwyd.*

Penybont *Dyfed, Powys,* ˌpenə-'bɒnt, pennăbónt

Pen-y-cae *Powys,* ˌpenə'kaɪ, pennăkí

Penydarren *Mid Glam.,* ˌpenə-'dærən, pennădárrĕn

Pen-y-fai *Mid Glam.,* ˌpenə'vaɪ, pennăví

Pen-y-fan *Powys,* ˌpenə'væn, pennăván

Pen-y-ffordd *Clwyd,* ˌpenə'fɔrð, pennăfórth

Penygelli *Gwynedd,* ˌpenə'geɬɪ, pennăgéhli

Penygenffordd *Powys,* ˌpenə-'genfɔrð, pennăgénforth

Penyghent *N. Yorks.,* 'penɪgent, pénnigent

Pen-y-gors *Mid Glam.,* ˌpenə'gɔrs, pennăgórss

Pen-y-graig *Mid Glam.,* ˌpenə-'graɪg, pennăgríg

Pen-y-groes *S. Glam.,* ˌpenə'grɔɪs, pennăgróyss

Penygwryd *Gwynedd,* ˌpenə-'guərɪd, pennăgóŏrid

Pen-y-lan *S. Glam.,* ˌpenə'læn, pennălán

Penyrheolgerrig *Mid Glam.,* 'penrɪul'gerɪg, pénri-ool-gérrig

Pen-y-waun *Mid Glam.,* ˌpenə-'waɪn, pennă-wín

Penzance *Cornwall,* pen'zæns, penzánss

Peock, *f.n.,* 'piək, peé-ŏk

Peover *Ches.,* 'pivər, peévĕr

Peowrie, *f.n.,* 'pauərɪ, pówri

Peper Harow *Surrey,* 'pepər 'hærou, péppĕr hárrō

Peppard Common *Oxon.,* 'pepɑrd 'kɒmən, péppaard kómmŏn

Peppiatt, *f.n.,* 'pepɪət, péppi-ăt

Pepys, *f.n.,* 'pepɪs, péppiss; pips, peeps; peps, pepps. *The first is appropriate for the family name of the Earl of Cottenham. The second was apparently that of the diarist, Samuel ∼, and this is the pronunciation used today by the ∼ Cockerell family, lineal descendants of the diarist's sister Paulina.*

Pepys Cockerell, *f.n.,* 'pips 'kɒkərəl, péeps kóckĕrĕl

Perceval, *f.n.,* 'pɜrsɪvəl, pérssĕvăl

Percuil Ferry *Cornwall,* 'pɑrkjul, pérkewl. *An older form is* **Porthcuel,** *q.v.*

Percy, *C.n. and f.n.,* 'pɜrsɪ, pérssi

Perdiswell Park *H. & W.,* 'pɜrdɪswəl, pérdisswĕl

Perdita, *C.n.,* 'pɜrdɪtə, pérdită

Perebourne, *f.n.,* 'perɪbɔrn, pérrĕborn

Perelman, *f.n.,* 'perəlmən, pérrĕlmăn

Peress, *f.n.,* 'peres, pérress

Pergamon Press, *publishers,* 'pɜrgəmən, pérgămŏn

Perham, *f.n.,* 'perəm, pérräm

Periton, *f.n.,* 'perɪtən, pérritŏn

Perkins, *f.n.,* 'pɜrkɪnz, pérkinz

Perks, *f.n.,* pɜrks, perks

Perne, *f.n.,* pɜrn, pern

Pernel, *f.n.,* pɜr'nel, pernéll

Perott, *f.n.,* 'perət, pérrŏt

Perou, *f.n.,* pə'ru, pĕro͝o

Perowne, *f.n.,* pə'roun, pĕrón

Perranarworthal *Cornwall,* ˌperənər'wɜrðl, perrănărwúrthl

Perranporth *Cornwall,* ˌperən-'pɔrθ, perrănpórth

Perranuthnoe *Cornwall,* ˌperə-'njuθnou, perrănéwthnō; ˌperə'nʌθnou, perrănúthnō. *Although the second is used extensively in the West Country, the first is the local pronunciation.*

Perranwell *Cornwall,* ˌperən'wel, perrănwéll

Perranzabuloe *Cornwall,* ˌperən-'zæbjulou, perrănzáb-yōōlō

Perren, *f.n.,* 'perɪn, pérrĕn

Perret, *f.n.,* 'pereɪ, pérray

Perrett, *f.n.,* 'perɪt, pérrĕt

Perrin, *f.n.,* 'perɪn, pérrin

Perring, *f.n.,* 'perɪŋ, pérring

Perrins, *f.n.,* 'perɪnz, pérrinz

Perris, *f.n.,* 'perɪs, pérriss

Perry, *f.n.,* 'perɪ, pérri

Pershouse, *f.n.,* 'pɜrshaus, pérss--howss

Persse, *f.n.,* pɜrs, perss

Perth *Tayside,* pɜrθ, perth

Pertwee, *f.n.,* 'pɑrtwɪ, pértwee

Perutz, *f.n.,* pə'ruts, pĕro͝ots

Pery, *f.n.,* 'pɛərɪ, páiri; 'pɪərɪ, peéri; 'perɪ, pérri. *The first is appropriate for the Earl of Limerick's family name.*

Peschek, *f.n.,* 'peʃek, pésheck

Pestel, *f.n.,* 'pestl, pésstl

Pestell, *f.n.,* pes'tel, pesstéll

Pestridge, *f.n.,* 'pestrɪdʒ, pésstrij

Petch, *f.n.,* petʃ, petch

Peterborough *Cambs.,* 'pitərbərə, peétĕrbŭră

Peterculter *Grampian,* ˌpitər-'kutər, peetĕrkoótĕr

Peterhead *Grampian,* ˌpitər'hed, peetĕr-héd

Peterkin, *f.n.,* 'pitərkɪn, peétĕrkin

Peterlee *Durham,* ˌpitər'li, peetĕr-leé

Peters, *f.n.,* 'pitərz, peétĕrz

Petersen, *f.n.,* 'pitərsən, peétĕrssĕn

Petersfinger *Wilts.*, 'pitərzfɪŋgər, péetĕrz-fing-gĕr

Petersham *London*, 'pitərʃəm, péetĕr-shăm

Peterstone super Ely *S. Glam.*, 'pitərstən ˌsupər 'ilɪ, péetĕrsstŏn soopĕr éeli

Peter Tavy *Devon*, 'pitər 'teɪvɪ, péetĕr táyvi

Petham *Kent*, 'petəm, péttăm

Pethen, *f.n.*, 'peθən, péthĕn

Petheram, *f.n.*, 'peðərəm, péthĕrăm

Petherbridge, *f.n.*, 'peθərbrɪdʒ, péthĕrbrij

Petherick, *f.n.*, 'peθərɪk, péthĕrick

Pethick-Lawrence, Barony of, 'peθɪk 'lɒrəns, péthick lórrĕnss

Petit, *f.n.*, 'petɪt, péttit

Peto, *f.n.*, 'pitoʊ, péetō

Petre, *f.n.*, 'pitər, péetĕr. *Appropriate also for Baron ~.*

Petrides, *f.n.*, pɪ'trɪdɪz, pĕtréedĕz

Petrie, Sir Flinders, *Egyptologist*, 'flɪndərz 'pitrɪ, flíndĕrz péetri

Petrie, *f.n.*, 'pitrɪ, péetri

Petrockstow *Devon*, 'petrɒkstoʊ, pétrocksstō

Petrox, saint, 'petrɒks, péttrocks

Pettener, *f.n.*, 'petənər, péttĕnĕr

Petteril, River, *Cumbria*, 'petrɪl, péttril

Pettican, *f.n.*, 'petɪkən, péttikăn

Pettifer, *f.n.*, 'petɪfər, péttifĕr

Pettigo *Co. Fermanagh*, 'petɪgoʊ, péttigō

Pettigrew, *f.n.*, 'petɪgru, péttigroo

Pettingell, *f.n.*, 'petɪŋgl, pétting-gl

Pettinger, *f.n.*, 'petɪndʒər, péttinjĕr

Pettistree *Suffolk*, 'petɪstri, péttisstree

Pettit, *f.n.*, 'petɪt, péttit

Pevensey *E. Sussex*, 'pevənzɪ, pévvĕnzi

Pevsner, Sir Nikolaus, *art historian*, 'nɪkələs 'pevznər, níckŏlăss pévznĕr

Pewsey *Wilts.*, 'pjuzɪ, péwzi

Pewsham *Wilts.*, 'pjuʃəm, péw-shăm

Peyre, *f.n.*, 'pɛər, pair

Peyton, *f.n.*, 'peɪtən, páytŏn

Pfammatter, *f.n.*, 'fæmətər, fámmătĕr

Phaidon Press, *publishers*, 'faɪdən, fídŏn

Phairkettle, *f.n.*, 'fɛərketl, fáirkettl

Pharay, *also spelt* **Fara**, *Orkney*, 'færə, fárră

Phayre, *f.n.*, fɛər, fair

Phelan, *f.n.*, 'filən, féelăn; 'feɪlən, fáylăn. *The first is normal in England, the second is the Northern Irish pronunciation.*

Phelops, *f.n.*, 'felɒps, féllops

Phelps, *f.n.*, felps, felps

Phemister, *f.n.*, 'femɪstər, fémmisstĕr

Philbin, *f.n.*, 'fɪlbɪn, fílbin

Philie, *f.n.*, 'fɪlɪ, fílli

Philiphaugh *Borders*, 'fɪlɪp'hɒx, fíllip-hóch

Philipson, *f.n.*, 'fɪlɪpsən, fíllipsŏn

Phillack *Cornwall*, 'fɪlək, fílläk

Philleigh *Cornwall*, 'fɪlɪ, fílli; 'fɪlɪ, fíllee

Philorth *Grampian*, fɪ'lɔrθ, filórth

Philp, *f.n.*, fɪlp, filp

Phipps, *f.n.*, fɪps, fipps

Phizacklea, *f.n.*, fɪ'zæklɪə, fizzácklià

Phoebe, *C.n.*, 'fibɪ, feébi

Phyllida, *C.n.*, 'fɪlɪdə, fíllidă

Phythian-Adams, *f.n.*, 'fɪθɪən 'ædəmz, fíthiăn áddămz

Piachaud, *f.n.*, 'piəʃoʊ, pée-ăshō

Picard, *f.n.*, 'pɪkɑrd, píckaard

Picarda, *f.n.*, pɪ'kɑrdə, pikaárdă

Piccadilly *London*, ˌpɪkə'dɪlɪ, pickădílli

Piché, *f.n.*, 'piʃeɪ, péeshay

Pichard, *f.n.*, 'pɪkɑrd, píckaard

Pickavance, *f.n.*, 'pɪkəvæns, píckăvanss

Pickaver, *f.n.*, pɪ'keɪvər, pikáyvĕr

Pickerell, *f.n.*, 'pɪkərəl, píckĕrĕl

Pickering, *f.n.*, 'pɪkərɪŋ, píckĕring

Pickett, *f.n.*, 'pɪkɪt, pickĕt

Pickford, *f.n.*, 'pɪkfərd, píckfŏrd

Pickles, *f.n.*, 'pɪklz, pícklz

Pickstock, *f.n.*, 'pɪkstɒk. píckstock

Pickthorne, *f.n.*, 'pɪkθɔrn, píck-thorn

Pickvance, *f.n.*, 'pɪkvæns, píckvanss

Pidding, *f.n.*, 'pɪdɪŋ, pídding

Piddinghoe *E. Sussex*, ˌpɪdɪŋ'hu, pidding-hoo

Piddletrenthide *Dorset*, ˌpɪdl'trentaɪd, piddltréntīd

Pidduck, *f.n.*, 'pɪdək, píddŭck

Pidley *Cambs.*, 'pɪdlɪ, pídli

Pidsley, *f.n.*, 'pɪdzlɪ, pídzli

Piears, *f.n.*, pɪərz, peerz

Piegza, *f.n.*, pɪ'egzə, pi-égză

Pielou, *f.n.*, pi'lu, peeloo

Pierce, *f.n.*, pɪərs, peerss

Piercebridge *Durham*, 'pɪərs-'brɪdʒ, péerss-brij

Piercy, *f.n.*, 'pɪərsɪ, péerssi. *Appropriate also for Baron ~.*

Pierpont, *f.n.*, 'pɪərpənt, péerpŏnt

Pierrepoint, *f.n.*, 'pɪərpɔɪnt, péerpoynt

Pierrepont, *f.n.*, 'pɪərpənt, péerpŏnt

Piers, *C.n.*, pɪərz, peerz

Pierssené, f.n., 'pɪərsneɪ, péerss-nay

Piggott, f.n., 'pɪgət, píggŏt

Pignéguy, f.n., pɪn'jeɪgɪ, pin-yáygi

Pignon, f.n., 'pɪnjõ, péen-yõng

Pigot, f.n., 'pɪgət, píggŏt

Pigou, f.n., 'pɪgu, píggoo

Pika, f.n., 'pɪkə, peékă

Pike, f.n., paɪk, pīk

Pikett, f.n., 'paɪkɪt, píkĕt

Pilbeam, f.n., 'pɪlbim, pílbeem

Pilbrow, f.n., 'pɪlbroʊ, pílbrō

Pilch, f.n., pɪltʃ, piltch

Pilcher, f.n., 'pɪltʃər, píltchĕr

Pilger, f.n., 'pɪldʒər, píljĕr

Pilley, f.n., 'pɪlɪ, pílli

Pillgwenlly Gwent, pɪɫ'gwenɫɪ, pihl-gwénhli

Pilling, f.n., 'pɪlɪŋ, pílling

Pillinger, f.n., 'pɪlɪndʒər, píllinjĕr

Pillow, f.n., 'pɪloʊ, píllō

Pimperne Dorset, 'pɪmpərn, pímpĕrn

Pinchbeck, f.n., 'pɪnʃbek, pínsh--beck; 'pɪntʃbek, píntch-beck

Pinchen, f.n., 'pɪnʃən, pínshĕn

Pinches, f.n., 'pɪnʃɪz, pínshĕz

Pincus, f.n., 'pɪŋkəs, pínkŭss

Pinel, f.n., pɪ'nel, pinéll

Pinero, f.n., pɪ'nɪəroʊ, pineérō; pɪ'nɛəroʊ, pináirō. The first is appropriate for Sir Arthur Wing ~, playwright.

Pinfield, f.n., 'pɪnfild, pínfeeld

Pinged Dyfed, 'pɪŋged, píng-ged

Pinhoe Devon, pɪn'hoʊ, pin-hó

Pinkerton, f.n., 'pɪŋkərtən, pínkĕrtŏn

Pinmachar S'clyde, pɪn'mæxər, pin-máchăr

Pinmill Suffolk, 'pɪnmɪl, pínmill

Pinnegar, f.n., 'pɪnɪgər, pínnĕgăr

Pinnell, f.n., pɪ'nel, pinéll

Pinniger, f.n., 'pɪnɪdʒər, pínnijĕr

Pinter, f.n., 'pɪntər, píntĕr. Appropriate for Harold ~, playwright.

Pinwhattle S'clyde, pɪn'hwætl, pin-wháttl

Pinwherry S'clyde, pɪn'hwerɪ, pin--whérri

Pinyoun, f.n., pɪn'jaʊn, pin-yówn; pɪn'joʊn, pin-yŏn

Piper, f.n., 'paɪpər, pípĕr

Pipewell Northants., 'pɪpwel, pípwel

Pipon, f.n., 'pɪpɒn, peépon

Pirant, f.n., 'pɪrənt, pírrănt

Piratin, f.n., pɪ'rætɪn, piráttin

Pirbright Surrey, 'pərbraɪt, pírbrīt

Pirie, f.n., 'pɪrɪ, pírri

Pirnie, f.n., 'pərnɪ, pírni

Pisciottani, f.n., ˌpɪskɪə'tɑnɪ, pisskiŏtáani

Pishill Oxon., 'pɪʃɪl, písh-il

Pistyll Gwynedd, 'pɪstɪɫ, písstihl

Pitblado, f.n., pɪt'bleɪdoʊ, pit-bláydō

Pitcairn, f.n., pɪt'kɛərn, pitkáirn

Pitcalzean House H'land, pɪt-'kæljən, pitkál-yĕn

Pitcruvie Fife, pɪt'kruvɪ, pit--kroóvi

Pitfichie Castle Grampian, pɪt-'fɪxɪ, pitfíchi

Pitfirrane Park Fife, pɪt'fɪrən, pitfírrăn

Pitfodels Grampian, pɪt'fɒdlz, pitfóddlz

Pitgaveny Grampian, pɪt'geɪvənɪ, pitgáyvĕni

Pithey, f.n., 'pɪθɪ, píthi; 'pɪðɪ, píthi

Pitlochry Tayside, pɪt'lɒxrɪ, pit-lóchri

Pitreavie Fife, pɪ'trɪvɪ, pitreévi

Pitscottie Fife, pɪt'skɒtɪ, pitskótti

Pitsea Essex, 'pɪtsi, pítsee

Pitsligo Grampian, pɪt'slaɪgoʊ, pitslígō

Pittenweem Fife, ˌpɪtən'wim, pittĕnweém

Pitteuchar Fife, pɪt'juxər, pit--yoóchăr

Pittodrie Grampian, pɪ'tɒdrɪ, pitóddri

Pittondrigh, f.n., 'pɪtəndraɪ, píttŏndri

Pizey, f.n., 'paɪzɪ, pízi

Pizzey, f.n., 'pɪzɪ, pízzi; 'pɪtsɪ, pítsi

Pladdies Co. Down, 'plædɪz, pláddiz

Plaid Cymru, Welsh National Party, 'plaɪd 'kʌmrɪ, plíd kúmri

Plainmoor Devon, 'pleɪnmʊər, pláynmoŏr

Plaisted, f.n., 'pleɪstɪd, pláysstĕd

Plaistow, f.n., 'pleɪstoʊ, pláysstō

Plaistow Derby., H. & W., 'pleɪstoʊ, pláysstō

Plaistow London, 'plɑstoʊ, plaásstō; 'plæstoʊ, plásstō. Appropriate for the ~ parliamentary division.

Plaistow Kent, 'plɑstoʊ, plaásstō; 'pleɪstoʊ, pláysstō

Plaistow W. Sussex, 'plæstoʊ, plásstō

Plaitford Hants, 'pleɪtfərd, pláytfŏrd

Plamenatz, f.n., 'plæmɪnæts, plámmĕnats

Planterose, f.n., 'plɑntəroʊz, plaántĕröz

Plaskow, f.n., 'plæskoʊ, plásskō

Plasnewydd S. Glam., plæs-'njuɪð, plass-néw-ith

Plastow, *f.n.*, 'plæstoʊ, plásstō
Plas-y-Brenin *Gwynedd*, 'plɑs ə
  'brenɪn, pláass ă brénnin
Plater, *f.n.*, 'pleɪtər, pláytĕr
Plath, *f.n.*, plæθ, plath
Platt, *f.n.*, plæt, platt
Platting *Gtr. M'chester*, 'plætɪŋ,
  plátting
Platts, *f.n.*, plæts, platts
Plaxtol *Kent*, 'plækstəl, pláckstŏl
Playle, *f.n.*, pleɪl, playl
Pleasance, *f.n.*, 'plezəns, plézz-
  änss
Pleasington *Lancs.*, 'plezɪŋtən,
  plézzingtŏn
Pleasley *Derby.*, 'plezlɪ, plézzli
Pleass, *f.n.*, plis, pleess; ples,
  pless
Pleshey *Essex*, 'pleʃɪ, pléshi
Pleydell, *f.n.*, 'pledl, pléddl;
  pleɪ'del, playdéll
Pleydell-Bouverie, *f.n.*, 'pledl
  'buvərɪ, pléddl boóvĕri. *Family
  name of the Earl of Radnor.*
Pliatzky, *f.n.*, plɪ'ætskɪ, pli-átski
Plimmer, *f.n.*, 'plɪmər, plímmĕr
Plinlimmon, *also spelt* Plynlimon,
  Dyfed, plɪn'lɪmən, plinlímmŏn.
  The Welsh form of the name is
  Pumlumon, *q.v.*
Plomer, *f.n.*, 'plumər, ploómĕr.
  Appropriate for William ∼,
  author.
Plomley, *f.n.*, 'plʌmlɪ, plúmli
Plouviez, *f.n.*, 'pluvɪeɪ, ploóvi-ay
Plowden, *f.n.*, 'plaʊdən, plówdĕn.
  Appropriate also for Baron ∼.
Plowman, *f.n.*, 'plaʊmən, plów-
  män
Plowright, *f.n.*, 'plaʊraɪt, plów-
  -rīt
Plugge, *f.n.*, plʌg, plug
Plumbe, *f.n.*, plʌm, plum
Plumbridge *Co. Tyrone*, plʌm-
  'brɪdʒ, plum-bríj
Plume, *f.n.*, plum, ploom
Plumer, Viscountcy of, 'plumər,
  ploómĕr
Plumer Barracks *Plymouth*,
  'plumər, ploómĕr
Plummer, *f.n.*, 'plʌmər, plúmmĕr
Plumptre, *f.n.*, 'plʌmtri, plúmtree
Plumtre, *f.n.*, 'plʌmtri, plúmtree
Plungar *Leics.*, 'plʌŋɡɑr, plúng-
  -gaar
Plunkett, *f.n.*, 'plʌŋkɪt, plúnkĕt
Pluscarden Priory *Grampian*,
  'plʌskərdən, plússkärdĕn
Plymen, *f.n.*, 'plaɪmən, plímĕn
Plymouth *Devon*, 'plɪməθ, plím-
  mŭth
Plymtree *Devon*, 'plɪmtri, plím-
  tree
Plynlimon *see* Plinlimmon

Pochin, *f.n.*, 'poʊtʃɪn, pótchin;
  'pʌtʃɪn, pútchin
Pocock, *f.n.*, 'poʊkɒk, pókock
Podds, *f.n.*, pɒdz, podz
Poderis, *f.n.*, pə'dɛərɪs, pŏdáiriss
Podevin, *f.n.*, 'poʊdəvɪn, pódĕvin
Podington *Beds.*, 'pɒdɪŋtən, pód-
  dingtŏn
Poel, *f.n.*, 'poʊel, pó-el
Poeton, *f.n.*, 'poʊɪtən, pó-ĕtŏn
Poett, *f.n.*, 'poʊɪt, pó-ĕt
Pogson, *f.n.*, 'pɒgsən, póggssŏn
Point Lynas *Anglesey*, pɔɪnt
  'laɪnəs, poynt línäss
Pointon, *f.n.*, 'pɔɪntən, póyntŏn
Poirier, *f.n.*, 'pɒrɪər, pórri-ĕr
Polak, *f.n.*, 'poʊlək, pólăk;
  'poʊlæk, pólack
Polan, *f.n.*, 'poʊlən, pólăn
Polapit *Cornwall*, 'pɒləpɪt, póllă-
  pit
Polbathic *Cornwall*, pɒl'bæθɪk,
  polbáthick
Polden Hills *Somerset*, 'poʊldən
  'hɪlz, póldĕn híllz
Poldhu *Cornwall*, pɒl'dju, poldéw
Pole, *f.n.*, poʊl, pōl; pul, pool
Polegate *E. Sussex*, 'poʊlgeɪt,
  pólgayt
Polesden Lacey *Surrey*, 'poʊlz-
  dən 'leɪsɪ, pólzdĕn láyssi
Polgigga *see* Poljigga
Pol Hill *Kent*, 'pɒl 'hɪl, pól hill
Poliakov, *f.n.*, 'pɒljəkɒf, pól-
  -yäkoff
Poling *W. Sussex*, 'poʊlɪŋ, póling
Poljigga, *also spelt* Polgigga,
  Cornwall, pɒl'dʒɪgə, poljíggă
Polkemmet *Lothian*, pɒl'kemɪt,
  polkémmĕt
Polkerris *Cornwall*, pɒl'kerɪs,
  polkérriss
Pollak, *f.n.*, 'pɒlək, póllăk
Pollard, *f.n.*, 'pɒlɑrd, póllaard
Pollock, *f.n.*, 'pɒlək, póllŏk
Pollokshields *S'clyde*, 'pɒlək-
  'ʃildz, póllŏk-sheéldz
Pollphail *S'clyde*, 'pɒlfeɪl, pólfayl
Polmadie *S'clyde*, ,pɒlmə'di,
  polmădeé
Polmont *Central*, 'poʊlmənt, pól-
  mŏnt
Polperro *Cornwall*, pɒl'peroʊ,
  polpérrō
Polruan *Cornwall*, pɒl'ruən,
  polroó-ăn
Polson, *f.n.*, 'poʊlsən, pólssŏn
Polstead *Suffolk*, 'poʊlsted,
  pólssted
Poltalloch *S'clyde*, pɒl'tæləx,
  poltálŏch
Poltimore *Devon*, 'poʊltɪmɔr, pól-
  timor. *Appropriate also for
  Baron* ∼.

Polton *Lothian*, 'poʊltən, póltěn
Polwarth, *f.n.*, 'pɒlwərθ, pólwărth
Polwarth *Lothian*, 'poʊlwərθ, pólwărth
Polwhele, *f.n.*, pɒl'wil, polwéel
Polwhele *Cornwall*, pɒl'wil, polwéel
Polygon *Southampton*, 'pɒlɪgən, póligŏn
Polzeath *Cornwall*, pɒl'zeθ, polzéth
Pomeroy, *f.n.*, 'poʊmrɔɪ, pómroy; 'pɒmərɔɪ, pómměroy. *The first is appropriate for the family name of Viscount Harberton.*
Pomeroy *Co. Tyrone*, 'pɒmərɔɪ, pómměroy
Pomfret, *f.n.*, 'pʌmfrɪt, púmfrět
Pompey, *popular name for Portsmouth*, 'pɒmpɪ, pómpi
Pomphrey, *f.n.*, 'pɒmfrɪ, pómfri
Ponfeigh *S'clyde*, pɒn'feɪ, ponfáy
Ponsanooth *Cornwall*, pɒnz'nuθ, ponz-noóth
Ponsford, *f.n.*, 'pɒnsfərd, pónssfŏrd
Ponsonby, *f.n.*, 'pʌnsənbɪ, púnssŏnbi; 'pɒnsənbɪ, pónssŏnbi
Ponsonby *Cumbria*, 'pʌnsənbɪ, púnssŏnbi; 'pɒnsənbɪ, pónssŏnbi
Ponsonby of Shulbrede, Baron, 'pʌnsənbɪ əv 'ʃulbrid, púnssŏnbi ŏv shoólbreed
Ponsonby of Sysonby, Baron, 'pʌnsənbɪ əv 'saɪzənbɪ, púnssŏnbi ŏv sízŏnbi
Pontardawe *W. Glam.*, ,pɒntər'daʊeɪ, pontărdów-ay
Pontarddulais *W. Glam.*, ,pɒntar-'ðɪlaɪs, pontaarthílliss. *The English form is* **Pontardulais**, *q.v.*
Pontardulais *W. Glam.*, ,pɒntər-'dɪlaɪs, pontărdílliss; ,pɒntər-'dɪləs, pontărdíllăss; ,pɒntər-'dʌləs, pontărdúllăss. *The Welsh form is* **Pontarddulais**, *q.v.*
Pontcysyllte *Clwyd*, ,pɒntkə'sʌɬteɪ, pontkŭssúhltay
Pont-dôl-goch *Powys*, ,pɒntdoʊl-'goʊx, pont-dōlgŏ́ch
Pontefract *W. Yorks.*, 'pɒntɪfrækt, póntěfrackt. *An old local form, which survives in the name of the liquorice sweets known as* '**Pomfret** *cakes*', *is pronounced* 'pʌmfrɪt, púmfrět *or* 'pɒmfrɪt, pómfrět
Ponteland *Northd.*, pɒnt'iлənd, pontéelănd
Ponterwyd *Dyfed*, pɒnt'ɛərwɪd, pontáirwid

Pontesbury *Salop*, 'pɒntɪzbərɪ, póntězbūri
Pontet, *f.n.*, 'pɒntɪt, póntět; 'pɒnteɪ, póntay
Pontfadog *Clwyd*, pɒnt'vædɒg, pontváddog
Pont-faen *Dyfed*, *Powys*, pɒnt-'vaɪn, pontvín
Pontfaen *Dyfed*, pɒnt'vaɪn, pontvín
Pontfenny *Dyfed*, pɒnt'venɪ, pontvénni
Ponthenry, *also spelt* **Pont Henry**, *Dyfed*, pɒnt'henrɪ, pont-hénri
Pontlase, Pontlasse *see* **Pontlassau**
Pontlassau, *also spelt* **Pontlase, Pontlasse**, *Mid Glam.*, pɒnt-'læseɪ, pontlássay
Pontllan-fraith *Gwent*, ,pɒntɬæn-'vraɪθ, pont-ḥlanvríth
Pont-lliw *W. Glam.*, pɒnt'ɬju, pont-ḥléw
Pontlottyn *Mid Glam.*, pɒnt'lɒtɪn, pontlóttin
Pontlyfni *Gwynedd*, pɒnt'lʌvnɪ, pont-lúvni
Pontneathvaughan *Powys*, ,pɒntniθ'vɔn, pont-neethváwn. *The Welsh form is* **Pontneddfechan**, *q.v.*
Pontneddfechan *Powys*, ,pɒntneð'vexən, pont-neṯhvéchăn. *The English form is* **Pontneathvaughan**, *q.v.*
Pontnewydd *Gwent*, pɒnt'newɪð, pontné-wiṯh
Pontnewynydd *Gwent*, ,pɒntnə-'wʌnɪð, pontněwúnniṯh
Ponton, Great *and* Little, *Lincs.*, 'pɒntən, póntŏn
Pontop *Durham*, 'pɒntɒp, póntop
Pontop Pike *Durham*, 'pɒntɒp 'paɪk, póntop pík
Pontrhydfendigaid *Dyfed*, ,pɒnt-hrɪdven'digaɪd, pontreed--vendéegïd
Pont-rhyd-y-fen *W. Glam.*, ,pɒnthrɪdə'ven, pontreedávén; ,pɒnthrɪdə'ven, pontridăvén
Pontrilas *H. & W.*, pɒnt'raɪləs, pontríläss
Pontrobert *Powys*, pɒnt'rɒbərt, pont-róbbĕrt
Pontsticill *Mid Glam.*, pɒnt'stɪkɪɬ, pontstíkihl
Pontyates *Dyfed*, pɒnt'jeɪts, pont--yáyts
Pontyberem *Dyfed*, ,pɒntə'berəm, pontăbérrĕm
Pontybodkin *Clwyd*, ,pɒntə'bɒd-kɪn, pontăbódkin
Pont-y-clun *Mid Glam.*, ,pɒntə-'klin, pontăkléen

Pontycymmer, *also spelt* **Ponty-cymer,** *Mid Glam.*, ˌpɒntə-ˈkʌmər, pontăkúmmĕr

Pont-y-gwaith *Mid Glam.*, ˌpɒntəˈgwaɪθ, pontăgwíth

Pontymister *Gwent*, ˌpɒntəˈmɪstər, pontămísstĕr

Pontymoile *Gwent*, ˌpɒntəˈmɔɪl, pontămóyl

Pontypool *Gwent*, ˌpɒntəˈpul, pontăpoól

Pontypridd *Mid Glam.*, ˌpɒntə-ˈprɪð, pontăpreéth

Pontyrhyl *Mid Glam.*, ˌpɒntəˈrɪl, pontăríll

Poock, *f.n.*, puk, pook

Pook, *f.n.*, puk, pook

Poole, *f.n.*, pul, pool

Poolewe *H'land*, pulˈju, poōléw

Popham, *f.n.*, ˈpɒpəm, póppăm

Popkin, *f.n.*, ˈpɒpkɪn, pópkin

Pople, *f.n.*, ˈpoupl, pōpl

Poplett, *f.n.*, ˈpɒplɪt, póplĕt

Porchester, Baron, ˈpɔrtʃɪstər, pórtchĕsstĕr

Porges, *f.n.*, ˈpɔrdʒɪz, pórjĕz

Poringland *Norfolk*, ˈpɒrɪŋlænd, páwring-land; ˈpɔrlænd, pór-land

Porkellis *Cornwall*, pɔrˈkelɪs, porkélliss

Portadown *Co. Armagh*, ˌpɔrtə-ˈdaun, portădówn

Portaferry *Co. Down*, ˌpɔrtəˈferɪ, portăférri

Portal, *f.n.*, ˈpɔrtl, pórtl

Portal of Hungerford, Viscount, ˈpɔrtl əv ˈhʌŋgərfərd, pórtl ŏv húng-gĕrfŏrd

Portarlington, Earl of, pɔrtˈɑrlɪŋtən, portaárlingtŏn

Portaskaig *S'clyde*, pɔrtˈæskeɪg, portásskayg

Portavadie, *also spelt* **Porta-vaidue,** *S'clyde*, ˌpɔrtəˈvædɪ, portăváddi

Portavoe *Co. Down*, ˌpɔrtəˈvou, portăvő

Portavogie *Co. Down*, ˌpɔrtə-ˈvougɪ, portăvógi

Portballintrae *Co. Antrim*, pɔrt-ˌbælɪnˈtreɪ, port-balintráy

Port Bannatyne *S'clyde*, pɔrt ˈbænətaɪn, port bánnătīn

Portbraddon *Co. Antrim*, pɔrt-ˈbrædən, port-bráddŏn

Portbury *Avon*, ˈpɔrtbərɪ, pórt-bŭri

Porteinon *see* **Port Eynon**

Porteous, *f.n.*, ˈpɔrtjəs, pórt-yŭss; ˈpɔrtɪəs, pórti-ŭss

Portesham *Dorset*, ˈpɔrtɪʃəm, pórtĕ-shăm

Port Eynon, *also spelt* **Porteynon, Porteinon,** *W. Glam.*, pɔrt ˈaɪnən, port ínŏn

Portglenone *Co. Antrim*, ˌpɔrtglə-ˈnoun, portglĕnőn

Porth, *f.n.*, pɔrθ, porth

Porthallow *Cornwall*, pɔrθˈælou, porth-álō

Porthcawl *Mid Glam.*, pɔrθˈkɔl, porthkáwl; pɔrθˈkaul, porth-kówl

Porthcuel Ferry *Cornwall*, ˈpɔrθ-kjul, pórthkewl. *The modern name is* **Percuil,** *q.v.*

Porthcurno *Cornwall*, pɔrθˈkɜrnou, porthkúrnō

Porth Dinllaen *Gwynedd*, ˌpɔrθ dɪnˈɬaɪn, porth din-ɬín. *Another form is* **Portin-llaen,** *q.v.*

Porthleven *Cornwall*, pɔrθˈlevən, porthlévvĕn

Porthmadog *Gwynedd*, pɔrθ-ˈmædɒg, porth-máddog

Porthoustock *Cornwall*, pɔrθ-ˈaustɒk, porth-ówsstock; ˈpraustɒk, prówsstock

Porthpean *Cornwall*, pɔrθˈpiən, porthpeé-ăn

Porthtowan *Cornwall*, pɔrθˈtauən, porthtów-ăn

Porth yr Aur *Gwynedd*, ˈpɔrθ ər ˈaɪər, pórth ŭr ír

Porth-y-rhyd *Dyfed*, ˌpɔrθəˈhrid, porth-ă-reéd

Portincaple *S'clyde*, ˈpɔrtɪnkæpl, pórtin-kappl

Portin-llaen *Gwynedd*, ˌpɔrtɪnˈɬaɪn, portin-ɬín. *Another form is* **Porth Dinllaen,** *q.v.*

Portishead *Avon*, ˈpɔrtɪshed, pórtiss-hed

Portland, Duke of, ˈpɔrtlənd, pórtlănd

Portlethen *Grampian*, pɔrtˈleθən, portléthĕn

Portloe *Cornwall*, pɔrtˈlou, portlő

Portmadoc *Gwynedd*, pɔrtˈmædək, portmáddŏk. *Former name of* **Porthmadog,** *q.v.*

Portmahomack *H'land*, ˌpɔrtmə-ˈhɒmək, portmă-hómmăk

Portman, *f.n.*, ˈpɔrtmən, pórtmăn

Portmeirion *Gwynedd*, pɔrt-ˈmerɪən, port-mérri-ŏn

Portnahaven *S'clyde*, ˌpɔrtnə-ˈhævən, portnă-hávvĕn

Portnoid, *f.n.*, ˈpɔrtnɔɪd, pórt-noyd

Portobello *Edinburgh*, ˌpɔrtə-ˈbelou, portŏbéllō

Portquin *Cornwall*, pɔrtˈkwɪn, portkwín

Portreath *Cornwall*, pɔr'triθ, portreeth
Portree *H'land*, pɔr'tri, portreé
Portrush *Co. Antrim*, pɔrt'rʌʃ, portrúsh
Portscatho *Cornwall*, pɔrt'skæθoʊ, portskáthō
Port Seton *Lothian*, pɔrt 'sitən, port seéton
Portskewett *Gwent*, pɔrt'skjuɪt, portskéw-ĕt
Portslade-by-Sea *E. Sussex*, 'pɔrtsleɪd baɪ 'si, pórtslayd bī seé
Portsmouth *Hants*, 'pɔrtsməθ, pórtsmŭth
Portsoy *Grampian*, pɔrt'sɔɪ, port-sóy
Portstewart *Co. Derry*, pɔrt-'stjʊərt, port-styoō-ärt
Port Talbot *W. Glam.*, pɔrt 'tɔlbət, port táwlbŏt; pɔrt 'tælbət, port tálbŏt; pɔr'tɔlbət, portáwlbŏt; pɔr'tælbət, portálbŏt
Portugheis, *f.n.*, pɔrtjʊ'geɪz, portyoōgáyz
Possell, *f.n.*, pə'sel, pŏsséll
Posta, *f.n.*, 'pɒstə, pósstä
Postcombe *Oxon.*, 'poʊstkəm, póstkŏm
Poster, *f.n.*, 'pɒstər, pósstĕr
Postgate, *f.n.*, 'poʊstgeɪt, póst-gayt
Postles, *f.n.*, 'pɒslz, pósslz
Postlethwaite, *f.n.*, 'pɒslθweɪt, póssl-thwayt
Postling *Kent*, 'poʊstlɪŋ, póstling
Poston, *f.n.*, 'pɒstən, pósstŏn
Postwick *Norfolk*, 'pɒzɪk, pózzick
Poton, *f.n.*, 'pɒtən, póttŏn
Potter Heigham *Norfolk*, 'pɒtər 'heɪəm, póttĕr háy-ăm; 'pɒtər 'haɪəm, póttĕr hí-ăm; 'pɒtər 'hæm, póttĕr hám
Potterspury *Northants.*, 'pɒtərz-pərɪ, póttĕrzpŭri
Pottinger, *f.n.*, 'pɒtɪndʒər, póttinjĕr
Pougher, *f.n.*, 'paʊər, pówĕr; 'pʌfər, púffĕr
Poughill *Cornwall*, 'pɒfɪl, póffil; 'pʌfɪl, púffil
Poughill *Devon*, 'paʊɪl, pów-il
Poulett, Earl, 'pɒlɪt, páwlĕt
Poulner *Hants*, 'paʊnər, pównĕr; 'paʊlnər, pówlnĕr
Poulsen, *f.n.*, 'poʊlsən, pŏlssĕn
Poulshot *Wilts.*, 'poʊlʃɒt, pŏl-shot
Poulson, *f.n.*, 'poʊlsən, pŏlssŏn
Poulter, *f.n.*, 'poʊltər, pŏltĕr
Poultney *Leics.*, 'poʊltnɪ, pŏltni
Poulton, *f.n.*, 'poʊltən, pŏltŏn

Poulton-le-Fylde *Lancs.*, 'pʊltən lə 'faɪld, poŏltŏn lĕ fíld
Pounder, *f.n.*, 'paʊndər, pówndĕr
Poundstock *Cornwall*, 'paʊndstɒk, pówndstock
Pounteney, *f.n.*, 'paʊntnɪ, pówntni
Pountney, *f.n.*, 'paʊntnɪ, pówntni
Poupart, *f.n.*, 'pupart, poōpaart; 'poʊpart, pŏpaart
Pouparts Junction *London*, 'pu-parts, poōpaarts
Povall, *f.n.*, 'poʊvl, póvl
Pover, *f.n.*, 'poʊvər, póvĕr
Povey, *f.n.*, 'poʊvɪ, póvi; pə'veɪ, pŏváy
Povey's Cross *Surrey*, 'poʊvɪz 'krɒs, póviz króss
Pow, *f.n.*, paʊ, pow
Powburn *Northd.*, 'paʊbɜrn, pówburn
Powe, *f.n.*, paʊ, pow
Powell, *f.n.*, 'paʊəl, pówĕl; 'poʊəl, pŏ-ĕl. *The first is appropriate for Dilys ~, film critic and broadcaster; the second for Anthony ~, author.*
Powerscourt, Viscount, 'pɔrzkɔrt, pórz-kort
Powerstock *Dorset*, 'paʊərstɒk, pówĕrstock
Powick *H. & W.*, 'poʊɪk, pŏ-ick
Powis, Earl of, 'poʊɪs, pŏ-iss
Powis, *f.n.*, 'paʊɪs, pówiss
Powis, *Grampian*, 'paʊɪs, pówiss
Powis Castle *Powys*, 'poʊɪs, pŏ-iss
Powlett, *f.n.*, 'pɔlɪt, páwlĕt
Powley, *f.n.*, 'poʊlɪ, póli; 'paʊlɪ, pówli
Pownall, *f.n.*, 'paʊnl, pównl
Powrie, *f.n.*, 'paʊərɪ, pówri
Powyke *see* **Beauchamp of Powyke**, Baron
Powys, *f.n.*, 'poʊɪs, pŏ-iss; 'paʊɪs, pówiss. *The first is appropriate for the family name of Baron Lilford; also for A. R. ~, church architect, John Cowper ~, poet and author, Llewelyn ~, author, Theodore Francis ~, author, and* **E.** ~ **Mathers,** *author and scholar.*
Powys *Co. name*, 'paʊɪs, pówiss
Poyntzpass *Co. Armagh*, pɔɪnts-'pas, poyntspaáss
Praa Sands, Praah Sands *see* **Prah Sands**
Prador, *f.n.*, 'pradɔr, praádor
Praed, *f.n.*, preɪd, prayd
Pragnell, *f.n.*, 'prægnəl, prágnĕl
Prah Sands, *also spelt* **Praa, Praah**, *Cornwall*, 'preɪ 'sændz, práy sándz
Prangnell, *f.n.*, 'præŋnəl, práng-nĕl

Prashar, *f.n.*, prə'ʃɑr, pră-shá'ar
Prater, *f.n.*, 'preɪtər, práytĕr
Pratley, *f.n.*, 'prætlɪ, prátli
Prawer, *f.n.*, 'prɑvər, praávĕr
Praze *Cornwall*, preɪz, prayz
Predannack *Cornwall*, 'predənæk, préddănack; 'prednæk, préd-
-nack
Preece, *f.n.*, pris, preess
Preedy, *f.n.*, 'pridɪ, preédi
Preesall *Lancs.*, 'prizl, preézl
Preger, *f.n.*, 'preɪgər, práygĕr
Prehen *Co. Derry*, prɪ'hen, prĕhén
Preidel, *f.n.*, 'praɪdel, prídel
Prem, *f.n.*, prem, prem
Premru, *f.n.*, 'premru, prémroo
Prendergast, *f.n.*, 'prendərgæst, préndĕrgasst
Prendwick *Northd.*, 'prendɪk, préndick
Prentice, *f.n.*, 'prentɪs, préntiss
Prentis, *f.n.*, 'prentɪs, préntiss
Prentiss, *f.n.*, 'prentɪs, préntiss
Prescelly Mountains, *also spelt*
Prescely, *Dyfed*, pre'selɪ, pre-sséli
Preshaw *Hants*, 'preʃɔ, préshaw
Pressey, *f.n.*, 'presɪ, préssi
Prestatyn *Clwyd*, pres'tætɪn, presstáttin
Presteigne *Powys*, pres'tin, pressteén
Prestige, *f.n.*, 'prestɪdʒ, présstij
Preston *Herts.*, *Lancs.*, 'prestən, présstŏn
Prestonpans *Lothian*, 'prestən-'pænz, présstŏnpánz
Prestwick *Northd.*, 'prestɪk, présstick
Prestwick *S'clyde*, 'prestwɪk, présstwick. *Appropriate also for*
~ *Airport.*
Pretius, *f.n.*, 'preʃəs, préshŭss
Pretty, *f.n.*, 'prɪtɪ, prítti; 'pretɪ, prétti
Pretyman, *f.n.*, 'prɪtɪmən, príttimăn
Prevatt, *f.n.*, 'prɪvət, prívvăt
Prevezer, *f.n.*, prɪ'vizər, prĕvéezĕr
Previté, *f.n.*, prɪ'vitɪ, prĕvéeti; 'prevɪtɪ, prévviti
Prevost, *f.n.*, prɪ'voʊ, prĕvó; 'prevəst, prévvŏst; 'prevoʊ, prévvō
Prewer, *f.n.*, 'pruər, proó-ĕr
Preye, *f.n.*, preɪ, pray
Price, *f.n.*, praɪs, príss
Priday, *f.n.*, 'praɪdeɪ, príday
Prideaux, *f.n.*, 'prɪdoʊ, príddō
Prideaux *Cornwall*, 'prɪdəks, príddŭks
Prideaux-Brune, *f.n.*, 'prɪdoʊ 'brun, príddō broón
Pridham, *f.n.*, 'prɪdəm, príddăm

Priechenfried, *f.n.*, 'prikənfrid, preékĕnfreed
Priestland, *f.n.*, 'pristlənd, preéstländ
Priestley, *f.n.*, 'pristlɪ, preésstli
Princes Risborough *Bucks.*, 'prɪnsɪz 'rɪzbərə, prínssĕz rízbŏrŏ
Princetown *Devon*, *Mid Glam.*, 'prɪnstaʊn, prínsstown
Pringle, *f.n.*, 'prɪŋgl, príng-gl
Prinknash Abbey *Glos.*, 'prɪnɪdʒ, prínnij
Prins, *f.n.*, prɪns, prinss
Prinsep, *f.n.*, 'prɪnsep, prínssep
Prioleau, *f.n.*, 'prɪəloʊ, preé-ōlō
Prion *Powys*, 'prɪɒn, preé-on
Prior, *f.n.*, 'praɪər, prí-ŏr
Priske, *f.n.*, prɪsk, prissk
Pritchard, *f.n.*, 'prɪtʃərd, prítchärd; 'prɪtʃɑrd, prítchaard
Pritlove, *f.n.*, 'prɪtlʌv, prítluv
Privett, *Hants*, 'prɪvɪt, prívvĕt
Probert, *f.n.*, 'prɒbərt, próbbĕrt; 'proʊbərt, próbĕrt
Probus *Cornwall*, 'proʊbəs, próbŭss
Probyn, *f.n.*, 'proʊbɪn, próbin
Prochazka, *f.n.*, prɒ'xæskə, prochásskă
Procope, *f.n.*, 'prɒkəpeɪ, próckŏpay
Procter, *f.n.*, 'prɒktər, prócktĕr
Prodrick, *f.n.*, 'prɒdrɪk, pródrick
Profumo, *f.n.*, prə'fjumoʊ, prŏféwmō
Progin, *f.n.*, 'proʊdʒɪn, prójin
Prolze, *f.n.*, proʊlts, prōlts
Proniewicz, *f.n.*, 'prɒnəvɪtʃ, prónnŏvitch
Prosen, *f.n.*, 'proʊzən, prózĕn
Prosser, *f.n.*, 'prɒsər, próssĕr
Protasus, saint, prə'teɪzəs, prŏtáyzüss
Prothero, *f.n.*, 'prɒðəroʊ, próthĕrō; 'prʌðəroʊ, prúthĕrō
Protheroe, *f.n.*, 'prɒðəroʊ, próthĕrō; 'prʌðəroʊ, prúthĕrō
Protus, saint, 'proʊtəs, prótüss
Prout, *f.n.*, praʊt, prowt
Provan, *f.n.*, 'prɒvən, próvvăn; 'proʊvən, próvăn
Provan *Glasgow*, 'prɒvən, próvvăn
Provis, *f.n.*, 'proʊvɪs, próviss
Prowse, *f.n.*, praʊs, prowss; praʊz, prowz
Prudhoe *Northd.*, 'prʌdoʊ, prúddō; 'prʌdhoʊ, prúd-hō
Prue, *f.n.*, pru, proo
Pruslin, *f.n.*, 'prʌslɪn, prússlin
Prusmann, *f.n.*, 'prʌsmən, prússmăn
Pryce, *f.n.*, praɪs, príss
Prynne, *f.n.*, prɪn, prinn

Prys, *f.n.*, pris, preess
Prytherch, *f.n.*, 'prʌðərx, prú-
thĕrch; 'prʌðərk, prúthĕrk;
'prɪðrk, príthick. *The first is the*
Welsh pronunciation.
Puckey, *f.n.*, 'pʌkɪ, púcki
Puddefoot, *f.n.*, 'pʌdɪfʊt, púddĕ-
fŏot; 'pʊdɪfʊt, pŏodĕfŏot
Puddephat, *f.n.*, 'pʌdɪfæt, púddĕ-
fat
Puddephatt, *f.n.*, 'pʌdɪfæt,
púddĕfat; 'pʊdɪfæt, pŏodĕfat
Puddletown *Dorset*, 'pʌdltaʊn,
púddltown
Puddy, *f.n.*, 'pʌdɪ, púddi
Pudney, *f.n.*, 'pʌdnɪ, púdni
Pudsey *W. Yorks.*, 'pʌdsɪ, púdssi
Puffett, *f.n.*, 'pʌfɪt, púffĕt
Puffin Island, *also* **St. Seiriol**
Island *q.v.*, *Gwynedd*, 'pʌfɪn,
púffin
Pugh, *f.n.*, pju, pew
Pughe, *f.n.*, pju, pew
Pugin, *f.n.*, 'pjudʒɪn, péwjin
Pugmire, *f.n.*, 'pʌgmaɪər, púgmīr
Pulay, *f.n.*, 'puleɪ, poólay
Puleston, *f.n.*, 'pulstən, poólsstŏn
Pulfer, *f.n.*, 'pʊlfər, poŏlfĕr
Pullein, *f.n.*, 'pʊlɪn, poŏlĕn
Pullen, *f.n.*, 'pʊlɪn, poŏlĕn
Pulling, *f.n.*, 'pʊlɪŋ, poŏling
Pullinger, *f.n.*, 'pʊlɪndʒər,
poŏlinjĕr
Pulloxhill *Beds.*, 'pʊləkshɪl,
poŏlŏks-hil
Pulman, *f.n.*, 'pʊlmən, poŏlmăn
Pulteney, *f.n.*, 'pʌltnɪ, púltni;
'pʊʊltnɪ, pŏltni
Pulteney Bridge *Bath*, 'pʌltənɪ,
púltĕni
Pulvertaft, *f.n.*, 'pʌlvərtæft,
púlvĕrtafft
Pumlumon *Dyfed*, pɪm'lɪmən,
pimlímmŏn. *See also* **Plinlim-**
mon.
Pumpherston *Lothian*, 'pʌmfər-
stən, púmfĕrstŏn
Pumphrey, *f.n.*, 'pʌmfrɪ, púmfri
Pumpsaint *Dyfed*, 'pɪmpsaɪnt,
pímpsīnt
Puncheston *Dyfed*, 'pʌnʃɪstən,
púnshĕsstŏn
Puncknowle *Dorset*, 'pʌnl, púnnl
Punshon, *f.n.*, 'pʌnʃən, púnshŏn
Purbrick, *f.n.*, 'pɜrbrɪk, púrbrick
Purcell, *f.n.*, 'pɜrsl, púrssl; pɜr'sel,
pursséll. *The first is appropriate*
for the 17th-c. composer, Henry
~.
Purchese, *f.n.*, pɜr'tʃiz, pur-
tchéez
Purdie, *f.n.*, 'pɜrdɪ, púrdi
Purdom, *f.n.*, 'pɜrdəm, púrdŏm
Purdon, *f.n.*, 'pɜrdən, púrdŏn

Purdue, *f.n.*, 'pɜrdju, púrdew
Purdy, *f.n.*, 'pɜrdɪ, púrdi
Purdysburn *Co. Down*, 'pɜrdɪz-
bɜrn, púrdizburn
Purefoy, *f.n.*, 'pjʊərfɔɪ, pyŏŏrfoy
Purfleet *Essex*, 'pɜrflit, púrfleet
Purgavie, *f.n.*, pɜr'geɪvɪ, purgáyvi
Puriton *Somerset*, 'pjʊərɪtən,
pyŏŏritŏn
Purleigh *Essex*, 'pɜrlɪ, púrli
Purnell, *f.n.*, pɜr'nel, purnéll
Pursey, *f.n.*, 'pɜrzɪ, púrzi
Purves, *f.n.*, 'pɜrvɪs, púrvĕss;
pɜrvz, purvz
Purvey, *f.n.*, 'pɜrvɪ, púrvi
Pusey, *f.n.*, 'pjuzɪ, péwzi
Putnam, *f.n.*, 'pʌtnəm, pútt-năm
Putney *London*, 'pʌtnɪ, púttni
Putson *H. & W.*, 'pʌtsən, púttsŏn
Putt, *f.n.*, pʌt, putt
Putteridge Bury *Herts.*, 'pʌtərɪdʒ
'berɪ, púttĕrij bérri
Pwll *Dyfed*, puɬ, poohl
Pwllcrochan *Dyfed*, puɬ'krɒxən,
poohlkróchăn
Pwll-gwaun *Mid Glam.*, puɬ-
'gwaɪn, poohl-gwín
Pwllheli *Gwynedd*, puɬ'helɪ,
poohl-hélli; pu'ɬelɪ, poohlélli
Pwll-Meyric *Gwent*, puɬ'maɪrɪk,
poohl-mírick
Pyburn, *f.n.*, 'paɪbɜrn, píburn
Pybus, *f.n.*, 'paɪbəs, píbüss
Pyecombe *W. Sussex*, 'paɪkum,
píkoom
Pyer, *f.n.*, 'paɪər, pí-ĕr
Pyke, *f.n.*, paɪk, pīk
Pyle *Mid Glam.*, paɪl, pīl
Pylle *Somerset*, pɪl, pill; paɪl, pīl
Pym, *f.n.*, pɪm, pim
Pyman, *f.n.*, 'paɪmən, pímăn
Pymore *Cambs.*, 'paɪmɔr, pímor
Pyper, *f.n.*, 'paɪpər, pípĕr
Pyrah, *f.n.*, 'paɪərə, píră
Pyrford *Surrey*, 'pɜrfərd, púrförd
Pyrgo Park *Essex*, 'pɜrgoʊ, púrgō
Pytchley *Northants.*, 'paɪtʃlɪ,
pítchli

Q

Quaddell, *f.n.*, kwə'del, kwŏdéll
Quaddy, *f.n.*, 'kwɒdɪ, kwóddi
Quadring *Lincs.*, 'kweɪdrɪŋ,
kwáydring
Quaglino's Hotel & Restaurant
London, kwæg'linoʊz, kwag-
leénōz
Quaid, *f.n.*, kweɪd, kwayd
Quaife, *f.n.*, kweɪf, kwayf

Quain, f.n., kweın, kwayn. *Appropriate also for the ~ professorship of English in the University of London.*
Quant, f.n., kwɒnt, kwont
Quantock Hills *Somerset*, 'kwɒntɒk, kwóntock
Quantrill, f.n., 'kwɒntrıl, kwóntril
Quarendon, f.n., 'kwɒrəndən, kwórrĕndŏn
Quarff *Shetland*, kwɑrf, kwaarf
Quarles, f.n., kwɔrlz, kwawrlz. *Appropriate for Francis ~, 16th-c. poet.*
Quarles *Norfolk*, kwɔrlz, kwawrlz
Quarley *Hants*, 'kwɔrlı, kwáwrli
Quarmby, f.n., 'kwɔrmbı, kwáwrmbi
Quarndon *Derby.*, 'kwɔrndən, kwáwrndŏn
Quarr Abbey *I. of Wight*, kwɔr, kwawr
Quarrell, f.n., 'kwɒrəl, kwórrĕl
Quartermaine, f.n., 'kwɔrtərmeın, kwáwrtĕrmayn
Quartley, f.n., 'kwɔrtlı, kwáwrtli
Quass, f.n., kwɒs, kwoss
Quastel, f.n., 'kwɒstel, kwósstel
Quatermain, f.n., 'kwɒtərmeın, kwáwtĕrmayn
Quatermass, f.n., 'kweıtərmæs, kwáytĕrmass
Quatt *Salop*, kwɒt, kwott
Quay, f.n., kweı, kway
Quaye, f.n., kweı, kway
Quayle, f.n., kweıl, kwayl
Quealy, f.n., 'kwılı, kweéli
Quedgeley *Glos.*, 'kwedʒlı, kwéjjli
Queenborough *Kent*, 'kwinbərə, kweénbŭră. *Appropriate also for the Barony of ~.*
Queenslie *S'clyde*, 'kwinz'li, kweénz-leé
Quelch, f.n., kwelʃ, kwelsh
Quemerford *Wilts.*, 'kʌmərfərd, kúmmĕrfŏrd
Queniborough *Leics.*, 'kwenıbərə, kwénnibŭră
Quenington *Glos.*, 'kwenıŋtən, kwénningtŏn. *Appropriate also for Viscount ~.*
Quennell, f.n., kwı'nel, kwĕnéll
Quentin, *C.n. and* f.n., 'kwentın, kwéntin
Querée, f.n., 'kerı, kérri
Queripel, f.n., 'kwerıpel, kwérripel
Quernmore *Lancs.*, 'kwɔrmər, kwáwrmĕr; 'kwɑrmər, kwáarmĕr
Quertier, f.n., 'kɜrtıeı, kérti-ay
Quesnel, f.n., kwı'nel, kwĕnéll; 'keınl, káynl
Quested, f.n., 'kwestıd, kwésstĕd

Quethiock *Cornwall*, 'kweðık, kwéthick; 'kweθık, kwéthick; 'kwıðık, kwíthick
Quibell, f.n., kwı'bel, kwibéll; 'kwıbl, kwíbbl; 'kwaıbl, kwíbl; kwaı'bel, kwıbéll. *The third is appropriate for the Barony of ~ of Scunthorpe.*
Quicke, f.n., kwık, kwick
Quigley, f.n., 'kwıglı, kwígli
Quiller-Couch, Sir Arthur, *author*, 'kwılər 'kutʃ, kwillĕr koótch
Quilliam, f.n., 'kwıljəm, kwíl-yăm
Quilter, f.n., 'kwıltər, kwíltĕr
Quin, f.n., kwın, kwin
Quinain, f.n., kwı'neın, kwináyn
Quinan, f.n., 'kwaınən, kwínăn
Quinault, f.n., 'kwınəlt, kwínnŭlt
Quincey, f.n., 'kwınsı, kwínssi
Quincy, f.n., 'kwınsı, kwínssi
Quinion, f.n., 'kwınıən, kwínni-ŏn
Quinlan, f.n., 'kwınlən, kwínlăn
Quinnell, f.n., kwı'nel, kwinéll
Quintana, f.n., kwın'tɑnə, kwıntáană
Quinton, f.n., 'kwıntən, kwíntŏn
Quinton *Co. Down*, 'kwıntən, kwíntŏn
Quirk, f.n., kwɜrk, kwirk
Quirke, f.n., kwɜrk, kwirk
Quitak, f.n., 'kwıtæk, kwíttack
Quixall, f.n., 'kwıksɔl, kwícksawl
Quoich, Loch *and* River, *H'land*, kɔıx, koych
Quoile, River, *Co. Down*, kɔıl, koyl
Quorn *Leics.*, kwɔrn, kwawrn. *Appropriate also for the ~ Hunt.*
Quothquan *S'clyde*, 'kwɒθ'kwɒn, kwóth-kwón
Quoyburray *Orkney*, 'kwaıbʌrı, kwíburri
Quoyloo *Orkney*, 'kwaılu, kwíloo
Quy, f.n., kwaı, kwī
Quy *Cambs.*, kwaı, kwī

R

Raad, f.n., rɑd, raad
Raans Manor *Bucks.*, 'reınz, raynz
Raasay *Skye*, 'raseı, ráassay
Raban, f.n., 'reıbən, ráybăn
Rabbetts, f.n., rə'bets, răbétts
Rabin, f.n., 'reıbın, ráybin
Rabinovitch, f.n., rə'bınəvıtʃ, răbínnŏvitch
Rabinowitz, f.n., rə'bınəwıts, răbínnŏwits

Rachman, *f.n.*, 'rækmən, ráck-măn

Racionzer, *f.n.*, ˌræsɪ'ɒnzər, rassi-ónzĕr

Radcliffe, *f.n.*, 'rædklɪf, rádkliff

Rademon *Co. Down*, rə'demən, rădémmŏn

Radernie *Fife*, rə'dɜrnɪ, rădérni

Radford, *f.n.*, 'rædfərd, rádfŏrd

Radford Semele *Warwicks.*, 'rædfərd 'semɪlɪ, rádfŏrd sémmĕli

Radice, *f.n.*, rə'dɪtʃɪ, rădeétchi; rə'dɪtʃeɪ, rădeétchay

Radin, *f.n.*, 'reɪdɪn, ráydin

Radleian, *one educated at Radley College*, ræd'liən, radleé-ăn

Radley, *f.n.*, 'rædlɪ, rádli

Radnor *Powys*, 'rædnər, rádnŏr. *Appropriate also for the Earl of ~*.

Rado, *f.n.*, 'reɪdoʊ, ráydō

Radyr *S. Glam.*, 'rædər, ráddĕr

Rae, *f.n.*, reɪ, ray

Rael, *f.n.*, reɪl, rayl

Raffan, *f.n.*, 'ræfən, ráffăn

Raffell, *f.n.*, ræ'fel, rafféll

Rafford *Grampian*, 'ræfərd, ráffŏrd

Raffrey *Co. Down*, 'ræfrɪ, ráffri

Ragan, *f.n.*, 'reɪgən, ráygăn

Ragg, *f.n.*, ræg, rag

Raggett, *f.n.*, 'rægɪt, rággĕt

Raghan, *f.n.*, 'reɪgən, ráygăn

Raglan *Gwent*, 'ræglən, ráglăn. *Appropriate also for Baron ~*.

Ragosin, *f.n.*, 'rægəzɪn, rággōzin

Rahere, *founder of St. Bartholomew the Great and of St. Bartholomew's Hospital*, 'reɪhɪər, ráy-heer; rə'hɪər, ră-héer; 'rɑhɪər, ráa-heer

Rahilly, *f.n.*, 'rɑɪlɪ, raá-illi

Raholp *Co. Down*, rə'hɒlp, ră-hólp

Raikes, *f.n.*, reɪks, rayks

Rainbow, *f.n.*, 'reɪnboʊ, ráynbō

Raine, *f.n.*, reɪn, rayn

Rainger, *f.n.*, 'reɪndʒər, ráynjĕr

Rainier, *f.n.*, 'reɪnɪeɪ, ráyni-ay; 'reɪnjər, ráyn-yĕr

Rainow *Ches.*, 'reɪnoʊ, ráynō

Rainsberry, *f.n.*, 'reɪnzbərɪ, ráynzbĕri

Rainsford, *f.n.*, 'reɪnzfərd, ráynzfŏrd

Rainworth *Notts.*, 'reɪnwɜrθ, ráynwurth

Rais, *f.n.*, reɪs, rayss

Raishbrook, *f.n.*, 'reɪʃbrʊk, ráysh-brŏok

Raisman, *f.n.*, 'reɪzmən, ráyzmăn

Raison, *f.n.*, 'reɪzən, ráyzŏn

Raistrick, *f.n.*, 'reɪstrɪk, ráysstrick

Raitt, *f.n.*, reɪt, rayt

Raitz, *f.n.*, raɪts, rīts

Ralegh, *f.n.*, *also spelt* **Raleigh,** 'rɒlɪ, ráwli; 'rɑlɪ, raáli; 'rælɪ, ráli. *Sir Walter ~, 16th-c. adventurer, although his name is usually spelt* **Raleigh** *today, never used this spelling himself, and the indications are that his own pronunciation was the first. His treatment today, even among scholars, seems to vary according to taste. The third is appropriate for the* **Raleigh** *bicycle.*

Ralli, *f.n.*, 'rælɪ, ráli

Ralling, *f.n.*, 'rælɪŋ, ráling

Ralls, *f.n.*, rɔlz, rawlz

Raloo *Co. Antrim*, rə'lu, rălóo

Ralph, *C.n.*, rælf, ralf; reɪf, rayf; ræf, raff. *The first is appropriate for Sir ~ Richardson, actor, the second for Dr ~ Vaughan Williams, composer.*

Ralph, *f.n.*, rælf, ralf

Ralph Gore *yachting trophy*, 'reɪf 'gɔr, ráyf gór

Ralphs, *f.n.*, rælfs, ralfs

Ralston, *f.n.*, 'rɔlstən, ráwlsstŏn; 'rælstən, rálsstŏn

Ralston *S'clyde*, 'rɔlstən, ráwls-stŏn

Ramage, *f.n.*, 'ræmɪdʒ, rámmij

Rambaut, *f.n.*, 'rɒmboʊ, rómbō; 'rɑmboʊ, raámbō

Rambert, *Dame* **Marie,** *ballet director*, 'mɑrɪ 'rɑbɛər, maáree raáng-bair. *This is Dame Marie's pronunciation. The Ballet Rambert is often called* 'rɒmbɛər, rómbair *in popular usage.*

Rame *Cornwall*, reɪm, raym. *Appropriate also for ~ Head.*

Ramelson, *f.n.*, 'ræmlsən, rámls-sŏn

Ramore Head *Co. Antrim*, rə'mɔr, rămór

Rampisham *Dorset*, 'ræmpɪʃəm, rámpi-shăm

Rampton *Cambs.*, 'ræmptən, rámptŏn

Ramsay, *f.n.*, 'ræmzɪ, rámzi. *Appropriate also for Baron ~*.

Ramsbotham, *f.n.*, 'ræmzbɒθəm, rámzboth-ăm; 'ræmzbɒtəm, rámzbottăm. *The first is appropriate for Viscount Soulbury's family name.*

Ramseyer, *f.n.*, 'ræmseɪər, rámssay-ĕr

Ramsgate *Kent*, 'ræmzgeɪt, rámzgayt

Ramshaw, *f.n.*, 'ræmʃɔ, rám-shaw

Ramus, *f.n.*, 'reıməs, ráymŭss
Ramuz, *f.n.*, 'reımʌz, ráymuz
Ranalow, *f.n.*, 'rænəloʊ, ránnălō
Rance, *f.n.*, ræns, ranss
Ranchev, *f.n.*, 'ræntʃev, rántchev
Randall, *f.n.*, 'rændl, rándl
Randalstown *Co. Antrim*,
'rændlztaʊn, rándlztown
Randel, *f.n.*, 'rændl, rándl
Randles, *f.n.*, 'rændlz, rándlz
Randolph, *C.n. and f.n.*, 'rændɒlf,
rándolf
Rands, *f.n.*, rændz, randz
Ranelagh, *f.n.*, rænılə, ránnělă
Ranelagh Gardens *London*,
'rænılə, ránnělă
Ranfurly, Earl of, 'rænfərlı, rán-
fŭrli
Rangag, Loch, *H'land*, 'rængæg,
rán-gag
Ranger, *f.n.*, 'reındʒər, ráynjěr
Rankeillour, Nether *and* Over,
Fife, ræŋ'kilər, rankéelŭr.
Appropriate also for Baron ∼.
Rankin, *f.n.*, 'ræŋkın, ránkin
Rankine, *f.n.*, 'ræŋkın, ránkin
Rankov, *f.n.*, 'ræŋkɒf, ránkoff
Rannoch *H'land*, 'rænəx, ránnŏch
Ransome, *f.n.*, 'rænsəm, ránssŏm
Ranulph, *C.n.*, 'rænʌlf, ránnulf
Raper, *f.n.*, 'reıpər, ráypěr
Raphael, *f.n.*, 'reıfl, ráyfl; 'ræfeıl,
ráffayl; 'ræfeıəl, ráffay-ěl;
'ræfıəl, ráffi-ěl; 'reıfjəl, ráyf-yěl.
*The third is appropriate for
Frederic* ∼, *author.*
Raphael Park *Essex*, 'reıfl, ráyfl
Rapoport, *f.n.*, 'ræpoʊpɔrt, ráppō-
port
Rapp, *f.n.*, ræp, rap
Rappitt, *f.n.*, 'ræpıt, ráppit
Rasharkin *Co. Antrim*, rə'ʃarkın,
ră-shaárkin
Rashee *Co. Antrim*, rə'ʃi, ră-sheé
Rashleigh, *f.n.*, 'ræʃli, ráshlee
Rasmussen, *f.n.*, ræs'musən,
rassmoóssěn
Rassal Ashwood *H'land*, 'ræsl
'æʃwʊd, rássl áshwoōd
Ratcheugh *Northd.*, 'rætʃəf,
rátchŭf
Ratcliff, *f.n.*, 'rætklıf, rátkliff
Ratcliffe, *f.n.*, 'rætklıf, rátkliff
Ratendone, Viscount, 'rætəndʌn,
ráttěndun
Rath, *f.n.*, ræθ, rath
Rathbone, *f.n.*, 'ræθboʊn, ráth-
bōn; 'ræθbən, ráthbŏn
Rathcavan, Baron, ræθ'kævən,
rathkávvăn
Rathcreedan, Baron, ræθ'kridən,
rathkréedăn
Rathdonnel, *f.n.*, ræθ'dɒnl, rath-
dónnl

Rathe, *f.n.*, reıθ, rayth
Rathen *Grampian*, 'reıθən, ráy-
thěn
Rathfriland *Co. Down*, ræθ'fraı-
lənd, rathfríländ
Rathlin *Co. Antrim*, 'ræθlın,
ráthlin
Rathmore, *f.n.*, ræθ'mɔr, rathmór
Ratho *Lothian*, 'raθoʊ, raáthō
Rathven *Grampian*, 'ræθvən,
ráthvěn
Ratigan, *f.n.*, 'rætıgən, ráttigăn
Ratlinghope *Salop*, 'rætʃəp,
rátchŏp
Rattale, *f.n.*, 'rætl, ráttl
Rattenbury, *f.n.*, 'rætənbərı,
ráttěnbŭri
Rattigan, *f.n.*, 'rætıgən, ráttigăn
Rattle, *f.n.*, 'rætl, ráttl
Rattray, *f.n.*, 'rætrı, ráttri
Rattray *Tayside*, 'rætrı, ráttri
Raughton Head *Cumbria*, 'raftən
'hed, raáftŏn héd; 'rɒftən 'hed,
rófftŏn héd
Raunds *Northants.*, rɔndz,
rawndz
Ravelston *Lothian*, 'rævlstən,
rávvlstŏn
Ravendale, East, *Humberside*,
'reıvəndeıl, ráyvěndayl
Ravenglass *Cumbria*, 'reıvənglɑs,
ráyvěn-glaass
Raveningham *Norfolk*, 'rævən-
ıŋəm, rávvěning-ăm; 'rævıŋəm,
rávving-ăm; 'rænıŋəm, ránning-
-ăm. *The third is particularly
associated with* ∼ *Hall.*
Ravensbourne, River, *Kent*,
'reıvənzbɔrn, ráyvěnz-born
Ravensdale, Baron, 'reıvənzdeıl,
ráyvěnzdayl
Ravenstruther *S'clyde*, 'reıvən-
strʌðər, ráyvěn-struthěr
Raverat, *f.n.*, 'rɑvərɑ, raávěraa
Ravetta, *f.n.*, rə'vetə, răvéttă
Ravetz, *f.n.*, 'rævıts, rávvěts
Ravillious, *f.n.*, rə'vılıəs, răvílli-
-ŭss
Raw, *f.n.*, rɔ, raw
Rawlings, *f.n.*, 'rɔlıŋz, ráwlingz
Rawlins, *f.n.*, 'rɔlınz, ráwlinz
Raworth, *f.n.*, 'reıwərθ, ráy-wŭrth
Rawreth *Essex*, 'rɔrəθ, ráwrěth
Rawson, *f.n.*, 'rɔsən, ráwssŏn
Rawsthorne, *f.n.*, 'rɔsθɔrn, ráwss-
-thorn
Rawtenstall *Lancs.*, 'rɔtənstɔl,
ráwtěnstawl; 'rɒtənstɔl, róttěn-
stawl
Rawthey, River, *Cumbria*, 'rɔðı,
ráwthi
Raybould, *f.n.*, 'reıboʊld, ráy-
bōld
Rayel, *f.n.*, 'reıəl, ráy-ěl

Rayleigh *Essex*, 'reɪlɪ, ráyli. *Appropriate also for Baron* ∼.
Raymont, *f.n.*, 'reɪmɒnt, ráymont
Rayner, *f.n.*, 'reɪnər, ráynĕr
Raynham, *f.n.*, 'reɪnəm, ráynăm
Raynsford, *f.n.*, 'reɪnzfərd, ráynzfŏrd
Rayson, *f.n.*, 'reɪsən, ráyssŏn
Razzall, *f.n.*, 'ræzl, rázzl
Rea, *f.n.*, reɪ, ray; rɪ, ree. *The second is appropriate for Baron* ∼.
Read, *f.n.*, rid, reed
Reade, *f.n.*, rid, reed
Reader, *f.n.*, 'ridər, réedĕr
Readhead, *f.n.*, 'redhed, réd-hed
Reading *Berks.*, 'redɪŋ, rédding. *Appropriate also for the Marquess of* ∼.
Readman, *f.n.*, 'redmən, rédmăn
Reagh, Island, *Co. Down*, reɪ, ray
Reakes, *f.n.*, riks, reeks
Reaney, *f.n.*, 'reɪnɪ, ráyni; 'rinɪ, réeni. *The first is appropriate for P. H.* ∼, *author of 'A Dictionary of British Surnames'.*
Rearden, *f.n.*, 'rɪərdən, réerdĕn
Reason, *f.n.*, 'rizən, réezŏn
Reavell, *f.n.*, 'revl, révvl
Reavey, *f.n.*, 'rivɪ, réevi
Reavgli, *f.n.*, 'rivglɪ, réevgli
Reay, *f.n.*, reɪ, ray
Reay *H'land*, reɪ, ray. *Appropriate also for Baron* ∼.
Rebak, *f.n.*, 'ribæk, réeback
Rebbeck, *f.n.*, 'rebek, rébbeck
Rebel, *f.n.*, rɪ'bel, rĕbéll
Recknell, *f.n.*, 'reknəl, récknĕl
Reculver *Kent*, rɪ'kʌlvər, rĕkúlvĕr
Redadder, River, *Borders*, 'redədər, réddădĕr
Redcliffe-Maud, Barony of, 'redklɪf 'mɔd, rédklíff máwd
Reddick, *f.n.*, 'redɪk, réddick
Rede *Suffolk*, rid, reed
Redelinghuyes, *f.n.*, 'redlɪŋhjuz, rédling-hewz
Redenhall *Norfolk*, 'redənhɔl, réddĕn-hawl
Redesdale, Baron, 'rɪdzdeɪl, réedzdayl
Redfern, *f.n.*, 'redfɜrn, rédfern
Redgorton *Tayside*, 'red'gɔrtən, réd-górtŏn
Redhead, *f.n.*, 'redhed, réd-hed
Redheugh *Tyne & Wear*, 'redhjuf, réd-hewf; 'redjuf, réddewf
Redman, *f.n.*, 'redmən, rédmăn
Redmond, *f.n.*, 'redmənd, rédmŏnd
Redmoss *Grampian*, 'red'mɒs, réd-móss
Redrup, *f.n.*, 'redrʊp, rédrŏŏp

Redruth *Cornwall*, red'ruθ, redróoth
Rée, *f.n.*, reɪ, ray
Reed, *f.n.*, rid, reed
Reekie, *f.n.*, 'rikɪ, réeki
Reepham, *Lincs.*, *Norfolk*, 'rifəm, réefăm
Rees, *f.n.*, ris, reess
Reese, *f.n.*, ris, reess
Reeves, *f.n.*, rivz, reevz
Reffell, *f.n.*, 'refl, réffl
Regen, *f.n.*, 'rigən, réegĕn
Reibbit, *f.n.*, 'raɪbɪt, ríbit
Reibel, *f.n.*, 'raɪbl, ríbl
Reich, *f.n.*, raɪk, rīk
Reichel, *f.n.*, 'raɪxl, ríchl
Reid, *f.n.*, rid, reed
Reigate *Surrey*, 'raɪgɪt, rígit; 'raɪgeɪt, rígayt
Reighton *N. Yorks.*, 'ritən, réetŏn
Reilly, *f.n.*, 'raɪlɪ, ríli
Reinagle, G. P., *painter* (*1802–35*), 'raɪnəgl, rínaagl
Reindorp, *f.n.*, 'raɪndɔrp, ríndorp
Reiner, *f.n.*, 'reɪnər, ráynĕr; 'raɪnər, rínĕr
Reinold, *f.n.*, 'raɪnoʊld, rínōld
Reiss, *f.n.*, raɪs, rīss
Reiss *H'land*, ris, reess
Reiter, *f.n.*, 'raɪtər, rítĕr
Reith, *f.n.*, riθ, reeth. *Appropriate also for Baron* ∼.
Reizenstein, **Franz**, *pianist and composer*, 'frænz 'raɪzənstaɪn, fránz rízĕnstīn
Rejerrah *Cornwall*, rɪ'dʒerə, rĕjérră
Relubbas *Cornwall*, rɪ'lʌbəs, rĕlúbbăss
Relugas *Grampian*, rɪ'lugəs, rĕloʻogăss
Remedios, *f.n.*, rə'meɪdɪɒs, rĕmáydi-oss
Remer, *f.n.*, 'rimər, réemĕr
Remes, *f.n.*, rimz, reemz
Remfry, *f.n.*, 'remfrɪ, rémfri
Renals, *f.n.*, 'renlz, rénnlz
Renault, *f.n.*, 'renoʊ, rénnō. *Appropriate for Mary* ∼, *author.*
Rencher, *f.n.*, 'rentʃər, réntchĕr
Rendall, *f.n.*, 'rendl, réndl
Rendcomb *Glos.*, 'rendkəm, réndkŏm
Rendell, *f.n.*, 'rendl, réndl; ren'del, rendéll
René, *C.n.*, reneɪ, rénnay; 'rəneɪ, rĕnay; rə'neɪ, rĕnáy
Renée, *C.n.*, reneɪ, rénnay; 'rəneɪ, rĕnay; rə'neɪ, rĕnáy; 'rinɪ, réeni
Reney, *f.n.*, 'reneɪ, rénnay
Renfrew *S'clyde*, 'renfru, rénfroo
Renhold *Beds.*, 'renld, rénnld

Renier, *f.n.*, rə'nɪər, rĕneér
Renishaw *Derby.*, 'renɪʃɔ, rénni-
-shaw. *Appropriate also for* ~
Hall.
Renish Point *W. Isles,* 'renɪʃ,
rénnish
Rennell, *f.n.*, 'renl, rénnl. *Appro-
priate also for Baron* ~.
Renney, *f.n.*, 'renɪ, rénni
Rennie, *f.n.*, 'renɪ, rénni
Renold, *f.n.*, 'renld, rénnld
Renshaw, *f.n.*, 'renʃɔ, rén-shaw
Renton, *f.n.*, 'rentən, réntŏn
Rentoul, *f.n.*, ren'tul, rentoól;
'rentʊl, réntoŏl
Renwick, *f.n.*, 'renɪk, rénnick.
Appropriate also for Baron ~.
Renwick *Cumbria,* 'renɪk, rén-
nick; 'renwɪk, rénwick
Reoch, *f.n.*, 'rɪɒx, rée-o*ch*
Rescobie *Tayside,* rɪ'skoʊbɪ,
rĕsskŏbi
Reside, *f.n.*, rɪ'zaɪd, rĕzíd
Resolis *H'land,* rɪ'soʊlɪs, rĕssŏ-
liss
Resolven *W. Glam.*, rɪ'zɒlvən,
rĕzólvĕn
Restalrig *Edinburgh,* 'reslrɪg,
résslrig
Restieaux, *f.n.*, 'restɪoʊ, résti-ō
Restormel Castle *Cornwall,*
rɪs'tɔrməl, rĕstórmĕl
Restronguet *Cornwall,* rɪs'trɒŋgɪt,
rĕstróng-gĕt
Retallick, *f.n.*, rɪ'tælɪk, rĕtálick
Reuel, *f.n.*, rʊəl, roŏ-ĕl
Reuter, *f.n.*, 'rɔɪtər, róytĕr
Revans, *f.n.*, 'revənz, révvănz
Revell, *f.n.*, 'revl, révvl
Revelstoke *Devon,* 'revlstoʊk,
révvl-stōk. *Appropriate also for
Baron* ~.
Revesby *Lincs.*, 'rivzbɪ, réevzbi
Revie, *f.n.*, 'rɪvɪ, réevi
Revill, *f.n.*, 'revɪl, révvil; 'revl,
révvl
Revis, *f.n.*, 'revɪs, révviss
Rew, *f.n.*, ru, roo
Rewe *Devon,* ru, roo
Rey, *f.n.*, reɪ, ray. *Appropriate for
Margaret* ~, *sculptor.*
Reydon *Suffolk,* 'reɪdən, ráydŏn
Reymerston *Norfolk,* 'remərstən,
rémmĕrsstŏn
Reynard, *f.n.*, 'renərd, rénnărd;
'renɑrd, rénnaard; 'reɪnɑrd,
ráynaard
Reynders, *f.n.*, 'raɪndərz, ríndĕrz
Reyner, *f.n.*, 'renər, rénnĕr;
'reɪnər, ráynĕr
Reynish, *f.n.*, 'reɪnɪʃ, ráynish
Reynolds, *f.n.*, 'renldz, rénnldz
Reynoldston *W.Glam.*, 'renldstən,
rénnldstŏn

Reyntiens, *f.n.*, 'rentjənz, rént-
-yĕnz. *Appropriate for Patrick*
~, *stained-glass artist.*
Reyrolle, *f.n.*, 'reɪroʊl, ráy-rōl
Rezler, *f.n.*, 'rezlər, rézlĕr
Rhae, *f.n.*, reɪ, ray
Rhandir-mwyn *Dyfed,* 'hrændɪər-
'mʊɪn, rándeer-moŏ-in
Rhayader *Powys,* 'hraɪədər, rí-
-ădĕr. *Appropriate also for the
Barony of* ~.
Rhee, *f.n.*, ri, ree
Rhees, *f.n.*, ris, reess
Rheidol, River, *Dyfed,* 'hraɪdɒl,
rídol
Rhenigidale *W. Isles,* 'renɪgɪdeɪl,
rénnigidayl
Rhenish Tower *Lynmouth
(Devon),* 'renɪʃ, rénnish
Rhewl *Clwyd,* 'reʊl, ré-oŏl
Rhian, *Welsh C.n.*, 'hriən, rée-
-ăn
Rhiannon, *Welsh C.n.*, hri'ænən,
ree-ánnŏn
Rhianydd, *Welsh C.n.*, hri'ænɪð,
ree-ánni*th*
Rhiconich *H'land,* ri'koʊnɪx,
reekŏni*ch*
Rhigos *Mid Glam.*, 'hrigɒs, rée-
goss; 'rɪkɒs, ríckoss. *The second
is confined to local use.*
Rhind, *f.n.*, raɪnd, rīnd; rɪnd,
rinnd
Rhinns of Galloway, *also spelt*
Rinns, *D. & G.*, 'rɪnz əv 'gælə-
weɪ, rínnz ŏv gálŏ-way
Rhinns of Islay, *also spelt* **Rinns,**
S'clyde, 'rɪnz əv 'aɪlə, rínnz ŏv
ílă
Rhinns of Kells, *also spelt* **Rinns,**
D. & G., 'rɪnz əv 'kelz, rínnz ŏv
kéllz
Rhinog Fach *Gwynedd,* 'hrinɒg
'vax, réenog vaa*ch*
Rhinog Fawr *Gwynedd,* 'hrinɒg
'vaʊər, réenog vówr
Rhiwbina *S. Glam.*, ru'baɪnə,
roobínă; ˌhriu'baɪnə, ree-
-oobínă
Rhiwderyn *Gwent,* ˌhriu'derɪn,
ree-oodérrin
Rhiwlas *Clwyd, Gwynedd,* rɪ'uləs,
ri-oŏlăss
Rhodes, *f.n.*, roʊdz, rōdz
Rhondda *Mid Glam.*, 'hrɒnðə,
rónthă
Rhoose *S. Glam.*, rus, rooss
Rhoscolyn *Gwynedd,* hroʊs'kɒlɪn,
rōsskóllin
Rhoscrowther, *also spelt* **Rhos-
crowdder,** *Dyfed,* rɒs'kraʊðər,
ross-krów*th*ĕr
Rhos-ddu *Clwyd,* hroʊs'ðiː, rōss-
-*th*eé

Rhosesmor *Clwyd*, hroʊs'esmɔr, rōsséssmor

Rhosgadfan *Gwynedd*, hroʊs-'gædvən, rōssgádvăn

Rhosier, *f.n.*, 'hrɒsjɛər, róss-yair

Rhosllanerchrugog *Clwyd*, 'hroʊs-'ɬænərx'rigɒg, rōss-<u>hl</u>ánnĕr<u>ch</u>-reégog

Rhos-maen *Dyfed*, hroʊs'maɪn, rōssmín

Rhos-meirch *Gwynedd*, hroʊs-'maɪərx, rōssmír<u>ch</u>

Rhosneigr *Gwynedd*, hroʊs'naɪgər, rōssnígĕr

Rhossili *W. Glam.*, hrɒ'sɪlɪ, ros-sílli

Rhostryfan *Gwynedd*, hroʊs-'trʌvən, rōsstrúvvăn

Rhostyllen *Clwyd*, hroʊs'tʌɬɪn, rōsstú<u>hl</u>ĕn

Rhowniar, Outward Bound school, *Gwynedd*, 'raʊnɪər, równi-ăr

Rhos-y-bol *Gwynedd*, ˌhroʊsə'bɒl, rōssăbóll

Rhosymedre *Clwyd*, ˌhroʊsə-'medreɪ, rōssămédray

Rhu *S'clyde*, ru, roo

Rhuallt *Clwyd*, 'rɪæɬt, reé-a<u>hl</u>t

Rhudde, *f.n.*, rʌd, rudd

Rhuddlan *Clwyd*, 'hrɪðlæn, rí<u>th</u>lan

Rhum, *also spelt* **Rum,** *H'land*, rʌm, rum

Rhuthun *Clwyd*, 'hrɪθɪn, ríthin. *The English form is* **Ruthin,** *q.v.*

Rhyd-ddu *Gwynedd*, hrɪd'ði, reed--<u>th</u>eé

Rhydderch, *f.n.*, 'hrʌðərx, rú<u>th</u>ĕr<u>ch</u>

Rhydding *W. Glam.*, 'rɪdɪŋ, rídding

Rhydfelen *Mid Glam.*, hrɪd'velɪn, reedvéllĕn

Rhydlafar Hospital *S. Glam.*, hrɪd'lævər, reedlávvär

Rhydlewis, *also spelt* **Rhyd Lewis,** *Dyfed*, hrɪd'luɪs, reed--loó-iss

Rhydowen *Dyfed*, hrɪd'oʊɪn, reedó-ĕn

Rhydwen, River, *Gwynedd*, 'hrɪdwen, reédwen

Rhyd-y-felin *Dyfed*, ˌhrɪdə'velɪn, reedăvéllin

Rhyd-y-fro *W. Glam.*, ˌhrɪdə'vroʊ, reedăvrǒ

Rhyd-y-main *Gwynedd*, ˌhrɪdə-'maɪn, reedămín

Rhyd-y-mwyn *Clwyd*, ˌhrɪdə-'mʊɪn, reedămoō-in

Rhyl *Clwyd*, hrɪl, rill

Rhymney *Mid Glam.*, 'rʌmnɪ, rúmni

Rhynd *Tayside*, rɪnd, rinnd

Rhys, *f.n.*, ris, rees; raɪs, rīss. *Although the first is usual in Wales, the second is appropriate for Baron Dynevor's family name.*

Riach, *f.n.*, 'rɪəx, reé-ă<u>ch</u>

Riall, *f.n.*, 'raɪəl, rí-äl

Ribbesford *H. & W.*, 'rɪbzfərd, ríbzfŏrd

Riccall *N. Yorks.*, 'rɪkɔl, ríckawl

Riccarton *S'clyde*, 'rɪkərtən, ríckärtŏn

Rice, *f.n.*, raɪs, rīss

Richard, *C.n. and f.n.*, 'rɪtʃərd, rítchărd

Richards, *f.n.*, 'rɪtʃərdz, rítchărdz

Richardson, *f.n.*, 'rɪtʃərdsən, rítchărdssŏn

Riche, *f.n.*, rɪtʃ, ritch

Richens, *f.n.*, 'rɪtʃənz, rítchĕnz

Richer, *f.n.*, 'rɪtʃər, rítchĕr

Richhill *Co. Armagh*, rɪtʃ'hɪl, ritch-híll

Richmond *London, N. Yorks., S. Yorks.*, 'rɪtʃmənd, rítchmŏnd

Rickard, *f.n.*, 'rɪkɑrd, ríckaard

Rickards, *f.n.*, 'rɪkɑrdz, ríckaardz

Rickarton *Grampian*, 'rɪkərtən, ríckärtŏn

Rickett, *f.n.*, 'rɪkɪt, ríckĕt

Ricketts, *f.n.*, 'rɪkɪts, ríckĕts

Rickmansworth *Herts.*, 'rɪkmənzwərθ, ríckmänzwurth

Ricôt, *f.n.*, 'rɪkoʊ, ríckō; 'rɪkoʊ, reékō

Riddell, *f.n.*, 'rɪdl, ríddl; rɪ'del, ridéll

Riddiough, *f.n.*, 'rɪdjoʊ, ríd-yō

Riddoch, *f.n.*, 'rɪdɒx, ríddo<u>ch</u>

Rideal, *f.n.*, rɪ'dil, rideél

Ridealgh, *f.n.*, 'rɪdɪælʃ, ríddi-alsh; 'raɪdældʒ, rídalj

Rideau, Baron, 'rɪdoʊ, reédō

Ridehalgh, *f.n.*, 'raɪdhælʃ, ríd--halsh; 'rɪdɪhælʃ, ríddi-halsh

Rideout, *f.n.*, 'raɪdaʊt, rídowt

Rider, *f.n.*, 'raɪdər, rídĕr

Ridgeway, *f.n.*, 'rɪdʒweɪ, ríj-way

Ridgway, *f.n.*, 'rɪdʒweɪ, ríj-way

Riding, *f.n.*, 'raɪdɪŋ, ríding

Ridout, *f.n.*, 'rɪdaʊt, ríddowt; 'raɪdaʊt, rídowt

Ridsdale, *f.n.*, 'rɪdzdeɪl, rídzdayl

Ridsdel, *f.n.*, 'rɪdzdəl, rídzdĕl

Ridz, *f.n.*, rɪdz, riddz

Riera, *f.n.*, rɪ'ɛərə, ree-äirä

Riesco, *f.n.*, rɪ'eskoʊ, ri-ésskō

Rietty, *f.n.*, rɪ'etɪ, ri-étti

Rieu, *f.n.*, rɪ'u, ri-oó; 'riu, reé-oo. *The first is appropriate for Dr Emile Victor ～, former Editor of the Penguin Classics.*

Rievaulx, *f.n.*, 'rɪvəz, rívvăz
Rievaulx *N. Yorks.*, 'rɪvoʊ, reévō;
   'rɪvəz, rívvăz. *Both are appropriate for* ~ *Abbey.*
Rifkind, *f.n.*, 'rɪfkɪnd, ríffkinnd
Rigal, *f.n.*, 'rɪgl, reégl
Rigby, *f.n.*, 'rɪgbɪ, rígbi
Rigg, *f.n.*, rɪg, rigg
Riggs, *f.n.*, rɪgz, riggz
Rigler, *f.n.*, 'rɪglər, rígglĕr
Rignold, *f.n.*, 'rɪgnoʊld, ríg-nōld
Rimbault, *f.n.*, 'rɪmboʊlt, rím-bōlt
Rimell, *f.n.*, 'raɪml, ríml
Rimer, *f.n.*, 'raɪmər, rímĕr
Rimington *Lancs.*, 'rɪmɪŋtən, rímmingtŏn
Ringdufferin *Co. Down*, rɪŋ-'dʌfərɪn, ringdúffĕrin
Ringhaddy *Co. Down*, rɪŋ'hædɪ, ring-háddi
Ring's End *Cambs.*, rɪŋz 'end, ringz énd
Rinsey Head *Cornwall*, 'rɪnzɪ, rínzi
Rintoul, *f.n.*, rɪn'tul, rintóol;
   'rɪntul, ríntool. *The first is the normal Scottish pronunciation.*
Riou, *f.n.*, 'riu, reé-oo
Ripon *N. Yorks.*, 'rɪpən, ríppŏn
Rippon, *f.n.*, 'rɪpən, ríppŏn
Risbridger, *f.n.*, 'rɪsbrɪdʒər, ríssbrijjĕr
Risca *Gwent*, 'rɪskə, rísskă
Riseley *Beds.*, 'raɪzlɪ, rízli
Risman, *f.n.*, 'rɪzmən, rízzmăn
Rison, *f.n.*, 'raɪsən, ríssŏn
Ritchford, *f.n.*, 'rɪtʃfərd, rítchfŏrd
Ritchie, *f.n.*, 'rɪtʃɪ, rítchi
Ritchie-Calder, Barony of, 'rɪtʃɪ 'kɔldər, rítchi káwldĕr
Rittener, *f.n.*, 'rɪtnər, rítt-nĕr
Rittermann, *f.n.*, 'rɪtərmən, ríttĕr-măn
Ritzema, *f.n.*, 'rɪtsɪmə, rítsĕmă;
   rɪd'zimə, ridzeémă; rɪt'simə, ritseémă
Rive, *f.n.*, raɪv, rīv; rɪv, reev
Rivelin *S. Yorks.*, 'rɪvəlɪn, rívvĕlin
Rivers, *f.n.*, 'rɪvərz, rívvĕrz
Rivet, *f.n.*, 'rɪveɪ, reévay
Rivett, *f.n.*, rɪ'vet, rivétt
Riviere, *f.n.*, 'rɪvɪɛər, rívvi-air;
   rɪv'jɛər, riv-yáir; rɪ'vɪər, rivveér
Rivière, *f.n.*, 'rɪvɪɛər, rívvi-air;
   rɪv'jɛər, riv-yáir; rɪ'vɪər, rivveér
Rivis, *f.n.*, 'rɪvɪs, rívviss
Rivvett, *f.n.*, 'rɪvɪt, rívvĕt
Rizden, *f.n.*, 'rɪzdən, rízdĕn
Roach, *f.n.*, roʊtʃ, rōtch
Roaf, *f.n.*, roʊf, rōf
Roag, Loch, *W. Isles*, 'roʊæg, rṓ-ag

Roanhead *Grampian*, 'rɒnhed, rónn-hed; 'roʊnhed, rṓn-hed
Roast, *f.n.*, roʊst, rōst
Roath *Cardiff*, roʊθ, rōth
Robartes, *f.n.*, rə'bɑrts, rŏbaárts
Robarts, *f.n.*, rə'bɑrts, rŏbaárts
Robathan, *f.n.*, 'roʊbəθən, rṓbăthăn
Robay, *f.n.*, 'roʊbeɪ, rṓbay
Robb Caledon Shipbuilders Ltd., 'rɒb 'kælɪdən, róbb kálĕdŏn
Robbie, *f.n.*, rɒbɪ, róbbi
Robbins, *f.n.*, 'rɒbɪnz, róbbinz
Robens, *f.n.*, 'roʊbənz, rṓbĕnz.
   Appropriate also for Baron ~.
Roberton, *f.n.*, 'rɒbərtən, róbbĕr-tŏn
Roberts, *f.n.*, 'rɒbərts, róbbĕrts
Robertson, *f.n.*, 'rɒbərtsən, róbbĕrtsŏn
Robeston Wathen *Dyfed*, 'rɒbɪstən 'wɒðən, róbbĕstŏn wóthĕn
Robey, *f.n.*, 'roʊbɪ, rṓbi
Robieson, *f.n.*, 'rɒbɪsən, róbbissŏn
Robin, *C.n.*, 'rɒbɪn, róbbin
Robins, *f.n.*, 'rɒbɪnz, róbbinz;
   'roʊbɪnz, rṓbinz
Robinson, *f.n.*, 'rɒbɪnsən, róbbins-sŏn
Roblou, *f.n.*, 'rɒbloʊ, róbblō
Roborough *Devon*, 'roʊbərə, rṓbŭră. *Appropriate also for Baron* ~.
Robotham, *f.n.*, rə'boʊθəm, rŏbṓthăm
Robsart, *f.n.*, 'rɒbsɑrt, róbsaart.
   Appropriate for Amy ~, *wife of Robert Dudley, Earl of Leicester.*
Robson, *f.n.*, 'rɒbsən, róbssŏn;
   'roʊbsən, rṓbssŏn. *The first is appropriate for Dame Flora* ~, *actress.*
Roby *Merseyside*, 'roʊbɪ, rṓbi
Rocester *Staffs.*, 'roʊstər, rṓsstĕr
Roch, *f.n.*, roʊtʃ, rōtch; rɒtʃ, rotch
Roch *Dyfed*, roʊtʃ, rōtch. *Appropriate also for* ~ *Castle.*
Rochdale *Gtr. M'chester*, 'rɒtʃdeɪl, rótchdayl
Roche, *f.n.*, roʊtʃ, rōtch; roʊʃ, rōsh; rɒʃ, rosh. *The first is appropriate for the Barony of* ~.
Roche *Cornwall*, roʊtʃ, rōtch
Rochester *Kent*, 'rɒtʃɪstər, rótchĕstĕr
Rochford *Essex*, 'rɒtʃfərd, rótch-fŏrd
Rochfort, *f.n.*, 'rɒtʃfərt, rótchfŏrt
Rockbeare *Devon*, 'rɒkbɪər, róck-beer; 'rɒkbər, róckbĕr
Rodbaston *Staffs.*, 'rɒdbəstən, ródbăstŏn

Roddam, *f.n.*, 'rɒdəm, róddăm
Roddis, *f.n.*, 'rɒdɪs, róddiss
Rodel *W. Isles*, 'roʊdl, ródl
Rodger, *f.n.*, 'rɒdʒər, rójjĕr
Rodgers, *f.n.*, 'rɒdʒərz, rójjĕrz
Rodick, *f.n.*, 'rɒdɪk, róddick
Roding *Essex*, 'roʊdɪŋ, róding;
'ruðɪŋ, róothing. *The second,
the historical pronunciation, has
gradually given way, although
not entirely succumbed, to the
former. The group of villages
known as The Rodings includes
Abbess ~, Aythorpe ~, Beau-
champ ~, Berners ~, High ~,
Leaden ~, Margaret ~, and
White ~ or Roothing. Except
in the last case, where Roothing
has been retained in the name of
the civil parish, it appears that
Roding is now accepted as the
standard spelling.*
Rodmersham *Kent*, 'rɒdmərʃəm,
ródmĕr-shăm
Rodnight, *f.n.*, 'rɒdnaɪt, ródnīt
Rodon, *f.n.*, 'roʊdən, ródŏn
Roe, *f.n.*, roʊ, rō
Roedean *School E. Sussex*,
'roʊdin, ródeen
Roeg, *f.n.*, roʊg, rōg
Roehampton *London*, roʊ'hæmp-
tən, rō-hámptŏn
Roemmele, *f.n.*, 'rɒmɪlɪ, rómmĕli
Roetter, *f.n.*, 'roʊtər, rótĕr
Rofe, *f.n.*, roʊf, rōf
Roffe, *f.n.*, rɒf, roff
Roffey, *f.n.*, 'rɒfɪ, róffi
Rogaly, *f.n.*, roʊ'geɪlɪ, rōgáyli
Rogart *H'land*, 'roʊgərt, rōgărt
Roger, *C.n. and f.n.*, 'rɒdʒər,
rójjĕr
Rogers, *f.n.*, 'rɒdʒərz, rójjĕrz
Rogerstone *Gwent*, 'rɒdʒərstən,
rójjĕrstŏn
Roget, *f.n.*, 'roʊʒeɪ, rózhay
Rohan, *f.n.*, 'roʊən, ró-ăn
Rohrer, *f.n.*, 'rɔrər, ráwrĕr
Roissetter, *f.n.*, 'rɒsɪtər, róssitĕr
Rokeby *Durham*, 'roʊkbɪ, rókbi
Rokison, *f.n.*, 'roʊkɪsən, rókissŏn
Roland, *C.n. and f.n.*, 'roʊlənd,
rólănd
Rolfe, *f.n.*, roʊf, rōf; rɒlf, rolf.
*The first is appropriate for John
~, 16th–17th-c. colonist and
husband of Pocahontas, and for
Frederick ~, Baron Corvo,
19th-c. author.*
Roll, *f.n.*, roʊl, rōl; rɒl, rol
Rollason, *f.n.*, 'rɒləsən, róllăssŏn
Rolle, Richard, *14th-c. hermit and
author*, roʊl, rōl
Rollesby *Norfolk*, 'roʊlzbɪ,
rólzbi

Rolleston, *f.n.*, 'roʊlstən, rólsstŏn
Rolleston *Notts.*, 'roʊlstən,
rólsstŏn
Rollestone *Wilts.*, 'roʊlstən,
rólsstŏn
Rollins, *f.n.*, 'rɒlɪnz, róllinz
Rollo, *f.n.*, 'rɒloʊ, róllō. *Appro-
priate also for Baron ~.*
Rolls, *f.n.*, roʊlz, rōlz
Rolston, *f.n.*, 'roʊlstən, rólsstŏn
Rolt, *f.n.*, roʊlt, rōlt
Rolvenden *Kent*, 'rɒlvəndən,
rólvĕndĕn
Romanby *N. Yorks.*, 'roʊmənbɪ,
rómănbi
Romanes, *f.n.*, roʊ'mɑnɪz,
rōmaániz; roʊ'mænɪs, rōmán-
nĕss. *The first is appropriate for
the ~ Lectureship, Univ. of
Oxford.*
Rombaut, *f.n.*, 'rɒmboʊ, rómbō
Romeike, *f.n.*, roʊ'mikɪ, rōméeki
Romer, *f.n.*, 'roʊmər, rómĕr
Romford, *f.n.*, 'rʌmfərd, rúmfŏrd;
'rɒmfərd, rómfŏrd
Romford *London*, 'rɒmfərd, róm-
fŏrd; 'rʌmfərd, rúmfŏrd
Romilly, *f.n.*, 'rɒmɪlɪ, rómmili.
Appropriate also for Baron ~.
Romney, Earl of, 'rʌmnɪ, rúmni
Romney, *f.n.*, 'rʌmnɪ, rúmni;
'rɒmnɪ, rómni
Romney, New *and* Old, *Kent*,
'rɒmnɪ, rómni; 'rʌmnɪ, rúmni
Romney Marsh *Kent*, 'rɒmnɪ
'mɑrʃ, rómni maársh
Romsey *Hants*, 'rʌmzɪ, rúmzi.
Appropriate also for Baron ~.
Romsley *H. & W.*, 'rɒmzlɪ,
rómzli
Rona *W. Isles*, 'roʊnə, rónă
Ronald, *C.n. and f.n.*, 'rɒnld,
rónnld
Ronaldsay, North *and* South,
Orkney, 'rɒnldseɪ, rónnld-say;
'rɒnldʃeɪ, rónnld-shay
Ronaldshay, Earl of, 'rɒnldʃeɪ,
rónnld-shay
Ronaldsway Airport, *I. of Man*,
'rɒnldzweɪ, rónnldzway
Ronan, saint, 'roʊnən, rónăn
Ronane, *f.n.*, rɒ'neɪn, ronnáyn
Ronas Voe *Shetland*, 'roʊnəs
'voʊ, rónäss vō
Ronay, *f.n.*, 'rɒneɪ, rónnay
Ronayne, *f.n.*, roʊ'neɪn, rōnáyn
Roney, *f.n.*, 'roʊnɪ, róni
Ronson, *f.n.*, 'rɒnsən, rónssŏn
Rook, *f.n.*, rʊk, rŏŏk
Rooley, *f.n.*, 'rulɪ, róoli
Room, *f.n.*, rum, room
Roome, *f.n.*, rum, room
Rooney, *f.n.*, 'runɪ, róoni
Roope, *f.n.*, rup, roop

Rooper, *f.n.,* 'roʊpər, róopĕr
Roos *Humberside,* rus, rooss
Roose, *f.n.,* rus, rooss
RoosmaleCocq, *f.n.,* 'roʊzmələ-'koʊk, róozmă-lĕkók
Rooss, *f.n.,* rus, rooss
Root, *f.n.,* rut, root
Rootes, *f.n.,* ruts, roots
Rootham, *f.n.,* 'rutəm, róotăm
Roper, *f.n.,* 'roʊpər, róopĕr
Ropley *Hants,* 'rɒplɪ, róppli
Ropner, *f.n.,* 'rɒpnər, rópnĕr
Roques, *f.n.,* roʊks, rōks
Rosalie, *C.n.,* 'roʊzəlɪ, rózăli; 'rɒzəlɪ, rózzäli
Rosbotham, *f.n.,* 'rɒsbɒtəm, róssbottăm
Roscroggan *Cornwall,* rɒs'krɒgən, rosskróggăn
Rose, *f.n.,* roʊz, rōz
Rosebery, Earl of, 'roʊzbərɪ, rózbĕri
Rosehearty *Grampian,* roʊz-'hɑrtɪ, rōz-haárti
Roseingrave, *f.n.,* 'roʊzɪngreɪv, rózin-grayv. *Specifically the 17th–18th-c. family of musicians.*
Rosemarkie *H'land,* roʊz'mɑrkɪ, rōzmaárki
Rosen, *f.n.,* 'roʊzən, rózĕn
Rosenberg, *f.n.,* 'roʊzənbərg, rózĕnberg
Rosenthal, *f.n.,* 'roʊzəntɑl, rózĕntaal; 'roʊzənθɔl, rózĕn-thawl
Rosetta *Co. Down,* rə'zetə, rózéttă
Roseveare, *f.n.,* 'roʊzvɪər, rózveer
Roseworthy *Cornwall,* roʊz-'wɜrðɪ, rōzwúrthi
Rosherville *Kent,* 'roʊʃərvɪl, róshĕrvil; 'rɒzərvɪl, rózzĕrvil
Rosier, *f.n.,* 'roʊzɪər, rózi-ĕr
Roskell, *f.n.,* 'rɒskl, rósskl
Roskestal *Cornwall,* rɒs'kestl, rosskésstl
Roslea *Co. Fermanagh,* rɒs'leɪ, rossláy
Roslin *Lothian,* 'rɒzlɪn, rózzlin
Rosneath *S'clyde,* 'roʊz'niθ, róz-néeth
Ross, *f.n.,* rɒs, ross
Ross and Cromarty *H'land,* 'rɒs ənd 'krɒmərtɪ, róss ănd krómmärti
Rossall, *f.n.,* 'rɒsl, róssl
Rossall School *Fleetwood* (*Lancs.*), 'rɒsl, róssl
Rossallian, *one educated at* Rossall *School,* rɒ'seɪlɪən, rossáyliăn
Rossendale *Lancs.,* 'rɒsəndeɪl, róssĕndayl

Rosser, *f.n.,* 'rɒsər, róssĕr
Rossetti, *f.n.,* rə'zetɪ, rözétti; rə'setɪ, rössétti. *Both are accepted usage for the family of Dante Gabriel ~, 19th-c. poet and painter.*
Rossiter, *f.n.,* 'rɒsɪtər, róssitĕr
Rosslyn, Earl of, 'rɒslɪn, rósslin
Rosslyn Chapel *Lothian,* 'rɒzlɪn, rózzlin
Rost, *f.n.,* rɒst, rosst
Rostal, *f.n.,* 'rɒstæl, rósstal
Rostrevor, *f.n.,* rɒs'trevər, rosstrévvŏr
Rostrevor *Co. Down,* rɒs'trevər, rosstrévvŏr
Rosudgeon *Cornwall,* rə'sʌdʒən, rössújjŏn
Rosyth *Fife,* rə'saɪθ, rössíth
Rotblat, *f.n.,* 'rɒtblæt, rótblat
Rotdon *Merseyside,* 'rɒtdɒn, rótdon
Roth, *f.n.,* rɒθ, roth; roʊθ, rōth
Rotha, *f.n.,* 'roʊθə, róthă
Rothamsted *Herts.,* 'rɒθəmsted, róthämsted
Rothay, River, *Cumbria,* 'rɒθeɪ, róthay
Rothbury *Northd.,* 'rɒθbərɪ, róth-bŭri
Rothe, *f.n.,* roʊθ, rōth
Rothenstein, *f.n.,* 'roʊθənstaɪn, róthĕnstīn. *Appropriate for Sir William ~, portrait painter, Sir John ~, erstwhile Director of the Tate Gallery, and Michael ~, painter and print-maker.*
Rother, Rivers, 'rɒðər, róthĕr. *Appropriate for the following rivers: Derby.–S. Yorks.; Hants–W. Sussex; E. Sussex–Kent. Also for the ~ Valley parliamentary division, and the administrative division of E. Sussex.*
Rothera, *f.n.,* 'rɒðərə, róthĕră
Rotherfield *E. Sussex,* 'rɒðərfild, róthĕrfeeld
Rotherfield Peppard *Oxon.,* 'rɒðərfild 'pepərd, róthĕrfeeld péppaard
Rotherhithe *London,* 'rɒðərhaɪð, róthĕr-hīth
Rotherham, *f.n.,* 'rɒðərəm, róthĕräm
Rotherham *S. Yorks.,* 'rɒðərəm, róthĕräm
Rothermere, Viscount, 'rɒðərmɪər, róthĕrmeer
Rotherwick, Baron, 'rɒðərwɪk, róthĕrwick
Rothes *Fife,* 'rɒθɪs, róthĕss; 'rɒθɪz, róthĕz. *The second is appropriate for the Earl of ~.*

Rothes *Grampian*, 'rɒθɪs, róthĕss
Rothesay *S'clyde*, 'rɒθsɪ, róthssi
Rothholz, *f.n.*, 'rɒθhoʊlts, róth-
-hōlts
Rothiemay *Grampian*, ˌrɒθɪ'meɪ,
rothimáy
Rothiemurchus *H'land*, ˌrɒθɪ-
'mɜrkəs, rothimúrkŭss
Rothienorman *Grampian*, ˌrɒθɪ-
'nɔrmən, rothinórmăn
Rothley *Leics.*, 'roʊθlɪ, rŏthli
Rothney, *f.n.*, 'rɒθnɪ, róthni
Rothschild, Baron, 'rɒθstʃaɪld,
róths-child
Rothwell, *f.n.*, 'rɒθwəl, róthwĕl
Rothwell *Lincs.*, *W. Yorks.*,
'rɒθwel, róthwell
Rothwell *Northants.*, 'rɒθwel,
róthwell; 'roʊəl, rŏ-ĕl
Rottingdean *E. Sussex*, 'rɒtɪŋdin,
rótting-deen
Roubicek, *f.n.*, 'rubɪtʃek, roóbi-
tcheck
Roucan *D. & G.*, 'rukən, roókăn
Roud, *f.n.*, raʊd, rowd
Roudham *Norfolk*, 'raʊdəm, rów-
dăm
Roudsea Wood *Lancs.*, 'raʊdzɪ,
rówdzi
Rough, *f.n.*, rʌf, ruff
Rougham *Norfolk*, *Suffolk*, 'rʌfəm,
rúffăm
Roughan, *f.n.*, 'roʊən, rŏ-ăn
Roughdown *Hants*, 'raʊdaʊn,
rówdown
Roughlee *Lancs.*, 'rʌf'li, rúff-leé
Rought, *f.n.*, rɔt, rawt; raʊt, rowt
Roughton, *f.n.*, 'raʊtən, rówtŏn
Roughton *Lincs.*, 'rutən, roótŏn
Roughton *Salop*, 'raʊtən, rówtŏn
Rough Tor *Cornwall*, 'raʊ 'tɔr,
rów tór
Rouken Glen *S'clyde*, 'rukən
'glen, roókĕn glén
Roulston, *f.n.*, 'roʊlstən, rŏlsstŏn
Roundhay Park *W. Yorks.*,
'raʊndeɪ, równday
Rountree, *f.n.*, 'raʊntri, równtree
Rous, *f.n.*, raʊs, rowss. *Appropri-
ate also for Baron ~.*
Rousay *Orkney*, 'raʊzeɪ, rówzay
Rousdon *Devon*, 'ruzdən, roóz-
dŏn; 'raʊzdən, rówzdŏn
Rouse, *f.n.*, raʊs, rowss
Rousham *Oxon.*, 'raʊʃəm, rów-
-shăm; 'raʊsəm, rówssăm
Rousky *Co. Tyrone*, 'ruskɪ,
roósski
Rous Lench *H. & W.*, 'raʊs 'lenʃ,
rówss lénsh
Rouson, *f.n.*, 'raʊsən, rówssŏn
Roussak, *f.n.*, 'rusæk, roóssack
Roussel, *f.n.*, ru'sel, roōsséll
Rout, *f.n.*, raʊt, rowt

Routh, *f.n.*, raʊθ, rowth
Routier, *f.n.*, 'rutɪeɪ, roóti-ay
Routledge, *f.n.*, 'raʊtlɪdʒ, rówt-
lĕj; 'rʌtlɪdʒ, rútlĕj
Routledge and Kegan Paul, *pub-
lishers*, 'raʊtlɪdʒ ənd 'kigən 'pɔl,
rówtlĕj ănd keégăn páwl
Routley, *f.n.*, 'raʊtlɪ, rówtli
Rowallan, Baron, roʊ'ælən, rō-
-álăn
Rowan, *f.n.*, 'roʊən, rŏ-ăn;
'raʊən, rówăn. *The second is
usual in Scotland.*
Rowan Gallery *London*, 'roʊən,
rŏ-ăn
Rowardennan *Central*, ˌraʊər-
'denən, rowărdénnăn
Rowarth *Derby.*, 'raʊərθ, rówărth
Rowbotham, *f.n.*, 'roʊbɒtəm, rŏ-
bottăm
Rowde *Wilts.*, raʊd, rowd
Rowden, *f.n.*, 'raʊdən, rówdĕn
Rowdon, *f.n.*, 'roʊdən, rŏdŏn
Rowe, *f.n.*, roʊ, rō
Rowell, *f.n.*, 'raʊəl, rówĕl
Rowena, *C.n.*, roʊ'inə, rō-eénă
Rowett Research Institute *Bucks-
burn* (*Grampian*), 'raʊɪt, rówĕt
Rowhedge *Essex*, 'roʊhedʒ, rŏ-
-hej; 'raʊhedʒ, rów-hej
Rowland, *f.n.*, 'roʊlənd, rŏlănd
Rowlatts Hill *Leics.*, 'raʊləts 'hɪl,
rówlăts hill
Rowledge, *f.n.*, 'roʊlɪdʒ, rŏlĕj
Rowledge *Surrey*, 'raʊlɪdʒ, rów-
lĕj
Rowlett, *f.n.*, 'raʊlɪt, rówlĕt
Rowlette, *f.n.*, roʊ'let, rōlétt
Rowley, Barony of, 'roʊlɪ, rŏli
Rowley, *f.n.*, 'roʊlɪ, rŏli
Rowley Mile *Newmarket* (*Suffolk*),
'roʊlɪ, rŏli
Rowley Regis *W. Midlands*,
'raʊlɪ 'ridʒɪs, rówli reéjiss
Rowling, *f.n.*, 'roʊlɪŋ, rŏling
Rowlinson, *f.n.*, 'roʊlɪnsən,
rŏlinssŏn
Rowner *Hants*, 'raʊnər, równĕr
Rowney, *f.n.*, 'raʊnɪ, równi;
'roʊnɪ, rŏni
Rowntree, *f.n.*, 'raʊntri, równtree
Rowridge *I. of Wight*, 'raʊrɪdʒ,
rów-rij
Rowse, *f.n.*, raʊs, rowss
Rowsell, *f.n.*, 'raʊsl, rówssl
Rowsley *Derby.*, 'roʊzlɪ, rŏzli
Rowson, *f.n.*, 'raʊsən, rówssŏn;
'roʊsən, rŏssŏn
Rowston *Lincs.*, 'raʊstən, róws-
stŏn
Rowton, *f.n.*, 'raʊtən, rówtŏn
Rowton *Salop*, 'raʊtən, rówtŏn.
*Appropriate also for ~ Castle in
Shropshire.*

Roxburgh, *f.n.*, 'rɒksbərə, rócks-
bŭră
Roxburgh *Borders*, 'rɒksbərə,
rócksbŭră
Roxburghe, Duke of, 'rɒksbərə,
rócksbŭră
Roxwell *Essex*, 'rɒkswel, rócks-
wel
Royall, *f.n.*, 'rɔɪəl, róy-ăl
Royce, *f.n.*, rɔɪs, royss
Royle, *f.n.*, rɔɪl, royl
Royse, *f.n.*, rɔɪs, royss
Royston, *f.n.*, 'rɔɪstən, róysstŏn
Royston *Herts., Somerset,
S. Yorks.*, 'rɔɪstən, róysstŏn
Royton *Gtr. M'chester*, 'rɔɪtən,
róytŏn
Rozentals, *f.n.*, rou'zentlz,
rōzéntlz
Ruabon *Clwyd*, ru'æbən, roo-
-ábbŏn
Ruane, *f.n.*, ru'eɪn, rōō-áyn
Ruanlanihorne *Cornwall*, ‚ruən-
'lænɪhɔrn, roo-ănlánnihorn
Ruanne, *f.n.*, ru'æn, roo-ánn
Ruardean *Glos.*, 'ruərdin, rōōr-
deen
Rubach, *f.n.*, 'rubax, roóbaa<u>ch</u>
Rubbra, Edmund, *composer*,
'rʌbrə, rúbbră
Rubery *H. & W.*, 'rubərɪ, roóbĕri
Rubidge, *f.n.*, 'rubɪdʒ, roóbij
Rubin, *f.n.*, 'rubɪn, roobin
Rubislaw *Grampian*, 'rubslɔ,
roóbsslaw; 'rubɪslɔ, roóbisslaw
Rubra, *f.n.*, 'rubrə, roóbră
Ruchazie *S'clyde*, rʌx'heɪzɪ, ru<u>ch</u>-
-háyzi
Ruchill *S'clyde*, 'rʌxɪl, rú<u>ch</u>il
Ruchlaw *Lothian*, 'rʌxlɔ, rú<u>ch</u>law
Rucker, *f.n.*, 'rukər, rōōkĕr
Ruckinge *Kent*, 'rʌkɪndʒ, rúckinj
Rudd, *f.n.*, rʌd, rudd
Ruddell, *f.n.*, 'rʌdl, rúddl
Rudgard, *f.n.*, 'rʌdgard, rúd-
-gaard
Rudge, *f.n.*, rʌdʒ, rujj
Rudgwick *W. Sussex*, 'rʌdʒwɪk,
rújwick; 'rʌdʒɪk, rújjick
Rudhall *H. & W.*, 'rʌdɔl, rúdd-
awl
Rudham, *f.n.*, 'rʌdəm, rúddăm
Rudkin, *f.n.*, 'rʌdkɪn, rúdkin
Rudolphi, *f.n.*, ru'dɒlfɪ, rōōdólfi
Rudry *Mid Glam.*, 'rʌdrɪ, rúddri
Rudyard *Staffs.*, 'rʌdʒərd, rújjărd
Ruff, *f.n.*, rʌf, ruff
Ruffe, *f.n.*, rʌf, ruff
Rufforth *N. Yorks.*, 'rʌfərθ, rúf-
fŏrth
Rugbeian, *one educated at Rugby
School*, rʌg'biən, rugbee-ăn
Rugby *Warwicks.*, 'rʌgbɪ, rúgbi
Rugeley *Staffs.*, 'rudʒlɪ, roójli

Ruggles-Brise, *f.n.*, 'rʌglz 'braɪz,
rúgglz bríz
Ruhrmund, *f.n.*, 'ruərmənd, rōōr-
mŭnd
Ruishton *Somerset*, 'ruɪʃtən, róo-
-ishtŏn
Ruislip *London*, 'raɪslɪp, rísslip
Rum *see* Rhum
Rumbelow, *f.n.*, 'rʌmbəlou, rúm-
bĕlō
Rumbold, *f.n.*, 'rʌmbould, rúm-
bōld
Rumens, *f.n.*, 'rumənz, roóměnz
Rumney, *f.n.*, 'rʌmnɪ, rúmni
Rumney *S. Glam.*, 'rʌmnɪ, rúmni
Rumsam, *f.n.*, 'rʌmsəm, rúmssăm
Rumsey, *f.n.*, 'rʌmzɪ, rúmzi
Runacre, *f.n.*, 'rʌnəkər, rúnnăkĕr
Runacres, *f.n.*, 'rʌnəkərz, rún-
năkĕrz
Runcie, *f.n.*, 'rʌnsɪ, rúnssi
Runciman, Viscount, 'rʌnsɪmən,
rúnssimăn
Rundall, *f.n.*, 'rʌndl, rúndl
Runge, *f.n.*, rʌndʒ, runj
Runkerry *Co. Antrim*, rʌn'kerɪ,
run-kérri
Runnalls, *f.n.*, 'rʌnlz, rúnnlz
Runtz, *f.n.*, rʌnts, runts
Rupp, *f.n.*, rʌp, rupp
Ruse, *f.n.*, rus, rooss
Rushall *H. & W., W. Midlands*,
'rʌʃɔl, rúshawl
Rushall *Norfolk*, 'rʌʃhɔl, rúsh-
-hawl
Rushall *Wilts.*, 'rʌʃəl, rúshăl
Rushdie, **Salman**, *author*, sæl'man
'ruʃdɪ, salmaán rōóshdi
Rushen *I. of Man*, 'rʌʃən, rúshěn
Rusholme *Gtr. M'chester*, 'rʌʃ-
houm, rúsh-hōm. *Appropriate
also for the Barony of* ∼.
Rushyford *Durham*, 'rʌʃɪ'fɔrd,
rúshi-fórd
Ruskin, *f.n.*, 'rʌskɪn, rússkin
Rusland *Cumbria*, 'rʌslənd, rúss-
lănd
Russell, *f.n.*, 'rʌsl, rússl
Russell of Killowen, Baron, 'rʌsl
əv kɪ'louɪn, rússl ŏv kiló-ěn
Rusthall *Kent*, 'rʌsthɔl, rúst-hawl
Ruswarp *N. Yorks.*, 'rʌsərp,
rússărp
Rutherford, *f.n.*, 'rʌðərfərd,
rú<u>th</u>ĕrfŏrd
Rutherglen *S'clyde*, 'rʌðərglən,
rú<u>th</u>ĕrglĕn
Ruthin *Clwyd, S. Glam.*, 'rɪθɪn,
ríthin
Ruthrieston *Grampian*, 'rʌðərstən,
rú<u>th</u>ĕrstŏn
Ruthven, Baron, 'rɪvən, rívvěn
Ruthven, *f.n.*, 'rɪvən, rívvěn;
'ruθvən, roóthvěn

Ruthven, Loch, *H'land*, 'rʌθvən, rúthvĕn

Ruthven of Canberra, Viscount, 'rɪvən əv 'kænbərə, rívvĕn ŏv kánbĕră

Ruthwaite *Cumbria*, 'rʌθweɪt, rúthwayt; 'rʌθət, rúth-ăt

Ruthwell *D. & G.*, 'rʌθwəl, rúth-wĕl; 'rʌðwəl, rúṯhwĕl; 'rɪðl, ríṯhl

Rutland, *f.n.*, 'rʌtlənd, rútlănd

Rutland *Leics.*, 'rʌtlənd, rútlănd

Ruyton-Eleven-Towns *Salop*, 'raɪtən ɪ'levəntaʊnz, rī́tŏn--ĕlévvĕntownz

Ryall, *f.n.*, 'raɪəl, rī́-ăl

Ryan, *f.n.*, 'raɪən, rī́-ăn

Ryarsh *Kent*, 'raɪɑrʃ, rī́-aarsh

Rydal *Cumbria*, 'raɪdl, rídl. *Appropriate also for* ~ *Water*.

Rydz, *f.n.*, rɪdz, ridz

Ryhope *Tyne & Wear*, 'raɪəp, rī́-ŏp

Rykwert, *f.n.*, 'rɪkwərt, ríckwĕrt

Ryland, *f.n.*, 'raɪlənd, rílănd

Rylands, *f.n.*, 'raɪləndz, ríländz

Rylett, *f.n.*, 'raɪlɪt, rílĕt

Ryme Intrinseca *Dorset*, 'raɪm ɪn'trɪnsɪkə, rím intrínssĕkă

Rynd, *f.n.*, rɪnd, rinnd

Ryrie, *f.n.*, 'raɪərɪ, ríri

Rysanek, *f.n.*, 'raɪsənek, ríssăneck

Ryton, *f.n.*, 'raɪtən, rítŏn

Ryton *Durham*, 'raɪtən, rítŏn

Ryton-on-Dunsmore *Warwicks.*, 'raɪtən ɒn 'dʌnzmər, rítŏn on dúnzmor

Ryves, *f.n.*, raɪvz, rīvz

S

Saatchi, *f.n.*, 'sɑtʃɪ, saátchi

Sabbagh, *f.n.*, 'sæbɑ, sábbaa

Sabel, *f.n.*, 'seɪbl, sáybl

Sabelli, *f.n.*, sə'belɪ, săbélli

Sabeston, *f.n.*, 'sæbɪstən, sábbĕs-tŏn

Sabin, *f.n.*, 'seɪbɪn, sáybin; 'sæbɪn, sábbin

Sabina, *C.n.*, sə'binə, săbée̅nă

Sabine, *f.n.*, 'sæbaɪn, sábbīn

Sabit, *f.n.*, 'sæbɪt, sábbit

Sach, *f.n.*, seɪtʃ, saytch; seɪʃ, saysh

Sacher, *f.n.*, 'sækər, sáckĕr

Sachs, *f.n.*, sæks, sacks

Sackley, *f.n.*, 'sæklɪ, sáckli

Sackur, *f.n.*, 'sækər, sáckŭr

Sackville-West, Vita, *poet and novelist (1892–1962)*, 'vitə 'sækvɪl 'west, vée̅tă sáckvil wést

Sacombe *Herts.*, 'seɪkəm, sáykŏm

Sacriston Heugh *Durham*, 'sækrɪs-tən 'hjuf, sáckristŏn héwf

Sadberge *Durham*, 'sædbɜrdʒ, sádberj

Saddell Abbey *S'clyde*, 'sædl, sáddl

Sadie, *f.n.*, 'seɪdɪ, sáydi

Sadleir, *f.n.*, 'sædlər, sádlĕr

Saffell, *f.n.*, 'sæfl, sáffl; sə'fel, săféll

Saffron Walden *Essex*, 'sæfrən 'wɔldən, sáffrŏn wáwldĕn

Sagar, *f.n.*, 'seɪgər, sáygăr

Sager, *f.n.*, 'seɪgər, sáygĕr

Saggar, *f.n.*, 'sægɑr, sággaar

Saham Toney *Norfolk*, 'seɪəm 'toʊnɪ, sáy-ăm tŏ́ni

Saich, *f.n.*, seɪʃ, saysh

Saighton *Ches.*, 'seɪtən, sáytŏn

Sainsbury, *f.n.*, 'seɪnzbərɪ, sáynz-bŭri. *Appropriate also for Baron* ~.

Saint, *f.n.*, seɪnt, saynt

St. Albans *Herts.*, snt 'ɔlbənz, sĭnt áwlbănz. *Appropriate also for the Duke of* ~.

St. Aldate's *Oxford*, snt 'ɔldɪts, sĭnt áwldits; snt 'oʊldz, sĭnt ṓldz

St. Aldwyn, Earl, snt 'ɔldwɪn, sĭnt áwldwin

St. Andrews *Fife*, snt 'ændruz, sĭnt ándrooz. *Appropriate also for the Earl of* ~.

St. Anthony in Meneage *Cornwall*, snt 'æntənɪ ɪn mɪ'nig, sĭnt ántŏni in mĕnée̅g; snt 'æntənɪ ɪn mɪ'neɪg, sĭnt ántŏni in mĕnáyg

St. Asaph *Clwyd*, snt 'æsəf, sĭnt ássăf

St. Athan *S. Glam.*, snt 'æθən, sĭnt áthăn

St. Aubyn, *f.n.*, snt 'ɔbɪn, sĭnt áwbin

St. Audries *Somerset*, snt 'ɔdrɪz, sĭnt áwdriz

St. Austell *Cornwall*, snt 'ɔstl, sĭnt áwsstl; snt 'ɔsl, sĭnt áwssl

St. Bathans Abbey *Borders*, snt 'bæθənz, sĭnt báthănz

St. Benet's Abbey *Norfolk*, snt 'benɪts, sĭnt bénnĕts

St. Breock *Cornwall*, snt 'briək, sĭnt brée̅-ŏk

St. Breward *Cornwall*, snt 'bruərd, sĭnt brŏ́o-ărd

St. Briavels *Glos.*, snt 'brevlz, sĭnt brévvlz

St. Budeaux *Devon*, snt 'bjudoʊ, sĭnt béwdō

St. Chloe *Glos.*, snt 'kloʊɪ, sĭnt klṓ-i

St. Clair, *f.n.*, snt 'klɛər, sĭnt
kláir; 'sıŋklɛər, sínklair

St. Clair-Erskine, *f.n.*, snt 'klɛər
'ɜrskın, sĭnt kláir érsskin.
*Family name of the Earl of
Rosslyn.*

St. Clare, *f.n.*, 'sıŋklər, sínklăr

St. Clears *Dyfed*, snt 'klɛərz, sĭnt
kláirz

St. Clement Danes *London*, snt
'klemənt 'deınz, sĭnt klémměnt
dáynz

St. Clements *Cornwall*, snt 'kle-
mənts, sĭnt klémměnts

St. Clether *Cornwall*, snt 'kleðər,
sĭnt kléthěr

St. Cloud *H. & W.*, snt 'klu, sĭnt
kloo

St. Columb Major *and* Minor
Cornwall, snt 'kʌləm, sĭnt kúl-
lŭm; snt 'kɒləm, sĭnt kóllŭm

St. Cyres, Viscount, snt 'saıərz,
sĭnt sírz

St. Dennis *Cornwall*, snt 'denıs,
sĭnt dénniss

St. Dogmaels *Dyfed*, snt 'dɒg-
məlz, sĭnt dógmělz

St. Dogwells *Dyfed*, snt 'dɒgwəlz,
sĭnt dógwělz

St. Dominick *Cornwall*, snt
'dɒmınık, sĭnt dómminick

St. Donat's *S. Glam.*, snt 'dɒnəts,
sĭnt dónnăts. *Appropriate also
for ~ Castle.*

St. Endellion *Cornwall*, snt
en'delıən, sĭnt endélliŏn

St. Enoder *Cornwall*, snt 'enədər,
sĭnt énnŏděr

St. Enodoc *Cornwall*, snt 'enədɒk,
sĭnt énnŏdock

St. Erth *Cornwall*, snt 'ɜrθ, sĭnt
érth

St. Eval *Cornwall*, snt 'evl, sĭnt
évvl

St. Ewe *Cornwall*, snt 'ju, sĭnt
yoo

St. Fagan's *S. Glam.*, snt 'fægənz,
sĭnt fággänz

Saintfield *Co. Down*, 'seıntfild,
sáyntfeeld

St. Fillan's *Tayside*, snt 'fılənz,
sĭnt fíllänz

St. Gennys *Cornwall*, snt 'genıs,
sĭnt génniss

St. Germans, Earl of, snt 'dʒɜr-
mənz, sĭnt jérmänz

St. Giles' Cathedral *Edinburgh*,
snt 'dʒaılz, sĭnt jílz. *Traditionally, no optional possessive -s is
used in the spelling, nor* ız, *-ěz in
the pronunciation.*

St. Gorran, *also spelt* **St. Goran,**
Cornwall, snt 'gɒrən, sĭnt górrăn

St. Govan's Head *Dyfed*, snt
'gɒvənz, sĭnt góvvänz; snt
'gʌvənz, sĭnt gúvvänz. *The first
is the Welsh pronunciation. The
second tends to be heard on the
English side of the Bristol
Channel.*

St. Helier *London*, snt 'heljər, sĭnt
héll-yěr

St. Hilary *Cornwall, S. Glam.*,
snt 'hılərı, sĭnt hílläri

St. Ippolyts, *also spelt* **St. Ippol-
litts,** *Herts.*, snt 'ıpəlıts, sĭnt
íppŏlits

St. Issey *Cornwall*, snt 'ızı, sĭnt
ízzi

St. Ive *Cornwall*, snt 'iv, sĭnt éev

St. Ives *Cambs., Cornwall*, snt
'aıvz, sĭnt ívz

St. James's, Court of, snt
'dʒeımzız, sĭnt jáymziz

St. John, *f.n.*, 'sındʒən, sínjŏn;
snt 'dʒɒn, sĭnt jón. *The first is
appropriate for Viscount Bolingbroke's family name.*

St. John of Bletso, Baron,
'sındʒən əv 'bletsou, sínjŏn ŏv
blétsō

St. John of Lydiard Tregoze,
Baron, 'sındʒən əv 'lıdıərd
trə'gɒz, sínjŏn ŏv líddi-ärd
trěgózz

St. John's Point *H'land*, snt
'dʒɒnz 'pɔınt, sĭnt jónz póynt

St. Juliot *Cornwall*, snt 'dʒulıət,
sĭnt jooli-ŏt; snt 'dʒılt, sĭnt jílt

St. Just, Baron, snt 'dʒʌst, sĭnt
júst

St. Just in Penwith *Cornwall*, snt
'dʒʌst ın pen'wıθ, sĭnt júst in
penwíth

St. Keverne *Cornwall*, snt 'kev-
ərn, sĭnt kévvěrn

St. Keyne *Cornwall*, snt 'keın,
sĭnt káyn; snt 'kin, sĭnt kéen

St. Kilda *W. Isles*, snt 'kıldə, sĭnt
kíldă

St. Leger, *f.n.*, snt 'ledʒər, sĭnt
léjjěr; 'selındʒər, séllinjěr. *The
first is appropriate for Viscount
Doneraile's family name, the
second for the Yorkshire branch
of the family.*

St. Levan *Cornwall*, snt 'levən,
sĭnt lévvăn. *Appropriate also for
Baron ~.*

St. Loyes *Devon*, snt 'lɔız, sĭnt
lóyz

St. Lythan's *S. Glam.*, snt 'lıðənz,
sĭnt líthänz

St. Mabyn *Cornwall*, snt 'meıbın,
sĭnt máybin

St. Machar's Cathedral *Aberdeen*,
snt 'mæxərz, sĭnt máchărz

St. MacNissi's College *Co. Antrim*, 'seɪnt mək'nɪsɪz, sáynt măk-neéssiz

St. Martin in Meneage *Cornwall*, snt 'mɑrtɪn ɪn mɪ'nɪg, sĭnt maártin in mĕneég; snt 'mɑrtɪn ɪn mɪ'neɪg, sĭnt maártin in mĕnáyg

St. Martin's le Grand *London*, snt 'mɑrtɪnz lə 'grænd, sĭnt maártinz lĕ gránd

St. Mary Axe *City of London*, snt 'mɛərɪ 'æks, sĭnt máiri ácks; 'sɪmərɪ 'æks, símmări ácks

St. Marylebone *see* **Marylebone**

St. Mary-le-Strand *London*, snt 'mɛərɪ lə 'strænd, sĭnt máiri lĕ stránd

St. Mary Woolnoth *City of London Guild Church*, snt 'mɛərɪ 'wʊlnɒθ, sĭnt máiri woŏlnoth

St. Maur, *f.n.*, 'sɪmɔr, seémor

St. Mawes *Cornwall*, snt 'mɔz, sĭnt máwz

St. Mawgan in Meneage *Cornwall*, snt 'mɔgən ɪn mɪ'nɪg, sĭnt máwgăn in mĕneég; snt 'mɔgən ɪn mɪ'neɪg, sĭnt máwgăn in mĕnáyg

St. Mawgan-in-Pydar *Cornwall*, snt 'mɔgən ɪn 'paɪdɑr, sĭnt máwgăn in pídaar

St. Merryn *Cornwall*, snt 'merɪn, sĭnt mérrin

St. Mewan *Cornwall*, snt 'mjuən, sĭnt méw-ăn

St. Michael Penkevil *Cornwall*, snt 'maɪkl peŋ'kɪvl, sĭnt míkl penkívvl

St. Monance *Fife*, snt 'moʊnəns, sĭnt mónănss

St. Neot *Cornwall*, snt 'nɪət, sĭnt neé-ŏt

St. Neots *Cambs.*, snt 'nɪəts, sĭnt neé-ŏts

St. Ninian's Cathedral *Perth*, snt 'nɪnɪənz, sĭnt nínni-ănz

St. Olaves *Norfolk*, snt 'ɒlɪvz, sĭnt óllivz

Sainton, *f.n.*, 'seɪntən, sáyntŏn

St. Oswald, Baron, snt 'ɒzwəld, sĭnt ózwăld

St. Osyth *Essex*, snt 'oʊzɪθ, sĭnt ózith; snt 'oʊsɪθ, sĭnt óssith

St. Pancras *London*, snt 'pæŋkrəs, sĭnt pánkrăss

St. Paul's Walden Bury *Herts.*, snt 'pɔlz 'wɔldən 'berɪ, sĭnt páwlz wáwldĕn bérri

St. Peter-at-Gowts *Lincoln church*, snt 'pitər ət 'gaʊts, sĭnt peétĕr ăt gówts

St. Pierre *Gwent*, snt pɪ'ɛər, sĭnt pi-áir. *Appropriate also for the*

~ *Golf Course, nr. Chepstow, Gwent.*

St. Pinnock *Cornwall*, snt 'pɪnək, sĭnt pínnŏk

St. Rollox *Glasgow*, snt 'rɒləks, sĭnt róllŏks

St. Romaine, *f.n.*, snt rə'meɪn, sĭnt rŏmáyn

St. Salvator's College *Univ. of St. Andrews*, snt sæl'veɪtərz, sĭnt salváytŏrz

St. Seiriol Island, *also* **Puffin Island** *q.v.*, *Gwynedd*, snt 'saɪərɪɒl, sĭnt sĭri-oll

St. Teath *Cornwall*, snt 'teθ, sĭnt téth

St. Teilo Priory *Cardiff*, snt 'taɪloʊ, sĭnt tílō

St. Tudy *Cornwall*, snt 'tjudɪ, sĭnt téwdi

St. Vigeans *Tayside*, snt 'vɪdʒənz, sĭnt víjjănz

St. Weonards *H. & W.*, snt 'wenərdz, sĭnt wénnărdz

St. Werburgh *Bristol*, snt 'wɜrbərg, sĭnt wérburg

St. Wynifred's Well *Clwyd*, snt 'wɪnɪfrədz, sĭnt wínnifrĕdz

Sala, George Augustus Henry, *19th-c. journalist and author*, 'sɑlə, saálă

Salaman, *f.n.*, 'sæləmæn, sálăman; 'sæləmən, sálămăn

Salamé, *f.n.*, 'sæləmeɪ, sálămay

Salant, *f.n.*, 'seɪlənt, sáylănt

Salberg, *f.n.*, 'sɔlbərg, sáwlberg

Salcey Forest *Northants.*, 'sɔlsɪ, sáwlssi

Salcombe *Devon*, 'sɒlkəm, sáwlkŏm; 'sɒlkəm, sólkŏm

Sale *Gtr. M'chester*, seɪl, sayl

Sales, *f.n.*, seɪlz, saylz

Salew, *f.n.*, sə'lu, sălóo

Salford *Beds.*, 'sæfərd, sáffŏrd

Salford *Gtr. M'chester*, 'sɒlfərd, sólfŏrd; 'sɔlfərd, sáwlfŏrd

Salfords *Surrey*, 'sælfərdz, sálfŏrdz

Salhouse *Norfolk*, 'sæləs, sálŭss; 'sælhaʊs, sál-howss

Saline *Fife*, 'sælɪn, sálin

Salisbury *Wilts.*, 'sɔlzbərɪ, sáwlzbŭri; 'sɔlzbrɪ, sáwlzbri. *The first is appropriate for the Marquess of* ~.

Salisse, *f.n.*, sə'lis, săleéss

Salkeld, *f.n.*, 'sɔlkeld, sáwlkeld

Salkeld *Cumbria*, 'sɔlkeld, sáwlkeld; 'sæfəld, sáffĕld

Salkield, *f.n.*, 'sɔlkɪld, sáwlkeeld

Sall, *also spelt* **Salle**, *Norfolk*, sɔl, sawl

Sallagh *Co. Antrim*, 'sælə, sálă

Salle *see* **Sall**

Sallis, *f.n.*, 'sælɪs, sáliss
Salmon, *f.n.*, 'sæmən, sámmŏn
Salmonby *Lincs.*, 'sæmənbɪ, sám-
mŏnbi; 'sælmənbɪ, sál-mŏnbi
Salmond, *f.n.*, 'sæmənd, sám-
mŏnd
Salop, *alternative name and
abbrev. for Shropshire*, 'sæləp,
sálŏp
Salopian, *one educated at* Shrews-
bury *School*, sə'loupɪən, sălŏp-
iăn
Saloway, *f.n.*, 'sæləweɪ, sálŏ-way
Salpeter, *f.n.*, 'sælpɪtər, sálpeetĕr
Salsburgh *S'clyde*, 'sɔlzbərə,
sáwlzbŭră
Salt, *f.n.*, sɔlt, sawlt; sɒlt, sollt
Saltaire *W. Yorks.*, sɔl'teər, sawl-
táir
Salter, *f.n.*, 'sɔltər, sáwltĕr;
'sɒltər, sólltĕr
Saltersford *Ches.*, 'sɔltərzfərd,
sáwltĕrzfŏrd. *Appropriate also
for Baron* ~.
Saltfleetby *Lincs.*, 'sɔltflɪtbɪ,
sáwltfleetbi; 'sɒləbɪ, sóllăbi
Salthouse *Norfolk*, 'sɔlthaus,
sáwlt-howss
Saltley *W. Midlands*, 'sɔltlɪ,
sáwltli
Saltoun, *f.n.*, 'sɔltən, sáwltŏn;
'sæltən, sáltŏn. *The first is
appropriate for Baroness* ~.
Saltoun, East *and* West, *Lothian*,
'sɔltən, sáwltŏn
Salusbury, *f.n.*, 'sɔlzbərɪ, sáwlz-
bŭri
Salvesen, *f.n.*, 'sælvɪsən, sálvĕssĕn
Salveson, *f.n.*, 'sælvɪsən, sálvĕssŏn
Salway, *f.n.*, 'sɔlweɪ, sáwlway
Salwick *Lancs.*, 'sælɪk, sálick;
'sælwɪk, sálwick
Salzedo, *f.n.*, sæl'zeɪdou, salzáydō
Samares, *f.n.*, 'sæməreɪ, sámmă-
ray
Sambles, *f.n.*, 'sæmblz, sámblz
Samett, *f.n.*, 'sæmɪt, sámmĕt
Samlesbury *Lancs.*, 'sæmzbərɪ,
sámzbŭri; 'samzbərɪ, saámz-
bŭri
Sammes, *f.n.*, sæmz, samz
Sampford Courtenay *Devon*,
'sæmpfərd 'kɔrtnɪ, sámpfŏrd
kórtni
Sampford Spiney *Devon*, 'sæmp-
fərd 'spaɪnɪ, sámpfŏrd spíni
Sampson, *f.n.*, 'sæmpsən, sámps-
sŏn
Samson Island *I. of Scilly*,
'sæmsən, sámssŏn
Samuels, *f.n.*, 'sæmjuəlz, sám-
-yōō-ĕlz
Samuely, *f.n.*, ˌsæmjuˈelɪ, sam-
-yōō-élli

Sancreed *Cornwall*, sæŋ'krid,
sankréed
Sandaig *S'clyde*, 'sændeɪg,
sándayg
Sandars, *f.n.*, 'sændərz, sándărz
Sanday *Orkney*, 'sændeɪ, sánday
Sandbach, *f.n.*, 'sændbætʃ, sándbatch
Sandbach *Ches.*, 'sændbætʃ,
sándbatch
Sandell, *f.n.*, 'sændl, sándl
Sandelson, *f.n.*, 'sændlsən,
sándlssŏn
Sander, *f.n.*, 'sændər, sándĕr
Sanders, *f.n.*, 'sandərz, saándĕrz;
'sændərz, sándĕrz; 'sɒndərz,
sáwndĕrz
Sanderson, *f.n.*, 'sandərsən,
saándĕrsson; 'sændərsən,
sándĕrssŏn
Sanderson of Ayot, Barony of,
'sændərsən əv 'eɪət, sándĕrssŏn
ŏv áy-ŏt
Sandes, *f.n.*, sændz, sandz
Sandford, *f.n.*, 'sændfərd, sánd-
fŏrd; 'sændfɔrd, sánd-ford;
'sænərd, sánnŏrd
Sandhaven *Grampian*, 'sænd-
heɪvən, sánd-hayvĕn
Sandhurst Royal Military Aca-
demy *Berks.*, 'sændhərst, sánd-
hurst
Sandiacre *Derby.*, 'sændɪeɪkər,
sándi-aykĕr
Sandilands, *f.n.*, 'sændɪləndz,
sándilăndz
Sandness *Shetland*, 'sændnes,
sándness
Sandow, *f.n.*, 'sændou, sándō
Sandridge *Herts.*, 'sandrɪdʒ,
saándrij
Sandringham *Norfolk*, 'sændrɪŋ-
əm, sándring-ăm
Sandry, *f.n.*, 'sændrɪ, sándri
Sands, *f.n.*, sændz, sandz
Sandwich *Kent*, 'sændwɪtʃ, sánd-
witch
Sandy, *f.n.*, 'sændɪ, sándi
Sandy *Beds.*, 'sændɪ, sándi
Sandyknowe Crags *Borders*,
'sændɪnau, sándinŏw
Sandys, *f.n.*, sændz, sandz.
Appropriate also for Baron ~.
Sanford, *f.n.*, 'sænfərd, sánfŏrd
Sanger, *f.n.*, 'sæŋər, sáng-ĕr
Sangster, *f.n.*, 'sæŋstər, sángstĕr
Sanquhar *D. & G.*, 'sæŋkər,
sánkăr. *Appropriate also for the
Earl of* ~.
Sansom, *f.n.*, 'sænsəm, sánssŏm
Sapcote *Leics.*, 'sæpkout, sápkŏt
Saphier, *f.n.*, 'sæfɪər, sáffeer
Sapiston *Suffolk*, 'sæpɪstən, sáp-
pistŏn

Sapley *Cambs.*, 'sæplı, sáppli
Sapte, *f.n.*, sæpt, sapt
Sarell, *f.n.*, 'særəl, sárrĕl
Sargant, *f.n.*, 'sɑrdʒənt, saʹarjănt
Sargeaunt, *f.n.*, 'sɑrdʒənt, saʹar-
  jĕnt
Sargent, *f.n.*, 'sɑrdʒənt, saʹarjĕnt
Sargisson, *f.n.*, 'sɑrdʒɪsən, saʹar-
  jissŏn
Sarisbury *Hants*, 'sɑrzbərı, saʹarz-
  bŭri; 'sɛɑrzbərı, sáirzbŭri
Sarnau *Dyfed, Gwynedd, Powys*,
  'sɑrnaɪ, saʹarnī
Sarony, *f.n.*, sə'roʊnɪ, sărŏ́ni
Sarratt *Herts.*, 'særət, sárrăt
Sarre *Kent*, sɑr, saar
Sarson, *f.n.*, 'sɑrsən, saʹarssŏn
Sarstedt, *f.n.*, 'sɑrsted, saʹarssted
Sartoris, *f.n.*, 'sɑrtərɪs, saʹartŏriss
Sartorius, *f.n.*, 'sɑrtərɪs, saʹartŏriss
Sarum *Roman name for* Salisbury,
  'sɛɑrəm, sáirŭm
Sasse, *f.n.*, sæs, sass
Sassoon, *f.n.*, sə'sun, sássoʹon
Satchwell, *f.n.*, 'sætʃwel, sátchwel
Satow, *f.n.*, 'satoʊ, saʹatō
Satterleigh *Devon*, 'sætərlı, sát-
  tĕrli
Sauchiehall Street *Glasgow*,
  ˌsɒxɪ'hɔl, soᴄhiháwl
Sauer, *f.n.*, sɔr, sor
Saughall, Great *and* Little, *Ches.*,
  'sɔkl, sáwkl
Saughton *Lothian*, 'sɒxtən,
  sóᴄhtŏn
Saughtree *Borders*, 'sɒxtri,
  sóᴄhtree
Saul *Co. Down, Glos.*, sɔl, sawl
Saulez, *f.n.*, 'sɔlɪ, sáwli; 'soʊlɪ,
  sóli
Saumarez, *f.n.*, 'sɒmərɪz, sóm-
  mărĕz; 'soʊmərɪ, sŏ́mări
Saundby, *f.n.*, 'sɔndbɪ, sáwndbi
Saunders, *f.n.*, 'sɔndərz, sáwn-
  dĕrz; 'sandərz, saʹandĕrz
Saundersfoot *Dyfed*, 'sɔndərzfʊt,
  sáwndĕrzfŏot
Saunderson, *f.n.*, 'sɔndərsən,
  sáwndĕrssŏn; 'sandərsən,
  saʹandĕrssŏn
Sauter, *f.n.*, 'soʊtər, sŏ́tĕr
Sauvage, *f.n.*, 'sævɪdʒ, sávvij;
  soʊ'vɑʒ, sōvaʹaᴢh
Sava, *f.n.*, 'savə, saʹavă
Savage, *f.n.*, 'sævɪdʒ, sávvij
Savernake *Wilts.*, 'sævərnæk,
  sávvĕrnack. *Appropriate also
  for Viscount* ∼.
Savidge, *f.n.*, 'sævɪdʒ, sávvij
Savigear, *f.n.*, 'sævɪgɪər, sávvigeer
Savile, *f.n.*, 'sævɪl, sávvil; 'sævl,
  sávvl
Savile Club *London*, 'sævɪl,
  sávvil; 'sævl, sávvl

Savile Row *London*, 'sævɪl 'roʊ,
  sávvil rŏ́; 'sævl 'roʊ, sávvl rŏ́
Savins, *f.n.*, 'sævɪnz, sávvinz
Savory, *f.n.*, 'seɪvərɪ, sáyvŏri
Saward, *f.n.*, 'seɪwərd, sáywărd
Sawbridgeworth *Herts.*, 'sɒbrɪdʒ-
  wərθ, sáwbrijwŭrth. *An old
  pronunciation was* 'sæpswərθ,
  sápswŭrth.
Saweard, *f.n.*, 'seɪwərd, sáywărd
Sawel *Co. Derry–Co. Tyrone*,
  'sɔəl, sáw-ĕl
Sawrey, *f.n.*, 'sɔrɪ, sáwri
Sawston *Cambs.*, 'sɔstən, sáwstŏn
Sawtry *Cambs.*, 'sɔtrɪ, sáwtri
Sawyer, *f.n.*, 'sɔjər, sáw-yĕr
Saxavord *Shetland*, 'sæksə'vɔrd,
  sácksăvórd
Saxilby *Lincs.*, 'sækslbɪ, sáckslbi
Saxmundham *Suffolk*, sæks-
  'mʌndəm, sacksmúndăm
Saxon, *f.n.*, 'sæksən, sácksŏn
Saxthorpe *Norfolk*, 'sæksθɔrp,
  sácks-thorp
Saxton, *f.n.*, 'sækstən, sáckstŏn
Saxty, *f.n.*, 'sækstɪ, sácksti
Sayce, *f.n.*, seɪs, sayss
Saye and Sele, Baron, 'seɪ ənd
  'sil, sáy ănd séel
Sayer, *f.n.*, sɛər, sair; 'seɪər,
  sáy-ĕr
Sayers, *f.n.*, sɛərz, sairz; 'seɪərz,
  sáy-ĕrz
Sayles, *f.n.*, seɪlz, saylz
Saynor, *f.n.*, 'seɪnər, sáynŏr
Sayres, *f.n.*, sɛərz, sairz
Saywell, *f.n.*, 'seɪwel, sáywel
Scadding, *f.n.*, 'skædɪŋ, skádding
Scadgell, *f.n.*, 'skædʒl, skájjl
Scafell *Cumbria*, 'skɔ'fel, skáw-
  -féll
Scalasaig *S'clyde*, 'skæləseɪg,
  skálăssayg
Scalford *Leics.*, 'skɔlfərd, skáwl-
  fŏrd; 'skɔfərd, skáwfŏrd
Scalloway *Shetland*, 'skæləwə,
  skálŏ-wă
Scalpay *H'land, W. Isles*, 'skælpeɪ,
  skálpay
Scammell, *f.n.*, 'skæml, skámml
Scannell, *f.n.*, 'skænl, skánnl
Scapa Flow *Orkney*, 'skɑpə 'floʊ,
  skaʹapă flŏ́
Scarba *S'clyde*, 'skɑrbə, skaʹarbă
Scarborough *N. Yorks.*, 'skɑr-
  bərə, skaʹarbŭră
Scarbrough, Earl of, 'skɑrbrə,
  skaʹarbră
Scardifield, *f.n.*, 'skɑrdɪfild,
  skaʹardifeeld
Scargill, *f.n.*, 'skɑrgɪl, skaʹar-gill
Scarinish *S'clyde*, 'skærɪnɪʃ,
  skárrinish; skæ'rɪnɪʃ, skarrín-
  nish

Scarisbrick, *f.n.*, 'skɛərzbrɪk, skáirzbrick

Scarisbrick *Lancs.*, 'skɛərzbrɪk, skáirzbrick

Scarlett, *f.n.*, 'skɑrlət, skaárlĕt

Scartho, *also spelt* Scarthoe, *Humberside*, 'skɑrθoʊ, skaár- -thō

Scarva *Co. Down*, 'skɑrvə, skaárvă

Scase, *f.n.*, skeɪs, skayss

Scaur, The, *Grampian*, skɔr, skor

Scavaig, Loch, *Skye*, 'skæveɪg, skávvayg

Scawen, *f.n.*, 'skɔən, skáw-ĕn

Sceales, *f.n.*, skilz, skeelz

Scears, *f.n.*, sɪərz, seerz

Sceats, *f.n.*, skits, skeets

Sceberras, *f.n.*, ˌʃebə'rɑs, sheb- bĕraáss

Scerri, *f.n.*, 'ʃerɪ, shérri

Scerry, *f.n.*, 'ʃerɪ, shérri

Schaffer, *f.n.*, 'ʃæfər, sháffĕr

Schapiro, *f.n.*, ʃə'pɪəroʊ, shăpéerō

Scharrer, *f.n.*, 'ʃɑrər, shaárĕr

Scharf, *f.n.*, ʃɑrf, shaarf

Schaschke, *f.n.*, 'ʃæskɪ, shásski

Schellenberg, *f.n.*, 'ʃelənbɜrg, shéllĕnberg

Scher, *f.n.*, ʃɜr, sher. *Appropriate for the Anna ~ Children's Theatre, Islington, London.*

Scherer, *f.n.*, 'ʃɛərər, sháirĕr; 'ʃerər, shérrĕr

Schidlof, *f.n.*, 'ʃɪdlɒf, shídloff

Schiehallion *Tayside*, ʃɪ'hæljən, shĕ-hál-yŏn

Schild, *f.n.*, ʃild, sheeld

Schilizzi, *f.n.*, skɪ'lɪtsɪ, skilítsi

Schiller, *f.n.*, 'ʃɪlər, shíllĕr

Schjelderup, *f.n.*, 'ʃeldrəp, shéldrŭp

Schlaen, *f.n.*, ʃleɪn, shlayn

Schlapp, *f.n.*, ʃlæp, shlapp

Schlazinger, *f.n.*, 'ʃlæzɪndʒər, shlázzinjĕr

Schlesinger, *f.n.*, 'ʃlesɪndʒər, shléssinjĕr

Schlie, *f.n.* sli, slee

Schmidt, *f.n.*, ʃmɪt, shmitt

Schofield, *f.n.*, 'skoʊfild, skṓ- feeld

Scholefield, *f.n.*, 'skoʊlfild, skṓlfeeld

Scholes, *f.n.*, skoʊlz, skōlz. *Appropriate for Percy ~, musicologist.*

Scholey, *f.n.*, 'skoʊlɪ, skṓli

Scholfield, *f.n.*, 'skoʊfild, skṓ- feeld; 'skoʊlfild, skṓlfeeld

Schon, *f.n.*, ʃɒn, shonn

Schonell, *f.n.*, ʃɒ'nel, shonnéll

Schonfield, *f.n.*, 'skɒnfild, skónn- feeld

Schooling, *f.n.*, 'skulɪŋ, skóoling

Schoutze, *f.n.*, 'ʃʊtseɪ, shóotsay

Schouvaloff, *f.n.*, ʃu'vɑlɒf, shoo- vaáloff

Schreiber, *f.n.*, 'ʃraɪbər, shríbĕr

Schroder, *f.n.*, 'ʃroʊdər, shrṓdĕr

Schulcz-Paull, *f.n.*, 'ʃʊlts 'pɔl, shóolts páwl

Schulten, *f.n.*, 'skultən, skóoltĕn

Schuster, *f.n.*, 'ʃʊstər, shóostĕr

Schwabe, *f.n.*, 'ʃwɑbə, shwaábĕ

Schwartz, *f.n.*, ʃwɔrts, shwawrts

Sciama, *f.n.*, 'ʃɑmə, shaámă

Sciberras, *f.n.*, ˌʃɪbə'rɑs, shib- bĕraáss

Sciennes, *f.n.*, ʃinz, sheenz

Scillonian, *native of the Isles of Scilly*, sɪ'loʊnɪən, silóniăn

Scilly, Isles of, 'sɪlɪ, sílli

Scissett *W. Yorks.*, sɪ'set, sissétt

Sclanders, *f.n.*, 'sklɑndərz, sklaándĕrz

Sclater, *f.n.*, 'sleɪtər, sláytĕr

Scobell, *f.n.*, skoʊ'bel, skōbéll

Scofield, *f.n.*, 'skoʊfild, skṓfeeld

Scole *Norfolk*, skoʊl, skōl

Scollan, *f.n.*, 'skɒlən, skóllăn

Scolt Head *Norfolk*, skɒlt, skollt

Scone *Tayside*, skun, skoon. *Appropriate also for Baron ~ and for the Stone of ~.*

Scoones, *f.n.*, skunz, skoonz

Scopes, *f.n.*, skoʊpz, skōps

Scopwick *Lincs.*, 'skɒpwɪk, skóp- wick

Scorer, *f.n.*, 'skɔrər, skáwrĕr

Scorgie, *f.n.*, 'skɔrdʒɪ, skórji

Scorrier *Cornwall*, 'skɒrɪər, skórri-ĕr

Scotby *Cumbria*, 'skɒtbɪ, skótbi

Scothern, *f.n.*, 'skɒθɜrn, skóthern; 'skɒθɜrn, skóthĕrn

Scothern *Lincs.*, 'skɒθɜrn, skóthern

Scotstoun *S'clyde*, 'skɒtstən, skótstōn

Scott, *f.n.*, skɒt, skott

Scottow *Norfolk*, 'skɒtoʊ, skóttō

Scougal, *f.n.*, 'skugl, skóogl

Scougall, *f.n.*, 'skugl, skóogl

Scoular, *f.n.*, 'skulər, skóolăr

Scoullar, *f.n.*, 'skulər, skóolăr

Scouller, *f.n.*, 'skulər, skóolĕr

Scouloudi, *f.n.*, sku'lʊdɪ, skōo- lóodi

Scourfield, *f.n.*, 'skaʊərfild, skówrfeeld

Scourie *H'land*, 'skaʊərɪ, skówri

Scovell, *f.n.*, skoʊ'vel, skōvéll

Scowcroft, *f.n.*, 'skoʊkrɒft, skṓ- -kroft

Scowen, *f.n.*, 'skoʊɪn, skṓ-ĕn

Scrabo *Co. Down*, 'skræboʊ, skrábbō

Scrafield *Lincs.*, 'skreɪfild, skráy-
feeld
Scresort, Loch, *H'land*, 'skrizərt,
skréezŏrt
Screveton *Notts.*, 'skritən, skrée-
tŏn
Scridain, Loch, *S'clyde*, 'skridən,
skréedăn
Scrimgeour, *f.n.*, 'skrɪmdʒər,
skrímjĕr
Scrivelsby *Lincs.*, 'skrɪvlzbɪ,
skrívvlzbi; 'skrilzbɪ, skréelzbi
Scrivener, *f.n.*, 'skrɪvənər, skrív-
vĕnĕr
Scroggie, *f.n.*, 'skrɒgɪ, skróggi
Scroggs, *f.n.*, skrɒgz, skroggz
Scrooby *Notts.*, 'skrubɪ, skroóbi
Scrope, *f.n.*, skrup, skroop
Scrubey, *f.n.*, 'skrubɪ, skroóbi
Scruby, *f.n.*, 'skrubɪ, skroóbi
Scruton, *f.n.*, 'skrutən, skroótŏn
Scrymgeour, *f.n.*, 'skrɪmdʒər,
skrímjĕr
Scudamore, *f.n.*, 'skjudəmər,
skéwdămor
Scull, *f.n.*, skʌl, skull
Scullion, *f.n.*, 'skʌljən, skúll-yŏn
Sculpher, *f.n.*, 'skʌlfər, skúllfĕr
Scunthorpe *Lincs.*, 'skʌnθɔrp,
skúnthorp
Scupham, *f.n.*, 'skʌfəm, skúffäm
Scuse, *f.n.*, skjus, skewss
Scutt, *f.n.*, skʌt, skutt
Seabright, *f.n.*, 'sibraɪt, seé-brīt
Seacy, *f.n.*, 'sisɪ, seéssi
Seaford *E. Sussex*, si'fɔrd, seefórd
Seaforde *Co. Down*, 'sifɔrd, seé-
ford
Seager, *f.n.*, 'sigər, seégĕr
Seago, *f.n.*, 'sigoʊ, seégō
Seagoe *Co. Armagh*, 'sigoʊ, seégō
Seagrave, *f.n.*, 'sigreɪv, seé-grayv
Seaham *Durham*, 'siəm, seé-ăm
Seahouses *Northd.*, 'sihaʊzɪz,
seé-howzĕz
Seaman, *f.n.*, 'simən, seémăn
Sea Palling *Norfolk*, si 'pɔlɪŋ,
see páwling
Searchfield, *f.n.*, 'sɜrtʃfild, sértch-
feeld
Searcy, *f.n.*, 'sɪərsɪ, seérssi
Searell, *f.n.*, 'serəl, sérrĕl
Searight, *f.n.*, 'siraɪt, seé-rīt
Searle, *f.n.*, sɜrl, serl
Sears, *f.n.*, sɪərz, seerz
Seasalter *Kent*, 'sisɔltər, seé-
-sawltĕr
Seascale *Cumbria*, 'siskeɪl, seé-
-skayl
Seathwaite *Cumbria*, 'siθweɪt,
seé-thwayt
Seaton, *f.n.*, 'sitən, seétŏn
Seaton Carew *Cleveland*, 'sitən
kə'ru, seétŏn kăroó

Seaton Delaval *Northd.*, 'sitən
'deləvəl, seétŏn délläväl
Seaville *Cumbria*, 'sevɪl, sévvil
Seavington *Somerset*, 'sevɪŋtən,
sévvingtŏn
Sebergham *Cumbria*, 'sebərəm,
sébbĕräm
Secchie, *f.n.*, 'sekɪ, sécki
Secombe, *f.n.*, 'sikəm, seékŏm
Secondé, *f.n.*, sɪ'kɒndɪ, sĕkóndi
Secord, *f.n.*, 'sikɔrd, seékord
Secretan, *f.n.*, 'sekrɪtən, séckrĕtăn
Secrett, *f.n.*, 'sikrɪt, seékrĕt
Sedbergh *Cumbria*, 'sedbər, séd-
bĕr; 'sedbɑrg, sédberg. *The
first is appropriate for ~
School.*
Sedberghian, *one educated at
Sedbergh School*, sed'bɑrgɪən,
sedbérgiăn
Seddon, *f.n.*, 'sedən, séddŏn
Sedgehill *Wilts.*, 'sedʒhɪl, séj-hil;
'sedʒl, séjjl
Sedgwick, *f.n.*, 'sedʒwɪk, séjwick
Sedlescombe *E. Sussex*, 'sedlz-
kəm, séddlzkŏm
Seear, *f.n.*, 'sɪər, seé-ăr. *Appro-
priate also for Baroness ~.*
Seend *Wilts.*, sind, seend
Segal, *f.n.*, 'sigl, seégl. *Appro-
priate also for Baron ~.*
Segar, *f.n.*, 'sigər, seégăr
Seghill *Northd.*, 'seghɪl,ség-hil
Segontium, *Roman site at
Caernarvon*, sɪ'gɒntɪəm,
sĕgónti-ŭm
Segrave, *f.n.*, 'sigreɪv, seégrayv.
*See also Baron Mowbray, ~
and Stourton.*
Segrue, *f.n.*, 'sigru, seégroo
Seif, *f.n.*, sif, seef
Seifert, *f.n.*, 'sifərt, seéfĕrt
Seigal, *f.n.*, 'sigl, seégl
Seighford *Staffs.*, 'sifərd, seéfŏrd;
'saɪfərd, sífŏrd
Seignior, *f.n.*, 'sinjər, seén-yŏr
Seil *S'clyde*, sil, seel
Seilebost *W. Isles*, 'ʃeɪlɪbɒst,
sháylibosst
Seilern, *f.n.*, 'saɪlɜrn, sílern
Seiont, River, *Gwynedd*, 'saɪɒnt,
sí-ont
Seiriol, *Welsh C.n.*, 'saɪərɪɒl, síri-
-ol
Seisdon *Staffs.*, 'sizdən, seézdŏn
Seivad, *f.n.*, 'sivæd, seévad
Seivwright, *f.n.*, 'sɪvraɪt, sívvrīt
Sekers, *f.n.*, 'sekərz, séckĕrz
Selham *W. Sussex*, 'siləm, seé-
lăm; 'seləm, séllăm
Seligman, *f.n.*, 'selɪgmən, séllig-
măn
Seligmann, *f.n.*, 'selɪgmən, séllig-
măn

Selkirk *Borders*, 'selkərk, sélkirk
Sellack *H. & W.*, 'selək, séllăk
Sellar, *f.n.*, 'selər, séllăr
Sellars, *f.n.*, 'selərz, séllărz
Sellas, *f.n.*, 'seləs, séllăss
Sellers, *f.n.*, 'selərz, séllĕrz
Selley, *f.n.*, 'seli, sélli
Sellick, *f.n.*, 'selik, séllick
Sellindge *Kent*, 'selindʒ, séllinj
Selly Oak *W. Midlands*, 'seli 'oʊk, sélli ṓk
Selmeston *E. Sussex*, 'selmztən, sélmztŏn
Selous, *f.n.*, sə'lu, sĕlóo
Selsey *Glos., W. Sussex*, 'selzi, sélzi
Selsey Bill *W. Sussex*, 'selzi 'bil, sélzi bíll; 'selsi 'bil, sélssi bíll
Selwick *Orkney*, 'selwik, sélwick
Selwyn, *f.n.*, 'selwin, sélwin
Semer *Suffolk*, 'simər, séemĕr
Semer Water, *also spelt* **Semmer Water**, *N. Yorks.*, 'semər 'wɔtər, sémmĕr wáwtĕr
Semington *Wilts.*, 'semiŋtən, sémmingtŏn
Semmer Water *see* **Semer Water**
Sempill, Baroness, 'sempl, sémpl
Sendall, *f.n.*, 'sendɔl, séndawl
Senghenydd *Mid Glam.*, seŋ-'henið, seng-hénnith
Sennen *Cornwall*, 'senən, sénnĕn
Sensier, *f.n.*, 'sensiər, sénsseer; 'sãsiei, saangssi-ay
Serena, *C.n.*, si'rinə, sĕréenă
Sereny, *f.n.*, si'rini, sĕréeni
Sergison, *f.n.*, 'sardʒisən, saárjis-sŏn
Serota, *f.n.*, sə'roʊtə, sĕrótă. *Appropriate also for Baroness* ~.
Serpell, *f.n.*, 'sərpl, sérpl
Servaes, *f.n.*, sər'veiz, sĕrváyz
Seskinore *Co. Tyrone*, ‚seskɪ'nɔr, sesskinór
Seton, *f.n.*, 'sitən, séetŏn
Setoun, *f.n.*, 'sitən, séetŏn
Sever, *f.n.*, 'sevər, sévvĕr
Severn, River, *Powys–Salop–H. & W.–Glos.*, 'severn, sévvĕrn
Severs, *f.n.*, 'sevərz, sévvĕrz
Sevier, *f.n.*, 'sevjər, sév-yĕr; si'viər, sĕvéer
Seville, *f.n.*, 'sevil, sévvil; 'sevl, sévvl
Seward, *f.n.*, 'sjuərd, syṓo-ărd; 'siwərd, sée-wărd
Sewell, *f.n.*, 'sjuəl, séw-ĕl
Sewerby *Humberside*, 'suərbi, sóo-ĕrbi
Sewing, *f.n.*, 'siwiŋ, sée-wing
Sexton, *f.n.*, 'sekstən, séckstŏn
Seyd, *f.n.*, said, sïd
Seyers, *f.n.*, sɛərz, sairz

Seyler, Athene, *actress*, ə'θini 'sailər, ăthéeni sïlĕr
Seymour, *f.n.*, 'simər, séemŭr; 'simər, séemor; 'seimər, sáymŭr. *The first is appropriate for the family name of the Duke of Somerset and of the Marquess of Hertford.*
Seys, *f.n.*, seis, sayss; seiz, sayz
Sezincote *Glos.*, 'sizənkət, seézĕn-kŏt; 'sizinkət, seézin-kŏt; 'sezinkət, sézzin-kŏt
Sgiwen *see* **Skewen**
Sgurr Alasdair *Skye*, 'skuər 'ælistər, skṓor álistär
Sgurr Biorach *Skye*, 'skuər 'birəx, skṓor bírrăch
Sgurr Dearg *Skye*, 'skuər 'derig, skṓor dérrĕg
Sgurr na Banachdich *Skye*, 'skuər nə 'bænəxdix, skṓor nă bánnăchdich
Sgurr nan Eag *Skye*, 'skuər nən 'eik, skṓor năn áyk
Sgurr nan Gillean *Skye*, 'skuər nən 'giljən, skṓor năn geél-yăn
Sgurr na Stri *Skye*, 'skuər nə 'stri, skṓor nă streé
Shackell, *f.n.*, 'ʃækl, sháckl
Shacklady, *f.n.*, 'ʃækleidi, sháck-laydi
Shackleton, *f.n.*, 'ʃækltən, sháckltŏn. *Appropriate also for Baron* ~.
Shackman, *f.n.*, 'ʃækmən, sháckmăn
Shaen, *f.n.*, ʃein, shayn
Shaer, *f.n.*, ʃɛər, shair
Shaffer, *f.n.*, 'ʃæfər, sháffĕr
Shafir, Shulamith, *pianist*, 'ʃuləmiθ ʃæ'fiər, shoolămith shafféer
Shaftesbury *Dorset*, 'ʃaftsbəri, shaáftsbŭri. *Appropriate also for the Earl of* ~.
Shairp, *f.n.*, ʃarp, shaarp
Shakerley, *f.n.*, 'ʃækərli, sháckĕrli
Shakerley *Gtr. M'chester*, 'ʃækərli, sháckĕrli
Shakerly, *f.n.*, 'ʃækərli, sháckĕrli
Shakeshaft, *f.n.*, 'ʃeikʃaft, sháyk-shaaft
Shakespeare, *f.n.*, 'ʃeikspiər, sháykspeer
Shalden *Hants*, 'ʃɔldən, sháwldĕn; 'ʃɒldən, shólldĕn
Shaldon *Devon*, 'ʃɔldən, sháwldŏn; 'ʃɒldən, shólldŏn
Shalfleet *I. of Wight*, 'ʃælflit, shál-fleet
Shalford *Essex, Surrey*, 'ʃælfərd, shálfŏrd
Shallcross, *f.n.*, 'ʃælkrɒs, shál-kross

Shalmsford Street *Kent*, 'ʃælmz-fərd strit, shálmzförd street
Shanbally *Co. Down*, 'ʃænbælɪ, shánbali
Shankill *Co. Antrim*, 'ʃæŋkɪl, shánkil
Shanklin, *f.n.*, 'ʃæŋklɪn, shánklin
Shanklin *I. of Wight*, 'ʃæŋklɪn, shánklin
Shankly, *f.n.*, 'ʃæŋklɪ, shánkli
Shanley, *f.n.*, 'ʃænlɪ, shánli
Shannagh *Co. Down*, 'ʃænə, shánnă
Shannon, *f.n.*, 'ʃænən, shánnŏn
Shantallow *Co. Derry*, ʃæn'tælʊ, shantálō
Shap *Cumbria*, ʃæp, shap
Shapinsay *Orkney*, 'ʃæpɪnseɪ, sháppinssay
Shapiro, *f.n.*, ʃə'pɪərʊ, shăpéerō
Shapland, *f.n.*, 'ʃæplənd, shápländ
Shapley, *f.n.*, 'ʃæplɪ, shápli
Sharman, *f.n.*, 'ʃɑrmən, sha'armän
Sharp, *f.n.*, ʃɑrp, shaarp
Sharpe, *f.n.*, ʃɑrp, shaarp
Sharpenhoe *Beds.*, 'ʃɑrpənʊ, sha'arpénō
Sharples, *f.n.*, 'ʃɑrplz, sha'arplz
Sharpley, *f.n.*, 'ʃɑrplɪ, sha'arpli
Sharpness *Glos.*, 'ʃɑrp'nes, sha'arpnéss
Shasby, *f.n.*, 'ʃæzbɪ, sházbi
Shaughnessy, *f.n.*, 'ʃɔnəsɪ, sháwnéssi. *Appropriate also for Baron* ~.
Shaugh Prior *Devon*, 'ʃɔ 'praɪər, sháw prí-ör
Shavington *Ches.*, 'ʃævɪŋtən, shávvingtŏn
Shaw, *f.n.*, ʃɔ, shaw
Shawcross, *f.n.*, 'ʃɔkrɒs, sháwkross. *Appropriate also for Baron* ~.
Shawell *Leics.*, 'ʃɑwəl, sha'a-wĕl
Shea, *f.n.*, ʃeɪ, shay
Shead, *f.n.*, ʃed, shed; ʃid, sheed
Sheaf, River, *Derby.–S. Yorks.*, ʃif, sheef
Sheaff, *f.n.*, ʃif, sheef
Sheard, *f.n.*, ʃeərd, shaird; ʃɪərd, sheerd; ʃɑrd, sherd
Shearer, *f.n.*, 'ʃɪərər, sheérĕr
Shearlock, *f.n.*, 'ʃɪərlɒk, sheérlock
Shearman, *f.n.*, 'ʃɪərmən, sheér-män; 'ʃɑrmən, shérmän
Shearn, *f.n.*, ʃɑrn, shern
Shears, *f.n.*, ʃɪərz, sheerz
Shearsby *Leics.*, 'ʃɪərzbɪ, sheérzbi
Shebbear *Devon*, 'ʃebɪər, shéb-beer
Shebbeare, *f.n.*, 'ʃebɪər, shébbeer
Sheehy, *f.n.*, 'ʃihɪ, sheéhi
Sheen, *f.n.*, ʃin, sheen
Sheene, *f.n.*, ʃin, sheen

Sheepscombe *Glos.*, 'ʃepskəm, shépskŏm
Sheffield, *f.n.*, 'ʃefild, shéffeeld
Sheffield *S. Yorks.*, 'ʃefild, shéf-feeld. *Appropriate also for Baron* ~.
Sheiham, *f.n.*, 'ʃaɪəm, shí-ăm
Shelburne, Earldom of, 'ʃelbərn, shélbŭrn
Sheldon, *f.n.*, 'ʃeldən, shéldŏn
Shelfanger *Norfolk*, 'ʃelfæŋgər, shélfang-gĕr
Shelford, Great *and* Little, *Cambs.*, 'ʃelfərd, shélförd
Shelland *Suffolk*, 'ʃelənd, shél-länd
Shelley, *f.n.*, 'ʃelɪ, shélli
Shelmerdine, *f.n.*, 'ʃelmərdin, shélmĕrdeen
Shelock, *f.n.*, 'ʃilɒk, sheélock; 'ʃelɒk, shéllock
Shelton, *f.n.*, 'ʃeltən, shéltŏn
Shelvey, *f.n.*, 'ʃelvɪ, shélvi
Shemming, *f.n.*, 'ʃemɪŋ, shémming
Shephalbury *Herts.*, 'ʃeplbərɪ, shépplbŭri
Shephall *Herts.*, 'ʃepl, shéppl
Shepheard, *f.n.*, 'ʃepərd, shéppĕrd
Shepherd, *f.n.*, 'ʃepərd, shéppĕrd
Shepherdine *Avon*, 'ʃepərdaɪn, shéppĕrdīn
Sheppard, *f.n.*, 'ʃepərd, shéppärd
Shepreth *Cambs.*, 'ʃeprəθ, shép-rĕth
Shepshed *Leics.*, 'ʃepʃed, shép--shed
Shepton Beauchamp *Somerset*, 'ʃeptən 'bitʃəm, shéptŏn beé-tchăm
Shepton Mallet *Somerset*, 'ʃeptən 'mælɪt, shéptŏn málĕt
Sher, *f.n.*, ʃɑr, sher
Shera, *f.n.*, 'ʃɪərə, sheéră
Sheraton, *f.n.*, 'ʃerətən, shérrătŏn. *Appropriate for Thomas* ~, *18th-c. cabinet-maker and furniture designer.*
Sherborne *Dorset*, 'ʃɑrbərn, shér-bŭrn. *Appropriate also for Baron* ~.
Shere *Surrey*, ʃɪər, sheer
Sheret, *f.n.*, 'ʃerɪt, shérrĕt
Sherfield, Baron, 'ʃɑrfild, shér-feeld
Sherfield-on-Loddon *Hants.*, 'ʃɑrfild ɒn 'lɒdən, shérfeeld on lóddŏn
Shergold, *f.n.*, 'ʃɑrgʊld, shér-gōld
Sheridan, *f.n.*, 'ʃerɪdən, shérridăn
Sheridan, Richard Brinsley, *18-c. dramatist*, 'rɪtʃərd 'brɪnzlɪ 'ʃerɪdən, rítchärd brínzli shérri-dăn

Sheriffmuir *Central*, 'ʃerɪf'mjʊər, shérriff-myo͞or
Sheringham *Norfolk*, 'ʃerɪŋəm, shérring-ăm
Sherlaw, *C.n.*, 'ʃɔrlɔ, shérlaw
Sherlock, *f.n.*, 'ʃɜrlɒk, shérlock
Shermanbury *W. Sussex*, 'ʃɜrmənbərɪ, shérmănbŭri
Sherrin, *f.n.*, 'ʃerɪn, shérrin
Shetland Islands, 'ʃetlənd, shétlănd
Shettleston *S'clyde*, 'ʃetlstən, shéttlstŏn
Sheviock *Cornwall*, 'ʃevɪək, shévvi-ŏk
Shew, *f.n.*, ʃu, shoo
Shewell-Cooper, *f.n.*, 'ʃuəl 'kupər, shoo-ĕl koͦopĕr
Shewen, *f.n.*, 'ʃuɪn, shoͦo-ĕn
Shewey, *f.n.*, 'ʃoʊɪ, shŏ-i
Shiant Isles *W. Isles*, 'ʃiənt, shée-ănt
Shide *I. of Wight*, ʃaɪd, shīd
Shields, *f.n.*, ʃildz, sheeldz
Shields, North *and* South, *Tyne & Wear*, ʃildz, sheeldz
Shihwarg, *f.n.*, ʃi'vɑrg, shiva'arg
Shillaker, *f.n.*, 'ʃɪleɪkər, shíllaykĕr
Shillidy, *f.n.*, 'ʃɪlɪdɪ, shíllidi
Shilling, *f.n.*, 'ʃɪlɪŋ, shílling
Shillingford *Devon*, 'ʃɪlɪŋfərd, shílling-fŏrd
Shillinglaw, *f.n.*, 'ʃɪlɪŋlɔ, shílling-law
Shimell, *f.n.*, 'ʃɪml, shímml
Shimna, River, *Co. Down*, 'ʃɪmnə, shímnă
Shincliffe *Durham*, 'ʃɪŋklɪf, shínkliff
Shinebourne, *f.n.*, 'ʃaɪnbɔrn, shínborn
Shinkwin, *f.n.*, 'ʃɪŋkwɪn, shínkwin
Shinwell, *f.n.*, 'ʃɪnwəl, shínwĕl; 'ʃɪnwel, shínwell
Shipbourne *Kent*, 'ʃɪbərn, shíbbŭrn
Shipdham *Norfolk*, 'ʃɪpdəm, shípdăm; 'ʃɪpəm, shíppăm
Shiplake *Oxon.*, 'ʃɪpleɪk, shíplayk
Shipley, *f.n.*, 'ʃɪplɪ, shípli
Shipp, *f.n.*, ʃɪp, ship
Shippea Hill *Suffolk*, 'ʃɪpɪ 'hɪl, shíppi híll
Shipston-on-Stour *Warwicks.*, 'ʃɪpstən ɒn 'staʊər, shípstŏn on stówr
Shipton Bellinger *Hants*, 'ʃɪptən 'belɪndʒər, shíptŏn béllinjĕr
Shipton Oliffe *Glos.*, 'ʃɪptən 'ɒlɪf, shíptŏn óliff
Shiremoor *Tyne & Wear*, 'ʃaɪərmʊər, shír-moͦor
Shirley, *C.n. and f.n.*, 'ʃɜrlɪ, shírli
Shirreff, *f.n.*, 'ʃɪrɪf, shírrĕf; 'ʃerɪf, shérrĕf

Shiskine *S'clyde*, 'ʃɪskɪn, shísskin
Shivas, *f.n.*, 'ʃivəs, shéevăss
Shlaen, *f.n.*, ʃleɪn, shlayn
Shobbrook, *f.n.*, 'ʃɒbrʊk, shóbbroͦok
Shobrooke *Devon*, 'ʃoʊbrʊk, shŏbroͦok
Shockett, *f.n.*, 'ʃɒkɪt, shóckĕt
Shocklach *Ches.*, 'ʃɒklɪtʃ, shócklitch
Shoeburyness *Essex*, 'ʃubərɪ'nes, shoͦobŭrinéss
Shoemake, *f.n.*, 'ʃumeɪk, shoͦomayk
Sholden *Kent*, 'ʃoʊldən, shŏldĕn
Sholing *Hants*, 'ʃoʊlɪŋ, shŏling
Sholto, *f.n.*, 'ʃɒltoʊ, shóltō
Shone, *f.n.*, ʃoʊn, shōn
Shonfield, *f.n.*, 'ʃɒnfɪld, shónnfeeld
Shooter, *f.n.*, 'ʃutər, shoͦotĕr
Shoreham *Kent*, 'ʃɔrəm, sháwrăm
Shoreham-by-Sea *W. Sussex*, 'ʃɔrəm baɪ 'si, sháwrăm bī sée
Short, *f.n.*, ʃɔrt, short
Shortlanesend *Cornwall*, ,ʃɔrtleɪnz'end, short-laynzénd
Shorto, *f.n.*, 'ʃɔrtoʊ, shórtō
Shorwell *I. of Wight*, 'ʃɔrwel, shórwel
Shotesham All Saints *Norfolk*, 'ʃɒtsəm ɔl 'seɪnts, shóttsăm awl sáynts
Shotesham St. Mary *Norfolk*, 'ʃɒtsəm snt 'mɛərɪ, shóttsăm sīnt máiri
Shottisham *Suffolk*, 'ʃɒtsəm, shóttsăm
Shotwick *Ches.*, 'ʃɒtwɪk, shótwick
Shouksmith, *f.n.*, 'ʃʊksmɪθ, shoͦok-smith
Shouldham *Norfolk*, 'ʃoʊldəm, shŏldăm
Shouldham Thorpe *Norfolk*, 'ʃoʊldəm 'θɔrp, shŏldăm thórp
Shouler, *f.n.*, 'ʃulər, shoͦolĕr
Shoults, *f.n.*, ʃoʊlts, shōlts
Shove, Fredegond, *poet and author*, 'fredɪgɒnd 'ʃoʊv, frédĕgond shŏv
Showell, *f.n.*, 'ʃoʊəl, shŏ-ĕl
Shrawardine *Salop*, 'ʃreɪwərdaɪn, shráy-wăr-dīn
Shrewsbury *Salop*, 'ʃroʊzbərɪ, shrŏzbŭri; 'ʃruzbərɪ, shroͦozbŭri. *The first is appropriate for the Earl of ~ and for the public school, but both are used in the town.*
Shrewton *Wilts.*, 'ʃrutən, shroͦotŏn
Shrimpton, *f.n.*, 'ʃrɪmptən, shrímptŏn
Shrivenham *Oxon.*, 'ʃrɪvənəm, shrívvĕnăm

Shrodells Wing *Watford General Hospital, Herts.*, ʃroʊ'delz, shrōdéllz
Shroton *Dorset*, 'ʃroʊtən, shrótŏn
Shryane, *f.n.*, 'ʃraɪən, shrí-ăn
Shuard, *f.n.*, 'ʃuɑrd, shoo-aard
Shube, *f.n.*, ʃub, shoob
Shuckburgh, *f.n.*, 'ʃʌkbərə, shúckbŭră
Shuckburgh, Lower *and* Upper, *Warwicks.*, 'ʃʌkbərə, shúckbŭră
Shudy Camps *Cambs.*, 'ʃudɪ 'kæmps, shoódi kámps
Shukman, *f.n.*, 'ʃʊkmən, shoŏkmăn
Shuldham, *f.n.*, 'ʃuldəm, shoóldăm
Shulman, *f.n.*, 'ʃulmən, shoólmăn
Shults, *f.n.*, ʃʌlts, shullts
Shurey, *f.n.*, 'ʃʊərɪ, shoŏri
Shurmer, *f.n.*, 'ʃɜrmər, shúrmĕr
Shurrery *H'land*, 'ʃʌrərɪ, shúrrĕri
Shute, Baron, ʃut, shoot
Sian, *Welsh C.n.*, ʃɑn, shaan
Sibbett, *f.n.*, 'sɪbɪt, síbbĕt
Sibdon Carwood *Salop*, 'sɪbdən 'kɑrwʊd, síbdŏn kaárwoŏd
Sible Hedingham *Essex*, 'sɪbl 'hedɪŋəm, síbbl hédding-ăm
Sibley, *f.n.*, 'sɪblɪ, síbbli
Sibree Hall *Coventry*, 'saɪbrɪ, síbri
Sibson, *f.n.*, 'sɪbsən, síbssŏn
Sibun, *f.n.*, 'saɪbən, síbŭn
Sich, *f.n.*, sɪtʃ, sitch
Sichell, *f.n.*, 'sɪtʃl, sítchl; 'sɪʃl, síshl
Sickert, *f.n.*, 'sɪkərt, síckĕrt. *Appropriate for Walter* ~, *painter and author.*
Sicklesmere *Suffolk*, 'sɪklzmɪər, sícklzmeer
Sicklinghall *N. Yorks.*, 'sɪklɪŋhɔl, síckling-hawl
Sidaway, *f.n.*, 'sɪdəweɪ, síddă-way
Sidcup *London*, 'sɪdkʌp, sídkup; 'sɪdkəp, sídkŭp
Siddall, *f.n.*, 'sɪdɔl, síddawl
Sidebotham, *f.n.*, 'saɪdbɒtəm, sídbottăm
Sidebottom, *f.n.*, 'sɪdbɒtəm, seédbottŏm; ˌsɪdɪbə'toʊm, siddibŏtŏm; 'saɪdbɒtəm, sídbottŏm
Sidestrand *Norfolk*, 'saɪdstrænd, sídstrand; 'saɪdɪstrænd, sídĕsstrand
Sidey, *f.n.*, 'saɪdɪ, sídi
Sidford *Devon*, sɪd'fɔrd, sidfórd; 'sɪdfɔrd, sídford
Sidgreaves, *f.n.*, 'sɪdgrɪvz, sídgreevz
Sidlesham *W. Sussex*, 'sɪdlsəm, síddlssăm

Sidmouth *Devon*, 'sɪdməθ, sídmŭth
Sidor, *f.n.*, 'saɪdɔr, sídor
Siebert, *f.n.*, 'sibərt, seébĕrt
Sieff, *f.n.*, sif, seef. *Appropriate also for Baron* ~.
Sieman, *f.n.*, 'simən, seémăn
Siemons, *f.n.*, 'simənz, seémŏnz
Sier, *f.n.*, sɪər, seer; 'saɪər, sír
Sieve, *f.n.*, siv, seev
Sieveking, *f.n.*, 'sivkɪŋ, seévking
Sievewright, *f.n.*, 'sɪvraɪt, sívv-rīt
Sievier, *f.n.*, 'sɪvjər, seév-yĕr
Sievwright, *f.n.*, 'sɪvraɪt, seévrīt
Sigal, *f.n.*, 'sɪgl, seégl
Siggins, *f.n.*, 'sɪgɪnz, sígginz
Sigsworth, *f.n.*, 'sɪgzwɜrθ, síggzwurth
Silchester *Hants*, 'sɪltʃɪstər, síltchĕstĕr
Sileby *Leics.*, 'saɪlbɪ, sílbi
Silhillian, *native of* **Solihull**, sɪl'hɪlɪən, silhílli-ăn
Silkin, *f.n.*, 'sɪlkɪn, sílkin. *Appropriate also for the Barony of* ~.
Silkstone *S. Yorks.*, 'sɪlkstoʊn, sílksstōn
Sill, *f.n.*, sɪl, sill
Sillars, *f.n.*, 'sɪlərz, síllărz
Sillence, *f.n.*, sɪ'lens, sillénss; 'saɪləns, sílĕnss
Sillita, *f.n.*, 'sɪlɪtə, síllită
Sillito, *f.n.*, 'sɪlɪtoʊ, síllitō
Sillitoe, *f.n.*, 'sɪlɪtoʊ, síllitō
Sillitto, *f.n.*, 'sɪlɪtoʊ, síllitō
Silloth *Cumbria*, 'sɪləθ, síllŏth
Sillyearn *Grampian*, ˌsɪlɪ'ɜrn, silli-érn
Silsoe *Beds.*, 'sɪlsoʊ, sílssō. *Appropriate also for Baron* ~.
Silver, *f.n.*, 'sɪlvər, sílvĕr
Silverman, *f.n.*, 'sɪlvərmən, sílvĕrmăn
Silverstone, *f.n.*, 'sɪlvərstoʊn, sílvĕrsstōn
Silverstone *Northants.*, 'sɪlvərstoʊn, sílvĕrsstōn
Silvertown *London*, 'sɪlvərtaʊn, sílvĕrtown
Silvester, *f.n.*, sɪl'vestər, silvéstĕr
Silvey, *f.n.*, 'sɪlvɪ, sílvi
Simak, *f.n.*, 'simæk, seémack
Simche, *f.n.*, 'sɪmtʃɪ, símtchi
Simeons, *f.n.*, 'sɪmɪənz, símmi-ŏnz
Simey, *f.n.*, 'saɪmɪ, sími
Simister, *f.n.*, 'sɪmɪstər, símmistĕr
Simmonds, *f.n.*, 'sɪməndz, símmŏndz; 'sɪmənz, símmŏnz
Simmons, *f.n.*, 'sɪmənz, símmŏnz
Simms, *f.n.*, sɪmz, simmz
Simon, *C.n. and f.n.*, 'saɪmən, símŏn. *Appropriate also for Viscount* ~.

Simond, *f.n.,* 'saɪmənd, símŏnd
Simonds, *f.n.,* 'sɪməndz, símmŏndz; 'saɪməndz, símŏndz. *The first is appropriate for the Viscountcy of* ∼.
Simonis, *f.n.,* sɪ'moʊnɪs, simmóniss
Simon of Glaisdale, Baron, 'saɪmən əv 'gleɪzdeɪl, símŏn ŏv gláyzdayl
Simon of Wythenshawe, Baron, 'saɪmən əv 'wɪðənʃɔ, símŏn ŏv wíthĕnshaw
Simons, *f.n.,* 'saɪmənz, símŏnz
Simonsbath *Somerset,* 'sɪmənzbɑθ, símmŏnzbaath
Simonstone *Lancs.,* 'sɪmənstoʊn, símmŏnsstŏn
Simpson, *f.n.,* 'sɪmpsən, símpsŏn
Sims, *f.n.,* sɪmz, simmz
Sinclair, *f.n.,* 'sɪŋkleər, sínklair; 'sɪŋklər, sínklăr. *The first is appropriate for Baron* ∼. *The second is usual in Scotland.*
Sinclair of Cleeve, Baron, 'sɪŋklər əv 'kliv, sínklĕr ŏv kléev
Sindlesham *Berks.,* 'sɪndlʃəm, síndl-shăm
Sinead, *Irish C.n.,* ʃɪ'neəd, shinné-äd
Singer, *f.n.,* 'sɪŋər, síng-ĕr
Singleton, *f.n.,* 'sɪŋgltən, síng-gltŏn
Siniawski, *f.n.,* ˌsɪnɪ'æfskɪ, sinni-áfski
Sinnatt, *f.n.,* 'sɪnət, sínnăt
Sinodun Hill *Oxon.,* 'sɪnədən, sínnŏdŭn
Sinstadt, *f.n.,* 'sɪnstæt, sínstat
Sion Mills *Co. Tyrone,* 'saɪən 'mɪlz, sí-ŏn míllz
Sired, *f.n.,* 'saɪərɪd, síréd
Sirett, *f.n.,* 'sɪrɪt, sírrĕt
Sirhowy *Gwent,* sər'haʊɪ, sir-hówi
Siriol, *Welsh C.n.,* 'sɪrɪɒl, sírri-ol
Sirrell, *f.n.,* 'sɪrəl, sírrĕl
Sisam, *f.n.,* 'saɪsəm, síssăm
Sisland *Norfolk,* 'saɪzlənd, sízländ
Sisley, *f.n.,* 'sɪzlɪ, sízzli. *Appropriate also in English usage for the Anglo-French painter, Alfred* ∼.
Sissinghurst *Kent,* 'sɪsɪŋhərst, síssing-hurst. *Appropriate also for* ∼ *Castle.*
Siston *Avon,* 'saɪstən, sísstŏn; 'saɪsən, síssŏn
Sisum, *f.n.,* 'saɪsəm, síssŭm
Sitch, *f.n.,* sɪtʃ, sitch
Sithney *Cornwall,* 'sɪθnɪ, síthni
Sitwell, Sir Sacheverell, *author,* sə'ʃevərəl 'sɪtwəl, săshévvĕrĕl sítwĕl

Sizer, *f.n.,* 'saɪzər, sízĕr
Sizergh Castle *Cumbria,* 'saɪzər, sízĕr
Sizewell *Suffolk,* 'saɪzwəl, sízwĕl
Skakle, *f.n.,* 'skekl, skéckl
Skamacre, *f.n.,* 'skæmeɪkər, skámmaykĕr
Skara Brae *Orkney,* 'skærə 'breɪ, skárră bráy
Skea, *f.n.,* ski, skee
Skeabost *Skye,* 'skeɪbɒst, skáybosst
Skeaping, *f.n.,* 'skipɪŋ, skéeping
Skeat, *f.n.,* skit, skeet
Skeats, *f.n.,* skits, skeets
Skeavington, *f.n.,* 'skevɪŋtən, skévvingtŏn
Skegoniel *Co. Antrim,* ˌskegə'nil, skeggŏnéel
Skelhorn, *f.n.,* 'skelhɔrn, skélhorn
Skell, River, *N. Yorks.,* skel, skell
Skellern, *f.n.,* 'skelərn, skéllĕrn
Skelmersdale *Lancs.,* 'skelmərzdeɪl, skélmĕrzdayl. *Appropriate also for Baron* ∼.
Skelmorlie *S'clyde,* 'skelmərlɪ, skélmŏrli
Skelsey, *f.n.,* 'skelsɪ, skélssi
Skelton, *f.n.,* 'skeltən, skéltŏn
Skelton *Cumbria,* 'skeltən, skéltŏn
Skelwith *Cumbria,* 'skelɪθ, skéllith
Skemp, *f.n.,* skemp, skemp
Skempton, *f.n.,* 'skemptən, skémptŏn
Skene, *f.n.,* skin, skeen
Skernaghan Point *Co. Antrim,* 'skɜrnəxən, skérnăchăn
Sker Point *Mid Glam.,* skeər, skair
Skerritt, *f.n.,* 'skerɪt, skérrit
Skerrow, Loch, *D. & G.,* 'skeroʊ, skérrō
Skerryvore *W. Isles,* ˌskerɪ'vɔr, skerrivór
Sketch, *f.n.,* sketʃ, sketch
Skewen, *also spelt* **Sgiwen,** *W. Glam.,* 'skjuɪn, skéw-ĕn
Skeyton *Norfolk,* 'skaɪtən, skítŏn
Skidelsky, *f.n.,* skɪ'delskɪ, skidélski
Skidmore, *f.n.,* 'skɪdmɔr, skídmor
Skilbeck, *f.n.,* 'skɪlbek, skílbeck
Skinburness *Cumbria,* ˌskɪnbər'nes, skinbürnéss
Skinnard, *f.n.,* 'skɪnɑrd, skínnaard
Skinner, *f.n.,* 'skɪnər, skínnĕr
Skiport, Loch, *W. Isles,* 'skɪpərt, skíppŏrt
Skirlaugh, North *and* South, *Humberside,* 'skɜrloʊ, skírlō
Skirling *Borders,* 'skɜrlɪŋ, skírling
Skirrow, *f.n.,* 'skɪroʊ, skírrō
Skirsa *H'land,* 'skɜrzə, skírză

Skliros, *f.n.*, 'sklıǝrɒs, skleéross
Skokholm, *also spelt* **Skokham**, *Dyfed*, 'skɒkhoʋm, skóck-hŏm; 'skoʋkǝm, skókăm
Skomer Island *Dyfed*, 'skoʋmǝr, skómĕr
Skone, *f.n.*, skoʋn, skōn
Skrimgeour, *f.n.*, 'skrımdʒǝr, skrímjŭr
Skrimshire, *f.n.*, 'skrımʃaıǝr, skrímshir
Skrine, *f.n.*, skrin, skreen; skraın, skrīn
Skues, *f.n.*, skjuz, skewz
Skye *H'land*, skaı, skī
Skyrme, *f.n.*, skǝrm, skirm
Slaap, *f.n.*, slɑp, slaap
Sladden, *f.n.*, 'slædǝn, sláddĕn
Slade, *f.n.*, sleıd, slayd
Sladen, *f.n.*, 'sleıdǝn, sláydĕn
Slaithwaite *W. Yorks.*, 'slæθweıt, sláthwayt; 'slaʋıt, slów-it
Slamannan *Central*, slǝ'mænǝn, slămánnăn
Slamin, *f.n.*, 'slæmın, slámmin
Slapin, Loch, *Skye*, 'slapın, slaápin
Slater, *f.n.*, 'sleıtǝr, sláytĕr
Slatter, *f.n.*, 'slætǝr, sláttĕr
Slattery, *f.n.*, 'slætǝrı, sláttĕri
Slaugham *W. Sussex*, 'slæfǝm, sláffăm; 'slɑfǝm, slaáfăm
Slaughdon *Suffolk*, 'slɔdǝn, sláwdŏn
Slaughter, *f.n.*, 'slɔtǝr, sláwtĕr
Slaughter, Lower *and* Upper, *Glos.*, 'slɔtǝr, sláwtĕr
Slawith *N. Yorks.*, 'slaʋıθ, slów-ith
Sleaford *Lincs.*, 'slifǝrd, sleéfŏrd
Sleat *Skye*, sleıt, slayt
Sleath, *f.n.*, sliθ, sleeth
Slebech *Dyfed*, 'slebetʃ, slébbetch
Sledmere *Humberside*, 'sledmıǝr, slédmeer
Sleeman, *f.n.*, 'slimǝn, sleémăn
Sleigh, *f.n.*, sleı, slay; sli, slee
Sleights *N. Yorks.*, slaıts, slīts
Slemish *Co. Antrim*, 'slemıʃ, slémmish
Slessenger, *f.n.*, 'slesındʒǝr, sléssĕnjĕr
Slessor, *f.n.*, 'slesǝr, sléssŏr
Slevin, *f.n.*, 'slevın, slévvin
Slieu Lhean *I. of Man*, 'slju 'len, slèw lén
Slievebane *Co. Antrim*, sliv'bæn, sleevbán
Slieve Bearnagh *Co. Down*, sliv 'bɛǝrnǝ, sleev báirnă
Slieve Donard *Co. Down*, sliv 'dɒnǝrd, sleev dónnărd
Slieve-na-Man *Co. Down*, ‚slivnǝ-'mæn, sleevnămán

Sligachan *Skye*, 'sligǝxǝn, sleé-găchăn
Sligo, Marquess of, 'slaıgoʋ, slígō
Slimon, *f.n.*, 'slımǝn, slímmŏn
Sloan, *f.n.*, sloʋn, slōn
Sloane, *f.n.*, sloʋn, slōn
Slochd *H'land*, slɒx, sloch
Slocombe, *f.n.*, 'sloʋkǝm, slókŏm
Sloman, *f.n.*, 'sloʋmǝn, slómăn
Sloperton Cottage *Wilts.*, 'sloʋpǝrtǝn 'kɒtıdʒ, slópĕrtŏn kóttij. *Home of the poet Thomas Moore (1779–1852) for some years.*
Slough *Berks*, slaʋ, slow
Slowey, *f.n.*, 'sloʋı, slṓ-i
Sloy, Loch, *S'clyde*, slɔı, sloy
Slydell, *f.n.*, slaı'del, slīdéll
Slynn, *f.n.*, slın, slin
Smaje, *f.n.*, smeıdʒ, smayj
Smale, *f.n.*, smeıl, smayl
Smalley, *f.n.*, 'smɔlı, smáwli
Smalley *Derby.*, 'smɒlı, smáwli
Smallpeice, *f.n.*, 'smɒlpıs, smáwlpeess
Smarden *Kent*, 'smɑrdǝn, smaárdĕn; 'smɑrden, smaárden
Smart, *f.n.*, smɑrt, smaart
Smeaton, *f.n.*, 'smitǝn, smeétŏn
Smedley, *f.n.*, 'smedlı, smédli
Smeeth *Kent*, smið, smeeth
Smeeton, *f.n.*, 'smitǝn, smeétŏn
Smellie, *f.n.*, 'smelı, smélli
Smeterlin, *f.n.*, 'smetǝrlın, smét-tĕrlin
Smethurst, *f.n.*, 'smeθǝrst, sméth-urst; 'smeθhǝrst, sméth-hurst
Smethwick *W. Midlands*, 'smeðık, sméthick
Smibert, *f.n.*, 'smaıbǝrt, smíbĕrt
Smieton, *f.n.*, 'smitǝn, smeétŏn
Smillie, *f.n.*, 'smaılı, smíli
Smily, *f.n.*, 'smaılı, smíli
Smirke, *f.n.*, smǝrk, smirk
Smith, *f.n.*, smıθ, smith
Smithaleigh *Devon*, 'smıðǝli, smíthălee
Smithells, *f.n.*, 'smıðlz, smíthlz
Smithers, *f.n.*, 'smıðǝrz, smíthĕrz
Smithfield *Cumbria*, 'smıθfild, smíthfeeld
Smitton, *f.n.*, 'smıtǝn, smíttŏn
Smolen, *f.n.*, 'smɒlen, smóllenn
Smollett, *f.n.*, 'smɒlıt, smóllĕt
Smurthwaite, *f.n.*, 'smǝrθweıt, smúrthwayt
Smyrl, *f.n.*, smǝrl, smurl
Smyth, *f.n.*, smıθ, smith; smaıθ, smīth; smaıð, smith. *The second is appropriate for Dame Ethel ~, composer and conductor. The first is the usual Irish pronunciation.*

Smythe, *f.n.*, smaɪð, smĭth; smaɪθ, smīth

Smythson, *f.n.*, 'smaɪðsən, smĭthssŏn

Snabdough *Northd.*, 'snæbdʌf, snábduff

Snaefell *I. of Man*, 'sneɪ'fel, snáy-féll

Snagge, *f.n.*, snæg, snag

Snailum, *f.n.*, 'sneɪləm, snáylŭm

Snaith, *f.n.*, sneɪθ, snayth

Snashall, *f.n.*, 'snæʃl, snáshl

Snatchwood *Gwent*, 'snætʃwʊd, snátchwŏŏd

Snaveley, *f.n.*, 'sneɪvlɪ, snáyvli

Snead, *f.n.*, snid, sneed

Sneezum, *f.n.*, 'snizəm, sneézŭm

Sneinton *Notts.*, 'snentən, snéntŏn

Snelling, *f.n.*, 'snelɪŋ, snélling

Snettisham *Norfolk*, 'snetɪʃəm, snétti-shäm; 'snetsəm, snétsäm; 'snetɪsəm, snéttissäm; snet-ʃəm, snét-shäm

Snewin, *f.n.*, 'snjuɪn, snéw-in

Snewing, *f.n.*, 'snjuɪŋ, snéw-ing

Sneyd, *f.n.*, snid, sneed

Sneyd *Staffs.*, snid, sneed

Snizort *H'land*, 'snaɪzərt, snízŏrt

Snizort, Loch, *H'land*, 'snaɪzərt, snízŏrt

Snoad, *f.n.*, snoʊd, snōd

Snodgrass, *f.n.*, 'snɒdgrɑs, snódgraass

Snodin, *f.n.*, 'snoʊdɪn, snódin

Snodland *Kent*, 'snɒdlənd, snódländ

Snoswell, *f.n.*, 'snɒzwəl, snózzwĕl

Snow, *f.n.*, snoʊ, snō

Snowdon *Gwynedd*, 'snoʊdən, snódŏn. *Appropriate also for the Earl of* ~.

Snowdonia *Gwynedd*, snoʊ'doʊnɪə, snōdóniă

Snowdown Colliery *Kent*, 'snoʊdaʊn, snódown

Snoxall, *f.n.*, 'snɒksɔl, snóckssawl

Snoxell, *f.n.*, 'snɒksl, snóckssl

Soal, *f.n.*, soʊl, sōl

Soames, *f.n.*, soʊmz, sōmz. *Appropriate also for Baron* ~.

Soane, *f.n.*, soʊn, sōn

Soar *Mid Glam.*, *Powys*, 'soʊɑr, só-aar

Soar, River, *Warwicks.–Leics.*, sɔr, sor

Soay *H'land*, *W. Isles*, 'soʊeɪ, só-ay; 'soʊə, só-ă

Sobas, *f.n.*, 'soʊbæs, sóbass

Sobell, *f.n.*, 'soʊbel, sóbell

Sobiotto, *f.n.*, soʊ'bjɒtoʊ, sōbyóttō

Sodor and Man, bishopric, 'soʊdər ənd 'mæn, sódŏr ănd mán

Sofaer, *f.n.*, soʊ'fɛər, sōfáir

Sofer, *f.n.*, 'soʊfər, sófĕr

Soham *Cambs.*, 'soʊəm, só-äm

Sohier, *f.n.*, 'soʊjər, só-yĕr

Soke of Peterborough *Cambs.*, 'soʊk əv 'pitərbərə, sók ŏv péetĕrbŭră

Soley, *f.n.*, 'soʊlɪ, sóli

Solent sea channel, 'soʊlənt, sólĕnt

Solihull *W. Midlands*, ,soʊlɪ'hʌl, sōli-húll

Sollars, *f.n.*, 'sɒlərz, sóllărz

Sollas, *f.n.*, 'sɒləs, sólläss

Sollas *W. Isles*, 'sɒləs, sólläss

Solon, *f.n.*, 'soʊlɒn, sólon; 'soʊlən, sólŏn

Solsgirth *Tayside*, 'sɒlzgзrθ, sólz-girth

Solti, Sir Georg, *conductor*, 'dзɔrdз 'ʃɒltɪ, jórj shólti

Solva *Dyfed*, 'sɒlvə, sólvă

Solway Firth *part of Irish Sea*, 'sɒlweɪ, sólway

Somerby *Lincs.*, 'sʌmərbɪ, súmmĕrbi

Somercotes *Derby.*, 'sʌmərkoʊts, súmmĕrkōts

Somerfield, *f.n.*, 'sʌmərfild, súmmĕrfeeld

Somerhough, *f.n.*, 'sʌmərhɒf, súmmĕrhoff

Somerleyton *Suffolk*, 'sʌmərleɪtən, súmmĕrlaytŏn. *Appropriate also for Baron* ~.

Somers, *f.n.*, 'sʌmərz, súmmĕrz. *Appropriate also for Baron* ~.

Somersby *Lincs.*, 'sʌmərzbɪ, súmmĕrzbi

Somerset, *f.n.*, 'sʌmərsɪt, súmmĕrssĕt

Somerset *Co. name.* 'sʌmərsɪt, mĕrssĕt; 'sʌmərset, súmmĕrsset. *The first is appropriate for the Duke of* ~.

Somersham *Cambs.*, 'sʌmərʃəm, súmmĕr-shäm

Somerton, *f.n.*, 'sʌmərtən, súmmĕrtŏn. *Appropriate also for Viscount* ~.

Somerton *Somerset*, 'sʌmərtən, súmmĕrtŏn

Somerton, East *and* West, *Norfolk*, 'sʌmərtən, súmmĕrtŏn

Somervell, *f.n.*, 'sʌmərvəl, súmmĕrvĕl

Somerville, *f.n.*, 'sʌmərvɪl, súmmĕrvil

Sompting *W. Sussex*, 'sʌmptɪŋ, súmpting; 'sɒmptɪŋ, sómpting

Sondes, Earl, sɒndz, sondz

Sonnex, *f.n.*, 'sɒneks, sónnecks

Sonning *Berks.*, 'sʌnɪŋ, súnning; 'sɒnɪŋ, sónning

Soper, *f.n.,* 'soupər, sṓpĕr. *Appropriate also for Baron* ~.

Sopley *Hants,* 'sɒpli, sóppli

Soref, *f.n.,* 'sɒrɪf, sórrĕf

Sorensen, *f.n.,* 'sɒrənsən, sórrĕnssĕn

Sorley, *f.n.,* 'sɔrlɪ, sórli

Sorrell, *f.n.,* 'sɒrəl, sórrĕl; sə'rel, sŏréll

Soskice, *f.n.,* 'sɒskɪs, sósskiss

Sotham, *f.n.,* 'sʌðəm, súthăm

Sothcott, *f.n.,* 'sɒθkɒt, sóthkott

Sotheby's, *auctioneers,* 'sʌðəbɪz, súthĕbiz

Sothers, *f.n.,* 'sʌðərz, súthĕrz

Sotterley *Suffolk,* 'sɒtərlɪ, sóttĕrli

Soudley *Glos.,* 'sudlɪ, sóodli

Souez, *f.n.,* 'suɪz, sóo-ĕz

Soughton *Clwyd,* 'sɔtən, sáwtŏn. *The Welsh form of this name is* **Sychdyn,** *q.v.*

Soul, *f.n.,* sul, sool

Soulbury *Bucks.,* 'soulbərɪ, sṓlbŭri. *Appropriate also for Viscount* ~.

Soulby, *f.n.,* 'soulbɪ, sṓlbi

Soulby *Cumbria,* 'soulbɪ, sṓlbi

Souldern *Oxon.,* 'souldərn, sṓldĕrn

Souldrop *Beds.,* 'souldrɒp, sṓldrop

Soulsby, *f.n.,* 'soulzbɪ, sṓlzbi

Sound of Mull, *sea passage,* 'saund əv 'mʌl, sównd ŏv múll

Souness, *f.n.,* 'sunɪs, sóonĕss

Sourin *Orkney,* 'sauərɪn, sówrin

Sourton *Devon,* 'sɔrtən, sórtŏn

Souster, *f.n.,* 'sustər, sóostĕr

Soutar, *f.n.,* 'sutər, sóotĕr

Souter, *f.n.,* 'sutər, sóotĕr

Souter Point *Tyne & Wear,* 'sutər 'pɔɪnt, sóotĕr póynt

Southall, *f.n.,* 'sʌðɔl, súthawl; 'sʌðl, súthl

Southall *London,* 'sauθɔl, sówth--awl

Southam, *f.n.,* 'sauðəm, sówthăm

Southam *Warwicks.,* 'sauðəm, sówthăm

Southampton *Hants,* sauθ'hæmptən, sowth-hámptŏn; sau-'θæmptən, sowthámptŏn

South Baddesley *Hants,* 'sauθ 'bædɪzlɪ, sówth báddĕzli; 'sauθ 'bædzlɪ, sówth bádzli

Southborough *Kent,* 'sauθbərə, sówthbŭră. *Appropriate also for Baron* ~.

Southby, *f.n.,* 'sauθbɪ, sówthbi

South Cerney *Glos.,* 'sauθ 'sɜrnɪ, sówth sérni

Southcombe, *f.n.,* 'sauθkəm, sówthkŏm

South Croxton *Leics.,* 'sauθ 'krousən, sówth krṓssŏn; 'sauθ 'kroustən, sówth krṓsstŏn; 'sauθ 'krouzən, sówth krṓzŏn

Southerndown *Mid Glam.,* 'sʌðərndaun, súthĕrndown

Southerness *D. & G.,* ,sʌðər'nes, suthĕrnéss

Southers, *f.n.,* 'sʌðərz, súthĕrz

Southerwood, *f.n.,* 'sʌðərwud, súthĕrwŏŏd

Southery *Norfolk,* 'sʌðərɪ, súthĕri

Southesk, Earl of, sauθ'esk, sowthésk

Southey, *f.n.,* 'sauðɪ, sówthi; 'sʌðɪ, súthi. *The first is appropriate for Robert* ~, *Poet Laureate.*

Southey *S. Yorks.,* 'sauðɪ, sówthi

Southgate, *f.n.,* 'sauθgeɪt, sówthgayt; 'sauθgɪt, sówthgit

South Heighton *E. Sussex,* 'sauθ 'heɪtən, sówth háytŏn

South Hiendley *W. Yorks.,* 'sauθ 'hindlɪ, sówth héendli

South Hykeham *Lincs.,* 'sauθ 'haɪkəm, sówth híkăm

South Kirby *W. Yorks.,* 'sauθ 'kɜrbɪ, sówth kírbi

Southleigh *Devon,* 'sauθ'li, sówth-lée; 'saulɪ, sówlee

South Leverton *Notts.,* 'sauθ 'levərtən, sówth lévvĕrtŏn

South Malling *E. Sussex,* 'sauθ 'mɔlɪŋ, sówth máwling

South Merstham *Surrey,* 'sauθ 'mɜrstəm, sówth mérstăm

Southminster *Essex,* 'sauθ-'mɪnstər, sówthmínstĕr

Southoe *Cambs.,* 'sauθou, sówthṓ; 'sauðou, sówthṓ

Southorn, *f.n.,* 'sʌðɔrn, súthorn

Southowram *W. Yorks.,* sauθ-'auərəm, sowth-ówrăm

Southrepps *Norfolk,* 'sauθreps, sówthrepps

Southrey *Lincs.,* 'sʌðrɪ, súthri

Southron, *f.n.,* 'sʌðrən, súthrŏn

South Ronaldsay *Orkney,* 'sauθ 'rɒnldseɪ, sówth rónnld-say; 'sauθ 'rɒnldʃeɪ, sówth rónnld--shay

Southrop *Glos.,* 'sʌðərəp, súthĕrŏp

South Shields *Tyne & Wear,* 'sauθ 'ʃildz, sówth shéeldz

South Walsham *Norfolk,* 'sauθ 'wɒlʃəm, sówth wáwl-shăm

Southwark, *f.n.,* 'sʌðərk, súthărk

Southwark *London,* 'sʌðərk, súthărk. *Appropriate also for* ~ *Cathedral.*

Southwell, *f.n.*, 'sʌðl, súthl; 'saʊθwəl, sówthwĕl. *The first is appropriate for Viscount* ~.
Southwell *Dorset*, 'sʌðl, súthl
Southwell *Notts.*, 'sʌðl, súthl; 'saʊθwəl, sówthwĕl. *Hence also for the Lord Bishop of* ~.
Southwick *Hants*, 'sʌðɪk, súthick; 'saʊθwɪk, sówthwick
Southwick *Northants.*, 'sʌðɪk, súthick
Southwick *W. Sussex*, 'saʊθwɪk, sówthwick
Southwold *Suffolk*, 'saʊθwoʊld, sówth-wōld
Soutra *Lothian*, 'sutrə, sóotră
Souttar, *f.n.*, 'sutər, sóotăr
Soward, *f.n.*, 'saʊərd, sówărd
Sowden, *f.n.*, 'soʊdən, sṓdĕn
Sowe, River, *Coventry*, saʊ, sow
Sowels, *f.n.*, 'soʊəlz, sṓ-ĕlz
Sowerbucks, *f.n.*, 'soʊərbʌks, sṓ-ĕrbucks
Sowerbutts, *f.n.*, 'saʊərbʌts, sówĕrbutts
Sowerby, *f.n.*, 'soʊərbɪ, sṓ-ĕrbi; 'saʊərbɪ, sówĕrbi
Sowerby *N. Yorks.*, 'saʊərbɪ, sówĕrbi
Sowerby Bridge *W. Yorks.*, 'soʊərbɪ 'brɪdʒ, sṓ-ĕrbi bríj; 'saʊərbɪ 'brɪdʒ, sówĕrbi bríj
Sowerby parliamentary division *W. Yorks.*, 'soʊərbɪ, sṓ-ĕrbi; 'saʊərbɪ, sówĕrbi
Sowle, *f.n.*, soʊl, sōl
Sowler, *f.n.*, 'saʊlər, sówlĕr
Sowood, *f.n.*, 'soʊwʊd, sṓ-wŏŏd
Sowrey, *f.n.*, 'saʊərɪ, sówri
Sowry, *f.n.*, 'saʊərɪ, sówri
Sowton *Devon*, 'saʊtən, sówtŏn
Spadeadam Waste *Cumbria*, speɪd'ædəm, spaydáddăm
Spalding *Lincs.*, 'spɔldɪŋ, spáwlding
Spaldwick *Cambs.*, 'spɔldwɪk, spáwldwick
Spalford *Notts.*, 'spɔlfərd, spáwlfŏrd; 'spɒlfərd, spólfŏrd
Spamount *Co. Tyrone*, 'spɑmaʊnt, spaámownt
Spanier, *f.n.*, 'spænjeɪ, spán-yay
Spanoghe, *f.n.*, 'spænoʊg, spánnōg
Spanswick, *f.n.*, 'spænzwɪk, spánz-wick
Sparey, *f.n.*, 'speərɪ, spáiri
Sparham, *f.n.*, 'spɑrəm, spaárăm
Sparham *Norfolk*, 'spærəm, spárrăm
Spark, *f.n.*, spɑrk, spaark
Sparrar, *f.n.*, 'spærər, spárrăr
Sparsholt *Hants*, 'spɑrʃoʊlt, spaár-shōlt

Spaull, *f.n.*, spɔl, spawl
Speaight, *f.n.*, speɪt, spayt
Spean, River, *H'land*, 'spiən, speé-ăn
Spean Bridge *H'land*, 'spiən 'brɪdʒ, speé-ăn bríj
Spearing, *f.n.*, 'spɪərɪŋ, speéring
Spearman, *f.n.*, 'spɪərmən, speérmăn
Spears, *f.n.*, spɪərz, speerz
Speight, *f.n.*, speɪt, spayt
Speir, *f.n.*, spɪər, speer
Speirs, *f.n.*, spɪərz, speerz
Speke *Merseyside*, spik, speek
Spence, *f.n.*, spens, spenss
Spenceley, *f.n.*, 'spenslɪ, spénssli
Spencer, *f.n.*, 'spensər, spénssĕr. *Appropriate also for Earl* ~.
Spender, *f.n.*, 'spendər, spéndĕr
Spens, *f.n.*, spenz, spenz. *Appropriate also for Baron* ~.
Spenser, *f.n.*, 'spensər, spénssĕr
Sperrin Mountains *Co. Derry–Co. Tyrone*, 'sperɪn, spérrin
Spetisbury *Dorset*, 'spetsbərɪ, spétsbŭri
Spey, Loch *and* River, *H'land*, speɪ, spay
Speybridge *H'land*, 'speɪ'brɪdʒ, spáy-bríj
Speyer, *f.n.*, speər, spair
Speymouth *Grampian*, 'speɪmaʊθ, spáymowth
Spice, *f.n.*, spaɪs, spīss
Spicer, *f.n.*, 'spaɪsər, spíssĕr
Spiegl, *f.n.*, 'spigl, speégl
Spier, *f.n.*, spɪər, speer
Spiers, *f.n.*, spaɪərz, spīrz
Spillane, *f.n.*, spɪ'leɪn, spilláyn
Spiller, *f.n.*, 'spɪlər, spíllĕr
Spilsbury, *f.n.*, 'spɪlzbərɪ, spíllzbŭri
Spiridion, *f.n.*, spɪ'rɪdɪən, spiríddi-ŏn
Spiritus, *f.n.*, 'spɪrɪtəs, spírrĭtŭss
Spitalfields *London*, 'spɪtlfɪldz, spíttlfeeldz
Spital Tongues *Tyne & Wear*, 'spɪtl 'tʌŋz, spíttl túngz
Spithead *Portsmouth Harbour*, 'spɪt'hed, spít-héd
Spittal, *f.n.*, 'spɪtl, spíttl
Spittal of Glenshee *Tayside*, 'spɪtl əv glen'ʃi, spíttl ŏv glen-sheé
Spivey, *f.n.*, 'spaɪvɪ, spívi
Splott *Cardiff*, 'splɒt, splótt
Spofforth, *f.n.*, 'spɒfərθ, spóffŏrth
Spofforth *N. Yorks.*, 'spɒfərθ, spóffŏrth
Spon, *f.n.*, spɒn, sponn
Spondon *Derby.*, 'spɒndən, spóndŏn
Spooner, *f.n.*, 'spunər, spoónĕr

Sporle *Norfolk*, spɔrl, sporl
Spottiswoode, *f.n.*, 'spɒtɪswʊd, spóttiswōōd; 'spɒtswʊd, spótswōōd. *The first is appropriate for the publishers Eyre and* ~.
Spouse, *f.n.*, spaʊz, spowz
Sprague, *f.n.*, spreɪg, sprayg
Spread, *f.n.*, spred, spred
Spreadborough, *f.n.*, 'spredbərə, sprédbŭră
Spriggs, *f.n.*, sprɪgz, spriggz
Springall, *f.n.*, 'sprɪŋɔl, spríng-awl
Springburn *S'clyde*, 'sprɪŋbɜrn, spríngburn
Springett, *f.n.*, 'sprɪŋɪt, spríng-ĕt
Springfield *Co. Antrim*, 'sprɪŋfɪld, springfeeld
Sproson, *f.n.*, 'sprousən, spróssŏn
Sproughton *Suffolk*, 'sprɔtən, spráwtŏn
Sproul-Cran, *f.n.*, 'spraʊl 'kræn, sprówl kránn
Sproule, *f.n.*, sprouǀ, sprōl; sprul, sprool
Sprouston *Borders*, 'spraʊstən, sprówsstŏn
Sprowston *Norfolk*, 'sprʌʊstən, sprówsstŏn
Sproxton, *f.n.*, 'sprɒkstən, spróckstŏn
Spungin, *f.n.*, 'spʌŋgɪn, spúng-gin
Spurling, *f.n.*, 'spɜrlɪŋ, spúrling
Spurrell, *f.n.*, 'spʌrəl, spúrrĕl
Spurrier, *f.n.*, 'spʌrɪər, spúrri-ĕr
Squier, *f.n.*, 'skwaɪər, skwīr
Squire, *f.n.*, 'skwaɪər, skwīr
Squires, *f.n.*, 'skwaɪərz, skwīrz
Stacey, *f.n.*, 'steɪsɪ, stáyssi
Stadlen, *f.n.*, 'stædlən, stádlĕn
Staffa *S'clyde*, 'stæfə, stáffă
Stafford *Staffs.*, 'stæfərd, stáffŏrd
Stagg, *f.n.*, stæg, stag
Staiman, *f.n.*, 'steɪmən, stáymăn
Stainby *Lincs.*, 'steɪnbɪ, stáynbi
Stainer, *f.n.*, 'steɪnər, stáynĕr
Staines *Surrey*, steɪnz, staynz
Stainthorpe, *f.n.*, 'steɪnθɔrp, stáyn-thorp
Staithes *N. Yorks.*, steɪðz, staythz
Stakehill *Gtr. M'chester*, 'steɪk-'hɪl, stáyk-híll
Stalbridge *Dorset*, 'stɔlbrɪdʒ, stáwlbrij
Stalham *Norfolk*, 'stæləm, stálăm
Stalisfield *Kent*, 'stælɪsfɪld, stálissfeeld
Stalker, *f.n.*, 'stɔkər, stáwkĕr; 'stælkər, stál-kĕr
Stallard, *f.n.*, 'stælɑrd, stálaard
Stallingborough *Humberside*, 'stalɪŋbərə, staálingbŭră
Stallworthy, *f.n.*, 'stɔlwɜrðɪ, stáwlwurthi

Stallybrass, *f.n.*, 'stælɪbrɑs, stálibraass
Stalman, *f.n.*, 'stælmən, stálmăn
Stalybridge *Gtr. M'chester*, 'steɪlɪbrɪdʒ, stáylibrij
Stamfordham *Northd.*, 'stæmfərdəm, stámfŏrdăm; 'stænərtən, stánnĕrtŏn
Stamp, *f.n.*, stæmp, stamp
Stancliffe, *f.n.*, 'stænklɪf, stán-kliff
Standaloft, *f.n.*, 'stændəlɒft, stándăloft
Standedge *W. Yorks.*, 'stæned3, stánnej
Standeven, *f.n.*, 'stændivən, stándeevĕn
Standing, *f.n.*, 'stændɪŋ, stánding
Stanford, *f.n.*, 'stænfərd, stánfŏrd
Stanford-le-Hope *Essex*, 'stænfərdlɪ'houp, stánfŏrdli-hóp
Stangar, *f.n.*, 'stæŋər, stáng-ăr
Stangboom, *f.n.*, 'stæŋbum, stángboom
Stangroom, *f.n.*, 'stæŋrʊm, stáng-rōōm; stæn'grum, stan-gróom
Stanhill *Lancs.*, 'stænhɪl, stánhil
Stanhoe *Norfolk*, 'stænou, stánnō
Stanhope, *f.n.*, 'stænəp, stánnŏp. *Appropriate also for the Earldom of* ~.
Stanhope *Durham*, 'stænəp, stánnŏp
Stanier, *f.n.*, 'stænɪər, stánni-ĕr
Staniland, *f.n.*, 'stænɪlənd, stánniländ
Stanion *Northants.*, 'stænjən, stán-yŏn
Stanks *W. Yorks.*, stæŋks, stanks
Stanley, *C.n. and f.n.*, 'stænlɪ, stánli
Stanley of Alderley, Baron, 'stænlɪ əv 'ɔldərlɪ, stánli ŏv áwldĕrli
Stannard, *f.n.*, 'stænɑrd, stánnaard; 'stænərd, stánnărd
Stansfield, *f.n.*, 'stænzfɪld, stánzfeeld
Stansgate, Viscountcy of, 'stænzgeɪt, stánzgayt
Stansted Airport *Essex*, 'stænsted, stánssted
Stansted Mountfitchet *Essex*, 'stænsted maʊnt'fɪtʃɪt, stánssted mowntfítchĕt
Stanton, *f.n.*, 'stæntən, stántŏn; 'stantən, staántŏn
Stanton *Glos.*, 'stantən, staántŏn
Stanton-by-Bridge *Derby.*, 'stæntən baɪ 'brɪdʒ, stántŏn bī brij
Stanwick, *f.n.*, 'stænɪk, stánnick
Stanwick *Northants.*, 'stænɪk, stánnick

Stanwick St. John *N. Yorks.*, 'stænɪk snt 'dʒɒn, stánnick sĭnt jón

Stanwix *Cumbria*, 'stænɪks, stánnicks

Stapleford *Cambs., Herts., Notts.*, 'steɪplfərd, stáyplfŏrd

Stapleford *Leics.*, 'stæplfərd, stápplfŏrd

Stapley, *f.n.*, 'stæplɪ, stápli; 'steɪplɪ, stáypli

Staploe *Beds.*, 'steɪploʊ, stáyp-lō

Stareton *Warwicks.*, 'stɑrtən, staártŏn

Stark, *f.n.*, stɑrk, staark

Starkey, *f.n.*, 'stɑrkɪ, staárki

Starlaw *Lothian*, 'stɑr'lɔ, staár-láw

Startin, *f.n.*, 'stɑrtɪn, staártin

Statham, *f.n.*, 'steɪθəm, stáythăm; 'steɪðəm, stáyt͟hăm

Stathe *Somerset*, steɪð, stayt͟h

Stathern *Leics.*, 'stæθərn, stát-hern

Staton, *f.n.*, 'steɪtən, stáytŏn

Staub, *f.n.*, stɔb, stawb

Staudinger, *f.n.*, 'staʊdɪŋər, stówding-ĕr

Staughton, Great, *Cambs.*, 'stɔtən, stáwtŏn

Staughton, Little, *Beds.*, 'stɔtən, stáwtŏn

Staughton Green *Cambs.*, 'stɔtən 'grin, stáwtŏn gréen

Staughton Highway *Cambs.*, 'stɔtən 'haɪweɪ, stáwtŏn hí-way

Staughton Moor *Cambs.*, 'stɔtən 'mʊər, stáwtŏn mŏŏr

Staunton, *f.n.*, 'stɔntən, stáwntŏn

Stave, *f.n.*, steɪv, stayv

Staveacre, *f.n.*, 'steɪveɪkər, stáyvaykĕr

Staveley *Cumbria, Derby., N. Yorks.*, 'steɪvlɪ, stáyvli. *Appropriate for both places of the name in Cumbria.*

Staverton *Glos., Northants.*, 'stævərtən, stávvĕrtŏn

Stavordale Priory *Somerset*, 'stævərdeɪl, stávvŏrdayl

Staward *Northd.*, 'stawərd, staáwărd

Stawell *Somerset*, stɔl, stawl

Staxigoe *H'land*, 'stæksɪgjoʊ, stácksig-yō

Stayt, *f.n.*, steɪt, stayt

Staythorpe *Notts.*, 'steɪθɔrp, stáy-thorp

Stead, *f.n.*, sted, sted; stid, steed

Steadman, *f.n.*, 'stedmən, stédmăn

Steart *Somerset*, 'stiərt, steé-ărt

Stechford *W. Midlands*, 'stetʃfərd, stétchfŏrd

Steck, *f.n.*, stek, steck

Steddall, *f.n.*, 'stedɔl, stéddawl

Stedeford, *f.n.*, 'stedɪfərd, stéddĕford

Stedman, *f.n.*, 'stedmən, stédmăn

Steed, *f.n.*, stid, steed

Steegman, *f.n.*, 'stidʒmən, steéjmăn

Steele, *f.n.*, stil, steel

Steen, *f.n.*, stin, steen

Steep Holme Island *Avon*, 'stip hoʊm, steép hōm

Steer, *f.n.*, stɪər, steer

Stein, *f.n.*, staɪn, stīn; stin, steen

Steinberg, *f.n.*, 'staɪnbərg, stĭn-berg

Steine, The Old, *Brighton*, stin, steen

Steinitz, *f.n.*, 'staɪnɪts, stĭnits

Steley, *f.n.*, 'stelɪ, stélli

Stelling Minnis *Kent*, 'stelɪŋ 'mɪnɪz, stélling mínniz

Stenalees *Cornwall*, ˌstenə'liz, stennăleéz

Stenhousemuir *Central*, 'stenhaʊs'mjʊər, sténhowss-myŏŏr

Stenigot *Lincs.*, 'stenɪgɒt, sténnigot

Stenning, *f.n.*, 'stenɪŋ, sténning

Stentiford, *f.n.*, 'stentɪfərd, sténtifŏrd

Stepaside *Dyfed, Powys*, ˌstepə'saɪd, steppássíd; 'stepəsaɪd, stéppássíd

Stephen, *C.n.*, 'stivən, steévĕn

Stephens, *f.n.*, 'stivənz, steévĕnz

Stephenson, *f.n.*, 'stivənsən, steévĕnssŏn

Steptoe, *f.n.*, 'steptoʊ, stéptō

Sterke, *f.n.*, stɑrk, staark

Sterling, *f.n.*, 'stɜrlɪŋ, stérling

Stern, *f.n.*, stɜrn, stern

Sterndale-Bennett, *f.n.*, 'stɜrndeɪl 'benɪt, stérndayl bénnĕt. *Appropriate also for the composer Sir William Sterndale Bennett (1816–75).*

Sterner, *f.n.*, 'stɜrnər, stérnĕr

Sternfeld, *f.n.*, 'stɜrnfeld, stérnfeld

Steuart, *f.n.*, 'stjuərt, stéw-ărt; 'stjʊərt, styŏŏ-ărt

Stevas, *f.n.*, 'stivæs, steévass; 'stivəs, steévăss

Stevens, *f.n.*, 'stivənz, steévĕnz

Stevenson, *f.n.*, 'stivənsən, steévĕnssŏn

Stevenston *S'clyde*, 'stivənztən, steévĕnztŏn

Steventon *Berks., Hants*, 'stivəntən, steévĕntŏn

Stevington *Beds.*, 'stevɪŋtən, stévvingtŏn

Steward, *f.n.*, 'stjuərd, stéw-ărd; 'stjʊərd, styŏŏ-ărd

Stewart, *f.n.*, 'stjuərt, stéw-ărt; 'stjuərt, styŏŏ-ărt

Steyn, *f.n.*, staɪn, stīn

Steyne *I. of Wight*, stin, steen

Steyne, The, *Worthing* (*W. Sussex*) ðə 'stin, thĕ steén

Steyning *W. Sussex*, 'stenɪŋ, sténning

Steynor, *f.n.*, 'stinər, steénŏr

Stickells, *f.n.*, 'stɪklz, stícklz

Sticklepath *Devon*, 'stɪklpaθ, stícklpaath

Stiebel, *f.n.*, 'stibl, steébl

Stiffkey *Norfolk*, 'stɪfkɪ, stíffki; 'stukɪ, stoóki; 'stjukɪ, stéwki. *The two latter are rarely heard today.*

Stillwell, *f.n.*, 'stɪlwel, stíllwel

Stilton *Cambs.*, 'stɪltən, stíltŏn

Stinchar, River, *S'clyde*, 'stɪnʃər, stínshăr

Stiperstones *Salop*, 'staɪpər-stoʊnz, stípĕrsstŏnz

Stirling, *f.n.*, 'stɜrlɪŋ, stírling

Stirling *Central, Grampian*, 'stɜrlɪŋ, stírling

Stirtloe *Cambs.*, 'stɜrtloʊ, stírt-lō

Stirton, *f.n.*, 'stɜrtən, stírtŏn

Stisted *Essex*, 'staɪsted, stí-sted

Stithians *Cornwall*, 'stɪðɪənz, stíthi-änz

Stiven, *f.n.*, 'stɪvən, stívvĕn

Stivichall, *also spelt* **Styvechale,** *W. Midlands*, 'staɪtʃl, stítchl; 'staɪtʃəl, stítchawl

Stobart, *f.n.*, 'stoʊbɑrt, stŏbaart

Stobo *Borders*, 'stoʊboʊ, stŏbō

Stoborough *Dorset*, 'stoʊbərə, stŏbŭră

Stock, *f.n.*, stɒk, stock

Stocking, *f.n.*, 'stɒkɪŋ, stócking

Stockins, *f.n.*, 'stɒkɪnz, stóckinz

Stockleigh Pomeroy *Devon*, 'stɒklɪ 'pɒmərɔɪ, stóckli póm-mĕroy

Stockley, *f.n.*, 'stɒklɪ, stóckli

Stockport *Ches.*, 'stɒkpɔrt, stóck-port

Stocks, *f.n.*, stɒks, stocks

Stocksbridge *S. Yorks.*, 'stɒks-brɪdʒ, stócks-brij

Stockton-on-Tees *Durham*, 'stɒktən ɒn 'tiz, stócktŏn-on--teéz

Stockwell, *f.n.*, 'stɒkwel, stóck-well; 'stɒkwəl, stóckwĕl

Stodart, *f.n.*, 'stɒdərt, stóddărt; 'stoʊdɑrt, stŏdaart; stoʊ'dɑrt, stōdáart

Stoddart, *f.n.*, 'stɒdərt, stóddărt; 'stɒdɑrt, stóddaart

Stody *Norfolk*, 'stʌdɪ, stúddi

Stoer, *f.n.*, stɔr, stor

Stoer *H'land*, 'stoʊər, stŏ-ĕr

Stoessiger, *f.n.*, 'stesɪdʒər, stés-sijĕr

Stogdon, *f.n.*, 'stɒgdən, stógdŏn

Stogumber *Somerset*, stoʊ'gʌmbər, stōgúmbĕr; 'stɒgəmbər, stóggŭmbĕr

Stogursey *Somerset*, stoʊ'gɜrzɪ, stōgúrzi

Stohl, *f.n.*, stoʊl, stōl

Stoic, *one educated at Stowe School*, 'stoʊɪk, stŏ-ick

Stoke Bruern *Northants.*, 'stoʊk 'bruərn, stŏk broó-ĕrn

Stoke d'Abernon *Surrey*, 'stoʊk 'dæbərnən, stŏk dábbĕrnŏn

Stoke Damerel *Devon*, 'stoʊk 'dæmərəl, stŏk dámmĕrĕl

Stoke Gifford *Avon*, 'stoʊk 'gɪfərd, stŏk gíffŏrd

Stoke-in-Teignhead, *also spelt* **Stokeinteignhead,** *Devon*, 'stoʊk ɪn 'tinhed, stŏk in teénhed

Stoke Mandeville *Bucks.*, 'stoʊk 'mændɪvɪl, stŏk mándĕvil

Stokenham *Devon*, ,stoʊkən'hæm, stŏkĕnhám; 'stoʊkənəm, stŏkĕnăm

Stoke-on-Trent *Staffs.*, 'stoʊk ɒn 'trent, stŏk on trént

Stoke Pero *Somerset*, 'stoʊk 'pɪəroʊ, stŏk peérŏ

Stoker, *f.n.*, 'stoʊkər, stŏkĕr

Stokes, *f.n.*, stoʊks, stōks

Stokoe, *f.n.*, 'stoʊkoʊ, stŏkō

Stoll, *f.n.*, stɒl, stoll

Stoller, *f.n.*, 'stɒlər, stóllĕr

Stollery, *f.n.*, 'stɒlərɪ, stóllĕri

Stolz, *f.n.*, stɒlts, stollts

Stonar *Kent*, 'stɒnər, stónnăr

Stonards Brow *Surrey*, 'stɒnərdz 'braʊ, stónnărdz brów

Stonborough, *f.n.*, 'stoʊnbərə, stŏnbŭră

Stone, *f.n.*, stoʊn, stōn

Stonea *Cambs.*, 'stoʊnɪ, stŏni

Ston Easton *Somerset*, stɒn 'istən, ston eésstŏn

Stonebridge, *f.n.*, 'stoʊnbrɪdʒ, stŏnbrij

Stonebyres *S'clyde*, 'stoʊnbaɪərz, stŏnbīrz

Stoneclough *Gtr. M'chester*, 'stoʊnklʌf, stŏn-kluff

Stonedge *Derby.*, 'stoʊnedʒ, stŏnej; 'stænedʒ, stánnej

Stonehaven *Grampian*, stoʊn-'heɪvən, stōn-háyvĕn; steɪn'haɪ, stayn-hí. *The first is appropriate also for Viscount ~.*

Stonehenge *Wilts.*, 'stoʊn'hendʒ, stŏn-hénj

Stoneleigh *Surrey*, 'stoʊn'li, stŏn-leé

Stoneleigh *Warwicks.*, 'stoʊnlɪ, stónli. *Appropriate also for ~ Abbey.*

Stonely *Cambs.*, 'stoʊnlɪ, stónli

Stoner, *f.n.*, 'stoʊnər, stóněr

Stoney, *f.n.*, 'stoʊnɪ, stóni

Stoney Houghton, *also spelt* **Stony Houghton,** *Derby.*, 'stoʊnɪ 'hʌftən, stóni húftŏn

Stonham *Suffolk*, 'stɒnəm, stónnăm

Stonham Aspal *Suffolk*, 'stɒnəm 'æspɔl, stónnăm ásspawl

Stonier, *f.n.*, 'stoʊnɪər, stóni-ĕr

Stonnall *Staffs.*, 'stɒnl, stónnl

Stonor, *f.n.*, 'stoʊnɔr, stónor; 'stɒnər, stónnŏr. *The first is appropriate for the family name of Baron Camoys.*

Stonor *Oxon.*, 'stoʊnər, stónŏr

Stooke, *f.n.*, stʊk, stŏŏk

Stopham *W. Sussex*, 'stɒpəm, stóppăm

Stopher, *f.n.*, 'stoʊfər, stófĕr

Stoppard, *f.n.*, 'stɒpɑrd, stóppaard

Storace, *f.n.*, 'stɒrɪs, stórrăss

Stordy, *f.n.*, 'stɔrdɪ, stórdi

Storey, *f.n.*, 'stɔrɪ, stáwri

Storm, *f.n.*, stɔrm, storm

Stormont, *f.n.*, 'stɔrmənt, stórmŏnt

Stormont *Tayside*, 'stɔrmənt, stórmŏnt. *Appropriate also for Viscount ~.*

Stormont Castle *Co. Down*, 'stɔrmənt, stórmŏnt

Stormontfield *Tayside*, 'stɔrməntfild, stórmŏntfeeld

Stormonth, *f.n.*, 'stɔrmənt, stórmŏnt

Stornoway *W. Isles*, 'stɔrnəweɪ, stórnŏ-way

Storr, *f.n.*, stɔr, stor

Storr, The, *Skye*, stɔr, stor

Storrier, *f.n.*, 'stɒrɪər, stórri-ĕr

Storrs, *f.n.*, stɔrz, storz

Stothard, *f.n.*, 'stɒðard, stóthaard; 'stɒðərd, stóthărd

Stothert, *f.n.*, 'stɒðərt, stóthĕrt

Stott, *f.n.*, stɒt, stott

Stottesdon *Salop*, 'stɒtɪzdən, stóttĕzdŏn

Stoughton, *f.n.*, 'stɔtən, stáwtŏn; 'staʊtən, stówtŏn; 'stoʊtən, stŏtŏn. *The third is appropriate for the publisher Hodder & ~.*

Stoughton *Leics.*, *W. Sussex*, 'stoʊtən, stŏtŏn

Stoughton *Surrey*, 'staʊtən, stówtŏn. *Appropriate also for ~ Barracks.*

Stoughton, Middle *and* West, *Somerset*, 'stɔtən, stáwtŏn

Stoughton Cross *Somerset*, 'stɔtən 'krɒs, stáwtŏn króss

Stoulton *H. & W.*, 'stoʊltən, stŏltŏn

Stour, Rivers, *H. & W.*, *Oxon.– Warwicks.*, 'staʊər, stowr; 'stoʊər, stŏ-ĕr

Stour, River, *Kent*, stʊər, stŏŏr; 'staʊər, stowr. *Although the first is much more usual for the name of the river, see treatment of neighbouring* **Stourmouth.**

Stour, River, *Suffolk–Essex*, stʊər, stŏŏr. *This is the river associated with Constable.*

Stourbridge *W. Midlands*, 'staʊərbrɪdʒ, stówrbrij; 'stoʊərbrɪdʒ, stŏ-ĕrbrij

Stourbridge Common *Cambs.*, 'staʊərbrɪdʒ 'kɒmən, stówrbrij kómmŏn

Stourhead House *Wilts.*, 'stɔrhed, stór-hed; 'staʊərhed, stówr-hed

Stourmouth *Kent*, 'staʊərmaʊθ, stówrmowth; 'stʊərmaʊθ, stŏŏrmowth. *Although the first of these is more usual locally for the place name, it is interesting that the neighbouring River Stour is more often pronounced* stʊər, stŏŏr.

Stourport-on-Severn *H. & W.*, 'staʊərpɔrt ɒn 'sevərn, stówrport on sévvĕrn; 'stʊərpɔrt ɒn 'sevərn, stŏŏrport on sévvĕrn

Stour Provost *Dorset*, 'staʊər 'prɒvəst, stówr próvvŏst

Stour Row *see* **Stower Row**

Stourton, *f.n.*, 'stɜrtən, stúrtŏn. *See also Baron* **Mowbray, Segrave and ~.**

Stourton *H. & W.*, 'stɔrtən, stórtŏn

Stourton *Wilts.*, 'stɜrtən, stúrtŏn; 'stɔrtən, stórtŏn

Stourton Caundle *Dorset*, 'stɔrtən 'kɒndl, stórtŏn káwndl; 'stɜrtən 'kɒndl, stúrtŏn káwndl

Stout, *f.n.*, staʊt, stowt

Stoute, *f.n.*, staʊt, stowt

Stovell, *f.n.*, stə'vel, stŏvéll; stoʊ'vel, stŏvéll; 'stoʊvl, stŏvl

Stoven *Suffolk*, 'stʌvən, stúvvĕn

Stovold, *f.n.*, 'stoʊvɒld, stŏvold; 'stɒvoʊld, stóvvōld

Stow, *f.n.*, stoʊ, stŏ

Stow Bedon *Norfolk*, stoʊ 'bidən, stŏ beedŏn

Stowell, *f.n.*, 'stoʊəl, stŏ-ĕl

Stowell *Somerset*, 'stoʊəl, stŏ-ĕl; stoʊl, stŏl

Stower Row, *also spelt* **Stour Row,** *Dorset*, 'staʊər 'roʊ, stówr rŏ

Stowey *Avon*, 'stoʊɪ, stŏ-i

Stowford *Devon*, 'stoʊfərd, stŏ-fŏrd

Stow Longa *Cambs.*, 'stoʊ 'lɒŋgə, stŏ lóng-gă

Stow Maries *Essex*, stoʊ 'mɑrız, stŏ maáriz

Stowmarket *Suffolk*, 'stoʊmɑrkɪt, stŏmaarkĕt

Stow-on-the-Wold *Glos.*, 'stoʊ ɒn ðə 'woʊld, stŏ on the̱ wŏld

Stowting *Kent*, 'staʊtɪŋ, stówting

Strabane *Co. Tyrone*, strə'bæn, străbán. *Appropriate also for Viscount ~.*

Strabolgi, Baron, strə'boʊgɪ, străbŏgi

Stracathro *Tayside*, strə'kæθroʊ, străkáthrŏ

Strachan, *f.n.*, 'stræxən, stráchăn; strɒn, strawn

Strachan *Grampian*, strɒn, strawn

Strachey, *f.n.*, 'streɪtʃɪ, stráytchi; 'stræxɪ, stráchi

Strachie, *f.n.*, 'streɪtʃɪ, stráytchi. *Appropriate also for the Barony of ~.*

Strachur *S'clyde*, strə'xɜr, străchúr

Stradbroke *Suffolk*, 'strædbroʊk, strádbrŏŏk. *Appropriate also for the Earl of ~.*

Stradey Park rugby ground *Llanelli (Dyfed)*, 'strædɪ 'pɑrk, stráddi paárk

Stradishall *Suffolk*, 'strædɪʃɔl, stráddi-shawl

Stradling, *f.n.*, 'strædlɪŋ, strádling

Stradwick, *f.n.*, 'strædwɪk, strádwick

Strahan, *f.n.*, strɒn, strawn

Straiton *S'clyde*, 'streɪtən, stráytŏn

Straker, *f.n.*, 'streɪkər, stráykĕr

Strakosch, *f.n.*, 'strækɒʃ, stráckosh

Straloch *Tayside*, strə'lɒx, strălóch

Strange, *f.n.*, streɪndʒ, straynj

Strange of Knokin, Baron, 'streɪndʒ əv 'nɒkɪn, stráynj ŏv nóckin

Stranger, *f.n.*, 'streɪndʒər, stráynjĕr

Strangeways *Gtr. M'chester*, 'streɪndʒweɪz, stráynjwayz

Strangford *H. & W.*, 'stræŋfərd, strángfŏrd

Strangways, *f.n.*, 'stræŋweɪz, stráng-wayz

Stranmillis *Co. Antrim*, stræn-'mɪlɪs, stranmílliss

Stranocum *Co. Antrim*, stræn'oʊkəm, stranŏkŭm

Stranraer, *f.n.*, stræn'rɑr, stran-raár

Stranraer *D. & G.*, strən'rɑr, străn-raár

Strata Florida *Dyfed*, 'stræt ə 'flɒrɪdə, strắttă flórridă. *The Welsh form is* **Ystrad Fflur**, *q.v.*

Stratfieldsaye House *Hants*, 'strætfɪldseɪ, strátfeeldssay

Stratford-atte-Bowe *London*, 'strætfərd ætɪ 'boʊ, strátfŏrd atti bŏ́; 'strætfərd ætɪ 'boʊɪ, strátfŏrd atti bŏ́-i; 'strætfərd ætə 'boʊə, strátfŏrd attĕ bŏ́-ĕ. *The first is a modern pronunciation of the historic name. The others are perhaps more familiar to students of Chaucer.*

Stratford-upon-Avon *Warwicks.*, 'strætfərd əpɒn 'eɪvən, strátfŏrd ŭpon áyvŏn

Strath, *f.n.*, strɑθ, straath

Strathalmond, Baron, stræθ-'ɑmənd, strath-aámŏnd

Strathardle *Tayside*, stræθ'ɑrdl, strathaárdl

Strathaven *S'clyde*, 'streɪvən, stráyvĕn

Strathblane *Central*, stræθ'bleɪn, strathbláyn

Strathclyde *admin. region of Scotland*, stræθ'klaɪd, strath-klíd. *Appropriate also for Baron ~ and for the University of ~.*

Strathcona, Baron, stræθ'koʊnə, strathkŏ́nă

Strathdee, *f.n.*, stræθ'di, strathdeé

Strathearn *Tayside*, stræθ'ɜrn, strathérn

Stratheden, Baron, stræθ'idən, stratheédĕn

Stratherrick *H'land*, stræθ'erɪk, strathérrick

Strathfillan *Central*, stræθ'fɪlən, strathfíllăn

Strathkinness *Fife*, stræθ'kɪnɪs, strathkínnĕss

Strathleven *S'clyde*, stræθ'livən, strathleévĕn

Strathmiglo *Fife*, stræθ'mɪgloʊ, strathmíglŏ

Strathmore *H'land–Central*, stræθ'mɔr, strathmór

Strathmore and Kinghorne, Earl of, stræθ'mɔr ənd 'kɪŋhɔrn, strathmór ănd kíng-horn

Strathnaver *H'land*, stræθ'neɪvər, strathnáyvĕr

Strathpeffer *H'land*, stræθ'pefər, strathpéffĕr

The form stræθ-, strath-, *used to indicate the unstressed prefix* **Strath**-, *is that used in careful speech. Its occurrence as* strəθ-, străth- *is equally frequent and acceptable.*

Strathspey *H'land–Grampian*, stræθ'speɪ, strath-spáy. *Appropriate also for Baron* ∼.
Strathtay *Tayside*, stræθ'teɪ, strathtáy
Straton, *f.n.*, 'strætən, stráttŏn
Straughan, *f.n.*, strɔn, strawn
Strauli, *f.n.*, 'strɔlɪ, stráwli
Strauss, *f.n.*, straʊs, strowss
Strauther, *f.n.*, 'strɔðər, stráwthĕr
Streat, *f.n.*, strit, street
Streatfeild, *f.n.*, 'stretfɪld, strétfeeld
Streatham *London*, 'stretəm, stréttăm
Streather, *f.n.*, 'streðər, stréthĕr
Streatlam *Durham*, 'stritləm, stréetlăm
Streatley *Beds.*, 'stretlɪ, stréttli
Streatley *Berks.*, 'stritlɪ, stréetli
Stredwick, *f.n.*, 'stredwɪk, strédwick
Street, *f.n.*, strit, street
Streethay *Staffs.*, 'striteɪ, stréet-hay
Strensall *N. Yorks.*, 'strensl, strénssl
Strethall *Essex*, 'strethɔl, strét-hawl
Stretham *Cambs.*, 'stretəm, stréttăm
Stretton Sugwas *H. & W.*, 'stretən 'sʌgəs, stréttŏn súggăss
Strevens, *f.n.*, 'strevənz, strévvĕnz
Strichen *Grampian*, 'strɪxən, stríchĕn
Stride, *f.n.*, straɪd, strīd
Striguil Castle *Gwent*, 'strɪgɪl, stríggil
Stringer, *f.n.*, 'strɪŋər, stríng-ĕr
Striven, Loch, *S'clyde*, 'strɪvən, strívvĕn
Strode, *f.n.*, straʊd, strōd
Strollamus *H'land*, 'strɒləməs, stróllămŭss
Stroma *H'land*, 'straʊmə, strŏ́mă
Stromeferry *H'land*, straʊm'ferɪ, strōm-férri
Stromness *Orkney*, 'strɒmnes, strómness; strʌmnes, strúmness
Stronachlachar *Central*, 'strɒnəx-'læxər, strónnăch-láchăr
Strong, *f.n.*, strɒŋ, strong
Stronge, *f.n.*, strɒŋ, strong
Strongitharm, *f.n.*, 'strɒŋɪθɑrm, stróng-ithaarm
Stronsay *Orkney*, 'strɒnzeɪ, strónzay
Strontian *H'land*, strɒn'tiən, strontée-ăn
Strood *Kent*, strud, strood
Stross, *f.n.*, strɒs, stross
Strother, *f.n.*, 'strʌðər, strúthĕr

Stroud, *f.n.*, straʊd, strowd
Stroud *Glos.*, *Hants*, straʊd, strowd
Stroud Green *London*, 'straʊd 'grin, strówd gréen
Stroudley, *f.n.*, 'straʊdlɪ, strówdli
Strouthous, *f.n.*, 'strʌðəz, strúthŏz
Strowan, *f.n.*, 'straʊən, strŏ́-ăn
Strowan *Tayside*, 'straʊən, strów-ăn; 'struən, strŏ́o-ăn
Stroxton *Lincs.*, 'strɒsən, stráwssŏn; 'straʊsən, strŏ́ssŏn
Stroyan, *f.n.*, 'strɔɪən, stróyăn
Struan *Tayside*, 'struən, strŏ́o-ăn
Strube, *cartoonist*, 'strubɪ, strŏ́obi
Strule, River, *Co. Tyrone*, strul, strool
Strumpshaw *Norfolk*, 'strʌmpʃə, strúmp-shă
Struve, *f.n.*, 'struvɪ, strŏ́ovi
Stuart, *f.n.*, 'stjuərt, stéw-ărt; 'stjuərt, styŏ́o-ărt
Stuart of Findhorn, Viscount, 'stjuərt əv 'fɪndhɔrn, styŏ́o-ărt ŏv fíndhorn
Stubbs, *f.n.*, stʌbz, stubbz
Stuchbury, *f.n.*, 'stʌtʃbrɪ, stútch-bri
Stuchell, *f.n.*, 'stʊtʃl, stŏ́otchl
Stuck, *f.n.*, stʌk, stuck
Stucke, *f.n.*, stjuk, stewk
Stucley, *f.n.*, 'stjuklɪ, stéwkli
Studd, *f.n.*, stʌd, studd
Studdal *Kent*, 'stʌdl, stúddl
Studdert, *f.n.*, 'stʌdərt, stúddĕrt
Studholme, *f.n.*, 'stʌdhoʊm, stúd-hōm
Studley *Warwicks.*, 'stʌdlɪ, stúdli
Studt, *f.n.*, stʌt, stutt
Stukeley, Great *and* Little, *Cambs.*, 'stjuklɪ, stéwkli
Stunell, *f.n.*, stə'nel, stŭnéll
Stunt, *f.n.*, stʌnt, stunt
Stuntney *Cambs.*, 'stʌntnɪ, stúntni
Sturdee, *f.n.*, 'stɜrdɪ, stúrdi
Sturdy, *f.n.*, 'stɜrdɪ, stúrdi
Sturgate *Lincs.*, 'stɜrgeɪt, stúrgayt
Sturge, *f.n.*, 'stɜrdʒ, sturj
Sturley, *f.n.*, 'stɜrlɪ, stúrli
Sturmer, *f.n.*, 'stɜrmər, stúrmĕr
Sturminster Marshall *Dorset*, 'stɜrmɪnstər 'mɑrʃl, stúrminstĕr maárshl
Sturminster Newton *Dorset*, 'stɜrmɪnstər 'njutən, stúrminstĕr néwtŏn
Sturridge, *f.n.*, 'stʌrɪdʒ, stúrrij
Sturrock, *f.n.*, 'stʌrək, stúrrŏk
Sturry *Kent*, 'stʌrɪ, stúrri
Sturt, *f.n.*, stɜrt, sturt
Sturtevant, *f.n.*, 'stɜrtɪvənt, stúrtĕvănt

Sturtivant, f.n., 'stɜrtɪvənt, stúrtivănt

Sturton Humberside, 'stɜrtən, stúrtŏn

Stuttaford, f.n., 'stʌtəfərd, stúttăfŏrd

Styal Ches., 'staɪəl, stí-ăl

Styche, f.n., staɪtʃ, stītch

Styche Hall Salop, staɪtʃ, stītch

Styles, f.n., staɪlz, stīlz

Styvechale see Stivichall

Suart, f.n., 'sjuərt, séw-ărt

Suchet, f.n., 'suʃeɪ, sooshay

Sudbourne Suffolk, 'sʌdbɔrn, súdborn

Sudbury, f.n., 'sʌdbərɪ, súdbŭri

Suddaby, f.n., 'sʌdəbɪ, súddăbi

Suddes, f.n., 'sʌdɪs, súddĕss

Sudeley, Baron, 'sjudlɪ, séwdli

Sudley, Baron, 'sʌdlɪ, súdli

Suenson, f.n., 'suənsən, sóo--ĕnssŏn

Sueter, f.n., 'sjutər, séwtĕr; 'sutər, sóotĕr

Suffield, f.n., 'sʌfild, súffeeld

Suffolk Co. name, 'sʌfək, súffŏk

Sugden, f.n., 'sʌgdən, súgg-dĕn

Suggate, f.n., 'sʌgeɪt, súggayt

Suggett, f.n., 'sʌgɪt, súggĕt

Sugrew, f.n., 'sugru, sóogroo

Sugrue, f.n., 'sugru, sóogroo

Sugwas Pool H. & W., 'sʌgəs 'pul, súggăss poól

Suilven H'land, 'sʊlvən, soʻolvĕn

Suirdale, Viscount, 'ʃɜrdl, shúrdl

Suitters, f.n., 'sutərz, sóotĕrz

Sulby I. of Man, 'sʌlbɪ, súllbi

Suleiman, f.n., 'suleɪmæn, sóolayman

Sule Skerry Orkney, 'sul 'skerɪ, soʻol skérri

Sulham Berks., 'sʌləm, súllăm

Sulhamstead, also spelt Sulhampstead, Berks., sʌl'hæmpstɪd, sullhámpstĕd

Sullivan, f.n., 'sʌlɪvən, súllivăn

Sullom Voe Shetland, 'suləm 'voʊ, sóolŏm vó

Sully S. Glam., 'sʌlɪ, súlli

Sulwen, Welsh C.n., 'sɪlwən, séelwĕn

Sumbler, f.n., 'sʌmblər, súmblĕr

Sumburgh Head Shetland, 'sʌmbərə, súmbŭră

Summerfield, f.n., 'sʌmərfild, súmmĕrfeeld

Summers, f.n., 'sʌmərz, súmmĕrz

Sumption, f.n., 'sʌmpʃən, súmp-shŏn

Sumsion, f.n., 'sʌmʃən, súm-shŏn

Sunart, Loch, H'land, 'sunərt, sóonărt

Sunderland Tyne & Wear, 'sʌndərlənd, súndĕrlănd

Sundquist, f.n., 'sʌndkwɪst, súndkwist

Surbiton London, 'sɜrbɪtən, súrbitŏn

Surfleet, f.n., 'sɜrflɪt, súrfleet

Surgenor, f.n., 'sɜrdʒɪnɔr, súrjĕnor; 'sɜrdʒɪnər, súrjĕnŏr

Surguy, f.n., 'sɜrgaɪ, súrgī

Surlingham Norfolk, 'sɜrlɪŋəm, súrling-ăm

Surplice, f.n., 'sɜrplɪs, súrpliss

Surrey, f.n., 'sʌrɪ, súrri

Surrey Co. name, 'sʌrɪ, súrri

Surridge, f.n., 'sʌrɪdʒ, súrrij

Survaes, f.n., 'sɜrveɪz, súrvayz

Suss, f.n., sʌs, suss

Sussams, f.n., 'sʌsəmz, sússămz

Susser, f.n., 'sʌsər, sússĕr

Sussex, East and West, Co. names, 'sʌsɪks, sússĕks

Susskind, f.n., 'suskɪnd, soʻosskinnd. Appropriate for Walter ~ and Peter ~, conductors.

Sutcliffe, f.n., 'sʌtklɪf, sútkliff

Suter, f.n., 'sutər, sóotĕr

Sutherland, f.n., 'sʌðərlənd, súthĕrlănd

Sutherland H'land, 'sʌðərlənd, súthĕrlănd. Appropriate also for the Duke of ~ and the Countess of ~.

Sutlieff, f.n., 'sʌtlif, súttleef

Sutro, f.n., 'sutroʊ, sóotrō

Sutter, f.n., 'sʌtər, súttĕr

Suttie, f.n., 'sʌtɪ, sútti

Suttle, f.n., 'sʌtl, súttl

Sutton, f.n., 'sʌtən, súttŏn

Sutton Coldfield W. Midlands, 'sʌtən 'koʊldfild, súttŏn kóldfeeld

Sutton Courtenay Oxon., 'sʌtən 'kɔrtnɪ, súttŏn kórtni

Sutton Poyntz Dorset, 'sʌtən 'pɔɪnts, súttŏn póynts

Sutton Scotney Hants, 'sʌtən 'skɒtnɪ, súttŏn skótni

Sutton Veny Wilts., 'sʌtən 'vɪnɪ, súttŏn veéni

Suzman, f.n., 'suzmən, sóozmăn

Swaby Lincs., 'sweɪbɪ, swáybi

Swadlincote Derby., 'swɒdlɪŋkoʊt, swódlinkŏt

Swaebe, f.n., 'sweɪbɪ, swáybi

Swaffer, Hannen, journalist arꜙꙺd dramatic critic, 'hænən 'swɒfər, hánnĕn swóffĕr

Swaffham Norfolk, 'swɒfəm, swóffăm

Swaffham Bulbeck Cambs., 'swɒfəm 'bʊlbek, swóffăm bóolbeck

Swaffham Prior Cambs., 'swɒfəm 'praɪər, swóffăm prí-ŏr

Swafield *Norfolk*, 'sweɪfild, swáy-feeld

Swalcliffe *Oxon.*, 'sweɪklɪf, swáykliff

Swales, *f.n.*, sweɪlz, swaylz

Swalwell *Tyne & Wear*, 'swɒlwel, swólwel

Swan, *f.n.*, swɒn, swonn

Swanage *Dorset*, 'swɒnɪdʒ, swónnij

Swanborough *E. Sussex*, 'swɒnbərə, swónnbŭră

Swanbourne *Bucks.*, 'swɒnbɔrn, swónnborn

Swanley *Kent*, 'swɒnlɪ, swónli

Swann, *f.n.*, swɒn, swonn

Swannell, *f.n.*, 'swɒnl, swónnl

Swanscombe *Kent*, 'swɒnzkəm, swónzkŏm

Swansea *W. Glam.*, 'swɒnzɪ, swónzi. *Appropriate also for Baron ∼.*

Swanson, *f.n.*, 'swɒnsən, swónssŏn

Swanton Novers *Norfolk*, 'swɒntən 'nouvərz, swónntŏn nóvĕrz

Swanwick, *f.n.*, 'swɒnɪk, swónnick

Swanwick *Derby.*, 'swɒnɪk, swónnick

Swanzy, *f.n.*, 'swɒnzɪ, swónzi

Swardeston *Norfolk*, 'swɔrstən, swáwrsstŏn

Swarkestone, *also spelt* **Swarkeston,** *Derby.*, 'swɔrkstən, swáwrkstŏn

Swarland *Northd.*, 'swɔrlənd, swáwrländ

Swatman, *f.n.*, 'swɒtmən, swótmăn

Swaton *Lincs.*, 'sweɪtən, swáytŏn

Swatragh *Co. Derry*, 'swɒtrə, swótră

Swavesey *Cambs.*, 'sweɪvzɪ, swáyvzi; 'sweɪvəzɪ, swáyvĕzi

Sweatman, *f.n.*, 'swetmən, swétmăn

Sweet, *f.n.*, swit, sweet

Sweetland, *f.n.*, 'switlənd, sweetländ

Sweetman, *f.n.*, 'switmən, sweetmăn

Swefling *Suffolk*, 'sweflɪŋ, swéffling

Swenarton, *f.n.*, 'swenərtən, swénnărtŏn

Swenerton, *f.n.*, 'swenərtən, swénnĕrtŏn

Swetman, *f.n.*, 'swetmən, swétmăn

Swillies Channel *Gwynedd*, 'swɪlɪz, swílliz

Swillington *W. Yorks.*, 'swɪlɪŋtən, swílling-tŏn

Swimbridge, *also spelt* **Swymbridge,** *Devon*, 'swɪmbrɪdʒ, swímbrij

Swimer, *f.n.*, 'swaɪmər, swímĕr

Swinburne, *f.n.*, 'swɪnbərn, swínburn

Swindall, *f.n.*, 'swɪndɔl, swíndawl

Swindell, *f.n.*, 'swɪndel, swíndell

Swindells, *f.n.*, swɪn'delz, swindéllz; 'swɪndlz, swíndlz

Swinderby *Lincs.*, 'swɪndərbɪ, swíndĕrbi

Swindon *Wilts.*, 'swɪndən, swíndŏn

Swine *Humberside*, swaɪn, swīn

Swiney, *f.n.*, 'swaɪnɪ, swíni; 'swɪnɪ, swínni

Swiney *H'land*, 'swɪnɪ, sweéni

Swingler, *f.n.*, 'swɪŋglər, swíng-glĕr

Swinnerton, *f.n.*, 'swɪnərtən, swínnĕrtŏn

Swinnow *W. Yorks.*, 'swɪnou, swínnō

Swire, *f.n.*, 'swaɪər, swīr

Swithin, saint, 'swɪðɪn, swíthin; 'swɪθɪn, swíthin

Swithland *Leics.*, 'swɪðlənd, swíthländ

Switzer, *f.n.*, 'swɪtsər, swítsĕr

Swona, island, *Pentland Firth*, 'swounə, swónă

Sword, *f.n.*, sɔrd, sord

Swordale *W. Isles*, 'sɔrdeɪl, sórdayl

Sworder, *f.n.*, 'sɔrdər, sórdĕr

Swymbridge *see* **Swimbridge**

Swyre *Dorset*, 'swaɪər, swīr

Sycharth *Clwyd*, 'sʌxɑrθ, súch-aarth

Sychdyn *Clwyd*, 'sʌxdɪn, súchdin. *The English form of this name is* **Soughton,** *q.v.*

Sychnant Pass, *Gwynedd*, 'sʌxnənt, súchnănt

Sydee, *f.n.*, 'saɪdɪ, sídee

Sydenham *London, Co. Down.*, 'sɪdənəm, síddĕnăm

Syderstone *Norfolk*, 'saɪdərstoun, sídĕrsstŏn

Sydie, *f.n.*, 'saɪdɪ, sídi

Sydling St. Nicholas *Dorset*, 'sɪdlɪŋ snt 'nɪkələs, síddling sĭnt níckŏlăss

Syers, *f.n.*, 'saɪərz, sí-ĕrz

Syerston *Notts.*, 'saɪərstən, sí-ĕrsstŏn

Syfret, *f.n.*, 'saɪfrɪt, sífrĕt

Sygrove, *f.n.*, 'saɪgrouv, sígrōv

Sykes, *f.n.*, saɪks, sīks

Sylvester, *f.n.*, sɪl'vestər, silvéstĕr

Symbister *Shetland*, 'sɪmbɪstər, símbisstĕr

Syme, *f.n.*, saɪm, sīm
Symene, River, *Dorset*, saɪ'mɪnɪ, sīmeeni
Symes, *f.n.*, saɪmz, sīmz
Symington, *f.n.*, 'saɪmɪŋtən, sīmingtŏn
Symington *S'clyde*, 'saɪmɪŋtən, sīmingtŏn
Symon, *f.n.*, 'saɪmən, sīmŏn
Symonds, *f.n.*, 'sɪməndz, sím-mŏndz; 'saɪməndz, sīmŏndz. *The first is appropriate for John Addington ~, 19th-c. author and translator.*
Symondsbury *Dorset*, 'sɪmənzbərɪ, símmŏnzbŭri
Symond's Yat *H. & W.*, 'sɪməndz 'jæt, símmŏndz yát
Symons, *f.n.*, 'sɪmənz, símmŏnz; 'saɪmənz, sīmŏnz. *The first is that of the authors A. J. A. ~ and Julian ~, and of Arthur ~, poet and critic.*
Synge, *f.n.*, sɪŋ, sing
Syon House *London*, 'saɪən, sī-ŏn
Syrad, *f.n.*, 'saɪəræd, sīrad
Syrett, *f.n.*, 'saɪərɪt, sīrĕt
Syrus, *f.n.*, 'saɪərʊs, sīrŏoss
Sysonby, Baron, 'saɪzənbɪ, sízŏnbi
Syston *Leics.*, 'saɪstən, sísstŏn
Sytchampton *H. & W.*, 'sɪtʃhæmp-tən, sítch-hamptŏn
Sywell *Northants.*, 'saɪwel, sī-wel
Szasz, *f.n.*, sæz, sazz
Szemerey, *f.n.*, 'zemərɪ, zémmĕri
Szerelmey, *f.n.*, sə'relmɪ, sĕrélmi
Szudek, *f.n.*, 'ʃudek, shŏodeck

T

Taaffe, *f.n.*, tæf, taff
Tabberer, *f.n.*, 'tæbərər, tábbĕrĕr
Tabern, *f.n.*, 'tæbərn, tábbĕrn
Taberner, *f.n.*, 'tæbərnər, tábbĕr-nĕr; tə'bərnər, tăbérnĕr
Tabley *Ches.*, 'tæblɪ, tábbli
Tabor, *f.n.*, 'teɪbər, táybor
Tabori, *f.n.*, tə'bɔrɪ, tăbáwri
Tachbrook Mallory *Warwicks.*, 'tætʃbrʊk 'mælərɪ, tátchbrŏok málŏri
Tack, *f.n.*, tæk, tack
Tacolneston *Norfolk*, 'tæklstən, tácklstŏn
Tadcaster *N. Yorks.*, 'tædkæstər, tádkasstĕr
Taf, River, *Dyfed*, tɑv, taav. *The English form is* Taff, *q.v.*
Tafarnau Bach *Gwent*, tə'vɑrnaɪ 'bɑx, tăvaárnī baách

Taff, River, *Dyfed*, tæf, taff. *The Welsh form is* Taf, *q.v.*
Taff, River, *Powys–Mid Glam.– S. Glam.*, tæf, taff
Taffinder, *f.n.*, 'tæfɪndər, táffindĕr
Tagliaferro, *f.n.*, ˌtɑlɪə'ferʊ, taaliăférrŏ
Tahourdin, *f.n.*, 'taʊərdɪn, tówĕr-din
Tailyour, *f.n.*, 'teɪljɔr, táyl-yor
Tain *H'land*, teɪn, tayn
Tainsh, *f.n.*, teɪnʃ, taynsh
Tainton, *f.n.*, 'teɪntən, táyntŏn
Tait, *f.n.*, teɪt, tayt
Takeley *Essex*, 'teɪklɪ, táykli
Talachddu *Powys*, tə'læxðɪ, tălách-thi
Talacre *Clwyd*, tæl'ækreɪ, taláck-ray. *Also appropriate for the Mostyns of ~.*
Talaton *Devon*, 'tælətən, tálătŏn
Talbot, *f.n.*, 'tɔlbət, táwlbŏt; 'tɒlbət, tóllbŏt
Talbut, *f.n.*, 'tɔlbət, táwlbŭt; 'tɒlbət, tóllbŭt
Talerddig *Powys*, tæ'lɛərðɪg, taláirthig
Talfan, *Welsh C.n.*, 'tælvən, tálvän
Talfourd, *f.n.*, 'tælfərd, tálfŏrd
Talfryn, *f.n.*, 'tælvrɪn, tálvrin
Talgarth *Powys*, 'tælgɑrθ, tál-gaarth
Taliesin, *Welsh bardic name*, tæl-'jesɪn, tal-yéssin
Talisker *Skye*, 'tælɪskər, táliskĕr
Talkin *Cumbria*, 'tɔkɪn, táwkin
Talland Bay *Cornwall*, 'tælənd, tálănd
Tallantire *Cumbria*, 'tæləntaɪər, tálăntīr
Talley *Dyfed*, 'tælɪ, táli
Tallington *Lincs.*, 'tælɪŋtən, tálingtŏn
Tallis, Thomas, *16th-c. composer*, 'tælɪs, táliss
Tallon, *f.n.*, 'tælən, tálŏn
Talog, *f.n.*, 'tælɒg, tálog
Talsarnau *Gwynedd*, tæl'sɑrnaɪ, tal-saárnī
Talwrn *Clwyd*, *Gwynedd*, 'tælʊərn, tálŏorn. *Appropriate for both places of the name in Clwyd.*
Talybont *Dyfed*, *Powys*, ˌtælə-'bɒnt, tălăbónt
Tal-y-bont *Gwynedd*, ˌtælə'bɒnt, tălăbónt. *Appropriate for all three places of the name in Gwynedd.*
Tal-y-llyn *Gwynedd*, ˌtælə'ɬɪn, tălă-hlín
Tal-y-sarn *Gwynedd*, ˌtælə'sɑrn, tălă-saárn
Talywaun *Gwent*, ˌtælə'waɪn, tălă-wín

Tamar, River, *Devon–Cornwall*, 'teɪmər, táymăr

Tamerton Foliott *Devon*, 'tæmərtən 'foʊlɪət, támmĕrtŏn fŏliŏt

Tames, *f.n.*, teɪmz, taymz

Tameside *Gtr. M'chester*, 'teɪmsaɪd, táymssīd

Tamsin, *C.n.*, 'tæmzɪn, támzin

Tamsyn, *C.n.*, 'tæmzɪn, támzin

Tamworth *Staffs.*, 'tæmwɜrθ, támwurth; 'tæmərθ, támmŭrth

Tanat, River, *Gwynedd–Powys*, 'tænət, tánnăt

Tancred, *f.n.*, 'tæŋkrɪd, tánkrĕd

Tandragee, *also spelt* Tanderagee, *Co. Armagh*, ,tændrə'gi, tandrăgeé

Tanerdy *Dyfed*, tæn'ɜrdɪ, tannérdi

Tangley *Hants*, 'tæŋlɪ, táng-li

Tangmere *W. Sussex*, 'tæŋmɪər, tángmeer

Tangye, *f.n.*, 'tæŋgɪ, táng-gi

Tanner, *f.n.*, 'tænər, tánnĕr

Tanqueray, *f.n.*, 'tæŋkərɪ, tánkĕri; 'tæŋkəreɪ, tánkĕray

Tansor *Northants.*, 'tænsɔr, tánssor

Tantallon Castle *Lothian*, tæn'tælən, tantálŏn

Tantobie *Durham*, tæn'toʊbɪ, tantóbi

Tan-y-bwlch *Gwynedd*, ,tænə'bʊlx, tannăboŏlch

Tanygrisiau *Gwynedd*, ,tænə'grɪsjaɪ, tannăgríssyī

Tan-y-maes *Gwynedd*, ,tænə'maɪs, tannămíss

Tan-yr-allt *Clwyd*, ,tænər'æɬt, tannăráhlt

Tappenden, *f.n.*, 'tæpəndən, táppĕndĕn

Tapply, *f.n.*, 'tæplɪ, tápli

Tapscott, *f.n.*, 'tæpskɒt, tápskott

Tapsell, *f.n.*, 'tæpsl, tápssl

Tapsfield, *f.n.*, 'tæpsfɪld, tápsfeeld

Tarbat *H'land*, 'tɑrbət, taárbăt. *Appropriate also for Viscount* ~.

Tarbatness *H'land*, 'tɑrbət'nes, taárbătnéss

Tarbolton *S'clyde*, tɑr'boʊltən, taarbŏltŏn

Tarbrax *S'clyde*, tɑr'bræks, taarbrácks

Tardebigge *H. & W.*, 'tɑrdəbɪg, taárdĕbig

Tarenig, River, *Powys*, tə'renɪg, tărénnig

Target, *f.n.*, 'tɑrdʒɪt, taárjĕt

Tarkowski, *f.n.*, tɑr'kɒfskɪ, taarkófski

Tarner, *f.n.*, 'tɑrnər, taárnĕr

Tarporley *Ches.*, 'tɑrpərlɪ, taárpŏrli; 'tɑrplɪ, taárpli

Tarradale *H'land*, 'tærədeɪl, tárrădayl

Tarran, *f.n.*, 'tærən, tárrăn

Tarrant Keynston *Dorset*, 'tærənt 'keɪnstən, tárrănt káynsstŏn

Tarring *W. Sussex*, 'tærɪŋ, tárring

Tarrinzean and Mauchline, Lady, tə'rɪŋən ənd 'mɔxlɪn, tăríng-ăn ănd máwchlin

Tarskavaig *Skye*, 'tɑrskəvɪg, taársskăvig

Tartaraghan *Co. Armagh*, tɑr'tærəhən, taartárrăhăn

Tarves *Grampian*, 'tɑrvɪs, taárvĕss

Tasburgh *Norfolk*, 'teɪzbərə, táyzbŭră

Tasker, *f.n.*, 'tæskər, tásskĕr

Tassagh *Co. Armagh*, 'tæsə, tássă

Tate, *f.n.*, teɪt, tayt. *Appropriate also for the* ~ *Gallery, London.*

Tatem, *f.n.*, 'teɪtəm, táytĕm

Tatenhill *Staffs.*, 'teɪtənhɪl, táytĕnhil

Tatham, *f.n.*, 'teɪθəm, táy-thăm; 'teɪðəm, táy-thăm; 'tætəm, táttăm

Tatham *Lancs.*, 'teɪtəm, táytăm

Tatt, *f.n.*, tæt, tatt

Tattersall, *f.n.*, 'tætərsɔl, táttĕrsawl; 'tætərsl, táttĕrssl

Tattershall *Lincs.*, 'tætərʃl, táttĕr-shl

Tattingstone *Suffolk*, 'tætɪŋstən, táttingstŏn

Taubman, *f.n.*, 'tɔbmən, táwbmăn

Taunton *Somerset*, 'tɔntən, táwntŏn; 'tɑntən, taántŏn

Taupin, *f.n.*, 'tɔpɪn, táwpin

Tausky, Vilem, *conductor*, 'vɪləm 'taʊskɪ, villĕm tówski

Tavaré, *f.n.*, 'tævəreɪ, távvăray

Tavener, *f.n.*, 'tævənər, távvĕnĕr

Taverham *Norfolk*, 'teɪvərəm, táyvĕrăm

Taverne, *f.n.*, tə'vɜrn, tăvérn

Tavy, River, *Devon*, 'teɪvɪ, táyvi

Tawe, River, *Powys–W. Glam.*, 'taʊeɪ, tów-ay

Tawell, *f.n.*, tɔl, tawl; 'tɔəl, táw-ĕl

Tay, Loch *and* River, *Tayside*, teɪ, tay

Tayar, *f.n.*, 'taɪər, tí-ăr

Taylor, *f.n.*, 'teɪlər, táylŏr

Taylor of Gryfe, Baron, 'teɪlər əv 'graɪf, táylŏr ŏv gríf

Taylour, *f.n.*, 'teɪlər, táylŏr

Taynuilt *S'clyde*, teɪ'nʊlt, taynoŏlt

Tayport *Fife*, 'teɪpɔrt, táyport

Tayside, Baron, 'teɪsaɪd, táy-sīd

Teaffe, *f.n.*, tɑf, taaf
Teague, *f.n.*, tig, teeg
Tealby *Lincs.*, 'tilbɪ, téelbi
Tean, River, *Staffs.*, tin, teen.
  Appropriate also for Upper ~
  and Lower ~, Staffs.
Teape, *f.n.*, tip, teep
Tear, *f.n.*, tɪər, teer
Teare, *f.n.*, tɪər, teer
Tearlath, *Gaelic C.n.*, 'tʃɛərləx,
  cháirlách
Tearle, *f.n.*, tɜrl, terl
Teasdale, *f.n.*, 'tizdeɪl, téezdayl
Teastler, *f.n.*, 'tistlər, téestlĕr
Tebay, *f.n.*, tɪ'beɪ, tĕbáy
Tebay *Cumbria*, 'tibɪ, téebi
Tebbit, *f.n.*, 'tebɪt, tébbit
Tebbs, *f.n.*, tebz, tebbz
Tebbutt, *f.n.*, 'tebət, tébbŭt
Tebby, *f.n.*, 'tebɪ, tébbi
Tebworth *Beds.*, 'tebwərθ, téb-
  wŭrth
Tecwyn, *Welsh C.n.*, 'tekwɪn,
  téckwin
Tedburn St. Mary *Devon*, 'ted-
  bɜrn snt 'mɛərɪ, tédburn sĭnt
  máiri
Tedder of Glenguin, Baron,
  'tedər əv glen'gwɪn, téddĕr ŏv
  glen-gwín
Teear, *f.n.*, 'tɪər, tée-ăr
Teed, *f.n.*, tid, teed
Teetgen, *f.n.*, 'tidʒən, téejĕn
Teevan, *f.n.*, 'tivən, téevăn
Tegel, *f.n.*, 'tigl, téegl
Tegetmeier, *f.n.*, 'tegɪtmaɪər,
  téggĕtmīr
Teggin, *f.n.*, 'tegɪn, téggin
Tei, *f.n.*, teɪ, tay
Teich, *f.n.*, taɪk, tīk
Teichman, *f.n.*, 'taɪʃmən, tĭsh-
  măn
Teifi, River, *also spelt* **Teivy,**
  Dyfed, 'taɪvɪ, tívi
Teifion, *Welsh C.n.*, 'taɪvɪən, tívi-
  -ŏn
Teigh *Leics.*, ti, tee
Teign, River, *Devon*, tin, teen; tɪn,
  tin
Teigngrace *Devon*, 'tingreɪs, téen-
  -grayss
Teignmouth *Devon*, 'tɪnməθ,
  tínmŭth; 'tinməθ, téenmŭth.
  The first is appropriate for
  Baron ~.
Teise, River, *Kent*, tiz, teez
Teivy, River, *see* **Teifi**
Teleri, *Welsh C.n.*, tɪ'lerɪ, tĕlérri
Telfer, *f.n.*, 'telfər, télfĕr
Telscombe *E. Sussex*, 'telskəm,
  télsskŏm
Temair *see* **Aberdeen and ~,**
  Marquess of
Temme, *f.n.*, 'temɪ, témmi

Temperton, *f.n.*, 'tempərtən,
  témpĕrtŏn
Temple, *f.n.*, 'templ, témpl
Temple Guiting *Glos.*, 'templ
  'gaɪtɪŋ, témpl gíting
Templepatrick *Co. Antrim*,
  'templ'pætrɪk, témpl-pátrick
Temple Sowerby *Cumbria*,
  'templ 'saʊərbɪ, témpl sówĕrbi;
  'templ 'sɔrbɪ, témpl sórbi
Tenby *Dyfed*, 'tenbɪ, ténbi
Tendeter, *f.n.*, ten'detər, ten-
  déttĕr
Ten Kate, *f.n.*, ten 'kɑtə, ten
  káatĕ
Tenniel, Sir John, *cartoonist*,
  'tenjəl, tén-yĕl
Tennyson, *f.n.*, 'tenɪsən, ténnissŏn
Tennyson Jesse, Fryn, *novelist*,
  'frɪn 'tenɪsən 'dʒes, frín ténnis-
  sŏn jéss
Tenterden *Kent*, 'tentərdən,
  téntĕrdĕn
Ter, River, *Essex*, tɑr, taar
Terally *D. & G.*, tɪ'rælɪ, tĕráli
Tereshchuk, *f.n.*, 'terəʃʊk, térrĕ-
  shŏŏk
Terling *Essex*, 'tɑrlɪŋ, táarling;
  'tɜrlɪŋ, térling
Terraine, *f.n.*, tɪ'reɪn, tĕráyn
Terregles *D. & G.*, tɪ'reglz,
  tĕrégglz
Terrell, *f.n.*, 'terəl, térrĕl
Terrington, *f.n.*, 'terɪŋtən, térring-
  tŏn
Terrot, *f.n.*, 'terət, térrŏt
Terson, *f.n.*, 'tɜrsən, térssŏn
Terry, *f.n.*, 'terɪ, térri
Tertis, *f.n.*, 'tɜrtɪs, tértiss
Terwick *W. Sussex*, 'terɪk, térrick
Tester, *f.n.*, 'testər, tésstĕr
Teston *Kent*, 'tisən, téessŏn
Tettenhall *W. Midlands*, 'tetənhɔl,
  téttĕnhawl
Tetzner, *f.n.*, 'tetsnər, tétsnĕr
Teulon, *f.n.*, 'tjulən, téwlŏn
Teversal *Notts.*, 'tevərsl, tévvĕrssl
Teversham *Cambs.*, 'tevərʃəm,
  tévvĕr-shăm
Teviot, Baron, 'tevɪət, tévvi-ŏt
Teviot, River, *Borders*, 'tivɪət,
  téevi-ŏt
Teviotdale *Borders*, 'tivɪətdeɪl,
  téevi-ŏtdayl
Tewkesbury *Glos.*, 'tjuksbərɪ,
  téwksbŭri
Teynham *Kent*, 'teɪnəm, táynăm;
  'tenəm, ténnăm. *The second is*
  appropriate for Baron ~.
Teyte, Dame **Maggie,** *soprano*
  (1888–1976), 'mægɪ 'teɪt, mággi
  táyt
Thaarup, *f.n.*, 'tɑrʊp, taárŏŏp
Thacker, *f.n.*, 'θækər, tháckĕr

Thackeray, *f.n.*, 'θækərɪ, tháckĕri
Thackley *W. Yorks.*, 'θæklɪ, tháckli
Thackrah, *f.n.*, 'θækrə, tháckră
Thackwray, *f.n.*, 'θækreɪ, tháckray
Thain, *f.n.*, θeɪn, thayn
Thakeham *W. Sussex*, 'θeɪkəm, tháykăm
Thalben-Ball, George, *organist*, 'θælbən 'bɔl, thálbĕn báwl
Thame *Oxon.*, teɪm, taym
Thames, River, *London*, temz, temz
Thanet, Isle of, *Kent*, 'θænɪt, thánnĕt
Thankerton *S'clyde*, 'θæŋkərtən, thánkĕrtŏn
Thatcher, *f.n.*, 'θætʃər, thátchĕr
Thavenot, *f.n.*, 'tævənoʊ, táv-věnō; 'tævənɒt, távvĕnot
Theakstone, *f.n.*, 'θikstoʊn, theékstŏn
Theale *Berks.*, θil, theel
Theiler, *f.n.*, 'taɪlər, tílĕr
Thellusson, *f.n.*, 'teləsən, téllŭssŏn
Thelnetham *Suffolk*, θel'niθəm, thelneéthăm; 'θelnəθəm, thél-nĕthăm
Thelwall *Ches.*, 'θelwɔl, thél-wawl
Themerson, *f.n.*, 'temərsən, témmĕrssŏn
Theobald, *f.n.*, 'θiəbɔld, theé--ŏbawld; 'tɪbəld, tíbbăld. *The second is appropriate for Lewis ~, 17th–18th-c. Shakespearian critic.*
Theobalds Park *Herts.*, 'θiəbɔldz, theé-ŏbawldz
Theobald's Road *London*, 'θiəbɔldz, theé-ŏbawldz; 'tɪbəldz, tíbbăldz
Thesiger, *f.n.*, 'θesɪdʒər, théssijĕr
Theunissen, *f.n.*, 'tenɪsən, ténnis-sĕn
Thevenard, *f.n.*, 'tevənɑrd, tév-věnaard
Thew, *f.n.*, θju, thew
Thewes, *f.n.*, θjuz, thewz
Theydon Bois *Essex*, 'θeɪdən 'bɔɪz, tháydŏn bóyz
Thick, *f.n.*, θɪk, thick
Thicke, *f.n.*, θɪk, thick
Thicknesse, *f.n.*, 'θɪknɪs, thíck-nĕss
Thiebault, *f.n.*, 'θiəbɔlt, theé--ĕbawlt
Thiman, *f.n.*, 'timən, teémän
Thirde, *f.n.*, θɜrd, third
Thirer, *f.n.*, 'θaɪrər, thírĕr
Thirkell, *f.n.*, 'θɜrkl, thírkl
Thirkettle, *f.n.*, 'θɜrketl, thírkettl
Thirsk *N. Yorks.*, θɜrsk, thirsk
Thoday, *f.n.*, 'θoʊdeɪ, thóday
Thody, *f.n.*, 'θoʊdɪ, thódi

Tholthorpe *N. Yorks.*, 'θɔlθɔrp, tháwlthorp; 'tɒlθɔrp, tólthorp
Thom, *f.n.*, tɒm, tom
Thomae, *f.n.*, 'toʊmeɪ, tómay
Thomas, *C.n. and f.n.*, 'tɒməs, tómmăss
Thomas, Dylan, *poet*, 'dɪlən 'tɒməs, díllăn tómmăss. *Although the Welsh pronunciation is more nearly* 'dʌlən, *dúllăn, the poet himself recommended the anglicized pronunciation of his Christian name.*
Thomason, *f.n.*, 'tɒməsən, tóm-măssŏn
Thompson, *f.n.*, 'tɒmsən, tómssŏn; 'tɒmpsən, tómpssŏn
Thomson, *f.n.*, 'tɒmsən, tómssŏn
Thomson of Monifieth, Baron, 'tɒmsən əv ˌmʌnɪ'fiθ, tómssŏn ŏv munnifeéth
Thonger, *f.n.*, 'θɒŋər, thóng-ĕr; 'θɒŋgər, thóng-gĕr
Thonock *Lincs.*, 'θɒnək, thónnŏk
Thorburn, *f.n.*, 'θɔrbɜrn, thórburn
Thorby, *f.n.*, 'θɔrbɪ, thórbi
Thoresby *Notts.*, 'θɔrzbɪ, thórzbi
Thorley, *f.n.*, 'θɔrlɪ, thórli
Thorn, *f.n.*, θɔrn, thorn
Thornaby-on-Tees *N. Yorks.*, 'θɔrnəbɪ ɒn 'tiz, thórnăbi-on--teéz
Thorndike, *f.n.*, 'θɔrndaɪk, thórn-dík
Thorne, *f.n.*, θɔrn, thorn
Thorne *S. Yorks.*, θɔrn, thorn
Thorne Gyme *S. Yorks.*, 'θɔrn 'gaɪm, thórn gím
Thorneloe, *f.n.*, 'θɔrnɪloʊ, thórnĕlō
Thorness *I. of Wight*, θɔr'nes, thornéss
Thorngumbald *Humberside*, 'θɔrŋgəmbɔld, thórng-gŭm-bawld
Thornham *Norfolk*, 'θɔrnəm, thórnăm
Thornham Magna *Suffolk*, 'θɔrnəm 'mægnə, thórnăm mágnă
Thornham Parva *Suffolk*, 'θɔrnəm 'pɑrvə, thórnăm paárvă
Thornhaugh *Cambs.*, 'θɔrnhɔ, thórn-haw
Thornhill, *f.n.*, 'θɔrnhɪl, thórn-hil
Thorning, *f.n.*, 'θɔrnɪŋ, thórning
Thornley, *f.n.*, 'θɔrnlɪ, thórnli
Thornliebank *S'clyde*, 'θɔrnlɪ-ˈbæŋk, thórnlibánk
Thornton, *f.n.*, 'θɔrntən, thórntŏn
Thornton Heath *London*, 'θɔrntən 'hiθ, thórntŏn heéth
Thornton Hough *Merseyside*, 'θɔrntən 'hʌf, thórntŏn húff

Thorogood, *f.n.*, 'θʌrəgʊd, thúrrŏ-gōŏd

Thorold, *C.n. and f.n.*, 'θɒrəld, thórrŏld; 'θʌrəld, thúrrŏld; 'θɒrоʊld,thórrŏld. *The first is appropriate for ~ Dickinson, film director.*

Thorp, *f.n.*, θɔrp, thorp

Thorpe Davie, Cedric, *composer*, 'sedrɪk 'θɔrp 'deɪvɪ, sédrick thórp dáyvi

Thorpe-le-Soken *Essex*, 'θɔrp lə 'soʊkən, thórp lĕ sŏkĕn

Thorpe Morieux *Suffolk*, 'θɔrp mə'ru, thórp mŏroó

Thorrington *Essex*, 'θɒrɪŋtən, thórringtŏn

Thouless, *f.n.*, 'θaʊles, thówless

Thousell, *f.n.*, 'θaʊsl, thówssl

Thovez, *f.n.*, 'θoʊvɪz, thŏvĕz

Thow, *f.n.*, θaʊ, thow

Threapland *Cumbria*, 'θrɪplənd, threépländ

Threave Castle *D. & G.*, θriv, threev

Threekingham *Lincs.*, 'θrekɪŋəm, thrécking-äm

Threlfall, *f.n.*, 'θrelfɔl, thrélfawl

Threlkeld *Cumbria*, 'θrelkeld, thrélkeld

Thriplow, *also spelt* **Triplow,** *Cambs.*, 'trɪploʊ, tríplō. **Triplow** *is the ecclesiastical spelling.*

Thripp, *f.n.*, θrɪp, thripp

Throapham *S. Yorks.*, 'θroʊpəm, thrŏpäm

Througham *Glos.*, 'θrʌfəm, thrúf-fäm

Throwley *Kent*, 'θraʊlɪ, thrówli

Thrupp, *f.n.*, θrʌp, thrupp

Thrybergh *S. Yorks.*, 'θraɪbər, thríbĕr; 'θraɪbərə, thríbĕrä

Thubron, *f.n.*, 'θjubrən, théwbrŏn

Thuillier, *f.n.*, 'twɪljər, twill-yĕr

Thurgarton *Norfolk, Notts.*, 'θɜrgərtən, thúrgărtŏn

Thurgoland *S. Yorks.*, 'θɜrgoʊlænd, thúrgōland

Thurgood, *f.n.*, 'θɜrgʊd, thúrgŏŏd

Thurleigh *Beds.*, θɜr'laɪ, thur-lí

Thurley, *f.n.*, 'θɜrlɪ, thúrli

Thurling, *f.n.*, 'θɜrlɪŋ, thúrling

Thurloxton *Somerset*, θɜr'lɒkstən, thurlóckstŏn

Thurmaston *Leics.*, 'θɜrməstən, thúrmässtŏn

Thurne *Norfolk*, θɜrn, thurn

Thurnham *Kent*, 'θɜrnəm, thúrn-äm

Thurnscoe *S. Yorks.*, 'θɜrnzkoʊ, thúrnzkŏ

Thurso *H'land*, 'θɜrsoʊ, thúrssō. *Appropriate also for Viscount ~.*

Thurston, *f.n.*, 'θɜrstən, thúrsstŏn

Thurstonfield *Cumbria*, 'θrʌstən-fild, thrússtŏnfeeld

Thwing *Humberside*, twɪŋ, twing; θwɪŋ, thwing

Thynne, *f.n.*, θɪn, thin

Tiarks, *f.n.*, 'tiɑrks, teé-aarks

Tibbermore *Tayside*, ‚tɪbər'mɔr, tibbĕrmór

Tibenham *Norfolk*, 'tɪbənəm, tíbbĕnäm

Ticciati, *f.n.*, tɪ'tʃɑtɪ, titcháati

Tice, *f.n.*, taɪs, tīss

Ticehurst, *f.n.*, 'taɪshərst, tíss-hurst

Tichborne *Hants*, 'tɪtʃbɔrn, títchborn

Tichelar, *f.n.*, 'tɪtʃələr, títchĕlaar

Ticher, *f.n.*, 'tɪtʃər, títchĕr

Tickell, *f.n.*, tɪ'kel, tickéll

Tickhill *S. Yorks.*, 'tɪkhɪl, tíckhil

Tickle, *f.n.*, 'tɪkl, tíckl

Ticknall *Derby.*, 'tɪknəl, tícknäl

Ticktum, *f.n.*, 'tɪktəm, tícktŭm

Tidball, *f.n.*, 'tɪdbɔl, tídbawl

Tideford *Cornwall*, 'tɪdɪfərd, tíddĕförd

Tidenham *Glos.*, 'tɪdənəm, tíddĕnäm

Tideswell *Derby.*, 'taɪdzwel, tídzwel; 'tɪdzl, tíddzl

Tidmarsh, *f.n.*, 'tɪdmɑrʃ, tídmaarsh

Tiernan, *f.n.*, 'tɪərnən, teérnän

Tierney, *f.n.*, 'tɪərnɪ, teérni

Tietjen, *f.n.*, 'titʃən, teétchĕn

Tievebulliagh *Co. Antrim*, tiv-'bʊljə, teev-bŏŏl-yä

Tievenagh *Co. Tyrone*, 'tivənə, teévĕnä

Tiffin, *f.n.*, 'tɪfɪn, tíffin

Tigar, *f.n.*, 'taɪgər, tígär

Tighe, *f.n.*, taɪ, tī

Tighnabruaich *S'clyde*, ‚taɪnə-'bruəx, tīnăbroó-ă*ch*; ‚tɪnə-'bruəx, tinnăbroó-á*ch*

Tilbe, *f.n.*, 'tɪlbɪ, tílbi

Tilbury, *f.n.*, 'tɪlbərɪ, tílbŭri

Tilbury *Essex*, 'tɪlbərɪ, tílbŭri

Tiley, *f.n.*, 'taɪlɪ, tíli

Tiller, *f.n.*, 'tɪlər, tíllĕr

Tillett, *f.n.*, 'tɪlɪt, tíllĕt

Tilley, *f.n.*, 'tɪlɪ, tílli

Tillicoultry *Central*, ‚tɪlɪ'kutrɪ, tillikoótri

Tilling, *f.n.*, 'tɪlɪŋ, tílling

Tillyard, *f.n.*, 'tɪljɑrd, tíll-yaard

Tillysburn *Co. Antrim*, ‚tɪlɪz'bɜrn, tillizbúrn

Tilmanstone *Kent*, 'tɪlmənstoʊn, tílmänsstŏn

Tilshead *Wilts.*, 'tɪlzhed, tíllz-hed

Timberscombe *Somerset*, 'tɪm-bərzkum, tímbĕrzkoom

Timewell, *f.n.*, 'taɪmwəl, tímwĕl
Timmins, *f.n.*, 'tɪmɪnz, tímminz
Timpson, *f.n.*, 'tɪmpsən, tímpssŏn
Tinbergen, *f.n.*, 'tɪnbɜrgən, tín-
bergĕn
Tindall, *f.n.*, 'tɪndl, tínndl; 'tɪndɔl,
tíndawl
Tindell, *f.n.*, 'tɪndel, tĭndel; 'tɪndl,
tínndl
Tinegate, *f.n.*, 'taɪngeɪt, tín-gayt
Tingay, *f.n.*, 'tɪŋgeɪ, tíng-gay
Tingewick *Bucks.*, 'tɪndʒwɪk,
tínjwick
Tingey, *f.n.*, 'tɪŋgɪ, tíng-gi
Tingrith *Beds.*, 'tɪŋgrɪθ, tíng-
-grith
Tingwall *Shetland*, 'tɪŋwəl, tíng-
-wăl
Tinhay *Devon*, 'tɪnheɪ, tín-hay
Tink, *f.n.*, 'tɪŋk, tink
Tinne, *f.n.*, 'tɪnɪ, tínni
Tintagel *Cornwall*, tɪn'tædʒl,
tintájjl
Tintern Abbey *Gwent*, 'tɪntərn,
tíntĕrn
Tintern Parva *Gwent*, 'tɪntərn
'pɑrvə, tíntĕrn paárvă
Tinwald *D. & G.*, 'tɪnl, tínnl
Tiplady, *f.n.*, 'tɪpleɪdɪ, típlaydi
Tippett, *f.n.*, 'tɪpɪt, típpĕt. *Appro-
priate for Sir Michael* ∼,
composer.
Tipping, *f.n.*, 'tɪpɪŋ, típping
Tipton St. John *Devon*, 'tɪptən snt
'dʒɒn, típtŏn sĭnt jón
Tirabad *Powys*, tɪər'æbæd, teeráb-
bad
Tirbutt, *f.n.*, 'tɜrbət, tírbŭt
Tirebuck, *f.n.*, 'taɪərbʌk, tírbuck
Tiree, *also spelt* **Tyree,** *S'clyde*,
taɪ'ri, tī-rée
Tirpentwys *Gwent*, tɪər'pentʊɪs,
teerpéntōo-iss
Tir-phil *Mid Glam.*, tɪər'fɪl, teer-
-fíll
Tir-y-berth *Mid Glam.*, ˌtɪrə-
'bɛərθ, tirrăbáirth
Tir-y-dail *Dyfed*, ˌtɪərə'daɪl, teeră-
díl
Tisi, *f.n.*, 'tɪzɪ, téezi
Tissot, James, *Anglo-French
painter, 1836–1902*, 'tisoʊ,
téessō
Tithby, *also spelt* **Tythby,** *Notts.*,
'tɪðbɪ, títhbi
Titheradge, *f.n.*, 'tɪðərɪdʒ, títhĕrij
Titley *H. & W.*, 'tɪtlɪ, títli
Titmus, *f.n.*, 'tɪtməs, títmŭss
Titshall, *f.n.*, 'tɪtsl, títtsl
Tittensor *Staffs.*, 'tɪtənsər, títtĕns-
sŏr
Tittleshall *Norfolk*, 'tɪtlʃɔl, títtl-
-shawl
Titus, *f.n.*, 'taɪtəs, títŭss

Tiumpan Head *W. Isles*, 'tjʊmpən,
tyōompăn
Tiverton *Devon*, 'tɪvərtən, tívvĕr-
tŏn
Tivetshall *Norfolk*, 'tɪvɪtshɔl,
tívvĕts-hawl
Tividale *W. Midlands*, 'tɪvɪdeɪl,
tívvidayl
Tixall *Staffs.*, 'tɪksɔl, tícksawl
Tizard, *f.n.*, 'tɪzɑrd, tízzaard;
'tɪzərd, tízzärd
Tjaden, *f.n.*, 'tʃɑdən, chaáděn
Tobermore *Co. Derry*, ˌtʌbər'mɔr,
tubbĕrmór
Tobermory *S'clyde*, ˌtoʊbər'mɔrɪ,
tōbĕrmáwri
Tobias, *f.n.*, tə'baɪəs, tōbí-ăss
Tobin, *f.n.*, 'toʊbɪn, tóbin
Toch, *f.n.*, tɒk, tock; tɒʃ, tosh
Tocher, *f.n.*, 'tɒxər, tóchĕr
Tockholes *Lancs.*, 'tɒkhoʊlz,
tóckhōlz
Tockwith *N. Yorks.*, 'tɒkwɪθ,
tóckwith
Todd, *f.n.*, tɒd, todd
Todds, *f.n.*, tɒdz, toddz
Todmorden *W. Yorks.*, 'tɒdmər-
dən, tódmŏrdĕn; 'tɒdmɔrdən,
tódmordĕn
Toghill, *f.n.*, 'tɒghɪl, tóg-hil
Toker, *f.n.*, 'toʊkər, tókĕr
Tokyngton *London*, 'toʊkɪŋtən,
tókingtŏn
Tolcarne *Cornwall*, tɒl'kɑrn, tol-
kaárn
Tolgullow *Cornwall*, tɒl'gʌloʊ,
tolgúllō
Tolkien, J. R. R., *author and
scholar*, 'tɒlkin, tólkeen
Toll, *f.n.*, tɒl, tol
Tolladay, *f.n.*, 'tɒlədeɪ, tóllăday
Tollady, *f.n.*, 'tɒlədɪ, tóllădi
Tollemache, *f.n.*, 'tɒlmæʃ, tól-
mash; 'tɒlmɑʃ, tólmaash. *The
first is appropriate for Baron* ∼.
Tollerton, *f.n.*, 'tɒlərtən, tóllĕrtŏn
Tollerton *Notts., N. Yorks.*,
'tɒlərtən, tóllĕrtŏn
Tollesbury *Essex*, 'toʊlzbərɪ, tólz-
bŭri
Tollesby *Cleveland*, 'toʊlzbɪ,
tólzbi
Tolleshunt d'Arcy *Essex*, 'toʊlz-
hʌnt 'dɑrsɪ, tólz-hunt daárssi
Tolleshunt Knights *Essex*, 'toʊlz-
hʌnt 'naɪts, tólz-hunt níts
Tolleshunt Major *Essex*, 'toʊlz-
hʌnt 'meɪdʒər, tólz-hunt
máyjŏr
Tol-Pedn-Penwith *Cornwall*,
tɒl'pednpen'wɪθ, tolpéddn-
-penwíth
Tolpuddle *Dorset*, 'tɒlpʌdl, tól-
puddl; 'tɒlpɪdl, tólpíddl

Tolskithy *Cornwall*, tɒl'skıθı, tolsskíthi
Tolt Hill *I. of Wight*, tɔt, tawt
Tolworth *London*, 'tɒlwərθ, tól-wŭrth; 'toʊlwərθ, tólwŭrth
Tomalin, *f.n.*, 'tɒməlın, tómmălin
Toman, *f.n.*, 'toʊmən, tőmăn
Tomatin *H'land*, tə'mætın, tŏmát-tin
Tombs, *f.n.*, tumz, toomz
Tombstone, *f.n.*, 'tumstoʊn, toʻomstŏn
Tomelty, *f.n.*, 'tɒmltı, tómmlti
Tomes, *f.n.*, toʊmz, tōmz
Tomich *H'land*, 'tɒmıx, tómmich
Tominey, *f.n.*, 'tɒmını, tómmini
Tomintoul *Grampian*, ˌtɒmın'taʊl, tommintówl
Tomlinson, *f.n.*, 'tɒmlınsən, tómlinssŏn
Tomnahurich *H'land*, ˌtɒmnə-'hʊərıx, tomnă-hőőrich
Tomnavoulin *Grampian*, ˌtɒmnə-'vulın, tomnăvoʻolin
Tomney, *f.n.*, 'tɒmnı, tómni
Tompion, Thomas, *17th-c. clock--maker*, 'tɒmpıən, tómpi-ŏn
Toms, *f.n.*, 'tɒmz, tommz
Tonbridge *Kent*, 'tʌnbrıdʒ, túnbrij
Ton-du *Mid Glam.*, tɒn'dı, tondeé
Tone, River, *Somerset*, toʊn, tōn
Toner, *f.n.*, 'toʊnər, tőněr
Tonfanau *Gwynedd*, tɒn'vænaı, tonvánnī
Tong, *f.n.*, tɒŋ, tong
Tonge, *f.n.*, tɒŋ, tong; tɒndʒ, tonj; tʌŋ, tung
Tonge *Kent*, *Gtr. M'chester*, tɒŋ, tong
Tonge-cum-Breightmet *Gtr. M'chester*, 'tɒŋ kʌm 'breıtmət, tóng kum bráytmět; 'tɒŋ kʌm 'braıtmət, tóng kum brítmět
Tonge Fold *Gtr. M'chester*, 'tɒŋ 'foʊld, tóng főld
Tongland, *also spelt* **Tongueland**, *D. & G.*, 'tʌŋlənd, túng-lănd
Tongue, *f.n.*, tʌŋ, tung
Tongue *H'land*, tʌŋ, tung
Tongueland *see* **Tongland**
Tongwynlais *S. Glam.*, tɒn'gwın-laıs, ton-gwín-liss
Tonmawr *W. Glam.*, 'tɒnmaʊər, tónmowr
Tonna *W. Glam.*, 'tɒnə, tónnă
Tonpentre *Mid Glam.*, tɒn'pentreı, tonpéntray
Tonwell *Herts.*, 'tʌnl, túnnl
Tonypandy *Mid Glam.*, ˌtɒnə-'pændı, tonnăpándi
Tonyrefail *Mid Glam.*, ˌtɒnə-'revaıl, tonnărévvīl
Tonysguboriau *Mid Glam.*, ˌtɒnəskı'bɒrıaı, tonnŭskibórri-ī

Toobe, *f.n.*, 'tubi, toʻobee
Tooher, *f.n.*, 'tuər, toʻo-ĕr
Toombs, *f.n.*, tumz, toomz
Toomebridge *Co. Antrim*, tum-'brıdʒ, toom-bríj
Toop, *f.n.*, tup, toop
Toot Baldon *Oxon.*, 'tut 'bɔldən, toʻot báwldŏn
Tooth, *f.n.*, tuθ, tooth
Toothill, *f.n.*, 'tuthıl, toʻot-hil
Tooting Graveney *London*, 'tutıŋ 'greıvnı, toʻoting gráyv-ni
Toovey, *f.n.*, 'tuvı, toʻovi
Topliss, *f.n.*, 'tɒplıs, tópliss
Topolski, *f.n.*, tə'pɒlskı, tŏpólski
Toppesfield *Essex*, 'tɒpısfıld, tóppĕssfeeld; 'tɒpsfıld, tóps-feeld
Topping, *f.n.*, 'tɒpıŋ, tópping
Topsham *Devon*, 'tɒpsəm, tóps-săm; 'tɒpʃəm, tóp-shăm
Tor Achilty *H'land*, 'tɔr 'æxıltı, tór áchilti
Tordoff, *f.n.*, 'tɔrdɒf, tórdoff
Torell, *f.n.*, 'tɒrəl, tórrĕl
Torksey *Lincs.*, 'tɔrksı, tórksi
Torlesse, *f.n.*, 'tɔrləs, tórlĕss
Torley, *f.n.*, 'tɔrlı, tórli
Tormarton *Avon*, 'tɔrmɑrtən, tór-maartŏn
Tormore *S'clyde*, tɔr'mɔr, tormór
Torness *Lothian*, tɔr'nes, tornéss
Torney, *f.n.*, 'tɔrnı, tórni
Torosay *Mull*, 'tɒrəseı, tórrŏssay
Torpantau *Powys*, tɔr'pæntaı, tor-pántī
Torpenhow *Cumbria*, trı'penə, tripénnă; 'tɔrpənhaʊ, tórpĕn--how
Torphichen *Lothian*, tɔr'fıxən, torfíchĕn. *Appropriate also for Baron ~.*
Torphins *Grampian*, tɔr'fınz, tor-fínz
Torpoint *Cornwall*, tɔr'pɔınt, torpóynt
Torquay *Devon*, tɔr'ki, torkeé
Torquil, *C.n.*, 'tɔrkwıl, tórkwil
Torrance, *f.n.*, 'tɒrəns, tórrănss
Torrens, *f.n.*, 'tɒrənz, tórrĕnz
Torrie, *f.n.*, 'tɒrı, tórri
Torthorwald *D. & G.*, tər'θɒrəld, tŏr-thórrăld; tər'θɒrwəld, tŏr--thórwăld
Torvill, *f.n.*, 'tɔrvıl, tórvil
Torwoodlee *Borders*, ˌtɔrwʊd'li, torwŏŏdleé
Tory, *f.n.*, 'tɒrı, táwri
Toseland, *f.n.*, 'toʊzılənd, tőzĕ-lănd
Toseland *Cambs.*, 'toʊzlənd, tőzlănd
Tosh, *f.n.*, tɒʃ, tosh
Tossell, *f.n.*, 'tɒsl, tóssl

Tosside *Lancs.–N. Yorks. border*,
'tɒsaɪd, tóssíd; 'tɒsɪd, tóssid;
'tɒsɪt, tóssit

Totham, Great *and* Little, *Essex*,
'tɒtəm, tóttăm

Tothill, *f.n.*, 'tɒthɪl, tótt-hil; 'tɒtɪl,
tóttil

Totley *S. Yorks.*, 'tɒtlɪ, tóttli

Totnes *Devon*, 'tɒtnɪs, tótnĕss

Toton *Notts.*, 'tɒutən, tŏtŏn

Tottenham *London*, 'tɒtənəm,
tóttĕnăm

Totternhoe *Beds.*, 'tɒtərnhoʊ,
tóttĕrnhō

Tottman, *f.n.*, 'tɒtmən, tóttmăn

Totton *Hants*, 'tɒtən, tóttŏn

Touch, *f.n.*, taʊtʃ, towtch

Touch *Fife*, tux, tooch

Touche, *f.n.*, tuʃ, toosh

Touchet, *f.n.*, 'tʌtʃɪt, tútchĕt

Tough, *f.n.*, tux, tooch; tʌf, tuff

Tough *Grampian*, tux, tooch

Touhey, *f.n.*, 'tuɪ, tóo-i

Toulmin, *f.n.*, 'tulmɪn, toolmin

Toulson, *f.n.*, 'tulsən, toolssŏn

Toulston *N. Yorks.*, 'toulstən,
tŏlsstŏn

Tourle, *f.n.*, tɜrl, turl; tuərl, toōrl

Tourneur, Turnour *or* **Turner**,
Cyril, *16th–17th-c. dramatist*,
'tɜrnər, túrnĕr

Tours, *f.n.*, tuərz, toōrz

Tourtel, *f.n.*, tɔr'tel, tortéll

Tovell, *f.n.*, 'touvl, tŏvl

Tovey, *f.n.*, 'touvi, tŏvi; 'tʌvɪ,
túvvi. *The first is appropriate
for Sir Donald Francis ~,
writer on music; the second
for Baron ~, Admiral of the
Fleet.*

Tovil *Kent*, 'tɒvɪl, tóvvil; 'tɒvl,
tóvvl

Toward Point *S'clyde*, 'tauərd,
tów-ărd

Towb, *f.n.*, taub, towb

Towcester *Northants.*, 'toustər,
tŏsstĕr

Towednack *Cornwall*, tə'wednək,
tŏ-wédnăk

Towell, *f.n.*, 'tauəl, tówĕl

Towers, *f.n.*, 'tauərz, tówĕrz

Towgood, *f.n.*, 'tougud, tŏgoōd

Tow Law *Durham*, 'tau 'lɔ, tów
láw

Towle, *f.n.*, toul, tōl

Towler, *f.n.*, 'taulər, tówlĕr

Towndrow, *f.n.*, 'taundrou,
tówndrō

Townend, *f.n.*, 'taunend, tównend

Townsend, *f.n.*, 'taunzend, tównzend

Townsend Thoresen Car Ferries
Ltd. G.B., 'taunzend 'tɒrəsən,
tównzend tórrĕssĕn

Townshend, *f.n.*, 'taunzend,
tównzend. *Appropriate also for
Marquess ~.*

Townshend *Cornwall*, 'taunz'end,
tównz-énd

Townson, *f.n.*, 'taunsən, tównssŏn

Towse, *f.n.*, tauz, towz

Towy, River, *Dyfed*, 'tauɪ, tówi

Towyn, *C.n.*, 'touɪn, tŏ-in

Towyn *Clwyd*, 'tauɪn, tów-in

Toxteth *Merseyside*, 'tɒkstəθ,
tóckstĕth

Toynbee, *f.n.*, 'tɔɪnbɪ, tóynbi

Toyne, *f.n.*, tɔɪn, toyn

Trabichoff, *f.n.*, 'træbɪtʃɒf, trábbi-
tchoff

Tracey, *f.n.*, 'treɪsɪ, tráyssi

Tradescant, *f.n.*, trə'deskənt,
trădésskănt. *Appropriate for
John ~, naturalist (1608–62),
and hence for ~ Gardens,
Lambeth.*

Trafalgar, Viscount, trə'fælgər,
trăfálgăr. *The sixth Earl Nelson
advocated this pronunciation
although mentioning that previous holders of the title had
preferred* ˌtræfl'gɑr, trafflgaʹar

Trafalgar House *nr. Salisbury*,
ˌtræfl'gɑr, trafflgaʹar; trə'fælgər,
trăfálgăr

Traherne, *f.n.*, trə'hɜrn, tră-hérn

Trallong *Powys*, 'træɫɒŋ, tráhlong

Trampleasure, *f.n.*, 'træmpleʒər,
trám-plezhĕr

Train, *f.n.*, treɪn, trayn

Tranchell, *f.n.*, 'træŋkl, tránkl;
'træntʃel, trántchel

Tranent *Lothian*, trə'nent, trănént

Tranmire of Upsall, Baron, 'træn-
maɪər əv 'ʌpsl, tránmïr ŏv úpssl

Trant, *f.n.*, trænt, trannt

Tranter, *f.n.*, 'træntər, tránntĕr

Traprain, Viscount, trə'preɪn,
trăpráyn

Traquair, *f.n.*, trə'kweər, trăkwáir

Traquair *Borders*, trə'kweər, trăkwáir

Trathen, *f.n.*, 'treɪθən, tráythĕn

Travers, *f.n.*, 'trævərz, trávvĕrz

Traverse, *f.n.*, 'trævərs, trávvĕrss

Traversi, *f.n.*, trə'vɜrsɪ, trăvérssi

Travess, *f.n.*, trə'ves, trăvéss

Travis, *f.n.*, 'trævɪs, trávviss

Trawscoed *Dyfed*, 'trauskɔɪd,
trówsskoyd

Trawsfynydd *Gwynedd*, traus-
'vʌnɪð, trowssvúnnith

Traynor, *f.n.*, 'treɪnər, tráynŏr

Treacher, *f.n.*, 'tritʃər, trèetchĕr

Treacy, *f.n.*, 'treɪsɪ, tráyssi

Treadwell, *f.n.*, 'tredwəl, trédwĕl

Trealaw *Mid Glam.*, trɪ'ælau,
tri-álow

Treales *Lancs.*, treɪlz, traylz
Trearddur Bay *Gwynedd*, treɪ-
  'arðɪər 'beɪ, tray-aárt͟heer báy
Trease, *f.n.*, triz, treez
Trebanos *W. Glam.*, trɪ'bænɒs,
  trĕbánnoss
Trebarwith *Cornwall*, trɪ'bɑrwɪθ,
  trĕbaárwith
Trebble, *f.n.*, 'trebl, trébbl
Trebehor *Cornwall*, trɪ'bɪər, trĕ-
  beér
Trebey, *f.n.*, 'trɪbɪ, treébi
Trebilcock, *f.n.*, trɪ'bɪlkoʊ, trĕ-
  bílkŏ; trɪ'bɪlkɒk, trĕbílkock
Trebullet *Cornwall*, trɪ'bʊlɪt,
  trĕboōlĕt
Trebursye *Cornwall*, trɪ'bɜrzɪ,
  trĕbúrzi
Trecastle *Powys*, trɪ'kæsl, trĕ-
  kássl
Tredegar *Gwent*, trɪ'dɪgər, trĕ-
  deégăr
Tredell, *f.n.*, trɪ'del, trĕdéll
Tredennick, *f.n.*, trɪ'denɪk, trĕ-
  dénnick
Tredree, *f.n.*, 'tredri, trédree
Tree, *f.n.*, tri, tree
Trefdraeth, *also spelt* **Trevdraeth**,
  Dyfed, 'trevdraɪθ, trévdrīth
Trefeglwys *Powys*, trɪv'eglʊɪs,
  trĕvégloō-iss
Trefgarne, Baron, 'trefgɑrn,
  tréffgaarn
Trefilan *Dyfed*, trɪv'ilæn, trĕveé-
  lan
Tre-fin *see* **Trevine**
Trefnant *Clwyd*, 'trevnænt, trév-
  nant
Trefonen *Salop*, trɪ'vɒnɪn, trĕ-
  vónnĕn
Trefor, *Welsh C.n.*, 'trevər, trévvŏr
Treforest *Mid Glam.*, trɪ'fɒrɪst,
  trĕfórrĕst
Trefriw *Gwynedd*, 'trevrɪu,
  trévri-oo
Trefusis, *f.n.*, trɪ'fjusɪs, trĕféwssiss
Tregadillett *Cornwall*, ˌtregə'dɪlɪt,
  treggădíllĕt
Tregaminian *Cornwall*, ˌtregə-
  'mɪnɪən, treggămínni-ăn
Treganthe *Cornwall*, trɪ'gænθɪ,
  trĕgánthi
Tregare *Gwent*, trɪ'gɛər, trĕgáir
Tregaron *Dyfed*, trɪ'gærən, trĕ-
  gárrŏn
Tregavethan *Cornwall*, ˌtregə-
  'veθən, treggăvéthăn
Tregear, *f.n.*, trɪ'gɪər, trĕgeér
Tregellas, *f.n.*, trɪ'geləs, trĕgélläss
Tregelles, *f.n.*, trɪ'gelɪs, trĕgéllĕss
Tregenza, *f.n.*, trɪ'genzə, trĕgénză
Tregeseal *Cornwall*, ˌtregə'sɪəl,
  treggĕsseé-ăl; ˌtregə'sil, treggĕs-
  seél

Treglown, *f.n.*, trɪ'gloʊn, trĕglŏn;
  trɪ'gloʊn, treeglŏn
Tregolls *Cornwall*, trɪ'gɒlz, trĕ-
  góllz
Tregonetha *Cornwall*, ˌtregə'neθə,
  treggŏnéthă
Tregoning, *f.n.*, trɪ'gɒnɪŋ, trĕgón-
  ning
Tregony *Cornwall*, 'tregənɪ, trég-
  gŏni
Tregrehan *Cornwall*, tre'greɪn,
  tregráyn
Tregurrian *Cornwall*, trɪ'gʌrɪən,
  trĕgúrri-ăn
Tregynon *Powys*, trɪ'gʌnən, trĕ-
  gúnnŏn
Trehafod *Mid Glam.*, trɪ'hævəd,
  trĕ-hávvŏd
Trehane, *f.n.*, trɪ'heɪn, trĕháyn
Treharris *Mid Glam.*, trɪ'hærɪs,
  trĕ-hárriss
Trehearne, *f.n.*, trɪ'hɜrn, trĕ-hérn
Treherbert *Mid Glam.*, trɪ'hɜrbərt,
  trĕ-hérbĕrt
Treig, Loch *and* River, *H'land*,
  trig, treeg
Treitel, *f.n.*, 'traɪtl, trítl
Trekenner *Cornwall*, trɪ'kenər,
  trĕkénnĕr
Trelawney, *f.n.*, trɪ'lɔnɪ, trĕláwni
Trelawny, *f.n.*, trɪ'lɔnɪ, trĕláwni
Trelawnyd *Clwyd*, trɪ'laʊnɪd,
  trĕlównid
Trelease, *f.n.*, trɪ'lis, trĕleéss
Treleaven, *f.n.*, trɪ'levən, trĕ-
  lévvĕn
Tre-lech a'r Betws *Dyfed*, trɪ'leɪx
  ɑr 'betʊs, trĕláych aar béttooss
Treleigh *Cornwall*, trɪ'leɪ, trĕláy
Trelewis *Mid Glam.*, trɪ'luɪs,
  trĕloó-iss; trɪ'ljuɪs, trĕléw-iss
Treligga *Cornwall*, trɪ'lɪgə, trĕ-
  líggă
Treliving, *f.n.*, trɪ'lɪvɪŋ, trĕlívving
Trelleck *Gwent*, 'trelek, trélleck
Treloar, *f.n.*, trɪ'lɔr, trĕlór
Treluggan *Cornwall*, trɪ'lʌgən,
  trĕlúggăn
Tremain, *f.n.*, trɪ'meɪn, trĕmáyn
Trematon *Cornwall*, 'tremətən,
  trémmătŏn
Tremeer, *f.n.*, trɪ'mɪər, trĕmeér
Tremeirchion *Clwyd*, trɪ-
  'maɪərxɪɒn, trĕmírchi-on
Tremenheere, *f.n.*, 'tremənhɪər,
  trémmĕnheer
Tremethick, *f.n.*, trə'meθɪk,
  trĕméthick
Tremills, *f.n.*, 'tremlz, trémmlz
Tremlett, *f.n.*, 'tremlɪt, trémlĕt
Trenaman, *f.n.*, trɪ'nɑmən, trĕ-
  naámăn
Trenance *Cornwall*, trɪ'næns,
  trĕnánss

Trenant *Cornwall*, trı'nænt, trĕ-nánt

Trenchard, Viscount, 'trenʃərd, trén-shărd

Trencrom Hill *Cornwall*, tren-'krɒm, tren-krómm

Treneglos *Cornwall*, trı'neglɒs, trĕnégloss

Trengrouse, *f.n.*, 'trengrouz, tréng-grōz

Trengwainton *Cornwall*, trən-'gweıntən, trĕn-gwáyntŏn

Trenowth *Cornwall*, trı'nauθ, trĕnówth

Trent, River, *Staffs.–Derby.– –Notts.–Humberside*, trent, trent

Trentham *Staffs.*, 'trentəm, tréntăm

Trentishoe *Devon*, 'trentıshou, tréntiss-hō

Treorchy *Mid Glam.*, trı'ɔrkı, tri-órki

Treppass, *f.n.*, trı'pæs, trĕpáss

Trepte, *f.n.*, 'treptı, tréptí

Trerice Manor *Cornwall*, trı'raıs, trĕríss

Trerise, *f.n.*, trı'raız, trĕríz

Trerule Foot *Cornwall*, trı'rul 'fʊt, trĕrool fŏŏt

Tresardern, *f.n.*, 'tresərdərn, tréssărdern

Tresco *I. of Scilly*, 'treskou, trésskō

Tresham, *f.n.*, 'treʃəm, tréshăm

Tresham *Avon*, 'treʃəm, tréshăm

Treshnish Isles *S'clyde*, 'treʃnıʃ, tréshnish

Tresillian *Cornwall*, trı'sılıən, tréssilli-ăn

Tresman, *f.n.*, 'trezmən, trézmăn

Tresmeer *Cornwall*, trez'mıər, trezméer

Treswithian *Cornwall*, trı'swıðıən, trĕ-swíthi-ăn

Tretchikoff, *f.n.*, 'tretʃıkɒf, trétchikoff

Trethewey, *f.n.*, trı'θjuı, trĕthéw-i

Trethewey, *f.n.* trı'θjuı, trĕthéw-i

Trethowan, *f.n.*, trı'θauən, trĕthówăn; trı'θouən, trĕthó-ăn

Treuddyn *Clwyd*, 'traıðın, tríthin

Trevan, *f.n.*, trı'væn, trĕván

Trevarrack *Cornwall*, trı'værək, trĕvárrăk

Trevaskis, *f.n.*, trı'væskıs, trĕvásskiss

Trevdraeth *see* **Trefdraeth**

Trevella *Cornwall*, trı'velə, trĕvéllă

Trevelyan, *f.n.*, trı'vıljən, trĕvíl--yăn; trı'veljən, trĕvél-yăn. *The first is the usual Cornish*

pronunciation, the second the Northumbrian. The first is appropriate for George Macaulay ∼, *historian, and for Baron* ∼, *diplomatist.*

Trevena *Cornwall*, trı'vinə, trĕveénă

Treverbyn *Cornwall*, trı'vɜrbın, trĕvérbin

Treves, *f.n.*, trivz, treevz

Trevethick, *f.n.*, trı'veθık, trĕvéthick

Trevethin, Baron, trı'veθın, trĕvéthin

Trevett, *f.n.*, 'trevıt, trévvĕt

Trevine, *also spelt* **Tre-fin**, *Dyfed*, trı'vin, trĕveén

Trevivian, *f.n.*, trı'vıvıən, trĕvívvi--ăn

Trevor, *C.n. and f.n.*, 'trevər, trévvŏr

Trevose Head *Cornwall*, trı'vouz, trĕvṓz

Trew *Co. Tyrone*, tru, troo

Trewavas, *f.n.*, trı'wævəs, trĕ--wávvăss

Treweek, *f.n.*, trı'wik, trĕ-weék

Trewellard *Cornwall*, trı'welərd, trĕ-wéllărd

Trewhela, *f.n.*, trı'hwelə, trĕ--whéllă

Trewidland *Cornwall*, trı'wıdlənd, trĕ-wídländ

Trewin, *f.n.*, trı'wın, trĕ-wín

Trewoon *Cornwall*, 'truən, tro̓o-ŏn

Trewyddfa *W. Glam.*, trı'wıðvə, trĕ-with-vă

Treyarnon Bay *Cornwall*, trı-'jɑrnən, trĕ-yaárnŏn

Trickett, *f.n.*, 'trıkıt, trícket

Trier, *f.n.*, trıər, treer

Trillick *Co. Tyrone*, 'trılık, trillick

Trillo, *Welsh saint*, 'trıɫou, tríhlō

Trillo, *f.n.*, 'trılou, trilllō

Trimingham *Norfolk*, 'trımıŋəm, trímming-ăm

Trimlestown, Baron, 'trımlztən, trímmlztŏn

Trimsaran *Dyfed*, trım'særən, trim-sárrăn

Trinafour *Tayside*, ˌtrınə'fuər, trinnăfo̓or

Trinaman, *f.n.*, 'trınəmən, trínnă-măn; trı'nɑmən, trinaámăn

Trinant *Gwent*, 'trınænt, trínnant

Tring, *f.n.*, trıŋ, tring

Tring, *Herts.*, trıŋ, tring

Triplow *see* **Thriplow**

Tripp, *f.n.*, trıp, trip

Trippier, *f.n.*, 'trıpıər, tríppi-ĕr

Trispen *Cornwall*, 'trıspən, tríss-pĕn

Tristram, *C.n. and f.n.*, 'trıstrəm, trísstrăm

Tritton, f.n., 'trɪtən, tríttŏn
Trocchi, f.n., 'trɒkɪ, trócki
Troedrhiw-fuwch Mid Glam.,
    'trɔɪdhrɪu'vjux,tróydri-oo-véwch
Troedrhiw-gwair Gwent, 'trɔɪd-
    hrɪu'gwaɪər, tróydri-oo-gwír
Troed-yr-aur Dyfed, 'trɔɪdər'aɪər,
    tróydǎrír
Troed-y-rhiw Mid Glam., 'trɔɪd-
    ərɪ'u, tróydǎri-óo
Trofarth Clwyd, 'trouvɑrθ,
    tróvaarth
Trollope, f.n., 'trɒləp, tróllŏp
Tron Edinburgh, Glasgow, trɒn,
    tronn
Trossachs, The, Central, 'trɒsəxs,
    tróssǎchs
Trostre Gwent, 'trɒstreɪ, trósstray
Troth, f.n., trɒθ, troth
Trotter, f.n., 'trɒtər, tróttĕr
Trottiscliffe Kent, 'trɒzlɪ, trózzli
Troubridge, f.n., 'trubrɪdʒ, tróobrij
Troughton, f.n., 'trautən, trówtŏn
Troup, f.n., trup, troop
Troway Derby., 'trouɪ, trŏ-i
Trowbridge Wilts., 'troubrɪdʒ,
    trŏbrij
Trowell, f.n., 'trauəl, trówĕl;
    'trouəl, trŏ-ĕl
Trowell Notts., 'trauəl, trówĕl
Trower, f.n., 'trauər, trówĕr
Trowsdale, f.n., 'trauzdeɪl,
    trówzdayl
Trowse Norfolk, trous, trŏss
Troy, f.n., trɔɪ, troy
Truckle, f.n., 'trʌkl, trúckl
Trudgill, f.n., 'trʌdgɪl, trúd-gill
Trueman, f.n.. 'trumən, tróomǎn
Truesdale, f.n., 'truzdeɪl, tróoz-
    -dayl
Trueta, f.n., tru'etə, troo-éttǎ
Trufitt, f.n., 'trufɪt, tróofit
Truim, River, H'land, 'truɪm,
    tróo-im
Truman, f.n., 'trumən, tróomǎn
Trunch Norfolk, 'trʌnʃ, trunsh
Truro Cornwall, 'truərou, tróorō
Truscott, f.n., 'trʌskət, trússkŏt;
    'trʌskɒt, trússkott
Trusham Devon, 'trʌsəm, trússǎm;
    'trɪsəm, tríssǎm
Trustan Co. Fermanagh, 'trʌstən,
    trússtǎn
Trusthorpe Lincs., 'trʌsθɔrp,
    trúss-thorp
Trusthorpe Gowt Lincs., 'trʌsθɔrp
    'gaut, trúss-thorp gówt
Trustram, C.n., 'trʌstrəm, trús-
    strǎm
Truzzi, f.n., 'trʌzɪ, trúzzi
Try, f.n., traɪ, trī
Tryfan Gwynedd, 'trʌvən, trúvvǎn
Tryon, f.n., 'traɪən, trí-ŏn. Appro-
    priate also for Baron ~.

Trysull Staffs., 'trisl, tréessl; 'trizl,
    tréezl
Trythall, f.n., 'traɪθəl, trí-thawl
Tschaikov, f.n., 'tʃaɪkɒf, chíkoff
Tschiffely, A. F., author, tʃɪ'feɪlɪ,
    chifáyli
Tschirren, f.n., 'tʃɪrən, chírrĕn
Tubb, f.n., tʌb, tubb
Tuchet-Jesson, f.n., 'tʌtʃɪt
    'dʒesən, tútchĕt jéssŏn
Tuchner, f.n., 'tʌknər, túcknĕr
Tuck, f.n., tʌk, tuck
Tucker, f.n., 'tʌkər, túckĕr
Tuckett, f.n., 'tʌkɪt, túckĕt
Tuddenham, f.n., 'tʌdənəm,
    túddĕnǎm
Tudley Kent, 'tjudlɪ, téwdli;
    'tudlɪ, toodli
Tudhoe Durham, 'tʌdou, túddō
Tudhope, f.n., 'tjudəp, téwdŏp
Tudsbery, f.n., 'tʌdzbərɪ, túdz-
    bĕri
Tudur, Welsh C.n., 'tɪdɪər, tíddeer
Tudweiliog Gwynedd, tɪd'waɪljɒg,
    tidwíl-yog
Tueart, f.n., 'tjuərt, téw-ärt;
    'tjuərt, tyŏo-ärt
Tue Brook Merseyside, 'tju bruk,
    téw brŏok
Tufano, f.n., tu'fɑnou, tŏofa'anō
Tuffin, f.n., 'tʌfɪn, túffin
Tuffnell, f.n., 'tʌfnəl, túffnĕl
Tugendhat, f.n., 'tugənhɑt,
    tŏogĕn-haat
Tuggal see Tughall
Tughall, also spelt Tuggal,
    Northd., 'tʌgl, túggl. Tuggal is
    an older spelling, used in his
    title by the late Baron Beveridge
    of ~.
Tugwell, f.n., 'tʌgwəl, túgwĕl
Tuite, f.n., tjut, tewt; 'tjuɪt, téw-it
Tuke, f.n., tjuk, tewk
Tuker, f.n., 'tjukər, téwkĕr
Tulchan Lodge Tayside, 'tʌlxən,
    túlchǎn
Tulk, f.n., tʌlk, tulk
Tullibardine, Marquess of, ˌtʌlɪ-
    'bɑrdɪn, tullibaárdin
Tulliemet Tayside, ˌtʌlɪ'met,
    tullimét
Tulloch H'land, 'tʌləx, túllŏch
Tully Carnet Belfast, 'tʌlɪ 'kɑrnɪt,
    túlli kaárnĕt
Tummel, Loch and River, Tay-
    side, 'tʌml, túmml
Tunesi, f.n., tju'nesɪ, tewnéssi
Tungate, f.n., 'tʌŋgeɪt, túng-gayt
Tungay, f.n., 'tʌŋgeɪ, túng-gay
Tunnard, f.n., 'tʌnərd, túnnärd
Tunnell, f.n., tə'nel, tŭnéll
Tunstall Norfolk, 'tʌnstəl, túns-
    stawl
Tunstall Staffs., 'tʌnstəl, túnsstǎl

Tunstead *Norfolk*, 'tʌnstɪd, túnsstĕd
Tuohey, *f.n.*, 'tuɪ, toó-i
Tuohy, *f.n.*, 'tuɪ, toó-i
Tupper, *f.n.*, 'tʌpər, túppĕr
Tuppholme, *f.n.*, 'tʌphoʊm, túpp-hōm
Turgis Green *Hants*, 'tɜrdʒɪs 'grin, túrjiss greén
Turjansky, *f.n.*, tuər'jænskɪ, toōr-yánski
Turl, *f.n.*, tɜrl, turl
Turley, *f.n.*, 'tɜrlɪ, túrli
Turnbull, *f.n.*, 'tɜrnbʊl, túrnboōl
Turnell, *f.n.*, tər'nel, tŭrnéll
Turner, *f.n.*, 'tɜrnər, túrnĕr
Turnhouse *Lothian*, 'tɜrnhaʊs, túrn-howss
Turnill, *f.n.*, 'tɜrnɪl, túrnil
Turnour, *f.n.*, 'tɜrnər, túrnŭr
Turnour, Cyril, *see* Tourneur, Cyril
Turquand, *f.n.*, tɜr'kwænd, turkwánd; 'tɜrkwənd, túrkwănd; tɜr'kɒŋ, turkóng
Turrell, *f.n.*, 'tʌrəl, túrrĕl
Turriff *Grampian*, 'tʌrɪf, túrrif
Turvey, *f.n.*, 'tɜrvɪ, túrvi
Turweston *Bucks.*, tər'westən, tŭrwésstŏn
Tusa, *f.n.*, 'tjusə, téwssă
Tushielaw *Borders*, ,tʌʃɪ'lɔ, tushi-láw
Tuson, *f.n.*, 'tjusən, téwssŏn
Tussaud, *f.n.*, 'tusoʊ, toóssō. *Although members of the family themselves use this pronunciation, they expect and accept the popular versions for Madame ~'s exhibition, q.v.*
Tussaud's, Madame, *waxworks exhibition*, tə'sɔdz, tŭssáwdz; tə'soʊdz, tŭssōdz
Tustain, *f.n.*, 'tʌsteɪn, tússtayn
Tutaev, *f.n.*, tu'taɪef, tootí-eff
Tutill, *f.n.*, 'tutɪl, tootíl
Tuttiett, *f.n.*, 'tʌtjet, tút-yet
Tuxford *Notts.*, 'tʌksfərd, túcksfŏrd
Tuyrrell, *f.n.*, 'tɪrəl, tírrĕl
Tuzo, *f.n.*, 'tjuzoʊ, téwzō
Twechar *S'clyde*, 'twexər, twéchăr
Tweddel, *f.n.*, 'twedl, twéddl
Tweed, River, *Scotland*, twid, tweed
Tweeddale, Marquess of, 'twiddeɪl, twéed-dayl
Tweedsmuir, Baron, 'twidzmjʊər, tweédz-myoōr
Twentyman, *f.n.*, 'twentɪmən, twéntimän
Tweseldown *Hants*, 'twizldaʊn, tweézldown

Twidell, *f.n.*, twɪ'del, twidéll; 'twɪdl, twíddl
Twidle, *f.n.*, 'twaɪdl, twídl
Twigworth *Glos.*, 'twɪgwɜrθ, twígwurth
Twiname, *f.n.*, 'twaɪnəm, twínăm
Twine, *f.n.*, twaɪn, twīn
Twineham *W. Sussex*, 'twaɪnəm, twínăm
Twinhoe *Avon*, 'twɪnoʊ, twínnō
Twining, *f.n.*, 'twaɪnɪŋ, twíning
Twisleton-Wykeham-Fiennes, *f.n.*, 'twɪsltən 'wɪkəm 'faɪnz, twissltŏn wíckăm fínz. *Family name of Baron Saye and Sele.*
Twisly *E. Sussex*, twɪz'laɪ, twizz-lí
Twitchett, *f.n.*, 'twɪtʃɪt, twítchĕt
Twizell *Durham*, 'twaɪzl, twízl
Twohy, *f.n.*, 'tuɪ, toó-i
Twomey, *f.n.*, 'tumɪ, toómi
Twomley, *f.n.*, 'twɒmlɪ, twómli
Twyman, *f.n.*, 'twaɪmən, twímăn
Twynholm *D. & G.*, 'twaɪnəm, twínŏm
Twyn-yr-Odyn *S. Glam.*, 'tuɪn ər 'ɒdɪn, toó-in ŭr óddin
Tyacke, *f.n.*, 'taɪæk, tí-ack
Tyberton *H. & W.*, 'tɪbərtən, tíbbĕrtŏn
Tyburn *W. Midlands*, 'taɪbərn, tíbŭrn
Tycoch Study Centre *Swansea*, 'tikoʊx, teékōch
Ty-croes *Dyfed*, ti'krɔɪs, tee-króyss
Tydd Gote *Lincs.*, 'tɪd 'goʊt, tídd gŏt
Tydd St. Giles *Cambs.*, 'tɪd snt 'dʒaɪlz, tídd sĭnt jílz
Tydd St. Mary *Norfolk*, 'tɪd snt 'meərɪ, tídd sĭnt máiri
Tydeman, *f.n.*, 'taɪdmən, tídimän; 'taɪdmən, tídmän
Tye, *f.n.*, taɪ, tī
Tyersal *W. Yorks.*, 'taɪərsl, tí-ĕrssl
Ty-hyll Bridge *Gwynedd*, ti 'hɪɬ, tee híhl
Tyla-gwyn *Mid Glam.*, ,tʌlə'gwɪn, tullăgwin
Tyldesley, *f.n.*, 'tɪldzlɪ, tíldzli
Tyldesley *Gtr. M'chester*, 'tɪldzlɪ, tíldzli; 'tɪlzlɪ, tíllzli
Tylecote, *f.n.*, 'taɪlkoʊt, tílkōt
Tylee, *f.n.*, 'taɪlɪ, tílee
Tyler, *f.n.*, 'taɪlər, tílĕr
Tylney Hall *Hants*, 'tɪlnɪ, tíllni
Tylorstown *Mid Glam.*, 'taɪlərztaʊn, tílŏrztown
Tylwch *Powys*, 'tʌlʊx, túllōoch
Ty-mawr *Clwyd*, ti'maʊər, teemówr
Tymiec, *f.n.*, 'tɪmɪek, tímmi-eck
Tynan, *f.n.*, 'taɪnən, tínăn

Tynan Co. Armagh, 'taɪnən, tĭnăn

Tyndale, William, translator of the New Testament, 'tɪndl, tíndl

Tyndrum Central, taɪn'drʌm, tĭndrúm

Tyne, Rivers, Lothian, Northd.– Tyne & Wear, taɪn, tīn

Tynemouth Tyne & Wear, 'taɪn-maʊθ, tĭnmowth; 'tɪnməθ. tínmŭth

Tynewydd Mid Glam., ti'newɪð, teené-wiṯẖ

Tyninghame Lothian, 'tɪnɪŋhəm, tínning-hăm

Tynte, f.n., tɪnt, tint

Tyntesfield Avon, 'tɪntsfɪld, tíntsfeeld

Tynwald, Manx legislative assembly, 'tɪnwəld, tínwăld

Tynygongl Gwynedd, ˌtɪnə'gɒŋl, tinnăgóng-ĕl

Tyree, also spelt **Tiree,** S'clyde, taɪ'ri, tī-reé

Tyrell, f.n., 'tɪrəl, tírrĕl

Tyrella Co. Down, tɪ'relə, tiréllă

Tyrer, f.n., 'taɪərər, tírĕr

Tyrie, f.n., 'tɪrɪ, tírri

Tyringham, f.n., 'tɪrɪŋəm, tírring-ăm

Tyrone Co. name, tɪ'roʊn, tirŏn. Appropriate also for the Earl of ~.

Tyrrell, f.n., 'tɪrəl, tírrĕl

Tyrwhitt, f.n., 'tɪrɪt, tírrit

Tyseley W. Midlands, 'taɪzlɪ, tízli

Tysilio, Welsh saint, tə'sɪljoʊ, tŭssil-yō

Tysoe, Lower, Middle, and Upper, Warwicks., 'taɪsoʊ, tíssō

Tyssen, f.n., 'taɪsən, tíssĕn

Tysser, f.n., 'taɪsər, tíssĕr

Tyte, f.n., taɪt, tīt

Tythby, also spelt **Tithby,** Notts., 'tɪðbɪ, títhbi

Tytler, f.n., 'taɪtlər, títlĕr

Tywardreath Cornwall, ˌtaɪwər'dreθ, tī-wărdréth

Tywyn Gwynedd, 'taʊɪn, tów-in

Tyzack, f.n., 'taɪzæk, tízack; 'tɪzæk, tízzack

U

Ubbelohde, f.n., 'ʌbəloʊd, úbbĕlōd

Ubberley Staffs., 'ʌbərlɪ, úbbĕrli

Uber, f.n., 'jubər, yóobĕr

Ubley Avon, 'ʌblɪ. úbbli

Ubsdell, f.n., 'ʌbzdəl, úbzdĕl

Ubysz, f.n., 'jubɪʃ, yoóbish

Udal, f.n., 'judl, yoodl

Udale, f.n., 'judeɪl, yoódayl; ju'deɪl, yoodáyl

Udall, f.n., 'judl, yoódl; 'judəl, yoódawl; 'judæl, yoódal; ju'dæl, yoodál; ju'dɔl, yoodáwl

Udell, f.n., ju'del, yōodéll

Uden, f.n., 'judən, yoódĕn

Udimore E. Sussex, 'judɪmɔr, yoódimor; 'ʌdɪmər, úddimor

Udny Grampian, 'ʌdnɪ, úddni

Uffculme Devon, 'ʌfkəm, úffkŭm

Ugglebarnby N. Yorks.. 'ʌgl-'barnbɪ, úggl-baárnbi

Ugley Essex, 'ʌglɪ, úggli

Uglow, f.n., 'ʌgloʊ, úgglō; 'jugloʊ, yoóglō. The first is usual in Cornwall.

Ugthorpe N. Yorks., 'ʌgθɔrp, úg-thorp

Uig H'land, 'uɪg, oó-ig

Uisgean Mull, 'uʃgən, oŏsh-găn

Uist, North and South, W. Isles, 'juɪst, yoó-ist; 'uɪst, oó-ist

Ulbster H'land, 'ʌlbstər, úlbstĕr

Ulceby Humberside, 'ʌlsəbɪ, úlssĕbi; 'ʌlsbɪ, úlssbi

Ulceby Lincs., 'ʌlsbɪ, úlssbi

Ulcombe Kent, 'ʌlkəm, úlkŏm

Uldale Cumbria, 'ʌldeɪl, úldayl

Uley Glos., 'julɪ, yoóli

Ulgham Northd., 'ʌfəm, úffăm

Ulick, C.n., 'julɪk, yoólick

Ullapool H'land, 'ʌləpul, úllăpool

Ulleskelf N. Yorks., 'ʌləskelf, úllĕskelf

Ullesthorpe Leics., 'ʌləsθɔrp, úllĕss-thorp

Ullman, f.n., 'ʊlmən, oŏlmăn

Ullock, f.n., 'ʌlək, úllŏk

Ullswater Cumbria, 'ʌlzwɔtər, úlzwawtĕr. Appropriate also for Viscount ~.

Ulnes Walton Lancs., 'ʌlzwɔltən, úlzwawltŏn

Ulph, f.n., ʌlf, ulf

Ulva S'clyde, 'ʌlvə, úlvă

Ulverston Cumbria, 'ʌlvərstən, úlvĕrsstŏn

Umberleigh Devon, 'ʌmbərlɪ, úmbĕrli

Umfreville, f.n., 'ʌmfrɪvɪl, úmfrĕvil

Uncles, f.n., 'ʌŋklz, únklz

Underdown, f.n., 'ʌndərdaʊn, úndĕrdown

Underhill, f.n., 'ʌndərhɪl, úndĕr-hil

Underwood, f.n., 'ʌndərwʊd, úndĕrwŏod

Undery, f.n., 'ʌndərɪ, úndĕri-

Ungar, *f.n.*, 'ʌŋgər, úng-găr

Ungoed, *Welsh C.n.*, 'ɪŋgɔɪd, íng-goyd

Ungoed, *f.n.*, 'ɪŋgɔɪd, íng-goyd; 'ʌŋgɔɪd, úng-goyd

Uniacke, *f.n.*, 'juːnɪæk, yóoni-ack

Unst *Shetland*, ʌnst, unsst

Unstone *Derby.*, 'ʌnstən, únsstŏn

Unthank, *f.n.*, 'ʌnθæŋk, únthank

Unthank *Cumbria*, 'ʌnθæŋk, únthank

Unwin, *f.n.*, 'ʌnwɪn, únwin. *Appropriate for George Allen and* ~, *publishers.*

Upavon *Wilts.*, 'ʌpeɪvən, úppayvŏn

Upend *Cambs.*, 'ʌpend, úppend

Up Exe *Devon*, 'ʌp eks, úp ecks

Up Holland *Lancs.*, ʌp 'hɒlənd, up hólländ

Upjohn, *f.n.*, 'ʌpdʒɒn, úpjon

Upleadon *H. & W.*, ʌp'ledən, upléddŏn

Uplowman *Devon*, ʌp'loumən, uplómăn

Up Marden *W. Sussex*, ʌp mardən, úp maardĕn

Up Ottery *Devon*, ʌp 'ɒtərɪ, up óttĕri

Uppark *W. Sussex*, 'ʌppɑrk, úp--paark

Upper Benefield *Northants.*, 'ʌpər 'benɪfɪld, úppĕr bénnifeeld

Upper Broughton *Notts.*, 'ʌpər 'brɔtən, úppĕr bráwtŏn

Upperdine, *f.n.*, 'ʌpərdaɪn, úppĕrdīn

Upper Hardres *Kent*, 'ʌpər 'hɑrdz, úppĕr haárdz

Upper Haugh *S. Yorks.*, 'ʌpər 'hɔf, úppĕr háwf

Upper Heyford, *also sometimes called* Heyford Warren, *Oxon.*, 'ʌpər 'heɪfərd, úppĕr háyfŏrd

Upper Hiendley *W. Yorks.*, 'ʌpər 'hindlɪ, úppĕr heéndli

Upperlands *Co. Derry*, 'ʌpərləndz, úppĕrlăndz

Upper Shuckburgh *Warwicks.*, 'ʌpər 'ʃʌkbərə, úppĕr shúckbŭră

Upper Slaughter *Glos.*, 'ʌpər 'slɔtər, úppĕr sláwtĕr

Upper Tean *Staffs.*, 'ʌpər 'tin, úppĕr teén

Upper Wyche *H. & W.*, 'ʌpər 'wɪtʃ, úppĕr wítch

Uprichard, *f.n.*, ju'prɪtʃɑrd, yooprítchaard; ju'prɪtʃərd, yooprítchărd; ʌp'rɪtʃərd, upprítchărd

Upshire *Essex*, 'ʌpʃaɪər, úp-shīr; 'ʌpʃər, úp-shĕr

Upton, *f.n.*, 'ʌptən, úptŏn

Upton Hellions *Devon*, 'ʌptən 'helɪənz, úptŏn hélli-ŏnz

Upware *Cambs.*, 'ʌpwɛər, úpwair

Upwell *Cambs.–Norfolk border*, 'ʌpwel, úpwel

Upwey *Dorset*, 'ʌpweɪ, úpway

Urban, *f.n.*, 'ɜrbən, úrbăn

Urch, *f.n.*, ɜrtʃ, urtch

Urchfont *Wilts.*, 'ɜrtʃfɒnt, úrtchfont

Urdd Gobaith Cymru, *Welsh League of Youth*, 'ɪərð 'gɒbaɪθ 'kʌmrɪ, eérth góbbĭth kúmri

Ure, *f.n.*, juər, yoŏr

Uren, *f.n.*, juə'ren, yoŏrén

Uridge, *f.n.*, 'juərɪdʒ, yoŏrij

Urmston *Gtr. M'chester*, 'ɜrmstən, úrmsstŏn

Urquhart, *f.n.*, 'ɜrxərt, úrchărt; 'ɜrkərt, úrkărt

Urrard House *Tayside*, 'ʌrərd, úrrärd

Urray *H'land*, 'ʌrɪ, úrri

Urswick *Cumbria*, 'ɜrzwɪk, úrzwick; 'ɜrzɪk, úrzick; 'ɒsɪk, óssick

Urwick, *f.n.*, 'ɜrwɪk, úrwick

Ury, *f.n.*, 'juərɪ, yoŏri

Usan *Tayside*, 'uzən, óozăn

Usborne, *f.n.*, 'ʌzbɔrn, úzzborn

Ushaw *Durham*, 'ʌʃə, úsh-ă; 'ʌʃɔ, úsh-aw

Usher, *f.n.*, 'ʌʃər, úsh-ĕr

Usherwood, *f.n.*, 'ʌʃərwʊd, úshĕrwŏod

Usk *Gwent*, ʌsk, ussk. *Appropriate also for* ~ *Priory.*

Usk, *River, Powys–Gwent*, ʌsk, ussk

Uskmouth *Gwent*, 'ʌskmauθ, ússkmowth

Ussleby *Lincs.*, 'ʌslbɪ, ússlbi

Ussher, *f.n.*, 'ʌʃər, úsh-ĕr

Ustinov, *f.n.*, 'justɪnɒf, yoóstinoff; 'ustɪnɒf, oóstinoff. *Peter* ~, *film producer, actor and playwright, submits to either pronunciation.*

Uswayford *Northd.*, 'ʌzweɪfɔrd, úzzwayford

Usworth *Tyne & Wear*, 'ʌzwɜrθ, úzzwurth

Uthwatt, *f.n.*, 'ʌθwɒt, úth-wott. *Appropriate also for the Barony of* ~.

Utiger, *f.n.*, 'jutɪgər, yoótigĕr

Utting, *f.n.*, 'ʌtɪŋ, útting

Uttoxeter *Staffs.*, ju'tɒksɪtər, yootóckssĕtĕr; ʌ'tɒksɪtər, uttóckssĕtĕr; 'ʌksɪtər, úckssĕtĕr. *There are other less common variants.*

Uvarov, *f.n.*, ju'vɑrɒf, yoova'aroff; 'juvərɒf, yoovăroff
Uwins, *f.n.*, 'juɪnz, yoo-inz
Uxbridge *London*, 'ʌksbrɪdʒ, úcksbrij
Uyeasound *Shetland*, 'juəsaʋnd, yoo-ässownd
Uziell, *f.n.*, 'juzɪel, yoozi-el
Uzmaston *Dyfed*, 'ʌzməsən, úzzmässŏn

V

Vache, The, *Bucks.*, ðə 'vætʃ, thĕ vátch
Vachell, *f.n.*, 'veɪtʃl, váytchl; 'vætʃl, vátchl
Vachell, Horace Annesley, *author*, 'hɒrɪs 'ænzlɪ 'veɪtʃl, hórriss ánzli váytchl
Vacher, *f.n.*, 'væʃər, váshĕr. *Appropriate in particular for the printers of ~'s Parliamentary Companion.*
Vaesen, *f.n.*, 'veɪzən, váyzĕn
Vaila *Shetland*, 'veɪlə, váylă
Vaillant, *f.n.*, 'væljənt, vál-yănt; 'vaɪjɒŋ, ví-yong
Vaizey, *f.n.*, 'veɪzɪ, váyzi
Valency, *f.n.*, və'lensɪ, vălénssi
Valency, *River, Cornwall*, və'lensɪ, vălénssi
Valentin, *f.n.*, 'væləntɪn, válĕntin
Valentine, *C.n. and f.n.*, 'vælən-taɪn, válĕntīn
Valerio, *f.n.*, və'lɛərɪoʋ, vălái̇rio͝
Valetort, *f.n.*, 'vælɪtɔrt, válĕtort
Vallance, *f.n.*, 'væləns, válănss
Vallancey, *f.n.*, væ'lænsɪ, valánssi
Vallans, *f.n.*, 'væləns, válănss
Vallaquie *see* **Dunrossil** of ~, Viscount
Valle Crucis Abbey *Clwyd*, 'vælɪ 'krusɪs, váli kroóssiss
Vallely, *f.n.*, 'væləlɪ, válĕli
Valley *Gwynedd*, 'vælɪ, váli
Vallier, *f.n.*, 'væljeɪ, vál-yay
Vallins, *f.n.*, 'vælɪnz, válinz
Van Asch, *f.n.*, væn 'æʃ, van ásh
van Barthold, *f.n.*, væn 'bɑrtoʋld, van baártŏld
Vanbrugh, *f.n.*, 'vænbrə, vánbră
Vanburgh, *f.n.*, 'vænbrə, vánbră
Vance, *f.n.*, væns, vanss; vɑns, vaanss
Van Cutsem, *f.n.*, væn 'kʌtsəm, van kúttsĕm
Vandam, *f.n.*, væn'dæm, vandám
Van Damm, *f.n.*, væn 'dæm, van dám

Vanden-Bempde-Johnstone, *f.n.*, 'vændən 'bemptɪ 'dʒɒnstən, vándĕn bémptɪ jónstŏn. *Family name of Baron Derwent.*
Van den Bergh, *f.n.*, 'vændən-bɜrg, vándĕnberg
Vandepeer, *f.n.*, ˌvændə'pɪər, vandĕpéer
van der Beek, *f.n.*, ˌvændər'bik, vandĕrbeék
van der Burgh, *f.n.*, 'vændərbɜrg, vándĕrburg
Vanderbyl, *f.n.*, 'vændərbaɪl, vándĕrbīl
Van Der Gucht, *f.n.*, 'vændərgut, vándĕrgoot
Van der Pant, *f.n.*, 'vændərpænt, vándĕrpant
Vanderplank, *f.n.*, 'vændərplæŋk, vándĕrplank
Van der Pump, *f.n.*, 'vændər-pʌmp, vándĕrpump
van der Riet, *f.n.*, 'vændərit, vándĕreet
Vanderspar, *f.n.*, 'vændərspar, vándĕrspaar
van der Sprenkel, *f.n.*, ˌvændər 'spreŋkl, vandĕr sprénkl
Van der Weyer, *f.n.*, ˌvændər 'weɪər, vandĕr wáy-ĕr
Vandyck, *f.n.*, væn'daɪk, vandík
Van Dyck, *f.n.*, væn 'daɪk, van dík
Van Eyssen, *f.n.*, væn 'aɪsən, van íssĕn
Vange *Essex*, vændʒ, vanj
van Geloven, *f.n.*, ˌvæn gə'loʋvən, van gĕlóvĕn
van Greenaway, *f.n.*, væn 'grinə-weɪ, van greénă-way
van Gyseghem, *f.n.*, væn 'gaɪzə-gəm, van gízĕgĕm
Van Kampen, *f.n.*, væn 'kæmpən, van kámpĕn
Van Moppes, *f.n.*, væn 'mɒpɪz, van móppĕz
Vanneck, *f.n.*, væn'ek, vannéck
Van Praagh, *f.n.*, væn 'prɑg, van praág
Van Riemsdijk, *f.n.*, væn 'rimz-daɪk, van reémzdík
Vans Colina, *f.n.*, ˌvænz kə'linə, vanz kŏleénă
Vansittart, *f.n.*, væn'sɪtərt, van-síttărt. *Appropriate also for the Barony of ~.*
van Straten, *f.n.*, væn 'strɑtən, van straátĕn
van Straubenzee, *f.n.*, ˌvæn strɔ-'benzɪ, van strawbénzi
Van Thal, *f.n.*, væn 'tɔl, van táwl
Van Wyck, *f.n.*, væn 'waɪk, van wík
Varah, *f.n.*, 'vɑrə, va'ără
Varcoe, *f.n.*, 'vɑrkoʋ, va'arkō

Varley, *f.n.*, 'vɑrlı, vaárli
Varndell, *f.n.*, vɑrn'del, vaarndéll
Varnel, *f.n.*, vɑr'nel, vaarnéll
Varteg *Gwent*, 'vɑrteg, vaárteg
Vas, *f.n.*, vɑs, vaass
Vasey, *f.n.*, 'veizi, váyzi
Vaternish *see* Waternish
Vatersay *W. Isles*, 'vætərsei, váttĕrssay
Vaughan, *f.n.*, vɔn, vawn
Vaughan Williams, Ralph, *composer*, 'reif ,vɔn 'wiljəmz, ráyf vawn wílyămz
Vaus, *f.n.*, vɔs, vawss
Vautor, Thomas, *16th–17th-c. composer*, 'voutər, vŏtor
Vaux, *f.n.*, vɔks, vawks; voυ, vō; vɒks, vocks
Vaux of Harrowden, Baron, 'vɔks əv 'hæroυdən, váwks ŏv hárrō-dĕn
Vauxhall *London, West Midlands*, 'vɒksɔl, vócksawl; 'vɒkshɔl, vócks-hawl
Vavasour, *f.n.*, 'vævəsər, vávvăs-sŭr
Vavasseur, *f.n.*, ,vævə'sзr, vavvăs-sŭr
Vayne, *f.n.*, vein, vayn
Vaynol *Gwynedd*, 'vainɒl, vínoll
Vaynor *Mid Glam.*, 'veinɔr, váynor; 'vainɔr, vínor
Vear, *f.n.*, viər, veer
Veasey, *f.n.*, 'vizi, veézi
Vedast, saint, 'vidæst, veédasst
Vedrenne, *f.n.*, vi'dren, vĕdrén
Veitch, *f.n.*, vitʃ, veetch
Vel, *f.n.*, vel, vell
Velindre *Dyfed*, ve'lindrei, velíndray; ve'lindrə, velíndrĕ. *Cf.* Felindre. *The first is the Welsh pronunciation, appropriate for both places of the name in Dyfed, although the steel-works near Newcastle Emlyn is usually known by the second, anglicized, pronunciation.*
Velindre *Powys*, ve'lindrei, velíndray
Vellenoweth, *f.n.*, 'velənoυiθ, véllĕnō-ĕth; 'velnoυθ, vélnŏth; ,velə'naυiθ, vellĕnów-ĕth; 'velənaυθ, véllĕnowth; 'velnəθ, vélnŏth
Vementry *Shetland*, 'veməntri, vémmĕntri
Venables, *f.n.*, 'venəblz, vénnăblz
Vendryes, *f.n.*, ven'dris, ven-dreéss
Venediger, *f.n.*, vi'nedidзər, vĕnéddijĕr
Veness, *f.n.*, vi'nes, vĕnéss
Vennachar, Loch, *Central*, 'venəxər, vénnăchăr ·

Venner, *f.n.*, 'venər, vénnĕr
Venning, *f.n.*, 'veniŋ, vénning
Venour, *f.n.*, 'venər, vénnŭr; vi'nuər, vĕnoŏr
Ventham, *f.n.*, 'venθəm, vén-thăm
Ver, River, *Herts.*, vзr, ver
Verco, *f.n.*, 'vзrkoυ, vérkō
Vercoe, *f.n.*, 'vзrkoυ, vérkō
Vercow, *f.n.*, vər'koυ, vĕrkô
Vercowe, *f.n.*, vər'koυ, vĕrkô
Vereker, *f.n.*, 'verikər, vérrĕkĕr
Verey, *f.n.*, 'viəri, veéri
Verinder, *f.n.*, 'verindər, vérrindĕr
Verity, *C.n. and f.n.*, 'veriti, vérriti
Verlander, *f.n.*, vər'lændər, vĕr-lándĕr; 'vзrləndər, vérländĕr
Vernède, *f.n.*, vər'neid, vĕrnáyd
Verney, *f.n.*, 'vзrni, vérni
Vernon, *C.n. and f.n.*, 'vзrnən, vérnŏn
Verrall, *f.n.*, 'verəl, vérräl
Verrells, *f.n.*, 'verəlz, vérrĕlz
Verschoyle, *f.n.*, 'vзrskɔil, vérs-skoyl
Verstappen, *f.n.*, vər'stæpən, vĕrstáppĕn
Vertigan, *f.n.*, 'vзrtigən, vértigăn
Verulam, Earl of, 'verυləm, vérrŏŏläm
Verulamium, *Roman site near St. Albans*, ,verυ'leimiəm, ver-rŏŏláymiŭm
Veryan *Cornwall*, 'veriən, vérri-ăn
Vesey, *f.n.*, 'vizi, veézi
Vesian, *f.n.*, 'veziən, vézzi-ăn
Vesselo, *f.n.*, vi'seloυ, vĕsséllō
Vevers, *f.n.*, 'vivərz, veévĕrz
Veysey, *f.n.*, 'veizi, váyzi
Vezin, *f.n.*, 'vizin, veézin
Via Gellia *Derby.*, 'vaiə 'dзeliə, ví-ă jélli-ă
Vialls, *f.n.*, 'vaiəlz, ví-älz; 'vaiɔlz, ví-awlz
Viant, *f.n.*, 'vaiənt, ví-ănt
Vibart, *f.n.*, 'vaibərt, víbărt
Vidal, *f.n.*, 'vaidl, vídl
Videan, *f.n.*, 'vidiən, víddi-ăn
Vidler, *f.n.*, 'vidlər, víddlĕr
Vieler, *f.n.*, 'vilər, veélĕr
Vigar, *f.n.*, 'vaigər, vígăr; 'vaigɑr, vígaar
Vigay, *f.n.*, 'vaigei, vígay
Vigers, *f.n.*, 'vaigərz, vígĕrz
Viggers, *f.n.*, 'vigərz, víggĕrz
Vigne, *f.n.*, vain, vīn
Vignes, *f.n.*, vinz, veenz
Vignoles, *f.n.*, 'vinjoυlz, vín-yōlz; 'vinjoυlz, veen-yōlz; 'vinjool, veen-yōl; vin'joυlz, vin-yôlz; 'vinjɒlz, veen-yollz
Vigo Inn *Kent*, 'vaigoυ, vígō
Vigor, *f.n.*, 'vaigər, vígor
Vigrow, *f.n.*, 'vigroυ, veégrō

Vigurs, *f.n.*, 'vaɪgərz, vígŭrz; 'vɪgərz, víggŭrz

Viles, *f.n.*, vaɪlz, vīlz

Villiers, *f.n.*, 'vɪlərz, víllĕrz; 'vɪljərz, víl-yĕrz. *The first is appropriate for the family name of the Earl of Clarendon and of the Earl of Jersey, for Viscount ~ and for Baron de ~.*

Vinall, *f.n.*, 'vaɪnl, vínl

Vinaver, *f.n.*, vɪ'nɑvər, vináavĕr

Vincent, *C.n. and f.n.*, 'vɪnsənt, vínssĕnt

Vincze, *f.n.*, vɪnts, vints

Vine, *f.n.*, vaɪn, vīn

Viner, *f.n.*, 'vaɪnər, vínĕr

Vinerian, *pertaining to Viner,* vaɪ'nɪərɪən, vīneéri-ăn. *Appropriate for the ~ common law professorship and fellowships at the University of Oxford.*

Viney Hill *Glos.*, 'vaɪnɪ 'hɪl, víni híll

Vintcent, *f.n.*, 'vɪnsənt, vínssĕnt

Vinter, *f.n.*, 'vɪntər, víntĕr

Vintner, *f.n.*, 'vɪntnər, víntnĕr

Viollet, *f.n.*, 'vaɪələt, vī-ŏlĕt

Vipont, *f.n.*, 'vaɪpɒnt, vípont

Virago Press, *publishers,* vɪ'rɑgoʊ, viráagō

Virginia Water *Surrey*, vər'dʒɪnɪə 'wɔtər, vŭrjínni-ă wáwtĕr

Vivary Park *Taunton*, 'vaɪvərɪ, vívări

Viveash, *f.n.*, 'vaɪvæʃ, vívash

Vivian, *f.n.*, 'vɪvɪən, vívvi-ăn

Vivis, *f.n.*, 'vɪvɪs, véeviss

Vizard, *f.n.*, 'vɪzɑrd, vízzaard

Vizetelly, *f.n.*, ˌvɪzə'telɪ, vizĕtélli

Voce, *f.n.*, voʊs, vōss

Voelcker, *f.n.*, 'voʊlkər, vŏlkĕr

Vogel, *f.n.*, 'voʊgl, vŏgl

Vogt, *f.n.*, voʊkt, vōkt; voʊt, vōt; vɒt, vott

Vogue Beloth *Cornwall*, 'voʊg bɪ'lɒθ, vŏg bĕlóth

Voigt, *f.n.*, vɔɪt, voyt

Voisey, *f.n.*, 'vɔɪzɪ, vóyzi

Volante, *f.n.*, və'læntɪ, vŏlánti

Volckman, *f.n.*, 'vɒlkmən, vóllkmăn

Volk, *f.n.*, vɒlk, vollk; voʊlk, vōlk. *The first is appropriate for ~'s Railway at Brighton.*

Volze, *f.n.*, voʊlz, vōlz

Von der Heyde, *f.n.*, 'vɒndərhaɪd, vóndĕr-hīd

Von Stranz, *f.n.*, vɒn 'strænz, von stránz

Vores, *f.n.*, vɔrz, vorz

Vortigern, *5th-c. king of the Britons*, 'vɔrtɪgərn, vórtigĕrn

Vos, *f.n.*, vɒs, voss

Vosburgh, *f.n.*, 'vɒsbərə, vóssbŭră

Voss, *f.n.*, vɒs, voss

Vought, *f.n.*, vɔt, vawt

Voules, *f.n.*, voʊlz, vōlz; vaʊlz, vowlz

Vowden, *f.n.*, 'vaʊdən, vówdĕn

Vowles, *f.n.*, voʊlz, vōlz; vaʊlz, vowlz

Voysey, *f.n.*, 'vɔɪzɪ, vóyzi

Vroncysyllte *see* **Froncysyllte**

Vuller, *f.n.*, 'vʊlər, vŏolĕr

Vulliamy, *f.n.*, 'vʌljəmɪ, vúl-yămi. *Appropriate for Benjamin Lewis ~, 18th-c. clock-maker.*

Vychan, *f.n.*, 'vʌxən, vúchăn

Vyrnwy, Lake *and* River, *Powys*, 'vɜrnʊɪ, vúrnŏō-i

Vyse, *f.n.*, vaɪz, vīz

Vyvyan, *C.n. and f.n.*, 'vɪvɪən, vívvi-ăn

W

Wacey, *f.n.*, 'weɪsɪ, wáyssi

Wach, *f.n.*, wɒtʃ, wotch

Wacher, *f.n.*, 'weɪtʃər, wáytchĕr

Wacton *Norfolk*, 'wæktən, wácktŏn

Waddell, *f.n.*, 'wɒdl, wóddl; wə'del, wŏdéll

Waddesdon *Bucks.*, 'wɒdzdən, wódzdŏn

Waddicor, *f.n.*, 'wɒdɪkər, wóddikor

Waddilove, *f.n.*, 'wɒdɪlʌv, wóddiluv

Waddon *London*, 'wɒdən, wóddŏn

Wade, *f.n.*, weɪd, wayd

Wadebridge *Cornwall*, 'weɪdbrɪdʒ, wáydbrij

Wadeford *Somerset*, 'wɒdfərd, wódfŏrd

Wade-Gery, *f.n.*, 'weɪd 'gɪərɪ, wáyd geéri

Wadenhoe *Northants.*, 'wɒdənhoʊ, wódděn-hō

Wadey, *f.n.*, 'weɪdɪ, wáydi

Wadham College *Univ. of Oxford*, 'wɒdəm, wóddăm

Wadsley, *f.n.*, 'wɒdzlɪ, wódzli

Wadsworth, *f.n.*, 'wɒdzwərθ, wódzwŭrth

Waechter, *f.n.*, 'veɪktər, váyktĕr

Waenfawr, *also spelt* **Waunfawr**, *Dyfed*, 'waɪnvaʊər, wínvowr

Wagg, *f.n.*, wæg, wagg

Waghen *see* **Wawne**

Wagner, *f.n.*, 'wægnər, wágnĕr

Wahab, *f.n.*, wɒb, wawb

Waight, *f.n.*, weɪt, wayt

Wainfleet *Lincs.*, 'weɪnflɪt, wáynfleet

Wainwright, *f.n.*, 'weɪnraɪt, wáyn-rīt

Waites, *f.n.*, weɪts, wayts

Waith, *f.n.*, weɪθ, wayth

Waithman, *f.n.*, 'weɪθmən, wáyth-män

Wake, *f.n.*, weɪk, wayk

Wakefield, *f.n.*, 'weɪkfɪld, wáyk-feeld

Wakefield *W. Yorks.*, 'weɪkfɪld, wáykfeeld

Wakeling, *f.n.*, 'weɪklɪŋ, wáykling

Wakering, Great *and* Little, *Essex*, 'weɪkərɪŋ, wáykĕring

Wakes Colne *Essex*, 'weɪks 'koʊn, wáyks kṓn

Wakley, *f.n.*, 'wækli, wáckli; 'weɪklɪ, wáykli. *The first is considered appropriate for Thomas* ~, *19th-c. surgeon, founder of* 'The Lancet'.

Walberswick *Suffolk*, 'wɔlbərzwɪk, wáwlbĕrzwick

Walcot, *f.n.*, 'wɔlkɒt, wáwlkott

Walcote *Leics.*, 'wɔlkoʊt, wáwl-kōt

Waldegrave, *f.n.*, 'wɔlgreɪv, wáwlgrayv; 'wɔldɪgreɪv, wáwl-dĕgrayv. *The first is appropriate for Earl* ~.

Walden, *f.n.*, 'wɔldən, wáwldĕn; 'wɒldən, wóldĕn

Walder, *f.n.*, 'wɔldər, wáwldĕr

Walderslade *Kent*, 'wɔldərsleɪd, wáwldĕrsslayd

Waldo, *C.n.*, 'wɔldoʊ, wáwldō; 'wɒldoʊ, wólldō

Waldron, *f.n.*, 'wɔldrən, wáwldrŏn

Waleran, Barony of, 'wɔlrən, wáwlrăn

Walesby *Lincs.*, *Notts.*, 'weɪlzbɪ, wáylzbi

Waley, *f.n.*, 'weɪlɪ, wáyli

Walford, *f.n.*, 'wɔlfərd, wáwlfŏrd; wɒllfərd, wólfŏrd

Walhampton *Hants*, 'wɔl'hæmptən, wáwl-hámptŏn

Walkden *Gtr. M'chester*, 'wɔkdən, wáwkdĕn

Walke, *f.n.*, wɔk, wawk

Walker, *f.n.*, 'wɔkər, wáwkĕr

Walkerdine, *f.n.*, 'wɔkərdin, wáwkĕrdeen

Walkern *Herts.*, 'wɔkərn, wáw-kĕrn

Walkham, River, *Devon*, 'wɔlkəm, wáwlkăm

Walkley *S. Yorks.*, 'wɔklɪ, wáwkli

Wall, *f.n.*, wɔl, wawl

Walla, *f.n.*, 'wɒlə, wóllă

Wallace, *f.n.*, 'wɒlɪs, wólliss

Wallach, *f.n.*, 'wɒlək, wóllăk; 'wɒlə, wóllă

Wallage, *f.n.*, 'wɒlɪdʒ, wóllij

Wallasey *Merseyside*, 'wɒləsɪ, wóllăssi

Waller, *f.n.*, 'wɒlər, wóllĕr; 'wɔlər, wáwlĕr

Walles, *f.n.*, 'wɒlɪs, wólliss

Wallich, *f.n.*, 'wɒlɪk, wóllick

Walliker, *f.n.*, 'wɒlɪkər, wóllikĕr

Wallinger, *f.n.*, 'wɒlɪndʒər, wóllin-jĕr

Wallington *Clwyd*, *Hants*, *Herts.*, *London*, 'wɒlɪŋtən, wóllingtŏn

Wallis, *f.n.*, 'wɒlɪs, wólliss

Wallop, *f.n.*, 'wɒləp, wóllŏp

Wallop, Middle, Nether, *and* Over, *Hants*, 'wɒləp, wóllŏp

Wallsend *Tyne & Wear*, 'wɒlz-end, wáwlzénd

Walmer *Kent*, 'wɔlmər, wáwlmĕr

Walmersley *Gtr. M'chester*, 'wɒmzlɪ, wáwmzli

Walmesley, *f.n.*, 'wɒmzlɪ, wáwm-zli

Walmisley, *f.n.*, 'wɒmzlɪ, wáwm-zli

Walmsley, *f.n.*, 'wɒmzlɪ, wáwmzli

Walne, *f.n.*, wɒn, wawn

Walney, Isle of, *Cumbria*, 'wɔlnɪ, wáwlni

Walond, William, *18th-c. composer and organist*, 'wɒlənd, wóllŏnd

Walpole, *f.n.*, 'wɒlpoʊl, wáwlpōl; 'wɒlpoʊl, wóllpōl. *The first is appropriate for Baron* ~.

Walpole Highway *Norfolk*, 'wɒlpoʊl 'haɪweɪ, wáwlpōl hí-way; 'wɒlpoʊl 'haɪweɪ, wóllpōl hí-way

Walrond, *f.n.*, 'wɔlrənd, wáwl-rŏnd

Walsall *W. Midlands*, 'wɔlsl, wáwlssl; 'wɔlsɔl, wáwlssawl; 'wɒsl, wáwssl

Walsden *W. Yorks.*, 'wɒlzdən, wáwlzdĕn

Walsh, *f.n.*, wɒlʃ, wawlsh; wɒlʃ, wollsh; welʃ, welsh

Walsham, North *and* South, *Norfolk*, 'wɒlʃəm, wáwl-shăm

Walsingham, Baron, 'wɒlsɪŋəm, wáwlssing-ăm

Walsingham, Great *and* Little, *Norfolk*, 'wɒlzɪŋəm, wáwlzing--ăm

Walsoken *Cambs.*, wɒl'soʊkən, wawlssŏkĕn

Walston, *f.n.*, 'wɒlstən, wáwlsstŏn. *Appropriate also for Baron* ~.

Walsworth, *f.n.*, 'wɔlzwərθ, wáwlzwŭrth

Walter, *C.n. and f.n.*, 'wɔltər, wáwltĕr; 'wɒltər, wólltĕr

Walters, *f.n.*, 'wɔltərz, wáwltĕrz; 'wɒltərz, wólltĕrz

Waltham, *f.n.*, 'wɔlθəm, wáwl-
-thăm
Waltham *Humberside,* 'wɔlθəm,
wáwl-thăm
Waltham, Great *and* Little, *Essex,*
'wɔltəm, wáwltăm
Waltham, North, *Hants,* 'wɔlθəm,
wáwl-thăm
Waltham Abbey *Essex,* 'wɔlθəm
'æbɪ, wáwl-thăm ábbi
Waltham Cross *Herts.,* 'wɔlθəm
'krɒs, wáwl-thăm króss
Waltham Forest *London,* 'wɔlθəm
'fɒrɪst, wáwl-thăm fórrĕst
Waltham-on-the-Wolds *Leics.,*
'wɔlθəm ɒn ðə 'wouldz, wáwl-
-thăm on thĕ wŏldz
Waltham St. Lawrence *Berks.,*
'wɔlθəm snt 'lɒrəns, wáwl-thăm
sĭnt lórrĕnss
Walthamstow *London,* 'wɔlθəm-
stou, wáwl-thămsstŏ
Walthew, *f.n.*, 'wɔlθju, wáwl-thew
Walton, *f.n.*, 'wɔltən, wáwltŏn;
'wɒltən, wólltŏn
Walton-le-Dale *Lancs.,* 'wɔltən
lɪ'deɪl, wáwltŏn l dáyl
Walton-on-the-Naze *Essex,*
'wɔltən ɒn ðə 'neɪz, wáwltŏn on
thĕ náyz
Walton-on-Thames *Surrey,*
'wɔltən ɒn 'temz, wáwltŏn on
témz
Walwick *Northd.,* 'wɒlɪk, wóllick;
'wɔlwɪk, wáwlwick
Walwyn, *f.n.*, 'wɔlwɪn, wáwlwin
Wamil Hall *Suffolk,* 'wɒmɪl,
wómmil
Wamphray Water *D. & G.,* 'wɒm-
freɪ, wómfray
Wanborough *Wilts.,* 'wɒnbrə,
wónnbră
Wand, *f.n.*, wɒnd, wonnd
Wandor, *f.n.*, 'wɒndər, wónndŏr
Wands, *f.n.*, wɒndz, wonndz
Wandsworth *London,* 'wɒndz-
wərθ, wónndzwŭrth
Wanhills, *f.n.*, 'wɒnhɪlz, wónn-
-hilz
Wanklyn, *f.n.*, 'wæŋklɪn, wánklin
Wanlip *Leics.,* 'wɒnlɪp, wónn-lip
Wanlockhead *D. & G.,* ,wɒnlɒk-
'hed, wonnlock-héd
Wann, *f.n.*, wɒn, wonn
Wannop, *f.n.*, 'wɒnəp, wónnŏp
Wansbeck, River, *Northd.,*
'wɒnzbek, wónnzbeck
Wansbeck parliamentary divi-
sion *Northd.,* 'wɒnzbek, wónnz-
beck
Wansborough, *f.n.*, 'wɒnzbərə,
wónnzbŭră
Wansbrough, *f.n.*, 'wɒnzbrə,
wónnzbră

Wansey, *f.n.*, 'wɒnzɪ, wónnzi
Wansford *Cambs.,* 'wɒnzfərd,
wónnzfŏrd
Wanstall, *f.n.*, 'wɒnstɔl, wónns-
-stawl
Wanstead *London,* 'wɒnsted,
wónnssted
Wantage, *f.n.*, 'wɒntɪdʒ, wónntij
Wantage *Oxon.,* 'wɒntɪdʒ, wónn-
tij
Wantisden *Suffolk,* 'wɒntsdən,
wónntsdĕn
Wapping *London,* 'wɒpɪŋ, wóp-
ping
Wapping Old Stairs *London,*
,wɒpɪŋ 'ould stɛərz, wopping
ŏld stairz
Warbeck, *f.n.*, 'wɔrbek, wáwr-
beck
Warboys *Cambs.,* 'wɔrbɔɪz,
wáwrboyz
Warbstow *Cornwall,* 'wɔrbstou,
wáwrbsstŏ
Warburg, *f.n.*, 'wɔrbərg, wáwr-
burg
Warburg Institute *London,* 'wɔr-
bərg, wáwrburg
Warburton, *f.n.*, 'wɔrbərtən,
wáwrbŭrtŏn
Warcop *Cumbria,* 'wɔrkəp, wáwr-
kŏp
Ward, *f.n.*, wɔrd, wawrd
Wardell, *f.n.*, wɔr'del, wawrdéll
Wardhaugh, *f.n.*, 'wɔrdhɔ,
wáwrd-haw
Wardrop, *f.n.*, 'wɔrdrəp, wáwr-
drŏp
Wardy Hill *Cambs.,* 'wɔrdɪ 'hɪl,
wáwrdi híll
Wareing, *f.n.*, 'wɛərɪŋ, wáiring
Waren Burn *Northd.,* 'wɛərən,
wáirĕn
Warenford *Northd.,* 'wɛərənfɔrd,
wáirĕn-ford
Waren Mills *Northd.,* 'wɛərən
'mɪlz, wáirĕn millz
Warenton *Northd.,* 'wɛərəntən,
wáirĕntŏn
Wargrave *Berks.,* 'wɔrgreɪv,
wáwr-grayv
Warham, William, *15th–16th-c.*
Archbishop of Canterbury,
'wɒrəm, wórrăm
Waring, *f.n.*, 'wɛərɪŋ, wáiring
Waringstown *Co. Down,* 'wɛərɪŋz-
taun, wáiringztown
Wark *Northd.,* wɔrk, wawrk
Warkleigh *Devon,* 'wɔrklɪ, wáwrk-
li
Warkworth, *f.n.*, 'wɔrkwərθ,
wáwrkwŭrth
Warkworth *Northd.,* 'wɔrkwərθ,
wáwrkwŭrth. *Appropriate also*
for Baron ∼.

Warleggan, *also spelt* **Warleggon,** *Cornwall,* wɔr'legən, wawr-léggăn

Warley *Staffs., W. Yorks.,* 'wɔrlɪ, wáwrli

Warley, Great *and* Little, *Essex,* 'wɔrlɪ, wáwrli

Warley Common *Essex,* 'wɔrlɪ 'kɒmən, wáwrli kómmŏn

Warlock, *f.n.,* 'wɔrlɒk, wáwrlock

Warman, *f.n.,* 'wɔrmən, wáwrmăn

Warmington *Northants.,* 'wɔrmɪŋtən, wáwrmingtŏn

Warmsworth *S. Yorks.,* 'wɔrmzwɜrθ, wáwrmzwurth

Warmwell *Dorset,* 'wɔrmwel, wáwrmwel

Warncken, *f.n.,* 'wɔrŋkɪn, wáwrnkĕn

Warner, *f.n.,* 'wɔrnər, wáwrnĕr

Warnham, *f.n.,* 'wɔrnəm, wáwrnăm

Warninglid *W. Sussex,* 'wɑrnɪŋlɪd, wáarning-lidd

Warnock, *f.n.,* 'wɔrnɒk, wáwrnock

Warr, *f.n.,* wɔr, wawr

Warrack, *f.n.,* 'wɒrək, wórrăck

Warre, *f.n.,* wɔr, wawr

Warrell, *f.n.,* 'wɒrəl, wórrĕl

Warren, *f.n.,* 'wɒrən, wórrĕn

Warrender, *f.n.,* 'wɒrɪndər, wórrĕndĕr

Warrick, *f.n.,* 'wɒrɪk, wórrick

Warrin, *f.n.,* 'wɒrɪn, wórrin

Warsash *Hants,* 'wɔrsæʃ, wáwrs-sash; 'wɔrzæʃ, wáwrzash

Warschauer, *f.n.,* 'wɒʃər, wóshĕr

Warsop *Notts.,* 'wɔrsɒp, wáwrssop

Warter, *f.n.,* 'wɔrtər, wáwrtĕr

Wartle *Grampian,* 'wɔrtl, wáwrtl

Wartling *E. Sussex,* 'wɔrtlɪŋ, wáwrtling

Warton, *f.n.,* 'wɔrtən, wáwrtŏn

Warwick, *f.n.,* 'wɒrɪk, wórrick

Warwick *Cumbria, Warwicks.,* 'wɒrɪk, wórrick. *Appropriate also for the Earl of* ~.

Wasdale, *also spelt* **Wastdale,** *Cumbria,* 'wɒsdl, wóssdl. **Wastdale** *is the ecclesiastical spelling.*

Wasdale Head, *also spelt* **Wastdale Head,** *Cumbria,* 'wɒsdl 'hed, wóssdl héd

Wash, *f.n.,* wɒʃ, wosh

Washbourne, *f.n.,* 'wɒʃbɔrn, wóshborn

Wass, *f.n.,* wɒs, woss

Wasserstein, *f.n.,* 'wæsərstin, wássĕr-steen

Wasson, *f.n.,* 'wɒsən, wóssŏn

Wastdale *see* **Wasdale**

Wastell, *f.n.,* 'wɒstl, wósstl

Wastie, *f.n.,* 'wæstɪ, wássti

Wastwater *Cumbria,* 'wɒstwɔtər, wósstwawtĕr

Watchet *Somerset,* 'wɒtʃɪt, wótchĕt

Watendlath *Cumbria,* wɒ'tendləθ, wotténdlăth

Waterden *Norfolk,* 'wɒtərdən, wáwtĕrdĕn

Waterford, Marquess of, 'wɒtərfərd, wáwtĕrfŏrd

Waterlooville *Hants,* ,wɒtərlu'vɪl, wawtĕrloo-víll

Waterman, *f.n.,* 'wɒtərmən, wáwtĕrmăn

Waternish, *also spelt* **Vaternish,** *H'land,* 'wɒtərnɪʃ, wáwtĕrnish

Waterrow *Somerset,* 'wɒtərou, wáwtĕrō

Waters, *f.n.,* 'wɒtərz, wáwtĕrz

Watford *Herts.,* 'wɒtfərd, wóttfŏrd

Wath *N. Yorks.,* wɒθ, woth

Wathen, *f.n.,* 'wɒθən, wóthĕn

Watherston, *f.n.,* 'wɒθərstən, wóthĕrstŏn

Wathes, *f.n.,* 'wɒθɪz, wóthĕz

Wath upon Dearne *S. Yorks.,* 'wɒθ əpɒn 'dɜrn, wóth ŭpon dérn; 'wæθ əpɒn 'dɜrn, wáth ŭpon dérn

Watkin, *f.n.,* 'wɒtkɪn, wóttkin

Watkins, *f.n.,* 'wɒtkɪnz, wóttkinz

Watling, *f.n.,* 'wɒtlɪŋ, wóttling

Watling Street, *Roman military road, Kent–N. Wales,* 'wɒtlɪŋ strit, wóttling street

Watmough, *f.n.,* 'wɒtmou, wóttmō

Watney, *f.n.,* 'wɒtnɪ, wóttni

Watrous, *f.n.,* 'wɒtrəs, wóttrŭss

Watson, *f.n.,* 'wɒtsən, wóttssŏn

Watt, *f.n.,* wɒt, wott

Watten *H'land,* 'wɒtən, wóttĕn; 'wætən, wáttĕn

Watters, *f.n.,* 'wɒtərz, wáwtĕrz; 'wɒtərz, wóttĕrz

Watthews, *f.n.,* 'wɒθjuz, wáw-thewz

Wattis, *f.n.,* 'wɒtɪs, wóttiss

Wattisfield *Suffolk,* 'wɒtɪsfɪld, wóttisfeeld

Wattisham *Suffolk,* 'wɒtɪʃəm, wótti-shăm

Watton *Norfolk,* 'wɒtən, wóttŏn

Watts, *f.n.,* wɒts, wotts

Wattstown *Mid Glam.,* 'wɒtstaun, wóttstown

Wauchope, *f.n.,* 'wɒxəp, wóchŏp; 'wɔkəp, wáwkŏp

Waugh, *f.n.,* wɔ, waw; wɒx, woch, wɒf, woff; wɑf, waaf. *The first is appropriate for Auberon,* 'ɔbərən, áwbĕrŏn, *and Evelyn,* 'ivlɪn, éevlin, *authors.*

Waunarlwydd *W. Glam.*, waın-
'arlʊıð, wīnaárlōō-ith
Waunfawr *see* Waenfawr
Waun-lwydd *Gwent*, waın'lʊıð,
wīn-lōō-ith
Waun-pound *Gwent*, waın'paʊnd,
wīnpównd
Wauthier, *f.n.*, 'vʊʊtjeı, vôt-yay
Wavell, *f.n.*, 'weıvl, wáyvl
Wavendon *Bucks.*, 'wævəndən,
wávvĕndŏn
Waveney, River, *Norfolk–Suffolk*,
'weıvənı, wáyvĕni
Waverley *Surrey*, 'weıvərlı, wáy-
vĕrli. *Appropriate also for
Viscount* ∼.
Waverton *Ches.*, 'weıvərtən,
wáyvĕrtŏn
Wavertree *Merseyside*, 'weıvərtri,
wáyvĕrtree
Wawne, *also spelt* Waghen,
Humberside, wɔn, wawn
Weacombe *Somerset*, 'wikəm,
weékŏm
Weal, *f.n.*, wil, weel
Wealdstone *London*, 'wildstʊʊn,
weéldsstŏn
Wealeson, *f.n.*, 'wilsən, weélssŏn
Wealleans, *f.n.*, 'wilənz, weélĕnz
Wear, River, *Durham–Tyne &
Wear*, wıər, weer
Weardale *Durham*, 'wıərdeıl,
weérdayl
Wearde *Cornwall*, wɛərd, waird
Weare Giffard *Devon*, 'wıər
'dʒıfərd, weér jiffárd
Wearing, *f.n.*, 'wɛərıŋ, wáiring
Wearn, *f.n.*, wɜrn, wern
Wearne, *f.n.*, wɜrn, wern
Wearne *Somerset*, wɛərn, wairn;
wıərn, weern; wɜrn, wern
Weasenham AllSaints *Norfolk*,
'wizənəm ɔl 'seınts, weézĕnăm
awl sáynts
Weasenham St. Peter *Norfolk*,
'wizənəm snt 'pitər, weézĕnăm
sĭnt peétĕr
Weaste *Gtr. M'chester*, wist, weest
Weaverham *Ches.*, 'wivərhæm,
weévĕr-ham
Webb, *f.n.*, web, webb
Webber, *f.n.*, 'webər, wébbĕr
Weber, *f.n.*, 'webər, wébbĕr;
'wibər, weébĕr; 'weıbər, wáybĕr
Webster, *f.n.*, 'webstər, wébsstĕr
Weddell, *f.n.*, 'wedl, wéddl;
wı'del, wĕdéll
Wedderburn, *f.n.*, 'wedərbɜrn,
wéddĕrburn
Wedgewood, *f.n.*, 'wedʒwʊd,
wéjwōōd
Wedgwood, *f.n.*, 'wedʒwʊd,
wéjwōōd. *Appropriate for Josiah
and Thomas* ∼, *18th-c. potters.*

Wednesbury *W. Midlands*, 'wenz-
bərı, wénzbŭri; 'wedʒbərı,
wéjbŭri
Wednesfield *W. Midlands*, 'wens-
fild, wénssfeeld; 'wedʒfild,
wéjfeeld
Weeks, *f.n.*, wiks, weeks
Weelkes, Thomas, *16th-c.
organist and composer*, wılks,
wilks; wilks, weelks. *The first is
now more common among
Weelkes scholars, who base this
on variant spellings in old
documents.*
Weem *Tayside*, wim, weem
Wegener, *f.n.*, 'wegənər, wéggĕnĕr
Wegg, *f.n.*, weg, wegg
Wegner, *f.n.*, 'veıgnər, váygnĕr
Weguelin, *f.n.*, 'wegəlın, wéggĕlin
Weidenfeld and Nicolson,
George, *publishers*, 'vaıdənfelt
ənd 'nıklsən, vídĕnfelt ănd
nícklssŏn
Weigal, *f.n.*, 'waıgl, wígl
Weigall, *f.n.*, 'waıgɔl, wígawl;
'waıgl, wígl
Weigh, *f.n.*, weı, way
Weighell, *f.n.*, 'weıəl, wáy-ĕl;
wil, weel
Weighill, *f.n.*, 'weıhıl, wáyhil
Weight, *f.n.*, weıt, wayt
Weightman, *f.n.*, 'weıtmən, wáyt-
măn
Weil, *f.n.*, wil, weel; vaıl, vīl
Weiland, *f.n.*, 'wilənd, weélănd
Wein, *f.n.*, win, ween
Weiner, *f.n.*, 'waınər, wínĕr
Weinreich-Haste, *f.n.*, 'waınraık
'heıst, wínrīk háyst
Weinstock *f.n.*, 'waınstɒk, wín-
-stock
Weipers, *f.n.*, 'waıpərz, wípĕrz
Weir, *f.n.*, wıər, weer
Weis, *f.n.*, wis, weess
Weisdale *Shetland*, 'wizdeıl,
weézdayl
Weisner, *f.n.*, 'wiznər, weéznĕr
Weiss, *f.n.*, vaıs, vīss
Weist, *f.n.*, wist, weesst
Weitz, *f.n.*, wits, weets
Weitzman, *f.n.*, 'waıtsmən, wíts-
măn
Welbourne, *f.n.*, 'welbɔrn, wél-
born
Welch, *f.n.*, weltʃ, weltch; welʃ,
welsh
Weldon, *f.n.*, 'weldən, wéldŏn
Wellbeloved, *f.n.*, 'welbılʌvd,
wélbĕluvd
Weller, *f.n.*, 'welər, wéllĕr
Wellesbourne *Warwicks.*, 'welz-
bɔrn, wélzborn
Wellesley, *f.n.*, 'welzlı, wélzli.
Appropriate also for Viscount ∼.

Wellesz, Egon, *composer and musicologist,* 'eıgɒn 'velıs, áygon véllĕss

Wellingborough *Northants.,* 'welıŋbərə, wéllingbŭră

Wellington, *f.n.,* 'welıŋtən, wéllingtŏn

Wellington *Cumbria, H. & W., Salop, Somerset,* 'welıŋtən, wéllingtŏn. *Appropriate also for the Duke of* ~.

Wellman, *f.n.,* 'welmən, wélmăn

Wells, *f.n.,* welz, wellz

Wells-Pestell, *f.n.,* 'welz pes'tel, wéllz pestéll

Welltog Island *Gwynedd,* 'wełtɒg, wéhltog

Wellwood, *f.n.,* 'welwʊd, wél-wŏŏd

Welnetham *see* **Whelnetham**

Welney *Norfolk,* 'welnı, wélni

Welsh, *f.n.,* welʃ, welsh

Welshpool *Powys,* 'welʃpul, wélshpool; 'welʃ'pul, wélsh-poól

Welwick *Humberside,* 'welık, wéllick

Welwyn *Herts.,* 'welın, wéllin

Welwyn Garden City *Herts.,* 'welın ,gɑrdən 'sıtı, wéllin gaar-dĕn sítti

Wem *Salop,* wem, wemm

Wembley *London,* 'wemblı, wémbli

Wemyss *Fife,* wimz, weemz. *Appropriate also for the Earl of* ~.

Wemyss Bay *S'clyde,* 'wimz 'beı, wéemz báy

Wendon, *f.n.,* 'wendən, wéndŏn

Wendover *Bucks.,* 'wendoʊvər, wéndōvĕr

Wendron *Cornwall,* 'wendrən, wéndrŏn

Wendy-cum-Shingay *Cambs.,* 'wendı kʌm 'ʃıŋgı, wéndi kum shíng-gi

Wenger, *f.n.,* 'weŋər, wéng-ĕr

Wenninger, *f.n.,* 'wenındʒər, wénninjĕr

Wensley *N. Yorks.,* 'wenzlı, wénzli

Wensleydale *N. Yorks.,* 'wenzlı-deıl, wénzlidayl. *Appropriate also for* ~ *cheese and for the* ~ *breed of sheep.*

Wensum, River, *Norfolk,* 'wen-səm, wénssŭm

Wentworth, *f.n.,* 'wentwərθ, wéntwŭrth; 'wentwɜrθ, wént-wurth

Wentz, *f.n.,* wents, wents

Wentzel, *f.n.,* 'wentsl, wéntssl

Wenvoe *S. Glam.,* 'wenvoʊ, wénvō

Weobley *H. & W.,* 'weblı, wébli

Weoley Castle *W. Midlands,* 'wıəlı, weé-ŏli

Werner, *f.n.,* 'wɜrnər, wérnĕr; 'wɔrnər, wáwrnĕr

Werneth *Gtr. M'chester,* 'wɜrnəθ, wérnĕth

Wernher, *f.n.,* 'wɜrnər, wérnĕr

Wernick, *f.n.,* 'wɜrnık, wérnick

Wesham *Lancs.,* 'wesəm, wéssăm

Wesil, *f.n.,* 'wesl, wéssl

Weske, *f.n.,* wesk, wesk

Wesker, *f.n.,* 'weskər, wéskĕr

Wesley, *f.n.,* 'weslı, wéssli; 'wezlı, wézli. *The first is appropriate for John* ~, *18th-c. evangelist and leader of Methodism, and his brother Charles.*

Wesleyan, *pertaining to John and Charles* **Wesley,** 'weslıən, wéssli-ăn

Wess, *f.n.,* wes, wess

Westaby, *f.n.,* 'westəbı, wéstăbi

Westacott, *f.n.,* 'westəkɒt, wéstă-kot

Westall, *f.n.,* 'westɔl, wéstawl

West Alvington *Devon,* 'west 'ɔlvıŋtən, wést áwlvingtŏn

West Bradley *Somerset,* 'west 'brædlı, wést brádli

West Bromwich *W. Midlands,* 'west 'brɒmıtʃ, wést brómmitch

Westbrook, *f.n.,* 'westbrʊk, wéstbrŏŏk

Westbury-on-Trym *Avon,* 'west-bərı ɒn 'trım, wéstbŭri on trím

West Calder *Lothian,* 'west 'kɔldər, wést káwldĕr

West Challow *Oxon.,* 'west 'tʃæloʊ, wést chálō

Westcott, *f.n.,* 'westkət, wéstkŏt; 'weskət, wéskŏt

Westenra, *f.n.,* 'westənrə, wés-tĕnră

Wester Fearn *H'land,* 'westər 'fɑrn, wéstĕr férn

West Freugh *D. & G.,* 'west 'frux, . wést froóch

Westgate, *f.n.,* 'westgeıt, wést-gayt; 'westgıt, wéstgit

West Grinstead *W. Sussex,* 'west 'grınstıd, wést grínsstĕd

Westham *E. Sussex,* 'westhæm, wést-ham

West Hartlepool *Cleveland,* 'west 'hɑrtlıpul, wést haártlipool

West Heslerton *N. Yorks.,* 'west 'heslərtən, wést hésslĕrtŏn

West Hoathly *W. Sussex,* 'west hoʊθ'laı, wést hōth-lí

West Horsley *Surrey,* 'west 'hɔrzlı, wést hórzli

Westhoughton *Gtr. M'chester,* 'west'hɔtən, wést-háwtŏn

Westleton *Suffolk*, 'wesltən, wéssltŏn
Westley *Suffolk*, 'westlı, wéstli
Westley Waterless *Cambs.*, 'westlı 'wɔtərlıs, wéstli wáwtĕrlĕss
West Lockinge *Oxon.*, 'west 'lɒkındʒ, wést lóckinj
West Lothian *Lothian*, 'west 'loʊðıən, wést lṓthiän
West Malling *Kent*, 'west 'mɔlıŋ, wést máwling
West Meon *Hants*, 'west 'miən, wést meé-ŏn
West Mersea *Essex*, 'west 'mɜrzı, wést mérzi
Westmeston *E. Sussex*, west-'mestən, westméstŏn
Westminster *London*, 'west-mınstər, wéstminstĕr
West Molesey *Surrey*, 'west 'moʊlzı, wést mốlzi
Westmorland *former Co. name*, 'westmərlənd, wéstmŏrländ. *Appropriate also for the Earl of* ∼.
Westoby, *f.n.*, 'westəbı, wéstŏbi; wes'toʊbı, westŏ́bi
Weston, *f.n.*, 'westən, wéstŏn
Weston Bampfylde *Somerset*, 'westən 'bæmfıld, wéstŏn bámfeeld
Weston Colville *Cambs.*, 'westən 'koʊlvıl, wéstŏn kṓlvil
Weston Favell *Northants.*, 'westən 'feıvl, wéstŏn fáyvl
Westoning *Beds.*, 'westənıŋ, wéstŏning
Weston-super-Mare *Avon*, 'westən ˌsupər 'mɛər, wéstŏn soopĕr máir; 'westən ˌsjupər 'mɛər, wéstŏn sewpĕr máir; 'westən ˌsjupər 'mɛərı, wéstŏn sewpĕr máiri
Weston Zoyland *Somerset*, 'westən 'zɔılənd, wéstŏn zóyländ
Westray *Orkney*, 'westreı, wéstray
Westrope, *f.n.*, 'westroʊp, wést--rōp
Westruther *Borders*, 'westrʌðər, wéstruthĕr
West Somerton *Norfolk*, 'west 'sʌmərtən, wést súmmĕrtŏn
West Stoughton *Somerset*, 'west 'stɔtən, wést stáwtŏn
West Walton Highway *Norfolk*, 'west 'wɔltən 'haıweı, wést wáwltŏn hí-way; 'west 'wɒltən 'haıweı, wést wólltŏn hí-way
Westward *Cumbria*, west'wɔrd, west-wáwrd
Westwater, *f.n.*, 'westwɔtər, wéstwawtĕr

West Wickham *Cambs.*, 'west 'wıkəm, wést wickăm
Westwoodside *Humberside*, 'westwʊdsaıd, wéstwŏŏd-sīd
West Wratting *Cambs.*, 'west 'rætıŋ, wést rátting
West Wycombe *Bucks.*, 'west 'wıkəm, wést wíckŏm
Wetherby *W. Yorks.*, 'weðərbı, wéthĕrbi
Wetton, *f.n.*, 'wetən, wéttŏn
Wetwang *Humberside*, 'wetwæŋ, wétwang
Wevill, *f.n.*, 'wevıl, wévvil
Wexler, *f.n.*, 'wekslər, wékslĕr
Weybourne *Norfolk*, 'webərn, wébbŭrn
Weybridge *Surrey*, 'weıbrıdʒ, wáybrij
Weyman, *f.n.*, 'waımən, wímăn. *Appropriate for Stanley J.* ∼, *author.*
Weymouth *Dorset*, 'weıməθ, wáy-mūth. *Appropriate also for Viscount* ∼.
Whaddon *Cambs.*, 'wɒdən, wóddŏn
Whaley Bridge *Derby.*, 'weılı 'brıdʒ, wáyli brij
Whalley, *f.n.*, 'wɒlı, whólli; 'hwɒlı, wháwli; 'weılı, wáyli
Whalley *Lancs.*, 'hwɒlı, wháwli
Whalley Range *Gtr. M'chester*, 'wɒlı 'reındʒ, wólli ráynj
Whalsay *Shetland*, 'hwɔlseı, wháwlssay
Whannel, *f.n.*, 'hwɒnl, whónnl; wɒ'nel, wonnéll
Whaplode *Lincs.*, 'hwɒploʊd, whóp-lōd
Wharam, *f.n.*, 'hwɛərəm, wháirăm
Wharfe, River, *N. & W. Yorks.*, wɔrf, wawrf
Wharncliffe, Earl of. 'wɔrnklıf, wórn-kliff
Wharram le Street *N. Yorks.*, 'wɒrəm lə 'strıt, wórrăm lĕ stréet
Wharram Percy *N. Yorks.*, 'wɒrəm 'pɜrsı, wórrăm pérssi
Whateley, *f.n.*, 'hweıtlı, wháytli
Whatham, *f.n.*, 'wɒðəm, wóthăm; 'wɒtəm, wóttăm; 'wɒθəm, wóthăm
Whatley, *f.n.*, 'hwɒtlı, whóttli
Whatling, *f.n.*, 'hwɒtlıŋ, whóttling
Whatmore, *f.n.*, 'hwɒtmɔr, whótt-mor
Whatmough, *f.n.*, 'hwɒtmoʊ, whóttmō; 'wɒtmʌf, wóttmuff; 'wɒtmʊf, wóttmŏŏf
Whatsley, *f.n.*, 'wɒtslı, wóttsli
Whatstandwell *Derby.*, wɒt-'stændwel, wottstándwel

Whatton, *f.n.*, 'wɒtən, wóttŏn
Whatton *Notts.*, 'wɒtən, wóttŏn
Wheadon, *f.n.*, 'widən, weédŏn
Wheal Rose *Cornwall*, 'wil 'rouz,
 weél rŏz
Wheare, *f.n.*, hwɛər, whair
Wheatacre *Norfolk*, 'hwɪtəkər,
 whíttäkĕr
Wheathampstead *Herts.*, 'hwet-
 əmsted, whéttämssted; 'hwitəm-
 sted, wheétämssted
Wheatley, *f.n.*, 'hwitlı, wheétli
Wheatstone, *f.n.*, 'hwitstən,
 wheétstŏn
Wheeler, *f.n.*, 'hwilər, wheélĕr
Whelan, *f.n.*, 'hwilən, wheélän
Wheldon, *f.n.*, 'weldən, wéldŏn
Wheldale *W. Yorks.*, 'weldeıl,
 wéldayl
Whelen, *f.n.*, 'hwilən, wheélĕn
Whelleans, *f.n.*, 'wilənz, weélĕnz
Whelnetham, *also spelt* Wel-
 netham, *Suffolk*, wel'niθəm,
 welneéthäm; 'welnetəm, wél-
 nettäm
Whernside, mt., *Cumbria–N.
 Yorks.*, 'wɜrnssid, wérnssîd
Wherstead *Suffolk*, 'wɜrsted,
 wérssted
Wherwell *Hants.*, 'hwɜrwel, whér-
 -wel
Wheway, *f.n.*, 'hwiweı, wheéway
Whewell, *f.n.*, 'hjuəl, héw-ĕl
Whibley, *f.n.*, 'hwɪblı, whíbbli
Whichcote, *f.n.*, 'hwɪtʃkout,
 whítch-kŏt
Whicher, *f.n.*, 'wɪtʃər, wítchĕr
Whicker, *f.n.*, 'wɪkər, wíckĕr
Whiddett, *f.n.*, wı'det, widétt
Whiffen, *f.n.*, 'wɪfɪn, wíffĕn
Whiffin, *f.n.*, 'wɪfɪn, wíffin
Whiffing, *f.n.*, 'wɪfɪŋ, wíffing
Whigham, *f.n.*, 'hwɪgəm, whíggäm
Whilding, *f.n.*, 'hwaıldıŋ, whílding
Whiligh *E. Sussex*, 'hwaılaı, whí-lī
Whincup, *f.n.*, 'wɪŋkəp, wínkŭp
Whinerey, *f.n.*, 'hwɪnərı, whinnĕri
Whipsnade *Beds.*, 'hwɪpsneıd,
 whíp-snayd
Whissendine *Leics.*, 'hwɪsəndaın,
 whíssĕndîn
Whistlefield *S'clyde*, 'hwɪslfild,
 whísslfeeld
Whitaker, *f.n.*, 'hwɪtəkər, whít-
 täkĕr. *Appropriate for* ~'s
 Almanac.
Whitbread, *f.n.*, 'hwɪtbred, whítt-
 bred
Whitby, *f.n.*, 'hwɪtbı, whíttbi
Whitby *N. Yorks.*, 'hwɪtbı, whíttbi
Whitcher, *f.n.*, 'wɪtʃər, wítchĕr
Whitchurch Canonicorum *Dorset*,
 'hwɪt-tʃɜrtʃ kə,nɒnı'kɔrəm,
 whít-churtch känonnikáwrŭm

White, *f.n.*, hwaıt, whīt
Whiteabbey *Co. Antrim*, hwaıt-
 'æbı, whītábbi
Whiteadder, River, *Borders–
 -Northd.*,' hwɪtədər, whíttädĕr
Whitear, *f.n.*, 'hwɪtɪər, whítti-är
Whitebridge *H'land*, 'hwaıtbrıdʒ,
 whítbrij
White Colne *Essex*, 'hwaıt 'koun,
 whīt kŏn
Whitefield, *f.n.*, 'hwɪtfild, whítt-
 feeld; 'hwaıtfild, whítfeeld. *The
 first is appropriate for George
 ~, 18th-c. preacher and evangelist, and hence for the ~
 Memorial Church in London.*
Whitefield *Gtr. M'chester*, 'hwaıtfild, whítfeeld
White Friargate *Hull*, 'waıtfrə-
 geıt, wít-frägayt
Whitehall *London*, 'hwaıthɔl,
 whít-hawl; 'hwaıt'hɔl, whít-
 -háwl
Whitehaugh *Grampian*, hwaıt'hɔ,
 whīt-háw
Whitehaven *Cumbria*, 'hwaıt-
 heıvən, whít-hayvĕn
Whitehead, *f.n.*, 'hwaıthed, whít-
 -hed
Whitehead *Co. Antrim*, hwaıt-
 'hed, whīt-héd
Whitehorn, *f.n.*, 'hwaıthɔrn, whít-
 -horn
Whitehough *Derby.*, 'hwaıthʌf,
 whít-huff
Whitehouse, *f.n.*, 'hwaıthaus,
 whít-howss
Whitehouse *Co. Antrim*, 'hwaıthaus, whít-howss
Whiteley, *f.n.*, 'hwaıtlı, whítli
Whitelock, *f.n.*, 'hwaıtlɒk, whít-
 lock
Whitemoor *Cornwall*, 'hwaıtmuər,
 whítmŏŏr
Whitemore, *f.n.*, 'hwaıtmɔr, whít-
 mor
Whiten Head *H'land*, 'hwaıtən
 'hed, whítĕn héd
Whiteside, *f.n.*, 'hwaıtsaıd, whít-
 sîd
Whiteslea Lodge *Norfolk*,
 'hwaıtsli, whítsslee
Whitestone *Devon*, 'hwɪtstən,
 whíttstŏn
White Stone *H. & W.*, 'hwaıt
 stoun, whīt stŏn
White Waltham *Berks.*, 'hwaıt
 'wɔlθəm, whīt wáwl-thäm;
 'hwaıt 'wɔltəm, whīt wáwltäm
Whitfield, *f.n.*, 'hwɪtfild, whítt-
 feeld
Whitfield *Kent*, 'wɪtfild, wíttfeeld
Whithorn *D. & G.*, 'hwɪthɔrn,
 whítt-horn

Whiting, *f.n.*, 'hwaɪtɪŋ, whīting
Whiting Bay *S'clyde*, 'hwaɪtɪŋ 'beɪ,
    whīting báy
Whitla Hall *Queen's University*,
    Belfast, 'hwɪtlə, whíttlä
Whitley, *f.n.*, 'hwɪtlɪ, whíttli
Whitlock, *f.n.*, 'hwɪtlɒk, whíttlock
Whitmore, *f.n.*, 'hwɪtmɔr, whítt-
    mor
Whitney, *f.n.*, 'hwɪtnɪ, whíttni
Whitred, *f.n.*, 'hwɪtrɪd, whíttrĕd
Whitrow, *f.n.*, 'wɪtroʊ, wíttrō
Whittaker, *f.n.*, 'hwɪtəkər, whít-
    tăkĕr
Whittenbury, *f.n.*, 'hwɪtənbərɪ,
    whíttĕnbŭri
Whittingehame *Lothian*, 'hwɪt-
    ɪndʒəm, whíttinjäm
Whittingham *Lancs.*, 'hwɪtɪnhəm,
    whíttin-hăm
Whittingham *Northd.*, 'hwɪtɪndʒ-
    əm, whíttinjäm
Whittle, *f.n.*, 'hwɪtl, whíttl
Whittle-le-Woods *Lancs.*, 'hwɪtl
    lə 'wʊdz, whíttl lĕ wŏŏdz
Whittlesford *Cambs.*, 'wɪtlzfərd,
    wíttlzfŏrd
Whittock, *f.n.*, 'hwɪtək, whíttŏk
Whitton, *f.n.*, 'hwɪtən, whíttŏn
Whitty, *f.n.*, 'hwɪtɪ, whíttī
Whitwick *Leics.*, 'hwɪtɪk, whíttick
Whitworth, *f.n.*, 'hwɪtwɜrθ,
    whítt-wurth
Whoberley *W. Midlands*, 'woʊ-
    bərlɪ, wŏbĕrli
Whone, *f.n.*, woʊn, wōn
Whorlow, *f.n.*, 'wɜrloʊ, wúrlō
Whyberd, *f.n.*, 'waɪbərd, wíberd
Whybrow, *f.n.*, 'hwaɪbraʊ,
    whíbrow
Whyke *W. Sussex*, wɪk, wick
Whyman, *f.n.*, 'waɪmən, wímän
Whymant, *f.n.*, 'waɪmənt, wímănt
Whymper, *f.n.*, 'hwɪmpər, whím-
    pĕr
Whyte, *f.n.*, hwaɪt, whīt
Whyteleaf *Surrey*, 'hwaɪtlif, whīt-
    leef
Whytham, *f.n.*, 'hwaɪtəm, whítăm
Whythorne, Thomas, *16th-c.*
    composer, 'hwaɪthɔrn, whít-
    -horn. *The name also appears*
    spelt Whithorne.
Wibaut, *f.n.*, 'viboʊ, veébō
Wibsey *W. Yorks.*, 'wɪpsɪ, wípssi;
    'wɪbzɪ, wíbzi
Wichelo, *f.n.*, 'wɪtʃɪloʊ, witchĕlō
Wichnor *Staffs.*, 'wɪtʃnɔr, witchnor
Wick *H'land*, wɪk, wick
Wicken, *f.n.*, 'wɪkɪn, wíckĕn
Wicken *Cambs.*, 'wɪkɪn, wíckĕn
Wickhambreaux, *also spelt*
    Wickhambreux, *Kent*, 'wɪkəm-
    bru, wíckămbroo

Wickhambrook *Suffolk*, 'wɪkəm-
    brʊk, wíckămbrŏŏk
Wickhamford *H. & W.*, 'wɪkəm-
    'fɔrd, wickămfórd
Wickham Market *Suffolk*, 'wɪkəm
    'mɑrkɪt, wickăm maárkĕt
Wickham Skeith *Suffolk*, 'wɪkəm
    'skiθ, wickăm skeéth
Wickins, *f.n.*, 'wɪkɪnz, wíckinz
Wicks, *f.n.*, wɪks, wicks
Wickwar *Avon*, 'wɪkwɔr, wíck-
    wawr
Wicor *Hants*, 'wɪkər, wickŏr
Widecombe *Devon*, 'wɪdɪkəm,
    wíddĕkŏm
Wideford Hill *Orkney*, 'waɪdfərd,
    wídfŏrd
Widemouth Bay *Cornwall*, 'wɪd-
    məθ 'beɪ, widmŭth báy
Wideopen *Tyne & Wear*, 'waɪd-
    oʊpən, wídōpĕn
Wideson, *f.n.*, 'waɪdsən, wíds-
    sŏn
Widgery, *f.n.*, 'wɪdʒərɪ, wíjjĕri
Widlake, *f.n.*, 'wɪdleɪk, wídlayk
Widley *Hants*, 'wɪdlɪ, wídli
Widnall, *f.n.*, 'wɪdnəl, widnäl
Widnes *Ches.*, 'wɪdnɪs, wídnĕss
Widnesian *native of Widnes*,
    wɪd'nɪzɪən, widneézi-ăn
Wiegold, *f.n.*, 'waɪgoʊld, wígōld
Wieler, *f.n.*, 'wilər, weélĕr
Wien, *f.n.*, win, ween
Wiesenthal, *f.n.*, 'visəntɑl, veéss-
    ĕntaal
Wigan, *f.n.*, 'wɪgən, wíggăn
Wigan *Gtr. M'chester*, 'wɪgən,
    wíggăn
Wigdor, *f.n.*, 'wɪgdɔr, wigdor
Wigfull, *f.n.*, 'wɪgfəl, wigfŭl
Wiggall, *f.n.*, 'wɪgɔl, wíggawl
Wiggins, *f.n.*, 'wɪgɪnz, wígginz
Wigham, *f.n.*, 'wɪgəm, wíggăm
Wight, I. of, waɪt, wīt
Wightman, *f.n.*, 'waɪtmən, wít-
    män
Wighton, *f.n.*, 'waɪtən, wítŏn
Wightwick, *f.n.*, 'wɪtɪk, wíttick
Wightwick *W. Midlands*, 'wɪtɪk,
    wíttick
Wigley, *f.n.*, 'wɪglɪ, wígli
Wigmore, *f.n.*, 'wɪgmɔr, wígmor
Wigoder, *f.n.*, 'wɪgədər, wiggŏdĕr
Wigram, *f.n.*, 'wɪgrəm, wígrăm.
    Appropriate also for Baron ~.
Wigtown *D. & G.*, 'wɪgtaʊn, wíg-
    town; 'wɪgtən, wígtŏn
Wigzell, *f.n.*, 'wɪgzl, wigzl
Wilbarston *Northants.*, wɪl'bɑr-
    stən, wilbaársstŏn
Wilberforce, *f.n.*, 'wɪlbərfɔrs,
    wilbĕrforss
Wilbraham, *f.n.*, 'wɪlbrəhəm,
    wílbrăhăm; 'wɪlbrəm, wílbrăm

Wilbraham, Great *and* Little, *Cambs.*, 'wɪlbrəm, wilbrăm; 'wɪlbrəhæm, wilbrăham
Wilburton *Cambs.*, wɪl'bɜrtən, wilbúrtŏn
Wilbye, John, *16th–17th-c. madrigal composer*, 'wɪlbɪ, wílbi. *A contemporary reference to him as Wilbee seems to discount the view held by some that the second syllable should rhyme with 'high'.*
Wilcox, *f.n.*, 'wɪlkɒks, wílkocks
Wild, *f.n.*, waɪld, wild
Wildash, *f.n.*, 'waɪldæʃ, wíldash
Wilde, *f.n.*, waɪld, wild
Wildeman, *f.n.*, 'waɪldmən, wíld-măn
Wildenstein Gallery *London*, 'wɪldənstaɪn, wílldĕnsstīn
Wilder, *f.n.*, 'waɪldər, wíldĕr
Wilderhope *Salop*, 'wɪldərhoʊp, wílldĕr-hŏp
Wilderspool *Ches.*, 'wɪldərzpul, wílldĕrzpool
Wilding, *f.n.*, 'waɪldɪŋ, wílding
Wildman, *f.n.*, 'waɪldmən, wíld-măn
Wilen, *f.n.*, vɪ'leɪn, viláyn
Wilenski, *f.n.*, wɪ'lenskɪ, wilénski
Wiles, *f.n.*, waɪlz, wilz
Wiliam, *f.n.*, 'wɪljəm, wíl-yăm
Wilkes, *f.n.*, wɪlks, wilks
Wilkie, *f.n.*, 'wɪlkɪ, wílki
Wilkinson, *f.n.*, 'wɪlkɪnsən, wílkinssŏn
Willapark Point *Cornwall*, 'wɪləpark 'pɔɪnt, willăpaark póynt
Willard, *f.n.*, 'wɪlɑrd, willaard
Willcocks, *f.n.*, 'wɪlkɒks, wílkocks
Willcox, *f.n.*, 'wɪlkɒks, wílkocks
Willenhall *W. Midlands*, 'wɪlənhɔl, willĕnhawl
Willes, *f.n.*, wɪlz, willz
Willesden *London*, 'wɪlzdən, wilzdĕn
Willey, *f.n.*, 'wɪlɪ, wílli
Williams, *f.n.*, 'wɪljəmz, wíl-yămz
Williamscot *Oxon.*, 'wɪlskət, wílsskŏt
Willicomb, *f.n.*, 'wɪlɪkəm, willikŏm
Willies, *f.n.*, 'wɪlɪz, williz; 'wɪlɪs, williss
Willingale, *f.n.*, 'wɪlɪŋgeɪl, willing-gayl
Willingham, *f.n.*, 'wɪlɪŋəm, willing-ăm
Willis, *f.n.*, 'wɪlɪs, williss
Willison, *f.n.*, 'wɪlɪsən, wíllissŏn
Willmott, *f.n.*, 'wɪlmət, wílmŏt; 'wɪlmɒt, wilmott
Willoughby, *f.n.*, 'wɪləbɪ, wíllŏbi

Willoughby de Broke, Baron, 'wɪləbɪ də 'brʊk, wíllŏbi dĕ brŏŏk
Willoughby de Eresby, Baron, 'wɪləbɪ 'dɪərzbɪ, wíllŏbi déerzbi
Wills, *f.n.*, wɪlz, willz
Wills Neck *Somerset*, 'wɪlz 'nek, willz néck
Willson, *f.n.*, 'wɪlsən, wilssŏn
Willum, *f.n.*, 'wɪləm, wíllŭm
Wilmcote *Warwicks.*, 'wɪlmkoʊt, wilmkŏt
Wilmslow *Ches.*, 'wɪlmzloʊ, wílmzlŏ; 'wɪmzloʊ, wímzlŏ
Wilnecote *Staffs.*, 'wɪlnɪkət, wilnĕkŏt; 'wɪŋkət, wínkŏt
Wilpshire *Lancs.*, 'wɪlpʃər, wílp-shĕr
Wilshamstead *Beds.*, 'wɪlʃəmstɪd, wíl-shămsstĕd. *Also spelt* **Wilstead**, *q.v.*
Wilshaw, *f.n.*, 'wɪlʃɔ, wíl-shaw
Wilshin, *f.n.*, 'wɪlʃɪn, wíl-shin
Wilson, *f.n.*, 'wɪlsən, wilssŏn
Wilstead *Beds.*, 'wɪlstɪd, wílsstĕd. *Also spelt* **Wilshamstead**, *q.v.*
Wiltshire, *f.n.*, 'wɪlt-ʃər, wílt-shĕr
Wiltshire *Co. name*, 'wɪlt-ʃər, wílt-shĕr; 'wɪlʃər, wíl-shĕr
Wimbledon *London*, 'wɪmbldən, wímbldŏn
Wimbotsham *Norfolk*, 'wɪmbət-ʃəm, wímbŏt-shăm
Wimhurst, *f.n.*, 'wɪmhɜrst, wímhurst
Wincanton *Somerset*, wɪn'kæntən, win-kántŏn
Winch, *f.n.*, wɪntʃ, wintch
Winchburgh *Lothian*, 'wɪnʃbərə, wínshbŭră
Winchcombe *Glos.*, 'wɪnʃkəm, wínshkŏm
Winchelsea *E. Sussex*, 'wɪntʃlsɪ, wíntchlssee
Winchelsey, *f.n.*, 'wɪntʃlsɪ, wíntchlssi
Winchester *Hants*, 'wɪntʃɪstər, wíntchĕstĕr
Winchilsea, Earl of, 'wɪntʃlsɪ, wíntchlssi
Winchwen *W. Glam.*, 'wɪnʃwen, wínsh-wen
Winckless, *f.n.*, 'wɪŋkles, wínkless
Wincle *Ches.*, 'wɪŋkl, wínkl
Wincott, *f.n.*, 'wɪŋkət, wínkŏt
Windeatt, *f.n.*, 'wɪndɪət, wíndi-ăt
Windebank, *f.n.*, 'wɪndɪbæŋk, wíndĕbank
Winder, *f.n.*, 'wɪndər, wíndĕr
Windermere *Cumbria*, 'wɪndərmɪər, wíndĕrmeer
Winders, *f.n.*, 'wɪndərz, wíndĕrz
Windess, *f.n.*, 'wɪndɪs, wíndĕss
Windeyer, *f.n.*, 'wɪndɪər, wíndi-ĕr

Winding, *f.n.*, 'waɪndɪŋ, wínding
Windle, *f.n.*, 'wɪndl, wíndl
Windlesham *Surrey*, 'wɪndlʃəm, wíndl-shăm. *Appropriate also for Baron* ~.
Windley, *f.n.*, 'wɪndlɪ, wíndli
Windram, *f.n.*, 'wɪndrəm, wíndrăm
Windrush, River, *Glos.–Oxon.*, 'wɪndrʌʃ, wíndrush
Windscale *Cumbria*, 'wɪndskeɪl, wíndskayl
Windsor, *f.n.*, 'wɪnzər, wínzŏr
Windsor *Berks.*, 'wɪndzər, wíndzŏr
Windus, *f.n.*, 'wɪndəs, wíndŭss
Windygates *Fife*, 'wɪndɪgeɪts, wíndigayts
Wine, *f.n.*, waɪn, wīn
Winearls, *f.n.*, 'wɪnərlz, wínnĕrlz
Wineham *W. Sussex*, waɪn'hæm, wīn-hám
Winestead *Humberside*, 'waɪnsted, wínssted
Winfrith *Dorset*, 'wɪnfrɪθ, wínfrith
Winfrith Heath *Dorset*, 'wɪnfrɪθ 'hiθ, wínfrith héeth
Winfrith Newburgh *Dorset*, 'wɪnfrɪθ 'njubərg, winfrith néwburg
Wing, *f.n.*, wɪŋ, wing
Wing *Bucks.*, wɪŋ, wing
Wingerworth *Derby.*, 'wɪŋərwɜrθ, wíng-ĕr-wurth
Winget, *f.n.*, 'wɪŋɪt, wíng-ĕt
Wingham, *f.n.*, 'wɪŋəm, wíng-ăm
Wingrove, *f.n.*, 'wɪŋgroʊv, wíng--grōv
Winkle, *f.n.*, 'wɪŋkl, wínkl
Winkleigh *Devon*, 'wɪŋklɪ, wínkli
Winlaton *Tyne & Wear*, wɪn-'leɪtən, winláytŏn; 'wɪnletən, wínlettŏn
Winn, *f.n.*, wɪn, winn
Winnall *Hants*, 'wɪnl, wínnl
Winsborough, *f.n.*, 'wɪnzbrə, wínzbră
Winser, *f.n.*, 'wɪnzər, wínzĕr
Winsham *Somerset*, 'wɪnsəm, wínssăm
Winshill *Staffs.*, 'wɪnzhɪl, wínz-hil
Winslade, *f.n.*, 'wɪnsleɪd, wínsslayd
Winsor, *f.n.*, 'wɪnzər, wínzŏr
Winspear, *f.n.*, 'wɪnspɪər, wínsspeer
Winstanley, *f.n.*, 'wɪnstənlɪ, wínsstănli; wɪn'stænlɪ, winsstánli
Winstanley *Gtr. M'chester*, 'wɪnstənlɪ, wínsstănli; wɪn-'stænlɪ, winsstánli
Winstock, *f.n.*, 'wɪnstɒk, wínsstock
Winter, *f.n.*, 'wɪntər, wíntĕr

Winterbourne Whitechurch *Dorset*, 'wɪntərbɔrn 'hwɪt-tʃɜrtʃ, wínterborn whit-churtch
Winterbotham, *f.n.*, 'wɪntərbɒtəm, wíntĕrbottăm
Winterbottom, *f.n.*, 'wɪntərbɒtəm, wíntĕrbottŏm
Winterflood, *f.n.*, 'wɪntərflʌd, wíntĕrfludd
Winther, *f.n.*, 'wɪntər, wíntĕr
Wintle, *f.n.*, 'wɪntl, wíntl
Wintour, *f.n.*, 'wɪntər, wíntŭr
Wintringham, *f.n.*, 'wɪntrɪŋəm, wíntring-ăm
Winward, *f.n.*, 'wɪnwərd, wínwărd
Winwick *Cambs.*, 'wɪnɪk, wínnick
Wippell, *f.n.*, 'wɪpl, wíppl
Wirksworth *Derby.*, 'wɜrkswərθ, wírkswŭrth
Wirral *Merseyside–Ches.*, 'wɪrəl, wírrăl
Wirswall *Ches.*, 'wɜrzwəl, wírzwăl
Wirth, *f.n.*, wɜrθ, wirth
Wisbech *Cambs.*, 'wɪzbitʃ, wízbeetch
Wisdom, *f.n.*, 'wɪzdəm, wízdŏm
Wise, *f.n.*, waɪz, wīz
Wiseton *Notts.*, 'waɪstən, wísstŏn
Wishart, *f.n.*, 'wɪʃərt, wíshărt
Wishaw *S'clyde*, *Warwicks.*, 'wɪʃɔ, wíshaw
Wisher, *f.n.*, 'wɪʃər, wíshĕr
Wiske, River, *N. Yorks.*, wɪsk, wisk
Wiskemann, *f.n.*, 'wɪskəmən, wísskĕmän
Wisley *Surrey*, 'wɪzlɪ, wízzli
Wissington *see* **Wiston** *Suffolk*
Wistaston *Ches.*, 'wɪstəstən, wísstässtŏn
Wiston *Dyfed*, 'wɪsən, wíssŏn
Wiston *S'clyde*, 'wɪstən, wísstŏn
Wiston, *also spelt* **Wissington**, *Suffolk* 'wɪstən, wísstŏn
Wiston *W. Sussex*, 'wɪstən, wísstŏn; 'wɪsən, wíssŏn
Wistow *Cambs.*, *Leics.*, *N. Yorks.*, 'wɪstoʊ, wísstō
Wistreich, *f.n.*, 'wɪstraɪk, wísstrīk
Wistrich, *f.n.*, 'wɪstrɪtʃ, wísstritch
Witcham *Cambs.*, 'wɪtʃəm, wítchăm
Witchell, *f.n.*, 'wɪtʃl, wítchl
Witham, *f.n.*, 'wɪtəm, wíttăm
Witham *Essex*, 'wɪtəm, wíttăm
Witham, River, *Leics.–Lincs.*, 'wɪðəm, wíthăm
Witham Friary *Somerset*, 'wɪtəm 'fraɪərɪ, wíttăm frī-ări; 'wɪðəm 'fraɪərɪ, wíthăm frī-ări
Withe, *f.n.*, wɪð, with
Withern *Lincs.*, 'wɪðərn, wíthĕrn
Withernsea *Humberside*, 'wɪðərnsi, wíthĕrnssee

Witherow, *f.n.*, 'wɪðərou, wíthērō
Withers, *f.n.*, 'wɪðərz, wíthĕrz
Witherspoon, *f.n.*, 'wɪðərspun, wíthĕrsspoon
Withington *Gtr. M'chester*, 'wɪðɪŋtən, wíthingtŏn
Withnall, *f.n.*, 'wɪθnəl, wíthnăl
Withnell *Lancs.*, 'wɪθnəl, wíthnĕl
Withy, *f.n.*, 'wɪðɪ, wíthi
Withycombe Raleigh *Devon*, 'wɪðɪkəm 'rɔlɪ, wíthikŏm ráwli
Withyham *E. Sussex*, wɪðɪ'hæm, withi-hám; 'wɪðɪhæm, wíthi--ham
Witt, *f.n.*, wɪt, witt
Wittenbach, *f.n.*, 'wɪtənbak, wíttĕnbaak
Wittersham *Kent*, 'wɪtərʃəm, wíttĕr-shäm
Wittkower, *f.n.*, 'wɪtkouvər, wíttkōvĕr
Wittle, *f.n.*, 'wɪtl, wíttl
Witton Gilbert *Durham*, 'wɪtən 'dʒɪlbərt, wíttŏn jílbĕrt; 'wɪtən 'gɪlbərt, wíttŏn gílbĕrt
Wiveliscombe *Somerset*, 'wɪvəlɪskəm, wívvĕlisskŏm; 'wɪlskəm, wílsskŏm
Wivelsfield *E. Sussex*, 'wɪvlzfɪld, wívvlzfeeld
Wivenhoe *Essex*, 'wɪvənhou, wívvĕn-hō
Wivenhoe Cross *Essex*, 'wɪvənhou 'krɒs, wívvĕn-hō króss
Wiverton *Notts.*, 'waɪvərtən, wívĕrtŏn; 'wɜrtən, wértŏn
Wiveton *Norfolk*, 'wɪvtən, wívtŏn; 'wɪvɪtən, wívvĕtŏn
Woan, *f.n.*, woun, wōn
Wober, *f.n.*, 'woubər, wóbĕr
Woburn *Beds.*, 'woubɜrn, wóburn; 'wubɜrn, wóoburn. *The second is used by the family of the Duke of Bedford and is therefore appropriate for* ~ *Abbey and Wild Animal Kingdom. The first is usual in the village.*
Woburn *Co. Down*, 'woubɜrn, wóburn
Woburn Press, *publishers*, 'woubɜrn, wóburn
Woburn Sands *Beds.–Bucks. border*, 'woubɜrn 'sændz, wóburn sándz; 'wubɜrn 'sændz, wóoburn sándz
Wodehouse, *f.n.*, 'wudhaus, wōod-howss; 'wudəs, wōodŭss. *The first is appropriate for P. G.* ~, *author.*
Wodell, *f.n.*, wɒ'del, woddéll
Wofford, *f.n.*, 'wɒfərd, wóffŏrd
Wofinden, *f.n.*, 'wufɪndən, wōofíndĕn
Woking *Surrey*, 'woukɪŋ, wóking

Wokingham *Berks.*, 'woukɪŋəm, wóking-ăm
Wolborough *Devon*, 'wulbərə, wōolbŭră
Woldingham *Surrey*, 'wouldɪŋəm, wólding-ăm
Woledge, *f.n.*, 'wulɪdʒ, wōolĕj
Wolfe, *f.n.*, wulf, wōolf
Wolfenden, *f.n.*, 'wulfəndən, wōolfĕndĕn
Wolferstan, *f.n.*, 'wulfərstən, wōolfĕrstän
Wolferton *Norfolk*, 'wulfərtən, wōolfĕrtŏn
Wolff, *f.n.*, wulf, wōolf
Wolfgang, *f.n.*, 'wulfgæŋ, wōolfgang
Wolfhampcote *Warwicks.*, 'wulfəmkət, wōolfămkŏt
Wolfrunian, *native of Wolverhampton*, wul'frunɪən, wōolfrooniăn
Wolfsthal, *f.n.*, 'wulfstal, wōolfstaal
Wollaston, *f.n.*, 'wuləstən, wōolässtŏn
Wollaston *Northants.*, 'wuləstən, wōolästŏn
Wollaton *Notts.*, 'wulətən, wōolätŏn
Wollescote *W. Midlands*, 'wulɪskout, wōolĕsskŏt
Wollstonecraft, *f.n.*, 'wulstənkraft, wōolstŏn-kraaft
Wolmer, *Viscount*, 'wulmər, wōolmĕr
Wolmer, *f.n.*, 'wulmər, wōolmĕr
Wolpert, *f.n.*, 'wulpərt, wōolpĕrt
Wolridge, *f.n.*, 'wulrɪdʒ, wōolrij
Wolseley, *f.n.*, 'wulzlɪ, wōolzli
Wolsey, *f.n.*, 'wulzɪ, wōolzi
Wolsingham *Durham*, 'wulzɪŋəm, wōolzing-ăm
Wolstanton *Staffs.*, wul'stæntən, wōolstántŏn
Wolstenbury *Hill E. Sussex*, 'wulstənbərɪ, wōolstĕnbŭri
Wolstencroft, *f.n.*, 'wulstənkrɒft, wōolstĕn-kroft
Wolstenholme, *f.n.*, 'wulstənhoum, wōolstĕnhŏm
Wolsty *Cumbria*, 'wulstɪ, wōolsti; 'wustɪ, wōossti
Wolterton *Norfolk*, 'wultərtən, wōoltĕrtŏn
Wolvercote *Oxon.*, 'wulvərkət, wōolvĕrkŏt
Wolverhampton *W. Midlands*, ˌwulvər'hæmptən, wōolvĕr--hámptŏn
Wolverley *H. & W.*, 'wulvərlɪ, wōolvĕrli
Wolverton, *Baron*, 'wulvərtən, wōolvĕrtŏn

Wolviston *Cleveland*, 'wʊlvɪstən, wŏŏlvisstŏn

Wombourn *Staffs.*, 'wɒmbərn, wómbŭrn

Wombridge *Salop*, 'wʌmbrɪdʒ, wúmbrij

Wombwell, *f.n.*, 'wumwəl, woŏm-wĕl; 'wʊmwəl, woŏmwĕl; 'wɒmwəl, wómwĕl

Wombwell *S. Yorks.*, 'wʊmwel, woŏmwell

Womenswold *Kent*, 'wɪmɪnz-woʊld, wímmĕnzwŏld; 'wimz-woʊld, weˇemzwŏld

Womersley, *f.n.*, 'wʊmərzlɪ, woˇomĕrzli; 'wɒmərzlɪ, wóm-mĕrzli

Wonersh *Surrey*, 'wɒnɜrʃ, wón-nersh

Wonnacott, *f.n.*, 'wɒnəkɒt, wónnăkott

Wontner, *f.n.*, 'wɒntnər, wónntnĕr

Wooburn *Bucks.*, 'wubɜrn, woˇo-burn

Wood, Haydn, *composer*, 'heɪdn 'wʊd, háydn woŏd

Woodall, *f.n.*, 'wʊdɔl, woˇodawl

Woodbridge, *f.n.*, 'wʊdbrɪdʒ, woˇodbrij

Woodbridge *Suffolk*, 'wʊdbrɪdʒ, woˇodbrij

Woodburn, East *and* West, *Northd.*, 'wʊdbɜrn, woˇodburn

Woodchester *Glos.*, 'wʊtʃɪstər, woˇotchĕstĕr

Woodforde-Finden, *f.n.*, 'wʊdfərd 'fɪndən, woˇodfŏrd fíndĕn

Woodford Halse *Northants.*, 'wʊdfərd 'hɒls, woˇodfŏrd hólss

Woodgate, *f.n.*, 'wʊdgeɪt, woˇod-gayt

Woodger, *f.n.*, 'wʊdʒər, woˇojĕr

Woodget, *f.n.*, 'wʊdgɪt, woˇod-gĕt

Woodhall, *f.n.*, 'wʊdhɔl, woˇod-hawl

Woodhatch, *f.n.*, 'wʊdhætʃ, woˇod-hatch

Woodhouse, *f.n.*, 'wʊdhaʊs, woˇod-howss

Woodiwiss, *f.n.*, 'wʊdɪwɪs, woˇodi-wiss

Woodland, *f.n.*, 'wʊdlənd, woˇod-lănd

Woodlesford *W. Yorks.*, 'wʊdlz-fərd, woˇodlzfŏrd

Woodley, *f.n.*, 'wʊdlɪ, woˇodli

Woodliff, *f.n.*, 'wʊdlɪf, woˇodliff

Woodman, *f.n.*, 'wʊdmən, woˇod-măn

Woodnesborough *Kent*, 'wʊdnəz-bərə, woˇodnĕzbŭră; 'wʊnzbərə, woˇonzbŭră; 'wɪnzbərə, wínzbŭră

Woodnutt, *f.n.*, 'wʊdnʌt, woˇod-nutt

Woodrooffe, *f.n.*, 'wʊdrəf, woˇodrŏf

Woods, *f.n.*, wʊdz, woŏdz

Woodstock *Oxon.*, 'wʊdstɒk, woˇodstock

Woodvale *Merseyside*, 'wʊdveɪl, woˇodvayl

Woodville, *f.n.*, 'wʊdvɪl, woˇodvil

Woodward, *f.n.*, 'wʊdwərd, woˇod-ward

Woof, *f.n.*, wʊf, woŏf

Woofferton *Salop*, 'wʊfərtən, woŏfĕrtŏn

Wookey *Somerset*, 'wʊkɪ, woŏki

Woolam, *f.n.*, 'wʊləm, woŏlăm

Woolard, *f.n.*, 'wʊlard, woŏlaard

Woolas, *f.n.*, 'wʊləs, woŏlăss

Woolaston *Glos.*, 'wʊləstən, woŏlăsstŏn

Woolavington *Somerset*, wʊl-'ævɪŋtən, woŏlávvington

Woolbeding *W. Sussex*, 'wʊl-bidɪŋ, woˇolbeeding

Woolcombe, *f.n.*, 'wʊlkəm, woˇol-kŏm

Wooldridge, *f.n.*, 'wʊldrɪdʒ, woˇoldrij

Wooler, *f.n.*, 'wʊlər, woˇolĕr

Woolf, *f.n.*, wʊlf, woˇolf

Woolfardisworthy nr. *Bideford* (*Devon*), *see* **Woolsery**

Woolfardisworthy nr. *Crediton* (*Devon*), 'wʊl'fardɪswɜrðɪ, woˇol-faˇardisswurthi

Woolford, *f.n.*, 'wʊlfərd, woˇolfŏrd

Woolhampton *Berks.*, wʊl'hæmp-tən, woˇol-hámptŏn

Woolhouse, *f.n.*, 'wʊlhaʊs, woˇol-howss

Wooll, *f.n.*, wʊl, woˇol

Woolland, *f.n.*, 'wʊlənd, woˇolănd

Woollard, *f.n.*, 'wʊlard, woˇolaard

Woollcombe, *f.n.*, 'wʊlkəm, woˇol-kŏm

Woolley, *f.n.*, 'wʊlɪ, woˇoli

Woolley *Cambs.*, 'wʊlɪ, woˇoli

Woolnough, *f.n.*, 'wʊlnoʊ, woˇolnŏ

Woolsery, *formerly spelt* **Woolfardisworthy**, nr. *Bideford* (*Devon*), 'wʊlzərɪ, woˇolzĕri

Woolsington *Tyne & Wear*, 'wʊlzɪŋtən, woˇolzingtŏn

Woolsthorpe *Lincs.*, 'wʊlzθərp, woˇolzthorp. *Appropriate for both places of this name in Lincs.*

Woolwich *London*, 'wʊlɪtʃ, woˇolitch; 'wʊlɪdʒ, woˇolij

Woon, *f.n.*, wun, woon

Woore *Salop*, wɔr, wawr

Woosnam, *f.n.*, 'wuznəm, woˇoz-năm

Wootton, *f.n.*, 'wʊtən, woˇotŏn

Wootton Wawen *Warwicks.*, 'wʊtən 'wɔən, woˇotŏn wáw-ĕn

Worbarrow Bay *Dorset*, 'wɔr-
bærou 'beɪ, wúrbarrō báy
Worcester, *f.n.*, 'wʊstər, wŏosstĕr
Worcester *H. & W.*, 'wʊstər,
wŏosstĕr
Worden, *f.n.*, 'wɔrdən, wáwrdĕn
Wordie, *f.n.*, 'wɜrdɪ, wúrdi
Wordingham, *f.n.*, 'wɜrdɪŋəm,
wúrding-ăm
Wordsworth, *f.n.*, 'wɜrdzwɜrθ,
wúrdzwurth; 'wɜrdzwərθ,
wúrdzwŭrth
Worfield *Salop*, 'wɜrfild, wúrfeeld
Worfolk, *f.n.*, 'wɜrfouk, wúrfōk
Worger, *f.n.*, 'wɔrgər, wáwrgĕr
Work, *f.n.*, wɜrk, wurk
Workington *Cumbria*, 'wɜrkɪŋtən,
wúrking-tŏn
Workman, *f.n.*, 'wɜrkmən, wúrk-
măn
Worland, *f.n.*, 'wɔrlənd, wáwr-
lănd
Worle *Avon*, wɜrl, wurl
Worledge, *f.n.*, 'wɜrlɪdʒ, wúrlĕj
Worley, *f.n.*, 'wɜrlɪ, wúrli
Worlingham *Suffolk*, 'wɜrlɪŋəm,
wúrling-ăm. *Appropriate also
for Baron* ~.
Worlington, East *and* West, *Devon*,
'wɜrlɪŋtən, wúrlingtŏn
Worlledge, *f.n.*, 'wɜrlɪdʒ, wúrlĕj
Worlock, *f.n.*, 'wɔrlɒk, wáwrlock
Wormald, *f.n.*, 'wɜrmɔld, wúrmăld
Wormegay *Norfolk*, 'wɜrmɪgeɪ,
wúrmĕgay
Wormelow *H. & W.*, 'wɜrmɪlou,
wúrmĕlō
Wormingford *Essex*, 'wɜrmɪŋfərd,
wúrmingfŏrd
Wormington, *f.n.*, 'wɔrmɪŋtən,
wáwrmingtŏn
Wormit *Fife*, 'wɜrmɪt, wúrmit
Wormleighton *Warwicks.*, 'wɜrm-
'leɪtən, wúrm-láytŏn
Wormley *Surrey*, 'wɜrmlɪ, wúrmli
Worn, *f.n.*, wɔrn, wawrn
Worne, *f.n.*, wɔrn, wawrn
Wornum, *f.n.*, 'wɜrnəm, wúrnŭm
Worplesdon *Surrey*, 'wɔrplzdən,
wáwrplzdŏn
Worrall, *f.n.*, 'wʌrəl, wúrrăl;
'wɒrəl, wórrăl
Worsall, High *and* Low, *N.
Yorks.*, 'wɜrsl, wúrssl
Worsley, *f.n.*, 'wɜrslɪ, wúrssli;
'wɜrzlɪ, wúrzli. *The first,
apparently much the more usual,
is appropriate for the maiden
name of HRH the Duchess of
Kent; the second for Baron* ~,
*subsidiary title of the Earl of
Yarborough.*
Worsley *Gtr. M'chester*, 'wɜrslɪ,
wúrssli

Worsley Mesnes *Gtr. M'chester*,
'wɜrslɪ 'meɪnz, wúrssli máynz
Worsnip, *f.n.*, 'wɜrsnɪp, wúrssnip
Worsnop, *f.n.*, 'wɜrznəp, wúrz-
nŏp
Worstead *Norfolk*, 'wʊsted,
wŏossted; 'wʊstɪd, wŏosstĕd
Worster, *f.n.*, 'wʊstər, wŏosstĕr
Worsthorne, *f.n.*, 'wɜrsθɔrn,
wúrss-thorn
Worswick, *f.n.*, 'wɜrswɪk, wúrss-
-wick; 'wɜrsɪk, wúrssick
Worth, *f.n.*, wɜrθ, wurth
Wortham *Suffolk*, 'wɜrðəm,
wúrthăm
Worthing *W. Sussex*, 'wɜrðɪŋ,
wúrthing
Worthington, *f.n.*, 'wɜrðɪŋtən,
wúrthingtŏn
Worthley, *f.n.*, 'wɜrθlɪ, wúrthli
Worth Matravers *Dorset*, 'wɜrθ
mə'trævərz, wúrth mătrávvĕrz
Worting *Hants*, 'wɜrtɪŋ, wúrting
Wortley, *f.n.*, 'wɜrtlɪ, wúrtli
Wortley *W. Yorks.*, 'wɜrtlɪ,
wúrtli
Worton *Wilts.*, 'wɜrtən, wúrtŏn
Wortwell *Norfolk*, 'wɜrtwəl,
wúrtwĕl
Wotherspoon, *f.n.*, 'wʌðərspun,
wúthĕrspoon; 'wɒðərspun,
wóthĕrspoon
Wothespoon, *f.n.*, 'wʌðəspun,
wúthĕsspoon; 'wɒðəspun,
wóthĕsspoon
Wotton, *f.n.*, 'wʊtən, wŏotŏn
Wotton-under-Edge *Glos.*, 'wʊtən
'ʌndrɪdʒ, wŏotŏn úndrĕj;
'wʊtən ˌʌndər 'edʒ, wŏotŏn
undĕr éjj
Woughton *Bucks.*, 'wʊftən, wŏof-
tŏn
Would, *f.n.*, wʊd, wŏod
Wouldham *Kent*, 'wʊldəm,
wŏoldăm
Wrafton *Devon*, 'ræftən, ráfftŏn
Wrangaton *Devon*, 'ræŋətən, ráng-
-ătŏn
Wrangham, *f.n.*, 'ræŋəm, ráng-ăm
Wrantage *Somerset*, 'rɒntɪdʒ,
raántij; 'ræntɪdʒ, rántij
Wrath, Cape, *H'land*, rɔθ, rawth;
rɑθ, raath; ræθ, rath; rɒθ, roth
Wrathall, *f.n.*, 'rɒθl, róthl
Wraxhall, *f.n.*, 'ræksl, rácksl
Wray, *f.n.*, reɪ, ray
Wraysbury *see* **Wyrardisbury**
Wrea Green *Lancs.*, 'reɪ 'grin,
ráy greén
Wreake, River, *Leics.*, rik, reek
Wreay *Cumbria*, 'rɪə, rée-ă
Wreford, *f.n.*, 'rɪfərd, réefŏrd
Wrekenton *Tyne & Wear*, 'rekɪn-
tən, réckĕntŏn

Wrekin, The, *Salop*, 'rikɪn, réekin.
*Appropriate also for the admin.
dist. of Shropshire.*

Wreningham *Norfolk*, 'renɪŋəm,
rénning-ăm

Wrentham *Suffolk*, 'renθəm,
rén-thăm

Wrexham *Clwyd*, 'reksəm, réck-
săm

Wrey, *f.n.*, reɪ, ray

Wreyland *Devon*, 'reɪlənd, ráy-
lănd

Wright, *f.n.*, raɪt, rīt

Wrighton, *f.n.*, 'raɪtən, rîtŏn

Wrigley, *f.n.*, 'rɪglɪ, riggli

Wriothesley, *f.n.*, 'raɪəθslɪ, rí-
-ŏthsli; 'rɒtslɪ, róttsli; 'rɒtɪslɪ,
róttĕssli; 'rɪθlɪ, ríthli; 'rɪzlɪ,
rízzli. *The name, now historic,
was the family name of the
Elizabethan Earls of Southampton. The first is the pronunciation used by at least one
descendant, the thirteenth Duke
of Bedford. To judge by various
works of reference, the others
were current, singly or severally,
in the fifteenth and sixteenth
centuries.*

Wrisberg, *f.n.*, 'rɪsbərg, ríssberg

Writhlington *Somerset*, 'rɪðlɪŋtən,
ríthlingtŏn

Wrixon, *f.n.*, 'rɪksən, ríckssŏn

Wrobel, *f.n.*, 'roʊbl, róbl

Wrose *W. Yorks.*, roʊz, rōz

Wrotham *Kent*, 'rutəm, róotăm

Wrottesley, *f.n.*, 'rɒtslɪ, róttsli.
Appropriate also for Baron ~.

Wrottesley *Staffs.*, 'rɒtslɪ, róttsli

Wroughton, *f.n.*, 'rɔtən, ráwtŏn

Wroughton *Wilts.*, 'rɔtən, ráwtŏn

Wroxall *Warwicks.*, 'rɒksɔl, róck-
sawl

Wulfrun Hall *Wolverhampton*,
'wʊlfrən, wóolfrŭn

Wulstan, *C.n. and f.n.*, 'wʊlstən,
wóolstăn

Wvendth, *f.n.*, wentθ, went-th

Wyatt, *f.n.*, 'waɪət, wī-ăt

Wyberg, *f.n.*, 'waɪbər, wíbĕr

Wyberton *Lincs.*, 'wɪbərtən,
wíbbĕrtŏn

Wyboston *Beds.*, 'waɪbəstən,
wíbŏstŏn

Wybrew, *f.n.*, 'waɪbru, wíbroo

Wybunbury *Ches.*, 'wɪmbrɪ, wím-
brɪ

Wychbold *H. & W.*, 'wɪtʃboʊld,
wítch-bōld

Wych Cross *E. Sussex*, 'wɪtʃ
'krɒs, wítch króss

Wyche, *f.n.*, waɪtʃ, wītch

Wyche, Lower *and* Upper, *H. &
W.*, wɪtʃ, witch

Wychnor Bridges *Staffs.*, 'wɪtʃnər
'brɪdʒɪz, witchnor brijjĕz

Wychwood Forest *Oxon.*, 'wɪtʃ-
wʊd, wítchwŏod

Wycliffe, *also spelt* **Wyclif**, John,
14th-c. religious reformer,
'wɪklɪf, wíckliff

Wycoller *Lancs.*, 'waɪkɒlər,
wíkollĕr

Wycombe *Bucks.*, 'wɪkəm,
wíckŏm

Wyddfa, Yr, *Gwynedd*, ər 'uɪðvə,
ŭr óo-ithvă. *This is the Welsh
name for* **Snowdon**.

Wye, River, *Gwent–Glos. border*,
waɪ, wī. *Its Welsh name is* **Gwy**,
q.v.

Wyfordby *Leics.*, 'waɪfərdbɪ,
wífŏrdbi

Wykeham, *f.n.*, 'wɪkəm, wíckăm

Wykeham *N. Yorks.*, 'waɪkəm,
wíkăm

Wykehamist, *one educated at*
Winchester *College*, 'wɪkəmɪst,
wíckămist

Wyken *W. Midlands*, 'waɪkən,
wíkĕn

Wyke Regis *Dorset*, 'waɪk 'ridʒɪs,
wík réejiss

Wykes, *f.n.*, waɪks, wīks

Wykey *Salop*, 'waɪkɪ, wíki

Wykham Hall *Banbury*, 'wɪkəm,
wíckăm

Wylam *Northd.*, 'waɪləm, wílăm

Wyld, *f.n.*, waɪld, wīld

Wylde, *f.n.*, waɪld, wīld

Wylfa *Gwynedd*, 'wɪlvə, wílvă

Wylie, *f.n.*, 'waɪlɪ, wíli

Wyllie, *f.n.*, 'waɪlɪ, wíli

Wylye *Wilts.*, 'waɪlɪ, wíli

Wymer, *f.n.*, 'waɪmər, wímĕr

Wymering *Hants*, 'wɪmərɪŋ,
wímmĕring

Wymeswold *Leics.*, 'waɪmz-
woʊld, wímzwōld

Wymington *Beds.*, 'wɪmɪŋtən,
wímmingtŏn

Wymondham *Leics.*, 'waɪməndəm,
wímŏndăm

Wymondham *Norfolk*, 'wɪndəm,
windăm

Wymondley, Great *and* Little,
Herts., 'waɪməndlɪ, wímŏndli

Wyn, *Welsh C.n.*, wɪn, win

Wynd, *f.n.*, waɪnd, wīnd

Wyndham, *f.n.*, 'wɪndəm, windăm

Wyness, *f.n.*, 'waɪnɪs, wíněss

Wynford, *f.n.*, 'wɪnfərd, winfŏrd

Wynn, *f.n.*, wɪn, winn

Wynne, *f.n.*, wɪn, winn

Wynward, *f.n.*, 'wɪnərd, wínnărd

Wynyard, *f.n.*, 'wɪnjərd, wín-yărd

Wynyard *Cleveland*, 'wɪnjərd,
wín-yărd

Wyrardisbury, *also spelt* **Wraysbury,** *Berks.*, 'reɪzbərɪ, ráyzbŭri
Wyre, River, *Lancs.*, 'waɪər, wīr
Wyreside *Lancs.*, 'waɪərsaɪd, wírssíd
Wyrley, Great *and* Little, *Staffs.*, 'wɜrlɪ, wúrli
Wyrley and Essington Canal *Staffs.*, 'wɜrlɪ ənd 'esɪŋtən, wúrli ănd éssing-tŏn
Wysall *Notts.*, 'waɪsl, wíssl
Wytch Farm *Dorset*, wɪtʃ, witch
Wythall *H. & W.*, 'wɪðəl, wíthawl
Wytham *Oxon.*, 'waɪtəm, wítăm
Wythburn *Cumbria*, 'waɪðbərn, wíthburn; 'waɪbɜrn, wíburn
Wythenshawe *Gtr. M'chester*, 'wɪðənʃə, withĕn-shaw
Wythop *Cumbria*, 'wɪðəp, wíthŏp
Wyton, *f.n.*, 'waɪtən, wítŏn
Wyton *Cambs.*, 'wɪtən, wíttŏn
Wyver, *f.n.*, 'waɪvər, wívĕr
Wyvis, Ben, *H'land*, 'wɪvɪs, wívviss; 'wivɪs, wéeviss

X

Xavier, *f.n.*, 'zeɪvjər, záyv-yĕr
Xerri, *f.n.*, 'ʃerɪ, shérri
Xiberras, *f.n.*, ˌʃɪbə'rɑs, shibbĕraáss
Xuereb, *f.n.*, 'ʃweɪrəb, shwáy-rĕb

Y

Yalden, *f.n.*, 'jɔldən, yáwldĕn
Yalding *Kent*, 'jɔldɪŋ, yáwlding
Yallop, *f.n.*, 'jæləp, yálŏp
Yar, River, *I. of Wight*, jɑr, yaar. *Appropriate for both rivers of this name on the I. of Wight.*
Yarborough, Earl of, 'jɑrbərə, yaárbŭră
Yarburgh *Lincs.*, 'jɑrbərə, yaárbŭră
Yare, River, *Norfolk*, jɛər, yair
Yarmouth *I. of Wight*, 'jɑrməθ, yaármŭth
Yarmouth, Great, *Norfolk*, 'jɑrməθ, yaármŭth
Yarrow *Borders*, 'jærou, yárrō
Yate *Avon*, jeɪt, yayt
Yates, *f.n.*, jeɪts, yayts
Yatton Keynell *Wilts.*, 'jætən 'kenl, yáttŏn kénnl
Yeabsley, *f.n.*, 'jebzlɪ, yébzli
Yeading *London*, 'jedɪŋ, yédding
Yeadon, *f.n.*, 'jidən, yéedŏn; 'jedən, yéddŏn

Yeadon *W. Yorks.*, 'jidən, yéedŏn
Yealand Conyers *Lancs.*, 'jelənd 'kɒnjərz, yélländ kón-yĕrz
Yealm, River, *Devon*, jæm, yamm
Yealmpton *Devon*, 'jæmtən, yámtŏn
Yeaman, *f.n.*, 'jeɪmən, yáymăn; 'jimən, yéemăn
Yeames, *f.n.*, jimz, yeemz; jeɪmz, yaymz
Yearby *Cleveland*, 'jɑrbɪ, yérbi
Yearsley, *f.n.*, 'jɪərzlɪ, yéerzli
Yeates, *f.n.*, jeɪts, yayts
Yeathouse *Cumbria*, 'jethaʊs, yét-howss
Yeatman, *f.n.*, 'jeɪtmən, yáytmăn
Yeats, *f.n.*, jeɪts, yayts
Yeavering *Northd.*, 'jevərɪŋ, yévvĕring
Yeaxlee, *f.n.*, 'jækslɪ, yácksli; 'jekslɪ, yécksli
Yell *Shetland*, jel, yell
Yelland, *f.n.*, 'jelənd, yélländ
Yelland *Devon*, 'jelənd, yélländ
Yelverton *Devon*, 'jelvərtən, yélvĕrtŏn
Yeo, *f.n.*, joʊ, yō
Yeoell, *f.n.*, 'joʊəl, yŏ-ĕl
Yeolmbridge *Cornwall*, 'joʊmbrɪdʒ, yŏmbrij
Yeovil *Somerset*, 'joʊvɪl, yŏvil
Yeowell, *f.n.*, 'joʊəl, yŏ-ĕl
Yerburgh, *f.n.*, 'jɑrbərə, yaárbŭră
Yerbury, *f.n.*, 'jɜrbərɪ, yérbŭri
Yester *Lothian*, 'jestər, yésstĕr
Yetholm, Kirk, *Borders*, 'jetəm, kɜrk, kirk yéttŏm
Yevele, Henry **de,** 14th-*c. master-mason and architect*, də 'jivəlɪ, dĕ yéevĕli
Yglesias, *f.n.*, ɪ'gleɪsɪəs, igláyssi-äss
Yielden *Beds.*, 'jɪldən, yéeldĕn
Yiend, *f.n.*, jend, yend
Yip, *f.n.*, jɪp, yip
Ynysangharad *Mid Glam.*, ˌʌnɪsæŋ'hærəd, únnissang-hárrăd
Ynys-ddu *Dyfed*, ˌʌnɪs'ðɪ, unniss-thée
Ynys-hir *Mid Glam.*, ˌʌnɪs'hɪər, unniss-héer
Ynys Llanddwyn *Anglesey*, 'ʌnɪs 'ɬænðʊɪn, únniss hlánthōo-in
Ynys Môn *Gwynedd*, 'ʌnɪs 'mɔn, únniss máwn. *This is the Welsh name for* **Anglesey.**
Ynysowen *Mid Glam.*, ˌʌnɪs'oʊɪn, únniss-ŏ-ĕn
Ynys Tawe *W. Glam.*, 'ʌnɪs 'taʊeɪ, únniss tów-ay
Ynys Welltog *Gwynedd*, 'weɬtɒg, únniss wéhltog
Ynys-wen *Mid Glam.*, ˌʌnɪs'wen, unniss-wén

Ynysybwl *Mid Glam.*, ˌʌnɪsəˈbʊl, unnissằbŏŏl
Yoker *S'clyde*, ˈjoʊkər, yŏkĕr
Yonge, *f.n.*, jʌŋ, yung
Yorath, *f.n.*, ˈjɔrəθ, yáwrằth
York, *f.n.*, jɔrk, york
York *N. Yorks.*, jɔrk, york
Yorke, *f.n.*, jɔrk, york
Youatt, *f.n.*, ˈjuət, yoó-ăt
Youde, *f.n.*, jud, yood
Youds, *f.n.*, jaʊdz, yowdz
Youel, *f.n.*, ˈjuəl, yoó-ĕl; ˈjuəl, yŏŏ-ĕl; jul, yool
Youell, *f.n.*, ˈjuəl, yoó-ĕl; ˈjuəl, yŏŏ-ĕl; jul, yool
Youens, *f.n.*, ˈjuɪnz, yoó-ĕnz
Youghal, *f.n.*, jɔl, yawl
Youings, *f.n.*, ˈjuɪŋz, yoó-ingz
Youldon, *f.n.*, ˈjuldən, yoóldŏn
Youlgrave, *also spelt* Youlgreave, *Derby.*, ˈjulgreɪv, yoólgrayv
Youlton *N. Yorks.*, ˈjultən, yoóltŏn
Youmans, *f.n.*, ˈjumənz, yoómănz
Young, *f.n.*, jʌŋ, yung
Younger, *f.n.*, ˈjʌŋgər, yùng-gĕr
Younger of Leckie, Viscount, ˈjʌŋgər əv ˈlekɪ, yúng-gĕr ŏv lécki
Younghusband, *f.n.*, ˈjʌŋhʌzbənd, yúng-huzbănd
Youngman, *f.n.*, ˈjʌŋmən, yúng-măn
Younkman, *f.n.*, ˈjʌŋkmən, yúnkmăn
Younson, *f.n.*, ˈjunsən, yoónssŏn
Youseman, *f.n.*, ˈjusmən, yoóssmăn
Yow, *f.n.*, jaʊ, yow
Yoxall, *f.n.*, ˈjɒksl, yócksl
Ypres, Earl of, ipr, eepr
Ypres Tower *Rye*, ipr, eepr
Yr Wyddfa *Gwynedd*, ər ˈuɪðvə, ŭr oó-ithvằ. *This is the Welsh name for* Snowdon.
Ysceifiog *Clwyd*, ʌsˈkaɪvjɒg, usskív-yog
Yspytty *Dyfed*, ʌsˈpʌtɪ, usspútti
Yspytty Ystwyth *Dyfed*, ʌsˈpʌtɪ ˈʌstwɪθ, usspútti ússtwith
Ystalyfera *W. Glam.*, ˌʌstələˈverə, usstằlăvérrằ
Ystrad *Mid Glam.*, ˈʌstrəd, ússtrăd
Ystrad, River, *Clwyd*, ˈʌstrəd, ússtrăd
Ystradfellte *Powys*, ˌʌstrədˈveltei, ussträd-véhltay
Ystrad Fflur *Dyfed*, ˈʌstrəd ˈflɪər, ússträd fleér. *The English form is* Strata Florida, *q.v.*
Ystradgynlais *Powys*, ˌʌstrədˈgʌnlaɪs, ussträd-gúnlïss
Ystrad Meurig *Dyfed*, ˈʌstrəd ˈmaɪərɪg, ússtrăd mírig

Ystrad Mynach *Mid Glam.*, ˈʌstrəd ˈmʌnəx, ússtrăd múnnằch
Ystrad Rhondda *Mid Glam.*, ˈʌstrəd ˈrɒnðə, ússträd rónthằ
Ystwyth, River, *Powys–Dyfed*, ˈʌstwɪθ, ússtwith
Ythan, River, *Grampian*, ˈaɪθən, íthăn
Ythanbank *Grampian*, ˈaɪθən-ˈbæŋk, íthăn-bánk
Ythanwells *Grampian*, ˈaɪθən-ˈwelz, íthăn-wéllz
Yudkin, *f.n.*, ˈjudkɪn, yoódkin
Yuille, *f.n.*, ˈjuɪl, yoó-il

Z

Zaehner, *f.n.*, ˈzeɪnər, záynĕr
Zalud, *f.n.*, ˈzælud, zálood
Zander, *f.n.*, ˈzændər, zándĕr
Zangwill, *f.n.*, ˈzæŋwɪl, záng-wil
Zara, *C.n.*, ˈzarə, zaˊără
Zealley, *f.n.*, ˈzilɪ, zéeli
Zeal Monachorum *Devon*, ˈzil mɒnəˈkɔrəm, zéel monnăkáwrŭm
Zeals *Wilts.*, zilz, zeelz
Zeeman, *f.n.*, ˈzimən, zéemän
Zelah *Cornwall*, ˈzilə, zéelă
Zennor *Cornwall*, ˈzenər, zénnŏr
Zerdin, *f.n.*, ˈzɜrdɪn, zérdin
Zetland, *alternative spelling of* Shetland, ˈzetlənd, zétländ. *Appropriate also for the Marquess of* ∼.
Zeuner, *f.n.*, ˈzɔɪnər, zóynĕr
Ziegler, *f.n.*, ˈziglər, zéeglĕr
Zilliacus, *f.n.*, ˌzilɪˈɑkəs, zilli-aˊakŭss
Ziman, *f.n.*, ˈzaɪmən, zímăn
Zinkeisen, *f.n.*, ˈzɪŋkaɪzən, zinkīzĕn. *Appropriate for Anna* ∼, *painter.*
Zinovieff, *f.n.*, zɪˈnɒvɪef, zinnóvvi-eff
Zoffany, John, *18th–19th-c. painter*, ˈzɒfənɪ, zóffăni
Zogolovitch, *f.n.*, zəˈgɒləvɪtʃ, zŏgólŏvitch
Zoller, *f.n.*, ˈzɒlər, zóllĕr
Zorian, *f.n.*, ˈzɔrɪən, záwri-ăn
Zorza, *f.n.*, ˈzɔrʒə, zórzhằ
Zouch *Notts.*, zɒtʃ, zotch
Zouche, Baron, zuʃ, zoosh
Zuckerman, *f.n.*, ˈzʊkərmən, zŏŏkĕrmăn. *Appropriate for Sir Solly* ∼, *scientist.*
Zuill, *f.n.*, jul, yool
Zussman, *f.n.*, ˈzʌsmən, zússmăn
Zwemmer, *f.n.*, ˈzwemər, zwémmĕr

CHANNEL ISLANDS APPENDIX

A

A'Court, *f.n.*, ˈeɪkɔrt, áykort
Ahier, *f.n.*, ˈɑjeɪ, aˊa-yay
Albiges, *f.n.*, ˌælbɪˈʒeɪ, albiẕháy
Alderney, ˈɔldərnɪ, áwldĕrni
Alexandre, *f.n.*, ˌælɪkˈzɒndr, alĕkzóndr
Allaire, *f.n.*, ˈælɛər, álair
Allenet, *f.n.*, ˈælɪneɪ, álinay
Alles, *f.n.*, ˈɔleɪ, áwlay
Allez, *f.n.*, ˈɔleɪ, áwlay
Allo, *f.n.*, ˈæloʊ, álō
Amourette, *f.n.*, ˌæmʊˈret, ammōo-rétt
Andrieux, *f.n.*, ˈændriɜ, ándree-ö
Anthoine, *f.n.*, ɔnˈtwɒn, awntwónn
Aubert, *f.n.*, ˈoʊbɛər, ôbair
Aubin, *f.n.*, ˈoʊbɪn, ôbin
Audrain, *f.n.*, ˈoʊdrɑ, ôdraa
Averty, *f.n.*, əˈvɜrtɪ, ăvérti
Avrill, *f.n.*, ˈævrɪl, ávril

B

Baal, *f.n.*, beɪl, bayl
Babbé, *f.n.*, bæˈbeɪ, babbáy
Bailhache, *f.n.*, ˈbælæʃ, bálash
Bailiff, *f.n.*, ˈbeɪlɪf, báylif
Balleine, *f.n.*, ˈbæleɪn, bálayn
Bannier, *f.n.*, ˈbænjeɪ, bán-yay
Barbé, *f.n.*, bɑrˈbeɪ, baarbáy
Bataille, *f.n.*, ˈbætaɪ, báttī
Batiste, *f.n.*, ˈbætist, bátteest
Baudains, *f.n.*, ˈboʊdæ, bôdang
Baudet, *f.n.*, ˈboʊdeɪ, bôday
Beaucamps, *f.n.*, ˈboʊkɒn, bôkon
Beauchamp, *f.n.*, ˈboʊʃɔ, bô-shaw
Beaugie, *f.n.*, ˈboʊʒeɪ, bôẕhi-ay
Beaulieu, *f.n.*, ˈboʊljɔ, bôl-yö
Beauport, *also spelt* **Beau Port,** *Jersey,* ˈboʊpɔr, bôpor; ˈboʊpɔrt, bôport
Bechelet, *f.n.*, ˈbeʃleɪ, béshlay
Becquet, *f.n.*, ˈbekeɪ, béckay
Beghin, *f.n.*, ˈbegæ, béggang
Benest, *f.n.*, ˈbeneɪ, bénnay
Bertaille, *f.n.*, ˈbɜrtaɪ, bértī
Berteau, *f.n.*, ˈbɜrtoʊ, bértō
Berthelot, *f.n.*, ˈbɜrtɪloʊ, bértĕlō
Besnard, *f.n.*, ˈbeɪnɑrd, báynaard
Besquet, *f.n.*, ˈbiskweɪ, béesskway
Beuzeval, *f.n.*, ˈbɜzvɒl, bôzvaal
Bichard, *f.n.*, ˈbɪʃɑr, bíshaar

Billot, *f.n.*, ˈbɪloʊ, bíllō
Binet, *f.n.*, ˈbɪneɪ, bínnay
Bisset, *f.n.*, ˈbɪsɪt, bíssĕt
Bisson, *f.n.*, ˈbɪsɒn, bísson; ˈbɪsɔ, bíssaw. *The first is a Guernsey pronunciation, the second a Jersey one.*
Blampied, *f.n.*, blɔmˈpieɪ, blămpeé-ay; ˈblɒmpieɪ, blómpee-ay. *The first is a Guernsey pronunciation, the second a Jersey one.*
Bliault, *f.n.*, ˈblioʊ, bleé-ō
Blondel, *f.n.*, ˈblɒndl, blóndl
Bois, *f.n.*, bwɑ, bwaa
Bonne Nuit *Jersey,* ˈbɒn ˈnwi, bón nweé
Bouchard, *f.n.*, ˈbʊʃɑrd, bōo-shaard
Boudin, *f.n.*, ˈbudæ, boˊodang
Bougeard, *f.n.*, ˈbuʒɑrd, boˊoẕhaard
Bougourd, *f.n.*, ˈbuguər, boˊogōōr
Bouley *Jersey,* ˈbulɪ, boˊoli
Bourgaize, *f.n.*, ˈbuərgeɪz, boˊorgayz
Brâche, *f.n.*, brɑʃ, braash
Braye *Alderney,* breɪ, bray
Brechou Island, *also spelt* **Brecqhou,** ˈbreku, bréckoo
Brecqhou, *f.n.*, ˈbreku, bréckoo
Brehaut, *f.n.*, breɪˈoʊ, bray-ô
Breuilly, *f.n.*, ˈbrui, broˊo-ee
Brouard, *f.n.*, ˈbruɑrd, broˊo-aard
Buesnel, *f.n.*, ˈbjunel, béwnel; ˈbjuznəl, béwznĕl
Burhou *islet, nr. Alderney,* bəˈru, bŭroˊo

C

Cabeldu, *f.n.*, ˈkæbldu, kábbl-doo
Cabot, *f.n.*, ˈkæboʊ, kábbō
Cadin, *f.n.*, ˈkædæ, káddang
Canichers, Les *and* Upper, *Guernsey,* ˈkænɪʃərz, kánnishĕrz
Carey, *f.n.*, ˈkɛərɪ, káiri
Carré, *f.n.*, ˈkɑreɪ, kaˊaray
Casquets *rocks, west of Alderney,* ˈkæskɪts, kásskĕts
Castel, *f.n.*, ˈkatel, kaˊatel
Castle Cornet *Guernsey,* ˈkɑsl ˈkɔrnɪt, kaˊassl kórnĕt
Cauvain, *f.n.*, ˈkoʊvæ, kôvang
Chevalier, *f.n.*, ʃɪˈvæljeɪ, shĕvál-yay

Cloche, *f.n.,* klɒʃ, klosh
Cohu, *f.n.,* 'koʊju, kổ-yoo
Colin, *f.n.,* 'kɒlæ̃, kóllang
Collas, *f.n.,* 'koʊləs, kổläss
Collenette, *f.n.,* 'kɒlɪnet, kóllĕ-net
Corbet, *f.n.,* 'kɔrbɪt, kórbĕt
Corbière Point *Jersey*, kɔr'bjɛər, korbyáir
Corbin, *f.n.,* 'kɔrbɪn, kórbin
Cordiere, *f.n.,* 'kɔrdɪɛər, kórdi-air
Corniere, *f.n.,* 'kɔrnɪɛər, kórni-air
Coutanche, *f.n.,* 'kutɒ̃ʃ, koʹo-tawnsh; 'kutɑ̃ʃ, koʹotaangsh.
The second is also appropriate for the Barony of ~.

D

Dallain, *f.n.,* 'dælæ̃, dálang
D'Eauthreau, *f.n.,* 'doʊtroʊ, dốtrō
De Caen, *f.n.,* də 'kɑ̃, dě kaʹang
De Carteret, *f.n.,* də ˌkɑrtə'ret, dě kaartĕrétt
Decaux, *f.n.,* də'koʊ, dĕkố
De Faye, *f.n.,* də 'feɪ, dě fáy
De Garis, *f.n.,* də 'gɑri, dě gaʹaree
De Gruchy, *f.n.,* də 'grɪʃɪ, dě gríshi; də 'gruʃɪ, dě grōʹoshi; də 'gruʃɪ, dě groʹoshi
De La Court, *f.n.,* ˌdelə'kɔr, dellăkór
De La Mare, *f.n.,* də lə 'mɛər, dě lă máir
De La Perrelle, *f.n.,* ˌdelə 'pɛərel, dellă páirel
De Louche, *f.n.,* də 'luʃ, dě loʹosh
De Mesquita, *f.n.,* də məs'kitə, dě mĕskéetä
De Moulpied, *f.n.,* də mul'pieɪ, dě moolpée-ay
De Putron, *f.n.,* də 'pjutrɒn, dě péwtron
Derouet, *f.n.,* 'dɛəroʊeɪ, dáiroōo-ay
De Ste Croix, *f.n.,* də sæn 'krwɑ, dě san krwaʹa; de snt 'krɔɪ, dě sĭnt króy
De Saumarez, *f.n.,* də 'sɒməreɪ, dě sómmăray
De Sausmarez, *f.n.,* də 'sɒməreɪ, dě sómmăray
Deslandes, *f.n.,* 'deɪlɒnd, dáy-lawnd
Desperques, *f.n.,* deɪ'pɜrk, day-pérk
De Veulle, *f.n.,* də 'vɜl, dě vốl
Digard, *f.n.,* 'dɪgɑr, diggaar
Ditot, *f.n.,* 'dɪtoʊ, díttō
Dixcart *Sark,* 'dikɑr, déekaar
Domaille, *f.n.,* 'doʊmaɪl, dốmīl

Dorey, *f.n.,* dɒrɪ, dórri; 'dɔrɪ, dáwri. *The first is a Guernsey pronunciation, the second a Jersey one.*
Dubras, *f.n.,* du'brɑ, doōobraʹa
Duchemin, *f.n.,* 'duʃmɪn, doʹoshmin
Du Feu, *f.n.,* du 'fɜ, doo fố
Du Heaume, *f.n.,* du 'hoʊm, doo hốm
Du Parcq, *f.n.,* du 'pɑrk, doo paʹark
Dupré, *f.n.,* du'preɪ, doopráy
Duquemin, *f.n.,* 'djukmɪn, déwkmin; 'dukmɪn, doʹokmin; 'dukmæ̃, doʹokmang. *The first two are Guernsey pronunciations, the third a Jersey one.*
Durell, *f.n.,* du'rel, doo-réll
Dutertre, *f.n.,* du'tɜrtr̩, dootértr

E

Ecobichon, *f.n.,* ˌekoʊ'biʃɔ, eckō-béeshaw
Ecrehou Islands, 'ekrɪhoʊ, éckrĕhō
Egré, *f.n.,* 'egreɪ, égray
Eker, *f.n.,* 'ikər, éekĕr
Enevoldsen, *f.n.,* en'vɒlsən, envólssĕn
Ereaut, *f.n.,* 'ɛəroʊ, áirō
Esnouf, *f.n.,* 'eɪnuf, áynoof
Etienne, *f.n.,* 'etjen, ét-yen

F

Falla, *f.n.,* 'fælɑ, fálaa
Fauvel, *f.n.,* 'foʊvel, fốvel
Ferbrashe, *f.n.,* 'fɛərbrʌʃ, fáirbrush
Filleul, *f.n.,* 'fɪljəl, fíl-yöl
Fiott, *f.n.,* 'fioʊ, fée-ō
Fosse, *f.n.,* fɒs, foss
Foullain, *f.n.,* 'fɒlæ̃, fóllang
Froome, *f.n.,* frum, froom
Frossard, *f.n.,* 'frɒsɑr, fróssaar

G

Gallichan, *f.n.,* 'gælɪʃɔ, gálishaw
Gallienne, *f.n.,* gæ'leɪn, galáyn
Garignon, *f.n.,* 'gærɪnjɔ, gárrin-yaw
Gaudin, *f.n.,* 'goʊdɪn, gốdin
Gaudion, *f.n.,* 'goʊdɪɒn, gốdi-on
Gautier, *f.n.,* goʊ'tieɪ, gōtée-ay
Gavet, *f.n.,* 'gæveɪ, gávvay

Gavey, *f.n.*, 'gæveɪ, gávvay
Gibault, *f.n.*, 'ʒɪbouʊ, zhíbbō
Girard, *f.n.*, 'ʒɪrɑr, zhírraar
Godel, *f.n.*, 'gɔdel, gáwdel
Gorey *Jersey*, gɔ'ri, gawreé
Gorin, *f.n.*, 'gɔræ̈, gáwra*ng*
Goubert, *f.n.*, 'gubɛər, goóbair
Gouyette, *f.n.*, 'gujet, goó-yet
Grandes Rocques *Guernsey*, 'grænd 'rɒk, gránd róck
Greffier, *f.n.*, 'grefjeɪ, gréff-yay
Greve de Lecq *Jersey*, 'greɪv də 'lek, gráyv dĕ léck
Grouville, *f.n.*, gru'vɪl, groovíll
Gruchy, *f.n.*, 'gruʃɪ, groóshi. *But cf.* De Gruchy.
Guegan, *f.n.*, 'gigən, geégăn
Guernsey, 'gɜrnzɪ, gérnzɪ
Guille, *f.n.*, gil, geel
Guillemette, *f.n.*, 'gɪlmet, gílmet
Guiton, *f.n.*, 'gɪtɔ, gíttaw

H

Hacquoil, *f.n.*, 'hækwɔɪl, háckwoyl
Hamon, *f.n.*, 'hæmɑ̃, hámaa*ng*; 'hæmɒn, hámmon. *The first is a Guernsey pronunciation, the second a Jersey one.*
Hautes Capelles *Guernsey*, 'houʊt kə'pel, hŏt kăpéll
Heaume, *f.n.*, jouʊm, yōm. *But cf.* Du Heaume.
Hegerat, *f.n.*, 'hegɑrɑ, héggĕraa
Herissier, *f.n.*, hɛə'rɪsjeɪ, hairíss--yay
Herivel, *f.n.*, 'herɪvel, hérrivel
Herm, hɜrm, herm
Hervé, *f.n.*, 'hɜrvi, hérvi
Hervieu, *f.n.*, 'hɛərvju, háirvew
Houguez, *f.n.*, 'hugeɪ, hoógay
Houiellebecq, *f.n.*, 'hulbek, hoólbeck
Hucquet, *f.n.*, 'hukeɪ, hoókay
Huelin, *f.n.*, 'hjulɪn, héwlin

I

Icart Point *Guernsey*, 'ikɑr, eékaar
Illien, *f.n.*, 'ɪljen, íll-yen
Ingrouille, *f.n.*, ɪn'gruil, in-groó-eel

J

Jamouneau, *f.n.*, ʒæ'munouʊ, zhammoónō
Jehen, *f.n.*, 'dʒiæn, jée-an; 'ʒiæn, zhée-an. *The first is a Guernsey pronunciation, the second a Jersey one.*

Jerbourg Point *Guernsey*, 'dʒɜrbɜrg 'pɔɪnt, jérburg póynt
Jerrom, *f.n.*, 'dʒerəm, jérrŏm
Jersey, 'dʒɜrzɪ, jérzi
Jethou *island nr. Guernsey*, 'dʒetu jéttoo
Jeune, *f.n.*, ʒɜn, zhön
Jory, *f.n.*, 'dʒɔrɪ, jáwri
Jouan, *f.n.*, 'ʒuɔ, zhoó-aw
Jouget, *f.n.*, 'ʒugeɪ, zhoógay
Journeaux, *f.n.*, 'ʒɔrnouʊ, zhórnō
Jurat, *f.n.*, 'dʒuərət, joŏrăt

K

Kergozou, *f.n.*, 'kɛərgouʊzu, káirgōzoo
Kerhoat, *f.n.*, 'kɛərhwɑ, káir--hwaa
Keyho, *f.n.*, 'keɪouʊ, káy-ō

L

Labey, *f.n.*, 'læbɪ, lábbi
La Corbière *Guernsey, Jersey*, ,lækɔr'bjɛər, lackorbyáir
La Coupée, *f.n.*, lɑ 'kupeɪ, laa koópay
Lainé, *f.n.*, 'leɪneɪ, láynay
La Maseline *Sark*, lɑ 'mæzəlin, laa mázzĕleen
La Moye Point *Guernsey, Jersey*, lə 'mɔɪ, lă móy
Lamy, *f.n.*, 'læmɪ, lámmi
Langlois, *f.n.*, 'lɒŋleɪ, lóng-lay; 'lɔŋgwɑ, láwn-gwaa. *The first is a Guernsey pronunciation, the second a Jersey one.*
Larbalestier, *f.n.*, lɑr'bɒlestɪeɪ, laarbólesti-ay
Laurens, *f.n.*, 'lɔrɔ, láwraw
La Villiaze *Guernsey*, ,lɑ vi'jɑz, laa vee-yaáz
Le Bailly, *f.n.*, lə 'baɪi, lĕ bí-ee
Le Bas, *f.n.*, lə 'bɑ, lĕ baá
Le Blancq, *f.n.*, lə 'blɔ, lĕ bláw
Le Boutillier, *f.n.*, lə 'butɪljeɪ, lĕ boótil-yay
Le Breton, *f.n.*, lə 'bretɒn, lĕ brétton
Le Brun, *f.n.*, lə 'brʌn, lĕ brúnn
Le Cappelain, *f.n.*, lə 'kæplæ̈, lĕ kápla*ng*
Le Chaminant, *f.n.*, lə 'ʃemɪnɔ, lĕ shémminaw
Le Chanu, *f.n.*, lə 'ʃænu, lĕ shánnoo
Le Cheminant, *f.n.*, lə 'ʃemɪnɑ̃, lĕ shémminaa*ng*
Le Clercq, *f.n.*, lə 'klɛər, lĕ kláir

Le Cocq, *f.n.*, lə 'koʊk, lĕ kók; lə 'kɒk, lĕ kóck. *The first is a Guernsey pronunciation, the second a Jersey one.*

Le Cornu, *f.n.*, lə 'kɔrnju, lĕ kórnew

Le Couteur, *f.n.*, lə 'kutər, lĕ koótĕr

Le Cras, *f.n.*, lə 'krɑ, lĕ kráa

Le Cuirot, *f.n.*, lə 'kwɪroʊ, lĕ kwírrō

Le Druillenec, *f.n.*, lə 'druɪlnek, lĕ droo-ilneck

Le Fauvic *Jersey,* lə 'foʊvɪk, lĕ fóvick

Le Febvre, *f.n.*, lə 'fɛːbr, lĕ fébbr

Le Feuvre, *f.n.*, lə 'fivər, lĕ feévĕr

Le Fondre, *f.n.*, lə 'fɔndreɪ, lĕ fáwndray

Le Gallais, *f.n.*, lə 'gæleɪ, lĕ gálay

Le Gallez, *f.n.*, lə 'gæleɪ, lĕ gálay

Le Gresley, *f.n.*, lə 'greɪlɪ, lĕ gráyli

Le Gros, *f.n.*, lə 'groʊ, lĕ grŏ

Le Hucquet, *f.n.*, lə 'hukeɪ, lĕ hoókay

Le Huray, *f.n.*, lə hju'reɪ, lĕ hew--ráy

Le Lacheur, *f.n.*, lə 'læʃər, lĕ láshĕr

Le Lievre, *f.n.*, lə 'livər, lĕ leévĕr

Le Machon, *f.n.*, lə 'mæʃə, lĕ máshă

Le Main, *f.n.*, lə 'mæ̃, lĕ máng

Le Maistre, *f.n.*, lə 'meɪtṛ, lĕ máytr

Le Maître, *f.n.*, lə 'meɪtṛ, lĕ máytr

Le Marchand, *f.n.*, lə 'mɑrʃə, lĕ maárshaw

Le Marquand, *f.n.*, lə 'mɑrkɑ̃, lĕ maárkaang; lə 'mɑrkə, lĕ maárkă. *The first is a Guernsey pronunciation, the second a Jersey one.*

Le Masurier, *f.n.*, lə mə'soʊrɪeɪ, lĕ mässoóri-ay; lə 'mæzʊərɪeɪ, lĕ mázoóri-ay. *The first is a Guernsey pronunciation, the second a Jersey one.*

Le Messurier, *f.n.*, lə 'meʒərər, lĕ mézhĕrĕr

Le Mesurier, *f.n.*, lə 'mezʊərɪeɪ, lĕ mézzoóri-ay

Le Moisne, *f.n.*, lə 'mwɑn, lĕ mwaán

Le Monnier, *f.n.*, lə 'mɒnjeɪ, lĕ món-yay

Le Montais, *f.n.*, lə 'mɒnteɪ, lĕ móntay

Lenfestey, *f.n.*, len'festɪ, lenfésti

Le Noury, *f.n.*, lə 'noʊrɪ, lĕ noŏri

Le Page, *f.n.*, lə 'peɪdʒ, lĕ páyj

Le Pelley, *f.n.*, lə 'peleɪ, lĕ péllay

Le Pennec, *f.n.*, lə 'penek, lĕ pénneck

Le Poidevin, *f.n.*, lə 'pedvɪn, lĕ pédvin; lə 'pɒdvæ̃, lĕ pódvang. *The first is a Guernsey pronunciation, the second a Jersey one.*

Le Prevost, *f.n.*, lə 'prevoʊ, lĕ prévvō

Le Quesne, *f.n.*, lə 'keɪn, lĕ káyn

Le Rendu, *f.n.*, lə 'rɔndu, lĕ ráwndoo

Le Riche, *f.n.*, lə 'rɪʃ, lĕ rísh

Le Rossignol, *f.n.*, lə 'rɒsɪnjɒl, lĕ róssin-yol

Le Ruez, *f.n.*, lə 'rueɪ, lĕ roó-ay

Le Sauteur, *f.n.*, lə 'soʊtər, lĕ sŏtur

Le Sauvage, *f.n.*, lə sɒ'vɑʒ, lĕ sovvaázh

Les Canichers *Guernsey,* leɪ 'kænɪʃərz, lay kánnishĕrz

Les Hanois Lighthouse *Guernsey,* leɪ 'hænwɑ, lay hán-waa

Les Mielles *Guernsey,* leɪ 'mjel, lay myéll

Les Mouriaux *Alderney,* leɪ 'moʊərɪoʊ, lay moŏri-ō

Le Sueur, *f.n.*, lə 'swər, lĕ swúr

Les Vauxbelets *Guernsey,* leɪ 'voʊbəleɪ, lay vŏbĕlay

Le Tissier, *f.n.*, lə 'tɪsjeɪ, lĕ tíss--yay

Le Tocq, *f.n.*, lə 'tɒk, lĕ tóck

Le Vesconte, *f.n.*, lə 'veɪkɒnt, lĕ váykont

Lihou Island, 'liu, leé-oo

Loveridge, *f.n.*, 'lʌvərɪdʒ, lúv-vĕrij

M

Machon, *f.n.*, 'mæʃɒn, máshon

Mahy, *f.n.*, 'mɑi, maá-ee

Marquand, *f.n.*, 'mɑrkɑ̃, maár-kaang. *But cf.* **Le Marquand.**

Marquis, *f.n.*, 'mɑrki, maárkee

Martel, *f.n.*, 'mɑrtel, maártel

Mauger, *f.n.*, 'meɪdʒər, máyjĕr

Mesny, *f.n.*, 'meɪnɪ, máyni

Michel, *f.n.*, 'mɪʃel, míshel

Miere, *f.n.*, 'miɛər, meé-air

Mignot, *f.n.*, 'mɪnjoʊ, mín-yō

Minquiers *reef, south of Jersey,* 'mɪŋkɪz, mínkiz; 'mækjeɪ, máng-kyay

Mollet, *f.n.*, 'mɒleɪ, móllay

Montais, *f.n.*, 'mɒnteɪ, móntay

Mont Orgeuil Castle *Jersey,* ˌmŏt ɔr'ɡɜɪ, mōngt orgŏ-i

Morin, *f.n.*, 'mɒræ̃, máwrang

Moulin Huet *Guernsey,* 'mulɪn wet, moólin wet

Mourant, *f.n.*, 'murɔ, moó-raw

N

Neveu, *f.n.*, 'nevju, névvew
Nicholle, *f.n.*, 'nɪkoʊl, níckōl
Noel, *f.n.*, noʊl, nōl
Noirmont Point *Jersey*, 'nwɑrmō, nwaármōng
Noyon, *f.n.*, 'nɔɪjɒn, nóy-yon

O

Oeillet, *f.n.*, 'ɔjeɪ, áw-yay
Ogier, *f.n.*, 'oʊʒɪər, ōzheer; oʊ'ʒɪjeɪ, ōzhée-yay. *The first is a Guernsey pronunciation, the second a Jersey one.*
Orange, *f.n.*, 'ɔrɒnʒ, áwrawnzh
Ouaisne *Jersey*, 'weɪneɪ, wáynay
Ozanne, *f.n.*, oʊ'zæn, ōzánn
Ozouf, *f.n.*, 'oʊzuf, ōzoof

P

Paisnel, *f.n.*, peɪ'nel, paynéll
Pallot, *f.n.*, 'pæloʊ, pálō
Parmentier, *f.n.*, ,pɑrmɒn'tɪər, paarmonteér
Perchard, *f.n.*, 'pɜrʃɑrd, pér-shaard
Perelle, *f.n.*, 'pɛərel, páirel
Perelle Bay *Guernsey*, 'pɛərel, páirel
Perrée, *f.n.*, pɛə'reɪ, pairáy
Petit, *f.n.*, 'petɪ, pétti
Petit Bot *Guernsey*, 'petɪ 'boʊ, pétti bố
Petit Port *Guernsey*, 'petɪ 'pɔr, pétti pór
Pettiquin, *f.n.*, 'petɪkæ̃, péttikang
Picot, *f.n.*, 'pɪkoʊ, píckō
Pigeon, *f.n.*, 'pɪʒɔ, péezhaw
Pinchemain, *f.n.*, 'pɪnʃmeɪn, pínshmayn
Pinel, *f.n.*, 'pɪnel, pínnel
Pirouet, *f.n.*, 'pɪroʊeɪ, pírrōo-ay
Pleinmont Point *Guernsey*, 'plaɪmɒn, plímon
Plémont *Jersey*, 'plemɔ, plémmaw
Poingdestre, *f.n.*, 'pɔɪndestər, póyndestĕr
Poree, *f.n.*, 'pɔreɪ, páwray
Potier, *f.n.*, 'pɒtjeɪ, pót-yay
Priaulx, *f.n.*, 'prioʊ, prée-ō
Procureur, *f.n.*, 'prɒkjʊərər, próck-yōorĕr

Q

Quellenec, *f.n.*, 'kelɪnek, kéllĕneck
Quentin, *f.n.*, 'kwentɪn, kwéntin

Queripel, *f.n.*, 'kerɪpel, kérripel
Quesnard Lighthouse *Alderney*, 'keɪnɑrd, káynaard
Quesnel, *f.n.*, 'keɪnel, káynel
Quevatre, *f.n.*, kɪ'vɑtr, kĕvaátr
Quinain, *f.n.*, kɪ'neɪn, kináyn
Quinquenel, *f.n.*, 'kæŋkɪnel, kánkinel
Quirot, *f.n.*, 'kwɪroʊ, kwírrō

R

Rabet, *f.n.*, 'ræbeɪ, rábbay
Rabey, *f.n.*, 'reɪbɪ, ráybi
Raimbault, *f.n.*, 'ræmboʊ, rámbō
Rault, *f.n.*, roʊlt, rōlt
Rebourg, *f.n.*, re'bʊərg, reb-boōrg
Rebours, *f.n.*, re'bʊər, rebboōr
Renier, *f.n.*, 'renjeɪ, rén-yay
Renouard, *f.n.*, 'renwɑr, rén-waar
Renouf, *f.n.*, re'nuf, rennoōf; 'renɒf, rénnoff. *The first is a Guernsey pronunciation, the second a Jersey one.*
Richard, *f.n.*, 'rɪʃɑr, ríshaar
Ricou, *f.n.*, 'rɪku, ríckoo
Rihoy, *f.n.*, 'rɪɔɪ, rée-oy
Rimeur, *f.n.*, 'rɪmər, rímmur
Robilliard, *f.n.*, roʊ'bɪlɪərd, rōbílli-ärd
Robin, *f.n.*, 'roʊbɪn, róbin
Roche, *f.n.*, roʊʃ, rōsh
Rocquaine Bay, *Guernsey*, roʊ-'keɪn, rōkáyn
Rohais, *f.n.*, 'roʊheɪz, rố-hayz
Romerill, *f.n.*, 'rɒmrɪl, rómril
Rouget, *f.n.*, ru'ʒeɪ, roozháy
Rousseau, *f.n.*, 'rusoʊ, roossō
Roussel, *f.n.*, ru'sel, roosséll
Routier, *f.n.*, 'rutɪeɪ, roóti-ay
Rozel *Jersey*, 'roʊzel, rốzel

S

St. Aubin *Jersey*, snt 'oʊbɪn, sĭnt ốbin; snt 'ɔbɪn, sĭnt áwbin
St. Brelade *Jersey*, snt brɪ'lɑd, sĭnt brĕlaád
St. Helier *Jersey*, snt 'helɪər, sĭnt hélli-ĕr
St. Ouen's *Jersey*, snt 'wɒnz, sĭnt wónnz
St. Peter Port *Guernsey*, snt 'pitər 'pɔrt, sĭnt péetĕr pórt
Salsac, *f.n.*, 'sælzæk, sálzack
Sangan, *f.n.*, 'sæŋen, sáng-en
Sark, sɑrk, saark
Sarre, *f.n.*, sɑr, saar

Savident, *f.n.*, 'sævɪdɒn, sávvidon
Sebire, *f.n.*, 'sebɪər, sébbeer
Simon, *f.n.*, 'sɪmɑ̃, símmaa*ng*;
　'sɪmɔ, simmaw. *The first is a*
　Guernsey pronunciation, the
　second a Jersey one.
Sohier, *f.n.*, 'sɔjeɪ, sáw-yay
Surcouf, *f.n.*, 'suərkuf, so͞or-
　koof
Syvret, *f.n.*, 'sɪvreɪ, sívray

T

Tabel, *f.n.*, 'teɪbel, táybel
Talibard, *f.n.*, 'tælɪbɑr, tálibaar
Tanguy, *f.n.*, 'tæŋɪ, táng-i; 'tæŋgɪ,
　táng-gi. *The first is a Guernsey*
　pronunciation, the second a
　Jersey one.
Tardif, *f.n.*, 'tɑrdɪf, taárdif
Tardivel, *f.n.*, 'tɑrdɪvel, taárdi-
　vel
Thoume, *f.n.*, tum, toom
Thoumine, *f.n.*, tu'min, tooméen
Tirel, *f.n.*, 'tɪrel, tírrel
Torode, *f.n.*, 'tɒroud, tórrōd
Tostevin, *f.n.*, 'tɒstɪvɪn, tósstĕ-
　vin
Tourtel, *f.n.*, 'tuərtel, to͞ortel
Touzeau, *f.n.*, 'tuzou, to͞ozō
Touzel, *f.n.*, 'tuzel, to͞ozel
Tregear, *f.n.*, trɪ'gɛər, trĕgáir
Trehorel, *f.n.*, 'treɪɔrel, tráy-
　-awrel
Troquer, *f.n.*, 'troukeɪ, trókay
Trouteaud, *f.n.*, tru'tou, trootó
Tulié, *f.n.*, ,tulɪ'eɪ, tooli-áy

U

Udle, *f.n.*, 'judl, yo͞odl
Upper Canichers *Guernsey*, 'ʌpər
　'kænɪʃərz, úppĕr kánnishĕrz

V

Vaillant, *f.n.*, 'veɪjə, váy-yă
Vallois, *f.n.*, 'vælwɑ, válwaa
Valpiéd, *f.n.*, 'vælpɪeɪ, válpi-ay
Vasselin, *f.n.*, 'væslæ̃, vásslan*g*
Vaudin, *f.n.*, 'voudɪn, vǒdin
Vautier, *f.n.*, 'voutjeɪ, vǒt-yay
Vazon Bay *Guernsey*, 'vɑzɒn,
　vaázon
Vibert, *f.n.*, 'vaɪbərt, víbĕrt;
　'vibɛər, veébair
Vidamour, *f.n.*, 'vɪdəmuər, víddă-
　mo͞or
Viel, *f.n.*, 'viel, veé-el
Vining, *f.n.*, 'vɪnɪŋ, vínning
Voisin, *f.n.*, 'vɔɪzɪn, vóyzin

Y

Yvette, *C.n. and f.n.*, i'vet, eevét
Yvonne, *C.n. and f.n.*, i'vɒn,
　eevónn

Z

Zabiela, *f.n.*, zæ'bɪlə, zabbíllă